KU-199-959

An Introduction to Developmental Psychology

Second Edition

BPS Textbooks in Psychology

BPS Blackwell presents a comprehensive and authoritative series covering everything a student needs in order to complete an undergraduate degree in psychology. Refreshingly written to consider more than North American research, this series is the first to give a truly international perspective. Written by the very best names in the field, the series offers an extensive range of titles from introductory level through to final year optional modules, and every text fully complies with the BPS syllabus in the topic. No other series bears the BPS seal of approval!

Each book is supported by a companion website, featuring additional resource materials for both instructors and students, designed to encourage critical thinking, and providing for all your course lecturing and testing needs.

For other titles in this series, please go to **www.bpsblackwell.co.uk**.

'Developmental psychology is an exciting field and the second edition of this introductory text covers an impressive breadth of topics and themes without sacrificing depth, yet it is readable, lively and engaging throughout. Students will find here excellent accounts of the theories, methods, findings and controversies that make developmental psychology such an intriguing and dynamic research area. An attractive feature of this textbook is that it conveys time and time again the relevance of developmental science to understanding the ways in which human beings grow, adjust and respond in our everyday worlds.'

Kevin Durkin, Professor, University of Strathclyde

'Alan Slater and Gavin Bremner have assembled an outstanding cast of leading international researchers who have written expert and authoritative introductions to all the core areas of Developmental Psychology. This book provides an ideal gateway for introductory level students to an exciting and rapidly growing body of research.'

Martyn Barrett, Professor of Psychology, University of Surrey

An Introduction
to Developmental
Psychology

SECOND EDITION

EDITED BY ALAN SLATER AND
GAVIN BREMNER

 **BPS BLACKWELL**

This edition first published 2011 by the British Psychological Society and Blackwell Publishing Ltd

© 2011 the British Psychological Society and Blackwell Publishing Ltd

© 2003 Blackwell Publishing Ltd

BPS Blackwell is an imprint of Blackwell Publishing, which was acquired by John Wiley & Sons Ltd in February 2007.

All effort has been made to trace and acknowledge ownership of copyright. The publisher would be glad to hear from any copyright holders whom it has not been possible to contact.

Front cover image: Ascending to stair, © Elif Gunyeli/iStock.

Images included on Part and Chapter opening pages are reproduced courtesy of Shutterstock, with the exception of images on chapter openers to: Chapter 2; Chapters 4 and 6 (reproduced by permission of Georgia King); Chapter 8 (reproduced by permission of Wendy Lawrenson); Chapter 9; Chapter 10; and Chapter 21 (reproduced with permission from Dr Gabor Stefanics).

Registered office
John Wiley & Sons Ltd, The Atrium, Southern Gate, Chichester, West Sussex, PO19 8SQ, United Kingdom. For details of our global editorial offices, for customer services and for information about how to apply for permission to reuse the copyright material in this book please see our website at www.wiley.com.

The right of Alan Slater and Gavin Bremner to be identified as the authors of this work has been asserted in accordance with the UK Copyright, Designs and Patents Act 1988.

Reprinted 2012, 2014, 2015(twice)

All rights reserved. No part of this publication may be reproduced, stored in a retrieval system, or transmitted, in any form or by any means, electronic, mechanical, photocopying, recording or otherwise, except as permitted by the UK Copyright, Designs and Patents Act 1988, without the prior permission of the publisher.

Wiley also publishes its books in a variety of electronic formats and by print-on-demand. Some content that appears in standard print versions of this book may not be available in other formats. For more information about Wiley products, visit us at www.wiley.com.

Designations used by companies to distinguish their products are often claimed as trademarks. All brand names and product names used in this book are trade names, service marks, trademarks or registered trademarks of their respective owners. The publisher is not associated with any product or vendor mentioned in this book. This publication is designed to provide accurate and authoritative information in regard to the subject matter covered. It is sold on the understanding that the publisher is not engaged in rendering professional services. If professional advice or other expert assistance is required, the services of a competent professional should be sought.

Library of Congress Cataloging in Publication Data
An introduction to developmental psychology / edited by Alan Slater and Gavin Bremner. — 2nd ed.
    p. cm.
   Includes bibliographical references and index.
    ISBN 978-1-4051-8652-0
  1. Developmental psychology.   I. Slater, Alan   II. Bremner, J. Gavin, 1949-
  BF713.I54   2011
  155—dc23

2011024400

A catalogue record for this book is available from the British Library.

Set in 11/12.5pt Dante MT by MPS Limited, a Macmillan Company, Chennai, India
Printed in Great Britain by Bell and Bain Ltd, Glasgow

The British Psychological Society's free Research Digest e-mail service rounds up the latest research and relates it to your syllabus in a user-friendly way. To subscribe go to www.researchdigest.org.uk or send a blank e-mail to subscribe-rd@lists.bps.org.uk

Commissioning Editor: Andrew McAleer
Assistant Editors: Georgia King and Katharine Earwaker
Marketing Managers: Fran Hunt and Jo Underwood
Project Editor: Juliet Booker

UNIVERSITY
OF
GLASGOW
LIBRARY

Brief Contents

Contents

Contributors

Gizelle Anzures, University of Toronto, Canada

Robert Atkins, Rutgers University, USA

Cagla Aydin, Cornell University, USA

Tanya Bergevin, Concordia University, Canada

J. Gavin Bremner, Lancaster University, UK

Peter Bryant, Oxford University, UK

William M. Bukowski, Concordia University, Canada

Stephen J. Ceci, Cornell University, USA

Nadia Chernyak, Cornell University, USA

Anandini Dar, Rutgers University, USA

Alyson Davis, Open University, UK

Margaret Anne Defeyter, Northumbria University, UK

Julian Elliott, Durham University, USA

Elisa A. Esposito, Teachers College, Columbia University, USA

William P. Fifer, New York State Psychiatric Institute, USA; Departments of Psychiatry and Pediatrics, Columbia University, USA

Stanka A. Fitneva, Cornell University, USA

Eirini Flouri, Institute of Education, University of London, UK

Alejo Freire, Children's Mental Health, Ontario, Canada

Elena L. Grigorenko, Yale University, USA; Moscow State University, Russia; Teachers College, Columbia University, USA

Leslie Morrison Gutman, Institute of Education, University of London, UK

Daniel Hart, Rutgers University, USA

Heather M. Hill, St Mary's University, Texas, USA

Ian Hocking, University of Christchurch Canterbury, UK

Scott P. Johnson, UCLA, USA

Stan A. Kuczaj II, University of Southern Mississippi, USA

Wendy Lawrenson, Open University, UK

Kang Lee, University of Toronto, Canada

Elizabeth Meins, University of Durham, UK

Richard Miners, Concordia University, Canada

Peter Mitchell, University of Nottingham, UK

Christine Moon, Pacific Lutheran University, Washington, USA

Darwin Muir, Queen's University, Canada

Sarah H. Norgate, Salford University, UK

H. Rudolph Schaffer, University of Strathclyde, UK (deceased)

Alan Slater, University of Exeter, UK

Peter K. Smith, Goldsmiths College, University of London, UK

Robert J. Sternberg, Tufts University, USA

Nyeema Watson, Rutgers University, USA

Naomi Winstone, University of Surrey, UK

Preface to Second Edition

Our aim in producing the second edition of this textbook is to offer a representative, comprehensive and completely up-to-date 'state of the art' account of human development from conception to adolescence. We appreciated that this needed to be an edited book rather than one written by the two editors, since one can be an expert in one or two fields of study, but not all! By making it an edited book that fulfilled our aims of a comprehensive textbook we first decided the areas that needed covering, specified in detail the topics for each chapter, and then invited some of the world's leading experts to write the chapters. Our invitations were received with enthusiasm, and we have been extremely gratified at the ways in which our authors have responded to our suggestions. The dangers of uneven writing levels, and possible lack of integration of the chapters were dealt with in two ways. First, we gave clear and extensive instructions to our authors as to content and style, and of course carefully edited the chapters. Second, the editorial and production staff at Wiley-Blackwell reviewed each chapter carefully to ensure that the book reads well and coherently as a whole, and is well and appropriately illustrated.

The book is organised chronologically and also thematically, into five parts, each concerned with different aspects of development and each containing three or more chapters. For the second edition many of our original authors have updated their chapters from the first edition, and we have added new chapters, based on the recommendation of reviewers. Here are brief comments on each part.

Part I: Introduction

In order to put child development into its modern context the student needs to be aware of the many ways that have been developed to explore development, and the theories that have developed from, and have guided this research. These are described in Chapters 1 and 2. One major topic that pervades almost all areas of development is the nature–nurture issue – to what extent do our genetic inheritance and our experiences across the life span influence and determine our development? This topic is explored in detail in Chapter 3.

Part II: Infancy

The Latin term 'infans' can be literally translated as 'the period without speech'. It is the advancement of the infant during this period, which we know as infancy, that is the starting point of child development, and the four chapters in Part II chart the course of this development. Although birth might seem to be the starting point of infant development, it is becoming increasingly recognised that developments prior to birth have considerable psychological implications. In Chapter 4 we have an account of biological and psychological development from conception to birth. In order to act upon the world infants have to have functioning sensory systems, have to acquire knowledge of the people and objects in their world, and they have to convert this growing knowledge into action. The story of how this development takes place is given in Chapter 5. Infant development takes place at many levels and in many contexts. Chapter 6 begins the story of the infant's development into a social world and considers the development of emotions, with a particular emphasis on the formation of attachments with others. The theme of social development is continued in Chapter 7 with an account of how the infant's early exchanges with others gradually turn into effective communication.

Part III: Childhood

As the period of infancy draws to a close, around 18 months from birth, the early competencies continue to develop and many new aspects of development begin to make their appearance. These many developments are charted in Part III, which covers social and cognitive development. Chapter 8 continues the themes covered in Chapter 7 and explores the developing child's awareness of self and of gender. According to 'the giant of developmental psychology', Jean Piaget, a new stage of thinking emerges around 7 years of age. The preceding cognitive abilities that lead to these changes, the changes themselves, and alternative accounts of them, are given in Chapter 9. Language development, probably a uniquely human accomplishment, is the focus of Chapter 10, and Chapter 11 describes how it is that children learn that others have thoughts, ideas, feelings and beliefs that are often different from their own – that is, how they develop a 'theory of mind'. In western education it is vital that children learn to read and write and develop an understanding of mathematics. How they do so, and the complexities of the tasks facing the child, is the focus of Chapter 12. A vital cognitive ability, one that underlies all development, is our memory. Memory development is discussed in Chapter 13, along with its social implications – in particular, how reliable is memory, how truthful are children, how suggestible are they, and do they make reliable eye witnesses? Development takes place within the social network that surrounds the child, and as childhood progresses beyond infancy, peer groups and peer relations become of great importance. This theme is explored in Chapter 14, which considers the topic of play and how it develops in the context of peer relations. Chapter 15 continues the theme of social interactions and asks how development of prosocial and antisocial behaviour takes place, and how the child's understanding of moral issues and concerns develops.

Part IV: Adolescence

The two chapters in Part IV give an account and overview of the major cognitive and social changes that take place in adolescence. In Chapter 16 the authors describe developments in perception and attention, memory, intelligence and reasoning. Piaget presented evidence that a major change in thinking develops in adolescence, known as *formal operational reasoning*. The authors describe and evaluate Piaget's account, and go beyond his theory to give alternative accounts of adolescent reasoning and thinking. Adolescence is often thought of as a period of turmoil as the individual copes with raging hormones and the changes that accompany the transition from child to adult. The many aspects of social development that accompany adolescence are considered in Chapter 17, including such themes as storm and stress, the role of the family and of peer groups, developing independence, and romantic relationships.

Part V: Practical Issues

There are, of course, many practical issues that accompany child development, and three of these important issues are considered here. Chapter 18 discusses the educational implications of what we have learned about children's development. Two major theoreticians whose work has had a major impact on educational thinking – Jean Piaget and Lev Vygotsky – are discussed in detail, along with many other issues, which include peers, educational practice, and the role of the parents. Although it is our hope that children will grow up in a happy, supportive environment, this is not always the case. Chapter 19 demonstrates how vital it is to develop an understanding of the effects different adverse experiences may have on children's development, but also to understand the other side of the coin, children's resilience in the face of these adverse events. One of the major social problems that can dramatically affect children's school experiences is that of bullying. It is, sadly, all too common for children who are bullied to experience great misery, and we have long been aware that programmes are necessary in order to reduce the effects of bullying. Chapter 20 describes bullies and their victims, and outlines effective school-based intervention programmes that can help to overcome some of the problems. Many of the chapters in this book focus exclusively on 'normally developing' children, that is, those who are following a typical pattern of development. However, much can be learned by studying the development of children whose development is atypical. Chapter 21 considers different senses in which development can be considered atypical, contrasting cases of delayed or accelerated development with cases in which development is qualitatively different or deficient in specific areas. It then goes on to review evidence regarding development of individuals with Williams syndrome, Down's syndrome, autism and ADHD, and also children with sensory deficits. Such studies are particularly important on two counts – their outcomes impact on practice and intervention with children with disabilities, and have implications for our understanding of development in general.

Pedagogical features and dedicated website

The book comes with a range of pedagogical features that contribute to the student's learning experience. Each chapter begins with an overview and the key concepts that are highlighted in the text. The chapters end with discussion points that focus on the important issues that have been raised, and with suggestions for further reading for those who wish to expand and develop their knowledge of the area. The book has a dedicated companion website (www.wiley.com/college/slater), which features author details, glossary, contents listing, and figures from the text that can be downloaded for PowerPoint presentations. For instructors who adopt the text there is password-protected access to 475 multiple-choice questions – 20 for each chapter – and for students a sample of 5 of these multiple-choice questions is given in the website. Other supplementary material, available only on the website, includes an alternative view of social development given in the chapter 'The Social Nature of Human Development' by Andy Lock (University of Massey, New Zealand) and John Shotter (University of New Hampshire, USA).

Overview

In summary, *Introduction to Developmental Psychology* has been written by a group of internationally known and respected authors who are at the forefront of research, and it gives an unrivalled high level of expertise and insight across all topics. The result is an outstanding and authoritative 'state-of-the-art' chronicle of human development from conception to adolescence, which gives a stimulating account of theories, findings and issues in this fascinating area. The text is designed for a broad range of readers, and in particular those with little prior exposure to psychology. The comprehensive coverage and emphasis on core topics in human development make it an excellent text for introductory students. We owe enormous thanks to our authors, and to Wiley-Blackwell.

Alan Slater and Gavin Bremner

Part I
Introduction

1 The Scope and Methods of Developmental Psychology

ALAN SLATER, SCOTT P. JOHNSON, AND DARWIN MUIR

KEY TERMS

affect • baby biographies • behaviourism • catharsis hypothesis • clinical method • cohort • continuous function - decreasing ability • continuous function -increasing ability • control group • correlational studies • cross-sectional design • dependent variable • developmental functions • discontinuous (step) function • ecological validity • electroencephalogram (EEG) • event-related potential (ERP) • event sampling • experimental group • experimental methods • extraversion • folk theories of development • Flynn effect • functional magnetic resonance imaging (fMRI) • Head Start • imaging methods • independent variable • intelligence test • intelligence quotient (IQ) • intelligence test • introversion • longitudinal design • marker task • maturation • mechanistic world view • medial temporal (MT) area • microgenetic method • moral judgement stages • observational studies • organismic world view • paradigm • personality trait • positron emission tomography (PET) • psychological tests • sequential design • social policy • stage-like changes in development • stages of moral reasoning • structured observation • Sure Start • theory of mind • time sampling • U-shaped functions

CHAPTER OUTLINE

OVERVIEW

The evidence base is the bedrock of the science of psychology, and developmental psychology is no exception. This chapter outlines the questions to which developmental psychologists seek answers, and shows that 'folk' theories of development often contradict each other and may find little support when research is done to test them.

The authors go on to present the different world views that form the basis for evidence-based accounts of human development, contrasting organismic and mechanistic views. This leads on to a discussion of research designs for studying age-related changes in development: longitudinal and cross-sectional designs are compared and the advantages and disadvantages of each are clearly stated.

This is followed by an account of some of the most frequently used research methods and the different forms of evidence that arise from observation, experimentation, psychological testing and correlational studies. In the case of many questions experimental research is more likely to yield results that can be interpreted in terms of cause and effect.

Having provided a detailed summary of research methodologies, the authors show how well-conducted research has radically changed our views about various aspects of development. Finally, they turn to a discussion of the most common developmental curves or functions that have emerged, that is, the ways in which humans typically grow and change as development proceeds. Not all development is gradual and continuous: it can be step-like, or show reversals and U-shaped or inverted U-shaped profiles.

Throughout the chapter the authors illustrate their points with fascinating examples drawn from current literature.

INTRODUCTION

Developmental psychology can be defined as the discipline that attempts to describe and explain the changes that occur over time in the thought, behaviour, reasoning, and functioning of a person due to biological, individual, and environmental influences. Developmental psychologists study children's development, and the development of human behaviour across the lifespan, from a variety of different perspectives. Thus, if one is studying different areas of development, different theoretical perspectives will be important and may influence the ways psychologists and students think about, and study, development.

In this chapter we first discuss the role of age-related factors in affecting development. Then we describe different *concepts of human development* and human nature that have helped to shape people's thinking about development. The issues raised in these sections will recur later in the chapter as we present psychological evidence relating to them. Next we will give an account of some of the *research designs* used to explore development, followed by a description of different *developmental methods*. Finally we will present some of the *developmental functions* that have emerged from the research.

STUDYING CHANGES WITH AGE

The newborn infant is a helpless creature, with limited means of communication and few skills. By 18–24 months – the end of the period of infancy – all this has changed. The child has formed relationships with others, has learned a lot about the physical world, and is about to undergo a vocabulary explosion as language development leaps ahead. By the time of adolescence the child is a mature, thinking individual actively striving to come to terms with a rapidly changing and complex society.

It is tempting to think that the many developments we find as childhood progresses are a result of age, but in this we must be careful. Increasing age, *by itself*, contributes nothing to development. What is important is the **maturation** and changes resulting from experience that intervene between the different ages and stages of childhood: the term maturation refers to *those aspects of development that are primarily under genetic control, and which are relatively uninfluenced by the environment*. An example could be puberty: although its onset can be affected by environmental factors, such as diet, the changes that occur are primarily genetically determined. With respect to environmental factors, we would not, for instance, expect a particular 4-year-old child to be more advanced in language development than a 2-year-old if, from the age of 2, the child had not been exposed to language at all. The normal 4-year-old will have been exposed to a multiplicity of agents, forces, and events in the previous two years, and will have had the opportunity actively to explore and experiment with the world.

> **maturation** aspects of development that are largely under genetic control, and hence largely uninfluenced by environmental factors.

Developmental psychologists study *age-related changes* in behaviour and development, but underlying their descriptions of these changes is the clear understanding that increasing age by itself causes nothing, and so we always need to look for the many factors that cause development to take place.

CONCEPTS OF HUMAN DEVELOPMENT

The assumptions and ideas we have about human nature will affect how we rear our own children and how we interpret the findings from studies of children. Our implicit, lay or **'folk' theories of development** often reflect the issues that psychologists investigate, with the aim of putting our understanding on a firmer, more scientific footing. We will begin by discussing two such views – 'punishment or praise?' – and then we will discuss some of the theoretical views that have influenced psychologists' thinking about development.

> **'folk' theories of development** ideas held about development that are not based upon scientific investigation.

'Folk' theories of development: Punishment or praise?

We all of us have theories and views on how children should be reared. These views result from our own upbringing, our peers' experiences, our parents' ideas, the media, and many other sources. These views will often influence how we bring up our own children and there is often *intergenerational continuity* of childcare practices. For example, there are several ways in which children become attached to their caregivers (see Chapter 6) and these 'styles of attachment' show continuity and stability across generations – from grandparents to parents to children (e.g., Benoit & Parker, 1994; Shaffer, Burt, Obradovic, Herbers & Masten, 2009).

Here are two opposing views about the usefulness of physical punishment – see which one you agree with!

Spare the rod and spoil the child

The dauphin, Louis, was born to King Henri IV of France in 1601 ('dauphin' means the eldest son of the king, and he became King Louis XIII at the age of 9). The king wrote to Louis' governess:

> I command you to whip him every time that he is willful or naughty, knowing by my own experience that nothing else did me so much good.
>
> *(From Wallace, Franklin & Keegan, 1994, p. 4)*

John Wesley (1703–91) was the founder of the religious Evangelical movement known as Methodism. He was the 15th of 19 children born to Samuel and Susanna Wesley. Here is part of a letter from Susanna Wesley (a woman of great piety) to her son John about how to rear children (cited in Sants & Barnes, 1985, p. 24):

> Let him have nothing he cries for; absolutely nothing, great or small; else you undo your own work ... make him do as he is bid, if you whip him ten times running to effect it. Let none persuade you it is cruelty to do this; it is cruelty not to do it. Break his will now, and his soul will live, and he will probably bless you to all eternity.

At that time infant mortality was very high (why else have 19 children?), and Susanna Wesley's views originate from a belief that children are born in a state of sin and it is therefore necessary to use all means to save their souls, almost from birth. A similar view was expressed by Theodore Dwight (1834, *The Father's Book*) – 'No child has ever been (born) destitute of an evil disposition – however sweet it appears.'

All sweetness and light: Like begets like

Compare these views with the following: 'Your baby is born to be a reasonable, friendly human being' (Benjamin Spock, from his book *Baby and Child Care*, 1946, cited in Sants & Barnes, 1985). Spock's book had a huge impact on American parents' rearing of their children. Here is an extract from the famous poem 'Children Learn What They Live' by Dorothy Lawe Nolte:

If a child lives with criticism she learns to condemn

If a child lives with hostility he learns to fight

BUT

If a child lives with approval she learns to like herself

If a child lives with acceptance and friendship he learns to find love in the world

In this and the previous section we have two opposing lay, or 'folk' theories about child rearing: (1) children need to be punished regularly in order to develop as pleasant, law-abiding citizens – failure to use harsh physical punishment carries with it the possibility, if not the certainty, that the child will grow up to be disobedient, and their very soul may be at risk; (2) the contrary view is that children are born inherently good, a view that carries the implication that the use of physical punishment might be unnecessary, perhaps even harmful.

We shall see later that research has given strong support to the latter view, but clearly the views and theories that parents and guardians have about child rearing will influence their own child-rearing practices. In much the same way that parents will be influenced by their 'folk' theories, developmental psychologists will be influenced by their theoretical leanings (which are not always based on a fully objective appraisal of the evidence!), and we discuss two of the most important of these next.

Defining development according to world views

Psychologists, and others who study children's development, also have different views of development. The manner in which development is defined, and the areas of development that are of interest to individual researchers, will lead them to use different methods of studying development. We will describe two such different views of development that have been offered by psychologists holding different *world views*.

paradigm literally, a pattern or sample, the term is now frequently applied to a theoretical or philosophical framework in any scientific discipline.

The eminent developmental psychologist Richard Lerner defines a world view (also called a **paradigm**, *model*, or *world hypothesis*) as 'a philosophical system of ideas that serves to organise a set or family of scientific theories and associated scientific methods' (1986, p. 42). They are beliefs we adopt, which are often not open to empirical test – that is, we simply believe them!

Lerner and others note that many developmental theories appear to fall under one of two basic world views: *organismic* and *mechanistic*. Only a superficial description of these two world views will be presented here (Lerner, 1986, Chapter 2, gives a detailed discussion, and Hultsch & Deutsch, 1981, give a concise summary). In Chapter 2 we describe some of the theories of development that 'fit into' these theoretical views.

organismic world view the idea that people are inherently active and continually interacting with the environment, and therefore helping to shape their own development. Piaget's theory is an example of this world view.

Organismic world view

According to the **organismic world view** a person is represented as a biological organism that is *inherently active and continually interacting with the environment, and therefore helping to shape its own development*. This world view emphasises the interaction between maturation and experience that leads to the development of new internal, psychological structures for processing environmental input (e.g., Gestsdottir & Lerner, 2008).

As Lerner states: 'The Organismic model stresses the integrated structural features of the organism. If the parts making up the whole become reorganised as a consequence of the organism's active construction of its own functioning, the structure of the organism may take on a new meaning; thus qualitatively distinct principles may be involved in human functioning at different points in life. These distinct, or new, levels of organization are termed stages . . .' (p. 57). An analogy is the qualitative change that occurs when molecules of two gases, hydrogen and oxygen, combine to form a liquid, water. Other qualitative changes happen to water when it changes from frozen (ice) to liquid (water) to steam (vapour). Depending on the temperature these qualitative changes in the state of water are easily reversed, but in human development the qualitative changes that take place are rarely, if ever, reversible – that is, each new stage represents an advance on the preceding stage and the individual does not regress to former stages.

The point is that the new stage is not simply reducible to components of the previous stage; it represents new characteristics not present in the previous stage. For example, the organism appears to pass through structural stages during foetal development (which is discussed in detail in Chapter 4). In the first stage (Period of the Ovum – first few weeks after conception) cells multiply and form clusters; in the second stage (Period of the Embryo – two to about eight weeks) the major body parts are formed by cell multiplication, specialisation and migration as well as cell death; in the last stage (Period of the Foetus) the body parts mature and begin to operate as an integrated system, for example, head orientation towards and away from stimulation, arm extensions and grasping, thumb sucking, startles to loud noises, and so on (Fifer, 2010; Hepper, 2007). Similar stages of psychological development beyond birth are postulated to occur as well.

Piaget is perhaps the best example of an organismic theorist, and his views are discussed in the next chapter, and also in Chapters 9 and 16. In brief, Piaget suggested that cognitive development occurs in stages and that the reasoning of the child at one stage is qualitatively different from that at the earlier and later stages. The job of the developmental psychologist subscribing to an organismic viewpoint is to determine *when* (i.e., at what ages) different psychological stages operate and *what* variables, processes, and/or laws represent the differences between stages and determine the transitions between them.

Mechanistic world view

According to the **mechanistic world view** a person can be represented as being like a machine (such as a computer), which is inherently passive until stimulated by the environment. Ultimately, human behaviour is reducible to the operation of fundamental behavioural units (e.g., habits) that are acquired in a gradual, cumulative manner. According to this view the frequency of behaviours can increase with age due to various learning processes and they can decrease with age when they no longer have any functional consequence, or lead to negative consequences (such as punishment). The developmentalist's job is to study the environmental factors, or principles of learning, which determine the way organisms respond to stimulation, and which result in increases, decreases, and changes in behaviour.

mechanistic world view the idea that a person can be represented as being like a machine (such as a computer), which is inherently passive until stimulated by the environment.

behaviourism the theoretical view, associated with J.B. Watson and B.F. Skinner, that sees directly observable behaviour as the proper focus of study, and that sees the developing child as a passive respondent to conditioning, reinforcement, and punishment.

Unlike the organismic view development is reflected by a more continuous growth function, rather than occurring in qualitatively different stages, and the child is passive rather than active in shaping its own development. **Behaviourists** represent this world view, and their views are discussed in Chapter 2.

WAYS OF STUDYING DEVELOPMENT

Developmental psychologists have a variety of strategies with which to study development. These various strategies can be subdivided into two broad, interrelated categories – designs that enable us to study age-related changes in behaviour, and the associated research methods that are used to collect the information or data about development. These are discussed under the next two broad headings – *Designs for studying age-related changes* and *Research methods*.

Designs for studying age-related changes

In all studies which describe behavioural changes with age, one of two general developmental designs, either the *cross-sectional* or the *longitudinal*, are used. Here we discuss the strengths and weaknesses of these designs. Many examples of research using these designs are presented later in this chapter, and throughout this book. There is a third approach – the *sequential design* – which often gives a partial solution for the limitations imposed by the use of only one method.

Cross-sectional designs

cross-sectional design a study where children of different ages are observed at a single point in time.

In a **cross-sectional design** people of different ages are tested once; thus, each point on the X-axis (the horizontal axis of graphs, such as those shown in Figures 1.1, 1.3, and 1.12) is represented by a different age group. This is the most common method employed by developmental researchers because it is the least time-consuming and provides a quick estimate of changes with age. However, it only describes age differences. There is no way to derive an estimate of the continuity or discontinuity of various processes over age (e.g., stability of personality; sudden shifts in language comprehension or production) because performance is averaged over *different* individuals at each age.

Longitudinal designs

longitudinal design a study where more than one observation of the same group of children is made at different points in their development.

In **longitudinal designs** people are tested repeatedly as they grow older. This method is powerful because each individual's development is measured over time, allowing one to assess *within-person* changes with age and *between-person* differences in age changes. In many cases the data are summarised by plotting the group average as a function of age; but, by looking at each individual's data, we can determine if there is a gradual change with age or a sudden shift in performance more characteristic of stage-like development (these and other types of developmental change are discussed later under *developmental functions*). There are many types of longitudinal designs. They may take place over a long period of time. An example is the Avon Longitudinal Study of Parents and Children (ALSPAC). This is a large-scale study of children born in Avon, UK, in the early 1990s, which recruited over 14,000 pregnant mothers-to-be, and is a major resource for the study of genetic and environmental factors contributing to long-term health and development. To date, ALSPAC findings have been reported in over 400 scientific publications (Golding, 2010). At the other extreme there are *microgenetic* studies in which typically only a few children are tested over a short period of time: examples of such studies are given in the next section.

Unfortunately, there are several problems with longitudinal designs as well, particularly studies such as ALSPAC. The cost is very high in several respects. They are time-consuming, and it may be difficult to schedule repeated visits of the same children, and the drop-out rate can be very high. If those who find the task difficult withdraw from the study, this *participant attrition*, with the accompanying *selective survivorship* of the remaining children in the sample, can produce a population bias that can give a misleading impression of development and may limit the generality of the results.

Another major problem can be the time it takes to complete a study – it equals the age span being tested. If, for example, the task is to map changes in performance on **IQ tests** between age 20 and 80, it would take 60 years to complete the study! And, after all that work, the results may only be true for the particular age **cohort** studied (those born at about the same time), producing yet another population bias. There is one final problem we can mention, which is the possible effects of repeated testing – children might get better over age simply because they have more practice on the tasks they are given! As a result, the data might not reflect typical development in the absence of this repeated practice.

> **cohort** a group of people who were raised in the same environment or who share certain demographic characteristics.

Microgenetic methods

A combination of procedures that are becoming increasingly popular are referred to as the **microgenetic method**. Developmental psychology is fundamentally concerned with change, and with the causes and consequences of change. However, most research, whether using cross-sectional, longitudinal or other designs, provides a snapshot of developmental changes, without describing the process of change itself (Flynn, Pine & Lewis, 2006). Microgenetic methods examine change *as it occurs*, and involve individual children being tested repeatedly, typically over a short period of time, so that the density of observations is high compared with the typical longitudinal study. Thus, the method provides detailed information about an individual, or individuals, over a period of transition. The microgenetic method has been used in many areas of development, which include arithmetic, theory of mind, locomotion, memory, analogical reasoning, strategy use, conscious and unconscious reasoning,

> **microgenetic method** a method that examines change as it occurs and involves individual children being tested repeatedly, typically over a short period of time so that the density of observations is high compared with the typical longitudinal study.

and, quite simply 'By examining change as it occurs this method can yield more precise descriptions than would otherwise be possible' (Flynn *et al.*, 2006, p. 154).

When longitudinal and cross-sectional results tell a different story

Usually researchers try to obtain both longitudinal and cross-sectional data on any topic. In general, we expect to obtain similar developmental functions from cross-sectional and longitudinal data, and usually this is the case. However, this does not always happen, and the two designs can sometimes give us dramatically different results. Two instances of conflicting results will be discussed; the first concerns the *length of time between measures* (the age scale) and the second concerns *cohort effects*.

Time between measures In designing a developmental study one must decide what intervals to use on the X-axis, that is, at what ages the children are to be tested or how often repeated tests will be administered. When studying infants, it is common to test them monthly or bi-weekly in longitudinal studies, depending on when we expect to see an age difference in performance appear. The transition point for changes in performance with age can be estimated using cross-sectional data. While this may be appropriate in most cases, sometimes different distances between test ages can result in very different developmental functions.

An interesting example involves physical growth, which usually is represented as a continuous, increasing growth curve. This is shown in Figure 1.1, where the

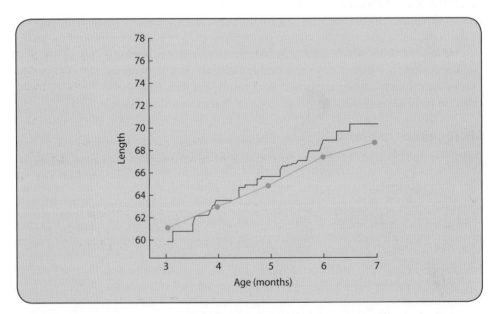

FIGURE 1.1 *A comparison of the continuous-growth function for length/height derived from averaged data from cross-sectional studies (the solid line connected by the filled circles) with the step-like function (sudden increases in length followed by periods of no growth) derived from daily measures on individual infants.*

filled circles connected by a solid line have been estimated from a normative study by Babson and Benda (1976) which is based on a combination of cross-sectional and longitudinal data. The function looks continuous, and the shape matches the monthly longitudinal data they reported for a few 'normally' growing individual infants. By contrast, a discontinuous step-like function was found by Lampl *et al.* (1992) when they made daily or weekly measures of the growth in the length of a small number of infants during the first 21 months from birth. Lampl *et al.* analysed individual growth functions and discovered that the main change in length occurred in sudden bursts followed by longer periods of no change, and they suggest that 90–95 per cent of development during infancy is growth free, and that throughout development continuous growth charts do not represent how individuals grow (Lampl & Thompson, 2007). Indeed, in daily measures, children were found to grow substantially, as much as 1 centimetre, in a sudden burst, in many cases overnight, and then not change for an average of 12 days. This is shown in Figure 1.1 where a summary of the growth pattern of one infant in Lampl *et al.*'s study is pictured by the thin line overlaying Babson and Benda's normative curve.

This may come as no great surprise to some parents who report that their babies seemed suddenly to outgrow their sleeper (or 'babygrow') overnight! The main point is that according to Lampl *et al.* changes in size occur in a discontinuous progression with the most common state being 'no change' at all. This developmental function is not revealed unless frequent measures are taken on individuals. It should be noted that if all of Lampl *et al.*'s data were collapsed across individuals and plotted as a function of monthly age groups, the curve probably would look like Babson and Benda's continuous age function.

Cohort effects A serious design problem, which is particularly relevant for studies covering a large age range, involves cohort effects. This is where there are changes across generations in the characteristic one is interested in. Here are a few examples of such effects.

- *Height:* the average height of the Western 20-year-old male has risen from around 5 ft 7 in (1.52 m) in the early 1900s to around 6 ft 0 in (1.83 m) by 2007. This has resulted from gradual improvements in diet which make foetal life in the womb and post-natal life healthier.
- *Attitudes:* There have been many changes in important psychological characteristics over generations. Consider, for example, current attitudes towards homosexuality – how do you think they have changed over the last 50 years?
- *Leisure activities:* Western children spend much more time in sedentary activities, such as watching television, playing video games, surfing the internet, etc. than their counterparts of 50 or 60 years ago.
- *Everyday life:* Huge changes have occurred in everyday life in recent generations which combine to produce substantial intergenerational psychological changes. In addition to changes in leisure activities consider the impact of better, more

FIGURE 1.2 *Watching television is now a common leisure activity for Western children.*

Source: Shutterstock.

intelligence quotient (IQ) an IQ score gives an indication of an individual's intelligence compared with other individuals of the same *chronological age*.

intelligence test Any test that aims to measure an individual's intellectual ability.

sequential design a combination of longitudinal and cross-sectional designs that examines the development of individuals from different age *cohorts*.

Flynn effect an increase in the average intelligence quotient (IQ) test scores over generations.

affordable cars and better transport in general, household appliances such as washing machines and televisions (Figure 1.2), electronic devices such as computers, mobile phones, iPods – the luxuries of yesteryear become today's necessities and, of course, electronic devices were not available a generation ago.

Intelligence: In much the same way that height has increased over generations, so too has measured intelligence (**intelligence quotient** or IQ as measured by **intelligence tests**). This means that the findings from early cross-sectional studies gave a different account of the development of intelligence across the life span than more recent studies – these findings are described in the next section.

Sequential designs

One possible way of investigating the different findings that might result from longitudinal and cross-sectional designs is with the use of what are called **sequential** or *age/cohort* designs. These studies involve a combination of designs, and are fairly rare (in large part because of the costs and time involved). We will illustrate this design with a schematic drawing of performance on one intelligence test (known as *visualisation performance* – the precise details of the test are not important for our purposes), adapted from Nesselroade *et al.*, 1972, which is shown in Figure 1.3. In this figure, adults in five different age groups (30, 37, 44, 51 and 58 years – the *cross-sectional* aspect of the study) were tested twice (seven years apart – the *longitudinal* part) giving us overlapping age groups.

The results show two effects. There is a *cohort effect*, resulting from testing different adults of different ages at about the same time: this is the lower performance by the older age groups, illustrated by the dotted line connecting the cross-sectional data. There is also a contrasting, *longitudinal effect*, where the same individuals tested at two ages show a slight improvement in performance over age, illustrated by the solid lines connecting each pair of longitudinal points for the five age groups. Thus, IQ scores have been increasing over generations, a phenomenon referred to as the **Flynn effect**.

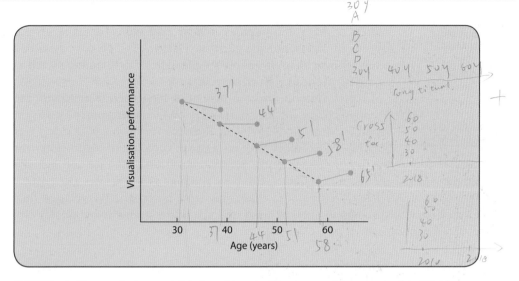

FIGURE 1.3 *The use of a sequential design with an intelligence test demonstrates that different results can emerge from cross-sectional findings (the cohort effect shown by the downward sloping dotted line) and longitudinal findings (the solid lines).*

However, when the same individuals are tested over time their scores remain relatively static. Thus, intelligence does not decline with age, but the environment has improved over successive generations. The Flynn effect is discussed in more detail later in this chapter, and also in Chapter 16.

Although sequential designs are not used often, when they are used they provide a measure of individual differences and reveal whether or not longitudinal and cross-sectional results agree. We now turn to an account of the different *research methods* which are used to collect data on children's development.

Research methods

The research designs that we have discussed always incorporate one or more developmental *research methods* in order to investigate development. Developmental psychologists employ a variety of methods, and here we will discuss some of the most important: **observational studies**, **experimental methods**, **psychological testing** and **correlational studies**.

Observational studies

Baby biographies Perhaps the simplest in form is the case study, which involves repeated observations of the same person over time. These observations are usually of infants, and are made by parents or caregivers who are close to the child. These are often called baby

observational studies studies in which behaviour is observed and recorded, and the researcher does not attempt to influence the individual's natural behaviour in any way.

experimental methods experimental methods control an individual's environment in systematic ways in an attempt to identify which variables influence the behaviour of interest.

psychological tests instruments for the quantitative assessment of some psychological attribute or attributes of a person.

correlational studies studies that examine whether two variables vary systematically in relation to each other, e.g. as height increases, will weight reliably increase also?

baby biographies
diaries detailing an infant's development, usually kept by the infant's parents or caregiver. Charles Darwin's biography of his eldest son's development is a well-known example.

diaries, or **baby biographies**, which may either describe several aspects of development, such as Darwin's biography described below, or may focus on a more specific type of development, such as emerging musicality (Forrester, 2010).

Charles Darwin wrote a delightful biographical sketch of the development of his first born son – William Erasmus Darwin (in Slater & Muir, 1999). William Erasmus (nicknamed 'Doddy') was born on 27 December 1839, but Darwin's account of his development was not published until 1877, by which time Charles and his wife Emma had had another nine children, five boys and four girls (Darwin, 1877/1999): thus Darwin was able to compare his eldest child with his others. We will give four extracts from this account in order to illustrate some of the strengths and weaknesses of such biographies:

Seeing: 'With respect to vision, – his eyes were fixed on a candle as early as the 9th day, and up to the 45th day nothing else seemed thus to fix them; but on the 49th day his attention was attracted by a brightly coloured tassel . . .'

Hearing: 'Although so sensitive to sound in a general way, he was not able even when 124 days easily to recognise whence a sound proceeded, so as to direct his eyes to the source.'

Anger: 'When two years and three months old, he became a great adept at throwing books or sticks, etc., at anyone who offended him; and so it was with some of my other sons. On the other hand, I could never see a trace of such an aptitude in my infant daughters; and *this makes me think that a tendency to throw objects is inherited by boys.*' (italics added)

Moral Sense: (When 2 years and 7½ months) 'I met him coming out of the dining room with his eyes unnaturally bright, and an odd unnatural or affected manner, so that I went into the room to see who was there, and found that he had been taking pounded sugar, which he had been told not to do. As he had never been in any way punished, his odd manner certainly was not due to fear and I suppose it was pleasurable excitement struggling with conscience. . . . *As this child was educated solely by working on his good feelings, he soon became as truthful, open, and tender, as anyone could desire.*' (italics added)

While such case studies provide a rich source of ideas and insights, they have many obvious weaknesses. Despite the fact that Darwin was one of the finest observers of natural behaviour who has ever lived, we now know that his account of the development of vision and hearing is wrong. As is described in Chapter 5 we know from careful experimentation that although vision at birth is poor it is sufficient for the infant to begin learning about the visual world: for instance, within hours from birth infants will prefer to look at their mother's face when hers is shown paired with that of a female stranger (Bushnell, 2003; see Figure 1.4). We also know that newborn infants can localise sounds at birth, an ability that Darwin was unable to detect in his son, even at 124 days (4 months). We will discuss auditory localisation later (under 'Developmental Functions').

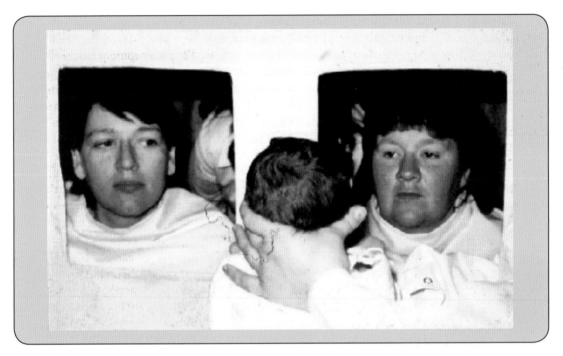

FIGURE 1.4 *Which one is mother? A few hours after birth newborn infants prefer to look at their mother's face.*
Source: Photograph by Ian Bushnell.

We can notice weaknesses in the italicised extracts from 'Anger' and 'Moral Sense': in both of these Darwin is expressing untested theoretical views which are derived either from observations of just a few children or from a 'folk theory of development' of the sort we discussed earlier. With respect to 'Anger', Darwin suggests that there may be inherited gender differences in acts of aggression, and indeed there is clear evidence that the majority of physically aggressive acts are committed by males. With respect to 'Moral Sense', note that Darwin is assuming that children brought up in the absence of physical punishment will display less anti-social behaviour in later life. We will comment on this later, in the section on 'Experimental Methods', but it turns out that Darwin was right: that is, the use of punishment is not a good way of changing behaviour, and children disciplined with the use of physical punishment are more likely to misbehave and become aggressive.

The weaknesses of such accounts include problems of generalisation – one or two children hardly constitute a representative sample of the population. Also, the observations tend to be unsystematic, and in many cases are retrospective – that is, events described long after their occurrence. Baby biographers may have strong theoretical biases which lead them to note anecdotes supporting their own theories.

The strengths of such accounts are primarily twofold: (1) the biographer can give a detailed account of subtle changes in behaviour because of their intimate knowledge of the child; (2) the observations can lead to the production of theories of child development, which can then be given a more systematic (often experimental) test.

Time and event sampling Time sampling is an observational method in which individuals are studied over a period of time, and at frequent brief intervals during this period a note is made – usually by an observer but sometimes by the individuals themselves – of whether or not certain behaviours of interest are occurring. For example, a researcher might watch a child over a 20-minute play period, noting every 30 seconds for a 5-second interval, whether the child is playing alone, playing with others, not playing, being aggressive, and so on.

> **Time sampling** an *observational study* that records an individual's behaviour at frequent intervals of time.

Here is one study to illustrate the use of this method. Lee and Larson (2000) sampled 56 high school seniors (17–18-year-olds) in Korea and 62 seniors (17-year-olds) in the United States. Each student was studied for one month and was provided with an electronic timer which gave a beep seven times a day at randomly spaced intervals over the period between approximately 7.00 am to 11.30 pm. Every time the beeper sounded the student was asked to note down (a) what they were doing, and (b) their affect state (i.e. whether they were happy, sad, etc.) as it was just before the beeper sounded. What they found was that the Korean students recorded many more times spent in schoolwork and much less time in other (e.g. recreational) activities than the American students. We know that academic stress heightens student anxiety levels (Leung *et al.*, 2010) and what Lee and Larson found that the Korean students experienced many more negative affect states (i.e. they were more depressed) than their American counterparts. This suggests that the Koreans' ordeal of studying in preparation for the competitive college entrance examinations was causing them considerable distress and depression.

> **affect** emotional state or feelings. Contrast with behaviour (what one does in a situation) and *cognition* (how one thinks about a situation).

This, and other time sampling studies, records the participants' behaviour at frequent intervals over a period of time, and simply notes what is happening at each recording period. (The aim is to get an idea of how frequently different behaviours occur during the total observation period.) However, there are two interrelated criticisms of time sampling. One is that the researcher may not get an accurate record of the amount of time spent in different behaviours – quite simply, many naturally occurring behaviours may not be happening when each behaviour sample is taken! The other is that many behaviours of interest may simply not occur, or might be missed, during the period that recording is taking place.

Event sampling is an alternative method that avoids these problems. As the name suggests, in this procedure the researchers actively select the type of event that they want to observe. This event is then recorded, usually *throughout* its time period (rather than at intervals as would be the case for time sampling) on a continuous basis – for this reason this type of event sampling is also known as *continuous sampling*, and it is the most common observation method used in child development research. There are innumerable events that are of interest to child psychologists. The following list, while long, is not exhaustive!

> **event sampling** an *observational study* which records what happens during particular events. Events studied include playing, bathtime, feeding, and reading.

> quarrels, anger episodes, fear episodes, frustration, success episodes, failure episodes, competition episodes, cooperation episodes, problem-solving, prosocial episodes, anti-social times, play with pets, play with others, solitary play, school recitations, toilet-training, discipline periods, first school day, bedtime activities, reading with mother, weaning, feeding, illness, vaccinations, school leisure times, mother–infant social engagements ...

Although these methods look like longitudinal designs their aim is to accumulate data systematically rather than to investigate change over time. A final point to note is that the baby biographies, referred to earlier, used both time and event sampling procedures, but not in a particularly systematic fashion.

The clinical method   The greatest developmental psychologist of all time, Jean Piaget, studied the development of his three children during their infancy. He kept very detailed records of their development, but instead of simply recording their development, which is typical of the baby biographers, he would note an interesting behaviour and then, in order to understand it better, he varied the task to note any changes in the infant's response. This technique, which is a combination of observation and loosely structured experimentation, is known as the **clinical method**. He also used this method extensively with other children, and an example of this method with children is given in Chapter 2. Here is a brief extract (Piaget, 1954, pp. 177–178) to illustrate the procedure – Piaget observed his son Laurent (aged 6 months 22 days) when reaching for objects:

clinical method
research method first used by Piaget whereby natural behaviour is observed and then the individual's environment is changed in order to understand better the behaviour of interest.

> Laurent tries to grasp a box of matches. When he is at the point of reaching it I place it on a book; he immediately withdraws his hand, then grasps the book itself. He remains puzzled until the box slides and thanks to this accident he dissociates it from its support.

Piaget's reasonable interpretation of this observation is that when one object is on top of, and hence touching, another object, his infant did not realise that there were two objects. In fact, it was not until he was 10 months old that he:

> immediately grasps matchboxes, erasers, etc., placed on a notebook or my hand; he therefore readily dissociates the object from the support (p. 178).

Experimental methods

The majority of investigations of child behaviour and development are experimental in nature. Behaviour does not occur, and development does not take place, without a *cause*. The aim of the experimenter is to specify, in as precise a manner as possible, the causal relationships between maturation, experience and learning, and behaviour. The essential aspect of experimental techniques is *control*. A situation is constructed which enables the experimenter to exert control over the causal variables

independent variable
a factor or variable in a study or experiment which can be systematically controlled and varied by the experimenter to see if there are changes in the child's response. The behaviour that changes is called the *dependent variable*.

dependent variable
the behaviour that is measured or observed in a study. Changes in the behaviour are dependent on, that is, caused by, changes to the *independent variable*.

that influence the behaviour of interest. One of these factors, which is called the **independent variable**, is varied in a systematic fashion, and objective measurements are made of any changes in the child's behaviour. The behaviour that is measured is called the **dependent variable** since (if all goes well!), changes in this behaviour are dependent upon, that is, caused by, changes in the independent variable. The following is a good example of application of the experimental method to a developmental phenomenon.

Why do infants grasp pictures of objects? Judy DeLoache and her colleagues have described one of the errors that children make with objects. This is where children seem to confuse objects with pictures and may try to pick up pictures as if they were the objects they depict.

FIGURE 1.5 *An example of a 3D toy car (top left) and three 2D representations of the car.*
Source: Photograph © Sophia Pierroutsakos. Reprinted with permission.

To illustrate the experimental method we will describe this effect. (DeLoache *et al.*, 1998). The famous Belgian experimental psychologist Albert Michotte (1881–1965) discussed the meaning of objects and the way in which a picture of an object represents the real object. Note that adults do not confuse objects with pictures except under special viewing conditions – perhaps looking with one eye, or being given *binocular stereoscopic images* (these are where slightly different images are presented to the two eyes so that they give the illusion of solidity and three-dimensionality). If someone were to ask us to pick up a pictured object we'd think them very strange! However, children often think differently.

DeLoache *et al.* (1998) tested 9-month-old infants and their *independent variable* was the extent to which the objects depicted in pictures looked like the real thing. They had four versions of pictorial representations, which were, in order of realism: (1) a highly realistic coloured photograph of real objects (such as a toy car); (2) a black-and-white photograph; [3] a coloured line drawing of the object; and (4) a black-and-white line drawing. All of the depicted objects measured approximately 3 cm × 3 cm, a size that matches the size of the infants' grasp. An illustration of these is given in Figure 1.5. Their *dependent variable* was the amount of manual investigation of the depicted objects, which included attempts at grasping them. The results are shown in Figure 1.6 and clearly show that the closer the depicted object is to the real object, the greater the amount of manual exploration. Sometimes, the pictured object is just too enticing! (Figure 1.7).

Deloache *et al.* had other experimental conditions. Their 1998 paper describes two experimental findings: a *cross-cultural* comparison – 9-month-old infants from two extremely different societies (the United States and the West African republic of

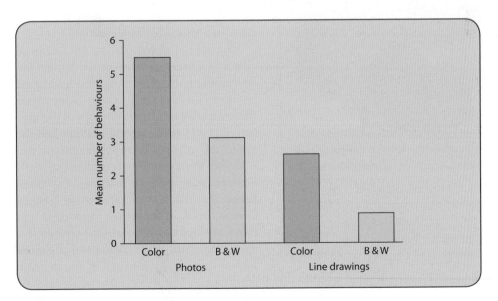

FIGURE 1.6 *Grasping and reaching behaviours were clearly related to how realistic the pictures were; the more the pictures looked like the real object, the more exploration they evoked.*

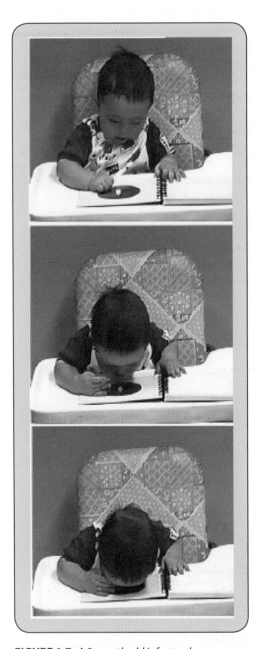

FIGURE 1.7 *A 9-month-old infant as he grasps and mouths a photograph of a baby bottle – the picture is just too enticing!*

Source: Photograph © Sophia Pierroutsakos. Reprinted with permission.

the Ivory Coast) produced the same reaching and grasping behaviour; a *cross-sectional* study, where different infants were tested at three different ages (9, 15 and 19 months) – the younger infants reached and grasped, by 15 months this behaviour was rare, and by 19 months of age they merely pointed at the pictures. Note that in this instance the *independent variable* is the age of the infants. In a further experimental condition 9-month-olds were presented with the realistic picture and the real object – in this condition none of the infants reached for the picture! Presumably, under these conditions the real object was clearly seen to be more realistic and graspable than the picture.

Deloache *et al.* interpret their intriguing results as indicating that the younger, 9-month-olds, do not understand the ways in which depicted objects are both similar to and different from real objects: when the real object is not present they treat the pictures as if they were real objects because in many ways they *look* like real objects. As they gain experience the infants develop a more sophisticated understanding of the relationship between the pictures and the objects they depict, and learn that pictures are *representations* of objects.

Deloache *et al.* are able to tell a convincing developmental story of the nature and development of infants' understanding of pictures and objects. In these experiments the independent variables – such as the realism of the pictorial representations and the age of the infants – were systematically varied, and the experimenters then carefully observed the babies' reaching responses. Sometimes this sort of experiment is called a **structured observation**, and there are those who would distinguish between this sort of experiment and those involving more formal or precise measures of the dependent variable. There is clearly an element of observation in many, perhaps most, experimental studies of children's development.

Psychological testing

Psychological tests can be defined as *instruments for the quantitative assessment of some psychological attribute or attributes of a person.* The developmental psychologist has available a wide variety of tests for measuring psychological functioning at all ages of childhood. These include tests of motor development, personality development, aptitudes (perhaps mechanical or musical or scholastic achievement), achievement, motivation, self-esteem, reading ability, general intelligence and many others.

Such tests are usually carefully standardised on large samples of children of the appropriate age groups, and norms (i.e. average scores and the range or spread of scores) for various age and gender groups are often available. Researchers, or testers, can compare their sample of children (or individual children) against the appropriate norms. Clear and precise instructions for administering and scoring the test items are usually included with the published test.

Types of test items   The type of item included in a particular test will depend both on the age group it is intended for and what is being measured. Tests of infant development usually consist of careful observations of the child when confronted with a number of standard situations: Can they stand alone? Can they build a tower of 5 bricks? and so on. Beyond about 2 years of age tests make increasing use of children's

> **structured observation**
> an *observational study* in which the *independent variable* is systematically controlled and varied, and the investigator then observes the child's behaviour. Similar to an experiment but the degree of control is less precise than in a laboratory setting.

FIGURE 1.8 *Building a brick tower – a test of infant development.*
Source: Shutterstock.

ability to use language, and the instructions given to the child are typically in a verbal form. Thus, in a test of intelligence the child might be asked to solve problems, to give the meanings of words, to say in what way(s) two or three words are similar in meaning, to trace a pathway through a maze, and so on.

Can test scores predict later development? Tests of ability and intelligence become increasingly accurate in predicting later behaviour (for example, school achievement) as children get older (Chapter 16 presents findings on the predictability of IQ scores in adolescence from scores obtained in earlier childhood). However, attempts to predict adult personality from measures of personality in earlier childhood have usually not been very successful. There are a couple of exceptions: children who are shy or bold as infants tend to become adults who are shy or bold; the child who fights with other children a lot is likely to become the adolescent who is judged by peers to be aggressive (see Chapter 15). In fact, aggression shows greater continuity across childhood and adolescence than any other facet of personality.

personality trait facet of a person's character that is relatively stable. Examples of personality traits include shyness, *extraversion*, and confidence.

However, the term *personality* is extremely difficult to define, and **personality traits** are difficult to measure precisely. One problem with measuring personality is that the most important personality traits – such as **extraversion**, **introversion**, sociability, suggestibility – are *social* in nature and may vary depending on the different types of social settings individuals find themselves in. Thus, although there may be some underlying stability of a shy/bold personality, the child who is sociable and outgoing with their family and friends may be shy and withdrawn in the classroom. Furthermore, changing life experiences alter behaviour and attitudes: an adolescent will be treated differently from a 7-year-old, and this will affect the way the individual behaves and responds.

extraversion a personality variable. Someone who scores highly on an extraversion scale will typically be an outgoing and confident person.

introversion a personality variable. Someone who scores highly on an introversion scale will typically be very quiet and reserved.

Uses of tests The uses of tests by developmental psychologists are many and varied. Tests are regularly used in *clinical* and *educational assessment*, to gain an understanding of an individual child and to see how they compare with others of the same age and gender.

Another use is to select groups of children for participation in an experiment, and then to evaluate the results of the experiment. Suppose a researcher is interested in evaluating a new scheme for teaching children to read. They may then wish to divide children into two groups of equal reading ability: to select these groups the researcher will give the children a standardised test of reading ability, and will perhaps also administer a test of general intelligence. On the basis of the test scores the children would be matched in terms of ability, usually in pairs. One of the matched pair will then be randomly assigned to the experimental and the other to the control group, resulting in two groups of children who are equated on the two variables of reading ability and intelligence. In this sort of experimental situation the group of children who receive the new reading scheme are often known as the **experimental group** (since they are to be experimented on!), and the other group, which simply receives the

experimental group the group of individuals who receive a particular treatment or manipulation. In order to measure the effectiveness of the treatment, their results are compared with those from a *control group* that does not receive the treatment.

FIGURE 1.9 *Teaching a young child to read.*

Source: Shutterstock.

usual, 'old' reading scheme, are the **control group**. When the two groups have had their different reading experiences they would then be assessed again on a standardised reading test: if the children in the experimental group now have higher reading scores than those in the control group we can perhaps conclude that the new reading scheme is a success!

> **control group** In order to evaluate the effectiveness of a particular treatment or manipulation, the control group is that group of individuals in an experiment who do not receive the treatment. Their behaviour is then compared with that of the *experimental group*, which does receive the treatment.

Correlational studies

Let us begin with a definition: a correlation coefficient is a statistic between $+1$ and -1 which indicates the extent to which two variables tend to be related or to vary together. A value close to $+1$ is a high positive correlation which tells us that the two variables are closely related. There are many instances of naturally occurring positive correlations: between height and weight (taller people tend to weigh more); between maths and English (students tend to be good, bad or indifferent at both!) There are innumerable instances of correlations that are close to zero (indicating no relationship): height is not correlated with academic performance; IQ is not correlated with sports achievement.

A correlation coefficient close to -1 is a high negative correlation which tells us that two variables are inversely related. There are fewer instances of negative correlations – perhaps amount of time spent watching television and school grades!

There are primarily two types of correlational studies that are of interest to the developmental psychologist, *concurrent* and *predictive*.

Concurrent studies A *concurrent* correlational study is where we are interested in the relationship between variables that are measured *at the same time*. An example of such a study would be to find out how similar the IQs of identical twins are. In this study we would give intelligence tests to pairs of identical twins and, if the correlation is high (which it almost certainly would be) this would tell us that if one twin had a high IQ the other one would also be bright; if one had a low IQ we could predict a low IQ for the other twin.

Predictive studies A *predictive* correlational study is one where we are interested in finding whether individuals retain their relative standing, or rank order, relative to others, over time. For example, does the bright child at age 5 turn out to be the gifted student at age 20?; does the outgoing child become an extraverted teenager?

Here is one example of a predictive correlational study, asking the question 'can we predict IQ in 3-year-olds from problem-solving in infancy?' This is a study carried out by Peter Willatts, a developmental psychologist at Dundee University, Scotland, UK. It begins with 9-month-old infants who were tested on what is called a *means-ends* problem-solving task. Each infant was shown an attractive toy which was placed out of reach on a cloth, and their job was then to grasp the cloth, pull it towards them – the means – in order to take the toy – the end. This doesn't sound too difficult, but babies only begin to string behaviours together to solve means-ends tasks around 7 or 8 months – at 9 months many can do it expertly (see Figure 1.10), but others are lagging behind. Willatts then gave the same infants the British Picture Vocabulary Test (BPVT) when they were 3 years 3 months old (the BPVT is the British version of the well-known American test the Peabody Picture Vocabulary Test, PPVT, which is a test of intelligence).

What Willatts found was that those 9-month-old infants who were best at the means-ends task tended to become the 3-year-olds with the higher IQs. The correlation was 0.64, and the relationship between the infants' scores at 9 months and their scores as children is shown in Figure 1.10. This figure is called a scattergram and is a graphical way of showing a correlation.

Correlational studies are thus important in telling us what sorts of abilities or psychological characteristics tend to go together (concurrent studies) and what abilities and characteristics predict later occurring behaviours (predictive studies).

Neurodevelopmental studies A particularly challenging task for developmental psychologists is to understand brain development and its relation to developments in perceptual, cognitive, social, and motor skills. This challenge is particularly acute for developmentalists because our subjects of interest – infants and children – can be difficult to test due to a general lack of cooperation or inability to cope with the methods, and also because the brain develops at a rapid pace early in life, making brain–behaviour links difficult to assess. Nevertheless, progress is being made with the judicious use of selective methods.

marker task a method designed to elicit a behaviour with a known neural basis.

Marker tasks A **marker task** refers to a method designed to elicit a behaviour with a known neural basis. Often the neural basis is discovered through experiments with animals, for which experiments on brain function present fewer ethical hurdles than experiments with

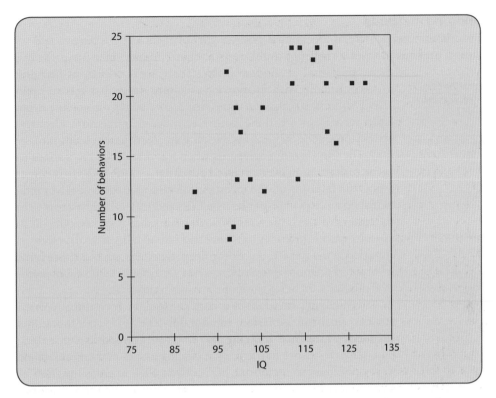

FIGURE 1.10 *Scattergram to show the relationship between the number of successful reaching behaviours at 9 months (vertical axis) and 3-year IQ (horizontal axis). The most successful infants turned out to be those with the higher IQs.*

Source: From Peter Willatts (1997).

humans. For example, much is known about the neural basis of visual function from experiments with monkeys. Visual attention in monkeys has been a subject of much investigation, and the neural underpinnings of different kinds of eye movements is fairly well known. It is thought that the visual system of rhesus macaques, a species of Old World monkeys, has a great deal of similarity to the human visual system, and researchers interested in the development of visual attention in humans have looked to the literature on monkeys for clues. Marker tasks have contributed much to this goal (Johnson, 1990). One prominent example comes from infants' ability to track moving objects using 'smooth pursuit' eye movements in which the point of gaze stays more or less locked on target as an object moves back and forth. Before 1-2 months of age, infants' tracking is jerky and frequently falls behind the object, necessitating numerous attempts to catch up to it. Johnson (1990) proposed that a specific area of the visual system known as the **medial temporal (MT) area** in the monkey has an analogue in the human, and development of this area and its connections with other parts of the visual system is responsible for the onset of smooth pursuit in humans. This is because damage to monkey MT causes deficits in motion tracking.

medial temporal (MT) area a specific area of the visual system. The development of this area and its connections with other parts of the visual system is responsible for the onset of smooth pursuit in humans.

Imaging methods

Recording brain activity in any animal poses a host of technical challenges, and no animal presents more of a challenge in this respect than a human child! Nevertheless, there are several methods available. There are two kinds of **imaging** used commonly with infants and children: those that record brain activity from the scalp, and those that record activity inside the head. Scalp recordings are done with electrodes that measure electrical activity produced by neurons, yielding an **electroencephalogram**, or *EEG*. The EEG is often measured when it is time-locked to a stimulus event, producing an **event-related potential**, or *ERP*. ERPs to different events can be compared to investigate developmental changes or individual differences in response. The EEG and ERP is highly sensitive to the timing of the brain's response to events, but it can be difficult to tap into specific brain regions with this method, because all activity is recorded at the surface. Accessing deep structures, such as those areas involved in memory or emotion, is not yet entirely feasible, but statistical methods are being developed to aid in this goal.

Two imaging methods are better suited to measuring cortical sources: **positron emission tomography**, or *PET*, and **functional magnetic resonance imaging**, or *fMRI*. PET works by measuring blood flow to tissues in the body, including tissues in the brain; blood flow is localised to regions of high activity. PET requires injection of a short-lived radioactive isotope, however, limiting its use to high-risk populations, and as such it is rarely used with infants and children. fMRI also measures blood flow, but involves no invasive procedures, instead recording by means of a strong magnetic field in which the participant is placed, which detects differences in oxygen concentration throughout the brain. fMRI has several disadvantages. It is expensive and it requires the participant to keep very still for lengthy periods, and the magnetic field itself is produced by a device that is very noisy – as loud as 120 dB. As such it is not suitable for widespread use with infants. At the time of this writing only a handful of published papers have reported fMRI data with infants and very young children, but it is increasingly being used with children aged 5 and older (Casey *et al.*, 2005).

imaging methods methods of recording brain activity.

electroencephalogram (EEG) a scalp recording done with electrodes that measure electrical activity produced by neurons.

event-related potential (ERP) scalp recordings in which brain activity is monitored during the presentation of specific perceptual events.

positron emission tomography (PET) an imaging method measuring cortical activity. PET works by measuring blood flow to tissues in the body, including tissues in the brain; blood flow is localised to regions of high activity.

functional magnetic resonance imaging (fMRI) an imaging method measuring cortical activity, which works by measuring blood flow, and involves no invasive procedures.

Choosing the method of study

It will be apparent that psychologists have available a great many research strategies and methods for observing, classifying, testing, and studying children's development. There are no hard and fast rules for determining which method should be used at a particular time, and the decision will depend on a number of considerations: the problem being investigated, the availability of participants, individual preferences of the researcher, and so on. In this section we will present the case for observation and the case for experimentation.

Observation versus experimentation As we have seen, observational studies are ideal for discovering questions to ask about various phases and aspects of children's development. Such studies can often lead to answers and theories, and they are often critical in allowing the researcher to generate hypotheses about aspects of development. We need always to remember that the child has a vast repertoire of behaviours that occur in natural settings. We can conclude that observational studies are ideal in studying children's behaviour and development in its natural context.

A common argument against the use of experimentation is that it often takes place in a highly controlled and unnatural setting: while experimental studies tell us a great deal about behaviour in such settings it sometimes happens that experimental findings have little bearing on real life – that is, it is often claimed that many experimental studies lack **ecological validity**. Typically, however, a great deal can be learned from experimental studies even when the experimental setting seems rather distant from real life. Additionally, it is clear that observational studies are less powerful than experimental studies when it comes to understanding the *causes of* development, or in testing hypotheses. To illustrate this point, we may find that children who are aggressive watch more violence on television. However, we cannot therefore infer that watching TV violence causes violent behaviour – it is possible that the relationship is the other way round, that is, that aggressive children seek out violence. To tease out the real cause–effect relationship we would need careful experimental studies in which the relevant variables were systematically varied.

> **ecological validity** the results obtained from a study are ecologically valid if they are meaningful in the real world.

Critical to the research process is the generation of hypotheses which can be systematically tested: hypotheses can be defined as *testable suppositions about the nature of reality.* In the example given above, one of the hypotheses tested by Judy Deloache and her team (1998) was 'infants will grasp more at pictured objects the more they resemble real objects', and this was tested by careful experimentation.

The well-controlled experiment allows relatively precise statements to be made about cause and effect. The degree of control required is often not easily attained in a natural setting, and experiments are often laboratory based, where a laboratory has no essential characteristics other than being a place in which the experimenter can exercise control over the relevant variables more easily than elsewhere. A laboratory may simply be a quiet room in a school or nursery, or it might be a purposely designed suite of rooms equipped with sophisticated equipment for measuring precise aspects of behaviour.

Experimentation allows us to explore avenues of research that could not easily be investigated by the use of observation alone. We have seen that Charles Darwin was quite wrong in his suggestion that the young infant's vision and hearing are extremely poor and our understanding of infants' development has only begun to emerge because of careful experimental findings – an account of some of these findings is given in Chapter 5.

BEYOND COMMON SENSE: THE IMPORTANCE OF RESEARCH EVIDENCE

Sometimes, when psychologists publish their findings we hear remarks such as 'What a waste of money! Everybody knows people behave like that!' Such comments assume that common observation is an adequate substitute for controlled observation and experimentation. However, everyday observation of human behaviour and 'folk' theories of development are notoriously unreliable, and in our impressions and interpretations of behaviour we are often unaware of the controlling and causative variables. We should also remember that there are often different and diametrically opposed 'folk' theories of development – see earlier in the chapter – and appropriate research evidence is needed to choose between them, or to show that they are all wrong!

Here are a few examples, some drawn from the accounts given earlier, which serve to convince us that systematic investigations are necessary to help us to understand human behaviour and development.

- We now know that babies can see reasonably well at birth, and that they can hear speech and other sounds even while in the womb. To paraphrase an eminent developmental psychologist, Annette Karmiloff-Smith (1994, p. 133): 'When two heavily pregnant women are talking to each other there are four people listening to the conversation.' Compare our current knowledge with Charles Darwin's assumption (given at the beginning of this chapter) that vision and hearing are almost non-functional at birth.

- Everybody 'knows' that children are more likely to do something for which they have been rewarded than *not* to do something for which they have been punished: we now know, from many experiments both with animals and humans, that punishment is a very ineffective way of controlling behaviour (Mazur, 1990). Contrast this view with the view implied by the expression discussed earlier: 'Spare the rod and spoil the child.' Psychological findings have influenced governments such that physical punishment of children in schools is banned by many states and countries, and some countries have banned parents from smacking their children.

- It has been widely held that a child's aggressive behaviours may be reduced by observing aggression through television programmes, movies and the like. This view has been called the **catharsis hypothesis**, the notion being that aggressive tendencies would be 'drained off' by the vicarious act of observing aggression. However, several decades of carefully designed experiments with children and adolescents have shown that observing aggression is likely to *increase,* rather than decrease, children's tendencies to behave aggressively towards others.

catharsis hypothesis the argument that watching aggressive tendencies in others will reduce your own feelings of aggression.

- We all know that tender loving care (TLC) is just as important as good nutrition in promoting favourable child development, but this was not always thought to be the case. In the 1920s and 1930s there was puzzlement as to why it was that children reared in orphanages, with a lack of care and attention, but with adequate nutrition, were 'failing to thrive' and there were high infant mortality rates. We now know that it was lack of affection and interaction with caring adults that resulted in these negative outcomes (see Chapter 6 for emotional development and attachments).

- No-one is surprised that the young child performs rather poorly on many tests of memory when compared with older children. The obvious reasons for the younger children's poorer performance is that they simply have a more limited memory capacity – that they have fewer 'slots' in which to put new information. Research has shown this view to be false: older children's better performance results from what they *do* to try and remember, and not from an increased memory capacity (Chapter 13 gives a detailed account of memory development).

- In the past it has often been assumed that infants almost exclusively needed their mother's care, and that alternative caregiving (fathers, older siblings or other relatives, child minders, day care) would have adverse effects on their development. We now know that infants' development can proceed normally if they have multiple caregivers, so long as they receive consistent and predictable care. This understanding was only recently established: for example, we know that infants can form multiple attachments, and that the mother is not necessarily the one with whom the infant has its closest bond. Many studies have demonstrated that adequate day care has no damaging effects on development.

- Some 50 years ago it was widely believed that language development began when infants spoke their first meaningful word, around 1 year of age. However, we now know that by this age infants have learned an enormous amount about their native language and, in normally hearing infants, this learning begins prior to birth. An account of language development is given in Chapter 10.

Social policy implications of child development research

In the latter part of the 20th century, and with increasing emphasis in the 21st century, developmental researchers have applied their vast store of knowledge to the implementation of **social policies** which are intended to improve children's well-being and to help them achieve their full potential. This is a world-wide endeavour, assisted by such bodies as the international Society for Research in Child Development (SRCD). In the previous section we have seen that child development research has implications for early visual development, discipline procedures, day care, and the provision of adequate psychological care.

Other social policy implications abound and include: the implementation, provision and assessment of early intervention schemes (such as the **Head Start** programme in the USA and its counterpart **Sure Start** in the UK – these are schemes aimed at alleviating the worst social and cognitive deficits that result from neglect and poverty in early childhood); programmes to reduce the amount of bullying in the school and its effects on the bullied; early detection and treatment of childhood disorders such as autism, dyslexia, and many others; combating the potential negative effects of parental divorce on children; detection and effective intervention in cases of child abuse and neglect; provision of effective health care for pregnant mothers-to-be and for young infants and children.

social policies actions, rules, and laws aimed at solving social problems or attaining social goals, in particular intended to improve existing conditions.

Head Start and Sure Start A federally supported programme in the United States with five components: (1) preschool enrichment education; (2) health screening and referral services; (3) nutrition education and hot meals; (4) social services; and (5) parent education and involvement. Research has indicated that children's cognitive and language development is enhanced during the period that they are participating in a Head Start programme. The British equivalent is called Sure Start.

You will be able to think of many other areas of concern relating to children's development. The essential point is that research into children's development is not simply the accumulation of information: it has a practical purpose, which is to understand better the development of the child in order to provide better attention to the requirements of children and families.

DEVELOPMENTAL FUNCTIONS: GROWING AND CHANGING

From the data that developmental psychologists collect, analyse and interpret, it is possible to describe a number of **developmental functions**, or developmental trends – that is, the ways in which humans typically grow and change with age. Developmental functions are presented in graphs similar to those in Figure 1.11. Usually, the measure of behaviour (or behavioural change) is represented on the vertical, Y-axis, and age or time is on the horizontal, X-axis. The practical value of such functions is that they allow us to detect unusual developmental patterns (e.g. developmental delays) and to intervene with treatment as and when appropriate. The theoretical value is that the data can be used to evaluate hypotheses derived from various theoretical perspectives by comparing *theoretical* schematic plots such as those in Figure 1.1 with *empirically derived* functions, where the latter are the data that are collected. Human development of course is extremely complex, and different aspects of development grow and change in different ways. Figure 1.11 shows five of the most commonly found functions, and we will give examples of development which match each of them.

> **developmental functions** typical trends in development; for example, we typically get more intelligent as we age.

Continuous function (a) – increasing ability

Perhaps the most common developmental function found in textbooks is the one shown in Figure 1.11(a) in which we simply get better, or increase in an ability or quantity with age. Examples include the negatively accelerating change in the height and weight of children which increase rapidly during the first few years of life, more gradually during childhood, and level off after adolescence. We should note that although height and weight are typically considered to be *continuous* in their development, research by Lampl *et al.* mentioned earlier (see Figure 1.1) suggests that changes in height might be *discontinuous* at times. Another example with a shorter timescale is the precision in reaching for and grasping an object, which gradually increases during the first year of life as infants practise and receive feedback from their errors. Intelligence is another example – as children grow older they become more intelligent, and this levels off during adolescence. We will return to the development of intelligence (and whether its development is continuous or discontinuous!) when we compare developmental functions.

> **continuous function – increasing ability** behaviour that improves with age. For example, during the first year of life the precision with which infants reach for objects increases.

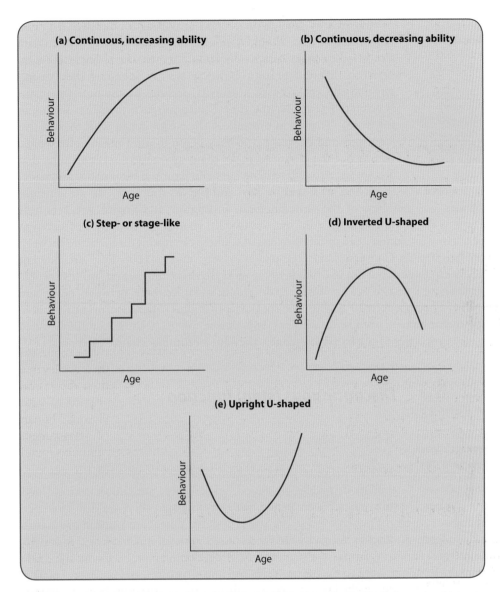

FIGURE 1.11 *Five of the most common developmental functions, illustrating the ways in which people typically grow and change with age: (a) continuous, increasing ability; (b) continuous, decreasing ability; (c) step- or stage-like; (d) inverted U-shaped; and (e) upright U-shaped. Usually (as here), the measure of behaviour, or changes in behaviour, is represented on the vertical, Y-axis, and age or time is on the horizontal, X-axis.*

Continuous function (b) – decreasing ability

It seems odd to think of aspects of development where we get *worse* rather than *better* as we grow up! As you can imagine there are few of these developmental functions. The clearest example is found in speech perception in early infancy (language development is discussed in detail in Chapter 10).

continuous function – decreasing ability behaviour that gets worse as we age. For example, young infants can initially distinguish non-native speech sounds very easily; however, for many sounds they lose this ability after their first year of life.

Research by Janet Werker and her colleagues has demonstrated that young infants, around 6 months of age, are able to discriminate almost every slight variation in sound (that is, the phonetic contrast between different phones, however similar sounding they seem), but that this broad-based sensitivity declines by the time the infant is around 1 year old (the time babies produce their first meaningful word). That is, as a result of their experience with their native language, and particularly as they begin to utter meaningful words, infants *lose* the ability to make many phonetic discriminations that are not used to differentiate between words in their native language.

For example, both the [k] sound in 'key' and the [k] sound in 'ski' are different phones, but members of the same phoneme in English, and English speakers hear them as the same sound. In contrast, the two [k] sounds are members of different phonemes in Chinese. As a result, speakers of Chinese can readily discriminate between the two sounds. Conversely, the [r] sound as in 'very' and the [l] in 'loud' are different phones in English but not in Chinese or Japanese, so that Chinese and Japanese people from about 1 year of age are unable to discriminate, for example, between 'berry' and 'belly'. Thus, speakers of English and speakers of Chinese differ in terms of their ability to discriminate sounds. As Werker (1989) puts it, infants become exquisitely tuned to the properties of the native language – they are 'becoming a native listener'.

discontinuous (step) function where development takes place in a series of stages, where each new stage appears to be *qualitatively* different from the preceding (and following) stages.

Discontinuous (step) function

A second, common function is where development takes place in a series of stages, where each new stage appears to be *qualitatively* different from the preceding (and following) stages (Figure 1.11(c)). It is easy to describe different major stages in the human lifespan such as infancy, preschool childhood, middle childhood, adolescence, adulthood, and old age: thus, infancy is the period 'without language', there are clear biological changes occurring at puberty, and so on. Stages of development are found in many areas of development. Piaget's theory (which is discussed in detail in Chapters 2, 9, and 16) is the most famous example of a stage theory of development. In his theory the child's thinking from one stage to the next involves different structures, and undergoes qualitative change: the young child will believe in Father Christmas, but this belief disappears around age 7; the adolescent, but not the younger child, is capable of abstract thought.

A stage-like progression of specific skills or processes also exists, such as in the development of mobility in the infant. Here the vertical, Y-axis on a graph could be distance travelled by an infant, which suddenly accelerates at different points in time matching the onset of various mobility accomplishments. Infants are relatively immobile during the first few months of life, begin to crawl around 6–8 months of age, stand up and toddle around furniture a few months later, and begin to walk on their own between 12–18 months of age (the time at which parents move all small objects out of the infant's reach!)

The onset of these mobility milestones seems to occur rather abruptly, and each one represents a qualitatively different type of locomotion suggesting a stage-like progression. Another example is the development of speech – an initial period of no word production is followed by a period of babbling beginning around 9 months of age when infants make speech-like sounds in a flowing 'conversation' which contains no words. Infants begin to use single words around 12 months of age, produce two- to three-word phrases at about 18 months, and, finally, produce complex grammatical sentences. These major milestones, which appear to be qualitatively different, also have been conceptualised as stages.

Many other step-like functions have been described, for example in the child's acquisition of a **theory of mind** (Chapter 11), in the **moral judgement stages** (Chapter 15).

> **theory of mind** the understanding that different people may have different emotions, feelings, thoughts, and beliefs from one's own.

U-shaped functions

Two other types of developmental functions are inverted and upright **U-shaped functions**. When we consider development across the lifespan, an *inverted U-shaped developmental function*, illustrated in Figure 1.11(d), is commonly observed. One example is the development of visual acuity which is poor at birth, increases rapidly during the first few months of life, and diminishes during the latter part of the lifespan. Inverted U-shaped functions can also be found during shorter time periods. For example, babbling is not present at birth, emerges around 6 months of age, and disappears without a trace a few months later (see Chapter 10). Of course, some might argue that it does emerge again during adulthood – perhaps during university lectures!

> **moral judgement stages** Piaget described two stages in the development of moral reasoning: heterono-mous and autonomous. Kohlberg described five stages: punishment and obedience orientation, instrumental morality, interpersonal normative morality, social system morality, and human rights and social welfare morality.

Inverted U-shaped functions are extremely common in development – we improve in the early years, stabilise or level off in adulthood, and get worse as we get older! Biological as well as psychological development often shows this function: thus, we reach our muscular and athletic peak in adolescence and early adulthood, and from about 30 years of age or thereabouts our abilities decline.

The other U-shaped function, shown in Figure 1.11(e) involves abilities which may be present early in life and disappear to re-emerge at a later age. One example is the ability of newborn infants to turn their heads and eyes towards sounds. This dramatic auditory localisa-

> **U-shaped functions** behaviour where abil-ity is initially very good, then decreases, and then increases again follows a U-shaped function of development. An inverted U-shaped func-tion follows the opposite trend, initially poor, then getting better, and then becoming poor again.

tion response is present at birth, diminishes or disappears at around 6 weeks of age, and re-appears again around 4 months of age (Muir *et al.*, 1994). Another example is the common observation that infants will display coordinated alternating step-like movements at birth, if they are supported in an upright position and held so that the soles of their feet are touching a solid surface. This amazing ability seems to disappear when infants are a few months old and re-appears again when they begin to stand and walk, around 12 months of age.

This 'stepping reflex' gives the impression that the baby is 'walking' (Zelazo, 1983), and it was only a few years ago that some 'experts' were encouraging parents to keep exercising this stepping response in very young infants with the assumption that they would then learn to walk earlier. In fact, it turns out that the stepping reflex is the remains of the kicking movements that appear near the end of pregnancy, and these serve two vital functions: (1) they prevent the legs from becoming locked or stiffened in the cramped space in the womb; and (2) they reposition the foetus so that it can be delivered in the normal manner. Although the stepping reflex, and later walking, use the same muscles, it turns out that they are qualitatively different, both in the underlying brain systems that control them and in the patterns of muscular coordination.

Comparing developmental functions

It can be useful to plot more than one developmental function on the same graph. Possible causal relationships may be suggested by doing so. In the case of the U-shaped auditory localisation function, Humphrey *et al.* (1988) compared the developmental functions for auditory localisation responses and orientation to schematic faces, from birth to 5 months of age, shown in Figure 1.12(a). When there is a minimum in the performance of head turning to off-centred sounds (i.e. it is very difficult to elicit), there is a maximum in looking time at the faces. They speculated that competition between the two stimulus–response systems occurred, with the most rapidly changing system, visual attention, predominating.

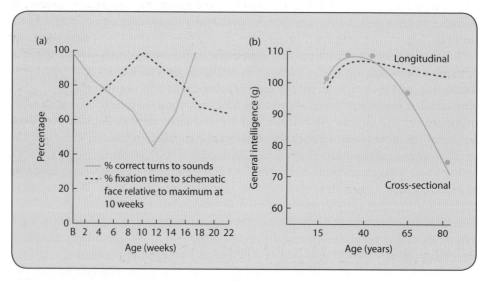

FIGURE 1.12 *Comparing developmental functions: (a) compares the developmental course of the U-shaped auditory localisation response function with that of the inverted U-shaped function for interest in a schematic face (reported in Humphrey et al., 1988); (b) shows the results from longitudinal (continuous function) and cross-sectional (inverted U-shaped function) studies of intellectual growth across a wide age span.*

Source: (a) ©1988, Canadian Psychological Association. Permission granted for use of material.

Uttal and Perlmutter (1989) provide a number of comparisons between developmental functions for older children and adults which illustrate possible causal relationships. One example has to do with the maintenance of typing speed by professional typists as they age. The developmental function tends to be flat over much of the life span. This is a puzzle because it is well known that as people age they have a slower reaction time, which should therefore slow down the typist's keystroke speed. It turns out that as keystroke speed declines, older typists increase their letter span (the number of words they code as a unit, which are then run off automatically by the fingers). This cognitive skill, which increases with practice, may compensate for the loss of keystroke speed.

We will make one final comparison, to do with the development of intelligence. Sometimes it is useful to think of intelligence as developing in a qualitative, stage-like manner (as in Figure 1.11(c)). However, sometimes it is convenient to think of intelligence as growing in a quantitative manner. This is the assumption that underlies most intelligence tests – as children get older they become able to solve, or answer, more and more of the items in the tests. With this latter assumption we find that children's measured intelligence (the raw scores they obtain on IQ tests) increases until adolescence, and then it levels off or stabilises. And then what happens? In the 1940s and 1950s there were many cross-sectional studies in which people of different ages, from young adults to the very elderly, were given the same intelligence tests. The clear finding was that the development of intelligence followed an inverted-U function (as in Figure 1.11(d)) – people simply got less intelligent as they approached middle- and old-age.

However, during the 1950s and 1960s the findings from longitudinal studies, in which the same people had been tested over many years, began to emerge. These findings were that intelligence did not decrease as people got older, rather scores on intelligence tests have simply been increasing over generations, most likely attributable to a number of factors which include improvements in nutrition, health and education, and smaller family size. As mentioned earlier, this is called the *Flynn effect*, named after James R. Flynn, the psychologist who documented it and described its implications (Flynn,1998, 2009; Lynn, 2009, and see Chapter 16). An idealised drawing of the findings from this work is shown in Figure 1.12(b), which illustrates the finding that the developmental functions of intellectual performance derived from *cross-sectional studies* decrease with age, while those derived from *longitudinal studies* may show little change with age.

SUMMARY AND CONCLUSIONS

Human development is extremely complex and multi-faceted. Not surprisingly, therefore, there are many ways of studying development and many different types of developmental functions that emerge from the research as scientists try to understand the ways in which children grow and change. Sometimes the story that is told gets confusing. For instance we have seen that the development of intelligence can be described as a continuously increasing function (the child simply gets better with age) – this is the assumption underlying intelligence tests. But sometimes it is better to think of the child's thinking as changing in a step-like, qualitative fashion, a view that is central to Piaget's theory of development. We have also seen that early research suggested that intelligence declined with age, but now we think that it doesn't (which is encouraging news for us all!).

As you read the remainder of the book you will find innumerable examples of longitudinal and cross-sectional studies, of the different developmental methods that are used, and of the different developmental functions that are found. It will be helpful to have a clear idea of these different designs, methods and functions. This basic understanding will help you understand better the ways in which researchers are gradually unlocking the secrets of children's development.

DISCUSSION POINTS

1. Think of the differing views that parents have about rearing their children. Is there scientific evidence for these 'folk' theories?

2. Consider the differences between organismic and mechanistic theories of development. How might these perspectives be helpful in understanding different areas of development?

3. What are the important differences between longitudinal and cross-sectional studies of development?

4. Why is it important to have both observational and experimental studies of development?

5. Think of ways in which the findings of developmental psychology go beyond common sense.

6. Consider the different developmental functions that describe how children grow and change. Why is it important to have these different functions?

SUGGESTIONS FOR FURTHER READING

Coolican, H. (2009). *Research methods and statistics in psychology* (5th edn). London: Hodder Education.

Harris, M. (2008). *Exploring developmental psychology*. London: Sage.

McNaughton, G., Rolfe, S., & Siraj-Blatchford, I. (2001). *Doing early childhood research: Theory and practice*. London: Open University Press.

Christensen, P., & James, A. (1999). *Research with children*. London: Routledge-Falmer.

Greig, A. D., & Taylor, J. (1998). *Doing research with children*. London: Sage.

Haslam, S. A., & McGarty, C. (1998). *Doing psychology*. London: Sage.

REFERENCES

Babson, T., & Benda, G. (1976). Growth graphs for the clinical assessment of infants of varying gestational age. *Journal of Pediatrics, 89*, 814–820.

Benoit, D., & Parker, K. (1994). Stability and transmission of attachment across three generations. *Child Development, 65*, 1444–1456.

Bushnell, I. W.R. (2003). Newborn face recognition. In O. Pascalis & A. Slater (Eds.) *Face: The development of face processing in infancy and early childhood* (pp. 41–53). New York: NOVA Science Publishers.

Casey, B.J., Tottenham, N., Liston, C., & Durston, S. (2005). Imaging the developing brain: What have we learned about cognitive development? *Trends in Cognitive Sciences, 9*, 104–110.

Darwin, C. (1877/1999). A biographical sketch of an infant. In A. Slater and D. Muir (Eds.), *The Blackwell reader in developmental psychology* (pp. 18–26). Oxford and Massachusetts: Blackwell.

Deloache, J.S., Pierroutsakos, S.L., Uttal, D.H., Rosengren, K.S., & Gottlieb, A. (1998). Grasping the nature of pictures. *Psychological Science, 9*, 205–210.

Fifer, W. (2010). Prenatal development and risks. In G. Bremner & T. Wachs (Eds.), *The Blackwell handbook of infant development*. Oxford: Wiley/Blackwell.

Flynn, E., Pine, K., & Lewis, C. (2006). The microgenetic method – Time for a change? *The Psychologist, 19*, 152–155.

Flynn, J.R. (1998). Searching for justice: The discovery of IQ gains over time. *American Psychologist, 54*, 5–20.

Flynn, J.R. (2009). Requiem for nutrition as the cause of IQ gains: Raven's gains in Britain 1938–2008. *Economics and Human Biology, 7*, 18–27.

Forrester, M.A. (2010). Emerging musicality during the pre-school years: A case study of one child. *Psychology of Music, 38*, 131–158.

Gestsdottir, S., & Lerner, R.M. (2008). Positive development in adolescence: The development and role of intentional self-regulation. *Human Development, 51*, 202–224.

Golding, J. (2010). Determinants of child health and development: The contribution of ALSPAC – a personal view of the birth cohort study. *Archives of Disease in Childhood, 95*, 319–322.

Hepper, P. (2007). Prenatal development. In A. Slater & M. Lewis (Eds), *Introduction to infant development* (2nd ed; pp. 41–62). Oxford: Oxford University Press.

Hultsch, D., & Deutsch, F. (1981). *Adult development and aging: A life-span perspective*. New York: McGraw-Hill.

Humphrey, G., Dodwell, P., Muir, D., & Humphrey, D. (1988). Can blind infants and children use sonar sensory aids? *Canadian Journal of Psychology, 42*, 94–119.

Johnson, M.H. (1990). Cortical maturation and the development of visual attention in early infancy. *Journal of Cognitive Neuroscience, 2*, 81–95.

Karmiloff-Smith, A. (1994). *Baby it's you*. London: Ebury.

Lampl, M., & Thompson, A.L. (2007). Growth charts do not describe individual growth biology. *American Journal of Human Biology, 19*, 643–653.

Lampl, M., Veldhuis, J., & Johnson, M. (1992). Saltation and stasis: A model of human growth. *Science, 258*, 801–803.

Lee, M., & Larson, R. (2000). The Korean 'examination hell': Long hours of studying, distress and depression. *Journal of Youth and Adolescence, 29*, 249–271.

Lerner, R. (1986). *Concepts and theories of human development* (2nd edn). New York: Random House.

Leung, G.S.M., Yeung, K.C., & Wong, D.F.K. (2010). Academic stressors and anxiety in children: The role of parental support. *Journal of Child and Family Studies, 19*, 90–100.

Lynn, R. (2009). What has caused the Flynn effect? Secular increases in the Developmental Quotients of children. *Intelligence, 37*, 16–24.

Mazur, J.E. (1990). *Learning and behavior* (2nd edn). New Jersey: Prentice Hall.

Muir, D., Humphrey, D., & Humphrey, K. (1994). Pattern and space perception in young infants. *Spatial Vision, 8*, 141–165.

Nesselroade, J., Schaie, K., & Baltes, P. (1972). Ontogenetic and generational components of structural and quantitative change in adult behavior. *Journal of Gerontology, 27*, 222–228.

Piaget, J. (1954). *The construction of reality in the child*. New York: Basic Books.

Sants, J., & Barnes, P. (1985). Childhood. In *Personality, development and learning* (Unit 2) [Open University second level course]. Milton Keynes: The Open University Press.

Shaffer, A., Burt, K.B., Obradovic, J., Herbers, J.E., & Masten, A.S. (2009). Intergenerational continuity in parenting quality: The mediating role of social competence. *Developmental Psychology, 45*, 1227–1240.

Slater, A., & Muir, D. (Eds) (1999). *The Blackwell reader in developmental psychology*. Oxford: Blackwell.

Uttal, D., & Perlmutter, M. (1989). Toward a broader conceptualization of development: The role of gains and losses across the life span. *Developmental Review, 9*, 101–132.

Wallace, D.B., Franklin, M.B., & Keegan, R.T. (1994). The observing eye: A century of baby diaries. *Human Development, 37*, 1–29.

Werker, J.F. (1989). Becoming a native listener. *American Scientist, 77*, 54–59.

Zelazo, P.R. (1983). The development of walking: New findings and old assumptions. *Journal of Motor Behavior, 15*, 99–137.

2 Theories and Issues in Child Development

Scott P. Johnson, Alan Slater and Ian Hocking

KEY TERMS

accommodation • animism • assimilation • behaviour genetics • bottom-up structures • castration complex • centration • cephalocaudal trend • chromosomes • classical conditioning • cognitive adaptations • concrete operations stage • connectionism • conservation tasks • constructivism • continuity versus discontinuity • critical period • dynamic systems theory • ego • egocentric • Electra complex • ethological approaches • formal operations stage • functional invariants • gender constancy • gender development • hierarchy of needs • humanistic theory • id • imprinting • information processing • introspectionism • law of effect • mechanistic world view • microgenetic studies • monotropy • motor milestones • nature–nurture issue • object unity • observational learning • Oedipus complex • operant conditioning • organismic world view • perception of causality • precocial species • preoperational stage • primary drives • proximodistal trend • psychoanalysis • psychoanalytic theory • psychosexual stages • psychosocial stages • reaction formation • reductionism • schemes • secondary drive • self-actualisation • sensorimotor stage • social cognitive theory • social learning theory • stability versus change • strange situation • strategies • superego • theory of development • top-down structures • zone of proximal development

CHAPTER OUTLINE

OVERVIEW

This chapter sets the theoretical background for the material in the chapters to follow. The coverage of theoretical approaches is broad, and will give the reader a good introduction to the diversity of explanations of children's development.

First, different theories of motor development are outlined, and the authors point to the advantages of dynamic systems theory according to which motor development is a product of the interplay between brain structure, the structure and dynamics of the body, and the structure of the environment.

Next, the chapter considers theories of cognitive development. Piaget's stage theory is central here, and receives a thorough treatment. His theory is contrasted with the information processing account. Whereas Piaget's theory treats early deficits in thought as due to lack of logical ability, information processing accounts identify processing deficits as the problem, in particular, limitations in memory.

A large number of theoretical approaches stress the social environment in some way or other. Vygotsky's theory treats higher cognitive structures as coming from the social world, becoming internalised as a result of interactions with knowledgeable others. Behaviourist theories are all based on the principle that the social world, and in particular the parents, shape the behaviour of the individual, and the best example of application of these accounts to child development is Albert Bandura's social learning theory.

Other theories have their origins in evolutionary theory, and the best example in developmental psychology is attachment theory, originally formulated by John Bowlby, according to which formation of a secure emotional attachment between infant and caregiver is a vital prerequisite for emotional stability. Attachment theory is closely related to psychoanalytic approaches, the prime example being Freud's theory of psychosexual development, according to which emotional problems in adulthood can be traced to problems the child encountered in one of the psychosexual stages. Humanistic theories bear certain similarities to psychoanalytic theory. For instance, Maslow's account proposes a hierarchy of needs that humans must achieve to reach a satisfactory adult state.

The authors summarise the sections on theories by pointing out, through examples, the fact that different theories are not necessarily mutually exclusive. Often, one theory explains some aspects of behaviour, while another theory fills in more of the story.

The chapter ends by summarising some key issues that will reappear in the pages that follow, namely the nature–nurture issue, stability versus change, and continuity versus discontinuity in development. Different theories very clearly say different things with respect to these distinctions, and the challenge for developmental psychology is to weigh these different accounts against each other.

THEORIES IN CHILD DEVELOPMENT

Es gibt nichts Praktischeres als eine gute Theorie.

Emmanuel Kant (1724–1804)

or …

There is nothing so practical as a good theory.

Kurt Lewin (1944, p. 195)

INTRODUCTION

Human development is rich, varied, and enormously complex. We should not expect, therefore, that any single theory of development will do justice to this complexity, and indeed no theory attempts to do this. Each theory attempts to account for only a limited range of development and it is often the case that within each area of development there are competing theoretical views, each attempting to account for the same aspects of development. We will see some of this complexity and conflict in our account of different theoretical views, and in Chapter 1 we have seen that different ways of studying children lead to different developmental functions, and these are linked with different theoretical views.

Before beginning our account of theories of development it is helpful to say what we mean by a theory, as this is a term that has many definitions.

theory of development a scheme or system of ideas that is based on evidence and attempts to explain, describe, and predict behaviour and development.

For our purposes a **theory of development** is a scheme or system of ideas that is based on evidence and attempts to explain, describe and predict behaviour and development. From this account it is clear that a theory attempts to bring order to what might otherwise be a chaotic mass of information – for this reason we can see why 'there is nothing so practical as a good theory'!

In every area of development there are at least two kinds of theory which we can call the minor and the major. What we are calling *minor* theories are those which deal only with very specific, narrow areas of development. So, for example, there are theories about the way in which eye movements develop, about the origins of pointing, and so on. *Major* theories are those which attempt to explain large areas of development, and it is these that are the focus of this chapter.

To make our account of theories more orderly and understandable, we have divided them into six broad groups:

- Motor development
- Cognitive development
- Social-cognitive development
- Evolution and ethology
- Psychoanalytic theories
- Humanistic theory

MOTOR DEVELOPMENT

motor milestones the basic motor skills acquired in infancy and early childhood, such as sitting unaided, standing, crawling, walking.

One of the most obvious signs of development in infancy is the baby achieving the various **motor milestones**. Parents are very proud of these acquisitions and they are a focus of parental conversations about their infants – 'Billy can sit now', 'Helen has just started to crawl', 'Jimmy can walk without help', 'Rachel loves to climb up stairs'. The development of motor skills has very important implications for other aspects of development. The ability to *act* on the world affects all other aspects of development, and each new accomplishment brings with it an increasing degree of independence. For example, when infants begin to crawl they become independently mobile and one of the major transitions in early development begins. These changes affect emotional and social development, communication, appreciation of heights, and an understanding of distance and space (Campos *et al.*, 2000).

Table 2.1 charts the sequence of development of various motor milestones during infancy. At birth the infant has a number of well-developed motor skills, which include sucking, looking, grasping, breathing, crying – skills that are vital for survival. However, the general impression of the newborn is one of uncoordinated inability and general weakness. Movements of the limbs appear jerky and uncoordinated, and it takes a few weeks before infants can lift their head from a prone position. The muscles are clearly unable to support the baby's weight in order to allow such basic activities as sitting, rolling over, or standing. By the end of infancy, around 18 months, all this has changed (Figure 2.1). The toddler can walk, run, climb, communicate in speech and gesture, and use the two hands in complex coordinated actions.

The questions that a theory of motor development needs to explain include the following: Do the early motor activities prepare the way for the more complex voluntary activities that follow, and if so, how do they do it? How do new motor patterns (such as pointing, running, speaking, tool use) develop since they appear to be qualitatively different from earlier patterns? As we shall see, the answers to these questions are complex.

If you look at Table 2.1 two things will become apparent. First is that the different motor milestones emerge in a regular sequence – sitting with support, sitting unaided, crawling, standing, walking, and climbing appear almost always in this order. The second is that there is a considerable age range in which individual infants achieve each skill – for example, some infants crawl at 5 months while others are as late as 11 months. These two aspects of motor development give separate support to the two major theories of motor development that we will discuss here – *maturational theories* and *dynamic systems theory*.

Maturational theories

One of the first psychologists to investigate human motor development was Arnold Gesell, who studied hundreds of hours of films of motor activity in longitudinal studies of children from birth to 9 years (e.g., Gesell & Ames, 1940). He concluded that motor development proceeded from the global to the specific in two directions. One direction is called the **cephalocaudal trend** and is from head to foot along the length of the body – that is, control of the head is first, then the arms and trunk, and finally control of the legs. The other direction of development is what is called the **proximodistal trend**, which is that motor control is from the centre of the body outwards to more peripheral segments – that is, the head, trunk, and

cephalocaudal trend
development that proceeds from head to foot along the length of the body.

proximodistal trend
the development of motor control in infancy which is from the centre of the body outwards to more peripheral segments.

Table 2.1 *The development of motor skills in infancy*

Age	Gross Motor Skills	Fine Motor Skills
1–3 months	Stepping reflex, lifts head, sits with support.	Grasps object if placed in hands, sucks, control of eye movements, the first smile.
2–4 months	When prone lifts head and uses arms for support.	Grasps cube when placed near hand.
5–8 months	Sits without support.	Reaches for and grasps object, using one hand.
5–10 months	Stands with support, and pulls self to stand.	Points at object of interest, grasps with thumb and finger ('pincer grip').
5–11 months	Crawls.	Grasps spoon, gradually learns to direct food to mouth!
10–14 months	Stands alone, and walks alone.	Puts objects into small containers, builds 'tower' of cubes. Produces first meaningful word.
13–18 months	Walks backwards and sideways, runs, climbs, walks up stairs.	Holds crayon with fingers, scribbles energetically.
18–30 months	Runs easily, jumps, skips, rides and steers tricycle, walks on tiptoe.	Vocabulary and articulation increases rapidly, picks up small objects (e.g. candy/sweets).

pelvic girdle are brought under control before the elbow, wrist, knee, and ankle joints, which in turn lead to finer control over hands and fingers.

These two invariant sequences of development, together with the regular sequence with which the motor milestones are achieved, led Gesell to the view that *maturation* alone shapes motor development – development is controlled by a maturational timetable linked particularly to the central nervous system and also to muscular development. Each animal species has its own sequence, and experience has little, if any, effect on motor development.

One of the first researchers to question Gesell's hypothesis was Myrtle McGraw (1945). She tested pairs of twins where one member of each pair received enriched motor training (in reaching, climbing stairs, and other motor skills) and found that in the trained twin motor development was considerably accelerated when compared with the 'untrained' twin.

FIGURE 2.1 *The 18-month-old can walk, run, climb and has the fine motor skills to feed themselves.*

In addition to McGraw's findings there are other considerations which suggest that a purely maturational account of motor development can be largely dismissed. Here are just two such considerations. First, the fact that motor skills develop in a regular sequence does not prove a genetic cause. Consider advanced skills such as learning to play a sport, typing, driving, and playing the piano. In these instances we can see an invariant sequence of development, as we progress from simple actions to more complex integrated skilful behaviour, but nobody would suggest that these skills are genetically determined! Second, a maturational theory does not account for the considerable individual differences in the acquisition of various motor skills.

Clearly, a different theoretical account of motor development is needed, and here we describe one of the most recent of these, known as the **dynamic systems theory** of motor development.

> **dynamic systems theory** a theoretical approach applied to many areas of development which views the individual as interacting dynamically in a complex system in which all parts interact.

Dynamic systems theory

What has become apparent is that infants (and children) develop skills in different ways. As an example, there are some infants who simply do not like to crawl and these will often stand and walk before they crawl, indicating that the motor milestones referred to earlier are not set in stone. Those infants who do crawl will acquire it in their own individual ways – some will shuffle on their bellies before crawling on hands and knees, others will skip the belly-crawling stage, and still other infants will forgo the crawling stage entirely, and after several months of sitting and shuffling may stand and then walk (Adolph & Joh, 2007). In addition to these observations there are what are called microgenetic studies of motor development in which experimenters observe individual infants or children from the time they first attempt a new skill, such as walking or crawling, until it is performed effortlessly (e.g., Gill, Adolph & Vereijken, 2009). From these studies it becomes clear that infants' acquisition of a new motor skill is much the same as that of adults learning a new motor skill – the beginnings are usually fumbling and poor, there is trial and error learning and great concentration, all gradually leading to the accomplished skilful activity, which then is usually used in the development of yet new motor skills.

According to the dynamic systems theory all new motor development is the result of a dynamic and continual interaction of three major factors: (1) nervous system development; (2) the capabilities and biomechanics of the body; (3) environmental constraints and support (Thelen & Spencer, 1998). We can illustrate this dynamic interplay by considering three separate studies on infant kicking, reaching and sitting, and walking.

Infant kicking

Esther Thelen (1999) tested 24 three-month-olds on a foot-kicking task in which each infant was placed in a crib in a supine (lying on their back) position and a soft elastic ankle cuff was attached to one leg, and the cuff, in turn, was attached by a cord to an overhead brightly coloured mobile. By kicking the leg the babies could make the mobile dance around and they quickly learned to make this exciting event happen. In this condition the *other* leg – the one that was not connected to the mobile movements – either moved independently or alternately with the attached leg (Figure 2.2).

Then Thelen changed the arrangement by yoking the legs together. She did this by putting ankle cuffs on both legs, and joining the two together with a strip of Velcro. What happened then was that the infants initially tried to kick the legs separately – because moving the legs alternately is the more natural action – but gradually learned to kick both together to get the mobile to move.

This study shows that the infants were able to change their pattern of interlimb coordination to solve a novel, experimentally imposed task.

Infant reaching

Thelen and Spencer (1998) followed the same four infants from 3 weeks to 1 year (a longitudinal study) in order to explore the development of successful reaching. Their aim was to look at the interrelationship between different motor systems. What they found was that infants acquired stable control over the head several weeks before the onset of reaching, then there was a reorganisation of muscle patterns so that the infants could stabilise the head and shoulder. These developments gave the infants a stable base from which to reach, and successful reaching followed. This is an indication that infants need a stable posture before they can attain the goal of reaching successfully, and is a clear demonstration that new motor skills are learned through a process of modifying and developing their already existing abilities.

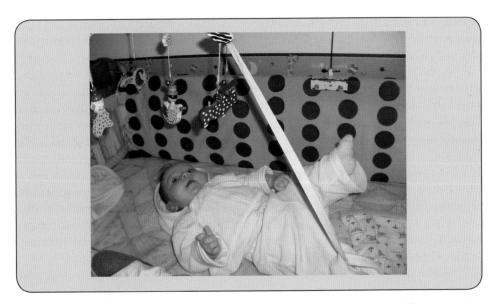

FIGURE 2.2 *The ankle ribbon attached to the baby's foot causes the mobile to jiggle about when she kicks her legs. This is an example of operant conditioning, the infant learns the contingency between kicking and reward.*

Source: Carolyn Rovee-Collier, reprinted with permission.

Infant walking

Newborn infants are extremely top heavy, with big heads and weak legs. Over the coming years their body weight is gradually redistributed and their centre of mass gradually moves downwards until it finishes slightly above the navel. Adolph and Avolio (2000, p. 1148) put it rather nicely – 'It is as if infants' bodies are growing to fit their comparatively large heads'! This means that as infants and children grow they need constantly to adjust and adapt their motor activities to accommodate the naturally occurring changes to their body dimensions. There can be few clearer demonstrations that the motor system is dynamic and constantly changing than this simple fact.

Adolph and Avolio give a nice demonstration of the way in which infants can make adjustments over a very short period of time. They tested 14-month-olds by having them wear saddlebags slung over each shoulder. The saddle bags increased the infants' chest circumference by the same amount in each of two conditions: *feather-weight* – filled with pillow-stuffing, weighing the negligible amount of 120 g – and *lead-weight* – the not so negligible amount of between 2.2 and 3.0 kg, which increased their body weight by 25 per cent and raised their centre of mass (raising the centre of mass leads to increased instability, and is similar to a backpacker carrying a heavy pack). They found that the lead-weight infants were more cautious, and made prolonged exploratory movements – swaying, touching and leaning – before attempting to walk down a slope. That is, these infants were testing their new-found body dimensions and weight, and adjusted their judgements of what they could and could not do. These findings again demonstrate that infants do not have a fixed and rigid understanding of their own abilities, and have the dynamic flexibility to adjust their abilities as they approach each novel motor problem.

Overview

Despite the apparent appeal of maturational theories of motor development, research over the last 20 years has demonstrated that motor skills are learned, both during infancy and throughout life. The apparently invariant ordering of the motor mile-stones is partly dictated by logical necessity – you can't run before you can walk! – and is not necessarily invariant (you *can* walk before you can crawl!) From a consideration of the studies described above it becomes clear that motor development cannot be accounted for by any maturational theory. These and other findings contribute to the 'emerging view of infants as active participants in their own motor-skill acquisition, in which developmental change is empowered through infants' everyday problem-solving activities' (Thelen, 1999, p. 103).

The emphasis on children as active participants in their own development is an essential characteristic of the theoretical views offered by 'The Giant of Developmental Psychology', Jean Piaget, whose claim was that children's ability to act on the world underlies their cognitive development, and we now turn our attention to his views.

COGNITIVE DEVELOPMENT

Piaget's theory of development

Everyone knows that Piaget was the most important figure the field has ever known … [he] transformed the field of developmental psychology.

(Flavell, 1996, p. 200)

Once psychologists looked at development through Piaget's eyes, they never saw children in quite the same way.

(Miller, 1993, p. 81)

A towering figure internationally.

(Bliss, 2010, p. 446)

Piaget's contribution to our understanding of children's development has been quite extraordinary, and his influence is reflected in this book – in particular Chapters 5 (infancy), 9 (early and middle childhood), 16 (adolescence), and 18 (education), and in these chapters alternatives to Piaget's account of development are also given. In order to see why he had such an impact we will first describe the state of developmental psychology before Piaget, and then describe some of the fundamental aspects of human development that he described which changed our view of development. We follow this with a brief account of the *stages of development* that he described, and finally give an overview of his enormous contribution to developmental psychology.

Developmental psychology before Piaget

Before Piaget revolutionised our understanding of children's development psychology was dominated by the influence of the two diametrically opposed theoretical views of *behaviourism* and **psychoanalysis**. Both of these views are discussed later, and for the moment we will restrict our comments to note that, despite the fact that they are strikingly opposed, they share one essential feature, which is that the child is seen as the passive recipient of their upbringing – development results from such things as the severity of toilet training, and of rewards and punishments. Neither approach gives much credit to the child in shaping their own course of development. With Piaget, all this changed . . .

> **psychoanalysis** the theoretical view, first developed by Sigmund Freud, that much of our behaviour is determined by unconscious factors.

Fundamental aspects of human development, according to Piaget

Children are active agents in shaping their own development, they are not simply blank slates who passively and unthinkingly respond to whatever the environment offers them. That is, children's behaviour and development is motivated largely *intrinsically* (internally) rather than *extrinsically*.

For Piaget, children learn to adapt to their environments and as a result of their **cognitive adaptations** they become better able to understand their world. Adaptation is something that all living organisms have evolved to do and as children adapt they gradually construct more advanced understandings of their worlds.

> **cognitive adaptations** children's developing cognitive awareness of the world. As a result of cognitive adaptations they become better able to understand their world.

These more advanced understandings of the world reflect themselves in the appearance, during development, of new stages of development. Piaget's theory is therefore the best example of the **organismic world view** that we discussed in Chapter 1, which portrays children as inherently active, continually interacting with the environment, in such a way as to shape their own development.

Since children are active in developing or constructing their worlds Piaget's theory is often referred to as a *constructivist theory.* In the next sections we will first discuss the ways in which children adapt to their environments, and next give an account of the stages of development that Piaget put forward.

Adaptation: Assimilation and accommodation

In order to adapt to the world two important processes are necessary. **Assimilation** is what happens when we treat new objects, people and events as if they were familiar – that is, we *assimilate* the new to our already-existing schemes of thought. Examples would be: we meet a new policeman (or doctor, professor . . .) and treat them as we habitually treat policemen, doctors or professors. Assimilation occurs from the earliest days – the infant is offered a new toy and puts it in their

> **assimilation** the process through which children incorporate new experiences into their preexisting *schemes* – that is, they *assimilate* the new to their already-existing schemes of thought. An important process in Piaget's theory.

accommodation the cognitive process through which children adapt to new experiences by modifying their preexisting *schemes*. An important process in Piaget's theory.

schemas mental structures in the child's thinking that provide representations and plans for enacting behaviours.

functional invariants processes that do not change during development, such as *accommodation* and *assimilation* in Piaget's theory.

sensorimotor stage in Piaget's theory, the first stage of *cognitive development*, whereby thought is based primarily on perception and action and internalised thinking is largely absent. This stage is characteristic of infants from birth to about 2 years old.

preoperational stage a stage of development described by Piaget in which children under the age of approximately 7 years are unable to coordinate aspects of problems in order to solve them.

concrete operations stage the third Piagetian stage of development in which reasoning is said to become more logical, systematic, and rational in its application to concrete objects.

formal operations stage the fourth Piagetian stage in which the individual acquires the capacity for abstract scientific thought. This includes the ability to theorise about impossible events and items.

mouth to use the familiar activity of sucking; the child meets a new teacher and treats them in the same way they treat teachers.

Accommodation is where individuals have to modify or change their **schemas**, or ways of thinking, in order to adjust to a new situation. For example: infants might be presented with a toy that is larger than those they have previously handled, and so will have to adjust their fingers and grasp to hold it; when children meet a new teacher who is different from their previous teachers they have to adjust their way of thinking to understand the new person. It is worth stressing that assimilation and accommodation always occur together during infancy and the examples given above are both cases of assimilation and accommodation occurring together.

Throughout life the processes of assimilation and accommodation are always active as we constantly strive to adapt to the world we encounter. These processes, therefore, are what can be called **functional invariants** in that they don't change during development. What do change are the cognitive structures (often called schemas) that allow the child to comprehend the world at progressively higher levels of understanding. According to Piaget's view there are different levels of cognitive understanding that take the child from the activity-based sensorimotor functioning in infancy to the abstract levels of thought found in adolescence.

The four stages of cognitive development

Children move through four broad stages of development, each of which is characterised by qualitatively different ways of thinking (Piaget, 1962). These stages are the **sensorimotor stage** of infancy, the **preoperational stage** of early childhood, the **concrete operations stage** of middle childhood, and the **formal operations stage** of adolescence and beyond. We will give a brief account of each of these stages, together with the approximate ages at which they are found – note that these ages are only approximate and individual children's development will often be slower or quicker.

Sensorimotor stage (birth to 2 years)

This is one of the most impressive and dramatic areas of development. The child changes from the helpless newborn to the thinking and knowing toddler, that is, to the cognitive individual with a 'mind'. These changes take place as a result of the infant's actions on the objects and people in its environments, and this stage is the development of *thought in action*. As a result, infants learn to solve problems, such as pulling a cloth to obtain an out-of-reach toy, and they learn that objects continue to exist even though they cannot be seen or heard. As the stage draws to a close the infant, now a toddler whose language is developing rapidly, is able to reason through thought as well as through sensorimotor activities.

Preoperational stage (2 to 7 years)

Preschool children can solve a number of practical, concrete problems by the intelligent use of means-end problem solving, the use of tools, requesting objects, asking for things to happen, and other means. They can communicate well and represent information and ideas by means of symbols – in drawing, symbolic play, gesture, drawing, and particularly speech.

These abilities continue to develop considerably during the preoperational stage, but there are some striking limitations to children's thinking during this period. Children tend to be **egocentric** (find it difficult to see things from another's point of view). They display **animism** in their thinking (they tend to attribute life and lifelike qualities to inanimate objects, particularly those that move and are active, such as the wind and the clouds, and sometimes trees and other objects. Here is Piaget asking a child about the sun, which follows you around as you move: *Piaget* – 'Is it alive?' *Child* – 'Of course, otherwise it wouldn't follow us, it couldn't shine' (Piaget, 1960, p. 215). Their thinking tends to be illogical, and at times seems quite magical – it is at this stage that children believe in Santa Claus! What underlies children's thinking during the preoperational stage is the lack of a logical framework for thought, and this appears during the concrete operations stage.

egocentric an egocentric child is one who finds it difficult to see things from another person's point of view. Not to be confused with egotistical.

animism a characteristic of children's thinking in Piaget's *preoperational stage* in which they tend to attribute life and lifelike qualities to inanimate objects, particularly those that move and are active.

Concrete operations stage (7 to 11 years)

One major characteristic of preoperational thought is called **centration** – the focusing or centering of attention on one aspect of a situation to the exclusion of others. This is clearly demonstrated in Piaget's **conservation tasks**. A typical conservation problem is the conservation of number. In this problem the child is shown two rows of candies/sweets, in one-to-one correspondence and with each having six candies. The child is simply asked 'Look what I do' and is not questioned about the number in each row. Then, while the child watches, one of the candies is added to one row so that it has seven. Next, the other row is stretched out so that it *looks* as though it has more, but in reality it has less.

centration the focusing or centring of attention on one aspect of a situation to the exclusion of others.

conservation tasks tasks that examine children's ability to understand that physical attributes of objects, such as their mass and weight, do not vary when the object changes shape.

Then the child is asked 'Which row would you like?' Preoperational children will usually ask for the longer row – they focus on the increase in length and ignore the addition of one candy/sweet to the other row. However, the child at the concrete operations level knows that one has been added to the shorter row, and since nothing has been added or subtracted by the action of stretching out the other row, knows that the shorter row contains more – and will therefore ask for the shorter row. If you have access to a 4- and a 7-year-old and are allowed to give them candies/sweets then this is an interesting experiment to do with both of them – the younger child will want the longer row, and the older child the shorter, and neither understands the reasoning of the other!

In addition to mastering conservation, the concrete operational child becomes better at a number of tasks that share the same underlying logic, and these are discussed in detail in Chapter 9.

The formal operations stage (from about 11 years)

The concrete operations child becomes able to solve many problems involving the physical world, but the major limitation in their thinking is to do with the realm of possibilities. When children enter the final stage of cognitive development – the *formal operations stage* – this limitation is removed. The adolescent now becomes able to reason in the way that scientists do – to manipulate variables to find out what causes things to happen – and is also introduced to the realm of possibilities and hypothetical thought. Adolescents (and adults) spend many hours discussing abstract matters – Does God exist? – Why do we need politics? – Should abortion be allowed? – What is the meaning of life? A more detailed account of adolescent thinking is given in Chapter 16.

Overview

In Piaget's theory we have a comprehensive and detailed account of cognitive development from birth to adulthood. Cognitive development proceeds through a series of stages, each more complex than the last, and each building on the achievements of the previous one. In many respects, aspects of Piaget's theory seem obvious – of course children are active in shaping their own development. But it was many years before his theories began to make an impact on American and British psychology. This was primarily due to three factors. First, American and British psychology was dominated by the theoretical school of thought known as behaviourism, which offered the **mechanistic world view** that the child is inherently passive until stimulated by the environment and so the opposing view offered by Piaget took time to be accepted. Second, Piaget only ever wrote in French, which made his work less accessible to English-speaking psychologists. And, third, while Piaget was a brilliant thinker, his writings are often extraordinarily complex and difficult to understand!

Piaget's full impact awaited the arrival of one man who could summarise, synthesise and present his theoretical views in a way that was comprehensible and available to the English-speaking world. This was John H. Flavell whose *The Developmental Psychology of Jean Piaget* appeared in 1963 (and in the foreword to this book Piaget wrote 'I am not an easy author; hence it must have required an immense effort at comprehension and intellectual empathy to have produced the clear and straightforward presentation that is found here'). More recently, Flavell (1996) wrote an assessment of Piaget's contribution, entitled 'Piaget's legacy' and quotes an anonymous reviewer of his article – 'The impact of Piaget on developmental psychology is . . . too monumental to embrace and at the same time too omnipresent to detect', to which Flavell simply adds the words 'I agree'.

INFORMATION PROCESSING APPROACHES

....

Information processing approaches view the human mind as a complex system through which information flows. Information processing accounts of human cognition include current views of memory formation, with terms such as *encoding,* *storage*, *retrieval*, **strategies**, *metamemory*, and this account is given in Chapter 13. A brief account of information processing explanations of cognitive changes in adolescence is given in Chapter 16.

Information processing theories are rooted in three 20th-century innovations. The first is the rapid and continuing advances in computer technology. The second is the view, revolutionary at the time, that an organism's behaviour cannot be understood without knowing the structure of the perceiver's environment – for example, the structure of light reflected from objects (Gibson, 1979). The third is **constructivism**, a theory about how perception 'fills in' information that cannot be seen or heard directly, such as inferring the parts of an object that are hidden from view via processes of inference. Piaget's theory is also regarded as a 'constructivist' view, because the child is proposed to *construct* their knowledge from existing perceptual and cognitive skills. Gibson's theory is also a constructive view, but primarily concerned with how we construct our perceptual, rather than cognitive, world. Gibson's theory and constructivism were opposed to a theoretical viewpoint that was dominant at mid-century, *behaviourism*, whose principal tenet was that our knowledge of an organism is limited exclusively to what we can observe, and a position that avoided discussions of what goes on *inside* the mind. Investigations of both perception and cognition and their development, therefore, were severely constrained and, ultimately, unsatisfying – hence the need for new theoretical approaches.

Information processing theories, therefore, focus on the information available in the external environment, and the means by which the child receives and interprets this information. This way of thinking can provide clarity with respect to understanding many aspects of cognitive development. The task of the developing child is to use their perceptual systems – vision, hearing, touch, and so forth – to explore the world and obtain information about its properties. The information must be attended to, encoded, stored, retrieved, and acted upon to build knowledge of objects and their characteristics.

In contrast to Piaget's theory, information processing theories are not the product of one person's work, but instead represent a number of scientists working with a common set of assumptions. In the following sections we provide some recent examples.

Cognitive development in infancy

According to the information processing approach, cognitive development proceeds in **bottom-up** fashion beginning with the 'input,' or uptake of information by the child, and building complex systems of knowledge from simpler origins. (This is opposed to **top-down** fashion in which the state of the system is specified or presumed, and then working to discover its components and their development, a view more consistent with nativist theory.) For young infants, sensory and perceptual skills are relatively immature, and this may impose limits on knowledge acquisition. An important part of a

information processing the view that cognitive processes are explained in terms of inputs and outputs and that the human mind is a system through which information flows.

strategies knowledge used to solve particular problems.

constructivism Piaget's theoretical view that infants are not born with knowledge about the world, but instead gradually construct knowledge and the ability to represent reality mentally.

bottom-up a cognitive development process beginning with the 'input' or uptake of information by the child, and building complex systems of knowledge from simpler origins.

top-down a cognitive development process in which the state of the system is specified or presumed, and then working to discover its components and their development, a view more consistent with nativist theory.

research agenda, therefore, is investigations of how infants assemble the building blocks of knowledge.

A prominent example of this approach comes from the work of Les Cohen and colleagues, who asked how infants come to perceive *causality*, as when one object bumps into another and causes it to move. Two parameters are especially important to perceive causality: temporal and physical proximity. When a billiard ball strikes another and makes it move, for instance, the second ball moves immediately upon contact. When an event is arranged so that the second ball moves after a brief delay (violating temporal proximity) or before being contacted by the first ball (violating physical proximity), 6-month-old infants did not seem to perceive the event as causal (Leslie, 1984). (This was learned by reversing the events and observing infants for evidence that they saw a reversal of the causal relation). Cohen and Amsel (1998) repeated this experiment and tested younger infants, and discovered that 4-month-olds perceived the 'components' of each event – that is, the motions of the individual objects – but not

perception of causality perception of the causal nature of interactions between objects and between people. For instance, when one object collides with another it causes it to move.

their causal relation. In information processing terms, the younger infants processed the *lower-order* units involved in the event but not the *higher-order* relations, and this suggests that development of causal perception between 4 and 6 months consists in noticing the higher-order, complex relations among objects and their motions.

A second example of the information processing approach comes from the work of Scott Johnson and colleagues, who asked how infants perceive **object unity**, as when two parts of an object are visible but its centre is hidden by another object – do infants perceive the visible parts to be connected? As in the case of causal perception,

object unity when two parts of an object are visible but its centre is hidden by another object – do infants perceive the visible parts to be connected?

younger infants perceive the components but not the wholes – in this case, they perceive the parts of a partly hidden object but do not see it as a single unit (Johnson, 2004). Amso and Johnson (2006) found that unity perception depends on the extent to which infants actually look at the object parts, as opposed to other parts of the scene (this was ascertained by measuring infants' eye movements with an eye tracker device). Development of object perception, in particular object unity, therefore, consists again in detecting the higher-order relations among lower-order components.

Cognitive development in childhood

In childhood, the task of building knowledge often comes down to determining which of the many 'strategies' are available to solve particular problems. This idea has been investigated rigorously by Robert Siegler and colleagues in the area of mathematics instruction. A typical approach to this question involves examination of arithmetic strategies (learning to add by memorisation, counting on the fingers, and so forth) repeatedly in individual children as the school year progresses, and recording speed, accuracy, and strategy use. A number of strategic changes have been noted: incorporation of new strategies, identification of efficient strategies, more efficient execution of each strategy, and more adaptive choices among strategies (Siegler & Shipley, 1995). There are stable individual differences in strategy choice, but children typically use multiple strategies at all points of assessment. Children hone their choices with experience and thus come to solve problems more quickly and accurately. A more detailed account of Siegler's view of development is given in Chapter 9.

Connectionism and brain development

Information processing theory also takes advantage of two new advances in cognitive science: the use of **connectionist models** and methods for recording brain activity in infants and children. Each is discussed in turn.

connectionism a modern theoretical approach that developed from *information processing* accounts in which computers are programmed to simulate the action of the brain and nerve cells (*neurons*).

Connectionist models are computer programs designed to emulate (model) some aspect of human cognition, including cognitive development. The word 'connectionist' refers to the structure of the model, which consists of a number of processing units that are connected and that influence one another by a flow of activations. This is analogous to the brain, which likewise consists of processing units (neurons) that are connected and activate one another (across synapses). Connectionist models take in information, appropriately coded in a way that the computer can process, and provide a response, coded in a way that a human can understand. In between input and output are units, typically numbered in the dozens to the thousands, which process the information. The model learns by changing the activation strengths and connections among units. It is provided with multiple opportunities to process the information, and often some sort of feedback on how it is doing between trials, as impetus to improve performance. Because there is no knowledge built into a model, it is effectively a 'blank slate', and as such represents a model for learning in the human child. Initially the model has to guess at how it is to respond, but given enough training and feedback, it is capable of learning remarkably sophisticated kinds of information.

Connectionist models have been used to examine many aspects of perceptual and cognitive development. There is no single model of cognitive development *per se*, but instead modellers will choose a particular problem to emulate, design a model and a learning regimen, and probe the time course and nature of learning as it occurs. Two examples, relevant to infant development studies discussed previously, merit mention. In the first, Cohen *et al.* (2002) described a model of infant cognitive development that learned to discriminate the temporal and physical parameters that lead infants to perceive causality, and appeared to represent 'truly' causal events (to humans) uniquely, as more than the 'sum of the parts' (as do humans). In the second, Schlesinger *et al.* (2007) devised a model of infants' gaze patterns based on the idea of different brain systems that respond to specific visual features in an input image: luminance, motion, colour, and orientation. The model computed 'salience' based on competition among features, known to occur in real brains (Gottlieb *et al.*, 1998), and it directed its attention toward regions in the input of highest salience. The question was how infants learn to direct their attention to a partly hidden object, as part of the more general question of perception of object unity. The model learned to 'find' the object quickly and suggests that gaze control and salience, and the development of neural structures that support them, are a vital component of object perception in infancy. Other models of cognitive development incorporate a role for social interaction, physical growth, genes and gene expression, and the development of circuits and networks in the brain, and as such epitomise both a major theoretical advancement and a more realistic representation of human development (Westermann *et al.*, 2007).

Summary

The theories and research we have described are motivated by multiple notions of information: the information available in the stimulus, the uptake of that information, the processing of the information by the individual, and the individual's response. Understanding of information at these different levels is a central task of information processing theory, and multiple methods are used in pursuit of this goal: empirical studies of infants and children (including close observations of behaviours at a 'microgenetic' scale), connectionist models, and recordings of brain activity.

Comparing information-processing approaches with Piaget's approach

Piaget's theory and information-processing approaches have quite a lot in common. Both attempt to specify children's abilities and limitations as development proceeds, and both try to explain how new levels of understanding develop from earlier, less advanced ones. More importantly, Piaget's theory and information processing theories share a focus on 'active' participation by the child in their own development. In both views, children learn by doing, by trying new strategies (and discarding many) and discovering the consequences, and learn by directing their attention appropriately.

However, they differ in several important ways. Information processing approaches place great importance on the role of processing limitations (another computing analogy) in limiting children's thinking and reasoning at any point in time, and also emphasise the development of stategies and procedures for helping to overcome these limitations – clear accounts of these with respect to memory development are given in Chapters 13 and 16. Piaget's theory does not discuss processing limitations, but rather discusses developmental changes in terms of the child gradually constructing logical frameworks for thought, such as *concrete operations* and *formal operations*.

Another important difference is that information processing accounts see development as unfolding in a continuous fashion, rather than in qualitatively different stages as Piaget suggested. To see how this difference might work consider the child who moves from Piaget's *preoperational stage* to the *concrete operations stage*. When presented with a conservation of number task the preoperational child centres attention on one aspect of the changed array – the increase in length – and ignores the other, equally important, aspect, which is that, in the example given above, a candy/sweet has been added to the shorter row. When the child is able to overcome this limitation they move to the qualitatively different level of thinking that characterises the stage of concrete operations. An information processing account, on the other hand, would simply say that the child's processing capacity has increased so that they are now able to hold two things in mind simultaneously, so that what underlies the apparently *qualitative* change in thinking is actually a *quantitative* change in processing capacity.

SOCIAL-COGNITIVE DEVELOPMENT

Whereas Piaget tended to focus on the individual child attempting to make sense of the world (given some basic tools) other researchers have been interested in the interaction between the child and their community – the social environment.

Vygotsky

Born in the same year as Piaget, the Russian psychologist Lev Semenovich Vygotsky (1896–1934) was one of the first to recognise the importance of knowledgeable adults in the child's environment. For him, the development of intellectual abilities is influenced by a *didactic* relationship (one based on instructive dialogue) with more advanced individuals. One fascinating facet of his work is the claim that higher mental abilities are first encountered and used competently in social interactions, only later being internalised and possessed as individual thought processes. For instance, language is used socially to quite a level of competence before it is internalised, reorganising thought in the process.

Thus, a major theme in Vygotsky's theories is that social interaction plays a fundamental role in cognitive development. He argued that there is a gap between what the child knows and what they can be taught. At a given stage of development the child has a certain level of understanding, a temporary maximum. A little beyond this point lies the **zone of proximal development** (**ZPD**). This zone can be seen as representing problems and ideas that are just a little too difficult for the child to understand on their own. It can, however, be explored and understood with the help of an adult. Thus the adult can guide the child because they have a firmer grasp of the more complex thinking involved.

Vygotsky died young (from tuberculosis) but he left an impressive amount of work (over 100 published articles and books) which continues to have an impact on developmental psychology. A comparison of Vygotsky's views with those of Piaget is given in Chapter 9, and his contribution to education is discussed in detail in Chapter 18.

zone of proximal development (ZPD) the distance between the actual developmental level as determined by independent problem solving and the level of potential development as determined through problem solving under adult guidance or in collaboration with more able *peers*.

introspectionism an approach to psychology common in the nineteenth century in which observers were asked to reflect on their thoughts, feelings, and perceptions.

classical conditioning a method of learning first investigated by the Russian physiologist Ivan Pavlov in the early part of the 20th century. In this form of conditioning, certain behaviours can be elicited by a neutral (normally unstimulating) stimulus because of its learned association with a more powerful stimulus.

Behaviourism and social learning theory

Early behaviourism

Towards the end of the nineteenth century, psychology experienced a swing away from the subjective perspective of **introspectionism** (the analysis of self-reported perceptions) towards a more objective method. This scientific approach to psychology had its roots in the work of Vygotsky's countryman, Ivan Petrovich Pavlov (1849–1936). Pavlov developed a grand theory of learning called **classical conditioning**. According to this theory, certain behaviours can be elicited by a neutral (normally unstimulating) stimulus simply because of its learned association with a more powerful stimulus. For example, when food was presented to dogs at the same time as a bell, the bell would eventually cause a salivation response when presented on its own. The dogs learned an *association* between the two. This principle of conditioning is applicable to much human behaviour – you might find yourself salivating when the dinner bell sounds!

law of effect law or rule devised by the American psychologist Edward Lee Thorndike which states that the likelihood of an action being repeated is increased if it leads to a pleasant outcome, and decreased if it leads to an unpleasant outcome.

Many psychologists seized upon his ideas. Because of its fundamental nature, Pavlov's work had the potential to explain all forms of human behaviour and its development. It was combined with other theoretical notions such as Thorndike's **law of effect** (the likelihood of an action being repeated is increased if it leads to reward, and decreased if it leads to punishment) and *behaviourism* was born. With this, the pendulum swing towards objectivity was complete. In its most radical form – as espoused by early behaviourist John Watson (1878–1958) – behaviourism denies the role of the mind as an object of study and reduces all behaviour to chains of stimuli (from the environment) and the resulting response (the behaviour). Some took this very seriously indeed, and ascribed the mind's 'inner voice' to a sub-vocal tremor of the larynx. One behaviourist administered himself a muscle-relaxing nerve toxin in order to find out, but, despite his condition, his mind remained active along with his scientific zeal.

The early behaviourists' view of child development is quite simple. The infant is born with little more than the machinery of conditioning and infancy and childhood consists of constant warping and moulding under pressure of the environment. The child is passive and receptive and can be shaped in any direction. This view was clearly expressed by Watson (1970, p. 94):

reductionism the claim that complex behaviours and skills such as language and problem-solving are formed from simpler processes, such as neural activity and conditioning, and can ultimately be understood in these simpler terms.

Give me a dozen healthy infants, well-formed, and my own specified world to bring them up in and I'll guarantee to take any one at random and train him to become any type of specialist I might select – doctor, lawyer, merchant-chief and yes, even beggar-man and thief, regardless of his talents, penchants, tendencies, abilities, vocations, and race of his ancestors.

Any behaviours – even the most elaborate, like language – are towers built upon the foundations of very simple, repeated connections between a stimulus and its response. This has been termed a **reductionist** perspective because it reduces ostensibly complex phenomena to simpler core processes.

operant conditioning a form of conditioning investigated by B.F. Skinner. The training, or shaping, of an animal or human by reinforcing them for producing the desired behaviour (or a close approximation to it) and/or either ignoring or punishing undesirable behaviours in order to stop them.

B.F. Skinner's behaviourism

Any discussion of behaviourism would not be complete without the inclusion of Burrhus Frederic Skinner (1904–90). He had an effect on his area of psychology perhaps greater than any other individual (and during his lifetime was regularly in the list of the most famous 10 Americans). Whilst the early behaviourists emphasised the passive nature of the child, Skinner envisioned a more active role. **Operant conditioning** differs from *classical conditioning* because children operate (emit behaviours) on their environments. It is still the case that the child's development is dominated by their environment, but Skinner's viewpoint allowed for more flexible and generative patterns of behaviour. According to Skinner's view it is possible to shape the animal's or child's behaviour by manipulating the reinforcement received.

We can see the role of reinforcement in this brief account of infant behaviour (Skinner, 1961, p. 418):

> One reinforcer to which babies often respond is the flashing on and off of a table lamp. Whenever the baby lifts its hand, flash the light. In a short time a well-defined response will be generated. (Human babies are just as 'smart' as dogs or pigeons in this respect.) Incidentally, the baby will enjoy the experience.

It is certainly the case that our behaviour is guided by reward and punishment, and behaviourism continues to be used in the control of behaviour. Skinner gave an account of how parents may unwittingly promote undesirable behaviours, such as aggression, crying or shouting in their children. If, for example, the mother only gives the child attention when it is misbehaving, then her positive reinforcement of attention is likely to promote the very behaviour she does not want! The remedy is this (Skinner, 1961, p. 419):

> The remedy in such a case is simply for the mother to make sure that she responds with attention and affection to most if not all the responses of the child which are . . . acceptable . . . and that she never reinforces the annoying forms of behavior.

Social learning theory

Whereas behaviourism had important but rather vague things to say about the child's acquisition of behaviour patterns, the work of Albert Bandura (1925–) examined particular behaviours in more detail. His behaviourism was less mechanistic than that of Skinner. He did not focus only on observable behaviour, but posited processing that occurred within the mind – a construct specifically denied by his behaviourist colleagues. His approach was initially named *sociobehaviourism*, then **social learning theory**.

During the 1960s Bandura carried out a series of experiments on childhood aggression. In one, some children were divided into two groups. The first ('control') group saw an adult playing with toys, one of which was an inflatable 'Bobo' doll. The second ('experimental') group saw the same adult, this time playing aggressively with the toys, hitting the doll with a hammer. When allowed to play individually, Bandura observed that children from the experimental group behaved in a more aggressive way towards their own Bobo doll.

So, without obvious reinforcement, a particular aggressive behaviour had been learned. Bandura termed this **observational learning** or 'vicarious conditioning'. In some sense, the child had *mentally* assumed the role of the observed person and taken note of any reinforcement. Bandura concluded that children imitate the actions of

social learning theory
associated with Albert Bandura. The application of *behaviourism* to social and cognitive learning that emphasises the importance of *observational learning*, that is, learning by observation and then copying (imitating) the observed acts.

observational learning
situation in which people (especially children) learn by observing others and then copying (imitating) the observed acts.

others, based on perceived reinforcement. He followed up the Bobo-doll experiment with investigations into cartoon and film violence. The findings were clear: children imitated the aggressive behaviour.

Bandura's approach kept the essential components of behaviourism – that we learn by reinforcement and punishment of behaviour, in accord with the *law of effect* – and added the important dimension of learning by observation. Adults and others in the child's life provide models, and in humans learning by imitation is extremely common in all areas of social and cognitive development. Over the last 40 years social learning theory has become increasingly cognitive in its account of human learning

social cognitive theory
a theory that emphasises social factors in cognitive development.

and by the mid-1980s Bandura had developed the **social cognitive theory** of human functioning. This theory is a development of social learning theory and emphasises humans' ability to exercise control over the nature and quality of their lives, and to be 'self-reflective about one's capabilities, quality of functioning, and the meaning and purpose of one's life pursuits' (Bandura, 2001, p. 1). Although not designed as a theory of child development, social cognitive theory is currently being used to introduce social change in successful attempts to ameliorate global problems such as population explosions (Bandura, 2009).

ETHOLOGY AND EVOLUTION

Evolution

The theoretical basis of any evolutionary theory of development is, of course, evolution itself. The present form of the theory is largely identical to that developed by its founder, Charles Robert Darwin (Darwin was born on 12 February 1809 – the same day as Abraham Lincoln – and died on 19 April 1882). Perhaps the most important unit in evolution is the *gene*, which is the basic genetic material out of which **chromosomes** are formed. The term gene is also used in a vague way

chromosomes strands of DNA (deoxyribonucleic acid) and protein that contain the genes and provide the genetic blueprint for the animal or plant.

when talking about any heritable characteristic of an organism: eye colour, intelligence, or an inherited behaviour. When a set of genes leads to an overall advantage for an organism, the organism tends to produce more copies of itself. Those genes, therefore, will become more frequent in the *gene pool*. When a set of genes leads to an overall disadvantage, those genes will become less frequent. This means that as evolution proceeds any gene still in the gene pool will tend to be advantageous. The difficult concept to master is to remember this should apply to behaviours as well as physical characteristics.

ethological approaches
approaches which emphasise the evolutionary origins of many behaviours that are important for survival, such as *imprinting*.

Evolutionary theories of child development that emphasise the genetic basis of many behaviours, and point to the adaptive and survival value of these behaviours, are known as **ethological approaches**.

The ethological approach

The origins of ethology can be traced back to Darwin, and its modern foundations were laid by two European zoologists, Konrad Lorenz (1903–89) and Niko Tinbergen (1907–88), who pioneered the genetic analysis of development: they both shared the 1973 Nobel prize in Physiology or Medicine. They reasoned that certain behaviours in the young of many species would be genetic in origin because they (i) promote survival and (ii) are found in many species, including humans. One such behaviour is **imprinting**, which refers to the tendency of the newborn or newly hatched of **precocial species** of animals (which includes ducks, geese, sheep, horses) to follow the first moving objects they see. This behaviour involves the formation of an attachment between the infant and the mother (Figure 2.3). Clearly, imprinting is *adaptive* (adds to survival value) because it leads to a physical proximity between parent and offspring. As a consequence, the parent is always at hand to feed, give warmth, protect from predators and generally attend to the offspring.

Lorenz is famous for his experiments with young geese (goslings). He demonstrated that if the first moving object they saw after hatching was him then the unwitting goslings would imprint on him and follow him around (and even, as adults, attempt to mate with him!).

imprinting a process soon after birth or hatching in which the young of *precocial species* of animals (which includes ducks, geese, sheep, horses) follow the first moving objects they see.

precocial species those species of animals where the young are able to locomote almost immediately after birth or hatching. These include ducks, geese, sheep, and horses. The young will often *imprint* on and follow their mother, an instinctive response which has clear survival value for the young.

FIGURE 2.3 *Newly hatched chicks will follow their mother and siblings.*
Source: © Jan de Wild/Shutterstock.

There are two implications of ethology's conception of behaviours. The first is that, for the most part, they require an external stimulus or target. For example, imprinting needs a target 'parent' – if this target does not exist, imprinting will either not take place, or will take place with an inappropriate target (cf. Lorenz's goslings). The second implication is one of time. Originally, ethologists envisioned a **critical period**, this being the length of time for the behaviour to grow to maturity in the presence of the right conditions (e.g. language developing in a rich linguistic environment). When this critical period expires, the behaviour cannot develop. These days, the evidence points towards a *sensitive* rather than critical period; behaviours may take root beyond this sensitive time period, but their development may be difficult and ultimately retarded.

critical period a limited period, usually early in an animal's life, in which the young have to be exposed to a particular skill or experience in order for it to be learned.

EMOTIONAL DEVELOPMENT

Attachment theory – John Bowlby and Mary Ainsworth

Mother love in infancy and childhood is as important for mental health as are vitamins and proteins for physical health.

(Bowlby, 1952)

The British physician and psychoanalyst John Bowlby was inspired by observations of imprinting, and was one of the first to offer an ethological and evolutionary interpretation of human development. The concluding comment to his 1952 book (given above) is one of the most widely quoted within developmental psychology. His contribution to our understanding of attachment formation in infancy and childhood continues to have an immense impact, and here we will give a very brief account of his views, and that of his American colleague Mary Ainsworth.

Prior to Bowlby the prevailing belief, stemming from behaviourism is that the attachment of infants to their caregivers was a **secondary drive**, that is, because the mother (or **primary caregiver**) satisfies the baby's **primary drives** (these include hunger, thirst and the need for warmth) she acquires secondary reinforcing properties. However, Bowlby pointed out that the need for attachment was itself a primary drive (as the quote given above indicates, which is the conclusion to his 1952 report to the World Health Organization).

Several lines of evidence have since supported this conclusion. In the 1950s and 1960s Harry Harlow and his colleagues (e.g. Harlow & Zimmerman, 1959) separated baby monkeys from their real mothers and offered them two surrogate (substitute) 'mothers'. One of these was made of wire, but had a nipple attached which provided food (and hence satisfied the primary drives of hunger and thirst). The other was made of soft cloth and provided no nutrition. What

primary drives basic needs which include hunger, thirst, and the need for warmth. Bowlby and others have argued that an infant's need for attachment is also a primary drive.

secondary drive a term used to refer to the fact that an object can acquire reinforcing properties by being associated with the satisfaction of an individual's *primary drives.*

they found is that the baby monkeys fed from the 'wire mother', but cuddled up to the 'soft cloth mother', and ran to 'her' when frightened by loud sounds. It therefore seemed reasonable to conclude that the 'soft cloth mother' provided what we can call *contact comfort*, and satisfied a basic or primary need.

Bowlby argued that there is an innate, instinctual drive in humans to form attachments that is as strong as any other primary drive or need. He put forward the principle of **monotropy**, which is the claim that the infant has a need to form an attachment with one significant person (usually the mother). This claim was later found to be overstated, because Rudolph Schaffer and Peggy Emerson (1964) found that infants often formed multiple attachments, and that in some cases their strongest attachment was to people such as the father, a grandparent, or peers, who did not fulfil basic caregiving activities, but who did engage in satisfying interactions ('quality time') with them (see Figure 2.4).

monotropy the view that the infant has a basic need to form an attachment with one significant person, usually the mother. A central claim in Bowlby's early theory of attachment formation.

Bowlby believed that the attachment system between infant and caregiver became organised and consolidated in the second half of the infant's first year from birth, and became particularly apparent when the infant began to crawl. At this time, infants tend to use the mother as a 'safe base' from which to begin their explorations of the world, and it then becomes possible to measure how infants react to their mother's departure and to her return. For these measures we are indebted to Mary Ainsworth, who trained with Bowlby, and who invented what is commonly called the **strange situation**. In this situation a baby (usually around a year old) and their mother enter an experimental room in which there are several toys. The mother sits on a chair and after a short while a stranger enters, at which point the mother leaves, only to return a few minutes later. An observer then notes the infant's response to several events – when the stranger enters, when the mother leaves and when she returns.

strange situation measure, devised by Ainsworth, of the level of attachment a child has with their parent.

FIGURE 2.4 *Infants will usually form multiple attachments.*

Using the strange situation Ainsworth discovered that there are several attachment 'styles' that differ in degree of security. A detailed account of these attachment styles and of Bowlby's and Ainsworth's contribution in developing what is called *attachment theory* is given in detail in Chapter 6. For the moment we can conclude that their importance has been in demonstrating the importance of early secure attachments and showing that these attachments are as basic and important as any other human drive or motivation.

PSYCHOANALYTIC THEORIES

Sigmund Freud – The founder of psychoanalysis

For generations almost every branch of human knowledge will be enriched and illuminated by the imagination of Freud.

(Jane Harrison, 1850–1928)

His place is not, as he claimed, with Copernicus and Darwin, but with Hans Christian Anderson and the Brother Grimm, tellers of fairy tales.

(Hans Eysenck, 1916–97)

As will be apparent from the above, not everyone agrees that Freud's contribution to knowledge has been entirely positive! Freud claimed that much of our behaviour is determined by unconscious forces of which we are not directly aware. In presenting his **psychoanalytic theory** he suggested that there are three main structures to personality: the **id**, the **ego**, and the **superego**. The *id* is present in the newborn infant and consists of impulses, emotions and desires. It demands instant gratification of all its wishes and needs. As this is impractical the *ego* develops to act as a practical interface or mediator between reality and the desires of the id. The final structure to develop is the *superego*, which is the sense of duty and responsibility – in many ways the conscience.

The ego and the superego develop as the individual progresses through the five **psychosexual stages** – oral, anal, phallic, latency and genital – and these are described next.

The five psychosexual stages

Oral stage (approximately birth to 1 year)

The infant's greatest satisfaction is derived from stimulation of the lips, tongue, and mouth. Sucking is the chief source of pleasure for the young infant.

psychoanalytic theory most prominently associated with Sigmund Freud. Freud suggested that there are three main personality structures: the *ego*, the *id* and the *superego*.

id in Freud's theory, a primitive collection of urges with which an individual begins life. The id is responsible for an individual's 'primitive' instincts, such as eating and reproducing.

ego in Freud's theory, the ego can be thought of as the rational thought that evolved to control the urges of the *id* in order to meet the demands of reality and maintain social approval and esteem.

superego in Freud's theory, a collection of ideals, an individual's morality. This is what we refer to as our conscience and it is often in conflict with our *id*.

psychosexual stages Freud argued that there were five stages of human development: oral (0–1 year), anal (1–3 years), phallic (3–6 years), latency (6 years–adolescence), and genital (adolescence onwards).

Anal stage (approximately 1 to 3 years)

During this stage toilet or potty training takes place and the child gains the greatest psychosexual pleasure from exercising control over the anus and by retaining and eliminating faeces.

Phallic stage (approximately 3 to 6 years)

This is the time when children obtain their greatest pleasure from stimulating the genitals. At this time boys experience the **Oedipus complex**. This expression derives from the Greek myth in which Oedipus became infatuated with his mother. In the Freudian account the young boy develops sexual feelings towards his mother but realises that his father is a major competitor for her (sexual) affections! He then fears castration at the hands of his father (the **castration complex**) and in order to resolve this complex he adopts the ideals of his father and the superego (the conscience) develops. If we return to Greek mythology, the noblewoman Electra remained obsessively bound, or fixated to the memory of her father Agamemnon. In the Freudian account, for little girls the **Electra complex** is when they develop feelings towards their father and fear retribution at the hands of their mother. They resolve this by empathising with their mother, adopting the ideals she offers, and so the girl's superego develops.

Oedipus complex an important stage of development in Freud's *psychoanalytic theory*. This expression derives from the Greek myth in which Oedipus became infatuated with his mother. In the Freudian account, the young boy develops sexual feelings toward his mother but realises that his father is a major competitor for her (sexual) affections.

castration complex in Freud's *psychoanalitic theory* where the young boy fears castration at the hands of his father.

Electra complex in Freud's *psycholanalytic theory* this is where little girls develop feelings towards their father and fear retribution at the hands of their mother.

Latency and genital stages (approximately 6 years to adolescence)

From around 6 years the torments of infancy and early childhood subside and the child's sexual awakening goes into a resting period (*latency*, from around 6 years to puberty and adolescence). Then, at adolescence, sexual feelings become more apparent and urgent and the genital stage appears. In the latter 'true' sexual feelings emerge and the adolescent strives to cope with awakening desires.

Problems with Freudian theory

One of the main claims of Freudian theory is that much of what motivates us is determined unconsciously. By their very nature unconscious processes cannot be measured and so it is often claimed that belief in Freudian ideas is precisely that – beliefs rather than evidence-based claims. It is certainly the case that Freud's views are almost impossible to test. To illustrate this consider the Freudian notion of **reaction formation**. If you are harshly toilet trained as a child then the Freudian prediction would be that you become 'anally retentive', that is, you become excessively neat and tidy. However, if in some way you recognise this in yourself (maybe even unconsciously) then you can react against it (i.e. *reaction formation* occurs) and you actively become very untidy! What this means is that you can react against your upbringing and reverse the effects, which means in turn that it

reaction formation a term used in *psychoanalytic theory*. The individual may react, often unconsciously, to negative aspects of their personality.

is impossible to predict the child's development despite the fact that the first 6 years from birth are supposedly critical in determining later personality formation.

Psychoanalysis, then and now: An overview

Freudian theory has been of immense importance in pointing out two possibilities. One is that early childhood can be immensely important in affecting and determining later development (a position also adopted by people such as Bowlby, whose views are given above), and the other is that we can be driven by unconscious needs and desires of which we are not aware. Thus, if we did not go through one of the childhood psychosexual stages very well, this could reflect itself in later adult disorders such as neurotic symptoms, but we would not be aware of the causes of the problem. The only way to come to terms with this would be intensive sessions of psychoanalysis (see Figure 2.5) in which the analyst tries to discover what it is that went wrong in your childhood that is causing your current problems.

The theory is largely unsupported by scientific evidence. Thus, there is little evidence that the Oedipus and Electra complexes occur. Additionally, if events occurring in early childhood can have different outcomes (as a result of reaction formation) then it is impossible to make clear predictions about the effects of early experiences. Nevertheless, there are many who believe that psychoanalytic theories are important in understanding human development, and there have been many theoreticians who have offered variations and alternatives to Freud's proposals. We briefly consider two of these next, Anna Freud and Erik Erikson (psychoanalytic accounts of the development of self and of adolescence are given in Chapters 8 and 17).

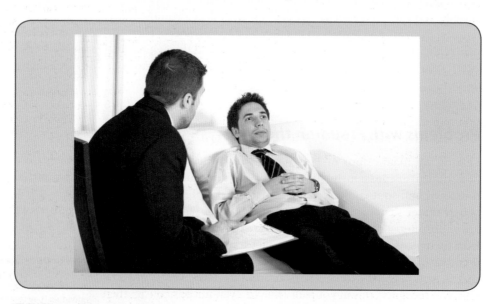

FIGURE 2.5 *The psychoanalyst tries to discover what it is that went wrong in your childhood that is causing your current problems.*
Source: © Blaj Gabriel/Shutterstock.

Modern psychoanalysts – Anna Freud and Erik Erikson

Anna Freud (1895–1982) was the youngest of Sigmund Freud's children. She grew up with an interest in psychoanalysis, and is often referred to as 'the founder of child psychoanalysis'. She felt that adolescence and puberty presented a series of challenges. During this period of ego struggle, through meeting these challenges the ego matures and becomes better able to defend itself. For Erik Erikson (1902–94), like Anna Freud, personality formation was not largely complete by age 6 or 7 as Sigmund Freud suggested. Rather, stages of psychological conflict and adjustment occur throughout the lifespan. Whereas Freud felt that the child's personality was determined largely by parents and by unconscious forces, Erikson gave much greater emphasis to the role of the broader social world which includes relatives, friends, society and culture. For this reason Erikson's stages are called **psychosocial** rather than *psychosexual*. The work of Anna Freud and Erikson as it applies to adolescent development is discussed in more detail in Chapter 17.

psychosocial stages
stages of development put forward by Erik Erikson. The child goes from the stage of 'basic trust' in early infancy to the final stage in adult life of maturity with a sense of integrity and self-worth.

HUMANISTIC THEORY – ABRAHAM MASLOW

Humanistic theories focus on the individual's own subjective experiences, motives, and desires. In general, they differ from psychoanalytic views in putting much less emphasis on the role of the unconscious in determining behaviour. Humanists argue that we are not driven by unconscious needs, neither are we driven by external environmental pulls such as reinforcement and rewards. Rather, humans have free will and are motivated to fulfil their potential. The inner need or desire to fulfil one's potential is known as **self-actualisation**. The drive for self-actualisation is not restricted to childhood but is applicable across the life span, and a leading proponent of the humanistic view was Abraham Maslow (1908–70).

humanistic theory theory which emphasises that humans have free will and are motivated to fulfil their potential.

self-actualisation fulfilment of needs beyond those deemed necessary for survival.

Abraham Maslow's hierarchy of needs

Maslow suggested that there is a **hierarchy of needs** or motives that determine our behaviour. The hierarchy is given below (Figure 2.6) and extends from the basic needs for survival through the search for self-actualisation. To see how Maslow's hierarchy might work, imagine the following scenario (based on Dworetsky, 1995, p. 43). You are a young man or woman who arrives as an emigrant/immigrant to a foreign country, broke and homeless. Your first aim would be

hierarchy of needs
stages of needs or desires in Abraham Maslow's *humanistic theory* which go from the basic physiological needs for food and water to the ultimate desire for *self-actualisation* or the desire to fulfil one's potential.

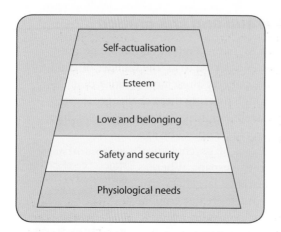

FIGURE 2.6 *Maslow's hierarchy of needs.*

to ensure that your basic physiological needs for food, water and warmth were satisfied. Next would be finding a place where you feel safe and secure. You are then able to begin to search for ways of satisfying your psychological needs, to develop relationships with people so you feel that you belong. Your sense of self-esteem develops as you feel needed by others, and your final goal would be to attain self-actualisation – this is equivalent to achieving your full potential, perhaps in education, sport, music, rearing children, and many other types of activity and attainment.

Maslow's theory was not intended as a theory of children's development – the hierarchy of needs is applicable at all ages from early childhood on, and children achieve goals and fulfil their potential as do adults. It is worth noting that, sadly, there are over 200 million child slaves in the world today – children who work in the fields, in domestic slavery, in bars, restaurants, on building sites, in sweatshops perhaps making expensive (or cheap) clothes and shoes for Western consumption, and in many countries the prettiest children are raised in brothels. For countries in the developing world child slave labour makes good sense – children are a renewable resource, they don't form unions, they are cheap and trainable. These children enter a lifetime sentence of hard labour and ill health for the 'crime' of poverty – their needs lower in Maslow's hierarchy are met but self-actualisation is a myth not an attainable possibility.

PUTTING IT ALL TOGETHER – DIFFERENT THEORIES FOR DIFFERENT NEEDS

In this chapter we have given a sample of the many different theories that have been developed to explain human development. As is abundantly obvious, child development is enormously complex, and we should not expect any theory, however 'grand' to attempt to account for more than one or two selected areas of development. Thus, there are theories that focus specifically on motor, perceptual, cognitive, emotional, social, or personality development.

However, it is important to remember that in the child themselves all aspects of development are interrelated. For example, each new motor acquisition in infancy opens up new ways of exploring the world, which in turn affects infants' awareness of the world and their cognitive and social development. New cognitive achievements affect the child's social development since they allow the child to interact with others at an increasingly more sophisticated level of understanding. Cognitive and social developments give increased opportunities for children to develop their potentials, and hence allow for the possibility of self-actualisation.

The essential point is that theories typically focus on specific areas of development, but development itself is multi-faceted and all aspects of change are integrally linked. To illustrate this interrelatedness of different aspects of development we will focus on one area of development where different theoretical views make their own different contributions, the topic of **gender development**.

Gender development

Gender development concerns the important question of how it is that children grow up knowing that they are either a boy or a girl. Psychologists from several different theoretical traditions have offered accounts of how this happens, and here we give very brief accounts of cognitive, behaviourist/social learning, psychoanalytic and biological explanations.

gender development the developing understanding by a child that it is either a girl or a boy and that there are gender-appropriate behaviours associated with this difference.

A cognitive account

A cognitive view of gender development was offered over 40 years ago by the American psychologist Lawrence Kohlberg (1966, see also Chapter 15 for his theory of the development of moral reasoning). According to Kohlberg's account of gender development the child gradually comes to realise that she/he is a girl or a boy and that this is unchangeable – once a girl (or boy) always a girl (or boy), a realisation that is known as **gender constancy**. Most children come to this realisation some time after 3 years, and almost all know it by age 7 (Tobin et al., 2010; Wehren & De Lisi, 1983). Kohlberg's theory suggests that once children understand which gender they are they will develop appropriate gender-role behaviours. That is, knowing you are a girl or a boy helps the child to organise their behaviour to be gender-appropriate.

gender constancy the awareness, in early childhood, that one is either a boy or a girl, and that this is unchangeable – once a girl (boy), always a girl (boy).

A social learning account

Social learning accounts of gender development are based on the work of Albert Bandura, whose views we discussed earlier, and these in turn are developed from behaviourist theories of learning. In this account the child is reinforced for what the parents and others perceive as being gender-appropriate behaviour (girls play with dolls, boys don't cry). Additionally, children imitate significant others and learn to observe same-gender models to see how to behave. In this way, through observation, imitation and reinforcement children's gender roles are shaped.

A psychoanalytic view

In the Freudian version of psychoanalytic theory a girl's identification with her mother, and a boy's with his father, develop from the resolution of the Electra and Oedipus complexes, as described above. As a result of this identification girls and boys form female and male identities (respectively!) and take on their same-gender parent's views and behaviour as their own.

Biological determinants

The accounts described so far all emphasise the role of *nurture* in promoting gender development. But remember that the physical aspects of gender are biologically determined by the type of chromosomes we inherit at conception (see Chapter 4). Here we will describe a case history (which is described in more detail in Chapter 8) to highlight the role of *nature* (genetic and biological) in gender determination.

Bruce Reimer was one of two identical twins born on 22 August 1965. The twins developed urinary problems and at 8 months Bruce (and his twin brother Brian) were taken to a clinic for circumcision. What happened to Bruce was that he 'had his penis accidentally burned to ablation during phimosis repair by cautery' (Diamond & Sigmundson, 1999, p. 58). What this medical terminology means is that the incompetent physician destroyed Bruce's penis.

At the time one of the most influential views on gender development was expressed by the psychologist John Money (e.g. Money & Ehrhardt, 1972), and was that individuals are psychosexually and gender neutral at birth, and that experience (*nurture*) is the sole determinant of their development. A decision was therefore made to carry out gender-reassignment surgery (to create a vagina and female genital appearance), and to rear Bruce as Brenda. This case is described in earlier textbooks on child development as clear evidence that nurture determined gender roles, and Money's theoretical views achieved widespread acceptance, even to the point that some were arguing that if a genetic male had a small penis (in extreme instances this is referred to as a *micropenis*) then 'Often it is wiser to rear a genetic male as a female' (Donahoe & Hendren, 1976, p. 396).

But it all went drastically wrong. Even soon after the operation 'Brenda' began rejecting girl things, like refusing to wear dresses. Somewhere between the ages of 9 and 11 Brenda 'figured that I was a guy'. At school 'she' persisted in standing up to urinate in the girls' bathroom. She made several suicide attempts and finally learned the truth. At this time Brenda refused to carry on as a female and insisted on gender reassignment (which included a mastectomy and phallus reconstruction) to his biologically determined gender, and called himself David. He later married an older woman and adopted her children. This case is one that gives strong support for the view that prenatal and early-infantile hormones have a strong influence on gender development and other gender dimorphism characteristics.

Overview

These different accounts of gender development all have their appeal. It is clear that social influences and children's cognitive awareness influence their gender-related behaviour. But it is also clear that biological (genetic/hormonal) influences are important. Many, perhaps most, *transsexuals* (those who elect for gender reassignment, often through surgical procedures) will say that they have felt that they were a girl in a boy's body (or vice versa) for as long as they can remember, even though they may never have been reinforced for gender-inappropriate behaviour. What is clear is that we have different theoretical views and there are multiple causes of gender development in children. Perhaps biological factors provide the basic differences, and cognitive and social factors add the fine detail to create behavioural differences.

ISSUES IN CHILD DEVELOPMENT

There are many issues, controversies and debates in the study of child development, and we will see the most important of these in the pages of this book. Many of these topics are specific to a particular area or areas of development, but there are others that affect almost all aspects of growth and here we briefly describe three of these – the **nature–nurture issue**, **stability versus change**, **continuity versus discontinuity**.

The nature–nurture issue

We are all of us a product of the *interaction* of the two broad factors of *nature* – inheritence or genetic factors – and *nurture* – environmental influences. For example, it is argued that humans are genetically predisposed to acquire language, but which language we acquire is determined by the language(s) we hear and learn. It is important to note that without both factors no development could occur! Nevertheless, people differ in their abilities, temperaments, personalities and a host of other characteristics, and psychologists and **behaviour geneticists** have attempted to estimate the relative contributions of nature and nurture to these individual variations between people. Are certain behavioural characteristics such as gender development (as discussed in the previous section), intelligence, and personality more influenced by heredity or by the environment? A detailed account of these attempts, and of the nature–nurture issue in general, is given in Chapter 3.

nature–nurture issue ongoing debate on whether development is the result of an individual's genes (nature) or the kinds of experiences they have throughout their life (nurture).

stability versus change the question of whether individuals are stable in the sense of maintaining their rank order across age, e.g. does the bright 2-year-old become a bright 10-year-old?

continuity versus discontinuity whether development is *continuous*, and therefore an accumulation of 'more of the same', or *discontinuous* and marked by qualitative changes. Piaget's theory is an example of a *discontinuous* theory of development.

behaviour genetics the study of how genetic factors influence behaviour and, more generally, differences between individuals.

Stability versus change

It is often claimed that 'the child is father to the man' (or 'the child is mother to the woman'), meaning that early experiences influence current and later development. This view suggests that certain aspects of children's development display stability, in the sense that they are consistent and predictable across time. It turns out that development is characterised by both stability and change – for example, personality characteristics such as shyness, and the tendency to be aggressive tend to be stable, while others such as *approach* (the tendency to extreme friendliness and lack of caution with strangers) and *sluggishness* (reacting passively to changing circumstances) are unstable (as discussed in Chapter 15).

Continuity versus discontinuity

In Chapter 1 we described two 'world views' which are called *organismic* and *mechanistic*. Organismic theories, such as Piaget's, emphasise that some of the most interesting changes in human development – such as those that accompany major changes in thinking, puberty, and other life transitions such as first going to school, going to college, getting married, etc. – are characterised by discontinuity, by qualitatively different ways of thinking and behaving. Mechanistic theories, as exemplified by behaviourist views, emphasise continuity – that development is reflected by a more continuous growth function, rather than occurring in qualitatively different stages. What complicates things is that, as we have seen, it is often possible to think of the same aspect of development (such as intelligence) as being both continuous and discontinuous. Sternberg and Okagaki (1989, p. 158) state the case as follows:

> as it stands, the continuity–discontinuity debate is largely misconceived and . . . we should . . . be thinking in terms of ways in which development is simultaneously continuous and discontinuous with respect to different dimensions of analysis.

SUMMARY AND CONCLUSIONS

Although these three issues will appear regularly in the chapters of this book it is important to keep in mind that human development requires both nature and nurture, it displays aspects of stability and also change, and it is both continuous and discontinuous.

In the rest of this book you will find many examples of theories and theoretical approaches – mostly the ones that we have described in this chapter, but also a few new ones. Always remember that a theory has specific applications – that is, attempts to account for a limited area of development – and we should not ask too much of any one. It would be a mistake to criticise Piaget, Freud, and Bowlby for paying too little attention, respectively, to social development, the role of conscious awareness, and cognitive development, because this was not their aim! All of these theoreticians, the others described here, and yet others whose work will appear in later chapters, have helped to mould our understanding of children's development and make it the exciting, dynamic topic of enquiry that it is today.

DISCUSSION POINTS

1. Considering the evidence presented here, list as many aspects of motor development (a) that may not depend on experience, (b) that probably do depend on experience.

2. Discuss ways in which Piaget's account of development differs from (a) maturational accounts, and (b) accounts that portray development as moulded by the environment.

3. Think of differences between Piaget's theory and information processing theories of development.

4. Skinner's theory of learning through reinforcement seems quite plausible in many ways. Think about what makes the account plausible, and also about the aspects of development that it does not explain.

5. In what ways has Albert Bandura's social learning theory and social cognitive theory advanced our understanding of factors influencing development?

6. Is the psychoanalytic approach to development a theory or just a compelling story?

7. How plausible is it that Maslow was able to establish a hierarchy of needs simply from interviews about sexuality?

8. The view presented here is that different theoretical approaches to development can exist side by side, complementing each other. Consider whether there are limits to this view. For instance, are there some approaches that are so opposed that they cannot coexist?

SUGGESTIONS FOR FURTHER READING

Bremner, G., & Slater, A. (2004). *Theories of infant development*. Oxford and Massachusetts: Blackwell.

Fancher, R.E. (1990). *Pioneers of psychology* (2nd edn). New York & London: W.W. Norton.

Green, M., & Piel, J.A. (2002). *Theories of human development: a comparative approach*. Massachusetts: Allyn and Bacon.

Harris, M. (2008). *Exploring developmental psychology: understanding theory and methods*. Washington, DC & London: Sage.

Thomas, R.M. (2000). *Recent theories of human development*. Washington, DC & London: Sage.

Thomas, R.M. (2005). *Comparing theories of child development*. Belmont, CA: Wadsworth Publishers.

REFERENCES

Adolph, K.E., & Avolio, A.M. (2000). Walking infants adapt locomotion to changing body dimensions. *Journal of Experimental Psychology: Human Perception and Performance, 26,* 1148–1166.

Adolph, K.E., & Joh, A.S. (2007). Motor development: how infants get in the act. In A. Slater & M. Lewis (Eds.), *Introduction to infant development* (pp.63–80). Oxford: Oxford University Press.

Amso, D., & Johnson, S.P. (2006). Learning by selection: Visual search and object perception in young infants. *Developmental Psychology, 6,* 1236–1245.

Bandura, A. (2001). Social Cognitive Theory: An agentic perspective. *Annual Review of Psychology, 52,* 1–26.

Bandura, A. (2009). Social cognitive theory goes global. *The Psychologist, 22,* 504–506.

Bliss, J. (2010). Recollections of Jean Piaget. *The Psychologist, 23,* 444–446.

Bowlby, J. (1952). *Maternal care and mental health*. Geneva: World Health Organisation.

Campos, J.J., Anderson, D.I., Barbu-Roth, M.A., Hubbard, E.M., Hertenstein, M.J., & Witherington, D. (2000). Travel broadens the mind. *Infancy*, *1*, 149–219.

Cohen, L.B., & Amsel, G. (1998). Precursors to infants' perception of causality. *Infant Behavior & Development*, *21*, 713–731.

Cohen, L.B., Chaput, H.H., & Cashon, C.H. (2002). A constructivist model of infant cognition. *Cognitive Development*, *17*, 1323–1343.

Diamond, M., & Sigmundson, H.K. (1999). Sex reassignment at birth. In S.J. Ceci & W.M. Williams (Eds.), *The nature–nurture debate: The essential readings* (pp. 55–80). Oxford and Massachusetts: Blackwell.

Donahoe, P.K., & Hendren, W.H.I. (1976), Evaluation of the newborn with ambiguous genitalia. *Pediatric Clinics of North America*, *23*, 361–370.

Dworetsky, J.P. (1995). *Human development: A lifespan approach*. New York: West Publishing.

Flavell, J.H. (1963). *The developmental psychology of Jean Piaget*. Toronto, New York and London: Van Nostrand.

Flavell, J.H. (1996). Piaget's legacy. *Psychological Science*, *7*, 200–203.

Gesell, A., & Ames, L. (1940). The ontogenetic organization of prone behavior in human infancy. *Journal of Genetic Psychology*, *56*, 247–263.

Gibson, J.J. (1979). *The ecological approach to visual perception*. Hillsdale, NJ: Erlbaum.

Gill, S.V., Adolph, K.E., & Vereijken, B. (2009). Change in action: How infants learn to walk down slopes. *Developmental Science*, *12*, 888–902.

Gottlieb, J.P., Kusunoki, M., & Goldberg, M.E. (1998). The representation of visual salience in monkey parietal cortex. *Nature*, *391*, 481–484.

Harlow, H., & Zimmerman, R.R. (1959). Affectional responses in the infant monkey. *Science*, *130*, 421–432.

Johnson, S.P. (2004). Development of perceptual completion in infancy. *Psychological Science*, *15*, 769–775.

Kohlberg, L. (1966). A cognitive-developmental analysis of children's sex-role concepts and attitudes. In E.E. Macoby (Ed.), *The development of sex differences* (pp. 81–173). Stanford, CA: Stanford University Press.

Leslie, A.M. (1984). Spatiotemporal continuity and the perception of causality in infants. *Perception*, *13*, 287–305.

Lewin, K. (1944). The dynamics of group action. *Educational Leadership*, *1*, 195–200.

McGraw, M. (1945). *Neuromuscular maturation of the human infant*. New York: Hafner.

Money, J., & Ehrhardt, A.A. (1972). *Man and woman/boy and girl*. Baltimore, MD: Johns Hopkins University Press.

Miller, P.H. (1993). *Theories of developmental psychology* (3rd edn). Englewood Cliffs, NJ: Prentice-Hall.

Piaget, J. (1960). *The child's conception of the world*. London: Routledge.

Piaget, J. (1962). The stages of the intellectual development of the child. *Bulletin of the Menninger Clinic*, *26*, 120–128. Reprinted in A. Slater & D. Muir (1999). (Eds.), *The Blackwell reader in developmental psychology*, pp. 35–42. Oxford and Massachusetts: Blackwell.

Schaffer, H.R., & Emerson, P.E. (1964). *The development of social attachments in infancy*. Monographs of the Society for Research in Child Development, 29, No 94.

Schlesinger, M., Amso, D., & Johnson, S.P. (2007). The neural basis for visual selective attention in young infants: A computational account. *Adaptive Behavior*, *15*, 135–148.

Siegler, R.S., & Shipley, C. (1995). Variation, selection, and cognitive change. In T. Simon & G. Halford (Eds.), *Developing cognitive competence: New approaches to process modeling* (pp. 31–76). Hillsdale, NJ: Erlbaum.

Skinner, B.F. (1961). *Cumulative record*. London: Methuen.

Sternberg, R.J. & Okagaki, L. (1989). Continuity and discontinuity in intellectual development are not a matter of 'either–or'. *Human Development*, *32*, 158–166.

Thelen, E. (1999). Three-month-old infants can learn task-specific patterns of interlimb coordination. In K. Lee (Ed.), *Childhood cognitive development: the essential readings* (pp. 91–105). Oxford: Blackwell.

Thelen, E., & Spencer, J.P. (1998). Postural control during reaching in young infants: A dynamic systems approach. *Neuroscience and Biobehavioral Reviews*, *22*, 507–514.

Tobin, D.D., Menon, M., Menon, M., Spatta, B.C., Hodges, E.V.E., & Perry, D.G. (2010). The intrapsychics of gender: A model of self-socialization. *Psychological Review*, *117*, 601–622.

Watson, J.B. (1970). *Behaviorism*. New York: Norton.

Wehren, A., & De Lisi, R. (1983). The development of gender understanding: judgements and explanations. *Child Development*, *54*, 1568–1578.

Westermann, G., Mareschal, D., Johnson, M.H., Sirois, S., Spratling, M.W., & Thomas, M.S.C. (2007). Neuroconstructivism. *Developmental Science*, *10*, 75–83.

3 The Nature–Nurture Issue (an Illustration Using Behaviour-Genetic Research on Cognitive Development)

Elisa A. Esposito, Elena L. Grigorenko, and Robert J. Sternberg

KEY TERMS

alleles • alternative splicing • autosomes • behaviour genetics • chromosome • chronological age (CA) • cognitive functioning • components of phenotypic variance • differential psychology • dizygotic (fraternal) twins • empiricism • environmentalism • environmentality • epigenetic theory • familial resemblance • fluid intelligence • g • gene–environment correlation • gene expression • genetic determinism • genetic variant • genotype • heritability • intelligence quotient (IQ) • intelligence test • mental age (MA) • meta-analysis • monozygotic (identical) twins • nativism • nature–nurture issue • nucleotides • nurture • phenotype • socio-economic status (SES) • standardised test • transcription • translation

CHAPTER OUTLINE

BOX 3.1   INTELLIGENCE AND INTELLIGENCE TESTS: A PRECHAPTER INTERLUDE

Alan Slater

The Start of It All: The First Intelligence Test

The first intelligence test along modern lines was created by the Frenchman Alfred Binet in 1905. Binet had been set the task by the Parisian school authorities of devising a test that would select those children who were unlikely to learn much from being in ordinary schools, so that they could then be given special education (see Figure 3.1). Binet's test gave different questions to children of different ages and was based on their general knowledge, and their ability to reason and solve problems. His test consisted of some 30 items, ranging from the ability to touch parts of one's face to more abstract concepts. It was sufficiently successful that it correlated well with teachers' estimates of children's ability such that those who scored highly were judged to be "bright," whereas those who did poorly were judged "dull" or retarded. A modern version of Binet's test is still much used today – the Stanford-Binet test.

Mental Age and Intelligence Quotient (IQ)

Binet introduced the concept of *mental age (MA)*, which can be defined as *an individual's level of mental ability relative to others*. If a child with a real or **chronological age (CA)** of 5 years succeeded at problems usually solved by 7-year-olds, their MA would be 7 while their CA is 5 and the child is judged to be bright. Conversely, if a 5-year-old succeeded only at the level of a 3-year-old their MA is below average and they are likely to have learning difficulties at school.

> **chronological age (CA)** a person's actual age, as opposed to their *mental age*.

A few years later (1912), William Stern introduced the term *intelligence quotient (IQ)*, and in its original formulation it was simply calculated as a child's MA divided by the child's CA multiplied by 100:

$$IQ = \frac{MA}{CA} \times 100$$

We can see from this formulation that those children who are exactly average for their age have an IQ of 100; if MA is below CA then the IQ is below 100; if MA is above CA then the child is bright and IQ is above 100.

Intelligence Tests

There are four important things to note about IQ tests and IQ scores. (1) The simple formula given above is no longer used, but the purpose of IQ tests is always to compare people's (children's or adults') scores with those from people of the same population and of approximately the same age. (2) The average IQ at a given time is always 100. To ensure this it means that tests are carefully **standardised** every few years to ensure that the population varies around this mean. This means that test makers provide a conversion chart so that an individual's raw score (i.e. the number of items passed) can be expressed as an IQ score. (3) Children's and adults' raw scores tend to increase from one generation to the next, hence the need for regular standardisation of tests – a

> **standardised test** a test of a psychological characteristic, such as personality, aptitude, or intelligence, that has been *standardised* on a representative sample of the population.

(Continued)

fuller discussion of this, and the possible reasons for the changes, is given in Chapter 1. (4) The items on IQ tests invariably proceed from the simple to the complex, so that an individual's raw score (and hence their IQ) is derived from the number of items passed before they make mistakes.

There are now several widely used IQ tests, and hundreds of tests of specific abilities. Three well-known tests are: (1) the *Stanford-Binet* for the ages of 2 to adulthood; (2) the Wechsler scales (the *Wechsler Preschool and Primary Scale of Intelligence – WPPSI –* for ages 4 to 6.5; the *Wechsler Intelligence Scale for Children – WISC –* 6 to 16 (see Table 15.1, p.000); the *Wechsler Adult Intelligence Scale – WAIS*); (3) the *Differential Ability Scales – DAS –* from infancy to adolescence.

What is Intelligence – One Ability or Several?

To a large extent how intelligence is defined determines how it is measured. We can probably agree that intelligence involves verbal abilities, memory, problem-solving skills, and the ability to adapt and change to meet life's demands. Unfortunately, however, the agreement stops there! The concepts of mental age and IQ suggest that intelligence is a single general ability, and there are those who argue that a general intelligence ability (often referred to simply as '**g**') underlies performance on all intelligence tests. Others suggest that intelligence is made up of a number of specific abilities or subskills. Still others have argued that performance on intelligence tests is unrelated to our ability to 'live our lives intelligently'. One commentator has remarked: 'Tests have very modest correlations with performance in skills that society deems important' (Deese, 1993, p.113).

g the term used to denote general intelligence. Note that it is always written as g and never G.

In line with this view, Steve Ceci and Jeff Liker (1986) tested 30 'avid racetrack patrons' for their ability to use a sophisticated multiplicative model to handicap races – an important ability if you make a living from horse races! They found no relationship (correlation) between this ability and IQ (the handicappers' IQs ranged from 83 to 130), leading them to the conclusion that 'IQ is unrelated to real-world forms of cognitive complexity' (p. 255). In additional research Steve Ceci found little relationship between IQ and income, leading him to the reasonable conclusion that 'it's better to be born rich than smart'!

Nevertheless, we have known for many years that occupation is related to IQ: teachers, doctors, accountants, pharmacists, lawyers, and those in similar occupations have a mean IQ above 120; people in semi- or low-skilled occupations such as barber, farmhand, or labourer have a mean IQ below 100. Perhaps we can conclude that intelligence, as measured by intelligence tests, is genuinely measuring something that is worthwhile, and there are many who would argue that 'intelligence is a useful and powerful construct' (Kline, 1991, p.145).

Intelligence test items

The inability of psychologists and others to agree on a definition of intelligence has led some to produce the circular definition that 'intelligence is what intelligence tests measure' – at least this avoids a lot of controversy! So, how do intelligence tests measure intelligence?

Many tests divide intelligence into two broad abilities, verbal and performance subscales. You would be likely to find the following sorts of items.

Verbal subscales

Similarities The child is asked to say in what way things might be similar. For example, 'In what ways do blue, green, and yellow go together?' and (an item suitable for an older child) '. . . justice, democracy, freedom.'

(Continued)

Comprehension This subscale measures the child's common sense and understanding. For example: 'Why do people need to pay taxes?'

Recall of digits The tester reads out sequences of digits and after each sequence the child calls it back. For example: '6 – 9 – 4' and later (much later!) '4 – 7 – 8 – 5 – 1 – 7 – 2 – 4 – 8 – 3.' The average digit span for adults is about seven items (so very few people would give perfect recall of the second list of digits), and it increases during childhood.

You might wonder why this item is given under the heading 'verbal subscales'! This is simply because digit span correlates well with verbal rather than performance subscales – the child with the higher digit span is likely to have the greater verbal skills.

Performance subscales

Block design The child is given a set of blocks with coloured patterns on them, and asked to use them to make patterns that the tester shows.

Copying The child is shown a drawing and asked to copy it on a sheet of paper. The drawings are initially simple (perhaps an outline of a triangle, or three vertical lines) and become progressively more complex geometric shapes.

Controversies and Issues in Intelligence

We have seen some of the controversies already: How many types of intelligence are there? How useful is what intelligence tests measure? Here we will consider one more controversial issue: How much of our intelligence is shaped by genetic factors and how much by our environment?

In fact, it has long been recognized that genes and environment are not additive, in the sense that *x* per cent of intelligence is caused by genes and *y* per cent by the environment. Rather, they *interact* with each other in causing the development of all human characteristics, including intelligence. Accordingly, scientists try to produce estimates of *heritability*, which is asking the question *how much of the variation in intelligence between individuals in a population is caused by genetic factors?*

The importance of this issue lies in its societal, racial, economic, and political implications. If heritability is high, then some racial groups and classes of children who score poorly, on average, on IQ tests might be thought to do so for reasons that are primarily of genetic origin. Conversely, if heritability is low, these differences in IQ scores may be primarily environmentally determined and it becomes important to enhance the cognitive environment of the disadvantaged in order to provide an intellectually stimulating environment.

A detailed account of the nature–nurture issue and estimates of heritability is provided in this chapter.

FIGURE 3.1 *A child taking an intelligence test.*
Source: Sciencephoto.com

OVERVIEW

The question of the origins of individual differences has concerned philosophers and scientists for centuries. Just as in the case of questions about the origins of ability, controversy has raged concerning the degree to which genetic and environmental factors determine the differences in ability between individuals. This is the nature–nurture issue described at the end of Chapter 2, and in this chapter the authors review the methods used to investigate the origins of individual differences and the evidence that emerges from the *behaviour-genetic* approach.

The first step towards getting to grips with the behaviour-genetic approach is to master the basic terminology, and an early part of the chapter explains terms such as *genotype, phenotype, genetic variant, components of phenotypic variance* and *familial resemblance*. The authors go on to consider the factors that contribute to individual differences, the concepts used in investigating the effects of these factors, and how different research approaches contribute to our understanding of the interaction between effects of genes and environment. The chapter considers evidence arising from twin studies and problems interpreting the concepts of *heritability* and *environmentality*.

One thing that this chapter makes very clear is that there is no simple answer regarding the contribution of genetic and environmental factors to the development of differences between people. Rather, there is a highly complex interplay between factors. Thus, it is not enough to have plotted the human genome, and we have to go on to understand how genes are expressed in cognition, and the authors point to the expanding field of *epigenetics* as holding the ultimate key.

WHY DO PEOPLE DIFFER IN THE WAY THEY THINK?

Why do people differ in the way they think? Why are some people smarter than others? Why do children's abilities resemble their parents' abilities? Why do children in one family differ in the way they learn compared with children in other families and, moreover, compared with each other? Why do people vary in intelligence? Why do people's levels of intelligence vary as they develop? These are the kinds of questions we address in this chapter.

The observation of differences in cognitive abilities between people has many explanations, depending on the context and the goal of the given discussion. For example, consider how different professionals might seek to understand differences in two people's performance on an IQ test. Nutritionists might inquire whether both people have been well nourished over the course of their lifetime; the nutritionists might even ask if both people had breakfast on the day of the test, and if so, what it was. Psychophysiologists might think about differences in nerve conduction velocities. Psychologists might seek to understand previous learning experiences, motivation, and genetic endowments. In this chapter, we will speak from a behaviour- and molecular-genetic point of view, considering both the genetic and environmental sources of individual differences in **cognition**.

The goal of this chapter is to explore sources of observed differences in cognitive functioning as informed by behaviour-genetic research. The design of the chapter is as follows. First we describe the phenomenon of individual differences in cognition. We then show how this phenomenon is studied using a behaviour-genetic approach. Finally, we summarise the current state of knowledge regarding the sources of individual differences in cognition.

> **cognition** mental activity, such as attention, memory, problem-solving, thinking, intelligence.

THE BEHAVIOUR-GENETIC APPROACH TO STUDYING INDIVIDUAL DIFFERENCES

The concept of individual differences

If we enter a randomly selected classroom in any non-specialised school in any corner of the world and look at the children in this classroom, at first glance we will notice how different these children are (see Figure 3.2). They are different in height and weight, their bodies are formed differently, and their noses and eyes have different shapes. Then, if we look at the class yearbook or talk to a teacher, we will discover that all of these children differ as well in terms of their academic performance and abilities. In other words, in any randomly chosen group of children (or adults, for that matter), we will find a significant amount of variation in virtually any trait we observe. Almost everything that can be measured or counted in human beings demonstrates variation around the mean (average) value in a given population. The concept traditionally used to describe such variation in human traits (e.g. height, weight, facial features, academic performance) is that of *individual differences*.

The existence of individual differences in the ways people think and learn attracted the attention of philosophers many centuries ago. These philosophers proposed theories to account for the sources of variation between people. The assumption made was quite simple: If people vary in the way they think, there should be some natural explanation of this variation. Two hypotheses dominated philosophical thinking and still dominate much thinking today: (1) People are born to be the way they are (**genetic determinism**) or (2) people learn to be the way they are (**environmentalism**).

> **genetic determinism** the hypothesis that people become who they are as a consequence of their genetic code.

> **environmentalism** the hypothesis that people learn to be the way they are, that the person we become is a consequence of the experiences we have had throughout life.

There have been many attempts to verify both hypotheses, both philosophical and scientific. Here, we concentrate on the scientific endeavours. As a result of massive scientific effort, much information

FIGURE 3.2 *In any randomly chosen group of children there will be a significant amount of variation in virtually any trait we observe.*
Source: Shutterstock.

has been accumulated. The consensus today, however, is that there is not just a single source of individual differences. Rather, the appearance of variation between people (sometimes called *interindividual variation*) in any population is the product of a complex interplay of two forces, globally referred to as genes and environment.

Genes and environment

The paradigm

How did the idea come about that genes and environments may be relevant to cognition? The idea to look for measurable links between genes, environment, and cognitive functioning is relatively new, but its philosophical framework was formulated many centuries ago. The roots of this idea are in the well-known **nature versus nurture** controversy that has been around for ages. The main idea (albeit a misformulated one) underlying this controversy is that genes and environment act separately. Within the framework of the nature–nurture controversy, genes and environments are viewed as independent forces; the extreme polar examples of this controversy are the assumptions that genes determine one's fate, at the one extreme, or that it is environments that completely shape one's individuality, at the other.

The nature–nurture controversy has many faces, including the **nativism–empiricism** issue in the psychology of sensation and perception and the issue of maturation versus learning in developmental psychology. In the psychology of learning and cognition, this controversy presents itself as the issue of environmental equipotentiality (i.e. we all have the same potential to learn and benefit from environmental experiences) versus biological preparedness (i.e. we are genetically different in our ability to learn from our environments; for more details, see Kimble (1994). At the end of the 19th century, a British scientist, Francis Galton (1869), narrowed the nature–nurture controversy down to an opposition between heredity and environment. With the discovery of genes as units of heredity, the controversy took its current form as the 'genes versus environment' debate. It is crucial to point out here that the formulation of a 'genes versus environment' controversy at all is extremely misleading. Genes do not exist in a vacuum – they exist in each of the cells of our bodies. Because it would be impossible for a person to exist without ever interacting with their environment in some way, this controversy presents an impossible premise. Scientists have shifted from viewing genes and environment as opposing forces, to understanding the genome as a dynamic structure (Robinson, 2004), which we will illustrate during a later discussion of epigenetics. Yet, despite its inaccuracies, the motivation for formulating the nature–nurture opposition is clear: Knowing that people differ in the ways that they think, scientists wanted to understand *why* they differ and, subsequently, what (if anything) can be done to minimise (or maximise) these differences. In other words, knowing that there is variation in cognitive functions between people, scientists want to understand the sources of this variation and how to control them.

Studies investigating sources of variability in behavioural traits presently are being conducted in different fields, among which are developmental psychology, **differential psychology** (that branch of psychology which deals with individual differences between people), quantitative genetics, molecular genetics, psychiatric genetics, behaviour genetics, and others. For the sake of brevity, in this chapter we will refer to all these studies as behaviour-genetic studies, and will focus on them in the body of this chapter.

> **nativism** the belief that psychological abilities are the product of genetic inheritance – we are simply the product of our genes.

> **empiricism** the belief that psychological abilities are acquired primarily through experience.

> **differential psychology** the branch of psychology that deals with individual differences between people.

Learning the terminology

Five definitions are essential at the outset for the terms phenotype, genotype, genetic variant, components of the phenotypic variance, and familial resemblance.

Phenotype

One of the most important concepts for this chapter is that of phenotype. **Phenotype** refers to the apparent, observable, measurable

> **phenotype** the apparent, observable, measurable characteristics of the individual.

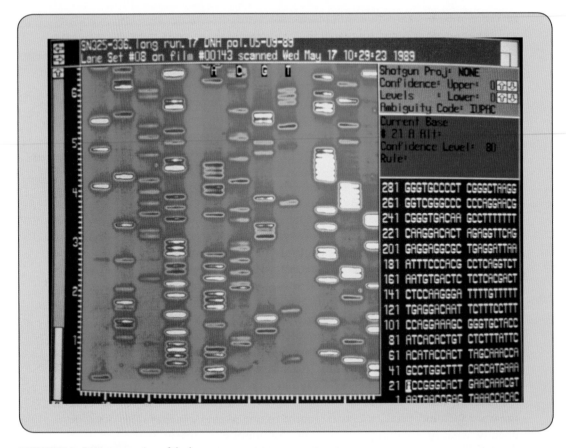

FIGURE 3.3 *DNA sequencing of the human genome.*

Source: © Peter Menzel/Science Photo Library.

characteristics of the individual. Behaviour is a phenotype. Cognition is a phenotype. Because a phenotype literally refers to traits that can be measured, increasingly sophisticated technologies allow researchers to consider phenotypes that were initially unavailable for study. For example, instead of simply measuring IQ as a phenotype of interest, researchers can use different imaging techniques to measure brain size or patterns of neural activation. Imagine designing a study in which you measure frontal lobe activation patterns in lieu of the broader phenotype of mental giftedness. In this example, brain activation is an *endophenotype* – a phenotype within a phenotype. When a given phenotype (e.g. IQ) is measured in a population of individuals and characteristics of the distribution of this measure are obtained, the variance of this distribution is referred to as *phenotypic variance*. The concept of phenotypic variance as a behaviour-genetic concept is analogous to that of individual differences in psychology.

genotype the genetic composition of the individual.

Genotype

Another important concept is the concept of genotype. **Genotype** refers to *the genetic material of the individual*. More specifically, genotype denotes an individual's nucleotide (see p. 93) sequence. This distinction will become more important later in our discussion, but for now it is enough to understand that a genotype is purely a descriptive measure; it tells us which genes are present, but does not give any direct indication of how those genes are behaving. Consider the following analogy: like a genotype, a score on an IQ test is descriptive – it informs us of which capacities are present and to what degree, but it doesn't provide any conclusions as to how the person's mind works.

Genetic variant

A popular misconception – one perpetuated by the mass media – is that there are 'genes' for specific traits, and individuals either have 'a gene' or not. As humans, the vast majority of our DNA is identical, and our species is defined by a series of genes that *all humans possess* (see Figure 3.3). One might ask, then, how genes contribute to individual differences at all if we are indeed largely identical, and here is where we draw the crucial fine lines: Everyone has the same set of genes (i.e. the human genome), but different individuals possess slightly different *versions* of those genes, called **genetic variants** or **alleles**. The best way to understand this concept is to think about faces. Everyone has two eyes, a nose, and a mouth. These features are often only minimally different between individuals of similar ethnic backgrounds. However, those subtle differences are what make us unique – what allow us instantly to recognise the faces of people we know, and even to tell identical twins apart! Although certain research may refer to 'candidate genes' in relation to specific disorders or traits, it is the variants *within* individual genes that result in phenotypic variability.

> **genetic variant** the contribution of different versions of the human genome to individual differences.

> **alleles** genes for the same characteristic located in the same place on a pair of *chromosomes.*

Causal components of the phenotypic variance

The importance of the phenotype–genotype distinction is that it presents the relationship between observable and unobservable characteristics: an observable trait (phenotype) is not a perfect indicator of the individual's latent qualities (genotype). These differences between the phenotype and the corresponding genotype can be accounted for by environmental influences. For example, *monozygotic (identical) twins* (see Figure 3.4) have identical genotypes, yet one may have a higher IQ than the other because of differences in environment.

> **components of phenotypic variance** Components of phenotypic variance are those parts of the total trait variance that can be attributed to different sources of individual differences in a phenotype.

An individual has a given genotype and is exposed to a given environment at a given point of time, so that a person has one 'overall' phenotype at a given time. The phrase 'at any given time' implies that the individual's environment varies over time. The degree to which environmental changes influence the phenotypic value depends on what is being measured. For example, whereas the measurement of a person's height does not depend on daily environment, the measurement of a person's verbal ability might vary daily, depending on the person's mental alertness or general state of mind.

In a somewhat more sophisticated form, this model may also include an interactive term, referring to possible interactions (combinations) of genetic and environmental effects. For example, suppose children who have genetic variants predisposing

FIGURE 3.4 *These identical (monozygotic or MZ) twins share the same genes. Identical twins who are reared in the same home have their genes and environments in common, and an important comparison is between the similarities in IQ (or other measure of phenotypic variation) between identical twins reared together and those reared apart. Nonidentical (dizygotic, fraternal, or DZ) twins have half of their genes in common.*
Source: Shutterstock.

for high levels of a trait (i.e. an absolute pitch) and who are immersed in the strong environment of a music school will develop high-level skills, whereas children with other genetic variants, while at a music school, will, on average, not develop such high levels of skills. Then genetic and environmental factors, as mediated by the parents, are interacting to affect the children's cognitive development. It is important to realise that attempts to quantify the gene–environment interaction can be made only for groups of individuals, because an interaction is only observable using group-based inferential statistics. We have no way of quantifying the interaction for individuals.

The model may also involve gene–environment covariation, which means that sometimes genes and environment produce effects that are indistinguishable from each other (this phenomenon is discussed later, under the heading of 'gene–environment correlations'). To take a simplified case, suppose that children with a certain set of genetic variants that predispose them to musical talents all beg their parents to buy them instruments and music lessons, whereas children without this set of genetic variants do not. The parents agree to the request. Do we attribute the resulting musical outcomes to genes or environment? Well, in a certain sense, we can attribute them to both. The genes influenced the children to behave in a certain way that encouraged the parents to allow the children to play instruments. But the buying of the instruments and lessons was certainly environmental; without it, their musical skills might not have come to fruition. Genes and environment covaried to produce a given effect.

The reader might ask why ideas about genetic and environmental effects, as well as their interaction and covariation, apply at the population level and not at the individual level. The answer to this question is provided in the next section.

Familial resemblance

There are two methods for determining each of the components of phenotypic variance: (1) measuring the response to genetic selection, and (2) assessing the resemblance between relatives (**familial resemblance**). The first method assumes the breeding of organisms selectively for a given trait and then measuring the outcome of the genetic experiments. The structure of modern human society is such that, as a result of our ethical norms and values, we do not wish to do such targeted breeding with humans. What we can do, however, is utilise the second method. We can benefit from so-called natural experiments and assess resemblances between relatives, finding spontaneously occurring situations in which (1) genetic influences are either controlled or randomised so that the effects of the environment can be studied or (2) environmental influences are controlled so that the effects of genes can be studied. So, what is the rationale behind quantifying familial resemblance?

We start with the fact that relatives share genes. **Monozygotic (identical) twins** share all of their genes. A parent and their offspring have half of their genes in common. Two siblings share, on average, half of their genes. **Dizygotic (fraternal) twins**, like regular siblings, also share half of their genes. Half-siblings have a quarter of their genes in common, on average, and so on. Moreover, relatives who live in one home share the family environment. Thus, both genetic and environmental hypotheses predict similarity between relatives living together. This similarity is usually measured by the covariance or correlation on a given trait between relatives.

For example, the correlation of IQs between pairs of unrelated individuals picked at random is about 0 (i.e. 0 within error of measurement). This absence of a positive correlation makes sense because such individuals share neither genes nor environment, and hence their scores do not resemble each other. Other relationships, however, yield both genes and environment in common. For example, in one analysis, the correlation for IQ between identical twins reared together is 0.86 and between fraternal twins reared together is 0.60. The correlation between the IQs of siblings reared together is 0.47, and the correlation between cousins is 0.15 (Chipuer *et al.*, 1990). In other words, for a given trait (e.g. IQ), the correlation between relatives could be explained by the genetic variance and the environmental variance resulting from the genetic and environmental influences shared by relatives.

familial resemblance the resemblance between relatives whose genetic relationship to each other is known.

monozygotic (identical) twins genetically identical twins, developed from one ovum and one sperm which divides into two shortly after conception. Such twins have the same genetic make-up.

dizygotic (fraternal) twins individuals who are conceived at the same time but result from two eggs being fertilised by different sperm. Thus, they are like regular siblings and share half of their genes.

The simplest illustration of how components of phenotypic variance can be determined from studying relatives comes from studying identical and fraternal twins. Identical twins reared together share 100 per cent of their genes and 100 per cent of their family environment. Fraternal twins reared together share only 50 per cent of their genes and 100 per cent of their family environment.

Thus, the components of phenotypic variance can be determined by combining various types of relatives and comparing the measures of their similarity on a trait. Behaviour-genetic studies use a variety of methods (e.g. the family method, twin method, adoption/separation method) in which the degree of resemblance between relatives of different degrees is assessed.

In the above section, we defined the fundamental terms of the chapter. In addition, we summarised the reasoning behind quantifying phenotypic variance and stated that the components of phenotypic variance could be estimated based on the assessment of trait similarity in relatives who share various degrees of genetic similarity. Now, with the necessary background reviewed, the rest of the discussion will centre around the following questions:

- What are the factors that determine interindividual variation in cognitive functioning?
- What are the major concepts used to study these factors?
- How have different research paradigms contributed to our understanding of the effects of genes and environments on cognitive functioning?

THE FORCES DETERMINING INDIVIDUAL DIFFERENCES IN COGNITION

Current behavioural-genetic conceptualisations of the forces determining individual differences in cognition distinguish three major groups of factors: genetic, environmental, and interactional. Let us consider each of them separately.

Genetic influences (G): Types and effects

Every normal human cell has two copies of each **chromosome**, one inherited from the mother and one from the father. Chromosomes are made of genetic material, called DNA, organised into genes, which are templates for the synthesis of the proteins vital to the functioning of the organism. There are 23 pairs of chromosomes in all human cells, except for sperm or egg cells, where this number is halved so that each egg and each sperm receives only one copy of each chromosome. Twenty-two chromosomal pairs are identical in male and female organisms; these chromosomes are called **autosomes**. Autosomes look similar in males and females. The twenty-third pair determines sex. Sex chromosomes in men and women are very different. Females have two (large) X chromosomes; males have a single X and a (smaller) Y. Every gene exists in two copies, maternal and paternal (with the exception, of course, of the Y chromosome), as is the case for chromosomes. These gene copies (gene instantiations) are referred to as alleles.

DNA is composed of four **nucleotides**: adenosine (A), thymine (T), cytosine (C), and guanine (G), which act like a genetic 'alphabet' and encode information. These nucleotides are also referred to as *base pairs* because at any location on the genome, A is always directly across from (or paired with) T, and C is always paired with G. An individual's genotype refers to the sequence of these four 'letters'. When a cell needs to synthesise a particular protein, a series of enzymes 'read' the gene and make a copy of the information in a process known as **transcription**. This copy, called *messenger RNA (mRNA)*, leaves the nucleus and enters the cytosol, where specific organelles use the genetic information to synthesise a protein. Turning an mRNA transcript into a protein is called **translation**. Once a gene is transcribed, we say it has been *expressed*. **Gene expression**, in the form of mRNA transcripts and their resulting proteins, results in a phenotype. These processes are fairly straightforward, but they fail to account for an important detail. If each gene codes for a single protein, why are there many more proteins than there are genes?

Genes can code for more than one protein by utilising **alternative splicing**, in which chunks of the mRNA transcript are removed and/or rearranged before leaving the nucleus to be translated into protein. In other words, a single gene can be expressed in numerous ways – as different versions of a protein (e.g. a serotonin receptor with differently shaped binding sites), or as different proteins altogether. To complicate things further, proteins can change their shape *after* they are translated and they typically interact with each other in huge, complex networks. As evident from even this brief description, the distance between the information coded in an individual's DNA and a behavioural phenotype, such as intelligence, is large and filled with intermediaries. These levels of complexity illustrate that there is room for modification at many points in the pathway from genes to behaviour. Because of this, we must draw another crucial distinction: genes are *probabilistic*, not *deterministic*. Throughout this chapter, we will see that genes do have a significant effect on cognitive skills and general intelligence, but any phenotype is the result of something much more complex than possessing a particular allele.

autosomes the 22 pairs of human *chromosomes*, with the exception of the sex chromosomes.

nucleotides the structural units of DNA which act like a genetic 'alphabet' and encode information. Molecules that when joined together make up the structural units of RNA and DNA.

transcription a process of creating an equivalent RNA copy of a sequence of DNA.

translation turning an mRNA transcript into a protein.

Gene expression the process by which information from a gene is used in the synthesis of a functional gene product.

alternative splicing a process used to code for more than one protein in genes – in which chunks of the mRNA transcript are removed and/or rearranged before leaving the nucleus to be translated into protein.

Additive genetic effects

Additive genetic effects refer to the combined effects of alleles both within and between genes. If a trait is controlled by a number of genes, the additive genetic effect is calculated as a sum of the contributions from every allele, each of which independently contributes a small amount to phenotypic diversity. When alleles do not interact, their joint effect on a trait is equal to a simple sum of their individual effects. Today most behaviour geneticists believe that human intelligence relies on the effects of alleles in dozens of genes; thus, many different genes make small (or very small) individual contributions to the trait of intelligence.

Non-additive genetic effects

The two main types of genetic non-additivity are *dominance* and *epistasis*. Dominance refers to types of interactions between alleles within a gene, whereas epistasis refers to types of interactions between different genes. As we will show below, both dominant and epistatic effects appear to be important in determining variation in cognitive abilities, in general, and in IQ in particular.

Environmental influences (E): Types and effects

Behaviour-genetic researchers divide environmental variance into *shared* and *non-shared* components.

FIGURE 3.5 *Children raised in disadvantaged circumstances, such as this orphanage in Gulu, Uganda, have fewer opportunities to develop higher cognitive abilities than do children brought up in a more stimulating and enriched home environment.*

Source: Sciencephoto.com

Shared environmental effects

All children in a family share the same environment to the degree that, on average, psychosocial environmental characteristics (e.g. social class and parenting styles) differ from those in other families. Shared environmental effects make children reared in the same family more similar than children reared in different families. Scarr (1997) has suggested viewing between-family differences as differences in opportunities. For example, children from low **socio-economic status (SES)** class are thought of as having fewer opportunities to develop higher cognitive abilities than do children from higher SES class as a result of both more stimulating home environment and the correlated school and after-school activities experienced by the higher SES children (Figure 3.5).

> **socio-economic status (SES)** a scale that gives an indication of someone's social class and income bracket.

Non-shared environmental effects

Non-shared environmental variance refers to those aspects of the environment that make children in the same family different. Parents, no matter how hard they try, do not treat all their children in exactly the same way. Examples of within-family environment variance include a wide range of conditions, from prenatal to psychosocial events that affect one sibling differently from another sibling.

When the two are brought together: Gene–environment effects (G × E)

It long has been realised that any model that sharply distinguishes the effects of 'genes' and 'environments' is a simplified model that ignores several processes that are important in the appearance of variation between individuals. Two concepts depicting these processes have been suggested.

Gene–environment correlations

In most cases (with the exception of children given up for adoption or adverse social circumstances that result in externally caused family destruction), parents bestow upon their children not only their genes but also their related immediate environments and experiences. This phenomenon is referred to as *passive* **gene–environment correlation** (or covariance), as discussed earlier. One example of evidence supporting passive gene-environment correlation is the finding that social disadvantage tends to correlate with lower levels of IQ. To take the example a step further, consider children who inherit the genes that predispose them to high IQ and who may also experience the stimulating influence of a family environment that promotes reading. Possibly, the tendency of parents to read to their children a lot may be associated with the same genes that control high IQ.

> **gene–environment correlation** the ways in which children's genetic inheritance affects the environment they experience, and vice versa (also known as *environment–gene correlation*).

There are also other types of gene–environment correlations. *Evocative* correlations arise because the ways in which people respond to children are influenced by the children's own characteristics (Plomin *et al.*, 1977). It is possible that high-IQ children elicit different responses from their caregivers than do children of low intelligence. The example given earlier in this chapter – of children begging their parents for a musical instrument – is an example of evocative gene–environment correlation (covariation).

Active correlations arise as a result of the increased control over the environment that is experienced by growing children. Children themselves shape and organise their environments. For example, children with lower levels of intelligence tend to spend less time engaged in activities that would further stimulate their intellectual development.

Scarr and McCartney (1983) hypothesised that the roles of passive, evocative, and active correlations shift in their significance over the course of development, with the effects of the passive type declining, of the active type increasing, and of the evocative remaining equally important throughout the lifespan. Effects that are outcomes of gene–environment correlations are bidirectional – the observed differences resulting from differential levels of intelligence may in turn influence the child's later development.

meta-analysis an analysis of many studies on the same topic in order to draw general or overall conclusions.

Detection of genotype–environment correlations requires large sample sizes. As of today, only one **meta-analysis**, combining data from five adoption studies, has sufficient power for an analysis of the importance of passive genotype-environment correlation for IQ (Loehlin & DeFries, 1987). It was concluded that passive correlation may account for as much as 30 per cent of the overall variance in IQ. However, none of the subsequent behaviour-genetic studies has yet replicated this finding.

Genotype × environment interaction

Gene–environment interaction, mentioned earlier, refers to conditions in which genetically influenced characteristics mediate individual responsiveness to the encountered environment. G × E refers to the genetic control of sensitivity to environmental differences (Neale & Cardon, 1992). For example, individuals who are genetically susceptible to a disease will be free of the condition as long as the environment does not contain the pathogen; resistant individuals, those individuals who do not have the mutant gene, will be free of the disease even in a pathogenic environment. Thus, the appearance of the pathogen in the environment will have a very different impact on the phenotype of susceptible individuals as compared with its effect on the phenotype of resistant individuals. In the context of our discussion, if it were found that genetic predispositions for higher levels of cognitive abilities were actualised to a greater extent in some environments than in others, this finding would be interpreted as indicative of a genotype–environment interaction.

Although there are many examples of gene–environment interactions in biology and medicine (Rutter & Pickles, 1991), there is limited evidence of G × E interactions for variation in cognitive abilities within the normal range. In a widely cited paper, Turkheimer and colleagues (2003) found that among 7-year-old twin pairs, the proportions of variance in IQ score explained by genetic and environmental factors was substantially moderated by SES. Among the most impoverished families included in the study, approximately 60 per cent of the variance of total cognitive ability was explained by shared environmental factors, whereas additive genetic factors accounted for almost no variability in IQ scores. Conversely, additive genetic factors accounted for the vast majority (almost 80%) of phenotypic variance among the most affluent families. The interaction of genetic factors and socio-economic status in general cognitive ability was recently replicated in an adolescent sample, although the results were less dramatic. In wealthier families, additive genetic and shared environmental factors accounted for 55 per cent and 35 per cent of trait variance, respectively. The direction of this effect was reversed among lower-income families, with only 39 per cent of phenotypic variance explained by genetic factors and 45 per cent accounted for by shared environment (Harden et al., 2007). A recent attempt to replicate these findings in an adult sample failed to yield a significant interaction (Sluis et al., 2008).

When interpreting the results of G × E studies, several factors must be considered. First, most designs have rather weak power for detecting interactions, which may be small compared to the main effects of genes and environment (Wahlsten, 1990). In other words, the interactions may have been there, but undetectable by the research. Second, genotype–environment interactions for cognitive abilities, if they existed, might not be linear and might be localised in their effects. In other words, these interactions might be important at the extremes of the range of environments, but not in the typical range of environments (Turkheimer & Gottesman, 1991). For example, genotype–environment interactions might be significant within the range of environments that are thought to impede intellectual development (e.g. malnutrition, poverty, abuse, highly authoritarian parenting), but would be virtually undetectable in average non-problematic families.

Finally, and most importantly, even significant interactions do not say anything about the *mechanisms* producing phenotypic variability. It may be possible that significant interactions at the extreme ends of the socio-economic spectrum actually represent two distinct gene–environment correlations. In other words, children and adolescents from poor and affluent families may be genetically different from each other. Alternatively, the results could be interpreted in terms of environmental differences: Greater overall variability in scores could inflate the relative importance of environmental factors among less advantaged children and adolescents (Turkheimer et al., 2003).

In previous sections we introduced the concept of individual differences, translated this into the behaviour-genetic concept of phenotype, showed how phenotypic variation on a trait in a population could be described in terms of genetic, environmental, and interactive factors, and then described all of these factors. In the next section, we discuss two other important concepts, heritability and environmentality.

THE RELATIVE IMPACT OF GENES ON COGNITION: QUANTITATIVE GENETIC STUDIES

Heritability and environmentality

Heritability

heritability the extent to which variations within a population are genetically determined.

The concept of **heritability** (h^2), or the proportion of trait variance (phenotypic variance) due to genetic factors, is used to quantify the genetic contribution to phenotype. Heritability is the ratio of genetic variation to total variation in the trait under consideration.

environmentality the extent to which variations within a population are caused by environmental factors. Often expressed as e^2.

Environmentality

Environmentality (e^2) is defined as the aggregate estimate of the proportion of environmental variance in the phenotype (or $1 - h^2$). Thus, heritability plus environmentality sum to 1.

Heritability of cognitive abilities

Intelligence has been the most widely studied trait in the field of behaviour genetics, so for the sake of brevity, we will summarise several decades worth of research: both meta-analyses and reviews of the literature suggest that the heritability estimate for IQ is approximately 0.50, with a range from 0.40 to 0.80 (Deary *et al.*, 2006; Devlin *et al.*, 1997; Patrick, 2000; Plomin & Spinath, 2004). Despite the apparent 'half-and-half' contributions of genetic and environmental factors to variability in IQ, longitudinal twin and adoption studies have demonstrated that the continuity of general cognitive abilities over time is primarily accounted for by genetic factors (Bartels *et al.*, 2002; Patrick, 2000).

Interpreting heritability and environmentality

Both the heritability and environmentality statistics have a number of properties that are frequently misunderstood (Plomin *et al.*, 2008; Sternberg & Grigorenko, 1997, 1999). In considering the value of these statistics, it is important to remember several things.

Heritability and environmentality are estimated variance components, not measured effects

Neither heritability nor environmentality estimates point to measurable genetic or environmental effects. In other words, h^2 does not translate into an understanding of the biological mechanisms underlying it; obtaining a global estimate of the genotypic effect that is reflected by h^2 does not buy us an understanding of the biological mechanisms behind intellectual development. The same is true for e^2: the estimate of environmentality has yet to be linked to measured characteristics of environment that can explain observed variation in cognition.

Heritability and environmentality are not constants, and their estimates are not precise

Both heritability and environmentality refer to a particular phenotype measured in a given population at a given time. These estimates may vary from population to population and from time to time. Both h^2 and e^2 values vary across age: h^2 generally increases with age, whereas e^2 declines with age, reflecting both changes in the age-specific breakdown of genetic/environmental influences on the trait and changes in age-to-age genetic effects. Both h^2 and e^2 are estimated with a certain degree of precision involving a range of error that is a function of both sample size and type of relatives from which the estimate is obtained.

Heritability and environmentality apply to a population, not to one individual

These concepts apply to populations, not to individuals; hence, they do not say anything regarding the strength of either genetic or environmental effects in an individual's intellectual functioning. If we state that IQ has a heritability of 0.50, we mean that 50 per cent of the variation in IQ observed in a given population at this time in the population's history is accounted for by genetic differences among the population's members. We do not mean that an individual whose IQ is 110 got 55 IQ points as a result of genes and the other 55 as a result of the influences of the environment. However, if an individual from this population were about 20 IQ points smarter than the average, one could estimate (roughly) that about 50 per cent of this deviation would be explainable by genetic effects and the other 50 per cent due to the influence of the environment.

Heritability and environmentality do not say much about means

Almost every result and conclusion obtained in the field of behaviour-genetic research relates to the *causes* of human *differences* and does not deal with the processes that account for the development of the typical expression of a trait in a particular population. Heritability research is concerned with what makes people vary around the mean of the group, population, race, or species from which they are sampled, not with what makes people score at a given level.

Suppose, for example, it were found that differences in the ability to write poetry had a significant component only of genetic (and not environmental) variation among citizens of the country Ursulandia. What would this finding tell us about the role of Ursulu culture in determining this ability? This finding could suggest two different things. It might suggest that the culture was uniform for everyone (e.g. poetry education is either compulsory and equal for everybody or absent for all), so that only genetic effects could account for variability in the ability to write poetry. Or it might mean that cultural changes were adopted by everyone so rapidly that environmental effects were not apparent. For example, let us assume that Ursulandia has undergone a war resulting in the simultaneous worsening of living standards for most of the population; the rapid nature of this change might result in a levelling of the profiles of various environments. Perhaps instead of teaching children how to write poetry, schools, as a result of societal hardship, a lack of financial support, and a shortage

FIGURE 3.6 *Often time constraints mean that teachers can only concentrate on teaching the basics such as grammar, and maths.*
Source: Shutterstock.

of teachers, might be forced to concentrate on teaching grammar. In other words, differential levels of poetry education as a source of environmental variability in the ability to write poetry would be absent.

Taking into account the above, it is important to understand the incorrectness of such statements as 'The ability to write poetry is genetic'; the precisely correct statement based on behaviour-genetic analysis would instead be 'Individual differences in the ability to write poetry, in this population at this point in time, are mainly genetic.' It is crucial to be aware of which conclusions are justified and which are not on the basis of behaviour-genetic data.

Heritability and environmentality do not refer to modification or intervention

In early behaviour-genetic work, it sometimes has been asserted that the degree to which a studied trait was inherited carried important implications for the quantification of the impact of environmental interventions (Jensen, 1969). Today, it is recognised that this assertion is wrong. First, intervention influences the mean of the observed variable and can raise the mean and the scores going into it. The mechanism controlling the appearance of individual differences for a given trait might not be altered, however. For example, an intervention may increase a group's average score on a measure of reading ability, but if the individuals in the group continue to vary around the new mean in a similar way, the heritability estimate for this trait will remain unchanged.

Second, the causes of variation derived from behaviour-genetic studies relate to a particular population of individuals at a given time. Results of these studies might change as a result of the influence of factors altering the gene frequencies in the population, the expression of genes in the population, or frequencies and structures of different environments. In any case, then, any conclusions pertain only to a given population at a given time. This logic can be easily illustrated by an example from the evolutionary history of the human species. In a given population, gene frequencies have been altered multiple times as a result of rapid decreases in the size of a population due to wars, hunger, or epidemics. The relocation of a population or rapid changes in climate resulted in changed expressions of genes. Cultural developments led to better schooling, reflecting a structural environmental change. This schooling gradually became accessible to the majority of populations, reflecting a change in the frequency of schooling.

Third, even when it is shown that genetic effects are important, the possibility of the existence of a rare crucial environmental factor cannot be entirely excluded. An example of such factor is a brain injury that could result in severe mental retardation in an individual with a normal genetic endowment for intelligence. Similarly, a rare gene with a major effect may hold the key to understanding cognitive development. Due to its rarity, this gene might account for only a relatively small amount of the *total* variation in cognition, but, when present in an individual, might *almost completely* determine the course of cognitive development for that individual.

Although its interpretations are limited, the heritability statistic was the driving force in the field of behavioural genetics when researchers were limited to studying the effects of genes based on familial resemblance of behavioural phenotypes. Today, the genome is no longer an unobservable trait; advances in technology have shifted the field from asking 'what is the relative importance of genetic influences?' to '*which genes* are important?'

FINDING THE GENES THAT IMPACT COGNITION: MOLECULAR GENETICS STUDIES

Researchers use two different methodologies when attempting to localise a phenotype of interest in the genome, linkage and association studies.

Linkage and association studies

Linkage studies
Researchers use linkage studies to identify a specific location or region of the genome that corresponds to a phenotype of interest. These designs are carried out exclusively

among related individuals, and do not identify specific genes or genetic variants. A major limitation of linkage studies is their low resolution; they can only consider fairly large chromosomal regions. However, linkage studies remain a useful strategy that serves as a starting point for research. In other words, this research paradigm allows researchers to narrow down the entire genome to a series of 'most likely suspects' that can be examined in subsequent assays.

Association studies

Whereas linkage studies are exploratory in nature, association studies are hypothesis driven and examine whether a particular genetic variant is related to the phenotype of interest. These studies often use case-control designs, evaluating whether the putative variant is more reliably present in individuals with the phenotype of interest compared to control subjects.

To date, six genome-wide scans for genes contributing to intelligence and cognition have been published (Butcher *et al.*, 2008; Buyske *et al.*, 2006; Dick *et al.*, 2006; Luciano *et al.*, 2006; Posthuma *et al.*, 2005; Wainwright *et al.*, 2006). Overall, the results are quite variable, but there are several chromosomal regions that have been implicated in multiple studies. Specifically, the findings coincide in regions on chromosomes 14q (for three out of six studies), 2q (for four out six studies), and 6p (for five out of six studies). These overlapping regions may contain genes that could explain some of the variance in IQ, but several issues warrant caution when interpreting these results. First, the studies did not measure intelligence or its corollaries (e.g. achievement) consistently; only one study (Butcher *et al.*, 2008) utilised an indicator of general intelligence, making it difficult to interpret the overlapping identified regions as associated with variability in intelligence *per se*. Second, considerable overlap between samples and the use of genetic data that has already been analysed for subsamples in other studies raise concerns about the statistical reliability of the findings. Although none of these studies revealed specific candidate genes, the results warrant further investigation of the genes at these putative loci.

Candidate genes

The apolipoprotein E gene (*APOE*) is located on chromosome 19q13 and its product is responsible for breaking down lipoproteins (protein-lipid complexes). Research on this gene has focused on neuronal development and repair; this research, in turn, is directly related to work on Alzheimer's disease (AD) (Blackman *et al.*, 2005; Buttini *et al.*, 1999; Rapoport *et al.*, 2008; Teasdale *et al.*, 2005; Teter & Ashford, 2002). Three variants of *APOE* have been studied extensively: *ApoE2*, *ApoE3*, and *ApoE4*. These variants code for three different *isoforms*, or variants (Apo-ε2, Apo-ε3, and Apo-ε4) of the protein that differ only by single amino acid substitutions; despite this small difference, these substitutions are associated with dramatic physiological outcomes. Of these three isoforms, Apo-ε2 and Apo-ε4 are considered abnormal proteins. This discussion will focus on the *ApoE4* allele because it has been associated with AD, impaired cognitive function, and neuronal deficiencies. A meta-analysis which pooled data from 38 studies demonstrated that among older individuals, possession of the

ApoE4 allele is associated with poorer performance on tests of global cognitive function, episodic memory, and executive function (Small *et al.*, 2004). Young, healthy adults with the *ApoE4* variant display altered patterns of brain activity both at rest and during cognitive challenges (Scarmeas & Stern, 2006). Another study found that the presence of this allele in children was associated with a thinner cortex in the area of the brain where the morphological changes related to AD tend to occur first (Shaw *et al.*, 2007). In sum, data from these three studies suggest that the *ApoE4* variant plays a significant role in cognitive functioning, especially related to cognitive decline later in life. Although the evidence for *ApoE4*'s involvement in neural and cognitive processes appears robust, it was not significantly associated with general cognitive ability using a case-control design (Turic *et al.*, 2001). Also, it appears that even in familial AD, only a relatively small portion of variation in memory is attributable to *APOE* (Lee *et al.*, 2004). Research by Payton and colleagues (2006) suggests that the *ApoE4* allele alone has no effect on cognitive functioning, but an epistatic interaction with another risk variant (an allele in the Cathepsin D gene (*CTSD*)) results in significantly lower scores on cognitive tasks compared with those of individuals who possess only one of the risk alleles. Although this finding complicates the picture, it also suggests that perhaps the true effect of *ApoE4* on cognition has not yet been captured with simple models that only evaluate the direct association between the variant and phenotype of interest. Thus, understanding this variation and its connection to individual differences in cognition and, subsequently, to the acquisition of AD or not, is of great interest to researchers in a variety of fields.

Likewise, the connections between a protein and its respective isoforms, brain structure, and cognition are of great interest to researchers studying the gene for catechol-O-methyl transferase (COMT). At a specific location in this gene (codon 158), a single nucleotide substitution (G-to-A), results in the addition of the amino acid methionine (Met) instead of valine (Val) to the amino acid chain during translation. This *polymorphism* (so named because multiple alleles of this gene exist in the population) is known as Val158Met. The Met allele results in a fourfold decrease in enzymatic activity in the prefrontal cortex (Lachman *et al.*, 1996), which results in slower inactivation of dopamine in this region (Tunbridge *et al.*, 2004; Winterer & Goldman, 2003). This decreased enzymatic activity means that dopamine remains in the synapse longer, and this increase in synaptic dopamine levels may directly result in more efficient processing in the prefrontal cortex (Winterer & Goldman, 2003), more advanced functioning of several other cognitive processes (e.g. executive function and memory), and higher IQ (Barnett *et al.*, 2007; Shashi *et al.*, 2006; Tunbridge *et al.*, 2006). Although the literature generally supports this connection, the relationship between a genetic variant and a behavioural phenotype is rarely simple, and this is no exception. Not all cognitive tasks are similarly affected by dopamine levels; thus the Met variant may confer an advantage only under certain circumstances (MacDonald *et al.*, 2007; H.-Y. Tan *et al.*, 2007).

Other polymorphisms on the *COMT* gene, as well as other genes (e.g. *DRD2*), also affect the rate at which dopamine is metabolised (Palmatier *et al.*, 2004; Reuter *et al.*, 2005). Research by Stein and colleagues (2006) suggests that the Val and Met variants have differential impacts (risk and protective) on both cognitive and psychological functions. And although research findings seem consistent with regard to the impact of these alleles on behavioural phenotypes, this impact does not always hold true for brain activation patterns (Bishop *et al.*, 2008). There are also mixed reports regarding the connection between the Val158Met polymorphism and cognition across the life span (de Frias *et al.*, 2005; Harris *et al.*, 2005). Again, there is a strong argument in the literature for the involvement of the *COMT* gene in general cognition, but findings are often confounded by the tasks used to assess cognitive functioning and warrant further research.

Likewise, there is an intriguing story involving another Val to Met substitution (Val66Met), in yet a different gene, the brain-derived neurotrophic factor gene, *BDNF*. The BDNF protein is found in the central and peripheral nervous systems, where it is involved in both the survival of existing neurons and synapses as well as the growth and differentiation of new ones. In the brain, it is expressed widely, and is notably present in areas implicated in numerous cognitive functions: the hippocampus, cortex, and basal forebrain. This polymorphism has been reported to be associated with cognitive functioning, but the pattern of the results is curiously inconsistent. Specifically, a substantial portion of the reports indicate that the Met allele, which is associated with a reduced secretion of BDNF, detrimentally impacts long-term memory via its influence on the decreased presence of BDNF in the hippocampus, but does not greatly affect IQ, short-term memory, or other cognitive processes (Egan *et al.*, 2003). The impact of the Met allele on long-term memory has been supported by several other studies (Dempster *et al.*, 2005; Echeverria *et al.*, 2005; Hariri *et al.*, 2003; Y.L. Tan *et al.*, 2005) and was not reproduced in only one study (Strauss *et al.*, 2004). Despite support for the hypothesis that the Met allele exerts a domain-specific effect impacting the hippocampus (Hansell *et al.*, 2007), the hypothesis has been challenged by findings suggesting the Met allele may be associated with impaired performance on IQ-related tasks (Tsai *et al.*, 2004), both long-term and short-term memory tasks (Echeverria *et al.*, 2005; Rybakowski *et al.*, 2003; Rybakowski *et al.*, 2006), and indica-tors of **fluid intelligence** and processing speed (Miyajima *et al.*, 2008).

fluid intelligence
intellectual ability that cannot be taught easily, general ability to grasp new concepts and to think and reason abstractly.

In addition, it has been shown that the Met allele significantly reduces hippocampal and cerebral neocortex volume and that these effects appear independent of age and gender (Bueller *et al.*, 2006; Frodl *et al.*, 2007; Pezawas *et al.*, 2004). On the contrary, other studies have indicated that Met homozygotes (individuals with two copies of the Met allele) score significantly higher than heterozygotes (those with one Met and one Val allele) and Val homozygotes on a measure of general cognitive ability (e.g. Harris *et al.*, 2006). The Met allele also appears to be playing a protective role in certain neurological conditions and is associated with improved non-verbal reasoning skills in the elderly (Oroszi *et al.*, 2006; Zivadinov *et al.*, 2007).

In summary, there is a lot to sort out here. Although the importance of genetic factors to the development of intelligence and intelligence-related cognitive processing is widely acknowledged, the identification and confirmation of the specific genes that form these genetic factors has proven difficult. While positive evidence of association has been reported for several interesting genes, thus far there has not been widespread success in replicating reported associations. Even though the field appears to be accepting of the role of specific genes such as *APOE*, *COMT*, and *BDNF*, the specific neurocognitive processes underlying their involvement continue to be a matter of debate. In general, it is assumed that the effect sizes of specific genes involved in complex human traits are small (Greenwood & Parasuraman, 2003). With such a diverse pattern of findings, it has been rather difficult to systematically distinguish between false positive findings, the effects of single genes on multiple cognitive processes (*pleiotropic effects*), and the role of the *g*-factor (the underlying factor of intelligence; Starr *et al.*, 2008).

As mentioned above, very few studies actually limit themselves to 'true' indicators of the *g*-factor (i.e. some kind of summative indicator of multiple intelligence-related measures). Most studies employ and analyse a variety of intelligence-related indicators. Thus, similar to the findings obtained from genome scans, the field unequivocally supports the idea of the involvement of genetic factors in the development of intelligence and abilities, but it is far from able to generate a cohesive picture of the genetic machinery behind these factors.

HOW DO GENES INFLUENCE COGNITION? FUNCTIONAL PARADIGMS

In the previous section, we reviewed contributions from the field of molecular genetics, but our discussion was limited to the questions of 'which genes or genetic variants matter to cognition?' and 'what specific phenotypes are associated with these genes?' We will now move beyond the genotype and begin to examine the pathways from genes to cognition, specifically examining gene expression and epigenetics.

Gene expression profiling

Why study gene expression? If you can sequence an entire person's genome, what more do you need to know? Consider the following: In every cell of your body, your genome consists of the exact same base pair sequence, yet you are made up of differentiated cells and tissues that have unique properties and functions. Each of these tissues selectively expresses a subset of the genome. Can you imagine what would happen if any gene could be transcribed in any tissue? It would be chaos – your bones would synthesise neurotransmitters and your brain would start growing hair! Although this statement is obviously an exaggeration, it is meant to highlight the fact that gene expression is the main character driving the genetic 'story.' We mentioned earlier in the chapter that genes are probabilistic; if we think of genes as outlining a set of possibilities for any individual, we can think of gene expression as a snapshot of that person's reality.

The pathway from genes to cognition starts with the DNA structure (the genotype), followed by the mRNA transcript, the protein products, the brain, and behaviour. There are two important things to consider when examining gene expression. First, which genes – and which *version* of those genes – are being transcribed? Unlike

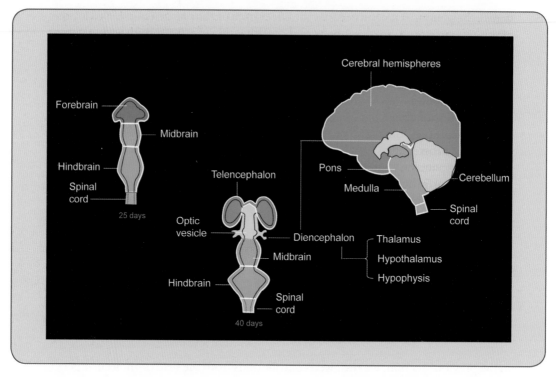

FIGURE 3.7 *Foetal brain development.* A fully developed brain is at right. During the 4th week (25 days) the neural tube begins to differentiate into a spinal cord, forebrain, midbrain and hindbrain. During the 6th week (40 days) the forebrain differentiates into the telencephalon and diencephalon. The telencephalon develops into the hippocampus, basal ganglia, amygdala and the cerebral cortex. The diencephalon develops into the thalamus, hypothalamus and hypophysis.

Source: © Francis Leroy, Biocosmos/Science Photo Library.

genotyping, studies of gene expression can capture whether or not genes are being alternatively spliced. Within a developmental framework, it is particularly interesting to examine which genes are being expressed at specific points in the lifespan. The mechanisms for the timing of gene expression are generally not coded for in the DNA (transcription is activated by environmental factors or the products of earlier gene expression), so gene expression studies have an advantage over genotyping alone when studying developmental phenomena. Second, it is important to know the rate at which genes are being transcribed. Because expression analysis is a 'snapshot' of gene activity, research uses the number of mRNA transcripts as an indicator of the rate of transcription. As psychologists, our primary interest is how genes are expressed in the brain, though, studying this directly in humans is limited to postmortem studies.

A recent study by Johnson and colleagues (2009) examined gene expression across multiple regions in the human foetal brain (see Figure 3.7). Of all of the genes expressed in the brain, approximately one third were differentially expressed across sampled regions, and 28 per cent of all genes were alternatively spliced. In other words, the genome was behaving quite differently in different areas of the developing brain! Of genes more highly expressed within the hippocampus and neocortex, the vast majority serve a regulatory function. Across analyses of both individual genes and gene networks that were differentially expressed between sampled brain regions, researchers found several genes that have previously been implicated in speech and language disorders, developmental dyslexia, and autism. The authors also examined the co-expression of multiple genes, finding networks that contribute primarily to axon guidance, receptor activity and signalling, and signal transduction in the neo-cortex, basal cortex, and hippocampus. The complex patterns of gene expression and alternative splicing across various areas of the foetal brain provide insight into the importance of both timing and location of gene expression for the development of area specialisation in the brain.

Although research in this area is limited, the above study wonderfully illustrates that the genotype itself makes a very limited contribution to our understanding of the role of genetics and cognition. The variant of any given gene that an individual possesses provides a developmental constraint, but the behavioural phenotype is also a function of *when* and *where* that gene is expressed in the brain during development, in addition to *how* it works together with complex networks of other genes. As complex as these questions are, there is another important one that we have yet to answer: What regulates gene expression?

THE DYNAMIC GENOME: EPIGENETICS

The term **epigenetics** refers to modifications to the genome that alter gene expression without affecting the base pair sequence. Epigenetic mechanisms include, among others, the addition or removal of a molecule, usually a methyl group (the addition of a methyl group is called *methylation*), to the DNA helix itself or to the protein complexes associated with the DNA polymer. Epigenetic modifications alter the likelihood that a particular gene will be transcribed, sometimes silencing it completely. These molecules are added to the genome in response to environmental cues, ranging from diet (e.g. Barres *et al.*, 2009) to early life experience (e.g. McGowan *et al.*, 2009; Weaver *et al.*, 2005). Monozygotic twins, although identical at the genotypic level, develop increasingly divergent methylation patterns as they get older (Fraga *et al.*, 2005). Whereas our earlier discussion of gene–environment interactions relied entirely on inferential statistics, epigenetics allows us to observe the molecular basis of these interactions. This is the essence of the dynamic genome: *Our genes can be changed by our environment.*

epigenetic theory a theory of development concerning changes in phenotype (appearance) resulting from the dynamic interaction between genetic and environmental forces.

In animal studies, epigenetic mechanisms have been demonstrated to regulate synaptic plasticity, spatial memory, and emotional memory (for a review, see Graff & Mansuy, 2008). Expression of the *BDNF* gene, regardless of whether an individual possesses the Val or Met allele, is regulated by epigenetic mechanisms. Changes in the electrical charge of the cytosol in neurons, caused by shifts in ion concentration, serve to increase *BDNF* expression. In general, increased expression of this gene is related to less methylation; methylation decreases the probability of transcription. This activity-dependent increase in expression is caused by the demethylation (removal of methyl groups) of a specific region in the gene (Martinowich *et al.*, 2003). DNA methylation is also responsible for key processes that regulate the development of the central nervous system (Liu *et al.*, 2009).

The *APP* gene, which codes for amyloid precursor protein (APP; a protein found in cell membranes) has been implicated in familial AD. This gene is overexpressed in AD, and studies of brain tissue from individuals affected by the disorder have found that the *APP* gene is hypomethylated, meaning that there are fewer methyl groups than would be normally observed (West *et al.*, 1995). However, hypomethylation of this gene in the cerebral cortex also occurs as a function of aging in the normal population (Tohgi *et al.*, 1999). This age-related decrease in methylation co-occurs with normal cognitive decline later in life (Liu *et al.*, 2009). Although it is difficult to draw firm conclusions from the research (most of which is conducted on clinical samples), it is enough to suggest that the methylation status of the *APP* gene may contribute to the maintenance of normal cognitive functioning and warrants further research.

Epigenetics is a rapidly expanding field that is helping to generate a more comprehensive understanding of the genetic and environmental contributions to cognition. While most research consists of studies on animals and clinical populations, methylation appears to be the driving force behind memory formation (Levenson & Sweatt, 2005). As the field moves forward, research will continue to shed light on the mechanisms by which genes affect general cognitive ability.

SUMMARY AND CONCLUSIONS

Despite its popularity, the 'nature–nurture' debate over intelligence is no longer relevant. As the field of behavioural genetics has moved forward, increasingly more interesting and complex questions are being asked as we begin to understand the enormous complexities of the role that genes play in general cognitive ability. There are several key points that should be taken away from this chapter:

- Genes are probabilistic, not deterministic. They code for proteins, not behaviours.
- Phenotypes are always the result of both genes and environment. Genes do not exist in a vacuum, and recent research in the field of epigenetics demonstrates that environmental influences are often responsible for gene expression.
- Pathways from genes to cognitive abilities are complex and as yet unclear. Multiple genes work together in networks that influence development and functioning at the cellular level of the brain.
- The field of developmental psychology is unique in its acknowledgment of change across multiple domains – neurological, physical, cognitive, and emotional. Studies in each of these domains frequently acknowledge the importance of both genetic and environmental characteristics, and the study

of behaviour- and molecular-genetics allows scientists to get a closer (usually sub-microscopic!) look at how these genetic and environmental factors contribute to developmental outcomes. In this chapter we have used cognition to illustrate fundamental concepts of genetic research, and have provided a background in popular research paradigms in the field. As genetic research continues to contribute to the field of psychology, it is vital that we move away from over-simplified misconceptions of genes that code for behaviours, and embrace the intricacies of the pathways leading from genes to behaviour. Understanding genes – even if it's only understanding what genes *don't* do – allows us to better grasp the bidirectional influences of the individual and their environment on development over time.

DISCUSSION POINTS

1. Define the concepts of heritability and environmentality, and indicate how they reflect genetic and environmental contributions to individual differences.

2. Discuss the importance and the limitations of twin studies in gaining an understanding of the contributions of genes and environment to human development.

3. Think of ways in which heritability (genetic contribution to individual differences) can be high for a particular ability, but the ability is still highly influenced by the environment.

4. Consider why it is so important to consider processes of gene expression.

5. Consider some of the ways in which genetic and environmental factors can interact in causing development.

6. What do we know about the heritability of general versus specific cognitive abilities?

SUGGESTIONS FOR FURTHER READING

Atkinson, P., Glasner, P., & Lock, M. (Eds.) (2009). *The handbook of genetics & society: Mapping the new genomic era (genetics and society)*. New York, NY: Routledge.

Ceci, S.J., & William, W.M. (1999). *The nature/nurture debate: Essential readings*. Cambridge, MA, and Oxford: Blackwell.

Gottesman, I.I. (2008). Milestones in the history of behavioral genetics: Participant observer. *Acta Psychologica Sinica*, 40, 1042–1050.

Plomin, R. (1994). *Genetics and experience: The developmental interplay between nature and nurture*. Newbury Park, CA: Sage.

Sternberg, R.J., & Grigerenko, E.L. (Eds.) (1997). *Intelligence, heredity, and environment*. New York: Cambridge University Press.

Sternberg, R.J., & Grigerenko, E.L. (Eds.) (2001). *Environmental effects on intellectual functioning*. Mahwah, NJ: Erlbaum.

REFERENCES

Barnett, J.H., Heron, J., Ring, S.M., Golding, J., Goldman, D., Xu, K., *et al.* (2007). Gender-specific effects of the catechol-O-methyltransferase Val(108)/(158)Met polymorphism on cognitive function in children. *American Journal of Psychiatry, 164,* 142–149.

Barres, R., Osler, M.E., Yan, J., Rune, A., Fritz, T., Caidahl, K., *et al.* (2009). Non-CpG methylation of the PGC-1 alpha Promoter through DNMT3B controls mitochondrial density. *Cell Metabolism, 10*(3), 189–198.

Bartels, M., Rietveld, M.J.H., Van Baal, G.C.M., & Boomsma, D.I. (2002). Genetic and environmental influences on the development of intelligence. *Behavior Genetics, 32*(4), 237–249.

Bishop, S.J., Fossella, J., Croucher, C.J., & Duncan, J. (2008). COMT Val158Met genotype affects recruitment of neural mechanisms supporting fluid intelligence. *Cerebral Cortex, 18,* 2132–2140.

Blackman, J.A., Worley, G., & Strittmatter, W.J. (2005). Apolipoprotein E and brain injury: Implications for children. *Developmental Medicine & Child Neurology, 47,* 64–70.

Bueller, J.A., Aftab, M., Sen, S., Gomez-Hassan, D., Burmeister, M., & Zubieta, J.K. (2006). BDNF Val66Met allele is associated with reduced hippocampal volume in healthy subjects. *Biological Psychiatry, 59,* 812–815.

Butcher, L.M., Davis, O.S.P., Craig, I.W., & Plomin, R. (2008). Genome-wide quantitative trait locus association scan of general cognitive ability using pooled DNA and 500K single nucleotide polymorphism microarrays. *Genes, Brain and Behavior, 7,* 435–446.

Buttini, M., Orth, M., Bellosta, S., Akeefe, H., Pitas, R.E., Wyss-Coray, T., *et al.* (1999). Expression of human apolipoprotein E3 or E4 in the brains of Apoe-/- mice: Isoform-specific effects on neurodegeneration. *Journal of Neuroscience, 19,* 4867–4880.

Buyske, S., Bates, M.E., Gharani, N., Matise, T.C., Tischfield, J.A., & Manowitz, P. (2006). Cognitive traits link to human chromosomal regions. *Behavior Genetics, 36,* 65–76.

Ceci, S. & Liker, J. (1986). A day at the races: A study of IQ, expertise and cognitive complexity. *Journal of Experimental Psychology, 115,* 255–266.

Chipuer, H.M., Rovine, M., & Plomin, R. (1990). LISREL modeling: Genetic and environmental influences on IQ revisited. *Intelligence, 14,* 11–29.

de Frias, C.M., Annerbrink, K., Westberg, L., Eriksson, E., Adolfsson, R., & Nilsson, L.-G. (2005). Catechol-O-Methyltransferase Val158Met polymorphism is associated with cognitive performance in nondemented adults. *Journal of Cognitive Neuroscience, 17,* 1018–1025.

Deary, I.J., Spinath, F.M., & Bates, T.C. (2006). Genetics of intelligence. *European Journal of Human Genetics, 14,* 690–700.

Deese, J. (1993). Human abilities versus intelligence. *Intelligence, 17,* 107–116.

Dempster, E., Toulopoulou, T., McDonald, C., Bramon, E., Walshe, M., Filbey, F., *et al.* (2005). Association between BDNF Val66Met genotype and episodic memory. *American Journal of Medical Genetics. Neuropsychiatric Genetics, 134,* 73–75.

Devlin, B., Daniels, M., & Roeder, K. (1997). The heritability of IQ. *Nature, 388,* 468–471.

Dick, D.M., Aliev, F., Bierut, L., Goate, A., Rice, J., Hinrichs, A., *et al.* (2006). Linkage analyses of IQ in the collaborative study on the genetics of alcoholism (COGA) sample. *Behavior Genetics, 36,* 77–86.

Echeverria, D., Woods, J.S., Heyer, N.J., Rohlman, D.S., Farin, F.M., Bittner, A.C.J., *et al.* (2005). Chronic low level mercury exposure, BDNF polymorphism, and associations with cognitive and motor function. *Neurotoxicology and Teratology, 27,* 781–796.

Egan, M.F., Kojima, M., Callicott, J.H., Goldberg, T.E., Kolachana, B.S., Bertolino, A., *et al.* (2003). The BDNF Val66Met polymorphism affects activity-dependent secretion of BDNF and human memory and hippocampal function. *Cell, 112,* 257–269.

Fraga, M.F., Ballestar, E., Paz, M.F., Ropero, S., Setien, F., Ballestart, M.L., *et al.* (2005). Epigenetic differences arise during the lifetime of monozygotic twins. *Proceedings of the National Academy of Sciences of the United States of America, 102*(30), 10604–10609.

Frodl, T., Schule, C., Schmitt, G., Born, C., Baghai, T., Zill, P., *et al.* (2007). Association of the brain-derived neurotrophic factor Val66Met polymorphism with reduced hippocampal volumes in major depression. *Archives of General Psychiatry, 64*, 410–416.

Galton, F. (1869). *Hereditary genius: An inquiry into its laws and consequences.* London: Macmillan.

Graff, J., & Mansuy, I.A. (2008). Epigenetic codes in cognition and behaviour. *Behavioural Brain Research, 192*(1), 70–87.

Greenwood, P.M., & Parasuraman, R. (2003). Normal genetic variation, cognition, and aging. *Behavioral & Cognitive Neuroscience Reviews, 2*, 278–306.

Hansell, N.K., James, M.R., Duffy, D.L., Birley, A.J., Luciano, M., Geffen, G.M., *et al.* (2007). Effect of the BDNF V166M polymorphism on working memory in healthy adolescents. *Genes, Brain, & Behavior, 6*, 260–268.

Harden, K.P., Turkheimer, E., & Loehlin, J.C. (2007). Genotype by environment interaction in adolescents' cognitive aptitude. *Behavior Genetics, 37*, 273–283.

Hariri, A.R., Goldberg, T.E., Mattay, V.S., Kolachana, B.S., Callicott, J.H., Egan, M.F., *et al.* (2003). Brain-derived neurotrophic factor Val66Met polymorphism affects human memory-related hippocampal activity and predicts memory performance. *Journal of Neuroscience, 23*, 6690–6694.

Harris, S.E., Fox, H., Wright, A.F., Hayward, C., Starr, J.M., Whalley, L.J., *et al.* (2006). The brain-derived neurotrophic factor Val66Met polymorphism is associated with age-related change in reasoning skills. *Molecular Psychiatry, 11*, 505–513.

Harris, S.E., Wright, A.F., Hayward, C., Starr, J.M., Whalley, L.J., & Deary, I.J. (2005). The functional COMT polymorphism, Val 158 Met, is associated with logical memory and the personality trait intellect/imagination in a cohort of healthy 79 year olds. *Neuroscience Letters, 385*, 1–6.

Jensen, A.R. (1969). How much can we boost IQ and scholastic achievement? *Harvard Educational Review, 39*, 1–123.

Johnson, M.B., Kawasawa, Y.I., Mason, C.E., Krsnik, Z., Coppola, G., Bogdanovic, D., *et al.* (2009). Functional and evolutionary insights into human brain development through global transcriptome analysis. *Neuron, 62*, 494–509.

Kimble, G.E. (1994). Evolution of the nature–nurture issue in the history of psychology. In R. Plomin & G.E. McClearn (Eds.) *Nature, nurture, and psychology* (pp. 3–26). Washington, DC: American Psychological Association.

Kline, P. (1991). *Intelligence: The psychometric view.* London: Routledge.

Lachman, H.M., Papolos, D.F., Saito, T., Yu, Y.M., Szumlanski, C.L., & Weinshilboum, R.M. (1996). Human catechol-O-methyltransferase pharmacogenetics: Description of a functional polymorphism and its potential application to neuropsychiatric disorders. *Pharmacogenetics, 6*, 243–250.

Lee, J.H., Flaquer, A., Stern, Y., Tycko, B., & Mayeux, R. (2004). Genetic influences on memory performance in familial Alzheimer disease. *Neurology, 62*, 414–421.

Levenson, J.M., & Sweatt, J.D. (2005). Epigenetic mechanisms in memory formation. *Nature Reviews Neuroscience, 6*, 108–118.

Liu, L., van Groen, T., Kadish, I., & Tollefsbol, T.O. (2009). DNA methylation impacts on learning and memory in aging. *Neurobiology of Aging, 30*, 549–560.

Loehlin, J.C., & DeFries, J.C. (1987). Genotype-environment correlation and IQ. *Behavior Genetics, 17*, 263–277.

Luciano, M., Wright, M.J., Duffy, D.L., Wainwright, M.A., Zhu, G., Evans, D.M., *et al.* (2006). Genome-wide scan of IQ finds significant linkage to a quantitative trait locus on 2q. *Behavior Genetics, 36*, 45–55.

MacDonald, A.W., Carter, C.S., Flory, J.D., Ferrell, R.E., & Manuck, S.B. (2007). COMT Val158Met and executive control: A test of the benefit of specific deficits to translational research. *Journal of Abnormal Psychology, 116,* 306–312.

Martinowich, K., Hattori, D., Wu, H., Fouse, S., He, F., Hu, Y., *et al.* (2003). DNA methylation-related chromatin remodeling in activity dependent BDNF gene regulation. *Science, 302,* 890–893.

McGowan, P.O., Sasaki, A., D'Alessio, A.C., Dymov, S., Labonte, B., Szyf, M., *et al.* (2009). Epigenetic regulation of the glucocorticoid receptor in human brain associates with childhood abuse. *Nature Neuroscience, 12,* 342–348.

Miyajima, F., Ollier, W., Mayes, A., Jackson, A., Thacker, N., Rabbitt, P., *et al.* (2008). Brain-derived neurotrophic factor polymorphism Val66Met influences cognitive abilities in the elderly. *Genes, Brain and Behavior, 7*(4), 411–417.

Neale, M.C., & Cardon, L.R. (Eds.). (1992). *Methodology for genetic studies of twins and families.* Dordrecht: Kluwer Academic Press.

Oroszi, G., Lapteva, L., Davis, E., Yarboro, C.H., Weickert, T., Roebuck-Spencer, T., *et al.* (2006). The Met66 allele of the functional Val66Met polymorphism in the brain-derived neurotrophic factor gene confers protection against neurocognitive dysfunction in systemic lupus erythematosus. *Annals of the Rheumatic Diseases, 65,* 1330–1335.

Palmatier, M.A., Pakstis, A.J., Speed, W., Paschou, P., Goldman, D., Odunsi, A., *et al.* (2004). COMT haplotypes suggest P2 promoter region relevance for schizophrenia. *Molecular Psychiatry, 9,* 1359–4184.

Patrick, C.L. (2000). Genetic and environmental influences on the development of cognitive abilities: Evidence from the field of developmental behavior genetics. *Journal of School Psychology, 38*(1), 79–108.

Payton, A., Van den Boogerd, E., Davidson, Y., Gibbons, L., Ollier, W., Rabbitt, P., *et al.* (2006). Influence and interactions of cathepsin D, HLA-DRB1 and APOE on cognitive abilities in an older non-demented population. *Genes, Brain & Behavior, 5,* 23–31.

Pezawas, L., Verchinski, B.A., Mattay, V.S., Callicott, J.H., Kolachana, B.S., Straub, R.E., *et al.* (2004). The brain-derived neurotrophic factor Val66Met polymorphism and variation in human cortical morphology. *Journal of Neuroscience, 24,* 10099–10102.

Plomin, R., DeFries, J.C., & Loehlin, J.C. (1977). Genotype–environment interaction and correlation in the analysis of human behavior. *Psychological Bulletin, 84,* 309–322.

Plomin, R., DeFries, J.C., McClearn, G.E., & McGuffin, P. (2008). *Behavioral Genetics* (5th edn). New York: Worth.

Plomin, R., & Spinath, F.M. (2004). Intelligence: Genetics, Genes, and Genomics. *Journal of Personality and Social Psychology, 86*(1), 112–129.

Posthuma, D., Luciano, M., Geus, E.J., Wright, M.J., Slagboom, P.E., Montgomery, G.W., *et al.* (2005). A genomewide scan for intelligence identifies quantitative trait loci on 2q and 6p. *American Journal of Human Genetics, 77,* 318–326.

Rapoport, M., Wolf, U., Herrmann, N., Kiss, A., Shammi, P., Reis, M., *et al.* (2008). Traumatic brain injury, Apolipoprotein E-epsilon4, and cognition in older adults: A two-year longitudinal study. *Journal of Neuropsychiatry & Clinical Neurosciences, 20,* 68–73.

Reuter, M., Peters, K., Schroeter, K., Koebke, W., Lenardon, D., Bloch, B., *et al.* (2005). The influence of the dopaminergic system on cognitive functioning: A molecular genetic approach. *Behavioural Brain Research, 164,* 93–99.

Robinson, G.E. (2004). Genomics. Beyond nature and nurture. *Science, 304,* 397–399.

Rutter, M., & Pickles, A. (1991). Person–environment interaction: Concepts, mehcanisms, and implications for data analysis. In T.D. Wachs & R. Plomin (Eds.) *Conceptualization and measurement of organism–environment interaction* (pp. 105–141). Washington, DC: American Psychological Association.

Rybakowski, J.K., Borkowska, A., Czerski, P.M., Skibinska, M., & Hauser, J. (2003). Polymorphism of the brain-derived neurotrophic factor gene and performance on a cognitive prefrontal test in bipolar patients. *Bipolar Disorders, 5,* 468–472.

Rybakowski, J.K., Borkowska, A., Skibinska, M., Szczepankiewicz, A., Kapelski, P., Leszczynska-Rodziewicz, A., *et al.* (2006). Prefrontal cognition in schizophrenia and bipolar illness in relation to Val66Met polymorphism of the brain-derived neurotrophic factor gene. *Psychiatry & Clinical Neurosciences, 60,* 70–76.

Scarmeas, N., & Stern, Y. (2006). Imaging studies and APOE genotype in persons at risk for Alzheimer's disease. *Current Psychiatry Reports, 8,* 11–17.

Scarr, S. (1997). Behavior-genetic and socialization theories of intelligence: Truce and reconciliation. In R.J. Sternberg & E.L. Grigorenko (Eds.) *Intelligence, heredity, and environment* (pp. 3–41). New York: Cambridge University Press.

Scarr, S., & McCartney, K. (1983). How people create their own environments: A theory of genotype-environment effects. *Child Development, 54,* 424–435.

Shashi, V., Keshavan, M.S., Howard, T.D., Berry, M.N., Basehore, M.J., Lewandowski, E., *et al.* (2006). Cognitive correlates of a functional COMT polymorphism in children with 22q11.2 deletion syndrome. *Clinical Genetics, 69,* 234–238.

Shaw, P., Lerch, J.P., Pruessner, J.C., Taylor, K.N., Rose, A.B., Greenstein, D., *et al.* (2007). Cortical morphology in children and adolescents with different apolipoprotein E gene polymorphisms: An observational study. *Lancet Neurology, 6,* 494–500.

Sluis, S. v. d., Willemsen, G., Geus, E.J.C. d., Boomsma, D.I., & Posthuma, D. (2008). Gene–environment interaction in adults' IQ scores: Measure of past and present environment. *Behavior Genetics, 38,* 348–360.

Small, B.J., Rosnick, C.B., Fratiglioni, L., & Backman, L. (2004). Apolipoprotein E and cognitive performance: A meta-analysis. *Psychology & Aging, 14,* 592–600.

Starr, J.M., Fox, H., Harris, S.E., Deary, I.J., & Whalley, L.J. (2008). GSTz1 genotype and cognitive ability. *Psychiatric Genetics, 18,* 211–212.

Stein, D.J., Newman, T.K., Savitz, J., & Ramesar, R. (2006). Warriors versus worriers: The role of COMT gene variants. *Cns Spectrums, 11,* 745–758.

Sternberg, R.J., & Grigorenko, E.L. (1997). Interventions for cognitive development in children 0–3 years old. In M.E. Young (Ed.) *Early child development: Investing in our children's future* (pp. 127–156). Amsterdam–Tokyo: Elsevier.

Sternberg, R.J., & Grigorenko, E.L. (1999). Myths in psychology and education regarding the gene–environment debate. *Teachers College Record, 100,* 536–553.

Strauss, J., Barr, C.L., George, C.J., Ryan, C.M., King, N., Shaikh, S., *et al.* (2004). BDNF and COMT polymorphisms: Relation to memory phenotypes in young adults with childhood-onset mood disorder. *NeuroMolecular Medicine, 5,* 181–192.

Tan, H.-Y., Chen, Q., Goldberg, T.E., Mattay, V.S., Meyer-Lindenberg, A., Weinberger, D.R., *et al.* (2007). Catechol-O-methyltransferase Val158Met modulation of prefrontal-parietal-striatal brain systems during arithmetic and temporal transformations in working memory. *Journal of Neuroscience, 27,* 13393–13401.

Tan, Y.L., Zhou, D.F., Cao, L.Y., Zou, Y.Z., Wu, G.Y., & Zhang, X.Y. (2005). Effect of the BDNF Val66Met genotype on episodic memory in schizophrenia. *Schizophrenia Research, 77,* 355–356.

Teasdale, G.M., Murray, G.D., & Nicoll, J.A. (2005). The association between APOE epsilon4, age and outcome after head injury: A prospective cohort study. *Brain, 128,* 2556–2561.

Teter, B., & Ashford, J.W. (2002). Neuroplasticity in Alzheimer's disease. *Journal of Neuroscience Research*, 70, 402–437.

Tohgi, H., Utsugisawa, K., Nagane, Y., Yoshimura, M., Genda, Y., & Ukitsu, M. (1999). Reduction with age in methylcytosine in the promoter region −224 approximately −101 of the amyloid precursor protein gene in autopsy human cortex. *Molecular Brain Research*, 70, 288–292.

Tsai, S.J., Hong, C.J., Yu, Y.W., & Chen, T.J. (2004). Association study of a brain-derived neurotrophic factor (BDNF) Val66Met polymorphism and personality trait and intelligence in healthy young females. *Neuropsychobiology*, 49, 13–16.

Tunbridge, E.M., Bannerman, D.M., Sharp, T., & Harrison, P.J. (2004). Catechol-O-methyltransferase inhibition improves setshifting performance and elevates stimulated dopamine release in the rat prefrontal cortex. *Journal of Neuroscience*, 24, 5331–5335.

Tunbridge, E.M., Harrison, P.J., & Weinberger, D.R. (2006). Catechol-o-methyltransferase, cognition, and psychosis: Val158Met and beyond. *Bioliological Psychiatry*, 60, 141–151.

Turic, D., Fisher, P.J., Plomin, R., & Owen, M.J. (2001). No association between apolipoprotein E polymorphisms and general cognitive ability in children. *Neuroscience Letters*, 299, 97–100.

Turkheimer, E., & Gottesman, I.I. (1991). Individual differences and the canalization of human behavior. *Developmental Psychology*, 27, 18–22.

Turkheimer, E., Haley, A., Waldron, M., D'Onofrio, B., & Gottesman, II (2003). Socioeconomic status modifies heritability of IQ in young children. *Psychological Science*, 14(6), 623–628.

Wahlsten, D. (1990). Insensitivity of the analysis of variance to heredity–environment interaction. *Behavioral and Brain Sciences*, 13, 109–161.

Wainwright, M.A., Wright, M.J., Luciano, M., Montgomery, G.W., Geffen, G.M., & Martin, N.G. (2006). A linkage study of academic skills defined by the Queensland Core Skills Test. *Behavior Genetics*, 36, 56–64.

Weaver, I.C., Champagne, F.A., Brown, S.E., Dymov, S., Sharma, S., Meaney, M.J., et al. (2005). Reversal of maternal programming of stress responses in adult offspring through methyl supplementation: Altering epigenetic marking later in life. *Journal of Neuroscience*, 25, 11045–11054.

West, R.L., Lee, J.M., & Maroun, L.E. (1995). Hypomethylation of the amyloid precursor protein gene in the brain of an Alzheimer's disease patient. *Journal of Molecular Neuroscience*, 6, 141–146.

Winterer, G., & Goldman, D. (2003). Genetics of human prefrontal function. *Brain Research Reviews*, 43, 134–163.

Zivadinov, R., Weinstock-Guttman, B., Benedict, R., Tamano-Blanco, M., Hussein, S., Abdelrahman, N., et al. (2007). Preservation of gray matter volume in multiple sclerosis patients with the Met allele of the rs6265 (Val66Met) SNP of brain-derived neurotrophic factor. *Human Molecular Genetics*, 16, 2659–2668.

Part II
Infancy

4 Prenatal Development

CHRISTINE MOON AND WILLIAM P. FIFER

KEY TERMS

apoptosis • autosomal genetic disorders • axon • cerebral cortex • chemosensory development • circadian rhythm • cochlea • colostrum • cranial-caudal • developmental programming • ectoderm • embryo • foetus • gyri • meiotic cell division • myelin • myelination • neonates • neural plate • neural tube • neurogenesis • neurons • organogenesis • perinatal • postnatal development • prenatal development • preterm • rods and cones • rooting reflex • sulci • synapse • synaptogenesis • term • transnatal learning (perinatal learning) • trimester • ultradian • rhythm • vestibular system

CHAPTER OUTLINE

OVERVIEW

It is tempting to treat birth as the beginning of psychological development because we can readily observe a newborn baby, so immature at birth and yet growing and changing before our eyes in the next weeks. In recent years, however, we have come to understand that birth is an important milestone in a developmental trajectory that begins in the womb about 266 days or 38 weeks before the baby becomes accessible to us. New technologies are allowing us to study development in the womb as never before, and prenatal research itself is maturing at a rapid rate.

Investigations of development of the brain and spinal cord reveal fascinating self-organising processes through which nerve cells appear, migrate, and become appropriately interconnected, forming pathways between the brain and peripheral organs. A major change within the brain concerns the development of the cerebral cortex, which is fairly mature by 27 weeks and exerts increasing control over the foetus's activities.

Early in development, the foetus is engaged in almost constant movement. Later in prenatal development, however, clear sleep/wake cycles become established as behaviour comes increasingly under cortical control. Many of the movements that the foetus engages in are likely to be important for the development of motor systems. For instance, approaching *term* or the end of gestation, foetal breathing becomes increasingly frequent and is probably important for lung development in preparation for birth.

The senses become functional between 8 weeks, which marks the end of the *embryonic period* and **organogenesis**, and 26 weeks, marking the beginning of the last *trimester* of pregnancy. Touch develops first, followed by the *chemical senses* of taste and smell, the *vestibular* sense, audition, and, finally, vision. With the exception of vision, the foetal brain's sensory systems all receive signals arising outside the brain itself as the foetus moves their body, brings their

> **organogenesis** the process of organ formation in very early development. In humans this is from first cell divisions until about 10 weeks.

hands into contact with their face, ingests amniotic fluid, and is impacted by sound waves, including those of the mother's voice. Vision is the exception because there is very little patterned light in the womb; and yet, the visual and auditory systems develop in parallel throughout gestation. An important difference between the two systems is that the external signals to the auditory system allow for prenatal learning and recognition memory. There is striking evidence that the foetus actually learns about their mother's voice and ambient language prior to birth.

This chapter addresses risks to foetal psychological development. These include both genetic and environmental factors. In the first category, chromosomal defects lead to problems such as Down's syndrome. In the environmental category, heavy maternal alcohol intake can have dramatic effects on foetal development and may lead to cognitive and behavioural impairments in the child. Maternal smoking can also have detrimental effects, particularly on foetal growth rate, and adequate nutrition is important for normal physical and psychological development.

The chapter ends by pointing out the important continuities that exist between developmental processes prior to and following birth. For instance, it seems likely that individual differences in temperament are to a large extent established before the infant is born. Continuing developments in technology for measuring foetal behaviour are liable to uncover progressively more of the detail regarding relationships between foetal development and infant behaviour.

FIGURE 4.1 *There is striking evidence that the foetus learns about the mother's voice and ambient language prior to birth. Source:* Shutterstock.

prenatal development
the development of
human individuals
before they are born.

foetus in human *pre-natal development*, the
organism 12 weeks after
conception until birth.

embryo the develop-ing organism during the
period when organs are
forming. In humans from
first cell divisions until
about 10 weeks.

neonate an infant less
than a month old.

postnatal develop-ment the development
of a human individual
after he or she is born,
particularly during early
infancy.

INTRODUCTION

For most of the last century, knowledge of human **prenatal psy-chological development** came from indirect methods of investiga-tion such as presenting loud sounds near the mother's abdomen and
detecting movement on the surface of her abdomen or by asking
her to report whether the **foetus** moved (for details see Lecanuet
et al., 1995.) Some indirect methods continue to be essential; one
example is making inferences about human neurobehavioural devel-opment from non-human animal models of prenatal changes in
brain and behaviour. We also continue to gain knowledge, especially
about abnormal development, from studies of human **embryos** and
foetuses who die and are investigated during autopsy. Another cur-rent indirect measure is testing the perception and memory of **neo-nates** who have a minimum of **postnatal** experience. In addition to
the indirect methods, we now can use direct methods of investigation
such as measurement of autonomic nervous system activity with or
without external stimulation to garner information about the typical
path of human development and also
about individual paths or *phenotypes*,
that is, characteristics, capacities,
and patterns of activity. An impor-tant direct measure of autonomic
nervous system activity is placing a
foetal ultrasound cardiotocograph
sensor around the maternal abdo-men that can electronically record
foetal heart rate. This method also
provides information about move-ment. In addition, foetal ultrasound
has become an important imaging
tool that allows observation and
recording of behaviour (see Figure
4.2). More recently it has become
possible to image and record foetal
brain activity using functional mag-netic resonance imaging (fMRI) and
magnetoencephalography (MEG).

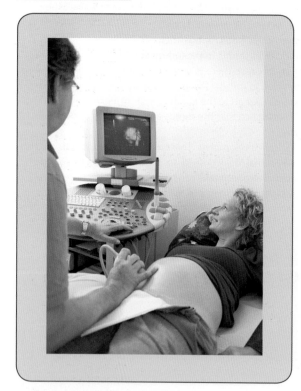

FIGURE 4.2 *Foetal ultrasound has become an
important imaging tool that allows observation and
recording of behaviour.*
Source: Shutterstock.

Through research on neurobeha-vioural development in the womb,
the roots of human psychological
development are being uncovered.
Throughout life, normal develop-ment demands constant and complex
interactions between genes, environ-ment, and the emerging organism.

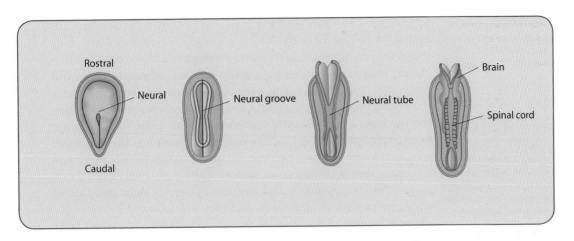

FIGURE 4.3 *The development of the neural tube into the spinal cord and primitive brain.*

Source: Adapted from J. H. Martin (2003), *Neuroanatomy Text and Atlas* (3rd ed.). Stamford, CT: Appleton & Lange.

Fuller appreciation now exists regarding the long-term implications of foetal adaptation to a changing uterine environment that is unique for each maternal/child dyad. The impact of prenatal experience occurs on multiple levels, from biochemical factors influencing gene expression in the foetus's neuronal circuitry to characteristics of the mother's lifestyle affecting the foetal environment. Exquisitely timed, complex interactions between the genes and environmental input affect acquisition of neuronal identity, guidance of **axons** to target, induction of connections between cells or **synaptogenesis**, and also programmed cell death or **apoptosis**. At another level, sensory systems are being sculpted by environmental input. The complexity and need for intrauterine stimulation is just beginning to be appreciated. In what follows, we describe foetal neurobehavioural development throughout gestation and, in particular, we focus on the role of the uterine environment in facilitating and directing foetal growth and behaviour.

THE BRAIN, THE SPINAL CORD AND THE EMERGENCE OF MIND

Processes and sequencing of brain development

During the embryonic period, the central nervous system begins as cells of **ectoderm**, one of three germ layers (the others are endoderm and mesoderm). The germ layers are the foundation for organ

axon the tail-like part of a **neuron** which transmits impulses (the actual message) away from the cell body.

synapses the connections between *neurons* which enable them to transmit information.

synaptogenesis the building of connections (**synapses**) between nerve cells.

apoptosis programmed cell death.

neurons nerve cells within the central nervous system which transmit information in the form of electrochemical impulses.

ectoderm the outermost of the three primary germ layers of an *embryo*. The central nervous system and skin, among other structures, develop from ectoderm.

neural plate a thickening of endoderm cells that will give rise to the brain.

neural tube a hollow structure in the embryo that gives rise to the brain and spinal column.

cranial-caudal the direction beginning with the head end and moving toward the opposite end or feet in humans.

neurogenesis the birth of neurons.

formation. The endoderm thickens and becomes the **neural plate** by day 18 of gestation. By then it is already differentiated into cells that will become forebrain (cerebral hemispheres, thalamus, hypothalamus), midbrain (superior and inferior colliculi, substantia nigra), and hindbrain (medulla oblongata, pons.) The neural plate folds to become the **neural tube**, and by the end of the first month the embryonic body has the basic **cranial-caudal** organisation (see Figure 4.3). Cells are born (**neurogenesis**) and begin extensive migration to their eventual locations where they will become, for example, specialised neurons of the brain or cells of the spinal cord. (Kandel *et al.*, 2000; Schoenwolf *et al.*, 2009). Neurogenesis and migration continue right up to about the sixth month of pregnancy, and they are followed by extensive changes in individual cells that program them for the myriad tasks awaiting the emerging brain. Despite their ultimate high level of specialisation, the 10^{10} nerve cells that will comprise the brain originate from one single layer of identical cells in the wall of the neural tube.

There is a hierarchy of control systems within the nervous system that basically determines what the foetus is doing and when. The hierarchical structure becomes more complex as the unborn infant develops. The larger the behavioural repertoire is, the greater is the need for organisation by the nervous system. Initially, behaviours are of a reflexive nature, and the circuitry controlling them may consist only of a few sensory cells directly connected to some motor cells – these may be found in the spinal cord and work independently of the brain. The types of behaviour mediated by the spinal cord are likely to be early reflexive movements such as moving when the area around the lips is touched, starting around 7–8 weeks of pregnancy. By birth, the full complement of infant reflexes will be in place, and they will be modifiable by experience as in habituation to repeated stimulation.

Development of the cerebral cortex

cerebral cortex the area of the brain that is associated with complex tasks such as memory, language, and thoughts and the control and integration of movement and the senses.

For memory, language, thought, and control and integration of movement with the senses, the primary part of the brain responsible is the **cerebral cortex**, the outer six-layer 'crust' of the hemispheres that is about as thick as a credit card. For the first two or three months of pregnancy there is relatively little development in this crust. It is not surprising therefore that behaviours emerging before this time, for example, early foetal movements, are largely reflexive and probably controlled via simpler circuits that begin to arise in the midbrain. The cerebral hemispheres begin to develop from the forebrain at about 9 weeks and rapidly increase in size, expanding to form different regions that will later become highly specialised, and by mid-pregnancy, the cerebral hemispheres have expanded to cover the rest of the brain. By the fourth month of pregnancy, the cells in the cerebral hemispheres begin to proliferate and migrate. Cell migration is unique in the cortex; cells migrate and find their ultimate destinations in the innermost of the six layers, first with successive migrating neurons passing them on their way to the outer layers nearer the skull.

By 6 months, the surface of the cortex is no longer smooth because rapid cell proliferation has caused the characteristic infolding that is necessary for the large surface area of the cortex to be accommodated within the skull. **Sulci** (valleys) and **gyri** (ridges) have appeared, and the frontal, parietal, and occipital lobes can be differentiated. Additional sulci and gyri develop until birth, but emergence from the womb doesn't mark the end of rapid brain development. It continues in the months after birth as well. As the higher centres of the brain develop, and more neural inputs become active, increasingly sophisticated messages can be sent from the brain. The process of inhibition becomes functional, and this is an important advance in complexity. With inhibition, when the foetus's brain sends a nerve impulse to the muscles, instead of only being able to cause movement, it can now begin to modify it. Consequently, this eventually leads to better control and refinement of movement. A by-product of this process is that at about 15 weeks there is a bit of a lull in activity. This is followed by a period of reorganisation of behaviours. Reflexive neuronal circuits are still in place, but these circuits are now controlled by more sophisticated nerve cells in the new higher brain centres.

> **sulci** the deep narrow grooves of the outer surface of the brain.

> **gyri** the prominent ridges on the outer surface of the brain.

By 27 weeks, the numbers of cells in the cerebral cortex are thought to be mature, but at birth the brain is only about 25 per cent of its adult volume. Additional volume comes from increases in cell body size and proliferation of dendritic spines during *synaptogenesis*. Most of the growth, however, comes from the **myelination** of nerve fibres. The formation of **myelin**, a fatty insulator, around the nerve fibres is very important in neural development. The myelin prevents leakage of the messages travelling along the nerve, and it also makes it possible for messages to travel faster and more efficiently. Myelination begins in the sixth month of foetal life, continues through childhood, and is not entirely complete until the third decade of life (see Figure 4.4).

> **myelin** a fatty insulator which prevents leakage of the messages travelling along the nerves, and increases the speed of neural transmission.

> **myelination** The process by which *myelin* is formed around the *neurons*. Myelination begins in the sixth month of life in the *foetus* but continues through childhood.

Despite the immaturity of the foetal nervous system, by about 24 weeks foetuses do have a limited capacity to learn. They respond to the environment and begin to show a very basic form of memory – habituation of responding to repeated auditory stimulation. By birth, the cerebral cortex consists of a large number of well-defined primary motor and sensory zones. The frontal lobes of the left and right hemisphere are generally thought to be associated with movement. The parietal lobes are concerned with sensation. The temporal lobes are important for hearing, memory, and a sense of self and time. The occipital lobes form the visual centre of the brain. The association cortex areas surround the primary sensory areas, and their development occurs over a much longer period because they are concerned with higher cognitive and integrative functions that develop with experience and with the emerging mind.

Behavioural organisation

Foetus behaviour becomes progressively more organised as gestation proceeds. At 34 weeks, they are no longer the continually moving creatures of 13 weeks; instead

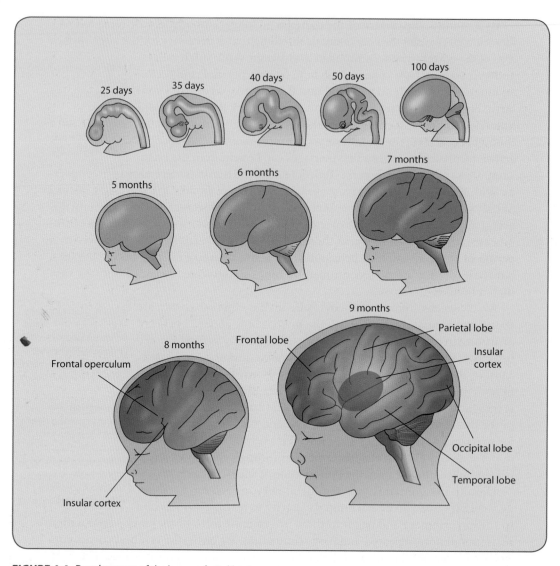

FIGURE 4.4 *Development of the human foetal brain.*

Source: Adapted from J. H. Martin (2003), *Neuroanatomy Text and Atlas* (3rd ed., p. 51). Stamford, CT: Appleton & Lange.

they have distinct patterns of rest and activity. In fact, two dominant patterns of behaviour have now emerged. Foetuses now spend most of their time either in quiet sleep or active sleep. By this stage, foetuses spend about 20 to 30 per cent of their time in a quiet, motionless sleep-like state with a steady heartbeat and breathing movements that are rhythmic, when they occur. For most of the rest of the time they are similarly not awake but are in a state like newborn active sleep with many different body movements and their eyes moving rapidly back and forth, periodically open. Heart rate and breathing patterns tend to be irregular, and they will be responsive to the sensory stimuli that they are naturally exposed to in their uterine environment.

During periods of active sleep foetuses may be more reactive to sounds and touch. Early neuronal networks are being stimulated or 'exercised', both by external stimuli and also volleys of activity that the brain generates without external stimulation. It is thought that this level of brain activity is probably necessary for adequate development and further maturation of the vital organs and the nervous system. Foetuses make fewer general body movements now – these movements probably only occur about 15 per cent of the time. They also make breathing movements fairly frequently (about 30 per cent of the time), which are important for lung development in readiness for birth.

In contrast to one month ago, 38-week-old (**term**) foetuses no longer spend quite as much time in a state of active sleep (Figure 4.5). Because their brain has matured in the last month, more inhibitory pathways have developed, further reducing the amount of movement they make. Consequently, foetuses will have longer periods when they are resting quietly in deep sleep (Nijhuis, 1992). On the whole, foetus activity and rest periods alternate cyclically throughout the day. Already, the length of one entire activity–rest cycle has lengthened from that seen one month ago, and now probably lasts about 80 to 100 minutes (Visser, 1992). However, superimposed on this cyclical rhythm are maternal physiological factors such as hormone levels, breathing, heart rate, and uterine activity (Mirmiran & Swaab, 1992). Variations in some or all of these factors are thought to affect foetus behaviour over the course of the day. In general there is a peak in activity occurring when the mother is asleep, in the late evening, and a relative lull in activity in the early hours of the morning (Patrick *et al.*, 1982).

term the end of pregnancy.

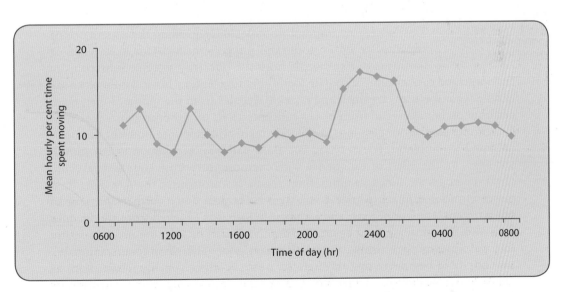

FIGURE 4.5 *Foetal movement at 38–39 weeks, plotted as the average per cent time spent moving in a 24-hour interval.*

Source: Adapted from Patrick *et al.* (1982).

SENSATIONS

Touch

The emergence of the senses follows a set mammalian pattern of development, and we will describe them in their sequence . Emergence is further organised in a cranial-caudal direction. The first system to function is touch. By about 8 weeks, if the area around the lips is stroked by a hairlike wire, foetuses will respond by moving. Within two weeks foetuses will curl their fingers in a reflexive grasp when their palm is touched. Then two weeks later their toes will curl when the soles of their feet are touched. Initially foetuses move their head and neck away from the source of facial touch, often with their mouth open; later in gestation, they will move toward the touch. This is the pre-cursor of the **rooting reflex**, which helps babies to find the nipple for nursing. Once foetuses start to move around they will be touching the uterine wall, the umbilical cord, and also themselves. Foetuses will touch their own face more frequently than any other body part. So the foetus is provided with a wide breadth of physical sensations, which probably helps to promote further development of the physical sensation of touch (see de Vries & Hopkins, 2005).

rooting reflex the reflex that causes newborn babies to respond to one of their cheeks being touched by turning their head in that direction.

The chemosensory system

chemosensory system encompasses both the gustatory (taste) and olfactory (smell) senses.

The gustatory (taste) and olfactory (smell) senses are called the **chemosensory system** because the sensory receptors in the mouth and nose respond to molecules of the substances that contact them. Taste receptors respond to molecules signalling the experience of sweet, salty, bitter, sour, and umami (meaty.) Our experience of flavour is due to signals from the olfactory system. Substances in amniotic fluid can certainly stimulate foetal chemoreceptors, but it is difficult to say exactly what foetuses can smell and taste. Molecules from the mother's diet, from perfume on her skin, and from heavy concentrations of airborne substances such as cigarette smoke can pass into her bloodstream and then into both the amniotic fluid and foetal blood. Foetal blood is a third pathway, in addition to the mouth and nose, for the effect of experience with chemosensory stimulants (Schaal *et al.*, 1995). Foetuses swallows amniotic fluid regularly throughout the day. This fluid passes into the stomach where it will then be broken down further and sent to other organs, the brain, liver, and kidneys, before it is expelled from the bladder back into the amniotic fluid again. During the fourth month, the plugs of tissue that were previously blocking the nostrils have gone, and when foetuses 'inhale', amniotic fluid begins passing through the nose. Foetuses actually inhale twice as much fluid as they swallow (Duenholter & Pritchard, 1976), so the sensory receptors within the nose are continuously being bathed in amniotic fluid. Certain foods in a woman's diet such as garlic can cause a noticeable odour in the delivery room after the amniotic membranes have ruptured. During the second half of pregnancy, the constitution of amniotic fluid becomes increasingly dependent on foetal urination. This may be particularly important for stimulation of the chemosensory system since it contains large amounts of ammonia-smelling urea in addition to molecules that have passed through the foetal digestive system.

In another chemosensory route, odour and taste molecules from the food, drink, lotions, or inhalants consumed by the mother will pass into her bloodstream. These will then travel via the placenta into the foetal circulation system. Unlike substances in the amniotic fluid, those within the blood have not been broken down or metabolised and are relatively undiluted and consequently more intense. Foetal blood will flow in tiny capillaries through the nose and mouth and therefore have ample opportunity to bind with olfactory and gustatory receptors. It appears that nearly all babies, whether before or after birth, show a preference for sweet substances over bitter. If the amniotic fluid tastes sweet then the foetus will swallow more regularly than if it contains bitter substances (Hepper, 1992). Not surpris-

FIGURE 4.6 *Exposure to alcohol while in the womb has been shown to increase foetal swallowing and may cause preference for alcohol later in life.*
Source: Shutterstock.

ingly, after a meal and when glucose levels rise within the maternal bloodstream and the amniotic fluid, there is more breathing and swallowing. The amniotic fluid probably tastes sweeter as a result of the additional glucose. Swallowing by foetuses will also regulate the volume of the amniotic fluid.

While some of the foetus's ability to detect and prefer certain flavours to others may be genetically determined, other preferences may be learned *in utero*. Newborn infants turn their heads in the direction of odorants that have been present in their mother's diet such as anise, garlic, and carrot juice. Exposure to alcohol while in the womb has been shown to increase foetal swallowing and may cause preferences for alcohol later in life (Molina *et al.*, 1995). It appears that preferences for smells may be individually tailored for babies, depending on what flavours and smells they have been exposed to during life in the womb. Newborns are selectively responsive to their own amniotic fluid and to their own mother's **colostrum** and breast milk, likely due to prenatal experience with characteristic odorants. This has been particularly supported by studies suggesting that if a mother dramatically changes her diet after her pregnancy, the infant may have a more difficult time learning to suckle (Hepper, 1988). See Schaal, 2005, for a thorough review.

colostrum the breast fluid that precedes true milk. It is rich in minerals and antibodies, and it helps populate the newborn's gut with 'good' bacteria.

The vestibular system

As described above, foetuses do a lot of moving around *in utero*, constantly changing position within the warm amniotic fluid that cushions them from the outside world. Additionally, since mothers are moving about for much of the day, foetuses are also subjected to constant passive motion and will experience positional changes relative to gravity, depending on whether the mother is standing up, sitting, or lying down. This information is sensed by the **vestibular** apparatus consisting of three semi-circular canals, set at right angles to each other within the foetus's inner ear. These canals are fluid-filled and when the foetus moves (or is moved) the fluid within at least one of the canals will also move, stimulating tiny hairs within the canal lining. Depending on the direction and plane of movement, one semi-circular canal may be stimulated more than another. This information is then sent to the brain to be processed and information about motion and position extracted.

vestibular system the sensory system that contributes to balance and spatial orientation.

Although it is difficult to elicit responses to vestibular stimulation in babies *in utero* (Hepper, 1992), this does not mean that this system is not functioning. By 25 weeks, foetuses will show a righting reflex (Hooker, 1952), and it is possible that the vestibular system is in some way responsible for most babies lying head down prior to delivery. We do not know exactly how much information about position and motion foetuses are actually processing at this time. We do know that the system is actively being stimulated, and that this stimulation is very important for many aspects of normal foetal growth and development. Vestibular stimulation plays an important role in changing arousal states and this will become more apparent as time goes on. Initially, during the pregnancy, foetuses are often quiet when the mother is moving about a lot and causing a lot of vestibular stimulation. In contrast, when the mother is lying down at night, foetuses are receiving minimal vestibular stimulation and are often at their most active. Once foetuses are born, the parents will probably rock the baby when they are fussy or to put them to sleep. Again, the vestibular system is being stimulated and may play a role in eliciting changes in the arousal state of the child. The level of vestibular stimulation received by foetuses during the pregnancy is particularly high resulting in a level of stimulation to the vestibular system that will probably not be matched until babies start to walk independently (Hofer, 1981). Studies of **preterm** infants (who are deprived of the vestibular stimulation that would have been provided by their mother's movement) show lags in neurobehavioural development that may in part be due to a lack of vestibular stimulation. Early research on preterm infants showed that weight gain, visual responsiveness, and even later expressive language development are improved if the incubator is gently rocked (Masi, 1979). Along the same lines, if preterm babies are put on waterbeds instead of mattresses, the rocking movement of the water may compensate for the vestibular stimulation that they lack from being out of the womb too early and appears to result in better sleep organisation (Korner et al., 1983). More recently, daily one-hour sessions of Kangaroo Care, skin-to-skin contact between the mother and her hospitalised preterm infant, over 24 days has been shown to favourably affect maturation of the autonomic nervous system and **circadian rhythms** (24-hour

preterm born prematurely. Human infants are regarded as preterm if they are born before 38 weeks of pregnancy.

circadian rhythm bodily cycles within the body that occur on a 24-hour cycle, such as patterns of sleeping/waking.

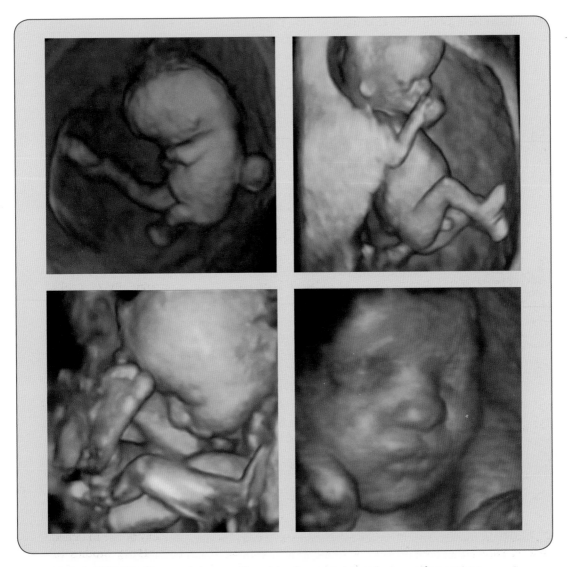

FIGURE 4.7 *Noninvasive ultrasound pictures of foetal development at various stages of pregnancy, using 3D technology.*

Source: Dr. Armin Breinl, Austria. Reproduced with permission.

cycles, e.g. sleep-wake patterns) by the time of assessment at 37 weeks gestational age (Feldman & Eidelman, 2003).

The visual system

Pregnancy is a time for structural formation of the basic components of the visual system, from the development of the eyes to the specialised areas in the brain that receive and process visual input. As mentioned above, there is little visual stimulation in the developing baby's prenatal world. The interior of the womb is dark; only the brightest of lights can filter through a naked abdomen and this would provide a reddish glow with no light–dark contrast or edges necessary for the visual system to function. The eyelids are fused shut shortly after their formation and do not open until 5–7 months of gestation, further reducing the amount of light reaching the developing retina. Since premature infant experience with ambient light is implicated in subtle visual deficits, this period of darkness may be necessary for proper development (Fielder & Moseley, 2000). In contrast, after a term birth, visual development can proceed normally only when the system is adequately stimulated.

Development of the eyes

At about 5 weeks postconception, two balloon-like structures form on either side at the front of the brain. These are the future eyes. As they develop they become separated from the brain by a small stalk; this is where the nerve fibres will travel between the eye and brain. A few days later, the 'balloons' infold to form a two-layered cup, and the retina develops from this cup. The mature retina is a complex neural structure made of many layers, whose function is to capture the light entering the eye and to convert it into electrical impulses or messages that can be transmitted to the brain. The cells that perform this task are the **rods and cones**, and they develop from the inner wall of the optic cup. The outer wall forms a pigment-containing layer that actually absorbs the light. This outer wall also goes on to develop the nutritive network of blood vessels needed by the rods and cones.

rods and cones light-sensitive cells found in the retina of the eye which translate light into electrical signals that are then transferred to the brain so that the image can be interpreted.

The lens of the eye begins to form at about 2 months of pregnancy. The eyelids and muscles that move the eyes are also beginning to form around this time. The circular ring of pigmented muscle, the iris, begins to develop. By 3 months the eyelids have fused together. The cornea, the clear, curved part of the eye, is forming different layers; the organisation of the cells and fibres in these layers is crucial in providing a strong but transparent window to the eye. By 6 months, all the muscles that move the eyeball are in place. Eye movements usually begin between weeks 16–23, even though not all the muscles may be fully formed. The eyes will sometimes make slow rolling movements, or faster movements that may be smooth or jerky in nature. It is known that even premature babies, as immature as 26 weeks gestation, are able to distinguish light from dark and are soon able to make tracking eye movements to follow an attractive moving object.

Development of the visual pathway

There is simultaneous development of the visual pathway (see Figure 4.8) connecting the light-sensitive cells in the eye (rods and cones) to the brain. This pathway deals with the transmission and interpretation of the electrical impulses encoding the visual information that enters the eye. There is a series of relay stations that form between the eye and cerebral cortex, connecting cells from one level to the next. In humans, the lateral geniculate nucleus (LGN) of the thalamus (a structure in the forebrain) has evolved to be one such relay station. By 9 weeks of pregnancy, shortly after the period of the embryo, the optic nerve has already penetrated the neural tube from its stalk, and there is a partial crossing over of the fibres of the optic nerve, that

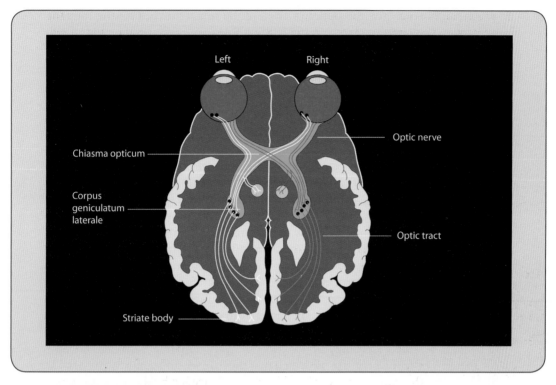

FIGURE 4.8 *The visual pathway.*

Source: © Francis Leroy, Biocosmos/Science Photo Library.

is, some fibres from the right eye go to the right side of the brain, and others go to the left, and vice versa. This allows for information from both eyes to be integrated. This crossing is complete by 15 weeks of pregnancy. By the end of the first **trimester**, the nerve fibres interconnect with cells in the LGN, an area of the brain that is highly developed in primates. At about 5 months, the cells in this structure take on a very particular arrangement: six stripes appear. The cells within the stripes are highly specialised to deal with particular types of visual information and will be part of the 'what' and 'where' visual pathways for object perception. Cells in two of the stripes respond maximally to moving stimuli and gross form, whereas the cells in the other four stripes are concerned with the transmission of information about colour and fine detail. It is remarkable that this cell differentiation awaits a task that cannot begin until four months later at birth, and even then the visual system will be insufficiently developed to fully process colour or fine detail.

> **trimester** a period of three months. The course of human pregnancy is divided into three trimesters.

Development of the visual cortex

As the nerve fibres pass on from the LGN they go to the visual cortex, an area at the back of the brain in the occipital lobes. The visual cortex is organised like a map of the two retinas. Each point on the retina represents a point in space within the field of vision, and because of the optics of the eye the image formed on the retina is upside down; similarly, an object on the left will form an image on the right of the retina. The visual cortex makes sense of this information, turning the image right way up. Since the optic nerves from each eye partially cross, the left side of the field of vision of each eye is represented on the right side of the brain, and vice versa. An area known as the striate cortex in the occipital lobe is the part of the brain concerned with many aspects of basic visual function. The surrounding brain areas are involved with perceptual processes, that is, the interpretation of sensory information, and their development is less well known, but they are thought to begin formation somewhat later in the last trimester. The development of the cerebral cortex is characterised by the formation of layers of varying cell densities and by about 7 months, the striate cortex attains the definitive laminar structure seen in the adult.

At this time, foetuses' eyelids are no longer fused closed. Foetuses will spend some time with their eyes open and will now be making blinking movements. Externally, foetuses' eyes will look fully formed. There are still some minor immaturities in the gross structures of the eyes, but the major source of immaturity in foetuses' visual system is within the neural structures of the eye, the retina, and the pathways to the brain. Nonetheless, if foetuses were born now at 28 weeks, they would have some vision, even at this early age. Babies of this age can easily distinguish between light and dark (Taylor et al., 1987) and have the ability to discriminate form to some extent (Dubowitz et al., 1998). Certainly by 30 weeks of age, premature newborns are able to see patterns of fairly large size, provided that they are of sufficiently high contrast (e.g., black stripes on a white background) and fairly close to their eyes (Grose & Harding, 1990). Foetuses do have the basic 'equipment' to be able to see, even though this ability is really not in use until birth when development of the visual system continues at a rapid pace. At birth babies are relatively near-sighted, but this is perfect for the task in hand, looking at the faces of the people who are holding them. The ability to focus on objects across the room will develop in the first months of life (see Chapter 5).

The auditory system

The development of the auditory system (see Figure 4.9) begins at about 6 weeks of pregnancy. At this time, two small, inward-facing bubbles appear on either side of the back of the brain. These become the inner ear and will later contain the auditory and balance organs. The middle ear tube has also begun to develop from the pharynx or oral cavity area above the trachea. At 7 weeks, the external part of the ear along with the canal leading into the ear and the eardrum develop from a groove between the mouth and the heart. At this stage, the external part of the ear looks rather like a 'wrinkled mouth'. By 8 weeks of pregnancy, the inner ear begins to develop the semicircular canals that will eventually house the organs that are able to sense balance and position. A week later, the **cochlea** in the inner ear forms one coil, the first step in the formation of the spiral shell-like structures that will be the auditory organs. By 10 weeks, sensory cells

cochlea the inner ear, a structure encased in bone that contains the receptors for sound.

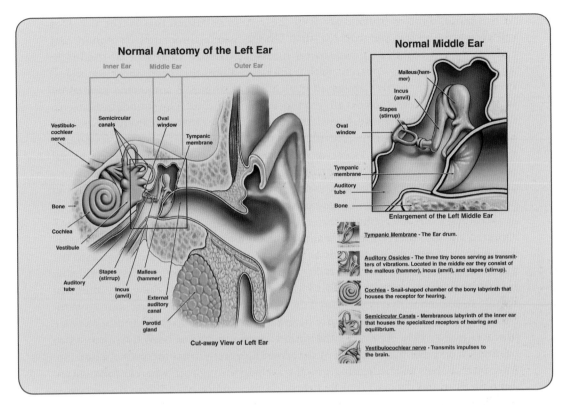

FIGURE 4.9 *Normal anatomy of the ear.*

Source: © Nucleus Medical Art, Visuals Unlimited/Science Photo Library.

are present in the semi-circular canals. The middle ear forms two soft structures that later become two of the three bones that conduct sound from the outer to the inner ear. The foetal ears will look like simple skin folds now.

By 14 weeks, the vestibular system begins to work. This system will be receiving high levels of stimulation at this time, and the baby is almost constantly moving about, not only because of their own constant activity but also in response to maternal movement. The cochlea has become more coiled and now contains sensory cells, and the auditory nerve attaches to the cochlear duct. By 20 weeks the third bone of the ear is present and all three have begun to harden. This process is likely to improve the ability of the middle ear to conduct sound. Cochlear function is considered to begin around 24 weeks (Pujol *et al.*, 1991). At this time, the external ear is adult-shaped, but continues to grow in size until 9 years of age. Its function is to collect the sound from the external environment and channel it into the ear canal.

Responses to sounds

The auditory system becomes mature enough between 23 and 25 weeks to detect vibroacoustic stimulation, as demonstrated by foetal movement (Kisilevsky, 1995).

At this point, a major immaturity is in the system's sensors, that is, the tiny hair cell receptors within the cochlea that vibrate when stimulated by sound and convert these vibrations into electrical messages that are then sent to the brain. Another immaturity is apparent within the nerve fibres that carry these messages. Consequently, the foetus's ability to hear different sounds is somewhat limited by these factors. However, almost all frequencies can be heard. The sounds available to the foetus have to pass through various maternal tissues that effectively cut out the higher frequencies; consequently, the sounds that reach the foetus are predominantly low-frequency ones. However, even with this limitation, the uterine sound environment is rich with sound including the background noises of the mother's pulsing heartbeat, which changes constantly as both mother and foetus move and when maternal pulse and blood pressure change. On recordings made during labour by threading a tiny microphone through the cervix after amniotic membranes have ruptured and also on recordings made in the fluid-filled wombs of pregnant sheep, the loudness of heartbeats depends on the location of the microphone relative to the maternal uterine artery (Abrams et al., 1995). This variability in loudness is probably true for foetuses as their head shifts locations. Borborygmi are the gastrointestinal sounds associated with digestion, and these, too, are part of the foetal sound experience. But by far the most frequently heard and loudest sound is the mother's voice (Abrams et al., 1995). As rich as the sound environment has been documented to be, there is no unambiguous way of determining exactly what foetuses are hearing. After birth, babies will be hearing sound travelling through air, whereas foetuses are listening to sound that has travelled through the amniotic fluid with no air spaces on either side of the eardrum. Furthermore, the rest of the auditory system is still immature, and so we do not know how well these sounds are converted into electrical signals by the cochlear hair cell receptors or what the foetus's brain makes of these messages. Foetal motor and heart rate responses to externally delivered sounds begin to be measurable at the beginning of the third trimester or 262–7 weeks, and they become reliably detectable around 30 weeks. See Lecanuet et al., 1995, for a review.

Very loud sounds will result in a very fast heart rate. As foetuses get older, their response will change based on the sound intensity, how deeply they are sleeping, and how familiar they are with the sounds (Lecanuet, 1996). Foetuses will also respond to some sounds by moving their limbs, or sometimes by stopping their movement if they are in the middle of a high-activity period. One study has shown that foetuses will actually startle and empty their bladders following the loudest of sounds (Zimmer, Chao et al., 1993). Responding to a change in auditory stimulation has been reported for foetuses as young as 26 weeks (Zimmer, Fifer et al., 1993.) Sounds are thought to shape permanent changes in the auditory system, and these are probably required for normal brain development. Permanent changes are also reflected in newborn perceptual capacities and sound preferences as a newborn. Areas of the brain devoted to processing and remembering 'multimodal' stimulation are probably also affected, since during some sound experiences several senses are activated at once. For example, when a mother speaks, her diaphragm moves, resulting in movement of the foetus, consequently those pathways that sense pressure, touch, and balance are also stimulated along with the auditory system.

PRENATAL AND TRANSNATAL AUDITORY LEARNING

Because there are few methods for measuring their behaviour, it is difficult to determine when foetuses have learned and when that learning has been retained into the postnatal period (**transnatal learning**). One way of doing it during the foetal period is to present a stimulus repeatedly and measure whether there is a reduction in responding that cannot be attributed to sensory adaptation or response system fatigue (Zelazo *et al.*, 1991). Habituation experiments typically take place over a period of minutes during which learning is shown by increasingly less responding.

transnatal learning learning that occurs during the *prenatal* period which is remembered during the *postnatal* period.

Further evidence of learning is shown in dishabituation, a return to a higher level of responding when a novel stimulus is presented after habituation. This demonstrates that organisms retain stimulus characteristics long enough to compare them with a new exemplar. In a study of habituation, foetuses from 32–37 weeks of age habituated their cardiac defensive response (cardiac accelerations) to repeated high intensity vibroacoustic stimulation, but those at younger ages required significantly more trials to habituate (Morokuma *et al.*, 2004.) In a more recent study using low-intensity auditory stimulation to investigate heart rate orienting responses (decelerations), most 35–37-week-old foetuses habituated and dishabituated, but at 32–34 weeks gestational age, the habituation responses were more variable and there was no dishabituation (Morokuma *et al.*, 2008.) This suggests that 35 weeks marks an important advance in learning ability. Another way to use habituation to investigate foetal learning is to habituate the foetus to a stimulus and then test subsequent habituation to the same stimulus at later times. If learning has occurred, fewer trials to reach habituation should be required. In such a study, retention was demonstrated at 10 minutes and at 24 hours for term foetuses (van Heteren *et al.*, 2000). Full-term neonates have revealed themselves to be adept learners and it is likely that much of this capacity was already present at the end of gestation prior to birth. For a review, see Moon & Fifer, 2000.

If we accept that foetuses can learn about sounds that they hear *in utero*, then it becomes reasonable to ask whether there is any indication that newborns respond differentially to sounds that occurred during the prenatal period either naturally or through deliberate exposure. One candidate natural prenatal sound is the rhythm of a heartbeat. Salk (1962, 1973) reported that playing recordings of a heartbeat sound for groups of newborns in a hospital nursery resulted in greater weight gain and reduced crying time. Other researchers have also found that intrauterine sounds calm neonates (Murooka *et al.*, 1976; Rosner & Doherty, 1979). Based partially upon this research, commercial products using heartbeat sounds have been devised for pacifying young infants (Murooka, 1974). Other research has, however, called the soothing effect of heartbeat sounds into question. There have been failures to replicate (Detterman, 1978; Tulloch *et al.*, 1964). There have also been many experiments with sounds other than heartbeats that show that a neonatal arousal response to sound depends upon many variables including broad characteristics of the stimulus, the infant's initial state of arousal, and the experimenter's choice of response (Detterman, 1978; Gerber, 1985). One study has demonstrated that heartbeat sounds acted as a reinforcer for the infants. That is, they changed their patterns of sucking on a pacifier when specific changes in sucking behaviour were required in order to hear a recording of heatbeat sounds. (DeCasper & Sigafoos, 1983).

Learning about mother's voice and language

Although the maternal voice has been noted to be a prominent sound, and it is more intense than other voices, it is not more intelligible. All voices on intrauterine recordings are muffled, largely because the higher frequency sound waves travel relatively poorly through the maternal body to reach the foetus (Abrams *et al.*, 1995). Several studies support the hypothesis that newborns prefer a low-pass filtered recording of the maternal voice compared to an unfiltered recording of her voice (DeCasper & Spence, 1986; Fifer & Moon, 1995; Spence & Freeman, 1996). This preference for the prenatal version of mother's voice strongly suggests that newborns can learn about sounds available in the womb and that early postnatal responding is influenced by this experience. Selective responses to particular stimuli like the familiar maternal voice and familiar odours may be biologically adaptive and beneficial to mammalian newborns because they make it less likely that the immature nervous system will be overwhelmed with information. (Schaal, 2005.)

The salience of mother's voice to infants shortly after birth has been the focus of several experiments in which responding to the maternal voice has been compared to stranger female voices. In one study done within two hours after birth, infants reacted with more movement when mother was speaking compared with strangers (Querleu *et al.*, 1984; described in Moon & Fifer, 2000). Well-controlled studies of neonates have used recordings of mothers' and stranger females' voices in a procedure in which sucking on a pacifier activated a voice recording (DeCasper & Fifer, 1980; Fifer & Moon, 1989). Infants sucked to activate the recording of the maternal voice proportionately more frequently than the unfamiliar voice. Additional supporting evidence comes from a study of differential newborn brain activity to the maternal voice (deRegnier *et al.*, 2000). Interestingly, recordings from preterm infants' brains do not show the same degree of differentiation of voices (deRegnier *et al.*, 2002). Father's voice has received little attention from researchers compared to mother, and although newborns apparently discriminate between the paternal and a stranger male voice (DeCasper & Prescott, 1984; Ockleford *et al.*, 1988), a preference has not been documented (DeCasper & Prescott, 1984).

In addition to demonstrating preferences for listening to particular voices, newborns have shown that they respond differentially to languages. Within the first four days after birth, infants discriminate the language that their mother speaks compared to a foreign language (Mehler *et al.*, 1988), and 2-day-olds have demonstrated a preference for the maternal language compared to a foreign language (Moon *et al.*, 1993). The rhythmic structure of the two comparison languages appears to be important in neonates' ability to classify utterances (Nazzi *et al.*, 1998). In the experiments with voices and languages described above, it is not possible to rule out the effect of postnatal experience. Remarkably, there is only one published experiment that is a direct test of the hypothesis that prenatal learning is retained after birth. DeCasper and Spence (1986) asked women to read a particular three-minute speech passage out loud two times a day during the last 6 weeks of pregnancy, and their babies' preferences were tested as newborns. Infants activated the tape recording of the prenatal story more frequently than the novel story, and notably, for half of the newborns, the familiar story was recognised even though the recording was made by an unfamiliar voice, suggesting that the infants recognised speech patterns unique to reading a story out loud, not to specific words or a particular person's voice. This is one experiment in which postnatal experience with the auditory stimulus can be ruled out as an explanation for newborn response to a prenatal event. This result is further supported by a test of learning by term foetuses whose mothers had read a story passage out loud for several weeks before testing. Foetal heart rates differed when recordings of the familiar and a novel passage were played on a loudspeaker in the laboratory (DeCasper *et al.*, 1994).

Summary

Taken altogether, the studies of transnatal learning suggest that (1) the foetus can learn and that prenatal experience affects postnatal brain activity and behaviour; (2) the maternal voice may provide a perceptual bridge into postnatal life; and (3) we still know very little about the extent, limits, and underlying mechanisms of both prenatal and transnatal learning.

RISKS TO FOETAL DEVELOPMENT

Perinatal complications (detectable around the time of birth) can have their origins in parental preconception conditions, as well as in gene–environment interactions throughout embryogenesis and gestation. Genetic factors are thought to account for roughly 10–15 per cent of congenital defects, while environmental agents acting alone – such as alcohol, excess quantities of vitamin A, and radiation – are thought to cause another 10 per cent of them. The rest of congenital anomalies are believed to be the result of multifactoral causation, that is, the result of genes and environment interacting together (Ashmead & Reed, 1997; Milunsky & Milunsky, 1998).

perinatal the period just before and after birth.

In chromosomal defects, whole *chromosomes* or parts of them are missing or duplicated. Overall, chromosomal abnormalities are seen in 1/200 live births and in 50–70 per cent of first-trimester miscarriages (Ashmead & Reed, 1997; Robinson *et al.*, 1998). Abnormal numbers of chromosomes are usually caused by an error in the separation of chromosomes into appropriate daughter cells during **meiotic division**. For reasons still only partially understood, there

meiotic cell division the type of cell division that occurs in sexually reproducing organisms which halves the number of *chromosomes* in reproductive cells (sperm and ova).

is a dramatic increase in the risk of chromosomal anomalies with advancing maternal age. For example, risk of Down's syndrome at age 20 is 1/2,000; at age 30, it is 1/1,000; by age 37, it is 1/200 (Davidson & Zeesman, 1994; Hsu, 1998). We are learning that the effect of advancing age on atypical development is not limited to mother. Age in the father has been shown to be a factor in impairment of social function, the extremes of which are schizophrenia and autism. There are a number of ways in which aging could affect the father's DNA, most prominently an increased likelihood of a mutation in one of the complex of genes that affect the development of the nervous system components involved in social functioning (Weiser *et al.*, 2008.)

Disorders can result from an inherited single gene abnormality. The risk of an affected individual having a child with the disorder depends on their partner's status with respect to the genetic mutation, and, therefore, on how rare the disease is. Examples of **autosomal genetic disorders** are: sickle cell disease, cystic fibrosis, Tay-Sachs disease, Huntington's disease, and Marfan syndrome (Ashmead & Reed, 1997). Certain ethnic groups are at greater risk for specific genetic disorders. For example, in Ashkenazi Jews (Jews of Eastern European descent), 1 in 30 is a carrier of Tay-Sachs disease. Another example is sickle cell anaemia; approximately 8 in 100 African Americans from North America are carriers of the sickle cell gene (Davidson & Zeesman, 1994). Rates for these disorders are much lower in other groups.

> **autosomal genetic disorders** disorders resulting from a mutation in a gene in one of the non-sex *chromosomes.* Well-known examples are cystic fibrosis (a recessive type) and achondroplasia (dwarfism, a dominant type).

Effects of exposure to psychoactive substances

Heavy maternal alcohol consumption profoundly influences foetal and child development. Adverse foetal outcomes include increased risk for spontaneous abortion, stillbirth, premature placental separation, intrauterine growth restriction, and, some studies suggest, preterm birth – itself a risk factor for future health problems, poor development, and newborn mortality. For children who survive, the effects include elevated risk for sudden infant death syndrome (SIDS) (Iyasu *et al.*, 2002), mild to severe physical anomalies (Day *et al.*, 1990) and cognitive and behavioural impairments (Kodituwakku, 2007). Alcohol has detrimental effects on development and function of the placenta, which is crucial for survival and normal development of the foetus (Burd *et al.*, 2007.)

Despite major efforts to warn pregnant women of the dangers cigarette smoking poses for their foetus, smoking is still one of the most preventable risk factors for an unsuccessful pregnancy outcome (Cnattingius, 2004). On average, babies born to smokers weigh 100–200 g less than those of non-smokers and have twice the risk for foetal growth restriction (Horta *et al.*, 1997; Walsh, 1994). Furthermore, independent of the risks for lower birthweight, smoking is associated with risk for prematurity and perinatal complications, such as premature detachment of the placenta (Andres, 1996; Kyrklund-Blomberg & Cnattingius, 1998). Cigarette smoking also is associated with a two- to threefold increase for SIDS (Golding, 1997). Finally, more subtle effects of foetal exposure to maternal smoke have been found during infancy and childhood. Behavioural problems and cognitive weaknesses, including problems with attention, visuoperceptual processing, and speech processing have been associated with smoking during pregnancy (Fried & Watkinson, 2000; Fried *et al.*, 1992; Key *et al.*, 2007; Weitzman *et al.*, 2002). The strong effects that active smoking exerts on pregnancy outcomes have led to research on maternal exposure to environmental tobacco smoke (ETS), and there are data showing that ETS is related to adverse influences on early development. including low birthweight (Windham *et al.*, 1999) and pediatric asthma (Dietert & Zelikoff, 2008).

Nutrition and foetal development

Specific nutritional requirements must be met for healthy foetal development. For example, adequate amounts of calcium are needed for foetal bone, muscle, and transmitter production; sufficient supplies of iron are necessary for foetal red blood cell and tissue production (Judge, 1997). Research from epidemiological and animal studies indicates that independent of gross congenital anomalies, women's food intake and/or weight gain during pregnancy may subtly affect foetal development in ways that have implications for the child's future medical and mental health, with some effects appearing only in adulthood. Adult disease that is associated with specific prenatal challenges during particular time windows is called **developmental programming** (Nijland *et al.*, 2008.) For example, in several large samples, low birthweight has been linked to an increased risk for future cardiovascular disease (CVD), and for factors associated with CVD such as high blood pressure (Clark *et al.*,1998; Law *et al.*,1993; Moore *et al.*, 1999; Rich-Edwards *et al.*,1997). To account for this association, researchers hypothesise that aspects of the foetus's cardiovascular functioning are 'programmed' *in utero* by maternal nutritional and/or hormonal factors (Barker, 1995). New research also indicates that women's nutrition during pregnancy and baby's birthweight also might be markers for physiological processes that place the infant at risk for future breast cancer (Michels *et al.*, 1996; Morgan *et al.*, 1999) and mental illness (Casper, 2004; Susser *et al.*, 1999). Specifically, epidemiological studies suggest that higher birthweight is associated with an increased risk for breast cancer (Morgan *et al.*, 1999). Studies based on the offspring of Dutch women pregnant during the Nazi food embargo ('the Dutch Hunger Winter') suggest that extreme undernutrition (fewer than 1000 calories a day) during first and second trimesters (and thus occurring during rapid brain reorganisation) is associated with those at risk of having schizophrenia, antisocial personality disorder or a mood disorder (Neugebauer *et al.*, 1999). Although the mechanisms underlying these associations are not yet known, it is likely that future research will clarify the impact of variations in maternal nutrition and newborn weight on the child's physical and mental health.

> **developmental programming** the hypothesis that prenatal conditions have detrimental effects on health into adulthood.

Effects of maternal stress

Similar to the developmental programming effects of maternal suboptimal nutrition, maternal psychosocial stress during pregnancy has long been linked to negative birth outcomes such as low birthweight and prematurity as well as alterations in foetal neurobehavioural development (Istvan, 1986; Lobel, 1994; Lobel *et al.*, 1992; Stott & Latchford, 1976). Further support for a link between maternal stress and foetal development comes from other studies indicating that over the course of gestation, maternal psychological variables such as stress and anxiety, act via alterations in maternal physiology (Monk *et al.*, 2000). In a recent study, contrary to what we might expect, foetuses of pregnant women who reported greater pregnancy-specific stress showed prenatal cardiac and cardiac-somatic coupling effects that were indicative of *greater* maturation and neural integration. The same study found that newborns of mothers with greater stress were more mature on information-processing measures (DiPietro *et al.*, 2010). These results replicate an earlier study showing that mild to moderate maternal psychological stress during pregnancy and the first year resulted in greater motor and mental maturity in their infants at age 2 (DiPietro *et al.* (2006). This may seem counter-intuitive, but the pregnant women in the study were not exposed to large, unmanageable amounts of stress. Perhaps some stress is actually beneficial for foetal development, but overwhelming, 'toxic' maternal stress is detrimental. It is clear that maternal stress during pregnancy has implications for child development, but future research is needed to clarify its role.

PRENATAL DEVELOPMENT OF POSTNATAL FUNCTIONS: THE BRIDGE TO INFANCY

Most of the reflex behaviours that babies demonstrate after they are born, including breathing, rooting, sucking, and swallowing, are part of the foetal repertoire. Other reflexes that have less obvious functional significance for present-day humans include the toe-curling reflex, the finger-grasping reflex, and the startle reflex. These reflexes all disappear within the first year of life. Another reflexive behaviour that has received considerable attention is the stepping reflex. If resistance is provided to their feet, foetuses will make stepping movements placing one foot in front of the other. This reflex usually disappears in the first two months after birth. There is some argument as to whether this activity is a kicking motion (Thelen, 1986) or whether it is the precursor of early walking (Zelazo, 1983). It has also been suggested that this reflex may help in the birthing process itself (Kitzinger, 1990).

There are now several studies that suggest more fundamental psychobiological continuities between foetal and infant development. For example, work from Kagan and colleagues suggested that low resting heart rate during the prenatal period predicts lower levels of crying and motoric responses to novelty at 4 months old (Snidman *et al.*, 1995). By observing foetal movement on ultrasound images, another group of researchers found that foetuses, who move at certain rates during active sleep, move at the same relative rate at 2 and 4 weeks postpartum (Groome *et al.*, 1999).

Groome and his colleagues have also observed that the duration of quiet sleep epochs provides a stable measure of behavioural state development between the prenatal and postnatal periods (Groome *et al.,* 1999). Other research suggests that a relatively greater number of weak body movements, as opposed to strong, full-body ones, were positively associated with the amount of crying during the first three months of life (St. James-Roberts and Menon-Johansson, 1999). The authors speculate that an inability to inhibit responsiveness is the common underlying characteristic linking increased foetal body movements and greater crying. In an extensive study of foetal to newborn continuities, indices of foetal neurobehaviour accounted for a large amount of the variability in infant temperament differences (DiPietro *et al.,* 1996). In general, higher foetal activity resulted in increased fussiness and inconsistent behaviour while more predictable increases and decreases in the amount of foetal activity resulted in lower scores on these variables.

SUMMARY AND CONCLUSIONS

An important developmental question is whether we can point to characteristics of a person that remain stable over time. Continuity of an individual's behaviour from foetal to postnatal life is often difficult to confirm, whether due to differences in (1) rapidly developing brain/behaviour infrastructure; (2) intra- and extrauterine constraints and supports for activity; or (3) amount and patterns of sensory stimulation, for example, fluid vs. air transmission of sound and chemosensory stimulation, and marked differences in visual and vestibular stimulation. To give a specific example, it is difficult to measure how one individual might differ from another in the continuity of their reaction to being moved (vestibular stimulation) during and after gestation because it is hard to generate motion that is the same during the two periods. If neonates respond differently to motion stimulation compared to how they responded while in the womb, is it because there is no continuity in their response or because the motion itself is different? To add to the complexity of investigating continuity in behaviour, at birth there are abrupt transformations in physiological requirements or motivation, for example, hunger, temperature variation, and maintaining oxygen levels. These abrupt changes make it difficult to measure developmental continuity. The triggers for and characteristics of circadian and **ultradian** (less than 24-hour) **rhythms** are clearly altered at birth, for example, oral feeding intervals and light–dark cycles vs. maternal-generated patterns of physiological, physical, and hormonal activity. Technological advances have been made, for example, 3D ultrasound imaging and improved detection of foetal heart and blood-flow patterns, that may serve as markers for continuities in attentional capacities, temperament, or risk status. For example, prenatal heart rate variability and its pattern of maturation are related to measures of mental and psychomotor development in toddlers (Di Pietro *et al.,* 2007). However, other serious methodological hurdles remain, such as limited access to the maternal/foetal dyad and control over and accurate measurement of

ultradian rhythm rhythms or cycles that repeat in less than a 24-hour period.

foetal vs. infant sensory input. There is promise in emerging research methods for direct measurement of foetal brain activity that are shedding light on foetal to new-born trajectories in brain development. Continued improvements in technology and experimental methods should lead to creative new approaches to investigation of the foetal origins of human behaviour and development.

DISCUSSION POINTS

1. Think about the similarities and differences existing between environments pre and post birth.
2. List the forms of sensory information that the foetus picks up and consider how this information may affect sensory development.
3. What different functions are served by foetal behaviours?
4. In the foetal period, is development of all sensory systems dependent on input to these systems?
5. Think about the auditory environment of the foetus and compare it to the auditory environment of the newborn.
6. List the different environmental factors that constitute risks to foetal development.
7. Think of reasons why some foetal behaviours disappear after birth while others are maintained.

SUGGESTIONS FOR FURTHER READING

Hopkins, B. & Johnson, S.P. (2005) *Prenatal development of postnatal functions*. Westport, CT: Praeger.

Lecanuet, J-P (1996). Fetal sensory competencies. *European Journal of Obstetrics and Gynecology and Reproductive Biology*, 68, 1–23.

Lecanuet, J-P., Fifer, W.P, Krasnegor, N.A, & Smotherman, W.P. (Eds.). (1995). *Fetal development: A psychobiological perspective*. Hillsdale, NJ: Erlbaum.

Nathanielsz, P. (2001). *The prenatal prescription*. New York: HarperCollins.

Nilsson, L., Wigzel, H., & Holborn, M. (2006) *Life*. New York: Harry N. Abrams.

Spear N.E. & Molina J.C. (2005) Fetal or infantile exposure to ethanol promotes ethanol ingestion in adolescence and adulthood: A theoretical review. *Alcoholism: Clinical and Experimental Research*, 29(6), 909–929.

REFERENCES

Abrams, R.M., Gerhardt, K.J., & Peters, A.J.M. (1995). Transmission of sound and vibration to the fetus. In J. Lecanuet, W. Fifer, N. Krasnegor, & W. Smotherman (Eds.) *Fetal development: A psychobiological perspective* (pp. 315–30). Hillsdale, NJ: Erlbaum.

Andres, R.L. (1996). The association of cigarette smoking with *placenta previa* and *abruptio placentae*. *Seminars in Perinatology, 20*, 154–159.

Ashmead, G.G., & Reed, G.B. (Eds.) (1997). *Essentials of maternal and fetal medicine*. New York: Chapman & Hall.

Barker, D.J. (1995). Fetal origins of coronary heart disease. *British Medical Journal, 311*, 171–174.

Casper, R.C. (2004). Nutrients, neurodevelopment and mood. *Current Psychiatry Reports, 6*(6), 425–429.

Cnattingius, S. (2004). The epidemiology of smoking during pregnancy: Smoking prevalence, maternal characteristics, and pregnancy outcomes. *Nicotine and Tobacco Research, 6*(Supplement 2), S125–S140.

Burd, L., Roberts, D., Olson, M., & Odendaal, H. (2007). Ethanol and the placenta: A review. *The Journal of Maternal-Fetal and Neonatal Medicine, 20*(5), 3613–3675.

Clark, P.M., Atton, C., Law, C.M., Shiell, A., Godfrey, K., & Barker, D.J. (1998). Weight gain in pregnancy, tricept skinfold thickness, and blood pressure in offspring. *Obstetrics and Gynecology, 91*, 103–7.

Davidson, R.G., & Zeesman, S. (1994). Genetic aspects. In G. Koren (Ed.) *Maternal-fetal toxicology* (pp. 575–600). New York: Marcel Dekker.

Day, N.L., Richardson, G., Robles, R., Sambamoorthi, U., Taylor, P., Scher, *et al.* (1990) Effect of prenatal alcohol exposure on growth and morphology of offspring at 8 months of age. *Pediatrics, 85*, 7487–52.

DeCasper, A.J. and W.P. Fifer (1980). Of human bonding: Newborns prefer their mothers' voices. *Science, 208*(4448), 11741–11776.

DeCasper, A.J., Lecanuet, J-P, Busnel, M-C, Granier-Deferre, C., & Maugeais, R. (1994) Fetal reactions to recurrent maternal speech. *Infant Behavior and Development, 17*(2), 1591–1564.

DeCasper, A.J., & Prescott, P.A. (1984). Human newborns' perception of male voices: Preference, discrimination, and reinforcing value. *Developmental Psychobiology, 17*(5), 4814–4891.

DeCasper, A.J., & Sigafoos, A.D. (1983). The intrauterine heartbeat: A potent reinforcer for newborns. *Infant Behavior and Development, 6*, 192–195.

DeCasper, A.J., & Spence, M.J. (1986). Prenatal maternal speech influences newborns' perception of speech sounds. *Infant Behavior and Development, 9*, 1331–50.

deRegnier, R.A., Nelson, C.A., Thomas, K.M., Wewerka, S., & Georgieff, M.K. (2000) Neurophysiologic evaluation of auditory recognition memory in healthy newborn infants and infants of diabetic mothers. *Journal of Pediatrics, 137*(6), 777–784.

deRegnier, R.A., Wewerka, S., Georgieff, M.K., Mattia, F., & Nelson (2002). Influences of postconceptional age and postnatal experience on the development of auditory recognition memory in the newborn infant. *Developmental Psychobiology, 41*, 2162–2125.

Detterman, D.K. (1978). The effect of heartbeat sounds on neonatal crying. *Infant Behavior and Development, 1*, 364–368.

de Vries, J.I.P., & Hopkins, B. (2005). Fetal movements and postures: What do they mean for postnatal development? In B. Hopkins & S.P. Johnson (Eds.) *Prenatal Development of Postnatal Functions*. Westport, CT: Praeger.

Dietert, R.R. & Zelikoff, J.T. (2008). Early-life environment, developmental immunotoxicology, and the risk of pediatric allergic disease including asthma. *Birth Defects Research (Part B), 83*, 5475–5460.

DiPietro, J.A., Bornstein, M.H., Hahn, C-S., Costigan, K., & Aristide, A-B. (2007). Fetal heart rate and variability: Stability and prediction to developmental outcomes in early childhood. *Child Development, 78*(6), 1788–1798.

DiPietro, J.A., Kivlighan, K.T., Costigan, K.A., Rubin, S.E., Shiffler, D.E., Henderson, J.L., *et al.* (2010) Prenatal antecedents of newborn neurological maturation. *Child Development, 81*(1), 115–130.

DiPietro, J.A., Novak, M.F., Costigan, K.A., Atella, L.D., & Reusing, S.P. (2006). Maternal psychological distress during pregnancy in relation to child development at age two. *Child Development*, *77*(3), 5735–5787.

DiPietro, J.A., Hodgson, K.A., Costigan, S.C., & Johnson, T.R.B. (1996). Development of fetal movement–fetal heart rate coupling from 20 weeks through term. *Early Human Development*, *44*, 139–151.

Dubowitz, L., Mercuri, E., & Dubowitz, V. (1998). An optimality score for the neurologic examination of the term newborn. *Journal of Pediatrics*, *133*(3), 406–416.

Duenholter, J.H., & Pritchard, J.A. (1976). Fetal respiration: Quantitative measurements of amniotic fluid inspired near term by human and rhesus fetuses. *American Journal of Obstetrics and Gynecology*, *125*, 306–309.

Feldman, R., & Eidelman, A.I. (2003). Skin-to-skin contact (Kangaroo Care) accelerates autonomic and neurobehavioural maturation in preterm infants. *Developmental Medicine & Child Neurology*, *45*, 2742–2781.

Fielder, A.R., & Moseley, M.J. (2000). Environmental light and the preterm infant. *Seminars in Perinatology*, *24*, 291–298.

Fifer, W.P., & Moon, C. (1989). Psychobiology of newborn auditory preferences. *Seminars in Perinatology*, *13*, 4304–4333.

Fifer, W.P., & Moon, C. (1995). The effects of fetal experience with sound. In J.P. Lecanuet, W.P. Fifer, N.A. Krasnegor, & W.P. Smotherman (Eds.) *Fetal Development: A Psychobiological Perspective*. Hillsdale, NJ: Erlbaum.

Fried, P.A., & Watkinson, B. (2000). Visuoperceptual functioning differs in 9–12-year-olds prenatally exposed to cigarettes and marihuana. *Neurotoxicology and Teratology*, *22*, 11–29.

Fried, P.A., Watkinson, B., & Gary, R. (1992). A follow-up study of attentional behavior in 6-year-old children exposed prenatally to marihuana, cigarettes, and alcohol. *Neurotoxicology and Teratology*, *14*, 299–311.

Gerber, S.E. (1985). Stimulus, response, and state variables in the testing of neonates. *Ear and Hearing*, *6*(1), 151–159.

Golding, J. (1997). Sudden infant death syndrome and parental smoking: A literature review. *Paediatrics and Perinatal Epidemiology*, *11*, 67–77.

Groome, L.J., Swiber, M.J., Holland, S.B., Bentz, L.S., Atterbury, J.L., & Trimm, I.R.F. (1999). Spontaneous motor activity in the perinatal infant before and after birth: Stability in individual differences. *Developmental Psychobiology*, *35*, 15–24.

Grose, J., & Harding, G.F.A. (1990). The development of refractive error and pattern reversal VEPs in pre-term infants. *Clinical Vision Sciences*, *5*, 375–382.

Hepper, P.G. (1988). Adaptive fetal behavior: Prenatal exposure affects postnatal preferences. *Animal Behavior*, *36*, 935–936.

Hepper, P.G. (1992). Fetal psychology: An embryonic science. In J. Nijhuis (Ed.) *Fetal behavior: Developmental and perinatal aspects* (pp. 129–56). New York: Oxford University Press.

Hofer, M.A. (1981). *The roots of human behavior*. San Francisco: W.H. Freeman.

Hooker, D. (1952). *The prenatal origin of behavior*. Kansas: University of Kansas Press.

Horta, B.L., Victora, C.G., Menezes, A.M., Halpern, R., & Barros, F.C. (1997). Low birthweight, preterm births and intrauterine growth retardation in relation to maternal smoking. *Pediatrics and Perinatal Epidemiology*, *11*, 140–151.

Hsu, L.Y.F. (1998). Prenatal diagnosis of chromosomal abnormalities through amniocentesis. In A. Milunsky (Ed.) *Genetic disorders and the fetus: Diagnosis, prevention, and treatment* (pp. 179–248). Baltimore, MD: Johns Hopkins University Press.

Istvan, J. (1986). Stress, anxiety and birth outcomes: A critical review of the evidence. *Psychological Bulletin*, 100(3), 331–348.

Iyasu, S., Randall. L.L., Welty, T.K., Kinney, H.C., , Mandell, F., McClain, M., *et al.* (2002). Risk for sudden infant death syndrome among northern plains Indians. *The Journal of the American Medical Association*, 288(21), 27171–723.

Judge, N.E. (1997). The physiology of pregnancy. In G.G. Ashmead (Ed.) *Essentials of maternal fetal medicine* (pp. 26–40). New York: Chapman & Hall.

Kandel, E.R., Schwartz, J.H., & Jessell, T.M. (2000). *Principles of neural science*. New York: McGraw-Hill.

Key, A.P.F., Ferguson, M., Molfese, D.L., Peach, K., Lehman, C., & Molfese, V.J. (2007) Smoking during pregnancy affects speech-processing ability in newborn infants. *Environmental Health Perspectives*, 115, 6236–29.

Kitzinger, S. (1990). *The complete book of pregnancy and childbirth*. New York: Alfred A. Knopf.

Kisilevsky, B. (1995). The influence of stimulus and subject variables on human fetal responses to sound and vibration. In J-P Lecanuet, W.P. Fifer, N.A. Krasnegor, & W.P. Smotherman (Eds.) *Fetal Development: A Psychobiological Perspective*. Hillsdale, NJ: Erlbaum.

Kodituwakku, P.W. (2007). Defining the behavioral phenotype in children with fetal alcohol spectrum disorders. *Neuroscience & Biobehavioral Reviews*, 31(2), 192–201.

Korner, A.F., Schneider, P., & Forrest, T. (1983). Effects of vestibular-proprioceptive stimulation on the neurobehavioral development of preterm infants: A pilot study. *Neuropediatrics*, 14, 170–175.

Kyrklund-Blomberg, N.B., & Cnattingius, S. (1998). Preterm birth and maternal smoking: Risks related to gestational age and onset of delivery. *American Journal of Obstetrics and Gynecology*, 179, 1051–1055.

Law, C.M., de Swiet, M., Osmond, C., Fayers, P.M., Barker, D.J.P., Cruddas, A.M., *et al.* (1993). Initiation of hypertension *in utero* and its amplification throughout life. *British Medical Journal*, 306, 24–27.

Lecanuet, J-P (1996). Fetal sensory competencies. *European Journal of Obstetrics and Gynecology and Reproductive Biology*, 68, 1–23.

Lecanuet, J-P., Granier-Deferre, C., & Busnel, M-C. (1995). Human fetal auditory perception. In J-P Lecanuet, W.P. Fifer, N.A. Krasnegor, & W.P. Smotherman (Eds.) *Fetal development: A psychobiological perspective*. Hillsdale, NJ: Erlbaum.

Lobel, M. (1994). Conceptualizations, measurement, and effects of prenatal maternal stress on birth outcomes. *Journal of Behavioral Medicine*, 17(3), 225–272.

Lobel, M., Dunkel-Schetter, C., & Scrimshaw, S.C. (1992). Prenatal maternal stress and prematurity: A prospective study of socioeconomically disadvantaged women. *Health Psychology*, 11(1), 32–40.

Martin, J.H. (2003). *Neuroanatomy text and atlas* (3rd edn). Stamford, CT: Appleton & Lange.

Masi, W. (1979). Supplemental stimulation of the premature infant. In T.M. Field (Ed.) *Infants born at risk* (pp. 367–388). New York: Scientific Publications.

Mehler, J., Jusczyk, P., Lambertz, G., Halsted, N., Bertoncini, J., & Amiel-Tison, C. (1988) A precursor of language acquisition in young infants. *Cognition*, 29, 1431–1478.

Michels, K.B., Trichopoulos, D., Adami, H.O., Hsieh, C., & Lan, S.J. (1996). Birthweight as a risk factor for breast cancer. *Lancet*, 348, 1542–1546.

Milunsky, A., & Milunsky, J. (1998). Genetic counseling: Preconception, prenatal, and perinatal. In A. Milunsky (Ed.) *Genetic disorders and the fetus: Diagnosis, prevention, and treatment* (pp. 1–52). Baltimore, MD: Johns Hopkins University Press.

Mirmiran, M., & Swaab, D.F. (1992). Effects of perinatal medicine on brain development. In J. Nijhuis (Ed.) *Fetal behavior: Developmental and perinatal aspects* (pp. 112–28). New York: Oxford University Press.

Molina, J.C., Chotro, M.G., & Dominguez, H.D. (1995). Fetal alcohol learning resulting from contamination of the prenatal environment. In J. Lecanuet, W. Fifer, N. Krasnegor, & W. Smotherman (Eds.) *Fetal development: A psychobiological perspective* (pp. 419–438). Hillsdale, NJ: Erlbaum.

Monk, C., Fifer, W.P., Sloan, R.P., Myers, M.M., Trien, L., & Hurtado, A. (2000). Maternal stress responses and anxiety during pregnancy: Effects on fetal heart rate. *Developmental Psychobiology, 36*, 67–77.

Moon, C., & Fifer, W.P. (2000). Evidence of transnatal auditory learning. *Journal of Perinatology, 20*, S37–S44.

Moon, C., Panneton Cooper, R.P., & Fifer, W.P. (1993). Two-day-olds prefer their native language. *Infant Behavior and Development, 16*(4), 495–500.

Moore, V.M., Cockington, R.A., Ryan, P., & Robinson, J.S. (1999). The relationship between birth weight and blood pressure amplifies from childhood to adulthood. *Journal of Hypertension, 17*, 883–8.

Morgan, I., Damber, L., Tavelin, B., & Hogberg, U. (1999). Characteristics of pregnancy and birth and malignancy in the offspring. *Cancer Causes Control, 10*, 85–94.

Morokuma, S., Doria, V., Ierrullo, A., Kinukawa, N., Fukushima, K., Arulkumaran, S., *et al.* (2008). Developmental change in fetal response to repeated low-intensity sound. *Developmental Science, 11*(1), 47–52.

Morokuma, S., Fukushima, K., Kawai, N., Tomonaga, M., Satoh, S., & Nakano, H. (2004). Fetal habituation correlates with functional brain development. *Behavioural Brain Research, 153*(2), 459–463.

Murooka, H. (1974). *Lullaby from the womb.* Hollywood, CA: Capitol Records.

Murooka, H., Koie, Y., & Suda, N. (1976). Analyse des sons intra-uterins et leurs effects tranquil-lisants sur le nouveau-ne. *Journal de Gynécologie Obstétrique et Biologie de la Reproduction, 5*(3): 3673–3676.

Nazzi, T., Bertoncini, J., & Mehler, J. (1998). Language discrimination by newborns: Towards an understanding of the role of rhythm. *Journal of Experimental Psychology: Human Perception and Performance, 24*(3), 256–766.

Neugebauer, R., Hoek, H.W., & Susser, E. (1999). Prenatal exposure to wartime famine and development of antisocial personality disorder in early adulthood. *Journal of American Medical Association, 282*, 455–462.

Nijhuis, J.G. (1992). The third trimester. In J. Nijhuis (Ed.) *Fetal behavior: Developmental and perinatal aspects* (pp. 26–40). New York: Oxford University Press.

Nijland, M.J., Ford, S.P., & Nathanielsz, P.W. (2008). Prenatal origins of adult disease. *Current Opinion in Obstetrics and Gynecology, 20*(2), 1321–1338.

Ockleford, E.M., Vince, M.A., Layton, C., & Reader, M.R. (1988) Responses of neonates to parents' and others' voices. *Early Human Development, 18*(1), 273–276.

Patrick, J., Campbell, K., Carmichael, L., Natale, R., & Richardson, B. (1982). Patterns of gross fetal body movements over 24 observation intervals in the last 10 weeks of pregnancy. *American Journal of Obstetrics and Gynecology, 136*, 471–477.

Pujol, R., Lavigne-Rebillard, M., & Uziel, A. (1991) Development of the human cochlea. *Acta Oto-Laryngologica, Supplementum, 482*, 71–72.

Querleu, D., Lefebvre, C., Titran, M., Renard, X., Morillion, M., & Crepin, G. (1984). Réactivité du nouveau-né de moins de deux heures de vie á la voix maternelle. *Journal de Gynécologie Obstétrique et Biologie Reproductive, 13*, 125–135.

Rich-Edwards, J.W., Stampfer, M.J., Manson, J.E., Rosner, B., Hankinson, S.E., Colditz, G.A., *et al.* (1997). Birthweight and the risk of cardiovascular disease in adult women. *British Medical Journal, 315*, 396–400.

Robinson, A., Linden, M.G., & Bender, B.G. (1998). Prenatal diagnosis of sex chromosome abnormalities. In A. Milunsky (Ed.) *Genetic disorders of the fetus* (pp. 249–285). Baltimore, MD: Johns Hopkins University Press.

Rosner, B.S., & Doherty, N.E. (1979). The response of neonates to intra-uterine sounds. *Developmental Medicine and Child Neurology, 21*, 723–729.

St. James-Roberts, I., & Menon-Johansson, P. (1999). Predicting infant crying from fetal movement data: An exploratory study. *Early Human Development, 54*(1), 55–62.

Salk, L. (1962). Mothers' heartbeat as an imprinting stimulus. *Transactions of the New York Academy of Sciences, 24*(7), 7537–7563.

Salk, L. (1973). The role of the heartbeat in the relations between mother and infant. *Scientific American 228*, 242–249.

Schaal, B. (2005). From amnion to colostrum to mild: Odor bridging in early developmental transitions. In B. Hopkins and S.P. Johnson (Eds.) *Prenatal development of postnatal functions*. Westport, CT: Praeger.

Schaal, B., Orgeur, P., & Rognon, C. (1995). Odor sensing in the human fetus: Anatomical, functional and chemoecological bases. In J. Lecanuet, W. Fifer, N. Krasnegor, & W. Smotherman (Eds.) *Fetal development: A psychobiological perspective* (pp. 205–238). Hillsdale, NJ: Erlbaum.

Schoenwolf, G.C., Bleyl, S.B., Brauer, P.R., & Francis-West, P.H. (2009). Larsen's Human Embryology (4th edn). Philadelphia: Elsevier.

Snidman, N., Kagan, J., Riordan, L., & Shannon, D.C. (1995). Cardiac function and behavioral reactivity during infancy. *Psychophysiology, 32*, 199–207.

Spence, M.J. and Freeman, M.S. (1996). Newborn infants prefer the maternal low-pass filtered voice, but not the maternal whispered voice. *Infant Behavior and Development, 19*(2), 199–212.

Stott, D.H., & Latchford, B.A. (1976). Prenatal antecedents of child health, development, and behavior. *Journal of American Academic Child Psychiatry, 15*(1), 161–191.

Susser, E.B., Brown, A., & Matte, T.D. (1999). Prenatal factors and adult mental and physical health. *Canadian Journal of Psychiatry, 44*, 326–334.

Taylor, M.J., Menzies, R., MacMillan, L.J., & Whyte, H.E. (1987). VEPs in normal full-term and premature neonates: Longitudinal versus cross-sectional data. *Electroencephalography and Clinical Neurophysiology, 68*, 20–27.

Thelen, E. (1986). Treadmill-elicited stepping in seven-month-old infants. *Child Development, 57*, 1498–1506.

Tulloch, J.D. Brown, B.S., Jacobs, H.L., Purgh, D.G. & Greene, W.A. (1964), Normal heart beat sound and the behavior of newborn infants – A replication study. *Psychosomatic Medicine, 26*, 6616–6670.

van Heteren, C.F., Boekkooi, P.F., Jongsma, H.W., & Nijhuis, J.G. (2000). Fetal learning and memory. *The Lancet, 356*, 1169–1170.

Visser, G.H.A. (1992). The second trimester. In J. Nijhuis (Ed.) *Fetal behavior: Developmental and perinatal aspects* (pp. 17–25). New York: Oxford University Press.

Walsh, R.A. (1994). Effects of maternal smoking on adverse pregnancy outcomes: Examination of the criteria of causation. *Human Biology, 66*, 1059–1092.

Weiser, M., Reichenberg, A., Werbeloff, N., Kleinhaus, K., Lubin, G., Shmushkevitch, M., *et al.* (2008). Advanced parental age at birth is associated with poorer social functioning in adolescent males: Shedding light on a core symptom of schizophrenia and autism. *Schizophrenia Bulletin, 34*(6), 1042–1046.

Weitzman, M., Byrd, R.S., Alligne, C.A., & Moss, M. (2002). The effects of tobacco exposure on children's behavioral and cognitive functioning: Implications for clinical and public health policy and future research. *Neurotoxicology and Teratology, 24*(3), 397–406.

Windham, G.C., Eaton, A., & Hopkins, B. (1999). Evidence for an association between environ-mental tobacco smoke exposure and birthweight: A meta-analysis and new data. *Paediatrics and Perinatal Epidemiology, 13*, 35–57.

Zelazo, P.R. (1983). The development of walking: New findings and old assumptions. *Journal of Motor Behavior, 15*, 99–137.

Zelazo, P.R., Weiss, M.J.S., & Tarquinio, N. (1991). Habituation and recovery of neonatal orienting to auditory stimuli. In M. Salomon & P. Zelazo (Eds.) *Newborn attention: Biological constraints and the effect of experience* (pp.120–141). Norwood: Ablex.

Zimmer, E.Z ., Chao, C.R., Guy, G.P., Marks, F., & Fifer, W.P. (1993). Vibroacoustic stimulation evokes fetal micturition. *Obstetrics and Gynecology, 81*, 178–180.

Zimmer, E.Z., Fifer, W.P., Kim, Y-I., Rey, H.R., Chao, C.R. & Myers, M.M. (1993). Response of the premature fetus to stimulation by speech sounds. *Early Human Development, 33*, 207–215.

5 Perception, Knowledge, and Action in Infancy

J. Gavin Bremner

KEY TERMS

A not B error • clinical method • cognition • cognitive development • core knowledge • executive functioning • frontal cortex • habituation • infant-directed speech (motherese) • innate mechanism • intonation • mental representation • nativism • object permanence • object unity • prototypical face • response perseveration • retinal image size • shape constancy • size constancy • subitising • subjective contour • violation of expectation technique • visual accommodation • visual acuity • visual preference method

CHAPTER OUTLINE

OVERVIEW

This chapter reviews evidence bearing on fundamental questions about infants' ability to perceive and understand the physical and social world. Infancy researchers have devised a number of ingenious techniques that make it possible to discover a great deal about infants' perceptual and cognitive abilities, and these studies reveal that even very young infants are surprisingly advanced.

Although young infants are unable to resolve fine visual detail, even newborns have a surprisingly well developed ability to perceive the structure of the world, making visual discriminations between shapes and apparently perceiving the world as an arrangement of objects in three-dimensional space, much as adults do. However, the ability to fill in gaps in perception, such as when one object partly hides another, does not appear to be there at birth, but develops by around 4 months.

Young infants' perception of people is also highly advanced. From birth, they recognise facial configurations as special and learn to discriminate parents from strangers within hours from birth. The fact that newborns imitate facial gestures adds to the evidence that infants are capable of processing faces. Similarly, auditory perception is well developed, and there is even evidence of auditory learning prior to birth.

The chapter then considers research on infants' cognitive development, where the focus is on understanding of the perceived world. From around the age of 4 months, infants appear to be aware of the permanence of objects and the rules that govern the movement of one object relative to another. Most of the evidence pointing to this is based on simple measures of looking time; infants look longer at events that violate some physical principle, and longer looking is interpreted as recognition by the infant that the event was impossible. However, tests based on more complex behaviours reveal less positive findings. For instance, 6-month-old infants fail to search for hidden objects, and older infants make characteristic search errors, which suggest that their understanding of the world is relatively limited.

The likely resolution of the conflicting data arising from these different methods of investigation is that young infants are aware of an objective world of permanent objects, but that they are unable to use this knowledge to guide their actions in that world. Seen this way, early cognitive development is more to do with constructing relationships between knowledge and action than with constructing knowledge itself.

INTRODUCTION

Questions about the perceptual and cognitive abilities of infants are of interest in their own right and are also particularly important because infancy is in many ways a starting point for later development. Although this statement needs some qualification in the sense that a great deal of development takes place prior to birth (see Chapter 4), the moment of birth marks the infant's emergence into the world that they will inhabit for some 80 years. Although some continuities exist between the environment of the foetus and that of the newborn infant, there are a whole range of entirely new experiences. In particular, for the first time the visual sense is provided with patterned light stimuli that change and move both in themselves and in response to movements of the infant. A fundamental question concerns what the newborn makes of such stimuli (Figure 5.1). Are they just meaningless patterns of light, or can infants identify them as arising from the objects and people in their surrounding world, much as we do? Not surprisingly, a major focus of infancy research has been to do with these starting states, and the reader will see how evidence of this sort

FIGURE 5.1 *A young infant exploring the visual world.*
Source: Shutterstock.

cognitive development
the development of behaviours that relate to perception, attention, thinking, remembering, and problem-solving.

mental representation
an internal description of aspects of reality that persists in the absence of these aspects of reality.

relates directly to questions arising in Chapter 3 concerning the origins of knowledge, specifically the issue of *nativism* vs. *empiricism*.

In addition to investigating infants' perceptual abilities, we can also ask what they understand of the events that they perceive. These questions lie in the domain of **cognitive development**. Traditionally, a key aspect of the distinction between perception and cognition was the concept of **mental representation**. When we view a world of objects, this is a matter of perception, whereas when we call to mind an environment that is not present we are engaged in internal processes through which this environment is mentally represented. Although there is a lot to be said for this distinction (and the concept of representation will crop up again in this chapter) its application to infancy has not been so productive as once seemed likely. This is in large part because, prior to gaining the ability to reflect on absent environments, infants have to learn how to perceive and act appropriately in their here-and-now environment. In the pages that follow, I shall review evidence indicating that, right from birth, infants perceive the world in a sophisticated way, and that in the early months they develop perceptual abilities that 'fill in the gaps' in perception so that invisible parts of objects are perceived, and objects that are temporarily hidden are treated as continuing in existence. Additionally, there is now a very large body of evidence indicating that from about 3 months on, infants have a well-developed awareness of the physical properties of objects and relationships between objects. However, I shall also point to evidence indicating that these abilities are not initially used successfully to guide the infant's actions; though the motor abilities are present, in some important respects the links between knowledge and action do not seem to be in place, and some interesting errors in action result.

VISUAL PERCEPTION FROM BIRTH TO SIX MONTHS

Early limitations of vision: Are they really a problem?

We know that newborns' vision is significantly poorer than that of older individuals. **Visual acuity**, which is basically a measure of the fineness of detail that can be resolved, is probably around 1/30th the level of perfect adult acuity (Van Hof-van Duin & Mohn, 1985). Additionally, young infants have poor control over focusing the eyes (**visual accommodation**), something that is necessary for the creation of a sharp retinal image of objects at different distances from the viewer. These limitations are short lived, because both acuity and accommodation improve rapidly during the first 6 months. Nevertheless, you would be forgiven for concluding that the early limitations paint a pessimistic picture regarding visual perception of the world at birth and soon after. However, poor visual acuity and focusing only limits the fineness of detail that can be resolved: although much of the detail of the visual world may not be available to young infants, these limitations should not affect perception of the larger scale structure of objects, and provided we present sufficiently large stimuli at an appropriate distance from the infant, it is perfectly possible to investigate just what young infants are capable of perceiving.

> **Visual acuity** the ability to make fine discriminations between the elements in the visual array.

> **visual accommodation** the ability to focus on objects irrespective of their distance from the eye. Therefore, as an object moves closer toward us, it does not appear to go in and out of focus.

How can we investigate infant perception?

Given that we know that there is potentially an ability to be detected, how can we go about measuring it? If we were working with adults, we could present different stimuli and ask participants whether or not they discriminated some particular variation between them. But we cannot ask infants these questions, so our approach has to be rather less direct. Around the beginning of the 1960s, some techniques were developed that opened up exciting possibilities.

The visual preference method

The spontaneous **visual preference method** simply involves presenting infants with two different stimuli and measuring whether they look consistently longer at one than the other (Figure 5.2). Such a looking time difference is defined as a visual preference, and if one thinks about it, such a preference implies discrimination: without discrimination there would be no basis for the preference. Of course, one has to be sure that a looking preference is not simply a tendency to look in one direction. Thus, the two stimuli are presented over a series of trials in which their left–right locations are systematically varied.

> **visual preference method** to determine whether infants have preferences for certain stimuli, they are shown two objects (usually 2-D pictures) side by side, and the amount of time they spend looking at each one is then compared.

Habituation techniques

If an infant is presented with the same stimulus over a series of presentations, the time spent looking at it declines. This phenomenon, the technical term for which is **habituation**, is often described as an early example of boredom, but that description runs the risk of diverting the reader from the important psychological implications of the phenomenon. If the infant looks for shorter periods over trials, this implies that progressively more of the stimulus has been committed to memory, thus if infants habituate they must have a form of visual memory. Additionally, we can

> **habituation/ dishabituation** the process by which attention to a stimulus gradually declines over time and recovers when a new stimulus is presented.

FIGURE 5.2 *The spontaneous visual preference method involves presenting infants with two different stimuli and measuring whether they look consistently longer at one than the other.*

use this phenomenon to investigate visual discrimination. If, after habituation to one stimulus (say a cross), we present a different stimulus (say a circle), we would predict that if infants can discriminate between the two they should recognise the circle as novel and hence look longer at it. If, on the other hand, they cannot discriminate between the two stimuli, looking should remain as low as it was before the stimulus swap. A more sensitive variant on this technique involves habituation to one stimulus followed by paired presentation of familiar and novel stimuli.

The measure in this case is the proportion of time spent looking at each of the two stimuli, and the prediction is that if infants discriminate the two they should look longer at the novel stimulus. Recently, methods based on simple accumulated looking time have increasingly been supplemented by more sophisticated methods such as eye tracking or measures of brain activity. We shall encounter examples of use of these methods later in the chapter. However, it is still the case that methods based on simple looking duration provide the bulk of evidence regarding infant perception and cognition.

Shape perception in newborns

As already indicated, despite the poor visual acuity of young infants, we can still investigate shape perception provided we present sufficiently large stimuli at an appropriate viewing distance. And it turns out that even newborns are capable of perceiving differences between simple shapes such as crosses, triangles, squares, and circles. Slater and colleagues (1983) habituated newborns to one of these four simple shapes and then tested their looking at the familiar (habituated) one when it was shown paired with a new shape. Infants looked longer at the stimulus that they had not been habituated to, indicating that they discriminated between them and treated as novel the stimulus to which they had not had prior exposure.

The components of shape

This was an exciting result, but it poses the problem of whether infants are discriminating between the forms as such or simply on the basis of the presence of a single feature in one stimulus (for instance, the pointed apex of the triangle) and its absence in the other. Thus, some of the subsequent work took a rather different approach, starting with the lowest level components of a shape and working

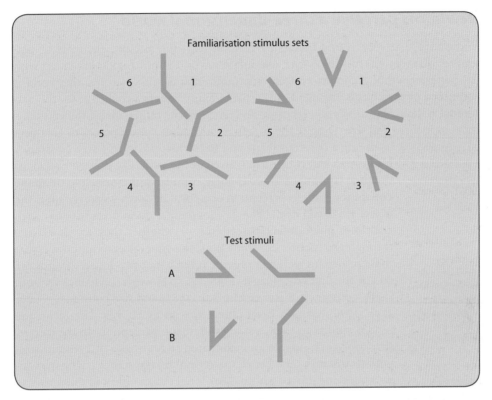

FIGURE 5.3 *During familiarisation trials infants see either the set of obtuse or the set of acute angles, with stimulus orientation varied across presentation, so that the only constant feature is the angular relationship. They are then tested for a novelty preference between acute and obtuse figures.*

Source: Slater *et al.* (1991). Reprinted by permission of Elsevier.

upwards. For instance, Slater *et al.* (1988) showed that newborns could discriminate between different line orientations. Going a step higher, Cohen and Younger (1984) investigated whether infants could discriminate between different angular relationships between lines. Their finding was that although 4-month-olds discriminated on this basis, 6-week-olds did not, discriminating instead on the basis of the orientation of the constituent lines. However, this is not the end of the story. Any figure consisting of a pair of intersecting lines contains both an angular relation and two lines in specific orientations, and it seems that during habituation young infants have a tendency to process on the basis of the simplest variable, in this case line orientation. The way around this problem is to habituate infants to a constant angular relationship but to vary the overall orientation of the figure so that the angle is the only constant during habituation (see Figure 5.3). When Slater *et al.* (1991) did this, they found that newborns discriminated on the basis of angular relationship. This finding indicates that even newborn infants perceive simple shapes as a whole, and not just as a collection of parts.

Newborns perceive a three-dimensional world

Knowledge that very young infants perceive at least the angular elements of patterns is of great interest. However, the infant's world is not totally inhabited with flat patterns; although adults typically surround infants with pictures, the world is composed of 3D objects arranged in 3D space. This presents a challenge for the perceptual system, because as objects move and reorient, the retinal image they produce changes in form and size. Despite these changes, the adult viewer perceives an object as having a constant shape and size. The principle of **size constancy** leads to an object being perceived as the same size however much its distance from the viewer changes. Similarly, the principle of **shape constancy** leads to perception of a constant form whatever angle the object is viewed from. The developmental question is whether such principles guide infant perception, or whether they are developed through experience. For some time, the general assumption was that these principles were not present at birth, but developed towards the end of the first year (Piaget, 1936/1954). However, evidence for both shape constancy (Slater & Morison, 1985) and size constancy (Slater et al., 1990) has now been obtained with newborns. The technique used is similar to that in studies of shape perception. In the case of size constancy, infants are habituated to an object of constant size, with its distance (and hence the **retinal image size**) varying over trials. Following this, newborns look longer at an object of different size than at the same object at a new distance (and hence with a new retinal image size). This happens even though the new object is placed at a distance that leads it to produce the same retinal image size as the old object at one of its habituation distances. In other words, infants respond to a change in true size but not to a change in retinal image size, an impressive ability by any account. Just as in the case of line orientation versus angular intersection discrimination, it appears that very young infants tend to respond to lower order stimulus variables , in this case retinal size. But if we vary retinal size during habituation, we prevent infants from responding to this variable, and this reveals their ability to process the only constant feature of habituation trials – true size. By 4 months of age infants respond primarily to real size and not to retinal image size (Granrud, 2006).

size constancy understanding that an object remains the same size despite its *retinal image size* changing as it moves closer to or away from us.

shape constancy understanding that an object remains the same shape even though its *retinal image shape* changes when it is viewed from different angles.

retinal image size the size of a visually perceived object on the retina of the eyes. This image will vary depending on the real size of the object and its distance from the observer.

Perceptual development in the first six months

So far we have seen that newborn visual perception, though not well tuned to detect fine detail, is in other respects much like adult perception. However, current evidence suggests that there are some important aspects of perception that emerge during the first few months of life.

Perception of object unity

If you look at the top half of Figure 5.4, you will probably interpret what you see as a complete rod behind a box; the adult visual system 'fills in' the invisible parts of the partly hidden rod. This is referred to as *object unity*, that is, perceiving a complete object despite the fact that parts of it cannot be seen. An important question is whether infants perceive object unity in this way. Kellman and Spelke (1983) tested this by habituating 4-month-olds to the display at the top of Figure 5.4, a rod moving back and forth behind a box, and they then measured looking at the two displays at the bottom of the figure, the complete rod versus the parts which they had literally seen. The rationale was that if the infants had perceived the complete rod during habituation, it would be familiar and so they would look more at the separate parts, whereas if they had perceived only the parts, they would look longer at the complete rod because it would be novel.

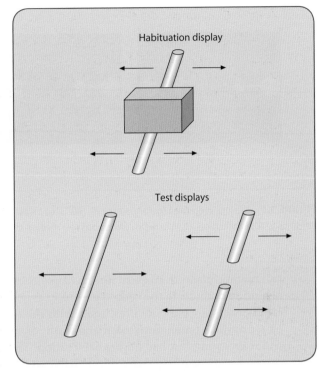

FIGURE 5.4 *Displays presented by Kellman and Spelke (1983).*
Source: Kellman and Spelke (1983). Reprinted by permission of Elsevier.

Kellman and Spelke found that infants looked longer at the separate parts than at the complete rod, and they concluded that 4-month-olds perceive object unity in displays of this sort. It is important to note that there was no spontaneous preference for the rod parts over the whole, so there is no way to explain these result other than in terms of object unity perceived during habituation. Interestingly, the effect only occurs if the rod moves, and it seems likely that *common motion* is one principle infants use to perceive object unity – by 'common motion' is meant the fact that the upper and lower portions of the rod moved at the same time and in the same direction.

Newborns' perception of these displays seems to be fundamentally different (Slater *et al.*, 1996). Instead of looking longer at the rod parts after habituation, they look longer at the complete rod. Slater *et al.* (1990) concluded that, unlike 4-month-olds, newborns do not perceive object unity, instead being limited to perception of what is literally in view. Subsequent work (Johnson & Aslin, 1995) showed that 2-month-olds showed the same result as 4-month-olds, though only if the occluding box was made quite narrow so that the amount of object invisible was relatively small. All this presents a picture of gradual emergence of object unity during the early months.

Just as we can ask if infants 'fill in' the hidden centre part of the rod in the object unity task, we can ask whether, when an object moves behind an occluder, they fill in the invisible part of its trajectory. On the face of it, this involves a greater processing load because unlike the rod behind the box, there is a period when the object is totally invisible. Johnson, Bremner *et al.* (2003) investigated trajectory continuity by

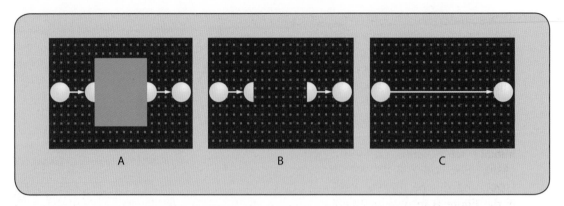

A   B   C

FIGURE 5.5 *Displays presented by Johnson* et al. *(2003) to investigate infants' perception of trajectory continuity. A: Habituation display, B: Discontinuous test display, C: Continuous test display.*

habituating infants to an event in which an object moved back and forth, disappearing behind an occluder in the central part of its trajectory (see Figure 5.5). Following this experience, they presented test trials with the occluder absent, in which the object either moved continuously back and forth, or moved discontinuously, disappearing and reappearing as it had during habituation. The rationale was that if they had perceived a *continuous* trajectory during habituation, they would look longer at the *discontinuous* test trial because it was novel, whereas if they perceived a *discontinuous* trajectory during habituation, they would look longer at the *continuous* test trial. It turned out that 6-month-olds perceived trajectory continuity, whereas 4-month-olds only did so when the occluder was very narrow, and 2-month-olds perceived the trajectory to be discontinuous even with the narrow occluder. Further work indicates that 4-month-olds perceive trajectory continuity when either the time out of sight or the distance out of sight is short (Bremner *et al.*, 2005). Also, this is one area in which precise eye-tracking measures (measures of exactly where the infants are looking) have been used to verify simple looking duration measures. Johnson, Amso *et al.* (2003) measured anticipatory eye movements to the point of object emergence once it had disappeared behind a wide occluder, and found few such anticipations by 4-month-olds but frequent ones by 6-month-olds. This fits well with the 4- and 6-month-old evidence gained by Johnson, Bremner *et al.* (2003), and confirms the presence of a developmental progression that lags that of development of object unity by about 2 months.

Perception of subjective contours

subjective contour
when only parts of an object are presented, the remaining contours are 'filled in' in order that the complete shape can be perceived.

Another form of perceptual organisation that involves filling in invisible parts can be seen in Figure 5.6. You will probably see a lilac square partially occluding four black disks. However, there is no square there of course, only four disks with quadrants missing ('pacmen'). The arrangements of the missing quadrants creates the illusion of a complete square, although there are no contours connecting these four 'corners'. For obvious reasons this is called a **subjective contour**.

Perception of subjective contours can be investigated in infants by habituating them to something like that in Figure 5.6 and then measuring looking at a real square versus some other shape. The rationale is that if they perceive the subjective square, the real square presented on test trials should be familiar, and so they will look longer at the other test shape. And this is what was found, initially with 7-month-olds (Bertenthal *et al.*, 1980), and later with 3-month-olds (Ghim, 1990), and this perception is particularly strong if the figure is in motion (Yoshino *et al.*, 2010). Interestingly, 7-month-olds (Csibra, 2001) and even 4-month-olds (Bremner *et al.*, submitted) perceive this illusory figure as an occluding surface, treating it in the same way as the occluder in trajectory continuity studies. So far, however, the ability to perceive illusory figures has not been shown to exist at birth, so again it seems likely that this ability develops shortly after birth.

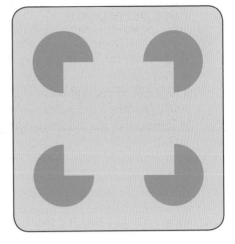

FIGURE 5.6 *Subjective contours. The arrangement and orientation of missing segments from the circles creates the percept of a complete square.*

Summary

The evidence reviewed in this section indicates that newborns and young infants are capable of perceiving objects and shapes and apply the perceptual constancies that are necessary for perception of an objective, three-dimensional world. Newborn abilities appear to be limited to the 'here and now' of perception, but during the first four months infants develop the ability to fill in gaps in perception in order to perceive object unity and subjective contours.

INFANTS' PERCEPTION OF PEOPLE

As well as being surrounded with inanimate objects, from birth infants are embedded in a social world, and important questions exist concerning their ability to perceive people. These questions are of interest in their own right but are also vital in relation to accounts of the infant's social and emotional development. For instance, if an infant is to form an emotional attachment to a specific person (see Chapter 6) they must have some means of identifying the individual as a person and of discriminating between that individual and others. One might expect such recognition and discrimination to be a simple matter, given how much interest infants take in people. However, people provide highly complex dynamic information to both the visual and auditory systems, so it is by no means a foregone conclusion that young infants will be well equipped for person perception.

Face perception

Fantz (1961) carried out a classic study of face perception, in which he presented infants with the schematic stimuli shown in Figure 5.7. One stimulus contained facial features in the correct configuration, another presented them in a jumbled array, and the third provided no specific features but the same overall amount of stimulus brightness. Even in the first month, infants showed a small but consistent spontaneous preference for the facial configuration, and Fantz concluded that even the youngest infants had the ability to perceive a facial configuration in this schematic stimulus. However, there were a number of criticisms of this early study. The main one that should concern us is that the facial arrangement contained more information around the edge of the stimulus. This might not seem to matter, but there is evidence that young infants tend to scan around the periphery of complex stimuli. Given this tendency, they may have looked longer at the facial arrangement simply because there was more to look at around its edge.

Subsequent work applied better controls in the design of the stimuli, and revised the estimated age regarding the emergence of face perception to at least 4 months (Wilcox, 1969), though later, this was revised downwards again to 2 months (Maurer & Barrera, 1981). There is, however, always the chance that negative results obtained with younger infants are due to the fact that the technique used is not the most suitable for very young infants. And in parallel with this work was another study using a different technique with newborns. Instead of using the visual preference technique, Goren, Sarty, and Wu (1975) moved schematic stimuli back and forth in the visual field of newborns, and found that they followed the facial arrangement further and for longer than a jumbled face. This different form of visual preference strongly suggests that a form of face perception is present at birth. Why does this technique appear to work better than the spontaneous visual preference technique? Probably the crucial

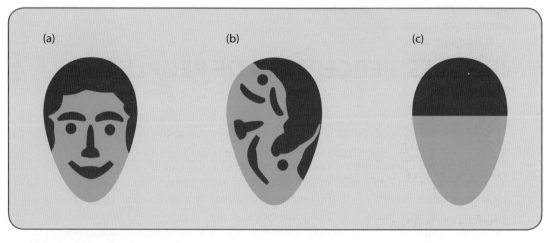

FIGURE 5.7 *Face stimuli used by Fantz (1961): a) facial arrangement, b) jumbled facial features, c) control stimulus with same overall brightness as other two.*

Source: Fantz, 1961. Reproduced by permission of Scientific American.

factor is the movement of the stimuli. It seems likely that if infants are equipped with a system for perceiving faces, it will be tuned to detecting and discriminating between real faces, which of course are rarely static.

Discriminating between faces

The question of most relevance in relation to infants' social and emotional development concerns at what age infants are able to discriminate between faces, in particular between their parents' faces and those of others. The tendency has been to tackle this question by investigating infants' responses to real faces. Typically, infants are presented with a familiar and an unfamiliar face side by side, with a view to measuring any spontaneous visual preference. Although use of real faces has the advantage of increased realism, it carries with it a number of difficulties, as we shall see.

Several studies have obtained evidence for discrimination between the mother's and a female stranger's face by young infants (Carpenter, 1974; Maurer & Salapatek, 1976) and even newborns with only a few hours contact with their mother (Bushnell, 2001; Field et al., 1984). In all cases, infants showed a visual preference for their mother's face. However, this finding is quite hard to interpret without applying quite strict controls. For instance, infants are capable of identifying their mother by sense of smell, and this, rather than visual recognition, could have directed looking to their mother. Bushnell et al. (1989) reduced the likelihood of this by providing a strong smelling perfume to act as an olfactory mask. Another problem is that in most studies the mother presumably recognised her infant and so may have produced more dynamic facial expressions, something that could have attracted more looking without any implication that the infant identified their mother. However, Walton et al. (1992) effectively ruled out this possibility by presenting videotaped images of the mother's and a stranger's faces. Because these images were captured while both mother and stranger were looking at a camera (and one baby's 'stranger' mother was another baby's real mother), it is clear that the infants' longer looking at mother than stranger was a genuine visual preference for her face.

It thus appears clear that, even within a day of birth, newborns are capable of discriminating between their mother's and a female stranger's face. What remains unclear, however, is the basis on which this discrimination is made. Although most investigators have gone to considerable lengths to match mothers and strangers on colouring, hair colour and style, it is still possible that discriminations are made on gross differences of this sort rather than on recognition of the mother's face as a whole. However, the evidence on face perception indicates that, even at birth, there is a distinct possibility that discrimination is based on configurational differences, that is, differences in the spacing of the eyes, the relationship between eyes and nose, and so on.

Preference for attractive faces

One intriguing recent finding is that 2-month-old infants (Langlois et al., 1991) and even newborns (Slater et al., 1998) will look longer at a face rated attractive by adults than they will at faces rated less attractive. We can begin to make sense of this finding

prototypical face the most typical example of a face. Produced when many different faces are averaged.

innate mechanism a mechanism or ability that does not need to be learned, something we are born knowing.

by considering another finding; if one averages a set of faces to produce a **prototypical face** (see Figure 5.8), adults rate the product more attractive than the individual faces that make up the overall average. Possibly, then, attractiveness preferences have their origins in preferences for prototypes. It is fairly unlikely that infants have a concept of attractiveness, but they may possess an **innate** 'face recognition system' that triggers attention to faces and which is maximally stimulated by a prototypical face.

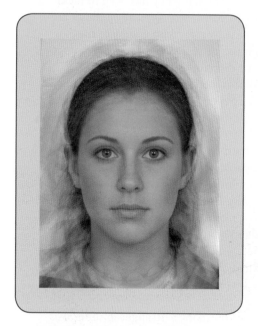

FIGURE 5.8 *An averaged female face.*

Source: Reproduced with permission from the Face Research Lab (faceresearch.org)

Perceptual narrowing and the other species/race effect

Although most of the evidence covered so far points towards innate perceptual processes for face recognition and very rapid establishment of discriminations, there are interesting findings that point to longer term effects of experience. Specifically, it appears that very general abilities become more narrowly tuned (known as perceptual narrowing) as a result of experience. For instance, 6-month-olds are able to discriminate Barbary Macaque monkey faces, whereas, like adults, 9-month-olds have lost this ability (Pascalis *et al.*, 2002). Also, 3-month-olds discriminate faces in other races, but this ability is gradually lost in the subsequent 6 months (Kelly *et al.*, 2009). Finally, preference for female faces is not present at birth, and when it develops it only appears for same-race faces (Quinn *et al.*, 2008). One interpretation of these effects is that infants are born with a very general system for recognising faces, possibly tuned to a very general prototype, and permitting discrimination of faces in other species and other races, but that experience with a specific race leads to this being replaced by a more specific face system tuned to the race the infant encounters (Slater, Quinn *et al.*, 2010). As we shall see, very similar effects are evident in the case of speech perception.

Imitation

The conventional view put forward many years ago by Piaget was that imitation was impossible until infants were capable of representing self and other, a capacity which was thought to develop late in infancy (Piaget, 1936/1954, see later in this chapter). However, it now seems clear that even newborns are capable of imitating facial and manual gestures. Meltzoff and Moore (1977) were the first to report well-controlled studies of imitation in early infancy. It is tricky to carry out work of this sort. In order to provide a fair test of the phenomenon, investigators must focus on gestures that the infant is capable of producing spontaneously, and so we are faced with the problem of establishing whether the infant is truly imitating or simply exercising a gesture that they produce frequently anyway. Thus, if one focused purely on tongue protrusion, apparent agreement between the modelled act and the infant's response might simply reflect the high spontaneous rate of tongue protrusion by young infants.

Meltzoff and Moore surmounted this problem by presenting different facial gestures (see Figure 5.9) and asking raters who were blind to the gesture modelled to judge the gesture that infants were making. Working with data from infants within their first month, judges showed a significant tendency to identify the gesture made by the infant as matching the one the adult had been modelling. Later they found similar evidence with newborns (Meltzoff & Moore, 1983).

Although these claims were highly controversial at the time (and to some extent continue to be controversial, e.g. Anisfeld et al, 2001), the findings have now been replicated in many laboratories and neonatal imitation appears to be a real phenomenon. In addition to its relevance regarding infants' social awareness, the ability to

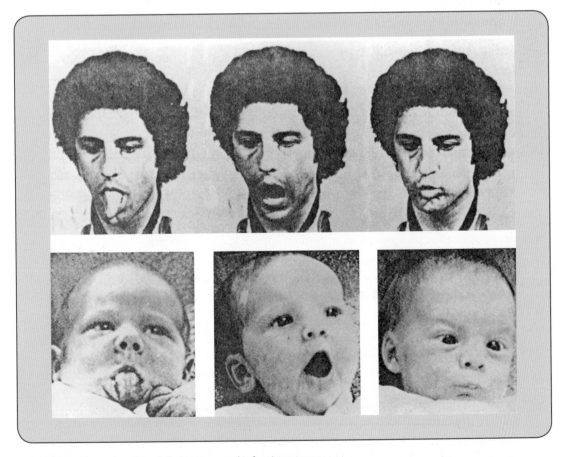

FIGURE 5.9 *Examples of modelled gesture and infant's response.*

Source: Meltzoff and Moore (1977). Reproduced by permission of Science.

imitate implies a great deal regarding infants' face perception. After all, in order to imitate a facial gesture, infants have to be able to perceive the internal parts of the face making the gesture, and be able to make matches to the corresponding parts of their own face.

Voice perception

Evidence presented in Chapter 4 makes it clear that even prior to birth the foetus picks up auditory information. Kisilevsky *et al.* (1992) found that from 26 weeks gestation onwards, foetal heart rate changed consistently in relation to auditory stimulation, and Hepper (1992) obtained evidence for foetal responsiveness to sounds at only 12 weeks gestation.

Research with young infants reveals some remarkable abilities to discriminate speech sounds. Newborns reveal the ability to discriminate between certain speech syllables (Moon *et al.*, 1992; Moon & Fifer, 1990). Additionally, unlike adults, very young infants appear to discriminate speech distinctions that exist in other languages but not in their own (Eilers *et al.*, 1982; Trehub, 1976), later narrowing their discriminative capabilities to distinctions contained in their own language (Eimas *et al.*, 1971). A particularly nice example of this can be seen in the case of linguistic tone. Over 70 per cent of languages are 'tone languages' in which the tone or pitch affects meaning. It turns out that young infants are sensitive to linguistic tone, but only those exposed to a tone language maintain this ability (Mattock & Burnham, 2006). Changes in infants' speech discrimination abilities are also discussed in Chapters 1 and 10.

Some investigators saw this as evidence for a language acquisition device; newborns were receptive to all languages and later became focused on the one to which they were exposed. However, some of the magic was taken out of these findings when it was shown that other species, including chinchilla rabbits, made similar speech sound discriminations to very young infants! It seems likely then that human language evolved to suit the characteristics of the auditory system, characteristics that have much in common across species. However, the evidence for the progressive narrowing of discriminations to those existing in the language infants are exposed to does suggest the presence of an important speech learning process.

Voice and speech discrimination

Just as in the case of facial discrimination, it turns out that newborn infants show an attentional preference for their mother's voice compared to that of a female stranger of similar age (DeCasper & Fifer, 1980). Because these infants were only 3 days old with only 12 hours' contact with their mother, we might assume that, as with face discrimination, we are dealing with a very rapid learning process (Figure 5.10). However, hearing is different from vision in the sense that there is scope for learning prior to birth. If foetuses are responsive to sounds do they learn about sounds? This whole topic is treated in detail in Chapter 4, but it is worth commenting on this here to complete the picture. It has been demonstrated that speech sounds, particularly those produced by the mother, are available in the uterine environment, and a fascinating study by DeCasper and Spence (1986) indicates that the unborn child learns about auditory information. In their study mothers were asked to read a prose passage repeatedly, prior to the birth of their infant. Once the infants were born, they were exposed to this passage again and a novel one. They showed an attentional preference for the pre-exposed passage even though both were read by the mother, or even when both were read by another speaker. Nobody is claiming that these infants discriminated between these passages in terms of meaning. But the finding is exciting nevertheless, indicating that foetuses and newborn infants are capable of encoding speech in sufficient detail to extract differences in rhythm and/or **intonation** between the two passages, independent of the reader's tone of voice.

FIGURE 5.10 *A mother talking to her newborn infant.*
Source: Shutterstock.

> **intonation** the rhythmic pattern of speech. For example, the meaning of a sentence is changed when the ending has a raised pitch, e.g. 'He didn't come' versus 'He didn't come?'

Preference for infant-directed speech

When parents speak to infants, they typically use a form of speech in which intonation patterns are exaggerated, that is, there is more rise and fall in the pitch of the voice than when addressing other adults. It has been shown that infants prefer to hear this speech over adult-directed speech (Fernald, 1982). This form of speech is often called *motherese*, or **infant-directed speech**, and it is further discussed in Chapters 7 and 10. However, the term motherese is a bit of a misnomer, because similar preferences emerge even when the speaker is male (Pegg *et al.*, 1992). It seems likely that infant-directed speech not only attracts the infant's attention, but presents clearer examples of speech from which the infant is more capable of learning relationships between words, and objects and actions.

> **infant-directed speech (motherese)** the speech that adults and children over 4 years old use when addressing an infant.

Summary

Current evidence indicates that the ability to perceive faces is present at birth, and that discrimination between mothers' and strangers' faces develops within the first days after birth. Preference for 'attractive' faces appears at birth and is probably linked to the infant's internal model of the prototypical face. The existence of neonatal imitation of facial gestures further reinforces the conclusion that newborns are capable of perceiving the internal detail and configuration of the human face. Voice and speech perception is also well developed in early infancy, and it is likely that voice discrimination actually develops prior to birth. Further development of voice perception is likely to be supported by parents' spontaneous production of infant-directed speech which contains exaggerated pitch contours that both attract their infant's attention and are likely to support speech perception.

INFANTS' KNOWLEDGE OF THE WORLD

The conventional view is that cognitive processes involve mental representations of the world. This sets **cognition** apart from perception, because cognitive processes can act on representations of aspects of the world that are not available to the senses, whereas perception is limited to the 'here and now'. In recent years, the clarity of this distinction has been somewhat watered down. For instance, take Kellman and Spelke's 'rod and box' study illustrated in Figure 5.4. The fact that 4-month-olds appear to 'fill in' the invisible parts of the rod could be taken either as evidence of a high level *perceptual* process, or of the ability to form a mental representation of the absent part (and hence a *cognitive* ability), and the choice of account is determined very much by the investigator's theoretical orientation. And the same applies in the case of trajectory continuity (see Figure 5.5) in which case the infants have to fill in an object that is totally invisible for part of its trajectory. Nevertheless, there is a large body of work dating since early last century that is aimed specifically at investigating infants' knowledge and representations of the world.

cognition psychological processes that involve mental representations and thus that go beyond perception.

Jean Piaget and the development of object permanence

Piaget's (1936/1954) view was that infants were not born with knowledge of the world, but instead gradually constructed knowledge and the ability to represent reality mentally – this theoretical view is known as *constructivism* (see Chapter 2). Note that this view is not necessarily incompatible with the evidence cited earlier pointing to sophisticated perception of the world at birth, because Piaget was making his claims primarily about *knowledge* or understanding, rather than perception. A key aspect of Piaget's account related to the development of mental representation, specifically, the ability to maintain a representation of objects that are out of sight, leading to awareness of their permanence. According to him, prior to the age of 9 months, infants do not exhibit **object permanence**, and although this appears in simple form at 9 months, it does not develop fully until near the end of the second year of life.

object permanence the ability to understand that even if an object is no longer visible, it continues to exist.

Piaget reported a multitude of convincing observations to substantiate his claims, and although these were from his own three children as infants, the main phenomena have replicated readily in controlled laboratory investigations involving large numbers of infants. His principal examples involved infants' responses to an object being hidden. Prior to 9 months, he found that infants made no response when an object was hidden; even if they were very interested in it and thus highly motivated to retrieve it, their actions towards it ceased when it went out of sight. It was as though out of sight was out of mind, which is more or less Piaget's claim. Not being able to represent the hidden object, there was no way that the young infant could hold it in mind.

Search onset and the A not B error

In contrast, by 9 months the infant's reaction to disappearance had changed. Now, if an object was hidden, the 9-month-old would search for it successfully. To Piaget, this indicated the beginnings of the ability to represent the absent object. However, Piaget always went on to complicate the task, to test the extent of the infant's ability (note that this is the essence of the clinical method, which is described in more detail in Chapters 1 and 2). He found that after having searched successfully at one location (A) infants failed to take account of its disappearance at a new location (B); even though its disappearance at the new location was perfectly obvious (the infants saw it being hidden there!), infants continued to search at the old place. For obvious reasons this has become known as the **A not B error**. Piaget took this as evidence that their representation of the hidden object was not yet fully objective; they repeated an old action to 'recreate' the object, as if their own actions, rather than objective knowledge of where it had gone, defined its existence.

A not B error an object-searching error that is often made by 8–12-month-olds. Infants making this error will look for an object where they have most often found it (location A) rather than where they last saw it hidden (location B).

LATER WORK ON INFANT COGNITION

Persuasive though Piaget's observations were, over the past 20 or 30 years a substantial body of work has emerged suggesting strongly that, well before Piaget would have recognised, infants have an awareness of object permanence and an advanced general understanding of the physical world. One of the limitations of Piaget's techniques was that in many cases he relied on measuring the infant's actions towards objects, such as reaching, and because we know that motor skill develops with age, investigators sought ways of investigating infant knowledge in ways that did not rely so heavily on complex actions.

violation of expectation technique infants are shown an event and are then shown two new events, one of which is consistent with everyday reality (possible), and the other inconsistent (impossible). Infants will typically look longer at the impossible event because it violates their expectancies.

The violation of expectation technique

The technique used in most recent studies of young infants' ability is called the **violation of expectation technique**, and bears similarities to the habituation–novelty technique described earlier. Infants are familiarised with an event sequence, and are then presented with two test trials that are variants on the original, one involving a possible event and the other involving an impossible event. Infants' looking at the two test events is measured, but in this case longer looking at one event does not just indicate discrimination between the events. In these studies, if infants look longer at the impossible event this is taken as evidence that they have detected that it violates a principle of everyday reality. As we shall see, such a conclusion is strengthened by the fact that all these studies incorporate careful controls to rule out the possibility that longer looking is due to perceptual novelty.

Evidence of object knowledge: The 'drawbridge study' and others

An example should make the technique clear. Baillargeon *et al.* (1985) familiarised 5-month-old infants with a repeated event in which a flap (the drawbridge) rotated from flat on the table with its free edge near to the infant, through 180^0 so that it was again flat on the table with its free edge away from the infant, and then back through 180^0 to its starting point. Following these trials, infants were presented with two types of test trial (see Figure 5.11). In both cases, a block was introduced in the path of the flap, such that it would impede its full rotation. In the *possible* test event, the

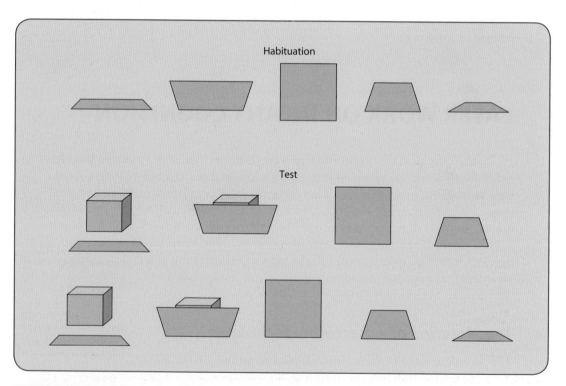

FIGURE 5.11 *Habituation and test displays used by Baillargeon, Spelke and Wasserman, (1985).*
Source: Baillargeon, Spelke and Wasserman, (1985). Reprinted with permission of Elsevier Science.

flap rotated to hide the block and stopped at the point at which it would contact the block, and then rotated back to its starting point. In the *impossible* test event, the flap rotated 180°, appearing to move through and annihilate the block in the process. What is particularly neat about this study is that, in terms of perceptual familiarity, the *impossible* event is most similar to the familiarisation event (i.e. in both instances the flap or 'drawbridge' rotates through 180°, and so if infants were processing at a simple perceptual level, we would expect them to look at the *possible* event because it is superficially more novel. However, what Baillargeon *et al.* (1985) actually found was that infants looked longer at the impossible event. Their conclusion is that 5-month-old infants have knowledge of object permanence (they know that the block continues to exist when hidden by the flap) and know about the conditions under which one object will impede the movement of another.

Another even more striking demonstration comes from the results of a study by Baillargeon (1986), illustrated in Figure 5.12. Infants were familiarised with an event in which a truck ran down a track and passed behind a screen, re-emerging at the other side. Prior to each trial, the screen was lifted revealing the unobstructed track. Following familiarisation, two test events were presented; an event in which, prior to the truck's movement, the screen was lifted to reveal a block placed *behind* the track, and one in which the screen was lifted to reveal a block placed *on* the track: the screen was then lowered so that the block could no longer be seen. On the test trials that followed, in both cases the truck then rolled down the track as usual, re-emerging

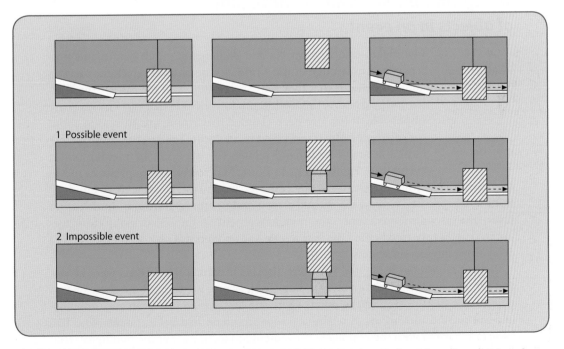

1 Possible event

2 Impossible event

FIGURE 5.12 *Displays presented by Baillargeon (1986). The habituation event is show above the possible and impossible test events.*

Source: Baillargeon (1986). © 1986, with permission from Elsevier Science.

from the screen as before, an impossible event when the block was placed on the track beforehand. Baillargeon found that 6- and 8-month-olds looked longer at the imposs-ible test event, a finding replicated by Baillargeon and DeVos (1991) with 4-month-olds. Again, the conclusion is that infants are capable of detecting the impossibility of the truck moving through the block. Given that the block is hidden when the truck event takes place, this requires knowledge of object permanence as well as knowl-edge of the solidity and impenetrability of objects.

It appears that even 2-month-olds have some ability of this sort. Spelke *et al.* (1992) familiarised infants to an event in which a ball rolled behind a screen, whereupon the screen was raised to reveal the ball resting against an end wall. On test trials, an obstruction was introduced behind the screen between the ball and the end wall, and the possible event involved the screen lifting to reveal the ball resting against the obstruction, whereas the impossible event involved it being revealed beyond the obstruction against the wall. These very young infants looked longer at the latter event, despite the fact that the ball rested where it had on familiarisation trials. One simplification in this task was that the top of the obstruction was visible above the screen. Thus, it can be argued that success at this task does not require full object per-manence because at least part of the obstruction could be seen throughout. Again, however, the conclusion is that these 2-month-olds realise that the ball cannot move through the obstruction.

Young infants reason about the number of objects in an event

core knowledge basic information about the world, particularly knowledge about the physical properties of objects, available to the very young infant and probably *innate*

Investigators such as Spelke and Baillargeon argue that infants pos-sess **core knowledge** of the world, on the basis of which they reason about the events that they see (Spelke, 2007). In the case of the stud-ies outlined above, this leads them to conclude that certain events are impossible. It has also been claimed that young infants reason about the *number* of objects involved in an event. Spelke *et al.* (1995) famil-iarised 3- and 4-month-old infants to two types of moving object events (see Figure 5.13). In both, two screens were present, and in one case – the continuous event – an object moved behind the first screen, re-emerged from it, disappeared behind the second screen and re-emerged from it. In the other case – the discontinuous event – the middle segment of the object's trajectory was omitted; it disappeared behind the first screen and an identical object emerged after a delay from the second screen.

Infants were then presented with test displays in which the screens were absent and the movements either involved a single object moving the full distance, or two objects, the first moving to the point where the first screen had been and stopping, and the second moving from where the second screen had been. Infants who had been familiarised with the *continuous* movement looked longer at the two-object test, and those that had been familiarised with the *discontinuous* event, looked longer at the single object movement. The conclusion was that infants reasoned that there was one object involved in the continuous event and two objects involved in the discontinuous

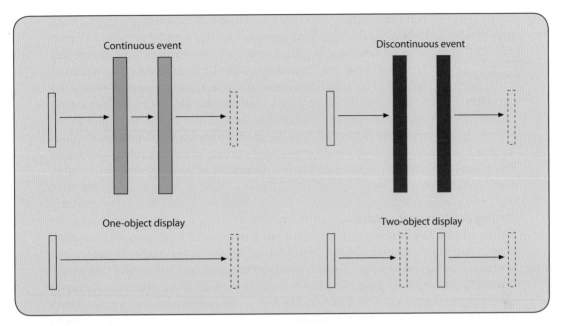

FIGURE 5.13 *Displays presented by Spelke* et al. *(1995). Habituation displays (top half of figure) are either continuous or discontinuous, and test events involve either one or two objects.*

Source: Spelke et al. (1995). Reproduced with permission from *The British Journal of Psychology,* © The British Psychological Society.

event, and so on test trials they looked at the event involving the number of objects that differed from their expectation.

Wilcox and Baillargeon (1998) used a particularly ingenious technique to detect whether infants reason about numerosity on the basis of object features. They presented 7- to 9-month-olds with a moving object event in which an object disappeared behind a screen and a different object re-emerged from the other side. In one event, the screen was wide enough to conceal both objects at once, whereas in another event, the screen was only just wider than one object. Wilcox and Baillargeon found that infants looked longer at the narrow screen event, and their conclusion is that on the basis of the featural differences between objects, the infants reasoned that two were involved and that both could not be hidden behind the narrow screen.

Young infants discriminate different numbers of items

Over 20 years ago, Starkey and Cooper (1980) habituated 4- to 7-month-old infants to patterns of a particular number of dots (either two or three) and then tested for *dishabituation* to the other number (three or two). They also included a large number condition in which there were either four or six dots. Infants dishabituated to number change in the small number but not in the large number condition. This suggested that infants are capable of discriminating between arrays in terms of numerosity, though only in the case of small numbers. Starkey and Cooper were of the view

subitising the ability to perceive directly the number of items without consciously counting them or using another form of calculation. This ability only applies to very small numbers.

that numerical competence was based on **subitising**, which can be defined as the ability to perceive directly a small number of items without counting or carrying out any calculation. This ability only applies to very small numbers, which fits the results they obtained. Starkey *et al.* (1990) replicated this effect using arrays of widely differing everyday objects, thus showing that the ability did not simply apply to arrays of identical dots. Infants also appear to be able to discriminate between larger numbers, although in this case they appear to be using a distinct system for detecting approximate differences that only works when the ratio between smaller and larger number is large (Feigenson *et al.*, 2004; Xu & Spelke, 2000).

Young infants can count!

More recently, Wynn (1992, 1995) carried out a number of ingenious studies aimed at assessing not just whether infants could discriminate on the basis of number, but whether they had knowledge of addition and subtraction operations. Her task is indicated in Figure 5.14. In the addition task, 4- and 5-month-old infants were presented with a single object, a screen was raised to hide it, whereupon a hand appeared with a second object and placed it behind the screen (the addition operation). The screen was then lowered for the test trial to reveal either one object (original array, but impossible given the addition of the second object) or two objects (novel array but correct given the addition). In the subtraction task, initially two objects were presented, and the hand removed one once they were screened. Thus, in this case on the test trial the single object outcome is correct and the two-object outcome is incorrect. Infants looked longer at the single object in the addition case and longer at the double object in the subtraction case. In other words, they looked longer at the unexpected event, as if registering that it was impossible.

Wynn concluded that young infants have an understanding of addition and subtraction, but recognised that this could be a very approximate system in which any larger or smaller number would be accepted as the result of addition and subtraction respectively. Thus, she conducted a further study in which 4-month-olds were exposed to the 1 + 1 addition task and on test trials were presented with either two or three objects. Infants looked longer at the three-object outcome, and Wynn concluded that their knowledge of addition was quite precise, to the extent that they expected exactly two objects, and just not more objects, to result from a 1 + 1 operation. This conclusion attributes a great deal of knowledge to young infants, and continues to be controversial. For instance, Wakeley *et al.* (2000) failed to replicate Wynn's finding that infants' numerical expectations are very precise.

However, this is one case in which the use of eye tracking is beginning to prove useful. It turns out that in the case of the two-object outcome of subtraction, infants look significantly longer at the object that should no longer be there (Slater, Bremner *et al.*, 2010), a finding that is in keeping with Wynn's account. Additionally, there is some neuroscientific evidence in keeping with Wynn's interpretation. Berger, Tzur, and Posner (2006) demonstrated that when infants saw an incorrect numerical outcome, they produced brain activity that matched that obtained from adults when they encounter incorrect outcomes.

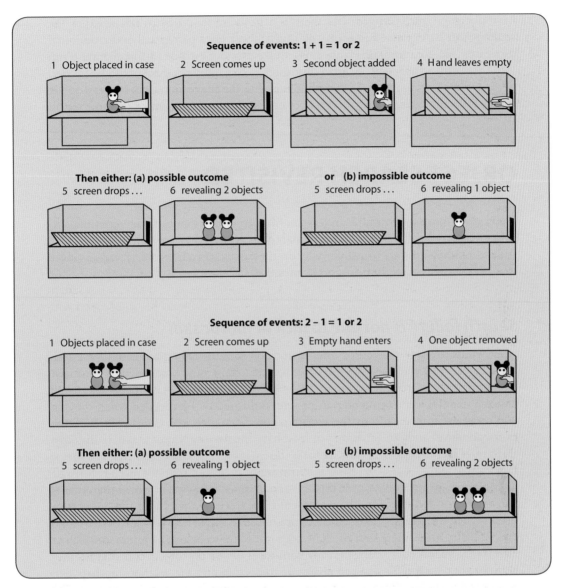

FIGURE 5.14 *Event sequences presented by Wynn (1992): addition events above, subtraction events below.*

Source: Wynn (1992). Reprinted with permission from *Nature,* copyright 1992 Macmillan Magazines Limited and Professor K. Wynn.

Summary

The evidence reported in this section provides compelling evidence that quite young infants understand object permanence and the rules that constrain the movement of one object relative to another, and also that they have some basic awareness of number and numerical operations, relating to small numbers in particular. And there is much other evidence bearing on other aspects of awareness of the physical world that yields a similar picture of early competence. It should be noted, however, that these results have not gone unchallenged, and there is a growing tendency to ask whether the findings can be explained in terms of much lower level perceptual and attentional processes (see, for example, Haith, 1998). It is beyond the scope of this chapter to go into these critical accounts in detail. But there is one question that should be tackled here, namely how to reconcile these findings with the suggestion from Piaget's object search tasks that object permanence does not begin to emerge until 8 or 9 months.

OBJECT SEARCH REVISITED

If infants of around 4 months understand that an object that is hidden continues to exist, why do they fail to search for hidden objects until they are 8 or 9 months old? And when they do start to search, why do they make search errors of various sorts that persist right through to around 18 months?

Search failure is not due to lack of motor skill

An obvious possible reason for infants under 8 months failing to search for a hidden object is that they lack the motor skill of reaching. However, it seems clear that this is not the explanation. Bower and Wishart (1972) showed that infants who failed to retrieve an object from under an opaque upturned cup succeeded when the cup was transparent. In each case, the action required was identical, and success with the transparent case indicates that they at least have the necessary motor skill to dislodge the cup. It seems clear from this that it is the invisibility of the object that is a major factor preventing successful retrieval. However, it turns out that not just *any* form of invisibility leads to problems for this age group, since it has been shown that infants will reach out and grasp an object suspended in front of them after the lights have been turned off and the object is therefore invisible (Bower & Wishart, 1972; Hood and Willatts, 1986). Here, out of sight does not seem to be out of mind, and Bower claims that infants have problems only with cases where one object conceals another because they have difficulty perceiving or understanding the relationship between object and occluder. This view is partly in keeping with Piaget's account, because he claimed that it was through constructing the relationship between hidden object and occluder that infants began to represent the hidden object. The difference, however, is that Bower claimed that very young infants possess object permanence, *before* they understand relationships between objects and occluders.

Seeking an explanation of the A not B error

Over the years, a great deal of research effort has gone into attempts to explain the A not B error. As indicated earlier, infants of about 9 months search successfully for an object hidden in one position (A) but when the object is hidden in a new position (B), they continue to search back in the old location (A).

Response perseveration?

Could the error simply arise because infants carry on with a response habit established during hiding trials at A? Maybe when the object is hidden in a new place, they do not attend fully and repeat the old response, a phenomenon referred to as **response perseveration**. If this were all there was to it, we would expect them to correct their error on subsequent trials, realising the need to attend more closely. However, although some infants correct themselves quickly, others will make a string of errors over many trials – persisting in searching at the 'A' location.

> **response perseveration**
> repeating a previously learned response usually when it is no longer appropriate.

Curiously, it turns out that infants make errors even if they have only *seen* the object hidden and revealed at the A location, and have not been given the opportunity to reach for it (Butterworth, 1974; Evans, 1973; Landers, 1971). Under these circumstances, they have executed no action to A, but on being allowed to search for the first time on B trials, they search at A! Thus, it does not seem that response perseveration can easily explain the error.

Memory limitations?

It has frequently been pointed out that absent minded adults often search for objects in customary places despite just having put them elsewhere. Adults do not have problems in representing hidden objects; in this case the problem is to do with memory of the past history of the object in question. Note, however, that these adult errors tend to occur when the individual is not fully attentive, and as Piaget pointed out, infants make these errors even when they *are* fully attentive. This, however, does not rule out a memory explanation, it being quite possible that infants have more profound memory limitations than adults. Harris (1973) showed that infants rarely made errors if they were allowed to search immediately for the hidden object at B, and this led him to suggest that the phenomenon was memory based. It was not a matter of simply forgetting about the object entirely, because infants search accurately at A, and continue to search there on B trials. Instead, Harris suggested that interference occurred between memory of the object at the first location and memory of it at the new location, such that information about its prior location often predominated over the more recent information about its new location.

There is a major problem for any memory account. Piaget (1936/1954) noted that errors occurred even when the object was fully in view at the B location. Additionally, Butterworth (1977) and Harris (1974) both obtained errors when the object was placed under a transparent cover at B. Some suggested that these errors arose partly due to infants' difficulty understanding transparent covers. However, Bremner and Knowles (1984) obtained errors even when the object was fully visible and uncovered at A. In this study, provided there was a covered location at A, infants made errors at much the usual rate even though the object was in full view and fully accessible at B. It is difficult to see in what way memory for the new location of the object can enter into this form of the task. These errors with the object in view indicate just what a powerful phenomenon we are dealing with. Although making the object visible under a cup helped younger infants to begin to search, making the object visible in the B location does not help them to search accurately after successful search at A.

Place A as a container One possibility is that through seeing an object hidden and finding it, infants quickly learn to treat place A as a container, and that it is this knowledge rather than knowledge about the specific object hidden that leads to search errors (Bremner, 1985). And if we consider infants' everyday experience it is quite possible that their ideas about containers are to some extent magical. For instance, they start each day with a full toy box and progressively empty it, and yet the next day it is full again. This account has certain advantages. For instance, errors with the object in view at place B are not surprising if the infant is exploring place A for further objects. Recently, Topál *et al.* (2008) suggest that infants misinterpret the investigator's communicative act in hiding the object at A, using it as a cue to treat place A as a container of objects. When hiding took place without overt communication between investigator and infant this effect was not obtained and errors were reduced on B trials.

Frontal cortex immaturity

frontal cortex one of the four main lobes of the *cerebral cortex*. It is involved in emotional experiences and many cognitive abilities, such as problem-solving, planning, and judgment.

executive functions the process whereby behaviour is directed and controlled in order that the desired goal will be achieved.

There is strong evidence that an area of the brain known as the **frontal cortex** (see Figure 5.15, frontal lobe) is involved in planning and guidance of action, processes that are often referred to as **executive functions**. Diamond (1985, 1988) claims that immaturity of frontal cortex in early infancy leads to deficits in infants' ability to use certain types of information to guide action. Specifically, she argues that infants are unable to use their memory of the absent object to inhibit an old response (search at A) that is now inappropriate.

This account is a combination of the memory and response perseveration accounts presented above. In this respect, it is a significant advance on previous models in recognising that it is probably a *combination* of factors that leads to error. However, the same problems that provide difficulty for single factor accounts apply here as well.

This model does not predict errors in searching at the 'B' location after simply observing the object being hidden at A, and yet such errors occur, in circumstances under which there is no prior response to inhibit. Similarly, this model does not predict errors when the object is visible at B, because there is no memory load in this case, and yet such errors occur.

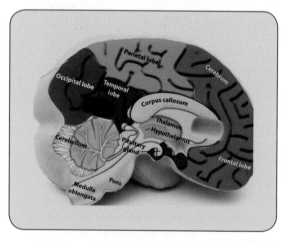

FIGURE 5.15 *Longitudinal section through a model human brain showing position of Frontal lobe (cortex).*
Source: Shutterstock.

Converting knowledge to action

The answer to our dilemma may be that we need to identify a more general role of frontal cortex in using high-level information to guide action. The evidence presented earlier in this chapter strongly suggests that quite young infants have knowledge of object permanence and the rules governing object movement. However, research using object search tasks shows that they are unable to use this information to guide action. Thus, when faced with the A not B task, infants are aware of the continued presence of the object, but are simply unable to use this information to guide action (Bremner, 2010; Willatts, 1997). Thus, initial success at finding the object at A is based on trial and error manipulation of the cover at which it disappeared rather than on knowledge of the existence of the object, and they repeat this action whenever and wherever the object disappears, and even if the object is placed in view at the B location. Development of frontal cortex involves formation of links between object knowledge and action, leading to accurate search based on knowledge of the object's position rather than trial and error.

There is some evidence in keeping with this interpretation. Ahmed and Ruffman (1998) showed that infants who made A not B errors nevertheless showed evidence in a non-search A not B task of knowing where the object was on both A and B trials. If, after seeing the object hidden and retrieved from A, infants saw it hidden at B, they looked longer if it was then retrieved from A than if it was retrieved from B. Thus, they appear to know where the object is wherever it is hidden, and are capable of holding that location in memory for quite some time. But they are unable to use that information to guide their manual search and may instead rely on social cues from adults (Topál *et al.* 2008).

SUMMARY AND CONCLUSIONS

Early knowledge

The evidence reviewed in the early parts of this chapter indicates that even at birth, infants are capable of discriminating patterns and shapes and perceiving an objective world. In addition, they have special perceptual abilities regarding human faces and voices, they learn to discriminate between people in the first few hours of life, and are capable of imitating facial gestures. These abilities appear to be limited to the 'here and now' of perception, and it is a few months before infants show the ability to fill in the gaps in perception, for instance by perceiving the invisible part of an object in object unity tasks (Figure 5.4), perceiving the continuity of an object's trajectory (Figure 5.5), or perceiving subjective contours (Figure 5.6). Additionally, evidence from ingenious *violation of expectation* studies reveals that around this time young infants show impressive awareness of the rules governing objects, including object permanence and the impenetrability of one object by another – they are budding physicists.

Early knowledge does not guide action

Set against this impressive array of early abilities, strong evidence remains indicating that, whatever form this early knowledge takes, it does not appear to guide action successfully. Even though they are capable of the necessary action, infants do not search for hidden objects until they are 8 or 9 months old, and even then they make characteristic search errors, in particular the A not B error. The best way at present of reconciling these conflicting bodies of evidence is to conclude that although young infants possess quite advanced knowledge of the world, either this knowledge is not sufficiently engrained to guide action or the necessary links between knowledge and action have not been developed.

Remodelling the Piagetian account

Recent evidence indicates that some aspects of Piaget's account of infancy require modification. Contrary to his view, it appears that young infants perceive an objective world and are at some level aware of object permanence and of the basic rules governing relationships between objects. Although the recent accounts identify further elaboration of knowledge throughout the first year of life, Piaget's view that the infant begins life without knowledge of the world now seems untenable. However, Piaget's evidence suggests a clear developmental sequence in infants' ability to act on the world. As we have seen, this is not simply a matter of motor development; 6-month-old infants are motorically capable of what is required to retrieve a hidden object and yet they do not search. Thus, it may be concluded that the Piagetian account remains relatively intact if we shift the emphasis in one major way. Instead of conceptualising infant development as primarily to do with constructing knowledge of the world, we should treat infants as possessing much of this knowledge from the start. But instead they are faced with the task of constructing links between this knowledge and action. It is here that the Piagetian concept of *construction through action on the world* is likely to remain very useful in reaching an understanding of development during the early months and years.

DISCUSSION POINTS

1. Considering the evidence, think of as many ways as you can in which newborns' perception of the world is (a) similar to and (b) different from that of adults.

2. Are you more convinced by claims about infants' knowledge of objects that are based on infants' manual action (for instance, object search) than claims based on longer looking at an event that violates a principle of reality?

3. Select a study using the violation of expectation technique and see if you can think of an alternative explanation of the results that does not assume high-level knowledge of the world on the part of the infant.

4. Think of what awareness of self and others infants must possess to explain their ability to imitate facial gestures.

5. Given evidence that foetuses can pick up sounds from their mother and the external environment, consider what sort of information infants might have already learned by the time they are born.

6. Consider Piaget's concept of constructing knowledge through action on the world. Is this concept still valid?

SUGGESTIONS FOR FURTHER READING

Bremner, J.G., & Wachs, T. (2010). *Wiley-Blackwell handbook of infant development* (2nd edn). Oxford: Wiley-Blackwell.

Slater, A., & Lewis, M. (2007). *Introduction to infant development* (2nd edn). Oxford: Oxford University Press.

Field, T. (2007). *The amazing infant*. Oxford: Blackwell.

Bremner, J.G. (1994). *Infancy* (2nd edn). Oxford: Blackwell.

Bremner, J.G., & Slater, A. (Eds.) (2004). *Theories of infant development*. Oxford: Blackwell.

REFERENCES

Ahmed, A., & Ruffman, T. (1998). Why do infants make A not B errors in a search task, yet show memory for the location of hidden objects in a nonsearch task? *Developmental Psychology, 34*, 441–453.

Anisfeld, M., Turkewitz, G., Rose, S.A., Rosenberg, F.R., Sheiber, F.J., Couturier-Fagan, D.A., *et al.* (2001). No compelling evidence that newborns imitate oral gestures. *Infancy, 2*, 111–122.

Baillargeon, R. (1986). Representing the existence and the location of hidden objects: Object permanence in 6- and 8-month-old infants, *Cognition, 23*, 21–41.

Baillargeon, R., & DeVos, J. (1991). Object permanence in young infants: Further evidence. *Child Development, 62*, 1227–1246.

Baillargeon, R., Spelke, E.S., & Wasserman, S. (1985). Object permanence in five-month-old infants. *Cognition, 20*, 191–208.

Berger, A., Tzur, G., & Posner, M. (2006). Infant brains detect arithmetic errors. *Proceedings of the National Academy of Sciences, 103*, 12649–12653.

Bertenthal, B.J., Campos, J.J., & Haith, M.M. (1980). Development of visual organization: The perception of subjective contours. *Child Development, 51*, 1075–1080.

Bower, T.G.R., & Wishart, J.G. (1972). The effects of motor skill on object permanence. *Cognition, 1*, 165–172.

Bremner, J.G. (1985). Object tracking and search in infancy: A review of data and a theoretical evaluation. *Developmental Review, 5*, 371–396.

Bremner, J.G. (2010). Cognitive development: Knowledge of the physical world. In J.G. Bremner & T. Wachs (Eds.) *Wiley-Blackwell handbook of infant development* (2nd edn; pp. 204–242). Oxford: Wiley-Blackwell.

Bremner, J.G., Johnson, S.P., Slater, A.M., Mason, U., Foster, K., Cheshire, A., *et al.* (2005). Conditions for young infants' perception of object trajectories. *Child Development, 74*, 1029–1043.

Bremner, J.G., & Knowles, L.S. (1984). Piagetian stage IV errors with an object that is directly accessible both visually and manually, *Perception, 13*, 307–314.

Bremner, J.G., Slater, A.M., Johnson, S.P., Mason, U., & Spring, J. (submitted). Illusory contours are perceived as occluding contours by 4-month-old infants. *Developmental Psychology*.

Bushnell, I.W.R. (2001). Mother's face recognition in newborn infants: Learning and memory. *Infant and Child Development, 10*, 67–74.

Bushnell, I.W.R., Sai, F., & Mullin, J.T. (1989). Neonatal recognition of the mother's face. *British Journal of Developmental Psychology, 7*, 3–15.

Butterworth, G. (1974). *The development of the object concept in human infants.* Unpublished D.Phil. thesis, University of Oxford.

Butterworth, G. (1977). Object disappearance and error in Piaget's stage IV task. *Journal of Experimental Child Psychology, 23,* 3891–401.

Carpenter, G.C. (1974). Mother's face and the newborn. *New Scientist, 61,* 742–744.

Cohen, L.B., & Younger, B.A. (1984). Infant perception of angular relations. *Infant Behavior & Development, 7,* 37–47.

Csibra, G. (2001). Illusory contour figures are perceived as occluding surfaces by 8-month-old infants. *Developmental Science, 4,* F7–F11.

DeCasper, A.J., & Fifer, W. (1980). Of human bonding: Newborns prefer their mothers' voices. *Science, 208,* 1174–1176.

DeCasper, A.J., & Spence, M.J. (1986). Prenatal maternal speech influences newborns' perception of speech sounds. *Infant Behavior & Development, 9,* 133–150.

Diamond, A. (1985). Development of the ability to use recall to guide action, as indicated by infants' performance on A not B. *Child Development, 56,* 868–883.

Diamond, A. (1988). Abilities and neural mechanisms underlying A performance. *Child Development, 59,* 523–527.

Eilers, R.E., Gavin, W.J., & Oller, D.K. (1982). Cross-linguistic perception in infancy: Early effects of linguistic experience. *Journal of Child Language, 9,* 289–302.

Eimas, P.D., Siqueland, E.R., Jusczyk, P.W., & Vigorito, J. (1971). Speech perception in infants. *Science, 171,* 303–306.

Evans, W.F. (1973). *The stage IV error in Piaget's theory of object concept development.* Unpublished dissertation, University of Houston.

Fantz, R.L. (1961). The origin of form perception. *Scientific American, 204,* 66–72.

Feigenson, L., Dehaene, S., & Spelke, E. (2004). Core systems of number. *Trends in Cognitive Sciences, 8,* 307–314.

Fernald, A. (1982). *Acoustic determinants of infant preference for 'motherese'* [doctoral dissertation, University of Oregon]. *Dissertation Abstracts International, 43,* 545B.

Field, T., Cohen, D., Garcia, R., & Greenberg, R. (1984). Mother–stranger face discrimination by the newborn. *Infant Behavior & Development, 7,* 19–26.

Ghim, H.R. (1990). Evidence for perceptual organization in infants: Perception of subjective contours by young infants. *Infant Behavior & Development, 13,* 221–248.

Goren, C., Sarty, M., & Wu, P. (1975). Visual following and pattern discrimination of face-like stimuli by newborn infants. *Pediatrics, 56,* 544–549.

Granrud, C.E., (2006). Size constancy in infants: 4-month-olds' responses to physical versus retinal size. *Journal of Experimental Psychology: Human Perception and Performance, 32,* 1398–1404.

Haith, M.M. (1998). Who put the cog in cognition? Is rich interpretation too costly? *Infant Behavior & Development, 21,* 167–179.

Harris, P.L. (1973). Perseverative errors in search by young infants. *Child Development, 44,* 28–33.

Harris, P.L. (1974). Perseverative search at a visibly empty place by young infants. *Journal of Experimental Child Psychology, 18,* 535–542.

Hepper, P.G. (1992). Fetal psychology: an embryonic science. In J.G. Nijhuis (Ed.), *Fetal behaviour: Developmental and perinatal aspects* (pp. 129–156). Oxford: Oxford University Press.

Hood, B., & Willatts, P. (1986). Reaching in the dark to an object's remembered position: Evidence for object permanence in five-month-old infants. *British Journal of Developmental Psychology, 4,* 57–65.

Johnson, S.P., Amso, D., & Slemmer, J.A. (2003). Development of object concepts in infancy: Evidence for early learning in an eye-tracking paradigm. *Proceedings of the National Academy of Sciences (USA), 100,* 10568–10573.

Johnson, S.P., & Aslin, R.N. (1995). Perception of object unity in 2-month-old infants. *Developmental Psychology, 31*, 739–745.

Johnson, S.P., Bremner, J.G., Slater, A.M., Mason, U.C., Foster, K., & Cheshire, A. (2003). Infants' perception of object trajectories. *Child Development, 74*, 94–108.

Kellman, P.J., & Spelke, E.R. (1983). Perception of partly occluded objects in infancy. *Cognitive Psychology, 15*, 483–524.

Kelly, D.J., Liu, S., Lee, K., Quinn, P.C., Pascalis, O., Slater, A.M., *et al.* (2009). Development of the other-race effect during infancy: Evidence toward universality? *Journal of Experimental Child Psychology, 104*, 105–114.

Kisilevsky, B.S., Muir, D.W., & Low, J.A. (1992). Maturation of human fetal responses to vibro-acoustic stimulation. *Child Development, 63*, 1497–1508.

Landers, W.F. (1971). The effect of differential experience on infants' performance in a Piagetian stage IV object concept task. *Developmental Psychology, 5*, 48–54.

Langlois, J.H., Ritter, J.M., Roggman, L.A., & Vaughn, L.S. (1991). Facial diversity and infant preferences for attractive faces. *Developmental Psychology, 27*, 79–84.

Mattock, K., & Burnham, D. (2006). Chinese and English infants' tone perception: Evidence for perceptual reorganisation. *Infancy, 3*, 241–265.

Maurer, D., & Barrera, M. (1981). Infants' perception of natural and distorted arrangements of a schematic face. *Child Development, 52*, 196–202.

Maurer, D., & Salapatek, P. (1976). Developmental changes in the scanning of faces by young infants. *Child Development, 47*, 523–527.

Meltzoff, A.N., & Moore, M.K. (1977). Imitation of facial and manual gestures by human neonates. *Science, 198*, 75–78.

Meltzoff, A.N., & Moore, M.K. (1983). Newborn infants imitate adult facial gestures. *Child Development, 54*, 702–709.

Moon, C., Bever, T.G., & Fifer, W.P. (1992). Canonical and non-canonical syllable discrimination by two-day-old infants. *Journal of Child Language, 19*, 1–17.

Moon, C., & Fifer, W.P. (1990). Syllables as signals for two-day-old infants. *Infant Behavior & Development, 13*, 377–390.

Pascalis, O., de Haan, M., & Nelson, C.A. (2002). Is face processing species-specific during the first year of life? *Science, 296*, 1321–1323.

Pegg, J.E., Werker, J.F., & McLeod, P.J. (1992). Preference for infant-directed over adult directed speech: Evidence from seven-week-old infants. *Infant Behavior & Development, 15*, 325–345.

Piaget, J. (1936/1954). *The construction of reality in the child* (trans M. Cook; originally published in French in 1936). New York: Basic Books.

Quinn, P.C., Uttley, L., Lee, K., Gibson, A., Smith, M., Slater, A., *et al.* (2008). Infants preference for female faces occurs for same- but not other-race faces. *British Journal of Neuropsychology, 2*, 15–26.

Slater, A.M., Bremner, J.G., Johnson, S.P., & Hayes, R.A. (2010). The role of perceptual processes in infant addition/subtraction experiments. In L.M. Oakes, C.H. Cashon, M. Cassaola, & D.H. Rakison (Eds.) *Early perceptual and cognitive development* (pp. 85–110). Oxford: Oxford University Press.

Slater, A., Johnson, S. P., Brown, E., & Badenoch, M. (1996). Newborn infants' perception of partly occluded objects. *Infant Behavior and Development, 19*, 145–148.

Slater, A., Mattock, A., & Brown, E. (1990). Size constancy at birth: Newborn infants' responses to retinal and real sizes. *Journal of Experimental Child Psychology, 49*, 314–322.

Slater, A., Mattock, A., Brown, E., & Bremner, J.G. (1991). Form perception at birth: Cohen and Younger (1984) revisited. *Journal of Experimental Child Psychology, 51*, 395–406.

Slater, A., & Morison, V. (1985). Shape constancy and slant perception at birth. *Perception, 14*, 337–344.

Slater, A., Morison, V., & Rose, D. (1983). Perception of shape by the newborn baby. *British Journal of Developmental Psychology, 1*, 135–142.

Slater, A., Morison, V., & Somers, M. (1988). Orientation discrimination and cortical function in the human newborn. *Perception, 17*, 597–602.

Slater, A., Quinn, P.C., Kelly, D.J., Lee, K., Longmore, C.A., McDonald, P., *et al.* (2010). The shaping of the face space in early infancy: Becoming a native face processor. *Child Development Perspectives, 4*(3), 205–211.

Slater, A., von der Schulenburg, C., Brown, E., Badenoch, M., Butterworth, G., Parsons, S., *et al.* (1998). Newborn infants prefer attractive faces. *Infant Behavior & Development, 21*, 345–354.

Spelke, E.S. (2007). Core knowledge. *Developmental Science, 10*, 89–96.

Spelke, E.S., Breinlinger, K., Macomber, J., & Jacobson, K. (1992). Origins of knowledge. *Psychological Review, 99*, 605–632.

Spelke, E.S., Kestenbaum, R., Simons, D.J., & Wein, D. (1995). Spatiotemporal continuity, smoothness of motion and object identity in infancy. *British Journal of Developmental Psychology, 13*, 113–142.

Starkey, P., & Cooper, R.G. (1980). Perception of number by human infants. *Science, 210*, 1033–1035.

Starkey, P., Spelke, E.S., & Gelman, R. (1990). Numerical abstraction by human infants. *Cognition, 36*, 97–128.

Topál, J., Gergely, G., Miklósi, A., Erdöhegzi, Á., & Csibra, G. (2008). Infants' perseverative search errors are induced by pragmatic misinterpretation. *Science, 321*, 1831–1833.

Trehub, S.E. (1976). The discrimination of foreign speech consonants by infants and adults. *Child Development, 47*, 46–472.

Van Hof-van Duin, J., & Mohn, G. (1986). The development of visual acuity in normal fullterm and preterm infants. *Vision Research, 26*, 909–916.

Wakeley, A., Rivera, S., & Langer, J. (2000). Can young infants add and subtract? *Child Development, 71*, 1525–1534.

Walton, G.E., Bower, N.J.A., & Bower, T.G.R. (1992). Recognition of familiar faces by newborns. *Infant Behavior & Development, 15*, 265–269.

Wilcox, B.M. (1969). Visual preferences of human infants for representations of the human face. *Journal of Experimental Child Psychology, 7*, 10–20.

Wilcox, T., & Baillargeon, R. (1998). Object individuation in infancy: The use of featural information in reasoning about occlusion events. *Cognitive Psychology, 37*, 97–155.

Willatts, P. (1997). Beyond the 'couch potato' infant: How infants use their knowledge to regulate action, solve problems, and achieve goals. In G. Bremner, A. Slater, & G. Butterworth (Eds.) *Infant development: Recent advances*. Hove: Psychology Press.

Wynn, K. (1992). Addition and subtraction by human infants. *Nature, 358*, 749–750.

Wynn, K. (1995). Origins of numerical knowledge. *Mathematical Cognition, 1*, 35–60.

Xu, F., & Spelke, E.S. (2000). Large number discrimination in 6-month-old infants. *Cognition, 74*, B1–Bll.

Yoshino, D., Idesawa, M., Kanazawa, S., & Yamaguchi, M.K. (2010). Infant perception of the rotating Kanizsa square. *Infant Behavior & Development, 33*, 196–208.

6 Emotional Development and Attachment Relationships

Elizabeth Meins

KEY TERMS

Adult Attachment Interview • affect • attunement • appearance–reality distinction • attachment behaviour • autonomous attachment • dismissing attachment • emotion • emotion regulation • emotional ambiguity • false belief • innate • innate mechanism • insecure-avoidant • insecure-resistant • maternal deprivation • meta-analysis • mind-mindedness • peers • preoccupied attachment • primary drives • psychopathology • script • secondary drive • securely attached • social referencing • strange situation procedure • stranger anxiety • unresolved attachment • visual cliff

CHAPTER OUTLINE

OVERVIEW

Feelings of emotions accompany all of our activities, and yet the topic of emotion is often neglected. Even from birth, infants display a wide range of emotional expressions, and it seems likely that emotional expression is innate. Most of the arguments about innateness concern simple emotions such as happiness, sadness, fear, and anger. However, it has been claimed that more complex emotions such as shyness and embarrassment can be detected in the first year of life.

There is also evidence that infants perceive facial expressions of emotions and that, even at birth, they show emotional resonance by expressing the same emotions in response. The ability to perceive the emotions of others makes it possible to learn a good deal about the world through seeing how adults respond to particular events. Known as *social referencing*, this allows infants to detect the emotional significance of a situation, such as the danger of a vertical drop. Emotional awareness is also seen in infant–parent interaction, with infants showing distress if parents stop responding as expected.

The emergence of language provides additional evidence regarding children's emotional world, because even very early utterances include emotion words such as 'happy' and 'scary'. It has been claimed that the rich use of emotion words indicates a well developed understanding of emotions early in development.

Research on emotional awareness in early school-age children includes work on children's ability to feel more than one emotion simultaneously. Presented with stories involving a conflict of emotions, 6-year-olds tend to deny the possibility of emotional conflict whereas 10-year-olds are much more likely to recognise that experience of two conflicting emotions is possible. During this period, children also show growing recognition that in certain situations another individual may feel a different emotion from them, and they become better able to identify the causes of others' emotions

The focus of the chapter then shifts to attachment relationships. Work in this area is rooted in Bowlby's theory that attachment is a primary drive to maintain proximity to the primary caregiver. The author reviews work stemming from Ainsworth's classification of attachment security, and the assessment of internal working models of attachment relationships.

Both attachment security and emotional development are likely to relate closely to parental sensitivity and parents' emotional characteristics, and there is fascinating evidence for inter-generational transfer of attachment patterns. The way in which parents represent their own childhood attachment experiences relates to the type of attachment their infant forms.

INTRODUCTION

In introductory texts on developmental psychology, a chapter on the development of the child's emotional engagement with and understanding of the world is commonly conspicuous by its absence. This oversight is curious, since emotional development would appear to underlie many other aspects of developmental psychology, and has serious implications for how we conduct research with children. For example, the results of a study on the development of a cognitive ability such as problem-solving will only be valid if we can be confident that children's performance was not influenced by shyness, anxiety or lack of interest or motivation. Consequently, it is important for all of us to be aware of the emotional context in which research is carried out, and the emotional maturity and engagement of each individual child.

FIGURE 6.1 *Early emotional attachment between infant and mother.*

Source: Shutterstock.

The aim of this chapter is to provide an introductory overview of emotional development and attachment relationships, and to consider research that has investigated links between these areas. The chapter reviews certain key theoretical positions and empirical findings, but since the individual literatures on emotional development and attachment are vast and complex, it is impossible to cover everything. Rather, the chapter begins with a broad review of the literature on emotional development from birth (Figure 6.1) to adolescence, and then focuses on how researchers have investigated one particular kind of emotion: the child's feelings of attachment toward the caregiver. The final section describes the relatively new area of research on relations between attachment and emotional development.

EMOTIONAL DEVELOPMENT

Children's emotional development can broadly be divided into three areas. First, research has investigated infants' and young children's ability to *recognise* different facial emotional expressions and to convey their own emotions. Second, various tasks have been designed to test children's *understanding* of emotions. When do children realise that certain situations are likely to elicit particular emotional responses? At what point do children recognise that our emotions lead us to behave in certain ways? Finally, researchers have addressed how children become able to *regulate* their emotions, shedding light on factors that may lead to individual differences in the extent to which children can control their feelings.

Are expressions of emotion innate?

Darwin (1872) argued that the ability to communicate emotions through a wide repertoire of facial expressions is **innate**. More recent researchers have attempted to investigate this claim in two ways: (a) by establishing whether different emotional facial expressions are universally understood; and (b) by observing whether newborn infants spontaneously produce recognisable facial expressions.

Cross-cultural evidence

There is good evidence for the universality of human facial expressions of emotion. For example, Ekman and Friesen (1971) found remarkable cross-cultural similarity in adults' interpretations of facial expressions. They tested a group of Fore people from New Guinea (who had never had contact with Westerners) on a task that required them to choose a photograph of the facial expression that matched the emotional context. The facial expressions in the photographs were posed by Western adults and children, and yet the Fore could easily select the correct photographs for happiness, anger, disgust, and sadness, although they found surprised and fearful expressions somewhat difficult to distinguish. Similarly, Americans were equally skilled in correctly judging the emotional facial expressions of the Fore (Ekman, 1973). Cross-cultural work such as this demonstrates that human understanding of how emotions are conveyed through facial expressions is universal, but, as Harris (1989) pointed out, this does not necessarily mean that understanding emotional expressions is innate, since it is possible that all cultures learn about facial expressions merely by copying those of others in specific emotional contexts.

Expression of emotion in infancy

More convincing evidence of the innate quality of emotional expression comes from the observation that infants from birth spontaneously display a wide repertoire of emotions through their facial expressions. Emotions are often divided into those that are **basic emotions** (happiness, interest, surprise, disgust, sadness, distress, anger, fear) and those that are **complex emotions** (pride, shyness, jealousy, guilt, shame, embarrassment).

emotion emotion ranges from simple emotions such as happiness, sadness, fear, and anger, to more complex emotions such as self-consciousness and jealousy.

Adults are skillful in accurately reading infants' expressions. For example, Izard *et al.* (1980) reported that adults could accurately judge whether the facial expressions of 1- to 9-month-old infants arose because of a pleasant experience, such as interacting with their mothers, or a painful or unpleasant event, such as being given an injection or a nasty tasking substance (see Figure 6.2). However, adults are less accurate in discriminating infants' negative facial expressions indicative of fear, anger, sadness or disgust (Oster et al., 1992). This appears not to be due to a lack of subtlety in young infants' expression, but to the fact that the facial expressions arising from these different emotions are quite similar. Figure 6.3 shows diagrammatic depictions of some emotions. Try to label each expression. How confident are you in your discrimination of the negative emotional expressions? To find out if you are correct see p. 209.

Fascinating research in support of the notion that there is a biological basis for infants' emotional facial expressions has been published more recently. Oster (2003) investigated whether adults are capable of accurately interpreting the emotional expressions of infants with craniofacial anomalies caused by conditions such as cleft palate. Oster found that adults were just as accurate at judging facial expressions of distress, interest, and happiness in the infants with craniofacial anomalies as in infants with no facial disfigurement. This suggests that multiple facial cues are used to signal emotion and that the ability to convey and accurately interpret emotional expressions is impressively robust.

FIGURE 6.2 *An infant's reaction after being given either a sweet solution or an unpleasant (but harmless) solution, guess which is which!*

Source: Slater, Field and Hernandez-Reif (2007), reprinted with permission.

Infants indisputably display basic emotions very early in life, but there is considerable debate about when complex emotions emerge. Many influential accounts (e.g. Dunn, 1994; Harris, 1989; Izard, 1994) assume that complex emotions are not evident until the second year of life, but others maintain that the behaviour of very young infants betrays feelings of more complex emotions (see Draghi-Lorenz *et al.*, 2001, and Lewis, 2007, for reviews). For example, Reddy and colleagues (Draghi-Lorenz *et al.*, 2005; Reddy, 2000) provided evidence that infants as young as 2 to 4 months of age display coyness, shyness, and embarrassment. However, the notion that complex emotions emerge so early in life remains controversial because such emotions appear to require quite sophisticated cognitive understanding, such as recognising that one's behaviour may have fallen short of expected standards. While it seems reasonable to conclude that basic emotions are innate and the consequences of evolutionary adaptation, it is more difficult to make such claims about these more complex emotions.

FIGURE 6.3 *Exaggeratedly drawn facial expressions of emotion.*

Infant discrimination of facial expressions

Even if one accepts that infants can demonstrate complex emotions, this ability tells us very little about whether they can discriminate emotions in other people, and therefore whether they have any fundamental *understanding* of emotions. In order to address this question, researchers have employed the *habituation–dishabituation* technique (see Chapter 5) to assess infants' discrimination of a variety of facial expressions. Barrera and Maurer (1981) reported that 3-month-olds could distinguish between photographs of people smiling and frowning, and Caron *et al.*

(1982) found that 4- to 7-month-olds could distinguish between expressions of happiness and surprise. Even more astounding is Field *et al.*'s (1982) finding that neonates could discriminate between happy, sad, and surprised expressions posed by a live model. However, although infants appear capable of quite impressive feats of sensory discrimination, this does not necessarily mean that they can understand that there is *meaning* in emotional facial expressions. In order to begin to make such a claim, one needs to analyse how infants respond to different facial expressions.

Can young infants empathise with others' emotions?

Some results from Field *et al.*'s (1982) study suggest that these very young infants may be empathising with the emotion they see being portrayed. In addition to investigating infants' responses to the emotional expressions, Field *et al.* had adult judges assess which emotional expression they thought the infant was viewing purely by watching the infant's response during the procedure. The adults could do this at levels above chance because the infants actually appeared to imitate the facial expression they were watching, and did not merely view the stimuli passively (see Figure 6.4). By 6 months, infants can respond to

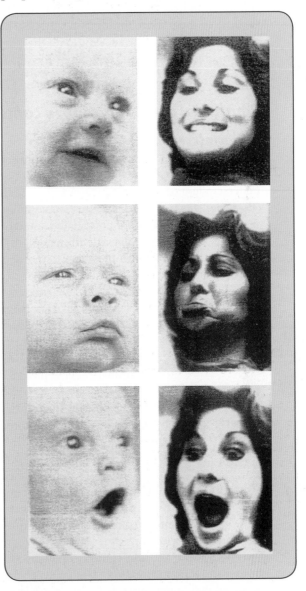

FIGURE 6.4 *Modelled and matching expressions of adult and neonate.*

Source: Field, T., Woodson, R., Greenberg, R., & Cohen, D. (1982). Discrimination and imitation of facial expressions by neonates. *Science, 218,* 179–181. Reprinted with permission from AAAS.

expressions in more sophisticated and appropriate ways, crying and frowning at angry and sad faces (Kreutzer & Charlesworth, 1973). But once again, there are problems with making strong claims that this research demonstrates an understanding of emotion in young infants. Infants' responses to these emotional expressions were measured in a non-emotional context, where changes in facial cues were unrelated to events, and their responses may have been mere imitation. The infant's response, therefore, still does not indicate an understanding that expressions relate to emotional feelings. Because of these shortcomings, one can only be confident that infants understand the relation between people's feelings and their facial expressions if a study manipulates the emotional context, and not merely the visual cues present in emotional expressions.

Emotional discrimination in context

Social referencing

The phenomenon of **social referencing**, whereby infants look to their caregiver to glean information on how they should act, provides an excellent way to assess infants' understanding of other people's emotional expressions. In a classic study, Sorce *et al.* (1985) investigated whether infants could utilise their caregivers' facial expressions to appraise a potentially dangerous situation. Using Gibson and Walk's (1960) '**visual cliff**' paradigm (see Figure 6.5), mothers coaxed their 12-month-olds close to the 'deep' side before posing a happy or fearful expression. Sorce *et al.* (1985) reported that none of the infants crossed over to the deep side if the mother posed a fearful expression; on the contrary, such facial expressions tended to result in infants retreating or showing distress. Conversely, when their mothers looked happy, three quarters of the infants crossed to the deep side.

social referencing infants and young children look to their caregiver for 'advice' when faced with a difficult or uncertain situation and seek social cues (such as smiling or frowning) to guide their actions.

visual cliff a piece of apparatus used to study depth perception in infants, consisting of a glass table with a checkerboard pattern immediately beneath the glass on one half (shallow side) and on the floor below on the other half (deep side).

Studies such as those above suggest that infants are not only able to discriminate between facial expressions, but can modify their own emotional response and behaviour in accordance with the emotion conveyed by the mother's facial expression. Indeed, some researchers credit infants with even more sophisticated understanding of facial expressions. Murray and Trevarthen (1985) investigated whether 2-month-old infants were sensitive to the appropriateness of the timing and patterning of their mothers' facial expressions. In this study, infants and mothers communicated via a video system, so that it was possible to assess how infants responded when face to face interactions with their mothers were put out of synchrony. Infants' responses to interactions in real time were compared with those when the mother's behaviour was made non-contingent by showing infants a replay of the mother's face from earlier in the session. Under such circumstances, Murray and Trevarthen reported that infants quickly began to disengage from the interaction, looking away, and in some cases showing distress. The authors argued that infants can identify when the 'rules' of interaction are violated, leading them to conclude that infants have *expectations* of what their mothers should do and which emotions they should show in response to their own behaviour. It should be noted, however, that these

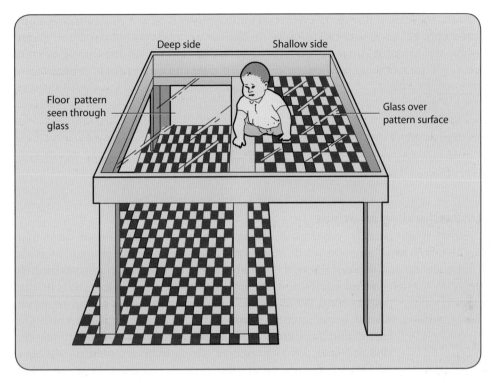

FIGURE 6.5 *Gibson and Walk's (1960) visual cliff apparatus.*

Source: Gibson, E.J. & Walk, R.D. (1960). The "visual cliff", *Scientific American*, 202: 80–92. Used by permission of *Scientific American*.

conclusions should be treated with a degree of caution, since other researchers (e.g. Rochat, Neisser, & Marian, 1998) have encountered problems in replicating Murray and Trevarthen's results.

Beyond infancy: Linguistic expression of emotion

As in all areas of developmental psychology, the onset of language enables one to pinpoint more precisely the exact level of emotional understanding a child has reached. Children begin to talk about emotions at a surprisingly young age, and parents readily give anecdotal accounts of their children using emotion words in the second year of life. Bretherton *et al.* (1981) reported on a search of published diaries and accounts of children's acquisition of emotion words that showed some children begin to use emotion words as young as 18 months of age, with a rapid increase in children's emotional vocabularies during the third year of life. In a follow-up study, Bretherton and Beeghly (1982) found that 28-month-olds could use emotion words to explain and comment on their own and other people's current behaviour:

'Bees everywhere. Scared me!'

'You sad, Daddy?'

The children in this study even used emotion words in a decontextualised fashion to predict an emotional response in the future, and showed that they understood the causal relation between behaviour and emotional response. Examples included the following predictions about their own and other people's future emotional responses:

'Daddy be mad? '

'Santa will be happy if I pee in the potty'

'No watch the Hulk. I afraid' [several hours before the television programme *The Incredible Hulk* was due to be shown].

Understanding emotions

Bretherton and Beeghly (1982) made strong claims on the basis of their data, arguing that the use of emotion words implies that children really understand emotions. Consequently, they opposed the view that early social understanding consists exclusively of **script** knowledge (whereby children do not understand the emotions involved, but know the 'script' for how to act in a given situation), which later becomes replaced by a true understanding of psychological functioning. Bretherton and Beeghly's account is persuasive, and the evidence does point to children having quite a sophisticated understanding of their own and other people's emotional lives well before they reach their third birthday. Clearly, though, everyday experience tells us that there are differences between the emotional responses of infants and young children and those of older children and adults. The question now is how such differences can be characterised. One way in which researchers have approached this question is to investigate children's understanding of **emotional ambiguity** – the realisation that a person's feelings may not be clear-cut or match your own emotional response. Another approach is to explore when children integrate their knowledge about emotions with that of other internal states such as thoughts and beliefs.

> **script** a generalised framework for commonly experienced events or situations, with a stored representation of what one would expect to happen in such situations.

> **emotional ambiguity** the realisation that a person's feelings may not be clear-cut or match your own emotional response.

Denham (1986) used a puppet task to investigate whether 2- and 3-year-old children are able to predict a person's emotional responses in a non-*egocentric* (first discussed by Piaget, see Chapters 2 and 9) manner. Mothers had provided information on their children's preferences (e.g. their child's favourite food) and responses to various events (e.g. if the child was happy or sad to go to nursery, or would be pleased or afraid to see their doctor). In the task, the puppet voiced the emotional reaction that was the *opposite* of how the child was reported to respond. For example, if the child was happy to go to nursery, the puppet would say in a sad voice: 'I hate it here. I miss my mummy.' The child was then asked to choose from an array of happy, sad, angry, and scared faces the facial expression that matched how the puppet was feeling. Denham reported that 2- and 3-year-olds were able to predict the puppet's response at levels above chance, although there was considerable variation in children's performance on the task.

There is even evidence that infants as young as 18 months can appreciate that another person might like something that they themselves dislike. In Repacholi and

Gopnik's (1997) study, infants watched an experimenter taste two kinds of food (raw broccoli and a popular brand of children's crackers). In one condition, the experimenter showed the opposite preference to that of the 18-month-olds (saying 'Mmm' while tasting the broccoli, and 'Eww!' while tasting the crackers). When the experimenter later asked the infant for some food, 18-month-olds were able to use her previous emotional reaction to give her the food to which she had previously shown a positive response. Thus, infants gave the experimenter broccoli even though they themselves preferred the crackers.

Differing emotional responses to the same event

Gnepp *et al.* (1987) also investigated whether children recognised that it was possible for different people to feel different emotions about the same situation. In contrast to Denham's (1986) procedure where the puppet's tone of voice provided the child with a clue to the correct emotional response, this task assessed 5- to 8-year-olds' spontaneous recognition that some events were emotionally unequivocal, whereas others would elicit different emotions in different people (see Table 6.1). The older children were found to be better at discriminating between equivocal and unequivocal situations, but the younger children rarely gave mixed positive/negative responses to the equivocal situations. By age 8, children had begun to realise that different children might react in different ways in the emotionally equivocal situations, such that one child might be terrified of dogs, while another child may love dogs. However, even the 8-year-olds only gave mixed responses to the equivocal situations about half of the time.

Cognition and emotion

Harris *et al.* (1989) investigated whether children could use their knowledge about a person's preferences and beliefs to predict their emotional reaction to a situation.

Table 6.1 *The emotional situations used in Gnepp et al.'s (1987) Study*

Equivocal situations
Child gets an egg sandwich for lunch
A butterfly lands on the child's arm
Mum tells child to brush teeth
Child is approached by a small dog while playing
Child gets tomatoes with dinner
Mum asks child to do a job for her
A cat sits down next to child on front porch
Parents ask child to sing a song for their friends

Unequivocal situations
All the lights go off when child is playing alone
Child drops and breaks favourite toy
Parents give child a new toy
Child runs a race and loses
Parents let child stay up late to watch TV
Best friend comes over and asks child to play

In this study, children learnt about a toy animal's preference for a particular food or drink. A mischievous toy animal then played a trick by replacing the favoured food or drink with the one that was disliked. For example, the animal might love milk and hate Coca Cola®, but is unaware that the milk in the carton had been replaced with Coca Cola. Crucially, the containers were opaque so that their true contents could not be seen. The child was then asked to predict how the animal would feel (a) when they first saw the container, and (b) when they opened it to discover its actual contents. If children can use their knowledge about the animal's belief state to predict how it will feel, they should report that the animal will be happy when it first sees the milk carton (since it loves milk and does not know the carton actually contains the hated Coca Cola), but sad when the true contents are discovered.

false belief incorrectly believing something to be the case when it is not. Often used in *theory of mind* research.

Harris *et al.* (1989) reported that 4-year-olds typically performed badly on this **false belief** and emotion task when predicting the animal's initial emotional response. Despite the fact that children of this age are able to represent false beliefs (see Chapter 11 on children's theory of mind abilities), they could not use this capacity to predict the likely emotional response, and thus appeared unable to integrate their understanding of beliefs and emotions. However, by age 6, children performed well, and were also able to justify their response with reference to how the animal's belief state would determine their initial emotional response. This lag between understanding false belief and integrating this understanding in order to make appropriate emotional attributions has been replicated in a number of studies, using a range of different emotions (Bradmetz & Schneider, 1999; de Rosnay *et al.*, 2004; Hadwin & Perner, 1991).

Emotional conflicts

Harris (1983) investigated whether 6- and 10-year-olds understood that it was possible to feel more than one emotion simultaneously. Children were told stories, each involving an emotional conflict, whereby the protagonist would be likely to feel two emotions at the same time. For example, one story was as follows:

> Late one night there is a bark outside the door. It's Lassie your dog. She has been lost all day and she has come home, but she has cut her ear in a fight.

After each story, children were asked whether they would feel any of four emotions: happiness, fear, anger, sadness. For example, the above story was meant to elicit a mixture of happiness that Lassie has come back, tinged with sadness about her injury. The other stories detailed happy/angry conflicts (e.g. opening a present, but having it snatched away by a sibling) and happy/afraid conflicts (e.g. seeing a monster on TV after being allowed to stay up late). Harris found an age-related shift in children's ability to acknowledge the emotional conflict in the stories. Moreover, the design of the study allowed Harris to rule out a number of obvious explanations, unrelated to emotional understanding, for this shift. First, the poor performance of the 6-year-olds could not be explained in terms of their memory for the stories' events. Second, when the two events in the stories were presented separately so that there was no emotional conflict, there were no age-related differences in children's ability to predict the correct emotional response, showing that the results on the conflict stories were not due to the younger children's ignorance of which emotion is elicited by each separate component of the story. Rather, the age-related shift appeared to arise because the 6-year-olds were more likely to believe that emotional conflicts were impossible. This conclusion is borne out by their responses when they were explicitly asked whether one could feel happy and sad at the same time. Of the 6-year-olds, 79 per cent asserted that this was not possible, compared with 33 per cent of the 10-year-olds. The children's justifications for such a belief show that they typically maintained that emotional conflicts were logically impossible ('Because they're the opposite of each other; it's either good or it's bad') or behaviourally impossible ('Because you can't make your face go down and up'). One should note, however, that a substantial minority (a third) of 10-year-olds still denied that it was possible to feel two emotions simultaneously, showing that age cannot fully explain the observed increase in children's understanding of emotional conflicts. We should note that this is one variation on the **appearance–reality distinction** that is also discussed in Chapter 9.

> **appearance–reality distinction** an awareness that things are not always what they appear to be.

Summary

In summary, it seems that although children quickly become skilled at reading people's emotions from their facial expressions and at talking about emotions, their understanding of the rich complexities of human emotion continues to develop throughout the primary school years. Indeed, one could argue that the ability to sympathise and empathise develops throughout the lifespan, leading to considerable individual differences in adults' emotional understanding.

Hiding your true feelings

Anyone with experience of looking after young children will know that they are very bad at hiding their true feelings (Figure 6.6). Witness the child who broadcasts to the whole bus how ugly the woman opposite is, or tells Daddy how disgusting lunch is, or who fails to hide the fact that the birthday present really doesn't live up to expectations! It is therefore somewhat surprising to learn that children as young as 3 years show some ability to control their expression of mild negative emotions in a test situation (Cole, 1986), and by age 6, children are able to understand the difference between real and apparent emotions. For example, Harris *et al.*

FIGURE 6.6 *Young children can be very bad at hiding their true feelings.*
Source: Shutterstock.

(1986) compared the performance of 4-, 6-, and 10-year-olds in predicting how a story character would look and how the character would really feel in a situation where it was appropriate to hide one's emotion (e.g. hiding the fact that you feel ill because you want to go to a party).

Harris *et al.* (1986) found that all of the age groups were capable of recognising that one can mask one's true feeling by posing a conflicting facial expression, although there was an age-related increase in how well children could justify and explain the distinction between real and apparent emotions. One should, however, bear in mind that the younger children's poorer performance when asked to justify their responses might be related to their comparatively less sophisticated understanding and use of language. Nevertheless, this study suggests that preschool children are capable of making quite sophisticated judgements on whether a person's facial expression is always an accurate portrayal of their true feelings.

One reason why children may understand that true emotions can be hidden or attenuated at a relatively young age is that hiding one's emotions is often explicitly dealt with in children's general socialisation. For example, in the scenarios given at the beginning of this section, it is highly likely that the reaction of adults or older children will help young children to learn that it is not always socially permissible or desirable to voice one's true negative feelings about a person's ugliness, standard of cuisine, or choice of gift. Indeed, there is evidence that, as early as the second year of life, children have begun to regulate their displays of emotion by, for example, tightly compressing their lips to control their feelings of anger (e.g. Malatesta *et al.*, 1989). One could argue that children's ability to control their feelings will be encouraged, particularly for socially undesirable emotions, and there is evidence to support this position. For example, Morency and Krauss (1982) found that children are less able to deceive someone of their pleasant feelings compared with their unpleasant feelings. Interestingly, by as young as 5 years of age, children have even learnt that generally positive emotions, such as pride in one's achievements, can be seen to be socially undesirable showing off or gloating (*hubris*), and will therefore attempt to hide how proud they feel (Reissland & Harris, 1991).

Emotion in the family

Given that children tend to express their emotions most freely in the home environment, and the intuition that parents' ability to read and deal with their children's emotions is central to emotional development, it is surprising that so little systematic investigation of children's understanding of intra-familial emotions has been conducted. There are, however, some notable exceptions. Dunn and colleagues have investigated how families discuss emotion and whether differences in the emotional content of such discussion relate to children's understanding of emotion. Dunn, Brown, and Beardsall (1991) reported marked differences in the frequency with which both 3-year-olds and their mothers talked about emotions, with some families never mentioning emotions during the observational period. Moreover, this tendency to discuss people's feelings and the causes of such emotions was related to children's subsequent understanding of the emotional states of story characters (Dunn, Brown, Slomkowski, *et al.*, 1991) and emotional conflicts (Brown & Dunn, 1996). More recently, de Rosnay *et al.* (2004) reported that mothers' tendency to describe their children with reference to mental characteristics (rather than their physical appearance or behavioural tendencies) was related to children's performance on the false belief and emotion task (described in the 'Cognition and Emotion' section above). Children were more likely to understand the relation between false belief and emotion if their mothers focused on their mental characteristics when describing them.

While the data in these studies are *correlational*, and cannot therefore be used as proof of early discussion of emotion improving children's later understanding of emotion, they highlight clear

FIGURE 6.7 *Children who demonstrate happy emotional responses during play show better emotional understanding.*
Source: Shutterstock.

consistencies in children's tendency to engage with human emotions. In more recent work, Dunn and colleagues (e.g. Hughes, Dunn, & White, 1998) reported that children who are rated as being 'hard to manage' and who demonstrate behaviour problems showed poorer emotional understanding than control group children. Denham (1986) also reported links between young children's understanding of emotions as assessed on a task and their naturalistic behaviour during play. For example, superior task performance was related to more prosocial behaviour (e.g. helping, sharing, comforting) with their **peers** during play. Moreover, children who demonstrated predominantly happy emotional responses during play (Figure 6.7) showed better emotion understanding on the task, whereas negative emotional behaviours (anger, hurt) were associated with poorer emotion understanding. This suggests that emotional understanding may be related to children's ability to form harmonious close relationships with others.

> **peer** companion of approximately the same age and developmental level.

Understanding the causes of people's feelings

Other research on emotion in the family has focused on children's understanding of the *causes* of people's feelings. Harter (1982, 1983) reported that 83 per cent of 4- to 11-year-olds cited themselves as the cause of parental anger, with 65 per cent believing themselves to induce parental happiness, 49 per cent parental sadness, and 41 per cent parental fear. Citing themselves as the cause of their parents' emotions was more common in younger children, a finding that was replicated by Covell and Abramovitch (1987). This later study also extended Harter's findings by questioning 5- to 15-year-olds about the causes of their own emotions, as well as those of their mothers. Covell and Abramovitch found that the youngest group of children (aged 5 and 6 years) were more likely to reference *only* themselves as the cause of their mothers' anger and happiness. Across all ages, children were likely causally to attribute their own anger, rather than their happiness or sadness, to their families.

Clearly, these results have important implications for real life and how parents interact with their children on a day-to-day basis. In particular, the fact that young children appear to take sole responsibility for whether their mothers are happy or angry gives some cause for concern, especially if families are undergoing stress, for example during parental conflict or divorce. Some naturalistic studies have shown that children's distress in response to angry exchanges is more marked if they come from families where there has been serious family conflict (Cummings *et al.*, 1981, 1984). Unsurprisingly, overt parental conflict appears to be particularly detrimental, and is related to emotional and behavioural problems in the child (Jenkins & Smith, 1991). Experience of severe parental conflict may also exacerbate children's feelings of responsibility for their mother's emotional well-being. For example, Cummings, Pellegrini, and Notarius (1989) reported that children whose parents had a history of physical violence would actually intervene in a staged quarrel between their mother and another individual. Even though the children in this study were only between 2 and 5 years old, they attempted to defend or comfort their mothers. These findings on the deleterious effects of parental conflict on children's emotional development, coupled with the ever-rising divorce rate, highlight the need for further investigations into why young children feel such a burden of emotional responsibility, and whether such misattributions of the causes of parental emotions may be one reason why periods of intense family emotion have a negative impact on children's understanding of emotion.

This research involving more extreme emotional situations highlights the question of how commonplace individual differences in children's social environment influence their emotional development. For example, there is considerable variation in emotional sophistication between children of the same age, with some showing precocious skill in reading and analysing emotions while others are somewhat slower in grasping the fundamentals of emotional understanding. Similarly, some children will be more emotionally resilient than others. Why do such individual differences arise? One possible explanation is that individual differences in emotional development may relate to the type of attachment relationship the child forms to the primary caregiver (usually the mother) in infancy. Infant–caregiver attachment is the focus of the second part of this chapter.

ATTACHMENT RELATIONSHIPS

Bowlby's theory of attachment

Attachment as an innate drive

The infant's expression of emotion and the caregiver's response to these emotions lies at the heart of John Bowlby's theory of attachment. Bowlby's (1958, 1969/1982, 1973, 1980) theory was influenced by an eclectic range of disciplines, including Freudian psychoanalysis, ethology, and the biological sciences. Before Bowlby, the predominant view of infant–mother attachment was that it was a '**secondary drive**' or by-product of the infant associating the mother with providing for physiological needs, such as hunger (Figure 6.8). In contrast, Bowlby argued that attachment was an innate **primary drive** in the infant. Although the theory underwent several revisions over a period of many years, this argument remained fundamental. Thus, in the original theory (Bowlby, 1958), the focus was on how instinctual behaviours such as crying, clinging, and smiling served to elicit a reciprocal attachment response from the caregiver:

> There matures in the early months of life of the human infant a complex and nicely balanced equipment of instinctual responses, the function of which is to ensure that he obtains parental care sufficient for his survival. To this end the equipment includes responses which promote his close proximity to a parent and … evoke parental activity.
>
> *(Bowlby, 1958, p. 346)*

In contrast, in the 1969 version of his theory (the first volume of his trilogy *Attachment and Loss*), Bowlby sought to highlight the dynamics of attachment behaviour, with a move toward explaining the infant–mother tie in terms of a *goal-corrected system* which was triggered by environmental cues rather than innate instinctual behaviours. But regardless of whether attachment behaviour is instinctual or goal-corrected, it results in the infant maintaining proximity to the caregiver.

Bowlby recognised that the establishment of an attachment relationship was not dependent purely upon the social and emotional interplay between infant and caregiver. Since attachment behaviour is seen primarily when the infant is separated from the caregiver, it is clearly dependent upon the infant's level of cognitive development in terms of being able to represent an object that is not physically present (*object permanence* – see Chapter 5). Bowlby based his argument on Piaget's (1955) contention that this level of object permanence is not acquired until the infant is approximately 8 months of age (although see Chapter 5 for alternative accounts). Consequently, while infants are capable of recognising familiar people before this age, they will not miss the attachment figure, and thus demonstrate attachment behaviour,

FIGURE 6.8 *Early theories of infant–mother attachment suggested that it was a secondary drive resulting from the mother satisfying the infant's primary drives, such as hunger.*

Source: Shutterstock.

until they have reached the level of cognitive sophistication that allows them to represent absent objects and people.

The phases of attachment

stranger anxiety unhappiness felt by many infants when they encounter an unfamiliar person. Stranger anxiety begins to emerge at around 7 months of age.

Bowlby therefore proposed that attachments develop in phases. Initially, infants are in the pre-attachment phase (0–2 months) and typically show little differentiation in their social responses to familiar and unfamiliar people. During the second phase (2–7 months), the foundations of attachment are being laid, with infants beginning to recognise their caregivers, although they do not yet show attachment behaviours upon separation. Clear-cut attachments are seen after 7 months, when infants protest at being separated from their caregivers and become wary of strangers (so-called **stranger anxiety**). The final phase of attachment (from around 2 years) is reached when the attachment relationship has evolved into a goal-corrected partnership between infant and caregiver. This phase is marked by the child's increased independence and recognition of the caregiver's needs and motives that sometimes make separation necessary. From this phase onwards, the child relies on representations or internal working models of attachment relationships to guide their future social interactions.

Adult Attachment Interview a semi-structured interview in which adults are asked to describe their childhood relationships with mother and father, and to recall times when they were separated from their parents or felt upset or rejected.

Early infant–caregiver attachment relationships and internal working models are the aspects of Bowlby's theory that have received greatest attention, with researchers developing two of the most widely used instruments in developmental psychology to investigate Bowlby's theoretical claims: the **strange situation procedure** to assess the goal-corrected system, and the **Adult Attachment Interview** to assess internal working models.

Mary Ainsworth and the strange situation procedure

Bowlby's theory was concerned mainly with the making and breaking of attachment ties, probably because his experiences of working as a child psychiatrist exposed him to the negative consequences for emotional development of severe **maternal deprivation**, such as long-term separation or being orphaned. Nowadays, however, researchers are generally less concerned with *whether* a child has formed an attachment, since a child who experiences any degree of continuity of care will become attached to the person who provides that care. Research interest now focuses on the quality or *security* of the attachment relationship. This shift in emphasis was due to the pioneering empirical work of Mary Ainsworth.

maternal deprivation a term to describe the deprivation infants experience as a result of long-term separation from their mother, or from being orphaned.

Ainsworth became interested in Bowlby's ideas on attachment after working with him in London during the 1950s. When she later went to live with the Ganda people in Uganda, she set about making systematic observations of infant–mother interactions in order to investigate Bowlby's goal-corrected attachment systems in operation. What was striking about these observations (Ainsworth, 1963, 1967) was the lack of uniformity in infants' attachment behaviour, in terms of its frequency, strength, and degree of organisation. Moreover, such differences were not specific to Gandan infants, since she replicated these findings in a sample of American children when she moved to Baltimore. Such variation in attachment behaviour was not accounted for in Bowlby's theory, and this led Ainsworth to investigate the question of individual differences in attachment.

The richness of the data she had collected over a period of many years, and her experience of working with Bowlby, put Ainsworth in a unique position to develop attachment as an empirical field of research. Ainsworth's contribution meant that attachment issues became part of mainstream developmental psychology, rather than being confined to child psychiatry. She achieved this by investigating the development of attachments under normal family circumstances and by developing a quick and effective way of assessing attachment patterns in the developmental laboratory. Although this *strange situation procedure* (Ainsworth & Wittig, 1969) circumvented the need for researchers to conduct lengthy observations in the home, it was not developed purely for research convenience, but because there are problems in trying to evaluate attachment behaviour in the home environment. For example, if a child becomes extremely distressed upon the mother going into another room in their own home environment, this may indicate a *less* than optimal attachment, since if a child feels secure, such a separation should not result in severe distress. Ainsworth's extensive experience of observing infant–mother interactions enabled her to identify the situations that were most crucial in attachment terms, and therefore formed the basis of the strange situation procedure. (See Marvin's interview with Ainsworth (Ainsworth & Marvin, 1995) for a fascinating insight into how the strange situation evolved.)

securely attached descriptive of children who find comfort and consolation in the presence of a parent or caregiver, and who seek comfort from that person after a separation or other aversive event.

Different attachment types

The strange situation is typically conducted when the infant is between 1 and 2 years of age and assesses infants' responses to separations from, and subsequent reunions with, their mothers, and their reactions to an unfamiliar woman (the so-called 'stranger'). In the testing room, there are two chairs (one for the mother and one for the stranger) and a range of toys with which the infant can play. As Table 6.2 shows, the episodes are ordered so that the infant's attention should shift from exploration of the environment to attachment behaviour toward the caregiver as the strange situation proceeds. Infants' responses during the two reunion episodes are most crucial, and form the basis for assessing an infant's security of attachment. The coding scheme for attachment security was developed by Ainsworth *et al.* (1978) and describes infant behaviour according to four indices: proximity-seeking, contact-maintenance, resistance, and avoidance. Ainsworth *et al.*'s (1978) original coding scheme identified three major categories of attachment: **securely attached** infants (Type B); **insecure-avoidant** (Type A); and **insecure-resistant** (Type C).

insecure-avoidant in the strange situation measure, used to describe infants who appear indifferent toward their caregiver, and treat the stranger and caregiver in very similar ways.

insecure-resistant in the strange situation measure, used to describe infants who are over-involved with the caregiver, showing attachment behaviour even during the pre-separation episodes, with little exploration or interest in the environment.

Table 6.2 *The strange situation procedure*

1.	Mother and baby introduced into room
2.	Mother and baby alone, baby free to explore (3 minutes)
3.	Female stranger enters, sits down, talks to mother and then tries to engage the baby in play (3 minutes)
4.	Mother leaves. Stranger and baby alone (up to 3 minutes*)
5.	First reunion. Mother returns and stranger leaves unobtrusively. Mother settles baby if necessary, and tries to withdraw to her chair (3 minutes)
6.	Mother leaves. Baby alone (up to 3 minutes*)
7.	Stranger returns and tries to settle baby if necessary, and then withdraws to her chair (up to 3 minutes*)
8.	Second reunion. Mother returns and stranger leaves unobtrusively. Mother settles baby if necessary, and tries to withdraw to her chair (3 minutes)

*If the mother feels that her child is becoming overly upset, these episodes may be terminated before the full 3 minutes has elapsed.

Secure attachments If one sees the dynamics of the attachment relationship as a balance between exploratory behaviour directed toward the environment and attachment behaviour directed toward the caregiver (see Figure 6.9), securely attached infants have got the balance right. The caregiver's presence in the pre-separation episodes affords them the security to turn their attention to exploration and play, confident in the knowledge that the caregiver will be available for comfort or support should it be needed. However, the separation episodes trigger securely attached infants' attachment behaviour, leading them to seek comfort, contact, proximity or interaction with the caregiver when they return. *Securely attached* infants may or may not become distressed by being separated from their caregivers, making infants' response to separation a relatively poor indicator of attachment security. But regardless of their response to separation, securely attached children are marked by their positive and quick response to the caregiver's return, shown by their readiness to greet, approach, and interact with the caregiver.

Insecure attachments In contrast, the two patterns of insecure attachment have the balance of infant attachment tipped to either extreme. *Insecure-avoidant* infants show high levels of environment-directed behaviour to the detriment of attachment behaviour, whereas *insecure-resistant* infants are overly preoccupied with the caregiver to the detriment of exploration and play. Consequently, insecure-avoidant infants show little if any proximity-seeking, and even tend to avoid the caregiver, by averting gaze or turning or moving away, if the caregiver takes the initiative in making contact. Throughout the whole strange situation, insecure-avoidant infants appear indifferent

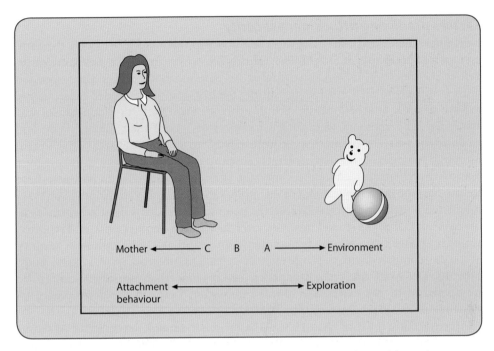

FIGURE 6.9 *Attachment as a balance of behaviour directed toward mother and the environment.*
Source: Adapted from Meins (1997), with permission.

toward the caregiver, and treat the stranger and caregiver in very similar ways; indeed, these infants may show less avoidance of the stranger than of the caregiver. Conversely, *insecure-resistant* infants are over-involved with the caregiver, showing attachment behaviour even during the pre-separation episodes, with little exploration or interest in the environment. These infants tend to become extremely distressed upon separation, but the over-activation of their attachment system hampers their ability to be comforted by the caregiver upon reunion. This leads to angry or petulant behaviour, with the infant resisting contact with and comfort from the caregiver, which in extreme cases manifests itself as tantrum behaviour where the caregiver may be hit or kicked.

Insecure-disorganised infants (Type D) In addition to Ainsworth *et al.*'s (1978) original categories, Main and Solomon (1986, 1990) established a fourth category, Type D, for infants whose behaviour appeared not to match that of any of the A, B or C categories. These *insecure-disorganised* infants seem disoriented during the strange situation procedure, and show no clear strategy for coping with separations from and reunions with their caregivers. The insecure-disorganised infant may simultaneously demonstrate contradictory behaviours during the reunion episodes, such as proximity-seeking coupled with obvious avoidance (e.g. backing towards the caregiver or approaching with head sharply averted). These infants may also respond to reunion with fearful, stereotypical or odd behaviours, such as rocking themselves, ear-pulling or freezing. Main and Hesse (1990) argued that, although the classification criteria for disorganisation are diverse, the characteristic disorganised behaviours all share a lack of coherence in the infant's response to attachment distress and betray the 'contradiction or inhibition of action as it is being undertaken' (p. 173).

Factors predicting attachment security

Individual differences in the caregiver's sensitivity to the infant's cues were the earliest reported predictors of attachment security. Ainsworth and colleagues (Ainsworth, Bell, & Stayton, 1971, 1974; Ainsworth *et al.*, 1978) found that mothers who responded most sensitively to their infants' cues during the first year of life tended subsequently to have securely attached infants. The insecure-avoidant pattern of attachment was associated with mothers who tended to reject or ignore their infants' cues, and inconsistent patterns of mothering were related to insecure-resistant attachment. Although subsequent research has largely supported this link between early caregiver sensitivity and later attachment security, the strength of the relation between these factors has not been replicated. For example, De Wolff and van IJzendoorn (1997) conducted a **meta-analysis** to explore the parental antecedents of attachment security using data from 21 studies involving over 1000 infant–mother pairs, and reported a moderate effect size for the relation between sensitivity and attachment security ($r = 0.24$), compared with the large effect ($r = 0.85$) in Ainsworth *et al.*'s (1978) study. This led De Wolff and van IJzendoorn to conclude that 'sensitivity cannot be considered to be the exclusive and most important factor in the development of attachment' (p. 585).

More recently, my own research team has begun to rethink the construct of sensitivity, returning to Ainsworth *et al.*'s (1971, 1974) original definitions in order to gain a better understanding of predictors of attachment security. In this research, we were particularly influenced by Ainsworth's focus on the caregiver's ability not merely to respond to the infant, but to respond in a way that was consistent with the infant's cue. For example, Ainsworth *et al.* (1971) described how mothers of securely attached infants appeared 'capable of perceiving things from [the child's] point of view' (p. 43), whereas maternal *insensitivity* involved the mother attempting to 'socialize with the baby when he is hungry, play with him when he is tired, and feed him when he is trying to initiate social interaction' (Ainsworth *et al.*, 1974, p. 129). Meins *et al.* (2001) thus argued that the critical aspect of sensitivity was the caregiver's ability to 'read' the infant's signals accurately so that the response could be matched to the specific cue from the child. In order to test this proposal, Meins *et al.* (2001) obtained measures of mothers' ability to read their 6-month-olds' signals appropriately (so-called **mind-mindedness**), and investigated the comparative strength of mind-mindedness versus general maternal sensitivity in predicting subsequent infant–mother attachment security. Meins *et al.* reported that maternal mind-mindedness was a better predictor of attachment security 6 months later than was maternal sensitivity, with mind-mindedness accounting for almost twice the variance in attachment security than that accounted for by sensitivity.

mind-mindedness
caregivers who are able to 'read' their infant's signals appropriately. Maternal mind-mindedness is a good predictor of attachment security.

The origins of disorganised attachment

An increasing amount of research attention is being paid to the origins of disorganised attachment, perhaps due to the fact that early disorganisation has been identified as a risk factor for later **psychopathology** (Fearon *et al.*, 2010; van IJzendoorn *et al.*, 1999), with studies identifying a link between disorganised attachment in infancy and (a) behaviour problems in later childhood (Lyons-Ruth *et al.*, 1993; Munson *et al.*, 2001; Shaw *et al.*, 1996); and (b) dissociative disorders in early adulthood (Carlson, 1998; Lyons-Ruth, 2003; Ogawa *et al.*, 1997).

> **psychopathology** a psychological imbalance such that the individual has difficulties in functioning in the real world.

In their seminal work on disorganisation, Main and Hesse (1990; Hesse & Main, 2000) argued that these infants have been unable to establish an organised pattern of attachment because they have been frightened by the caregivers or have experienced their caregivers themselves showing fearful behaviour. This is supported by findings that have linked insecure-disorganised attachment to infant maltreatment or hostile caregiving (Carlson, Cicchetti, Barnett, & Braunwald, 1989; Lyons-Ruth *et al.*, 1991), maternal depression (Radke-Yarrow *et al.*, 1995), and maternal histories of loss through separation, divorce, and death (Lyons-Ruth *et al.*, 1991). However, in their meta-analytic review, van IJzendoorn *et al.* (1999) reported that 15 per cent of infants in non-clinical middle class American samples are classified as insecure-disorganised, suggesting that pathological parenting practices cannot fully account for disorganised attachment in the infant. As highlighted by Bernier and Meins (2008), the origins of attachment disorganisation are highly complex, involving factors ranging from infants' genetic make-up to parents' experiences of loss or abuse, and much remains to be learned about why some infants are unable to form an organised attachment relationship with the caregiver.

Another factor that has well-replicated predictive links to the infant–caregiver attachment relationship, both at the level of security/insecurity and organisation/disorganisation, is the caregiver's representations or internal working models of their own attachment experiences as assessed using the Adult Attachment Interview.

Internal working models and the adult attachment interview

Attachment theory proposes that children use their early experiences with their caregivers to form internal working models (Bowlby, 1969/1982, 1980) which incorporate representations of themselves, their caregivers, and their relationships with others. The child will then use these internal working models as templates for interacting with others. Consequently, because of the sensitive, loving support that securely attached children's caregivers have supplied, these children are self-confident and have a model of themselves as being worthy; they therefore expect others to behave in a sensitive and supportive fashion. Conversely, given the patterns of interaction typically experienced by avoidant and resistant infants, insecurely attached children expect people to be rejecting, or inconsistent and ambivalent when interacting with them.

Attachment categories in adults

Individuals' representations of their early childhood experiences with attachment figures are assessed using the Adult Attachment Interview (AAI: George *et al.*, 1996),

autonomous attachment adults who give a coherent, well-balanced account of their attachment experiences, showing a clear valuing of close personal relationships.

dismissing attachment adults who deny the importance of attachment experiences and insist they cannot recall childhood events and emotions, or provide idealised representations of their attachment relationships that they are unable to corroborate with real life events.

preoccupied attachment adults who are unable to move on from their childhood experiences, and are still over-involved with issues relating to their early attachment relationships.

unresolved attachment adults who have not been able to resolve feelings relating to the death of a loved one or to abuse that they may have suffered.

a semi-structured interview in which adults are asked to describe their childhood relationships with mother and father, and to recall times when they were separated from their parents or felt upset or rejected. Specific questions also deal with experiences of loss and abuse. According to their responses during the AAI, adults are placed into one of four attachment categories: *autonomous, dismissing, preoccupied, unresolved*. Adults' attachment classifications are based not upon the nature of their actual childhood experiences, but on the way they represent these experiences, be they good or bad. **Autonomous** adults are able to give coherent, well-balanced accounts of their attachment experiences, showing a clear valuing of close personal relationships. These adults may have experienced problems in childhood, or even had very difficult or abusive upbringings, but they can talk openly about negative experiences and seem to have managed to resolve any early difficulties and conflicts. In contrast to the open and balanced way in which autonomous adults talk about childhood experiences, adults in the remaining three categories have difficulties in talking about attachment relationships. **Dismissing** adults deny the importance of attachment experiences and insist they cannot recall childhood events and emotions, or provide idealised representations of their attachment relationships that they are unable to corroborate with real life events. Conversely, **preoccupied** adults are unable to move on from their childhood experiences, and are still over-involved with issues relating to their early attachment relationships. The final **unresolved** category is reserved for adults who have not been able to resolve feelings relating to the death of a loved one or to abuse they may have suffered.

Relationship between AAI classifications and infant–parent attachments

These AAI classifications have been found to relate systematically to the security of the infant–parent attachment relationship. Autonomous parents are more likely to have securely attached infants, and parents in the three non-autonomous groups (dismissing, preoccupied and unresolved) are more likely to form insecure attachment relationships with their infants. This relation has been identified both for patterns of infant–mother (e.g. Fonagy *et al.*, 1991; Levine *et al.*, 1991) and infant–father (Steele *et al.*, 1996) attachment. In addition, unresolved maternal AAI classification has been identified as a predictor of insecure-disorganised attachment (Main & Hesse, 1990; van IJzendoorn, 1995). Thus, the way in which a parent represents their own childhood attachment experiences is related to the types of relationship formed with their own children.

Links between attachment and emotional development

The infant's earliest mode of engaging with the world centres on conveying emotions: fear, discomfort, pain, contentment, happiness. Given that caregivers' responses to such emotional cues and their representations of their own childhood emotional experiences are known to be such strong predictors of infant attachment security, it is surprising that so little research has been conducted on the relation between security and children's emotional development. There are two main ways in which links between attachment and emotional development have been addressed. First, research has investigated whether infants' early emotional experiences predict attachment security. Second, researchers have explored whether the security of the infant–caregiver attachment relationship predicts children's subsequent emotional development.

Emotion regulation and attachment security

Research in this area has focused mainly on how caregivers' responses to infants' emotional cues predict later attachment security. Mothers of *insecure-avoidant* infants have been found to withdraw when their infants express negative emotions (Escher-Graeub & Grossmann, 1983). Conversely, mothers of *insecure-resistant* infants typically find it difficult to comfort their infants effectively, meaning that their responses result in prolonging their infants' feelings of distress (Ainsworth *et al.*, 1978). Cassidy (1994) proposed that caregivers may enable their children to develop good emotional coping and *regulation* strategies by virtue of their willingness to acknowledge and respond to their children's emotions. She argued that secure attachment is marked by the openness with which the caregiver recognises and discusses the full spectrum of emotions, which in

> **emotional regulation**
> adjusting one's emotional state to a suitable level of intensity. This prevents emotional 'overload' and allows one to function in a consistent manner.

turn teaches the child that emotions do not need to be suppressed and can be dealt with effectively. Insecure-avoidant attachment is associated with caregivers failing to respond to their infants' negative emotions because of their tendency to bias interactions in favour of positive emotional expressions. In contrast, insecure-resistant attachment is associated with the caregiver heightening the infant's negative affect. Cassidy maintained that mothers of insecure-resistant children need to emphasise the importance of the attachment relationship, and therefore adopt strategies that fail to help the child efficiently regulate negative emotion, thus prolonging the need for contact with the caregiver.

Affect attunement

Cassidy's views are consistent with other theoretical positions, such as Stern's (1985) characterisation of sensitive parenting in terms of **affect attunement**. Stern described the sensitive mother as someone who is attuned to all of her infant's emotions, accepting and sharing in their affective content. Insensitive mothers undermatch or overmatch their infants' emotional signals because of their own perceptual biases.

> **affect attunement**
> characteristic of the sensitive mother who is attuned to all of her infant's emotions, accepting and sharing in their affective content.

In support of these approaches, Pauli-Pott and Mertesacker (2009) reported that mismatches between maternal and infant affect at 4 months (e.g. mother shows positive affect while her infant demonstrates neutral or negative affect) predicted insecure infant–mother attachment at 18 months. Similarly, mind-mindedness is operationalised in terms of the caregiver's tendency accurately to interpret the infant's cognitions and emotions, and has been found to predict later attachment security (Meins *et al.*, 2001). Thus, comments such as a mother stating that her infant is surprised if startled in response to a jack-in-the-box, or is happy when she smiles, are associated with subsequent secure attachment. In contrast, insecure attachment is related to mothers misreading their infants' internal states by, for example, commenting that the infant is scared when there is no cue to such an emotion in the infant's overt behaviour. In recent work (Meins *et al.*, 2009), we have found that these inappropriate mind-related comments are particularly common in mothers of insecure-resistant infants, with mothers in this group being more likely to comment inappropriately on their infants' thoughts and feelings than their counterparts in the secure, insecure-avoidant, and insecure-disorganised groups.

Interestingly, evidence suggests that mothers in the insecure-avoidant and insecure-resistant groups are aware of over-controlling and under-controlling strategies in coping with their children's negative emotions. Berlin and Cassidy (2003) followed up a sample of infants who had been assessed in the strange situation in infancy, questioning the mothers when the children were aged 3 about how they dealt with their child's emotional expressiveness. Berlin and Cassidy found that insecure-avoidant group mothers reported the greatest control of their 3-year-olds' negative emotional expressiveness (e.g. expressing anger or fear), whereas mothers in the insecure-resistant group reported the least control of their children's expressing negative emotions. These findings suggest that the maternal behaviours associated with avoidant and resistant attachment that have been observed in infancy are stable and persist into the preschool years.

Security-related differences in the way in which children regulate their emotions are also in line with Cassidy's (1994) approach. Spangler and Grossmann (1993) took physiological measures of infant distress during the strange situation procedure and compared these with infants' outward shows of upset and negative affect. The physiological measures showed that insecure-avoidant group infants were as distressed or more distressed than their secure group counterparts, despite the absence of *overt* behavioural distress observed in insecure-avoidant group infants. Spangler and Grossmann therefore concluded that insecure-avoidant infants mask or dampen their expression of negative emotions as a means of coping with the fact that caregivers are likely to reject their bids for contact and comfort when they are distressed.

Belsky, Spritz, and Crnic (1996) reported that 3-year-olds who had been securely attached in infancy were more likely to remember the positive emotional events that they had witnessed in a puppet show, whereas insecurely attached children tended to remember the negative events. Similarly, Kirsch and Cassidy (1997) found that both secure and insecure-resistant attachment in infancy were associated at age 3 with better recall for a story in which a mother responded sensitively to her child than to one in which she rejected her child. In contrast, insecure-avoidant infants showed no difference in their recall of the responsive versus rejecting stories. Kirsch and Cassidy also reported that 3-year-olds classified as insecure in infancy were more likely than those in the secure group to look away from drawings depicting mother–child engagement. These findings suggest that the positive experiences of secure infants with their caregivers may result in these children attending more to positive emotional events because they are consistent with their attachment history.

Summary

In summary, theoretical and empirical research suggests that caregivers' responses to their infants' emotional cues, particularly their tendency to interpret the infant's emotions accurately and to recognise the infant's negative emotions, are related to attachment security. Specifically, accurate interpretation and open communication about negative emotions by caregivers predict a secure infant–caregiver attachment relationship. However, much less is known about how the security of the attachment relationship in infancy predicts children's later emotional development. Questions focusing on the inter-relations between attachment experiences, individual differences in caregiver characteristics and family interaction, and children's emotional development thus represent a rich area of untapped research. A priority for the future should be to address such questions to provide a clearer picture of how children acquire and develop their understanding of the building blocks of human emotional experience, and how parents and adults may help or hinder this process.

> Figure 6.3, p. 188: The expressions are [from left to right and top to bottom]: fear; anger; surprise; sadness; disgust; happiness; neutral.

SUMMARY AND CONCLUSIONS

Emotional competence in infancy

- Emotional facial expressions are understood cross-culturally, and neonates spontaneously produce recognisable facial expressions. These findings suggest that communicating emotions through facial expressions is innate.
- There is evidence that infants can discriminate between different facial expressions from birth.
- During the first year of life, infants begin to use other people's emotional responses to appraise how to act.

Later emotional competence

- Children begin to talk about emotions during the second year of life, and by 28 months their linguistic expression of emotions is quite sophisticated.
- In comparison with their linguistic emotional expression, children's understanding of more complex emotional events does not develop until much later, with some 10-year-olds still having problems in acknowledging the existence of emotional conflicts.
- Differences in family interaction (e.g. parental conflict) impact negatively on children's understanding of emotion.

Attachment theory

- Bowlby's attachment theory proposed that all infants have an innate drive to form an attachment to the caregiver.
- Ainsworth highlighted different patterns of attachment, and introduced the concept of *security* of attachment, assessed using the 'strange situation' procedure.
- Main and Solomon introduced a fourth attachment category (insecure-disorganised) that has been linked to parental psychopathology and poor psychological outcomes in the child.
- Differences in caregivers' mind-mindedness and sensitivity have been found to predict infant–caregiver attachment security.
- Children use their early experiences with their caregivers to form internal working models of their attachment relationships, which are utilised as templates for interacting with others throughout life.
- Parents' internal working models of attachment relationships are assessed using the adult attachment interview, and there is considerable evidence for inter-generational transfer of attachment patterns.

Attachment and emotional development

- Security of attachment relates to children's emotional regulation, but few studies have been conducted on the links between early attachment patterns and later emotional development.

DISCUSSION POINTS

1. What evidence would you need to be convinced that expressions of emotion are innate? Are there some emotions that cannot be innate?
2. We know that newborns mirror the emotional expressions of adults. How could we tell whether this is evidence for emotional understanding or simply imitation of the facial expression without any understanding?
3. Consider the different forms of evidence presented here for emotional awareness, and assess which are the stronger forms and which the weaker?
4. What abilities must children have to be able to identify that someone else's emotional reaction to a situation differs from theirs?
5. Bowlby argued that attachment behaviour was aimed at maintaining proximity between infant and caretaker. Think of the different ways in which infants could achieve proximity and how these are liable to change with age.
6. Do you think that the evidence on cultural differences in predominant attachment type weakens the argument that secure attachment is important?
7. Consider the evidence indicating that attachment patterns are transmitted from one generation to the next. Does this seem plausible and, if so, are there ways in which the cycle might be broken?

SUGGESTIONS FOR FURTHER READING

Bretherton, I. (1992). The origins of attachment theory: John Bowlby and Mary Ainsworth. *Developmental Psychology, 28,* 759–775.

Bowlby, J. (1969/1982). *Attachment and loss, vol. 1: Attachment* (2nd edn). London: Hogarth Press.

Cassidy, J., & Shaver, P.R. (Eds.) (2008). *Handbook of attachment: Theory, research, and clinical applications* (2nd edn). New York: Guildford Press.

Ekman, P., & Davidson, R.J. (Eds.) (1994). *The nature of emotion: Fundamental questions.* Oxford: Oxford University Press.

Fox, N. (Ed.) (1994). *The development of emotion regulation: Biological and behavioral constraints* (pp. 228–250). Monographs of the Society for Research in Child Development, 59 (2–3, Serial No. 240).

Harris, P.L. (1989). *Children and emotion.* Oxford: Blackwell.

Meins, E. (1997). *Security of attachment and the social development of cognition.* Hove: Psychology Press.

Solomon, J., & George, C. (1999). *Attachment disorganization.* New York: The Guilford Press.

REFERENCES

Ainsworth, M.D.S. (1963). The development of infant–mother interaction among the Ganda. In B.M. Foss (Ed.) *Determinants of infant behaviour* (Vol. 2). London: Methuen; New York: Wiley.

Ainsworth, M.D.S. (1967). *Infancy in Uganda: Infant care and the growth of love.* Baltimore, MD: Johns Hopkins University Press.

Ainsworth, M.D.S., Bell, S.M., & Stayton, D.J. (1971). Individual differences in Strange Situation behavior of one year olds. In H.R. Schaffer (Ed.) *The origins of human social relations.* New York: Academic Press.

Ainsworth, M.D.S., Bell, S.M., & Stayton, D.J. (1974). Infant–mother attachment and social development: Socialisation as a product of reciprocal responsiveness to signals. In M.P. M. Richards (Ed.) *The introduction of the child into a social world.* London: Cambridge University Press.

Ainsworth, M.D.S., Blehar, M.C., Waters, E., & Wall, S. (1978). *Patterns of attachment: Assessed in the strange situation and at home.* Hillsdale, N.J.: Lawrence Erlbaum.

Ainsworth, M.D.S., & Marvin, R.S. (1995). On the shaping of attachment theory and research: An interview with Mary D.S. Ainsworth (Fall 1994). In *Caregiving, cultural, and cognitive perspectives on secure-base behavior and working models: New growing points in attachment theory and research* (pp. 3–21). Monographs of the Society for Research in Child Development, 60 (2–3, Serial No. 244).

Ainsworth, M.D.S., & Wittig, B.A. (1969). Attachment and exploratory behavior of one year olds in a strange situation. In B.M. Foss (Ed.) *Determinants of infant behaviour, vol. 4.* New York: Barnes and Noble.

Barrera, M.E., & Maurer, D. (1981). The perception of facial expressions by the three-month-olds. *Child Development, 52,* 714–716.

Berlin, L.J., & Cassidy, J. (2003). Mothers' self-reported control of their preschool children's emotional expressiveness: A longitudinal study of associations with infant–mother attachment and children's emotion regulation. *Social Development, 12,* 477–495.

Bernier, A., & Meins, E. (2008). A threshold approach to understanding the origins of attachment disorganization. *Developmental Psychology, 44,* 969–982.

Belsky, J., Spritz, B., & Crnic, K. (1996). Infant attachment security and affective-cognitive informa-tion processing at age 3. *Psychological Science*, *7*, 111–114.

Bowlby, J. (1958). The nature of the child's tie to his mother. *International Journal of Psycho-Analysis*, *41*, 251–269.

Bowlby, J. (1969/1982). *Attachment and loss, vol. 1: Attachment* (2nd edn. New York: Basic Books.

Bowlby, J. (1973). *Attachment and loss, vol. 2: Separation*. New York: Basic Books.

Bowlby, J. (1980). *Attachment and loss, vol. 3: Loss: Sadness and depression*. New York: Basic Books.

Bradmetz, J., & Schneider, R. (1999). Is Little Red Riding Hood afraid of her grandmother? Cognitive vs. emotional response to a false belief. *British Journal of Developmental Psychology*, *17*, 501–514.

Bretherton, I., & Beeghly, M. (1982). Talking about internal states: The acquisition of an explicit theory of mind. *Developmental Psychology*, *18*, 906–921.

Bretherton, I., McNew, S., & Beeghly-Smith, M. (1981). Early person knowledge as expressed in gestural and verbal communication: When do infants acquire a 'theory of mind'? In M.E. Lamb & L.R. Sherrod (Eds.) *Infant social cognition*. Hillsdale, NJ: Erlbaum.

Brown, J.R., & Dunn, J. (1996). Continuities in emotion understanding from three to six years. *Child Development*, *67*, 789–802.

Carlson, E.A. (1998). A prospective longitudinal study of attachment disorganization/ disorientation. *Child Development*, *69*, 1107–1128.

Carlson, V., Cicchetti, D., Barnett, D., & Braunwald, K. (1989). Disorganized/disoriented attach-ment relationships in maltreated infants. *Developmental Psychology*, *25*, 525–531.

Caron, A.J., Caron, R.F., & Myers, R.S. (1982). Abstraction of invariant face expressions in infancy. *Child Development*, *53*, 1008–1015.

Cassidy, J. (1994). Emotion regulation: Influences of attachment relationships. In N. Fox (Ed.) *The development of emotion regulation: Biological and behavioral constraints* (pp. 228–250). Monographs of the Society for Research in Child Development, 59 (2–3, Serial No. 240).

Cole, P.M. (1986). Children's spontaneous control of facial expression. *Child Development*, *63*, 314–324.

Covell, K., & Abramovitch, R. (1987). Understanding emotion in the family: Children's and parents' attributions of happiness, sadness, and anger. *Child Development*, *58*, 985–991.

Cummings, E.M., Pellegrini, D.S., & Notarius, C.I. (1989). Children's responses to angry adult behavior as a function of marital distress and history of intraparent hostility. *Child Development*, *60*, 1035–1043.

Cummings, E.M., Zahn-Waxler, C., & Radke-Yarrow, M. (1981). Young children's response to expressions of anger and affection by others in the family. *Child Development*, *52*, 1275–1282.

Cummings, E.M., Zahn-Waxler, C., & Radke-Yarrow, M. (1984). Developmental changes in chil-dren's reactions to anger in the home. *Journal of Child Psychology and Psychiatry*, *25*, 63–74.

Darwin, C. (1872). *The expression of emotions in man and animals*. London: John Murray.

Denham, S.A. (1986). Social cognition, prosocial behavior, and emotion in preschoolers: Contextual validation. *Child Development*, *57*, 194–201.

de Rosnay, M., Pons, F., Harris, P.L., & Morrell, J.M.B. (2004). A lag between understanding false belief and emotion attribution in young children: Relationships with linguistic ability and mothers' mental-state language. *British Journal of Developmental Psychology*, *22*, 197–218.

De Wolff, M.S., & van IJzendoorn, M.H. (1997). Sensitivity and attachment: A meta-analysis on parental antecedents of infant attachment. *Child Development*, *68*, 571–591.

Draghi-Lorenz, R., Reddy, V., & Costall, A. (2001). Rethinking the development of 'nonbasic' emo-tions: A critical review of existing theories. *Developmental Review*, *21*, 263–304.

Draghi-Lorenz, R. Reddy, V., & Morris, P. (2005). Young infants can be perceived as shy, coy, bashful, embarrassed. *Infant and Child Development*, *14*, 63–83.

Dunn, J. (1994). Experience and understanding of emotions, relationships, and membership of a particular culture. In P. Ekman & R.J. Davidson (Eds.) *The nature of emotion: Fundamental questions* (pp. 352–355). Oxford: Oxford University Press.

Dunn, J., Brown, J., & Beardsall, L. (1991). Family talk about feeling states and children's later understanding of others' emotions. *Developmental Psychology, 27*, 448–455.

Dunn, J., Brown, J., Slomkowski, C., Tesla, C., & Youngblade, L. (1991). Young children's understanding of other people's feelings and beliefs: Individual differences and their antecedents. *Child Development, 62*, 1352–1366.

Ekman, P. (1973). Cross-cultural studies of facial expression. In P. Ekman (Ed.) *Darwin and facial expression*. New York: Academic Press.

Ekman, P., & Friesen, W. (1971). Constants across culture in the face and emotion. *Journal of Personality and Social Psychology, 17*, 124–129.

Escher-Graeub, D., & Grossmann, K.E. (1983). *Attachment security in the second year of life: The Regensburg cross-sectional study* [research report]. Regensburg: University of Regensburg.

Fearon, R.P., Bakermans-Kranenburg, M.J., & van IJzendoorn, M.J. (2010). The significance of insecure attachment and disorganization in the development of children's externalizing behavior: A meta-analytic study. *Child Development, 81*, 435–456.

Field, T., Woodson, R., Greenberg, R., & Cohen, D. (1982). Discrimination and imitation of facial expressions by neonates. *Science, 218*, 179–181.

Fonagy, P., Steele, H., & Steele, M. (1991). Maternal representations of attachment during pregnancy predict organization of infant-mother attachment at one year of age. *Child Development, 62*, 891–905.

George, C., Kaplan, N., & Main, M. (1996). *Adult attachment interview protocol* (3rd edn) Unpublished manuscript, University of California, Berkeley.

Gibson, E.J., & Walk, R.D. (1960). The 'visual cliff'. *Scientific American, 202*, 80–92.

Gnepp, J., McKee, E., & Domanic, J.A. (1987). Children's use of situational information to infer emotion: Understanding emotionally equivocal situations. *Developmental Psychology, 23*, 114–123.

Hadwin, J., & Perner, J. (1991). Pleased and surprised: Children's cognitive theory of emotion. *British Journal of Developmental Psychology, 9*, 215–234.

Harris, P.L. (1983). Children's understanding of the link between situation and emotion. *Journal of Experimental Child Psychology, 36*, 490–509.

Harris, P.L. (1989). *Children and emotion*. Oxford: Blackwell.

Harris, P.L., Donnelly, K., Guz, G.R., & Pitt-Watson, R. (1986). Children's understanding of the distinction between real and apparent emotion. *Child Development, 57*, 895–909.

Harris, P.L., Johnson, C.N., Hutton, D., Andrews, G., & Cooke, T. (1989). Young children's theory-of-mind and emotion. *Cognition and Emotion, 3*, 379–400.

Harter, S. (1982). A cognitive-developmental approach to children's understanding of affect and trait labels. In F.C. Serafica (Ed.) *Social-cognitive development in context* (pp. 27–61). New York: Guilford.

Harter, S. (1983). Children's understanding of multiple emotions: A cognitive-developmental approach. In W.F. Overton (Ed.) *The relationship between social and cognitive development* (pp. 147–194). Hillsdale, NJ: Erlbaum.

Hesse, E., & Main, M. (2000). Disorganized infant, child, and adult attachment: Collapse in behavioural and attentional strategies. *Journal of the American Psychoanalytic Association, 48*, 1017–1127.

Hughes, C., Dunn, J., & White, A. (1998). Trick or treat? Uneven understanding of mind and emotion and executive dysfunction in 'hard-to-manage' preschoolers. *Journal of Child Psychology and Psychiatry, 39*, 981–994.

Izard, C.E. (1994). Intersystem connections. In P. Ekman, & R.J. Davidson (Eds.) *The nature of emotion: Fundamental questions* (pp. 356–361). Oxford: Oxford University Press.

Izard, C.E., Huebner, R.R., Risser, D., McGinnes, G.C., & Dougherty, L.M. (1980). The young infant's ability to produce discrete emotional expressions. *Developmental Psychology, 16*, 132–40.

Jenkins, J.M., & Smith, M.A. (1991). Marital disharmony and children's behaviour problems: Aspects of a poor marriage that affect children adversely. *Journal of Child Psychology and Psychiatry, 32*, 793–810.

Kirsch, S.J., & Cassidy, J. (1997). Preschoolers' attention to and memory for attachment-relevant information. *Child Development, 68*, 1143–1153.

Kreutzer, M.A., & Charlesworth, W.R. (1973, March). *Infants' reactions to different expressions of emotion.* Paper presented at the meeting of the Society for Research in Child Development, Philadelphia.

Levine, L.V., Tuber, S.B., Slade, H., & Ward, M.J. (1991). Mothers' mental representations and their relationship to mother–infant attachment. *Bulletin of the Menninger Clinic, 55*, 454–469.

Lewis, M. (2007). Early emotional development. In A. Slater & M. Lewis (Eds.) *Introduction to infant development,* pp. 216–232. Oxford: Oxford University Press.

Lyons-Ruth, K. (2003). Dissociation and the parent–infant dialogue: A longitudinal perspective from attachment research. *Journal of the American Psychoanalytic Association, 51*, 883–911.

Lyons-Ruth, K., Alpern, L., & Repacholi, B. (1993). Disorganized infant attachment classification and maternal psychosocial problems as predictors of hostile-aggressive behaviour in the preschool classroom. *Child Development, 64*, 527–585.

Lyons-Ruth, K., Repacholi, B., McLeod, S., & Silva, E. (1991). Disorganized attachment behavior in infancy: Short-term stability, maternal and infant correlates and risk-related subtypes. *Development and Psychopathology, 3*, 377–396.

Main, M., & Hesse, E. (1990). Parents' unresolved traumatic experiences are related to infant disorganized attachment status: Is frightened and/or frightening parental behaviour the linking mechanism? In M.T. Greenberg, D. Cicchetti, & E.M. Cummings (Eds.) *Attachment in the preschool years* (pp. 161–182). Chicago: University of Chicago Press.

Main, M., & Solomon, J. (1986). Discovery of a disorganized/disoriented attachment pattern. In T.B. Brazelton & M.W. Yogman (Eds.) *Affective development in infancy.* Norwood, NJ: Ablex.

Main, M., & Solomon, J. (1990). Procedures for identifying infants as disorganized/disoriented during the Ainsworth Strange Situation. In M.T. Greenberg, D. Cicchetti, & E.M. Cummings (Eds.) *Attachment in the preschool years* (pp. 121–160). Chicago: University of Chicago Press.

Malatesta, C.Z., Culver, C., Tesman, J.R., & Shepard, B. (1989). *The development of emotion expression during the first two years of life.* Monographs of the Society for Research in Child Development, 54(1–2), no. 219.

Meins, E., Arnott, B., de Rosnay, M., Fernyhough, C., Leekam, S.R., Vittorini, L., et al. (2009). Mind-mindedness predicts four-way attachment security and mothers' accuracy in describing infants' responses to emotionally challenging situations. Manuscript submitted for publication.

Meins, E., Fernyhough, C., Fradley, E., & Tuckey, M. (2001). Rethinking maternal sensitivity: Mothers' comments on infants' mental processes predict security of attachment at 12 months. *Journal of Child Psychology and Psychiatry, 42*, 637–648.

Morency, N.L., & Krauss, R.M. (1982). Children's nonverbal encoding and decoding of affect. In R.S. Feldman (Ed.) *Development of nonverbal behavior in children.* New York: Springer-Verlag.

Munson, J.A., McMahon, R.J., & Spieker, S.J. (2001). Structure and variability in the developmental trajectory of children's externalizing problems: Impact of infant attachment, maternal depressive symptomatology, and child sex. *Development and Psychopathology, 13*, 277–296.

Murray, L., & Trevarthen, C.B. (1985). Emotional regulation of interactions between 2-month-olds and their mothers. In T.M. Field & N.A. Fox (Eds.) *Social perception in infants*. New Jersey: Ablex.

Ogawa, J.R., Sroufe, L.A., Weinfield, N.S., Carlson, E.A., & Egeland, B. (1997). Development and the fragmented self: Longitudinal study of dissociative symptomatology in a nonclinical sample. *Development and Psychopathology, 9*, 855–879.

Oster, H. (2003). Emotion in the infant's face – Insights from the study of infants with facial anomalies. In P. Ekman, J.J. Campos, R.J. Davidson, & F.B.M. DeWaal (Eds.) *Emotions inside out – 130 years after Darwin's The expression of the emotions in man and animals*. New York: New York Academic Sciences.

Oster, H., Hegley, D., & Nagel, L. (1992). Adult judgments and fine-grained analysis of infant facial expressions: Testing the validity of a priori coding formulas. *Developmental Psychology, 28*, 1115–1131.

Pauli-Pott, U., & Mertesacker, B. (2009). Affect expression in mother–infant interaction and subsequent attachment development. *Infant Behavior and Development, 32*, 208–215.

Piaget, J. (1955). *The child's construction of reality*. London: Routledge and Kegan Paul.

Radke-Yarrow, M., McCann, K., DeMulder, E., Belmont, B., Martinez, P., & Richardson, D.T. (1995). Attachment in the context of high-risk conditions. *Development and Psychopathology, 7*, 247–265.

Reddy, V. (2000). Coyness in early infancy. *Developmental Science, 3*, 186–192.

Reissland, N., & Harris, P.L. (1991). Children's use of display rules in pride-eliciting situations. *British Journal of Developmental Psychology, 9*, 431–435.

Repacholi, B.M., & Gopnik, A. (1997). Early reasoning about desires: Evidence from 14- and 18-month-olds. *Developmental Psychology, 33*, 12–21.

Rochat, P., Neisser, U., & Marian, V. (1998). Are young infants sensitive to interpersonal contingency? *Infant Behavior and Development, 21*, 355–366.

Shaw, D.S., Owens, E.B., Vondra, J.I., & Keenan, K. (1996). Early risk factors and pathways in the development of early disruptive behavior problems. *Development and Psychopathology, 8*, 679–699.

Slater, A., Field, T., & Hernandez-Reif, M. (2007). The development of the senses. In A. Slater & M. Lewis (Eds.) *Introduction to infant development*, pp. 81–99. Oxford: Oxford University Press.

Sorce, J., Emde, R., Campos, J., & Klinnert, M. (1985). Maternal emotional signalling: Its effect on visual cliff behavior of 1-year-olds. *Developmental Psychology, 21*, 195–200.

Spangler, G., & Grossmann, K.E. (1993). Biobehavioral organization in securely and insecurely attached infants. *Child Development, 64*, 1439–1450.

Steele, H., Steele, M., & Fonagy, P. (1996). Associations among attachment classifications of mothers, fathers, and their infants. *Child Development, 67*, 541–555.

Stern, D.N. (1985). *The interpersonal world of the infant: A view from psychoanalysis and developmental psychology*. New York: Basic.

van IJzendoorn, M.H. (1995). Adult attachment representations, parental responsiveness, and infant attachment: A meta-analysis on the predictive validity of the Adult Attachment Interview. *Psychological Bulletin, 117*, 1–17.

van IJzendoorn, M.H., Schuengel, C., & Bakermans-Kranenburg, M.J. (1999). Disorganized attachment in early childhood: Meta-analysis of precursors, concomitants, and sequelae. *Development and Psychopathology, 11*, 225–249.

7 Social Interaction and the Beginnings of Communication

H. Rudolph Schaffer[1]

KEY TERMS

autism • egocentrism • emotion • emotion regulation • infant-directed speech (motherese) • innate mechanism • non-nutritive sucking • nutritive sucking • object permanence • prosody • social referencing • social signaling devices • still-face procedure • theory of mind • turn-taking • visual preference technique

[1]Rudolph Schaffer passed away on 23rd February 2008. He was one of Britain's foremost developmental psychologists during a career spanning five decades, and was acclaimed for his work on children's attachments and fear of separation. He was the founding editor of the international journal *Social Development*, which continues as a lasting monument to his enormous contribution. His chapter, which appeared in the first edition of this book, has been updated by the editors.

CHAPTER OUTLINE

OVERVIEW

Psychological development invariably takes place in the context of interacting with other people. Infants are born with a strong predisposition to recognise, identify with, and form social relationships with others, and this constitutes the starting point from which social interactions with others take place. The chapter traces the development of these social interactions from birth and for the first two years. Learning about early interactions is not only a goal in its own right, but also helps us to gain insight into the development of such functions as language, attachment, cognitive achievements and emotional regulation. The progressive changes occurring in infants' social behaviour during the first two years are considered as falling in five developmental stages:

1. The regularisation of the infant's biological functions and their harmonising with parental requirements.
2. The regulation of mutual attention and responsiveness in face-to-face exchanges.
3. Objects become incorporated into social interactions.
4. The infant develops more flexible and symmetrical relationships.
5. Verbal and other symbolic means help the infant to relate to others and to reflect on social exchanges.

As development proceeds the initially helpless and utterly dependent newborn baby becomes a toddler who is able to act in cooperative, prosocial ways, and has developed sophisticated ways of communicating with people that make possible the reciprocal interchange of ideas and intentions.

INTRODUCTION

Psychological development invariably takes place in the context of interacting with other people. This is as true of the newborn baby as of the older child – in one sense more so because the baby is so utterly dependent on the attention and care of adults, and in another sense less so because early interactions are in certain respects one-sided affairs and not yet truly reciprocal in nature. At all ages, however, a child's psychological functions derive their meaning from the social context in which the child is reared, and the nature, content, and rate of development are all closely related to the kind of interpersonal experiences that the child encounters therein. Learning about early interactions is thus not only a goal in its own right, but also helps us to gain insight into the development of such functions as language, attachment, cognitive achievements, and **emotion regulation.**

Changes in social interactions in early development

Drastic changes occur in the nature of social interactions in the course of early development. Compare newborn babies with 2-year-old toddlers. The former still treat all individuals as interchangeable, having little ability to recognise specific persons, other than the mother, as discussed below. As yet they cannot understand that other people are independent agents, with thoughts and feelings of their own. Communicating with others is dependent on primitive actions such as crying, which are not employed intentionally but which others need to interpret. From the second year on, on the other hand, a great range of socio-cognitive abilities is in place: for example, toddlers not only know their caretakers but have developed intense feelings of attachment towards them; have begun to view others as independent, intentional beings; are able, under certain conditions at least, to act in a cooperative, prosocial manner; and have developed sophisticated ways of communicating with people that makes possible the interchange of ideas and intentions. And yet even at the earliest age children's interactions with their caretakers give the impression, more often than not, of being 'well coordinated', 'meshed', 'smooth'; that is, from the beginning there is a certain order which characterises most of a child's social encounters. How that order is brought about, how it changes with age, why occasionally it breaks down – these are questions which developmental psychologists have tried to answer, both to gain theoretical insight into the nature of childhood and to provide practical help to those caring for children.

Much effort has been devoted to describing the way in which social interactions manifest themselves in the early years, to analysing the processes on which they depend and to converting such intuitive impressions as 'smoothness' into objective terms. In undertaking these cold-blooded scientific efforts it is easy, however, to overlook one essential point: interacting with others is often a highly emotional business, that can be a source of intense pleasure or of great sorrow (Figure 7.1). It is there that children first learn to understand the nature of **emotions**, both their own and those of others, and to regulate and control these feelings and express them in ways regarded as socially desirable, known as emotion regulation. To what extent these early learning experiences influence children's later emotional development remains largely a matter of conjecture, but it is likely that they influence the attachment bond that forms between the mother and her infant (see Chapter 6). Here, we shall discuss them in their own right as they occur in the first two years or so rather than in terms of any possible implications they may have for later life.

FIGURE 7.1 *Interacting with others is often a highly emotional business.*

Source: Shutterstock.

Table 7.1 *Stages in parent–infant interaction*

Stage		Starting age	Developmental task
1.	Biological regulation	Birth	To regularise the infant's basic biological processes such as feeding and waking–sleeping states, and harmonise them with parental requirements.
2.	Face-to-face exchanges	2 months	To regulate mutual attention and responsiveness in face-to-face situations.
3.	Topic sharing	5 months	To incorporate objects into social interactions and ensure joint attention and action to them.
4.	Reciprocity	8 months	To initiate actions directed at others, and develop more flexible and symmetrical relationships.
5.	Symbolic representation	12 months	To develop verbal and other symbolic means of relating to others and reflect upon social exchanges.

A DEVELOPMENTAL FRAMEWORK

The basic question to which we need to find an answer is how the separate activities of two individuals, parent and child, become coordinated in such a way that they form a unitary entity – a feed, a game, a conversation, or any other joint activity that is dependent on the behaviour of both participants. We shall examine what has been learned so far within the framework outlined in Table 7.1. This presents a developmental scheme which traces the progressive changes occurring in infants' social behaviour during the first two years of life and gives an outline of the tasks which infant and parent must jointly cope with at each developmental stage.

PREFERENCE FOR HUMANS IS PRESENT AT BIRTH

Before considering the infant's interactions with others it is worth describing research findings which demonstrate that infants' exposure to, and preference for, humans, develops prenatally and is found soon after birth.

All of the sensory modalities other than vision are functioning and responsive to stimulation in the prenatal period. The auditory modality is particularly sensitive to human speech sounds in the last *trimester* (the last three months) of pregnancy (Hepper, 2007), and newborn babies prefer to listen to speech compared to many non-speech sounds (Vouloumanos *et al.*, 2010). Impressive auditory abilities are found soon after birth, which give clear evidence of *prenatal learning*: 2-day-old infants born to native-speaking French and Spanish mothers will prefer to listen to unknown adults speaking French or Spanish, respectively (Moon *et al.*, 1993); French newborn babies produce cries with a rising melody contour, while German newborn babies cry with a falling melody contour, intonation contours that mimic the **prosody** of the native lan-

prosody the intona-tions, stress, and rhythm of speech that are used to communicate meanings.

guage speech sounds they have heard prenatally (Mampe *et al.*, 2009). Recognition of voices is also found in the neonatal period and recognition and preference for their mother's voice is evident at this very early age (DeCasper & Fifer, 1980; DeCasper *et al.*, 1994).

Visual experience begins at birth and processing of visual information begins with a vengeance. By far the most attention-worthy visual aspect of the external environment at this stage is the human face. By using the **visual preference technique**, i.e. by simultaneously confronting an infant with two stimuli and measuring the amount of attention paid to each, Fantz (1961) was able to demonstrate that infants are equipped from the beginning with certain perceptual biases, as a result of which they are predisposed to attend to faces above all else. Using the visual preference technique several researchers have found that newborn infants are able to differentiate the mother's face from that of a stranger, and will prefer to look at their mother, within hours from birth (Bushnell, 2003). Initially, it may be that newborn babies only have limited abilities to visually scan faces: a 1-month-old infant may scan only the external boundaries and neglect the rest, but by 2 months, however, attention is clearly paid to internal features, as can be seen in Figure 7.2.

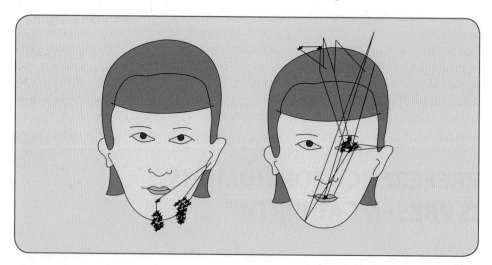

FIGURE 7.2 *Visual scanning lines of a human face by a 1-month-old (left) and a 2-month-old infant (right).*

Source: A. Fogel and G.F. Melson (1988). Reproduced with permission.

Nevertheless, there is evidence that even very young infants may see faces *as* faces and respond to them accordingly. For example, even newborn infants will imitate facial gestures, such as tongue protrusion or mouth opening, which they see an adult displaying (Meltzoff & Moore, 1977) which is linked to the suggestion that imitation serves a social identity function and allows infants to see the behaviours of others as 'like me' (Meltzoff, 2007). Additionally, just as adults interact better with an adult who engages them in eye contact, even newborn infants will look longer at faces with direct gaze, compared with averted gaze (Farroni *et al.*, 2006), and when even very young (4-month-old) infants see a face that establishes direct, mutual gaze, brain areas are activated that correspond to similar brain activity in adults (Grossmann *et al.*, 2008).

The several findings described in this section give strong support for the view that infants are born with a strong predisposition to recognise, identify with, and form social relationships with others.

INITIAL ENCOUNTERS

Let us consider one of the very first situations in which an infant comes upon another person: the feeding situation. For it to go 'smoothly' and be 'successful' feeding requires mutual adjustment of both child and adult, and this can be observed at two levels: a macro- and a micro-level.

Macro-level adjustments

The former refers to the feeding schedule which infant and mother need to settle between them. On the one hand infants have certain internal periodicities which determine their hunger rhythms; on the other hand mothers have particular preferences as to how their daily lives are arranged, and ideally mutual adjustment should take place between these two sets of requirements. Mothers must clearly learn to 'read' their infant's requirements and adjust feeding times accordingly; however, even quite young infants already have the ability to adapt their rhythms to others' demands, as demonstrated in a classical study by Marquis (1941). This investigated the hourly changes in activity of two groups of infants during the first 10 days of life, one of which was fed regularly every three hours and the other every four hours. After just a few days each group showed a peak of restlessness just before its respective feeding time – something which became particularly obvious when the three-hour group was shifted to a four-hour schedule and so the infants had to wait an extra hour for the feed. The infants, that is, had learned to adjust to the particular contingencies with which their respective environments confronted them.

Micro-level adjustments

As to the micro level, let us consider what happens from moment to moment when a mother feeds her baby. An infant's sucking has been shown (e.g. by Wolff, 1968) to

non-nutritive sucking infant sucking that does not provide nourishment, as when the baby is sucking on a dummy or pacifier.

be a highly complex behaviour pattern: for example, there are differences in patterns of sucking between times when it does not provide nutrition (i.e. when a dummy or pacifier is put in the baby's mouth, known as **non-nutritive sucking**) and those when it does, known as **nutritive sucking**; in the latter case there are even differences in sucking patterns between breast and bottle feeding (Moral *et al.*, 2010).

nutritive sucking infant sucking that provides nourishment, as when the baby is breast or bottle fed.

To complicate things further, nutritive sucking is closely coordinated with such other aspects of feeding as breathing and swallowing, and for another, and like non-nutritive sucking, it is organised in temporal sequences which normally take the form of a *burst–pause* pattern: sucks, that is, tend to occur in series of bursts, with pauses interspersed between bursts. It is, in other words, a *high-frequency micro-rhythm* – an extremely intricate, innately organised response that turns out to be well adapted not only for the immediate business in hand of taking in food but also for interacting with the person doing the feeding. This becomes apparent when the mother's behaviour is investigated and related to what the infant is doing. As Kaye (1977) has shown, mothers tend to interact with their infants during a feed in precise synchrony with the burst–pause pattern of sucking. As illustrated in Figure 7.3, during a sucking burst the mother is generally quiet and inactive; during pauses, on the other hand, she will jiggle, stroke, and talk to the infant, thereby setting up a **turn-taking** pattern in which first one and then the other partner is principal actor while the other is spectator. The mother thus fits in with the infant's natural sucking rhythm, accepts the opportunity to intervene offered by pauses between bouts of sucks, and in this way sets up a turn-taking pattern and introduces her infant to a way of interacting that is typical of many social situations which the child will encounter subsequently.

turn-taking the understanding that during a communicative exchange each participant takes turns to communicate in an alternating fashion.

Two conditions of early social interactions

Thus, early social interactions depend on two conditions, referring respectively to the characteristics which infants and mothers contribute:

1. The *temporal organisation of the infant's behaviour*, seen here in the burst–pause pattern of sucking. Such an on–off arrangement lends itself well to social interaction because of the opportunities it offers for adults' intervention; it can thus be regarded as one aspect of infants' *social preadaptedness* in

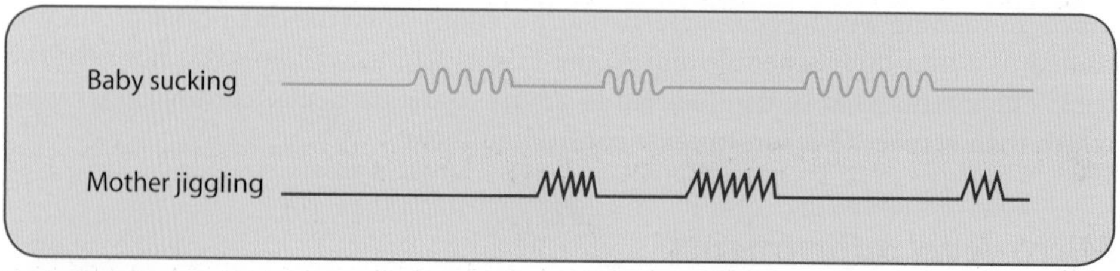

Baby sucking

Mother jiggling

FIGURE 7.3 *Baby's sucking bursts interspersed by mother's activity.*
Source: Schaffer, 1996. Reprinted with permission.

that the inborn nature of the infant's response organisation facilitates the to-and-fro interchange with another person.

2. *The adult's sensitivity* to the signals that the infant provides. By its means she can allow herself to be paced by the burst–pause pattern and respond to the onset of pauses as though they were a signal to her to play her complementary part in the exchange. Thus, by fitting in with the infant's behavioural organisation, and treating the child's behaviour as though it were already intentionally communicative, mothers provide their infants from a very early age with the chance of learning something about the format of social interaction generally, and so of acquiring in due course the skills necessary to act as a full partner.

Both adult and child, from the very beginning, thus play their part in bringing about the coordination of their separate activities and weaving them into one interactive stream. How they do so will change with the child's age: initially, as we saw in the case of feeding, their dialogue is really a *pseudo-dialogue*, for as yet infants cannot appreciate the communicative function of their behaviour and it is therefore up to the mother to make their encounter into an interactive one. Only in the course of subsequent development, as a result of further social experience and cognitive maturity, will infants begin to learn about the rules which govern social interactions and thus become capable of playing a more equal role to that of the adult.

Individual differences

Let us note, however, that even at this early age there are already marked individual differences in the way adult–child pairs achieve coordination. For one thing, not all parents are equally sensitive to their infants' signals: those less so are likely to make the infant's task of learning about the social world a more difficult and prolonged one (Bigelow *et al.*, 2010). And for another, not all infants are equally easy to be sensitive to: the behaviour of some may be so disorganised as to be unpredictable, making caretakers' task to 'read' their children an uncertain and difficult one. This applies, for example, to premature children (Eckerman & Oehler, 1992), who in the early months may show abnormally high or low thresholds to stimulation and have difficulty in paying and maintaining attention; similarly some categories of mentally handicapped infants act in ways that adults may find lacking in clear communicative messages (Field, 1987, and see also Chapter 21). Under such circumstances the 'smoothness' of interaction becomes a much harder objective for adult and child to achieve.

FACE-TO-FACE EXCHANGES

In the earliest weeks of life infants' interactions with others are mainly concerned with the regulation of biological functions such as feeding and sleeping. Somewhere around two months, however, infants increasingly turn from the inner to the outer world; as

FIGURE 7.4 *A variety of signals – visual, vocal, bodily –*
are used to communicate with each other.

Source: Shutterstock.

a result of a sharp increase in visual efficiency they now become much more aware of and interested in their external environment, and especially so in other people. Social interactions consequently are primarily face-to-face affairs: parent and infant looking at each other, smiling at each other, having fun together. The regulation of mutual attention and responsiveness now becomes the main developmental theme.

What actually goes on when mother and infant are in a face-to-face situation – one where there is no 'business' to transact like feeding but where only gazing at each other and playfully vocalising together takes up all their interest? Studies of these encounters are useful in that they shed light on the way in which infants come to learn something about the rules which govern social intercourse, and especially so if the interactions are filmed and subjected to *microanalytic techniques* in order to reveal just how the considerable variety of signals – visual, vocal, bodily – which they exchange are integrated into coherent patterns of communicative significance to the other person (Figure 7.4).

Mutual gazing

Take mutual gazing – probably the most versatile of all interactive patterns – which can be the prelude to further interactions such as smiling, vocalising or bodily games but which, as every lover knows, can also exist in its own right as an intensely pleasurable and moving experience. Indeed, when one analyses the mother's looking behaviour one finds it to resemble very closely the way lovers act, in that she will gaze at her infant almost continuously as though totally absorbed, thereby constantly monitoring the child's actions and enabling her immediately to adjust the timing, nature and intensity of her stimulation in the light of the infant's behaviour. Thus, when the infant's attention is on her, the mother will do her best to provide 'interesting' stimulation such as exaggerated facial displays or rhythmic and repetitive vocalisations; during the infant's looking away periods, on the other hand, she will respect the child's need for time-out by keeping quiet but also watchful, ready to help the infant to resume the next cycle of activity. We have here another example of maternal sensitivity, in that the mother is constantly prepared for interaction but leaves it to the infant to determine when interaction actually takes place.

To-and-fro gaze-on/gaze-off cycles

Infants' gazing in face-to-face situations is not continuous but assumes a to-and-fro pattern, which has been ascribed to certain biologically based cycles of attention–non-attention (Feldman, 2007; Lester *et al.*, 1985). However this may be, the regularity of the cycles makes the infant more predictable to the adult partner; their function, moreover, is to modulate the infant's arousal level and ensure that the excitement obtained from looking at another person can be kept within bounds by periodic time-out periods. Thus, even quite young infants already have the capacity to control the social situation by deciding when to engage with the other person, and with increasing age infants become ever more sophisticated in their visual strategies for seeking or excluding stimulation. The rate of gaze-on/gaze-off cycles, for example, has been found to double in the first six months, indicating a growing ability to get rid of stimulation and yet readily return to it; at the same time there is also an increase in the use of peripheral vision as a means of remaining in contact with the other person (Kaye & Fogel, 1980).

Vocal exchanges

In the vocal exchanges of mothers and infants, as in the feeding situation, turn-taking has been found to be a prominent feature. This is, of course, an essential aspect of adult conversations, for when information is exchanged it is necessary that one person talks while the other listens, and that their roles are then switched smoothly and without overlap. This usually takes place at a split-second level; it is therefore interesting to note that the same can already be observed in the vocal to-and-fro of mothers and infants, even though the latter are still at a pre-verbal level and are not in fact conveying any information as such in their vocalisations (Schaffer, 1984). Infant and adult, that is, alternate their contributions, rarely clashing and managing the exchange of speaker–listener roles with great precision. Yet, unlike the conversations of two adults, there is an asymmetry in the way in which the two partners take responsibility for managing the to-and-fro, for this is brought about primarily by the mother skilfully inserting her contributions in the pauses between the bursts of vocalisations produced by the infant. The mother, that is, allows herself to be paced by the infant; being highly attentive she can ensure that there is no clash, and in this way is able to provide the exchange with all the appearance of a conversation. As with feeding, we see again that the interaction is based, on the one hand, on the infant's spontaneous burst–pause patterns and, on the other hand, on the mother's sensitivity to this pattern. However, the experience of participating in such social formats provides the child with the opportunity of learning how to conduct them and, eventually, how to play an equal role in maintaining them.

Infants learn quickly about interactions!

That infants very quickly do learn about the nature of interactions is well illustrated by experiments in which the customary conduct of the adult partner is deliberately distorted. In the so-called **still-face procedure** mothers are asked not to respond to their infant as they normally do

still-face procedure
used to examine how changes to infants' social surroundings affect their behaviour. Mothers are asked not to respond to their infants as they normally would, but to remain silent and expressionless.

but to remain silent and expressionless (e.g. Chow *et al.*, 2010: Muir & Nadel, 1998). Infants as young as 2 or 3 months can already show signs of disturbance under such circumstances – gazing warily at the mother, alternately giving brief smiles and sobering, looking away for lengthening periods when their overtures are not reciprocated, and eventually withdrawing altogether or becoming overtly distressed. This may continue for a while even when the mother resumes her normal responsiveness. The infant, it seems, has acquired certain expectancies as to what transpires in a face-to-face situation, and is consequently disturbed when these expectancies are not met.

The exchange of emotional expressions

One of the more important experiences that infants are deprived of in the still-face situation is the exchange of emotional expressions. Among adults these are an essential part of any social interaction: the facial and vocal cues that one's partners provide can serve as an important guide to their feelings and thus constitute a most useful communicative device. The same normally applies in infant–mother exchanges: indeed, as videotaped sessions show, the facial displays mothers provide tend to be grossly exaggerated in comparison with their behaviour with another adult (see Figure 7.5) – as though quite unconsciously compensating for the limited information processing capacity of young children and ensuring that the infant's attention remains on them as long as possible.

The mother's face, as well as her voice, conveys messages about the mother's underlying emotional state and attitude – pleasure or displeasure, approval or disapproval, and so on – and before the onset of speech these cues are therefore a most important source of interpersonal information. As research has shown, by at least 5 months of age infants are able reliably to differentiate emotions such as anger, fear and sadness, and what a mother does with her face and voice will thus from quite early on affect the way her baby responds to her (Ramsey-Rennels & Langlois, 2007).

FIGURE 7.5 *Mothers' facial displays to their infants tend to be exaggerated in comparison with their behaviour with another adult. Source:* Shutterstock.

Infants send emotional messages

Young infants are not only capable of receiving emotional messages; they can also from the very beginning send such messages. According to a great deal of evidence (Izard, 1994), every individual, irrespective of race or culture, is equipped from birth with a number of basic emotions, each of which is expressed in a distinct manner and associated with a specific feeling tone. Some are present from birth; others emerge later, at a time of the life cycle when they first become adaptive to the individual. There is still no general agreement as to the number and identity of these emotions; however, here it is worth singling out two that are clearly discernible from early on and have considerable communicative significance – *distress* and *joy*. The former gives rise to a distinctive facial expression involving such features as frowning and a turned down mouth, and is linked to what is surely one of the most essential signalling devices infants bring into the world with them, namely crying. As detailed analyses have shown (e.g. by Wolff, 1969), there are in fact three distinct types of cry, associated respectively with hunger, anger and pain, each of which carries different information and which mothers soon become adept at recognising. The emotion of joy, too, is linked to a particular response pattern (including the smile!). While present from birth it is only from about 6 weeks of age that smiling appears primarily in response to other people, and by increasing infants' attractiveness helps to ensure that adults will attend to children and take pleasure in their company.

Social signalling

Smiling and crying are **social signalling devices** with which infants are equipped from birth and which serve to ensure their survival. They are thus further examples of the fact that infants arrive in the world pre-adapted for social interaction and, by virtue of possessing **innate** communicative patterns of such efficacy, help to bond the children to their caretakers. Initially, however, these devices are of a somewhat primitive nature – evoked in an automatic, reflex-like manner by crude stimuli. In the first few weeks, for instance, the smile is elicited merely by eye-like dots and not the full human face; similarly crying is a response to just a limited set of circumstances such as pain and hunger. Only subsequently will these devices evolve into much more complex, sophisticated communicative patterns – targeted at quite specific individuals, employed deliberately with certain aims in mind, and suppressed where not judged appropriate. Such improvement requires considerable cognitive learning and development; it also, however, requires a great deal of relevant experience with social partners: only if, for example, children have learned that their cry is regularly responded to by a caring adult will they in due course become capable of employing this device as an intentional signal; and only if, in repeated face-to-face situations, they have discovered the power of the smile will this response become part of their general social repertoire. One need only refer to descriptions of infants brought up under conditions of extreme deprivation, such as in institutions characterised by grossly deficient personal attention, to see how quickly responses such as crying and smiling can become extinguished (e.g. Dennis, 1973; Rutter *et al.*, 2010).

> **social signalling devices** devices such as smiling and crying that signify someone's emotional state.

INCORPORATING OBJECTS IN SOCIAL INTERACTIONS

At around 4–5 months of age a notable change occurs in infants' orientation to the environment: they switch their main preoccupation from faces to objects. This is primarily because at that age infants discover the use of their hands and become proficient at grasping, handling and manipulating things; as a result a new world opens up for them. The parent's face has become familiar and is no longer as fascinating: according to one study (Kaye & Fogel, 1980) a drop in visual attention to the mother occurs from 70 per cent of session time at 6 weeks of age to 33 per cent at 26 weeks. Face-to-face interaction is no longer the sole vehicle of social exchange: increasingly the infant's contacts with others is structured around objects. How to bring about such *three-party, triadic contacts* is the new task confronting parent and child.

The problem of limited attentional capacity

Initially at least, this is not easily accomplished. The problem is that infants' attentional capacity is limited: they can attend to only one thing at a time and do not flexibly move from one focus to another. The 6-month-old infant, that is, plays with the parent *or* with a ball but cannot yet play ball *with* the parent. It is therefore up to the adult to convert an *infant–object* situation into an *infant–object–adult* situation: the adult, that is, needs to take the initiative in making the object a focus of *shared* attention and so convert it into a topic to which both partners can attend and around which the interaction of parent and child can take place. Such topic sharing is basic to every social interaction; its nature, however, varies according to age. Thus, in the early months the topic to which the two participants address themselves arises from within the dyad itself: it is changes in facial expression or vocal sounds that form the focus around which the interaction takes place. Later on, when verbal proficiency makes conversation possible, the shared topic may be a symbolic one, conjured up by the words used by the two participants. Before then, however, it is the balls, rattles, buttons, spoons and bits of paper that the child finds so intriguing that need to be incorporated in social exchanges as shared topics.

The development of shared attention

There are a number of devices which we all use in everyday life in order to share with another person an interest in some aspect of the environment. They include direction of gaze, gestures such as pointing, object contact and referential language. The last of these has probably received most attention: words can stand for things, and by introducing them into a conversation one person can convey to another their interest of the moment. In infancy, however, the other devices, being non-verbal in nature, form the primary vehicle for attention sharing, even though it is not until the end of the first year that infants begin to understand their communicative function.

The development of pointing

Take pointing – a particularly useful way of indicating to someone else what in the environment one is interested in at the moment, and what one wants the other person to be interested in too. Pointing-like movements, with the arm and appropriately named index finger extended, can already be observed in infants as young as 4 months, but at that age there are no indications that the infant uses them in any indicative, let alone communicative, sense (Blake *et al.*, 1994). It is not until 10 or 12 months that pointing emerges as a gesture, elicited regularly by objects too far to reach or by books with attention-captivating pictures in them (Figure 7.6). Even then, however, the gesture is not yet used for communication: the infant points at the object but does not check whether the other person is following. Only in the second year will such *pointing-for-self* gradually be replaced by *pointing-for-others*: the infant can now attend to both object and partner, integrate the

FIGURE 7.6 *Infants begin to point as early as 9 months.*
Source: Photo by Karen Thorpe.

two in one communicative act and thus use the gesture in order to influence others (Schaffer, 1984). As to comprehending the meaning of another person's pointing, it is again not till the end of the first year that one can first find evidence for that. Up to about 9 months an infant will look at the extended finger but remain 'stuck' there, with no apparent appreciation of the indicative significance of the gesture. After 9 months infants begin to follow the direction of the finger to the relevant object, but only under 'easy' conditions, such as when finger and target are close together in the visual field, and it is not until the beginning of the second year that infants can locate most objects pointed out to them by another person and so share their topic of interest.

Following another person's gaze direction

Following another person's gaze direction is the other most common means of topic sharing. Here too there are indications that it is not until the end of the first year that infants become capable of understanding the significance of such an action and begin to look where the other person is looking, though again this ability emerges first under 'easy' conditions, when person and object are both readily accessible (Butterworth, 2004). Until then it is up to the adult to take the initiative for topic-sharing by this means: mothers in particular tend closely to monitor their infant's focus of interest and, almost automatically, look where they are looking (Collis & Schaffer, 1975). What is significant about such topic-sharing is that it is often only a start to further interaction: having established the infant's focus of interest the mother may then point to it, name it, comment on it and perhaps fetch it for the child to play with.

From asymmetry to symmetry in social interactions

Once again we see that initially social interactions are largely asymmetrical in nature: it is very much up to the adult to ensure that they are indeed of an interactive nature. Just as the mother needs to fill in the pauses between bursts of sucks or bouts of vocalisations in order to embed the infant's individual behaviour in a *social* situation, so she must be prepared to follow the infant's gaze or early points and use these to construct a dialogue, based on the child's interests. And once again, a mother's sensitivity to her child's signals is crucial in terms of both timing and kind of response: thus, gazing can switch so rapidly that the adult can easily elaborate on an object no longer of interest to the infant, and talking about the object in incomprehensible adult terms will also do little to further the interaction or, for that matter, foster language acquisition. Where there is sensitive responsiveness, on the other hand, infants have the opportunity of finding out that their actions are of interest to the adult and that they can thereby elicit some sort of predictable reaction, thus encouraging them eventually to act *in order to* elicit such behaviour. Once an infant has learned that it has a part to play in bringing about the to-and-fro of social exchanges, interaction tends to become a much more symmetrical affair than hitherto.

Toward a theory of mind

The establishment of joint attention is significant because it represents the first real 'meeting of minds' with another person. When infants follow someone else's focus of attention, and even more so when they actively attempt to direct it, they show that they are able to view other people as independent, intentional beings, with interests of their own that do not necessarily coincide with the infant's interests. It is for this reason that the emergence of joint attention in the second half of the first year can be viewed as the forerunner of the **theory of mind** skills that fully appear two or three years later (see Chapter 11), and that its occurrence in infancy has been said to provide the foundation for all subsequent acts of communication and learning that involve some reference to the outside world (Carpenter *et al.*, 1998).

FROM INTERACTIONS TO RELATIONSHIPS

In the final third of the first year a positive blossoming of abilities takes place, in that a considerable range of capacities emerges during this period which together make the child's behaviour vastly more flexible, coordinated and purposive. Table 7.2 gives examples of these new achievements, and while these are largely based on the development of cognitive abilities they do have considerable social implications.

The development of object (and person!) permanence

Let us examine one of these cognitive abilities, the development of **object permanence**. This refers to the ability to remain aware of an object even in its absence – something which is absolutely fundamental to our conception of the world but which, as Piaget (1954) argued, the young infant does not possess. According to him, for the first eight or nine months infants behave on the basis of 'out of sight, out of mind': for example, the moment an object is hidden they cease to show any orientation towards it and

Table 7.2 *Examples of new capacities emerging around 8 months of age*

Invokes adult help in performing a task with an object
Obeys simple requests
Imitates demonstrated actions of objects
Points to objects and follows the pointing gesture of an adult
Plays peek-a-boo, hiding own face for another to watch
Holds cup to doll's mouth
Opens and closes book, looking at mother after each move
Follows adult's visual gaze
Shakes head and says 'no' in refusal
Begins to use conventional labels for objects; names, persons and pets
Demonstrates affection by hugging and kissing
Plays at carrying out adult activities (mopping floor, driving car, etc.)
Shows toes when these are named by mother
Plays 'appropriately' with cup, spoon and saucer

make no effort to look for it. Object permanence is one of the most fundamental achievements of infancy; it transforms the child's perception of the world and gives it a stability which it lacked before (for a more detailed account of object permanence see Chapter 5). This is perhaps most vividly seen in its social equivalent, *person permanence*: the realisation that people do not cease to exist when no longer in the infant's presence but can be remembered, missed, and searched for in their absence. In the early months infants separated from their mothers will contentedly accept the attention of complete strangers – even though they recognise them to be strange; from the second half year of life, however, they are able to cling to the image of the absent mother and will accordingly reject the unfamiliar substitute – a phenomenon referred to as *stranger anxiety*, which is found in some, but not all infants (e.g. de Rosnay *et al.*, 2006). What is more, the knowledge that people continue to exist when out of sight is clearly critical to the establishment of enduring relationships with them: the child must be able to count on the other person to be continuously accessible and not merely when they happen to be in the same environment. Thus, whereas previously infants' social *interactions*, taking place at particular times and places, made up their experience with other people, now it is enduring social *relationships* that constitute that experience and organise it to transcend time and place. Developmentally, this is a tremendous step forward. Attachments, for example, can now be formed to individuals who are not only familiar but who will form a focus around which the child's emotional life revolves (Schaffer, 1996, and see Chapter 6).

Learning to take the initiative

At the level of specific social interactions, too, there are changes as a result of the newly emerging abilities, and infants' cooperative activities develop considerably during the second year of life, and involve not only the mother but other family members and peers (Warneken & Tomasello, 2007).

These changes in interaction can be seen in the development of a greater symmetry in the respective roles of adult and child and can be well seen in the games that mothers and infants play, such as give-and-take, peekaboo and patacake (Gustafson *et al.*, 1979).

Such games involve oft-repeated, conventionalised routines requiring the participation of both partners according to certain set rules that usually include turn-taking, role exchange and repetition of rounds, and which thus provide infants with the opportunity to acquire and display the social skills that they need for interacting with people in a wide range of situations. For example, in give-and-take games the infant's participation up to 8 months or so tends to be limited to 'take': the mother offers the toy, the infant takes it and the sequence ends there. After that age the infant comes to realise that there are further moves: first at the request of the mother, but then spontaneously, the infant hands the toy back, having come to appreciate that each action forms part of a wider sequence, that is, the 'game', and that the roles of giver and taker are both reciprocal and exchangeable. In addition, instead of always being dependent on the mother to start the game infants may come to take the initiative by offering her the toy, thereby clearly indicating that they are no longer wholly dependent on others to structure their experience.

Social referencing

The increasingly flexible and purposive behaviour of infants can be seen in other situations too. Take the **social referencing** phenomenon: young infants, confronted by a strange object, will stare fixedly at it for a brief while and then take some form of action – approach or withdrawal. From the age of 9 or 10 months, however, infants will not merely look at the object but also at the mother (or even a stranger: Sternberg, 2008) – referring to her, that is, in order to check out her reaction and seek cues from her expression that will guide their appraisal of the situation. Infants show thereby that they can now integrate information from multiple sources and, instead of reacting impulsively, are able to produce a much more purposive and complex plan of action. Or take the way in which infants become capable of making use of the mother in order to achieve some goal, such as getting access to or working a toy (Mosier & Rogoff, 1994). It is once again in the final third of the first year that this ability becomes notable – at a time, that is, when according to Piaget (1954) the child becomes capable of differentiating means from ends and understanding the connection between these two. As a result, instead of merely stretching out a hand for an out of reach toy infants are able to call for or gesture to the mother to fetch the toy, using her as the means for obtaining the desired end. Intentional initiation of interactions, understanding of their reciprocal nature, the consequently greater symmetry of all social exchanges and their organisation into relationships, are thus the developmental achievements which characterise infants' behaviour with others which begin to develop as they approach the end of the first year, and continue to develop in the second year and beyond.

COMMUNICATING WITH SYMBOLS

In the second year of life other drastic changes take place in the way in which children relate to other people, for increasingly from then on their interactions take a verbal form. The first words usually appear somewhere around 1 year of age, but just as pointing is initially employed for the self rather than for communicative purposes so words are at first merely labels that children attach to people or objects for their own purposes rather than to convey some meaning to another person. Talking, as a *social* device, is mostly found from the middle of the second year on; it occurs because children become capable of understanding the symbolic use of words, for example, that the sound *apple* can be used to stand for the real thing and that, moreover, other people share this system of representation.

From sensorimotor functioning to the use of symbols

As Piaget (1950) pointed out, the progression from sensorimotor functioning to the use of symbols in the second year is one of the major transitions in cognitive development. It can be seen in various spheres of the child's activity: play, for example, is no longer a matter of mere manipulation of things for the sake of their feel or sound but becomes imaginative and make-belief in nature. The child, that is, realises that a doll may be thought of as a baby or a piece of wood as a boat, and that one can talk on a toy telephone pretending there is someone listening (Figure 7.7). In the same way words are discovered to be more than mere sounds; they can be used to represent things even in their absence, so that an apple can be asked for or talked about although none is to be seen. Language, as a rule-governed way of using verbal symbols, eventually becomes a powerful tool of thought; for our purposes what matters is that it also, even in the early years of childhood, serves as a uniquely human interactive tool.

FIGURE 7.7 *In their second year, a child's play becomes imaginative and make-believe in nature. Source:* Shutterstock.

Talking to babies – is infant-directed speech necessary?

There is still much to be learned about the beginnings of language, and in particular about the role which social experience plays in the pre-linguistic period (a detailed account of language development is given in Chapter 10). It is noteworthy that, although infants do not begin to speak until around 12 months (although they have learned a great deal about their native language by this time: Hollich & Houston, 2007), for most of the first year, adults still talk to them, even in the earliest weeks of life. Rheingold and Adams (1980) observed nurses in a maternity hospital while caring for newborn babies and found that virtually everything they did was accompanied by talk. What is more, 23 per cent of their utterances were questions that the babies were obviously not expected to answer and 14 per cent were in the form of commands, none of which the babies could possibly carry out! It is almost certainly the case that by being inundated by talk, day in, day out, infants learn a great deal about their native language, and it is important that parents of pre-verbal infants involve their babies in conversation: young infants 'acquire considerable information about the nature and organization of their native language well before they actually begin to produce recognizable words' (Jusczyk, 2002, p.147), and this information can only be acquired by exposure to language.

When talking to infants and young children adults typically use a form of speech generally referred to as **infant-directed speech** or **motherese,** though it is by no means specific to mothers or even to parents. Some of the features of infant-directed speech are listed in Table 7.3; in sum, they make speech to young children simpler, briefer, more repetitive and more attention-worthy, the extent of such fine-tuning depending on the child's age and being carried out quite automatically and without prior planning. It is tempting to believe that such a style facilitates children's acquisition of language, and it is interesting to note that features of infant-directed speech such as simplifying, exaggeration and slowing down are found even in mothers' manual signing to deaf children (Masataka, 1996).

Although there is some evidence that infant-directed speech can facilitate aspects of language acquisition (e.g. Singh *et al.*, 2009), there are some interesting cultural variations which throw doubt on the notion that such early experience is a *necessary* precondition to language acquisition. For instance the Kaluli, a tribe living in an isolated part of Papua New Guinea, think of babies as 'having no understanding' and therefore rarely address them verbally in any way (although their infants will have exposure to language from hearing adults talking to each other). Nevertheless, despite this lack of infant-directed verbal experience, Kaluli children become speakers of their language within the normal range of development (Schieffelin & Ochs, 1983). For that matter, once their children do begin to talk Kaluli parents also do not use the particular style of child-directed talk found among Western adults and not only the Kaluli but various other cultures (e.g. Pye, 1986) make no use of it, and the fact that this happens with no obvious disadvantage to their children's language development makes it unlikely that it is quite the essential teaching device it was once thought to be (Soderstrom, 2007).

The desire to communicate

Of one thing there can be no doubt: children have a powerful desire to communicate with others, and when prevented from doing so in conventional ways will find

Table 7.3 *Some features of infant-directed speech*

Phonological characteristics	Syntactic characteristics	Semantic characteristics	Pragmatic characteristics
Clear enunciation	Short utterance length	Limited range of vocabulary	More directives
Higher pitch	Sentences well-formed, i.e. grammatically correct	'Baby talk' words	More questions
Exaggerated intonation		Reference mainly to here-and-now	More attention devices
Slower speech	Fewer subordinate clauses		Repetition of child's utterances
Longer pauses			

alternate means. This is clearly seen in deaf children: if they are signed to they will acquire language at the same rate as normally hearing children and will go through the same stages of language acquisition (e.g. Petitto *et al.*, 2004). If they are not signed to, using a conventional sign language, they are highly likely to develop their own non-verbal system of gestural signing, and do so apparently quite spontaneously without any indication of being influenced by teaching or imitation. As shown in a series of reports by Goldin-Meadow and colleagues (e.g. Goldin-Meadow, & Mylander, 1984; Goldin-Meadow *et al.*, 2007), such children, despite not being able to acquire spoken language naturally, even with a hearing aid, and despite not being exposed to a conventional sign language, will nevertheless construct for themselves a structured gestural system that enables them reasonably effectively to communicate to others their needs and wishes and thoughts. Prevented from following the conventional route to language learning, these children can nevertheless discover on their own other means of keeping in touch with people. What is more, the manual system they invent for themselves is in many respects comparable in content and structure to spoken language. Thus, the deaf children described by Goldin-Meadow *et al.* first developed single gestures to denote specific objects or events – just as hearing children begin by using single words; they then proceeded to link together gestures into 'sentences', and these gradually increased both in number and complexity. Though these gestural systems never became as complex and subtle as spoken language, they did provide a means of communication that was remarkably sophisticated for something that developed quite spontaneously.

Summary and conclusions: The development of effective communication

Effective communication, whether by verbal or by other means, involves a substantial range of skills, which are acquired only gradually in the course of the early years. Consider children's ability to participate in a conversation (McTear, 1985, and see Chapter 10). Initially, adult–child conversations tend to be asymmetrical in nature: the adult allows the child to set the topic, follows up that topic by commenting and enlarging on it in some way, and ensures in this way that continuity is maintained from one contribution to the other. Children's ability to pick up a topic introduced by the adult is at first limited: **egocentrically** they prefer to set their own agenda and both topic and temporal contingencies between adult and child speech are thus largely the responsibility of the adult (Bloom *et al.*, 1996). Yet very early on children become aware that adult communications require responses, and though mismatches may occur, children by the age of 2 already have a firm idea of the to-and-fro nature of a conversation, and will accordingly try to provide some sort of answer when a question is put to them. The rate and extent to which conversational skills develop depend largely on the parents' willingness to provide relevant experience: the more parents involve their children in conversations, and the more they facilitate the child's participation in them, the sooner the child will acquire the necessary skills. Thus, parents need to time their own contribution to the conversation in such a way that they leave plenty of time for the child's reply; in some cases they may even need to go further by filling

egocentrism the difficulty or inability of young children to distinguish between their own perspective and that of others.

in for the child when the latter fails to respond, thereby at least keeping the conversation in being, albeit in a one-sided manner, and also incidentally modelling for the child what the answer ought to have been. By employing techniques such as these parents help children to become increasingly competent participants, and conversations thus become lengthier, more explicit and more cohesive. Once again we see that, with increasing experience and maturity, the respective roles of adult and child gradually change towards a greater degree of symmetry.

SUMMARY AND CONCLUSIONS

In this chapter we have focused on the beginnings of social interactions – their emergence at the start of life and their characteristics during infancy. There is, of course, a lot more that must develop before the individual becomes a fully sophisticated social partner; however, the first steps are the vital ones and set the tone for all that follows.

autism a disorder that affects a person's ability to relate to others. Autistic individuals typically have problems with communication, forming attachments with other people (*attachment behaviour*), and lack a *theory of mind*. Autistic people usually avoid social contact and may seek a monotony of environment and action (resulting in repetitive stereotyped movements) which appear to provide some comfort. These problems are often referred to as *Wing's triad of impairments*. Occasionally, some autistic individuals demonstrate extreme talents (*savant skills*) in certain activities (e.g. the ability to accurately draw a building, or to mentally compute seven-figure prime numbers); however, these talents are uncommon. Autism is a rare condition (approximately 4 per 10,000 live births) that is usually inherited but can result from brain damage.

When development goes wrong

Just how important the first steps are can be seen by considering children who have, for one reason or another, failed to take them. One group of such children are those suffering from **autism**, in whom the most basic social abilities such as making eye contact with another person or establishing a focus of joint attention has failed properly to develop and in whom subsequent abilities such as verbal communication or the understanding of others' mental states may then also not emerge (Sigman, 1998 – autism is discussed in detail in Chapter 21). The cause of this disorder is not fully understood, although it is known that it is of genetic origin, inherent in the child's basic make-up, and thus present from birth. In other children, however, social development may be adversely affected by experiences following birth, as seen in institutionalised children reared under conditions of extreme interpersonal deprivation (Rutter *et al.*, 2010), where the lack of consistent, emotionally responsive caretaking results in children failing to develop whatever potential they have to become properly functioning members of society (Figure 7.8). It is clear that to reach that potential a child must have both the required inborn capacities to relate to other people and be raised in a supportive environment that allows these capacities to develop.

The complexity of the task facing the child

From an adult's point of view the mutual regulation that occurs when interacting with another person is such a natural, spontaneous function, carried out with split-second precision and generally without any conscious awareness, that it is not easy to appreciate just how complex an activity this really is. One benefit of studying its beginnings is to realise that we are dealing not with just one unitary ability but rather with a whole range of different skills – skills such as orienting to the other person's face and voice, attending to all relevant communicative cues, integrating these cues into meaningful messages, timing one's own messages to fit in with those of the partner, employing particular gestures or words to convey particular meanings, sharing a focus of attention to some aspect of the environment with the other person, making allowance for other people's different orientation to the same situation, matching their

FIGURE 7.8 *Severe interpersonal deprivation in childhood can result in failure to develop into properly functioning members of society.*
Source: Shutterstock.

emotional mood – and so forth. The various components must then be combined into organised wholes: part of the task the infant faces, that is, involves *intra*-personal coordination, where each component skill becomes one constituent of the ability to relate to another person. However, the other part involves *inter*-personal coordination, namely fitting one's behaviour to that of the other. Intra-personal coordination needs to go hand in hand with inter-personal coordination if the coming together of two individuals is to have a 'successful' outcome. The accomplishment of such a capacity in the early years of childhood is a very impressive undertaking.

DISCUSSION POINTS

1. Think about how early interactions change from being one-sided affairs to becoming truly reciprocal in nature.

2. What evidence suggests that infants arrive in the world preadapted for social interaction?

3. How do face-to-face interactions between the infant and caretaker develop over the first two years from birth?

4. How do infants overcome their initial limited attentional capacities to engage in reciprocal social interactions?

5. What are the major changes in social interactions that appear from around 8 months of age?

6. Why is the development of object and person permanence important in social development?

7. Consider the ways in which the infant develops effective communications using language and other symbols.

8. What sorts of sophisticated means of communication enable the 2-year-old to exchange ideas and intentions with others?

SUGGESTIONS FOR FURTHER READING

....

Dowling, M. (2010). *Young children's personal, social and emotional development*. London: Sage.

Slater, A. & Lewis, M. (2007), Introduction to infant development (2nd edn) (especially chapters 10–15). Oxford: Oxford University Press.

Goldberg, S. (2000). *Attachment and development*. London: Arnold.

Schaffer, H.R. (1996). *Social development*. Oxford: Blackwell.

Durkin, K. (1995). *Developmental social psychology*. Oxford: Blackwell.

Schaffer, H.R. (1984). *The child's entry into a social world*. London: Academic Press.

REFERENCES

....

Bigelow, A.E., MacLean, K., Proctor, J., Myatt, T., Gillis, R., & Power, M. (2010). Maternal sensitivity throughout infancy: Continuity and relation to attachment security. *Infant Behavior and Development, 33*, 50–60.

Blake, J., O'Rourke, P., & Borzellino, G. (1994). Form and function in the development of pointing and reaching gestures. *Infant Behavior and Development, 17*, 195–203.

Bloom, L., Margulis, O., Tinker, E., & Fujita, N. (1996). Early conversations and word learning: Contributions from child and adult. *Child Development, 67*, 3154–3175.

Bushnell, I.W.R. (2003). Newborn face recognition. In O. Pacalis & A. Slater (Eds.) *The development of face processing in infancy and early childhood: current perspectives*. New York: NOVA Science Publishers.

Butterworth, G.E. (2004). Joint visual attention in infancy. In G. Bremer & A. Slater (Eds.) *Theories of infant development* (pp. 317–354). Oxford: Blackwell Publishing.

Carpenter, M., Nagell, K., & Tomasello, M. (1998). *Social cognition, joint attention, and communicative competence from 9 to 15 months of age*. Monographs of the Society for Research in Child Development, 63(4, Serial No. 255).

Chow, S.M., Haltigan, J.D., & Messinger, D.S. (2010). Dynamic infant–parent affect coupling during the face-to-face/still-face. *Emotion, 10*, 101–104.

Collis, G.M., & Schaffer, H.R. (1975). Synchronization of visual attention in mother–infant pairs. *Journal of Child Psychology and Psychiatry, 16*, 315–320.

DeCasper, A.J., & Fifer, W.P. (1980). Of human bonding: Newborns prefer their mothers' voices. *Science, 208*, 1174–1176.

DeCasper, A.J., Lecanuet, J.-P., Bunuel, M.-C., Granier Deferre, C., & Maugeais, R. (1994). Foetal reactions to recurrent maternal speech. *Infant Behavior and Development, 17*, 159–164.

Dennis, W. (1973). *Children of the creche*. New York: Appleton-Century-Crofts.

de Rosnay, M., Cooper, P.J., Tisgaras, N., & Murray, L. (2006). Transmission of social anxiety from mother to infant: An experimental study using a social referencing paradigm. *Behaviour Research and Therapy, 44*, 1165–1175.

Eckerman, C.O., & Oehler, J.M. (1992). Very-low birthweight newborns and parents as early social partners. In S.L. Friedman & M.D. Sigman (Eds.) *The psychological development of low birthweight children*. Norwood, NJ: Ablex.

Fantz, R.L. (1961). The origin of form perception. *Scientific American, 204*, 66–72.

Farroni, T., Menon, E., & Johnson, M.H. (2006). Factors influencing newborns' preference for faces with eye contact. *Journal of Experimental Child Psychology, 95*, 298–308.

Feldman, R. (2007). Parent–infant synchrony: Biological foundations and developmental outcomes. *Current Directions in Psychological Science, 16,* 340–345.

Field, T. (1987). Affective and interactive disturbances in infants. In J.D. Osofsky (Ed.) *Handbook of infant development* (2nd edn). New York: Wiley.

Fogel, A., & Melson, G.F. (1988). *Child development.* St Paul, MN: West Publishing.

Goldin-Meadow, S., & Mylander, C. (1984). *Gestural communication in deaf children: The effects and noneffects of parental input on early language.* Monographs of the Society for Research in Child Development, 49(3–4, Serial No. 207).

Goldin-Meadow, S., Mylander, C., & Franklin, A. (2007). How children make language out of gesture: Morphological structure in gesture systems developed by American and Chinese deaf children. *Cognitive Psychology, 55,* 87–135.

Grossmann, T., Johnson, M.H., Lloyd-Fox, S., Blasi, A., Deligianni, F., Elwell, C., & Csibra, G. (2008). *Proceedings of the Royal Society B – Biological Sciences, 275,* 2803–2811.

Gustafson, G.E., Green, J.A., & West, M.J. (1979). The infant's changing role in mother–infant games: The growth of social skills. *Infant Behavior and Development, 2,* 301–308.

Hepper, P. (2007). Prenatal development. In A. Slater & M. Lewis (Eds.) *Introduction to infant development* (pp. 41–62). Oxford: Oxford University Press.

Hollich, G.J., & Houston, D.M. (2007). Language development: From speech perception to first words. In A. Slater & M. Lewis (Eds.) *Introduction to infant development* (2nd edn). Oxford: Oxford University Press.

Izard, C.E. (1994). Innate and universal facial expressions: Evidence from developmental and cross-cultural research. *Psychological Bulletin, 115,* 288–299.

Jusczyk, P.W. (2002). Language development: From speech perception to first words. In A. Slater & M. Lewis (Eds.) *Introduction to infant development* (1st edn; pp. 147–164). Oxford: Oxford University Press.

Kaye, K. (1977). Toward the origin of dialogue. In H.R. Schaffer (Ed.) *Studies in mother–infant interaction.* London: Academic Press.

Kaye, K., & Fogel, A. (1980). The temporal structure of face-to-face communication between mothers and infants. *Developmental Psychology, 14,* 454–464.

Lester, B.M., Hoffman, J., & Brazelton, T.B. (1985). The rhythmic structure of mother–infant interaction in term and preterm infants. *Child Development, 56,* 15–27.

Mampe, B., Friederici, A.D., Christophe, A., & Wermke, K. (2009). Newborns' cry melody is shaped by their native language. *Current Biology, 19,* 1994–1997.

Marquis, D.M. (1941). Learning in the neonate: The modification of behavior under three feeding schedules. *Journal of Experimental Psychology, 29,* 263–282.

Masataka, N. (1996). Perception of motherese in a signed language by 6-month-old deaf infants. *Developmental Psychology, 32,* 874–879.

McTear, M.F. (1985). *Children's conversations.* Oxford: Blackwell.

Meltzoff, A.N. (2007). The 'like me' framework for recognizing and becoming an intentional agent. *Acta Psychologica, 124,* 26–43.

Meltzoff, A.N., & Moore, M.K. (1977). Imitation of facial and manual gestures by human neonates. *Science, 198,* 75–78.

Moon, C., Cooper, R.P., & Fifer, W.P. (1993). Two-day-olds prefer their native language. *Infant Behavior and Development, 16,* 495–500.

Moral, A., Bolibar, I., Seguranyes, G., Ustrell, J.M., Sebastia, G., Martinez-Barba, C., & Rios, J. (2010). Mechanics of sucking: comparison between bottle feeding and breast feeding. *BMC Pediatrics, 10,* article 6.

Mosier, C.E., & Rogoff, B. (1994). Infants' instrumental use of their mothers to achieve their goals. *Child Development, 65*, 70–79.

Muir, D.W., & Nadel, J. (1998). Infant social perception. In A. Slater (Ed.) *Perceptual development: Visual, auditory and speech perception in infancy* (pp.247–285). Hove, East Sussex: Psychology Press.

Petitto, L.A., Holowaka, S., Sergio, L.E., Levy, B., & Ostro, D.J. (2004). Baby hands that move to the rhythm of language: Hearing babies acquiring sign languages babble silently on the hands. *Cognition, 93*, 43–73.

Piaget, J. (1950). *The psychology of intelligence*. London: Routledge & Kegan Paul.

Piaget, J. (1954). *The child's construction of reality*. London: Routledge & Kegan Paul.

Pye, C. (1986). Quiche Mayan speech to children. *Journal of Child Language, 13*, 85–100.

Ramsey-Rennels, J., & Lanlois, J.H. (2007). How infants perceive and process faces. In A. Slater & M. Lewis (Eds.) *Introduction to infant development* (2nd edn; pp. 191–232). Oxford: Oxford University Press.

Rheingold, H.L., & Adams, J.L. (1980). The significance of speech to newborns. *Developmental Psychology, 16*, 397–403.

Rutter, M., Sonuga-Barke, E.J., Beckett, C., Castle, J., Kreppner, J., Kumsta, R., *et al.* (2010). *Deprivation-specific psychological patterns: Effects of institutional deprivation*. Monographs of the Society for Research in Child Development, 75.

Schaffer, H.R. (1984). *The child's entry into a social world*. London: Academic Press.

Schaffer, H.R. (1996). *Social development*. Oxford: Blackwell.

Schieffelin, B.B., & Ochs, E. (1983). A cultural perspective on the transition from prelinguistic to linguistic communication. In R.M.Golinkoff (Ed.) *The transition from prelinguistic to linguistic communication*. Hillsdale, NJ: Erlbaum.

Sigman, M. (1998). Change and continuity in the development of children with autism. *Journal of Child Psychology and Psychiatry, 39*, 817–828.

Singh, L., Nestor, S., Parikh, C., & Yull, A. (2009). Influences of infant-directed speech on early word recognition. *Infancy, 14*, 654–666.

Soderstrom, M. (2007). Beyond babytalk: Re-evaluating the nature and content of speech input to preverbal infants. *Developmental Review, 27*, 501–532.

Sternberg, G. (2008). Selectivity in infant social referencing. *Infancy, 14*, 457–473.

Vouloumanos, A., Hauser, M.D., Werker, J.F., & Martin, A. (2010). The tuning of human neonates' preference for speech. *Child Development, 81*, 517–527.

Warneken, F., & Tomasello, M. (2007). Helping and cooperation at 14 months of age. *Infancy, 11*, 271–294.

Wolff, P.H. (1968). The serial organization of sucking in the young infant. *Pediatrics, 42*, 943–956.

Wolff, P.H. (1969). The natural history of crying and other vocalization in early infancy. In Foss, B.M. (Ed.) *Determinants of infant behaviour* (vol. 4). London: Methuen.

8 The Development of Self and Gender

WENDY LAWRENSON

KEY TERMS

absolute coding • attribution theory • categorical self • collectivist societies • Eight Stages of Man • Electra complex • existential self • gender constancy • hermaphrodite • hot cognition • identification • individualist societies • inferiority complex • Internal Working Model (IWM) • Material me • Oedipus complex • phallic stage • primary circular reactions • perceptual defence • personal modelling • phimosis • positional modelling • projection • relative coding • rouge test • secondary circular reactions • self-efficacy • self-esteem • Self-Esteem Inventory • Self Perception Profile • social learning theory • still-face procedure • strange situation • tachistoscope • tadpole stage • transsexual • Twenty-Statements Test (TST)

CHAPTER OUTLINE

OVERVIEW

We are all of us aware of our personal existence and of being a unique individual different from all other humans. In this chapter infants' gradual awareness of the developing sense of self is described, both as a sense of separateness from the physical world and of separateness from other people. From at least the age of 2 years, and possibly earlier, young children are able to compare themselves, both favourably and unfavourably, with others, and their developing theory of mind allows them to become aware that they may have different thoughts and feelings from others, and to imagine what it might be like to be someone else. This ability to compare oneself with others is linked to self-esteem – the overall evaluation or appraisal of one's own worth – and to self-efficacy – one's beliefs about one's abilities in different areas. The child also develops a sense of body image, which at first is incomplete since they will often try to go through a space that is much too narrow, or even try to sit on a miniature chair that is much too small!

An essential part of self-awareness is gender identity. Children soon become aware of their own gender and that this is, for most individuals, fixed and unchanging throughout life. Children's cognitive awareness of their gender identity is closely tied to what society considers to be gender-appropriate behaviour – I am a boy and therefore I do X or I am a girl and I do Y. The chapter describes well-defined gender roles of typical male and female behaviour, and how gender-appropriate behaviours often become strengthened through rewards and encouragement, while gender-inappropriate behaviours may be weakened through non-rewards. Nevertheless, there are cases where gender identity is not clear-cut, as in 'girlyboys' and transsexuals. The chapter describes a case of a boy who was raised as a girl, and the developmental problems that resulted from this gender reassignment.

For most children gender identity is important but not for all, and this comment also applies to developing a national identity, so that for many children this is important – I am English, Scottish, British, French, American, and so on – and these identities can come to the fore on certain occasions, benignly in events such as the soccer World Cup or the Olympic Games, but less so when there is civil strife or disputes between nations.

Throughout the chapter the sense of self developing within the child is viewed as unique and continuous. There is not, and can never be, a unitary theory which explains the amazing subtlety and complexity of the developing self and the author describes many of the ways in which these complexities appear in the developing child.

INTRODUCTION

The study of 'self' provides a wonderful opportunity to talk about the development of the child as a whole person with feelings, thoughts and behaviour rather than studying motor, affective, cognitive, and social development as separate parts and processes within the child. It also provides an opportunity to combine traditional approaches in developmental psychology with a more reflective approach and it is by reflecting upon 'self' in a personal manner that I shall begin.

EXISTENTIAL SELF

As a person I am conscious of being and I am aware of my personal existence. James (1890) referred to this as the **existential self**. As a child I remember moments of intense awareness of my existence when I was alone at bedtime watching the colour of the curtains fade as light fell into darkness. No-one could see me or touch me or talk to me and I was glad to be alone with my thoughts and feelings and my experiences of the world. As I lay between the crisp white sheets I could sense my body. It was mine and my thoughts and feelings happened within it and my experience of the world was created by it. To have any sense of self was to have my body. Subjective experience was the core of my experience of being a person. I knew which was my body and that it was not part of the sheets surrounding it.

existential self a sense of personal existence, uniqueness and autonomy which develops through the child's interactions with the social and physical world.

But how and when did thoughts of existence and being within a body begin? I don't remember the moment of 'self-awakening' when these reflections became possible. My conscious awareness of being an onlooker to the world, which would have entailed separating my body from the external world, must have begun very early. I have distinct memories of a sense of wonderment as I viewed what I could later label as 'very large fir trees' but my parents told me they were cut down less than a year after I was born due to heavy snow damage.

The development of self-agency

We know from studies of sensory deprivation that starving our bodies of sensation produces hallucinations and consequent distress (Heron, 1957). This is far removed from developmental psychology but it does make the point that we need external stimulation to promote a sense of 'being' and that we are a 'being' within a world that provides stimulation through our senses.

Whilst still in the womb the foetus can sense the physical world around and it is this stimulation through the child's senses which, according to Piaget (1953), facilitates the cognitive developmental progression from the child's inability to distinguish between its body and the surrounding world to a sense of separateness and a sense of agency.

The child's response to all kinds of stimuli received through the senses was acknowledged as early as 1897 by Wilhelm Wundt who said that immediately after birth the child reacts to all kinds of 'sense-stimuli most clearly to the impressions of touch and taste and with least certainty to those of sound'. He believed these were 'special forms of reaction-movements due to inherited reflexes' and amongst these he included the cry reflex when the child tasted sour or bitter substances or was affected by cold. Wundt suggested that the reflexive movements were accompanied by 'obscure sensations and feelings' presumably meaning that neither the observer nor the child could identify the 'new' feelings.

It is interesting that whilst Piaget focused upon the cognitive aspects of the child's response to the external world, Wundt focused upon the feelings associated with the child's movements. Clearly, both cognition and affect are important.

Cognitive responses to the external world

Let us look first at cognitive aspects of the child's stimulation by and responses to the external world. Piaget and Inhelder (1969, and see Chapters 9 and 16 for a fuller account of Piaget's theory) report that after the first month of reflexive responses, infants' responses are repeated again and again (**primary circular reactions**) although combined into more complex actions. By 4–8 months Piaget observed that infants are more responsive to the external world and seem to be aware that their behaviour has an effect upon objects around them. Rochat (1998) observed that from as early as 2 months the infant will wiggle its foot to effect movement of an attached mobile showing that exploration becomes more systematic and deliberate. By 8 months the **secondary circular reactions** become coordinated, in other words the child links its self-produced action with perceptual consequences (see Figure 8.1). A link is made between cause and effect with the infant capable of knowing how to produce a particular effect and developing an increasing sense of self-agency. This in turn enables the infant to develop a sense of its body as a differentiated entity or as separate from the external world.

> **primary circular reactions** the second stage in Piaget's period of sensorimotor development, from approximately 1 to 4 months. Repetitive actions based around the infant's body to exercise and coordinate reflexes that develop in the earlier period.

> **secondary circular reactions** the third stage in Piaget's period of sensorimotor development, from approximately 4–10 months. Infants repeat actions that have had an interesting effect on their environments, and manipulation and an understanding of the environment begins.

The child's external world comprises both objects and people and the child commandeers others to create desired effects. A rattle that is dropped may be picked up by an adult and given to the infant only to be dropped again for the adult to pick up and so the sequence is repeated again and again. The child seems to know how to produce a particular effect not just in relation to the physical world but also in relation to other people.

Infants are born to be sociable

From an early age the infant responds differently to people from objects (Stern, 1977) and the child enters the social world fully equipped to be sociable. Schaffer (1971) recognised the early sociability in the infant's preparedness to respond to social stimuli. These stimuli include the human face (Fantz, 1961), eyes or eye-like dots (Ahrens, 1954), attractive faces (Slater *et al.*, 1998), human-like movement (Simion *et al.*, 2008) and babytalk (high-pitched repetitive voices: Fernald, 1985). Additionally, there is a preparedness for others to respond to the sociability of the child, for example by being drawn to the child's cry (Ainsworth & Bell,

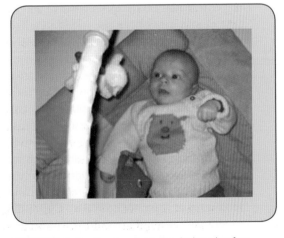

FIGURE 8.1 *Contingency learning: kicking her feet causes the mobile to move.*

1974), attracted to their cuteness or *Kindchenschema* (Lorenz, 1981) and responsive to their sucking pauses with looking and jiggling (Kaye & Brazelton, 1971). Early fumbling social interactions are quickly fine-tuned to become a synchronous caregiver–baby dance with both partners' movements and responses meshing with each other (Trevarthen, 1977).

Importantly from the infant's perspective, feedback is received from sociable others within this dance-like activity. In accord with Piaget's description of the secondary circular reaction stage of cognitive development, children seem to be aware that their behaviour has an effect on other people. Indeed, when a child's behaviour ceases to have an effect on the caregiver, visible signs of distress occur. Mesman, van Ijzendoorn and Bakermans-Kranenburg (2009) review the evidence demonstrating how in the *mother's blank face condition* (also known as the **still-face procedure**) during an otherwise rhythmic conversation-like exchange, the baby became distressed as evidenced by thrashing of arms and by frowning.

It is possible to deduce that in accord with Piaget's ideas, a link has been made in the child's mind between cause and effect, not only when the effect of the infant's actions is upon objects but also when it is upon people. Repetition or imitation by the mother or other adult is a particularly effective form of social feedback for the infant.

In the same way that children's realisation of their effects on the physical world helps them to develop a sense of separateness from the physical world, so too does children's realisation of their effects on others help them to develop a sense of separateness from others. From this it follows that there must also be a realisation by babies that they are not the only person.

An important cautionary note is needed. Whilst the young child may develop a sense of separateness from others, it does not necessarily follow that the child is aware of self and other as separate 'persons'. What we view as 'persons' may be separate 'objects' from the child so it is important to consider how a child's awareness of separate 'object' becomes an awareness of separate 'person'.

In doing this let us return to the emotional aspects of the children's response to the external world. Observations of very young babies' emotions show a rudimentary differentiation between positive and negative emotions so that by the end of the first month it has been suggested that lively rhythmical movements of babies' arms and legs indicate pleasurable feelings, whereas arrhythmical violent movements are symptoms of displeasurable feelings (Wundt, 1897). What is important for our study of self is how these emotions become associated with a growing sense of self. It is the psychodynamic theorists who take up the challenge.

In common with the cognitive theorists, Melanie Klein (1932) believed that at first babies cannot differentiate between themselves and their mother so that although the feelings experienced by babies are derived from sensations received from the mother they cannot grasp that they come from mother, a person different from themselves. Stern (1977) speculated that emotional aspects of a child's response to others is the key ingredient which transforms the child's schemas of people as objects to representations of separate person(s). Combining affective experiences with sensorimotor experiences permits encoding of internal representations of relationships and hence encoding of self and others as distinct. Whilst Stern analysed the richness of the social communication between caregiver and baby he did not make a direct link between this and the baby's emotional response to sociable others. Presumably, the emotional response arises within this rich social interchange.

THE DEVELOPMENT OF SELF-AWARENESS

Now that children can see themselves as separate from others there is a development of the ability to step outside oneself to look at oneself from the outside-in. James (1890) referred to this as 'me' or the self as known, which later became known as the **categorical self** (Lewis & Brooks-Gunn, 1979) and it contrasts with the previously described aspect of self, 'I', self as subject, self as knower or *existential self*. Furthermore, James saw the innermost part of 'me' as the **Material me**, a sense of embodiment (a sense of being related to a particular body). The child's recognition of his/her own body is indicative of the early growth of the self as known.

categorical self those aspects of self, e.g. gender and nationality, which define a person.

Material me according to William James, one of three constituents of self as a subject of experience (*existential self*). There is self-awareness of the body, clothes, close family, home and material possessions.

The rouge on the nose test

Studies of visual recognition confirm the growing awareness that children have about themselves as object. This was systematically explored by Lewis and Brooks Gunn (1979) who used an array of tasks, observations and measures but the most famous of all is the observation of a child playing in front of a mirror. The child's frequency of nose touching was noted whilst playing and then a dab of rouge was subtly rubbed onto the child's nose by the mother during a 'routine nose wipe' (this is commonly known as the **rouge test**; see Figure 8.2).

rouge test a small amount of rouge (or some other colour) is placed on the infant's nose before they are placed in front of a mirror. If the infant touches their own nose, as opposed to the reflection in the mirror, they are said to have acquired a self-concept.

Subsequent nose touching behaviour was noted whilst the child continued to play in front of the mirror. It was argued that if the child knew what they looked like, the change in appearance would be explored by touching the nose. At 15–18 months the child touched their nose to explore the rouge and this may be interpreted as indicative of visual self-recognition. However, knowledge of the direct contingency between the child's actions and the mirror image offers an alternative explanation of the findings. Other forms of evidence, for example, the use of appropriate personal pronouns to the child's own mirror image, struggles over possession, and use of possessive language such as 'that's mine' indicate that at roughly 2 years of age the child is able to recognise and respond to self, independent of contingency.

The fundamental problem in studying self-awareness is the same problem that besets developmental psychologists as they try to read the child's mind (see also Chapter 11

FIGURE 8.2 *The rouge test.*

on Acquiring a theory of mind). It is assumed that certain behaviours are indicators of 'self'. For example in Lewis *et al.*'s studies touching the nose is assumed to be a sign of visual recognition which in turn is assumed to be indicative of self-awareness. Whether it is a truly valid measure of the very personal experiential nature of self is difficult to ascertain. Long before the mirror studies of Brooks-Gunn, Wundt warned of the dangers of accepting as signs of self-consciousness:

any single symptoms such as the child's discrimination of parts of his body from objects of his environment, his use of the word "I", the recognition of his own image in the mirror or even first memories … since the objective observation of the child is not supplied at first with any certain criteria, it is impossible to determine the exact moment when self-consciousness begins.

(Wundt, 1897, p. 289).

Explaining the development of self-awareness

I am I and you are you and I am not you

We have discussed how children come to know their separateness from objects and their separateness from others through their actions and interactions with the world. An awareness of separateness presumes an awareness that there are others. It follows that as children come to know who they are, there is also an awareness of who they are not.

This was ably demonstrated by my 2-year-old son when on one bathtime occasion I had asked him to 'wash properly'. He angrily retorted 'I am I and you are you' (Figure 8.3). I was bowled over by the forcefulness of his retort, the confidence with which he spoke of his individuality and separateness from me, the ease with which he had used language to express his 'self' at such a young age and how he had used this to convince me that I too should be aware of his separateness. He was defining himself cognitively and affectively both in terms of who he was and who he was not. He had the cognitive ability to judge 'what was' and 'what was not' him. He had the emotional confidence to feel 'who he was' and 'who he was not'.

I am I and you are you and I am like you in some ways and not like you in other ways

One can speculate that the judgement made by my son was based upon his sense of existential self. He was aware that his existence was separate from mine. However

FIGURE 8.3 *I am I and you are you and I am not you.*

another way in which same/different judgements can be made is by comparison of attributes and it is likely that judgments about categorical self are made in this way.

Comparing oneself with others

Children's self descriptions often contain comparative statements – for example, 'I am taller than . . .', 'I have fair hair and he has dark hair' – and from these statements it is clear that attributes such as height, hair colour, age, and so on, are used as the basis for judgements about categorical self. Lawrenson and Bryant (1972) showed that pre-school children code **relatively** in preference to coding **absolutely** so it seems that from a young age making comparisons is the preferred mode of thinking. Further support for the dominance of this type of thinking comes from studies of concept formation. As early as 3–4 months babies can form category representations not only of things they frequently encounter, for example cats, dogs, chairs (Behl-Chadha, 1996) but also of abstract forms such as dot patterns (Younger & Gottlieb, 1988). Formation of categories involves storing information and later comparing other examples with the stored information. Thus making comparisons between elements of the baby's own world is a fundamental cognitive process and a baby's awareness of being categorically separate from others

relative coding/ absolute coding coding based on relative attributes, e.g. I am taller than him, I have fairer hair than her. Contrast with *absolute coding*, e.g. I am 5′5″ (1.7 m) tall, I have blond hair.

is facilitated by the cognitive comparison of selected attributes. But what attributes do they use? We know babies are drawn to certain features of their world, for example facial configurations (Fantz, 1961) and facial features (Ahrens, 1954), but research has not examined whether or not these features are the basis for self-related categorical judgements. There are several studies (Quinn, 2007; Quinn *et al.*, 2009) which show that young infants use information about the head region of animals to make categorical judgements (e.g. cat or dog?). Perhaps very young babies use features of the head region as one of the attributes to form their self judgements. The area is ripe for research. Ruble (1983) suggests that some attributes arising in a social situation are a natural basis for comparison, for example, preschool children comment upon being 'bigger/smaller', or 'older/younger' than other children. Other attributes, such as ability level or sports prowess, may become salient through comments made by significant others. Comparisons may be reinforced by parental encouragement and the language of others may become the inner speech and then the thoughts of the child (Vygotsky, 1978).

Further developing the focus upon language, Mead (1934) explained self-development as a cognitive process lodged in social experience and activity. He believed that communication, and not interaction *per se*, plays the pivotal role in self-development especially in the child's ability to represent self as object. The ideas are developed below.

I am I and although I am not you I can imagine what it is like to be you

In the preschool years children become increasingly aware of their own psychological properties and processes and also that other people have thoughts and feelings. The child's developing theory of mind (e.g. Shatz, 1994, and see Chapter 11) combines with their ability to remember the words of parents so that in pretend play, especially in role play, the child can both imitate the language of the parent (role of other) and respond as a child (role of self) to the language of the parent. Language provides a tool for shifting from one role to another and for trying out a range of roles. Some of the words used are likely to refer to personal attributes which may become the salient features for comparisons with others and ultimately for the development of a generalised view of self.

Now I am me will I always be me?

Mead's theory raises some contradictions about the nature of self. On the one hand Mead suggested that the process of trying out various roles in pretend play enables the child to select those features which ultimately crystallise into a sense of final 'generalised' self. On the other hand the notion of self as a social construction implies that as long as social interaction continues the process of self development must also continue, throughout the individual's life.

Some psychodynamic theorists favour the view that 'self' must ultimately and finally crystallise into a sense of being a unique whole self and that there is a continuity in this sense of self. Erikson (1959) supported this view with his emphasis upon identity formation with early roots in childhood conflicts that are finally resolved through important searching and reflection during adolescence. Anna Freud (1937) stressed the importance of maintaining the integrity of self and avoidance of self-fragmentation even to the extent of unconsciously deluding oneself through the use of psychological defence mechanisms, for example disowning negative self feelings and projecting them onto others, a defence mechanism known as **projection**.

In contrast Geertz (1984) argued that the notion of uniqueness of the individual is a Western cultural view and other cultures have very different views which emphasise sameness between people, especially between members of the same community: for example, in China people tend to view themselves as members of groups such as family and work groups. A closer look at the psychodynamics between family members including Western families reveals an apparent tension between **individualist** (uniqueness and difference) and **collectivist** (belonging and sameness) views of identity.

Through analysis of conversations, Edwards *et al.* (2006) viewed the complex relationships children share with their siblings. On the one hand there is a desire to be different from brothers and sisters, yet on the other hand there is a desire to be similar. There is a situation-dependent swing between feeling and wanting to be the same and feeling and wanting to be different. Thus, the view of self as unique, continuous, and ultimately crystallised is brought into question. Edwards' observations suggest there are a series of selves constructed through other people especially through siblings. Interestingly, in accord with our earlier view, these authors recognise the role of language in the constructions of multiple selves and suggest that in a person's internal world there may be many voices in dialogue with each other that may present with uncertain feelings and opposing demands.

> **projection** a psychological defence mechanism which derives from psychoanalysis in which the individuals see their own traits in others.

> **individualist societies** those in which there is an emphasis on the individualistic and uniqueness of individuals.

> **collectivist societies** those that emphasise the sameness and belongingness of individuals.

I AM ME BUT AM I WORTHY? THE STUDY OF SELF-ESTEEM – DEFINITION, MEASUREMENT AND ORIGIN

Whatever view of self we adopt there is no doubt that the language used by children about themselves has evaluative tones. For example children's self-descriptions in Rosenberg's (1979) studies are value laden and express aspects of self worth: 'I am rubbish at sport', 'I am good at drawing'. These kinds of comments are familiar to us and we have an intuitive understanding of the concept of **self-esteem** yet close analysis shows the difficulty of defining the concept. Typically, it is defined as the value that one puts upon oneself as indicated in the thoughts and feelings about oneself. Self-esteem seems to be viewed as a commodity with each one of us having more or less of this commodity. Closer inspection of both children's evaluative comments about themselves and introspections about one's own evaluations reveal that there can be simultaneous positive and negative evaluations of different aspects of self.

> **self-esteem** a person's overall evaluation or appraisal of his or her own worth.

Self Perception Profile designed by Harter (1983), aims to measure five specific domains of self-esteem: perceived athletic competence, behavioural conduct, physical appearance, scholastic competence, social acceptance and also overall self-worth.

Harter (1983, 1999) distinguished between five self-description domains: athletic competence, behavioural conduct, physical appearance, scholastic competence and social acceptance. Children (and adults) can feel good about themselves in one domain but not so good about themselves in another domain. She made a brave attempt to measure self-esteem within these five domains by using her **Self Perception Profile** which is presented in pictorial format for under 8-year-olds and verbal format for older children. For the younger children they are shown a series of picture pairs. One of the pictures in each pair allegedly shows a 'competent' child, e.g. a child who has almost completed a jig-saw puzzle and the other shows a 'less competent' child, e.g. a child who has completed just a small part of a jigsaw.

The children are asked to choose the picture within each pair which they think is most like themselves. For the older children the verbal equivalent involves making a choice between statements used to describe children who could do something and children who could not, for example, 'Some children do very well at sport' versus 'Some children don't feel they do very well at sport' (see Figures 8.4 and 8.5).

Children can further judge whether their choice of picture or statement is 'really true of me' or 'sort of true of me' and thus obtain a score in the range 1(high) to 4(low) on each self-description domain. Average scores (for each domain) are presented in a graphical profile. It has been suggested that the numerical average of the scores for each of the self-description domains gives an overall self-esteem measure but this is not the case. Additional measures of overall 'self-worth' (measured by responses to similarly structured questions requiring a choice between items such as 'Some children like the kind of person that they are' versus 'Some children don't like the kind of person that they are') often yields scores which deviate considerably from the average of domain specific scores. For example, the profile for one child in Harter's sample was scholastic competence: 3.8, athletic competence: 0.6, social acceptance: 2.8, behavioural conduct: 3.5, physical appearance: 2.3, giving an average of 2.5 which was considerably less than the overall self worth score: 3.6.

FIGURE 8.4 *Athletic competence may be part of one's self-description.*

Distinguishing between self-esteem and self-efficacy

A complicating factor is the importance that is attached to a domain, for example, the child may not be bothered if they bungle in the design and technology classes yet may be bothered by a pimple on the nose if physical attractiveness

FIGURE 8.5 *The child on the left, who has nearly finished her jigsaw, may be seen as more competent than the child on the right.*

Source: Vasta, R., Haith, M. & Miller, S., Child Psychology: The Modern Science (New York: Wiley, 1992), p. 487. Reprinted with permission of John Wiley & Sons, Inc.

is important. We have to be wary of imposing our own judgements about relative importance on the findings of studies. For example, we may think that academic prowess is a good contributor to overall self-worth because it is important to us but a child may be a member of a group in which poor academic performance is a sign of individual prowess. Thus, it is important to distinguish between **self-efficacy** (one's beliefs in one's ability in a particular area) and self-esteem: one could have very high self-esteem, yet be poor in certain areas that you don't really care about (Bandura, 1977).

> **self-efficacy** a person's evaluation of their ability to achieve a goal or an outcome in particular tasks.

It is important to make the distinction between quantification of self-esteem as if it were a commodity possessed and the subjective experience of self-esteem. The term itself is ambiguous. 'Self-esteem' has been used as a commodity that one does or does not have (Turner, 1980) or as an amount of a commodity in one of two categories: either high or low self-esteem (Coopersmith, 1967) or as a commodity ranging on a continuum from high to low self-esteem (Harter, 1983). These rather cold definitions contrast strongly with the feelings about worthiness which form the core of some psychodynamic theories.

Alfred Adler's view

An extreme but very interesting view was put forward by Alfred Adler (1927) who believed that all of us begin life with feelings of inferiority. According to this view the child has to try to overcome this **inferiority complex** by striving to achieve mastery in order to overcome the negative feelings and their perceived inferiority. The outcome of

> **inferiority complex** a feeling of self-worthlessness, and that one is inferior to others in some way(s).

striving is a temporary sense of superiority as mastery is achieved but feelings of superiority are quickly replaced by more feelings of inferiority so the striving has to begin again. This is the constant driving force. Note that a 'sense of superiority' is subtly different from a sense of self-worth as it suggests 'better than something', or 'better than someone else'.

I had asthma as a child at a time when inhalers were not available so the asthma prevented me from doing almost everything that I could see others doing. I used to wheeze heavily and wish that I could be brighter and more beautiful than other children but I wasn't. My mobility and physical capacities were limited but I don't think I felt as incapacitated as Adler. He was skinny, weak, and sickly. Having rickets he was unable to walk until he was four; he experienced a near death suffocation experience from a spasm of the glottis when he was five and was hit by a car twice when he was four or five years old, although not seriously hurt. He felt tormented by one of his brothers and rejected by his mother but his gregarious nature and tenacity ensured his popularity with others. Adler saw life as a series of challenges to be overcome – 'striving from a minus to a plus situation'.

You will remember how young children explore their physical and social world, thus receiving feedback and acting again upon the physical and social world, receiving feedback again and again. Through these transactions a sense of self-agency and hence a sense of separateness from objects and separateness from others develops. We can now add to this that early exploratory experiences provide the basis for feelings of self-worth or lack of self-worth.

Erikson's Eight Stages of Man

In his life-span developmental theory of personality, The **Eight Stages of Man**, Erikson (1959) described the social dynamics which create these value feelings as the child begins to explore the wider world. As one of eight life conflicts (named *learning autonomy versus shame*), the 2- to 3-year-old child has the potential through exploration of the world to develop either a sense of 'autonomy', a sense of 'shame' or a sense of 'self doubt'. Where expectations upon the child are realistic, exploration is successful and a sense of autonomy, 'I can do it and I am worthy' develops. If expectations upon the child are limited and opportunities for exploration are restricted, a sense of 'self-doubt' may develop. If expectations are too great and possibilities for exploration too vast, the child may try but fail and hence develop a sense of 'shame'. Shame and doubt are both negative feelings creating a sense of unworthiness.

Eight Stages of Man
eight distinct stages in life which, according to Erikson, are each characterised by a social challenge or conflict.

Self-esteem inventory

In searching for the origins of self-esteem, developmental psychologists moved away from reflecting upon the origins of the subjective experience of worthiness to more objective studies. A classic study by Coopersmith (1967) involved the administration of a **Self-Esteem Inventory** to 10–11-year-old boys. This was a checklist of 58 statements such as 'I'm pretty sure of myself' ' Most people are better liked than I am', each of which the boys decided were 'like' or 'unlike' them. It was intended to be a measure of global self-esteem examining how children saw themselves in relation to peers, parents, school, and personal interests. The measures were then correlated with a number of childhood indicators and it

Self-Esteem Inventory
a checklist of self-esteem items examining how children see themselves in relation to peers, parents, school and personal interests.

was found that the factors linked with high self-esteem included non-coercive dem-ocratic and consistent parenting, parents' acceptance of their children, clear and well-enforced demands, and respect for actions within well-defined limits. It was con-cluded that these were the antecedents of children's self-worth. Pervin (1993, p.189) wrote that, contrary to expectation, 'indicators of prestige (of the parents) such as wealth, amount of education, and job title did not have as overwhelming and as sig-nificant an effect on self-esteem as is often assumed'.

The suggestion by Coopersmith that factors such as democratic parenting were causal in their link to childhood self-esteem levels is flawed. Apart from the inap-propriateness of inferring causality from correlational studies (e.g. the link between high self-esteem and democratic parenting may have been due to another factor such as available parental leisure time), it is likely that the Self-Esteem Inventory is low in validity because of the subtle pressure on the boys to give socially desirable answers. There have been and continue to be many other attempts to measure self-esteem (e.g. Nadelman, 1982) but the problems of measuring this elusive concept remain and are humorously compared to the tale of the Blind Men and the Elephant. This is a famous Chinese or Indian legend in which six blind men had to describe an elephant after each had touched a different part of the animal – they each gave a different account, each one insisted that he alone was correct, but they were all wrong! In citing this legend Bosson *et al.* (2000) investigated seven different measures of self-esteem and found that the different measures did not correlate with each other, and they correlated only weakly with explicit (self-report) measures of self-esteem!

The assumption underlying many of the studies styled on Coopersmith's work was flawed. It is not possible to isolate a single causal variable that affects self-esteem or even to isolate a range of possible causes. The studies overlook the complex interac-tions between variables, the individual differences of children and most import-antly they ignore the nature of the transactions which take place between the child and others (Sameroff, 1991).

We need to shift our attention to the nature of these transactional processes involved in developing the inner sense of worthiness rather than looking for a cause(s) of behaviourally defined levels of self-esteem. Let us revisit some of the mechanisms previously described. Trevarthen (1977) reflected upon the synchronous meshing of the child's signals and responses with others' signals and responses in a dynamic continuous exchange. It is likely that a synchronous smooth exchange smooths the formation of a trusting relationship between child and caregiver. This harmonious transaction created by the active sociable child responding to and with the sensitive (nurturant, attentive and non-restrictive) parental care is associated with secure infant (Type B) behaviour in the **strange situation** (Ainsworth *et al.*, 1978, see Chapter 6). In contrast, the insecure-avoidant (Type A) child and insecure-resistant (Type C) child are more likely to have insensitive parenting, perhaps being cold, rejecting or failing to make their behaviour contingent upon the child's behaviour. It has been suggested that the important ingredients may be any or all of the following factors: warmth, sensitivity, acceptance, consistency, emotional responsiveness. In a longitudinal study, Goldberg *et al.* (1994) using videotaped recordings of behaviour in 'strange situations' found that Secure Type B children showed a full range of positive, negative and neut-ral emotions and mothers responded to all of these. In contrast, mothers of Type A children responded least often to their child's responses especially to the child's negative responses.

The relative amount and style of maternal responsiveness may be the magic ingredient in determining the way the child views themselves, views others and views relationships. The manner and timing of gazing into the child's eyes, of touching the child, the tone of voice and other subtle cues are likely to convey to the child the feelings that the caregiver has towards the child and whether or not they are loved. The feelings of others are introjected by the child. This is psychodynamic parlance for saying that the feelings of others become the feelings that the child has towards themselves so that the child who feels loved feels worthy of love and the child who feels unloved feels unworthy of love and therefore unworthy in general. This view is poetically expressed by Dorothy Law Nolte in 'Children Learn What They Live' sometimes known as 'If a Child Lives with . . .' (see Chapter 1). According to Bowlby (1969, 1973) and Bretherton (1993) these thoughts and feelings form the **internal working model (IWM)** which comprises three elements: a model of the self, a model of the 'other' and a model of the relationship between them. The IWM is the template for other relationships so that children, and later as adults, will have a blueprint for their expectations of self, other and relationships in the early formed model. As part of this the child's early sense of self worth will be one of the constituents of later relationships.

> **internal working model (IWM)** develops through day-to-day interactions with the primary caregiver(s) early in life, It comprises the child's picture of self, others and relationships (self in relation to others) and has both an affective (emotional) component and a cognitive component (mental representation).

THE POWER OF LANGUAGE

The subtlety of mutual body language is augmented by verbal language so that the views of others, especially 'significant' others becomes the view that the child has of him/herself (Cooley, 1902; Mead, 1934) Comments such as 'You are a good boy', 'Only naughty children do that', 'What pretty freckles you have' are often repeated many times and become the inner evaluative speech (Vygotsky, 1978) of the child. I remember as a young girl on a number of occasions enjoying being on my own sitting on the toilet, staring into space having an existential moment. I used to reflect that no-one could see me or touch me or hear me! No-one knew what I was thinking so I could just 'be' for a moment. In the next moment my thought was a realisation that I was not alone because God could read my thoughts. (I was a little girl in the 1940s with averagely religious parents) and then suddenly I remembered that my knickers were down so my moment of existential being was quickly supplanted with the thought that God would see me with my knickers down and that was naughty (Figure 8.6). Only naughty girls had their knickers down so I was a naughty girl. I was concerned about what others thought of me.

Rosenberg (1979) asked children how much they cared about what others, including parents, teachers, and peers, thought about them. For the young child parents were most important and for the adolescent peer judgements were most important. The power of language also aids children's ability to make evaluative comparisons (to code relatively) with others. This is demonstrated in children's self-descriptions such as 'she gets higher marks than I do'. Significant others also use comparative language: 'You eat up all your food but your brother does not', 'Other children are polite when they come here but you are not', 'Your father was always good at sums but . . .'.

Thus, through language, the judgements of others become the worthiness that the child feels. But one moment . . . is the feeling of worthiness simply about the feelings and thoughts of others transplanted through language to become the child's feelings and thoughts? Motivational and cognitive mechanisms play games with perception. In the 1940s and 1950s there was a rash of studies on perceptual sensitisation and **perceptual defence**. The idea was quite simply that you don't see what you don't want to see and you see what you want to see. The apparatus used in those days was a lumbering piece of equipment called a **tachistoscope** which enabled a stimulus to be flashed onto a screen for a exceedingly brief but controllable period of time (such experiments continue to be conducted, but presentation times are now computer controlled). It enabled the effects of motivational factors on perception to be studied. For example, Postman *et al.* (1948) found that people perceive words more quickly if they correspond to their personal values and if they relate to their needs. Bruner and Goodman (1947) asked children to adjust a circle of light to the size of a coin or to the size of a circular piece of cardboard. Adjusted light circles were larger when matching coins than when matching cardboard circles and the effect was greater for children who came from poorer families. In similar vein, Burkitt *et al.* (2003) showed that 4–11-year-olds draw positively characterised topics larger and negatively characterised topics smaller than a neutral topic. These studies add fuel to Barrett's (2005) **hot cognition** which is the label he uses to encapsulate the notion that emotion affects knowledge acquisition. We will revisit these ideas later.

FIGURE 8.6 *Only naughty girls had their knickers down!*

perceptual defence a defence mechanism in which the individual doesn't see, or hear, etc., stimuli or events that are personally threatening.

tachistoscope a device for presenting visual stimuli for very brief and precisely controlled times.

hot cognition the inextricable link between emotion (probably strong emotion) and cognition. Feelings influence thoughts and thoughts influence feelings.

Attribution theory

The study of self is well placed to make use of this important cognitive-emotional link in development. **Attribution theory** (Weiner, 1986) provides a convenient meeting

attribution theory a conglomerate of theories put forward by social psychologists aiming to encapsulate the allegedly systematic way in which individuals try to explain their own and others' behaviour.

ground for cognitive and affective explanations of the development of self-esteem. Conceived as a cognitive theory it states that a child (or adult) who is low in self-esteem will tend to attribute positive incidents, for example a good mark for homework, to external causes (the homework was easy), whereas they will attribute negative instances, for example a poor homework grade, to internal causes (I'm not clever enough). The child's negative thoughts about themselves are perpetuated by these thoughts. For a child high in self-esteem the same process of attribution but in reverse (attribution of success internally and attribution of failure externally) will confirm their high self-esteem. Although conceived as a cognitive theory, the explanation can easily incorporate emotional factors, namely that the child low in self-esteem emotionally blocks positive cognitions and the child high in self-esteem emotionally accepts the positive cognitions.

This is my body: The development of a sense of body image

The sense of embodiment or 'Material me' (James, 1890) begins with the baby's developing sense of separateness from objects and others and by the early recognition of their own body indicating the emergence of the categorical self or 'self as known'. The child is no longer profoundly egocentric (cognitive separation) and has separated or individuated (emotional separation) from the world around. The child begins to know themselves as an object, as a body whole with parts, as having body size and they begin to evaluate their body.

Body parts and whole

Our body has a shape, a size, many functional parts and a configuration of the parts as a whole. Thus, the child's body image is likely to comprise a mental representation of body shape, body size, functional parts and body configuration, and thoughts and feelings about the body as a whole.

Infants recognise and identify bodily attributes, for example, human facial configuration (Fantz, 1961), from an early age so this is likely to facilitate the development of body image. It has been argued that identification of body parts and the whole body configuration develop separately (Christie & Slaughter, 2007). Lis and Venuti (1990) tested 36 children aged 18–36 months. In a two-phase experiment the first involved testing the children's ability to identify body parts and the second involved attempting to complete a Manikin puzzle. They were asked to create a manikin when presented with the pieces in a logical order and then to create a manikin with the pieces presented all at once. It was found that although by 27 months most children completed the Manikin puzzle, they struggled with the trunk and often got the arms and legs confused. They were all good at completing faces, particularly positioning eyes and mouths. Interestingly there was no relationship between children's ability to identify body parts and their ability to complete the puzzle, which suggests that the identification of body parts and body whole configuration develop separately.

The tadpole stage in children's drawings

The problem with such studies is whether or not the investigators are truly measuring children's thoughts and feelings about their bodies. They are measuring body recognition and identification skills and this may be related to rather than a direct measure of the children's view of their own body. It is possible that children's drawing of the human body, especially when asked to draw themselves, provides a more valid measure of their thoughts and feelings about their bodies. Cox (1992) found in children's self portraits that they could draw faces before other parts of the body. Children's human figure drawings typically go through a **tadpole stage** (3–4 years) where there is no differentiation between the head and body. They often comprise a circle for the head or the head and body combined. Cox asked children to add a tummy button to their drawing and found that half the children put the tummy button in the face and half put it between the legs (see Figure 8.7).

> **tadpole stage** an early stage in children's drawings of the human figure in which there is no differentiation between the head and the body, and body parts such as the arms and legs are typically drawn as though they grow directly from the head, etc.

It may be that these pictures illustrate the children's views of themselves but drawing skill is likely to be an important factor influencing the productions so the drawings may not be indicative of their inner representations of their body. Other investigators have suggested alternative explanations for the multiplicity of tadpole drawings, for example, Kellogg's (1970) explanation that tadpoles are merely extensions of children's earlier scribbles. Freeman (1980) suggested that the tadpole drawings arise from planning difficulties associated with having to be familiar with societies' drawing conventions, having to recall the body parts and having to fit all the parts onto the

FIGURE 8.7 *The tadpole stage in children's drawings.*
Source: Cox (1992).

page. So we are left with a feeling of ambiguity about children's ability to form an inner representation of their body.

Are children drawing themselves?

There is also the question of whether or not children are drawing themselves. In other words is the drawing an attempted self representation or the representation of another person's body? In spite of the methodological difficulties, Piaget used children's drawings as a way of evidencing a child's representation of their body and from his studies he concluded a child's representation of their body progresses through a series of cognitive developmental stages. This theory suggests that with cognitive developmental 'improvements' the child will develop a more detailed and accurate view of their body. Certainly, drawings become more detailed and realistic but this does not necessarily indicate that the child's view of their body is becoming more accurate.

A simpler method is to ask the child about their body. Bannister and Agnew (1977) found that 5- to 9-year-old children recognised statements they had made about themselves and particularly statements made about their bodies. Similarly Rosenberg (1979) found physical features were frequently included amongst self-descriptions by 10-year-old children.

On reflecting upon the origin of the body whole/part representation it is necessary to draw upon resources beyond developmental psychology. There are many cited examples of people reporting phantom limbs, most commonly after amputation, and of children born with missing limbs, reporting that they actually have the missing limb. Social desirability may be a confounding factor but listening to the children describing their body parts it is uncannily convincing that the missing body part is truly part of their body representation. The explanation for these oddities may help to explain the development of the child's configurative body image. Ramachandran and Blakeslee (1998) argued that there exists a cortical map in the brain which represents the entire surface of the body and it is this which gives the child and adult a sense of whole body or body configuration even in the absence of some limbs.

Not all neuropsychologists agree with this determinist position, for example Kinsbourne (1995) believed that an infant gradually builds up representations in the brain through interaction with the environment and the feedback the body receives from the environment. The physical and sensory stimuli are coordinated by attentional processes in the brain and this gives rise to the body image representation. This theory gives biological substance to Piaget's constructivist theory which emphasises the active child's role in exploring the world, receiving feedback from the external world and forming a representation of the body through this process.

Body size image

My own observation is that children and adults spend longer talking about their body size than about their overall configuration. The configuration is assumed by most of us whereas even from a young age children are concerned with their height relative to others. Height is often perceived by children as an indicator of age and, interestingly, Argyle (1967) has shown that early perceived size relative to others tends to stick. Allegedly, children who feel small in comparison with others continue to feel small even after a growth spurt.

Brownell *et al.* (2007) have recently investigated 17–30-month-old children's body size self awareness in an article charmingly entitled 'So Big'. A comparison was made between children's performance on *Body size self awareness tasks* which encouraged them to consider properties of their own body size in relation to the outside world and their performance on *Size reasoning tasks* which involved making size judgements, but did not involve representation of their own body size.

Tasks which encouraged consideration of their own body size included

1. *Doll's clothes task* in which they were offered small doll's clothes to wear, and attempts to put the clothes on themselves as if they were full-sized were scored as errors.

2. *Door choice task* in which in a game of peek-a-boo the mother encouraged the child to go through a coloured screen through one of two doors. One door was too narrow even for the child's head to pass through and attempts to squeeze their bodies through the too-narrow door were scored as errors (Figure 8.8).

3. *Replica toys* in which after an initial play period with items such as a slide they were invited to resume play with scaled-down versions of the items, and attempts to use the replica toys as if they were full-sized versions were scored as errors.

The comparison size reasoning tasks included, amongst others, the item *Parents' doll's clothes task* in which children were invited to put the clothes on the parent, and attempts to put the too-small clothes on the parent were scored as errors.

There were significantly more errors in the tasks requiring self-awareness of body size than in the size reasoning tasks. Although the number of errors decreased with age all children at all ages made at least one body representation error. Thus, there is a continuing difficulty in developing a realistic body size image even by the age of two and a half. The authors suggest that this is because there are relatively few occasions in everyday life when the child needs to judge their body size.

FIGURE 8.8 *Young children will sometimes try to squeeze through a too-narrow opening.*

Source: Brownell *et al.* (2007). Reproduced with permission.

Although no theoretical framework is suggested for the explanation of the find-ings, a cognitive developmental explanation may be inferred from the authors' rea-soning. In accord with Piaget's ideas (although Piaget is not mentioned), Brownell *et al.* (2007) suggest that exploration is the child's key to developing a sense of their body as an object, and they imply that exploration may also provide opportunities to develop a sense of body size.

However, the validity of the measures must always be considered and the children must have made some interesting 'sense' (Donaldson, 1978) of Brownell *et al.*'s tasks. For example, when asked to put doll's clothes on themselves they may have thought this was very silly but felt compelled because of the power imbalance between inves-tigator and child to do as requested. When asked to go through one of the doors (one of which was too small for them) they may not only have thought about their current size but also thought how small they could make themselves.

This is a problem I am grappling with at the moment. In order to gain access to my roof void to investigate a roof leak I need to climb through a very small ceiling aperture. I am not only weighing up my size relative to the size of the hole but also wondering if I can make myself smaller by breathing in and tensing my muscles (Figure 8.9).

Children in Brownell *et al.*'s (2007) study may have been making similar complex judgements, or may have had problems in integrating visual information with appro-priate actions. A parallel finding was reported by DeLoache *et al.* (2004) who found that 18–30-month-old children often made serious attempts to carry out impossible actions on miniature objects, suggesting that the perception of object size and the organisation of actions on them are not properly integrated.

So far we have viewed body image as a cognitive concept but there is no doubt that we have very strong feelings about our bodies and these begin at an early age through the feedback received from the external world, especially from significant others. In literature there are examples of children comparing their small size with the largeness of adults (Figure 8.10). For example Jonathan Swift describes Gulliver's fear and disgust when visiting Brobdingnag, the land of the giants. He was fright-ened of being stepped on, amazed at the size of the skin pores and the size of a woman's nipple, disgusted by the volume of urination and the 'largeness' of the smell of giants.

Psychodynamic theorists are con-cerned with the feelings of the child especially with the unconscious sense of anxiety. Swift's literary ideas may be right, that the size of the adult whole body in relation to the smallness of the child engenders fear but Freud thought that the child was more concerned with the comparison between adult and

FIGURE 8.9 *Size testing: Trying to fit into a too-small space.*

children's body parts. Most notable is the alleged comparison made by the child of the difference between the size of a boy's penis and that of his father. Surprised at the enormity of it, the boy may feel inferior because his penis is small and seek to compensate for its smallness in other ways. Therein lies the potential to perceive size unrealistically and to distort our body size dimensions.

In addition to being especially aware of their height relative to other children and adults, children are particularly aware of their body build. In a study first conducted in USA and repeated in a London primary school (BBC Fat) with 24 5–8-year-old children it was found that they were more likely to select a photograph of an overweight child as the one they would least like as their friend, and it is clear that negative attitudes towards overweight body shapes develop from an early age (Dohnt & Tiggemann, 2006). These and other studies confirm popularly held views that at an early age overall size matters and being overweight is undesirable. These studies are about the judgements of other children, so what do we know about children's own body attractiveness ratings?

FIGURE 8.10 *So small … compared to adults.*
Source: Shutterstock.

PERCEPTION OF BODY ATTRACTIVENESS

It is not hard to find studies in this area, for example Thompson *et al.*'s (1997) survey of 9-year-olds indicates that there was greatest body dissatisfaction amongst females and white children than amongst males and black children with a heavier ideal size being chosen amongst black children than white children. Almost all wanted to be thinner than their current size. Humenikova and Gates (2008) measured perceived and ideal body size of Czechoslovakian and American 10–11-year-olds and found that American children had a thinner ideal body image than Czech children and were more dissatisfied with their body size.

Pelican *et al.* (2005) argue that significant others are particularly important in the development of body image, especially with regard to body shape and attractiveness. In accord with this, Birgeneau (2004) showed that judgements about the child's body begin in the earliest stages of a child's life. She gave photographs of gender-neutral average-sized and overweight infants to 229 men and women (mean age 29 years), Caucasian and African-American, parents and non-parents. Their judgements of personality and social characteristics showed a bias: 'Fat is bad' even in infancy.

Parents influence their children's body shape including size directly through the food they feed their children and the amount of physical exercise/play they encourage in their children. A host of correlational studies link parental influence with a child's view of their body attractiveness. For example, Smolak (2004) found a positive correlation between children's evaluation of their bodies and the parents' evaluation of their children's bodies. Keery *et al.* (2005) found that children's evaluation of their body shape and attractiveness was correlated with how much their fathers and older siblings teased them. Additionally, children who were teased by their parents were more likely to be teased by their siblings. Kelly *et al.* (2005) found that children were much more likely to develop a positive evaluation of their shape and attractiveness if parents talked to their children with regards to their bodies in terms of physical health rather than weight or weight control. In addition, Rosenblum and Lewis (1999) show that adolescents' (13–18-year-olds) body image has little to do with the perception of others but once developed remains constant through adolescence.

Unfortunately, in spite of the plethora of studies in this area, correlational studies tell us little about causality. Instead let us examine some of the processes by which children formulate their self-body judgements. We need not look far as the processes identified as key protagonists in the development of categorical self and of self-esteem will apply here too.

Early social relationships

First, early social relationships and the nature of transactions are important. It is likely that a child who is touched sensitively will begin to develop a positive feeling about its body. The subtlety of mutual body language is supplemented by verbal language so that the evaluative views of others, especially 'significant' others, become the evaluative view that the child has of themselves (Cooley, 1902; Mead, 1934). Evaluative verbal messages play an important part in conveying these viewpoints: 'You are clumsy', 'You are so pretty', 'Stop fidgeting and put your long legs under the table properly'. Further reference to Rosenberg's (1979) work shows how children are concerned about the views of others – initially parents then teachers and peers, especially the latter during adolescent years. The judgements of others become the worthiness that the child feels about their body. Additionally emotional and motivational factors influence a child's perception of their body so that existing feelings of low self-worth prevent the young person from seeing positive features. An extreme example of this is found in anorexia where the anorectic perceives their body as overweight in contradiction to the actual skinniness of their body.

personal modelling
occurs when the child feels emotionally attached to a person and wants to be like them.

Modelling and social comparison

Second, modelling and social comparison are important processes by which children acquire a sense of body image. Danzinger (1971) described two types of modelling: personal and positional modelling. **Personal modelling** occurs when the child feels emotionally attached to the person and wants to be like them. This is akin to the concept of **identification** used by the psychoanalytic theorists. **Positional modelling** occurs when the child perceives a similarity between themselves and the role model who may not be personally known to the child. This requires some form of cognitive representation and also requires the child to choose whether or not to copy the model. Evidence for copying aspects of body image is found in the study by Pike and Rodin (1991) who found that mothers of bulimic daughters often had eating disorders themselves or had begun dieting at an earlier age than those whose mothers did not have eating disorders. There is a similar finding with children/adolescents who have friends with eating disorders (Field *et al.*, 2001). Smolak (2002) found that children who played with toys such as Barbie dolls had a less positive body evaluation of themselves than those who did not. However, again this evidence is mostly correlational so establishing direction of cause and effect is difficult.

> **identification** a psychological process in which an individual identifies closely with another person, and may attempt to transform themselves to be like the other (usually admired or idolised) person.

> **positional modelling** occurs when the child perceives a similarity between themselves and the role model who may not be personally known to the child.

Clark and Tiggemann (2007) found that teenagers who discussed their body shape and attractiveness more with their peers had a less positive evaluation of their body than those who did not. However it could also be argued that these adolescents discuss their bodies more because they have a less positive evaluation and are preoccupied with it, rather than peers influencing their body image by either modelling or social comparison.

Emotionally charged cognitions, like Barrett's (2005) *hot cognition* may help us explain how we develop a positive or a negative view of our bodies.

Re-constructing the body and body image

Irrespective of the view children have of their bodies, there is potential for changing the appearance of the body. With increasing age more choice and control is possible, especially during adolescent years. Choices about the very young child's clothing will be made by significant adults and the age at which the child is allowed freedom of clothing choice will depend upon the nature of the relationship between parental figures and the child. I remember when I was 11 my mother permed my hair against my wishes. It went very frizzy and my sister called me 'fuzzy wuzzy bear' making me dreadfully unhappy. I have never curled my hair since then!

Once choice becomes possible it is likely that young people will aspire to achieve their ideal body image. Choice of clothes, physical changes to the body, which may include dieting to look slim, exercising to develop muscles, acquiring body tattoos, change of hairstyle, and so on, will directly influence the way the young person views themselves. Peer pressure and the desire for approval is strong so the style of clothes and general appearance that are chosen may be heavily influenced by what is perceived to be the socially desired physical appearance. A change in body image is partly due to the body changes but it is also mediated by the response of others.

The physical appearance is chosen because it has meaning for the young person, because it is intended to make a statement about that person's identity and to act as a signal to others, especially to peers. Thus, what began as a body form determined by biological factors becomes a vehicle for social signalling. Adoption of a style of clothing and general appearance often makes group allegiance clear, indicating both the groups to which the young person belongs and the groups to which they do not belong (Phoenix, 2005)

Although young children may have less choice than the adolescent, when they can make choices they act upon the same principle of conveying messages to other people through the clothes that they choose. In contrast to the plimsolls and Start-Rite shoes my mother chose for me, my sons used to put considerable pressure upon me to buy for them the latest designer brand trainers or surf shoes.

In sum, there is a remarkable development of the body image during childhood and adolescent years. It begins as an undifferentiated body image mixed up with the external world, becomes more differentiated as feedback is received from the physical and social world, and then has increasing potential to change as choices about physical appearance become more available.

GENDER IDENTITY DEVELOPMENT

'It's a boy' or 'it's a girl' is usually the first announcement about the newborn baby (at least where the parents have chosen not to be informed by earlier scans). The basis for the judgement lies in viewing whether or not there is a penis. At this point blue or pink knitting can begin and play items acquired. The categorisation of the baby into one or other of the gender groups elicits expectations in others and appropriate follow-on behaviour. Immediately, one can see that the roots of gender identity must lie in both biological determinants and social determinants. It all looks very simple – just add whether there is a penis or not with a spot of socialisation and the product is a boy or girl.

This beguiling simplicity hides a host of complexities but before addressing these we'll start with the psychoanalytic assumption that the basis for gender identity is

phallic stage a stage in Freud's *psychoanalytic theory* in which the young boy's interest centres on his penis and he develops feelings of sexual attraction towards his mother.

whether there is a penis or not. Freud (1905 / 1962) talked about parts of the body and functions of the body that nobody else dared mention and according to him at about three years of age, during the **phallic stage**, the boy's interest centres upon his penis and this interest gives rise to a feeling of sexual attraction towards his mother. These pleasurable feelings are associated with feelings of jealousy or resentment directed against the father, who thus becomes the rival for his mother's affection. The boy fears that his desires may be punished by the father with castration (the castration complex) so to resolve the conflict (known as the **Oedipus complex**) he identifies with his father. Through this unconscious mechanism he comes to feel that he is his father and thereby takes on masculine identity. This is a neat solution as he can fulfil his illicit desires by being his father and no longer fears castration by his father because he is his father. For girls there is an equivalent **Electra complex** in which instead of fearing castration she wishes she had a penis (penis envy) because it is superior to a clitoris. The girl feels that she has been punished already, renounces any desire to be masculine and thus presumably takes on a feminine identity instead. The theory is very unclear and somewhat demeaning for girls: additionally, there is little or no empirical support for either complex.

Evaluating Freudian theory

It's easy to reject the ideas because reflecting back one cannot remember these desires but of course this emotional turmoil is said to have taken place at an unconscious level. I cannot remember seeing a penis until I was 11, far too late for successful resolution of the Electra conflict!

Scientists abhor the theory because hypothetical constructs abound, testable hypotheses are difficult to form and it has been claimed that the theory can neither be proved nor disproved. Hidden feelings are notoriously not the subject matter for a true scientist, however, Kline (1981) tempered this view with a thorough review of Freudian theory establishing which parts could be scientifically verified and bringing together research which had verified aspects of the theory. The evidence presents a confusing picture in relation to the Oedipal and Electra conflicts. Apparently supporting the theory and working on the assumption that two parents are needed for successful resolution of the conflicts, we would expect single-parented children to have difficulty forming their gender identity. A number of studies of father-absent boys allegedly confirm this difficulty, for example, Hetherington and Deur (1971) found that boys whose fathers were absent before they were 4 were less 'masculine', but that absence after the age of 4 produced little effect on 'masculinity'. Apparently, contradicting the theory and working on the basis that both father and mother are needed for successful gender identity, one would expect children of homosexual parents to show inappropriate gender behaviour but this has not been found (Golombok et al., 1997). Gender development appears to be unrelated to parental sexual orientation (Fulcher et al., 2008).

These studies do raise questions about the validity of the measures of gender identity and force us to look at our definition of the term. So far I have not attempted a definition of gender identity and presumed that the reader would have a pretty good intuitive idea. In discussing the views of Freud, his emphasis was upon the affect or feeling part of being a boy or a girl. Although not mentioned in Freud's work there must also be a cognitive component of gender identity – how children think about their gender identity, how they classify themselves as a boy or girl. The cognitive classification is closely tied to gender appropriate behaviour – I am a boy and therefore I do X or I am a girl and I do Y. The behaviours are appropriate to the gender so that boys conform to the gender roles of a particular society and girls conform to their gender roles.

Boys and girls and shades of gender

Societies have well-defined gender roles and stereotypes of typical male and typical female behaviour and they are easy to access. Ask a group of mature students to let rip with gender stereotypes and contributions flow, emotions run high, everyone becomes animated and after the class students say what a wonderful time they have had. However, the serious side for our analysis is that any study which rests upon serious definitions of male and female gender-appropriate behaviour will be heavily influenced by the authors' preconceived ideas. For example in Hetherington's (1972) study 'masculinity' was defined as being more dependent upon peers, less involved in competitive and physical contact sports and being less assertive. Would this fit with your definition of masculinity?

There are further complications in that we take for granted that there are only two gender categories, boy or girl but perhaps there are shades of gender. Sex differences are not solely identified by having or not having a penis but also by relative levels of hormones, chromosomal differences, internal reproductive structures and the gonads. There is not necessarily a perfect correlation between these indicators as evidenced in examples of **hermaphrodites** or pseudo-hermaphrodites. These have been viewed as 'abnormal cases', the oddity and not the norm, but there is a realisation that a mixture of male and female biological attributes may reside in many children. Ehrensaft (2007) states that an increasing number of children are expressing themselves in gender-variant ways for example 'girlyboys' who are boys who accept themselves as boys but who cross culturally defined gender lines in their attitudes, behaviours and desires (Figure 8.11). For instance at Kampang Secondary school in Thailand a transgender toilet is provided for the 10–20 per cent of the children who identify themselves as **transsexuals**.

hermaphrodites an organism or individual with both male and female sexual organs.

transsexual an individual who identifies with a gender inconsistent or not culturally associated with their biological sex.

FIGURE 8.11 *Girlyboys.*

The boy who was raised as a girl

The way children think and feel about their gender identity does appear to have a biological basis as evidenced in the tragic case study of the boy whose circumcision went wrong (Colapinto, 2000; Money, 1974). On 22 August 1965, Janet Reimer gave birth to healthy twin boys, Bruce and Brian. As time passed concern was raised about how they urinated, and they were diagnosed with a condition known as **phimosis**, which is typically treated with circumcision. On 27 April 1966, in what was intended to be a routine circumcision, the doctors used an electrocautery needle, instead of a scalpel, to excise the 8-month-old Bruce's foreskin, but the procedure went horrifically wrong and his entire penis was burned off. On the advice of psychologist Dr. John Money, who was of the view that gender identity and assignment was entirely determined by nurture and not by nature, Bruce was castrated at

22 months, was renamed Brenda and reared as a girl. Until the age of 14 no-one told Brenda that she had been born as a boy, but when she was told what had happened she insisted on being gender-reassigned and became David Reimer.

phimosis a condition where the male foreskin cannot be fully retracted from the head of the penis, and typically causes problems with urinating. A treatment may be circumcision.

Money claimed that 'Brenda' developed as a 'real' girl with a clear female gender identity, but he was lying. The child's rearing as Brenda was not a success, and he did not identify as a girl:

> There is no way of knowing you are a boy or a girl. Nobody tells you are a boy or a girl. You know. It's in you and it's in your genetics, it's in your brain. No one has to tell you. I was never happy as Brenda . . . never. I would never go back to that. I would rather slit my throat. It did not work because it is life. You are not stupid . . . Eventually you are going to think who you are.

These were the words of David Reimer or was it Brenda Reimer or was it Bruce Reimer? David spoke of his unhappiness as a child, and he made two suicide attempts in his 20s:

> I tried to put make-up on but I looked like Bozo the clown. Can you imagine a guy trying to put make-up on himself. I tried but it was never going to work. I wore dresses on occasions. I never played with girls' things. I played with my brother's things. I did not like sharing but if I did not then I would have had nothing.

The emotion with which David spoke these words was palpable and with this information alone it would be easy to accept that gender identity is 'there' and that there is an existential sense of being gendered which stems from a biological basis, most probably from gender-specific hormonal changes whilst still in the womb.

Some tentative supportive evidence points to an area of the brain called the sexually dimorphic nucleus in the hypothalamus which is linked to gender identity. Gorski *et al.* (1978) found that this structure was three to eight times larger in the male rat than in the female rat. Swaab & Hofman, 1995, found that the nucleus was twice as large in heterosexual men as in homosexual men. There is evidence for ferrets, gerbils and sheep but there is the accompanying problem of extrapolating to humans and there are no data for children.

Whilst the biological explanation of gender identity is alluring and has some supportive scientific evidence, there is no doubt that other factors also contribute to the child's sense of gender identity. It could be argued that David's sense of being a boy was the result of being reared as a boy for 22 months before he was castrated. Money promoted the idea of *gender neutrality,* that how an infant is labelled and subsequently socialised is the major source of gender identity, but clearly he was wrong. David Reimer underwent treatment to reverse the reassignment, and he also married and became a stepfather to his wife's three children. However, he never had freedom from his problems and on 2 May 2004, at the age of 38, he took a shotgun from his home, sawed off its barrel, and on 5 May, he drove to the parking lot of a nearby grocery store and shot himself in the head, a suicide that finally ended his torture.

Rewarding gender-appropriate behaviours

Socialisation comprises many different processes. Strict learning theorists favour the view that gender-related behaviours are learned through operant conditioning. Gender-appropriate behaviours are strengthened through rewards and gender-inappropriate behaviours are weakened through non-rewards. Therefore, in our society we would expect approval for the girls' and boys' behaviour shown below.

The evidence that parents do reward gender-consistent behaviour and do not reward gender-inconsistent behaviour seems to apply more to fathers' responses than to mothers' responses. Langlois and Downs (1980) categorised fathers' responses to their 3–5-year-old children as either positive (e.g., attending to the child, giving praise, smiling, etc.) or negative (e.g. ignoring, interfering, and even ridiculing). On all indicators there were more positive responses for children when they played with a gender appropriate toy and for all indicators there were more negative responses when the child played with a gender-inappropriate toy (Figure 8.12).

FIGURE 8.12 *Parents tend to reward gender-appropriate behaviour.*

The investigators also showed that the tendency to reward gender-consistent behaviour and non-reward or even punish gender-inconsistent behaviour was stronger for boys than for girls. Block (1978) believed that differential reinforcement of gender appropriate and inappropriate behaviour continues through life rather than being confined to childhood so it is likely that the boy on the left may receive greater disapproval than the girl on the right in Figure 8.13.

The principles of operant conditioning were promoted by Skinner (1953) and in its strictest form of behaviourism, this type of learning was considered not to involve a cognitive component. The behaviour was either strengthened or weakened depending upon the reinforcement contingency. Although this mechanistic explanation of shaping behaviour may account for adopting some gender-appropriate behaviours, the explanation cannot account for changes in the way the child thinks and feels about themselves. Indeed the strictest behaviourists would not include the study of gender identity on their agenda as it would be considered far too woolly and non-measurable a concept to be worthy of study.

FIGURE 8.13 *It is likely that the boy on the left may receive greater disapproval than the girl on the right.*

Cognitive components of gender identity

The idea that gender identity can be explained without reference to cognition does not fit with the findings of Freeman (2007). She found that when parents of 3–5-year-old children were asked for their opinions about gender-typical and cross-gender play, most rejected common gender stereotypes. In contrast, when their children were asked to identify 'girl toys' and 'boy toys' and asked to predict their parents' reactions to their choices of gender-specific toys, the children predicted their parents would consistently approve of play with gender-appropriate toys and disapprove of play with cross-gender toys. Thus, it seems that children have begun to think about the appropriateness of their play. A cognitive component, a necessary component of gender identity has begun to form. Further evidence for the cognitive internalisation of gender appropriateness comes from the work of Bussey and Bandura (1992). In this study, 3–4-year-old children watched a video recording of children playing with gender-consistent and gender-inconsistent toys. They were asked to evaluate the behaviours and were also asked how they would feel if they were playing with the 'boy' toys and with the 'girl' toys. They disapproved of gender-inappropriate play in others and thought it would be wrong for them to play with the 'wrong' toys. Operant conditioning as a mechanism of learning cannot account for the development of these thoughts about gender appropriate and inappropriate behaviour. The presence of cognitive processes in learning was acknowledged by a behaviourist break-away group who became known as the **social learning theorists**. Not only did they acknowledge the

FIGURE 8.14 *A boy on a tractor would be seen as gender-appropriate behaviour.*

cognitive component in learning, they also acknowledged that learning typically takes place within a social context. Led by Bandura (1965), with his famous studies on aggression, the importance of observational learning was emphasised. Gender-appropriate behaviour is observed and copied from role models. In order for the behaviour to be copied, it is necessary for the child to selectively attend to the behaviour, form a mental representation of the behaviour and make a choice to copy that particular behaviour. Unlike operant conditioning this process involves cognitive processing and the child is actively involved in the process rather than being passively shaped by others (Figure 8.14).

We have mentioned the distinction between personal and positional modelling (Danzinger, 1971) and it is likely that both types of modelling occur in the development of gender identity. Children copy the gender behaviour of models they know and like and they will choose to copy the gender behaviour of models they may not know but perceive as similar to themselves. Role models may be encountered in the family, school, neighbourhood, in books, on television . . . the list is endless. There is a massive amount of gender role information in the child's social environment and the major question is how children make sense of this information. We can get our clues from the way mental representations are formed in general. Attention to information is selective, information needs to be organised, and this information informs behaviour. It follows that attention to gender information is selective, gender information needs to be organised and gender information informs behaviour.

There is some evidence to show that children selectively attend to gender-related information. Bussey and Bandura (1999) note that a young child prefers to play with toys traditionally associated with their gender. In the case study of the circumcision that went wrong, in spite of being reared as a girl, David Reimer said that he felt he was a boy and although he was given only girls' toys he preferred to share the boys' toys belonging to his brother. Note Bussey and Bandura's use of the phrase 'traditionally associated'. The processes which enable these 'traditional associations' to be implanted or constructed in the young child's mind warrant further analysis.

Construction of gender identity

It is probable that gender identity is constructed in ways that are similar to the development of self and to which we have already referred. Gender identity is after all part of the wider sense of self. Society dictates that gender is recorded and defined at birth, so children have no early choice – they have to construct a gendered self. In making comparisons between themselves and others they note attributes linked with gender (e.g. body features, mode of dress, play activities and associated toys). These comparisons are fuelled by the non-verbal and verbal messages received from others and the messages are replayed by the child during role play and during pretend play (Mead, 1934).

Focussing upon gender-related attributes, children form cognitive categories of 'boy' and 'girl'. Slabey and Frey (1975) showed children pictures of a young boy and a young girl and found that by 2 years they are able to correctly identify gender categories (gender labelling) and when asked 'Which one are you?' they can correctly place themselves in the right category. Further questioning revealed that an understanding of the continuity of gender (**gender constancy**, an awareness that one's gender does not change) develops by 3–4 years of age and a recognition of gender irrespective of changes in attributes, for example girls dressed in boy-style clothes (gender stability) develops by 7 years. This developmental progression may be interpreted as progression in logical thinking and in particular the development of conservation ability (Kohlberg, 1966; Piaget, 1953). Alternatively, it may be interpreted as information-processing development and the development of a conceptual framework as attributes are cognitively noted and sorted. From Bem's (1981) own work using a classification procedure, it was deduced that whilst children learn specific concepts and behaviours of being male or female, they also learn to perceive and organise different kinds of information in terms of gender schema or organised packages of information. These provide preconceived ideas about gender which help to organise new information but also act as blinkers to some new information.

It is especially interesting that Bem found gender was not always an important organisational concept for all children. Whilst society projects gender as a key feature it is not a key aspect of perceived self for every child. Furthermore, it is only in certain social situations that gender is perceived as relevant (David et al., 2004). This variability between children and the fluidity of self may also characterise other aspects of categorical self.

THE CHOSEN CATEGORICAL SELF

Whilst body image and gender identity may have an existential element of experiencing the body and experiencing gender, there is a strong categorical component in both and we can see a pattern emerging in the way in which subjective self-categories are constructed. There are common intermingling social, affective, and cognitive processes: social interaction especially with significant others, verbal and non-verbal communication within interactions, selecting and organising processes of cognition fuelled and partly directed by emotional and motivational processes – all of these help the child to assemble a view of self.

For most young children their subjective view of their body is important as evidenced in their multitude of physical descriptions (Rosenberg, 1979). As we have said, for many children gender identity is important but not for all (Bem, 1981). This prompts us to look further at the importance children attach to different aspects of themselves. Rosenberg's study of categorical self using the 'Who am I?' or **Twenty Statements Test (TST)** (Kuhn & McPartland, 1954) yields a variety of children's responses which can be classified into categories of physical attributes, family relationships, gender, nationality, religious and other beliefs, psychological characteristics, for example, I am a kind person. Personal replication of the study shows that individual children respond with their own list of categories elicited probably in each child's personal priority order. Responses are partly age dependent and probably partly language-ability dependent but may give an indication of what is important subjectively to a child at that point in time.

> **Twenty Statements Test (TST)** a tool to facilitate self-awareness. An individual asks the question 'Who am I?' 20 times and then reflects upon their responses in order to draw up a prioritised list of self-attributes.

Developing a national identity

For some children their list will include national identity but not all children will include this. There do not appear to be studies which consider a child's prioritisation of national identity relative to their overall sense of categorical self. Barrett (2005) gave children a set of cards on which gender, age and national categories ('English', 'Scottish', 'British', etc.) were written. In recognising and choosing all cards which described themselves it was shown that by 6 years of age, national identity commonly features as one aspect of chosen identity. Barrett argues that this shows national identity is important to children. Certainly his methodology is an improvement upon Carrington and Short's (2000) use of leading questions, for example, 'Are you British or something else?' However, Barrett's cards prompt the children and are unlikely to give a true picture of the subjective importance of national identity relative to other aspects of self. Nevertheless, the studies show that children correctly (as defined by society) recognise the name of their own national group and, in the context of the study, show some level of personal nationality ownership.

Barrett attempted to use adapted versions of traditional theories: cognitive developmental theory (Aboud & Amato, 2001; Piaget & Weil, 1951) and *social identity theory (STM)* (Duffy & Nesdale, 2009; Tajfel, 1978) to account for his wide-ranging developmental national identity findings but found the theories wanting. His alternative explanation is most interesting and fits snugly with the ideas put forward in the preceding sections of this chapter. He acknowledges the importance of constructive cognitive categorisation processes, social and emotional processes in the sense of belonging to a national group and acknowledges the interweaving of these processes, for example in 'hot cognition'. Whilst the methodology adopted in his studies makes it difficult to assess the subjective importance of national identity to children, Barrett does acknowledge there are individual differences in the relative importance of each chosen subjective identity category.

What is not apparent from Barrett's studies is the moment-to-moment shift in the importance of subjective national identity. For example, the two children shown in Figure 8.15 may be feeling and thinking of England in the context shown but may not list English identity in the TST nor consider their nationality at other times. As a child my awareness of being British was heightened on school trips to Paris but at other times I rarely thought of my national identity. It can be argued that a sense of national identity, like other self categories, is not simply a social category or a cognitive structure but is socially, cognitively and emotionally constructed by the child

FIGURE 8.15 *'Three lions on the shirt': Developing a sense of national identity.*

within a particular context. The idea of moment-to-moment shifts in the subjective sense of national identity fits with David *et al.*'s (2004) views of gendered self and it is a view we could adopt more widely. Perhaps we should move away from a fixed sense of categorical self as promoted in the 'generalised' sense of self (Mead, 1934) or identity formation (Erikson, 1959) and in place adopt a view of self as flexible, momentarily responsive and constructed.

Using children's spontaneous responses as the basis of future research we could ask how often particular categories arise? Does the distribution of categories change over time? What factors influence the ebb and flow of categories through time and situations/place? The research field is wide open.

We could adopt a compromise position that some aspects of subjective categorical self are pretty resistant to change and essential to a feeling of wholeness and stability, but others ebb and flow. For me the desire to be a mother and be 'good at books' was present at the earliest age and since my 20s the allied categories of 'mother' and 'psychologist' have been central to me. My children may have flown the nest but I am still a mother. I am not sure who I would be without these two subjective aspects of self, yet other categories matter less and flow in and out of my sense of self.

SUMMARY AND CONCLUSIONS

Through most of this chapter the sense of self developing within the child is viewed as unique and continuous. An early sense of separateness from the physical world develops as the child explores through motor actions, and a sense of separateness from other people develops through early social interactions. By about 15 months self-awareness seems to have developed, although care must be taken in the interpretation of studies. With increasing self awareness children come to know who they are and who they are not ('I am I and you are you'). A desire to be both the same and different from others is facilitated by the ability to imagine what it is like to be someone else and by the cognitive capacity to make comparisons.

A child's ability to look from the outside into their self enables the construction of subjective self categories. For many children the categories which are constructed include body image, gender, and nationality as aspects of their perceived self and the development of these subjective self-categories is discussed here. However, there are other categories, for example, perceived family membership, which could have been considered but as there is minimal research on these they have not been included here.

There is no unitary theory which explains the amazing subtlety and complexity of developing self. Both the child and others, especially significant others, are active players. The child reaches out through its motor actions and intrinsic sociable nature and in turn others respond to the child, thus facilitating the growth of a sense of self. There are multiple explanations including the shaping of the child through rewards and non-rewards, the provision of role models which the child can choose to copy, and the messages conveyed to a child via touch or what is said to the child. Undoubtedly, language is a powerful mediating tool in the construction of self. The messages of others will in part become the messages repeated by the child to the child about themselves. Cognitive processes within the child are selective, organising and inferential, thus they selectively attend to features about self.

The child attributes value to these features, thus fuelling the development of self-worth. Self-esteem is an inevitable aspect of self but is notoriously difficult to define and measure. It is the value that the child puts upon him/herself as a whole and upon specific aspects of self. Again there are multiple explanations of the development of self-esteem ranging from an idea that there is an intrinsic sense of inferiority within every child to consideration of the mediating role of language embedded in transactions with significant others.

The messages of significant others and the messages of society are conveyed through the language tool and it is this tool which gives self a flexibility and fluidity which needs to be considered alongside the view that self is unitary, stable, and continuous.

The chapter has attempted an integrated account of self but many exciting questions remain unanswered. Hopefully, the bringing together of so many research areas and theories will lead to more collaborative research in future.

One final point . . . I am still aware of my personal existence which changes over time and through new experiences, but through memory I maintain a sense of continuity. I remember and can re-experience the little girl feeling the crisp sheets on her body even though now as a mature woman I feel the heavy coverlet weighed down by books. For most children their subjective categorical self or selves may construct and reconstruct but the common core of existential self provides a sense of continuity.

DISCUSSION POINTS

1. By what means does a baby develop a sense of separateness from the world around?
2. What is 'categorical self'? What categories are used to define self? How are categories used to define self?
3. Consider whether 'self' as a unitary and stable concept is a construction of Western society.
4. What difficulties are encountered in the definition and measurement of self-esteem?
5. How important is the role of language in the development of self?
6. What methods would you use to investigate whether there is a link between a young child's perception of body size and their adolescent view of body size?
7. In what ways do social and cognitive processes influence the development of gender identity?
8. In what ways does national and ethnic identity develop through childhood and adolescence?

SUGGESTIONS FOR FURTHER READING

Barrett, M. (2006). *Children's knowledge, beliefs and feelings about nations and national groups.* Hove: Psychology Press.

Fivush, R., & Haden, C.A. (2003). *Memory and the construction of a narrative self: Developmental and cultural perspectives.* Hillsdale, NJ: Lawrence Erlbaum and Associates.

MacDonald, R.R., Hargreaves, D.J., & Miell, D. (2002). *Musical identities.* Oxford: Oxford University Press.

Maybin. J. (2008). *Children's voices: Talk, knowledge and identity.* Basingstoke: Palgrave Macmillan.

Nunnan, D., & Choi, J. (2010). *Reflective narratives and emergence of identity.* London: Routledge.

Wortham, S. (2005). *Learning identity: The joint emergence of social identification and academic learning.* Cambridge: Cambridge University Press.

REFERENCES

Aboud, F., & Amato, M. (2001). Developmental and socialization influences on intergroup bias. in R. Brown & S.I. Gaertner (Eds.) *Blackwell handbook of social psychology: intergroup processes.* Oxford: Blackwell.

Adler, A. (1927). *The practice and theory of individual psychology.* New York: Harcourt, Brace Jovanovich.

Ahrens, R. (1954). Beitrag zur entwicklung der physiognomie und mimikerkennes. *Zeitschrift fur Experimentalle und Angewandte Psychologie, 2,* 412–454.

Ainsworth, M.D.S., & Bell, S.M. (1974). Mother–infant interaction and the development of competence. In K.J. Connolly & J. Bruner (Eds.) *The growth of competence.* London and New York: Academic Press.

Ainsworth, M.D.S., Blehar, M.C., Waters, E., & Wall. S. (1978). *Patterns of attachment – a psychological study of the strange situation*. Hillsdale, NJ: Lawrence Erlbaum Associates.

Argyle, M. (1967). *The psychology of interpersonal behaviour*. Harmondsworth: Penguin.

Bandura, A. (1965). Influence of models' reinforcement contingencies on the acquisition of imitative responses. *Journal of Personality and Social Psychology*, *1*, 589–595.

Bandura, A. (1977). Self-efficacy – toward a unifying theory of behavioural change. *Psychological Review*, *84*, 191–215.

Bannister, D., & Agnew, J. (1977). The child's construing of self. In J. Cole (Ed.) *Nebraska Symposium on Motivation*. Lincoln, NE: University of Nebraska Press.

Barrett, M. (2005). Children's understanding of, and feelings about countries and national groups. In M. Barrett & E. Buchanan-Barrow, (Eds.) *Children's understanding of society*. Hove: Psychology Press.

Behl-Chadha, G. (1996). Basic-level and superordinate-like categorical representations in early infancy. *Cognition*, *60*, 105–141.

Bem, S.L. (1981). Gender schema theory: A cognitive account of sex typing, *Psychological Review*, *88*, 354–364.

Birgeneau, C.T.U. (2004). Body image in infancy: Adult body weight-related biases applied to infants. *Dissertation Abstracts International: Section B: The Sciences and Engineering*, *62*(11-B), 5362.

Block, J.H. (1978). Another look at sex differentiation in the socialization behaviors of mothers and fathers. In J. Sherman (Ed.) *Psychology of women: Future directions of research*. New York: Psychological Dimensions.

Bosson, J.K., Swann, W., & Pennebaker, J.W. (2000). Stalking the perfect measure of self esteem. The blind man and the elephant revisited. *Journal of Personality and Social Psychology*, *79*, 631–643.

Bowlby, J. (1969). *Attachment and loss, vol 1: Attachment*. New York: Basic Books.

Bowlby, J. (1973). *Attachment and loss, vol 2: Separation: Anxiety and anger*. New York: Basic Books.

Bretherton, I. (1993). From dialogue to internal working models: The co-construction of self relationships. In C.A. Nelson (Ed.) *Memory and affect in development: Minnesota symposia on child psychology*, *123* (pp. 1–41). Hillsdale, NJ: Lawrence Erlbaum Associates.

Brownell, C.A., Zerwas, S., & Ramani, G.B. (2007). 'So big': The development of body self-awareness in toddlers, *Child Development*, *78*, 1426–1440.

Bruner, J.S., & Goodman, C.C. (1947). Value and need as organising factors in perception. *Journal of Abnormal and Social Psychology*, *42*, 33–44.

Burkitt, E., Barrett, M., & Davis, A. (2003). The effect of affective characterizations on the size of children's drawings, *British Journal of Developmental Psychology*, *21*, 565–583.

Bussey, K., & Bandura, A. (1992). Self-regulatory mechanisms governing gender development. *Child Development*, *63*, 1236–1250.

Bussey, K., & Bandura, A. (1999). Social cognitive theory of gender development and differentiation. *Psychological Review*, *106*, 676–713.

Carrington, B., & Short, G. (2000). Citizenship and nationhood: The construction of British and American children. In M. Leicester, C. Modgil, & S. Modgil (Eds.) *Politics, education and citizenship*. London: Falmer Press.

Christie, T., & Slaughter, V. (2007). Early development of body representations. *Behavioral and Brain Sciences*, *30*, 203–204.

Clark, L.& Tiggemann, M. (2007). Sociocultural influences and body image in 9 to 12 year old girls: The role of appearance schemas. *Journal of Clinical Child and Adolescent Psychology*, *36*, 76–86.

Colapinto, J. (2000). *As Nature made him: The boy who was raised as a girl*. New York: Harper Collins.

Cooley, C.H. (1902). *Human nature and the social order*. New York: Scribner.

Coopersmith, S. (1967). *The antecedents of self esteem*. San Francisco: Freeman.

Cox, M.V. (1992). *Children's drawings*. Harmondsworth: Penguin.

Danzinger, K. (1971). *Socialization*. Harmondsworth: Penguin.

David, B., Grace, D., & Ryan, M.K. (2004). The gender wars: A self-categorisation theory perspective on the development of gender identity. In M. Bennett & F. Sani (Eds.) *The development of the social self* (pp. 135–157). Hove: Psychology Press.

DeLoache, J.S., Uttal, D.H., & Rosengren, K.S. (2004). Scale errors offer evidence for a perception-action dissociation early in life. *Science, 304*, 1027–1029.

Dohnt, H., & Tiggemann, M. (2006). The contribution of peer and media influences to the development of body satisfaction and self-esteem in young girls: A prospective study. *Developmental Psychology, 42*, 929–936.

Donaldson, M. (1978). *Children's minds*. London: Fontana.

Duffy, A.L., & Nesdale, D. (2009). Peer groups, social identity, and children's bullying behaviour. *Social Development, 18*, 121–139.

Edwards, R., Gadfield, L, Lucey, L., & Mauthner, M. (2006). *Sibling identity and relationships – sisters and brothers*. London: Routledge.

Ehrensaft, D. (2007). Raising girlyboys: A parent's perspective. *Studies in Gender and Sexuality, 8*, 269–302.

Erikson, E.H. (1959). *Identity and the life cycle*. Madison, CT: International Universities Press.

Fantz, R.H. (1961). The origin of form perception. *Scientific American, 204*, 66–72.

Fernald, A. (1985). Four-month-old infants prefer to listen to motherese. *Infant Behaviour and Development, 8*, 181–195.

Field, A.E., Camargo, C.A., Taylor, C.B., Berkey, C.S., Roberts, S.B., & Colditz, G.A. (2001). Peer, parent and media influences on the development of weight concerns among preadolescent and adolescent girls and boys. *Paediatrics, 107*, 54–60.

Freeman, N. (1980). *Strategies of representation in young children - Analysis of spatial skills and drawing processes*. London: Academic Press.

Freeman, N.K. (2007). Preschoolers' perceptions of gender appropriate toys and their parents' beliefs about genderized behaviors: Miscommunication, mixed messages, or hidden truths? *Early Childhood Education Journal, 34*, 357–366.

Freud, A. (1937). *The ego and the mechanisms of defence*. London: Hogarth Press and Institute of Psycho-Analysis.

Freud, S. (1905/1962). *Three essays on the theory of sexuality*. New York, NY: Avon.

Fulcher, M., Sutfin, E., & Patterson, C. (2008). Individual differences in gender development: Associations with parental sexual orientation. *Attitudes and Division of Labor in Sex Role, 58*, 330–341.

Geertz, C. (1984). From the natives' point of view: On the nature of anthropological understanding. In R. Schweder & R.A. LeVine (Eds.) *Culture theory: Essays on mind, self, emotion*. Cambridge: Cambridge University Press.

Goldberg, S., Mackay-Soroka, S., & Rochester, M. (1994). Affect, attachment, and maternal responsiveness. *Infant Behavior and Development, 17*, 335–339.

Golombok, S., Tasker, F., & Murray, C. (1997). Children raised in fatherless families from infancy: Family relationships and the socio-emotional development of children of lesbian and single heterosexual mothers. *Journal of Child Psychology and Psychiatry, 38*, 783–791.

Gorski, R.A., Gordon, J.H., Shryne, J.E., & Southam, A.M. (1978). Evidence for a morphological sex difference within the medial preoptic area of the rat brain. *Brain Research, 148*, 333–346.

Harter, S. (1983). Developmental perspectives on the self-system. In P.H. Mussen (Ed.) *Handbook of child psychology, vol. 4*. New York: Wiley.

Harter, S. (1999). *The construction of self*. Hove: The Guilford Press.

Heron, W. (1957). The pathology of boredom. *Scientific American, 196*, 52–69.

Hetherington, E.M. (1972). Father absence and personality development in daughters. *Developmental Psychology, 7*, 313–326.

Hetherington, E.M., & Deur, J.L. (1971). The effects of father absence on child development. *Young Children, 26*, 233–248.

Humenikova, L., & Gates, G.E. (2008). Body image perceptions in Western and post communist countries: A cross-cultural pilot study of children and parents. *Maternal Child Nutrition, 4*, 220–231.

James, W. (1890). *The principles of psychology*. New York: Holt, Rinehart and Winston.

Kaye, K., & Brazelton, T.B. (1971, March). Mother–infant interaction in the organisation of sucking. Paper presented to the Society for Research in Child Development, Minneapolis.

Keery, H., Boutelle, K., van den Berg, P., & Thompson, J.K. (2005). The impact of appearance-related teasing by family members. *Journal of Adolescent Health, 37*, 120–127.

Kellogg, R. (1970). *Analysing children's art*. Palo Alto, CA: Mayfield.

Kelly, A.M., Wall, M., Eisenberg, M.E., Story, M., & Neumark-Sztainer, D. (2005). Adolescent girls with high body satisfaction: Who are they and what can they teach us? *Journal of Adolescent Health, 37*, 391–396.

Kinsbourne, M. (1995). Awareness of one's own body: An attentional theory of its nature. In J.L. Bermudez, A. Marcel, & N. Amir (Eds.) *The body and the self* (pp. 205–223). Cambridge, MA: MIT Press.

Klein, M. (1932). *The psychoanalysis of children*. London: Hogarth.

Kline, P. (1981). *Fact and fantasy in Freudian theory* (2nd edn). London and New York: Methuen.

Kohlberg, L. (1966). A cognitive-developmental analysis of children's sex-role concepts and attitudes. In D.A. Goslin (Ed.) *Handbook of socialisation theory and research*. Chicago: Rand McNally.

Kuhn, H.H., & McPartland, T.S. (1954). An empirical investigation of self attitudes. *American Sociological Review, 47*, 647–652.

Langlois, J.H., & Downs, A.C. (1980). Mothers, fathers and peers as socialisation agents of sex-typed play behaviours in young children. *Child Development, 51*, 1237–1247.

Lawrenson, W., & Bryant, P.E. (1972). Absolute and relative codes in young children. *Journal of Child Psychology and Psychiatry, 13*, 25–35.

Lewis, M., & Brooks-Gunn, J. (1979). *Social cognition and the acquisition of self*. New York, NY: Plenum Press.

Lis, A., & Venuti, P. (1990). The development of body schemes in children aged 18–36 months. In L. Oppenheimer (Ed.) *The self concept*. New York: Springer-Verlag.

Lorenz, K.Z. (1981). *The foundations of ethology* (K. Lorenz & R.W. Kickert, Trans.). New York: Springer-Verlag.

Mead, G.H. (1934). *Mind, self and society*. Chicago, IL: University of Chicago Press.

Mesman, J., van Ijzendoorn, M.H., & Bakermans-Kranenburg, M.J. (2009). The many faces of the still-face paradigm: A review and meta-analysis. *Developmental Review, 29*, 120–162.

Money, J. (1974). Prenatal hormones and postnatal socialisation in gender identity differentiation. In J.K. Cole & R. Dienstbier (Eds.) *Nebraska symposium on motivation*. Lincoln, NE: University of Nebraska Press.

Nadelman, L. (1982). *Research manual in child development*. New York: Harper and Row.

Pelican, S., Vanden Heede, F., Holmes, B., Melcher, L.M., Wardlaw, M.K., & Raidl, M.M. (2005). The power of others to shape our identity: Body image, physical abilities and body weight. *Family and Consumer Sciences Research Journal, 34*, 56–79.

Pervin, L.A. (1993). *Personality: theory and research* (6th edn). New York: Wiley.

Phoenix, A. (2005). Young consumers. In S. Ding & K. Littleton (Eds.) *Children's personal and social development* (pp. 223–256). Oxford: Open University / Blackwell.

Piaget, J. (1953). *The origins of intelligence in the child*. London: Routledge and Kegan Paul.

Piaget, J., & Inhelder, B. (1969). *The psychology of the child*. London: Routledge and Kegan Paul.

Piaget, J., & Weil, A.M. (1951). The development in children of the idea of the homeland and of relations to other countries. *International Social Science Journal, 3*, 561–578.

Pike, K.M., & Rodin, J. (1991). Mothers, daughters and disordered eating. *Journal of Abnormal Psychology, 100*, 108–204.

Postman, L., Bruner, J.S., & McGinnies, E. (1948). Personal values as selective factors in perception. *Journal of Abnormal and Social Psychology, 43*, 142–154.

Quinn, P.C. (2007). Categorization. In A. Slater & M. Lewis (Eds.) *Introduction to infant development* (pp. 119–136). Oxford: Oxford University Press.

Quinn, P.C., Doran, M.M., Reiss, J.E., & Hoffman, J.E. (2009). Time course of visual attention in infant categorization of cats versus dogs: Evidence for a head bias as revealed through eye tracking. *Child Development, 80*, 151–161.

Ramachandran, V.S., & Blakeslee, S. (1998). *Phantoms in the brain: Probing the mysteries of the human mind*. Avon, UK: William Morrow.

Rochat, P. (1998). Self-perception and action in infancy. *Journal of Experimental Brain Research, 123*, 102–109.

Rosenberg, M. (1979). *Conceiving the self*. New York, Basic Books.

Rosenblum, G.D., & Lewis, M. (1999). The relations among body image, physical attractiveness, and body mass in adolescence. *Child Development, 70*, 50–64.

Ruble, D.N. (1983). The development of social-comparison processes and their role in achievement-related self-socialisation. In E.T. Higgins, D.N. Ruble, & W.W. Harrup (Eds.) *Social cognition and social development: A socio-cultural perspective*. Cambridge: Cambridge University Press.

Sameroff, A.J. (1991). The social context of development. In M. Woodhead, R. Carr, & P. Light (Eds.) *Becoming a person* (pp. 61–81). London: Routledge.

Schaffer, H.R. (1971). *The growth of sociability*. Harmondsworth: Penguin.

Shatz, M. (1994). *A toddler's life: Becoming a person*. New York: Oxford University Press.

Simion, F., Regolin, L., & Bulf, H. (2008). A predisposition for biological motion in the newborn baby. *Proceedings of the National Academy of Sciences USA, 105*, 809–813.

Skinner, B.F. (1953). *Science and human behaviour*. New York: Macmillan.

Slater, A., Von Der Schulenberg, C., Brown, E., Badenoch, M., Butterworth, G., Parsons, S., *et al.* (1998). Newborn infants prefer attractive faces. *Infant Behaviour and Development, l21*, 345–354.

Slabey, R.G., & Frey, K.G. (1975). Development of gender constancy and selective attention to same-sex models. *Child Development, 46*, 849–856.

Smolak, L. (2004). Body image in children and adolescents: Where do we go from here? *Body Image, 1*, 15–28.

Stern, D. (1977). *The first relationship: Infant and mother*. Fontana, CA: Open Books.

Swaab, D.F., & Hofman, M.A. (1995). Sexual differentiation of the human hypothalamus in relation to gender and sexual orientation. *Trends in Neuroscience, 18*, 264–270.

Tajfel, H. (1978). *Differentiation between social groups: Studies in the social psychology of intergroup relations*. London: Academic Press.

Thompson, S.H., Corwin, S.J., & Sargent, R.G. (1997). Ideal body size beliefs and weight concerns of fourth-grade children. *International Journal of Eating Disorders, 21*, 279–284.

Trevarthen, C. (1977). Descriptive analyses of infant communicative behaviour. In H.R. Schaffer (Ed.) *Studies in mother–infant interaction*. London: Academic Press.

Turner, J. (1980). *Made for life: Coping, competence and cognition*. London and New York: Methuen.

Vygotsky, L.S. (1978). *Mind in society: The development of higher psychological processes*. Cambridge, MA: Harvard University Press.

Weiner, B. (1986). *An attributional theory of motivation and emotion*. New York: Springer-Verlag.

Wundt, W.M. (1897). *Outlines of psychology* (Charles Hubbard Judd, Trans.). Stanford, CA: Stanford University Press.

Younger, B.A., & Gotlieb, S. (1988). Development of categorisation skills: Changes in the nature or structure of infant form categories. *Developmental Psychology, 24*, 611–619.

Part III
Childhood

9   Cognitive Development

Margaret Anne Defeyter

KEY TERMS

accommodation • adaptation • animism • appearance–reality distinction • assimilation • behaviourism • beginning of thought • categorisation • centration • class inclusion • concrete operations stage • conservation • constructivism • coordination of secondary schemes • deferred imitation • egocentrism • epistemology • equilibrium • false positive • guided participation • horizontal décalage • information processing • intuitive substage • microgenetic method • overlapping waves • phenomenism • preoperational stage • pretend play • primary circular reactions • private speech • rational imitation • realism • reflexive schemes • reversibility • scaffolding • schemes • secondary circular reactions • sensorimotor stage • seriation • symbolic function substage • tertiary circular reactions • theory of mind • three mountains task • transitive inference • vertical décalage • working memory • zone of proximal development

CHAPTER OUTLINE

OVERVIEW

There are many changes that take place in children's thinking in early and middle childhood. In particular, children change from a magical belief in characters such as Father Christmas to an ability to reason logically about the physical, concrete world. The first person to give a detailed description and theoretical account of these developments was the Swiss psychologist Jean Piaget – 'the giant of developmental psychology'. This chapter focuses on Piaget's theory with an account of stages of development and major changes in thinking in several areas of development:

- Egocentric thinking: a difficulty that children have in seeing things from others' point of view.
- Transitive inferences: understanding the relation between two (or more) premises (e.g. A > B, B > C) that leads to an inference that follows and is logically necessary (A > C).
- Class inclusion: the ability to coordinate and reason about parts and wholes simultaneously in recognising relations between classes and subclasses.
- Conservation: an understanding that certain properties of objects (such as number or weight) remain unchanged despite superficial transformations in appearance
- The appearance–reality distinction: an awareness that things are not always what they appear to be

Piaget's account of these changes has received many challenges, and it is also clear that by varying the tasks children can appear to display competence at very early ages. The author describes alternative theoretical accounts of cognitive development in childhood: Case's neo-Piagetian theory, Siegler's overlapping-waves theory, and Vygotsky's sociocultural theory.

INTRODUCTION

The Swiss psychologist Jean Piaget (1896–1980) has long been regarded as the 'giant of developmental psychology' (Hunt, 1969), and was 'a towering figure internationally' (Bliss, 2010). Some commentators have even gone so far as to endorse the statement that, 'assessing the impact of Piaget on developmental psychology is like assessing the impact of Shakespeare on English literature, or Aristotle on Philosophy – impossible' (e.g. Beilin, 1992, p.191; Lourenço & Machado, 1996, p.143). Such has been the prominence of Piaget's work that it has sparked a worldwide search for the authentic nature of the child's capacity for understanding.

Piaget's impact is reflected in several chapters of this book. A brief outline of his theory of intellectual development is given in Chapter 2, his account of infant development is described in Chapter 5, and his contribution to our understanding of changes in intelligence in adolescence is presented in Chapter 16. In addition, his contribution to educational practice is discussed in Chapter 18.

In this chapter we will discuss Piaget's cognitive-developmental theory with a particular emphasis on cognitive development during middle childhood. First, we focus on Piaget's cognitive-developmental theory and address, at each stage, a number of challenges to Piaget's theory. Then we explore a number of alternative theories, including Case's neo-Piagetian theory, Siegler's overlapping-waves theory, and Vygotsky's sociocultural theory.

PIAGET'S COGNITIVE-DEVELOPMENTAL THEORY

By the early 1960s Jean Piaget's theory of cognitive development dominated the study of child development. Like most researchers, Piaget's ideas were strongly influenced by his own history and background. From an early age Piaget showed a keen interest in Darwinian evolution; particularly in how various species change through adaptation to varied environmental conditions, and at age 10 he published his first scholarly article, on a rare albino sparrow, in a natural history journal. Later, influenced by an uncle, Piaget studied philosophy and was influenced by the field of **epistemology**. Briefly, epistemology is the study of the origins of knowledge and how we know what we know. Shortly after obtaining his degree, Piaget began to focus on the relationship between psychology and biological science and helped Alfred Binet develop standardised IQ tests for children (see Chapter 3). During the time he worked at the Alfred Binet Laboratories Piaget became interested in the incorrect answers that children provided to test questions, and discovered two very important findings. First, Piaget noted that children of the same age made similar errors and, second, he found that these errors differed from those of older and younger children.

> **epistemology** the study of the origins of knowledge and how we know what we know.

This mixture of disciplines and experiences led Piaget to combine the non-empirical approach of philosophy with the empirical, scientific approach of a naturalist in biology and led to a developmental theory that was fundamentally different in nature from **behaviourism.** According to Piaget everything that we know and understand is filtered through our current frame of reference. In other words, we construct new understandings of the world based on what we already know. Hence, Piaget's approach is often labelled as a **constructivist approach** as it depicts children as constructing their own knowledge.

Underlying structures and processes

Schemes

Piaget proposed that the basic unit of understanding was a **scheme**. A scheme can be defined as a cognitive structure that forms the basis of organising actions and mental representations so that we can understand and act upon the environment. Schemes make up our frames of reference through which we filter new information. Therefore, everything we know starts with the schemes we are born with. Three of the basic schemes we are born with are reflexive actions that can be performed on objects: sucking, looking, and grasping. As children grow older they begin to use schemes based on *internal* mental representations rather than using schemes based on physical activity (Lamb *et al.*, 2002). Piaget called these mental schemes **operations**.

Processes: Organisation and adaptation

In order to explain how children modify their schemes Piaget proposed two innate processes: *organisation* and **adaptation**. Organisation is the predisposition to group particular observations into coherent knowledge, and it occurs both within and across stages of development. For example, initially young infants have separate looking, grasping and sucking schemes. Over time these schemes become organised into a more complex multisensory cognitive system that allows the infant to look at an object, pick it up and suck it. This organisation enables the child to learn about the nature of these objects (e.g. their shape, texture and taste). However, in order to adapt to environmental demands we also need to incorporate new ideas.

adaptation Piaget believed that adaptation is composed of two processes, *assimilation* and *accommodation*, which work together to drive development forward.

Piaget believed that adaptation is composed of two processes, called **assimilation** and **accommodation** that work together to drive development forward. When faced with a new experience, infants/children try to *assimilate* this new information by incorporating the information into their existing schemes. For example, if a child believes all furry four legged animals are 'dogs' and then they encounter a breed of dog they have not seen before, they will probably apply a 'dog' label to the dog. The child will assimilate information about this 'new' breed of dog into their existing scheme. If the child then encounters a cat for the very first time they may apply a 'dog' label to the cat. As you can see from this example, assimilation allows us to generalise and apply what we know to many individual instances, although it may distort reality and not adapt to it. However, if the child is told that the cat is not a dog, or notices that the animal is considerably smaller than a dog and doesn't bark like a dog then the child needs to adjust their existing concept of four-legged animals (not all furry four-legged animals are dogs, some are cats) or generate a new scheme (*accommodation*). Thus, through the processes of accommodation and assimilation we adjust to reality rather than distort it.

Piaget's stages of cognitive development

Piaget's complementary processes of assimilation and accommodation comprise the **equilibration** process. According to Piaget we are, by nature, constantly motivated to be able to fully assimilate and accommodate to objects and situations in our environment; to reach a state of cognitive equilibrium. At times, however, so many new levels of understanding converge that we reach a major reorganisation in the structure of our thinking. Piaget called these shifts to new levels of thinking *stages*. Stages aren't simply quantitative additions to a child's knowledge and skills; rather

equilibration in Piagetian theory, a state in which children's schemes are in balance and are undisturbed by conflict.

they are defined as *qualitative shifts* in a child's way of thinking (see also Chapter 1 for an account of stage-like, or discontinuous, developmental functions).

Although Piaget provided typical ages for the four main stages and various sub-stages, the ages at which they are achieved will vary from one child to another. However, the order of progressing through stages is invariant, with each stage based on development in the previous stage. Piaget believed his stages were universal in two senses. First, he thought all people would develop through the same sequences of stages. Second, he thought that for any given stage children would be in that stage for all of their thinking and problem-solving strategies, whether in mathematical under-standing, problem-solving skills, social skills or other areas, although he recognised that there were transitional periods as children moved from one stage to the next, higher stage.

The sensorimotor stage: Birth to 2 years

The **sensorimotor stage** spans the first two years of life, and is divided into six sub-stages. During this period all that infants know is derived from information that comes in through the senses and the motoric actions that they can perform; hence the name 'sensorimotor'. It is important to note that for most of this stage young children are pre-verbal and therefore have no symbol use. Hence, young children must live in the present dependent upon sensorimotor input and the overt actions they can perform.

The first substage, the **reflexive schemes** substage, covers the period from birth to one month of age. During this substage infants use their innate reflexes (e.g. sucking, grasping) to explore their world. For example, if a nipple is placed near a newborn's mouth they will automatically open their mouth, seek to latch onto the breast and begin to suck. Whilst many of these innate reflexive schemes are designed to keep the infant alive, they also act as the building blocks for sensorimotor intelligence.

> **reflexive schemes** from birth to 1 month of age. In Piaget's theory the first substage of *sensorimotor* development, when infants use their innate reflexes (e.g., sucking, grasping) to explore their world.

In the second substage, termed **primary circular reactions** (1–4 months), there is a shift in the infant's voluntary control of behaviour. The infant starts to show a degree of coordination between the senses and their motor behaviour through the primary circular reactions. To illustrate, the infant accidentally discovers a new expe-rience as a result of their own motor activity (e.g. thumb sucking) and then repeats the event over and over again. The term *primary* is used because such repetitive behav-iours are focused almost exclusively around the infant's body and not the external world, while the term *circular* refers to the fact that the behaviour is repetitive. During this substage there is also some anticipation of events, although it is fairly limited. For example, a hungry infant may stop crying when approached by their mother because the infant anticipates being fed.

In the third substage, **secondary circular reactions**, which lasts from 4 to 10 months, there is a shift in the infant's voluntary control of behaviour as they become more aware of the external world. Infants now direct their behaviour to reaching and grasping objects (behaviours become secondary). Although the actions are still circular as the infant engages in repetitive behaviour (e.g. banging a cup on a table

coordination of secondary schemes from approximately 10–12 months. The fourth substage in Piaget's *sensorimotor* development, when infants begin to deliberately combine schemes to achieve specific goals.

tertiary circular reactions from approximately 12–18 months. The fifth substage in Piaget's account of *sensorimotor* development, when the child begins to search for novelty and uses trial and error to explore the characteristics and properties of objects, and develops new ways of solving problems.

beginning of thought from approximately 18–24 months. The final substage in Piaget's account of *sensorimotor* development, when children become able to form enduring mental representations.

deferred imitation the ability to copy or mimic the actions of others, some time after they have seen these actions, an important type of learning in humans, and facilitated by *mirror neurons*.

over and over again), the infant has begun to intentionally act on his environment.

During substage 4 (**coordination of secondary schemes**), which lasts from 10 to 12 months, the infant begins to deliberately combine schemes to achieve specific goals. In other words, they begin to engage in goal-directed behaviours. Perhaps the best example of this behaviour is demonstrated in the fact that infants in this substage solve *object permanence* tasks in which the infant has to co-ordinate two schemes (e.g. lifting a cover and grasping an object). See Chapter 5 for a detailed discussion of object permanence tasks.

In Substage 5, which lasts from 12 to 18 months, the child engages in **tertiary circular reactions**. The child has now begun to walk and begins to search for novelty. As children consolidate their understanding of causal relations between events (e.g. if a bowl is pushed off a table, it will crash onto the floor) they begin to systematically experiment with varying the means to test the end results. For example, they may see what happens if they push the bowl in another direction, or what happens if they push another object off a table. Such activities enable children to discover more about their world and new ways of solving problems.

During the final substage (18–24 months), the **beginning of thought**, children become able to form enduring mental representations. This capacity is clearly demonstrated in toddlers' ability to engage in **deferred imitation**. Deferred imitation is the capacity to imitate another person's behaviour some time after the behaviour was observed. Enduring mental representations also mean that children no longer have to go through the trial and error method; rather they can mentally experiment by performing the actions in their minds. Further evidence for symbol use is shown in toddlers' ability to engage in simple pretend play (Bosco *et al.*, 2006; Piaget, 1962), which develops further in the next substage (a detailed account of the development of play is given in Chapter 14).

Criticisms of Piaget's account There have been some strong criticisms of Piaget's account of development during the sensorimotor stage. The main criticism is that there is now a wealth of evidence that suggests both object permanence and deferred imitation occur much earlier in development than Piaget suggested. Piaget proposed that object permanence developed somewhere between 10 and 12 months of age. Baillargeon and colleagues, however, have shown convincing evidence that infants as young as 3.5 months of age understand that objects continue to exist when out of sight. As very young infants are not physically able to search for hidden objects, Baillargeon and colleagues used a violation of expectancy procedure (VOE). The basic premise underlying this procedure is that young infants will express surprise at objects or events that violate their expectancy. Thus, if infants possess the belief that objects continue to exist when out of sight, then an impossible event should evoke longer looking times than a possible event. To illustrate, Baillargeon (1987) first habituated 3.5-month-olds and 4.5-month-olds to the sight of a screen rotating through 180 degrees. Once infants had dishabituated to the event, a box was placed in the path of the screen. In the possible event the screen rotated upwards, occluded the box, but stopped when it reached the top of the box. In the impossible event the box rotated 180 degrees, just as if the box was not there. The results showed that 4.5-month-olds and some 3.5-month-olds looked significantly longer at the impossible event suggesting that the infant mentally represented the occluded box (see Chapter 5 and Figure 5.11 for more details). Similar findings have been shown for young infants' knowledge regarding occlusion of events (Aguiar & Baillargeon, 1999; and solidity of objects (Baillargeon & DeVos, 1991). Details of related experiments are given in Chapter 5.

There is also considerable evidence that infants are capable of deferred imitation much earlier than 18–24 months of age. For example, Meltzoff and Moore (1994) presented 6-week-old infants with one of two facial gestures, either mouth opening or tongue protrusion. Twenty-four hours later the infants saw the same experimenter who presented a passive face, and found that the infants imitated the gesture they had seen the previous day. This was a clear demonstration of deferred imitation: Piaget claimed that this ability did not appear until around 18 months, but Meltzoff and Moore's findings put its emergence at 6 weeks, and possibly even earlier.

The preoperational stage: 2 to 7 years

The preoperational stage is a stage that is characterised by an impressive increase in mental representation and accompanied by equally impressive limitations! This stage subdivides into the **symbolic function substage** (2–4 years) and the **intuitive substage** (4–7 years).

Symbolic function substage: 2 to 4 years In the symbolic substage children acquire the ability to mentally represent an object that is not physically present. This ability to engage in symbolic thought expands the child's mental world as they are no longer tied to the here and now and they no longer require sensory input to think of things. Evidence of symbolic function can be seen in **pretend play**. Early on the child requires a high level of similarity between external prop and referent in order to symbolise the referent. For example, children younger than 2 years will pretend to drink from a cup but refuse to pretend that a cup is a hat (Tomasello *et al.*, 1999). However, over time, children can use external props that are dissimilar to the referent (e.g. a banana to stand for a telephone, Leslie, 1987). Eventually, children can just *imagine* the referent and event (Rakoczy *et al.*, 2002; Striano *et al.*, 2001). Other examples of children engaging in symbolic thought can be seen in their use of language and their production of drawings. One of the most impressive examples of the symbolic function is in our use of language. At 16 months of age the average child comprehends over 150 words but in their early language they are restricted to producing one word at a time, and between 18 and 24 months their productions are typically restricted to two-word utterances. However, from around 2 years this word-length restriction

symbolic function substage the first substage in Piaget's *preoperational stage* of reasoning, in which children acquire the ability to mentally represent objects that are not physically present.

intuitive substage from approximately 4 to 7 years. The second part of Piaget's *preoperational stage* of thinking, when children begin to classify, order, and quantify in a more systematic manner.

pretend play 'make-believe play' in which the child may pretend to be other people or act out real-life situations.

becomes lifted and children learn an impressive nine words a day on average, so that they have a vocabulary of approximately 14,000 words by the time they are 6 years old (Hollich & Houston, 2007; see also Chapter 10).

Egocentrism

Aside from the notable acquisition of symbolic representation, Piaget also discussed what the preoperational child *cannot* do. According to Piaget the most important limitations shown by children in the symbolic function substage are **egocentrism** and

three mountains task
a task used by Piaget where the child is shown a model of three mountains and asked to choose the view that would be seen by someone in a different location from them- selves, and the preop- erational child typically chooses the view from their own location.

animism. Egocentrism is the tendency to perceive the world solely from one's own point of view, and is a concept that has been exten- sively studied under the heading of **theory of mind** (see Chapter 11). Thus, children often assume that other people will perceive and think about the world in the same way they do. Piaget and Inhelder (1956) investigated young children's egocentrism by devising the **three mountains task** (see Figure 9.1). The child is asked to walk around the model and view it from different perspectives. The child is then seated on one side of the table and the experimenter places the doll in different locations around the model. At each location the child is asked to draw or choose, from a set of different views of the model,

FIGURE 9.1 *The three mountains task. The child walks around the display and is then asked to choose from photographs to show what the scene would look like from different perspectives. Before age 6 or 7, most children select the photograph showing the scene from their own point of view.*

the view the doll would be able to see. Piaget found that rather than picking the view that the doll could see, they often picked the view they themselves could see. Indeed, Piaget found that children could not correctly identify the doll's view from the different locations or viewpoints until 9 or 10 years of age. This inability to take into account that another person can view the world differently can also be seen in young children's assumption that if they know something other people will too (Ruffman & Olsen, 1989).

In recent years, several criticisms have been made of the three mountains task. Research has shown that using familiar objects (e.g. trees and houses), and by asking children to rotate a small model of the display, rather than select from a set of pictures (decreasing the perceptual difficulty of the task), children as young as 3 or 4 years of age were able to identify the correct perspective for others (Borke, 1975; Newcombe & Huttenlocher, 1992). Of course, visual perspective taking is only one way to investigate whether young children have appreciation of others' perspectives. Research into young children's understanding of others' perspectives has shown that 14-month-olds appear to engage in what is called **rational imitation**: Gergely *et al.*, 2002, Figure 9.2). These researchers showed that when infants observed an adult turning on a light with their head, even though the adult's hands were free, the infants copied the behaviour after a week's delay: that is, they assumed that

rational imitation
where infants produce an action that they think the adult intended to do, rather than what the adult actually did.

because the adult's hands were free they had a reason for turning the light on with their head. However, if the adult turned on the light with their head and their hands were tied, the infants then used their hands to turn on the light. This finding demonstrates that 14-month-olds can infer others' intentions and perspectives. This ability is not confined to humans: even chimpanzees can imitate rationally! (Buttelmann *et al.*, 2007). Recently, researchers have shown that children as young as 18 months of age can sympathise with a stranger who is in a hurtful situation but showing no emotion (Vaish *et al.*, 2009). In this study the children saw an adult either destroying or taking away another adult's possessions, and the children showed concern and prosocial

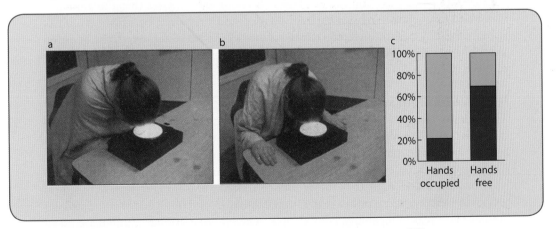

FIGURE 9.2 *Fourteen-month-olds were more likely to switch on the light with their hands if the adult model appeared to have her hands tied (left), than if her hands were free (right), that is they engaged in rational, rather than literal, imitation.*

Source: Gergely *et al.* (2002). Reproduced by permission of Nature.

behaviour towards the 'victim'. These findings suggest that even toddlers are able to engage in affective perspective taking!

In addition, a host of research under the *theory of mind* topic has shown that by 4 or 5 years of age, if not earlier, children understand that other people's mental states may differ from their own (e.g. Baillargeon *et al.*, 2010; Buttelmann *et al.*, 2009; Leslie, 2000; Wellman *et al.*, 2001; and see Chapter 11).

Animism

Another limitation of preoperational thought is animistic thinking – the belief that inanimate objects have lifelike qualities (such as thoughts, feelings, wishes) and are capable of independent action. A young girl might show animism by thinking that dropping her teddy bear down the stairs will cause her teddy pain, stating that it is raining because the clouds are feeling sad, or stating that the stairs made her fall down. Piaget discovered animistic thinking through interviewing children and asking questions such as, 'If you pricked a stone would it feel it?'; 'Why does the sun move?' (Piaget, 1960). Piaget suggested that young children's egocentric thinking prevents them from accommodating. As such they cannot adjust their schemes to accommodate the real-world state of affairs.

Many researchers now think that Piaget overestimated young children's animistic beliefs. Some of the main criticisms of Piaget's methodology are that Piaget used objects with which the children had little direct experience (e.g. extraterrestrial entities such as the sun, the clouds) and relied on verbal justifications, and have also criticised the wording of the interviews, which may have confused the children (e.g. Carey, 1985; Massey & Gelman, 1988; Richards & Siegler, 1984). Recently researchers have shown that, for familiar objects, 6–12-month-olds can sort pictures of objects into categories and can distinguish between animate and inanimate objects (e.g. Mandler & McDonough, 1998). And by the age of 2.5 years, children attribute wishes and likes to people and animals but hardly ever to objects (Hickling & Wellman, 2001). Overall, the developmental data contradict Piaget's account and suggest that the animate–inanimate distinction emerges early in infancy, and may even be innate (Farah & Rabinowitz, 2003). Although alternative accounts have been suggested, the question as to whether this capacity is inherent or acquired through experience has yet to be resolved (Gelman & Opfer, 2002; Mahon *et al.*, 2009).

Intuitive thought substage: 4 to 7 years

The *intuitive thought* substage roughly spans from age 4 to 7, and is characterised by a shift in children's reasoning. Children begin to classify, order, and quantify in a more systematic manner. Piaget called this substage intuitive because although a child can carry out such mental operations they remain largely unaware of the underlying principles and what they know. Hence a child's reasoning is largely based on perception and intuition, rather than rational thinking, and this leads to some striking limitations in reasoning ability. For example, when preoperational children are asked to arrange 10 sticks in order of length (a **seriation task**), some children sort the short

seriation task putting items in a coherent or logical order.

sticks into a pile and the longer ones into another pile, while others arrange one or two sticks according to length but are unable to correctly order all 10 sticks.

Cristism.

Researchers have challenged Piaget's account that children's successful solutions to seriation tasks are based on underlying changes to *mental* operations that develop during the next major stage of development (the **concrete operations stage**). Some researchers have suggested that the difficulty the preoperational child faces in verbal inference tests results from a lack of memory capacity. When researchers have employed procedures to ensure that children remember the information that they are given then young children can grasp **transitive inference** (e.g. Bryant & Trabasso, 1971).

> **transitive inference**
> the relation between two (or more) premises (e.g., A > B, B > C) that leads to an inference that is logically necessary (A > C).

Transitive inferences Transitive inference is the ability to seriate *mentally* between entities that can be organised into an ordinal series. For example, in a family of five people, the father may be the tallest, followed by the mother, then their three sons (Jasper, Scott, and Ronan, respectively). The size relations in the family can be represented as follows: F > M > J > S > R. Given this information we can make transitive inferences about the size relations between individual family members without them being physically present. For example, we can make the inference that Jasper is taller than Ronan.

Bryant & Trabasso (1971) conducted an experiment that showed that 4-year-old children could make transitive inferences as long as they were trained to remember the premises. Four- to six-year-olds were trained to remember the lengths of variously coloured rods presented in descending order of size. The rods were kept in a wooden block with holes drilled in it, with the rods reducing in size from the left- to the right-hand side of the block. Regardless of the length of the rod, the wooden block was designed so that each rod protruded the same amount above the surface of the block. During the training session children were presented with four different pairs made up from five different coloured rods (A > B, B > C, C > D, D > E). These pairs created a logical five-term series (A > B > C > D > E). Children were tested on their knowledge regarding the relative length of adjacent pairs (A > B, B > C, and so forth – note that they were asked about the relationship between the different colours, e.g. 'is the red one longer than the green one?' and not the relationship between the letters!) when the pairs of rods had been returned to the block. Following training children were asked questions about the relative length of non-adjacent pairs. Children were asked, 'Which is longer, A or C and C or E?' Children gave the correct answers to both of these questions showing that they had deduced that A > C and C > E.

By using a five-term series (A > B > C > D > E), rather than a three-term series (A > B > C), the researchers were able to ask the critical question, 'Which rod is longer, B or D?' . This question provides a true test of inferential ability because in a five-term series two components (B and D) have both been verbally labelled, during training, as 'longer than' and 'shorter than' adjacent rods A ,C, and E. Hence, a transitive inference is required to work out the relationship between B and D. Remember, this is the critical pair in determining whether the children could infer the correct relation between these two rods from their experience with the other pairs. The results showed that 4-, 5-, and 6-year-olds were able to make this transitive inference.

Hence, researchers have argued that children's failure during the preoperational stage resulted from their failure to remember all of the relevant information rather than not possessing the necessary logic needed to make the correct inference. However, an alternative hypothesis is that children correctly answered the inferential test question by simply remembering the presentation order of the coloured rods, as rods were presented in descending order of size. By manipulating Piaget's methodology in this manner, the procedure might have yielded **false positives**. In this case, children may simply pass the B–D test question by remembering that B is bigger than D because it was mentioned before D. Pears & Bryant (1990) tested this interpretation by presenting 4-year-olds with a transitive inference task where the order of premises was varied. The results showed that children's performance was still above chance level and numerous studies have replicated Bryant and Trabasso's (1971) findings.

false positive believing something to be true, when in fact it is false.

Hierarchical classification tasks The limitation of relying on the preoperational logic of young children is clearly illustrated in their performance on **class inclusion** tasks. These are tasks that involve part–whole relations in which one superordinate set of objects can be divided into two or more mutually exclusive subordinate sets. Typically, one of the subordinate sets contains more members than the other. For example, when a preoperational child is presented with a bunch of seven roses and two tulips they can easily state that there are more roses than tulips, as depicted in Figure 9.3. However, when asked if there are more

class inclusion the ability to coordinate and reason about parts and wholes simultaneously in recognising relations between classes and subclasses.

FIGURE 9.3 *A class inclusion problem: are there more roses or more flowers? Preoperational children will typically claim there are more roses.*

roses than flowers they typically state that there are more roses (Ginsburg & Opper, 1979). Piaget proposed that children have difficulty in focussing on a part of the set (e.g. roses) and, simultaneously, on the whole set (e.g. flowers). This idea is similar to Piaget's account of young children's failure to conserve.

More recently, researchers using simpler questions have found that children as young as 4 years of age were able to solve part–whole relations problems (e.g. Markman & Siebert, 1976; Smith, 1979). For example, Markman & Siebert (1976) found that children's performance is significantly improved by highlighting the part–whole relations between the objects by using collective terms (such as a bunch of flowers) rather than classes. Let's use the previous example of roses and tulips to look at a part–whole comparison question involving a collection of objects. 'Who would have more flowers, someone who owned the roses or someone who owned the bunch of flowers?' (Figure 9.3)

There is plenty of evidence that young children have formed a variety of global categories based on common natural kind, function and behaviour (e.g. Baldwin *et al.*, 1993; Gelman & Koenig, 2003; Gopnik & Nazzi, 2003). Importantly, they can make categorisation judgements based on non-observable properties. For example, when 2- to 5-year-olds are told that a bird has warm blood and a dinosaur has cold blood, they infer that a pterodactyl (labelled a dinosaur) has cold blood even though it looks more like a bird, has wings and can fly (see Figure 9.4) (Gopnik & Nazzi, 2003). These findings challenge Piaget's proposal that young children's thinking is governed by the way the way things appear. Rather, Gopnik and Gazzi suggest that preoperational children are able to draw inferences about category membership based on non-observable characteristics (e.g. categorising animals on the basis of whether they are warm blooded or cold blooded).

Cristism

Children's skill at categorising objects across the pre-school years is supported by gains in general knowledge and a rapid expansion in vocabulary. As children discover more about their world they form many *basic-level* **categories** (e.g. cat, dog, monkey) and by 2- to 3-years of age children can categorise an object according to a *superordinate* 'higher level' category (e.g. animal). In a study by Blewitt (1994) children were shown coloured drawings of familiar objects organised into sets of four pictures; two pictures from the target superordinate category and two pictures from another superordinate category. For example, children were shown a picture of a monkey, a turtle, an apple, and a pear. The researchers asked children to select exemplars of the target superordinate category, in this case animals, by asking children, 'Is there an animal here? Is there another animal here?' Then children were asked to categorise the same objects at a basic level category. 'Is there a turtle here? Is there a monkey here?'

> **categorisation** the grouping together of items that have some characteristic or characteristics in common.

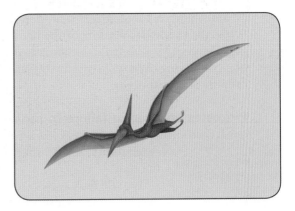

FIGURE 9.4 *Young children can infer that a pterodactyl has cold blood, even though it looks like a bird and can fly.*

Blewitt found that by that age of 2 children were able to include the same object into both a basic-level and a superordinate-level category. Hence, whilst young children's categorical knowledge is not as rich as that of older children, the capacity to classify in a hierarchal manner is present in early childhood (Mandler, 2007).

Conservation tasks Children who are able to conserve must recognise that certain characteristics of an object remain the same even when their appearance changes. For example, the child must realise that a piece of clay rolled into a ball which is subsequently rolled out to look like a sausage is still the same object and contains the same amount of clay as before. Although its superficial appearance has changed, its quantity has not. There are a series of *conservation tasks* and examples are provided in Figure 9.5. A frequently cited conservation task involves pouring the same amount of liquid into two identical drinking glasses (see Figure 9.6). Once the child has agreed that both glasses contain the same amount of liquid, the water from one glass is poured into a shorter, wider glass. Children are then asked whether there is the same amount of liquid in both glasses or whether one has more liquid. Below the ages of 6 or 7 children often reply that the taller glass contains more liquid. In other words they lack the knowledge that the volume of water is conserved. Bliss (2010, p. 446) describes a small girl who, when asked about the water-pouring task a week after being shown it said that all the glasses were full, and when asked how the liquids were poured from one beaker to another replied 'Both at the same time'. The girl then proceeded to pick up 'a pair of full glasses and in front of me tried with great conviction pouring each into the other. We both got drenched in coloured water'!

Let's look at two other examples, conservation of number and mass. In a conservation of number task the child might be shown two rows of counters or sweets/candies, with each laid out in one-to-one correspondence (see Figure 9.5). The child is then asked whether there is the same number in each row; all children will say 'yes'. The experimenter then makes one of the rows of counters longer by increasing the distance between each counter. The child is again asked whether there is the same number in each row. Even though no counters have been added or taken away, the non-conserving child often says there are more counters/sweets in the longer row. In a typical conservation of mass task, a child may be shown two balls of modelling clay, and agrees that there is the same amount of clay in each ball. While the child watches, one of the balls of clay is rolled out and becomes longer (see Figure 9.7). The child is then asked if there is still the same amount and a non-conserving child will typically say that there is more in the piece of clay that is cylindrical in shape.

Processes involved in failure to conserve Piaget proposed that the preoperational child's inability to conserve is characterised by three main limitations: **centration**, **reversibility**, and *focussing on the end state* rather than on the means to the end.

reversibility the ability to imagine a series of steps in both forward and reverse directions. Characteristic of thinking in Piaget's *concrete operations stage*.

We will look at centration by examining Piaget's account of what happens in the conservation of liquid task. According to Piaget one of the cognitive limitations the preoperational child faces in this conservation task results from the child being unable to engage in *decentration*. That is, the child cannot focus on two attributes, in this case

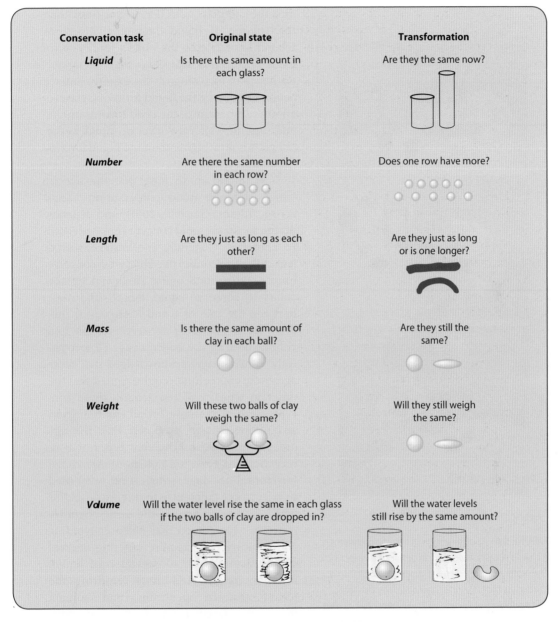

FIGURE 9.5 *Piaget's conservation tasks.*

Source: Piaget & Inhelder, 1956. Reprinted by permission of Psychology Press Limited, Hove, UK.

the height and the width of the glass, at the same time. Rather, the child engages in *centration* – the tendency to focus on one attribute (e.g. the height of the liquid in the glass) at a time, and hence judges that the taller glass contains more liquid.

Another limitation is the child's inability to understand *reversibility*. That is, they cannot mentally reverse the action of pouring the liquid from the short glass back

FIGURE 9.6 *A conservation of liquid experiment. A child is shown two identical glasses of water (top). The water from one of the glasses is poured into a third glass that is shorter and narrower (middle). The nonconserving child will now typically say that there is more in the taller, narrower glass (bottom).*

horizontal décalage refers to the non-synchronous development of children on Piagetian tasks (e.g. cases in which children may succeed on conservation of number tasks but not on conservation of continuous quantity).

into the tall glass, and hence work out that the volume of liquid has not changed. A related limitation is the child's tendency to focus on the *end state rather than the means.* Rather than focussing on the experimenter's action of pouring the liquid from one glass to another (the means), the child focuses on the end state in which the level of liquid in the tall glass is now higher than the liquid level in the shorter glass.

It is important to note that the age at which children attain conservation varies across culture (Gauvain, 2001), and depends on the substances and concept they are asked to conserve. Generally, in Western societies, children acquire the ability to conserve number at around age 6, followed by the ability to conserve liquid, length, and mass between the ages of 6 and 7. However, children are not able to conserve weight and volume until aged 9, and after age 11, respectively. Whilst Piaget acknowledged that these ages were approximations, he argued that the order in which children acquire these concepts remains constant for all children from all cultures. Piaget proposed that the age differences found on different types of conservation task reflected a phenomenon called **horizontal décalage**, which is the term used to refer to age differences in solving problems which appear to require the same cognitive processes. He argued that different types of conservation tasks require differing degrees of abstraction, with conservation of liquid, number, length, and mass requiring the fewest abstract operations, and volume the most. Hence, children attain conservation of mass prior to attaining conservation of volume. According to Piaget, the order of progression through different conservation tasks is constant, because knowledge of the simpler concept is essential in order for the child to attain the more abstract concept.

Throughout the last few decades many researchers have challenged Piaget's account of conservation. For example, Donaldson (1978) suggested that children build up a model of the world by formulating hypotheses, based on past experience, that help them build up expectations about future events. For example, in a number

FIGURE 9.7 *Conservation of mass. Having seen one ball of clay being rolled out the nonconserving child will typically say that there is more in the longer row.*

conservation task the experimenter initially asks the child: 'Are there the same number of counters in the two rows?' After the child has agreed that both rows contain the same number of counters, the experimenter then changes one of the rows and asks the same question again. One possibility is that the child expects a change because of the combination of an adult performing a deliberate action on one of the rows of counters and asking the subsequent question about number – in other words, 'why would she ask me the same question again if nothing has changed?' To test this proposal, McGarrigle & Donaldson (1974) used a 'naughty teddy' that accidentally muddled up the length of one of the rows of counters. The researchers predicted that when the physical manipulation occurred accidentally, the child might have less expectation that a real change had taken place. Their findings demonstrated that, compared to the classical Piagetian task, children were more likely to provide the correct answer, that is, to state that the number of counters had not changed.

Rochel Gelman (1972) devised a simpler conservation task than the classical Piagetian task, called 'the magic mice paradigm'. Three-year-old children were shown two plates; one with three toy mice placed upon it, and one with two toy mice. After covering both plates, children were asked to choose which plate was the 'winner' and which was the 'loser'. Each time the child identified the plate holding three mice as the winner they were given a prize. After a number of trials the experimenter surreptitiously altered the winning plate by either decreasing the number of mice to two, or changing the distance between the three mice to match the spacing of the plate containing two mice. When the child pulled the cover off the 'winning plate' they found that a transformation had taken place. According to Piaget, under such circumstances, children would choose the winning plate on the basis of row length or density. However, Gelman found that when the 'three mice' plate had simply been pushed together to match the spacing of the 'two mice' plate children were still able to correctly identify the 'winning' plate. On trials in which a mouse had been taken away, children were able to tell the experimenter that one mouse had been taken away. Furthermore, they stated that if one mouse was added to the 'losing' plate it would be like the earlier 'winning' plate. These findings suggest that children have some knowledge of conservation far earlier than Piaget suggested.

In fact, there is even a type of conservation of weight that can be found in infants. If infants are offered rods that differ in their length then, with practice, they will display differential preparation for their expected weights, expecting the longer rods to weigh more (Mash, 2007; Mounoud & Bower, 1974). If the rods are then switched so that their weights are changed (perhaps by having hollow rods, or ones weighted with lead) then the infant's arms will rise, or fall, if the rod is lighter or heavier than expected. Mounoud and Bower found that if 18-month-old infants saw a transformation to a longer rod, by folding it in two so that it was much shorter, they expected it to weigh the same as when it was longer. This appears to be a sensorimotor form of conservation of weight, and within Piagetian terminology this is an example of a **vertical décalage,** which is where what the child understands at one level or stage (in this case at the level of action) must be reconstructed at a later age on a different level of understanding (e.g. the level of verbal thought).

vertical décalage
within Piagetian terminology this is where the child has a level of understanding at one level (perhaps at the level of action) that has to be reconstructed at a later age at a different stage or level of understanding (perhaps at the level of thought).

Likewise, other researchers have found that making conservation tasks simpler results in children conserving at an earlier age than Piaget's theory suggests (e.g. Bruner, 1966; Halford, 1990; Sugarman, 1987). Nevertheless, although attentional and linguistic factors appear to play a significant role in children's failure on classical Piagetian conservation tasks, children do not seem to fully understand conservation until the school years. To illustrate this, here is a non-verbal conservation of number test that you can carry out if you have access to two children, say 4 and 8 years old. The only equipment you will need is 13 small rounded, coloured sweets/candies these must all be of the same colour because children often have colour preferences. First say to the children 'Look at what I do', then put two rows of six each in one-to-one correspondence as shown in Figure 9.5. Next, add one sweet/candy to one of the rows so that this one now has one more and is also longer. Next, stretch out the row that still has six sweets/candies so that it is slightly longer than the other and say to the children 'Which row would you like?' All being well the older conserving child will choose the shorter row because they *know* that it contains more, and the younger *non-conserving* child will choose the longer row because they '*know*' that it now contains more, and each will be surprised at the altruism of the other!

The appearance–reality distinction As discussed above, Piaget believed that young children tend to focus exclusively on the perceptual features of objects. This tendency would make it very difficult for these children to pass **appearance–reality** tasks in which appearance and reality diverge. A study by Rheta DeVries (1969) investigated children's ability to distinguish appearance from reality by allowing children to play with a cat called 'Maynard'. Initially children of all ages said that Maynard was a cat. After the children had played with the cat for a short period of time, the experimenters covered the front half of the cat with a screen and surreptitiously strapped a realistic mask of a ferocious dog onto the cat's head. Children were then presented with a full view of the cat and the experimenter asked a number of test questions, such as: 'What kind of animal is it now?', 'Can it bark?' Three-year-olds' answers revealed that they tended to focus solely on the cat's *appearance* rather than the *reality* (Maynard was still really a cat!) by saying that the cat had become a ferocious dog. Whilst the 4- and 5-year-olds did not believe that the cat could transform into a dog they did not always answer the test questions correctly. Indeed, it was not until age 6 that children answered all of the test questions correctly, by saying that it was *really* a cat but it *looked like* a dog.

John Flavell and colleagues (Flavell, 1993; Flavell *et al.*, 1986) reported similar findings in an appearance–reality task in which they presented children with objects that appeared to be one thing but were in reality another (e.g. a sponge that looked like a rock, a stone that looked like an egg; see Figure 9.8). After physically exploring the object, children were asked 'What does that look like?' and 'What is it really?' Four- and five-year-olds respond in an adult manner (i.e. the object looks like a rock but really is a sponge). The majority of 3-year-olds fail to differentiate between the object's appearance and reality. They typically make two kinds of error; a **phenomenism** error (i.e. saying that the object looks like a sponge and really is a sponge) or an intellectual **realism** error (i.e. stating that the object looks like a rock and really is a rock). Flavell and colleagues account for these findings by suggesting that 3-year-olds are not proficient at dual encoding, that is, the ability to represent an object in more than one way at the same time.

Recently, an innovative series of studies by DeLoache (2000) suggests that 3-year-olds but not 2.5-year-olds do possess the ability to represent an object in more than one way at the same time. In the scale model task, children were shown a model that provides information about the current location of a hidden object in a full-size room. First, children received an orientation task during which the experimenter points out the relation between the model and

phenomenism knowledge that is limited to appearances such that, in tasks that involve distinguishing reality from appearance, children report only appearance.

realism believing that things are as they appear and not what they might be, e.g. saying that a sponge that looks like a rock really is a rock.

FIGURE 9.8 *An appearance–reality test: A sponge that looks like a rock and a stone that looks like an egg.*

the full-size room. Second, children saw the experimenter hide a little Snoopy dog in the model (e.g. under a chair) and were told that big Snoopy will be hidden in the corresponding place in the full-size room. To succeed on this task, children have to understand the relation between the model and the room. In other words children have to understand that the model room is a symbolic representation of the full-size room (DeLoache, 2000). Three-year-old children were able to succeed on this task, giving strong evidence for the ability to have dual representations in early childhood.

Rice *et al.* (1997) extended the studies conducted by Flavell and colleagues by using a method that involved the children as co-conspirators in a deception. Children were invited to play a 'trick' on one of two experimenters. The child was introduced to two experimenters and shortly after one of the experimenters left the room. While the second experimenter was absent the first experimenter brought out a sponge that looked like a rock. Children were then administered the standard task from Flavell *et al.* (1986) and a trick task. The trick task was identical to the standard task except that children acted as co-conspirators in playing a trick on the second experimenter. Then the first experimenter asked the child a number of test questions: 'What is the object, really; what does it look like, and what will [the absent experimenter] think it is?' The results showed that only 29 per cent of the 3-year-olds passed the standard task, whereas 79 per cent of the 3-year-olds passed the trick task. Under this condition children said that the object looked like a rock but was really a sponge . . . Thus, this is further evidence that 3-year-olds are capable of forming dual representations of objects (e.g. distinguishing appearance from reality), this time under conditions in which their goal is to deceive another person!

Other researchers have suggested that young children's failure on these tasks may, in part, result from a difficulty in formulating the appearance–reality distinction into words (e.g. Huelsken *et al.*, 2001; Sapp, Lee & Muir, 2000). For example, Sapp *et al.* compared 3-year-olds' performance on Flavell's appearance–reality distinction using both the typical verbal response paradigm and a non-verbal response condition. The verbal response condition incorporated the standard verbal questions 'What does it look like?' and 'What is it really?', but the children were asked to respond non-verbally to an appearance request (e.g. they were asked to give the experimenter an object so that she could take a picture of a teddy bear with something that looks like a rock). Children were also asked to respond to a reality request (e.g. they were asked to give the experimenter an object so that she could wipe up some spilled water). The results showed that the majority of 3-year-olds gave correct responses to the test questions in the non-verbal condition. In contrast, many of the same children gave inappropriate answers when the verbal response paradigm was used.

The concrete operations stage: 7 to 11 Years

During this stage children's thought processes change yet again. They develop a new set of strategies called concrete operations. Piaget called these operations concrete because although children's thought is more logical and flexible, their reasoning is tied to concrete situations. They have attained the processes of decentration, compensation and reversibility and thus, can solve conservation problems. To illustrate, children not only begin to pass liquid conservation tasks but are aware that a change in one aspect (e.g. height) is compensated by a change in another aspect (e.g. width). Moreover, children often state that if the water is poured back into the original glass then the liquid in both glasses will be the same height (reversibility). This understanding of reversibility underlies many of the gains reported during this stage of development. Subsequent research has confirmed that children appear to acquire conservation of number, liquid, mass, length, weight, and volume in that order, which is the order Piaget proposed (e.g. Tomlinson-Keasey, 1978).

They can also seriate mentally, an ability named *transitive inference* (see earlier for a definition). For example, children may be presented with two pairings of three children of differing heights. In pair 1, the child sees that Jane is taller than Amanda, and in pair 2 the child sees that Amanda is taller than Claire. The child can then reason, without seeing the actual pairing, that Jane is taller than Claire. However, if the same problem is presented verbally, in an abstract form, simply by being told that 'Jane is taller than Amanda' and 'Amanda is taller than Claire', the child encounters difficulty in solving the problem. So whilst the concrete operational child can seriate mentally, it appears that the objects necessary for problem solution need to be physically present.

Between the ages of 7 and 10, children gain in their ability to classify objects and begin to pass Piaget's class inclusion problem. They can attend to relations between a general and two specific categories at the same time (e.g. Fischer & Roberts, 1986; Ni, 1998). For example, children can sort flowers into a major class and a subclass: yellow tulips, yellow daisies, yellow roses, red tulips, red daisies, and red roses while ignoring irrelevant properties such as the number of petals (Fischer & Roberts, 1986).

Whilst subsequent research has confirmed many of Piaget's observations about the concrete operations stage, other research has also shown that children's performance on tasks may be influenced by the context of the task. It has been demonstrated that culture and schooling affects children's performance on a number of Piagetian tasks. For example, children of the Hausa, a village society in Nigeria who rarely send their children to school, do not understand conservation tasks until around age 11 (Fahrmeier, 1978). Likewise, underprivileged children in Brazil receive hardly any formal schooling. Mostly, these children work as street vendors selling books to passers-by. Ceci and Roazzi (1994) showed that 6-to 9-year-old Brazilian street vendors demonstrate poor performance on formal class inclusion tasks, yet when the context of the task is changed so that it is relevant to street vending their performance improves. For example, the researchers presented these young street vendors with a problem in which the street vendors had four pieces of mint chewing gum and two pieces of grape chewing gum for sale, and simply asked the children whether it would be better to sell the mint chewing gum or all of the gum. Under such conditions the Brazilain street vendors outperformed children attending school.

Other researchers have examined the effect of how long children have been attending school. When children of the same age are tested on transitive inference problems, those that have been in school the longest perform best (Artman & Cahan,

1993). Such findings suggest that culture and context play an important role in children acquiring the forms of logic required to pass classical Piagetian tasks.

Overall evaluation of Piaget's theory

Piaget's contribution to the study of cognitive development was groundbreaking. Piaget demonstrated that young children think differently from adults and the questions he raised about how children develop continue to inspire today's developmental researchers (Desrochers, 2008). Although Piaget's theory remains highly influential, a number of weaknesses are now becoming apparent. Many researchers argue that the basic processes (e.g. assimilation, accommodation, and equilibrium) are vague (e.g. Siegler & Ellis, 1996) and tend to describe, rather than explain how change occurs.

Additionally, although Piaget was more interested in the sequence of change across development than the specific ages at which such change occurs (Lourenço & Machado, 1996), it is clear that Piaget often misjudged the ages at which children show evidence for understanding a particular concept. This may have resulted from the fact that he often failed to distinguish between competence and performance. As previously mentioned, recent research has shown there are many factors (e.g. memory capacity, context) other than understanding a concept that may be required to solve a task. Hence, it may be that children failed tasks not because they lacked competence but rather because they failed to demonstrate their competence on classical Piagetian tasks due to performance demands.

In this chapter we have also shown how culture and schooling affect cognitive development (e.g. Artman & Cahan, 1993). Such findings have led several researchers to argue that Piaget did not pay enough attention to the role of culture and social interaction in shaping cognitive development (e.g. Rogoff, 2003). In particular, the effect of schooling suggests that Piaget's assumption that children's learning is driven primarily by constructing their own knowledge by acting on the environment is too narrow. It is rather that teachers and adults guide children's learning by helping them focus on important issues or aspects of a situation, hence they are **scaffolding** the children's learning, an issue that is discussed in more detail in Chapter 18.

scaffolding the process whereby adults structure and simplify a child's environment in order to facilitate their learning.

Recent research has raised serious questions regarding the universality of Piaget's stages. In Piaget's conception, once a person has consolidated the skills and understanding of a particular stage, that person will be functioning cognitively in that stage regardless of the particular problem or domain of knowledge. However, many researchers (e.g. Siegler, 1981) propose that a child might use concrete-operational thinking on one task and use preoperational thinking on another. Although researchers have increasingly challenged Piaget's notion that broad stages of development exist (e.g. Flavell et al., 2002), there is still disagreement on how general or specific cognitive development actually is.

In the next section we will explore two developmental approaches to **information processing**. First we will discuss Robbie Case's (1992, 1998) neo-Piagetian theory that, like Piaget, sees development as proceeding through a series of stages. Second, we will examine Siegler's model of strategy choice (Siegler, 1996). Finally, we will describe Vygotsky's sociocultural theory.

CASE'S NEO-PIAGETIAN THEORY

Like Piaget, Case interpreted cognitive change occurring as a series of four stages or structural levels: *sensorimotor stage* (0–2 years), the *interrelational stage* (2–8 years), the *dimensional stage* (5–11 years) and the *vectorial stage* (11–19 years). However, unlike Piaget, Case adopted an information processing perspective to cognitive development in that he attributes changes within each stage and across stages to increases in central processing speed and **working memory** capacity. Hence, Case's theory of development is often referred to as a neo-Piagetian theory as it expands on Piaget's theory by providing an alternative theoretical account. Case attributed increases in working memory capacity to three factors: brain development, automatisation, and the formation of central conceptual structures. First, as children get older neurological changes within the brain result in increased working memory capacity. This means that as children get older they are able to attend to more operations in working memory at the same time (Case, 1985; Kail, 1990). However, at a given age there is a biological limit on how many operations can be stored in working memory. Second, as children get older they become more practised with Piagetian operations, and by repeatedly practising certain operations, their processing of these operations becomes more automatic. This increased efficiency in processing operations or schemes means that there are fewer demands on working memory, and free working memory capacity can be used for combining schemes and generating new schemes. A good analogy is learning to drive a motorcar. During the initial stages of learning to drive people focus on basic operations such as pressing in the clutch and changing gear. However, with practice this process eventually becomes automatic and requires less working memory space.

> **working memory**
> *short-term memory* store in which mental operations such as *rehearsal* and *categorisation* take place.

Third, Case proposed that increased processing efficiency, combined with increased free working memory capacity, allows children to generate central conceptual structures – semantic networks of concepts which represent children's knowledge in a particular cognitive domain (e.g. number, space). Case argues that when children form a new conceptual structure they move to the next stage of development.

To illustrate this, let us take another look at conservation of liquid tasks. In liquid conservation tasks children initially attend to one dimension (e.g. the height of liquid in the glass), and ignore the other dimension (the width of the glass). However, as children gain experience in pouring liquid from one container to another they notice that the height of liquid may change. As children become practised at pouring liquid from one container to another they may then notice that the width of liquid may change as well. Eventually children are able to combine these two observations into a conserving response. A similar developmental progression occurs for conservation of weight, mass, length, and so on. Once all of these schemes have become sufficiently automatic they are integrated into a *central conceptual structure* (networks of concepts) that enables them to effectively process information about a range of conservation tasks. Compared to Piaget's theory, Case's theory provides a far more satisfactory account of horizontal décalage. Simply, conservation tasks vary in their processing demands, with those tasks which require more working memory capacity being acquired later. The development of central conceptual structures, however, is not only affected by biological maturation (e.g. central processing speed and increased working memory capacity), but also through social and individual experience. Hence, a child who is particularly interested in reading but not drawing will display more advanced conceptual structures in reading.

SIEGLER'S OVERLAPPING WAVES THEORY

Siegler (1996, 2000) adopts an evolutionary perspective to account for child development. Unlike Piaget's theory, which depicts a child as thinking about a given task in a single way, Siegler suggests that when attempting to solve tasks (e.g. arithmetic, reading, number conservation) children may generate a variety of strategies (Chen & Siegler, 2000; Siegler, 1995; Siegler & Robinson, 1982; his approach is also discussed in Chapter 16). For example, on tests of number conservation Siegler (1995) draws our attention to the fact that while a 5-year-old child might often state that there are more counters in the longer row (the strategy described by Piaget), the very same child may use a different approach on another trial. For example, rather than judging amount based on the row length the child may decide to count the number of counters in each row.

overlapping waves a central concept in Siegler's theory of development in which at any one time the child has a number of strategies that can be used to solve problems. Over time less efficient strategies are replaced by more effective ones.

Siegler argues that children are most likely to use multiple strategies which compete with each other (hence **overlapping waves**) when they are still learning about how to solve a task. To illustrate this, Siegler and Robinson (1982) investigated the strategies used by 4- and 5-year-olds when attempting to solve addition problems using a *microgenetic* approach. Rather than using a cross-sectional approach, in which the performance of several different age groups is compared, the microgenetic approach involves testing children repeatedly over a short period of time, when change in children's performance is occurring. During this period of changing competence the density of observations is relatively high and observations are intensively analysed. Using a **microgenetic method** allows the researcher to examine the acquisition of new strategies on a trial by trial basis.

In Siegler and Robinson's study each child was asked to complete a number of addition problems over six sessions. The researchers found that the children tended to use four main strategies: (a) counting aloud using fingers; (b) counting on fingers without counting out loud; (c) counting out loud without using fingers; and (d) retrieving answers from memory. Analyses revealed that only 20 per cent of children consistently used one strategy for all of the addition problems. Furthermore, when children were given exactly the same addition problem in a second testing session, 30 per cent used a different (not necessarily more sophisticated) strategy in the second testing session. These findings suggest that when children are learning about how to solve a task they have available a range of different strategies to use at the same time, rather than just one. It also suggests that there is considerable variation in the adoption rate of new strategies.

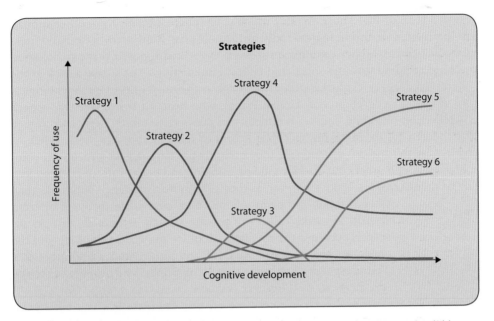

FIGURE 9.9 *To illustrate Siegler's overlapping waves theory. At any one point in time the child will have several strategies in order to solve a problem, and as cognitive development continues the use of less useful strategies will decline and more effective strategies will take their place.*

As children identify and experiment with different strategies they begin to real-ise that some are more effective in terms of accuracy and time than others. Hence, over time some strategies become more frequently used whilst strategies that are not frequently used tend to 'die off'. Siegler uses *overlapping waves* as a metaphor to illus-trate the increase and decrease of different strategies during this period of learning (see Figure 9.9). Overall, Siegler's model overcomes a number of problems that have been identified with Piaget's stage approach to cognitive development. It provides accounts both of the variation in children's thinking and also accounts for continuous change in children's thinking. However, the mechanisms that result in strategy vari-ation are not clear.

VYGOTSKY'S SOCIOCULTURAL PERSPECTIVE

Like Piaget, Vygotsky viewed the child as an active seeker of knowledge. However, Vygotsky emphasised that children's thinking is influenced by social and cultural contexts. He viewed children as being part of society and collaborators in their own learning with adults. According to this theory we share lower mental functions such as attention and memory with other animals and these functions develop during the first two years of life. Those abilities which differentiate humans from other animals are the mental or psychological tools we acquire that transform these basic mental capacities into higher cognitive processes. Vygotsky proposed that psychological tools are acquired through social and cultural interactions. Let's have a look at the role of language, as Vygotsky viewed language as the most important psychological tool in cognitive development. Unlike Piaget, who believed that egocentric speech is a reflection of young children's difficulty in perspective taking, Vygotsky argued that children engage in private speech as a form of self-guidance (e.g. Berk, 1992). As children master the use of language they not only use language as a means of communicating with others but also for guiding thinking and behaviour. At first children talk to themselves out loud. However, as they gain more experience with tasks (e.g.

private speech as children master language they can use internal self-directed speech to guide their thinking and planning.

categorisation, problem-solving) they internalise their self-directed speech. Vygotsky called this **private speech**. Eventually this private speech becomes the mediating tool for the child's thinking and the child uses private speech to think and plan (Duncan & Pratt, 1997). This perspective has been strongly supported by a number of studies (e.g. Berk, 2003; Winsler & Naglieri, 2003).

Unlike Piaget's stage theory, Vygotsky argued that children's learning takes place within a fuzzy range along the course of development; within the **zone of proximal development** (ZPD). According to Vygotsky the zone covers three developmental levels. The lower level is called the actual level of development and reflects what the learner can do unassisted; while the upper level of the zone is called the potential level of development and reflects what the learner cannot yet do. Everything between these levels is called the proximal development (i.e. it is proximal to the learner's last fully developed level).

Vygotsky drew attention to the fact that whether a child can successfully solve a problem or pass a task depends on many environmental factors (e.g. whether the child is helped by another person, whether the problem is worded clearly, and whether any cues are provided). While some tasks are not very challenging and the child can pass these unassisted, other tasks are more challenging and can only be passed with assistance. In the more challenging tasks adults can provide the child with guidance by breaking down the task into manageable pieces, offering direct instruction, etc. For this guidance to be of benefit to the learner it must fit the child's current level of performance. This type of teaching is referred to as *scaffolding*. As the child becomes more competent and begins to master the task the adult gradually withdraws assistance. The child internalises the language and behaviours used in these social interactions and it becomes part of their private speech, which in turn mediates their thinking and planning.

With the development of new skills at a higher level of mastery both the actual level and the potential level increases. Hence, the entire ZPD is dynamic and moves with development (Smagorinsky, 1995). Unlike Piaget's stage theory in which the child is at the same level of thinking across all domains, Vygotsky proposed that each domain (e.g. reading, mathematics) has its own dynamic zone. Hence, in a given domain one child's zone might be further along than another's, whereas in a different domain they might be the same.

Scaffolding, as a means of supporting the learner, may not be appropriate in all contexts. For example, adults often support and engage in social interactions involving pretend play but this instruction differs in nature from the direct instruction given when solving a problem-solving task. More recently, Rogoff (1998, 2003) has suggested the term **guided participation** as a way of capturing children's broad opportunities to learn through interaction with others. While Piaget viewed pretend play as a way for children to act out situations they didn't understand, Vygotsky saw pretend play as an area in which children advance themselves as they try out new skills. When children engage in pretend play, imaginary situations are created from internal ideas, rather than outside stimuli eliciting responses from the individual. In pretend play children often use one object to stand for another (e.g. a cardboard box for a boat). Gradually, they come to realise that a symbol (an object, an idea, or an action) can be differentiated from the referent to which it refers.

guided participation children's ability to learn from interaction with others.

Another major feature of pretend play is that it is rule-based. Children adhere to social and cultural norms that govern behaviour. For example, when pretending to participate in a tea party, children sit around a table with cups, saucers, and plates and typically pretend to drink tea and eat cakes or biscuits. Such play helps children internalise social and cultural norms that govern people's behaviour.

Overall evaluation of Vygotsky's theory

While Piaget has been criticised for emphasising the role of the individual while ignoring the role of culture in development, Vygotsky has been criticised for placing too much emphasis on the role of social interaction (Feldman & Fowler, 1997). It is probably fair to say that some learning occurs through social interaction (Gauvain & Rogoff, 1989) and some learning is individually constructed through discovery learning (Gallagher & Easley, 1978). Unlike Piaget, who highlighted the actions of the individual on the environment as driving forward development, Vygotsky placed more emphasis on the role of cultural and social factors, such as language.

SUMMARY AND CONCLUSIONS

There can be little doubt regarding the contribution of Piaget's theory to the field of cognitive development. However, although his theory remains influential, some weaknesses are now apparent. Researchers have shown that factors other than competence can influence performance on a task (e.g. the language used in asking the test question). Generally, research has demonstrated that infants and children are more cognitively competent than Piaget believed. For example, research by Baillargeon and colleagues (e.g. Baillargeon & DeVos, 1991) has shown object permanence in 3-month-olds (see Chapter 5). Likewise, Bryant & Trabasso (1971) have shown that children can make transitive inferences far earlier than Piaget suggested. Many argue that his basic processes, which include schemes, assimilation, accommodation, and equilibrium are metaphors and as such are impossible to test.

Other research has now brought into serious question the universality of Piaget's stages. Remember that according to Piaget, once a person has consolidated the understanding of a specific stage, that person will be functioning cognitively at that particular level regardless of the problem. However, Siegler (1981) has clearly demonstrated that children use different cognitive strategies across problems and sometimes even for the same problem. Finally, Piaget has been criticised for paying little attention to the role of social relationships in cognitive development.

Unlike Piaget who viewed development as coming from within and before learning, Vygotsky saw learning as coming first and bringing about development. Learning occurs within the ZPD as the child attains new skills with the aid of others. Through his theory Vygotksy placed greater emphasis on both the cultural and social influences on cognitive development than Piaget.

Case's neo-developmental theory adopts a stage-like approach but accounts for change both within and between stages to increases in working memory capacity and processing efficiency. This theory offers a theoretical account of horizontal déclage and provides an insightful account of how children's individual experiences effect development. As such, Case's theory provides a plausible account for unevenness in cognitive development without the need to invoke concepts like horizontal décalage.

In conclusion, the theories of cognitive development discussed within this chapter provide different accounts of the structures and processes underlying cognitive development. Although nowadays many researchers acknowledge that Piaget's theory has some severe limitations, it is fair to comment that Piaget played an instrumental role in changing the way that researchers view child development.

DISCUSSION POINTS

1. Think about the changes that take place in children's thinking around the ages of 3 to 6 years. How might these developments help children solve Piaget's concrete operational tasks?

2. What evidence suggests that young children are egocentric?

3. Can children make transitive inferences?

4. Think about Piaget's conservation problems. Why do you think that young children fail them, and what develops to enable the older child to succeed at these tasks?

5. What sort of weaknesses are apparent in Piaget's theory?

6. Does the evidence support the view that children go through qualitatively different stages in their cognitive development?

7. Do you think that alternative theoretical views, such as those by Case, Siegler, and Vygotsky, offer a better account of cognitive development than Piaget?

SUGGESTIONS FOR FURTHER READING

Eysenck, M.W., & Keane, M.T. (2010). *Cognitive psychology: A student's handbook* (6th edn). New York and East Sussex: Psychology Press.

Garton, A.F. (2004). *Exploring cognitive development: The child as problem solver.* Cambridge, MA. and Oxford: Blackwell.

Goswami, U. (2008). *Cognitive development: The learning brain.* New York and East Sussex: Psychology Press.

Lee, K. (Ed.) (2000). *Cognitive development: The essential readings.* Cambridge, MA. and Oxford: Blackwell.

Siegler, R.S., & Alibali, M.W. (2005). *Children's thinking* (4th edn). New Jersey: Pearson Education International.

REFERENCES

Aguiar, A., & Baillargeon, R. (1999). 2.5-month-old infants' reasoning about when objects should and should not be occluded. *Cognitive Psychology, 39,* 116–157.

Artman, L., & Cahan, S. (1993). Schooling and the development of transitive inference. *Developmental Psychology, 29,* 753–759.

Baillargeon, R. (1987). Object permanence in 3 1/2- and 4.1/2-month-old infants. *Developmental Psychology, 24*(5), 655–664.

Baillargeon, R., & DeVos, J. (1991). Object permanence in 3.3- and 4.5-month-old infants: Further evidence. *Child Development, 62,* 1227–1246.

Baillargeon, R., Scott, R.M., & He, Z. (2010). False-belief understanding in infants. *Trends in Cognitive Sciences, 14,* 110–118.

Baldwin, D.A., Markman, E.M., & Melartin, R.L. (1993). Infants' ability to draw inferences about nonobvious object properties: Evidence from exploratory play. *Cognitive Development, 64,* 711–728.

Beilin, H. (1992). Piaget's enduring contribution to developmental psychology. *Developmental Psychology, 28,* 191–204.

Berk. L.E. (1992). The extracurriculum. In P.W. Jackson (Ed.) *Handbook of research on curriculum* (pp. 1002–1043). New York: Macmillan.

Berk, L.E. (2003). Vygotsky, Lev. In L. Nadel (Ed.) *Encyclopaedia of cognitive science* (Vol. 6). London: Macmillan.

Blewitt, P. (1994). Understanding category hierarchies: The earliest levels of skill. *Child Development, 65,* 1279–1298.

Bliss, J. (2010). Recollections of Jean Piaget. *The Psychologist, 23,* 444–446.

Borke, H. (1975). Piaget's mountains revisited: Changes in the egocentric landscape. *Developmental Psychology, 11,* 240–243.

Bosco, F.M., Friedman, O., & Leslie, A.M. (2006). Recognition of pretend and real actions in play by one- and two-year-olds: Early success and why they fail. *Cognitive Development, 21,* 3–10.

Bruner, J.S. (1966). On cognitive growth. In J.S. Bruner, R.R. Oliver, & P.M. Greenheld (Eds.) *Studies in cognitiveg growth.* New York: Wiley.

Bryant, P.E., & Trabasso. T. (1971). Transitive inferences and memory in young children. *Nature, 232,* 456–458.

Buttelmann, D., Carpenter, M., Call, J., & Tomasello, M. (2007). Enculturated chimpanzees imitate rationally. *Developmental Science, 10,* F31–F38.

Buttelmann, D., Carpenter, M., & Tomasello, M. (2009). Eighteen-month-old infants show false belief understanding in an active helping paradigm. *Cognition, 112,* 337–342.

Carey, S. (1985). *Conceptual change in childhood.* Cambridge, MA: MIT Press.

Case. R. (1985). *Intellectual development: Birth to adulthood.* Orlando, FL: Academic Press.

Case, R. (1992). *The mind's staircase.* Hillsdale, NJ: Erlbaum.

Case, R. (1998). The development of central structures. In D. Kuhn & R. Siegler (Eds.) *Handbook of child psychology: Vol 2. Cognition, perception, and language* (5th edn; pp. 745–800). New York: Wiley.

Ceci, S.J., & Roazzi, A. (1994). The effects of context on cognition: Postcards from Brazil. In R.J. Sternberg (Ed.) *Mind in context* (pp. 74–101). New York: Cambridge University Press.

Chen, Z., & Siegler, R.S. (2000). *Across the great divide: Bridging the gap between understanding of toddlers' and older children's thinking.* Monographs of the Society for Research in Child Development, 65(2, Serial No. 261).

DeLoache, J.S. (2000). Dual representation and young children's use of scale models. *Child Development, 71,* 329–338.

Desrochers, S. (2008). From Piaget to specific Genevan developmental models. *Child Development Perspectives, 2,* 7–12.

De Vries, R. (1969). *Constancy of generic identity in the years three to six.* Monographs of the Society for Research in Child Development, 34(3, Serial No. 127).

Donaldson, M. (1978). *Children's Minds.* London: Fontana.

Duncan, R.M., & Pratt, M.W. (1997). Microgenetic change in the quantity and quality of preschoolers' private speech. *International Journal of Behavioural Development, 20,* 367.

Fahrmeier, E.D. (1978). The development of concrete operations among the Hausa. *Journal of Cross-Cultural Psychology, 9,* 23–44.

Farah, M.J., & Rabinowitz, C. (2003). Genetic and environmental influences on the organisation of semantic memory in the brain: Is 'living things' an innate category? *Cognitive Neuropsychology, 20,* 401–408.

Feldman, D.H., & Fowler, R.C. (1997). The nature(s) of developmental change: Piaget, Vygotsky, and the transition process. *New Ideas in Psychology, 3,* 195–210.

Fischer, K.W., & Roberts, R.J. (1986). *A developmental sequence of classifications skills and errors in preschool children.* Unpublished manuscript, Harvard University.

Flavell, J.H. (1993). The development of children's understanding of false belief and the appearance–reality distinction. *International Journal of Psychology, 28,* 595–604.

Flavell, J.H., Green, F.L., & Flavell, E.R. (1986). *Development of the appearance–reality distinction.* Monographs of the Society for Research in Child Development, 51(Serial No. 212).

Flavell, J.H., Miller, P.H., & Miller, S.A. (2002). *Cognitive development* (4th edn). Englewood Cliffs, NJ: Prentice-Hall.

Gallagher, S.K., & Easley, J.A. (Eds.). (1978). *Knowledge and development: Vol. 2. Piaget and education.* New York: Plenum.

Gauvain, M. (2001). *The social context of cognitive development.* New York: Guilford.

Gauvain, M., & Rogoff, B. (1989). Collaborative problem solving and children's planning skills. *Developmental Psychology, 25,* 139–151.

Gelman, R. (1972). The nature and development of early number concepts. In H.W. Reese (Ed.) *Advances in Child Development and Behavior* (Vol. 7). New York: Academic Press.

Gelman, S.A. & Koenigh, M.A. (2003). Theory-based categorisation in early childhood. In D.H. Rakison & L.M. Oakes (Eds.) *Early category and concept development: Making sense of the blooming, buzzing confusion* (pp. 330–359). New York: Oxford University Press.

Gelman, S.A., & Opfer, J.E. (2002). Development of the animate–inanimate distinction. In U. Goswami (Ed.) *Blackwell handbook of childhood cognitive development* (pp. 151–166). Malden, MA: Blackwell.

Gergely, G., Bekkering, H., & Kiraly, I. (2002). Rational imitation in preverbal infants. *Nature, 415*, 755.

Gopnik, A., & Nazzi, T. (2003). Words, kinds, and causal powers: A theory perspective on early naming and categorisation. In D.H. Rakison & L.M. Oakes (Eds.) *Early category and concept development: Making sense of the blooming, buzzing confusion* (pp. 303–329). New York: Oxford University Press.

Halford, G.S. (1990). Is children's reasoning logical or analogical. *Human Development, 33*, 356–361.

Hickling, A.K. & Wellman, H.M. (2001). The emergence of children's causal explanations and theories: Evidence from everyday conversation. *Developmental Psychology, 37*, 668–683.

Hollich, G.J., & Houston, D.M. (2007). Language development: from speech perception to first words. In A. Slater & M. Lewis (Eds.) *Introduction to infant development* (pp. 170–188). Oxford: Oxford University Press.

Huelsken, C., Sodian, B., *et al.* (2001). Distinguishing between appearance and reality in a dressing-up game–a problem of dual coding or preserving identity? *Zeitschrift für Entwicklungspsychologie und Paedagogische Psychologie, 33 (3)*, 129–137.

Hunt, J. McV. (1969). The impact and limitations of the giant of developmental psychology. In D. Elkind & J.H. Flavell (Eds.) *Studies in cognitive development: Essays in honor of Jean Piaget* (pp. 3–66). New York: Oxford University Press.

Kail, R. (1990). *The development of memory in children* (3rd edn). New York: Freeman.

Lamb, M.E., Bornstein, M.H., & Teti, D.M. (2002). *Development in infancy: An introduction*. Hillsdale, NJ: Lawrence Erlbaum Associates.

Leslie, A.M. (1987). Pretense and representations. The origins of 'theory of mind'. *Psychological Review, 94*, 412–426.

Leslie, A.M. (2000). How to acquire a 'representational theory of mind'. In D. Sperber & S. Davis (Eds.) *Metarepresentation: A multidisciplinary perspective* (pp. 197–223). Oxford: Oxford University Press.

Lourenço, O., & Machado, A. (1996). In defense of Piaget's theory: A reply to 10 common criticisms. *Psychological Review, 103*, 143–164.

Mahon, B.Z., Anzellotti, S., Schwarzback, J., Zampini, M., & Carazza, A. (2009). Category-specific organization in the brain does not require visual experience. *Neuron, 63*, 397–405.

Mandler, J.M. (2007). The conceptual foundations of animals and artifacts. In E. Margolis & S. Lawrence (Eds.) *Creations of the mind: Theories of artifacts and their representation*. Oxford: Oxford University Press.

Mandler, J.M., & McDonough, L. (1998). On developing a knowledge base in infancy. *Developmental Psychology, 34*, 1274–1288.

Markman, E.M., & Siebert, J. (1976). Classes and collections, internal organisation and resulting holistic properties. *Cognitive Psychology, 8*, 561–577.

Mash, C. (2007). Object representation in infants' coordination of manipulative force. *Infancy, 12*, 329–341.

Massey, C., & Gelman, R. (1988). Preschoolers decide whether pictured unfamiliar objects can move themselves. *Developmental Psychology, 24*, 307–317.

McGarrigle, J., & Donaldson, M. (1974). Conservation accidents. *Cognition, 3*, 341–350.

Meltzoff, A.N., & Moore, M.K. (1994). Imitation, memory, and the representation of persons. *Infant Behavior and Development, 17*, 83–99.

Mounoud, P. & Bower, T.G.R. (1974). Conservation of weight in infants. *Cognition, 3*, 29–40.

Newcombe, N., & Huttenlocher, J. (1992). Children's early ability to solve perspective-taking problems. *Developmental Psychology, 28*, 635–643.

Ni, Y. (1998). Cognitive structure, content knowledge, and classificatory reasoning. *Journal of Genetic Psychology, 159*, 280–296.

Pears, R., & Bryant, P. (1990). Transitive inferences by young children about spatial position. *British Journal of Psychology, 81*, 497–510.

Piaget, J. (1960). *The child's conception of the world*. London: Routledge.

Piaget, J. (1962). *Play, dreams and imitation in childhood*. New York: W.W. Norton.

Piaget, J., & Inhelder, B. (1956). *The child's conception of space*. New York: W.W. Norton.

Rakoczy, H., Tomasello, M., & Striano, T. (2002). How children turn objects into symbols: A cultural learning account. In L. Namy (Ed.) *Symbol use and symbol representation*. New York: Erlbaum.

Rice, C., Koinis, D., Sullivan, K., Tager-Flusberg, H., & Wimmer, E. (1997). When 3-year-olds pass the appearance–reality task. *Developmental Psychology, 33*, 54–61.

Richards, D.D., & Siegler, R.S. (1984). The effects of task requirements on children's life judgements. *Child Development, 55*, 1687–1696.

Rogoff, B. (1998). Cognition as a collaborative process. In D. Kuhn & R.S. Siegler (Eds.) *Handbook of child psychology: Vol 2. Cognition, perception and language* (5th edn; pp. 679–744). New York: Wiley.

Rogoff, B. (2003). *The cultural nature of human development*. New York: Oxford University Press.

Ruffman, T.K., & Olson, D.R. (1989). Children's ascriptions of knowledge to others. *Developmental Psychology, 25*, 601–606.

Sapp, F., Lee, K., & Muir, D. (2000). Three-year-olds' difficulty with the appearance–reality distinction: Is it real or is it apparent? *Developmental Psychology, 36*, 547–560.

Siegler, R.S. (1981). *Developmental sequences within and between concepts*. Monographs of the Society for Research in Child Development, 46(2, Serial No. 189).

Siegler, R.S. (1995). How does change occur? A microgenetic study of number conservation. *Cognitive Psychology, 28*, 225–273.

Siegler, R.S. (1996). *Emerging minds: The process of change in children's thinking*. New York: Oxford University Press.

Siegler, R.S. (2000). The rebirth of children's learning. *Child Development, 71*(1), 26–35.

Siegler, R.S., & Ellis, S. (1996). Piaget on childhood. *Psychological Science, 7*, 211–215.

Siegler, R.S., & Robinson, M. (1982). The development of numerical understandings. In H.W. Reese and L. P Lipsitt (Eds.) *Advances in Child Development and Behavior* (Vol. 16; pp. 241–312). New York: Academic Press.

Smagorinsky, P. (1995). The social construction of data: Methodological problems of investigating learning in the zone of proximal development. *Review of Educational Research, 65*, 191–212.

Smith, L.B. (1979). Perceptual development and category generalisation. *Child Development, 50*, 705–715.

Striano, T., Tomasello, M., & Rochat, P. (2001). Social and object support for early symbolic play. *Developmental Science, 4*, 442–455.

Sugarman, S. (1987). *Piaget's construction of the child's reality*. New York: Cambridge University Press.

Tomasello, M., Striano, T., & Rochat, P. (1999). Do children use objects as symbols? *British Journal of Developmental Psychology, 17*, 551–562.

Tomlinson-Keasey (1978). The structure of concrete operational thought. *Child Development, 50*, 1153–1163.

Vaish, A., Carpenter, M., & Tomasell, M. (2009). Sympathy through affective perspective taking and its relation to prosocial behaviour in toddlers. *Developmental Psychology, 45*, 534–543.

Wellman, H.M., Cross, D., & Watson, J. (2001). Meta-analysis of theory-of-mind development: The truth about false belief. *Child Development, 72*, 655–684.

Winsler, A., & Naglieri, J. (2003). Overt and covert verbal problem-solving strategies: Developmental trends in use, awareness, and relations with task performance in children aged 5 to 17. *Child Development, 74*, 659–678.

10 The Development of Language

HEATHER M. HILL AND STAN A. KUCZAJ II

KEY TERMS

babbling ● canonical ● categorical perception ● comprehension ● d-structure ● empiricism ● infant-directed speech (motherese) ● innate mechanism ● manual babbling ● maturation ● mirror neuron ● modulated babbling ● nativism ● overextension ● overgeneralisation ● overregularisation ● peer ● phoneme ● pragmatic system ● protoconversations ● protodeclarative ● proto-imperative ● reflexive vocalisations ● semantic system ● speech stream ● s-structure ● syntax ● turn-taking ● underextension

CHAPTER OUTLINE

OVERVIEW

The chapter begins by asking what human language is, and it is many things: a means of communication, a symbolic system, a rule-governed grammatical system, and it is productive in that we all can produce and comprehend sentences that have never previously been produced or heard. Language acquisition is discussed under four main headings.

- The abilities that enable us to communicate effectively comprise the *pragmatic system*, which involves a variety of cognitive and social skills.
- The development of the *phonological system* is described – from speech and word perception in infancy to the production of speech sounds, and the child's developing ability to articulate and pronounce words and speech.
- The development of the *syntactic system* gives an account of how children learn the grammatical structures and rules which allow us to produce grammatical sentences.
- The acquisition of *word meaning* – the semantic aspect of language development – is discussed in the next section.

Language acquisition does not proceed in isolation of other aspects of development, and the chapter discusses the relationship and interaction between language and cognitive development. The final section gives a brief account of some of the different theoretical views that attempt to explain language development.

INTRODUCTION

The apparent ease with which young children acquire their first language masks the inherent difficulty of the task. During the course of language acquisition, children must learn to perceive and produce particular types of sounds, associate thousands of words with the appropriate meanings, combine words to produce sentences, and discover the rules that govern the manner in which speakers of a language communicate with one another. Clearly, children learning language must sort through and make sense of an impressive amount of information.

In this chapter, we will consider the general characteristics of language acquisition and possible explanations for these characteristics. Evident in explanations of many biological and psychological phenomena, the debate between **nativists** and **empiricists** continues to be quite lively in the area of language development. Theoretical accounts of language acquisition are shaped by assumptions about the nature of human language. For example, if a theorist believes that human language is the result of learned associations of words (such as 'the' and 'boy'), their account of language acquisition will focus on how children learn such associations. However, a theorist who believes that human language depends on knowledge of abstract grammatical classes (such as *noun* and *verb*) will attempt to explain language acquisition in terms of such classes. Given the importance of assumptions about the nature of human language for theories of language acquisition, we will first consider the characteristics of human language.

WHAT IS HUMAN LANGUAGE?

A communication system

Human language is primarily a communication system, a means for speakers of

FIGURE 10.1 *The ability to communicate is not unique to the human species. Kittiwakes* (Rissa tridactyla) *greet each other when one returns to the cliff nesting site with cries of 'kit-i-waak' and entwining of their necks. The longer the returning bird has been absent from the nest, the longer this greeting ceremony.*

Source: Naturepl.com

a language to communicate with one another. The ability to communicate is not unique to the human species (Figure 10.1). Communication systems have been found in species as diverse as bees, lions, and dolphins. However, none of the communication systems of other species have been found to possess all of the characteristics found in human communication (Hauser, 1996; Kuczaj & Kirkpatrick, 1993). Human language is the most complex, diverse, and efficient means of communication known to any species on Earth. In fact, some have viewed language as a 'Special Gift', which has evolved solely in humans (as described by MacWhinney, 2005). Specifically, human language is *a symbolic, rule-governed system that is both abstract and productive, characteristics that enable its speakers to produce and comprehend a wide range of utterances.* However, our understanding of language, its characteristics, its development, its evolution, and its neural basis have indicated that language did not evolve from a single ability but from a multitude of abilities (as reviewed by MacWhinney, 2005). Some of these abilities will be highlighted in this chapter.

A symbolic system

Language is a symbolic system because words and parts of words (e.g. the English past tense suffix '-ed') represent meaning. The meaningful units of a language are symbols because they refer to things other than themselves. These symbols are conventional because speakers of a language use the same words to express the same meanings. For example, speakers of English use the word 'bird' to refer to the wide variety of creatures that comprise avians. The conventional nature of language symbols makes communication possible. If everyone chose their own symbols, communication would be difficult, if not impossible. At the same time, however, language symbols are *arbitrary* because there is no necessary relation between sounds and meanings. Consider the word 'bird' again. It is not necessary for this sound pattern to refer to the particular class of animals that it does. Speakers of English could just as easily refer to what we now call 'birds' as 'girts' or 'mantels'. The arbitrary nature of language symbols is readily apparent when we consider different human languages. Different languages use different sound combinations to refer to the same meaning. The English 'bird' is 'vogel' in German, 'ptaszek' in Polish, and 'oiseau' in French.

A rule-governed system

Language is a rule-governed system, meaning that each human language is constrained by a set of rules that reflects the regularities of the language. For example, in English, words such as 'the' and 'a' must precede the noun to which they refer: 'the dolphin ate a fish' is a correct English sentence, but 'dolphin the ate fish a' is not. The rule system of a language is abstract because it goes beyond the simple association of individual words and instead involves the manipulation of abstract classes of words. Thus, rather than saying that 'the' must precede 'dolphin', we may state that *articles* (the abstract class of words containing words such as 'the' and 'a') precede *nouns* (the abstract class of words containing words such as 'dolphin' and 'fish'). The abstract classes and the rules that manipulate them make possible the most important characteristic of human language, its productivity.

Language is productive

Human language is productive in the sense that a finite number of linguistic units (sounds, words, and the abstract classes that contain these units) and a finite number of rules are capable of yielding an infinite number of grammatical utterances. Even though no speaker of any human language will produce all of the sentences that their language makes possible, the capacity to do so means that speakers of human language are not limited to reproducing sentences that they have heard, but may instead produce and comprehend novel utterances. As a result, humans can communicate a wide variety of information. We are capable of communicating facts, opinions, and emotions, regardless of whether they occurred in the past, are occurring in the present, or will occur in the future. Language also makes it possible to discuss fantasies and hypothetical situations and events. Language facilitates learning, acquiring new knowledge, or clarifying previous information. The potential productivity of language and the richness of the human mind combine to make possible the communication of a very broad array of topics. This capability for communicative diversity makes human language unique among all known communicative systems. The abilities that enable us to communicate effectively are discussed next.

THE DEVELOPMENT OF THE PRAGMATIC SYSTEM

The abilities that enable us to communicate effectively and appropriately in a social context comprise the pragmatic system, which involves a variety of cognitive and social skills. For example, the abilities involved in **turn-taking**, initiating new topics and conversations, sustaining a dialogue, and repairing a faulty communication are all important aspects of the pragmatic system (Pan & Snow, 1999).

Turn-taking

Conversations take place when participants take turns responding to each other's queries or statements. Simply defined, turn-taking requires individuals to alternate between the roles of listener and speaker during the course of a conversation. Effective turn-taking requires that the listener recognise that a response is necessary, and realise when it is appropriate to make a response. Therefore, minimising the number of unnecessary interruptions is an important aspect of turn-taking because interruptions disrupt the flow and cohesiveness of a conversation.

Mother–infant interactions

Turn-taking behaviour makes its first appearance in the earliest interactions between mothers and infants. For example, nursing sometimes involves an early non-verbal type of turn-taking (Kaye, 1977). During nursing, infants pause between bursts of sucking. During these pauses, mothers sometimes jiggle the nipple or nudge the infant in order to stimulate the sucking response. Of course, young infants do not realise that they are taking turns when they rest after a sucking burst. Nonetheless, this form of interaction may set the stage for the development of other forms of turn-taking.

Turn-taking is also involved in other forms of mother–infant interactions. Touching and vocalisations are two modalities in which exchanges between mothers and their infants occur. Mothers and infants use touch to initiate exchanges, to soothe each other, or to communicate emotional states (Moszkowksi & Stack, 2007). Vocalisations may also be used to initiate and maintain games such as peek-a-boo and give-and-take with infants. For example, mothers tend to vocalise when their infants are not vocalising or after their infants have finished vocalising, which simulates a turn-taking event. These patterns of interactions have been called **proto-conversations**

proto-conversations interactions between adults and infants in which the adults tend to vocalise when the infants are not vocalising, or after the infant has finished vocalising.

(Bateson, 1975), and may be important precursors to the turn-taking observed in early conversations. In early proto-conversations, adults bear the burden of turn-taking. They must maintain the interaction by interpreting their infants' sounds and responding appropriately. However, sometime between 8 and 12 months, infants begin to take a more active role in turn-taking (Reddy, 1999). These later proto-conversations are *dyadic* interactions because they involve only the child and the adult. These dyadic interactions evolve into *triadic* interactions which involve the infant, an adult, and an object. Triadic interactions often involve **proto-imperatives** and **proto-declaratives** (Messinger & Fogel, 1998). A proto-imperative occurs when an infant points to an object and then alternates their gaze between the object and the adult until they obtain the desired object. A proto-declarative occurs when an infant uses pointing or looking to direct the adult's attention to an object. These actions allow infants to communicate their intentions more clearly while also facilitating their 'conversations' with others.

proto-imperative occurs when infants point to an object and then alternate their gaze between the object and the adult until they obtain the desired object.

proto-declarative occurs when infants use pointing or looking to direct an adult's attention toward an object.

Imitation

Turn-taking is also involved in infants' imitation of others (Masur & Rodemaker, 1999; Nelson, 1996). Although still controversial, some studies have indicated that very young infants are capable of imitation (for a review, see Meltzoff, in press; for a counter see Heyes, 2001). In fact, one study indicated that a greater frequency of vocal imitation at 12 months was related to early facial imitation at 3 months (i.e. tongue protrusion, Heimann, 1998). Other studies have also indicated that infants are capable of imitation at very early ages (Nagy, 2006) (Figure 10.2). One explanation for this early imitation is the discovery of a **mirror neuron** system in non-human primates (Ferrari *et al.*, 2003; Gallese *et al.*, 1996). Mirror neurons are a class of cells within the brain that respond to the execution of an action as well as to an observation of that action. It is clear that imitation in various play activities is an important precursor to the development of language (Kuczaj & Makecha, 2008; McCafferty, 2008; Nelson, 1996).

mirror neuron a distinctive class of neurons that fire or discharge both when an individual executes a motor act and when they see another individual performing a motor act.

FIGURE 10.2 *Even young infants are able to imitate, although it can sometimes be difficult to know who is imitating who!*

Children frequently use imitation in their conversations with other children or adults (e.g. Keenan, 1974; Kuczaj, 1982a). Imitation allows children to take a turn by repeating all or part of what the speaker has just said. The average 2-year-old takes only one to two turns per conversation (Brinton & Fujiki, 1984). In contrast, 3- to 5-year-old children are able to engage in conversations that contain as many as 12 turns (e.g. Garvey & Hogan, 1973). Finally, imitation may be a means by which children learn to increase the number of turns that they take in a conversation.

Initiating interactions

Infants must also learn to initiate interactions. Infants' first attempts to initiate interactions with an adult often focus on directing the adult's attention to the infant or to an object, such as with proto-imperatives and proto-declaratives. These first attempts are typically non-verbal. Instead of vocalising, infants as young as 8 months will point or reach toward an object in which they are interested (Masur, 1983; Werner & Kaplan, 1963). Although pointing seems to be a universal characteristic of human cultures (Butterworth, 1995; Call & Tomasello, 1994), infants point to objects before they understand that others may point out objects to them (Butterworth & Grover, 1990; Desrochers et al., 1995). As children learn to respond to the points of others, they also learn to better direct the attention of others. Thus, sometime between 12 and 18 months of age, infants learn to coordinate gestures, looks, and vocalisations in order to communicate their intents and wants to others (Franco & Butterworth, 1996; Tomasello, 1995) (Figure 10.3). As children acquire language, their attempts to initiate interactions become more verbal and less gestural (Foster, 1986).

Children younger than 2 years tend to talk about things that exist in the here and now. They are most likely to refer to familiar and visible objects or people. As their language skills increase, children come to discuss a much broader range of topics, including imaginary, possible, and hypothetical events (Kuczaj & Daly, 1979; Morford & Goldin-Meadow, 1997; O'Neill & Atance, 2000). For example, in a study performed with Japanese children (Komatsu, 2003), 5-year-old children were more likely to discuss their experiences with other children, games they played, and emotions they felt during their day at kindergarten with their mothers. Three-year-olds also discussed many of these same topics but were more likely to repeat topics or simply imitate their teacher's or classmate's actions. However, both ages were very active in their participation in the conversations.

FIGURE 10.3 *An 11-month-old using gestures and crying to indicate her desire to be picked up and comforted.*

Maintaining conversations

Appropriate turn-taking is an important aspect of conversation maintenance. Young children are likely to interrupt others, and so disrupt the conversational flow. Older children are more likely to wait until the other speaker has finished before attempting to gain their intended listener's attention (e.g. McLaughlin, 1998).

Children must also learn to add relevant information to the dialogue as well as learn when it is their turn to speak. Young children are likely to use their turns to refer to something completely different from the topic at hand, making sustained conversation difficult. This is true even if children are asked questions. Children under the age of two years typically answer only a third of the questions posed to them (Pan & Snow, 1999). By three years of age, children answer more than 50 per cent of the questions they are asked (Olson-Fulero & Conforti, 1983). Although parents may sometimes find this difficult to believe, children are more likely to *respond* to questions than they are to *ask* questions. As a result, most of their conversations with adults involve children being asked lots of questions (Hoff-Ginsberg, 1990).

By now, it should be clear that adults contribute a great deal to the structure and maintenance of conversations with young children. As one might expect, young children's conversations with their peers tends to be problematic. When children 'converse' with one another, topics are rarely consistently maintained (Blank & Franklin, 1980). Instead, young children's conversations with peers contain high proportions of imitations, repetitions, and sound play (Garvey, 1975; Keenan & Klein, 1975). However, if the conversation concerns a topic that is familiar to both children, even young children are able to sustain meaningful conversations (Nelson & Gruendel, 1979).

Repairing faulty conversations

In order to communicate effectively, children must learn when and how to repair conversations as miscommunications occur. In order to repair a miscommunication, one must both realise that a miscommunication has occurred and understand how to correct the problem. Sometimes all that is necessary is to repeat the original statement. Other times one must revise the original message in order for it to be understood.

Children as young as 1 year sometimes appear to recognise the failure of their non-verbal communicative attempts. For example, if infants do not receive the object they wanted, they may continue to point to the object until they are given it (Golinkoff, 1983). In such a case, the infant seems to be trying to repair the communicative failure by repeating the pointing. Of course, it is possible that the infant neither perceives the miscommunication nor is trying to repair it, but is instead simply producing a behaviour that has resulted in desired objects being provided in the infant's past experience. Regardless of the communicative intent of these early 'repairs,' young children do learn to use repetition to correct faulty communications. As they get older, children add revisions and substitutions to their increasing repertoire of strategies for repairing and maintaining conversations (Brinton *et al.*, 1986; Furrow & Lewis, 1987; Golinkoff, 1986; Gallagher, 1977, Tomasello *et al.*, 1984). For example, a child might revise a request by adding an additional word in order to clarify exactly what is being requested (e.g. 'I want the *big* box'). Similarly, a child might substitute a phrase to improve communication (e.g. 'the *thing* eats baby chicks' might become 'the *fox* eats baby chicks').

Adults play an important role in the development of this aspect of the pragmatic system. Adults often request children to repeat utterances or to clarify the portion of the conversation that they did not understand (e.g. Gallagher, 1981). These forms of interactions help children learn that utterances can be misunderstood, why particular utterances are not understood, and how to correct a miscommunication.

By the age of 3 years, children have learned to request clarification of messages that they do not understand. These early requests for clarifications are characterised by single word questions such as 'Huh?' or repetitions of portions of the adults' utterances (Gallagher, 1981; Ninio & Snow, 1996). As children become more proficient users of their language, they learn to more clearly question specific aspects of others' messages.

Children have learned many of the aspects of the pragmatic system before their fifth birthday, which is why 3-year-old and 4-year-old children are able to participate in the many delightful conversations that characterise the preschool years. Pragmatic skills are based on the acquisition of other aspects of their mother tongue, including the phonological system, the syntactic system, and the semantic system. We consider the acquisition of each of these systems in turn.

THE DEVELOPMENT OF THE PHONOLOGICAL SYSTEM

Phonology is the aspect of language that is concerned with *the perception and production of sounds that are used in language*. In order for effective communication to occur, children must learn which sounds are important in the language that they hear.

Speech perception

Speech segmentation

Deciphering the sounds of the language that they hear should be a formidable problem for infants. Like all of us, they are exposed to an undifferentiated series of speech sounds known as a **speech stream** (Jusczyk, 1997). Children must separate the speech stream into individual sounds and sound combinations in order to learn the relevant sounds of their language. Consider the following example, written without any word boundaries (from Slobin, 1979):

speech stream the undifferentiated series of words that are produced when we communicate.

wheredidyougowithgrandpa

Because it is in English, this uninterrupted string is relatively easy to separate into its component words. Now try the following example:

dedenlenereyegittinsen

This is the Turkish equivalent of the first example. Unless you are a Turkish speaker, knowing the meaning does not help to segment the string of sounds. Turkish speakers recognise that the example consists of the following components:

dede n le ne re ye git t in sen

Despite the inherent difficulty of the task, infants do learn to divide or segment the speech stream into meaningful units. Their attempts to do so may be facilitated by the nature of the speech that adults direct to infants. When compared to speech directed to adults, speech directed to infants has a higher pitch, more exaggerated pitch contours, a larger pitch range, and is more rhythmic (Trainor *et al.*, 2000): this if often called **infant-directed speech** or **motherese**. By the age of 7 months, infants are able to recognise familiar words in an uninterrupted speech stream (Jusczyk & Aslin, 1995). Thus, the capacity to segment the speech stream into words is present in infants at this age. By 7 months, they are also able to remember the words that they have segmented (Houston *et al.*, 1997). Young infants seem to use a variety of cues to determine when words begin and end in the speech stream, including strongly stressed syllables to indicate the onset of new words (Goodsit *et al.*, 1993; Jusczyk *et al.*, 1993). Infants also prefer to listen to human speech than to other sounds in their environment, which may also facilitate the difficult task of segmenting speech (Butterfield & Siperstein, 1974; Gibson & Spelke, 1983). Clearly, the ability to segment speech is a critical component in language acquisition. Supporting this idea are the findings of a recent study, which indicated that infants who were better at speech segmentation tasks before 12 months had a larger expressive vocabulary at 2 years and scored higher on language measures as preschoolers (Newman *et al.*, 2006).

Categorical perception of speech sounds

Human speech uses sound categories that are called **phonemes**. A phoneme is a set of sounds that are not physically identical to one another, but which speakers of a language treat as equivalent sounds. Human languages differ in terms of the number and types of phonemes that they employ. For example, both the [k] sound in 'key' and the [k] sound in 'ski' are members of the same phoneme in English. This means that the two [k] sounds are perceived as the same sound by English speakers despite the fact that the [k] sound in 'key' is aspirated (it concludes with a short puff of breath) and the [k] sound in 'ski' is unaspirated (it does not conclude with a short puff of breath). In contrast, the two [k] sounds are members of different phonemes in Chinese. As a result, speakers of Chinese can readily discriminate the two sounds. Thus, speakers of English and speakers of Chinese differ in terms of their ability to discriminate the two sounds.

phoneme the smallest unit of speech that can affect meaning

Infants discriminate between phonemes

In a pioneering study, Eimas *et al.* (1971) used habituation to test 1-month-old infants' ability to discriminate the syllables /ba/ and /pa/. The habituation technique involved the presentation of a stimulus (e.g. /ba/) until the infant ceased to pay attention to it. At this point, another stimulus (e.g. /pa/) was presented to the infant. If the infant paid attention to the new stimulus, then Eimas *et al.* assumed that the infant could distinguish between the new stimulus and the old stimulus.

Using this paradigm, Eimas *et al.* found that the infants could discriminate the phonemes /ba/ and /pa/. Remember that the sounds that constitute each phoneme represent a range of possible sounds. Thus, there is a set of physically distinct sounds that comprise the phoneme /ba/. There could be, for example, variations in the way a particular speaker produces the sound from one utterance to the next, or the sound as spoken by different speakers. Nonetheless, adult speakers of English find it very difficult to discriminate one /ba/ sound from another, even though they have no difficulty discriminating a /ba/ sound from a /pa/ sound. In other words, adults can readily distinguish sounds that are from different categories (e.g. /ba/ versus /pa/) but find it difficult to discriminate sounds from the same category (e.g. two different /ba/ sounds). Similarly, the 1-month-old infants studied by Eimas *et al.* could not discriminate one /ba/ sound from another, although they could distinguish a /ba/ sound from a /pa/ sound.

The ability of infants to discriminate phonemes has considerable implications (Eimas, 1985; Jusczyk, 1997). First, the fact that infants can discriminate sounds from different phonemes but cannot distinguish sounds from the same phoneme class suggests that even young infants engage in the **categorical perception** of speech sounds. Categorical perception is the process that allows us to distinguish sounds between categories (different phonemes) yet at the same time makes it difficult to distinguish sounds within a category (a particular phoneme such as /ba/). Second, the young age at which infants are able to discriminate phonemes suggests that categorical perception may be an **innate mechanism** for interpreting sounds. This mechanism may rest on general auditory processing skills rather than on skills specific to human speech (Jusczyk *et al.*, 1983). In other words, infants may be predisposed to categorise sounds which then may influence their perception of speech sounds. This possibility gains support from cross-species research in which non-human species such as chinchillas and macaque monkeys have demonstrated categorical perception of human speech sounds (Kuhl & Miller, 1975; Kuhl & Padden, 1982, 1983). If categorical perception of speech sounds depended on an innate knowledge of human phonemes, one would not expect species such as chinchillas and macaque monkeys to process human speech sounds categorically.

> **categorical perception**
> where perceptually discriminable stimuli are treated as belonging to the same category.

Becoming a native listener

The human ability to discriminate possible phonemes diminishes with age. At 6 months of age, infants are able to discriminate a wide range of phonemes, including those that adult speakers of the infant's native language cannot discriminate. Nonetheless, the discriminative capabilities of the 6-month-old infant are influenced by experience, specifically the language that they hear (Kuhl, 1992). The effects of experience become more pronounced with increasing age, so that by 12 months of age, infants remain able to discriminate the phonemes of the language they are learning, but are unlikely to discriminate the phonemes of other languages (Werker, 1989).

It seems, then, that children's acquisition of the phonemes of their native language depends on both the *innate predisposition* for categorical perception of sounds and *experience* with sounds used as phonemes in their native language(s). Children who are exposed to English hear sounds used as English phonemes, and learn this set of phonemes. Children who hear Chinese are exposed to sounds that function as Chinese phonemes, and so acquire the Chinese set of phonemes (Figure 10.4). Basically, children who hear sounds used as particular phonemes retain the ability to discriminate these phonemes. Experience with phonemes is not necessary for categorical perception *per se*, but experience is necessary for the infant to learn which categories are most relevant to the language being learned. In Werker's terms, the infant gradually becomes a 'native listener.'

FIGURE 10.4 *Children become 'native listeners' by learning which sounds are important in the language they hear. Children who hear Chinese learn the Chinese set of phonemes, whereas children who hear English acquire the English set.*
Source: Shutterstock.

Speech production

The ability to *produce* speech sounds lags behind the ability to *perceive* the same sounds. The sounds that infants can perceive at an early age are not reliably produced for months or even years. This developmental lag reflects the difficulty of learning to control the vocal cords, mouth, tongue, and lips, all of which are involved in the intentional production of speech sounds. Perhaps because of the **maturation** that is required for sound production, all children pass through the same phases of vocal production (Oller, 1980; Stark, 1980), as discussed below.

Reflexive vocalisations (birth–2 months)

The first sounds produced by infants are **reflexive vocalisations**, including cries, coughs, burps and sneezes. During the first month of life, infants produce more than one type of cry, raising the possibility that different infant cries might mean different things (Figure 10.5). These cry types are characterised by different mean fundamental frequencies, durations, and compositions of sounds (Rothgänger, 2003). However, if parents are asked to discriminate their young infant's cry types, they are unable to do so if the cries are tape recorded and played back to them in the absence of external context (Muller *et al.*, 1974). Even if infants are attempting to communicate with their cries, parents are more likely to respond to external context (e.g. a wet nappy/diaper) than to the type of cry itself. However, the characteristics of cries do change

reflexive vocalisations the first sounds produced by infants, including cries, coughs, burps, and sneezes.

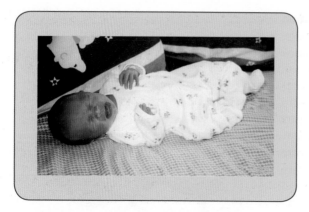

FIGURE 10.5 *The first author's son crying at 1 month!*

in response to the experience of various emotions and contexts, and individuals (infants and adults alike) do respond physiologically to these changes (Newman, 2007).

Cooing and laughing (2–4 months)

During this period, infants begin to laugh and to combine sounds with one another. For example, the *coo* sound emerges toward the end of the second month of life. This sound combines the [u] sound with other sounds, and is often produced while the infant is in what appears to be a happy state. The parent–infant interactions following infant cooing are usually pleasant in nature. Parents may coo back at their child, who may in turn coo back at the parent, and so on. The reciprocal cooing between infant and parent may help the infant to learn that communication involves taking turns.

babbling the first types of controlled vocalisations produced by infants typically between the ages of 4 and 6 months.

Babbling and vocal play (4–6 months)

Play with sounds (**babbling**) is the main characteristic of this period. As they gain control over their vocal cords, lips, tongue, and mouth, infants begin to produce a wide range of sounds and sound combinations.

Canonical babbling (6–10 months)

Infants begin to produce sound combinations that *sound* like words (hence the term **canonical**). However, there is no evidence that infants actually attach *meaning* to

canonical the usual, normal, or natural state of things. *Canonical babbling* refers to *babbling* sounds made by the infant around 6–10 months, when vowels and consonants are combined in such a way that they sound like words.

these sound combinations. During this period, infants continue their experimentation and play with sounds. The most common form of multisyllabic utterance during this period is the reduplicated babble, in which syllables are repeated (e.g. 'mamama').

Jespersen (1922) suggested that infants produce virtually all human speech sounds during the babbling period, but it is now known that this is not true (Locke, 1983). Nonetheless, babbling is a universal phenomenon that seems to be genetically determined. Infants tend to babble during the same age period and to produce a similar range of sounds during early babbling (Rothgänger, 2003). Many deaf children babble, as do hearing infants of deaf parents (Lenneberg *et al.*, 1965; Stoel-Gammon & Otomo, 1986). These results demonstrate that neither hearing human speech nor having others respond to infant vocalisations are necessary for early babbling to occur. However, vocal babbling is rare in deaf infants older than 7 months, suggesting that hearing speech sounds plays an important role in the continuation of babbling past its early stages (Oller & Eilers, 1988). More recently though, *gestural babbling* (sometimes referred to as **manual babbling**, which is the manual equivalent of vocal babbling) has been documented in deaf children and hearing children learning to sign (Petitto *et al.*, 2001). The presence of vocal and gestural babbling in hearing and non-hearing children has led to the proposition that a manual communication system may have evolved before our vocal-based system (Gentilucci & Corballis, 2006; also see Newman, 2007). Regardless of the modality of babbling, it is clear that some form of interaction is important for maintaining the infant's efforts to produce language sounds or gestures. For example, infants in institutions that provide little infant–adult interaction do not produce many vocalisations and may not even cry (Bowlby, 1951; Spitz, 1965).

> **manual babbling** the manual equivalent of vocal *babbling* which is found in deaf children and hearing children learning to sign.

Modulated babbling (10 months on)

This is the final period of babbling and language play. This period is characterised by a variety of sound combinations, stress and intonation patterns, and overlaps with the beginning of meaningful speech. While early babbling and vocal play may help infants to learn to purposely produce the sounds that are relevant for their language, **modulated babbling** may play an important role in the acquisition of the intonation patterns that are important for the infant's native language (Boysson-Bardies *et al.*, 1984; Thevenin *et al.*, 1985). For example, infants learning English must learn that different intonation patterns signal statements and questions. The statement 'The boy likes to dance with girls' ends with a flat intonation pattern. In contrast, the question 'Does the boy like to dance with girls?' ends with a rising intonation pattern. Modulated babbling may help infants learn to produce these different intonations. Regardless of the actual functions that babbling plays, it is clear that infants enjoy playing with speech sounds and intonation patterns, and that this play is a cornerstone for subsequent language development (Kuczaj, 1999a; Kuczaj & Makecha, 2008).

> **modulated babbling** the final period of babbling and language play, which appears from around 10 months on and is characterised by a variety of sound combinations, stress and intonation patterns, and overlaps with the beginning of meaningful speech.

The development of articulation

As they learn the phonological system of their language, children must learn to pronounce words correctly. Children are more likely to use words that they can pronounce (Ferguson, 1989; Ingram, 1986; Macken & Ferguson, 1983). This suggests that they are aware of the differences between their incorrect pronunciations and the correct ones (Berko & Brown, 1960; Kuczaj, 1983; Smith, 1973). For example, one 3-year-old child consistently deleted the [s] sound from the beginnings of words when it was followed by a consonant sound. Thus, 'I smell a skunk' was produced as 'I mell a kunk'. However, the child recognised that his form was the immature form, as illustrated in the following comment that the child made when asked to chose between one of his words ('neeze') and the correct word ('sneeze'): 'You talk like him. You say 'neeze' ('sneeze'). I can't say 'neeze' like you do. I say 'neeze'. I'll say 'neeze' like you when I get big' (Kuczaj, 1983, p.72).

As children learn to produce correct pronunciations, they may produce phonological distinctions that adults cannot perceive. Kornfield (1971) found that the 'gwass' for 'glass' and the 'gwass' for 'grass' produced by 2-year-old children were in fact slightly different sounds, even though adults equated the two 'gwasses'. Children consistently produced one 'gwass' for 'grass' and another 'gwass' for 'glass', suggesting that they were beginning to produce the two different sounds that would eventually yield 'grass' and 'glass'. However, it is not known if children can perceive the differences between the two pronunciations of 'gwass' if they are produced by another child.

The above examples suggest that children are aware that their incorrect pronunciations differ from those of adults, and that at least some children's pronunciations that are viewed as equivalent by adults may be functionally distinct for children. However, we do not know if children are aware of *how* their pronunciations differ from those of adults. Nor do we know the manner in which children's and adults' representations of pronunciations are related.

To sum up, the capacity to produce sounds and sound combinations reflects a combination of hereditary and environmental factors. The apparent universality of children's early sounds and babbling suggests that maturation plays an important role in these developments. However, children must hear adult sounds in order to determine the sounds and sound distinctions that are relevant for the language they are learning. Although it has proven difficult to demonstrate the relation of early sounds to later sounds, it seems likely that the entire course of sound production is important in that it enables children to practice and improve their articulatory skills (Vihman, 1996).

THE DEVELOPMENT OF THE SYNTACTIC SYSTEM

syntax the manner in which words and parts of words are related to one another to produce grammatical sentences: the production of sentences is governed by grammatical structures and rules.

s-structure the *syntax* of a sentence. However, one s-structure can have more than one meaning. In order to understand the intended meaning of a sentence, one must examine the *d-structure*.

d-structure the abstract representation of a sentence, or the actual meaning that the sentence is trying to convey.

Syntax deals with the manner in which words and parts of words are related to one another to produce grammatical sentences. Sentences are not created in a haphazard fashion. Instead, the production of sentences is governed by grammatical structures and rules. Chomsky (1957, 1982) suggested that the syntactic structure of every human language is the result of an interrelated set of elements. At one level is the **s-structure** (or surface structure), which roughly corresponds to the spoken sentence. At another level is the **d-structure** (or deep structure), which is a more abstract representation of a sentence. In order to understand the significance of the distinction between s-structure and d-structure, consider the following three sentences: 'The shooting of the hunters was awful', 'Mary is easy to please', and 'Mary is eager to please'. The first sentence is ambiguous. It could mean that the hunters were terrible marksman. Or it could mean that someone shot the hunters. The important point about this example is that one s-structure can have more than one meaning. The intended meaning is determined by the d-structure, which specifies that the hunters were either the ones doing the shooting or the ones being shot. The second and third sentence share similar s-structures: noun–verb–adjective–infinitive verb. However, the meaning of the two sentences is quite different. Mary is the subject of the verb 'to please' in 'Mary is eager to please', but in 'Mary is easy to please' the subject of 'to please' is whoever or whatever pleases Mary. Once again, the meaning of the s-structure is determined by the d-structure. For the past 40 years, the study of syntactic development has revolved in one way or another around debates about the relative roles of d-structures and s-structures.

The one-word period

Children's acquisition of syntax follows a relatively predictable pattern during the first two years of life. Sometime between 10 and 18 months of age, children begin to produce single word utterances. By examining the first one to 10 words produced by 8- to 16-month-old English-speaking and Chinese-speaking (Putonghua and Cantonese) children, recent cross-cultural research has indicated that first words generally include people-based terms (names – 'Mommy' or relational words – 'Auntie') followed by object nouns, which represent familiar, concrete objects found around the home, and action verbs (Tardif *et al.*, 2008). However, they also found that cultural differences affect the frequency in which certain types of words appear during the one-word period (Tardif *et al.*, 2008). For example, English-speaking children were more likely to produce object nouns (e.g. 'bottle', 'kitty') and animal sounds (e.g. 'Baa Baa', 'Grr') as one of their first three words whereas Chinese-speaking children rarely produced object nouns and never produced animal sounds. Instead, Chinese-speaking children were more likely to produce people-based terms (e.g. 'sister', 'grandma') or action verbs (e.g. 'hit', 'grab') as their first three words.

More than 80 years ago, DeLaguna (1927) suggested that the utterances of children in the one-word period are based on more complete thoughts than can be represented by a single word. According to DeLaguna, the single-word utterances that children produce actually represent simple complete sentences. In other words, although children in the one-word period are limited to producing single-word utterances, they are capable of conceiving of and comprehending more complete sentences. Thus, the child who says 'doggie' while pointing at his pet might mean 'there's my doggie', whereas the child who points to a toy dog that is on top of a shelf and says 'doggie' might mean 'I want the toy doggie'. In such a scenario, the s-structure 'doggie' has different d-structures.

What's in a word?

Most adults do interpret children's single-word utterances as if they mean more than the literal single word. However, Brown (1973) and Bloom (1973) both pointed out the dangers of such 'rich interpretation'. The basic problem is deciding exactly how much more a child means to produce than the single word contained in the s-structure. A child who says 'hot' while looking at a lit stove might mean 'that is hot', 'the stove we heat our food on is hot right now', or even 'if someone touches that hot stove, they will receive a bad burn'. While few of us would be willing to grant the young child the knowledge required to produce the second or third d-structure, the available information does not provide sufficient cues to determine exactly what a child means when a single word utterance is produced. Thus, assumptions about what children mean in the one-word period must be made with great caution (Barrett, 1986). As a result, the implication of the one-word period for syntactic development is unclear.

Despite the inherent ambiguity of children's one-word utterances, it is clear that children do comprehend more than they can produce. Golinkoff and Hirsh-Pasek (1995) presented 17-month-old infants with two videos, each of which portrayed two different scenes. For example, one video might show a dog licking a cat and the other video might show a cat licking a dog. While the videos were playing, the infants heard one of two sentences ('the dog is licking the cat' or 'the cat is licking the dog'). The infants looked longer at the video that corresponded to the sentence that they heard, suggesting that infants who can produce only a single word at a time nonetheless understand at least some aspects of word order.

The two-word period

The next major period of syntactic development is the two-word period. Between 18 and 24 months of age, most children begin to produce two words at a time. These words are not chosen randomly. Instead, children consistently use the words that convey the most meaning (e.g. nouns, verbs, and adjectives), and omit other sorts of words such as 'in', 'and', and 'of', and word endings such as the past tense '-ed' and the plural '-s'. Thus, children are likely to produce utterances such as 'mummy go' and 'kick ball'. Children's language environment increases the likelihood that they first learn and use high meaning words. Such words are more likely to be stressed in adult speech, and so are perceptually salient compared to other words (Brown, 1973; Gleitman & Wanner, 1982; Miller & Ervin, 1964). It seems, then, that children are most likely to use words that are highly salient in their environment, which turn out to be nouns, verbs, and adjectives. Children are also more likely to verbally produce words that they have initially produced as gestures and are faster in producing two-word combinations ('dog water') if they had previously combined a gesture with a word, such as pointing at a dog and saying water (Iverson & Goldin-Meadow, 2005).

Word order

Children's knowledge of language and their use of this knowledge are limited during the two-word period. For example, many children do not consistently use word order to mark semantic relations in the two-word period (Maratsos, 1983). Children learning English might say 'doggie lick' or 'lick doggie', regardless of whether the dog is licking or being licked. Children's use of consistent word order seems to reflect limited knowledge rather than general rules. For English, the most general way to relate an agent and an action is to place the agent before the action, as in 'doggie lick' when the dog is the one doing the licking. Young children are most likely to use the correct 'agent + action' word order in a limited sense. For example, children may use the 'agent + action' word order only when the agent is animate. Thus, they would be more likely to say 'doggie bark' than 'balloon pop' or 'hat fall' because 'doggie' is an animate noun and 'balloon' and 'hat' are not.

The manner in which speech in the two-word period is related to later syntactic development is a matter of considerable debate (Maratsos, 1999). Some (Bloom, 1990; Pinker, 1987) have argued that children learn syntax by linking semantic categories such as *agency* (the thing producing an action) and *action* (what something does) with syntactic categories such as subject (e.g. 'the boy') and verb (e.g. 'draws'). Others believe that children in this period lack certain aspects of d-structure, although there is little agreement about exactly what aspects of d-structure are missing (Hyams, 1989; Ingram, 1992; Radford, 1990). Relatively recent evidence suggests that 2-year-olds can successfully identify general rules regarding word order when novel verbs are used (Gertner *et al.*, 2006). Thus, children may be primed to learn patterns or 'rules' and novel words early on, suggesting that some syntactic knowledge may be present inherently – a generativist view. However, other researchers contend that syntactic knowledge is constructed through experience – a constructivist view (e.g. Dabrowska & Lieven, 2005; Rowland, 2007). So although it is clear that children in the two-word period are progressing toward a more mature understanding of syntax, it is not clear exactly *how much* they know nor *how* they know.

Later syntactic development

Children's syntactic knowledge increases dramatically following the two-word period, resulting in rapidly improving language skills. For example, one of the children studied by the second author was producing two-word utterances such as 'me happy' at 24 months of age. This same child produced the following sentence about a year later: 'I don't want to go to sleep and dream the dream I dreamed last night.' The difference between this child's language competence at 24 months and at 36 months of age is striking. This type of grammatical development is typical, as evidenced by the following two speech samples (obtained from one child at two different ages). In the first sample, the child is 24 months old.

Speech sample 1
Adult: It is hot.
Child: Hot. This hot. This hot this time.
Child: Mommy, help me. This hot.
Adult: Do you want a cinnamon one?
Child: Yes.
Adult: Okay.
Child: Cinnamon on them.
Adult: Cinnamon's already on them.
Child: Ow! Hot! This burn my hand.
Adult: You better be careful.

Child: Mommy, put butter on mine.
Adult: You want butter?
Child: Yes. Right there. Right there, mommy. Ow! I burn my hand. I burn my hand.

The following is another conversation involving the same child at 36 months of age:

Speech sample 2

Child: Mom fixed this for me and I don't like it.
Adult: You don't like bacon?
Child: No. Abe's gonna eat rest of it.
Adult: What?
Child: A coupon. Look. For McDonald's.
Adult: What kind of sandwich would you like?
Child: I like a mayonnaise sandwich.
Adult: Okay.
Child: (laughs). That is bad. Mom will come home and not like it.
Adult: What?
Child: This mess. I want a sandwich. Where is my sandwich? I don't want meat. I want not meat. Not peanut butter. Not cheese. Only mayonnaise.
Adult: Okay.
Child: And you will put it here. Okay? Put it right here so I can eat it.
Adult: Okay. I will after it's made.
Child: What kind you gonna make me? I don't want cheese. Only mayonnaise.

There are a number of differences in the speech produced by this child at 24 months and at 36 months of age. The child's utterances are longer (i.e. *mean length of utterances (MLU)* – the average number of morphemes, or the smallest units of meaningful sounds, produced) and more complex in the second speech sample than in the first speech sample. For example, the child uses a verb ending (the past tense '-ed'), a 'be' form ('is'), a modal auxiliary ('will'), and conjunctions ('and', 'so'). None of these forms were present in the first speech sample.

As is evident in our example, children learn to use a variety of linguistic forms and structures relatively quickly in the months following the two-word period. The speed with which children learn a vast amount of their language has perplexed scholars of language acquisition for some time.

overregularisation
when a previously learned rule is applied in the wrong situation. For example, a child learning English might say 'thinked' rather than 'thought' because the child is using the regular past tense rule.

The significance of overregularisation errors and creative generalisations

All languages have rules that govern the use of grammatical forms. As children learn syntax, they produce a variety of 'errors' that demonstrate that they are learning these rules. **Overregularisation** errors occur when children apply a rule to an exception to the rule. For example, a child learning English might say 'thinked' rather than 'thought' because the child is using the regular past tense rule (attach '-ed' to the end of the verb) rather than the correct exception to the rule ('thought'). Children who produce these sorts of errors are making reasonable and understandable mistakes. They are acting as if the rules they are learning do not have exceptions (languages contain exceptions to their rules because languages have evolved over long periods of time). Significantly, children who produce overregularisation errors are using forms that they have not heard. This suggests that they are using the rules of the language they are learning to produce novel words. Hence, children are already using language in a productive fashion. The extent to which children generalise the rules that they are learning depends on the ease of the language they are learning. Thus, children will cull information from the language they are learning, which they appropriate for their own use and production (Kuczaj & Borys, 1988).

Plurals

In English, singular nouns are made plural by adding the suffix '-s', as in 'cats' and 'dogs'. These nouns are called regular nouns. Other nouns have plural forms that are exceptions to this rule, and are called irregular forms. Examples of irregular plural forms include 'men' and 'mice'. Soon after children begin to produce correct regular plural forms such as 'dogs,' they also begin to produce overregularised forms such as 'foots' and 'mans' (Brown, 1973). These errors demonstrate that children have acquired a regular plural rule, but have not learned all the exceptions to the rule. Interestingly, children are unlikely to attach the plural suffix to mass nouns such as 'water' and 'air' (McNamara, 1982). Thus, children overregularise the plural to irregular count nouns (which refer to objects that can be counted) such as 'foot' and 'man' but not to mass nouns such as 'water' and 'air' (which cannot be counted). This finding suggests that young children can distinguish nouns that refer to countable objects from nouns that refer to entities that cannot be counted.

Past tense

In English, the suffix '-ed' is used to express past tense, as in 'called' and 'showed'. English also has many irregular past tense forms, such as ran and hit. As they learn the past tense, children often overregularise their use of '-ed', producing forms such as 'runned' and 'hitted' (Brown, 1973; Kuczaj, 1977; Maratsos, 2000). In fact, they produce such errors for many years. This is not surprising given that English has many irregular past tense forms and the fact that children must learn every exception to this regular rule.

Creative overgeneralisations

The progressive '-ing' form is the first suffix to be acquired by young children learning English (Brown, 1973). There are no irregular progressive forms in English, and so no opportunities for overregularisation errors. Nonetheless, children's use of the progressive does go beyond simply repeating what they have heard. Children (and adults) occasionally create new verbs by treating a noun as if it were a verb. For example, to search

FIGURE 10.6 *'I'm ballerining.' Children do not simply produce forms that they have heard others use. Instead, they overgeneralise, creating new forms (e.g., 'ballerining') based on the regularities in the language they hear.*
Source: Shutterstock.

overgeneralisation
creating a new verb by treating a noun as if it were a verb, for example 'I am ballereening', meaning 'I am dancing like a ballerina'.

for something on the web entails 'Googling'. Children also use the progressive with some of these novel forms, as in 'why is it weathering?' (referring to rain and thunder) and 'I'm ballereening' (dancing like a ballerina) (Kuczaj, 1978) (Figure 10.6). Both overregularisation errors and creative **overgeneralisations** demonstrate that children do not simply reproduce forms that they have heard others use. Instead, they create new forms ('runned,' 'ballereening') based on the regularities in the language that they hear.

How can syntactic development be explained?

Innate knowledge?

The speed with which children acquire syntax and the creativity that they exhibit at an early age must be explained by any theory that attempts to explain syntactic development. One of the most famous explanations focused on the notion that children are born with innate knowledge of language (Chomsky, 1972, 1987). Chomsky's arguments for innate knowledge rested on the following points:

1. Language requires the ability to relate d-structures to s-structures.

2. The environment only provides children with information about s-structures. As knowledge of d-structures is not available in the environment, such knowledge must be innate.

3. The sentences that children hear are complex and often ungrammatical.

4. Children receive little feedback about the grammatical correctness of their utterances.

5. Children acquire their first language relatively quickly and easily.

Do parents correct their child's language?

As we have seen, children do learn their first language relatively quickly and easily. Chomsky's claim that parents play little attention to their young children's syntax is also true. Parents are unlikely to correct their children's ungrammatical utterances (Brown & Hanlon, 1970; Hirsh-Pasek *et al.*, 1984). In fact, parents may actually reinforce ungrammatical utterances. For example, a mother responded to her child's statement 'No dinosaur no go here' with: 'That's right. We don't put dinosaurs there.' To further complicate matters, parents sometimes correct grammatical sentences because the meaning of the sentence is incorrect even though the syntax is perfect. For example, a child's grammatical statement that 'And Walt Disney comes on Tuesday' was corrected by the mother, who responded: 'No. He does not.'

Even when parents make a conscious effort to correct their child's ungrammatical constructions, they often encounter a resistant child. Braine (1971) reported the following interchange between himself and his daughter (Figure 10.7):

Daughter: Want other one spoon, daddy.
Father: You mean you want *the other spoon*.
Daughter: Yes, I want other one spoon, please, daddy.
Father: Can you say 'the other spoon'?
Daughter: Other . . . one . . . spoon.
Father: Say . . . 'other'.
Daughter: Other.
Father: Spoon.
Daughter: Spoon.
Father: Other spoon.
Daughter: Other spoon. Now give me other one spoon.

To the extent that parents' role in their children's syntactic development is limited to reinforcing their children's grammatical utterances and correcting children's ungrammatical utterances, Chomsky's claim that parents do not play significant roles in their children's syntactic development is supported by the data. However, even though young children produce utterances and constructions that they have not heard before (as evidenced by overregularisation errors and creative generalisations), they do in fact learn the language that they have heard their parents speak. Although overregularisation errors and creative generalisations demonstrate that imitation cannot be the primary method by which children learn syntax, children do imitate some of the speech that they hear (Kuczaj, 1982a; Ochs & Schieffelin, 1984). The parents' role in providing language models is an important one.

The language input to the child
Parents do a much better job of providing children with good examples of grammatical sentences than Chomsky supposed.

FIGURE 10.7 *"I want other one spoon, please, daddy".*
Source: Shutterstock.

Newport *et al.* (1975) found that mothers produced ungrammatical sentences *less than one-tenth of 1 per cent* of the time that they spoke to their young children. Parents usually speak to young children in short grammatical sentences (Farwell, 1975; Gleason & Weintraub, 1978), as do adults who have never had children. In fact, even 4-year-old children simplify the speech they direct to children younger than themselves (Shatz & Gelman, 1973).

Despite the fact that children hear a much more simplified version of language than do most adults, Chomsky still believes that innate knowledge of language is necessary for language acquisition. The reason is that no matter how simple the language input to the child is, it consists of s-structures. For Chomsky, d-structures must be innate, because spoken language can provide no direct information about this aspect of language. In his view, the role of experience is to provide information about s-structures. This information will be combined with the child's innate knowledge of language to yield the particular grammatical rules for the language the child is learning. A similar view has been offered by Pinker (1989), who proposed that children are born with knowledge of the categories of verb and noun. According to Pinker, children use the information from s-structure to sort out the precise manner in which their language uses nouns and verbs to express meaning in sentences.

The notion that children are born with knowledge of d-structures and possible types of grammatical categories is very controversial (Bloom, 1991; Tomasello, 1992). Although it seems clear that children are born with a very strong *predisposition* to learn a language, this does not necessarily mean that children are born with *innate knowledge* of language (see Maratsos, 1999). For example, research conducted on errors children make when producing questions emphasises the importance of constructing knowledge *rules* or *frames* from a basic set of experiences, which children then apply to familiar and novel situations (Dabrowska & Lieven, 2005; Rowland, 2007). However, the speed and accuracy with which children acquire and produce various utterances also suggests that some innate component must be present. Rather than specifying specific categories of knowledge, perhaps the innate predisposition consists of a set of mechanisms that help children to sort out the information that they hear. For example, recall the earlier discussion of categorical perception of phonemes. We are born with the ability to perceive phonemes, but we are not born with knowledge of particular phonemes or a general understanding of what phonemes are.

THE ACQUISITION OF WORD MEANING

comprehension in language development, the language children can understand, distinguished from *production*, which is the language they can produce. Comprehension almost always exceeds production.

Word meaning acquisition is a **comprehension**-based process. In order to learn a word, children must hear it being used. As children acquire their first words, they learn that words are meaningful sounds that can be used to represent something else (Bever, 1970; Dromi, 1999; Kuczaj, 1975, 1999b; Reddy, 1999). This process may begin in early infancy. Tincoff and Jusczyk (1999) presented 6-month-old infants with side-by-side videos of their parents. The infants looked longer at the video of the mother if the word 'mommy' was heard but looked longer at the video containing the father if the word 'daddy' was heard. This pattern did not occur if a strange man and woman were substituted for the mother and father. These results suggest that young infants are learning the meanings of at least some of the words in their environment.

Before their fourth birthday, children will learn to use words to represent and refer to real, possible and imaginary aspects of their world (Kuczaj & Daly, 1979; O'Neill & Atance, 2000) (Figure 10.8). Thus, the toddler who uses the word 'ball' only while holding a baseball becomes a 3-year-old who can use words to express complex thoughts such as 'if that dinosaur eats it, there won't be any more' (Kuczaj & Daly, 1979).

FIGURE 10.8 *16-month-old pretending to talk to Grandma: "Hi!".*

Guessing a word's meaning

The child's interpretation and memory of the situation in which the word was first encountered determines the child's initial guess about the word's meaning. The manner in which a child interprets a recently discovered word depends on the child's existing semantic system, their knowledge of the world, the level of their cognitive skills, and their ability to selectively attend to others' cues, such as eye gaze (Kuczaj, 1975, 1982b; 1999b; Masur, 1995; Nurmsoo & Bloom, 2008).

If a word that the child has just heard refers to an object, the child's attention might be drawn to the object while the word is being spoken, as when a parent points to a cow while saying 'there's a nice cow'. In such a case, the child must first understand that the parent intends to communicate something about the object to which the parent is pointing. If the child does comprehend the parent's intention, they are likely to guess that the word has something to do with the cow. Initially, children build their vocabulary by focusing on one-to-one correspondences between words and things. But concentrating on one-to-one correspondences does not make the child's task much easier. Consider a situation in which a child is shown a man riding an elephant and told to 'look at the elephant'. Prior to this, the child has neither heard the word 'elephant' nor seen an elephant. The possible meanings of 'elephant' in this situation are numerous. The child might guess that elephant means 'man riding elephant', 'long nose', 'big ears', 'big feet', 'animal under a man', and so on. As noted by Quine (1960) and Goodman (1983), there are many possible interpretations for every situation.

Given the number of possible interpretations that children might make about a word's meaning, it is not surprising that some of their initial guesses about the meanings of object words are incorrect. Children sometimes believe that a word refers to many

overextension extending the meaning of a word too broadly, for example using the word 'bird' to refer to birds, aeroplanes, and hot air balloons.

underextension extending the meaning of a word to too few instances, as when a child restricts their use of a word such as 'duck' to situations in which the child is playing with a toy while in the bath, therefore failing to refer to the animals at the park as 'ducks'.

more objects than it actually does. For example, the child might use the word 'bird' to refer to birds, aeroplanes, hot air balloons, falling leaves, and kites. The child who extends the meaning of a word too broadly is making an **overextension** error. The opposite extreme occurs when children extend the meaning of a word to too few instances, as when a child restricts their use of a word such as 'duck' to situations in which the child is playing with a toy duck while in the bath. Using a word too narrowly is called an **underextension** error.

The complexity of the task

Although children do make mistakes when attaching meaning to words, they make relatively few mistakes given the complexity of the task. In addition to the fact that words occur in situations that may be interpreted in numerous ways, many things may be referred to with a variety of words and linguistic forms. For example, the same creature might be called 'Susie', 'Mum', 'honey', 'sister', 'daughter', 'friend', 'doctor', and so on, depending on the speaker and the context. To further complicate matters, some categories are part of larger categories. For example, a person might be a Caucasian (a race included in the larger category *people*). A person is also a *mammal* (a category which includes people), an *animal* (a category that includes mammals), and a *terrestrial* (a category that includes animals). In addition, many words have more than one meaning. Hence, there is ample opportunity for children to be confused. Despite the complexity of the task, children somehow construct a vocabulary of approximately 14,000 words by the time they are 6 years old (Carey, 1978; Smith, 1926; Templin, 1957).

As children gain additional experience with a word and its uses, they must compare recently acquired information with that they have already stored in their semantic system. This process will allow children to eventually determine the correct meaning of the word. Regardless of the type of word being acquired, the basic processes of word meaning acquisition are the same. The child encounters the word in a situation. This information is interpreted in terms of the existing semantic system, the result being an initial guess about the meaning of the novel word. As a result of subsequent experiences and interpretations, this initial guess will be modified until the child has determined the correct meaning of the word. Building a semantic system requires the child to process vast amounts of information within a context in which words can mean virtually anything and are related to one another in myriad ways (Kuczaj, 1982b; Clark, 1993).

Is children's acquisition of word meaning constrained?

The complexity of the word learning task has led some researchers to suggest that children acquire words and meanings as quickly as they do because their choices are constrained. The notion of constraints on semantic development assumes that children neither consider all of the information available to them nor are overwhelmed by possible interpretations. Instead, both the types of information to be considered and the possible interpretations of this information are constrained by innate factors.

A number of constraints have been suggested to influence word meaning development (Clark, 1993; Golinkoff, Hirsh-Pasek, *et al.*, 1995; Golinkoff, Shuff-Bailey *et al.*, 1995; Markman, 1990; Soja *et al.*, 1991). The following are offered as examples:

- **Whole object constraint**: Assumes that children believe that words refer to whole objects rather than to parts of objects. Thus, the child who hears an adult say elephant while pointing to an elephant assumes that the adult is referring to the entire elephant rather than to some part of the elephant.

- **Mutual exclusivity constraint**: Assumes that children believe that there is a one-to-one correspondence between words and meanings. Thus, if a child knows that certain creatures are called 'dogs', they will not use 'dog' to refer to other types of objects or creatures. They will also assume that the things they call 'dog' can have no other name.

Although the notion of constraints seems to simplify the task the child faces in constructing a semantic system, there is little support for the notion that constraints are involved in word meaning acquisition (Gathercole & Min, 1997; Kuczaj, 1990, 1999b; Nelson, 1988). None of the hypothesised constraints has been shown to be an absolute predisposition (Behrend, 1995; Bloom, 1994; Bloom & Kelemen, 1995; Golinkoff, Shuff-Bailey *et al.*, 1995; Merriman *et al.*, 1995). In addition, many of the proposed constraints would actually make word meaning acquisition more difficult. For example, if the whole object constraint actually constrained children's acquisition of word meaning, why and how do they acquire so many words that refer to parts of objects? Similarly, if children are constrained to believe that word meanings are mutually exclusive, how do they ever learn that an 'elephant' is also a 'pachyderm', a 'mammal' and an 'animal'?

The importance of semantic relations

Children construct a **semantic system** rather than a list of independent words because words are related to one another rather than existing in isolation. The development of the semantic system is facilitated by children's acquisition of semantic relations.

> **semantic system** a system that categorises words in relation to their meaning.

We have already noted that children must learn that objects can be referred to by more than one word (a fact which even young children can learn, Mervis *et al.*, 1994). The child must also determine how words relate to one another. Some words are opposites ('hot'–'cold'), others form semantic dimensions ('hot', 'warm', 'cool', and 'cold'), and still others are structured in terms of subordinate–superordinate relations. For example, the word 'dog' is subordinate to the word 'mammal', which in turn is subordinate to the word 'animal'.

Semantic dimensions

As children learn the words contained in semantic sets such as 'hot', 'warm', 'cool', 'cold', or 'always', 'usually', 'sometimes', 'seldom', and 'never', words that express the far ends of the dimension ('hot'–'cold,' 'always'–'never') are learned before words that fall between the two extremes (Kuczaj, 1975, 1982b). The end points of semantic dimensions seem to be more salient to young children than are points between the two extremes. The salience of end points may be one reason that polar opposites are important aspects of the semantic system (Lyons, 1977).

As children discover the semantic relations that are necessary to structure their semantic system, they are better able to organise their growing vocabulary (Kuczaj, 1982b, 1999b). In addition, learning semantic relations helps children become aware of gaps in their vocabulary (Clark, 1993). For example, the child who knows that people have hair and that dogs have fur may wonder what one calls the stuff that covers a bird's body.

THE INTERACTION OF LANGUAGE AND COGNITIVE DEVELOPMENT

Before children begin to acquire words, they have formed concepts of the world. Children's first words are most likely to be those that express these early concepts because children search for ways to communicate what they know (Bowerman, 1981; Clark, 1973; Mervis, 1987). However, even the early development of the semantic system results in changes in children's concepts. As children construct their semantic system, they are building a rich and complex means to mentally represent their world. Hearing a novel word causes children to search for the meaning of the word, which often results in new concepts being learned (Balaban & Waxman, 1997; Kuczaj et al., 1989; Waxman, 1999; Waxman & Markow, 1995).

Kuczaj (1982b) suggested that children use two strategies when faced with gaps in their semantic and/or conceptual system. These strategies reflect the interrelationship of language and cognitive development:

- **Strategy 1 – acquiring a new word**: When acquiring a new word, search known concepts in case the word denotes a previously acquired concept. If no existing concept seems appropriate, attempt to construct a new one.
- **Strategy 2 – acquiring a new concept**: When acquiring a new concept, attempt to attach a known word to it. If no word seems appropriate, look for one.

In the process of building a semantic system, children acquire a world view that is shaped at least in part by the language they hear (Gellatly, 1995; Gopnik & Choi, 1995; Kuczaj, 1975, 1982b, Kuczaj et al., 1989; Nelson, 1996; Rattermann & Gentner, 1998). The development of the semantic system influences conceptual development by virtue of the manner in which language dissects and organises the world (Gopnik & Meltzoff, 1997; Kuczaj, 1999b).

SUMMARY AND CONCLUSIONS

The complexity of the task facing the language learning child has produced a variety of types of theoretical views that attempt to explain language development. Barrett (1999) categorised these views in terms of four general theoretical stances:

1. One stance is characterised by advocates of the notion that at least some aspects of language development are dependent on *innate capacities and knowledge* that are specific to language (e.g. Chomsky, 1986; Pinker, 1989; Ritchie & Bhatia, 1999). The most extreme nativist position proposes that both information processing skills specific to the acquisition of language and knowledge about certain aspects of language are believed to be passed from generation to generation via the genes. According to this view, knowledge of d-structures is not learned but innate.

2. A second theoretical stance also assumes that aspects of language development are strongly influenced by *innate information processing predispositions*, but does not assume that children are born with innate knowledge of language (Kuczaj, 1982c; Tomasello & Brooks, 1999). For example, children are born with the ability to discriminate phonemes but must learn which phonemes are important in the language they are acquiring.

The remaining two theoretical stances offer empiricist views and emphasise the importance of experience in language acquisition.

3. One of these stances assumes that children acquire language-specific concepts and representations because of their *experiences with language* rather than because the concepts and representations are innately specified (see Dabrowska & Lieven, 2005 for a recent review; Karmiloff-Smith, 1992). For example, in this view, children must learn that nouns are used to refer to objects, and so acquire the notion of noun from this sort of learning.

4. The remaining stance also emphasises the role of experience, but assumes that children acquire aspects of language because of *more general abilities* that play a role in cognitive development itself (Barrett, 1986). This theoretical position assumes that language development occurs in much the same way that other aspects of cognitive development do, and so minimises the notion that language development is a unique aspect of children's development.

As we have seen, the particular stance taken by a theorist depends on the aspect of language development with which they are concerned and their beliefs about the nature of language and its development. A true explanation of language development will require a combination of innate and environmental factors, and so researchers need to look beyond their 'favourite' theories to unravel the nature and evolution of language, a truly 'special gift' (MacWhinney, 2005).

DISCUSSION POINTS

1. What are the major characteristics of human language? Think about the ways in which language is a communication system, a symbolic system, a rule-governed system, and is productive.

2. What are the pragmatic abilities that enable children to communicate effectively, and how do they develop?

3. How does the phonological system develop, and why is it important to distinguish between the perception and production of speech?

4. What are the differences between the one-word and two-word stages of speech acquisition? Do one-word utterances stand for (or mean) a whole sentence?

5. What sort of attempts have been made to explain semantic development?

6. How do children learn the meaning of words?

7. How does language development interact with cognitive development?

SUGGESTIONS FOR FURTHER READING

Hoff, E., & Shatz, M. (Eds.) (2009). *Blackwell handbook of language development*. Cambridge, MA, and Oxford: Blackwell.

Hoff, E. (2009). *Language development, international edition* (4the edn). Belmont, CA: Wadsworth.

Holzman, M. (1997). *The language of children*. Cambridge, MA, and Oxford: Blackwell.

Norbury, C.F., Tomblin, J.B., & Bishop, D.V.M. (2008). *Understanding developmental language disorders*. London: Psychology Press.

Karmiloff, K., & Karmiloff-Smith, A. (2001). *Pathways to language: From fetus to adolescent*. Cambridge, MA: Harvard University Press.

Tomasello, M. & Bates. E. (2001). *Language development: The essential readings*. Cambridge, MA, and Oxford: Blackwell.

REFERENCES

Balaban, M., & Waxman, S. (1997). Do words facilitate object categorization in 9-month-old infants? *Journal of Experimental Psychology, 16*, 139–154.

Barrett, M.D. (1986). Early semantic representations and early word-usage. In S. Kuczaj & M.D. Barrett (Eds.) *The development of word meaning*. New York: Springer-Verlag.

Barrett, M.D. (1999). An introduction to the nature of language and to the central themes and issues in the study of language development. In M.D. Barrett (Ed.) *The Development of Language*, East Sussex, UK: Psychology Press.

Bateson, M. (1975). Mother–infant exchanges: The epigenesis of conversational interaction. *Annals of the New York Academy of Sciences, 263*, 101–113.

Behrend, D.A. (1995). Processes involved in the initial mapping of verb meanings. In M. Tomasello & W. Merriman (Eds.) *Beyond names for things*. Hillsdale, NJ: Erlbaum.

Berko, J., & Brown, R. (1960). Psycholinguistic research methods. In P. Mussen (Ed.) *Handbook on Research Methods in Child Development*, New York: Wiley.

Bever, T. (1970). The cognitive basis for linguistic structures. In J. Hayes (Ed.) *Cognition and the Development of Language*. New York: Wiley.

Blank, M., & Franklin, E. (1980). Dialogue with preschoolers – a cognitively-based system of assessment. *Applied Psycholinguistics, 1*, 127–150.

Bloom, L.M. (1973). *One word at a time: The use of single word utterances before syntax*. The Hague: Mouton.

Bloom, L.M. (1991). *Language development from two to three*. New York: Cambridge University Press.

Bloom, P. (1990). Syntactic distinctions in child language. *Journal of Child Language, 17*, 343–355.

Bloom, P. (1994) Possible names: The role of syntax-semantic mappings in the acquisition of nominals. In L. Gleitman and B. Landau (Eds.) *The Acquisition of the Lexicon*. Cambridge, MA: MIT Press.

Bloom, P., & Kelemen, D. (1995). Syntactic cues in the acquisition of collective nouns. *Cognition, 56*, 1–30.

Bowerman, M. (1981). Cross-cultural perspectives on language development. In H.C. Triandis & A. Heron (Eds.) *Handbook of Cross-cultural Psychology* (Vol. 4). Boston, MA: Alleyn and Bacon.

Bowlby, J. (1951). *Maternal care and mental health*. World Health Organization Monograph, 2.

Boysson-Bardies, B. de, Sagart, L., & Durand, C. (1984). Discernible differences in the babbling of infants according to target language. *Journal of Child Language, 11*, 1–15.

Braine, M.D.S. (1971) The acquisition of language in infant and child. In C. Reed (Ed.) *The Learning of Language*. New York: Appleton-Century-Crofts.

Brinton, B., & Fujiki, M. (1984) Development of topic manipulation skills in discourse. *Journal of Hearing and Speech Research, 27*, 350–358.

Brinton, B., Fujiki, M., Loeb, D., & Winkler, E. (1986) Development of conversational repair strategies in response to requests for clarification. *Journal of Hearing and Speech Research, 29*, 75–81.

Brown, R.W. (1973). *A first language: The early stages*. Cambridge, MA: Harvard University Press.

Brown, R.W., & Hanlon, C. (1970). Derivational complexity and order of acquisition. In J.R. Hayes (Ed.) *Cognition and the development of language*. New York: Wiley.

Butterfield, E., & Siperstein, G.N. (1974). Influence of contingent auditory stimulation upon non-nutritional suckle. In J. Bosma (Ed.) *Oral sensation and perception*. Sringfield, IL: Charles C. Thomas.

Butterworth, G. (1995). Origins of mind in perception and action. In C. Moore & P.J. Dunham (Eds.) *Joint attention: Its origins and role in development*. Hillsdale, NJ: Erlbaum.

Butterworth, G., & Grover, L. (1990). Joint visual attention, manual pointing, and preverbal communication in human infancy. In M. Jeannerod (Ed.) *Attention and Performance XIII*. Hillsdale, NJ: Erlbaum.

Call, J., & Tomasello, M. (1994). Production and comprehension of referential pointing by orangutans (*Pongo pygmaeus*). *Journal of Comparative Psychology, 108*, 307–317.

Carey, S. (1978). The child as a word learner. In M. Halle, J. Bresnan, & G. Miller (Eds.) *Linguistic theory and psychological reality*. Cambridge, MA: MIT Press.

Chomsky, N. (1957). *Syntactic structures*. The Hague: Mouton.

Chomsky, N. (1972). *Language and mind*. New York: Harcourt Brace Jovanovich.

Chomsky, N. (1982). *Some concepts and consequences of the theory of government and binding*. Cambridge, MA: MIT Press.

Chomsky, N. (1986). *Knowledge of language: Its nature, origins and use.* New York: Praeger.

Chomsky, N. (1987). *Language in a psychological setting*. Working papers in Linguistics, Number 22, Tokyo, Japan.

Clark, E.V. (1973). What's in a word? On the child's acquisition of semantics in his first language. In T.F. Moore (Ed.) *Cognitive Development and the Acquisition of Language*. New York: Academic Press.

Clark, E.V. (1993). *The lexicon in acquisition*. Cambridge: Cambridge University Press.

Dabrowska, E., & Lieven, E. (2005). Towards a lexically specific grammar of children's question constructions. *Cognitive Linguistics, 16*, 437–474.

DeLaguna, G. (1927). *Speech: Its function and development*. Bloomington, IN: Indiana University Press.

Desrochers, S., Morissette, P., & Ricard, M. (1995). Two perspectives on pointing in infancy. In C. Moore & P.J. Dunham (Eds.) *Joint attention: Its origin and role in development*. Hillsdale, NJ: Lawrence Erlbaum and Associates.

Dromi, E. (1999). Early lexical development. In M. Barrett (Ed.) *The development of language*. London: Psychology Press.

Eimas, P. (1985). The perception of speech in early infancy. *Scientific American, 252*, 46–61.

Eimas, P.D., Siqueland, E.R., Jusczyk, P.W., & Vigorito, J. (1971). Speech perception in infants. *Science, 171*, 303–306.

Farwell, C. (1975). The language spoken to children. *Human Development, 18*, 288–309.

Ferguson, C.A. (1989). Individual differences in language learning. In M. Rice & R. Schiefelbusch (Eds.) *The Teachability of Language*, Baltimore, MD: Brookes.

Ferrari, P.F., Gallese, V., Rizzolatti, G., & Fogassi, L. (2003). Mirror neurons responding to the observation of ingestive and communicative mouth actions in the monkey ventral premotor cortex. *European Journal of Neurosciences, 17*(8), 1703–1714.

Foster, S.H. (1986). Learning discourse topic management in the preschool years. *Journal of Child Language, 13*, 231–250.

Franco, F., & Butterworth, G. (1996). Pointing and social awareness: Declaring and requesting in the second year. *Journal of Child Language, 23*, 307–336.

Furrow, D., & Lewis, S. (1987). The role of the initial utterance in contingent query sequences: Its influence on responses to requests for clarification. *Journal of Child Language, 14*, 467–479.

Gallagher, T. (1977). Revision behaviors in the speech of normal children developing language. *Journal of Speech and Hearing Research, 20*, 303–318.

Gallagher, T. (1981). Contingent query sequences within adult–child discourse. *Journal of Child Language, 8*, 51–62.

Gallese, V., Fadiga, L., Fogassi, L., & Rizzolatti, G. (1996). Action recognition in the premotor cortex. *Brain, 119*(Pt. 2), 593–609.

Garvey, C. (1975). Requests and responses in children's speech. *Journal of Child Language, 2*, 41–63.

Garvey, C., & Hogan, R. (1973). Social speech and social interaction: Egocentrism revisited. *Child Development, 44*, 562–568.

Gathercole, V., & Min, H. (1997). Word meaning biases or language-specific effects? Evidence from English, Spanish, and Korean. *First Language, 17*, 31–56.

Gellatly, A. (1995). Colourful Whorfian ideas: Linguistic and cultural influences on the perception and cognition of colour, and on the investigation of them. *Mind and Language, 10*, 199–225.

Gentilucci, M., & Corballis, M.C. (2006). From manual gesture to speech: A gradual transition. *Neuroscience & Biobehavioral Reviews, 30*(7), 949–960.

Gertner, Y., Fisher, C., & Eisengart, J. (2006). Learning words and rules: Abstract knowledge of word order in early sentence comprehension. *Psychological Science, 17*(8), 684–691.

Gibson, E., & Spelke, E. (1983). The development of perception. In P.H. Mussen, J.H. Flavell, & E.M. Markman (Eds.) *Handbook of Child Psychology: Vol. 3. Cognitive Development*. New York: Wiley.

Gleason, J., & Weintraub, S. (1978). Input language and the acquisition of communicative competence. In K.E. Nelson (Ed.) *Children's Language* (Vol. 1). New York: Gardner Press.

Gleitman, L., & Wannner, E. (1982). The state of the art. In E. Wanner & L. Gleitman (Eds.) *Language acquisition: The state of the art*. Cambridge: Cambridge University Press.

Golinkoff, R.M. (1983). Infant social cognition: Self, people, and objects. In L. Lieben (Ed.) *Piaget and the foundations of knowledge* (pp. 57–78). Hillsdale, NJ: Lawrence Erlbaum and Associates.

Golinkoff, R.M. (1986). 'I beg your pardon?': The preverbal negotiation of failed messages. *Journal of Child Language, 13*, 455–463.

Golinkoff, R.M., & Hirsh-Pasek, K. (1995). Reinterpreting children's sentence comprehension: Toward a new framework. In P. Fletcher & B. MacWhinney (Eds.) *The handbook of child language*. Oxford: Blackwell.

Golinkoff, RM., Hirsh-Pasek, K., Mervis, C., Frawley, W., & Parillo, M. (1995). Lexical principles can be extended to the acquisition of verbs. In M. Tomasello & W. Merriman (Eds.) *Beyond Names for Things*. Hillsdale, NJ: Erlbaum.

Golinkoff, R.M., Shuff-Bailey, M., Olguin, R., & Ruan, W. (1995). Young children extend novel words at the basic level: Evidence for the principle of categorical scope. *Developmental Psychology, 31*, 494–507.

Goodman, N. (1983). *Fact, fiction, and forecast*. Cambridge, MA: Harvard University Press.

Goodsit, J., Morgan, J.L., & Kuhl, P.K. (1993). Perceptual strategies in prelingual speech segmentation. *Journal of Child Language, 20*, 229–252.

Gopnik, A., & Choi, S. (1995). Names, relational words, and cognitive development in English and Korean speakers: Nouns are not always learned before verbs. In M. Tomasello & W.E. Merriman (Eds.) *Beyond Names for Things: Young Children's Acquisition of Verbs*. Hillsdale, NJ: Erlbaum.

Gopnik, A., & Meltzoff, A. (1997). *Words, thoughts, and theories*. Cambridge, MA: MIT Press.

Hauser, M. (1996). *The evolution of communication*. Cambridge, MA: MIT Press.

Heimann, M. (1998). Imitation in neonates, older infants and in children with autism. Feedback to theory. In S. Braten (Ed.) *Intersubjective communication and emotion in early ontogeny* (pp. 89–104). Cambridge: Cambridge University Press.

Heyes, C. (2001). Causes and consequences of imitation. *Trends in Cognitive Sciences, 5*(6), 253–261.

Hirsh-Pasek, K., Treiman, R., & Schneiderman, M. (1984). Brown and Hanlon revisited: Mother's sensitivity to ungrammatical forms. *Journal of Child Language, 11*, 81–88.

Hoff-Ginsberg, E. (1990). Maternal speech and the child's development of syntax: A further look. *Journal of Child Language, 17*, 337–346.

Houston, D. Jusczyk, P.W., & Tager, J. (1997, November). *Talker-specificity and the persistence of infant's word representations*. Paper presented at the 22nd Annual Boston University Conference on Language Development, Boston, MA.

Hyams, N.M. (1989). The null-subject parameter in language acquisition. In O. Jaeggli & K.Safir (Eds.) *The null-subject parameter*. Dordrecht: Kluwer.

Ingram, D. (1986). Phonological development: Production. In P. Fletcher & M. Garman (Eds.) *Language acquisition* (2nd edn), Cambridge: Cambridge University Press.

Ingram, R. (1992). Review of S. Pinker, Learnability and cognition: The acquisition of argument structure. *Journal of Child Language, 19*, 205–211.

Iverson, J.M., & Goldin-Meadow, S. 2005. Gesture paves the way for language development. *Psychological Science, 16*(5), 367–371.

Jespersen, O. (1922). *Language: Its nature, development, and origin*. London: Allen & Unwin.

Jusczyk, P.W. (1997). *The discovery of spoken language*. Cambridge, MA: MIT Press.

Jusczyk, P.W., & Aslin, R.N. (1995). Infant's detection of sound patterns of words in fluent speech. *Cognitive Psychology, 29*, 1–23.

Jusczyk, P.W., Cutler, A., & Redanz, N. (1993). Preference for the predominant stress patterns of English words. *Child Development, 64*, 675–687.

Jusczyk, P.W., Pisoni, D.B., Reed, M., Fernald, A., & Myers, M. (1983). Infant's discrimination of the duration of a rapid spectrum change in nonspeech signals. *Science, 222,* 175–177.

Karmiloff-Smith, A. (1992). *Beyond modularity: A developmental perspective on cognitive science.* Cambridge, MA: MIT press.

Kaye, K. (1977). Towards the origin of dialogue. In H.R. Schaffer (Ed.) *Studies of Mother–Infant Interaction* (pp. 89–117). New York: Academic Press.

Keenan, E.O. (1974). Conversational competence in children. *Journal of Child Language, 1,* 163–183.

Keenan, E., & Klein, E. (1975). Coherence in children's discourse. *Journal of Psycholinguistic Research,* 4, 365–378.

Komatsu, K. 2003. Mother–child conversations about kindergarten friends, teachers and experiences: Conversation topics and the characteristics of children's speech. *Japanese Journal of Developmental Psychology, 14,* 294–303.

Kornfield, J.R. (1971). Theoretical issues in child phonology. In *Proceedings of the Seventh Annual Meeting of the Chicago Linguistic Society* (pp. 454–468), Chicago: University of Chicago.

Kuczaj, S. (1975). On the acquisition of a semantic system. *Journal of Verbal Learning and Verbal Behavior, 14,* 340–358.

Kuczaj, S. (1977). The acquisition of regular and irregular past tense forms. *Journal of Verbal Learning and Verbal Behavior, 16,* 589–600.

Kuczaj, S. (1978). Why do children fail to overgeneralize the progressive inflection? *Child Development, 5,* 167–171.

Kuczaj, S. (1982a). Language play and language acquisition. In H. Reese (Ed.) *Advances in Child Development and Child Behavior* (Vol. 17). New York: Academic Press.

Kuczaj, S. (1982b). The acquisition of word meaning in the context of the development of the semantic system. In C. Brainerd & M. Pressley (Eds.) *Progress in cognitive development research: Vol. 2. Verbal processes in children.* New York: Springer-Verlag.

Kuczaj, S. (1982c). On the nature of syntactic development. In S. Kuczaj (Ed.) *Language development: Vol. 1. Syntax and semantics.* Hillsdale, NJ: Erlbaum.

Kuczaj, S. (1983). 'I mell a kunk!'– Evidence that children have more complex representations of word pronunciations which they simplify. *Journal of Psycholinguistic Research, 12,* 69–73.

Kuczaj, S. (1990). Constraining constraint theories. *Cognitive Development, 5,* 341–344.

Kuczaj, S. (1999a). Is an evolutionary theory of language play possible? *Current Psychology of Cognition, 17,* 135–154.

Kuczaj, S. (1999b). The world of words: Thoughts on the development of a lexicon. In M. Barrett (Ed.) *The development of language.* London: Psychology Press.

Kuczaj, S., & Borys, R. (1988). The overgeneralization of morphological forms as a function of experience. *Language Sciences, 10,* 111–122.

Kuczaj, S., Borys, R., & Jones, M. (1989). On the interaction of language and thought: Some thoughts and developmental data. In A. Gellatly, D. Rogers, & J. Sloboda (Eds.) *Cognition and social worlds.* Oxford: Oxford University Press.

Kuczaj, S., & Daly, M. (1979). The development of hypothetical reference in the speech of young children. *Journal of Child Language, 6,* 563–580.

Kuczaj, S., & Kirkpatrick, V. (1993). Similarities and differences in human and animal language research: Toward a comparative psychology of language. In H. Roitblat, L. Herman, & P. Nachtigall (Ed.) *Language and communication: Comparative perspectives.* Hillsdale, NJ: Erlbaum.

Kuczaj, S., & Makecha, R. (2008). The role of play in the evolution and ontogeny of contextually flexible communication. In D.K. Oller & U. Griebel (Eds.) *Evolution of communicative flexibility.* Cambridge, MA: The MIT Press.

Kuhl, P. (1992). Speech prototypes: Studies on the nature, function, ontogeny and phylogeny of the 'centers' of speech categories. In Y. Tohkura, E. Vatikiotis-Bateson, & Y. Sagiska (Eds.) *Speech perception, production and linguistic structure.* Tokyo: Ohmsha.

Kuhl, P., & Miller, J. (1975). Speech perception by the chinchilla: Voiced-voiceless distinction in alveolar plosive consonants. *Science, 190,* 69–72.

Kuhl, P., & Padden, D. (1982). Enhanced discriminability at the phonetic boundaries for the voicing feature in macaques. *Perception and Psychophisics, 32,* 542–550.

Kuhl, P., & Padden, D. (1983). Enhanced discriminability at the phonetic boundaries for the place feature in macaques. *Journal of the Acoustic Society of America, 73,* 1003–1010.

Lenneberg, E., Rebelsky, F., & Nichols, I. (1965). The vocalizations of infants born to deaf and hearing parents. *Human Development, 8,* 23–47.

Locke, J.L. (1983). *Phonological acquisition and change.* New York: Academic Press.

Lyons, J. (1977). *Semantics, Vol. 1.* Cambridge: Cambridge University Press.

Macken, M., & Ferguson, C.A. (1983). Cognitive aspects of phonological development: Model, evidence, and issues. In K. Nelson (Ed.) *Children's language,* Hillsdale, NJ: Erlbaum.

MacWhinney, B. (2005). Language development. In M.H. Bornstein & M.E. Lamb (Eds.) *Developmental science: An advanced textbook* (5th edn; pp. 359–387). Mahwah, NJ: Lawrence Erlbaum and Associates.

Maratsos, M.P. (1983). Some current issues in the study of the acquisition of grammar. In J. Flavell & E. Markman (Eds.) *Handbook of Child Psychology: Vol. 3. Cognitive Development,* New York: Wiley.

Maratsos, M.P. (1999). Some aspects of innateness and complexity in grammatical acquisition. In M. Barrett (Ed.) *The Development of Language.* East Sussex: Psychology Press.

Maratsos, M.P. (2000). More overregularizations after all: New data and discussion of Marcus, Pinker, Ullman, Hollander, Rosen, and Xu. *Journal of Child Language, 27,* 183–212.

Markman, E.M. (1990). Constraints children place on word meanings. *Cognitive Science, 14,* 57–77.

Masur, E.F. (1983). Gestural development, dual-directional signaling, and the transition to words. *Journal of Psycholinguistic Research, 12,* 93–109.

Masur, E.F. (1995). Infants' early verbal imitation and their later lexical development. *Merrill-Palmer Quarterly, 41,* 286–306.

Masur, E.F., & Rodemaker, J.E. (1999). Mothers' and infants' spontaneous vocal, verbal, and action imitation during the second year. *Merrill-Palmer Quarterly, 45,* 392–412.

McLaughlin, S. (1998). *Introduction to language development.* San Diego, CA: Singular Publishing Group.

McCafferty, S.G. 2008. Mimesis and second language acquisition: A sociocultural perspective. *Studies in Second Language Acquisition, 30*(2), 147–167.

McNamara, J. (1982). *Names for things: A study of human learning.* Cambridge, MA: MIT Press.

Meltzoff, A.N., & Williamson, R.A. (2011). Imitation. In G. Bremner & T. Wachs (Eds.) *The Wiley-Blackwell handbook of infant development* (2nd edn; Vol. 1; pp.345–364). Oxford: Blackwell Publishers.

Merriman, W., Marazita, J., and Jarvis, L. (1995). Children's disposition to map new words onto new referents. In M. Tomasello & W. Merriman (Eds.) *Beyond names for things.* Hillsdale, NJ: Erlbaum.

Mervis, C.B. (1987). Child-based object categories and early lexical development. In U. Neisser (Ed.) *Concepts and conceptual knowledge.* Cambridge: Cambridge University Press.

Mervis, C.B., Golinkoff, R.M., & Bertrand, J. (1994). Two- year-olds readily learn multiple labels for the same category. *Child Development, 65,* 1163–1177.

Messinger, D.S., & Fogel, A. (1998). Give and take: The development of conventional infant gestures. *Merrill-Palmer Quarterly, 44,* 566–590.

Miller, W.R., & Ervin, S. (1964). *The development of grammar in child language*. The acquisition of language: Monographs of the Society for Research in Child Development, 29 (U. Bellugi & R. Brown, Eds.).

Morford, J.P., & Goldin-Meadow, S. (1997). From here and now to there and then: The development of displaced reference in homesign and English. *Child Development, 68*, 420–435.

Moszkowski, R., & Stack, D. (2007). Infant touching behaviour during mother–infant face-to-face interactions. *Infant & Child Development, 16*(3), 307–319.

Muller, E., Hollien, H., & Murry, T. (1974). Perceptual response to infant crying: Identification of cry types. *Journal of Child Language,* 1, 89–95.

Nagy, E. (2006). From imitation to conversation: The first dialogues with human neonates. *Infant & Child Development, 15*(3), 223–232.

Nelson, K. (1988). Constraints on word learning? *Cognitive Development, 3*, 221–246.

Nelson, K. (1996). *Language in cognitive development*. New York: Cambridge University Press.

Nelson, K.E., & Gruendel, J.M. (1979). At morning it's lunchtime: A scriptal view of children's dialogues. *Discourse Processes, 2*, 73–94.

Newman, J.D. (2007). Neural circuits underlying crying and cry responding in mammals. *Behavioural Brain Research, 182*(2), 155–165.

Newman, R., Ratner, N., Jusczyk, A., Jusczyk, P., & Dow, K. (2006). Infants' early ability to segment the conversational speech signal predicts later language development: A retrospective analysis. *Developmental Psychology, 42*(4), 643–655.

Newport, E.L., Gleitman, L.R., & Gleitman, H. (1975, September) *A study of mother's speech and child language acquisition*. Paper presented at the 7th Child Language Research Forum, Stanford University, Stanford, CA.

Ninio, A., & Snow, C. (1996). *Pragmatic development*. Boulder, CO: Westview.

Nurmsoo, E., & Bloom, P. (2008). Preschoolers' perspective taking in word learning: Do they blindly follow eye gaze? *Psychological Science, 19*, 211–215.

Ochs, E., & Schieffelin, B. (1984). Language acquisition and socialization. Three developmental stories and their implications. In R. Shweder & R. LeVine (Eds.) *Culture theory*. Cambridge: Cambridge University Press.

Oller, D. (1980). The emergence of speech sounds in infancy. In G. Yeni-Komshian, J, Kavanaugh, & C. Ferguson (Eds.) *Child phonology*. New York: Academic Press.

Oller, D., & Eilers, R. (1988). The role of audition in infant babbling. *Child Development, 59*, 441–449.

Olson-Fulero, L., & Conforti, J. (1983). Child responsiveness to mother questions of varying type and presentation. *Journal of Child Language,* 10, 495–520.

O'Neill, D., & Atance, C.M. (2000). 'Maybe my daddy give me a big piano': The development of children's use of modals to express uncertainty. *First Language, 20*, 29–54.

Pan, B.A., & Snow, C.E. (1999). The development of conversational and discourse skills. In M. Barrett (Ed.) *The development of language* (pp. 229–249). Hove: Psychology Press.

Petitto, L., Holokwa, S., Sergio, L.E., & Ostry, D. 2001. Language rhythms in baby hand movements. *Nature, 413*(6851), 35–36.

Pinker, S. (1987). The bootstrapping problem in language acquisition. In B. MacWhinney (Ed.) *Mechanisms of language acquisition*. Hillsdale, NJ: Erlbaum.

Pinker, S. (1989). *Learnability and cognition: The acquisition of argument structure*. Cambridge, MA: MIT press.

Quine, W.V. (1960). *Word and object*. Cambridge, MA: MIT Press.

Radford, A. (1990). *Syntactic theory and the acquisition of English syntax*. Oxford: Blackwell.

Reddy, V. (1999). Prelinguistic communication. In M. Barrett (Ed.) *The development of language* (pp. 25–50). Hove: Psychology Press.

Ritchie, W.C., & Bhatia, T.K. (Eds.) (1999). *Handbook of child language acquisition*. San Diego, CA: Academic Press.

Rothgänger, H. 2003. Analysis of the sounds of the child in the first year of age and a comparison to the language. *Early Human Development, 75*(1–2), 55–69.

Rattermann, M.J., & Gentner, D. (1998). The effect of language on similarity: The use of relational labels improves children's performance in a mapping task. In K. Holyoak, D. Gentner, & B. Kokinov (Eds.) *Advances in analogy research*. Sophia: New Bulgarian University.

Rowland, C. (2007). Explaining errors in children's questions. *Cognition, 104*(1), 106–134.

Shatz, M., & Gelman, R. (1973). *The development of communication skills: Modifications in the speech of young children as a function of a listener*. Monographs of the Society for Research in Child Development, 38 (Serial No. 152).

Slobin, D.I. (1979). *Psycholinguistics*. Dallas, TX: Scott, Foresman.

Smith, M. (1926). An investigation of the development of the sentence and the extent of vocabulary in young children. *University of Iowa Studies in Child Welfare, 3*(5).

Smith, N. (1973). *The acquisition of phonology: A case study*. Cambridge: Cambridge University Press.

Soja, N., Carey, S., & Spelke, E. (1991). Ontogenetic categories guide young children's inductions about word meaning: Object and substance terms. *Cognition, 38*, 179–211.

Spitz, R. (1965). *The first year of life*. New York: International Universities Press.

Stark, R.E. (1980). Stages of speech development during the first year of life. In G.H. Yeni-Komshian, J.F. Kavanagh, & C.A. Ferguson (Eds.) *Child phonology*. New York: Academic Press.

Stoel-Gammon, C., & Otomo, K. (1986). Babbling development of hearing impaired and normally hearing subjects. *Journal of Speech and Hearing Disorders, 51*, 33–41.

Tardif, T., Fletcher, P., Liang, W., Zhang, Z., Kaciroti, N., & Marchman, V.A. (2008). Baby's first 10 words. *Developmental Psychology, 44*(4), 929–938.

Templin, M.C. (1957). *Certain language skills in children: Their development and interrelationships*. Minneapolis: University of Minnesota Press.

Thevenin, D.M., Eilers, R.E., Oller, D., & Lavoie, L. (1985). Where's the drift in babbling drift? A cross-linguistic study. *Applied Psycholinguistics, 6*(1), 3–15.

Tincoff, R., & Jusczyk, P.W. (1999). Some beginnings of word comprehension in 6-month-olds. *Psychological Science, 10*, 172–175.

Tomasello, M. (1992). *First verbs: A case study of early grammatical development*. Cambridge: Cambridge University Press.

Tomasello, M. (1995). Joint attention as social cognition. In C. Moore & P.J. Dunham (Eds.) *Joint attention: Its origin and role in development*. Hillsdale, NJ: Lawrence Erlbaum Associates.

Tomasello, M. (Ed.) (1998). *The new psychology of language: Cognitive and functional approaches to language structure*. Mahwah, NJ: Lawrence Erlbaum and Associates.

Tomasello, M., Farrar, M.J., & Dines, J. (1984). Children's speech revisions for a familiar and an unfamiliar adult. *Journal of Speech and Hearing Research, 27*, 359–363.

Trainor, L.J., Austin, C.M., & Desjardins, R.N. (2000). Is infant-directed speech prosody a result of the vocal expression of emotion? *Psychological Science, 11*, 188–195.

Vihman, M.M. (1996). *Phonological development: The origins of language in the child*. Cambridge, MA: Blackwell.

Waxman, S. (1999). Specifying the scope of 13-month-old's expectations for novel words. *Cognition, 70*, 35–50.

Waxman, S., & Markow, D. (1995). Words as invitations to form categories: Evidence from 12- to 13-month-old infants. *Cognitive Psychology, 29*, 257–302.

Werker, J. (1989). Becoming a native listener. *American Scientist, 77*, 54–59.

Werner, H., & Kaplan, B. (1963). *Symbol formation*. New York: Wiley.

11 Acquiring a Theory of Mind

PETER MITCHELL

KEY TERMS

autism • chronological age (CA) • cognitive development • collectivist societies • competence • conceptual shift • cross-cultural study • deceptive box task • Down's syndrome • egocentric • false belief • hindsight bias • hunter–gatherer tribe • individualistic societies • instinct • intuitive psychology • intelligence quotient (IQ) • mental age (MA) • metacognition • modularity • performance limitations • posting version of the deceptive box test • representational ability • state change test • unexpected transfer test • violation of expectation (VoE) • Wing's triad of impairments

CHAPTER OUTLINE

OVERVIEW

The term *theory of mind* has been used to describe our everyday understanding of our own and others' minds. An understanding that others may hold beliefs that may be wrong (i.e. *false beliefs*) is seen as critical to an understanding of others' minds, and researchers have devised tests of false belief for assessing the development in children's understanding of the mind. These tests include the following:

* the unexpected transfer test of false belief;
* the deceptive box task;
* the state change test, and variations on this and other tests;
* the posting version of the deceptive box test.

Many children below about 4 years of age fail these tests, while older children pass. On the strength of these findings, some theorists have concluded that children negotiate a radical conceptual shift in their thinking around 4 years. The author suggests that a more plausible account is that children undergo a *gradual* change that allows them to disengage from a focus on current reality, and recent evidence suggests that if tasks are simplified even infants have some understanding of false belief. However, even adults have been found to fail certain types of false belief tasks!

INTRODUCTION

One of the most striking human qualities surrounds our ability to connect with other people. We exchange ideas, learn from each other, coordinate efforts, and influence one another. Certain non-human creatures can do some of these things too. But the way in which we do it is probably unique: Unlike other creatures, humans are able to marshal vast intellectual resources in an effort to connect with other people. In non-humans, social behaviour might have a great deal to do with **instinct**, in which case it would not be quite so insightful or creative. People experience a meeting of minds, and that feeling could be a special human privilege.

> **instinct** (1) behaviour that is genetic in its origin, e.g. human sexual desire; (2) a feeling or emotion that has no basis in fact, e.g. 'My instinct tells me he's not to be trusted'.

Early attunement to others' minds

The ability to connect with other minds is present early in development. Parents sense that their newborn has a unique set of feelings, desires, needs, pleasures, and temperamental characteristics. Before long, the relationship is cemented when the baby shows a range of social responses. In infancy and early childhood, the toddler ventures into the social realm of peers and has a repertoire of skills which allow play and cooperation, especially in the sphere of fantasy. In the way that they participate in joint activities and cooperate they show awareness of others' desires, motives, and

FIGURE 11.1 *Young children demonstrating social skills which allow play and cooperation.*

Source: Shutterstock.

beliefs, and will appear to anticipate others' reactions and behaviour. In brief, they spontaneously and easily seem to become attuned to other minds (Figure 11.1). This impressive beginning lays the foundations for the growth of a sophisticated **intuitive psychology**. In extreme cases, people can sometimes seem unnervingly telepathic in figuring out your thoughts.

There is a sense, then, in which we are able to read each others' minds – not through extrasensory perception. In short, other people are capable of diagnosing that you are ignorant or that you hold a **false belief**; people have an aptitude for inferring what you think.

Focusing on false beliefs: The unexpected transfer test

intuitive psychology the awareness some people have regarding others' desires, motives, and beliefs; they appear able to anticipate others' reactions and behaviour.

Why concentrate on ignorance and false belief? Why not concentrate on being amply informed? There are two reasons, one associated with the challenge of trying to find out whether a person is attuned to other minds and the other concerned with the special value of understanding about others' *false* beliefs.

If we ask a participant to make judgments about another person's true beliefs, they would respond correctly even in the absence of knowing anything about other minds. Imagine that we told the participant a story about Maxi, a little boy who stored a bar of chocolate safely in the cupboard, so that he can eat it when he returns from play. If we ask the participant where Maxi thinks the chocolate is or where he will look for it, they will correctly say 'cupboard'. But perhaps the participant is merely answering according to where they themselves would look for the chocolate. Asking about a person's true belief thus offers no opportunity to differentiate between a child who understands the mind and one who does not. Both children would answer in the same way, even though one is actually reporting where they themselves know the chocolate is.

unexpected transfer test a measure of *theory of mind* in which a child sees an object put in one place and it is later moved to another location without the child being aware of it. The theory-of-mind question is 'where will the child look for the object when they want to find it?'

A test of false belief is very different (see Figure 11.2, which shows the **unexpected transfer test** of false belief). Imagine that after Maxi went out to play, his mother moved the chocolate from the cupboard to the fridge after using some of it to bake a cake. Because this happens in Maxi's absence, and quite unexpectedly, he has unwittingly come to hold a false belief. By default, he would assume that the chocolate remained in the cupboard, where he left it. A competent

Scene 1: Maxi puts his chocolate in the cupboard

Scene 2: Later, Mum moves it to the fridge

FIGURE 11.2 *The unexpected transfer test of false belief, featuring Maxi, his bar of chocolate, and his mother.*

observing participant would predict that Maxi will look in the cupboard on his return; they would say that Maxi will search in the place he last saw his chocolate. In contrast, a participant who did not understand about minds would probably judge that Maxi will look in the place they themselves knew the chocolate was located – the fridge. Hence, a test of false belief is methodologically useful because it helps us to differentiate between those who do and do not understand that minds hold beliefs.

Another reason for focusing on false beliefs is because it is particularly important for children to be attuned to false as opposed to true beliefs. If we can accurately diagnose when a person holds a false belief, we can take steps to help them gain a true understanding. On the other hand, if we wanted to manipulate another person, we could misinform them in an attempt to instill a false belief. Hence there are Machiavellian as well as altruistic motivations involved in grappling with false belief.

WHEN DO CHILDREN BEGIN TO UNDERSTAND THAT PEOPLE HOLD BELIEFS?

Piaget characterised children below about 7 years of age as **egocentric**, so he would not have expected younger children to have any grasp of other people's mental states (see Chapter 9 for a description and evaluation of Piaget's account of the transition in children's thinking that occurs around 7 years of age). In Piaget's studies, children below age 7 wrongly judged that another person at a different vantage point had the same perspective as themselves. They also neglected to take account of a person's intention when apportioning blame or reward for a deed they had carried out. Moreover, their verbal communication was very poorly adapted to the informational needs of their listeners. With that background, Piaget would have been amazed at Wimmer and Perner's (1983) seminal discovery that from about 4 or 5 years, children set aside their own knowledge in making correct attributions of other people's false beliefs. These researchers presented children with the story about Maxi and his bar of chocolate. The results, along with those from a host of replication studies (see Wellman *et al.*, 2001), suggest there is a sharp increase in the number of children who answer correctly around the age of 4 years. Because the developmental trend was so striking,

conceptual shift a large qualitative change in an individual's *cognitive processes*.

representational ability the ability to form a mental representation of an event or an object.

Wimmer and Perner concluded, perhaps rather controversially, that children negotiate a radical **conceptual shift** around the time of their fourth birthday, which equips them with a **representational** theory of mind that allows them to acknowledge false belief. These children judged that Maxi would look for his chocolate in the place he last saw it – the cupboard. Younger children, in contrast, judged that he would look in the place they themselves knew it was located. In effect, when asked about Maxi's belief, they reported their own.

DO CHILDREN ACQUIRE A THEORY OF MIND?

Undoubtedly, children rapidly develop in their understanding of the mind at about 4 years of age. What form does this understanding take? Does it have the properties of an informal theory? In other words, do children acquire rules and principles from which they can explain and predict behaviour, just as a physicist has principles for explaining and predicting the motion of objects? That would be one way to do it. Another would be to use the power of your imagination to mentally simulate a person's mind (Harris, 1991). In effect, you could say to yourself, 'if I went out and Mum moved the chocolate in my absence, I would think it was still in the cupboard'. Just as an aviator uses a wind tunnel to simulate real conditions as a test for a prototype aircraft, so we might present a kind of thought experiment to our own mind to find out what we would think if we were in a particular situation. We could then treat the outcome of the mental simulation as telling us what another person would also think in that situation.

The deceptive box test

According to Gopnik (1993), understanding other minds by a process of simulation is implausible. She argues that being able to find out what someone else thinks by working out what you yourself would think in that situation depends on having reflective access to your own states of mind: this reflective access – effectively, thinking about how you are feeling or thinking – is often called **metacognition**. Gopnik and Astington (1988) found that children below about 4 years of age have just as much difficulty accessing their own states of belief as they have in estimating another person's. In their study, children were shown a tube (of popular sweets/candies usually sold in a small cardboard tube) and asked to guess what was inside. After children replied 'sweets', the experimenter opened the lid to reveal unexpectedly that there was only a pencil (Figure 11.3). The experimenter returned the lid with the pencil still inside and asked, 'When you first saw this tube, before we opened it, what did you think was inside?' Many children below about 4 years reported their current belief and said 'pencil'. In contrast, many older than 4 years correctly recalled that they had thought there were sweets in the tube. Gopnik and Astington also presented an unexpected transfer test based on Maxi and his bar of chocolate. The children who reported their current belief in this **deceptive box task** (pencil) tended to be the same who wrongly predicted that Maxi would look for his chocolate in its current location (the fridge). In contrast, the children who correctly recalled their prior false belief (sweets) tended to be the same who judged correctly that Maxi would look for his chocolate in the place he last saw it (the cupboard).

It seems that the children who were unable to acknowledge another person's false belief were not even attuned to their own prior beliefs. Gopnik (1993) argued that whether or not children could imagine what they would think in a different situation was not the issue. If children do not know their own mind, they

> **metacognition** knowledge of one's state of mind, reflective access to one's cognitive abilities, thinking about how one is feeling or thinking.

> **deceptive box task** in which a child sees that a box (usually of a well-known brand of sweets/candy) which they thought contained sweets/candies actually contains pencils, and when asked, 'What did you originally think was in the box?' children under the age of 4 will typically say 'pencils'.

FIGURE 11.3 *The deceptive box test of false belief. The tube of sweets unexpectedly contains a pencil.*

cannot use insights into their own mind as a basis for working out what another person thinks. Accordingly, their difficulty in understanding the mind seems to lie at a more fundamental level. Gopnik speculated that perhaps children had not yet acquired the principles that would allow them to explain and predict other people's behaviour. She suggests that children have to acquire a naive *theory* of the mind, a theory which gives access to their own states of belief as well as other people's. Once children have acquired this theory, they have a basis for making judgments about people's beliefs.

Advocates of the simulation account rebut Gopnik's argument by pointing out that having difficulty reporting your own prior belief is quite different from being able to access your *current* mental states. Indeed, we might have to conduct a mental simulation using our currently accessible mental states to work out what we used to think just as we have to perform simulation to work out what another person might be thinking (Goldman, 1993). Reporting what we used to think is perhaps not merely a matter of recall but a matter of reconstruction; and simulation might be the mechanism by which we achieve this. If so, then Gopnik might be wrong to say that children's difficulty reporting their own prior false belief lends support to the *theory account* in preference to a *simulation account* of how children (or adults) understand the mind.

IS THERE A DEVELOPMENTAL STAGE?

Some argue that there is a developmental stage in the sense that children move onto a radically different level of understanding at about 4 years of age once they acquire the principles for explaining and predicting other people's behaviour (e.g. Gopnik, 1993; Perner, 1991; but see the later section 'Signs of competence during infancy'). This fits neatly with the notion that competent children's understanding of the mind has the properties of a theory: some of the theoretical leaps in natural science are sudden. For example, the important parts of Einstein's theory of relativity are radically different from the theories and understanding that existed before. His contribution to theoretical physics was not of an incremental nature. Theoretical revolutions are a hallmark of scientific development, so it would be fitting if children's understanding of the mind were acquired in a kind of intellectual revolution. The apparently sudden emergence of children's correct judgments of false belief is consistent with such a possibility. (Chapters 1 and 2 discuss the differences between *stage-like* (qualitative), versus gradual (quantitative) *changes in development*).

The case for gradual change

Perhaps we should not be so hasty in ruling out the possibility of gradual development in acquiring an understanding of the mind. I shall now summarise evidence which suggests that children younger than 4 years might be capable of acknowledging false belief and also that sometimes older individuals, including adults, make systematic errors when trying to infer what another person is thinking. Success will thus be seen to depend not on the underlying competence of the participant, but on the demands placed on the participant's performance by the challenges presented by the particular task in question. Here, the assumption is that gradual changes that occur with development improve the probability that the child will give a correct judgement, but this will also depend on task demands.

Do children suddenly begin giving correct judgements of false belief?

When performing on a test of false belief (as with many of Piaget's tests of cognitive development, see Chapters 9 and 16) you can either answer correctly or incorrectly. The test is incapable of detecting degrees of performance that fall somewhere in between. For this reason, if development were gradual, the test of false belief would nonetheless make it appear as though development occurred in stages. Instead of focusing on whether the child passes or fails a test of false belief, we should enquire instead about the *probability* of the child passing at any given time. It might become apparent that the probability of a child answering correctly increases gradually between 3 and 5 years of age. And yet had we simply taken a snapshot of their erroneous performance in a single or small number of tests, we could easily be fooled into thinking that the child has not yet acquired the concept of mind. If development is gradual, conversely, we would expect there to be many instances where a child passes one test of false belief but fails another. What do the data tell us?

Even data reported by Gopnik and Astington (1988), which were presented as offering support for a stage-like shift in children's understanding, actually suggest that children are variable in their performance at about 4 years of age. Although children who passed one test of false belief tended also to pass another, there were very many instances of children passing one but failing the other. Moreover, giving a correct judgement in a test of false belief does not guarantee future success (Mayes *et al.*, 1996). Indeed, longitudinal studies indicate that the number of false belief tests that a child is likely to pass increases very gradually with age (Amsterlaw & Wellman, 2006; Flynn *et al.*, 2004).

This finding points to the possibility that 3-year-old children are capable of the same kind of processing as older children when it comes to working out what other people might be thinking, but tend to make errors in performance of the task. Hence, we need to recognise the distinction between **performance** and **competence** when interpreting errors made by children. If younger children engaged in the same kind of processing then a clue to this effect might be apparent in how long they take to respond to the question about another person's belief. Kikuno *et al.* (2007) found that children aged 3 and 4 years of age tended to take longer to answer questions about another person's false belief than they took to answer questions about the true state of reality. This is not surprising in that reporting the true state of

performance limitations limitations that are associated with the challenges presented by the task being asked, so that their performance may not reflect their underlying competence.

competence the child's underlying ability, which is often not reflected in their *performance* on tasks.

reality merely requires the child to recall information, whereas reporting what another person believes requires the child to work something out. Apparently, the children had not worked out what the protagonist was thinking automatically and only began to do that when prompted by the test question – hence the additional time they took to respond compared with when asked the question about the true state of reality.

Importantly, Kikuno *et al.* (2007) found that children took as long to reply to a question about the protagonist's belief whether their answer was correct or incorrect. This would be difficult to explain if, like Wimmer and Hartl (1991), we assumed that young children treated a question about belief as if it were a question about reality. Had that been the case then those who answered wrongly should have responded quickly; but they did not. Rather, the findings are more consistent with the possibility that children engaged in the same kind of processing irrespective of whether they got the answer right or wrong; seemingly, the younger children differed from older ones not in their level of competence but in being more prone to errors in performance.

It is very difficult to square all these findings with the claim that children undergo a radical conceptual shift that equips them to give correct judgments of false belief. Instead, it seems that whether or not children answer correctly can be described in terms of an age-related probability. What factors might determine whether children answer correctly?

Understanding the question asked

An obvious contender is the wording of the question. Lewis and Osborne (1990) suggested that whilst children aged 3 and 4 years might not differ from each other in how they understand the mind, they might differ drastically in how they interpret questions. In particular, the younger children might not be clear on the point in time that the question refers to. They might think that the experimenter is asking, 'What did you think was inside *after* we had opened the lid and showed you the pencil?' Lewis and Osborne offered clarification by explicitly asking children what they 'thought was inside before we opened the lid'. In this condition, significantly more children aged 3 gave a correct judgement compared with those asked a question of the kind used in previous research. Errors were not eradicated, but the modified question gave children a better chance of answering correctly.

Similarly, Siegal and Beattie (1991) modified Wimmer and Perner's (1983) question from the temporally ambiguous 'Where will Maxi look . . . ?' to: 'Where will Maxi look . . . *first of all*?' As in Lewis and Osborne (1990), children had a better chance of answering the question correctly with the new wording. Both Lewis and Osborne, and Siegal and Beattie, concluded that children's errors stemmed from difficulty comprehending the question rather than a deep seated conceptual deficit.

The state change test

Although misunderstanding the question seems to account for some of the errors children make, a study by Wimmer and Hartl (1991) suggest it is not the only important factor. They devised a new test they called the **state change test**, which is similar to a deceptive box test, and is shown in Figure 11.4. The child sees a tube of sweets/candy and guesses that it contains sweets when prompted to do so. The experimenter opens the tube to reveal that it does indeed contain sweets, but as the child watches, the experimenter empties the tube and replaces the sweets/candy with a pencil. He or she closes the lid and then asks the standard question, 'When you first saw the box, before we opened it, what did you think was inside?' In a sample of children aged 3 and 4 years, over 80 per cent gave a correct judgement of 'sweets'. In sharp contrast, only about 40 per cent of the same sample gave a correct judgement in a deceptive box task (see Figure 11.3), in which the tube

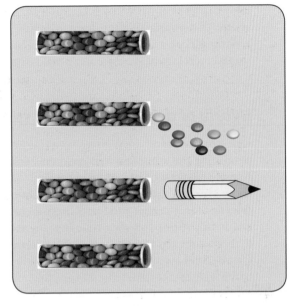

FIGURE 11.4 *The state change test of true belief. The sweets/candy tube initially contains sweets/candy, but these are replaced with a pencil as the child watches.*

contained a pencil from the beginning. In short, replacing the sweets with pencils as the child watched had a massive impact in helping them to answer correctly. Why?

One thing we know for sure is that it had nothing to do with the wording of the question. After all, the question was worded exactly the same in the deceptive box and the state change tests. Indeed, we might have predicted that children would give an incorrect answer in both tasks if they both contained the same vague question. Children's success in state change suggests that their problem does not lie entirely with the ambiguous temporal specification of the question. What enabled them to give a correct answer in state change?

Wimmer and Hartl (1991) offered an ingenious explanation, though further research has since proved this wrong also, as we shall see later. They quite plausibly suggested that any child who did not have a concept of the mind necessarily would not understand words that related to this concept – words such as *think*. As we know, failure to comprehend words seldom renders children mute! So how would they answer the question about what they used to think was inside the sweets/candies tube? According to Wimmer and Hartl, the simplest explanation is that children answer as if the word *think* had not been included in the question. Hence, 'What did you think was inside . . .?' would be interpreted as 'What was inside . . .?' The correct answer to the latter question is 'sweets' in the state change and 'Pencil' in the deceptive box, which is precisely how most younger children did answer. The authors suggested that when children acquire the concept of minds at about age 4, they are then equipped to understand the adult meaning of

state change test the child sees a tube or box of sweets/candy and the sweets/candies are removed and replaced by a pencil. The box is then closed again. The question asked is, 'When you first saw the box, before we opened it, what did you think was inside?' A large percentage of 3–4-year-old children give the correct response of sweets.

the word *think* and thereby successfully acknowledge false belief. Wimmer and Hartl accept that young children have a linguistic problem, but insist that this is merely a symptom of a deeper conceptual deficit. To understand development, our focus should therefore be on the conceptual rather than on the linguistic or conversational.

Hybrid of deceptive box and state change tests

Despite the elegance of Wimmer and Hartl's (1991) argument, and despite their success in refuting the argument that children's failure is explained by their non-comprehension of the question, subsequent research has proved Wimmer and Hartl to be wrong about children's lack of understanding about beliefs (Saltmarsh *et al.*, 1995). The fatal evidence for Wimmer and Hartl's argument followed the creation of a *hybrid* based on the deceptive box and state change tests, as shown in Figure 11.5. The sweets/candies tube was opened to reveal an atypical item (toothbrush) which was then exchanged for a second atypical item (pencil) as the child watched. As in the state change test, items were swapped in front of the child, but as in the deceptive box test, the sweets/candies tube never contained sweets. When asked 'When you first saw the box what was inside?', nearly all answered correctly by reporting the first content (toothbrush) but when asked 'When you first saw the box what did you think was inside?' most reported the current content (pencil). Hence, children who were unable to give a correct judgement of their own false belief (presumably, they originally thought the box contained sweets) were drawn to the current content and were not answering the question as if they had been asked 'What was inside?' This very clear finding unequivocally refutes Wimmer and Hartl, who would have predicted that children aged about 3 years would have given the same answer, irrespective of whether the question did or did not contain the word *think*. Granted, maybe those authors were correct to argue that children's difficulty cannot be explained purely as a misinterpretation of the question, for the reasons already stated, but seemingly they are not correct in saying that a deep seated conceptual deficit causes them to ignore the word *think*.

We are left trying to explain why young children easily give a correct judgement in Wimmer and Hartl's (1991) state change task. Perhaps it is not preposterous after all to suggest that children answer correctly for the correct reason. Perhaps they do understand both the word and the concept *think*, and a feature of the state change helps them to tune in to

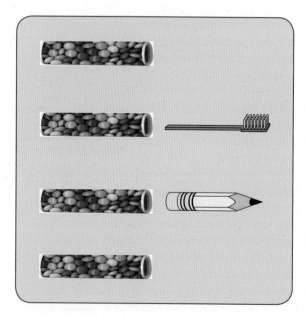

FIGURE 11.5 *Hybrid of deceptive box and state change tests.*

that concept. A conspicuous feature of the task is that children's initial belief that the tube contains sweets/candies is proved correct according to the physical evidence before their eyes on opening the tube. If a belief were supported with hard evidence, as in the state change test, perhaps it would be easier to acknowledge. In that case, can children be helped to acknowledge a *false belief* by endorsing that belief with a counterpart in reality?

The posting version of the deceptive box test

A task schematised in Figure 11.6 yielded evidence which suggests that children can indeed be helped to acknowledge false belief so long as that belief has a tangible counterpart. Children were asked to post a picture of what they thought a sweets tube contained when it was first introduced to them: the **posting version of the deceptive box test** (Mitchell & Lacohee, 1991). Children dutifully selected a picture of sweets/candies and placed it in a post box where it remained out of sight until the end of the procedure. The experimenter revealed the pencil in the tube and then closed the lid with the pencil still inside. Finally, the experimenter asked, 'When you posted your picture, what did you think was inside?' Under this condition, many more children correctly

FIGURE 11.6 *The posting version of the deceptive box task.*

acknowledged their prior false belief (sweets) compared with children who participated in a standard deceptive box procedure.

posting version of the deceptive box test a version of the *deceptive box task* where the child posts an illustration of what they think is in a box.

Did children in the posting task give correct judgements for the wrong reason (i.e. they might have thought they were being asked what was in the picture they posted, which of course was a picture of sweets/candies)? This seems unlikely when considering the results of a control condition, in which children posted a picture of their favourite cartoon character (e.g. Mickey Mouse) instead of the sweets/candies. If the children in the sweets posting condition answered 'sweets' because they wrongly thought they were being asked about the picture in the post box, then a tell-tale sign from the children in the cartoon posting condition – the control group – would be to answer 'Mickey Mouse', but none did so.

The results of the posting version of the deceptive box task suggest that children below age 4 might possess the concept of belief but have difficulty using it. What changes with age, seemingly, is the ease with which they can utilise their understanding.

SIGNS OF COMPETENCE DURING INFANCY: CAN INFANTS UNDERSTAND FALSE BELIEF?

The evidence seems to suggest that performance factors might mask early signs of competence in very young children's understanding of other people's minds. Specifically, it seems that whilst children below 3 years understand that minds hold beliefs about the world, amongst other things, they do not always demonstrate this level of competence under certain test conditions, perhaps because they have to remember too much of the information in the stories that are typically used. But if very young children really are competent, at least it should be possible to identify *some* conditions where this becomes apparent. Indeed, we might even expect to see signs of competence during infancy.

In support of this possibility, Onishi and Baillargeon (2005) found that children as young as 15 months showed signs of understanding false belief in a preferential looking procedure involving **violation of expectation** (**VoE**) (for a fuller account of VoE experiments see Chapter 5). The infants watched an actor hide a toy in one of two locations. Subsequently, a change occurred which resulted in the actor holding either a true or false belief about the location. Where would infants expect the actor to search for the object – in the place they knew the object was really located or in the location that the actor believes that the object is located? Although it was unrealistic to expect to gauge infants' understanding from their replies to verbally posed questions, it was nevertheless possible to evaluate understanding from their eye movements. If infants expected the actor to search based on their (the actor's) belief then infants should look longer when that expectation was violated, irrespective of whether the actor holds a true or false belief. Onishi and Baillargeon found that infants did indeed look longer when the expectation was violated. Hence, the infants seemed to be 'surprised' that the actor looked in the object's actual location in a circumstance where this should not have been possible because the actor harboured a false belief.

Further evidence that infants may be able to understand others' false beliefs is from a study by Buttelmann *et al.* (2009). In this study 18-month-olds were shown two boxes, each of which could be locked by putting a wooden pin into a hole in the front. There were two experimenters present, one female, E1 and one male, E2. The infants were shown how to lock and unlock the boxes and E2 played excitedly with a toy caterpillar which he then put into one of the boxes. The infants were then tested in one of two conditions: in the 'false belief' condition E2 made an excuse and left the room; while he was away E1 moved the caterpillar into the other box: in the other, 'true belief' condition, E1 also moved the caterpillar into the other box, but she did so while E1 was watching. In both conditions the boxes were then locked. Thus, in the 'false belief' condition E2 did not know that the caterpillar was in the other box, whereas in the 'true belief' condition he did. In both conditions (and in the 'false belief' condition after E2 had re-entered the room) E2 attempted to open the box where the caterpillar had originally been put, but appeared to fail, and asked the infants to help. The infants quickly chose a box, removed the pin, and opened the lid, but the box they opened was different in the two conditions! In the 'false belief' condition they assumed that the adult wanted to retrieve the caterpillar, so they opened the box where the toy was now located, but in the true belief condition they opened the box where the toy had originally been put, but was no longer located: that is, in this condition, because they knew that E2 had seen the location switch they assumed that he wanted to open that box for some reason other than to retrieve the caterpillar.

Buttelmann *et al.* concluded that 'These results represent by far the youngest age of false belief understanding in a task with an active behavioural measure' (2009, p. 337), and are a further illustration of a point that has been made both in this and other chapters, which is that infants' and children's *competence* can often be underestimated by measures of their *performance* when the latter makes too many demands on their abilities.

ADULTS' DIFFICULTY WITH FALSE BELIEFS

If the explanation for developmental change lies with *performance factors* rather than changing levels of *competence*, then sometimes we could expect to see older participants – even adults – systematically reporting their own knowledge when trying to diagnose another person's beliefs under certain conditions of performance. Surprisingly, evidence that adults sometimes have difficulty acknowledging false belief has been around for more than 30 years, but the full significance of the findings has only been recognised recently. The evidence is a phenomenon known as **hindsight bias**, which can be defined as 'the inclination to see events that have occurred as more predictable than they would have been before they actually took place'. In a classic study, Fischhoff (1975) told adult participants about a historical battle between British and Ghurkha armies that took place a couple of centuries ago. The participants heard about various factors that might advantage one or another army. For example, the British were well disciplined, well organised, had excellent equipment, and good logistics. On the other hand, the Ghurkhas knew the terrain intimately, had numerical superiority, and were renowned for their bravery and courage. The participants had to weigh up the advantages that favoured each army and then make a judgement on who they thought would have the best chance of winning. Incidentally, the participants were also told of the actual 'outcome' but were instructed to put that information out of their minds when arriving at a judgement. Despite the instruction, it became apparent that the participants were being heavily influenced by what they were led to believe was the true outcome. Those told that the British actually won tended to judge on balance that they thought the British had the best chance. Those told that the Ghurkhas actually won tended to judge that the Ghurkhas had the best chance.

hindsight bias the inclination to see events that have already happened as being more predictable than they were before they took place.

Although Fischhoff (1975) called this striking phenomenon *hindsight*, it was actually something more general. Indeed, it seems to be an example of systematic bias intruding on adults' judgements of beliefs. This became apparent in another part of Fischhoff's study in which the adult participants had to judge not who *they* thought would win, but what another group of people would think who were told everything except the actual outcome. Participants advised that the British actually won judged that the other group would favour the British, while participants advised that the Ghurkhas actually won judged that the other people would favour the Ghurkhas.

A subsequent study supports this interpretation (Mitchell *et al.*, 1996). Participants watched a video about a couple of protagonists, Kevin and Rebecca, set in their kitchen, which is schematised in Figure 11.7. There was a conspicuous jug on the

FIGURE 11.7 *The story about Kevin and Rebecca, designed to reveal adults' difficulties with false belief.*

shelf and Kevin noticed that it contained orange juice. Later that day, Kevin and Rebecca were together in their kitchen making lunch, when Kevin volunteered to prepare something to drink. Rebecca then announced that there is milk in the jug. At this point Kevin was the victim of conflicting information. He had previously seen orange juice in the jug but was told subsequently that it contained milk. The observing participants were invited to judge what Kevin now thought was inside the jug. Obviously, there is no way of determining the right answer. Although we might suppose that people believe what they see in preference to what they are told, this was a special circumstance. Rebecca's utterance was the most recent information, so it is possible that although the jug used to contain juice in the past, it now contains milk.

Half the participants heard only the information just presented while the rest were told additionally that Rebecca had poured out the juice and replaced it with milk. Effectively, half were told that Rebecca's utterance was true. However, it was made abundantly clear to the participants that this was privileged information, available only to them and not to Kevin the protagonist. Despite that edict, participants simply could not help but be influenced by their knowledge of the true content of the jug. Nearly all those told that there was really milk in the jug judged that he would believe the jug contained milk. In contrast, those given no additional information usually judged that Kevin would believe the jug contained juice, in accordance with what he had seen. In other words, their judgement of the believability of Rebecca's utterance was massively influenced by whether *they* knew it was true. It seems the participants were inclined to report what they assumed to be the actual current content of the jug when asked about Kevin's belief. In this respect, they bear a remarkable resemblance to children aged 3 years!

Converging evidence from Keysar *et al.* (2003) arose in a task where adult participants took turns as a 'speaker' in describing objects in an array to another participant, the 'listener'. Although the listener participants could see all objects in the array, some objects were hidden from the speaker. For example, there were two jars, and while the listener could see both, the speaker could only see one. The listener's task was to retrieve any object that the speaker intended and mistakes were surprisingly common, where listeners sometimes selected one of the jars that the speaker *could not see*. The listeners were fully informed about what the speaker could and could not see, but they sometimes lapsed by not taking this information into consideration when interpreting the speaker's message.

Apart from demonstrating a rather surprising lack of perspective-taking in adults, Keysar *et al.*'s study also raises the possibility that people do not automatically attune to other people's beliefs. Such a possibility was investigated by Apperly *et al.* (2006), who measured response times. The findings showed that participants took longer to respond to a question about a protagonist's false belief than they took to respond to a question about the true state of reality (cf. Kikuno *et al.*, 2007). It was not that making any judgement about belief necessarily takes longer, for participants were fast at making a judgement about belief when primed from the outset to think about the protagonist's belief. Hence, it seems that while participants could easily work out what a protagonist was thinking, this is something that they did not do automatically.

FACTORS THAT INFLUENCE DEVELOPMENT

Nature versus nurture

When making judgements about beliefs, we need to resist the lure of current reality and we must not fall victim to the hindsight bias, sometimes referred to as the 'curse of knowledge' (Birch & Bloom, 2007). Although the ability to do this is not all or nothing, success is more common among older than younger participants. Is age the only factor that determines success? If it were, then it would be a fair bet that development is an inevitable and predetermined **maturational unfolding** Another possibility, though, is that development is greatly influenced by social experience. How can we decide between these two possibilities? If social experience were an important influence, we would expect to find different rates of development depending on the particular milieu the child inhabited. The environment varies between families within a given society, and also between the cultures of different societies. Perhaps we should begin by asking whether the developmental trend seen in Western societies occurs in

hunter–gatherer tribe
a tribe of people who live in the traditional fashion of hunting and gathering. In such tribes, it is typical that the individual members will live in small communities and they depend upon one another for survival.

non-industrialised cultures. To address the question, Avis and Harris (1991) trekked out to the rain forest of the Cameroon and visited a traditional **hunter–gatherer tribe**. Participants were recruited from the tribe and cajoled into enacting a version of the unexpected transfer test. An older boy from the tribe volunteered to act as a confederate and cooked some mango in a pot as requested. While the fruit was cooking, he left the hut to have a chat with friends. In his absence, the observing child participant was assisted to empty the mango from the pot and put it in a jar. Subsequently, the older boy was returning to

eat the mango and at this point the observing young child was asked to predict where the older boy would look for his mango. Older members of the sample predicted that he would look in the place he last saw his mango (the pot) while younger children predicted that he would look in the place they themselves knew it was hidden, namely the jar. In other words, the younger children failed to acknowledge false belief. What was the specific age-trend? There were no accurate records of the date of birth of the participants, so their parents were asked to make their best estimate. The findings were approximately consistent with those reported in studies involving children from Western cultures. Children aged around 3 years tended to report current reality, while those aged around 5 years successfully acknowledged another person's false belief.

Nevertheless, it seems that more subtle differences in how people understand others' minds can vary between cultures. In a task based on Kevin's belief about whether a jug contained juice or milk (Mitchell *et al.*, 1996), participants from a **collectivistic** subculture judged that Kevin would believe what he was told by Rebecca irrespective of whether or not the participants had privileged information saying that Rebecca's utterance was true (Mitchell *et al.*, 2007). These participants also scored more highly than participants from **individualistic** subcultures in an independent measure of their tendency to trust other people. A collectivistic subculture stresses conformity, reliability and the importance of the collective, while an individualistic subculture stresses the importance of individuality and uniqueness. Interestingly, then, it seems that cultural values can impact upon one's level of trust in others which in turn perhaps impacts on how one evaluates what other people are thinking.

Are we equipped with a dedicated module in the brain for understanding other minds?

Fodor (1992) proposed a **modularity** view that we are born with a module for understanding minds and that such a module is active from the very beginning of life. The module supposedly undergoes refinement at about the age of 4 years, which allows children to pass a standard test of false belief. However, Fodor suggests that the module is demonstrably active at a younger age in tasks that have a different form from the standard test of false belief, although supporting evidence for his specific predictions is somewhat scant.

> **modularity** the view that we have separate modules for different abilities, e.g. face perception, understanding minds, numerical abilities.

Perhaps the most compelling case for modularity in understanding the mind is made by Leslie and Thaiss (1992). They borrowed a procedure called the false photo test developed by Zaitchik (1990) in the days before digital cameras became commonplace. The test is modelled on Wimmer and Perner's (1983) unexpected transfer test, except that children are not asked about Maxi's outdated belief; instead, they are asked about the outdated image in a photograph. In Scene 1, a doll sat on a box and the participant took a photo. Then, in Scene 2, the doll moved to the mat. Finally, participants were asked to anticipate which of the scenes would emerge in the developing photo.

Leslie and Thaiss (1992) presented the false photo test and also a standard false belief task to normally developing children and to children with autism. Of the normally developing children, those aged about 3 years tended to fail both tests, while older children tended to pass both. In sharp contrast, all individuals with autism *passed* the false photo test but a large majority *failed* the false belief test (see the 'Autism' section later in this chapter). Leslie and Thaiss concluded that children with autism lack the brain module needed for making judgements about beliefs, which is the reason why they specifically failed the test of false belief, but understand pictorial representation and so pass the false photo test. They suggested that normally developing young children, in contrast, possess the relevant module but at 3 years of age are yet to acquire the general processing skills to give a correct judgement in any task that has the form of a test of false belief. In other words, the reason they fail a test of false belief is not because it has mind-related content but because the form of the problem makes demands on processing that are beyond the performance abilities of a typical 3-year-old.

Another study converges with Leslie and Thaiss (1992) in suggesting that children have difficulty with the form of the task, even if it does not have mind-related content (Riggs *et al.*, 1998). Children were presented with an unexpected transfer task featuring

Maxi in his quest to find chocolate. In the story, Mum absent-mindedly puts the chocolate into a different place after grating some of it into a cake that she is making. In a novel condition participants were asked a counterfactual question: 'If Mum had not baked a cake, where would the chocolate be now?' Children who failed to reason counter to fact (they pointed to the current location of the chocolate) were nearly always the same children who failed to acknowledge Maxi's false belief. Conversely, children who succeeded in reasoning counter to fact were nearly always the same who succeeded in acknowledging Maxi's false belief. So long as children could acknowledge a counterfactual state, they had no further difficulty in identifying this as a false belief held by another person.

At the very least, the evidence suggests that whether or not children succeed in acknowledging false belief depends on more than the activity of a special brain module dedicated to the task. In the studies by Riggs *et al.* (1998) and Leslie and Thaiss (1992), children's difficulty in acknowledging false belief seems best explained by the general processing demands posed by the task. However, children with autism might have a more specific difficulty with false belief that is associated with their difficulty in connecting with other people. Children with autism and young children with typical development might thus fail tests of false belief for different reasons.

Perhaps the main problem with a modularity account is that it implies that calculating what other people think is something that we do automatically, but as we have already learned from research by Apperly *et al.* (2006), this seems not to be the case. Besides, cultural variation in understanding the mind (Mitchell *et al.*, 2007) is not easy to explain within a modularity account, because such an account would predict similar age-related developmental trends across cultures.

The role of the family: Siblings

If there are cultural variations in understanding minds, it would not be surprising if variations in development were also apparent within a culture but across different kinds of family. A variable of particular interest is the size of the family and especially how many siblings the child has. There are some reasons for thinking that having lots of siblings would be an advantage, but other reasons for thinking it would be an impediment! A child with many siblings would encounter the potentially beneficial experience of exposure to other points of view. Perhaps siblings typically assert their point of view in a somewhat unyielding manner. Obviously, this might be a socially uncomfortable or even annoying experience, but it could have cognitively beneficial spin-offs in terms of becoming better acquainted with other minds.

As mentioned, though, there are different reasons for supposing that having lots of siblings could be seen as a disadvantage. Perhaps children become attuned to other minds not through the experience of a clash of perspectives with siblings but by being informally tutored about the mind by wiser individuals, especially the parents. Perhaps children gain most benefit from having psychological states explained to them. For example: 'John isn't going out to play because he can't find his ball. He thought he put it in the garage but it isn't there.' In a family with lots of children, the potentially beneficial adult input would have to be divided, with the consequence that each child would not be receiving the optimum level of tutoring about the mind. A parallel can be drawn with the development of children's general intellectual abilities. Zajonc (1983) reported that the number of siblings correlates negatively with the child's **intelligence quotient** *(IQ)* score, as does birth order. The singleton tends to have higher IQ than the child with several siblings; the child who is first born tends to have higher IQ than the second born, who in turn has higher IQ than the third born, and so on. Note that these birth order IQ differences are very small, so if you have several younger brothers and sisters don't assume you're the brightest! Zajonc suggested that intellectual development depends partly on beneficial parental input, which becomes diluted as the family grows, and this is measurable as an adverse effect on the IQ scores of later-born children.

Perner *et al.* (1994) collected the relevant evidence and found that children aged 3 years who had siblings were more likely to pass a test of false

FIGURE 11.8 *Children with siblings are likely to have a more advanced theory of mind than only children.*
Source: Shutterstock.

belief than those of the same age but without siblings. Moreover, those with several siblings stood a better chance of giving a correct judgement than those with just one or two siblings (Figure 11.8). A study by Jenkins and Astington (1996) clarified things further. The apparently beneficial effect of having siblings was confined to those with older siblings. Children who only had younger siblings were no better in acknowledging false belief than those with none at all, while those with older siblings did show the kind of advantage reported by Perner *et al.*

Just because having siblings correlates with success in acknowledging false belief, this need not imply that the experience of interacting with siblings promotes an understanding of the mind. Perhaps the presence of siblings coincides with another as yet unspecified variable, and perhaps it is this that is crucial to development. Lewis, Freeman, Kyriakidou, Maridaki-Kassotaki and Berridge (1996) investigated such a possibility in a **cross-cultural study** that included Greek families. They recorded a wide range of variables concerning family structure, in addition to the number of siblings a child had. Lewis *et al.* confirmed that children with siblings were at an advantage in acknowledging false belief compared to those without. They also established that the advantage was stronger among those with older siblings than those with younger ones. The most

cross-cultural study a study which aims to examine differences that arise purely from culture.

important discovery, though, was that another social factor was even more strongly related with children's success in acknowledging false belief. Large families with many children also tended to be extended rather than nuclear. Consequently, there were numerous opportunities for adults to interact with the children, and indeed this was the best predictor of whether or not a child would succeed in acknowledging false belief. These findings give a hint to the effect that children are helped to acknowledge false belief if adults informally and perhaps even unwittingly offer tutoring on the characteristics of the mind.

The role of the family: Adults

Valuable as they are, the findings from Lewis *et al.* (1996) do not tell us exactly what features of adult input are beneficial. Much of the relevant information can be found in a study by Dunn *et al.* (1991). They observed individual differences in how mothers interacted with their toddlers aged 33 months. Some provided a narrative on the actions of people or on the characters in pretend scenarios that was embroidered with abundant references to psychological motives. For example, they might comment that Jane is looking in her toy box for her teddy bear because she thinks it is there and that she did not see her older brother put it behind the settee. Other mothers would give commentary on Jane's behaviour but without making reference to what Jane might be thinking. Hence, children of these parents did not hear much in the way of psychological explanations of human behaviour. Six months later, Dunn *et al.* tested the children for their ability to acknowledge false beliefs. The children who were *successful* tended to have parents who, six months previously, had been observed to give explanations of behaviour with reference to psychological states. We might say that these parents were 'mind minded' (see Chapter 6). The children who were *unsuccessful* tended to have parents who had seldom referred to psychological states.

In sum, the findings reported by Lewis *et al.* (1996) suggest that the correlation between having siblings and successfully acknowledging false belief could be coincidental to variations in adult input. The study by Dunn *et al.* effectively identifies the aspects of adult input which are likely to be especially beneficial. It raises the possibility that toddlers gain a great deal from verbal explanations in psychological terms by mind minded parents of why people behave as they do.

The characteristics of the child

Because the social environment appears to influence development in the ability to acknowledge beliefs, it does not follow that the intrinsic characteristics of the child are unimportant. The characteristics of the environment and the characteristics of the child probably interact in complex ways with respect to the influence they have on development. Indeed, the characteristics of the child are likely to shape the way people respond to them, which in turn will impact upon the extent to which social input is beneficial. Offering explanations to a child who has a fractious temperament might present a much greater challenge than offering explanations to one who has a calmer disposition. Notably, one characteristic within the child stands out above all others: **autism**. As we shall see in the next section, having autism seriously constrains the child's developing ability to understand other people's minds.

AUTISM

General aspects of autism are covered elsewhere in this book (see especially Chapter 21, which discusses several possible causes of the disorder). In the current chapter the aim is to examine the possibility that individuals with autism are lacking an understanding of the mind. Wing and Gould (1979) characterised autism as a triad of impairments (**Wing's triad of impairments**): social behaviour, communication and imagination.

Wing's triad of impairments impairments of (1) social relationships, (2) communication, and (3) imagination characteristic of *autistic* behaviour.

Lack of imagination

The lack of imagination is manifest in many ways but notably as impairment in the capacity to engage in pretend play (Figure 11.9). Leslie (1987) suggested that the kind of mental processing required for pretence is the same as that needed to understand states of belief. He suggests that the kind of disengagement from current reality that you need in order to acknowledge a false belief is precisely the same kind of disengagement you exhibit when indulging in pretend play. A person who did not have the ability to disengage from reality in pretence probably would not be able to disengage from reality in order to acknowledge a false belief. The finding that individuals with autism are impaired in pretence is in itself a striking clue to the possibility that they might be unable to attune to other minds.

Socialisation and communication deficits

Impairments in socialisation and communication also point to an underlying deficiency in understanding other minds. Without an understanding of the mind, an individual would perpetually be in danger of misjudging social

FIGURE 11.9 *Children engaging in pretend play. This ability is impaired in autistic children.*
Source: Shutterstock.

situations, of acting in an inappropriate way and of saying inappropriate things. Social skill depends on being able to diagnose other people's sensitivities, attitudes, and knowledge. Hence, difficulty in understanding the mind could present itself in the triad of impairments identified by Wing and Gould (1979), and these impairments are typically seen as defining of autism. In short, autism could be a manifestation of an impaired understanding of the mind.

Causes of autism

There is a distinct possibility that at least one of the causes of autism has genetic origin (Pickles *et al.*, 2000). Other causes could arise from accidental injury or virus infection. These various factors could lead to an abnormality in the brain that forms the neurological seat of autism.

Failure to understand the mind

There are reasons for thinking that children with autism might be delayed in developing an understanding of the mind. What does the evidence tell us? Baron-Cohen, Leslie and Frith (1985) sought an answer by presenting an unexpected transfer test of false belief to a group of 20 participants with autism, and found that 15 judged wrongly by reporting their own knowledge of the whereabouts of the item. Obviously, this result would only be noteworthy if the participants had a mental age above 4 years. We already know that normally developing individuals with a **chronological age** (and by implication a **mental age**) below 4 years tend to fail standard tests of false belief, so to find the same in young children with autism would be no surprise. Baron-Cohen *et al.* were thus careful to test their participants for mental age and discovered that even some members of the sample in their teens who had a verbal mental age well above 4 years failed to acknowledge false belief.

Down's syndrome (DS) a chromosomal condition caused by the presence of all or part of an extra 21st *chromosome*. Often Down's syndrome is associated with some impairment of cognitive ability and physical growth, and a particular set of facial characteristics.

Still, we should question whether the failure to acknowledge false belief is due to the autism or due to the associated learning difficulties. Apart from presenting the triad of impairments, many individuals with autism also have learning disabilities and this alone could account for their difficulty acknowledging false belief. Baron-Cohen *et al.* (1985) figured that if learning disabilities alone were sufficient for errors in acknowledging false belief, then children with **Down's syndrome (DS)** would also have problems. Accordingly, they tested individuals with DS who had a very similar intellectual profile to the autistic sample. In contrast to those with autism, however, most children with DS passed the test of false belief. The difficulty in acknowledging false belief therefore seemed to arise from autism rather than any associated learning disabilities. Some studies have required the participant to listen to a story and then answer questions at the end, while some have involved them directly, as in the deceptive box task (Perner *et al.*, 1989). The findings are largely consistent, suggesting that difficulty in acknowledging false belief is not confined to any particular version of the standard test for children with autism.

We are left with the impression that autism might be associated with a failure to understand the mind, which is measurable as failure to acknowledge false belief. However, what of the minority of individuals with autism who give a correct judgement of false belief? Is it possible that their success is a fluke or that they have been wrongly diagnosed? It seems to be no fluke, because some individuals with autism who pass a test of false belief do so reliably and repeatedly. Neither are there grounds for thinking they are all wrongly diagnosed. Baron-Cohen (1989) suspected that they might still have a subtle impairment that could be revealed by a more sophisticated test of understanding the mind. Instead of testing participants for their understanding of what a person thinks about an aspect of reality, he tested understanding of what a person thinks *another* person thinks about an aspect of reality – a more complex level of reasoning known as 'second order' belief attribution. Instead of asking where John thinks *his* chocolate is, Baron-Cohen asked where John thinks *Mary* thinks the chocolate is. Individuals with autism who passed a simple test of false belief failed this more complex test. As before, their poor performance was not commensurate with their relatively high verbal mental age. However, Bowler (1992) found that members of a sample of high functioning adults with autism reliably passed this sophisticated test of belief. Despite that, these individuals still presented the defining features of autism. Their ability to process simple and complex beliefs did not relieve them of the symptoms of autism. Consequently, it is invalid to argue that autism is the product of a failure to understand the mind as defined by an inability to acknowledge beliefs. Nonetheless, individuals with autism are likely to be developmentally delayed. Verbal mental age is a good predictor of whether or not a person with autism will succeed in acknowledging false belief, but it seems that verbal mental age has to be substantially higher in autism than in typically developing children (Happé, 1995). Whereas a verbal mental age of around 4 years is common for the onset of success in a standard test of false belief in typical development, it seems a minimal verbal mental age of 7 years is more often required in autistic development.

In order to pursue the 'theory of mind hypothesis of autism', Baron-Cohen *et al.* (1997) devised a new test based on the assumption that people with autism have difficulty understanding others, specifically because they are impaired in reading clues from others' eyes that disclose what they are thinking. To investigate this possibility, Back *et al.* (2007) presented participants with animated faces that displayed different emotional expressions, such as *surprised, don't trust* and *deciding*. Digital editing allowed freezing of the eyes so that no information was conveyed by this part of the face. Under that condition, very high functioning teenagers and adults with autism had less success in diagnosing the mental state being displayed than when information was conveyed by the eyes. Evidently, participants' success in the 'non-frozen' condition depended at least partly on participants being able to read information from the eyes, a finding that raises doubts over Baron-Cohen *et al.*'s account of impaired theory of mind in autism.

SUMMARY AND CONCLUSIONS

Researchers have devised several tests of false belief for assessing development in children's understanding of the mind. Many children below about 4 years of age fail these tests, while older children pass. It is possible that children undergo a gradual change that allows them to disengage from focusing on current reality. Certainly, there is evidence that even infants have a rudimentary understanding of others' minds. Modified tests that direct children away from current reality reveal early competence. On the other hand, even adults might never be fully rid of the allure of current reality and under special circumstances they too are shown systematically to report their *own* belief when trying to diagnose *another person's* belief.

The development in children's ability to acknowledge beliefs can be influenced by factors associated with the social environment, particularly characteristics of the parents' style of interaction with the child. However, the intrinsic characteristics of the child are also relevant and in extreme cases, as in autism, it seems that development is destined to be aberrant. Even so, there is no reason to think that individuals with autism are impervious to a beneficial environment. People with autism undergo developmental change, even if not quite so rapid as in typical development.

DISCUSSION POINTS

1. Why is it important for people to have a theory of mind?
2. Why is an understanding of false belief seen as important in testing children's theory of mind?
3. When do children begin to understand that people hold beliefs?
4. Think about the different tasks used to test children's theory of mind. Which of these, if any, seems to be the best?
5. What sorts of social and cognitive factors affect the development of a theory of mind?
6. Is there a radical (qualitative) conceptual shift in children's thinking around 4 years of age, or is there a gradual (quantitative) change?
7. What is the earliest age that children have been shown to understand false belief?
8. What evidence suggests that adults sometimes have difficulty with theory of mind tasks?

SUGGESTIONS FOR FURTHER READING

Doherty, M.J. (2008). *Theory of mind: How children understand others' thoughts and feelings*. Hove: Psychology Press.

Frith, U. (2008). *Autism: A very short introduction*. Oxford: Oxford University Press.

Mitchell, P. (1997). *Introduction to theory of mind: Children, autism and apes*. London: Arnold.

Mitchell, P., & Riggs, K. (2000). *Children's reasoning and the mind*. Psychology Press.

Mitchell, P., & Ziegler, F. (2007). *Fundamentals of development: The psychology of childhood*. Hove: Psychology Press.

REFERENCES

Amsterlaw, J., & Wellman, H.M. (2006). Theories of mind in transition: A microgenetic study of the development of false belief understanding. *Journal of Cognition and Development, 7*, 139–172.

Apperly, I.A., Simpson, A., Riggs, K.J., Samson, D., & Chiavarino, C. (2006). Is belief reasoning automatic? *Psychological Science, 17*, 841–844.

Avis, J., & Harris, P. (1991). Belief–desire reasoning among Baka children: Evidence for a universal conception of mind. *Child Development, 62*, 460–467.

Back, E., Ropar, D., & Mitchell, P. (2007). Do the eyes have it? Inferring mental states from animated faces in autism. *Child Development, 78*, 397–411.

Baron-Cohen, S. (1989). The autistic child's theory of mind: A case of specific developmental delay. *Journal of Child Psychology and Psychiatry, 30*, 285–297.

Baron-Cohen, S., Jolliffe, T., Mortimore, C., & Robertson, M. (1997). Another advanced test of theory of mind: Evidence from very high functioning adults with autism or Asperger syndrome. *Journal of Child Psychology and Psychiatry and Allied Disciplines, 38*, 813–822.

Baron-Cohen, S., Leslie, A.M., & Frith, U. (1985). Does the autistic child have a 'theory of mind'? *Cognition, 21*, 37–46.

Birch, S.A.J., & Bloom, P. (2007). The curse of knowledge in reasoning about false belief. *Psychological Science, 18*, 382–386.

Bowler, D.M. (1992). 'Theory of mind' in Asperger's syndrome. *Journal of Child Psychology and Psychiatry, 33*, 877–893.

Buttelmann, D., Carpenter, M., & Tomasello, M. (2009). Eighteen-month-old infants show false belief understanding in an active helping paradigm. *Cognition, 112*, 337–342.

Dunn, J., Brown, J., Slomkowski, C., Tesla, C., & Youngblade, L. (1991). Young children's understanding of other people's feelings and beliefs: Individual differences and their antecedents. *Child Development, 62*, 1352–1366.

Fischhoff, B. (1975). Hindsight is not equal to foresight: The effect of outcome knowledge on judgment under uncertainty. *Journal of Experimental Psychology: Human Perception and Performance, 1*, 288–299.

Flynn, E., O'Malley, C., & Wood, D. (2004). A longitudinal, microgenetic study of the emergence of false belief understanding and inhibition skills. *Developmental Science, 7*, 103–115.

Fodor, J.A. (1992). A theory of the child's theory of mind. *Cognition, 44*, 283–296.

Goldman, A.I. (1993). Competing accounts of belief-task performance. *Behavioral and Brain Sciences, 16*, 43–44.

Gopnik, A. (1993). How we know our minds: The illusion of first person knowledge of intentionality. *Behavioral and Brain Sciences, 16*, 1–14.

Gopnik, A., & Astington, J.W. (1988). Children's understanding of representational change, and its relation to the understanding of false belief and the appearance–reality distinction. *Child Development, 59*, 26–37.

Happe, F.G.E. (1995). The role of age and verbal ability in the theory of mind task performance of subjects with autism. *Child Development, 66*, 843–855.

Harris, P.L. (1991). The work of the imagination. In A. Whiten (Ed.) *Natural Theories of Mind* (pp. 283–304). Oxford: Basil Blackwell.

Jenkins, J.M., & Astington, J.W. (1996). Cognitive factors and family structure associated with theory of mind development in young children. *Developmental Psychology, 32*, 70–78.

Keysar, B., Lin, S.H., & Barr, D.J. (2003). Limits on theory of mind use in adults. *Cognition, 89*, 25–41.

Kikuno, H., Mitchell, P., & Ziegler, F. (2007). How do young children process beliefs about beliefs? Evidence from response latency. *Mind & Language, 22*, 297–316.

Leslie, A.M. (1987). Pretense and representation: The origins of 'theory of mind'. *Psychological Review, 94*, 412–426.

Leslie, A.M., & Thaiss, L. (1992). Domain specificity in conceptual development: Neuropsychological evidence from autism. *Cognition, 43*, 225–251.

Lewis, C., & Osborne, A. (1990). Three-year-olds' problems with false belief: Conceptual deficit or linguistic artefact? *Child Development, 61*, 1514–1519.

Lewis, C., Freeman, N.H., Kyriakidou, C., Maridaki-kassotaki K. & Berridge, D. (1996). Social influences on false belief access: Specific sibling influences or general apprenticeship. *Child Development, 67*, 2930–2947.

Mayes, L.C., Klin, A., Tercyak, K.P., Cicchetti, D.V., & Cohen, D.J. (1996). Test–retest reliability of false belief tasks. *Journal of Child Psychology and Psychiatry, 37*, 313–319.

Mitchell, P., & Lacohee, H. (1991). Children's early understanding of false belief. *Cognition, 39*, 107–127.

Mitchell, P., Robinson, E.J., Isaacs, J.E., & Nye, R.M. (1996). Contamination in reasoning about false belief: An instance of realist bias in adults but not children. *Cognition, 59*, 1–21.

Mitchell, P., Souglidou, M., Mills, L., & Ziegler, F. (2007). Seeing is believing: How participants in different subcultures judge people's credulity. *European Journal of Social Psychology, 37*, 573–585.

Onishi, K.H., & Baillargeon, R. (2005). Do 15-month-old infants understand false beliefs? *Science, 308*, 255–258.

Perner, J. (1991). *Understanding the representational mind*. London: MIT Press.

Perner, J., Ruffman, T., & Leekam, S.R. (1994). Theory of mind is contagious: You catch it from your sibs. *Child Development, 65*, 1228–1238.

Perner, J., Frith, U., Leslie, A.M., & Leekam, S.R. (1989). Exploration of the autistic child's theory of mind: Knowledge, belief and communication. *Child Development, 60*, 689–700.

Pickles, A., Starr, E., Kazak, S., Bolton, P., Papanikolaou, K., Bailey, A., *et al.* (2000). Variable expression of the autism broader phenotype: Findings from extended pedigrees. *Journal of Child Psychology and Psychiatry, 41*, 491–502.

Riggs, K.J., Peterson, D.M., Robinson, E.J., Mitchell, P. (1998). Are errors in false belief tasks symptomatic of a broader difficulty with counterfactuality? *Cognitive Development, 13*, 73–90.

Saltmarsh, R., Mitchell, P., & Robinson, E.J. (1995). Realism and children's early grasp of mental representation: Belief-based judgments in the state change task. *Cognition, 57*, 297–325.

Siegal, M., & Beattie, K. (1991). Where to look first for children's knowledge of false beliefs. *Cognition, 38*, 1–12.

Wellman, H.M., Cross, D., & Watson, J. (2001). Meta-analysis of theory-of-mind development: The truth about false belief. *Child Development, 72*, 655–684.

Wimmer, H., & Hartl, M. (1991). Against the Cartesian view on mind: Young children's difficulty with own false beliefs. *British Journal of Developmental Psychology, 9*, 125–138.

Wimmer, H., & Perner, J. (1983). Beliefs about beliefs: Representation and constraining function of wrong beliefs in young children's understanding of deception. *Cognition, 13*, 103–128.

Wing, L., & Gould, J. (1979). Severe impairments of social interaction and associated abnormalities in children: Epidemiology and classification. *Journal of Autism and Developmental Disorders, 9*, 11–29.

Zaitchik, D. (1990). When representations conflict with reality: The preschoolers' problem with false belief and 'false' photographs. *Cognition, 35*, 41–68.

Zajonc, R.B. (1983). Validating the confluence model. *Psychological Bulletin, 93*, 457–480.

12 Reading and Mathematics in Developmental Psychology

PETER BRYANT

KEY TERMS

abstraction principle ● alphabetic script ● cardinality ● conditional spelling rules ● conservation ● cultural tools ● derivational morphemes ● genitive ● habituation ● inflectional morphemes ● innate mechanism ● intelligence quotient (IQ) ● intrasyllabic units ● last-number-counted principle ● letter–sound associations ● mora ● morpheme ● morpho-phonemic ● one-to-one correspondence ● one-to-one principle ● onset ● order irrelevance principle ● ordinality ● orthography ● phoneme ● phonological skills ● procedural skills ● pseudo-word ● rhyme ● rime ● stable order principle ● syllabary ● syllable ● transitive inference ● universal counting principles

CHAPTER OUTLINE

OVERVIEW

Reading and mathematical skills are key aspects of children's development and they attract a great deal of research interest. This chapter describes research on the development of both of these forms of knowledge.

All reading and writing systems were originally devised by people and they differ between cultures. Thus, we can consider them as cultural tools which children usually have to acquire with help from other people. The chapter sets out the difficulties that children encounter when they begin to learn an alphabetic script. One problem is in dividing words into their constituent sounds: there is clear evidence that the ability to do so, called 'phonological awareness', is a key aspect of learning to read. Children are usually aware of relatively large phonological segments such as rimes ('cat' and 'hat' share the same rime) quite some time before they learn to read and write. However, they tend to learn about phonemes (the smallest units of sound that can affect meaning) at around the same time as they begin to read, and there is some evidence that learning to read plays an important role in the development of this phoneme awareness, which in turn helps the children establish the basic grapheme–phoneme associations and thus to understand and use the alphabet. Later on children have to learn more complex spelling rules, such as conditional spelling rules and morphemic spelling rules. The evidence on children's understanding of the split-digraph or silent 'e' conditional rule ('hope' 'plate' and 'bite' are all split digraphs) suggests that, although they are taught the rule, a lot of their learning of it comes from their own experiences in reading. They then generalise what they learn through reading to their spelling. Research suggests much the same two-stage process in children's learning of morphemic spelling rules (a morpheme is a unit of meaning.). English children are not usually taught about morphemic spelling. Instead they usually first learn a large number of specific spellings by rote, and then infer the morphemic spelling rules for themselves. Some of their initial inferences are wrong and lead to overgeneralisations, such as writing 'necsed' instead of 'next'. It seems that, although instruction would certainly help children with this aspect of reading and spelling, in the present educational system they have to work out morphemic spelling rules for themselves in a series of inferences.

The chapter then shifts its focus to children's acquisition of knowledge of the principles underlying number. Some investigators, most notably Gelman and Wynn, claim that infants are born with a basic understanding of number and even of addition and subtraction. An alternative argument, developed by Carey, is that children are born with an ability, which becomes increasingly effective over the first five years of life, to distinguish the numbers of very small sets. After they learn to count, they eventually coordinate the number words that they have newly learned with the knowledge that they had already gained about small sets, and as a result acquire a fully fledged understanding of number. The third main hypothesis is Piaget's who argued that children first have to understand one-to-one correspondence and ordinal series in order to learn about the cardinal and ordinal principles of number. This chapter criticises the evidence offered to support the first two theories for being based on an inadequate criterion for understanding cardinal number and argues that much of the evidence still favours Piaget's view that children construct their numerical understanding on the basis of one-to-one correspondence.

The general conclusion of the chapter is that children need to be taught about the cultural tools which are at the centre of learning to read and write, and learning about mathematics. However, this learning is also based on knowledge that children acquire informally and on their developing ability to make logical inferences and as a result to understand the abstract rules that they are being introduced to both in learning to read and in learning about mathematics.

INTRODUCTION

Reading and mathematics lie at the heart of almost everything that children do at school, but in other respects these two subjects may seem to have little in common. Mathematics is a strictly logical system: reading and spelling rules, in English at any rate, seem capricious and heterogeneous. Mathematics employs abstract symbols: reading and spelling are about words with meaning. Yet, the two forms of learning pose the same basic question for psychologists: how much of children's learning must depend on instruction and how much do they learn for themselves without formal help from others?

cultural tools any tools that help us to calculate, produce models, make predictions, and understand the world more fully, e.g. abacuses, slide rules, calculators, and computers.

Vygotsky's argument (Vygotsky, 1978, 1986; Vygotsky and Luria, 1993) about **cultural tools** has convinced most developmental psychologists that instruction must play a part in children's intellectual development. Vygotsky's starting point was his claim that mankind's intellectual power is enhanced by the inventions of previous generations. Abacuses, slide rules, calculators, and now computers help us to calculate, produce models, make predictions, and understand the world more fully than we could without these inventions, which Vygotsky called 'cultural tools' (Figure 12.1).

The original invention of each cultural tool, Vygotsky argued, always involved some intellectual barrier that mankind took a long time to surmount. How then can we expect children to re-invent, or even to understand, these inventions by themselves? They haven't the time or the ability to re-invent the inventions. This intellectual inheritance has to be passed on to them.

Many psychologists, however, and in particular Piaget (2001), maintain that children construct much of their knowledge for themselves. The distinction between Vygotsky and Piaget is important, but one has to tread carefully here. The difference between these two formidable figures was not so much in their views, for they had many views in common, but in emphasis. Both rejected the idea that children acquire new knowledge just by being told something. Both made the point that other people play an important role in promoting children's knowledge. Vygotsky, however, stressed the transmission of knowledge from one person to another, while Piaget concentrated on the children's own constructions. Piaget, who was mostly concerned with children's logical abilities, did

FIGURE 12.1 *According to Vygotsky, 'cultural tools' such as an abacus help us to calculate, produce models, make predictions and understand the world more fully.*
Source: Shutterstock.

not share Vygotsky's interest in the use and the power of human inventions. He argued, for example, that no one can understand standardised measures without an adequate grasp of the logic of measuring (Piaget *et al.*, 1960). You use rulers to compare quantities which cannot be compared directly, and you will not understand how these indirect comparisons work unless you can also make the logical inference that A = C when A = B, and B = C. This is a compelling argument, but it does not follow from it that learning about standardised units is a trivial matter, as Piaget was inclined to imply.

The issue of cultural tools and children's own constructions provokes an interesting set of questions. One concerns the role of children's own informal experiences. Another is about the need for instruction. A last question is about the effects of learning these basic skills on children's cognitive processes. No one disputes the fact that books, number systems and maps help us to acquire knowledge, but they may do more than that. They may also transform the way that we think, learn, and remember.

READING AND WRITING

One characteristic of cultural tools is that they can vary from culture to culture. Writing systems, or **orthographies**, as we shall call them, vary greatly. In some, such as English, individual letters for the most part represent **phonemes**, which are the smallest unit of sound that can affect the meaning of a word. Such scripts are called **alphabetic**. There are several different alphabetic scripts (e.g. Greek, Arabic, Roman), and there are radical differences among orthographies that use exactly the same script. Finnish and English, for example, are both written in Roman letters, but the relationship between sounds and letters in the two orthographies is different. This relationship is more regular in Finnish than in English. Each letter always represents the same sound in Finnish, but not in English, where, for example, the letter 'i' represents one sound 'pin' and quite another in 'pint'. In Finnish there is also a straightforward relationship between the length of a sound and the number of letters representing it. The rule is one letter for a short vowel or consonant and two letters for a long one. This is not the rule in English.

There are many viable scripts that are not alphabets. In Chinese, each character signals a **morpheme** (a unit of meaning). Most characters are complex structures, in which a part (the phonetic component) indicates something about the sound of the morpheme and another part (the radical component) something about the morpheme's meaning. The Japanese use two kinds of script. One, 'kanji', is based on the Chinese orthography. The other, 'kana', is a **syllabary**: every kana character represents a **mora**, which is the term for the rather simple Japanese **syllables**. To make matters even more complicated there are two different kana scripts.

orthography a writing system. Orthography is used to describe any aspect of print or, more loosely, spelling.

alphabetic script a writing system in which written symbols (letters) correspond to spoken sounds; generally, individual *phonemes* represent the individual letters of an alphabetic script.

morpheme a unit of meaning. The past verb 'cooked' has two morphemes, the stem 'cook' and the /t/ sound at the end of the word (the suffix), which tells you that it is about a past action.

syllabary the name given to a language that relies heavily on *syllables* for meaning.

mora a rhythmic unit in languages like Japanese and Tamil that can be either a syllable or part of a syllable. In English a mora roughly corresponds to a consonant–vowel syllable with a short vowel, e.g. 'the'.

syllable the smallest unit of a word whose pronunciation forms a rhythmic break when spoken.

All these scripts have stood the test of time and there is a good reason for their resilience. Many of their characteristics fit well with the language that they represent. There are, for example, few syllables in Japanese and so one does not need many characters for an effective Japanese syllabary. In English, in contrast, there are thousands of different syllables – far more than children could be expected to learn and remember – and that means that an English syllabary is out of the question. The English language needed the alphabetic solution: the Japanese language did not.

The difficulty of alphabetic scripts

The alphabetic solution is neat, but it comes at a price. The *solution* is to represent speech at the level of phonemes. This is a good and economic idea, because no language has many phonemes in it and thus one does not need many letters to represent them. In English, it is true, we do have a few more phonemes than we have alphabetic letters, but we have found ways round that problem (Nunes & Bryant, 2009). The alphabet is an effective way of representing English speech.

The *price* of the alphabetic solution is a psychological one. Phonemes, at first, pose an enormous problem to young children. It is hard at first for children even to realise that letters represent phonemes. Ferreiro and Tebersoky (1983) showed this in some ingenious research that they did with young Argentine children at the time when these children first realised that alphabetic letters indicate the sounds in words. In one of their tasks the experimenter showed the children a word and read it out to them, and then finally pointed to individual letters in the word, asking the children what sound each letter represented. The children who had only recently learned that written script works by representing sounds typically judged that each letter represented a syllable, not a phoneme.

The problem that children have with phonemes is deep seated. It is not solved just by learning the alphabet, which most children do soon after they go to school. They still have to learn how individual words can be broken down into phonemes and assembled from them, and there is a large amount of evidence that at first this is a barrier for them.

This evidence comes from work on children's explicit awareness of phonemes. Bruce (1964) asked young school-children what a word like 'sand' would sound like without the 's'. The children thus had to imagine a new word by removing a phoneme from the old one. Bruce found that none of the 5-year-old children succeeded with any of the 30 words that they were given. The 6-year-olds were not much better. The idea that words consist of a sequence of phonemes does not come easily to young children.

This initial difficulty with phonemes has been confirmed time and again. A team from the famous Haskins laboratory in America (Liberman *et al.*, 1974; Liberman *et al.*, 1989) introduced the 'tapping' task in which 4-, 5-, and 6-year-old children had to learn either to tap the number of phonemes (two taps for 'up', three for 'cat') or the number of syllables (two taps for 'donkey', three for 'elephant') in words read out to them. The youngest children, who had not yet learned to read, made hardly any progress at all in the phoneme task, but did quite well in the syllable task. The older children, too, fared better in the syllable than in the phoneme task, although their performance in the phoneme task was superior to that of the younger children.

Phonemic awareness and learning to read

The least surprising result here, and in Bruce's study, was that children get better with phonemes as they grow older. One expects children to become more effective at practically everything with the years. But there is an alternative to this 'developmental' explanation, which is that the improvement has nothing to do with age and much to do with instruction. The older children could have become aware of words as sequences of phonemes because of being taught about alphabetic letters.

One of the reasons why it took mankind so long to produce the alphabet in the first place may have been the difficulty of isolating the phoneme as a usable phonological unit. The inventors of the first alphabetic scripts took an impressive but difficult intellectual step when they recognised and harnessed phonemes in their new writing systems (Olson, 1994, 1996), and it would be unrealistic to expect generations of children to take this step on their own. They need instruction, and one of the effects of school instruction may be to make them aware of the existence of phonemes as well as of the correspondences between phonemes and graphemes.

If awareness of phonemes is the product of learning to read, illiterate adults should be as bad as young children at detecting and isolating phonemes. In the 1970s there was a crash literacy programme in Portugal to eradicate the alarming amount of illiteracy that existed then in rural communities. This allowed Morais and his colleagues (Morais *et al.*, 1979, 1986) to compare two groups of adults who were similar in every way, except that the people in one group had recently been through a literacy course and now could read, while those in the other had not taken a course and were still illiterate. Morais and colleagues gave both groups two tasks. One was a deletion task like Bruce's (1964). In another they had to add a sound to the beginning of the word: they were asked, for example, what 'urso' would sound like if it began with 'p'. The illiterate group was at a severe disadvantage in these tasks. Their relative failure suggests that the experience of learning to read an alphabetic script does make people aware of phonemes.

The connection between children's experience of learning to read and their growing awareness of phonemes suggests that they need this form of awareness to become successful readers. Ample evidence supports this suggestion (Bjaalid *et al.*, 1996; Demont & Gombert, 1996; Ehri, 1995; Lundberg *et al.*, 1980; Stanovich *et al.*, 1997; Vellutino & Scanlon, 1987; Wagner & Torgeson, 1987). There are now hundreds of studies of the relation between children's performance in phoneme tasks and their success in learning to read. As far as I know, all these studies have produced extremely strong positive relations: the more children have learned about phonemes the better they read and write, at the time when the phoneme measures are taken and later on too. This discovery is one of the most important achievements of modern psychology. It concludes the first part of the story that I am telling about children's reading.

Rhymes and rimes

Although the alphabetic script is based on the phoneme, some research suggests that children's awareness of *other* **phonological** *units*, besides the phoneme, plays a part in learning to read. Between the levels of the syllable and the phoneme lies a set of phonological

phonological skills
ability to detect and manipulate sounds at the phonetic, syllabic and intra-syllabic levels; being able to detect the individual sounds (phoneme, onsets and rimes, syllables) in words.

intrasyllabic units
units of speech that are
smaller than syllables
but larger than pho-
nemes. Onset and rime
are two examples of
intrasyllabic units.

onset the onset of a
syllable is the consonant,
cluster of consonants, or
vowel at the beginning
of a syllable. The onset
of 'hat' is 'h', and 'st' is the
onset of 'stair'.

rime the vowel sound
of a *syllable* plus any
consonants that follow.
The rime of 'hat' is 'at',
and the rime of 'stair'
is 'air'.

rhyme words rhyme
with each other when
they share a *rime* – 'cat'
and 'hat' rhyme because
they have the *rime* 'at' in
common.

units which linguists call **intrasyllabic**. These are usually smaller in size than the syllable and larger than the phoneme.

The most obvious, and probably the most important, are the units that linguists call **onset** and **rime**. The onset is the consonant (if there is one) or cluster of consonants at the beginning of a syllable. The rime is the syllable's vowel sound plus any consonant that follows. Thus 'c' is the onset and 'at' the rime in 'cat', and 'st' is the onset and 'ick' the rime in 'stick'. Monosyllabic words rhyme with each other when they share a rime: 'cat and 'hat' rhyme because they have a rime in common, and so do 'six' and 'picks'.

Most children are aware of rimes from an early age and often actively and spontaneously create, and play with, **rhymes** (Chukovsky, 1963; Dowker, 1989). We ourselves (Bryant *et al.*, 1990) have shown that 3-year-old children can solve rhyme oddity problems (i.e. can tell us which word in 'cat', 'hat', and 'pin' does not contain a sound that the other two have) reasonably well, but not perfectly.

Some time ago we ran two longitudinal studies (Bradley & Bryant, 1983; Bryant *et al.*, 1990), both of which showed that children's scores in rhyme oddity tasks, given to them before they went to school, predicted their success in reading over the next few years and also their ability to detect phonemes. These two relationships held even after we had controlled for the effects of differences in the children's *intelligence quotient (IQ)* and their social background. Other studies have also shown a good relationship between children's sensitivity to rhyme and their success in reading.

Of these two relationships, the second one, between rhyme and phoneme awareness, is the more straightforward. It suggests that children's awareness of phonemes is not just the product of reading instruction (the cultural tool argument), but also stems from their earlier experiences with other easier phonological units, such as onset and rime.

The other relationship, between rhyme and reading, has been confirmed many times (Baker *et al.*, 1998; Bowey *et al.*, 1992; Chaney, 1992; Cronin & Carver, 1998; Ellis & Large, 1987; Greaney *et al.*, 1997; Hansen & Bowey, 1994; Naslund & Schneider, 1996; Stahl & Murray, 1994; Walton, 1995). The reason for this relationship may seem less obvious, but it is at least as compelling, at any rate as far as English is concerned. English script is notoriously capricious at the level of the relationships between single letters and phonemes, but the relationship between sequences of letters and sequences of phonemes is a great deal more reliable. The letter sequence 'ight', for example, always represents the same sound, as in 'light', 'sight', 'might', and 'fight', even though the individual letters in the sequence, such as 'i' and 'g', represent different sounds in different words. This letter sequence represents the rime of the syllables that it appears in, and there is good statistical evidence that the relations between letter sequences and sounds is stronger in sequences that represent rimes than in other sequences (Kessler & Treiman, 1997; Treiman *et al.*, 1995). The close relationship with the size of the phonological segment and the reliability of its representation in writing is particularly strong in English but not so marked in other orthographies, such as Italian, in which grapheme–phoneme relations are a great deal more reliable. In a strikingly original and convincing theoretical review, Ziegler and Goswami (2005) called this difference between orthographies a difference in 'psycholinguisitic grain size', and argued that the grain size of each script will determine the way that it should be taught.

FIGURE 12.2 *Reading ability is a key aspect of children's development. How much of children's learning depends on instruction, and how much do children learn for themselves?*

Source: Shutterstock.

Summary

We started with the possibility that learning to read is simply a matter of skills imparted to children by their teachers – skills that enable children to master a cultural tool that depends on ways of analysing words which do not come naturally to them. We end with the conclusion that this idea is correct in part, but that there is more than this to children's use of phonology (Figure 12.2). Children also take advantage of phonological units that come much more easily to them. Rhyme is a natural part of their life long before they go to school, and yet they use this informal knowledge when learning to read. It even helps them come to grips with that stubbornly difficult intellectual hurdle, the phoneme.

CONDITIONAL SPELLING RULES

There is a great deal more to the English script and to many other alphabetic scripts than **letter–sound associations**. Many phonologically based spelling patterns are based on quite sophisticated, **conditional rules** (Nunes & Bryant, 2009). The final 'e' that lengthens and changes the quality of the preceding vowel ('hop' as opposed to ' hope') is an example, and so is the doubling of the final consonant that ensures the shortening of the preceding vowel ('hopping' as opposed to 'hoping'). These particular rules are well known and actively taught. Other conditional rules are not taught and any knowledge that experienced readers have of them is probably quite implicit. When, for example, the /k/ sound ends a syllable and is immediately preceded by a vowel, it is spelled as 'ck' if the vowel is short ('brick' 'luck') and as 'k' or 'ke' if the vowel is long ('steak' 'hike'). Few people are explicitly aware of this rule, but many obey it.

letter–sound associations where one letter represents one sound or phoneme

conditional spelling rules rules which determine that a letter, or a group of letters, represent one sound in one context and another sound in a different context.

Invented spelling

We know that children pay little or no attention to conditional rules at first. Instead they stick to letter–sound associations in a most literal manner. Read (1986), a distinguished American linguist, gave us the first systematic demonstration of children's initial concentration on letter–sound associations. For example, he reported a caption that an American child wrote under a picture 'Fes sowemeg ed wodr' which meant 'Fish swimming in water'. Every word is spelled wrongly here, but 'sowemeg' and 'wodr' capture the phonetic sequence of the spoken words remarkably well. Americans tend to convert the /t/ into a /d/ sound when it falls between two vowels and the boy's spelling represented this more accurately than conventional spelling does.

Read's work on what he called 'invented spelling' was revolutionary because it demonstrated that inexperienced children use their knowledge of letter–sound relationships in original and ingenious ways. He also showed certain stubborn weaknesses in these spellings. One was a frequent confusion between letter names and letter sounds. Read argued that a child who spells 'car' as 'cr' does so because the name of the letter 'r' corresponds to the rime of the word 'car'. This is an entirely understandable confusion. However, it is hard sometimes, particularly when vowels are concerned, to be sure whether children are confusing letter–names and letter–sounds or are making some other kind of error. A child who writes 'hope' as 'hop' may do so because of the name of the letter 'o' is the same as the sound of the vowel in that word (and this is what Read and others maintain). Another explanation is that the child knows that 'o' is actually the right spelling for the vowel sound, but has not yet realised that he must also put an 'e' at the end of the of the word to represent this vowel sound.

The split digraph (or the silent 'e')

This final 'e' rule is quite difficult for young children, despite the intensive instruction that they are given about it at school. It usually takes several years for them to learn the rule when writing real words. The most striking work on this was done by Marsh and his colleagues (Marsh & Desberg, 1983; Marsh *et al.*, 1980). They tested children's grasp of the final 'e' rule by giving them **pseudo-words** to read and to write. This was a good move: children who read the word 'rope' correctly may do so by rote learning of this word, but if they also read 'rofe' in the right way they must be doing so on the basis of a rule about the effect of the final, silent, 'e'. Marsh found that most children only pass the pseudo-word test by around the age of 10 years.

pseudo-words a non-existent but pronounce-able non-word, such as 'slosbon' or 'wug', often used in psychological experiments.

Recently we have confirmed Marsh's conclusion that children do have some initial difficulty with the final 'e' rule. In England they are first taught this rule at the end of their first year. Claire Davis and I (Davis & Bryant, 2006) asked over a hundred English children, whose ages ranged from 7 to 11 years, to read and write real words and also pseudo-words with long and short vowel sounds. The long vowel words that they had to read all ended in the silent 'e'. We found that the 7-year-old children did not do at all well in the pseudo-word reading and spelling tasks, but there was a marked improvement over the next few years. This change was strongest at first in reading, but between 9 and 11 years the children's spelling improved much more than their reading did.

This study was a longitudinal one, which allowed us to look at the relations between the different tasks over time. We found that between the age of 7 and 9 years the children's reading scores (of pseudo-words) in one session predicted their spelling scores in the next session, 12 months later, very well and much better than their spelling scores predicted their reading in the following session. This quite consistent pattern suggests that children's success in reading determines how well they learn this particular spelling rule and, perhaps, other spelling rules as well. In fact, an influential theory by Uta Frith (1985) about the development of reading and spelling had made a claim which fits well with the pattern of results that we have just described. She argued that children learn complex orthographic rules, largely by themselves, by reading text, and then use these rules in their spelling. The Davis and Bryant (2006) study strongly supports this claim.

Morphemic spelling rules: The case of English

Read's research on invented spelling provided us with another important result. Consider the characteristic invented spellings of 'kild' for 'killed', 'kist' for 'kissed', 'halpt' for 'helped', 'watid' for 'waited', and 'wotid' for 'wanted'. These follow the now familiar pattern of children using letter–sound correspondences in a literal way at first, but there is more to say about these particular mistakes. The children were ignoring a spelling rule based on *morphemic* structure. Spoken regular past verbs in English end in three different sounds, either /d/ or /t/ or /id/, but this ending is always spelled as 'ed'. The rule is a powerful reminder that many orthographies, including English, are not just phonemic scripts: they are **morpho-phonemic**, which means that the spelling rules are based not just on phonemes but also on morphemes and the way that they are spelled.

> **morpho-phonemic** a description of orthographies in which there are regular relationships between letters or groups of letters and morphemes as well as sounds.

Morphemes are units of meaning. The past verb 'packed', for example, has two morphemes, the stem 'pack' and the /t/ sound at the end which tells you that it is about a past action. 'Unpacked' is a three-morpheme word. Adding 'un' changes the word's meaning, which means that 'un' is a third morpheme. These added-on morphemes, 'un' and 'ed', are called affixes, and they come in two kinds. Inflectional morphemes, such as the '-ed' past verb ending or the plural 's' ending, tell you about the grammatical status of the word. **Derivational morphemes** 'like 'un-' or '-ness' change the meaning of the word.

> **derivational morphemes** affixes that create new words which are called 'derived' words. For example, 'health' is a noun which is created by adding the derivational suffix 'th' to the verb 'heal', and 'logical' is an adjective created by adding '-al' to the noun 'logic'.

Once one understands the significance of morphemes, English spelling loses much of its unpredictability. Morphemic rules explain why the same sounds in 'list' and 'kissed', and in 'freeze' and 'trees', are spelled differently. 'List' and 'freeze' are one-morpheme words and their end sounds are spelled according to normal grapheme–phoneme conventions. However, 'kissed' and 'trees' both contain two morphemes, a stem followed by an inflection: the past tense inflection is always

genitive a possessive word, for example the apostrophe + 's' in 'the boy's jumper' indicates that the jumper belongs to the boy.

spelled as 'ed' and the plural morpheme as 's'. The plural–possessive distinction is another morphemic rule. 'The boy's drink' and 'The boys drink' sound the same, but the apostrophe in the first phrase, and its absence in the second, tell us that 'boys/boy's' is plural in the first case and **genitive** (possessive) in the second. Many plural words, like 'trees' end in the sound /z/.

Morphemic spelling rules in Greek and French

Spelling rules based on morphemes are important in other scripts too – even in scripts that are regarded as highly regular. Modern Greek is so regular that if you know the letter–sound rules you can read any word in the language and know exactly how it is pronounced. However, there are more letters for vowels than there are vowels in Greek: there are alternative ways of spelling three of the five Greek vowel sounds, and so children have to learn which way to spell each of these three sounds in different words. Much of this learning depends on morphemes. All Greek nouns, adjectives and verbs end in **inflectional morphemes**, which have distinctive spellings and are often single vowels. For example, 'οι' and 'η' both represent the same sound, /i/, but this sound is always spelled as , 'οι' when it comes at the end of masculine plural nouns and as 'η' at the end of feminine singular nouns. This is plainly a morphemic spelling rule.

inflectional morphemes affixes whose presence, and also whose absence, provide essential information about words. For example, in English the presence of the suffix 's' at the end of a noun tells you that the noun is in the plural and its absence tells you that it is in the singular.

Morphemes are important in learning to spell French words as well (Figure 12.3). One example is the spelling of plurals, which the French represent in writing but not in speech. When they write the phrase 'les grandes maisons' they put the plural 's' inflection at the end of the adjective and noun, but when they say these words they do not pronounce these plural inflections. Thus, the plural adjective and the noun sound no different from the singular version of these words. The same is true of their verbs. They write the 'nt' ending to indicate the third-person plural, but they do not pronounce this plural inflection. The third-person singular 'aime' and plural 'aiment' sound the same but are spelled differently. French children, therefore, cannot rely just on letter–sound associations and it should help them to be aware of the morphemic structure of adjectives, nouns, and verbs in order to be able to spell them properly.

FIGURE 12.3 *Morphemes are important in learning to spell French words as well.*
Source: Shutterstock.

Morphemic spelling rules are difficult

Long after they have acquired a good working knowledge of letter–sound association, children continue to make errors with the conventional spelling of morphemes. We showed (Nunes *et al.*, 1997) that many English children as old as 10 years still ignore the 'ed' ending for regular past verbs and spell the endings of these verbs phonetically ('killd', 'kist'). Bryant *et al.* (1997) have established, to no one's surprise, that even 15-year-old children often put apostrophes in wrong places and fail to put them in the right places. We have even found (Kemp & Bryant, 2003) that many adults, as well as many children, do not completely understand the inflexible morphemic spelling rule that regular plural noun ending is always spelled as 's' even when its sound is actually /z/ (as in 'trees').

One reason for these difficulties could be that children are not at first aware of the morphemic structure of the words that they are trying to write. There is some support for this idea. Nunes *et al.* (1997) tested children's awareness of morphemes by giving them, in an oral task, pairs of related words such as 'writer–wrote' and then the first word of another pair, 'teacher'. The children had to produce the word that had the same relation to 'teacher' as 'wrote' had to 'writer'. Their scores in these morpheme tasks were strongly related to their success in spelling the endings of regular past verbs over a year later. Young children may fail to use the conventional spellings for morphemes because they simply do not know enough about morphemes.

There is another possible reason for their difficulties. We have evidence that children must go through a sequence of steps to learn morphemic spelling rules. Our longitudinal work on the 'ed' spelling showed that the youngest children ignore the conventional 'ed' ending completely and that many of the older ones used it correctly all the time. But in between these two states, we found another pattern. Children, who were just beginning to use the 'ed' ending with appropriate words such as 'kissed', also applied this spelling to inappropriate words. They often spelled irregular past verbs with an 'ed' ending. They wrote 'slept' as 'sleped' for example and 'heard' as 'heared'. More surprising – they used the ending with other parts of speech: they sometimes wrote 'next' as 'necsed' and ' ground' as 'grouned'.

There are parallels for this striking pattern in other languages. In Greek, children start by spelling different inflections that have the same sound in one way only (Bryant *et al.*, 1999; Chliounaki & Bryant, 2002). Although there are four different affixes with the /i/ sound, all spelled differently, young children typically apply one spelling (usually a single letter) to all of them. Later they adopt two or three spellings for this sound, but then put these new spellings on inappropriate as well as appropriate words. Although they are now better at spelling words which take the spellings that they have just adopted, they actually become worse with words that they used to spell correctly, because the new spellings are quite inappropriate for these particular words.

The phenomenon of children's spelling getting worse with some words at the same time as it gets better with others is surprisingly widespread. The apostrophe is a striking case (Bryant, 2002; Bryant *et al.*, 1997). We gave children of 8, 9 and 15 years sentences containing a word ending in /s/, which the children were asked to write. In half the cases this word was a singular possessive noun and in the other half a nominative or accusative plural. So, the first kind of words needed an apostrophe and the second did not. The youngest children hardly ever used the apostrophe, which meant that they spelled the plural endings nearly perfectly and the possessive endings wrongly most of the time. The older children used the apostrophe more often, and so their spelling of the possessive ending improved, but they used it with plural endings as well and this meant that their spelling of these endings actually got worse.

A final example comes from the way that French children learn to spell the unsounded plural affixes. At first (Fayol *et al.*, 1999; Totereau *et al.*, 1997) they leave them out altogether, but soon, as a result of intensive instruction, they learn about the 's' ending for plural nouns and adjectives. However, at the same time as they begin to use this ending with plural nouns they also begin to put 's' at the ends of plural verbs as well, which is quite wrong. Eventually, however, they learn about the 'nt' ending for plural verbs, but then they behave in a way that is closely similar to the behaviour of English children as they learn about the 'ed' ending and the apostrophe. While their spelling of plural verb endings gets better, their spelling of plural noun endings actually declines, because they begin to put 'nt' or 'ent' endings on plural nouns, for example, 'les merlent chantent' instead of 'les merles chantent'.

Two steps in learning morphemic spelling rules

These fascinating over-generalisations of newly learned spelling patterns may be an essential part of learning. This may be the underlying three-step sequence:

1. Children start by spelling a particular sound like the /t/ ending in one way only (kist, list).

2. They learn another way of spelling this ending ('ed') , and at first begin to use it without understanding when it is right to do so, and thus occasionally write 'list', for example, as 'lised'.

3. As a result of the feedback that they get when they use this new spelling, they learn the rule for its use.

The important point in this sequence is that children have to use the new spelling first before they can understand its underlying rule. They use it first and learn about it later.

We found further evidence for the idea that children first use a morphemic spelling sequence and then later on infer the underlying rule for it in a two-year longitudinal study of Greek children's spelling (Chliounaki & Bryant, 2007). The children were 6 years old at the beginning of the study and 8 years old at the end. During this time we asked the children to spell real words and pseudo-words. All these words were two-morpheme words which contained a stem followed by an inflection. Each inflection contained one of the three vowels for which there is more than one spelling in Greek. Recall that there is always a clear morphemic rule that determines the way that each of these vowels is spelled when the sound occurs in an inflection.

Our purpose was to find out how well children spell these inflections and the point of the comparison between real and pseudo-word spelling was that children might simply learn the spellings of particular familiar real words by rote without ever understanding the rule that underlies them. However, with pseudo-words they would have to know the relevant morphemic spelling rules (e.g. 'οι' for masculine plural, but 'η' for a feminine singular, noun ending in /i/). We found that the children spelled these inflections better in real words than in pseudo-words, which suggested that they might first learn the specific spellings of many real words by rote and might then infer the underlying rule for spelling inflections on the basis of this specific knowledge. The study produced another piece of evidence which supported the idea that children first form a bank of knowledge of specific spellings and then infer morphemic rules on the basis of this knowledge. Our study showed that children's knowledge of the spelling of inflections in real words (word-specific knowledge) strongly predicted their spelling of these inflections in pseudo-words (use of morphemic spelling rules) in later sessions. In contrast, the children's spelling of

FIGURE 12.4 *Children have to try out new spellings in order to learn about them.*
Source: Shutterstock.

pseudo-word inflection in the earlier sessions was not related to their spelling of real word inflections later on. This is good evidence that children's word specific knowledge is the basis for their learning of morphemic spelling rules and not the other way round.

Summary

The evidence that we have produced to show that children infer morphemic spelling rules for themselves comes from English and Greek children. In both these countries children are taught little or nothing about these rules at school. It is possible that they rely on their own inferences because that is all that they can do. This raises the question whether teaching would help them with this aspect of spelling and therefore whether it is possible to teach children about morphemes and spelling directly. The answer to these questions is a clear 'Yes': a series of intervention studies, described in a recent monograph (Nunes & Bryant, 2006) has established not just that children learn well from explicit teaching about morphemic spelling rules, but also that they enjoy doing so. Morphemes are, or at any rate can be, fun.

At the beginning of this chapter we asked about the relative importance of instruction and of the child's own contribution to learning how to read and to do mathematics. We have shown how instruction is indeed an essential part of the process of learning letter–sound associations. These associations involve a phonological unit, called the phoneme, which young children, and any other uninstructed human, find difficult to detect and isolate unless they are taught how to do so.

Children have to learn rules as well as associations, and here their own contribution is quite striking. Instruction may be necessary, but the most interesting outcome of research on learning morphemic spelling rules is its conclusion that children have try out new spellings in order to learn about them (Figure 12.4). This has been shown many times now in research on children's learning of morphemic rules. It may also be true of learning conditional phonological spelling rules.

NUMBER AND COUNTING

With number, as with reading, it is wise to consider what children need to learn before discussing how they manage to learn it. When children learn about number they have to come to terms with a mixture of universal, logical principles and of human inventions (cultural tools) that vary quite considerably from place to place.

Logic and number

Logical principles are the essential ingredients of number. Unless a system conforms to these principles, it cannot be called a number system. One is **cardinality**: any set of items with a particular number is equal in quantity to any other set with the same number of items in it. This may sound banal at first, but it is not. Cardinality is what makes the recognition of number more sophisticated and interesting than the recognition of particular patterns. To understand the cardinal properties of number, we must go beyond perceptual information. Two sets of objects have the same number despite looking completely different (four cars arranged in a square, four garages in a line) and a set of items stays numerically the same despite changes in its perceptual appearance (a group of children now in an orderly queue, later running around in a school playground).

> **cardinality** the numerical principle that states that any set of items with a particular number is equal in quantity to any other set with the same number of items in it.

A second principle is **ordinality**. Numbers come in an ordered scale of magnitude: 2 is more than 1 and 3 more than 2, and as a logical consequence 3 is more than 1. Thus the understanding of ordinality is a matter not just of knowing that numbers come in a certain order of magnitude, but also of being able to understand and make what are called *transitive inferences* (A>B, B>C: ∴ A>C).

> **ordinality** the numerical principle that states that numbers come in an ordered scale of magnitude: 2 is more than 1, and 3 is more than 2, and as a logical consequence 3 is more than 1.

These are essential characteristics of number. When we count, we use number words that are pure inventions but, whatever these words are, we must obey certain **universal counting principles**. Unless we do so, we are not really counting. Five such principles were set out by Gelman and Gallistel (1978). The first three are 'how to count' principles. The first is the **one-to-one principle**, which is that that one must count all the objects in a set once and once only: each one must be given just one number tag; the second is the **stable order principle**: one must count by producing the number words in a set order and in the same set order each time (1 always before 2 and 2 always before 3); the third is that the last number counted represents the value of the set. Gelman and Gallistel misleadingly called this the *cardinal principle*: it would be better to call it the **last-number-counted** principle.

The remaining two principles were the **abstraction principle** and the **order irrelevance principle**. The first of these states that the number in a set is quite independent of any of the qualities of the members in that set: the rules for counting a heterogeneous set of objects are the same as for counting a homogeneous one. The *order irrelevance principle* is that the order in which members of a set are counted makes no difference, and anyone who counts a set, for example, from left to right will come to the same answer as someone else who counts it from right to left.

Different counting systems

All counting systems must obey these principles. Nevertheless these systems vary across languages and across cultures (Saxe, 1981). The most obvious variation is in the words for numbers. Some languages lay linguistic traps: others do not.

In English, for example, words like 'eleven' and ' thirteen' are opaque: these words do not reveal the fact that they stand for 10 +1 and 10+3, in contrast with, for instance, 'one hundred and one'. 'Quatre-vingt-dix', the French word for 90 is not much better, and German children have to solve the problem that numbers between 20 and 99 start with the smaller denomination when spoken, but with the larger denomination when written.

Counting systems vary in another way too. We are so used to the decimal system that we tend to think of it as inevitable, but it is not. In the past, various cultures have used other base systems: the Mayans used a base-20 system for centuries and so, until quite recently, did the British for their currency (20 shillings to a pound). There are even number systems that have no base system at all. One is the system developed by the Oksapmin in Papua New Guinea (Saxe,1981) whose number words are names of body parts. Their counting starts with the word for the right thumb, which also means '1', and continues up the arm over the head (the word for the left eye is also the word for '16') and down eventually to the right hand. The base system of counting is undoubtedly an invention and it is a tool of great significance, because it makes numerical calculations much easier for human beings.

---

universal counting principles a set of principles that must be obeyed in order for our number system to work.

one-to-one principle the principle that when counting a set of objects, each object must be counted once and once only and that each must be given a unique number tag.

stable order principle the principle that number words must be produced in a set order: if you count 1–2–3 on one occasion, you must never then count 3–2–1 on another.

last-number-counted the principle that the last number counted represents the value for that set.

abstraction principle the principle that the number in a set is independent of any qualities of the members in that set.

order irrelevance principle the principle that the order in which members of a set are counted does not affect the number of items in the set.

The universal principles of number and of counting systems add up to a formidable list of logical requirements that children must follow to be able to make the simplest numerical calculations. When we put these together with the sophistication of the invented base systems and the vagaries of the language used in counting, we can see that that there are many difficulties on the way to learning about number. Some psychologists, however, have suggested that children have the help of a remarkable resource during this learning – an *innate* understanding of number. The evidence for this claim comes mostly from work with infants.

Infants' knowledge of number

The idea that humans are born with the ability to reason mathematically is taken extremely seriously these days. (Butterworth, 1999; Dehaene, 1997; Gelman & Gallistel, 1978; Gelman & Meck, 1983; Gelman *et al.*, 1986). Gelman and her colleagues used two kinds of evidence to support this hypothesis. The first was research on babies that was done by herself and her colleague Starkey, who used the technique of *habituation* in his experiments (Starkey & Cooper, 1980; Starkey *et al.*, 1990). Habituation experiments are based on the fact that babies show more interest in novel than in familiar objects (see Chapter 5).

Starkey and Cooper (1980) set up an experiment to see if 4-month-old babies can discriminate numbers. There were two phases in their experiment. In the first they showed the babies, over series of trials, a certain number of dots. In each trial the baby saw the same number of dots, but the perceptual arrangement of the dots (bunched up or spread out) varied from trial to trial. Some children were shown 'small' – either two or three dots – and others 'large' numbers – either four or six dots. During this first phase the babies' attention to the number displays usually decline. The aim of the second phase was to find out if a change in the number of dots would restore their interest. All the babies were shown a new number of dots in this phase.

When the numbers of dots were small, the babies looked at the displays with the new number of dots for a relatively long time and thus seemed to recognise a change in their number. Starkey and Cooper claimed, therefore, that infants do distinguish small numbers.

Many other studies have repeated and refined this result (e.g. Strauss & Curtis, 1981). Antell and Keating (1983) found that even neonates reacted in the same way, and van Loosbroek and Smitsman (1990) reported the same pattern in a study in which the objects in the displays moved all the time while the babies saw them.

However, the meaning of these results has been seriously questioned. The question is whether the experiments are about number. One research group (Mix *et al.*, 1997; Clearfield & Mix, 1999; Mix *et al.*, 2001) argues that infants made discriminations entirely on the basis of continuous quantity in these experiments. They claim that the infants in these habituation studies were aware of the total size taken up by the items in the display, and not of the number of items. None of the studies had included any control against this possibility.

Clearfield and Mix (1999) produced evidence for this alternative hypothesis. They compared the effects of:

1. varying the amount of material, while holding the number constant;
2. varying the number of items, while holding the total amount of material constant.

In the first case the change did provoke increased interest in the babies who saw it. But in the second case the babies showed no sign of revived interest in the second phase. The result supports the idea that the babies in Starkey's research might not have been attending to number. The issue of innate number discrimination is still open.

Infants' knowledge of addition and subtraction: Wynn's work

However, another set of experiments provided support for the idea of innate mathematical structures. Wynn (1992, 1998, 2000) looked at the understanding of adding and subtracting in babies as young as 6 months old (see Chapter 5 and Figure 5.14). She did this by enacting additions and subtractions in front of the baby, so that sometimes these led to the correct and at other times to the incorrect result. She argued that if babies can do the additions and subtractions, they should be surprised by incorrect outcomes and should look longer at them. In her first study she enacted addition (1 + 1) by:

1. Putting a Mickey Mouse on a platform in front of the child, then raising a screen in front of this toy, so that child could not see the toy.
2. Placing another Mickey Mouse behind the screen.
3. Lowering the screen so that the child could see how many toys there now were on the platform

The right outcome was 2 toys on the platform. On half the trials 2 toys were indeed there, but on the other half, by trickery, only 1 toy was left, and the child therefore saw an incorrect outcome.
She carried out her subtraction (2 − 1) in the same way:

1. Showed the child 2 toys on the platform.
2. Raised the screen to block the child's view of these toys.
3. Put her hand behind the screen and removed 1 of the 2 toys.
4. Lowered the screen, revealing 1 toy on some trials (the correct outcome), and 2 (the incorrect outcome) on others.

On some subtraction trials the children were presented with the correct outcome (1 toy there), and on others with an incorrect one (2 toys on the platform).
The results were positive. The infants did look longer at the wrong outcomes. Wynn recognised, however, that these results could be explained in another way. In this first experiment the incorrect outcome was always the same as the starting point in each of the problems (1 in the addition and 2 in the subtraction problems). The babies may have expected a change – any change – from the original state as a result

of the addition or subtraction, and may simply have been surprised to see everything unchanged.

So, Wynn carried out a second study with $1 + 1$ addition. Her procedure was exactly as before, except that the incorrect outcome, this time, was 3. Thus both the correct and the incorrect outcomes were different from the starting point. Wynn found that the infants still showed more interest in the new incorrect outcome ($1 + 1 = 3$) than in the correct one. She concluded that the babies must therefore have been able to work out the $1 + 1$ addition.

Criticisms of Wynn's work

These experiments have been criticised and they are still controversial. One relatively small criticism is that Wynn did not include subtraction in her second experiment. She did not, for example, give infants trials in which $3 - 1$ led to the incorrect outcome of 1, and thus both outcomes were different from the initial state. So, one cannot be sure that infants of this age have a genuine understanding of subtraction (Bryant, 1992).

Another criticism, made by Wakeley et al. (2000a, 2000b), is that in the crucial second experiment the infants could have attended more to the $1 + 1 = 3$ than to the $1 + 1 = 2$ outcome merely because they were more interested in larger numbers, or because it takes them more time to process 3 objects than 2 objects. Again the crucial test would be to introduce the $3 - 1 = 1$ outcome. In this case the incorrect outcome $3 - 1 = 1$ is less numerous than the correct outcome of $3 - 1 = 2$. So, a preference here for the incorrect outcome would go against the idea that children are just responding on the basis of numerosity.

Wakeley et al. carried out an experiment that repeated all four conditions of Wynn's first study and introduced the $3 - 1 = 1$ and $3 - 1 = 2$ sequences. They found no significant difference in the amount of attention that the infants paid to the $3 - 1 = 1$ and the $3 - 1 = 2$ outcomes. Worse still, when the experimenters repeated Wynn's original tasks, their results were different from hers. The babies did not look longer at the incorrect than at the correct outcomes.

Thus the research on addition/subtraction, like the habituation research, provides us with no convincing consistent evidence for innate mathematical knowledge. We must turn now to work with a different age group.

Principles before skills

procedural skills applying certain routines or procedures in order to solve certain problems, such as counting the number of objects in a set.

Gelman supported Starkey's conclusion about innate understanding of number, because she herself thinks that the understanding of her five counting principles is a basic, built in, part of our cognitive system. She acknowledges that children make mistakes when they count, but argues that this is a matter of **procedural skills**, which are never perfect. According to Gelman, however, knowledge of the principles is innate.

Her own work was mainly with older children. In a classic study, Gelman and Gallistel (1978) recorded how well children, aged between 2 and 5 years, count sets of objects. They gave the children sets that varied in number from 2 to 19, asked them to count each set, and recorded whether the children always produced number words in the same order and always counted each object once, and also whether they seemed to recognise that the last number counted signified the number of the set.

The main result was a large effect of set size. The children respected the counting principles with small number sets more than with large ones. Gelman and Gallistels's explanation was that children grasp the principles long before they can put them into effect consistently. They called this the 'principles-before-skills' hypothesis, and argued that children's mistakes with the larger sets are due to difficulties in applying the right procedures in increasingly difficult circumstances. For example, young children lose their way in one-to-one counting with large sets because of forgetting which items they have already counted.

Gelman and her colleagues (Gelman & Meck, 1983; Gelman *et al.*, 1986) tested this hypothesis by asking pre-school children to make judgements about a puppet which they saw counting. Sometimes the puppet counted correctly, but at other times it failed to respect the one-to-one principle or the last-number-counted principle. The experimenters wanted to see whether the children could spot these violations. The results of these puppet studies supported Gelman's claim that young children do have some understanding of the 'how to count' principles, as these were set out in her model.

These studies do show some understanding in young children of the process of counting, but they side-step some of the basic requirements for the understanding of number. Gelman's model and her empirical work leave out cardinal number, which is about relations between sets, because her research concentrates entirely on counting single sets. It also leaves out ordinal number, for there is nothing in the research about children's understanding of the increasing magnitude of numbers.

Thus, the claim for innate understanding of number is unimpressive. Research on number discrimination in babies may not be about number, and research on principles-before-skills leaves out some essential principles. We need to examine the alternative idea, which is that children acquire an understanding of number gradually and as a result of much experience.

Acquiring an understanding of number gradually: Carey's individuation hypothesis

One competing theory, which claims some innate knowledge but nevertheless argues that children acquire their understanding of number gradually and as a result of much experience, is Susan Carey's (2004) recent, but already well-known, hypothesis. She argues that children learn about number in several different ways, but her theory concentrates on only one of these ways, which is all that we shall discuss here. She claims that human infants are born with a 'parallel individuation' system, which makes it possible for them to recognise and represent very small numbers exactly. The system only operates for sets of 1, 2, and 3 objects and even within this restricted scope there is marked development over children's first three years.

Initially the system allows infants to recognise sets of 1 as having a distinct quantity. Children understand 1 as a quantity, though they do not at first know that the

word 'one' applies to this quantity. Later on children are able to discriminate and recognise – in Carey's term 'to individuate' – sets of 1 and 2 objects, and still later, around
the age of 3 to 4 years, sets of 1, 2, and 3 objects as distinct quantities. Young children
progress from being 'one-knowers', as Carey puts it, to becoming 'two-knowers' and
then 'three-knowers'.

During the same period, these children also learn number words and, though their
recognition of 1, 2, and 3 as distinct quantities does not in any way depend on this
verbal learning, they do manage to associate the right count words ('one', 'two', and
'three') with the right quantities.

Bootstrapping

This association in time between the development of parallel individuation and learning the count list eventually leads to what Carey (2004) calls 'bootstrapping', that is, the
children lifting themselves up by their own intellectual bootstraps. The bootstrapping,
according to Carey, takes place some time in children's fourth or fifth year of age and
therefore well before they go to school, and it takes two forms. First, with the help
of the constant order of number words in the count list, the children begin to learn
about the ordinal properties of numbers: 2 always comes after 1 in the count list and
is always more numerous than 1 by 1, and 3 is more numerous than 2, again by 1,
and always follows 2. Second, because the count list which the children learn goes well
beyond 3, they eventually infer that the number words represent a continuum of distinct
quantities which also stretches beyond 'three'. In Carey's words: 'The child . . . comes
to know the meaning of "five" through the bootstrapping process – i.e., that "five"
means one more than four, which is one more than three – by integrating representations of natural language quantifiers with the external serial ordered count list.' Carey
called this new understanding 'enriched parallel individuation' (Carey, 2004, p. 65).

Her main evidence for parallel individuation and enriched parallel individuation
came from experiments (Le Corre & Carey, 2007) in which she used a task, originally
developed by Wynn, called Give – a Number. In this, an experimenter asks the child
to give them a certain number of objects from the set of objects in front of the child:
'Could you take two cats out of the bowl and place them on the table?' Children sometimes put out the number asked for and sometimes just grab objects apparently randomly. Carey showed that different 3-, 4-, and 5-year-old children can be classified quite
convincingly as 'one-' 'two-' or 'three-knowers' or as 'counting-principle-knowers'.
The one-knowers do well when asked to provide one object but not when asked for
the other numbers while the two- and three-knowers can respectively provide up to 2
and 3 objects successfully. The 'counting-principle-knowers', in contrast, count quantities above 3 or 4.

This evidence fits well with Carey's interesting idea of a radical developmental
change from 'knowing' some small quantities to understanding that the number system can be extended to other numbers in the count list. The value of her work is
that it shows developmental changes in children's learning about the counting system.
These had been by-passed by both Piaget and his colleagues because their theory was
about the underlying logic needed for this learning and not about counting itself, and

also by Gelman, because her theory about counting principles was about innate or rapidly acquired structures and not about development. However, Carey's explanation of children's counting in terms of enriched parallel individuation suffers the limitation that we mentioned when discussing Gelman's work: Carey also has no proper measure of children's understanding of cardinality in its full sense. Just knowing that the last number that you counted is the number of the set is not enough.

Carey's theory has been subjected to much criticism for the role that it attributes to induction or analogy in the use of the 'next' principle and to language. Gelman and Butterworth (2005), for example, argue that groups of people who have very restricted number language still show understanding of larger quantities; their number knowledge is not restricted to small numerosities, as Carey suggested.

NUMBER AS A CULTURAL TOOL

The difficulty of establishing any hard evidence for the innate hypothesis makes it seem more likely that we spend a lot of our childhood acquiring mathematical knowledge and skills. But how do children acquire mathematics? One possible answer is that they learn mathematics by being taught about it. With cultural tools we can be sure that some instruction is needed. As we have seen, children cannot be left to re-invent these tools for themselves.

The decimal system

The decimal system is an obvious example of a cultural tool. Like other cultural tools, it does not come easily to young children (Fuson, 1988). One task that shows this is the Shop Task, described in Nunes & Bryant, (1996). The children are given money and are charged for items that they want to buy in a shop set up by the experimenters. In some trials they need pay in one denomination only – just in pence or just in 10p coins. In other trials they must mix denominations by combining 10p coins and pence to reach a sum such as 24. These mixed trials are a good test of their understanding of the base 10 system, because the whole point of the system is the combination of units with 10s, 10s with 100s, and so on. The mixed trials in our Shop Task were by far the hardest for the 5- and 6-year-old children, who usually go wrong by treating these trials as single denomination problems. They start counting out the 1p coins as pence, but then continue by counting the 10p coins as 1 penny each as well.

Cross-cultural differences in the difficulty of the decimal system
One explanation for English-speaking children's difficulty with the decimal system is a cultural one, and therefore absolutely consistent with the cultural tool approach. The teen and decade words are more opaque in European languages than in Asian languages. The Chinese, Japanese and Koreans do not have words such as 'eleven', 'twelve', 'thirteen', 'twenty', and 'thirty'; they say the equivalent of 'ten-one', 'ten-two',

'ten-three', 'two-ten', and 'three-ten'. Children from these Asian countries are also better at counting and at constructing numbers than European and American children. Miller and Stigler (1987) asked 4-, 5- and 6-year-old American and Taiwanese children to count up to just over a 100, and also to count sets of objects which were either arranged in a straight row or higgledy-piggledy. The Taiwanese children did better than the Americans in the free counting. The Americans tended to make mistakes when they got to the teen numbers while the Taiwanese coasted serenely through these particular numbers with hardly an error. When the children counted sets of concrete objects, the Americans and Taiwanese were similar in some ways, but different in others. Both groups of children made more mistakes with the randomly arranged objects than with the objects in a row, mainly because in the case of the random arrangements it was harder for them to remember which objects they had already counted. With both arrangements, the Americans too were just as good as the Taiwanese when it came to applying the one-to-one principle – counting each object once and only once. However, the Americans made many more mistakes that took the form of producing the wrong next number: they were much more likely than the Taiwanese to get the number sequence wrong.

We find the same Asian superiority when children construct numbers. Miura and colleagues devised a task in which children are given quantities of bricks that are either in units or joined together in groups of 10, and are asked to produce a certain number of bricks – 21, 34, 53. The question here is whether the children will laboriously count out units to reach the desired number, or whether they will take the quicker and more efficient option of combining 10s and units. Children from Asian countries adopted the sophisticated way of combining 10s and units much more often than children from European countries did (Miura et al., 1988; Miura et al., 1994).

The most plausible explanation for this European/Asian difference is the linguistic one. However, we must be cautious. We cannot yet rule out the possibility that some other cultural difference may have caused the difference (Towse & Saxton, 1997).

LOGIC IN THE UNDERSTANDING OF NUMBER

No one disputes the importance of logical reasoning in mathematics. The only argument is over the question whether children initially lack the necessary logical power and have to acquire it along the way. Piaget (1952, 1953; Piaget & Inhelder, 1974) claimed that children are at first held back by their lack of logic, and do have to acquire logical abilities in order to understand mathematics.

His view of young children's grasp of number was the direct opposite of the hypothesis of an innate number sense. He claimed that young children may know number words quite well, and yet do not actually understand what they are doing when they count. They do not, at first, understand what the number sequence means, because they have no idea of cardinality and ordinality.

Logic and cardinality

I will concentrate on cardinality here, because Piaget's work on this is more closely related to number than his work on ordinality is. Piaget's work on **conservation**, and particularly the work that he did together with his colleague Greco, was directly concerned with children's use and understanding of number words.

Greco (1962) gave 4- to 8-year-old children three versions of the conservation of number task. One of these was the traditional conservation task: the children saw two identical looking sets, judged correctly that the two sets were equal in number, then saw the appearance of one of the sets being altered, and were asked once again to compare the quantity of the two sets. The second task was the same, except that after the transformation the children had to count one of the sets and were then asked to infer the number of the second set. In the third task the children were required to count both sets after the transformation and then were asked whether they were equal in quantity.

Most of the children younger than 6 years failed the third task. Thus, the children counted both sets at the end of the third task, arrived at the same number, and yet still said that the more spread-out of the two sets had more objects in it than the other one did. They judged that one set with 'eight' objects in it was more numerous than another set, also with 'eight' objects, and that meant, according to Piaget and to Greco, that they do not know what the word 'eight' means.

A second important result was that slightly older children tended to get the first task (the traditional conservation problem) wrong, and yet were right in the second task in which they counted one set and then were asked to infer the number of objects in the second set. These children therefore judged that spreading out a set of objects alters its quantity (their mistaken judgement in the traditional task) but not its number in the sense of the number one would reach if one were to count the set.

Young children sometimes do not realise that same number = same quantity

Piaget and Greco explained these results by making a distinction between 'quantité' and 'quotité'. 'Quotité' is the understanding of the children who realise that two sets of objects have the same number, in the sense that counting each one leads to the same number word, and yet may think that there are more objects in the more spread-out set. They realised that the number words (quotité) stayed the same despite the perceptual transformation of one of the sets, and yet did not realise that the actual number (quantité) was also unaffected by this irrelevant, perceptual change.

The Greco experiment was about comparisons between sets. Other studies of such comparisons lead to much the same conclusion. Frye *et al.* (1989), Michie (1984) and Saxe (1979), in separate studies, asked children, who could count, to compare two sets of objects quantitatively. All reported a reluctance in these children to count in order to compare.

This failure to see that number can be used as a comparative measure was also demonstrated in a study by Sophian (1988). She showed 3- and 4-year-old children a puppet who counted two sets of objects. The children had to judge whether the puppet counted in the right way. In some trials the puppet had to compare the two sets and in other trials to find out how many objects there were in the two sets altogether. In the first condition the right thing to do was to count the two sets separately, while in the second it was to count them together. Sometimes the puppet did the right thing, and sometimes not.

The younger children were completely at sea in this experiment. They did badly when the puppet was asked to compare two different sets. They did not seem to know that one must count two sets separately in order to compare them. They cannot have understood the cardinal properties of the numbers that they knew so well. Their performance fits the Piagetian picture of quotité without quantité.

The importance of one-to-one correspondence

One way of making a number comparison is to use **one-to-one correspondence**. If two sets are in correspondence, in the sense that each object has its own counterpart in the other set, then the two sets are equal in number. One of the main pieces of evidence that Piaget cited for children's difficulties with cardinality was the difficulties that they have with one-to-one correspondence.

one-to-one corres-pondence two sets are in one-to-one correspondence if each object in one set has a counterpart in the other set. If the objects in two sets are in one-to-one correspondence, they are equal in number.

Piaget (1953, 1974) showed children a row of objects and asked them to lay out another row with the same number. The younger children did not pair off (or count) the items and usually equated the rows in terms of their length rather than of their number. Piaget and Inhelder (1966) and also Cowan and Daniels (1989) showed that children fail to use one-to-one correspondence to compare the number of items in two straight rows of counters laid side by side, even when every counter in each set is explicitly linked by a straight line to an equivalent counter in the other. Even this blatant cue has little effect on children's use of one-to-one correspondence.

Piaget concluded that young children have no understanding at all of one-to-one correspondence, but one must be cautious about this negative view, because there are grounds for thinking that children use one-to-one correspondence easily and effectively in another context. This context is sharing, which is something that children often do. Three studies (Desforges & Desforges, 1980; Frydman & Bryant, 1988; Miller, 1984) have shown that children as young as 4 years old share things competently between two or more recipients, usually on a repetitive 'one for A, one for B' basis. This sharing seems to be a temporal form of one-to-one correspondence.

Frydman and Bryant (1988) also looked at children's ability to relate number words to sharing. We asked some 4-year-old children to share out some 'sweets' (unifix bricks) between two recipients. When they had done this, we counted out aloud the number of sweets given to one recipient, and then asked the child how many sweets had been given to the other. The task divided the children into two almost equal groups. Just under a half of them correctly inferred that the second set contained the same number as the first. Just over half were unable to make that inference

It seems that young children do grasp one-to-one correspondence and cardinality when sharing before they go to school, but not all of them apply this understanding to number words. Some combine quotité with quantité: some do not. All of them probably grasp the mathematical significance of temporal one-to-one correspondence, but some do not yet apply this understanding to number words.

Conclusions about the beginnings of the understanding of number

The evidence for effective innate structures that are especially tuned to numerical principles is not strong. The research on infants is unreliable. The mistakes that pre-school children make in simple number tasks cannot be dismissed as mere procedural errors. Tasks in which these children have to compare quantities show serious gaps in young children's understanding of basic number principles. Young children do not at first realise that counting is a way of measuring the relative quantities of two different sets, and they are happy to maintain that two sets with the same number are nevertheless different in quantity. Even when they know that two sets are equal in quantity and they also know the number of items in one set, they sometimes fail to infer the number of items in the uncounted set. They plainly have a lot to learn.

At school they learn to reason additively and multiplicatively (which includes reasoning about fractions and proportions), and then to master aspects of mathematics, such as algebra, geometry, and calculus, that are at times quite complex and demanding. These relatively advanced aspects of mathematics are beyond the scope of this chapter. The reader is referred to Nunes and Bryant (1996) and to Nunes *et al.* (2009) for accounts of the psychological processes underlying this further mathematical learning.

SUMMARY AND CONCLUSIONS

The beginning of this chapter posed the question: how much of children's learning must depend on instruction and how much do they learn for themselves without formal help from others? The answer to this question is roughly the same for children learning to read and also to do mathematics. In both cases, we find that, either innately or through their own informal experiences, children do

FIGURE 12.5 *Children acquire some crucial knowledge, either innate or through their own formal experiences, of mathematics long before they go to school.*
Source: Shutterstock.

acquire some crucial knowledge, long before they go to school, which prepares them for the formal learning that they eventually have to do at school (Figure 12.5). This takes the form of an early awareness of phonology, initially through rhyme, in the case of reading, and of awareness and use of one-to-one correspondence in the case of mathematics. In both cases it takes them quite a long time to learn, with the help of formal instruction, how the cultural tools that they are taught at school relate to their initial knowledge. When we study how children eventually make this connection we must recognise the great importance both of their own informal knowledge and of the intellectual demands of the cultural tools which they learn from others.

DISCUSSION POINTS

1. Think about the relative contribution of instruction and the child's own constructions in the development of reading.
2. Why is rhyme so important in learning to read?
3. Think of ways in which cross-cultural studies of reading development can enhance our understanding of the reading process.
4. Think of the major challenges presented to a child learning to read an alphabetic script.
5. Evaluate the evidence for and against the proposition that infants have innate knowledge of number.
6. Consider how Carey's individuation hypothesis has contributed to understanding of early number knowledge.
7. Evaluate the evidence suggesting that children must acquire certain logical abilities before they can understand number.
8. What can we learn from cross-cultural studies of the development of numerical knowledge?

SUGGESTIONS FOR FURTHER READING

Butterworth, B. (1999). *The mathematical brain*. London: Macmillan.

Cain, K. (2010). *Reading development and difficulties*. Oxford: Wiley-Blackwell.

Cain, K., & Oakhill, J. (2007). *Comprehension problems in oral and written language: A cognitive perspective*. Hove: Guilford Press.

Dehaene, S. (1997). *The number sense*. London: Penguin.

Frydman, O., & Bryant, P.E. (1988). Sharing and understanding of number equivalence by young children. *Cognitive Development, 3*, 323–339.

Goswami, U., & Bryant, P. (1990). *Phonological skills and learning to read*. London: Erlbaum.

Nunes, T., & Bryant, P. (1996). *Children doing mathematics*. Oxford: Blackwell.

Nunes, T., & Bryant, P. (2009). *Children's reading and spelling: Beyond the first steps*. Chichester: Wiley-Blackwell.

REFERENCES

Antell, S.E., & Keating, D.P. (1983). Perception of numerical invariance in neonates. *Child Development, 54,* 695–701.

Baker, L., Fernandez-Fein, S., Scher, D., & Williams, H. (1998). Home experiences related to the development of word recognition. In J.L. Metsala & L.C. Ehri (Eds.) *Word recognition in beginning literacy* (pp. 263–287). Hillsdale, NJ: Erlbaum.

Bjaalid, I., Hoien, T., & Lundberg, I. (1996). The contribution of orthographic and phonological processes to word reading in Norwegian readers. *Reading and Writing, 8,* 189–198.

Bowey, J., Cain, M.T., & Ryan, S.M. (1992). A reading-level design study of phonological skills underlying fourth-grade children's word reading difficulties. *Child Development, 63,* 999–1011.

Bradley, L., & Bryant, P.E. (1983). Categorising sounds and learning to read—a causal connection. *Nature, 301,* 419–521.

Bruce, D.J. (1964). The analysis of word sounds. *British Journal of Educational Psychology, 34,* 158–170.

Bryant, P.E. (1992). Arithmetic in the cradle. *Nature, 358,* 712–713.

Bryant, P. (2002). Children's thoughts about reading and spelling. *Scientific Studies of Reading, 6,* 199–216.

Bryant, P., Devine, M., Ledward, A., & Nunes, T. (1997). Spelling with apostrophes and understanding possession. *British Journal of Educational Psychology, 67,* 93–112.

Bryant, P.E., MacLean, M., Bradley, L.L., & Crossland, J. (1990). Rhyme, alliteration, phoneme detection and learning to read. *Developmental Psychology, 26,* 429–438.

Bryant, P., Nunes, T., & Aidinis, A. (1999). Different morphemes, same spelling problems: Cross-linguistic developmental studies. In M. Harris & G. Hatano (Eds.) *Learning to read and write: a cross-linguistic perspective* (pp. 112–133). Cambridge: Cambridge University Press.

Butterworth, B. (1999). *The mathematical brain.* London: Macmillan.

Carey, S. (2004). Bootstrapping and the origin of concepts. *Daedalus, 133*(1), 59–69.

Chaney, C. (1992). Language development, metalinguistic skills and print awareness in 3-year-old children. *Applied Psycholinguistics, 15,* 485–514.

Chliounaki, K., & Bryant, P. (2002). Construction and learning to spell. *Cognitive Development, 17,* 1489–1499.

Chliounaki, K., & Bryant, P. (2007). How children learn about morphological spelling rules. *Child Development, 78*(4), 1360–1373.

Chukovsky, K. (1963). *From two to five.* Berkeley: University of California Press.

Clearfield, M.W., & Mix, K.S. (1999). Number vs contour length in infants' discrimination of small visual sets. *Psychological Science, 10,* 408–411.

Cowan, R., & Daniels, H. (1989). The children's use of counting and guidelines in judging relative numbers. *British Journal of Educational Psychology, 59,* 200–210.

Cronin, V., & Carver, P. (1998). Phonological sensitivity, rapid naming and beginning reading. *Applied Psycholinguistics, 19,* 447–461.

Davis, C., & Bryant, P. (2006). Causal connections in the acquisition of an orthographic rule: A test of Uta Frith's developmental hypothesis. *Journal of Child Psychology and Psychiatry, 47,* 849–856.

Dehaene, S. (1997). *The number sense.* London: Penguin.

Demont, E., & Gombert, J.E. (1996). Phonological awareness as a predictor of recoding skill and syntactic awareness as a predictor of comprehension skills. *British Journal of Educational Psychology, 66,* 315–332.

Desforges, A., & Desforges, G. (1980). Number-based strategies of sharing in young children. *Educational Studies, 6,* 97–109.

Dowker, A. (1989). Rhymes and alliteration in poems elicited from young children. *Journal of Child Language, 16*, 181–202.

Ehri, L.C. (1995). The emergence of word learning in beginning reading. In P. Owen & P. Pumfrey (Eds.) *Children learning to read: international concerns.* (pp. 9–31). New York: Falmer Press.

Ellis, N., & Large, B. (1987). The development of reading: As you seek so shall you find. *British Journal of Developmental Psychology, 78*, 1–28.

Fayol, M., Thenevin, M.G., Jarousse, J.P., & Totereau, C. (1999). From learning to teaching to learning French written morphology. In T. Nunes (ed.) *Learning to read: An integrated view from research and practice.* Dordrecht: Kluwer.

Ferreiro, E., & Teberosky, A. (1983). *Literacy before schooling.* Exeter, NH: Heinemann Educational Books.

Frith, U. (1985). Beneath the surface of developmental dyslexia. In K. Patterson, M. Coltheart, & J. Marshall (Eds.) *Surface dyslexia* (pp. 301–330). London: Lawrence Erlbaum and Associates.

Frydman, O., & Bryant, P.E. (1988). Sharing and the understanding of number equivalence by young children. *Cognitive Development, 3*, 323–339.

Frye, D., Braisby, N., Lowe, J., Maroudas, C., & Nicholls, J. (1989). Young children's understanding of counting and cardinality. *Child Development, 60*, 1158–1171.

Fuson, K.C. (1988). *Children's counting and concepts of number.* New York: Springer Verlag.

Gelman, R., & Butterworth, B. (2005). Number and Language: How are they related? *Trends in Cognitive Science, 9*, 6–10.

Gelman, R., & Gallistel, C.R. (1978). *The child's understanding of number.* Cambridge, MA: Harvard University Press.

Gelman, R., & Meck, E. (1983). Preschoolers' counting: Principles before skill. *Cognition, 13*, 343–360.

Gelman, R., Meck, E., & Merkin, S. (1986). Young children's numerical competence. *Cognitive Development, 1*, 1–30.

Greaney, K.T., Tunmer, W., & Chapman, J.W. (1997). Effects of rime-based orthographic analogy training on the word recognition skills of children with reading disability. *Journal of Educational Psychology, 89*, 645–651.

Greco, P. (1962). Quantité et quotité: Nouvelles recherches sur la correspondance terme-a-terme et la conservation des ensembles. In P. Greco & A. Morf (Eds.) *Structures numeriques elementaires: Etudes d'Epistemologie Genetique* (Vol 13; pp. 35–52). Paris: Presses Universitaires de France.

Hansen, J., & Bowey, J.A. (1994). Phonological analysis skills, verbal working memory and reading ability in 2nd grade children. *Child Development, 65*, 938–950.

Kessler, B., & Treiman, R. (1997). Syllable structure and the distribution of phonemes in English syllables. *Journal of Memory and Language, 37*, 295–311.

Kemp, N., & Bryant, P. (2003). Do beez buzz? Rule-based and frequency-based knowledge in learning to spell plural -s. *Child Development, 74*, 63–74.

Le Corre, M., & Carey, S. (2007). One, two, three, nothing more: An investigation of the conceptual sources of verbal number principles. *Cognition, 105*, 395–438.

Liberman, I.Y., Shankweiler, D., Fischer, F.W., & Carter, B. (1974). Explicit syllable and phoneme segmentation in the young child. *Journal of Experimental Child Psychology, 18*, 201–212.

Liberman, I.Y., Shankweiler, D., & Liberman, A. (1989). The alphabetic principle and learning to read. In D. Shankweiler & I.Y. Liberman (Eds.) *Phonology and reading disability* (pp. 1–34). Ann Arbor: The University of Michigan Press.

Lundberg, I., Oloffson, A., & Wall, S. (1980). Reading and spelling skills in the first school years predicted from phoneme awareness skills in kindergarten. *Scandinavian Journal of Psychology, 21*, 159–173.

Marsh, G., & Desberg, P. (1983). The development of strategies in the acquisition of symbolic skills. In D.R. Rogers & J.A. Sloboda (Eds.) *The Acquisition of Symbolic Skills* (pp. 149–154). New York: Plenum Press.

Marsh, G., Friedman, M.P., Welch, V., & Desberg, P. (1980). The development of strategies in spelling. In U. Frith (Ed.) *Cognitive Processes in Spelling* (pp. 339–355). London: Academic Press.

Michie, S. (1984). Why preschoolers are reluctant to count spontaneously. *British Journal of Developmental Psychology*, *2*, 347–358.

Miller, K.F. (1984). The child as the measurer of all things: Measurement procedures and the development of quantitative concepts. In C. Sophian (Ed.) *Origins of Cognitive Skills* (pp. 193–228). Hillsdale, NJ: Erlbaum.

Miller, K.F., & Stigler, J.W. (1987). Counting in Chinese: Cultural variation in a basic cognitive skill. *Cognitive Development*, *2*, 279-305.

Miura, I.T., Kim, C.C., Chang, C.-M., & Okamoto, Y. (1988). Effects of language characteristics on children's cognitive representation of number: Cross-national comparisons. *Child Development*, *59*, 1445–1450.

Miura, I.T., Okamoto, Y., Kim, C.C., Chang, C.-M., Steere, M., & Fayol, M. (1994). Comparisons of children's cognitive representation of number: China, France, Japan, Korea, Sweden and the United States. *International Journal of Behavioural Development*, *17*, 401–411.

Mix, K.S., Levine, S.C., & Huttenlocher, J. (1997). Numerical abstraction in infants: Another look. *Developmental Psychology*, *35*, 423–428.

Mix, K.S., Levine, S.C., & Huttenlocher, J. (2001) *Quantitative development in infancy and early childhood*. New York: Oxford University Press.

Morais, J., Bertelson, P., Cary, L., & Alegria, J. (1986). Literacy training and speech segmentation. *Cognition*, *24*, 45–64.

Morais, J., Cary, L., Alegria, J., & Bertelson, P. (1979). Does awareness of speech as a sequence of phones arise spontaneously? *Cognition*, *7*, 323–331.

Naslund, J.C., & Schneider, W. (1996). Kindergarten letter knowledge, phonological skills and memory processes: Relative effects on early literacy. *Journal of Experimental Psychology*, *62*, 30–59.

Nunes, T., & Bryant, P. (1996). *Children doing mathematics*. Oxford: Blackwell.

Nunes, T., & Bryant, P. (2006). *Improving literacy through teaching morphemes*. London: Routledge.

Nunes, T., & Bryant, P. (2009). *Children's reading and spelling: Beyond the first steps*. Chichester: Wiley-Blackwell.

Nunes, T., Bryant, P., & Bindman, M. (1997). Morphological spelling strategies: Developmental stages and processes. *Developmental Psychology*, *33*, 637–649.

Nunes, T., Bryant, P., & Watson, A. (2009, June). *Children's mathematical learning: A report to the Nuffield Foundation*. Retrieved 14 April 2011, from www.nuffieldfoundation.org/key-understandings-mathematics-learning.

Olson, D.R. (1994). *The world on paper*. Cambridge: Cambridge University Press.

Olson, D.R. (1996). Towards a psychology of literacy: On the relations between speech and writing. *Cognition*, *60*, 83–104.

Piaget, J. (1952). *The child's conception of number*. London: Routledge and Kegan Paul.

Piaget, J. (1953). How children form mathematical concepts. *Scientific American*, *189*, 74–79.

Piaget, J. (2001). *Studies in reflecting abstraction*. (R. Campbell Trans.). Hove: Psychology Press.

Piaget, J., & Inhelder, B. (1966). *Mental imagery in the child*. London: Routledge & Kegan Paul.

Piaget, J., & Inhelder, B. (1974). *The child's construction of quantities*. London: Routledge & Kegan Paul.

Piaget, J., Inhelder, B., & Szeminska, A. (1960). *The child's conception of geometry*. London: Routledge & Kegan Paul

Read, C. (1986). *Children's Creative Spelling*. London: Routledge & Kegan Paul.

Saxe, G. (1979). A developmental analysis of notational counting. *Child Development, 48*, 1512–1520.

Saxe, G. (1981). Body parts as numerals: A developmental analysis of numeration among the Oksapmin in Papua New Guinea. *Child Development, 52*, 306–316.

Sophian, C. (1988). Limitations on preschool children's knowledge about counting: Using counting to compare two sets. *Developmental Psychology, 24*, 634–640.

Stahl, S.A., & Murray, B.A. (1994). Defining phonological awareness and its relationship to early reading. *Journal of Educational Psychology, 86*, 221–234.

Stanovich, K.E., Siegel, L.S., & Gottardo, A. (1997). Converging evidence for phonological and surface subtypes of reading disability. *Journal of Educational Psychology, 89*, 114–127.

Starkey, P., & Cooper, R. (1980). Perception of numbers by human infants. *Science, 210*, 1033–1034.

Starkey, P., Spelke, E.S., & Gelman, R. (1990). Numerical abstraction by human infants. *Cognition, 36*, 97–128.

Strauss, M.S., & Curtis, L.E. (1981). Infant perception of number. *Child Development, 52*, 1146–1152.

Totereau, C., Thévenin M.-G., & Fayol, M. (1997). Acquisition de la morphologie du nombre à l'écrit en français. In: L. Rieben, M. Fayol & C.-A. Perfetti (Eds.) *Des orthographes et leur acquisition* (pp. 147–163). Lausanne: Delachaux et Niestlé.

Towse, J.N., & Saxton, M. (1997). Linguistic influences on children's number concepts: Methodological and theoretical considerations. *Journal of Experimental Child Psychology, 66*, 362–375.

Treiman, R., Mullenix, J., Bijeljac-Babic, R., & Richmond-Welty, E.D. (1995). The special role of rimes in the description, use and acquisition of English orthography. *Journal of Experimental Psychology – General, 124*, 107–136.

van Loosbroek, E., & Smitsman, A.W. (1990). Visual perception of numerosity in infancy. *Developmental Psychology, 26*, 916–922.

Vellutino, F.R., & Scanlon, D.M. (1987). Phonological coding phonological awareness and reading ability: Evidence from a longitudinal and experimental study. *Reading Research Quarterly, 30*, 854–875.

Vygotsky, L.S. (1978). *Mind in Society*. Cambridge, MA: Harvard University Press.

Vygotsky, L.S. (1986). *Thought and language*. Cambridge, MA: M.I.T. Press.

Vygotsky, L.S., & Luria, A.R. (1993). *Studies on the history of behaviour: Ape, primitive and child*. Hillsdale, NJ.: Lawrence Erlbaum and Associates.

Wakeley, A., Rivera, S., & Langer, J. (2000a). Can young infants add and subtract? *Child Development, 71*, 1525–1534.

Wakeley, A., Rivera, S., & Langer, J. (2000b). Not proved: Reply to Wynn. *Child Development, 71*, 1537–1539.

Walton, P.D. (1995). Rhyming ability, phoneme identity, letter–sound knowledge, and the use of orthographic analogy by pre-readers. *Journal of Educational Psychology, 87*, 587–597.

Wagner, R., & Torgeson, J.K. (1987). The nature of phonological processing and its causal role in the acquisition of reading skills. *Psychological Bulletin, 1101*, 192–212.

Wynn, K. (1992). Addition and subtraction by human infants. *Nature, 358*, 749–750.

Wynn, K. (1998). Psychological foundations of number: Numerical competence in human infants. *Trends in Cognitive Science, 2*, 296–303.

Wynn, K. (2000). Findings of addition and subtraction in infants are robust and consistent: Reply to Wakeley, Rivera and Langer. *Child Development, 71*, 1535–1536.

Ziegler, J. C., & Goswami, U. (2005). Reading acquisition, developmental dyslexia, and skilled reading across languages: A psycholinguistic grain theory. *Psychological Bulletin, 131*(1), 3–29.

13 Memory Development and Eyewitness Testimony

STEPHEN J. CECI, STANKA A. FITNEVA, CAGLA AYDIN, AND NADIA CHERNYAK

KEY TERMS

cluster effect • cognitive processes • demand characteristics • elaboration • encoding • episodic memory • explicit memory • implicit memory • infantile amnesia • long-term memory • metamemory • mnemonic strategy • organisation • paired-associate task • recall • recognition • rehearsal • retrieval demands • retroactive interference • script • semantic memory • short-term memory • suggestibility • theory of mind

CHAPTER OUTLINE

OVERVIEW

Memory, the retention of experience, is a ubiquitous cognitive process, and is essential for our functioning and development. There are three stages of the memory system. The first stage is called *encoding*. This stage determines how the events we witness are stored in memory, and how detailed is their representation. In the second, *storage* phase, encoded events enter *short-term memory* and may then enter into *long-term memory*. The final step in remembering involves the *retrieval* of stored information.

The authors discuss in detail three factors which change during development, and which influence the encoding, storage, and retrieval of information.

- The first factor is children's existing *knowledge*.
- The second is awareness and application of mnemonic *strategies* that facilitate remembering
- The third is *metamemory*, which refers to understanding the properties of memory and what strategy is needed in a given situation. Metamemory skills are extremely important to students engaged in the active learning of information.

The second part of the chapter looks at children's eyewitness testimony. How accurate is children's testimony when they are asked to be witnesses? A key notion here is *suggestibility*, or children's tendency to change their memories and beliefs in response to interrogation. The authors discuss the many factors that can lead both to false testimony, and also to accurate reports of past events.

INTRODUCTION

The Bronx case

In 1997 the *New York Times* reported that of a group of boys who attended Bronx Public School four were arrested for assaulting two young girls during recess. The four boys, aged 8 and 9, were charged with juvenile delinquency (Ojito, 1997). According to the statements taken from six aides and a parent volunteer – all of whom were said to be supervising the recess – a little girl approached a teacher's aide and told him that her friend had been pushed and shoved by the boys and that one of them had rubbed his body against her friend's body. A female aide interviewed the two girls. During this interview the alleged victim kept silent. 'Each and every time she was asked a question, her friend would speak up for her', the aide wrote in her report (Ojito, 1997). When the girls returned to their classroom, the friend repeated the story to her teacher. The principal called the boys in for questioning. They denied having rubbed their bodies against any of the girls.

Up to this point, neither of the girls nor any of the boys had mentioned a boy pulling his pants down and putting his penis into a girl's mouth. However, later that night, the girl in question told her 18-year-old sister that a boy had rubbed his genitals against her mouth. The girl's mother took her to the hospital and called the police. While the police investigation was going on, the principal wrote a letter to all the parents of children at the school assuring them that: 'I made a complete investigation by listening and speaking to our students. I have determined that no inappropriate behaviour took place at any time.' Whose story was right?

How reliable are children's reports?

Cases such as this one occur with all too great frequency. Courts and law enforcement professionals are faced with the daunting task of sorting out what actually happened. And when physical evidence is scarce, as is often the case in sexual offence investigations, they have to rely on the reports of alleged victims, perpetrators, and eyewitnesses to reconstruct the event. Thus, it becomes critical to evaluate the factors that might have influenced the reliability of those reports. The critical issues are whether the witnesses have any reason to distort the truth and whether their memories of the events are complete and reliable. In particular, the reliability of the alleged victim's report in the Bronx case can be evaluated if we could answer the following questions: What kept her from saying anything about the sexual assault at school? How did the circumstances at home prompt her report of sexual assault to her sister? What influence could have her friend's assertions had on her own memory for the event? What influence could have the repeated questioning by aides and teachers had on the accuracy of her statement?

Increasingly, officials dealing with cases involving child witnesses have turned to experts in the field of memory development for help in evaluating the reliability of the children's reports. Research in memory development addresses the questions of how everyday events are initially experienced, how they are represented in our brains, and how they are later retrieved. In this chapter we shall review some fundamental influences on children's memory development. The pressure to respond to the public need of establishing the credibility of child witnesses has moved the field to exploring a variety of factors that might influence children's reports. The key notion in this broader research is **suggestibility**, or the child's tendency to change their memories and beliefs in response to interrogation (Ceci & Bruck, 1993). Suggestibility is perceived as a dangerous characteristic of children because it allows memories to become tainted and inaccurate testimony to be given in court. In the second part of the chapter we shall survey the findings generated by this research agenda.

suggestibility a child's (or adult's) tendency to change their memories and beliefs, often in response to interrogation. This is likely to result in inaccurate recall of events.

THE DEVELOPMENT OF MEMORY

Memory, the ability to store, retain, and recall experience, is a ubiquitous *cognitive process*. Sometimes, e.g. for school, we intentionally commit facts to memory. Most of the time, however, we retain information without thinking that later we will be questioned about it. Indeed, we do not attend to our strolls through the park, coffee shop encounters, and trips abroad thinking about how we will later describe them to our friends. Still, our conversations are replete with references to such past experiences.

#1 06-11-2018 2:49PM Item(s) ch
ecked out to Proothi, Shammi.

TITLE
  BARCODE   DUE DATE
An introduction to developmental psycholog
y 30114015880704 13-11-18

Glasgow University

Library receipt

4hr & 24hr items ca

nnot be renewed

Recognition and recall

Researchers have developed a variety of methods to study remembering. Two common tests of memory are recognition and recall. After a person has been presented with study items or an event has occurred, they might be asked to identify the items they had been exposed to from a list of novel items and items that were present during the event. This test format measures **recognition** memory. Alternatively, the individual might be asked to retrieve details of the experienced event in an open format (e.g. 'Tell me what happened on the playground yesterday'). This is a test of **recall** memory. As you can imagine, it is much more difficult to recall events than to recognise them. Just try recalling the names of all classmates from a previous school; you may recall 75 per cent of them if you are exceptionally skilled. However, if you were presented with a list of all past classmates as well as some names of non-classmates, you would have little trouble correctly recognising the names of the actual classmates at close to 100 per cent accuracy. Recognition is easier because of the absence of retrieval demands – the task provides all of the retrieval cues needed by presenting the actual names (or shopping list items, etc.).

Recognition and recall measure **explicit memory,** that is, experience that is accessible to consciousness. However, on some occasions, our thoughts and actions are influenced by events that we cannot consciously remember. In these cases we say that we have **implicit memories** of these events (Schacter, 1987). Such memories require other types of measurement but as we are interested in children's verbal reports of past events, most of the studies we report use recognition and recall procedures to assess memory. The process that these procedures assess is complex and sometimes effortful. The likelihood that we can recall an event from our past depends on the skill with which we execute a set of tasks, initially during the event's occurrence, after it has ended, and later at the time of its retrieval. Psychologists who study human memory usually model these tasks as a flow of information from one stage of the memory system to another. The three main stages of the system are encoding, storage, and retrieval.

recognition after witnessing an event, or learning test items, a participant is shown a list of items and asked to identify (*recognise*) any that were present during the event or initial learning.

recall after witnessing an event, or learning test items, a participant is asked to describe anything about the event or the test items that they can remember, where the event or test items are no longer present

explicit memory memory for an experience or event that is easily accessible.

implicit memory memory for events that we cannot *consciously* remember.

THE MEMORY PROCESS

Encoding

The first phase of the memory system is called **encoding**. This stage determines how the event we witness is stored in memory and how detailed is its representation. There is selectivity in what gets encoded into the storage system, and not everything we experience

encoding the first stage in the memory system. Information that is attended to gets placed (*encoded*) in the memory storage system.

actually gets stored. In part, this selectivity in encoding reflects our limited attentional resources. We cannot attend to everything at one time: we generally attend only to certain aspects of an event and ignore other aspects. As an example, beginning drivers may invest their entire attentional capacity to keeping their car in the centre of the lane. They may have no attentional capacity left over to attend to peripheral information such as what songs were played on the radio or what signs were posted on the road. Thus, not everything that is 'out there' gets attended to and nothing that escapes attention gets encoded in memory. In addition to limited attentional capacity, there are a number of other factors that can potentially influence what enters the memory system. These include the amount of prior knowledge about the events, the duration and repetition of the original event, and the stress level at the time of encoding the original event.

Storage

In the second phase of the memory system, encoded events enter a **short-term memory** store. Not all of the memories survive the short-term memory's limited storage capacity, but those that do survive enter into **long-term memory** storage. The passage of time, the number of times that the event has been re-experienced (or mentally rehearsed), and the number and types of intervening experiences, which also become encoded and stored, can have a strong impact on the strength and organisation of the stored information. Memories can increase or decrease in strength as a function of how long they have been stored (usually shorter delays result in better recall) and as a function of the number of times that the original event has been recalled. (Repetition strengthens the memory for the features of the event that have been recalled.) The composition of a memory during the storage phase can also change due to expectancies, even ones created after the event. New expectancies generate pressure on old memories to be consistent with them. Long after we can no longer retrieve a memory, we use our expectations to reconstruct what was its likely content. Finally, intervening experiences may at times serve to solidify the initial memory (when they are congruent with the initial event) and at other times they may compete with and interfere with the stored memory (when they are inconsistent with the original event). Thus, all these factors influence the rate of memory decay and the accuracy of recollections.

> **short-term memory** encoded events enter the short-term memory first, and can then progress to the *long-term memory*.

> **long-term memory** items stored in the long-term memory have passed through the *short-term memory* and are now stored for an extended period of time.

Retrieval

The final step in remembering involves the **retrieval** of stored information. Retrieval is seldom perfect. In fact, there are times when the contents of the memory system are simply not accessible even though in principle they are available. A variety of cognitive as well as social factors influence the retrievability of stored memory, for example, motivation

> **retrieval demands** cognitive demands made when attempting to remember information.

to retrieve old memories, the willingness to cooperate with the examiner and the comprehension of what is important to recall. Some of these factors at times enhance recall, whereas at other times the same factors may decrease the accuracy of the recall. For example, memory retrieval is strongly influenced by context. The retrieval of a memory may be facilitated when the conditions prevalent at the time of retrieval parallel those that existed at the time of the original encoding. One of the best examples of this principle is provided by a study by Godden and Baddeley (1975). In this study, deep-sea divers were asked to learn lists of words while

FIGURE 13.1 *Deep-sea divers' recall of words was better while they were beneath the sea!*
Source: Shutterstock.

they were beneath the sea. Their later retrieval of these words was better when they were beneath the sea compared to when they were on land. In recent replications of this work, it has been shown that divers retrieve lists encoded on dry land better when they are put back on dry land, and they retrieve lists encoded under water better when they are put back under water at the time of retrieval (Figure 13.1). An extension of this finding is that when an interviewer provides cues that may reinstate the encoding context, accuracy of recall improves. Various types of cues can be given. Some involve reminding the subject about parts of the actual event, whereas others induce emotional or cognitive states that match those present at the time of encoding. Although these techniques may facilitate the recall of stored experience, they may also induce false recall if the cues suggest an event that was never experienced or call up an event different from the target one.

So, in summary, at every stage of remembering, encoding, storage, and retrieval, there are ways in which we can lose information about past experience. To start, not everything 'out there' that impinges on our senses actually gets encoded (because our attention is limited). Furthermore, of that portion that does get encoded, not all survives a lengthy storage period. And, finally, of that subset of encoded features that get encoded and stored, not all are retrievable. Adults have access to a variety of techniques, knowledge, and insights to minimise information loss at each stage of remembering. Young children need to acquire such techniques, as we will see.

Semantic and episodic memory

The encoding–storage–retrieval process applies to different kinds of remembering: from the acquisition of skills and factual knowledge to the learning of a foreign language and the spatial layout of a novel location. Among these different kinds of

semantic memory
long-term memory of all of our world knowledge, including concepts, algorithms, definitions of words and the relations between them.

episodic memory
memory for specific personally experienced events, including their temporal and spatial contexts.

remembering, an important distinction is drawn between **semantic** and **episodic memory** (Tulving, 1983). Semantic memory is defined as the long-term storage of all of our world knowledge, including concepts, algorithms, definitions of words and the relations between them. The semantic memory for 'market' for example includes the knowledge that it is a place for buying and selling goods. In contrast, episodic memory is conceptualised as memory of specific events, including their temporal and spatial contexts. Thus the episodic memory for 'market' would represent the trips to the market on Saturday and where you can find the best honey. As you will notice, most examples in this chapter are from research on episodic memory. This is because of the applicability of this research to the discussion of children's eyewitness testimony. In court, children are questioned about events of their lives rather than their conceptual knowledge. However, semantic memory researchers have arrived at similar conclusions about the problems of memory development discussed here.

THREE FACTORS THAT INFLUENCE THE DEVELOPMENT OF MEMORY: KNOWLEDGE, STRATEGIES, AND METAMEMORIES

mnemonic strategy
any strategy that helps to improve one's own memory. Mnemonic strategies include *elaboration, organisation,* and *rehearsal*.

metamemory understanding one's own memory and having an awareness of the ways in which memory works and can be improved.

We briefly pointed out factors that influence each of the three stages of memory: encoding, storage, and retrieval. Next we discuss in more detail three of these factors and how their maturation influences the development of memory. The first factor is children's existing knowledge (Bjorklund & Schneider, 1996; Chi & Ceci, 1987). The second factor is awareness and application of **mnemonic strategies** that facilitate remembering. The third factor is **metamemory**, which refers to understanding the properties of memory and what strategy is needed in a given situation. For instance, metamemory allows us to have insights into how our memories work, such as when we have memorised a list, what actions we need to take to maintain that list in memory.

Knowledge development

To a large extent, the ability to encode, store, and retrieve information directly depends on the knowledge that one possesses. Knowledge is the material that influences how we experience the flow of events and what we pay attention to. At the same time, it is the material that our experiences modify. Children differ from adults in the number of facts they have stored in their memories, in their understanding of the structure of events, and in their expectancies about the way the world works. Occasionally, children may have knowledge advantages in certain areas (for example, when they possess greater knowledge about cartoon characters than adults do). And occasionally, younger children's reduced knowledge inoculates them against suggestions (see Brainerd *et al.*, 2008). But, generally, knowledge increases as a function of age. In this section we will discuss the role of content knowledge on remembering.

Event representations or scripts

The most productive construct used to explain how knowledge influences memory is that of a **script** (Schank & Abelson, 1977). Scripts are generalised event representations. They are abstracted from the occurrences of similar events and, as conceptual structures, represent types of events of varying specificity. Scripts specify the structure of events by having 'slots' for the participants in the events and links between these slots. The links represent causal and temporal relations between the participants. For example, a script for 'Going to a Restaurant' has slots for the restaurant goers, the maître d'hôtel, the waitress, the menu, the table setting, and the different courses (Figure 13.2). The links between these slots denote the components of a 'Going to a Restaurant' event. These include the maître d'hôtel taking a party to its table, the use of a menu to make a selection, eating the entrée that was ordered, followed by dessert, and then paying the bill. The links are indexed so that the order of the components is specified and eating the dessert follows eating the entrée. The number of scripts a person possesses and the elaboration of these scripts can stand for their total amount of knowledge.

Top-down structures

Scripts are top-down structures: they lead to the automatic generation of expectations about the causal structure of an event and what or who fills the slots in the script. The top-down nature of scripts is evident in that the default slot fillers can fill in missing information or substitute ambiguous information both at the time an event is experienced and encoded and at the time of its retrieval. For example, when asked to recall a faded event, we may use our knowledge about what 'typically' happens to fill gaps in our memory. We may start a description of a dinner at a restaurant by saying

FIGURE 13.2 *Going to a restaurant is typically a scripted event, with the order and structure of the components being clearly known (e.g., the entrée comes before the dessert).*
Source: Shutterstock.

that we were taken to our table by the maître d'hôtel, even though we have no clear memory of how we entered the restaurant. Because being taken to a table is usually the first thing that happens at a restaurant, there is high probability that the description we provide of our evening is correct. We may also 'disambiguate' information in favour of the script-provided expectations. In some restaurants it is impossible to distinguish the maître d'hôtel from the waiters and some restaurants don't have one. In these cases, we might decide that the person who takes us to our table is the maître d'hôtel although there is no clear evidence for that. Again, given that most frequently it is the maître d'hôtel who takes a party to its table, we are probably going to be right.

Congruity and mismatch

When an event is highly congruent with our script-based knowledge, it is likely to be retrieved and retrieved accurately. When there is a mismatch between what is expected and what is actually experienced, it is not uncommon for this mismatch to be resolved by the expectation intruding into the experience record and preventing accurate retrieval. In the examples above, we might have in fact chosen our table ourselves and a waitress might have taken our party to a table. Scripts can be potent reminders of features and activities, but they also can lead to erroneous filling in of missing or expected features and activities. But the relationship between script-based knowledge and retrieval is not linear. If an event is highly incongruent with our script-based knowledge, it is also likely to be retrieved – presumably because of its bizarreness. Imagine, for example, that you interact with a red-haired individual. Presumably, your script of interacting with people provides you with an expectation that the people you meet have brown hair, the most typical hair colour in European nations. This expectation might lead you to not encode the hair colour of your new acquaintance (as atypical information, it is useless in predicting the features of other people you will meet), encode it wrongly (as a result of script interference), forget it easily (because it does not repeat), and to not retrieve it successfully (because of forgetting and script interference). Alternatively, you might form a long-lasting impression of the hair colour of this individual because of its deviance from the typical!

Memory is constructive

The idea that script-generated expectations influence memory is consistent with current theories emphasising that memory does not resemble a tape recorder or camera – devices that store and retrieve information veridically. These theories propose instead that the memory system is an integral part of the larger cognitive and social mechanisms underlying social interaction. There is abundant evidence to support this constructive view of memory. For example, children's memory for events that transpired during a doctor's visit is related to their knowledge of the types of activities that usually occur in a doctor's office (Ornstein et al., 1999) and their memory for chess positions is highly related to their knowledge of chess (Chi, 1978). Another example of this principle is provided by a study of preschool children's recall of a fire drill at their day care (Pillemer et al., 1994). Very young preschoolers, but not older ones, erroneously recollected some of the events because of their lack of understanding of the causal structure of the event. For instance, younger children recollected that they left the building and then heard the fire alarm. Older children did not make this error, presumably because they understood the procedures of a fire drill.

The relationship between age, scripted knowledge, and recall

The relationship between age, scripted knowledge, and recall is quite complex. Scripts develop with age but even very young children possess scripts for familiar events, and these scripts influence the way the children reconstruct past events (Flannagan & Hess, 1991; Hudson & Nelson, 1986). Once children of different ages have acquired a script, preschoolers may be more vulnerable to the negative effects of script-based knowledge than elementary school-aged children (Hudson & Nelson, 1986). Some work suggests that preschoolers' vulnerability to scripted information reflects their difficulty distinguishing 'special' events from 'scripted' events (Farrar & Goodman, 1992). It seems that with age, children become better able to tag unexpected events and to note that they are special; younger children are more likely to incorporate one-time special events into their scripts.

In order for scripted knowledge to influence the encoding, storage, and retrieval of an experience, that experience needs to be connected to the script. One way in which a particular life experience is identified as an instantiation of a script is through words. When you hear or think 'restaurant' you probably activate the script of 'Going to a Restaurant'. Word learning can be conceptualised as a process that helps get experience organised into meaningful chunks. Subsequently, words can be used to call up memories of events. The evidence for the hypothesis that limited language can impair the organisation and the recall of experience comes from a curious memory phenomenon, known as *childhood amnesia* (sometimes referred to as **infantile amnesia**). Childhood amnesia refers to the relative dearth of memories for events from the first three years of life compared to the amount of memories from other periods in life. One of the most salient characteristics of children younger than 3 years of age is that they have no or very impoverished linguistic skills. Around the age of 18–24 months, children go through a 'vocabulary spurt', a very quick growth in the size of their vocabulary. This point in language development is strongly associated with the dates of our first memories, as adults' earliest recollections are of events that took place shortly after this time in their lives. This suggests that language development can be one of the explanations for childhood amnesia and, therefore, that language is critically associated with remembering (Figure 13.3).

infantile amnesia
inability to remember events during early childhood (first 3 years). Also called *childhood amnesia*.

FIGURE 13.3 *In humans language is critically associated with remembering.*
Source: Shutterstock.

FIGURE 13.4 *Like dreams, fantasies, imagination, and Surrealist art, memory is not a copy of reality but an eclectic compilation of bits and pieces of different realities.*

Source: Salvador Dali, Persistence of Memory. DIGITAL IMAGE © 2011, The Museum of Modern Art/Scala, Florence.

Memory is constructive

In sum, the theoretical construct 'script', representing knowledge structure, helps explain why what a person 'remembers' does not always correspond to their actual experience. Memory, like dreams, is highly 'constructive': it elaborates, deletes, and shapes its contents (Figure 13.4). These transformations occur at the encoding, storage, and retrieval stages of the memory process. Thus, what gets retrieved is rarely a direct representation of the original event.

Strategy development

All of us have been asked and have applied effort to remember a poem, a telephone number, or an event. A strategy is a 'routine or procedure deliberately employed to achieve some end' (Wellman, 1988, p.5). Strategies that facilitate remembering are called *mnemonics*. We are going to review the development of three of the most popular mnemonics: rehearsal, organisation, and elaboration.

Rehearsal

rehearsal a *mnemonic strategy* that involves the repetition of the items or information that have to be remembered.

Rehearsal is the repetition of the items to be remembered. In an early investigation of children's use of strategies, Flavell *et al.* (1966) documented that children would repeat to themselves the items they had to remember. Although this strategy appears early in children's repertoire of mnemonic devices and its use is very robust throughout life, rehearsal patterns change with age. This was demonstrated when children were explicitly asked to repeat the words they have to remember (Ornstein *et al.*, 1975). The younger children in the study repeated only the last word that they had heard. In contrast, the older children repeated not only the last item but also the items preceding it.

Organisation

organisation a *mnemonic strategy* that reduces the load on memory by organising items into meaningful categories.

Organisation refers to the classification of the items to be remembered into meaningful groups or categories. The study of the organisation strategy has been motivated by the **cluster effect** in recall tests: subjects consistently retrieve objects that can be grouped together according to some principle (Bower, 1970). This finding motivated the hypothesis that imposing a structure on the set of stimuli to be remembered can guide later performance on memory tests. In tests of organisation, children are usually given time to group the items they have to remember in any way that might be helpful. Such tests show that children do not use the organisation strategy consistently until the age of 8 (Best & Ornstein, 1986). However, preschoolers *can* organise items on the basis of semantic meaning: they comply with explicit instructions to do so (Corsale & Ornstein, 1980).

cluster effect memory for test items is significantly improved if the items can be grouped together according to some category or principle, e.g. items of furniture; cutlery used to eat with; animals, etc.

Elaboration

Finally, **elaboration** refers to the action of making visual or verbal connections between the items to be remembered or between these items and salient objects in one's memory. Elaboration is a strategy that works well for the **paired-associate task**. In this task children have to remember pairs of unrelated items. In the recall test they are given one of the items as a cue and have to retrieve the other one. Using elaboration children create a representation in which the items to be remembered are meaningfully connected. For example, if children have to remember the pair 'fish–fork' they might imagine eating fish with a fork. Beuhring and Kee (1987) found out that 96 per cent of the increase in performance on the paired-associate task between fifth (10–11-year-olds) and twelfth (17–18-year-olds) graders is explained by the increased use of the elaboration strategy. The spontaneous use of this strategy does not appear until adolescence (Pressley & Levin, 1977).

elaboration a memory *mnemonic* that works by making connections between items that have to be remembered.

paired-associate task a memory test in which participants must remember pairs of unrelated items.

Other mnemonic devices

In addition to rehearsal, organisation, and elaboration there are a number of other mnemonics that can improve memory. For example, external cues (e.g. notes on the calendar, tying a thread on a finger) are extensively used to help recall. Even preschoolers know to leave a mark on the place a toy is hidden when told they would have to retrieve it later (Yussen, 1974). Ten-year-olds know to check the clock regularly when they are baking cupcakes and have to remember to turn off the oven (Ceci & Bronfenbrenner, 1985). Although very young children spontaneously perform actions that facilitate remembering, it is not clear when they start using these procedures deliberately for remembering (Wellman, 1988). Flavell (1970) has in fact suggested that children have a 'production' deficit, implying that they can use mnemonics but they do not apply them when they are necessary.

Utilisation deficiency

Another feature of the development of strategy use is that the initial use of a strategy might not accrue any benefit for its user. On the contrary, it might even decrease the efficiency of remembering. This leads to a U-shaped effect of the use of a strategy on actual memory. This effect has been called *utilisation deficiency* and documented by Miller and Bjorklund (e.g. Miller & Seier, 1994; Bjorklund *et al.*, 1992). Miller and her colleagues have identified this deficiency in selective memory tasks. In these tasks children have to remember a subset of the items present. Thus the appropriate strategy is to attend only to the subset of items they have to remember. Exploring the application of this simple strategy, DeMarie-Dreblow and Miller (1988) either instructed the children to remember six out of twelve items hidden behind doors or to remember all the items. The youngest children in this study aged 7 showed worse recall when asked to apply their attention selectively.

Knowing when to use a strategy

Research shows that the major reason for the utilisation deficiency is the effort required to produce the strategy and the limited resources of younger children. In the previously cited study, DeMarie-Dreblow and Miller (1988) enhanced children's memory capacity by allowing them to concentrate on memorisation while the experimenter opened the doors behind which the items were hidden. (In the previous condition the child themselves opened the doors.) Other causes of the utilisation deficiency are limited knowledge, inadequate metamemory, and failure to inhibit another strategy or to integrate the strategy with other mnemonic activities (Miller & Seier, 1994).

In general, the utilisation of a strategy does not necessarily improve performance. Children need to be able to tie a bow or a knot because an untied thread on a finger can easily slip off. They also need to recognise that tying a thread on one's finger can remind them to call up a friend but will not help with the memorisation of a poem. Thus not only the procedure defining a strategy needs to be mastered but also the identification of circumstances of its appropriate use. The discovery and mastery of strategies continues through life. Later, individual patterns of strategy use are strongly influenced by two factors. First, we become more knowledgeable about our memory. We come to realise that we are good at remembering some things, for example numbers and dates, and bad at others, for example faces. Second, work environments often require specific memory skills, for example good memory for numbers in accounting and good memory for faces in the service sector. These factors allow us to approach strategy use in a very deliberative way. Mastering a strategy can make up for discrepancies between our memory skills and the memory skills required by our life situations.

Metamemory development

Cognitive capacities (e.g. attention, working memory) are limited and oftentimes remembering is an effortful process. Thus effort allocation in remembering needs to be regulated. We need to be able to recognise the type of effort different situations require and to distinguish the situations in which applying effort will help us accomplish the memory task we have from the situations in which the memory tasks are just too hard to be accomplished. Metamemory refers to the awareness, monitoring, and regulation of the contents of memory, and it is the mechanism regulating effort allocation in the memory process. The better the regulatory mechanism, the more efficient memory should be. Thus, it is assumed that the development of metamemory leads to better remembering. Metamemory has two components (Flavell & Wellman, 1977; Schneider, 1999). The first one is *awareness of how memory works* (sometimes called *procedural metamemory*) for example awareness of what is easier or more difficult to remember and the circumstances that facilitate encoding and recall.

The second component is *memory monitoring* (sometimes called *declarative metamemory*) or knowledge about the appropriate use of mnemonics.

Awareness of how memory works

Researchers working on the first topic concentrate on how much overlap there is between the scientific findings about how memory works (e.g. the benefit of strategy use, the role of time delay in recall) and children's intuitive understanding of memory processes (Schneider, 1999). For example, Kreutzer *et al.* (1975) explored children's understanding of 14 properties of memory ranging from the strategies facilitating remembering to **retroactive interference** (i.e. the phenomenon that subsequent information can impair recall of the target information). For example, they asked children what they would do in order to remember to take their skates to school the next day, and how they would go about finding a lost jacket. The participants in Kreutzer *et al.*'s study were students from kindergarten (nursery school) to fifth grade (10–11-year-olds) classes. Generally, not until second grade (7–8-year-olds) did children show adequate performance on the tasks. Consequently, their understanding of how memory works develops quite late.

> **retroactive interference**
> the process through which information received after an event can interfere with and alter one's memory for the event.

On the other hand, researchers have documented that some more subtle aspects of metamemory can develop in earlier years as well. For example, even 3-year-old children can predict, fairly accurately, when they will or won't remember something they've encountered in the past (Balcomb & Gerken, 2008). Similarly, there is evidence to show that young children know basic truths about memory, such as the fact that smaller sets of items are easier to memorise than larger sets (Schneider & Pressley, 1997). Slightly older children (6-year-olds) can appreciate the fact that others can acquire false memories, and even have some intuitive understanding regarding this process (Jaswal & Dodson, 2009). Therefore, while a fully fledged understanding of memory may not develop until middle childhood, there is evidence to suggest that precursors to metamemory develop earlier on.

Memory monitoring

Declarative metamemory researchers concentrate on studying how children respond to instruction in the use of strategies. They look at whether children benefit from parents and teachers explicitly telling them how to approach a memory problem. For example, Larkina *et al.* (2008) found that children performed best on memory tasks when directed by their mothers to use effective strategies such as sorting the to-be-recalled items into appropriate categories. Rogoff & Gardner (1984) documented a similar trend: the adults in their study first provided examples of strategies to do the task and engaged the children in the process. Then, they monitored and provided feedback on their children's performance. In experimental situations, researchers also look at whether children benefit from feedback on the appropriate use of a strategy by measuring the application of the strategy to a novel problem (e.g. Ringel & Springer, 1980). For example, while the third graders (8–9-year-olds) in Ringel and Springer's (1980) study applied the strategy to the new task, the first graders (6–7-year-olds) did not. Young children are also susceptible to utilisation deficiencies (described earlier), which appear more often in younger (third grade, 8–9-year-olds) than older (seventh grade, 12–13-year-olds) children (Bjorklund *et al.*, 1997). Combined, the results from these studies suggest that metamemory skills are trainable rather late in childhood. A further limitation of metamemory enhancement approaches is that naturalistic observations show that parents and teachers rarely provide children with meta-memory information (Baker, 1994).

Why are young children poor in metamemory tasks?

Several explanations are offered for young children's relatively poor performance in metamemory tasks. First, interview techniques such as those used in Kreutzer *et al.*'s (1975) study rely on verbal competence and can therefore underestimate young children's performance on metamemory tasks (Schneider & Pressley, 1997). That is, children's usage of metamemory strategies may precede their ability to verbalise (or even explicitly understand) their importance (e.g. Friedman, 2007). Another possibility is that metamemory abilities involve a general understanding of the mind and how the mind may work, which does not develop in its entirety until age 5 (Lockl & Schneider, 2007). Finally, from a biological perspective, it is possible that brain regions implicated in metamemory (in particular the *right dorsolateral prefrontal cortex*) are not sufficiently developed in younger children.

The development of metamemory

The development of metamemory might depend on several other factors too. For one, exposure to memory tasks may aid in memory knowledge and awareness. Facing the challenges of remembering, children may spontaneously identify successful strategies, come to understand the benefit of applying strategies, and acquire knowledge about selecting the successful strategy in a new situation. However, we lack data to substantiate such a process. Another mechanism proposed to explain the develop-ment of metamemory is Vygotsky's theory of *cognitive development*, which emphasises the role of social context in cognitive growth (Vygotsky, 1962). In terms of this theory, the development of metamemory is a result of the socialisation process. Children acquire their understanding of memory through the guidance of adults who point out to them the requirements of the task at hand and to the relevant strategy. Thus, Vygotsky's theory provides motivation for training and intervention studies.

The relationship between metamemory and memory performance

Although it makes sense to hypothesise that metamemory influences remembering, notably through the application of mnemonic strategies, the empirical data on the connection between metamemory and memory have been mixed. While the rela-tionship between procedural metamemory and memory performance appears weak and unclear (Schneider, 1985), declarative metamemory appears strongly predictive of actual performance (Schneider & Pressley, 1997). As the majority of the studies looking at the relation between memory and metamemory are *correlational*, we can-not be sure whether memory improvement leads to the development of metamem-ory skills or whether the acquisition of metamemory spurs memory development. Metamemory is unquestionably important for memory performance. However, the intricacies of the relationship between metamemory and memory performance is still poorly understood.

Cross-cultural influences on memory

When studying memory development and processes, researchers are often faced with the question of universality. That is, does *every* person go through the same stages of memory development? Or alternatively, do people vary in how they encode, store, and retrieve memories? Does memory performance vary with culture, gender, age, and other factors?

The individualistic–collectivist divide

Han *et al.* (1998) asked preschool children from China, Korea, and the United States to recount various events in their lives such as their last birthday, or what they did after dinner the night before. While all three groups recalled objective aspects of the story to the same degree, American children's memories tended to be more detailed, specific, and emotional. Indeed, research has found that people belonging to individualistic cultures tend to have more specific and emotion-based memories than individuals belonging to interdependent or collectivist cultures, which instead emphasise the importance of group cohesion and collective identity. Other cross-cultural work has found that the earliest memories of people from collectivist cultures tend to be almost a year and a half later than the memories of those from more individualistic or independent cultures (Mullen, 1994), and that collectivist cultures tend to recall *fewer* story events when asked to read a story and then recall as many events as possible (Wang, 2009).

What causes cultural differences?

It is difficult to determine what drives these cultural differences, and whether these differences occur at the encoding, storage, or retrieval stage of the memory process. For example, in Han *et al.*'s study, it is not clear whether the Asian children's memories tended to be more general because they initially perceived the events in this manner, chose to keep only the general information in their memories, or felt the need to recount only general information when prompted. Of course, it is also possible that all three factors or some combination thereof play into this effect as well.

At the encoding level, Chua, Boland, & Nisbett (2005) tracked the eye movements of Chinese and American participants while they were viewing various scenes. They found that while Americans tended to focus more on individual objects in the foreground, Chinese participants stared more at the backgrounds and surroundings of those objects. This initial focus on background vs. focal objects may later affect what people remember and later recall. Similarly, Wang (2009) found that when reading a story, Asian-Americans tended to parse the information into fewer meaningful segments than European-Americans, suggesting that European-Americans perceived the story as a series of multiple specific events, while Asian-Americans grouped these specific events into several more general plot points. Therefore, people across cultures may in fact be processing the same exact events in qualitatively different ways.

The correlational nature of most cross-cultural work cannot fully tease apart the possibility that individuals belonging to collectivist cultures perceive the information in a different way or *choose* to focus on it in this manner. The latter possibility suggests that if prompted, it is also possible for Americans to form more general memories, and for Asians to form more specific ones. Indeed, researchers, have been able to 'prime' participants with individualist or collectivist-type thinking (e.g. by asking participants to write about themselves as either an individual or a member of a social group), and then subsequently test memory performance. These studies suggest that both culture and priming can affect the types of memories people recall (Wang & Ross, 2005).

Finally, culture can affect memory in the retrieval process as well. Because Asian cultures in general focus less on personal emotion states, it is possible that the Asian participants in these studies feel less need to communicate such states during memory recall tasks. Studies that have found cross-cultural differences in memory performance may be tapping into cultural beliefs about what is important to recall during memory performance tasks, and what is peripheral information. Mothers of American children tend to also prompt their children to elaborate on past events more than mothers of Asian children (see Leichtman *et al.*, 2003), thus sending the message that such elaboration is important to focus on, remember, and then later communicate to others. In contrast, Asian mothers tend to focus their children's attentions on cultural norms and societal expectations (Wang *et al.*, 2000). Mothers may therefore be instilling cultural values that are then reflected in children's own memory recalls. In this way, memory recall may be dependent on cultural expectations of what is important to recall rather than on memory ability itself. Finally, language may play a role in ability to retrieve memories. In general, memories are better recalled when asked to retrieve in the language that the memories were encoded in than in a different language (e.g. Schrauf & Rubin, 1998).

Other factors influencing memory performance

Largely, research has focused on culture and memory with regards to the individualistic–collectivist divide. However, other factors such as gender, birth order, education level, and socioeconomic status may all contribute to differences in memory performance. For example, females tend to recount more events during a memory recall test than males (e.g. Wang, 2009), and only-children's memories tend to be more specific and self-focused than those of children with siblings (Wang *et al.*, 1998). Because it is not possible to manipulate which culture children belong to, most cross-cultural studies leave many questions regarding culture and memory unanswered. For example, are gender differences in memory found as a result of physiological differences (e.g. sex differences in brain structures that subserve memory such as the *medial temporal lobe*), societal differences (e.g, are women encouraged to remember some things more than others?), or both? Which aspects of culture drive children's differences in memory performance? Future research may be able to find evidence for these important questions.

So far we have discussed how children's growing knowledge, mnemonic strategies, metamemory, and culture influence their remembering. These are the most prominent factors in the development of memory but not the only ones. (For example, general intelligence level has been also proven to affect how well one remembers, Bjorklund *et al.*, 1994.) The relative importance of each factor is yet to be determined. There are many interesting questions about memory that we have not addressed either because of lack of space or because there is no research on them. To start, why do some people in general have better memories than others? How are early childhood and adult memory performance related? In particular, how is early childhood experience with strategy and metamemory training related to memory performance later in life? These questions are not easy but they reveal how fascinating thinking about memory is. We now turn to the question of how memory development and other factors influence the accuracy of children's testimony.

CHILDREN'S EYEWITNESS TESTIMONY

As our opening vignette illustrated, children are often involved in criminal investigations (Figure 13.5). More and more often they are asked to testify when these cases reach the courts. Their testimonies influence verdicts and thus the lives of many people. Given the important consequences of children's presence in the courts, we need to ask how competent as a witness a child can be. The judicial systems of most countries require that every witness be able to distinguish between a truth and a lie and be able to retain and report information. The concern about children giving testimony is that their reports might be inaccurate for lack of either one of these abilities.

FIGURE 13.5 *Historically, children have been interrogated in a wide range of cases, as depicted in the famous painting, "And when did you last see your father?" by William Frederick Yeames, 1878.*
Source: Courtesy of National Museums, Liverpool.

Suggestibility

Suggestibility is children's proneness to give false reports of their experiences. Children's reports can be false because they can intentionally or unintentionally distort the truth about an event that they do remember accurately (where 'intentionally' refers to whether children realise the consequence of the distortion). The intentional distortion of truth is *lying* and the unintentional distortion *compliance*. Both behaviours aim to manipulate external forces: please people, avoid punishment, and decrease pressure. Children's reports can be false also due to vulnerabilities of their developing memory systems.

More precisely, we will use *suggestibility* to refer to the degree to which the encoding, storage, retrieval and reporting of events can be influenced by a range of cognitive and social factors (Ceci & Bruck, 1993). Cognitive factors are those related to properties of memory and social factors those related to properties of the situation that elicits the report. This definition of suggestibility accords with both the legal and everyday uses of the term. It connotes that subtle suggestions, expectations, stereotypes, and leading questions can unconsciously alter memories, as well as that explicit bribes, threats, and other forms of social inducement can lead to the conscious alteration of reports without affecting the underlying memory.

Ecological validity

Suggestibility research, as an outgrowth of memory development research, capitalises on the argument for *ecological validity*. The ecological validity argument dovetails with a larger argument having to do with the general relevance of laboratory research to behaviour that takes place outside the laboratory. Narrowly, the ecological validity argument is that aspects of the context can systematically differentiate behaviour. If researchers obtain results in one setting or context, there is no guarantee these results will generalise to a different context. Indeed, there is a venerable history in psychological research demonstrating context effects: people reason more effectively in one context than in another, despite the fact that the two reasoning tasks are isomorphic (for review, see Ceci, 1996). As we mentioned, Godden and Baddeley (1975) demonstrated that word lists learned by divers while under water were retrieved better when they were tested underwater than when tested on dry ground.

Since the 1980s the ecological validity argument has motivated two research programmes, both of which insist on looking at central events in children's lives that are analogous to crimes children are asked to testify about. These events usually involve potentially emotional experiences, e.g. touching, and/or misinformation (Figure 13.6). The debate between the two research programmes is on whether a child's testimony containing incriminating information can be fabricated (and thus lead to wrongful conviction) or whether it should be taken with all seriousness. The first programme maintains that children's reports of abuse or neglect are not amenable to manipulation and reflect real events. Some, like Goodman & Clarke-Stewart (1991), argue that this may be the case because of an evolutionary mechanism built in to protect children from life-threatening risks, thus giving privileged encoding to life-threatening events. Others argue that abuse events are simply a lot more salient and hence memorable.

Whatever the reason, these criticisms generated research that was taken as evidence that children were not, in fact, very suggestible when they were asked about body touching (e.g. 'The nurse kissed you, right?', 'The man took your picture, didn't he?'). The second research programme maintains that suggestibility is an ecologically valid concept in the sense of it being pervasive (Ceci, 1991). Basically, this research has argued that young children are suggestible about body touching and that children's reports of events such as medical procedures that involved ano-genital touching, which were followed by suggestive questioning, could come to contain potentially incriminating details (Bruck, Ceci, Francouer, & Renick, 1995).

FIGURE 13.6 *In order to study the reliability of children's accounts of stressful events, researchers investigate normally occurring events, such as immunisations, that are often naturally stressful.*
Source: Shutterstock.

The prevailing format of suggestibility experiments allows researchers to study a number of influences on children's reports. In a typical study, the participants are first exposed to an event, e.g. a visitor comes to the playground, or watch a sequence of slides. Next, they are exposed to false information about the event in which they have participated or which they have observed (e.g. that the man they had seen at the playground had a beard). This information is often embedded in an interviewer's question. For example, children can be asked 'What colour was his beard?', a question which presupposes that the man had a beard. Finally, they are questioned about their memories of the event. If children report a colour, their responses reflect suggestibility. 'What colour was his beard?' integrates the misinformation with the act of interrogation. More often, however, the misinformation and the interrogation events are separated. Using this procedure a researcher can study how new information alters an underlying memory by varying the number of times the misinformation is presented (i.e. the strength of the suggestion). Or, the researcher might manipulate the relation between the child and the interviewer to examine the place of compliance and lying in producing false reports. The straightforwardness and flexibility of the procedure have contributed to making suggestibility a prolific area of research. Indeed, the majority of studies we report have employed this design.

The relationship between suggestibility and memory development

Since suggestibility research is an offshoot of memory development research we could expect children's suggestibility to be influenced by the factors defining memory development. A couple of examples should suffice.

Strength of memory and suggestibility

A considerable amount of research has been done on the effect of memory strength on suggestibility. The reasoning is that it should be easier to implant a false suggestion if information about an event was weakly encoded or has degraded than if the memory about the event was strongly encoded and is well-preserved in storage. A straightforward way to manipulate the strength of a memory is through repetition. A number of studies on suggestibility have explored the effect of repeating erroneous information on children's reports. Most often the misleading suggestion is embedded in the experimenter's question and the question is repeated at several interviews (e.g. Poole & White, 1991, 1993). In other cases, the misinformation consists in asking the child repeatedly to imagine or think about a novel event or a novel feature of an experienced event (e.g. Ceci *et al.*, 1994). While some researchers have provided support for the proposal that there is a link between suggestibility and memory strength in children (Pezdek & Roe, 1997; Warren *et al.*, 1991) others have argued that there is no consistent relationship between a memory's strength and children's susceptibility to suggestion (Howe, 1991).

Scripts can produce false reports

The role of scripts in inducing false reports has been also extensively studied by suggestibility researchers. Leichtman & Ceci (1995), for example, gave preschool children stereotypical information about a clumsy character. Such information activates a script which, as we previously noted, has two effects. First, the script directs attention to behaviours consistent with it. Second, the actual behaviour of the character is fitted into the script. Leichtman and Ceci's study does not provide data about the first type of effects. But consistent with the second effect, children in the study used the 'clumsy character' script to attribute behaviours to the real character that were not actually observed but fitted his 'clumsy' personality. Thus, this study corroborates the thesis that expectations are actively used to interpret ambiguous information. It also illustrates that the use of scripts can lead to wrong interpretations.

Scripted knowledge can cause age changes in suggestibility

An extensive review of the suggestibility literature shows that younger children are more suggestible than older children. However, the deleterious effect of script information on memory leads to the paradoxical situation of older children being more suggestible. When younger children's scripted knowledge is insufficient or poorer than that of older children, older children might be expected to make more false inferences about events that were not witnessed but that are part of their scripts. Suggestibility researchers have documented this idea as well. For example, Lindberg (1991) erroneously told subjects that a film they were viewing depicted cheaters. Actually, in the film one student was asking another for the time. In this situation, sixth graders (11–12-year-olds) and college students tended to report more cheating than did third graders (8–9-year-olds). Younger children's scripts for cheating did not contain the scenario of asking for the time as a pretext for cheating, so their limited 'cheating' script made them less prone than older children to the erroneous suggestion. In this developmentally reverse trajectory the absence of knowledge actually benefits younger children's recall.

These examples clearly show how suggestibility research has built upon and expanded research on children's memory. The studies address issues of memory strength and knowledge representation but are set in contexts for which children's reports may be indeed solicited, e.g. someone's clumsiness and cheating. They barely can give a hint about the diversity of studies that emphasise memory factors as driving forces behind suggestibility effects.

Source-monitoring

Another aspect of memory development that is considered to influence suggestibility is the ability to keep track of the origins of one's beliefs. The idea is that if young children are able to identify the sources of their beliefs accurately, e.g. based on their own experience or imagination, or interviewer's post-event information, they will be less prone to misleading information by others. Referred to as 'source monitoring', this skill is considered a part of mental state understanding because it entails the understanding that people have different beliefs than one's own (Drummey & Newcombe, 2002). In fact, in parallel with **theory-of-mind development** (Chapter 11), children's source-monitoring skills develop gradually between the ages of 3 and 6. In general, studies looking directly at the association between suggestibility and source-monitoring used procedures such as: alerting children to sources of their knowledge before they are exposed to post-event information, putting contextual cues in retrieval questions, and explicitly warning about post-event misinformation (Bright-Paul *et al.*, 2005; Giles *et al.*, 2002; Holliday & Hayes, 2002; Thierry *et al.*, 2001). The findings show us that warnings or training on source information helps even 3- to 4-year-olds to resist suggestibility.

Social factors leading to false reports

Children's greater susceptibility to suggestion can be viewed as a direct outgrowth of their relatively weaker ability to accurately encode, store, retrieve, and monitor different types of information. But recently, researchers have also emphasised the importance of social factors in accounting for suggestibility effects in adults, and particularly in children. Based on what we know about the social development of children, it seems clear that social factors should play a large role in the creation of false reports.

Understanding the language used by the questioner

The social aspect of suggestibility is defined by the interaction between the child and another person. To understand the dynamics of this interaction, we first need to ask whether there is understanding between the speakers. As children's reports are usually prompted verbally and the child uses language to report their memories, it is crucial that the child understands the vocabulary used by the interrogator and that they possess the language skills necessary to express themselves unambiguously and in a way that does not allow misunderstandings to arise (Brennan & Brennan, 1988; Snyder *et al.*, 1993; Walker & Warren, 1997). For example, in one study (Goodman & Aman, 1990) some 3-year-old children inaccurately reported that a male experimenter

FIGURE 13.7 *To provide an accurate report it is crucial that the child understands the vocabulary used by the interrogator and that they possess the language to express themselves unambiguously.*

Source: Shutterstock.

had touched their 'private parts'. In response to the question 'Did he touch your private parts?', they answered 'yes' even though the experimenter had not. Upon further examination, the experimenters noted that the children simply did not know the meaning of the phrase 'private parts'. As Goodman and her colleagues note, if this term had been used inappropriately in an actual case, a misleading conclusion, eventually leading to a potential false allegation could have occurred (Goodman *et al.*, 1992). Thus, the child's level of linguistic comprehension and production skills influence their suggestibility-proneness (Figure 13.7). Children's answers to questions that they have incorrectly understood, in addition to adults' misunderstanding of their limited productions, may be incorporated into future interrogations, further increasing the likelihood of tainted reports.

Even when there is understanding between the speakers, other constraints in child–adult interactions might lead to children's false reports. Both children and adults approach a conversation with certain assumptions but these assumptions are often incompatible. For example, most children assume that if an adult asks a question, then a 'good' child should provide a response. Conversely, the adult assumes that if the child does not know the answer they will tell the interviewer 'I don't know' rather than guess and provide an inaccurate response. Although such misunderstandings appear even in adult–adult conversations, they are much more common in adult–child interactions. The major source of these misunderstandings is children's pragmatic language ability, such as understanding the intended meaning versus literal meaning (Beal & Belgrad, 1990). Newcombe and Dour (2001) employed a pragmatic competence scale to examine the relationship between children's conversational understanding and age-related differences in suggestibility. The findings revealed that suggestibility levels were mediated by the children's pragmatic language abilities.

Social pressure on the child

Children can be and often are motivated to please the experimenter, end the interview, and avoid some sort of punishment. Children see adult interviewers as omniscient and truthful and rarely question their statements or actions. Therefore, they may comply with the adult norms or what they perceive to be the adult's wishes.

Finally, children may lie in order to achieve a goal that is under the adult's control, e.g. get a prize or avoid reprimand. Furthermore, when children are part of an investigative interview, regardless of the coercive nature or unpleasantness of the interview, they are required to participate until the adult decides to terminate. Children are seldom allowed to end an interaction by saying 'I am not talking about this any more' or 'I want my attorney/lawyer present'. Children might and do express their discomfort and wishes to interrupt an unpleasant conversation with an adult but these are rarely taken seriously and respected (following the model of parent who knows what's best for the child). Thus when interacting with adults, and especially in the context of an investigative interview, children are under a lot of pressure and do not have at their disposal techniques that have the potential to ward off suggestive and coercive questioning methods.

To study the effect of social pressure, Ceci *et al.* (1987) conducted an experiment in which the misleading information was presented to the children either by another child or by an adult. The researchers found that the children who were misled by an adult were much more likely to incorporate the misleading information into their reports of the story they had heard than the children misled by another child. These results suggest that the authority of the speaker influences children's memory. Recent evidence, however, demonstrates that children are able to question and evaluate the credibility of authority figures in certain situations. For example, they think that in some domains adults might know less than children (Fitneva, in press), they respond to markings of uncertainty in speakers' utterances, and they doubt others' testimony if they are les informed than themselves (Robinson *et al.*, 2008).

Although children may be compliant, it is sometimes with much confusion. If one listens to the audio recordings of suggestibility experiments, one discovers long pauses in the interviews. Children's answers do not come spontaneously and there is often hesitation and a feeling of discomfort as they come to assent to the interviewer's questions. Thus, in contrast to children who have been repeatedly exposed to erroneous suggestions over long periods of time and who, as a result, come to harbour false beliefs that result in spontaneous answers, compliant children's disclosures frequently seem halting and confused.

Do children lie and deceive?

The pressures the child faces might lead to compliance as well as deception. But can children consciously and deliberately distort the truth with the deliberate goal of deceiving their interviewers? Historically, it was felt that young children were incapable of lying because this act required a level of cognitive sophistication beyond the capability of the young child (e.g. Piaget, 1926). Since the time of Piaget, much progress has been made in understanding the development and definitional features of lying (see Flanagan, 1992). With advances in our understanding of young children's cognitive sophistication, there is now evidence that even very young children sometimes do lie, with full appreciation of the differing perspectives of their listeners (Ceci *et al.*, 1993; McGough, 1994).

The most recent research on lying has attempted to approximate real-life crime contexts by weaving affect and motive into studies of recollection, and by using highly familiar contexts such as observing loved ones break toys or being kissed while in the bathtub. For example, Ceci *et al.* (1990) investigated children's responses to five motivations to lie or tell the truth: (1) avoiding punishment; (2) sustaining a game; (3) keeping a promise (e.g. to protect a loved one); (4) achieving personal gains (e.g. rewards, being

demand characteristics cues that are perceived as telling participants how they are expected to behave or respond in a research setting, i.e. social factors that 'demand' a certain sort of response.

accepted in a group); and (5) avoiding embarrassment. Generally, these studies demonstrate that, like adults, preschoolers are sensitive to the **demand characteristics** of a situation, and therefore succumb to a wide range of motives to lie or withhold information.

Different motivations do not produce comparable levels of lying though. For example, in one study an adult experimenter pretended to find a watch left behind by the teacher (Ceci *et al.*, 1990). After showing the watch to the child, the experimenter told the child that they were going to play a game of hiding it from the teacher. The child was told the game was a secret and was instructed not to talk to anybody about it. Later, the returning teacher asked the child who had taken her watch. Only 10 per cent of the preschoolers lied to sustain this game (see also Tate & Warren-Leubecker, 1990). However, when the motivational salience of the experimental procedure was increased by having a well-known adult coach the child to tell a lie about playing with a toy, then 35 per cent of 2- to 8-year-olds lied to sustain a secret game (Tate *et al.*, 1992). It appears that the degree to which children will lie to sustain a game is context-dependent, and that the use of stronger coaching will result in higher rates of deception.

The conclusion is that young children will consciously distort their reports of what they witnessed, and they will do so more in response to some motives (e.g. fear of reprisal and avoidance of embarrassment) than to others (to sustain a game, gain rewards). Subjects of all ages will lie when the motives are right. Children may be no different from adults in this regard. Thus, the argument that children are incapable of 'lying' should be discarded as should the insinuation that they are hopeless liars.

The interaction of cognitive and social mechanisms

Some researchers have attempted to determine the relative importance of social vs. cognitive factors in accounting for suggestibility effects (e.g. Ceci *et al.*, 1987). The results of these studies are inconsistent, and the issue as to the ascendance of one factor over the other remains unresolved. Still, the most feasible position on what causes false reports rests on the interaction of cognitive and social factors.

This interaction can have several forms. One possibility is that the degree to which social factors play a role in producing a false report has a cognitive basis. When memories are weak (or when there is no memory at all for the original event), children may be more compliant and willing to accept suggestions because there is no competing memory to challenge the suggestion. On the other hand, when memories are strong the child is less likely to incorporate misleading suggestions into memory. Another possibility is that social factors underpin the effectiveness of cognitive mechanisms in producing a false report. For example, a child may attend more to suggestions from an authority figure (a social factor), thus insuring greater encoding (a cognitive factor).

Finally, it is possible that a child's report may initially be the result of some social factor, but over time the report may become a part of the child's actual memory. Consider again the study in which preschool children were given stereotypical knowledge about a clumsy character called Sam Stone (Leichtman & Ceci, 1995). Children later used this knowledge to reconstruct what the character, Sam Stone, might have done, telling the interviewer 'Maybe Sam did it', or 'It could have been Sam'. Upon repeated post-event questioning, however, these children often became more and more convinced that the clumsy events had actually occurred, as opposed to might have occurred. In the legal arena, in response to strongly suggestive – even pressurised – interviews, children may initially realise that they are providing the interviewer with an erroneous account in order to please them (a social factor), but after repeated retellings to different interviewers, the erroneous account may become so deeply embedded as to be indistinguishable from an actual memory (a cognitive factor). Leichtman and Ceci (1995) demonstrated that often such children become highly resistant to being debriefed: they argue with the researchers and their parents when told that their reports are incorrect.

Another question that requires attention is whether there are age-related differences in the interaction of cognitive and social factors. Specifically, do younger children differ from older children and adults in terms of how quickly false reports, which may have been initially motivated by social factors, come to be believed, that is, a cognitive factor? Clearly, much more research is needed to gain comprehensive understanding of the conditions in which memories change.

Is suggestibility a personality trait?

Personality traits such as extraversion/introversion, agreeableness, and emotional stability are stable characteristics of individuals. Some traits persist with age; others are typical of a person's behaviour during a certain period of time but all are exhibited in a wide variety of circumstances. Is suggestibility a trait? Research data overwhelmingly show that younger children are more suggestible than older children and adults (Ceci & Bruck, 1993). A fairly large literature indicates that a variety of memory skills do improve with age (e.g. see reviews by Kail, 1989; Schneider & Pressley, 1997) and that younger children tend to lose information from storage more rapidly than older children do. These age-related differences suggest that younger children might form weaker memories in general and be more suggestible across the board.

Are suggestible children always suggestible?

If suggestibility is a personality trait then a person would exhibit this behaviour in a variety of situations. For example, we might expect that children can be influenced for events that personally concern them as well as events that they have only observed. We might also expect that they are as easily influenced by peers and strangers as by relatives. Unfortunately, most of the work that compares children's suggestibility in different situations does not allow us to address the question of whether suggestibility is a personality trait because different children participate in the different conditions of the experiment. For example, some children would be misled by another child and some by an adult (e.g. Ceci *et al.*, 1987). In order to assess the claim that suggestibility is a trait, we need to measure the proneness of the same children to produce false reports across several different situations.

Some recent work supports the hypothesis that suggestibility is a trait of individuals. Scullin and Warren (1999) presented 3- to 6-year-old children with three situations: a painting event, reading a story, and watching a video. The day after each event the children were interviewed about it. The researchers found that children who were suggestible about the painting event were also suggestible about the video event and that children who were suggestible about the video event were also suggestible about the reading event. These findings suggest that suggestibility might be a trait of individuals rather than a characteristic of particular situations.

Is suggestibility situation-dependent?

It is possible of course that suggestibility is a property of situations rather than individuals. It is easy to locate in the literature studies claiming that even young children are quite resistant to suggestion about traumatic, abuse-related events (e.g. Goodman & Clarke-Stewart, 1991; Saywitz et al., 1991), and some researchers claim that age differences in suggestibility are evident principally with non-participating children (i.e. bystanders as opposed to children who were the recipients of some action), and principally on non-sexual questions (Rudy & Goodman, 1991). To be sure, it may be the case that personal, salient events are harder to alter than neutral, sanitised ones, and there is some evidence that the stronger the memory trace, the more difficult it is to overwrite it (Pezdek & Roe, 1995). However, it would be misleading to imply that traumatic events are impervious to alteration. A large body of literature has demonstrated that this is not the case (e.g. Bruck, Ceci, Francoeur, & Renick, 1995; Bruck, Ceci, Francouer, & Barr, 1995; Wagenaar & Groenweg, 1990). For example, three studies of children's reports of a pediatric exam from three different labs have all obtained false reports from children alleging that an inappropriate behaviour took place during the exam (Bruck, Ceci, Francoeur, & Renick, 1995; Greenhoot et al., 1999; Saywitz et al., 1991). A careful reading of the scientific literature suggests that all types of memories are susceptible to alteration as a result of suggestive techniques (imagery inductions, leading questions, source confusions, stereotype inductions), and there are reliable age differences in suggestibility even for events that are stressful, painful, and potentially sexual, including ones where the child is a participant. The safest conclusion is probably that situations differ in degree and not in kind with regards to producing suggestibility effects. Suggestibility effects can and have been found for all types of events, but perhaps they are somewhat harder to get when the event is salient, persistent, and well understood by the child.

How well can we measure suggestibility?

Although the question about the existence of a suggestibility trait is far from settled, we are nearer to creating an instrument to measure an individual child's suggestibility. Scullin and Ceci (2001) developed a scale based on a story-telling event that is highly correlated with children's suggestibility. After viewing a brief videotape of a children's birthday party, the children were asked a series of questions some of which contained misleading information. At the end the children were told that they had missed some of the questions and the questionnaire was repeated. Two components of suggestibility were assessed: the tendency to incorporate the misleading information into children's answers to the questions ('yield'), and the tendency to shift answers, particularly ones that were originally correct, when the interviewer tells the child that they missed some ('shift'). Scullin and Ceci (2001) reported that 3-year-olds actually changed their answers less in response to negative feedback ('You missed some answers, so let's go over the questions again') than did older children. Shifting one's response when confronted with a conflicting claim ('you've missed some questions'), may require an ability to distinguish between what they said and what they think the interviewer wants them to say (Welch-Ross et al., 1997). In contrast, the tendency for children to yield, or respond affirmatively to misleading questions, appeared to remain relatively stable over the age span covered in this study.

The relationship between theory of mind and suggestibility

The ability to avoid an adult's suggestive questioning may also involve the unique understanding of others' mental states. For example, children who understand that people in general are capable of holding false beliefs may in turn understand that the experimenter's beliefs do not necessarily have to reflect reality. This so-called 'theory of mind' develops most rapidly between the ages of 3 and 5 (see Chapter 11). In an example of a standard theory-of-mind task, children are shown a box of crayons, which they then discover has sweets/candy inside. Children are asked to reason about what someone else will believe is in the box *prior* to seeing its contents (Gopnik & Astington, 1988). A child with a fully fledged theory-of-mind understanding should be able to reason that while the box in fact has sweets/candy inside, someone who hasn't seen its contents would *believe* it has crayons. Many other theory-of-mind measures have since been proposed (see Wellman et al., 2001; Wimmer & Perner, 1983). There are several parallels between an understanding of theory of mind and the ability to avoid adults' suggestibility. Both require cognitive control, or the ability to inhibit what *actually* occurred in order to reason about what someone *believes* may have occurred (see Scullin & Bonner, 2006). In other words, children must focus away from what they personally know about an event and reason instead about what the interrogator knows. Additionally, both abilities involve the understanding that one's knowledge can be limited. This type of reasoning might allow children to understand that the interrogator may have been misled, or may have inaccurate information about a given event. Therefore, they may be less likely to 'give in' to an adult's suggestive questioning. Not surprisingly, children who can accurately answer questions pertaining to theory of mind are also less prone to suggestibility (Bright-Paul et al., 2008).

SUMMARY AND CONCLUSIONS

In this chapter we mapped our understanding of how memory works and illustrated the practical importance of this knowledge by focusing on the problem of the reliability of children's eyewitness testimony. We discussed the role of knowledge, strategies, and metamemory in the improvement of children's ability to retain and report information. We also surveyed the causes of children's false testimonies. We did not focus on the biological underpinnings of memory, though a thorough treatment of this topic would also require discussion of its biological basis. However, doing so would have taken us beyond the scope of this chapter. In this section we would like to highlight what in our view are the three most important factors that are the important directions in current memory development research.

Alternatives to the encoding–storage–retrieval model of memory

We think that researchers will try to explore alternative models of memory (e.g. Glenberg, 1997). The current encoding–storage–retrieval model follows the information-processing tradition in psychology where cognitive processes are modelled in terms of inputs and outputs. This approach, however, ignores the functional significance of memory. What does memory bring to our lives? How did the evolution of memory change the lives of the organisms on Earth? These alternative approaches would allow us to move beyond studying memorisation and accuracy of memory. The questions they focus on are instead how memories form within the context of action, how they influence our behaviour, and how their change reflects the requirements of our environment and the needs of our actions.

Individual differences in suggestibility

We think that the issue of individual differences in suggestibility will continue to inspire future research. The stakes in this research are high because of the need to develop an instrument that can measure the trustworthiness of eyewitnesses' reports. As our review showed, recently researchers have discovered a greater consistency for suggestibility than might be expected if it was completely situational, because the same children who are the most suggestible in one situation appear to be the most suggestible in others, too (Scullin & Ceci, 2001; Scullin & Warren, 1999). This newer research does not imply that situational variables are unimportant, but rather that both situational and individual (trait) variables need to be considered. Much more research is needed to determine the relative contribution of individual and situational factors in producing false reports.

Ecological validity

The notion of 'ecological validity' will also continue to shape memory research. No single study captures the panoply of factors involved in an actual forensic case. (No study is designed to do this, either.) The goal of scientific research is to accumulate to the point where it provides the 'best light to go by when making decisions'. Not perfect light, but better light than other ways of knowing provide. Each new study is designed to fill in a missing piece in the literature, not to mimic a forensic case. Judges, juries, and law enforcement officials need to weigh and sift this evidence to decide how relevant it is for any particular case. In sum, the concern for ecological validity will continue to motivate the expansion of naturalistic and laboratory studies so that they combine to cover all relevant factors that can be expected to influence children's suggestibility in the everyday world.

DISCUSSION POINTS

1. Think about the distinction between recognition and recall. Can you explain why people often (rightly!) complain 'I can't remember names, but I never forget a face'?

2. What sort of items go into short-term memory, and which are likely to enter long-term memory?

3. Think about the difference between semantic and episodic memory.

4. Three factors that influence the development of memory are knowledge, strategies, and metamemory. What are the main characteristics of these different factors?

5. How do scripts, or scripted knowledge, influence the encoding, storage, and retrieval of an experience?

6. How competent as a witness can a child be, and what age changes are there in the accuracy of children's recall and testimony?

7. Why is suggestibility such an important factor in affecting the accuracy of children's testimony?

SUGGESTIONS FOR FURTHER READING

Bull, R. (Ed.) (2001). *Children and the law: The essential readings*. Oxford: Blackwell.

Ceci, S.J., & Bruck, M. (1999). *Jeopardy in the courtroom: A scientific analysis of children's testimony*. Washington, DC: APA Books.

Herbert, J.S., & Pascalis, O. (2007). Memory development. In A. Slater, & M. Lewis, *Introduction to infant development* (pp. 153–169). Oxford: Oxford University Press.

Schneider, W., & Lockl, K. (2008). Procedural metacognition in children: Evidence for developmental trends. In J. Dunlosky, & B. Bjork (Eds.) *A handbook of memory and metacognition*. Mahwah, NJ: Erlbaum.

Schneider, W., & Pressley, M. (1997). *Memory development between two and twenty*. Mahwah, NJ: Lawrence Erlbaum and Associates.

REFERENCES

Baker, L. (1994). Fostering metacognitive development. In H.W. Reese (Ed.) *Advances in Child Development and Behavior* (Vol. 25, pp. 201–239). San Diego, CA: Academic Press.

Balcomb, G.F., & Gerken, L. (2007). Three-year-old children can access their own memory to guide responses on a visual matching task. *Developmental Science, 11*, 750–760.

Beal, C.R., & Belgrad, S.L. (1990). The development of message evaluation skills in young children. *Cognitive Development, 61*, 705–712.

Best, D.L., & Ornstein, P.A. (1986). Children's generation and communication of mnemonic organization strategies. *Developmental Psychology, 22*, 845–853.

Beuhring, T., & Kee, D.W. (1987). Developmental relationships among metamemory, elaborative strategy use, and associative memory. *Journal of Experimental Child Psychology*, 44, 377–400.

Bjorklund, D.F., Coyle, T.R., & Gaultney, J.F. (1992). Developmental differences in the acquisition and maintenance of an organization strategy: Evidence for the utilization deficiency hypothesis. *Journal of Experimental Child Psychology*, 54, 434–448.

Bjorkland, D.F., Miller, P.H., Coyle, T.R., & Slawinski, J.L. (1997). Instructing children to use memory strategies: Evidence of utilization deficiency in memory training studies. *Developmental Review*, 17, 411–441.

Bjorklund, D.F., & Schneider, W. (1996). The interaction of knowledge, aptitude, and strategies in children's memory performance. In H.W. Reese (Ed.) *Advances in Child Development and Behavior* (Vol. 26, pp. 59–89). San Diego, CA: Academic Press.

Bjorklund, D.F., Schneider, W., Cassel, W.S. & Ashley, E. (1994). Training and extension of a memory strategy – evidence for utilization deficiencies in the acquisition of an organizational strategy in high-IQ and low-IQ children. *Child Development*, 65, 951–965.

Bower, G.H. (1970). Organizational factors in memory. *Cognitive Psychology*, 1, 18–46.

Brennan, M., & Brennan, R. (1988). *Strange language*. Wagga Wagga, New South Wales, Australia: Riverina Muury Institute of Higher Education.

Brainerd, C.J., Reyna, V.F., & Ceci, S.J. (2008). Developmental reversals in false memory: A review of data and theory. *Psychological Bulletin*, 134, 343–382.

Bright-Paul, A., Jarrold, C., & Wright, D.B. (2005). Age-appropriate cues facilitate source-monitoring and reduce suggestibility in 3-7-year-olds. *Cognitive Development*, 20, 1–18.

Bright-Paul, A., Jarrold, C., & Wright, D.B. (2008). Theory-of-mind development influences suggestibility and source monitoring. *Developmental Psychology*, 44, 1055–1068.

Bruck, M., Ceci, S.J., Francoeur, E., & Barr., R.J. (1995). 'I hardly cried when I got my shot!': Influencing children's reports about a visit to their pediatrician. *Child Development*, 66, 193–208.

Bruck, M., Ceci, S.J., Francoeur, E., & Renick, A. (1995). Anatomically detailed dolls do not facilitate preschoolers' reports of a pediatric examination involving genital touch. *Journal of Experimental Psychology: Applied*, 1, 95–109.

Ceci, S.J. (1991). Some overarching issues in the child suggestibility debate. In J.L. Doris (Ed.) *The suggestibility of children's recollections* (pp. 1–9). Washington, DC: American Psychological Association.

Ceci, S.J. (1996). *On intelligence: A bioecological treatise*. Cambridge, MA: Harvard University Press.

Ceci, S.J. (1997). False beliefs: Developmental and clinical implications. In D.L. Schacter, J.T. Coyle, G.D. Fischbach, M.M. Mesulam, & L.E. Sullivan (Eds.) *Memory distortion*. Cambridge, MA: Harvard University Press.

Ceci, S.J., & Bronfenbrenner, U. (1985). Don't forget to take the cupcakes out of the oven: Prospective memory, strategic time-monitoring, and context. *Child Development*, 56, 150–165.

Ceci, S.J., & Bruck, M. (1993). The suggestibility of the child witness: A historical review and synthesis. *Psychological Bulletin*, 113, 403–439.

Ceci, S.J., Crotteau-Huffman, M., Smith, E., & Loftus, E.W. (1994). Repeatedly thinking about non-events. *Consciousness and Cognition*, 3, 388–407.

Ceci, S.J., & DeSimone, M. (1992). 'I know that you know that I know who broke the toy': Recursivity in three-year-olds. In S.J. Ceci, M. DeSimone, & M. Putnick (Eds.) *Cognitive and social factors in preschoolers' deception* . Hillsdale, NJ: Erlbaum.

Ceci, S.J., DeSimone, M., Putnick, M., Lee, J.M., & Toglia, M. (1990, March). *Motives to lie*. Paper presented at Biennial Meeting of the American Psychology/Law Society, Williamsburg, VA.

Ceci, S.J., & Friedman, R.D. (in press). The suggestibility of children: Scientific research and legal implications. *Cornell Law Review*.

Ceci, S.J., Leichtman, M.D., & Putnick, M. (1993). *Cognitive and social factors in early deception.* Hillsdale, NJ: Lawrence Erlbaum and Associates.

Ceci, S.J., Ross, D., & Toglia, M. (1987). Age differences in suggestibility: Psycholegal implications. *Journal of Experimental Psychology: General, 117,* 38–49.

Chi, M. (1978). Knowledge structures and memory development. In R.S, Siegler (Ed.) *Children's thinking: What develops?* (pp. 73–96).Hillsdale, NJ: Erlbaum.

Chi, M.T.H., & Ceci, S.J. (1987). Content knowledge: Its role, representation, and restructuring in memory development. In H.W. Reese (Ed.) *Advances in Child Development and Behavior* (Vol. 20, pp. 91–142). San Diego, CA: Academic Press.

Chua, H.F., Boland, J.E., & Nisbett, R.E. (2005). Cultural variation in eye movements during scene perception. *Proceedings of the National Academy of Sciences, 102,* 12629–12633.

Corsale, K., & Ornstein, P.A. (1980). Developmental changes in children's use of semantic information in recall. *Journal of Experimental Child Psychology, 30,* 231–245.

DeMarie-Dreblow, D., & Miller, P.H. (1988). The development of children's strategies for selective attention: Evidence for a transitional period. *Child Development, 59,* 1504–1513.

Drummey, A.B., & Newcombe, N.S. (2002). Developmental changes in source memory. *Developmental Science, 5,* 502–513.

Farrar, M.J., & Goodman, G.S. (1992). Developmental changes in event memory. *Child Development, 63,* 173–187.

Fitneva, S.A. (2010). Children's representation of the relationship between child and adult knowledge. *Journal of Cognition and Development, 11,* 458–484.

Flanagan, O. (1992). Other minds, obligations, and honesty. In S.J. Ceci, M. DeSimone, & M. Putnick, (Eds.) *Cognitive and social factors in preschoolers' deception* (pp. 111–126). Hillsdale, NJ: Erlbaum.

Flannagan, T., & Hess, D. (1991, April). *Developmental differences in children's abilities to utilize scripts in promoting their recall for scenes.* Paper presented at Biennial Meeting of the Society for Research in Child Development, Seattle, WA.

Flavell, J.H. (1970). Developmental studies in mediated memory. In H.W. Reese & L.P. Lipsitt (Eds.) *Advances in Child Development and Behavior* (Vol. 20, pp. 91–142). New York: Academic Press.

Flavell, J.H., Beach, D.R., & Chinsky, J.M. (1966). Spontaneous verbal rehearsal in a memory task as a function of age. *Child Development, 37,* 283–299.

Flavell, J.H., & Wellman, H.M. (1977). Metamemory. In R.V. Kail & J.W. Hagen (Eds.) *Perspectives on the development of memory and cognition* (pp. 3–33). Hillsdale, NJ: Erlbaum.

Friedman, W.J. (2007). The development of temporal metamemory. *Child Development, 78,* 1472–1491.

Giles, J.W., Gopnik, A., & Heyman, G.D. (2002). Source monitoring reduces the suggestibility of preschool children. *Psychological Science, 13,* 288–291.

Glenberg, A.M. (1997).What memory is for. *Behavioral and Brain Sciences, 20,* 1–55.

Godden, D.R., & Baddeley, A.D. (1975). Context-dependent memory in two natural environments: On land and underwater. *British Journal of Psychology, 66,* 325–331.

Goodman, G., & Aman, C. (1990). Children's use of anatomically detailed dolls to recount an event. *Child Development, 61,* 1859–1871.

Goodman, G.S., Batterman-Faunce, J.M., & Kenney, R. (1992). Optimizing children's testimony: Research and social policy issues concerning allegations of child sexual abuse. In D. Cicchetti & S. Toth (Eds.) *Child abuse, child development, and social policy.* Norwood, NJ: Ablex.

Goodman, G.S., & Clarke-Stewart, A. (1991). Suggestibility in children's testimony: Implications for child sexual abuse investigations. In J.L. Doris (Ed.) *The suggestibility of children's recollections* (pp. 92–105). Washington, DC: American Psychological Association.

Goodman, G.S., Rudy, L., Bottoms, B., & Aman, C. (1990). Children's concerns and memory: Issues of ecological validity in the study of children's eyewitness testimony. In R. Fivush &

J. Hudson (Eds.) *Knowing and remembering in young children* (pp. 249–284). New York: Cambridge University Press.

Gopnik, A., & Astington, J.W. (1988). Children's understanding of representational change and its relation to the understanding of false belief and the appearance–reality distinction. *Child Development*, *59*, 26–37.

Greenhoot, A.F., Ornstein, P.A., Gordon, B.N., & Baker-Ward, L. (1999). Acting out the details of a pediatric check up: The impact of interview condition and behavioral style on children's memory reports. *Child Development*, *70*, 363–380.

Han, J.J., Leichtman, M.D., & Wang, Q. (1998). Autobiographical memory in Korean, Chinese, and American children. *Developmental Psychology*, *34*, 701–713.

Holliday, R.E., & Hayes, B.K. (2002). Automatic and intentional processes in children's recognition memory: The reversed misinformation effect. *Applied Cognitive Psychology*, *16*, 1–16.

Howe, M.L. (1991). Misleading children's story recall: Reminiscence of the facts. *Developmental Psychology*, *27*, 746–762.

Hudson, J., & Nelson, K. (1986). Repeated encounters of a similar kind: Effects of familiarity on children's autobiographic memory. *Cognitive Development*, *1*, 253–271.

Jaswal, V.K., & Dodson, C.D. (2009). Metamemory development: understanding the role of similarity in false memories. *Child Development*, *80*, 629–635.

Kail, R.V. (1989). *The development of memory in children* (2nd edn). New York: W.H. Freeman.

Kreutzer, M.A., Leonard, C., & Flavell, J.H. (1975). An interview study of children's knowledge about memory. *Monographs of the Society for Research in Child Development*, *40*(1), 1–60.

Larkina, M., Güler, O.E., Kleinknecht, E., & Bauer, P.J. (2008). Maternal provision of structure in a deliberate memory task in relation to their preschool children's recall. *Journal of Experimental Child Psychology*, *100*, 235–251.

Leichtman, M.D., & Ceci, S.J. (1995). The effects of stereotypes and suggestions on preschoolers' reports. *Developmental Psychology*, *31*, 568–578.

Leichtman, M.D., Wang, Q., & Pillemer, D.B. (2003). Cultural variations in interdependence and autobiographical memory: Lessons from Korea, China, India, and the United States. In R. Fivush & C.A. Haden (Eds.) *Autobiographical memory and the construction of a narrative self account* (pp. 73–98). Mahwah, NJ: Laurence Erlbaum and Associates.

Lindberg, M. (1991). A taxonomy of suggestibility and eyewitness memory: Age, memory process, and focus of analysis. In J.L. Doris (Ed.) *The suggestibility of children's recollections* (pp. 47–55). Washington, DC: American Psychological Association.

Lockl, K., & Schneider, W. (2007). Knowledge about the mind: Links between theory of mind and later metamemory. *Child Development*, *78*, 148–167.

McGough, L.S. (1994). *Child witnesses: Fragile voices in the American legal system*. New Haven, CT: Yale University Press.

Miller, P.H., & Seier, W.L. (1994). Strategy utilization deficiencies in children: When, where, and why. In H.W. Reese (Ed.) *Advances in child development and behavior* (Vol. 25; pp. 107–156). San Diego, CA: Academic Press.

Mullen, M.K. (1994). Earliest recollections of childhood: A demographic analysis. *Cognition*, *52*, 55–79.

Newcombe, P.A., & Dour, T. (2001). Conversational influences on young children's responses to misleading questions. *Journal of Applied Developmental Psychology*, *22*, 363–378.

Ojito, M. (1997). School officials skeptical of sexual assault charges, *New York Times*, 22 October, B3.

Ornstein, P.A., Naus, M., & Liberty, C. (1975). Rehearsal and organizational processes in children's memory. *Child Development*, *26*, 818–830.

Ornstein, P.A., Manning, E.L. & Pelphrey, K.A. (1999). Children's memory for pain. *Journal of Developmental and Behavioral Pediatrics*, *20*, 262–277.

Pezdek, K., & Roe, C. (1995). The effect of memory trace strength on suggestibility. *Journal of Experimental Child Psychology*, *60*, 116–128.

Pezdek, K. & Roe, C. (1997). The suggestibility of children's memory for being touched: Planting, erasing, and changing memories. *Law and Human Behavior*, *21*, 95–106.

Piaget, J. (1926). *The language and thought of the child*. London: Routledge, Kegan Paul.

Pillemer, D.B., Picariello, M.L., & Pruett, J.C. (1994). Very long-term memories of a salient pre-school event. *Applied Cognitive Psychology*, *8*, 95–106.

Poole, D., & White, L. (1991). Effects of question repetition on the eyewitness testimony of children and adults. *Developmental Psychology*, *27*, 975–986.

Poole, D., & White, L. (1993). Two years later: Effects of question repetition and retention interval on the eyewitness testimony of children and adults. *Developmental Psychology*, *29*, 844–853.

Pressley, M., & Levin, J.R. (1977). Task parameters affecting the efficacy of a visual imagery learning strategy in younger and older children. *Journal of Experimental Child Psychology*, *24*, 53–59.

Ringel, B.A., & Springer, C.J. (1980). On knowing how well one is remembering: The persistence of strategy use during transfer. *Journal of Experimental Child Psychology*, *29*, 322–333.

Robinson, E.J., Haigh, S.N., & Nurmsoo, E. (2008). Children's working understanding of knowledge sources: Confidence in knowledge gained from testimony. *Cognitive Development*, *23*, 105–118

Rogoff, B., & Gardner, W. (1984). Adult guidance in cognitive development. In B. Rogoff & J. Lave (Eds.) *Everyday cognition: Its development in social context*. (pp. 95–116). Cambridge, MA: Harvard University Press.

Rudy, L., & Goodman, G.S. (1991). Effects of participation on children's reports: Implications for children's testimony. *Developmental Psychology*, *27*, 527–538.

Saywitz, K., Goodman, G., Nicholas, G., & Moan, S. (1991). Children's memory of a physical examination involving genital touch: Implications for reports of child sexual abuse. *Journal of Consulting and Clinical Psychology*, *5*, 682–691.

Schacter, D.L. (1987). Implicit memory – history and current status. *Journal of Experimental Psychology – Learning, Memory and Cognition*, *13*, 501–518.

Schank, R.C., & Abelson, R.P. (1977). *Scripts, plans, goals, and understanding: An inquiry into human knowledge structures*. Hillsdale, NJ: Erlbaum.

Schneider, W. (1985). Developmental trends in the metamemory-memory behavior relationship: An integrative review. In D.L. Forrest-Pressley, G.E. MacKinnon, & T.G. Waller (Eds.) *Metacognition, cognition, and human performance*. San Diego: Academic Press.

Schneider, W. (1999). The development of metamemory in children. In D. Gopher & A. Koriat (Eds.) *Attention and performance XVII. Cognitive regulation of performance: Interaction of theory and application* (pp. 487–514). Cambridge, MA: MIT Press.

Schneider, W., & Pressley, M. (1997). *Memory development between 2 and 20* (2nd edn). Mahwah, NJ: Erlbaum.

Schrauf, R.W., & Rubin, D.C. (1998). Bilingual autobiographical memory in older adult immigrants: A test of cognitive explanations of the reminiscence bump and the linguistic encoding of memories. *Journal of Memory and Language*, *39*, 437–457.

Scullin, M.H., & Bonner, K.A. (2006). Theory of mind, inhibitory control, and preschool-age children's suggestibility in different interviewing contexts. *Journal of Experimental Child Psychology*, *93*, 120–138.

Scullin, M.H., & Ceci, S.J. (2001). A suggestibility scale for children. *Personality and Individual Differences*, *30*, 843–856.

Scullin, M.H., & Warren, H.K. (1999, July). *Individual differences and responsiveness to suggestive interviewing techniques in children*. Poster presented at the joint meeting of the American Psychology-Law Society and the European Association of Psychology and Law, Dublin, Ireland.

Snyder, L.S., Nathanson, R., & Saywitz, K. (1993). Children in court: The role of discourse processing and production. *Topics in Language Disorders, 13*, 39–58.

Tate, C.S., Warren, A.R., & Hess, T.M. (1992). Adults' liability for children's 'lie-ability': Can adults coach children to lie successfully? In S.J. Ceci, M.D. Leichtman, & M. Putnick (Eds.) *Cognitive and social factors in early deception* (pp. 69–87). Hillsdale, NJ: Lawrence Erlbaum and Associates.

Tate, C.S., & Warren-Leubecker, A.R. (1990, March). *Can young children lie convincingly if coached by adults?* Presented at the Do children lie? Narrowing the uncertainties symposium conducted at the biennial meeting of the American Psychology/Law Society, Williamsburg, VA.

Thierry, K.L., Spence, M.S., & Memon, A. (2001). Before misinformation is encountered: Source monitoring decreases child witness suggestibility. *Journal of Cognition and Development, 2*, 1–26.

Tulving, E.E. (1983). *Elements of episodic memory*. London: Oxford University Press.

Vygotsky, L.S. (1962). *Thought and language*. Cambridge, MA: MIT Press.

Wagenaar, V.A., & Groeneweg, J. (1990). The memory of concentration camp survivors. *Applied Cognitive Psychology, 4*, 77–87.

Walker, A.G., & Warren, A.R. (1997). The Language of the child abuse interview: Asking the questions, understanding the answers. In T. Ney (Eds.) *Allegations in child sexual abuse, assessment and case management*. New York: Brunner/Mazel.

Wang, Q. (2009). Are Asians forgetful? Perception, retention, and recall in episodic remembering. *Cognition, 111*, 123–131.

Wang, Q., Leichtman, M.D., & Davies, K.I. (2000). Sharing memories and telling stories: American and Chinese mothers and their 3-year-olds. *Memory, 8*, 159–177.

Wang, Q., Leichtman, M.D., & White, S.H. (1998). Childhood memory and self-description in young Chinese adults: The impact of growing up an only child. *Cognition, 69*, 73–103.

Wang, Q., & Ross, M. (2005). What we remember and what we tell: The effects of culture and self-priming on memory representations and narratives. *Memory, 13*, 594–606.

Warren, A., Hulse-Trotter, K., & Tubbs, E. (1991). Inducing resistance to suggestibility in children. *Law and Human Behavior, 15*, 273–285.

Welch-Ross, M.K., Diecidue, K., & Miller, S.A. (1997). Young children's understanding of conflicting mental representation predicts suggestibility. *Developmental Psychology, 33*, 43–53.

Wellman, H.M. (1988). Children's early development of memory strategies. In F.E. Weinert & M. Perlmutter (Eds.) *Memory development: Universal changes and individual differences* (pp. 1–29). Hillsdale, NJ: Erlbaum.

Wellman, H.M., Cross, D., & Watson, J. (2001). Meta-analysis of theory-of-mind development: The truth about false belief. *Child Development, 72*, 655–684.

Wimmer, H., & Perner, J. (1983). Beliefs about beliefs – representation and constraining function of wrong beliefs in young children's understanding of deception. *Cognition, 13*, 103–28.

Yussen, S.R. (1974). Determinants of visual attention and recall in observational learning by preschoolers and second graders. *Developmental Psychology, 10*, 93–100.

14 Play and the Beginnings of Peer Relationships

Peter K. Smith

KEY TERMS

associative activity • cooperative activity • dominance • ethnic identity • false belief • gender identity • imaginary companion • locus of control • paracosm • parallel activity • peer • play hierarchy • play tutoring • pretend play • psychopathology • racial prejudice • rough-and-tumble play • scaffolding • self-socialisation • sensorimotor play • sex-role stereotypes • social learning theory • sociodramatic play • sociogram • sociometric status • sociometry • standardisation • symbolic play • theory of mind

CHAPTER OUTLINE

OVERVIEW

We all know that children (and adults!) play, engaging in behaviour that is enjoyable, done for its own sake, and which may not have any obvious, immediate purposes. The chapter begins by distinguishing different types of play in early childhood: sensorimotor play, language play, and pretend or symbolic play Much play is social, and while it begins in infancy, typically in interaction with parents, it soon takes place largely with peers and siblings. Thus, the approach taken here is to treat play in the context of peer relationships.

Interest in peers can be seen even before the toddler is 2 years of age, and interaction with peers grows from that point on. Brothers and sisters are also important partners in social interaction and play, particularly if the age gap is small, and interaction with siblings can have an important role in social and cognitive development.

Once children are 2 or 3 years old, many of them go to nursery school or playgroup. During this period children develop a degree of independence from parents, and there is a great increase in social participation, that is, where children play interactively and cooperatively with peers. The chapter reviews evidence on the different forms of play observed in early childhood, which include social play, sociodramatic play, and physical activity play. Although play is often defined as behaviour that is done for its own sake, and with no obvious purpose, it is clear that it serves many functions. These include developing and maintaining peer friendships, enhancing social, language, and cognitive skills, and possibly contributing to motor development.

The chapter then moves on to social relationships in the peer group, with particular emphasis on the reason for social rejection and its consequences. Children rejected by peers are often aggressive, impulsive, non-cooperative, disruptive, and in general lacking in social skills. This can also be related to disruptive behaviours such as bullying, a topic that is the focus of Chapter 20. Closely related to this topic is friendship. Friendships are different from other peer relationships because they refer to some close association between two or more children, involving more intense, intimate relationships, more cooperation and conflict resolution. It is widely argued that having friends guards against loneliness, but while it is likely that having friends is important for a child's development, it is difficult to prove this.

The chapter then considers sex differences in play and social behaviour. Boys and girls differ substantially in play and social behaviour, and these differences start at preschool if not before. Different factors – biological, social and cognitive – lead to the establishment of these differences. This leads finally to the consideration of ethnicity, with an assessment of evidence regarding children's tendency to maintain segregation between racial and ethnic groups. Such segregation and recognition of differences between groups can easily develop into racial prejudice, although multiracial curricula in the school years can do much to counteract this.

INTRODUCTION

In this chapter we will look at the origins and development of peer relations – social relationships with same-age classmates, usually in school; and of friendships – what friendship is, and whether it is important in development. We will particularly examine the development of play in childhood, and the role of play in social relationships. We will conclude with some discussion of gender and ethnicity as factors in peer relationships. Other aspects of social relationships are discussed in Chapters 15, 17, 19, and 20.

EARLY PEER RELATIONSHIPS

In the first few years, parents and adults are very important in a child's life. They provide care and protection, and act as models for language use and for many kinds of behaviour. A few adults, usually including parents, act as attachment figures, providing security for the infant. However, by the time the child is about 2 years old, peers – other children of about the same age – are becoming increasing sources of interest (Figure 14.1). Even at this age, children seem to be especially interested in peers. In a study of 12–18-month-old infants, two mother–infant pairs who had not previously met shared a playroom together. The infants touched their mothers a lot (remaining in proximity to them, as we would expect from attachment theory, which is discussed in Chapter 6, but *looked* most at the peer, who clearly interested them (Lewis *et al.*, 1975).

Another study was made of French infants at 11 months and at 23 months (Tremblay-Leveau & Nadel, 1996). They put two toddlers together with a familiar experimenter in a playroom. The researchers used this triadic situation to see how an infant would react to being left out when the adult interacted with the other infant. Some social interaction did occur just between the toddlers; but, a toddler made much more effort to interact with the other toddler, if the latter was playing with the experimenter! At 11 months this made the first toddler five times more likely to try and get into interaction; and at 23 months, they were eight times more likely to do so.

Observations of under-2s in toddler groups – where mothers bring their infants to play together – show that the interactions between under-2s are brief, infrequent, and often consist of just looking at another child and perhaps smiling, showing a toy, or making

FIGURE 14.1 *Parents and adults are very important in children's lives, but by the time they are 2 years old other children of the same age are becoming increasing sources of interest.*
Source: Shutterstock.

a noise (Mueller & Brenner, 1977). Infants at this age have not yet learnt many skills of social interaction. They can interact with adults, who support the interaction by responding appropriately and at the right time; but – as we discuss for social pretend later – it takes a while for two infants to learn how to do this. There is some evidence that early peer experience in toddler groups or day nurseries can assist this development; in addition, infants who are securely attached to their mothers are more confident about exploring both objects and peers, and making new social relationships (Bretherton & Waters, 1985; Turner, 1991).

THE BEGINNINGS OF PLAY

The term 'play' refers to behaviour which is enjoyable, done for its own sake, but which does not have any obvious, immediate purpose. Examples of early play would be:

- an infant repeatedly dropping an object, even when handed it back;
- an infant banging objects together to make a noise;
- an infant babbling and cooing to themselves, while lying in a cot;
- an infant laying a teddy down 'in bed'.

Sensorimotor play

The first two of these would be **sensorimotor play**; the third, language play, the fourth, pretend play. Sensorimotor play refers to play with objects, making use of their properties (falling, making noises) to produce pleasurable effects – pleasurable for the infant, that is! The kinds of 'secondary circular reactions' described by Piaget (Chapter 9) as part of his sensorimotor period, appear to be playful in this way. This simple play with objects appears in the second half of the first year, but play with language and pretend play do not emerge until well into the second year, as sensorimotor development is completed.

sensorimotor play refers to play with objects, making use of their properties (falling, making noises) to produce pleasurable effects.

Pretend play

Psychologists have made a lot of study of **pretend play** – sometimes called make-believe play or, by Piaget, **symbolic play**. In pretend play, a child makes a non-literal use of an object or action – that is, it does not mean what it usually means (see Figure 14.2). Piaget (1951) was one of the first psychologists to describe the beginnings of pretend play in detail, by recording the behaviour of his children. He noted that at the age of 15 months, his daughter Jacqueline put her head down on a cloth, sucked her thumb, blinked her eyes – and laughed. He interpreted this as Jacqueline pretending to go to sleep; indeed, she did similar actions with her toy animals a month or so later.

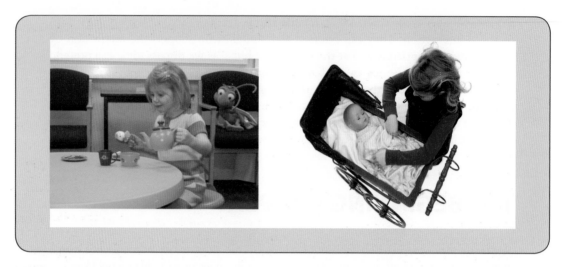

FIGURE 14.2 *In pretend play, children may act out real-life situations, e.g., putting a doll to bed or pretending to pour tea from an empty pot, or make believe that one object (e.g., a banana) is another (e.g., a phone).*
Source: © Heather Vickers (left); Shutterstock (right).

Characteristically, young children do pretend actions first with themselves, then with a doll or teddy – a process called 'decentration'.

standardisation the development of a test or procedure by administering it to a large group of individuals in order to develop uniform instructions and group norms.

A lot of early studies of pretend play were carried out by watching a child when they were put with some objects in a laboratory playroom. This had the advantage of a **standardised** procedure, but was rather unnatural. Basically, these were observations of solitary play. Such studies were put in perspective by Haight and Miller (1993). These investigators made video films of nine children playing at home; they started when the children were 12 months and continued until they were 48 months, a *longitudinal* study. While a minority of the pretend play they observed was solitary, the surprising finding they obtained was that about 75 per cent of pretend play was social – first with mothers or parents, later with friends (peers).

Howes and Matheson (1992) have described stages in the development of social pretence. It appears that the mother (or older partner, perhaps a sibling) has a **scaffolding** role – supporting the play a lot at first, by, for example, suggesting and demonstrating actions. For instance the mother might 'give teddy a bath' and then hand teddy to the infant. Thus a lot of early pretend play by the child is largely imitative; it tends to follow well-established 'scripts' or story lines, such as 'feeding the baby', or 'nursing the patient'. In addition, realistic props such as miniature cups, help to sustain pretend play. However as children get to 3 or 4 years, they are less reliant on older partners and realistic props. They take a more active role in initiating pretend play; they adapt less realistic objects (a block could be a cup, for example) or even just imagine the object completely; and they show an awareness of play conventions and competently negotiate roles within play sequences.

THE GROWTH OF SOCIAL PARTICIPATION

At 2 or 3 years of age, many children start going to a nursery school or playgroup (Figure 14.3). They have begun to develop some independence from adults, and are ready to interact with peers through play and other activities. From 2 to 4 years there is a great increase in what is called *social participation* – the extent to which children play interactively and cooperatively with others. This was first documented by Parten (1932) in her doctoral dissertation at the University of Minnesota – a classic study and one of the first generation of systematic studies of young children's social behaviour. Parten observed 2- to 4-year-olds in nursery classes; she described how they might be unoccupied, an onlooker on others' activities, or, if engaged in an activity, they could be solitary, in **parallel activity** with others or in **associative or cooperative activity** with others. These categories of social participation are defined in Table 14.1. Parten found that the first four categories declined with age, whereas associative and cooperative activity, the only ones involving substantial interaction with peers, increased with age.

associative or cooperative activity an activity in which children interact with one another, performing similar tasks.

parallel activity a type of activity where children play near each other with the same materials, but do not interact much.

If you watch preschool children, you will usually see just two or three children playing together, however, the size of groups of children playing together does tend to increase in older preschoolers and in the early school years. A study of more than 400 Israeli children aged 5–6 years in outdoor free play found a lot of group activity, with parallel activity becoming infrequent; while the size of groups in which children played increased (Hertz-Lazarowitz *et al.*, 1981). By the middle school years, boys especially are playing in large groups as team games such as football or basketball

Table 14.1 *Parten's categories of social participation*

Category	Description
Unoccupied	Child is not engaged in any activity
Onlooker	Child is just watching others, not joining in
Solitary	Child plays alone, away from others
Parallel	Child plays near other(s) with the same materials, but does not interact much, e.g. playing independently at the same sandpit
Associative	Child interacts with other(s) at an activity, doing similar things, e.g. each adding building blocks to the same tower
Cooperative	Child interacts with other(s) in complementary ways, e.g. one child gets blocks and hands them to another child, who builds the tower

FIGURE 14.3 *From 2–3 years of age many children go to a nursery school or playgroup, and have begun to develop some independence from adults.*
Source: Shutterstock.

become popular. At early adolescence the nature of children's groups alters, with large same-sex cliques or gangs becoming common, changing again in later adolescence as heterosexual relationships become more important.

Are siblings important?

Parents are much older than their infants. Harris (1998) argues that adults are more or less a 'different species' as far as infants are concerned! Peers are children of the same age – generally, within perhaps a year of one's own age. However, it is interesting to consider the impact of siblings (brothers and sisters). Not everyone has siblings, but the majority do. Usually, siblings differ in age by a few years. Although not exactly peers, they are often close enough in age, and similar enough in interests and developmental stages, to be an important social partner for the young child.

An older sibling may be ambivalent about a younger sibling, in a way in which a parent usually is not. Especially for the first-born child in the family, the new brother or sister displaces them from being the centre of attention in their parents' eyes. Although an older sibling can show great tolerance for younger ones, and act as an important model for more competent behaviour (such as pretend play), studies in many societies agree that they can also show hostility and ambivalence (Eibl-Eibesfeldt, 1989).

In the UK, Dunn and Kendrick (1982) carried out a detailed study of sibling relationships. They made observations in the homes of 40 first-born children living with both parents. At first visit, a new sibling was due in a month or so, and the first child was usually nearing their second birthday. After the birth of the sibling they made further visits, when the second child was about 1 month old, and again at 8 months and at 14 months. They found that many first-borns showed some signs of jealousy after the arrival of the new sibling. Much of this jealousy and ambivalence was directed towards parents, less as overt hostility to the infant, but some showed ambivalence or hostility, as the following extract of conversation shows:

> *Mother*: I don't know what we're going to do, do you? [Baby is crying]
> *Child*: Smack him.
> *Mother*: He's too little to smack.
> *Child*: Smack him.

Most of the first-born children also showed a lot of interest and affection towards their new sibling. Dunn and Kendrick (1982) felt that the sibling relationship was one in which a range of powerful emotions may be aroused – envy, but love as well.

Sibling relationships and the development of social understanding

The subtitle of Dunn and Kendrick's (1982) book is 'love, envy and understanding'. They argue that because the sibling relationship is both close and emotionally power-ful, it may be an optimal situation in which to learn understanding. Siblings seem to be learning how to frustrate, tease, placate, comfort or get their own way with their brother or sister. Dunn and Kendrick (1982) relate one incident in which Callum (14 months old) repeatedly reaches for and manipulates some magnetic letters that his 3-year-old sister Laura is playing with on a tray. Laura repeatedly says 'no' gently. Callum continues trying to reach the letters. Finally, Laura picks up the tray with the letters and takes it to a high table that Callum cannot reach. Callum is furious and starts to cry. He turns and goes straight to the sofa where Laura's comfort objects, a rag doll and a pacifier, are lying. He takes the doll and holds it tight, looking at Laura. Laura now gets very upset, starts crying, and runs to take the doll. Callum seems to have calculated how to annoy Laura so as to get his own back on her.

This behaviour suggests an ability to take account of the likely mental state of another, at a surprisingly early age since **theory of mind** abilities are often thought of as appearing at age 4 (but see the reference to Buttelmann et al., 2009, in Chapter 11, who suggest that this ability can be found at least as early as 18 months). In this incident, the younger sibling wished to have a negative effect on his older sister; but another incident shows empathic behaviour, with an intention to help the sibling by alleviating distress: Fifteen-month-old Len had previously learnt that he could make his parents laugh by pulling up his T-shirt, sticking out his tummy, and walking in an odd way. When his older brother fell off the climbing frame and cried vigorously, Len watched solemnly and then approached him with the funny walk, calling out to his brother.

Siblings and social and cognitive development

Observations such as these suggest a powerful role for siblings in social and cognitive development. Siblings will be getting practice in understanding others' feelings, and conflict resolution skills. Ross et al. (2006) found that siblings in the 3.5 to 12 years age range were able to reach or negotiate some sort of compromise in conflicts, about half the time, and to reach an agreeable win–loss outcome about one-fifth of the time. Several studies have found direct evidence that having an older sibling helps a younger sibling develop theory of mind skills. Ruffman et al. (1998) reported findings from four experiments with **false belief** tasks in England and Japan. In all four experi-ments the number of older siblings (0, 1, or 2) contributed linearly to false belief understanding, whereas number of younger siblings had no effect, so that the benefit was due to having older siblings.

A number of studies have used semi-naturalistic paradigms to look at sibling teaching; usually the older sibling is taught some task such as constructing a toy or how to play a game, and then is asked to teach the younger sibling (Howe et al., 2006). When the older sibling is of school age, they are more likely to use detailed verbal instructions, and to scaffold the process, whereas when the older sibling was still a preschooler, they more often used demonstration.

However, children can learn social cognitive skills with adults and peers, as well as with siblings. For example, Lewis *et al.* (1996) gave similar false belief tasks to 3- to 5-year-old children in Cyprus and Crete, where children lived with more extended families. They found significant effects not only for number of siblings, but more generally for the number of older children seen the day before. They argued for an 'apprenticeship' model, with children acquiring theory of mind from adults, older siblings, and other older children in their extended family or neighbourhood.

Only children

There has been a large body of research on only children. There are some studies which suggest advantages of having sibling(s), beyond the advantages for theory of mind development noted above (which are probably transient, as first order false belief tasks are consolidated by 5 years and also when children start school and meet many more peers). For example Kitzmann *et al.* (2002) compared the social competence of only children, and first- and second-borns in two-child families, at 6–12 years. They did not find any differences in self-concept, or loneliness, nor in self-rated number and quality of friendships. However, in terms of social preference (getting 'liked most' and not 'liked least' nominations from classmates, see below), second-borns were the most liked, and only children the least liked. Also only children were nominated most often as aggressive, victimised, and withdrawn. The authors concluded that 'having a sibling may be especially helpful for learning to manage conflict' (2002, p. 299).

Only children in China Some research on only children has taken place in China, where, because of the one-child policy in urban areas (Figure 14.4), many children are only children. Chen *et al.* (1994) studied 498 only children and 67 sibling children aged 8 and 10 years, from primary schools in Shanghai. They

FIGURE 14.4 *Because of the one-child policy in urban areas, many Chinese children are only children.*
Source: Shutterstock.

found no significant differences between these two groups, on sociometric assessments by peers, teacher ratings of school competence, or academic achievement. The authors attributed this to the fact that only children are in the majority in contemporary China; clearly, if most children are onlies, then it will be more difficult to get a general finding that only children are 'liked least'! Also, most children in China go to public day nurseries from an early age, and therefore get a lot of peer experience, which may substitute for lack of siblings in the only children.

The consensus of evidence appears to be that there are often non-significant findings in this area, but in some studies only children do less well on conflict resolution, and on theory of mind at 3 to 4 years, but they may do well on later achievement and intelligence scores (Falbo & Polit, 1986). Probably, there are many ways of achieving social skills and social-cognitive competence; for a lot of children, siblings are a help here, but for those without siblings, other routes are available.

Social play

A lot of the time that preschool children are together, they spend playing. Piaget (1951) described three main (though overlapping) stages in play – sensorimotor play with objects in infancy; symbolic play (fantasy or pretend play) from around 15 months to 6 years; and games with rules from around 6 years onwards; he linked these play stages to his stages of cognitive development (Chapter 9). Later, and developing Piaget's ideas, Smilansky (1968) postulated four stages in the development of play, shown in Table 14.2. Smilansky's main contribution was to add a stage of constructive play with objects – play which was more focused and mature than the sensorimotor play of infancy, but which was not pretend. Smilansky also popularised the idea of the importance of **sociodramatic play**; this is pretend play involving social role playing in an extended story sequence, for example playing doctors and nurses and patients, or spacemen and aliens, or parents and children (see Figure 14.5).

sociodramatic play *pretend play* involving social role-playing in an extended story sequence.

A play hierarchy

Rubin *et al.* (1978) felt it would be useful to combine Parten's scheme of social participation (Table 14.1) with Smilansky's scheme of play (Table 14.2) to create a **play hierarchy**. This nested category scheme

play hierarchy a scheme used for coding children's activities, based on social participation and level of play.

Table 14.2 *Smilansky's four-sequence developmental model of play*

Label	Description
Functional	Simple body movements or actions with objects, e.g. banging bricks
Constructive	Making things with objects, e.g. building a tower with bricks
Dramatic	Acting out roles in a pretend game, e.g. pretending to be a doctor
Games with rules	Playing in a game with publicly accepted rules, e.g. football, hopscotch

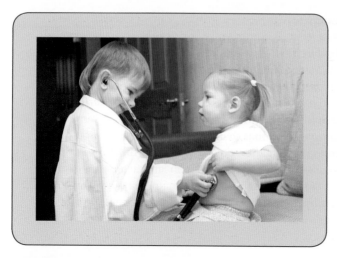

FIGURE 14.5 *Playing doctors and patients is an example of sociodramatic play – pretend play that involves social role-playing in an extended story sequence.*

Source: Shutterstock.

means that you can watch pre-school children and categorise their play according to both schemes, for example solitary practice play, or associative dramatic play. Categories higher up either scale were argued to be more mature. This scheme is useful for coding children's activities, but it has two limitations. First, it implies a developmental progression that is not universally accepted; some solitary play can be quite mature for example; and constructive play seems to co-exist with dramatic play rather than precede it. Second, it omits important kinds of play; particularly, physical activity play,

rough-and-tumble play a friendly type of play that involves play-fighting with a partner.

rough-and-tumble play (friendly play-fighting with a partner), and language play.

Social pretend and sociodramatic play

The role of the mother or other adult in encouraging pretend play has been shown in many studies. For example, Nielsen and Christie (2008) found that adult modelling of pretend play with children aged 27 to 41 months (using a doll's house and related props) increased pretend play by the children immediately afterwards, and that while some of this pretend was imitative, much was novel, suggesting a general facilitation of pretence.

Dunn (2004) argued that an older brother or sister may contribute a lot to a child's pretend play experiences. Based on her observations, she compared how mothers, and older siblings, might engage in pretend play with the younger sibling. Mothers almost always focused on object-based pretence, using objects as props; they would make relevant comments and suggestions, as 'interested spectators'. In contrast, the older siblings would take part in complementary role playing with their younger brother or sister. They would closely mesh their play, using talk and non-verbal actions.

From the age of 3 onwards, pretend play very commonly involves quite sophisticated social role-playing skills with peers. As mentioned earlier, the term 'sociodramatic play' was brought into prominence by Smilansky (1968). This refers to dramatic play, that is, the child is clearly enacting a role; and to social play. Smilansky used other criteria, such as a sustained narrative sequence lasting at least 10 minutes, but these further criteria were not widely used by others.

Pretend play and friendship

Children's pretence is more sustained and complex when they are playing with friends, compared to acquaintances (Howes, 1994). The mutuality and emotional commitment of friends may motivate children to sustain cooperative interaction. The work of Gottman and colleagues has examined the processes of developing and maintaining friendships in young children. Gottman (1983) observed pairs of children (aged 3 up to 9 years, and often previously unacquainted) playing in their homes, over several sessions. Often, children would establish a simple common-ground activity, such as colouring with crayons, that they could do side-by-side (a kind of 'parallel play'); they might 'escalate' this by 'information exchange' or 'self-disclosure', perhaps commenting on the other's activity, or saying something about what they liked or wished to do. If successful, the pair would move on to introducing a joint activity. Often, such joint activity would involve pretend.

For example, Gottman (1983, pp. 56–57) describes interactions between D (in his own house) and J (visiting), both young 4-year-olds. After some information exchange, J says 'pretend like those little roll cookies too, OK?' and D replies 'and make, um, make a, um, pancake, too'. Later D tries to introduce role play, and there is some negotiation:

D: I'm the mummy.
J: Who am I?
D: Um, the baby.
J: Daddy.
D: Sister.
J: I wanna be the daddy.
D: You're the sister.
J: Daddy.
D: You're the big sister!
J: Don't play house. I don't want to play house.

Despite J offering progressively higher status roles (but not equal to 'mummy'!), this negotiation ended in failure, and what Gottman calls a de-escalation. For a while they returned to pretend meal preparation.

Gottman describes the social skill of friendship formation as managing levels of closeness ('amity') and conflict, by escalating and when necessary de-escalating levels of play. Colouring side by side has low risks and low benefits (in friendship terms). Simple pretend (e.g. pretending blocks are cookies) is a step up; and role play a step further. Thus, in Gottman's model, pretend play has a central role in the development of friendship.

Sex differences in pretend play Some studies find that girls engage in more frequent and more sophisticated pretend play than boys. Bornstein *et al.* (1999) found that mothers tended to engage in symbolic play more frequently with daughters than with sons, and these mother–daughter interactions predicted peer fantasy play. Nevertheless, in a review, Göncü *et al.* (2002) concluded that findings are inconsistent, and dependent on the play environment, toys available, and the kinds of activities measured.

However there are sex differences in the themes of fantasy play. While girls' pretend play often involves domestic themes, boys' pretend play is often more physically vigorous, rough-and-tumble type activity, perhaps with super hero themes (Holland,

sex-role stereotypes
beliefs held about what
roles are most appropriate
for one sex or the other.

2003). Girls do seem to use their more mature language abilities in pretend play (Göncü *et al.*, 2002). The **sex-role stereotypicality** of the materials also influences boys' and girls' play. Boys' play with female-preferred toys, such as dolls, is less sophisticated than it is with male-preferred toys, such as blocks (Pellegrini & Perlmutter, 1989).

Imaginary companions

imaginary companion
a companion who does
not exist but who can
appear very real to
children.

The ultimate in imagination in childhood play is perhaps the **imaginary companion**, who may follow the child around, or need to be fed at mealtimes, or tucked up in bed with the child. Some one-quarter to one-half of children have some form of imaginary companion, especially between 3 and 8 years (they are mostly abandoned by age 10). These children tend to engage in a lot of sophisticated pretend play generally (Taylor *et al.*, 1993). Children are not confused about the imaginary status of imaginary companions and are aware they are different from real friends.

paracosm an imagined,
detailed fantasy world
invented by a child or
perhaps an adult, involv-
ing humans and/or
animals, or perhaps even
fantasy or alien creations.

Majors (2007) carried out a detailed exploration of imaginary companions of children aged 5 to 10 years, in the UK. Most imaginary companions were human, a few were animal (a duck; a pony). One child, John, had one imaginary companion and created an elaborate imaginary world (sometimes called a **paracosm**) around him. Majors found that the imaginary companions were significant and important for the children, and that they served several functions, including being a pleasurable retreat, dependable companions, wish fulfilment, and entertainment. For example, one girl said she needed her imaginary companions 'when I can't get to sleep or when I'm lonely and times when I'm feeling sad or there's no one to play with or talk to'. A boy who created a duck as an imaginary companion explained: 'I was swimming a width [in a swimming pool] and then I thought I would do another with my imaginary friend and I did and I needed it to be a swimming one so I chose a duck.' This boy's swimming had since improved a lot and it is possible the imaginary duck helped him.

Physical activity play

Although much play is with objects – especially play seen in laboratory playrooms with little space and many toys – in fact quite a lot of play involves gross physical activity, often without objects. In a review of what they argued was a neglected aspect of play, Pellegrini and Smith (1998) suggested there were three developmental phases in physical activity play. First were 'rhythmical stereotypes', bodily movements characteristic of babies such as kicking legs, waving arms. Then, during the preschool years there is a lot of 'exercise play' – running around, jumping, climbing – whole body movements which may be done alone or with others. Overlapping with and succeeding this is rough-and-tumble play, most common in the middle school years.

Rough-and-tumble play

Rough-and-tumble play, or play fighting, involves wrestling, grappling, kicking, tumbling and rolling on the ground, and chasing. These are activities which look like real fighting; in fact, they sometimes are mistaken by teachers and play-time supervisors, who may intervene to break up a 'fight' only to be told 'we were only playing, Miss!'. Rough-and-tumble play is common in the preschool years and especially in middle childhood. Observations in school playgrounds show that it takes up about 10 per cent of playground time (Humphreys & Smith, 1987) – though this does depend on factors such as how soft or hard the play surface is! Children enjoy play fighting, especially boys. It is characterised by laughter, self-handi-capping (a stronger child does not necessarily 'win'), restraint (not hitting or kicking hard or even making contact at all), and reversals (taking it in turns to be on top) (Figure 14.6).

FIGURE 14.6 *Rough-and-tumble play is common in the preschool years and in middle childhood.* Source: Shutterstock.

Sometimes playground supervisors clamp down on play fighting, because they think it often leads to real fighting. This appears to be a misconception, perhaps based on the behaviour of a small number of children. Both interviews with children, and observations in playgrounds, show that most of the time, rough-and-tumble play does not lead to real fighting (Schafer & Smith, 1996). Although the great majority of rough-and-tumble is really playful, occasionally things can go wrong and a fight develops or someone gets hurt. This could happen for two main reasons: one would be lack of social skills – a play signal such as a playful punch is misinterpreted; the other would be deliberate manipulation or cheating – one child deliberately abuses the play expectations of the other to inflict hurt while 'on top'. The likelihood of this happening seems more common in sociometrically rejected children (Pellegrini, 1994; we examine peer rejection later in this chapter); indeed, this behaviour could contribute to their dislike by classmates.

FUNCTIONS OF PLAY

Is play important in development? This has turned out to be a controversial question which has yet to be resolved. Most of the relevant research has been on play with objects – what Smilansky would call constructive play and dramatic play. In fact, most research effort has been put into possible functions of sociodramatic play. In her book on this topic, Smilansky (1968) argued that sociodramatic play was essential for normal development, and that if a child is deficient in it, intervention should be carried out in the preschool to encourage and enhance such play.

Is sociodramatic play important?

Smilansky had observed that immigrant children in Israeli preschools did not show much sociodramatic play; and were also behind in language and cognitive skills. Subsequently other studies in the USA and elsewhere documented similar findings for children from disadvantaged backgrounds. This may be because these parents did not encourage or 'scaffold' pretend play at home, and provided an unstimulating environment for their children. Of course, it might be that an unstimulating environment leads to both poor play skills, and poor linguistic and cognitive skills. Nevertheless, Smilansky and others hypothesised that sociodramatic play in itself contributed to development (or in the strong version of the argument, was essential for it), because of the rich practice in language skills, social negotiation and object transformation which such play entailed.

Play tutoring

As a result, a number of intervention studies were carried out to test the hypothesis. These could be done because Smilansky, and many other investigators, found that it is quite possible to get children to do more and better sociodramatic play, by having preschool teachers and staff model such play, encourage it, take children on visits (e.g. to hospitals, zoos), and provide suitable props and equipment. This was called **play tutoring**; it led to studies following the broad design shown in Table 14.3. Differences between pre- and post-test performance on various developmental tasks were compared, for children who received some kind of play tutoring and those who did not; the latter, the control group, was to allow for effects of age and general preschool experience. If the play tutored children improved more, this was felt to be strong evidence that sociodramatic play really was important.

play tutoring where parents or other adults, such as preschool teacher, model or *scaffold* types of play, such as social *pretend play* that may be limited or absent in the child's spontaneous play.

For quite some time through the 1970s and 1980s, a number of studies of this kind got positive results. Indeed, it seemed that almost whatever tests the researchers used, play tutored children improved more! This seemed too good to be true. Subsequently, some investigators argued that these earlier results were confounded

Table 14.3 *Design of play tutoring studies*

Play tutored group	Control group
Pre-tests carried out on social, cognitive, linguistic skills	
Children receive extra tutoring: support and encouragement in social pretend play	Children follow the normal curriculum with no special emphasis on social pretend play
Post-tests carried out on social, cognitive, linguistic skills	

by two main problems. First, the design in Table 14.3 is flawed. Generally the play tutored children got extra intervention from adults – more verbal and educational stimulation than the control group. Second, most studies did not use 'blind' testing, so that the testers knew which condition the child was in and might have been sub-consciously influenced by this. When further experiments were run to control for these two mistakes, the benefits of play tutoring were not found (Christie & Johnson, 1985; Smith, 1988, 2010). It seemed that the general adult stimulation was important, rather than specifically the pretend play.

More recently, it has been argued that pretend play is important for development of theory of mind skills (Harris, 2000). Pretend play and theory of mind do both get going properly at around 4 years of age, and pretend play does seem to exercise a child's understanding of a play partner's understanding – of the play convention, agreement on pretence, and so on. Also, children who score highly on theory of mind tasks tend to be good at pretend play (Taylor & Carlson, 1997). However, positive cor-relations might be due to a third variable, such as intelligence, and the link to theory of mind remains disputed (Smith, 2010).

An intervention study

Well-designed experimental studies might give more informative evidence. Dockett (1998) has reported an intervention study carried out in Australia, at a preschool in Sydney, over one term. There were 33 children aged around 4 years, of whom 15 attended in the mornings, and 18 in the afternoons. During three weeks of pre-test, each child was observed to record the quality of their play – particularly the amount and complexity of shared pretend play – and given theory of mind assessments. A four-week intervention was carried out with the morning group, taking pizzas as a theme which could involve both boys and girls. There was a visit to a pizza restaur-ant where the chef demonstrated how pizzas were made, followed by designing a pizza area in the preschool and centring a lot of play and activities around this. Teachers took opportunities to extend such play. The afternoon group acted as a control, following the normal curriculum. In a final three weeks of post-test, the play observations were repeated, and the theory-of-mind assessments were given both immediately after the intervention stopped (immediate post-test), and again three weeks later (delayed post-test). It was verified that the amount and complexity of shared pretend had increased in the intervention group, but not in the control group. During post-test (when the pizza activities had stopped), the intervention group chil-dren did more make-believe with objects, actions and situations, and talked more about pretend activities. Also, the intervention group children showed substantial and significant increases on the theory-of-mind tasks, and these increases were main-tained from the immediate post-test to the delayed post-test. Although the control group showed some slight increases on these tasks, these were small and not statist-ically significant. Dockett argued that the social negotiations and verbal commun-ications in the shared pretence had helped develop the theory-of-mind skills of the intervention group children; this study needs replication, bearing in mind the small sample size.

Dominance hierarchies

Less attention has been paid to physical activity play. Pellegrini and Smith (1998) discuss the evidence that physical activity play is useful for developing muscle strength and stamina. Particularly controversial is the role of rough-and-tumble play. It is not yet clear what function this play may have; but it appears similar to the kinds of play fighting seen in many species of mammals, kittens and puppies for example. Most likely, it helps develop physical strength for skills such as fighting, and especially as children approach adolescence, it may help children realise their own strength and that of others and establish their position in a **dominance** hierarchy. Dominance refers to being able to take precedence over another child, or beat them in a fight or conflict. A dominance hierarchy refers to children's recognition of an ordering with respect to dominance. Dominance relationships appear to become more important in adolescence, especially in boys' peer groups, and boys may use play fighting to test out others and try to improve their own status without actually fighting (Pellegrini, 2009; Pellegrini & Smith, 1998).

dominance getting one's own way or influencing others in interpersonal encounters.

SOCIAL STATUS AND SOCIOMETRY: THE MEASUREMENT OF SOCIAL RELATIONSHIPS IN THE PEER GROUP

We saw earlier how the work of Parten and others described social participation in preschool children. By the time they are in school, children mix with large peer groups, and social relationships are an important part of their life. Some children are sociable and popular, others are lonely, and others are disliked. How can we find out about these patterns of relationships?

This can be done by observation. For example Clark et al. (1969) observed nursery school children to record who was playing with whom, and constructed **sociograms** (an example is shown in Figure 14.7). The large concentric circles show the number of play partners a child has. Each symbol represents a child, with circles being girls, triangles boys. The number of lines joining two children represents the percentage of observations on which they were seen playing together. In the class shown here, there is one rather popular boy with four friends, central to a loose association of all the boys, except for two who are 'isolates' with no clear partners. There are three groups of girls, one of five girls loosely linked to the boys, another group of five, and a pair. This diagram allows one to see the social structure in a group of children at a glance.

The general technique here is called **sociometry**. Although observations can be used to get sociometric data, for reasons of time and

sociogram a visual representation of interpersonal relationships within a group. Often used in an educational context in order to help teachers and staff understand more about pupils' peer relationships.

sociometry a picture of the social structure in a group, derived from observation, questionnaire, or interview.

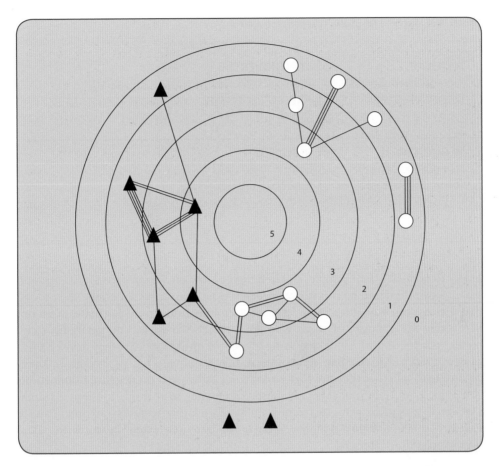

FIGURE 14.7 *A sociogram of a class of preschool (nursery school) children: circles represent girls, triangles boys.*

Source: Clarke *et al.,* 1969. Reprinted with permission.

also to get more information, interviews are often used. For example, each child might be asked 'Who are your best friends?' or 'Who are the three classmates you like most?' These *nomination* data can also be plotted on a sociogram. If Susan chooses Elisabeth as a best friend, but Elisabeth does not choose Susan, this can be indicated by an arrow from Susan to Elisabeth; if the choice is reciprocated, the arrow would point both ways on the sociogram.

It is also possible to ask children 'Who are the three classmates you like least?' There may be ethical objections to this, as such questions might bring about increased negative behaviour to unliked peers, but so far this has not been found (Mayeux *et al.*, 2007). The combined procedure – asking children for names of both liked most and liked least classmates – was used by Coie & Dodge (1983) in a seminal study which defined what are called 'sociometric status types'. These researchers found that they needed a two-dimensional rather than a one-dimensional model of social relationships. The older, one-dimensional model was from

sociometric status a categorisation of children as popular, controversial, rejected, neglected, or average, according to whether they are high or low on positive and negative nominations.

Table 14.4 *Sociometric status categories (based on Coie et al., 1983)*

POPULAR	CONTROVERSIAL
High on "liked most"	High on "liked most"
Low on "liked least"	High on "liked least"
AVERAGE	
NEGLECTED	REJECTED
Low on "liked most"	Low on "liked most"
Low on "liked least"	High on "liked least"

lonely to popular – for example, children high or low on Parten's social participation scale. A two-dimensional model was needed, Coie *et al.* argued, because they found that the children who got a lot of 'like most' nominations from classmates were not necessarily the opposite of those who got a lot of 'liked least' nominations; some pupils got a lot of both kinds, and some got few of either kind. So, they devised a five category model, of popular, controversial, rejected, neglected or average children, according to whether they are high or low on positive and on negative nominations (see Table 14.4). This model has been used extensively in peer relationships research. Meta-analyses show that there is some stability of sociometric status over time (Jiang & Cillessen, 2005). Stability is higher in older children, and when measures are taken over shorter time intervals.

Consequences of sociometric status

Does it matter which sociometric status group a child is in? A number of studies suggest possible problems with being in rejected status. In young children, poor social skills in joining play may lead to peer rejection. Dodge *et al.* (1983) looked at how 5-year-olds attempted to get into ongoing play between two other children. Children who were of popular status waited and watched, and then got to join in by making group-orientated statements; neglected children tended to stay at the waiting and watching stage, while rejected children tended to try disruptive actions such as interrupting the play. In an observational study of 8- to 9-year-olds in US playgrounds, Ladd (1983) found that rejected children spent less time in cooperative play and social conversation than did average or popular children, and more time arguing and fighting; they played in smaller groups, and with younger or with less popular companions. And at 11 to 13 years, a study by Wentzel and Asher (1995) found that rejected children often did poorly at school work; interestingly, neglected children were quite well motivated and liked by teachers.

Children can be disliked and peer rejected for different reasons, but the most common reason seems to be because of being aggressive and disruptive (as in the study by Pellegrini referred to earlier, in which rejected children often 'cheated' in play fighting). In a large study in the Netherlands of 5- to 7-year-old boys, nearly half the rejected children were categorised as 'aggressive-rejected', being impulsive, dishonest and non-cooperative. The next largest category was 'rejected-submissive', children who were shy but not particularly aggressive (Cillessen *et al.*, 1992). In the Wentzel and Asher study, it was only the aggressive-rejected children who had problematic academic profiles.

A social skills processing model

Children who are rejected in the middle school years may be in need of help – probably more than those who simply keep a low profile and are ignored or neglected. The findings above suggest that rejected children are lacking in some social skills. Dodge *et al.* (1986) suggested that the social skills of peer interaction can be envisaged as an exchange model, with five steps. Suppose child A is interacting with child B. The five steps for child A are:

1. Encode the incoming information – perceive what child B is doing.
2. Interpret this information.
3. Search for appropriate responses.
4. Evaluate these responses and select the best.
5. Enact that response.

Child B engages in a similar process with respect to child A.

Given this model, it might be possible to find out if rejected children lack skills at certain stages in the process. There is some evidence for this. For example, aggressive children have been found to misinterpret others' behaviour (stage 2) and to readily select aggressive responses (stage 4). Evidence relating to the model is reviewed by Crick and Dodge (1994).

Following the model that rejected (and perhaps, neglected) children lack social skills, attempts have been made by psychologists to help improve social skills by training children: for example, by providing training in sharing, negotiating, joining in, and being assertive but non-aggressive. Some of these methods have had some success; see Ladd *et al.* (2002) and Malik and Furman (1993) for reviews.

Different views on peer maladjustment and aggression

Not all behaviour labelled as maladjusted may be due to lack of social skills. Some rejected children may be simply reacting to exclusion by the popular cliques and would not necessarily be rejected or lacking in social skills in other situations outside the classroom. Also, some aggressive children may be quite skilled at manipulating others. A study of English children aged 7 to 11 years by Sutton *et al.* (1999) found that children nominated by others as ringleader bullies (Chapter 20) actually scored particularly highly on theory-of-mind tasks (Chapter 11); although these children did lack empathy, they were skilled at knowing how to hurt others with little risk of retaliation or detection by adults. At times, good social skills can be put to antisocial ends.

Escaping from rejected status

Sandstrom and Coie (1999) looked at factors involved in children escaping from 'rejected' status over a two-year period. Important factors for this were the child's own perception of their social status, participation in extracurricular activities, internal **locus of control**, and high parental monitoring. Interestingly, aggressive behaviour was *positively* related to status improvement amongst initially rejected boys; an indication that aggressive behaviour is not always maladaptive. Indeed the picture of rejected children becomes more complicated by adolescence; studies with adolescents suggest that aggressive pupils may associate together in antisocial cliques or gangs, which reject academic values. Such pupils may be disliked by many, but are liked or popular within their own group (Cairns *et al.*, 1988; and see Chapter 15).

locus of control people who develop an internal locus of control believe that they are responsible for their own failures and successes. Those with an external locus of control believe that external forces, such as luck or fate, determine their outcomes.

FRIENDSHIP

A related research area to that of sociometric status, is friendship. However, it is not quite the same; sociometric status refers to the general degree of being liked or disliked in the peer group, whereas friendship refers to some close association between two (or more) children. We tend to conceive of friendship as implying attachment and trust – psychological characteristics. For a preschool child, it is something more straightforward – if you ask 'what is a friend?', the child is likely to reply 'someone who plays with you'. Bigelow and La Gaipa (1980) studied understanding of friendship in 6- to 14-year-old children, in Canada and Scotland. They found three stages in expectations of friendship. From 6 to 8 years friendship was seen as based on common activities, living nearby, having similar expectations. From 9 to 10 years, shared values, rules, and sanctions became more important. From 11–12 years, a conception of friendship based on understanding and self-disclosure, as well as shared interests, emerged – similar to how adults usually describe friendship. These and other studies suggest that a shift from physical to more psychological ideas of friendship during the middle school years, with intimacy and commitment becoming important in adolescence.

Not surprisingly, friends tend to be similar in many respects. A study carried out in the Netherlands, with pupils aged 9 to 13 years, found that children were more similar to friends than to non-friends on a range of characteristics – such as being cooperative, or shy, or starting fights, being helpful or sociable. This was true, whether the characteristics were rated by the children themselves, or by classmates (Haselager *et al.*, 1998).

Most children have friends, and usually one or a few best friends. A question that has intrigued psychologists for some time is whether having a friend or friends is important for some aspects of healthy development and well-being. An American psychologist, Harry Stack Sullivan, had argued back in the 1950s that having at least one best friend or 'chum' was very important for pre-adolescent children, and that without this a child would feel lonely, lack feelings of competence or self-worth, and be more at risk of later maladjustment and poor mental health (Sullivan, 1953). We will look at some of the relevant evidence for this.

What is special about friends?

Part of the answer to the issue of what is important about friendship is to see how relations and activities with friends actually differ from those of non-friends. Newcomb and Bagwell (1995) reviewed a large number of studies and concluded that interactions between friends showed four features compared to interactions between non-friends:

- more intense social activity; friends play together more;
- more reciprocity and intimacy in interactions;
- although there may be conflicts with friends, as with non-friends, there is more frequent conflict resolution between friends;
- more effective task performance; in joint or cooperative tasks, friends help each other better and criticise each other more constructively.

An example of this kind of research comes from a study of 8-year-old Italian children (Fonzi *et al.*, 1997). Friendship pairs were compared with pairs of non-friends in two structured tasks designed to simulate real-life situations of potential conflict, for example where equipment had to be shared, or turns had to be taken (one task is shown in Figure 14.8). Friends were more effective about this in a number of ways: they made more proposals than non-friends, spent more time negotiating sharing arrangements, and were more able to make compromises. Those friendship pairs that were stable through the school year also showed more sensitivity in negotiations.

Hartup (1996) suggests that there are three important factors to consider:

- having friends;
- having high-status friends;
- having good quality friendships.

FIGURE 14.8 *A car-racing task where turns have to be taken.*

Source: Fonzi *et al.*, 1997, figure 1, p. 499. Reprinted by permission of the Society for Research in Child Development.

It may be that, while having a good friend may protect against loneliness, the other factors are also influential. For example, research on children who are victims of school bullying suggests that they may be low on all three of the above, but especially that if they have friends, these friends may also be low status (maybe victims too) and the friendships are of low quality – lacking trust and reciprocity; the result is that these friends either cannot or do not give much help when one is in trouble (for example, being bullied; see Chapter 20).

While it seems likely that having friends is important for a child's development, it is difficult to prove this. Parker and Asher (1987) reviewed a large number of relevant studies which had data on peer relationships and friendships in childhood, and three main kinds of later outcome: dropping out of school early; being involved in juvenile and adult crime; and adult **psychopathology** (mental health ratings, or needing psychiatric help of any kind). They found a consistent link between low peer acceptance (or having few friends) and dropping out of school early; and between aggressiveness at school and juvenile / adult crime. The data on effects of shyness / withdrawal and on predictors of adult psychopathology were less consistent, with any links unproven at present. Being correlational, these studies do not prove a causal effect, but they certainly suggest it.

psychopathology
a psychological imbalance such that the individual has difficulties in functioning in the real world.

Consequences of friendships for later well-being

An interesting study was carried out by Bagwell *et al.* (1998), in the mid-West United States. Some 12–13 years previously, the researchers had made a study of fifth grade

(10-year-old) students in school. Now, they contacted some of these students again as young adults (aged 23 years). The aim of the study was to see if friendships and peer rejection at school were related to adjustment in adult life. At school, 334 students had taken part, and were assessed twice over a one month interval. They were each asked to name their three best friends, and the three classmates they liked least, of the same sex. Subsequently two contrasting subgroups were formed: a *friended* subgroup who had a stable, mutual best friend at this time, and a *chumless* subgroup who did not receive any reciprocated friendship choice (out of three) at either assessment point. From these subgroups the researchers contacted and interviewed 30 from each as young adults, giving them questionnaires to assess life status, self-esteem, psychopathological symptoms, and quality of adult friendships. The main findings were that peer rejection at school was important for predicting poorer life status, such as job aspiration and performance, or extent of social activities; but it was friendship rather than peer rejection which predicted self-esteem as an adult. Both lack of friendship and peer rejection appeared to be predictors of psychopathological symptoms. The results suggest that both absence of a close friend in preadolescence and the experience of peer rejection have negative consequences for later well-being, but with each being stronger predictors of different aspects of later life. No one study can be conclusive here, but many researchers believe that having good friends is a causal factor of importance, and that children lacking friends need help of some kind to remedy this.

SEX DIFFERENCES IN PLAY AND SOCIAL BEHAVIOUR

Boys and girls obviously differ substantially in play and social behaviour, especially in the school years (Archer & Lloyd, 1986; Golombok & Fivush, 1994). This starts at preschool if not before. Observations of 2- to 4-year-olds have found that boys tend to prefer playing with transportation toys and blocks, and activities involving gross motor activity such as throwing or kicking balls, or rough-and-tumbling; girls tend to prefer dolls, and dressing-up or domestic play. Many activities, however, do not show a sex preference at this age.

Even in nursery school, children tend to select same-sex partners for play (see Figure 14.7 for example), and by the time children are getting into team games at about 6 or 7 years, sex segregation in the playground is much greater. Boys tend to prefer outdoor play and, later, team games; girls prefer indoor, more sedentary activities, and often play in pairs. Boys more frequently engage in both play-fighting and in actual aggressive behaviour. Girls tend to be more empathic, and remain more orientated towards adults (parents and teacher) longer into childhood. In a study of 10- to 11-year-old children in American playgrounds, Lever (1978) found that boys more often played in larger mixed-age groups, while girls were more often in smaller groups of same-age pairs. Boys liked playing competitive team games that were more complex in their rules and role-structure, and which seemed to emphasise 'political' skills of cooperation, competition and leadership in their social relations. Girls put more emphasis on intimacy and exclusiveness in their friendships.)

Maccoby (1998) has summarised these sorts of sex differences into three main phenomena:

- Segregation: a strong tendency for children to play with others of their own sex, from 3 years onwards.
- Differentiation: different styles of interaction in boys' and girls' groups.
- Asymmetry: boys' groups are both more cohesive and more exclusionary than girls' groups.

Explanations of sex differences

It seems almost certain that sex hormones have some effect on behaviour (Collaer & Hines, 1995). In normal foetal development male sex hormones predispose boys to become more physically active and interested in rough-and-tumble play. This is strongly suggested both by animal studies and also evidence from human children who are exposed accidentally to unusual concentrations of sex hormones. It is also consistent with evidence that such sex differences appear early in life, and in most human societies.

However, biological factors do not in themselves explain the process of sex-role identification, and the variations in sex roles in different societies. (Bandura (1969) argued that children are moulded into sex-roles by the behaviour of adults, especially parents and teachers. This **social learning theory** approach postulates that parents and others reward or reinforce sex-appropriate behaviour in children; for example they may encourage nurturant behaviour in girls, and discourage it in boys. Children may also observe the behaviour of same-sex models, and imitate them; for example, boys might observe and imitate the behaviour of male figures in TV films, in their playful and aggressive behaviour.

Barry et al. (1957) made a survey of the anthropological literature on child rearing in 110, mostly non-literate, societies. In more than 80 per cent of societies, girls more than boys were encouraged to be nurturant, whereas boys more than girls were subject to training for self-reliance and achievement. In many societies responsibility and obedience was also encouraged in girls more than boys. Pressure for sex-typing is especially strong in societies where male strength is important for hunting or herding; it is less strong in societies with small family groups, where sharing of tasks is inevitable.

While reinforcement does seem to have some effect, a number of studies suggest that it is not the whole story (Fagot, 1985). For example in nursery schools, teachers generally reinforce quiet, 'feminine' behaviours, and do not reinforce rough-and-tumble play. But this does not stop boys doing rough-and-tumble! In fact boys seem to be influenced by other boys, and girls by other girls. The cognitive-developmental approach in this area argues that the child's growing sense of **gender identity** – the awareness that one is a boy, or a girl

gender identity the awareness that one is a boy, or a girl.

(see Chapter 8) – is crucial. Children attend to and imitate same-sex models, and follow sex-appropriate activities, because they realise that this is what a child of their own sex usually does. Maccoby and Jacklin (1974) called this **self-socialisation** because it does not depend directly on external reinforcement.

> **self-socialisation** the idea that children attend to and imitate same-sex models, and follow sex-appropriate activities, because they realise that this is what a child of their own sex usually does.

Gender-typed beliefs

A study by Martin *et al.* (1999) illustrates this approach. They questioned and observed children aged 3 to 6 years of age in the USA. All children held gender-typed beliefs about what behaviours and play partners were appropriate for each sex, and these beliefs became stronger with age. They believed that other children would be more likely to approve of their behaviour when they played with same-sex peers, and this belief too became stronger with age. Children themselves preferred to play with same-sex peers; and those who held stronger beliefs about gender-appropriate behaviour also showed the most sex-segregated play preferences. Although both biology, and adult reinforcement, have influences on sex differences, it does seem as though the direct influence of the peer group is a very powerful one (Maccoby, 1998; Paterski *et al.*, 2010).

ETHNICITY

Besides differing by gender, people differ in terms of their racial or ethnic group; both are often obvious from physical characteristics such as hair and skin colour, and facial appearance. Besides country of origin, other important dimensions of difference are language (e.g. English Canadian and French Canadian) and religion (e.g. Muslim Indian and Hindu Indian). By 4 or 5 years children make basic discriminations, for example between black and white; and during the next few years more difficult ones, such as Anglo and Hispanic. By around 8 or 9 years, children understand that **ethnic identity** remains constant despite changes in age, or superficial attributes such as clothing.

> **ethnic identity** an awareness of which racial, national, linguistic, or religious group one belongs to.

Children seem to show some segregation by race, as well as by gender, for example in playground friendships. In a study in the United States by Finkelstein and Haskins (1983), 5-year-old black and white children showed marked segregation by race, which increased during a year in kindergarten. In older children, too, segregation by race is noticeable (Boulton & Smith, 1993). However, segregation by race seems to be less marked than segregation by sex in the middle school period. It is also not so evident amongst boys as girls, perhaps because boys play in larger groups than girls; when playing football, for example, ethnic group may be ignored in order to fill up a team with the requisite number of good players.

Development of racial attitudes

Preference is not the same as prejudice, which implies a negative evaluation of another person, on the basis of some general attribute (for example sex, race, or disability).

Racial prejudice a negative evaluation of someone as a consequence of their being in a certain racial or ethnic group.

Racial prejudice means a negative evaluation of someone as a consequence of their being in a certain racial or ethnic group. Prejudice can be measured by asking children to put photos of other children from different ethnic groups along a scale of liking (Aboud, 1988), or to assign positive adjectives such as 'work hard' and 'truthful', or negative adjectives such as 'stupid' or 'dirty', to all, some, one, or none of the photos representing different ethnic groups (Davey, 1983). These studies suggest that prejudice increases from 4 to 7 years, mainly at the expense of minority ethnic groups. During middle childhood, white children tend to remain prejudiced against black or minority group children, while the latter show a more mixed pattern but often become more positive to their own group. Aboud (1988) argued that from 4 to 7 years, children perceive other ethnic groups as dissimilar to themselves, and because of this tend to have negative evaluations of them. From 8 years onward, children become able to think more flexibly about ethnic differences, and in terms of individuals rather than groups, so that their earlier prejudice can be modified.

However, some more recent work suggests that children acquire racial attitudes before developing the ability to categorise by race (Hirschfeld, 2008; Quintana, 2010). According to this view, children first acquire racial attitudes (which may reflect society's biases against certain racial groups), and then the ability to sort and classify others into racial categories. Young infants show sensitivity to different-race faces (in terms of time spent looking at them, Kelly *et al.*, 2009); and a longitudinal study found that variations in parental socialisation as early as 18 months predict racial attitudes at 36 and 48 months (Katz, 2003). In Japan, Dunham *et al.* (2006) found that children show a racial bias toward African-origin persons early in life, even though they have not had any personal exposure to them.

Schools have been a focus for work to reduce racial prejudice in children. A multi-racial curriculum approach which emphasises the diversity of racial and cultural beliefs and practices and gives them equal evaluation may help in this process. Procedures such as Cooperative Group Work (Cowie *et al.*, 1994) bring together children of different race (and sex) together in common activities, and may help to reduce ethnic preference and prejudice in the classroom.

SUMMARY AND CONCLUSIONS

Although early important influences on the social development of the child are parents or caregivers, as the child enters school and progresses to middle childhood, the influence of peers becomes very important. Much play is social, and sociodramatic and rough-and-tumble play occupy much time in the kindergarten and early school years, moving into play with rules by middle childhood. Social participation and friendships with peers, and sociometric status in the peer group, probably are very influential for the course of later development. Children pay great attention to age-mates, and are influenced by them in terms of appropriate behaviour, sex segregation and choice of activities. In fact, Harris (1995, 1998) has argued that once children go to school, by far the dominant influence on behaviour is the peer group, rather than the parents; she believes that by then, the direct influence of parents is largely limited to genetic factors passed on, such as temperament.

Many researchers believe that the family continues to exert an influence, for example through patterns of attachment, management practices of parents (including a direct influence on the out-of-school peer network), and the effects of siblings. The older child, too, is increasingly aware of, and influenced by, the expectations of society for someone of their age, gender, ethnicity, and social background, as mediated by peers and by socialising influences such as schools, and the mass media. By adolescence, the separation from parents is becoming more complete, and the young person is moving towards a mature sense of identity and social being.

DISCUSSION POINTS

1. Describe how peer relationships begin.
2. How important are siblings for social and social-cognitive development?
3. What factors assist the development of pretend play?
4. Does play have an important or essential role in development?
5. How can we measure friendship?
6. How would you design a study to see if the quality of childhood friendships is important in later life?
7. What is meant by sociometric status, and why might it be important to measure?

SUGGESTIONS FOR FURTHER READING

Blatchford, P. (1998). *Social life in school*. London: Falmer Press.
Dunn, J. (2004). *Children's friendships: The beginnings of intimacy*. Malden, MA and Oxford: Blackwell.
Göncü, A., & Gaskins, S. (Eds.) (2007). *Play and development*. Mahwah, NJ: Lawrence Erlbaum and Associates.
Harris, P. (2000). *The work of the imagination*. Oxford: Blackwell.
Kupersmidt, J.B., & Dodge, K.A. (Eds.) (2004). *Children's peer relations*. Washington, DC: American Psychological Association.
Maccoby, E.E. (1998). *The two sexes: Growing up apart, coming together*. Cambridge, MA: Harvard University Press.
Pellegrini, A.D. (2009). *The role of play in human development*. Oxford: Oxford University Press.
Schneider, B. (2000). *Friends and enemies*. London: Arnold.

Singer, D.G., Golinkoff, R.M., & Hirsh-Pasek, K. (2006). *Play = learning*. Oxford and New York: Oxford University Press.

Smith, P.K. (2010). *Children and play*. Chichester: Wiley-Blackwell.

Smith, P.K., & Hart, C.H. (Eds.) (2011). *Wiley-Blackwell handbook of childhood social development* (2nd edn). Chichester: Wiley-Blackwell.

REFERENCES

Aboud, F. (1988). *Children and prejudice*. Oxford: Basil Blackwell.

Archer, J. & Lloyd, B. (1986). *Sex and gender*. Cambridge: Cambridge University Press.

Bagwell, C.L., Newcomb, A.F., & Bukowski, W.M. (1998). Preadolescent friendship and peer rejection as predictors of adult adjustment. *Child Development, 69*, 140–153.

Bandura, A. (1969). Social learning theory of identificatory processes. In D.A. Goslin (Ed.) *Handbook of socialization theory and research* (pp. 213–262). Chicago: Rand McNally.

Barry, H. III., Bacon, M.K., & Child, I.L. (1957). A cross-cultural survey of some sex differences in socialization. *Journal of Abnormal and Social Psychology, 55*, 327–332.

Bigelow, B.J., & La Gaipa, J.J. (1980). The development of friendship values and choice. In H.C. Foot, A.J. Chapman, & J.R. Smith (Eds.) *Friendship and social relations in children* (pp. 15–44). Chichester: Wiley.

Bornstein, M.H., Haynes, M., Pascual, L., Painter, K.M., & Galperin, C. (1999). Play in two societies: Pervasiveness of process, specificity of structure. *Child Development, 70*, 317–331.

Boulton, M.J., & Smith, P.K. (1993). Ethnic and gender partner and activity preferences in mixed-race schools in the UK: Playground observations. In C.H. Hart (Ed.) *Children on playgrounds* (pp. 210–237). New York: SUNY Press.

Bretherton, I., & Waters, E. (Eds.) (1985). *Growing points of attachment theory and research*. Monographs of the Society for Research in Child Development, 50(1–2).

Buttelmann, D., Carpenter, M., & Tomasello, M. (2009). Eighteen-month-old infants show false belief understanding in an active helping paradigm. *Cognition, 112*, 337–342.

Cairns, R.B., Cairns, B.D., Neckerman, H.J., Gest, S.D., & Gariepy, J.L. (1988). Social networks and aggressive behavior: Peer acceptance or peer rejection? *Developmental Psychology, 24*, 815–823.

Chen, X., Rubin, K.H., & Li, B. (1994). Only children and sibling children in urban China: A re-examination. *International Journal of Behavioral Development, 17*, 413–421.

Christie, J.F., & Johnson, E.P. (1985). Questioning the results of play training research. *Educational Psychology, 20*, 7–11.

Cillessen, A.H.N., Van IJzendoorn, H.W., Van Lieshout, C.F.M., & Hartup, W.W. (1992). Heterogeneity among peer-rejected boys: Subtypes and stabilities. *Child Development, 63*, 893–905.

Clark, A.H., Wyon, S.M., & Richards, M.P.M. (1969). Free-play in nursery school children. *Journal of Child Psychology and Psychiatry, 10*, 205–216.

Coie, J.D., & Dodge, K.A. (1983). Continuities and changes in children's social status: A five-year longitudinal study. *Merrill-Palmer Quarterly, 29*, 261–282.

Collaer, M.L., & Hines, M. (1995). Human behavioral sex differences: A role for gonadal hormones during early development? *Psychological Bulletin, 118*, 55–107.

Cowie, H., Smith, P.K., Boulton, M., & Laver, R. (1994). *Cooperative group work in the multi-ethnic classroom*. London: David Fulton.

Crick, N.R., & Dodge, K. (1994). A review and reformulation of social-information processing mechanisms in children's social adjustment. *Psychological Bulletin, 115*, 74–101.

Davey, A. (1983). *Learning to be prejudiced: Growing up in multi-ethnic Britain*. London: Edward Arnold.

Dockett, S. (1998). Constructing understandings through play in the early years. *International Journal of Early Years Education*, 6, 105–116.

Dodge, K.A., Pettit, G.S., McClaskey, C.L., & Brown, M.M. (1986). *Social competence in children*. Monographs of the Society for Research in Child Development, 51(2).

Dodge, K.A., Schlundt, D.C., Shocken, I., & Delugach, J.D. (1983). Social competence and children's sociometric status: The role of peer group entry strategies. *Merrill-Palmer Quarterly*, 29, 309–336.

Dunham, Y., Baron, A., & Banaji, M. (2006). From American city to Japanese village: A cross-cultural investigation of implicit race attitudes. *Child Development*, 77, 1268–1281.

Dunn, J. (2004). *Children's friendships: The beginnings of intimacy*. Malden, MA and Oxford: Blackwell.

Dunn, J., & Kendrick, C. (1982). *Siblings: Love, envy and understanding*. Oxford: Basil Blackwell.

Eibl-Eibesfeldt, I. (1989). *Human ethology*. New York: Aldine de Gruyter.

Fagot, B.I. (1985). Beyond the reinforcement principle: Another step toward understanding sex role development. *Developmental Psychology*, 21, 1097–1104.

Falbo, T., & Polit, D.F. (1986). Quantitative review of the only child literature: Research evidence and theory development. *Psychological Bulletin*, 100, 176–189.

Finkelstein, N.W., & Haskins, R. (1983). Kindergarten children prefer same-color peers. *Child Development*, 54, 502–8.

Fonzi, A., Schneider, B.H., Tani, F., & Tomada, G. (1997). Predicting children's friendship status from their dyadic interaction in structured situations of potential conflict. *Child Development*, 68, 496–506.

Golombok, S., & Fivush, R. (1994). *Gender development*. Cambridge: Cambridge University Press.

Göncü, A., Patt, M.B., & Kouba, E. (2002). Understanding young children's pretend play in context. In P.K. Smith & C.H. Hart (Eds.) *Blackwell handbook of childhood social development* (pp.418–437). Oxford: Blackwell.

Gottman, J.M. (1983). *How children become friends*. Monographs of the Society for Research in Child Development, 48(3, Serial No. 201).

Haight, W.L., & Miller, P.J. (1993). *Pretending at home: Early development in a sociocultural context*. Albany, NY: SUNY Press.

Harris, J.R. (1995). Where is the child's environment? A group socialization theory of development. *Psychological Review*, 102, 458–489.

Harris, J.R. (1998). *The nurture assumption*. London: Bloomsbury.

Harris, P.L. (2000). *The work of the imagination*. Oxford: Blackwell.

Hartup, W.W. (1996). The company they keep: Friendships and their developmental significance. *Child Development*, 67, 1–13.

Haselager, G.J.T., Hartup, W.W., van Lieshout, C.F.M., & Riksen-Walraven, J.M.A. (1998). Similarities between friends and nonfriends in middle childhood. *Child Development*, 69, 1198–1208.

Hertz-Lazarowitz, R., Feitelson, D., Zahavi, S., & Hartup, W.W. (1981). Social interaction and social organisation of Israeli five-to-seven-year olds. *International Journal of Behavioral Development*, 4, 143–155.

Hirschfeld, L.A. (2008). Children's developing conceptions of race. In S.M. Quintana & C. McKown (Eds.) *Handbook of race, racism, and the developing child* (pp. 37–54). Hoboken, NJ: Wiley.

Holland, P. (2003). *We don't play with guns here*. Philadelphia, PA: Open University Press.

Howe, N., Brody, M., & Recchia, H. (2006). Effects of task difficulty on sibling teaching in middle childhood. *Infant & Child Development*, 15, 455–470.

Howes, C. (1994). *The collaborative construction of pretend*. Albany, NY: SUNY Press.

Howes, C. & Matheson, C.C. (1992). Sequences in the development of competent play with peers: Social and pretend play. *Developmental Psychology*, 28, 961–974.

Humphreys, A., & Smith, P.K. (1987). Rough and tumble, friendship and dominance in school children: evidence for continuity and change with age. *Child Development, 58,* 201–212.

Jiang, X., & Cillessen, A.H.N. (2005). Stability of continuous measures of sociometric status: A meta-analysis. *Developmental Review, 25,* 1–25.

Katz, P.A. (2003). Racists or tolerant multiculturalists? How do they begin? *American Psychologist, 58,* 897–909.

Kelly, D.J., Liu, S.Y., Lee, K., Quinn, P.C., Pascalis, O., Slater, A.M., *et al.* (2009). Development of the other-race effect during infancy: Evidence towards universality? *Journal of Experimental Child Psychology, 104,* 105–114.

Kitzmann, J., Cohen, R., & Lockwood, R.L. (2002). Are only children missing out: Comparison of the peer-related social competence of only children and siblings. *Journal of Social and Personal Relationships, 19,* 299–316.

Ladd, G.W. (1983). Social networks of popular, average and rejected children in school settings. *Merrill-Palmer Quarterly, 29,* 283–307.

Ladd, G.W., Buhs, E.S., & Troop, W. (2002). Children's interpersonal skills and relationships in school settings: Adaptive significance and implications for school-based prevention and intervention programs. In P.K. Smith & C.H. Hart (Eds.) *Blackwell handbook of childhood social development* (pp. 394–415). Oxford, UK: Blackwell.

Lever, J. (1978). Sex differences in the complexity of children's play and games. *American Sociological Review, 43,* 471–483.

Lewis, C., Freeman, N.H., Kyriakidou, C., Maridaki-Kassotaki, K., & Berridge, D.M (1996). Social influences on false belief access: Specific sibling influences or general apprenticeship? *Child Development, 67,* 2930–2947.

Lewis, M., Young, G., Brooks, J., & Michalson, L. (1975). The beginning of friendship. In M. Lewis & L. Rosenblum (Eds.) *Friendship and peer relations* (pp. 27–65). New York: Wiley.

Maccoby, E.E. (1998). *The two sexes: Growing up apart, coming together.* Cambridge, MA: Harvard University Press.

Maccoby, E.E., & Jacklin, C.N. (1974). *The psychology of sex differences.* Stanford, CA: Stanford University Press.

Majors, K. (2007). *Children's imaginary companions and the purposes they serve: An interpretive phenomenological analysis.* Unpublished PhD thesis, Institute of Education, University of London, UK.

Malik, N., & Furman, W. (1993). Problems in children's peer relations: What can the clinician do? *Journal of Child Psychology and Psychiatry, 34,* 1303–1326.

Martin, C.L., Fabes, R.A., Evans, S.M., & Wyman, H. (1999). Social cognition on the playground: Children's beliefs about playing with girls versus boys and their relations to sex segregated play. *Journal of Social and Personal Relationships, 16,* 751–771.

Mayeux, L., Underwood, M., & Risser, S. (2007). Perspectives on the ethics of sociometric research with children: How children, peers and teachers help to inform the debate. *Merrill-Palmer Quarterly, 53,* 53–78.

Mueller, E., & Brenner, J. (1977). The origins of social skills and interaction among playgroup toddlers. *Child Development, 48,* 854–861.

Newcomb, A., & Bagwell, C. (1995). Children's friendship relations: A meta-analytic review. *Psychological Bulletin, 117,* 306–347.

Nielsen, M., & Christie, T. (2008). Adult modelling facilitates young children's generation of novel pretend acts. *Infant and Child Development, 17,* 151–162.

Parker, J.G., & Asher, S.R. (1987). Peer relations and later personal adjustment: Are low-accepted children at risk? *Psychological Bulletin, 102,* 357–389.

Parten, M.B. (1932). Social participation among preschool children. *Journal of Abnormal and Social Psychology*, 27, 243–269.

Paterski, V., Golombok, S., & Hines, M. (2010). Sex differences in social behaviour. In P.K. Smith & C.H. Hart (Eds.) *Wiley-Blackwell handbook of childhood social development* (2nd edn). Chichester: Wiley-Blackwell.

Pellegrini, A.D. (1994). The rough play of adolescent boys of differing sociometric status. *International Journal of Behavioral Development*, 17, 525–540.

Pellegrini, A.D. (2009). *The role of play in human development*. Oxford: Oxford University Press.

Pellegrini, A D., & Perlmutter, J.C. (1989). Classroom contextual effects on children's play. *Developmental Psychology*, 25, 289–296.

Pellegrini, A.D., & Smith, P.K. (1998). Physical activity play: The nature and function of a neglected aspect of play. *Child Development*, 69, 577–598.

Piaget, J. (1951). *Play, dreams and imitation in childhood*. London: Routledge & Kegan Paul.

Quintana, S.M. (2010). Ethnicity, race and children's social development. In P.K. Smith & C.H. Hart (Eds.) *Wiley-Blackwell handbook of childhood social development* (2nd edn). Chichester: Wiley-Blackwell.

Ross, H., Ross, M., Stein, N., & Trabasso, T. (2006). How siblings resolve their conflicts: The importance of first offers, planning, and limited opposition. *Child Development*, 77, 1730–1745.

Rubin, K.H., Watson, K.S., & Jambor, T.W. (1978). Free-play behaviors in preschool and kindergarten children. *Child Development*, 49, 534–536.

Ruffman, T., Perner, J., Naito, M., Parkin, L., & Clements, W.A. (1998). Older (but not younger) siblings facilitate false belief understanding. *Developmental Psychology*, 34, 161–174.

Sandstrom, M.J., & Coie, J.D. (1999). A developmental perspective on peer rejection: Mechanisms of stability and change. *Child Development*, 70, 955–966.

Schafer, M., & Smith, P.K. (1996). Teachers' perceptions of play fighting and real fighting in primary school. *Educational Research*, 38, 173–181.

Smilansky, S. (1968). *The effects of sociodramatic play on disadvantaged preschool children*. New York: Wiley.

Smith, P.K. (1988). Children's play and its role in early development: A reevaluation of the 'play ethos'. In A.D. Pellegrini (ed), *Psychological bases of early education*. Chichester: Wiley & Sons, pp. 207–226.

Smith, P.K. (2010). *Children and play*. Chichester: Wiley-Blackwell.

Sullivan, H.S. (1953). *The interpersonal theory of psychiatry*. New York: W.W. Norton.

Sutton, J., Smith, P.K., & Swettenham, J. (1999). Social cognition and bullying: Social inadequacy or skilled manipulation? *British Journal of Developmental Psychology*, 17, 435–450.

Taylor, M., Cartwright, B.S., & Carlson, S.M. (1993). A developmental investigation of children's imaginary companions. *Developmental Psychology*, 29, 276–285.

Taylor, M., & Carlson, S.M. (1997). The relation between individual differences in fantasy and theory of mind. *Child Development*, 68, 436–455.

Tremblay-Leveau, H., & Nadel, J. (1996). Exclusion in triads: Can it serve 'metacommunicative' knowledge in 11- and 23-month-old children? *British Journal of Developmental Psychology*, 14, 145–158.

Turner, P. (1991). Relations between attachment, gender, and behavior with peers in preschool. *Child Development*, 62, 1475–1488.

Wentzel, K.R., & Asher, S.R. (1995). The academic lives of neglected, rejected, popular, and controversial children. *Child Development*, 66, 754–763.

15 Prosocial Tendencies, Antisocial Behaviour, and Moral Development in Childhood

Daniel Hart, Nyeema Watson, Anandini Dar, and Robert Atkins

CHAPTER OUTLINE

OVERVIEW

Prosocial behaviour is essential for the maintenance of society and social groups within society. However, as we all know, antisocial behaviour is also common in society and gives rise to considerable concern among citizens and politicians. This chapter reviews evidence regarding the development of prosocial and antisocial behaviour from early childhood through to adolescence. From very early in development, children exhibit personality traits; for instance dispositions to act altruistically or aggressively, that can be mapped onto prosocial and antisocial dimensions.

The chapter goes on to consider the relationship between prosocial and antisocial behaviour and the development of social cognition in middle childhood, describing Piaget's and Kohlberg's accounts of the development of moral reasoning, and evaluating their strengths and weaknesses. One of the problems with these accounts is that children's moral judgements may differ from how they behave in reality, and thus the link to prosocial behaviour is not straightforward.

The chapter also includes discussion of the factors that influence the development of prosocial and antisocial behaviour, including social influences arising from parents, peers, and wider culture. This section includes consideration of evidence relating to the contentious issue of possible effects of television violence on childhood aggression. The conclusion is that television content is an important influence on children's behaviour, but that it can have a positive influence in promoting prosocial behaviour as well as the more commonly feared negative influence. Although much has been learned in this field, the chapter concludes by stating that there is still much to be learned, in particular, regarding how families and the media can foster prosocial behaviour.

INTRODUCTION

Social life changes dramatically in the transition from infancy to childhood. For infants, the social world is largely limited to interactions with parents and family members. This is so for obvious reasons. For example, the ability to communicate with others depends heavily on language skills, which are only in their nascent stages in infancy. The channels of communication that allow sophisticated, reciprocal exchanges between infants and caretakers – gestures, facial expressions, incompletely articulated words – require mutual experience in order to be decoded. The utterance 'Dah' from the mouth of a 14-month-old we have observed is correctly understood by his parents to mean 'dog,' but has little meaning to other adults. Not only do infants have difficulty in communicating with those outside their families, they are limited by immature motor skills from exploring new social contexts. Infants cannot walk around their neighbourhoods to make new friends, for instance.

Children, on the other hand, live in social worlds that are diverse and complicated. The ability to speak enables each child to communicate with every child and adult in the community. Children play with each other, seek friends out in their neighbourhoods, participate in social institutions such as schools, churches, teams, and community groups, look at billboards, listen to music, and watch television. The incredible range of social activities, relationships, and institutions in which the child is engaged require, and produce, forms of thought, *emotion*, and behaviour rarely seen in infancy.

The contrasts between infancy and childhood do not mean that at 18 months of age infants magically acquire capabilities that make them children. There is no single social skill, piece of knowledge, or type of interaction that divides the social world of infants and children, as every aspect of childhood has sophisticated precursors in infancy. However, the differences in social worlds noted earlier make some developmental tasks more apparent in childhood than in infancy. In this chapter, we use the development of **prosocial** and **antisocial behaviour** as a lens to reveal some of the most significant transformations to occur in social development over the course of childhood. Using prosocial and antisocial behaviour to focus our review means that other facets of social development are given short shrift. We cannot give full attention to the development of friendship, the formation of political views, or transformations in relationships with parents, to name just a few of the areas that receive little attention in this chapter. Our relative neglect of these topics permits us to look closely at the development of morality, aggression, altruism, and similar qualities that have been at the heart of the most important considerations of childhood in Western history.

prosocial behaviour
any behaviour that is enacted in order to benefit others.

antisocial behaviour
any behaviour that shows scant concern about other people's feelings and needs. There is little morality associated with this behaviour.

WHAT DO PROSOCIAL AND ANTISOCIAL MEAN?

Social interactions serve a variety of goals. Many social interactions seem intended to benefit others with no apparent instrumental benefit to the self: children are protected, the ill are cared for, donations to charities are made, help is offered to strangers, and so on. Without prosocial social interactions, no society or social group could survive. Similarly, no group can sustain itself over time if its members' social interactions with each other are principally aggressive and antisocial. Because prosocial and antisocial behaviour are both complex and key to every society's survival, understanding the nature of socially appropriate behaviour and the means necessary to foster its emergence are core issues for political philosophers, educators, government officials, and parents, as well as for those interested in child development.

It is easier to pronounce that prosocial and antisocial behaviours are essential for social organisation than it is to characterise precisely what these terms mean. The definitional task is made particularly difficult by the fact that behaviours considered prosocial or antisocial in one culture might be viewed quite differently in another. Even within a culture it can be difficult to determine whether a specific behaviour is genuinely prosocial. In the United States, for example, it was customary for many years for males to open doors for females. Whether this tradition promotes social organisation – by reducing uncertainty about who should proceed first towards a door – or poisons egalitarian interaction by reinforcing stereotypes that women have significant physical limitations is not immediately discernable from an observation of the act. Indeed, as this example illustrates, a full understanding of prosocial behaviour requires some knowledge of what an actor thinks and feels as the behaviour is executed. To open a door with the intention of reinforcing a status hierarchy that places males above females is an act that is inconsistent with the notion of prosocial behaviour. The centrality of intention and emotion in determining our interpretation of an act is also illustrated by the actions of mechanical and electronic devices. The actions of these devices are frequently helpful to us (computers 'remind' the authors about meetings, for example), but, lacking the requisite characteristics of appropriate emotion and intention, these devices are not viewed as prosocial actors.

For these reasons, our definitions of 'prosocial' and 'antisocial' integrate intentions. *Prosocial* refers to behaviour that is intended to promote the welfare of specific others or social groups, when this behaviour has no instrumental benefits (or some cost) for the actor (for a similar definition of prosocial behaviour, see Eisenberg, 1998). *Antisocial* connotes actions that harm specific individuals or social groups, either when such harm is intended or when the harm is foreseen but judged irrelevant (for a related definition, see Loeber, 1985). The kinds of thoughts and emotions that define our topics of prosocial and antisocial action can occur outside awareness (see Bargh & Chartrand, 1999, for a discussion of the automaticity of behaviour). In other words, while children and adolescents often do engage in extended introspection or conversation about what is good, moral, kind, mean, cruel, hurtful, and so on, much of their action in daily life occurs without conscious reflection on what should be done or how a situation makes one feel.

Continuity and transformation

Thought and emotion not only serve to define prosocial and antisocial behaviour, they are constructs that are used to explain why social development is characterised by both **continuity** and *transformation*. Continuity refers to the remarkable consistency in some facets of behaviour across childhood and adolescence. For example, the tendency for children to be aggressive shows considerable continuity: the child who fights with other children a lot is likely to be the adolescent who is judged by *peers* to be aggressive. However, not only are these children judged to be aggressive; their peers believe their aggression will persist and remain stable. Boxer and Tizak (2005) found that peers believe that aggressive

> **continuity in social development** some behaviours show a very strong consistency throughout development, for example the tendency for children to be aggressive shows considerable continuity.

children are likely to remain aggressive over time and in different contexts. The children who believe this are correct. In fact, aggression shows greater continuity across childhood and adolescence than any other facet of social development (see Espelage *et al.*, 2001, 2003; Huesmann & Guerra, 1997; Loeber & Stouthamer-Loeber, 1998 for a discussion of the continuity of aggression) (Figure 15.1). Long-term longitudinal studies have also shown gender differences, with males more likely than females to remain highly aggressive through adolescence (Huesmann, 2001). In the sections that follow, we shall describe research demonstrating that the continuity of behaviour

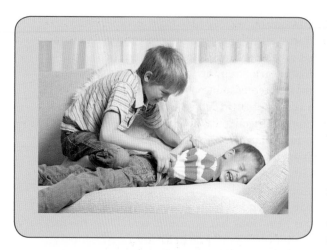

FIGURE 15.1 *Aggression shows greater continuity across childhood and adolescence than any other facet of social development.*

Source: Shutterstock.

across development is in part a consequence of characteristic patterns of emotion, emotion regulation, and cognition that are relatively stable over time.

Explanations for transformation, or qualitative change, in social behaviour across childhood also must rely on cognition and emotion. As most adults know, there is something profoundly different about reasoning with a 5-year-old about keeping a promise than discussing the same topic with a teenager. Adolescents think and feel differently from young children about the social world, and these differences are reflected in prosocial and antisocial behaviour.

Are prosocial and antisocial poles on the same dimension?

To this point, we have discussed prosocial and antisocial behaviour together, as if these two categories constitute the poles of a single dimension. A dimensional perspective implies that an act can be placed on a continuum from 'bad' antisocial behaviour to 'good' prosocial behaviour. Placing antisocial and prosocial behaviour on the same dimension implies that the same process gives rise to both. For example, one might

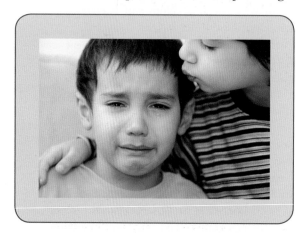

FIGURE 15.2 *Young children's social worlds include relationships with peers, and they display many prosocial behaviours such as comforting a friend in distress.*

Source: Shutterstock.

hypothesise that the personality trait of *sympathy* determines where on the continuum a child will be found; a child high in sympathy is presumed to act prosocially (Figure 15.2) while a child low in sympathy should act antisocially. In fact, this perspective is partially correct. In research with adults, Krueger *et al.* (2001) found that the personality tendency towards aggression was negatively correlated with prosocial behaviour and positively associated with antisocial behaviour. These and other research findings suggest that the factors that lead to prosocial behaviour are also associated in the opposite way with antisocial behaviour.

However, not all antisocial behaviour and prosocial behaviour can be explained using the same processes. Krueger *et al.* (2001) reported that behavioural genetic evidence – from examining patterns of similarity among monozygotic and dizygotic adult twins – indicates that antisocial behaviour may have deeper genetic roots than does prosocial behaviour. Later in the chapter we shall describe research demonstrating that children and adolescents who are extremely antisocial are best understood in terms of processes with little relevance for understanding dedicated, committed, moral behaviour. In other words, our view is that explaining why persons are at the extremes of the dimension requires consideration of psychological processes that are specific to each pole.

PREVIEW OF THE RESEARCH REVIEW

In the pages that follow, we shall describe the development of prosocial and antisocial behaviour, focusing primarily on development as it typically occurs in Western societies. Our account will begin with a description of behaviour, thought, and emotion among very young children, and end with an overview of prosocial and antisocial action in late childhood and the transition into adolescence. Important studies are described in some detail so that readers can judge for themselves the current state of research. We shall conclude with a discussion of how relationships and culture influence the course of development.

THE DEVELOPMENTAL TRAJECTORY OF PROSOCIAL AND ANTISOCIAL BEHAVIOUR AND THOUGHT

Toddlers

In contrast to infants, young children have the language and motor skills necessary to engage peers, older children, and adults in sustained social interaction. Three-year-olds talk, fight, play with their peers; they help one another and engage in long periods of synchronised interaction with adults; they think about what's wrong and what's fair; they experience sympathy and anger. The substantial differences in capacity between infants and young children to sustain social interaction means that infants and young children experience different social worlds. Infants' interact principally with their parents and family members. While young children obviously continue to have relationships with their parents, their social worlds begin to include relationships with peers, older children, teachers, and other adults. These relationships are contexts to learn about and to exhibit prosocial and antisocial action. Noteworthy as well is that in contrast to infants, young children are in direct contact with sources of cultural information. Many young children attend schools where information about culturally relevant prosocial and antisocial behaviour is transmitted. In some Western countries, children also receive messages about cultural expectations concerning prosocial and antisocial behaviour from television. In the United States, apart from attending school, watching television occupies more of children's time than any other activity (Committee on Communications, 1995) and there is no question but that television presents messages about antisocial and prosocial behaviour. In short, by the age of 3 children are capable of behaviour that we have labelled prosocial and antisocial, and have had ample opportunity to learn about it in social and cultural context.

Personality traits in social behaviour

Observers can easily discern characteristic patterns of behaviour in children 2 to 3 years of age. In other words, children clearly have *personality traits*. Personality traits are relatively stable dispositions to act in particular ways. It is certainly possible to distinguish among 3-year-olds by reference to personality traits: some are shy and others are outgoing; some are emotional, while others are calm; some are impulsive while others are controlled. As children develop stable patterns of behaviour, it is also possible to identify children who are characteristically antisocial and prosocial. Crick *et al.* (1997) examined aggression, one form of antisocial behaviour, in 3 and 4-year-old children in a preschool. Teachers were asked to rate children on items that tapped overt aggression (e.g. 'kicks or hits others') aggression in relation with others (e.g. 'tries to get others to dislike others') prosocial behaviour (e.g. 'is kind to others') and depression (e.g. 'looks sad'). Students in the preschool named three other students who 'they liked to play with the most' (p. 582) and three students 'they liked to play with the least.'

Several findings from this study are of interest for our goals in this chapter. First, children who were judged to be high in overt and relational aggression were low in prosocial behaviour. This is consistent with the dimensional perspective on prosocial and antisocial behaviour, according to which being high in one characteristic necessarily means being low on the other. Second, children judged to be especially aggressive by the teachers were prone to rejection by their peers ('play with the least'). This finding demonstrates that individual differences in antisocial behaviour are apparent to adults and to children by age 3; teachers and peers were selecting the *same* children in their identifications of those with difficulties in adjustment. Third, Crick *et al.* (1997) found that children who were judged to be high in negative emotions – high in depression – were more likely to be high in aggression than those low in negative emotions. This suggests that emotions, and emotion regulation, are important factors in understanding antisocial behaviour.

What leads to individual differences in antisocial and prosocial behaviour? Is today's prosocial 3-year-old likely to be prosocial in school? No simple answer can be offered for these important questions. However, we do know that the emergence of stable personality traits in early childhood reflects the interaction of genetic predispositions with early experiences. While predispositions to personality traits in the form of temperamental variations (for example, precursors to shyness can be identified in the first year of life) and social experience are present in infants, it appears necessary for these to become integrated over the first several years of life in order for observers to recognise personality traits.

What implications does the emergence of personality traits have for the development of prosocial and antisocial behaviour? As we shall discuss below, one very active line of investigation focuses on the organising effects of early personality on both poles of the dimension.

Personality traits and antisocial behaviour

There is a long history of research on antisocial behaviour in childhood, and a related interest in childhood antecedents of adolescent delinquent behaviour and adult criminality (see, for example, Glueck, 1982). We shall not review the history of this work, but instead will review some of the recent work on this topic.

One particularly informative study (Caspi *et al.*, 1995) has followed a group of children in Dunedin, New Zealand. A very valuable feature of this study is its sample. First, the sample of children studied is large, approximately 800 children, which makes it possible to detect relationships that might not be apparent in small samples. Second, the sample includes almost every child born in a single year in Dunedin, which means that the sample is not biased (towards wealthy families, for example). Because the sample is not biased, the results of the study of the individuals in the sample are more likely to generalise to other populations.

Caspi and his colleagues (Caspi *et al.*, 1995) began measuring personality when the children in the sample were 3 years of age. An examiner rated each child on 22 personality items, such as emotional lability ('extreme instability of emotional responses' (Caspi *et al.*, p. 58)), impulsivity ('explosive, uncontrolled behaviour'), self-reliance ('overt confidence'), and passivity ('placid, sluggish'), after observing the child responding to a series of cognitive tests. The 22 personality items were condensed into three scales, representing three traits: *lack of control, approach,* and *sluggishness.* The lack of control trait incorporates the items for emotional liability, negative emotions, and restlessness; broadly, it reflects problems in emotion regulation; approach is constituted of items suggesting *extraversion;* and sluggishness is reflected in items focusing on passivity.

Years later, when the children were adolescents, their parents provided ratings of them on scales tapping antisocial, delinquent behaviour such as bullying peers, teasing peers in order to hurt them, and so on. When correlations were calculated among the age 3 personality measures and the ratings of delinquency at ages 12, the results suggested that children who exhibited a lack of control in early childhood were more likely than other children to exhibit antisocial behaviour in adolescence. This suggests that antisocial behaviour is connected to personality. Particularly relevant is that it is the personality trait most directly relevant to emotion – lack of control – that is associated with later antisocial behaviour. That is, young children who had difficulty regulating emotion, and who were prone to experiencing negative emotions, were susceptible to the development of antisocial behaviour.

In a follow-up to the original study Caspi *et al.* (2003) presented evidence that linked the inability to regulate emotions in childhood not only to subsequent

FIGURE 15.3 *Child taking a personality test.*

Source: Shutterstock.

Big Five Inventory (BFI) personality outcomes measurement that assesses on extraversion, agreeableness, conscientiousness, emotional stability, and openness to experience.

antisocial behaviour in adolescence but also in adulthood. Surprisingly the study suffered little attrition with 96 per cent of the original study participants located for the follow-up. Personality outcomes measurements were gathered using self-reports using the Multidimensional Personality Questionnaire (Figure 15.3), which assessed three superfactors of personality: Negative Emotionality, Constraint and Positive Emotionality. Informant reports, by individuals who the study participants said knew them best, were also collected using a brief version of the **Big Five Inventory** (**BFI**) that assessed extraversion, agreeableness, conscientiousness, emotional stability, and openness to experience.

Comparing the adult personality outcomes of the original study participants at age 26 to their childhood scores at age 3, there was evidence that showed consistencies between behavioural qualities showed at both ages. Results showed that children who were rated as undercontrolled at age 3 scored highest on measurements for stress reaction and alienation and lowest on the measurement for harm avoidance. As adults they often responded with strong negative emotional reactions to many ordinary circumstances and had a tendency to experience frequent and intense negative emotional states, including distress and anger. These adults also obtained high scores on aggression, low scores on self-control and social closeness, and high on traits indexing negative emotionality. Not only do the participants' responses suggest the continuity of the antisocial traits previously seen in childhood and adolescence, but the informants added that those labelled as uncontrolled as children were antagonistic, unreliable, tense and narrow-minded adults. These findings highlight the importance of understanding the development, continuity, and long-lasting effects of antisocial and prosocial behaviour during childhood. As exciting as these findings are, it is extremely important to understand that early personality does not determine by itself whether antisocial behaviour will occur later in childhood and adolescence. There is a great deal of development that occurs between early and late childhood, and the changes that occur may shift children off – and in some cases onto – the path to antisocial behaviour.

Personality traits and prosocial behaviour

Personality traits and emotion regulation are important for prosocial behaviour as well as for antisocial behaviour. Some evidence for this claim can be adduced from investigations of the sample of children from New Zealand just discussed. Newman *et al.* (1997) grouped the 3-year-olds according to their temperament scores on the three dimensions described earlier. One of the five groups was composed of children who were impulsive and tended to have negative emotions; children in this group were labelled under-controlled (the nature of the other groups is not important for our discussion here). Eighteen years later, the participants nominated peers who rated the participants for a variety of characteristics, with a subset of these characteristics constituting a scale tapping prosocial tendencies (e.g. items included 'reliable,' 'trustworthy'). Newman and her colleagues found that children who belonged to the under-controlled group as 3-year-olds, in comparison to those in the other groups, were judged to be less prosocial at 21 years of age. This pattern suggests that positive emotions, self-control, and effective emotion-regulation in childhood form part of the foundation on which adult prosocial tendencies are built.

Extreme antisocial behaviour and breaks in the continuum

The two reports of research on the Dunedin study considered above suggest that antisocial and prosocial behaviour are poles of a single dimension, and can be understood to have roots in a single process, *emotion regulation*. One final study conducted with the Dunedin sample suggests that an account of consistently antisocial behaviour requires constructs that are *not* part of the process that gives rise to prosocial behaviour. Moffitt *et al.* (1996) identified boys in the sample who were consistently highly antisocial from age 5 to age 18 (this pattern is so rare among girls that it was impossible to identify a group to study even in the large Dunedin sample). These were children who were rated as much higher (1+ **standard deviation**) than average on scales tapping aggression and delinquency at the majority of seven measurement points (5, 7, 9, 11, 13, 15, and 18 years of age). Only 32 (7%) of the boys in the sample were consistently high in antisocial behaviour across childhood and adolescence;

standard deviation
statistical measure of the spread of scores from the mean.

chronic antisocial behaviour across childhood and adolescence is therefore very atypical. A second group of antisocial adolescents was formed of boys who were rated as much higher than average on the measures of adolescent delinquency, but who were not especially high on measures of antisocial behaviour in childhood. There were 108 boys from the sample (24%) in this group. Moffitt and her colleagues compared the two groups on the measures of age 3 temperament described in previous paragraphs. The results indicated that the boys who were consistently high in antisocial behaviour across childhood and adolescence had very difficult temperaments as 3-year-olds, while those who were only antisocial in adolescence were not noticeably different from other children in terms of age 3 temperament.

Not only were the children who were consistently antisocial extremely irritable as 3-year-olds, they showed evidence of **neuropsychological deficits** when tested with a battery of tests at age 13. These tests tapped areas of *cognitive functioning* that are affected by brain injury. For example, some of the tests tapped verbal functioning (e.g. a vocabulary test), while others assessed mental

neuropsychological deficits disorders that originate in the brain and that affect a person's behaviour or *cognitive functioning*.

flexibility (e.g. the Wisconsin Card Sort Test). Moffit *et al.* (1994) found that the consistently antisocial boys had scores that suggested neuropsychological problems. This finding is consistent with research with other samples, which has found considerable

attention deficit disorder (ADD or ADHD) the most common psychological disorder in childhood, affecting 3–5% of all school-aged children. These children have symptoms in the form of behavioural impairments – inattention, impulsivity, and hyperactivity.

evidence that extreme antisocial behaviour in childhood and adolescence is associated with **attention deficit disorder** (Hinshaw *et al.*, 1993). Though attention deficit disorder does not suggest any brain damage, other neurochemical imbalances may be involved which give rise to deficits in attention, overactivity and impulsiveness, causing behavioural problems (Sagvolden & Sergeant, 1998). Together these studies suggest that at least some extreme antisocial behaviour may have roots in neurological deficits and extreme temperamental irritability.

Note that these constructs do not have polar opposites that can be used (sensibly) to characterise consistently prosocial individuals. It would not make sense to suggest that genuinely moral people are characterised by an absence of neurological deficits – because such a description would accurately characterise almost everyone! In this sense, then, extremely antisocial children and adolescents may best be considered as a separate category with unique features.

Our account so far has focused on personality traits, particularly those related to emotion regulation, as they are related to prosocial and antisocial behaviour over the course of childhood and adolescence. The results of the studies that have been reviewed suggest the following: (1) there is continuity in prosocial and antisocial behaviour, with continuity in aggressive behaviour particularly high, though change in all facets occurs; (2) antisocial behaviour seems related to difficulties in regulating emotion, impulsivity, and high levels of negative *affect*; and (3) a small percentage of boys who are consistently antisocial may have extremely difficult temperaments and neurological deficits. What is missing in the account is a consideration of cognitive factors in antisocial and prosocial behaviour, and it is to these that we turn in the next section. Conveniently, much of the research on cognitive factors has focused on older children and adolescents, and consequently our discussion moves on from toddlers to middle childhood.

Middle childhood

Reasoning and judgement

Every discussion of the development of prosocial and antisocial behaviour must cover the work of Piaget (1932) and Kohlberg (1984), because they founded the developmental investigation of moral thinking. Piaget was the first to study in a systematic way the *moral judgements* of children. To elicit moral judgement from children, Piaget presented them with hypothetical **moral dilemmas** and then asked children to make judgements. For example, children were told about two boys, one of whom breaks fifteen teacups accidentally as he opens a door and the other who breaks a single cup while sneaking into a cupboard to obtain forbidden sweets. Children were then asked to judge which of the two boys was 'naughtier'. Piaget found that younger children tended to judge the first child's action more harshly than the second child's while older children showed the reverse.

moral dilemmas situations in which people must choose and justify a course of action or reasoning with respect to a moral issue.

From responses to dilemmas like this one and to queries concerning the rules of games, Piaget concluded that younger children's moral judgement was governed by unilateral respect for adults and adults' rules, with little understanding of reciprocity or the intentions of others. Consequently, young children judge that the greater damage in the tea-cup dilemmas constitutes a larger moral violation, because the intentions of the children will not be salient to the adults who observe the damage. With age, and Piaget believed in part as a result of interaction with peers, children develop a morality of cooperation and social exchange. This means that children come

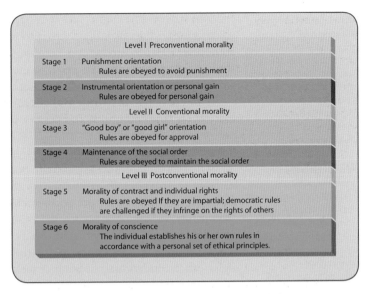

FIGURE 15.4 *Kohlberg's Stages of moral development, including the hypothesised sixth stage.*

Source: Adapted from Kohlberg, 1958.

to understand that intentions matter, that roles can be reversed, and that moral conflicts must be resolved through discussion and compromise with peers. This latter form of reasoning becomes more common in late childhood, somewhere around age 10.

Piaget's pioneering work was the starting point for Kohlberg's research on moral judgement, and it is Kohlberg's research that provides a backdrop for many of the recent investigations of moral judgement. Like Piaget, Kohlberg used moral dilemmas to elicit moral reasoning. The most famous of Kohlberg's dilemmas is about 'Heinz':

> In Europe, a woman was near death from a very bad disease, a special kind of cancer. There was one drug that the doctors thought might save her. It was a form of radium that a druggist in the same town had recently discovered. The drug was expensive to make, but the druggist was charging ten times what the drug cost him to make. He paid $200 for the radium and charged $2,000 for a small dose of the drug. The sick woman's husband, Heinz, went to everyone he knew to borrow the money, but he could get together only about $1,000, which was half of what it cost. He told the druggist that his wife was dying and asked him to sell it cheaper or let him pay later. But the druggist said, 'No, I discovered the drug and I'm going to make money from it.' Heinz got desperate and broke into the man's store to steal the drug for his wife.
>
> (Kohlberg, 1981, p. 12).

Children, adolescents, and adults were asked to judge whether Heinz's action was moral, and to justify their judgements. Kohlberg and his colleagues (Colby *et al.*, 1994) identified five *stages*, or patterns, of judgement revealed in reflections about the dilemmas (a sixth stage, not clearly evident in the research but theoretically relevant was also proposed – Figure 15.4). At the first of these stages, **heteronomous morality**,

heteronomous morality the stage of moral reasoning in which children believe that 'right' and 'wrong' are determined by powerful adult figures.

instrumental morality
the second of Kohlberg's moral judgement stages. In this stage individuals (usually children) become aware that other people have intentions and desires, and that there are two sides to every argument.

interpersonal normative morality this third stage of Kohlberg's moral judgement stages is sometimes referred to as the 'good boy/good girl orientation'. Individuals in this stage seek to be viewed as 'good' and feel guilt when it is likely that others will condemn their behaviour.

social system morality
the fourth of Kohlberg's *moral judgement stages*, also called the *law and order orientation stage*. In this stage individuals recognise that all members of society have intentions and pursue goals, but they understand that rules and laws are necessary in order for society to function and to prevent anarchy.

human rights and social welfare morality
Kohlberg's final stage of moral judgement, also called the *social contract orientation stage*. Individuals who have reached this stage make use of ethical principles to guide moral judgments.

children believe that 'right' and 'wrong' are determined by powerful adult figures; to act morally, then, is to follow the rules laid down by authorities ('Heinz was wrong because the police arrest people who steal'). Little consideration is given to the intentions or desires of individuals other than the self when making moral judgements.

At the Stage 2, **instrumental morality**, children become aware that others have intentions and desires, but this awareness influences moral judgement only when others' desires affect the pursuit of one's instrumental goals. Heinz might be judged to have acted morally if 'his wife helped him a lot around the house or at work'.

Stage 3, **interpersonal normative morality**, is characterised by an emergent concern for the perspectives of others towards the self. In contrast to Stage 2 at which the desires and intentions of others mattered only as they conflicted or advanced instrumental goals, at Stage 3 individuals are concerned with how the self is evaluated by these others. Individuals at Stage 3 seek to be viewed as 'good' and feel guilt when it is likely that others would condemn their behaviour. In Heinz's case, if he 'wants to be a good, loving husband' then he should steal the drug.

The appreciation of perspectives of others first evident at Stage 3 is expanded at Stage 4, **social system morality**. Individuals at Stage 4 understand that all members of a society have intentions and pursue goals. Accompanying this realisation is the understanding that rules and laws are necessary so that the pursuit of goals does not lead to anarchy. Moral judgement, then, focuses on the congruence of an individual's actions with the rules and laws necessary to preserve social harmony; Heinz might be judged in the wrong because 'if everyone stole property from others, then there would be no property rights, and society would disintegrate'.

Finally, at Stage 5, **human rights and social welfare morality**, individuals make use of ethical principles to guide moral judgements. For example, the rightness of an action might depend upon whether the action is consistent with the rules that individuals would accept for an ideal world. Heinz might be obligated to steal 'because in an ideal world, everyone would believe that the right to life supercedes the right to property'.

Kohlberg made a number of claims about the stages of moral judgement, and these claims have been scrutinised by philosophers, educators, and psychologists (for a particularly thoughtful review, see Lapsley, 1996). We shall review a few of the claims and the associated debate.

Age and stage

Kohlberg claimed that development across childhood and adolescence is characterised by sequential passage through the stages. Research indicates that Stages 1 and 2 are most characteristic of children with Stage 3 emerging among adolescents. Stage 4 increases in salience across adolescence, and Stage 5 appears in adulthood, although even then it remains fairly rare. Generally, longitudinal research (e.g. Colby *et al.*, 1994) indicates that individuals move up a single stage at a time (i.e. move from Stage 1 to Stage 2, not from Stage 1 to Stage 3) and that regression over time is rare (individuals who are characterised as being at Stage 3 are unlikely to use Stage 2 reasoning when tested years later). In another meta-analysis, Dawson (2002) suggests a strong positive linear relationship between educational attainment and moral stage, which further supports the sequentiality of the moral stages. The evidence that an educational environment has a progressive linear direction with respect to moral stages is compelling for development from lower stages to higher stages over the course of childhood and adolescence in Western cultures, and consequently there is little debate about this claim.

Judgement and action

One very common criticism of Kohlberg and Piaget is that the sorts of justifications offered for moral dilemmas are not associated with action. Most people can recall instances in which they acted in ways they knew were morally inappropriate, and it is this awareness that gives considerable credence to claims that the reflective judgment tapped by questions concerning hypothetical dilemmas has no influence on conduct. The relation of judgment to action is extremely complex and poorly understood; however, there is sufficient research to conclude that moral judgment stage *is* related to behaviour in moral contexts although this relation is weak (Lapsley, 1996). In short, those who reason at higher stages are more likely to act prosocially than those who reason at lower stages.

The loose connection between moral judgment and action means that it is impossible to predict accurately a person's behaviour in a specific situation from their moral stage. This is not altogether surprising: a person's behaviour in any one situation is determined by many psychological factors (emotions, perceptions, memories, as well as judgments) and by contextual factors (which persons are present and the actor's relationships with those persons, home versus the workplace, and so on). For these reasons behaviour is said to be multiply determined, and no single factor – such as moral stage – can be expected to direct behaviour. Moreover, as Blasi (1980) pointed out, moral stages represent ways of thinking about moral issues, not specific behavioural tendencies. Two persons at the same moral stage may reach different decisions about action. For example, at Stage 3, one person might conclude, 'Heinz should steal the drug if he wants to be a good loving husband' while another person at Stage 3 might assert that 'Heinz shouldn't steal the drug because people in his neighbourhood will think that he's untrustworthy'. Moreover, persons at different stages can choose the same action, but for different reasons. While the individual at Stage 3 wants to preserve the self's reputation by stealing for his wife, the individual at Stage 5 might be doing so as the result of a belief in a hierarchy of rights. For these reasons, the multiply-determined nature of behaviour and the complicated connection of moral stage to action, predictions from moral stage to moral behaviour are tenuous.

Comprehensiveness of moral stages

In much of Kohlberg's writing (e.g. 1981, 1984) there is an assumption that the stages of logical cognition outlined by Piaget are sufficient for an account of the development of

social cognition the comprehension of social situations.

intelligence and that the moral stages suffice for a broad understanding of **social cognition**. In other words, one can understand social interactions, moral emotions (guilt, shame), attitudes, and so on as deriving in one way or another from the five stages of moral judgment. However, much of the research of the past 20 years has demonstrated that the stages outlined by Kohlberg do not provide a comprehensive depiction of social cognitive development.

One line of investigation has demonstrated that young children's understanding of moral regulation is much more sophisticated than what is allowed by Stage 1 in Kohlberg's theory. Damon (1977) was one of the first to demonstrate that young children, at Kohlberg's Stage 1, reasoned in thoughtful ways about sharing in peer contexts. Damon suggested that he was able to detect moral sophistication overlooked by Kohlberg and Piaget by questioning children about familiar issues involving peers. Children have considerable experience sharing food and toys with their friends, and this experience is translated into implicit principles. In sharp contrast, young children have little experience with the kinds of issues posed by Kohlberg such as theft from stores and the importance of human life and consequently their reasoning on these issues is rather muddled. Research by Damon and many others has demonstrated convincingly that young children judge moral issues, weigh moral claims, and make moral judgments (Damon, 1999); there is much more to young children's moral understanding than was thought three decades ago.

Indeed, much recent research has sought to identify inferences and judgments made by very young children that are associated with moral behaviour. Two trends can be identified in this work. The first of these is moral cognition, best imagined to be a collection of non-conscious, automatically activated heuristics (Haidt, 2001). The assumption is that children's (and adults') moral judgments are made very quickly with essentially no conscious deliberation using rules that are specific to particular kinds of situations and contexts. This line of work suggests that it would be a mistake to expect to find the kind of consistency in reasoning postulated by Kohlberg's stages.

Second, researchers claim that these intuitions arise early and show relatively little developmental transformation. For example, Warneken and Tomasello (2006) had adult experimenters enact scenarios involving failure to achieve a goal. Eighteen-month-old humans observing these scenarios demonstrated the ability to infer the intended goal of the experimenters, and often provided the help necessary for the adults to achieve their goals. For example, in one scenario the seated experimenter dropped a marker on the floor and then reached for it unsuccessfully, frequently eliciting the assistance of the observing toddler. Because the toddler did not retrieve the marker in a parallel scenario in which the experimenter threw the marker – suggesting that the experimenter did not need it – Warneken and Tomasello concluded that even 18-month-old toddlers are capable of inferring the intentions of other people and providing assistance where warranted. The point is that even very young humans are capable of sophisticated inferences about the minds of others and can generate appropriate prosocial responses.

The discovery of early sophistication of some forms of moral cognition and prosocial behaviour is often linked to an evolutionary perspective. Many theorists posit that moral cognition – at least of the sort that rises early and operates automatically – is an **evolutionary adaptation** to the problems of living in social groups (e.g. Traulsen & Nowak, 2006). If true then forms of moral cognition and moral behaviour ought to be found in all social species. While this vast literature cannot be examined here, it suffices for this chapter to suggest that moral cognition and moral behaviour are found in some forms in other social species, though both cognition and behaviour seem less differentiated and robust than what is found in human children. For example, using the same scenarios enacting goal-directed failure described in the previous paragraph, Warneken and Tomasello found that human-raised chimpanzees made inferences about the minds of humans and responded prosocially – though the likelihood of prosocial responses was much lower than that observed in 18-month-old humans.

> **evolutionary adaptation** a process whereby a population becomes better suited to its habitat.

Distinguishing between moral and non-moral domains

Research of the last 20 years (for a review, see Turiel, 1998) has also demonstrated that children and adolescents make sharp distinctions between moral and non-moral domains, and consequently moral stages are unlikely to be used in reasoning about all social issues. Researchers have also argued that even within the moral domain there are types of judgments (e.g. about helping others (see Eisenberg & Fabes 1998, for a review), concerning obligations to the natural world (Kahn, 1999)) that are not well addressed by Kohlberg's scheme.

Finally, there is now a great deal of research indicating that one form of antisocial behaviour, aggression, is best understood in terms of the **attributions** children make rather than moral stages. Aggressive children are much more likely than non-aggressive children to attribute hostile intent to ambiguous situations (Coie & Dodge, 1998), especially when the aggressive child is emotionally aroused (Dodge & Somberg, 1987). A child who employs hostile attribution biases is more likely to perceive a threat of physical or emotional harm whether the circumstances are hostile or, in fact, clearly benign. The tendency to attribute hostile intentions to others is stable, and predicts future aggressive behaviour (Dodge et al., 1995). Furthermore, aggressive children when forced to make moral evaluations consider aggressive responses to be more acceptable (Deluty, 1983) and 'friendly' (Crick & Ladd, 1990) than do non-aggressive children. Children who are aggressive often do not view themselves as deviant or immoral, but rather assume that they are adhering to an acceptable societal standard of behaviour.

> **attribution** the belief one holds as to why people carry out a particular action or behaviour.

Universality

Finally, one of Kohlberg's boldest claims (1981) was that the moral stages that he used to characterise moral judgment development in the United States and could also be used to understand moral judgment in all other cultures (i.e. were **universal**). Supporters of Kohlberg's theory (e.g. Snarey, 1994) have reviewed studies from a variety of cultures that used Kohlberg's measure, and conclude that there is considerable evidence that Stages 2, 3, and 4 can be found in cultures radically different from the United States; there is less evidence for the presence of Stage 5 in non-Western cultures, however.

> **universality** the notion that certain developmental principles apply across all cultures.

While such reviews support claims that responses to the Kohlberg measure are similar across many cultures, the reviews do not lead to the conclusion that persons from different cultures reason in exactly the same way about moral issues. As we noted earlier, evidence has accumulated demonstrating that there is considerably more to social and moral reasoning than is represented by Kohlberg's stages; it is in these other areas the search for cross-cultural variability has had considerable success. Shweder *et al.* (1997), for instance, have demonstrated that adolescents and adults in India make frequent reference to notions of the divine in their moral justifications, in contrast to the emphasis on justice so characteristic of justifications of Westerners.

Moral judgement development and personality

In Western cultures, moral judgment sophistication, as reflected on Kohlberg's and similar measures, is associated with academic achievement, whether this is measured by grades in school or by standardised test (e.g. *IQ tests*). Given that Kohlberg's measure draws on some of the same skills necessary for academic success – comprehension of stories, verbal facility – this is an eminently reasonable association.

Particularly interesting is recent research that indicates that moral judgment is associated with *personality*. Earlier in the chapter, we reported that children who are able to regulate their emotions were less likely to become involved in antisocial behaviour. Hart and his colleagues (Hart *et al.*, 1997) found that children of this type passed through the stages of moral judgment development at a faster rate than other children. Their interpretation was that children who could regulate their emotions were better able to listen carefully to the moral arguments made by others, and consequently to benefit from the insights that others have about the adequacy of moral claims. In contrast, children who had difficulty regulating their emotions presumably became too anxious or too angry in discussions about moral conflicts to benefits from others' insights and suggestions.

Summary

There is both continuity and transformation in development across childhood. Young children who have difficulty regulating emotions are likely to retain this trait through adolescence. The consequences of poor emotion regulation are likely to be increased aggression, a tendency to attribute hostile intentions to others, and slow moral judgment development. There are dramatic changes in children's understanding of moral obligations. With age, children evidence increasingly sophisticated understanding of rights and responsibilities to others. Sophisticated moral reasoning is predictive of higher levels of prosocial action and a lower likelihood of behaving in an antisocial fashion.

SOCIAL INFLUENCES ON PROSOCIAL AND ANTISOCIAL DEVELOPMENT

Our review so far has focused on the psychological features within children that are the foundation for prosocial tendencies, antisocial behaviour, and moral development. These features – personality traits, emotion regulation, moral reasoning, and so on – are profoundly shaped by social influences. In the sections that follow, we review the effects of social relationships and culture on the constituents of prosocial and antisocial development.

DEVELOPMENT WITHIN RELATIONSHIPS

Parents

Psychologists have often noted that children bear remarkable psychological similarities to their siblings and parents. For example, impulsive children tend to have brothers and sisters who behave likewise and students who excel have parents who earned high grades. There are many exceptions to this general finding, of course, and no child is a duplicate of any other. Nonetheless, for most psychological characteristics, on average, children resemble their siblings and parents more than randomly selected non-family members.

Most typically, the similarity of children to their families has been interpreted to mean that through their social interactions, parents shape children in their own image. Parents who behave aggressively towards each other and their children, for example, are thought to be setting examples that children then imitate. An enormous body of research has accumulated over the past 50 years characterising the parenting behaviours that may lead children to resemble their families.

In recent years, however, many researchers, particularly those who advocate a *behavioural-genetic* approach to the study of development, have argued for a different interpretation of the resemblance of children to their families. These researchers point out that parents share genes with their children, and that many (if not most) psychological characteristics are influenced by genes (Turkheimer, 2000). In fact, behavioural geneticists have argued that the resemblance of children to their parents is more attributable to genes than it is to parents' systematic behaviour towards children (Turkheimer, 2000).

For our purposes in this chapter, the findings of *behaviour genetics* are cautionary. Until research is done on the influence of parents on adopted, biologically unrelated children – in which case parents do not share genes with their children – it is impossible to be certain that parenting patterns, not genes, influence prosocial and antisocial development. Our interpretations of this research must therefore be appropriately tentative.

Parents and personality

There is a clear relation between emotion regulation in parents and their children. Eisenberg *et al.* (1991) measured sympathy and negative emotions in children, and measured sympathy in the parents. The results indicated that sympathetic parents had children who were sympathetic. Kochanska (1991) studied a group of children between the ages of 2 and 10 years. At age 10, the children were asked to respond to stories like those used by Kohlberg. Moral sophistication at age 10 was related to both emotional regulation and parenting at age 2. Children prone to anxiety at 2 years

506 AN INTRODUCTION TO DEVELOPMENTAL PSYCHOLOGY

of age, and whose parents reasoned with them, were higher in sophistication at age 10 than children high in anxiety whose parents behaved autocratically. Interestingly, parental behaviour at age 2 seemed little related to moral sophistication at age 10 for the fearless children. Together these two studies suggest that parents who reason with and behave sympathetically towards their children are fostering the development of a prosocial personality. Kochanska's research suggests that children's personalities may affect how much influence parents have on children, although there is a need for future research to replicate this finding.

If democratic, warm, reasoning parenting is associated with an increased capacity for prosocial behaviour, then it comes as no surprise that autocratic, cold, harsh, inconsistent parenting is predictive of antisocial tendencies (Coie & Dodge, 1998). Parental physical abuse is particularly detrimental, as it interferes with the development of emotion regulation and sympathy, which in turn are internal resources that allow children to avoid aggression and antisocial behaviour (Dodge & Coie, 1998).

Parents and moral judgement

Families are traditionally assumed to influence moral development, and a number of studies have examined the influence of parents on moral judgment development. There is some research that indicates that the rate of moral judgment development is increased by warm supportive relationships with parents (e.g. Hart, 1988a, 1988b) and by family discussions that are supportive of children's comments (Walker & Taylor, 1991). Generally, then, studies of the influence of parents on moral judgment development are consistent with those assessing parents' roles on prosocial personality. Parents who are sympathetic, warm, and supportive of their children tend to have children who are able to regulate emotion effectively, sympathise with others, and judge moral issues with sophistication.

Peers

Peers and antisocial behaviour

Peers are powerful influences on the development of antisocial behaviour. Friends often draw children into delinquent activity, and children involved in antisocial activity are likely to choose like-minded peers. A child's network of peers is therefore a powerful context for initiation into and the consolidation of antisocial behaviour (Coie & Dodge, 1998).

Children's social relationships are influential in other ways as well. Particularly interesting are the consequences of *peer rejection*. Rejected children are those who are both influential (high impact) and disliked (identified by peers as undesirable interaction partners). Unsurprisingly, children who are very aggressive are often rejected by their peers, although there are exceptions to this generalisation (in fact, in some peer networks, for example within delinquent peer groups, it is possible to be aggressive and popular). More important, however, are a host of findings that suggest that peer rejection *increases* aggressive behaviour (Coie & Dodge, 1998). Apparently, the experience of rejection leads children to expect hostility in others, which has the effect of priming children to behave aggressively in peer contexts.

Peers and moral judgement

Surprisingly, little is known about the influence of peers on prosocial development (Eisenberg & Fabes, 1998). We do know that entry into voluntary community service (e.g. working in a shelter for homeless adults) is more common among older children and adolescents with peers engaged in similar activities than it is among those whose friends are not (Youniss & Yates, 1997). Whether this finding applies to younger children and is representative of other forms of prosocial action is not known, however (Figure 15.5).

Far more work has focused on peer influences on moral judgement development. There is a general consensus that moral judgment development is the result of individuals reflecting on moral claims, observing the behaviour of significant others, and negotiating with others when moral conflicts arise. Individuals formulate rules for moral conduct, apply these rules, and then revise them when the rules prove unsatisfactory to the self or to others. Piaget and Kohlberg – whose work was reviewed earlier in the chapter – argued that these processes are more likely to occur in peer relationships. This is because adult unilateral authority often dominates adult–child relationships thus precluding discussion about moral decisions, while the equality of peer relationships allows for mutual negotiation for the resolution of moral problems.

Research findings are consistent with this theoretical position. For example, Walker, Hennig, & Krettenauer (2000) examined the relation of discussions about moral issues among peers to subsequent moral judgment development. Walker and his colleagues found that children who attempted to understand fully their friends' perspectives experienced the most rapid moral judgment development. This finding suggests that effective peer collaboration facilitates development, a pattern consistent with the theories of Piaget and Kohlberg.

Apart from the correlation between parent and peer influence on children and adolescent moral judgment, Mahoney and Stattin (2000) in their study conducted in Sweden, discuss the role of leisure activities on adolescent antisocial behaviour. Their study of 703 14-year-olds indicated that some forms of adolescent leisure activities are correlated with antisocial behaviour. The participation of adolescents in structured activities linked to low antisocial behaviour, whereas involvement in relatively low structured activities (for e.g. the youth recreation centre) was associated with high levels of antisocial behaviour.

FIGURE 15.5 *Children's interactions with others may be contexts to learn about and to exhibit prosocial actions.*
Source: Shutterstock.

CULTURE AND DEVELOPMENT

Cultural variability

Cultural context is profoundly important for understanding prosocial and antisocial behaviour. For example, adolescents in the United States are about twice as likely to experience violent deaths than are youth in European countries (National Center for Educational Statistics, 1991). There is no evidence to indicate that American and European youth differ in important ways in personality or moral judgment, and consequently the dramatically different rates of violent death are not attributable to differences in personality. Nor would it be accurate to characterise this difference in violent death rates as an indication that European cultures are more prosocial than the United States, because on some indices of prosocial behaviour, such as volunteering for charitable causes, the United States is much higher (Greeley, 1997) than European countries. There is also considerable variation of the same sort within countries: in the United States, for example, homicide – an extreme antisocial behaviour – is much more common among adolescents living in poor urban areas than among those in affluent suburban neighborhoods (Federal Interagency Forum on Child and Family Statistics, 1999).

Cultural norms and social context are also essential for understanding the complicated developmental trajectories of prosocial and antisocial behaviour across childhood and adolescence. We have described the developments in personality and moral judgment that enable children to better regulate their emotions and consider moral claims. One might conclude from these trends that prosocial behaviour ought to increase regularly across childhood and adolescence, and generally this is so (Eisenberg & Fabes, 1998). This is not uniformly the case, however, and a consideration of one exception to the expected trend is illustrative.

Stanger *et al.* (1997) had a large sample of Dutch mothers rate their children and adolescents on measures of *aggression* (attacking others, screaming, temper tantrums) and *delinquency* (lying, swearing, vandalism – Figure 15.6). Aggression consistently declined between ages 4 and 17, a trend consistent with the growth of personality and moral

FIGURE 15.6 *An example of youth antisocial behaviour.*
Source: Shutterstock.

judgement over this age range. Interestingly, however, while the development of delinquency decreased from ages 4 to 10, it increased from age 10 to 17. The increase in delinquent behaviour is likely due to a number of social factors: the influence of peers, the freedom granted by many Western cultures to adolescents from parental and adult supervision, and so on.

When discussing cultural variability countries are often thought of as being either Western or Eastern cultures, but within a society itself there exists cultural heterogeneity. This cultural variability then becomes essential for understanding the importance of treatment and intervention in cases of severe antisocial behaviour such as drug abuse (Szapocznik *et al.*, 2007).

Media and development

One form of cultural influence on development that has received considerable attention is television. Television is pervasive in the lives of many children. For example, children in the United States are estimated to watch an average of three hours a day (Committee on Public Communications, 2001) (Figure 15.7), with children in Canada watching almost as much (Statistics Canada, 2001). Given our themes in this chapter – prosocial and antisocial development – it is reasonable to ask how moral life is portrayed in television programming.

American television presents a wide range of extremely violent, aggressive activity. For example, one analysis found that 66 per cent of programmes targeted towards American children contained violence (Federman, 1998). Because violence permeates television in the United States, a great deal of research has examined the association between television watching and childhood aggression. The evidence is clear: children who watch a lot of television tend to be more aggressive than children who watch little. It appears to have this effect for several reasons (Coie & Dodge, 1998). First, violent TV models aggressive actions that children imitate. Second, televised violence desensitises children to the dangers of aggression, because much of the violence depicted on television appears to have no harmful effects to innocent parties. Finally, televised violence heightens children's fears that the world is dangerous. Some researchers estimate

FIGURE 15.7 *In the United States and other Western countries, watching television occupies more of children's time than any other activity, apart from attending school. There is no question but that television presents messages about antisocial and prosocial behaviour.*

Source: Shutterstock.

that television is responsible for 10–20 per cent of the aggression observed in the United States (Comstock & Strasburger, 1993).

If television can make children aggressive, can it promote prosocial behaviour as well? Indeed, watching television with a prosocial theme increases altruistic behaviour, cooperation, and compliance with adult rules, an effect particularly evident in young children (Mares, 1996). We can conclude from the findings on aggression and prosocial behaviour that television is an important influence on children's development. The messages that societies present through the mass media – television, for example – are received by children and integrated into their thoughts and their actions. As web-based content aimed at children becomes increasingly common and supplements television, it is reasonable to assume that development will be shaped by media to an extent greater than what is observed today.

Culture and identity

While the transition from childhood to adolescence brings with it an increase in some forms of antisocial behaviour, as noted above, it is also a transition during which at least some adolescents construct moral identities. Moral identities refer to commitments to prosocial action (Figure 15.8) that are consistent with the self's goals and qualities (Hart *et al.*, 1998). There are 12- and 13-year-olds who are deeply involved in prosocial activities such as working in food banks, working with younger children, organising scout troops, and so on (Hart & Fegley, 1995). Interviews with these young adolescents suggest that their commitments reflect the integration of social relationships, personality characteristics, contacts with social institutions, and moral beliefs (Hart & Yates, 1998). This kind of integration is similar to that found among adult moral exemplars (Colby & Damon, 1995). However, the fusion of moral judgment, personality, and social experience typical of young adolescents committed to moral action does not seem to characterise adolescents who are frequently antisocial. In this sense, then, the formation of a moral identity in some at the transition of childhood to adolescence is a consequence of a process that is not easily understood for those who show a tendency towards antisocial behaviour. At the extremes, antisocial and prosocial tendencies seem to have different roots: the former in emotion regulation difficulties and frequently in neurological deficits, and for the latter in the formation of an identity that integrates personality, moral commitments, and social opportunities.

FIGURE 15.8 *Some adolescents construct moral identities, which are commitments to prosocial activities such as working in a voluntary capacity.*
Source: Shutterstock.

SUMMARY AND CONCLUSIONS

The development of prosocial and antisocial behaviour is a complex process, influenced by personality, emotions, judgment, social relationships, and culture. We have focused on two threads of the process, personality and judgment, and have described their development. Prosocial and antisocial development is shaped by social interactions and culture. While a great deal has been learned from 50 years of research, the most fascinating questions remain: To what extent can families foster prosocial behaviour in their children? How can the media be utilised to help children develop into productive citizens? Can the interactions among genes, biology, parenting, and culture be understood in sufficient detail to permit effective intervention? Answers to these and other important questions await the efforts of future researchers.

DISCUSSION POINTS

1. Discuss the importance of prosocial behaviour for the maintenance of social groups and wider society.
2. Consider the factors that contribute to continuity and change in social behaviours.
3. What are the causes of extreme antisocial behaviour?
4. What are the essential features of Kohlberg's five stages of moral reasoning, and has research supported his claims about these stages?
5. Consider evidence that human infants and some non-human species are able to read the intentions of others, and discuss the implication of this evidence for accounts of the development of prosocial behaviour.
6. Consider the ways in which culture and social context influence prosocial and antisocial behaviour.

SUGGESTIONS FOR FURTHER READING

Bornstein, M.H., Davidson, L., Keyes, C.M., Moore, K., & Smith, C. (2001). *Well-being: Positive development across the life course*. Hillsdale, NJ: Erlbaum.

Carlo, G., & Edwards, C.P. (2005). *Moral motivation through the life span*. Lincoln: University of Nebraska Press.

Craig, W. (2000). *Childhood social development: The essential readings*. Cambridge, MA, and Oxford: Blackwell.

Dodge, K.A. (2006). Translational science in action: Hostile attributional style and the development of aggressive behavior problems. *Development and Psychopathology, 18*(3), 791–814.

Eisenberg, N. (Ed.) (1998). *Handbook of child psychology: Vol. 3: Social, emotional, and personality development*. New York: Wiley.

Nucci, L. (1999). Education in the moral domain. New York: Cambridge University Press.

Smetana, J.G., Killen, M., & Smetana, J.G. (2006). *Handbook of moral development*. Mahwah, NJ: Lawrence Erlbaum and Associates.

REFERENCES

Bargh, J.A., & Chartrand, T.L. (1999). The unbearable automaticity of being. *American Psychologist*, *54*, 462–479.

Blasi, A. (1980). Bridging moral cognition and moral action: A critical review of the literature. *Psychological Bulletin*, *88*, 1–45.

Boxer, P., & Tizak, M.S. (2005). Children's beliefs about the continuity of aggression. *Aggressive behavior*, *31*, 172–188.

Caspi, A., Harrington, H., Milne, B., Amell, J.W., Theodore, R.F., & Moffitt T.E. (2003). Children's behavioral styles at age 3 are linked to their adult personality traits at age 26. *Journal of Personality*, *71*, 495–514.

Caspi, A., Henry, B., McGee, R.O., Moffitt, T.E., & Silva, P A. (1995). Temperamental origins of child and adolescent behavior problems: From age three to fifteen. *Child Development*, *66*, 55–68.

Coie, J.D., & Dodge, K.A. (1998). Aggression and antisocial behavior. In N. Eisenberg (Vol. Ed.) *Handbook of child psychology: Vol. 3: Social, emotional, and personality development* (5th edn; pp. 779–840). New York: Wiley.

Colby, A., Kohlberg, L., Gibbs, J., & Lieberman, M. (1994). A longitudinal study of moral judgment. In B. Puka (Ed.) *New research in moral development. Moral development: A compendium* (Vol. 5; pp. 1–124). New York: Garland.

Colby, A., & Damon, W. (1995). The development of extraordinary moral commitment. In M. Killen & D. Hart (Eds.) *Morality in everyday life: Developmental perspectives. Cambridge studies in social and emotional development* (pp. 342–370). New York, NY: Cambridge University Press.

Committee on Public Communications. (2001). Children, adolescents, and television. *Pediatrics*, *107*, 423–426.

Comstock G.C., & Strasburger, V.C. (1993). Media violence: Q & A. *Adolescent Medicine*, *4*, 505–509.

Crick, N.R., Casas, J.F., & Mosher, M. (1997). Relational and overt aggression in preschool. *Developmental Psychology*, *33*, 579–588.

Crick, N.R., & Ladd, G.W. (1990). Children's perceptions of the outcomes of aggressive strategies: Do the ends justify being mean? *Developmental Psychology*, *26*, 612–620.

Damon, W. (1977). *The Social World of the Child*. San Francisco, CA: Jossey-Bass.

Damon, W. (1999). The moral development of children. *Scientific American*, *281*, 72–79.

Dawson, T.H. (2002). New tools, new insights: Kohlberg's moral judgement stages re-visited. *International Journal of Behavioral Development*, *26*(2), 154–166.

Deluty, R.H. (1983). Children's evaluations of aggressive, assertive, and submissive responses. *Journal of Clinical Child Psychology*, *12*, 124–129.

Dodge, K.A., & Somberg, D.R. (1987). Hostile attributional biases among aggressive boys are exacerbated under conditions of threats to the self. *Child Development*, *58*, 213–224.

Dodge, K.A., Pettit, G.S., Bates, J.E, & Valente, E. (1995). Social information processing patterns partially mediate the effect of early physical abuse on later conduct problems. *Journal of Abnormal Psychology*, *104*, 632–643.

Eisenberg, N., & Fabes, R. (1998). Prosocial development. In N. Eisenberg (Vol. Ed.), *Handbook of child psychology: Vol. 3: Social, emotional, and personality development* (5th edn; pp. 701–778). New York: Wiley.

Eisenberg, N., Fabes, R.A., Schaller, M., Carlo, G., & Miller, P.A. (1991). The relations of parental characteristics and practices to children's vicarious emotional responding. *Child Development, 62*, 1393–1408.

Espelage, D.L., Bosworth, K., & Simon, T.R. (2001). Short-term stability and prospective correlates of bullying in middle-school students: An examination of potential demographic, psychosocial, and environmental influence. *Violence & Victims, 16*, 411–426.

Espelage, D.L., Holt, M.K., & Henkel, R.R. (2003). Examination of peer-group contextual effects on aggression during early adolescence. *Child Development, 74*, 205–220.

Federal Interagency Forum on Child and Family Statistics. (1999). *America's children: Key national indicators of well-being* (NECS Report No. 1999–2019). Washington, DC: US Government Printing Office.

Federman, J. (1998). *National television violence study. Vol 3*. Thousand Oaks, CA: Sage.

Glueck, S. (1982). *Family environment and delinquency*. Littleton, CO: F.B. Rothman.

Greeley, A. (1997). The other civic America: Religion and social capital. *The American Prospect* (32), 68–73.

Haidt, J. (2001). The emotional dog and its rational tail: A social intuitionist approach to moral judgment. *Psychological Review, 108*, 814–834.

Hart, D. (1988a). A longitudinal study of adolescents' socialization and identification as predictors of adult moral judgment development. *Merrill-Palmer Quarterly, 34*, 245–260.

Hart, D. (1988b). Development of personal identity in adolescence: A philosophical dilemma approach. *Merrill Palmer Quarterly, 34*, 105–114.

Hart, D., Atkins, R., & Ford, D. (1998). Urban America as a context for the development of moral identity in adolescence. *Journal of Social Issues, 54*, 513–530.

Hart, D., & Fegley, S. (1995). Prosocial behavior and caring in adolescence: Relations to self-understanding and social judgment. *Child Development, 66*, 1346–1359.

Hart, D., Hofmann, V., Edelstein, W., & Keller, M. (1997). The relation of childhood personality types to adolescent behavior and development: A longitudinal study of Icelandic children. *Developmental Psychology, 33*, 195–205.

Hart, D., & Yates, M. (1997). The interrelation of self and identity in adolescence: A developmental account. In R. Vasta (Ed.) *Annals of child development: A research annual, 12* (pp. 207–243). London, England UK: Jessica Kingsley Publishers.

Hinshaw, S.P., Lahey, B.B., & Hart, E.L. (1993). Issues of taxonomy and comorbidity in the development of conduct disorder. *Development and Psychopathology, 5*, 31–49.

Huesmann, L.R. (2001). *Gender and aggression*. Paper presented at the G. Stanley Hall Lecture Series, Williams College, Williamstown, MA.

Huesmann, L.R., & Guerra, N.G. (1997). Children's normative beliefs about aggression and aggressive behavior. *Journal of Personality & Social Psychology, 72*, 408–419.

Kahn, P.H. (1999). *The Human relationship with nature: Development and culture*. Cambridge, MA: MIT Press.

Kochanska, G. (1991). Socialization and temperament in the development of guilt and conscience. *Child Development, 62*, 1379–1392.

Kohlberg, L. (1958). *The development of modes of thinking and choices in years 10 to 16,* Ph.D. Dissertation, University of Chicago.

Kohlberg, L. (1981). *The philosophy of moral development: Moral stages and the idea of justice*. San Francisco, CA: Harper & Row.

Kohlberg, L. (1984). *The psychology of moral development: The nature and validity of moral stages*. San Francisco, CA: Harper & Row.

Krueger, R.F., Hicks, B.M., & McGue, M. (2001). Altruism and antisocial behavior: Independent tendencies, unique personality correlates, distinct etiologies. *Psychological Science, 12*(5), 397–402.

Lapsley, D. (1996). *Moral psychology*. Boulder, CO: Westview Press.

Loeber, R. (1985). Patterns and development of antisocial behavior. *Annals of Child Development,* *53*, 1431–1446.

Loeber, R., & Stouthamer-Loeber, M. (1998). Development of juvenile aggression and violence: Some common misconceptions and controversies. *American Psychologist, 53*, 242–259.

Mahoney, J. and Stattin, H. (2000). Leisure activities and adolescent antisocial behavior: The role of structure and social context. *Journal of Adolescence, 23*, 113–127.

Mares, M.L. (1996). *Positive effects of television on social behavior: A meta-analysis.* Unpublished manuscript. The Annenberg Public Policy Center, Philadelphia. Retrieved 4 April 2001, from www.appcpenn.org/appc/reports/rep3.pdf.

Moffitt, T.E., & Caspi, A., Dickson, N., Silva, P.A., & Stanton, W. (1996). Childhood-onset versus adolescent-onset antisocial conduct problems in males: Natural history from ages 3 to 18 years. *Development & Psychopathology, 8*, 399–424.

Moffitt, T.E., Lynam, D.R., & Silva, P.A. (1994). Neuropsychological tests predicting persistent male delinquency. *Criminology, 32*, 277–300.

National Center for Educational Statistics. (1991). *Education in states and nations: Indicators comparing US states with other industrialized countries in 1991* (NCES Report No. 96–160). Washington, DC: US Government Printing Office.

Newman, D.L., Caspi, A., Moffitt, T.E., & Silva, P.A. (1997). Antecedents of adult interpersonal functioning: Effects of individual differences in age 3 temperament. *Developmental Psychology, 33*, 206–217.

Piaget, J. (1932). *The moral judgment of the child.* New York: Harcourt, Brace.

Sagvolden, T., & Sergeant, J.A.(1998). Attention deficit/hyperactivity disorder – from brain dysfunctions to behaviour. *Behavioural Brain Research, 94*, 1–10.

Shweder, R.A., Much, N.C., Mahapatra, M., & Park, L. (1997). The 'big three' of morality (autonomy, community, divinity) and the 'big three' explanations of suffering. In A.M. Brandt & P. Rozin (Eds.) *Morality and health* (pp. 119–169). New York, NY: Routledge.

Snarey, J.R. (1994). Cross-cultural universality of social-moral development: A critical review of Kohlbergian research. In B. Puka (Ed.) *New research in moral development. Moral development: A compendium* (pp. 268–298). New York: Garland.

Stanger, C., Achenbach, T.M., & Verhulst, F.C. (1997). Accelerated longitudinal comparisons of aggressive versus delinquent behaviors. *Developmental Psychopathology, 9*, 43–58.

Statistics Canada. (2001). *Average hours per week of television viewing.* Retrieved 8 April 2001, from www.statcan.ca/english/Pgdb/People/Culture/arts23.htm.

Szapocznik, J., Prado, G., Burlew, A.K., Williams, R.A., & Santisteban, D.A. (2007). Drug abuse in African American and Hispanic asolescents: culture, development and behavior. *Annual Review of Clinical Psychology, 3*, 77–105.

Traulsen, A., & Nowak, M.A. (2006). Evolution of cooperation by multilevel selection. *Proceedings of the National Academy of Sciences, 103*(29), 10952–10955.

Turiel, E. (1998). The development of morality. In N. Eisenberg (Ed.) *Handbook of child psychology: Vol. 3: Social, emotional, and personality development* (5th edn; pp. 863–932). New York: Wiley.

Turkheimer, E. (2000). Three laws of behavior genetics and what they mean. *Current Directions in Psychological Science, 9*, 160–164.

Walker, L.J., Karl, H., Hennig, K.H., & Krettenauer, T. (2000). Parent and peer contexts for children's moral reasoning development. *Child Development, 71*, 1033–1048.

Walker L., & Taylor, J.H. (1991). Family interactions and the development of moral reasoning. *Child Development, 62*, 264–283.

Warneken, F., & Tomasello, M. (2006). Altruistic helping in human infants and young chimpanzees. *Science, 311*, 1301–1303.

Youniss, J., & Yates, M. (1997). *Community service and social responsibility in youth.* Chicago: University of Chicago Press.

Part IV
Adolescence

16 Cognitive Development in Adolescence

KANG LEE, GIZELLE ANZURES, AND ALEJO FREIRE

KEY TERMS

ambiguous figures • analogical reasoning • combinatory thought • configural processing • correlation coefficient • crystallised intelligence • deductive reasoning • domain-specific • elaboration • encoding switch hypothesis • featural processing • fluid intelligence • Flynn effect • formal operations stage • hypothetico-deductive reasoning • inductive reasoning • interpropositional thinking • intrapropositional thinking • intuitive scientists • metacognition • neo-cortex • percentile • second-order analogy • selective attention • speed of processing • standard deviation • standardised score • syllogism • transitivity task • working memory

CHAPTER OUTLINE

OVERVIEW

Decades of research indicate that important and sometimes fundamental changes in thinking occur during adolescence, and that adolescents become capable of sophisticated thinking. There are three interrelated components to thinking: the *process* by which adolescents perform basic and higher level intellectual functions, the *structure* in which their thoughts are organised, and the *content* of their thinking. The chapter discusses these topics by focusing on several aspects and theories of cognitive development:

- memory development;
- the development of intelligence;
- reasoning skills;
- formal operational thinking;
- alternatives to Piaget's theory of adolescent reasoning.

What has become clear is that adolescent thinking is qualitatively different from the thinking of young children. However, adolescents are still apprentices in thinking. They are yet to learn some sophisticated ways of thinking such as conducting truly scientific investigations and carrying out abstract logical reasoning. Nevertheless, the thinking skills acquired during adolescence lay the foundation for taking on the more complex and diverse problems of adulthood.

INTRODUCTION

This chapter is about thinking in adolescence. Now, if one were to believe what is often presented in the popular media, it might seem adolescents do not do much thinking at all. Consider how adolescents are typically portrayed in movies, television, and newspapers. At worst they are depicted as violent, heavily involved with drugs, promiscuous, and in general a menace to society. Even what is often considered normal is not very flattering: it is common to characterise young people as overly self-conscious, egotistic, and in a constant state of emotional turmoil. They are obsessed with whether their appearance looks 'cool' to others but are not concerned with their academic work. They hate school but love to party. They are impulsive and lack self-control. Neither view gives adolescents much credit for sophisticated thinking. But decades of research indicate that important and sometimes fundamental changes in thinking are occurring during this time.

In this chapter, we will use the word 'thinking' in a very broad sense. It includes not only such higher level intellectual functions as logical reasoning and problem-solving, but also some basic level intellectual functions such as perception, attention, and memory (Siegler, 1993). As well, readers need to keep in mind that when we mention 'adolescent thinking', the term refers to three interrelated aspects of thinking: the *process* by which adolescents perform basic and higher level intellectual functions, the *structure* in which adolescents' thoughts are organised, and the *content* of adolescents' thinking. For example, to understand adolescents' ability in

FIGURE 16.1 *Adolescent thinking is found in a range of tasks and activities.*

Source: Shutterstock.

problem-solving, one needs to know how they attack a problem from the beginning to its final solution (the process of thinking), how adolescents' problem-solving is related to their other cognitive abilities (the structure of thinking), and what information is specifically used during problem-solving (the content of thinking). This chapter will touch upon these issues with a focus on two main questions:

1. Do adolescents have a unique way of thinking?

2. What are the major characteristics of adolescents' thinking?

PERCEPTION AND ATTENTION

Perception

One area in which development is evident in adolescence is perception. As you have already read in Chapter 5, perception is one of the cognitive abilities that develop earliest in life: even newborns are very sensitive to environmental stimulation. By the end of toddlerhood, children's vision, hearing, and senses of smell, taste, and touch are all quite well developed. What aspects of perception, then, continue to develop throughout childhood and into adolescence? Perhaps the broadest generalisation to be made is that children's perception becomes increasingly flexible. Some examples will serve to illustrate what we mean by this statement. Consider the illustrations in Figure 16.2. These are called **ambiguous figures** because more than one object can be perceived in each drawing. However, in a study with 4- to 11-year-olds, Elkind and Scott (1962) found that the younger children usually reported only seeing one element in the illustrations rather than two. Often, only when an adult made the distinction between the two elements very explicit did the children indicate seeing both components. The older children in the study could readily perceive the figures in more than one way and alternate between them. This suggests that increased flexibility of thought in adolescence allows alternations between the different perspectives to be easily accomplished. In contrast, the relatively rigid perceptions of younger children make it more difficult to see the figures in multiple ways. A related demonstration of increasing flexibility of perception is obtained when considering Figure 16.2. Each illustration depicts an object composed of several other common objects. Similar to what is found in the case of ambiguous figures, young children tend to identify

ambiguous figure a figure that can be perceived in two (or more) different ways.

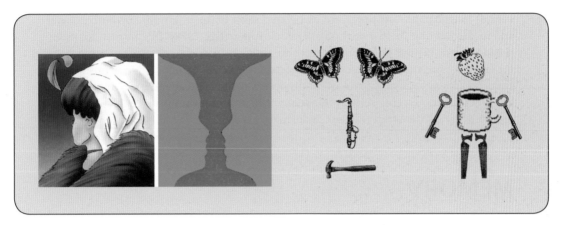

FIGURE 16.2 *Examples of (a) ambiguous figures; (b) composite objects.*

the component objects without perceiving the image 'gestalt', while adolescents can identify both components and wholes (Elkind *et al.*, 1964). In cases where young children do perceive the whole as well as components, they typically require a much longer inspection time to do so than what is required by older children.

Selective attention

Development is also evident in the adolescent's superior ability to allocate attentional resources. The ability for **selective attention** has been assessed using a central-incidental learning task. A set of cards, each showing two objects belonging to different categories, is used. For example, a set might consist of cards where each depicts one animal and one tool. The experimenter shows all the cards and gives the instruction to remember only one category of objects (the animals for example). In such a task, children are required to focus attention on the animals while selectively ignoring the tools appearing in the pictures. Later, however, they are asked to recall both the animals and tools. It is reasoned that children high in selective attention should be able to devote more of their attentional resources to the central task than the incidental task. More specifically, a child with high selective attention should show high retention for items in the *central* category (e.g. animals), but comparatively low memory of items in the *incidental* class (e.g. tools). In contrast, children with low selective attention may remember items in either category at a similar rate. What research has shown (e.g. Hagen, 1967) is that adolescents are more likely than younger children to remember a significantly higher number of items from the central class than the incidental class; in contrast, young children are more likely than adolescents to remember a comparable number of items from the two categories. There is also support for the interpretation that these differing patterns of results are due to differences in selective attention: whereas memory for central and incidental objects is positively correlated in young children, there is a negative correlation of these factors among adolescents (e.g. Miller & Weiss, 1981). In addition, when exposure to the central and the incidental objects is

> **selective attention** the ability to allocate attentional resources and to focus on (a) specific topic(s).

varied, longer exposure times are associated with better memory for both central and incidental objects in 9-year-olds (Hale & Alderman, 1978). In contrast, for older preadolescent 12-year-olds, longer exposure times are associated with better memory for central – but not for incidental – objects (Hale & Alderman, 1978). Thus, young children appear to divide their attention between the central and incidental objects, but older preadolescents selectively maintain their attention to the central objects as required by task demands (Hale & Alderman, 1978).

MEMORY

By early adulthood memory can be quite remarkable. An extreme example of this fact comes from a study by Bahrick *et al.* (1975). In this study, individuals recognised former high school classmates from yearbook photographs with 90 per cent accuracy, as long as 35 years after graduation and independently of class size. This incredible feat is a result of a rapid development in face processing abilities during childhood and adolescence, with adult-level recognition reached by about 16 years of age (Figure 16.3).

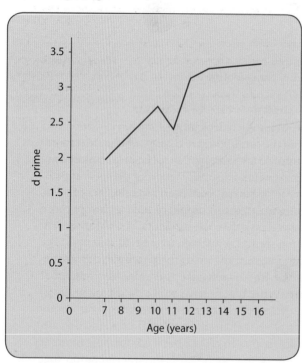

FIGURE 16.3 *Development of face recognition (adapted from Flin, 1985); d prime is an index of recognition.*

Source: Reproduced with permission from *The British Journal of Psychology*, © The British Psychological Society.

Whether there is a qualitative change in face processing between childhood and adolescence has been a focus of intense study. One proposal is a so-called **encoding switch hypothesis**. This hypothesis claims that young children rely more on information about faces that is not as 'good' for remembering them compared to the information about faces on which older children and adults place greater reliance. Carey and Diamond (1977) suggest that children prior to the age of 10 years primarily use information about individual features (e.g. eyes, nose, and mouth) in recognising faces, whereas older children and adults rely more on information about configuration, the spatial layout of face features. Face processing emphasising features is referred to as **featural processing**, whereas that emphasising configurations is called configurational or **configural processing**. There is some evidence consistent with Carey and Diamond's proposal: they found that children prior to age 10 years made identifications largely on the basis of paraphernalia items such as a hat or glasses. That is, shown an individual wearing a hat, and then later shown the same individual without a hat and a different person with the same hat, young children were more likely to say that the individual with the hat was the one they had seen previously. Carey and Diamond suggested that younger children's failure in recognising the right person was because they encoded non-essential, featural information for determining face identity, while adolescents succeeded because they encoded the critical, configural information. However, even face-processing abilities during adolescence are still developing considering their less than adult-like levels in face recognition memory (Carey *et al.*, 1980; Mondloch *et al.*, 2003).

Figure 16.2 also indicates another interesting finding. Notice that there is a drop in performance on face recognition tasks occurring at about age 11 years. This dip in recognition performance appears to be influenced by factors such as children's level of familiarity with the type of face stimuli used and the difficulty of the recognition task. For example, studies that used children's faces as stimuli and used fewer faces in the recognition task (i.e. imposing a smaller memory demand) found that the dip occurred at 11 years of age (Flin, 1980, 1985). However, another study that used adult faces and used more faces in the recognition task (i.e. imposing a larger memory demand) found that the dip occurred at 12 to 14 years of age (Carey *et al.*, 1980). While this 'dip' has not been found in every study carried out with children at these ages, it is reliable enough that several researchers have attempted to account for its occurrence. One intriguing proposal for which there is some support is that the dip coincides with hormonal changes associated with puberty. For example, Diamond *et al.* (1983) compared performance of girls aged 8 to 16 years in a face recognition task. They found that regardless of age, girls undergoing puberty performed more poorly than did either prepubescent or postpubescent girls. The issue of a temporary dip in face recognition as well as that of the encoding switch hypothesis remains controversial, and awaits further research and clarification (for excellent reviews of this literature, see Chung & Thomson, 1995; Lee *et al.*, in press).

Faces are just one type of stimulus for which adolescents show incredible memory skills. What about memory development more generally? Evidence indicates that development takes place in almost every aspect of memory. The three that will be highlighted here are short-term memory, long-term memory, and strategy use.

encoding switch hypothesis different information about faces is represented in memory by children at different ages. It is suggested that young children rely on information about individual features (e.g. eyes, nose, mouth) in recognising faces, whereas older children and adults use information about the configuration of the features.

featural processing a tendency to process the separate features of the face, as opposed to perceiving the relationship between the parts.

configural processing processing that pays particular attention to the overall configuration of the smaller elements within the object being perceived rather than the individual features or elements.

Short-term memory

As the name suggests, *short-term memory* refers to memory that is only required for a short amount of time and that is necessary to carry out the current task (indeed, short-term memory is also referred to as *working memory*). Experimentally, the capacity of

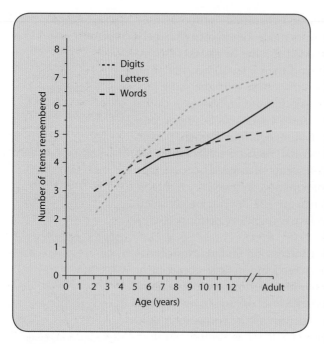

FIGURE 16.4 *Development of short-term memory.*

Source: Adapted from Schneider & Pressley, 1997. Reprinted by permission of Lawrence Erlbaum Associates Inc., Professors W. Schneider and G.M. Pressley.

short-term memory has been investigated using span tasks: a series of items is presented at a rate of 1 per second – for example letters, words, or digits – and the task is to repeat them in the same order as they were presented. Short-term memory has also been investigated using the spatial memory span task during which a certain number of blocks are presented on a computer screen. An examiner then taps the blocks in a particular sequence and participants are asked to reproduce the given sequence. A number of such studies have shown that short-term memory increases steadily throughout childhood and into adolescence (Figure 16.4). The figure shows the number of items of various types that can be remembered by children 2 to 12 years of age. For example, whereas a 5-year-old can remember between three and four of each class of item, a 12-year-old can remember an average of about seven digits, and between four and five letters or words. Relative to 13- to 17-year-olds and adults, younger children between 9 and 10 years of age also remember fewer items on tests of immediate recall, and 11- to 12-year-olds remember fewer items relative to 16- to 17-year-olds and adults (Conklin *et al.*, 2007; Luciana *et al.*, 2005). Such age-related improvements in immediate recall remain constant across varying retention intervals from 5 to 30 seconds of delay (Ryan, 1990).

There are a number of possible explanations for the developmental improvement in short-term memory. One possibility is simply that as children grow the capacity of short-term memory increases as a result of neurological changes. But it remains an open question whether this is indeed the case (Miller, 1956). The reason why this conclusion cannot be straightforwardly drawn becomes clear in considering Figure 16.4. As can be seen, the number of items remembered at a given age is in part determined by the nature of the items. So, for example, it is in general easier to remember a list of digits than a list of words. This should not be the case if what is changing in short-term memory is its capacity per se. Instead, this may reflect children's greater familiarity with numbers than with words. Or it may reflect practice, in that while sometimes we are required to keep a short sequence of random numbers in short-term memory (e.g. in calculating an arithmetic problem or dialling a phone number), it is rarer to have to remember a random string of words. Whatever the case, it is similarly possible that the developmental changes apparent in short-term memory studies reflect older children's greater familiarity and experience with words and numbers as a result of additional years of schooling. In other words while it is possible that the capacity of short-term memory is greater in adolescence than at earlier times, it is also possible that advances are a result of increases in general knowledge about the to-be-remembered materials. These possible explanations are discussed in more detail in Chapter 13.

In addition to the temporary storage of information, short-term memory has also been construed as a sort of work space for processing and manipulating both recent and old information – hence the term *working memory* (Baddeley & Hitch, 1974). Working memory is typically measured using a modified version of span tasks during which participants are presented with a specified sequence of items and asked to reproduce that sequence in the reverse order. Working memory can also be measured using a letter span task, in which an experimenter provides a list of randomly ordered letters and asks participants to repeat the letters in alphabetical order. Such tasks show better performance, and, thus, more sophisticated working memory, among older adolescents relative to younger adolescents (Conklin *et al.*, 2007; Luciana *et al.*, 2005).

Long-term memory

Long-term memory is more permanent than short-term memory, and includes such things as representations of people one has met and events one has experienced. It also includes knowledge acquired through schooling, such as multiplication tables and the location of different countries on a map. And, even though one is not really aware of the fact, long-term memory is what allows you to drive a car with little effort or why you do not have to consciously think about how to move your arms and legs once you have learned to swim. For all intents and purposes there are no limits on the capacity of long-term memory. This seems to be true even for young children, who may have quite detailed recollections of childhood friends or visits to grandma and grandpa's house. While its absolute capacity does not appear to change much, it is not the case that long-term memory of young children and adolescents is equivalent.

Speed of processing

One major type of development in long term memory is in **speed of processing**, with older children generally able to retrieve information from long-term memory more rapidly than can young children. One demonstration of this comes from a famous study by Keating and Bobbitt (1978). Keating and Bobbitt asked 9-, 13-, and 17-year-olds to sort two sets of index cards, each with two letters stencilled on it, as quickly as possible. The set used in the *physical-sorting* condition was sorted into cards with letters that were identical (e.g. AA, aa, BB, or bb) and cards that differed in physical appearance (e.g. Aa, bA, Ba, or Bb). In contrast, in the *name-sorting* condition similar stimuli were used to those in the physical-sorting condition. However, children were asked to sort cards into those with the

speed of processing
the time it takes for the brain to either receive or output information, or the speed with which a mental calculation can be carried out.

same name (e.g. AA, aa, BB, or bb) and those with a different name (e.g. Ab, bA, Ba, ba). Keating and Bobbitt reasoned that the name-sorting task should take longer because it required that the names of letters be retrieved from long-term memory, whereas the physical-sorting task was basically a perceptual task. Their other important assumption was that because in all other respects the two tasks were comparable, differences in the amount of time taken to complete the two tasks reflected the amount of time taken to retrieve letter names from long-term memory. As expected, they found that at all ages the name-sorting task took longer to complete than the physical-sorting task. In addition, the differences in time taken were greatest for the 9-year-olds, next largest for the 13-year-olds, and smallest for the 17-year-olds, consistent with the notion that speed of retrieving information from long-term memory improves throughout these years.

Memory strategies

Developmental differences between adolescents and younger children are also evident in the types of strategies used in order to remember information. This reflects adolescents' increased knowledge about ways to enhance their memory. Asked to remember the number sequence 3–6–5–2–5–1–1, a young child might use a *rehearsal* strategy, in which the sequence is repeated over and over. An older child might realise that the first three numbers are the same as the number of days in the year, that the next two numbers are a quarter of 100, and that the last two numbers are the same as the number of players in a soccer team. Now there are only three things to remember rather than seven. Although both instances show evidence of providing a deliberate aid to memory, the latter strategy is more effective. It is an example of an *elaboration* strategy, whereby information to be remembered is transformed in some way that makes it more meaningful and therefore easier to remember.

A different kind of elaboration is an *organisation* strategy. It is seen in older children's increased tendency to organise or *cluster* groups of items in memory when they are to be remembered; this is called the *cluster effect*. Presented with a list of items that includes subsets of different categories, for example animals, colours, and types of furniture, adolescents will more frequently use the information about categories to recall more items: when asked to recall as many items as they can from the list, they may begin with one category and name the items they remember from that category, then name items from the second category, and so on (Schneider, 1985). By actively imposing an organisation on material to be remembered, older children and adolescents become skilled at remembering seemingly chaotic and disorganised information.

A number of general findings about the development of strategy use have emerged in the literature. As the above examples indicate, more sophisticated strategy use for remembering information increases throughout childhood. It also seems to be the case that effective use of strategies to increase memory may especially proliferate in adolescence (e.g. Rohwer & Bean, 1973). Finally, it is important to point out that even when young children use elaboration strategies they will generally do so in only a limited way. That is, older children are much more likely to apply strategies more flexibly and broadly to aid memory in a wider range of tasks (Carr *et al.*, 1989).

INTELLIGENCE

Although psychologists have not reached a consensus about how to define intelligence, it is generally agreed that intelligence, or general intellectual ability, is the underlying potential for individuals to understand the world around them and to function successfully in it. Measures of adolescent intelligence are often obtained by using *intelligence tests*. One commonly used test is Wechsler's Intelligence Scale for Children (WISC; Wechsler, 1991). This test, now in its fourth edition, is suitable for use with children between 6 and 16 years of age. It has a *verbal scale* and a *performance scale*, which are purportedly tapping into different aspects of a child's intelligence (e.g. left and right hemispheric functioning, respectively). The verbal scale has six subscales that assess children's verbal intelligence on different dimensions and the performance scale has seven subscales that tap into children's non-verbal intelligence (see Table 16.1 for details). Adolescents' raw scores on these subscales are very informative and can tell us how adolescents' general intellectual abilities develop with age.

Rapid development

There are three important characteristics of adolescents' general intellectual ability. Figures 16.5(a) and 16.5(b) illustrate two of them. First, adolescents' performance on the subscales of the WISC suggests that their general intellectual abilities are significantly advanced compared to children younger than 10 years of age. As well, the abilities continue to develop rapidly during the entire adolescent period. Second, there are differences in the speed at which adolescents' intellectual abilities develop (as indicated by the steepness of the curves). Development is very sharp in some areas (e.g. vocabulary, suggesting rapid expansion of linguistic knowledge; coding,

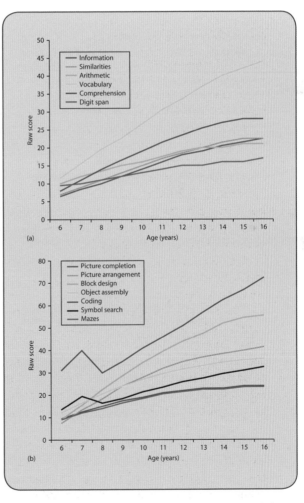

FIGURE 16.5 *Age trend of raw scores in (a) the WISC verbal scale; (b) the WISC performance scale*
Source: Adapted from Wechsler, 1991.

Table 16.1 *Items on the Wechsler Intelligence Scale for Children*

Verbal scale	Performance scale
1. General information: A sample of questions that most children have been exposed to (e.g. where does the sun rise? How many weeks are there in a year?).	1. Picture completion: Children are asked to point out which part is missing in a picture (e.g. a cat without whiskers).
2. Comprehension: Children are required to explain why certain practices are desirable or what course of action is preferred under certain circumstances (e.g. why one needs a driver's licence to drive a car? What is the thing to do if you lose a friend's book?).	2. Picture arrangement: Children are asked to arrange a series of pictures that are in a wrong order (e.g. pictures depicting a child going to school, and returning home, and getting up) back to the correct sequence.
3. Arithmetic: A series of mental arithmetic problems ranging from easy ones (e.g. how much does it cost to buy 2 kilograms of bananas when the cost is $65 per kilogram?) to hard ones that most of us dreaded when were in high school (e.g. Mr Davis drives at 50 km per hour and Mrs Davis drives at 100 km per hour but left a half hour later. After how many hours later will Mrs Davis catch up with Mr Davis?).	3. Block design: Children are required to arrange a number of blocks to form a pattern within a certain period of time.
4. Similarities: Children are asked to point out the similarities between pairs of words (e.g. in what way food and book are alike?).	4. Object assembly: The child must assemble jigsaw-like parts of a common object (e.g. a sailboat).
5. Vocabulary: Children are required to explain a series of increasingly difficult words (e.g. carpet, psychosis).	5. Coding: Children are asked to translate, as fast as possible, symbols to numbers based on a code given to them (e.g. @ = 1, * = 2 etc.)
6. Digit span: A series of numbers of increasing length are presented orally and children are asked to repeat them in the same or reversed order.	6. Mazes: The child must trace the correct route from a starting point to an exit on a series of mazes.
	7. Symbol search: Children must indicate whether a pair of symbols are present in a row of symbols.

suggesting rapid improvement in information processing speed). Performance in other areas, however, seems to level off after a period of rapid development between 6 and 10 years of age (e.g. digit span that taps into short-term memory; mazes that reflect speed of learning).

Stability of development

The third characteristic of adolescents' general intellectual abilities is that a particular adolescent's IQ score is relatively stable and does not change greatly as age increases: *IQ* is the abbreviation of *intelligence quotient*. This characteristic does not contradict the

previous statement about the rapid development of general intellectual abilities in adolescence. While an adolescent may develop rather significantly on a number of dimensions of intelligence, their IQ scores do not increase. This is because IQ scores are calculated based on age norms. That is, an individual's IQ only indicates how 'smart' the individual is in comparison with their own age group. For example, when an individual obtains an IQ score of 100, it means that half of the same aged peers have IQ scores higher than the individual and another half lower. The same score at a different age has the same meaning even though absolute general intellectual ability may be different.

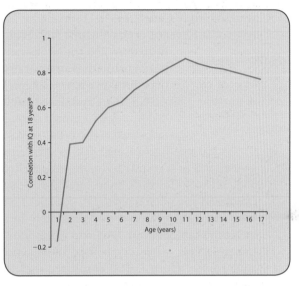

FIGURE 16.6 *Correlation between IQ scores at 18 years of age and those at earlier ages.*

Source: Adapted from Bayley, 1949. Reprinted with permission.

This third characteristic of adolescent intelligence suggests that the level of an adolescent's general intellectual abilities in relation to their peers is relatively stable from one age to another. For example, if Mike is ranked in the 90th **percentile** (i.e. his intellectual abilities are higher than 90 per cent of his age group) at 11 years of age, he will continue to rank at similar percentiles at later ages. Bayley (1949) reported that the IQ scores of 18-year-olds were very similar to their own IQ scores in adolescence. As shown in Figure 16.6, **correlation coefficients** between IQ scores at 18 years of age and IQ scores obtained between 11 and 17 years of age by the same individuals are all above 0.70. This result is in strong contrast to the poor correlation of IQ scores at 18 years with those obtained at much earlier ages (e.g. 0.4 at 3 years and 0.6 at 6 years; see Figure 16.6). One possibility is that children's general intellectual abilities are more unstable at younger ages than in later years. Fagan and Singer's (1983) findings seem to support this idea: when they reviewed a number of studies that measured children's IQ at 1 year and again at ages 3 through 6 years, the average correlation was only 0.14. There are other explanations for the high discrepancies in IQ scores in early childhood, but limitations of space do not permit us to go into further details. Interested readers should consult Slater *et al.* (1999) for an in-depth discussion about the controversy in the literature.

percentile location of an individual's development or achievement along a percentage scale.

correlation coefficients a statistical measure ranging from +1.00 to −1.00 that indicates the strength, as well as the direction, of the relationship between two variables.

Fluid and crystallised intelligence

Several researchers have suggested that the developmental pattern of adolescents' general intellectual abilities may be more complex than Figure 16.5 suggests. For example, Horn (1970) suggests that the developmental pattern of an individual's general intellectual ability depends on what type of intelligence is being measured. Based on earlier work (Horn & Cattell, 1967), Horn and his associates (Horn et al., 1981) assessed two types of intelligence, crystallised and fluid. **Fluid intelligence** is defined as a person's ability to think and reason abstractly as measured by culture-free reasoning tasks, such as those measuring the ability to see relations among objects or patterns in a series of items (e.g. what letter comes next in this series: ADGJMP?). **Crystallised intelligence** is the store of information, skills, and strategies acquired through education and prior experience. Many tasks used in the WISC verbal scale are examples of such tasks.

crystallised intelligence the store of information, skills, and strategies acquired through education and prior experience.

Typical intelligence tests fail to differentiate between the two types of intelligence, and as a result, IQ scores appear to be stable over time during and after adolescence. However, fluid intelligence has been found to improve throughout childhood and adolescence (Fry & Hale, 1996). In addition, when fluid and crystallised intelligence were tested separately in more than a dozen studies conducted in Horn's lab between 1966 and 1982, fluid intelligence was found to undergo a sharp decline, while crystallised intelligence increased rapidly beginning in late adolescence. Horn (1978) suggested that this pattern of development might be related to changes in the nervous system. Specifically, he proposed that the decline of fluid intelligence is associated with the deterioration of the part of the brain governing alertness and attention, the onset of which begins as early as adolescence. In contrast, crystallised intelligence is associated with information processing in the **neo-cortex**. As age increases, the neural connections that represent various information become more elaborated and more easily activated, which accounts for the increase in crystallised intelligence. According to Horn's theory, adolescence appears to be the critical developmental period that marks both the dawn of crystallised intelligence and the dust of fluid intelligence.

neo-cortex in evolutionary terms, the most recently developed area of the *cerebral cortex*.

Intergenerational IQ gains: We're brighter now!

However, there is no need to feel depressed about the demise of adolescents' fluid intelligence. What is lost is apparently compensated for by an almost equal improvement in crystallised intelligence (Horn, 1970). In addition, James Flynn (1984, 1998), after analysing archival IQ data from as early as the 1930s, discovered that American young children and adolescents made IQ score gains at the average rate of three IQ points per decade since 1932. What this means is that if we use the 1940s criteria to calculate the IQ scores of today's adolescents, those with an IQ score of 127 today would have had a score of 145 in 1939. In other words, a moderately smart young person in the year 2010 would have been considered a genius 70 years ago! Such substantial IQ gains are not limited to American children and adolescents; for example, British school children have gained 14 IQ points from the 1940s to the present day (Flynn, 2009). Also, data from 14 countries (Flynn, 1987) reveal that within a single generation (30 years) IQ gains in children, adolescents, and adults vary from 5 points to 25 points. Moreover, the biggest gains are from mental tests designed to measure fluid intelligence. After reviewing reports since his first discovery of generational IQ gains in 1980s, Flynn (1998) concluded that this so-called *Flynn effect* is a real, universal, and on-going effect. It is clear that genetic factors cannot account for the massive change in IQ scores on such a small timescale. The effect must be due to certain environmental factors. However, exactly what environmental factors are responsible for the effect is still hotly debated, but candidates include enhanced nutrition, improved health, better quality education, smaller family size, the increasing complexity of Western societies, which include the ubiquitous use of complex technological inventions such as computers, cell or mobile phones, video games, etc. (Flynn, 2009; Gauvain & Munroe, 2009; Rabbit, 2007; Wicherts *et al.*, 2010).

REASONING

Although 'reasoning' is not easily defined, it can be thought of approximately as the set of mental processes by which we draw conclusions on the basis of information known to us. For example, suppose you dislike getting wet in the rain. And suppose you know it is raining. Because both bits of information are known to you, you may reason that it is worthwhile to look for an umbrella before you go outside. As this example illustrates, reasoning is something we carry out on a frequent basis, often unaware of the fact we are doing so. But as anyone who has taken a course in formal logic knows, reasoning is rarely as clear or straightforward as in the above example. There are also many qualitatively different classes of reasoning. In this section we discuss three types of reasoning – deductive, inductive, and analogical.

Deductive and inductive reasoning

Much of the reasoning done by humans can be classified as either *deductive* or *inductive*. **Deductive reasoning** is the 'process of deriving inferences that make explicit what is implicit in the information available to us' (Small, 1990), while **inductive reasoning** is the use of specific examples to draw a general conclusion. One way to characterise the difference between them is that deductive reasoning involves drawing specific conclusions from general premises. In contrast, inductive reasoning draws a general conclusion from specific premises. A couple of examples will help to clarify this distinction.

deductive reasoning
the outcome of a specific example is calculated from a general principle, that is, deductive reasoning involves drawing specific conclusions from general premises.

inductive reasoning
creating a general principle or conclusion from specific examples, that is, drawing a general conclusion from specific premises.

syllogism comprises two statements (called premises) and a conclusion that is derived from these previous statements.

Deductive reasoning is often illustrated in the form of a **syllogism**. A syllogism is composed of two statements (called *premises*) and a conclusion that follows the premises. Suppose the first premise is 'all cows can fly', the second premise is 'Bertha is a cow', and the conclusion is 'Bertha can fly'. This is deductive reasoning. The next example illustrates a typical form of inductive reasoning. Suppose we are told 'Bertha the cow can fly', 'Mabel the cow can fly', and 'Trudy the cow can also fly' and 'Bertha, Mabel, and Trudy are the only cows living on Old MacDonald's farm'. It logically follows that 'all cows on the Old MacDonald farm can fly'.

Universal and particular quantifiers

Developmentally, Piaget held that true deductive and inductive reasoning could not be carried out until the stage of *formal operations* (see below), at which time adolescents could reason reliably, that is, in agreement with rules of logic. Subsequent research has indicated otherwise in a couple of respects. While it is true that reasoning improves with age it is not the case that adolescents reason reliably. Nor do adults for that matter. A study by Erickson (1978) serves to illustrate this point. First, we point out that premises and the conclusion in a syllogism can each have a *universal quantifier* or a *particular quantifier*. The word 'all' is typically used as a universal quantifier and 'some' as a particular quantifier. In addition, premises and conclusion can be stated in affirmative or negative form. The difference between universal and particular quantifiers is the difference between the statements 'all birds can fly' and 'some birds can fly'. The distinction between an affirmative and negative form is the difference between the statements 'all people are good' and 'all people are not good'.

What is important to point out for the present purposes is that it is generally easier to reason about *universal* premises than about *particulars*. In his study, Erickson had college students judge the validity of conclusions drawn from four types of abstract syllogisms, all with universal premises. He presented each type of problem in combination with four possible conclusions (i.e. universal-affirmative, universal-negative, particular-affirmative, particular-negative). What he found was that performance varied considerably depending on the form of the premises and conclusion. Consider the following example premises and two conclusions:

Premise 1 (P1): All C are B.
Premise 2 (P2): All B are A.
Conclusion 1 (C1): All A are C.
Conclusion 2 (C2): Some A are C.

In this case C1 is not valid and C2 is valid. However, subjects in Erickson's study tended to judge incorrectly both that C1 was valid (87%) and C2 not valid (95%).

Deductive reasoning

Thus, even as adults we often have difficulty distinguishing valid from invalid conclusions in cases of deductive reasoning. Nevertheless, it would be wrong to conclude that there is no development of deductive reasoning in childhood and adolescence. One reason the subjects in Erickson's study performed as poorly as they did was because all premises and conclusions were stated in abstract form. This becomes clear if we substitute 'all basketball players are tall' and 'all tall people are shy' for P1 and P2 respectively; the corresponding conclusions are 'all shy people are basketball players' (C1) and 'some shy people are basketball players' (C2). From P1 and P2 it follows that all basketball players are shy. Clearly this does not mean that all shy people are basketball players, as C1 states. But if all basketball players are shy, then it is also true that some shy people are basketball players, as C2 states.

The example above serves to illustrate what research has repeatedly shown: that for people of all ages deductive reasoning is facilitated by including concrete content rather than abstract symbols. Developmentally, what is important to note is that while even preschoolers show some evidence of deductive reasoning in cases where material is very familiar to them (Hawkins *et al.*, 1984), the reliance on content over logical form becomes increasingly diminished as childhood progresses and into adolescence (e.g. Overton *et al.*, 1987).

Although few studies have examined the development of inductive reasoning in childhood and adolescence, an informative study is one by Galotti *et al.* (1997). Galotti *et al.*, in two experiments, assessed deductive and inductive reasoning in kindergartners and second to sixth graders. They looked at understanding of syllogisms such as: 'All shakdees have three eyes. Myro is a shakdee. Does Myro have three eyes?' (deductive version); and 'Myro is a shakdee. Myro has three eyes. Do all shakdees have three eyes?' (inductive version). They asked children to state whether the conclusion was true. Importantly, they also asked them to rate their confidence in their responses, as well as to provide explanations for their answers. Galotti *et al.* found that beginning in the second grade, and clearly by the fourth grade, there was evidence that deductive reasoning problems were easier than inductive problems, in that they were answered more quickly and confidence ratings were higher than for the inductive reasoning problems. What this result suggests is that by the end of elementary school certain aspects of deductive and inductive reasoning are understood in an abstract sense; that is, it is increasingly understood that what is important is the logical form of the problem and not the content. This interpretation is supported by systematic changes in the types of explanations children provided for their responses: kindergarten children typically provided explanations that did not make reference to the logical form of the premises (for example by attempting to relate the conclusion to their real-world knowledge and responding on that basis), with the form of the premises mentioned progressively more at higher grades.

Analogical reasoning

Another type of reasoning is reasoning by analogy. **Analogical reasoning** requires abstraction of a relationship between two elements, and mapping of the relationship onto two other elements with a similar relationship. Although there are different types of analogies, one common type is often expressed in the general form 'A:B::C:D'. This shorthand is read as 'A is to B as C is to D', and states that the relationship of A to B is in some way equivalent or similar to the relationship of C to D. A very

analogical reasoning resolving a problem by comparing it to a similar problem that has been solved previously.

straightforward example is woman:man – girl:boy. Here, the relationships involved are related to genders and different parts of the lifespan. An analogy that is more abstract is food:body – book:mind.

In practice, even quite simple analogies such as the first example above are typically beyond the grasp of very young children. By age 9 or 10 such simple analogies are understood; however, analogical reasoning undergoes rapid development after this time. Specifically, researchers have identified at least three qualitatively distinct stages in analogical reasoning between approximately the ages of 9 and 18 (Sternberg & Rifkin, 1979; see Case, 1985). As mentioned, by age 9 or 10 years analogies with familiar elements and very clear relations among elements can be solved. By about 12 years of age relations among elements that are not obvious can be considered, but this is possible primarily in the case that the elements themselves are concrete rather than abstract

second-order analogy an analogy that requires the use of *crystallised intelligence*. In order to make the connections, one must be able to derive a relationship that is not inherent within the analogy.

entities, as in the second analogy above. By about 13 or 14 years of age, analogies wherein both the entities comprising the analogy and the relationship between the entities are abstract can be understood (e.g. task:completion::problem:solution). Even more complex analogies, referred to as **second-order analogies**, are not solved reliably until about 16 or 17 years of age. In general, then, the progression is from a very concrete understanding of analogies limited to very familiar content to a much more flexible and abstract understanding.

FORMAL OPERATIONAL THINKING

The term 'formal operational thinking' is used by Piaget to refer to the unique way of thinking in adolescence. Piaget theorised that the final stage of *cognitive development* is that of formal operation, by the end of which adolescents reach the highest level of thinking humanly possible.

According to Piaget, adolescent thinking is in some ways similar to that of children in the *concrete operations stage* (Chapter 9). Adolescents, like concrete operational children, think rationally and logically. Both are able to use mental operations to represent and manipulate ideas. They can use logical rules to infer new information based on given information, without actually observing the new information. For example, in a transitivity task, concrete and formal operational children can use the transitional logic (if a > b and b > c, then a > c) to draw a conclusion about who is the tallest after being told that Mary is taller than John and John is taller than Mike. They do not have to know Mary, John, and Mike, nor do they have to line up Mary against John and Mike to confirm who is actually the tallest. One of the major features of mental operations is *reversibility*. Due to this feature, school-aged children and adolescents can carry out many of their daily activities internally. They can mentally alter realities back and forth without actually changing them. For example, imagine that you pick up one of your parents' favourite vases, drop it, and see it shatter. Now reverse the sequence to return the vase back to its original form. You can do this effortlessly and repeatedly, to your heart's content. Now, break the vase for real and try to put it back together. On second thoughts, maybe that would be a bad idea!

Abstract thought

Despite some similarities, Piaget believed that adolescents are fundamentally different thinkers from concrete operational children. First, they think abstractly and use operations that are extracted from a number of concrete operations (i.e. operation of operations). Therefore, these operations are abstract, general, and content-free (hence the term 'formal). An analogy for the difference between concrete and formal operations is that between simple arithmetic calculations ($1 + 2 = 3$) and an algebraic equation ($X + Y = Z$). It is for this reason that concrete operational children pass number, length, liquid, mass, and volume *conservation tasks* at different ages, while adolescents can do them all: the concrete operational child needs a specific operation for each task, while the adolescent applies one rule to all conservation tasks. Piaget called this characteristic of adolescent thinking **interpropositional thinking**, contrasted with the **intrapropositional thinking** of concrete operational children. Adolescents' ability to think abstractly and globally perhaps leads to their struggles with big philosophical questions such as 'What is the meaning of life' and 'Does God exist?'

interpropositional thinking where the individual is able to relate one or more parts of a proposition to another part to arrive at a solution to a problem.

intrapropositional thinking the thought of the child in Piaget's *concrete operations stage of development*, which includes concrete content rather than abstract symbols.

Realms of possibility

Second, Piaget theorised that concrete and formal operational children conceptualise the relationship between reality and possibility differently. Concrete operational children are 'earthbound, concrete, and practical-minded' thinkers (Flavell *et al.*, 1993, p. 139). In contrast, adolescents treat reality as only one of many possibilities. Their minds can move freely in and out of many different realms of possibility. They apply logical thinking to the possible (what might exist), not just to the real (what does exist). For example, it would be very difficult for a concrete operation child to solve the following problems:

- If ants are bigger than dogs and dogs are bigger than elephants, which animals are the biggest?
- All goldfish are green. Wanda is a goldfish. What colour is Wanda?

Adolescents, in contrast, normally can answer these questions without any difficulty. The ability to think about what might be possible explains why for many people an interest in science-fiction emanates in the teenage years.

The adolescent as an apprentice scientist

Third, according to Piaget, adolescents are apprentice scientists who can come up with theories in an attempt to explain certain phenomena, generate hypotheses based

**hypothetico-deductive
reasoning** the ability to
develop theories in an
attempt to explain cer-
tain phenomena, gener-
ate hypotheses based
on these theories, and
systematically devise
tests to confirm or refute
these hypotheses.

on these theories, and systematically devise tests to confirm or refute
these hypotheses. In other words, adolescents can carry out **hypothetico-deductive reasoning**. Unlike formal operational thinkers, concrete operational children tend to have a single theory about how a
phenomenon in question operates. Although they do generate hypotheses to test their theories, only confirmatory evidence is accepted while
counter-evidence is ignored. For example, in a study by Karmiloff-
Smith and Inhelder (1975), both of whom were Piaget's research associates, children were presented with long wood blocks that weighed
differently at each end. Sometimes the weight differential was visible (an extra piece
of wood was glued to one end), while other times it was not visible (a metal piece was
inserted into one end). They were asked to balance the blocks on another piece of wood.
Many concrete operational children hypothesised that the blocks would balance in their
geometric middle. Children with this hypothesis repeatedly tried to balance the blocks
without success. They attributed their failure not to a faulty hypothesis but to some
anomalies in their procedure of testing. When they were asked to balance the blocks
with eyes closed, they succeeded in the task by using touch. However, once they opened
their eyes they refused to acknowledge their correct solution and stubbornly refused to
abandon their hypothesis. In contrast, adolescents tended to be more flexible about their
hypotheses; they would readily give up a hypothesis if the counter-evidence was strong.

Scientific problems

According to Piaget, adolescents' unique of way of thinking is manifested in how they
solve complex problems. In their book, the *Growth of Logical Thinking from Childhood to
Adolescence* (1958), Inhelder and Piaget documented their innovative experiments with
adolescents on more than a dozen scientific projects to illustrate various characteristics of formal operational thought. Here we only focus on two tasks to illustrate the
empirical evidence on which Piaget's theory of formal operational thought was based.

The balance scale problem

This problem was used by Piaget to illustrate how children develop the ability to think
systematically about multiple dimensions. Children are shown a simple balance scale,
with equally spaced pegs along each side. A number of same-sized weights can be placed
on the pegs. Children's task is to predict whether or not the balance scale will balance
when varying number of weights are placed at different distances from the fulcrum
(see Figure 16.7). The correct solution to this problem is to obtain the force torque of
each side (i.e. weight × distance). When the force torque on one side is greater than on
the other, the balance scale will tilt down on the side with greater weight. If the force
torque on either side is equivalent, the scale will balance. Piaget believed that, in order to
succeed in such a task, children must be able to think in a combinatory manner, that is,
taking more than one factor into consideration (weight and distance). Single-minded
thinking will lead to failure in some trials (e.g. only considering weight leads to the
false prediction that the scale in Figure 16.7 will fall on the right side; only considering
distance, in contrast, leads to the incorrect prediction that the scale will fall on the left

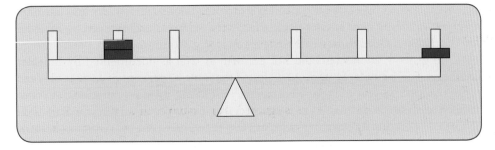

FIGURE 16.7 *The balance scale task.*

side). Piaget found that only adolescents can consider both weight and distance and succeed in predicting the behavior of the balance scale under various conditions.

The pendulum problem

To illustrate how children develop the ability to carry out hypothetico-deductive reasoning, Inhelder and Piaget presented children with the pendulum problem. This problem involves a wooden stand, various lengths of string, and several weights. The experimenter demonstrates how strings with different lengths and weights may produce different speeds of swinging when the weight is released at different heights. Children's task is to discover the law governing the pendulum's swinging speed. The correct response is that the length of the pendulum determines the speed; the shorter the string, the faster the pendulum swings. Inhelder and Piaget found that concrete operational children normally tried a few combinations of weights, lengths, and heights but in a random, unsystematic manner. In contrast, adolescents, especially older ones, proposed multiple hypotheses based on their observations. They isolated factors that could affect the pendulum speed, and tested the impact of each factor systematically. They first varied each factor alone while keeping other factors constant, then proceeded to test the effect of two or three factor combinations. From their observations of experiments with different factorial designs, they drew the conclusion that the speed of the pendulum varied only as a function of its length.

CONTROVERSIES ABOUT PIAGET'S THEORY AND RESEARCH REGARDING FORMAL OPERATIONAL THOUGHT

Do all adolescents reach this stage?

Piaget's theory and research on formal operational thinking has led to a considerable number of follow-up studies and heated theoretical debates about exactly how adolescents think. Consistent with Piaget's findings, Danner and Day (1977) found a large increase in formal operational reasoning from preadolescence to early and late adolescence. However, later studies using exactly the same tasks developed by Inhelder and Piaget often failed to replicate their findings (e.g. Commons *et al.*, 1982; Epstein, 1979). In general, adolescents did not perform as well as documented by Inhelder and Piaget. For example, Epstein (1979) found that only 32 per cent of 15-year-olds and 34 per cent of 18-year-olds showed evidence of using formal operations. A more detailed analysis shows that 33 per cent of 15-year-olds are at an intermediate level of formal operational reasoning, whereas less than 2 per cent of 15-year-olds show unequivocal formal operational reasoning (Bradmetz, 1999). Piaget seemed to have over-estimated adolescents' formal operational thinking.

Recall that Piaget suggested that the formal operational stage is the final level of cognitive development, by the end of which adolescents reach the highest level of logical thinking. Apparently, this conclusion is also flawed. For example, Capon and Kuhn (1979) and Keating (1980) found that only one-third of adolescents and adults passed formal operational tasks. Researchers now agree that formal operational thinking continues to develop well into adulthood and many adults may never reach this level of thinking.

Piaget contended that formal operational thinking is a pervasive form of thinking that emerges around 11 years of age and influences adolescents' performance in varying task domains. Follow-up studies showed that this claim is also inaccurate. Adolescents' ability to use formal operations appears to develop gradually. In early adolescence, formal operations are not fully developed, nor are they used consistently in different task domains. In late adolescence and adulthood, some, but not all, individuals become capable of consistently and skilfully using formal operational thought to solve problems (e.g. Kuhn *et al.*, 1977). However, it should be noted that relative to preadolescent children, older adolescents and young adults appear to be more susceptible to training in logical reasoning skills to improve formal operational thought (Kuhn *et al.*, 1979).

The role of experience

Piaget further claimed that formal operational thought is constructed by an adolescent themselves, and educational and cultural experiences play little role in its development. Many studies have disputed this conclusion. With the use of both limited (giving hints; e.g. Stone & Day, 1978) and extended training procedures (e.g. Case, 1974), researchers found that training was effective with children in late middle childhood and adolescents who did not show formal operational thinking in the pretest. Individuals' knowledge and expertise has also been shown to affect how effectively they use formal operations. One study (De Lisi & Staudt, 1980) showed that university students' performance in formal operational tasks depended on their major: those majoring in physics did well in the Piagetian tasks, while political-science students had better performance in tasks that required political reasoning. In addition, cultural experience also plays an important role in the development of formal operational thinking. A study conducted in Hong Kong and the United States (Douglas & Wong, 1977) found that Chinese adolescents responded in the Piagetian tasks at less advanced levels than their American counterparts; Chinese males performed better than Chinese females, perhaps due to the Chinese culture's differential socialisation processes for males and females. Cross-cultural studies also have revealed that adolescents and adults in cultures where scientific thinking is not emphasised tend to perform poorly in the standard Piagetian tasks (Dasen & Heron, 1981). This does not mean that they do not think in a complex manner. In fact, in situations that are adaptively meaningful to them, their cognitive ability is very sophisticated (e.g. Micronesian's ability to ride canoes in high seas without the aid of navigational instruments; Hutchins, 1993).

Cross-generational gains

A recent study (Flieller, 1999, and see also Lynn, 2009) further confirms the impact of environmental factors on cognitive development. Flieller (1999) compared data on five Piagetian tasks (Longeot, 1966) from 10- to 15-year-olds from two different generations (early 1970s versus mid-1990s). The five tasks were (1) weight and volume conservation tasks; (2) the pendulum problem; (3) a permutation task that requires children to identify how many ways different coloured tokens can be lined up; (4) a probability task in which children have to estimate odds of obtaining certain types of tokens drawn from a container; and (5) a mechanical curve task in which children have to draw curves produced by a pencil that is fastened to a rotating cylinder. These tasks are all adapted from those used by Inhelder and Piaget (1958) and are thought to test adolescents' formal operational thinking.

Flieller (1999) found that at equal age, today's adolescents exhibited a higher level of cognitive development than the adolescents of 20 or 30 years ago. For example, for the samples taken in 1972 and 1993, the cross-generational gain in the overall score is about 5 points (standardised score with a mean of 100 and a *standard deviation* of 15). What this means is that an adolescent who was ranked average in 1993 (i.e. a score of 100) in terms of formal operational thoughts would be ranked above average about 30 years ago (105). Flieller also observed that the amount of gain varied across tasks. Gains were greatest for **combinatory thought** (the permutation task) and quite large for the pendulum, probability, and mechanical curve tasks, but equivocal for the conservation tasks. A strong correlation was also found between the participants' IQ scores and their scores on these cognitive tasks. This suggests that the acceleration of cognitive development is related to the cross-generational gains in IQ scores; both are perhaps due to similar improvements in environmental factors over the last 30 years.

combinatory thought taking more than one factor into consideration.

BEYOND PIAGET'S THEORY

Despite the fact that empirical evidence fails to confirm the major predictions of Piaget's theory regarding adolescents' thinking, Piaget's contribution to research on adolescent cognitive development is undeniable. His theoretical and empirical work has inspired many researchers to work in the area and to ask the same questions that

Piaget asked almost a half century ago: How do adolescents think? Are adolescents fundamentally different thinkers? What are the characteristics of adolescent thought?

Adolescents as rule-based problem-solvers

One post-Piagetian approach to adolescent thinking is the *information processing* approach. This approach uses the computer as a metaphor to describe *cognitive processes*. Information processing theorists believe that adolescents' thinking is, in a nutshell, a process of obtaining information from the environment, storing information in the short-term and long-term memory systems, and using various rules and strategies to manipulate information. The goal of such a system is to derive new information and to guide actions.

To illustrate this approach, let us look at a study conducted by Siegler (1976). Siegler used the same balance scale task used by Inhelder and Piaget (1958) to test whether and how 5-, 9-, 13-, and 17-year-olds could solve this problem. However, he took an entirely different approach in analysing children's thinking processes. He believed that thinking is rule-based and children use specific rules for solving specific problems in a specific domain. Using a so-called task analysis method, Siegler identified several rules that children could possibly use to solve this problem. Rule I is to consider only the weights on each side. Rule II is to consider solely the weight factor, except in the case that the weights are equal, in which case distance is considered. Rule III is to consider weights and distances simultaneously; however, when the two factors conflict (i.e. one side has more weight and the other side has more distance), the child simply resorts to guessing. Rule IV is the most advanced rule, based on the force torque on each side.

Siegler presented children with different combinations of weights and distances on the balance scale. It was found that 89 per cent of the children followed one of the four rules (24% used Rule I, 18% used Rule II, 40% used Rule III, and 7% used Rule IV). Siegler reported that children used increasingly more complex rules as their age increased. Nearly all 5-year-olds used Rule I, most 9-year-olds used Rule II, and many 13- and 17-year-olds used Rule III. Inconsistent with Piaget's conclusion, few adolescents actually used Rule IV. Siegler used a flow chart to illustrate how children adopting a particular rule solve the balance beam tasks (see Figure 16.8).

Siegler (1981) has applied the same methodology to a number of additional Piagetian tasks and successfully obtained results consistent with the information processing approach. Based on his results and those of others (e.g. Klahr & Robinson, 1981), Siegler (1981) concluded that children and adolescents may not think using general-purpose formal operations that can be applied to problems across various domains. Rather, he claims their thinking is rule-based, and that these rules are **domain-specific**. That is, specific rules are only applicable to specific tasks in a specific domain. In different domains children's and adolescents' expertise may be different. Hence, they may use rules of different levels on different tasks.

domain-specific knowledge that can only be applied to specific situations that fall within the same domain.

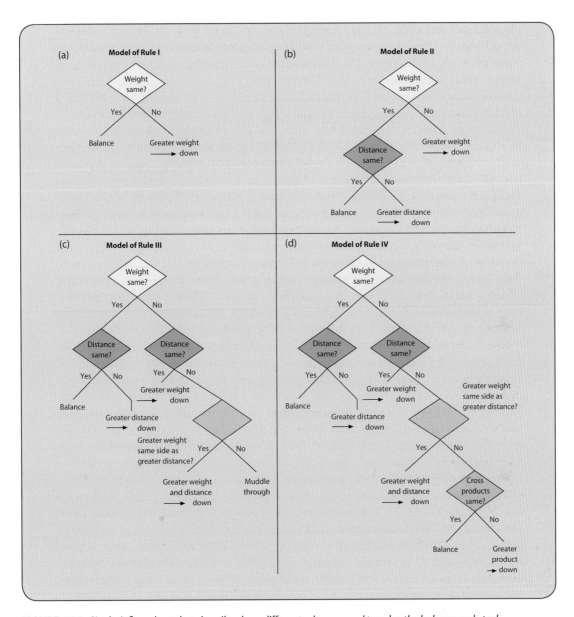

FIGURE 16.8 *Siegler's flow chart that describes how different rules are used to solve the balance scale task.*

Source: R.S. Siegler, "Information processing approaches to cognitive development." In W. Kessen (Ed.), *Handbook of child psychology*, Vol. 1 (New York: Wiley, 1983), p. 160. Reprinted by permission John Wiley & Sons, Ltd.

Adolescents as intuitive scientists

Another line of research on adolescents' thinking does not use the 'children process information like a computer' metaphor. Rather, children and adolescents are viewed as **intuitive scientists** (Karmiloff-Smith, 1992; Kuhn, 1989). The fundamental assumptions of this

intuitive scientists the idea that we are all capable of constructing commonsense theories to explain how the world works, and are able to conduct 'experiments' to test them.

approach are that children and adolescents are capable of both constructing theories to explain how the world operates in a law-like manner and conducting 'experiments' to confirm them. At this point, these notions do not depart significantly from those of Piaget. What makes this approach different from Piaget's theory is the assumption that cognitive development is domain-specific: there is no over-arching principle that a child of a particular age can use to solve all problems, and different domains call for different theories and different methods. Along this line of thinking, an adolescent may be an expert in solving problems in one domain (e.g. mathematics) but not in another (e.g. physics), and may never reach a sophisticated level of thinking in certain domains.

Unlike the information processing approach, the children-as-intuitive-scientists approach views children as naïve theorists, not as rule users. Thinking is not a rule-governed behaviour. Rather, it is a process guided by children's intuitive theoretical understanding of the world. As intuitive scientists, children divide problems they encounter into different domains (physical, biological, and psychological). For each domain they formulate an intuitive theory that consists of loosely organised assumptions. When children are called upon to explain a certain phenomenon in a particular domain, the intuitive theory for that domain is activated. While children's naïve theories are sometimes consistent with scientific theories, on many other occasions their theories are not supported by scientific evidence. Hence, errors are common.

For example, McCloskey and his colleagues conducted a series of studies to document the extent to which young children, adolescents, and university students understand the physical laws of motion. They presented participants with simple tasks that involved predicting the trajectory of a moving ball. In one study (Kaiser *et al.*, 1986), participants were shown a curved tube (Figure 16.9(a)) and asked to predict the path that a moving ball would take after it exits the tube. Only 44 per cent of 12-year-olds and 65 per cent of university students made correct predictions (Figure 16.9(a): the solid straight line). Many participants mistakenly thought the ball would travel in a curved path (Figure 16.9(a): the dotted line).

In a similar study (Kaiser *et al.*, 1985), preschoolers, first and second graders (6–8-year-olds), third and fourth graders (8–10-year-olds), fifth and sixth graders (10–12-year-olds), adolescents and university students were asked to predict how a moving ball would fall after rolling over the edge of a table. Most adolescents (79%) and all university students made correct predictions (i.e. the ball will continue to move forward as it falls; see Figure 16.9(b)), while most preschoolers and 6–8-year-olds and half of the 10–12-year-olds predicted erroneously that the ball would fall straight down. However, when participants were presented with a new situation in which the ball fell off a moving model aeroplane, most children, regardless of age, made incorrect predictions. They either thought that the ball would fall behind the dropping point or straight down (the correct response is that the ball travels the same path as the ball falling off the edge of a table; Figure 16.9(c): the solid line). Even 35 per cent of the university students made similar mistakes. Interestingly, when children and adults were shown the actual falling event after they made erroneous predictions, they were surprised by the outcomes but refused to admit that they had made a mistake. Rather, they explained the discrepancy away by suggesting, for example, that the experimenter released the ball later than the

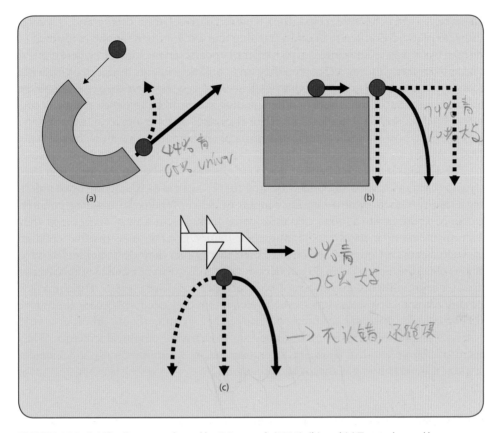

FIGURE 16.9 *(a) The C-curve task used by Kaiser* et al. *(1986). (b) and (c) Two tasks used by Kaiser* et al. *(1985).*

experimenter had indicated or that the ball was pushed just before falling. This result indicates that it is the erroneous theory of motion, not the lack of direct evidence, that led children and adolescents to make incorrect predictions. Overall, the studies by McCloskey and his associates suggest that many adolescents and some adults still hold at least a partially erroneous theory of motion. They are apparently not ready to relinquish a theory even in the face of counter-evidence.

Three common flaws in children's and adolescents' use of theories

Adolescents' reluctance to abandon an intuitive theory has also been found in areas other than physical motion (e.g. balance: Karmiloff-Smith & Inhelder, 1975; medicine: Kuhn, Amsel, & O'Loughlin, 1988; car mechanics: Schauble, 1991). Kuhn (1989), after reviewing a series of studies, identified three common flaws in children's and adolescents' use of theories. First, they tend to fail to separate theory and evidence. They seem to have difficulty in understanding that a theory needs to be confirmed or refuted by evidence. They find it even harder to understand the kind of evidence that is needed to refute a theory. Very often they carry out experiments in search of evidence that supports their theory rather than evidence that can test their theory. It should be noted, however, that the failure in differentiating theory from evidence mainly occurs with older children and adolescents when they already have a favoured theory and when several possible explanations exist for a phenomenon in question (Flavell *et al.*, 1993).

The second flaw of children's and adolescents' use of intuitive theory is that they tend to select evidence consistent with their theory instead of modifying or abandoning a theory in the face of mounting counter-evidence. When encountering counter-evidence, children and adolescents often ignore it or explain it away. Sometimes, they even manufacture evidence to support their theory. Overall, it seems that children and adolescents are often so attached to their theory that their eyes are blinded by it. In this regard, scientists often do not fair any better; they can be equally non-objective about a beloved theory in the face of counter-evidence (Kuhn, 1989). The third flaw of children and adolescents (and some adults) is that they need a plausible alternative theory in order to accept counter-evidence to their existing theory. In other words, having a theory seems to be more important than having empirical evidence. They seem to believe and live by a motto proclaimed by Karmiloff-Smith and Inhelder (1975): 'If you want to get ahead, get a theory.'

General characteristics of adolescent thinking

Despite theoretical debates and evidential discrepancies in the literature, and despite some weaknesses in adolescent thinking, many researchers agree that adolescent thinking is more sophisticated than that of younger children, as well as being fundamentally different. As Keating pointed out:

> across a wide range of content areas, from logical and mathematical topics, to moral reasoning, to interpersonal understanding, to social and political issues, to the nature of knowledge itself, there is substantial consistency in the ways in which adolescents, compared to children, respond to problems posed to them.
>
> *(Keating, 1990, p. 64)*

Keating (1980) summarised five major characteristics associated with the development of thinking in adolescence:

1. In contrast to childhood thinking that focuses on the here-and-now, adolescent thinking emphasises the world of possibility.

2. In adolescence the ability to carry out systematic hypothesis testing and scientific reasoning emerges.

3. Adolescents can think about the future by planning ahead.

4. Adolescents are also capable of introspecting about their own thought processes, that is, they can think about their thinking (or *metacognition*).

5. The content of adolescent thinking is expanded to include social, moral, and political issues, not only issues concerning the external world but also personal issues.

SUMMARY AND CONCLUSIONS

This chapter has been about thinking in adolescence. A large body of research has indicated that adolescent thinking is qualitatively different from the thinking of young children. This is true of the complex thinking involved in reasoning, for example, or in what we normally think of as 'intelligence'. It is also true, however, in areas you may not normally consider as part of 'thinking', for example perception and attention. Compared to the perceptions and attention of younger children, perception and attention in adolescence are more flexible. Increased flexibility is also evident in the advanced ways adolescents use strategies to enhance their memory relative to what young children are capable of. Reasoning and problem-solving can be carried out at a less concrete level than in younger years, ideas captured in Piaget's notions of formal operational thinking. Of course, adolescents are still apprentices in thinking. They are yet to learn some more sophisticated ways of thinking such as conducting truly scientific investigation and carrying out abstract logical reasoning. Nevertheless, the thinking skills acquired during adolescence lay the foundation for taking on the more complex and diverse problems of adulthood.

DISCUSSION POINTS

1. What is the difference between the process, structure, and content of adolescents' thoughts?

2. What aspects of perception and attention continue to develop throughout childhood and adolescence?

3. How does intelligence develop during adolescence?

4. What are the major features of formal operational reasoning?

5. Think about the criticisms of Piaget's theory of adolescent thinking. How adequate are alternative approaches?

6. In what ways might adolescents be considered 'intuitive scientists'?

SUGGESTIONS FOR FURTHER READING

Eysenck, M.W., & Keane, M.T. (2010). *Cognitive psychology: A student's handbook* (6th edn). New York and East Sussex: Psychology Press.

Garton, A.F. (2004). *Exploring cognitive development: The child as problem solver*. Cambridge, MA. and Oxford: Blackwell.

Goswami, U. (2008). *Cognitive development: The learning brain*. New York and East Sussex: Psychology Press.

Lee, K. (Ed.) (2000). *Cognitive development: The essential readings*. Cambridge, MA. and Oxford: Blackwell.

Siegler, R.S., & Alibali, M.W. (2005). *Children's thinking* (4th ed.). Boston, MA: Pearson Education International.

REFERENCES

Baddeley, A.D., & Hitch, G.J. (1974). Working memory. In G.H. Bower (Ed.) *The Psychology of Learning and Motivation* (Vol. 8, pp. 47–89). London: Academic Press.

Bahrick, H.P., Bahrick, P.O., & Wittlinger, R.P. (1975). Fifty years of memory for names and faces: A cross-sectional approach. *Journal of Experimental Psychology: General, 104*, 54–75.

Bayley, N. (1949). Consistency and variability in the growth of intelligence from birth to eighteen years. *Journal of Genetic Psychology, 75*, 165–196.

Bradmetz, J. (1999). Precursors of formal thought: A longitudinal study. *British Journal of Developmental Psychology, 17*, 61–81.

Capon, N., & Kuhn, D. (1979). Logical reasoning in the supermarket: Adult females' use of a proportional reasoning strategy in an everyday context. *Developmental Psychology, 15*, 450–452.

Carey, S., & Diamond, R. (1977). From piecemeal to configurational representation of faces. *Science, 195*, 312–314.

Carey, S., Diamond, R., & Woods, B. (1980). Development of face recognition – A maturational component? *Developmental Psychology, 16*, 257–269.

Carr, M., Kurtz, B.E., Schneider, W., Turner, L.A., & Borkowski, J.G. (1989). Strategy acquisition and transfer: Environmental influences on metacognitive development. *Developmental Psychology, 25*, 765–771.

Case, R. (1974). Structure and strictures: Some functional limitations on the course of cognitive growth. *Cognitive Psychology, 6*, 544–573.

Case, R. (1985). *Intellectual development: Birth to adulthood*. New York: Academic Press.

Chung, M., & Thomson, D.M. (1995). Development of face recognition. *British Journal of Psychology, 86*, 55–87.

Commons, M.L., Miller, P.M., & Kuhn, D. (1982). The relation between formal operational reasoning and academic course selection and performance among college freshman and sophomores. *Journal of Applied Developmental Psychology, 3*, 1–10.

Conklin, H.M., Luciana, M., Hooper, C.J., & Yarger, R.S. (2007). Working memory performance in typically developing children and adolescents: Behavioral evidence of protracted frontal lobe development. *Developmental Neuropsychology, 31*, 103–128.

Danner, F.W., & Day, M.C. (1977). Eliciting formal operations. *Child Development, 48*, 1600–1606.

Dasen, P.R., & Heron, A. (1981). Cross-cultural tests of Piaget's theory. In H. Triandis & A. Heron (Eds.) *Handbook of cross-cultural psychology: Vol. 4: Developmental psychology*. Boston, MA: Allyn & Bacon.

De Lisi, R., & Staudt, J. (1980). Individual differences in college students' performance on formal operations tasks. *Journal of Applied Developmental Psychology, 1*, 201–208.

Diamond, R., Carey, S., & Back, K.J. (1983). Genetic influences on the development of spatial skills during early adolescence. *Cognition, 13*, 167–185.

Douglas, J.D., & Wong, A.C. (1977). Formal operations: Age and sex differences in Chinese and American children. *Child Development, 48*, 689–692.

Elkind, D., Koegler, R.R., & Go, E. (1964). Studies in perceptual development. II: Part–whole perception. *Child Development, 35*, 81–90.

Elkind, D., & Scott, L. (1962). Studies in perceptual development. I: The decentering of perception. *Child Development, 33*, 619–630.

Epstein, H.T. (1979). Correlated brain and intelligence development in humans. In M.E. Hahn, C. Jensen, & B.C. Dudek (Eds.) *Development, and evolution of brain size: Behavioral implications*. New York: Academic Press.

Erickson, J.R. (1978). Research on syllogistic reasoning. In R. Revlin & R.E. Mayer (Eds.) *Human reasoning* (pp. 39–50). Washington, DC: Winston.

Fagan, J.F., & Singer, L.T. (1983). Infant recognition memory as a measure of intelligence. *Advances in Infancy Research, 2*, 31–78.

Flavell, J.H., Miller, P.H., & Miller, S.A. (1993). *Cognitive development* (3rd edn). Englewood Cliffs, NJ: Prentice Hall.

Flieller, A. (1999). Comparison of the development of formal thought in adolescent cohorts aged 10 to 15 years (1967–1996 and 1972–1993). *Developmental Psychology, 35*, 1048–1058.

Flin, R.H. (1980). Age effects in children's memory for unfamiliar faces. *Developmental Psychology, 16*, 373–374.

Flin, R.H. (1985). Development of face recognition: An encoding switch? *British Journal of Psychology, 76*, 123–134.

Flynn, J.R. (1984). The mean IQ of Americans: Massive gains 1932 to 1978. *Psychological Bulletin, 95*, 29–51.

Flynn, J.R. (1987). Massive IQ gains in 14 nations: What IQ tests really measure. *Psychological Bulletin, 101*, 171–191.

Flynn, J.R. (1998). Searching for justice: The discovery of IQ gains over time. *American Psychologist, 54*, 5–20.

Flynn, J.R. (2009). Requiem for nutrition as the cause of IQ gains: Raven's gains in Britain 1938–2008. *Economics and Human Biology, 7*, 18–27.

Fry, A.F., & Hale, S. (1996). Processing speed, working memory, and fluid intelligence: Evidence for a developmental cascade. *Psychological Science, 7*, 237–241.

Galotti, K.M., Komatsu, L.K., & Voelz, S. (1997). Children's differential performance on deductive and inductive syllogisms. *Developmental Psychology, 33*, 70–78.

Gauvain, M., & Munroe, R.L. (2009). Contributions of societal modernity to cognitive development: A comparison of four cultures. *Child Development, 80*, 1628–1642.

Hagen, J.W. (1967). The effect of distraction on selective attention. *Child Development, 38*, 685–694.

Hale, G.A., & Alderman, L.B. (1978). Children's selective attention with variation in amount of stimulus exposure. *Journal of Experimental Child Psychology, 26*, 320–327.

Hawkins, J., Pea, R.D., Glick, J., & Scribner, S. (1984). 'Merds that laugh don't like mushrooms': Evidence for deductive reasoning by preschoolers. *Developmental Psychology, 20*, 584–594.

Horn, J.L. (1970). Organization of data on life-span development of human abilities. In L. Goulet & P. Baltes (Eds.) *Life-span development psychology: Research and theory*. New York: Academic Press.

Horn, J.L. (1978). Human ability systems. In P.B. Baltes (Ed.) *Life-span development and behavior* (Vol. 1). New York: Academic Press.

Horn, J.L., & Cattell, R.B. (1967). Redefinement and test of the theory of fluid and crystallized intelligences. *Journal of Educational Psychology, 57*, 268–270.

Horn, J.L., Donaldson, G., & Engstrom, R. (1981). Apprehension, memory, and fluid intelligence decline in adulthood. *Research on Aging, 3*, 33–84.

Hutchins, E. (1993). Learning to navigate. In S. Chaiklin & J. Lave (Eds.) *Understanding practice: Perspectives on activity and context. Learning in doing: Social, cognitive and computational perspectives* (pp. 35–63). New York: Cambridge University Press.

Inhelder, B., & Piaget, J. (1958). *The growth of logical thinking from childhood to adolescence*. New York: Basic Books.

Kaiser, M.K., McCloskey, M., & Proffitt, D.R. (1986). Development of intuitive theories of motion: Curvilinear motion in the absence of external forces. *Developmental Psychology, 22*, 67–71.

Kaiser, M.K., Proffitt, D.R., & McCloskey, M. (1985). The development of beliefs about falling objects. *Perception and Psychophysics, 38*, 533–539.

Karmiloff-Smith, A. (1992). *Beyond modularity: A developmental perspective on cognitive science*. Cambridge, MA: MIT Press.

Karmiloff-Smith, A., & Inhelder, B. (1975). If you want to get ahead, get a theory. *Cognition, 3*, 195–212.

Keating, D.P. (1980). Thinking process in adolescence. In J. Adelson (Ed.) *Handbook of adolescent psychology*. New York: Wiley.

Keating, D.P. (1990). Adolescent thinking. In S.S. Feldman & G.R. Elliott (Eds.) *At the threshold: The developing adolescent* (pp. 54–89). Cambridge, MA: Harvard University Press.

Keating, D.P., & Bobbitt, B.L. (1978). Individual and developmental differences in cognitive processing components of mental ability. *Child Development, 49*, 155–167.

Klahr, D., & Robinson, M. (1981). Formal assessment of problem-solving and planning processes in preschool children. *Cognitive Psychology, 13*, 113–148.

Kuhn, D. (1989). Children and adults as intuitive scientists. *Psychological Review, 96*, 674–689.

Kuhn, D., Amsel, E., & O'Loughlin, M. (1988). *The development of scientific thinking skills*. San Diego, CA: Academic Press.

Kuhn, D., Ho, V., & Adams, C. (1979). Formal reasoning among pre- and late adolescents. *Child Development, 50*, 1128–1135.

Kuhn, D., Langer, J., Kohlberg, L., & Haan, N. (1977). The development of formal operations in logical and moral judgment. *Genetic Psychology Monographs, 95*, 97–188.

Lee, K., Anzures, G., Quinn, P.C., Pascalis, O., & Slater, A. (in press). Development of face processing expertise. In A. Calder, G. Rhodes, J.V. Haxby, & M. Johnson (Eds.) *Handbook of face perception*. Oxford: Wiley-Blackwell.

Longeot, F. (1966). Expérimentation d'une échelle individuelle du développement de la pensée logique [Experimentation of an individual scale of logical thought development]. *BINOP, 22*, 306–319.

Luciana, M., Conklin, H.M., Hooper, C.J., & Yarger, R.S. (2005). The development of nonverbal working memory and executive control processes in adolescents. *Child Development, 76*, 697–712.

Lynn, R. (2009). Fluid intelligence but not vocabulary has increased in Britain, 1979–2008. *Intelligence, 37*, 249–255.

Miller, G.A. (1956). The magical number seven, plus or minus two: Some limits on our capacity for processing information. *Psychological Review, 63*, 81–97.

Miller, P.H., & Weiss, M.G. (1981). Children's attention allocation, understanding of attention, and performance on the incidental learning task. *Child Development, 52,* 1183–1190.

Mondloch, C.J., Le Grand, R., & Maurer, D. (2003). Early visual experience is necessary for the development of some – but not all – aspects of face processing. In O. Pascalis & A. Slater (Eds.) *The development of face processing in infancy and early childhood: Current perspectives* (pp. 99–117). New York: Nova Science Publishers.

Overton, W.F., Ward, S.L., Noveck, I.A., Black, J., & O'Brien, D.P. (1987). Form and content in the development of deductive reasoning. *Developmental Psychology, 23,* 22–30.

Rabbit, P. (2007). IQ – The meek approach is best. *The Psychologist, 20,* 532.

Rohwer, W.D., & Bean, J.P. (1973). Sentence-effects and noun-pair learning: A developmental interaction during adolescence. *Journal of Experimental Child Psychology, 15,* 521–533.

Ryan, C.M. (1990). Age-related improvement in short-term memory efficiency during adolescence. *Developmental Neuropsychology, 6,* 193–205.

Schauble, L. (1991). Belief revision in children: The role of prior knowledge and strategies for generating evidence. *Journal of Experimental Child Psychology, 49,* 31–57.

Schneider, W. (1985). Developmental trends in the metamemory–memory behavior relationship: An integrative review. In D.L. Forrest-Pressley, G.E. MacKinnon, & T.G. Waller (Eds.) *Metacognition, cognition, and human performance* (Vol. 1; pp. 57–109). Orlando, FL: Academic Press.

Schneider, W., & Pressley, M. (1997). *Memory development between two and twenty* (2nd edn). Mahwah, NJ: Erlbaum.

Siegler, R.S. (1976). Three aspects of cognitive development. *Cognitive Psychology, 8,* 481–520.

Siegler, R.S. (1981). *Developmental sequences within and between concepts.* Monographs of the Society for Research in Child Development, 46(2, Serial No. 189).

Siegler, R.S. (1983). Information processing approaches to cognitive development. In W. Kessen (Ed.) *Handbook of child psychology* (Vol. 1). New York: Wiley.

Siegler, R.S. (1993). *Children's thinking* (3rd edn). Englewood Cliffs, NJ: Prentice Hall.

Slater, A., Carrick, R., Bell, C., & Roberts, E. (1999). Can measures of infant information processing predict later intellectual ability? In A. Slater & D. Muir (Eds.) *The Blackwell reader in developmental psychology* (pp. 55–64). Oxford: Blackwell.

Small, M.Y. (1990). *Cognitive development.* Toronto: Harcourt Brace Jovanovich.

Sternberg, R.J., & Rifkin, B. (1979). The development of analogical reasoning processes. *Journal of Experimental Child Psychology, 27,* 195–232.

Stone, C.A., & Day, M.C. (1978). Levels of availability of a formal operational strategy. *Child Development, 49,* 1054–1065.

Wechsler, D. (1991). *Wechsler intelligence scale for children* (4th edn). San Antonio: The Psychological Corporation.

Wicherts, J.M., Borsboom, D., & Dolan, C.V. (2010). Why national IQs do not support evolutionary theories of intelligence. *Personality and Individual Differences, 48,* 91–96.

17 Social Development

WILLIAM M. BUKOWSKI, TANYA BERGEVIN,
AND RICHARD MINERS

KEY TERMS

authoritarian parenting • authoritative parenting • autonomy • cross-cultural study • defence
mechanisms • digital culture • epigenetic principle • field theory • indulgent parenting
• libidinal forces • life space • moratorium • neglectful parenting • ontogeny • parenting styles
• peers • phylogeny • primary drives • recapitulation • zeitgeist

CHAPTER OUTLINE

OVERVIEW

Recognising the multifaceted nature of adolescence, this chapter approaches the topic by reviewing the contrasting accounts of five major figures in the field, along with the research that has followed in their wake.

According to G. Stanley Hall, adolescence is a time of storm and stress, a form of second birth through which individuals make a transition from the primitive ways of childhood to the refined values of adulthood. Fascinating though this picture may be, the chapter points out that adolescence is not typically as stormy and stressful as he portrays it.

The claim of Kurt Lewin's field theory is that interactional forces existing between individual and environment can predict individual behaviour, and Lewin suggests that adolescent problems can be understood as conflicts between competing forces. Such conflicts arise during adolescence in particular because individuals are in transition between child and adult group membership.

Anna Freud takes a psychoanalytic approach to adolescence, claiming that the upheavals of adolescence result from the growing challenge to the ego presented by developing sexuality. The prediction is that the onset of puberty should see an increase in 'moody' behaviour. It turns out that there is little evidence for this. However, boys' relationships with parents suffer during puberty. The strongest evidence concerns timing of puberty: early puberty in girls and late puberty in boys is associated with problems and conflict.

Peter Blos saw adolescence as part of a series of psychosexual stages during which personality development was completed. According to this account, a key factor in adolescence concerns the balance between the growing need for independence and the maintenance of parental bonds. The authors show how parental style has much to do with the success of this transition.

The work of Harry Stack Sullivan focuses particularly on peer relationships. Sullivan argues that behaviour can only be understood as the result of interaction processes between self and others, claiming that psychological growth is driven by the need to satisfy interpersonal needs. In adolescence the need is for romantic relationships and friendships with peers.

Erik Erikson sees adolescence as a transition to adult identity during which the individual goes through a period in which they do not have a stable sense of identity. Consequently, they may adhere to a wide range of beliefs and ideologies. Thus according to Erikson, a major focus in adolescence is development toward a stable identity and self-concept.

In reviewing these accounts and the evidence that stems from them, the chapter provides a convincing case for the need to consider many different factors in explaining developmental processes during adolescence.

INTRODUCTION

Adolescence is a time of action and movement (Collins & Steinberg, 2006). Compared with the childhood period, adolescence is a time of 'newness' and change. These changes are seen in the person, the dyad, and the environment. Life's realities change and even become virtual and electronic. Social and personality development in adolescence is mutifaceted and dynamic. It involves several highly interrelated forms of development that involve a broad range of behaviours, feelings, thoughts, and health-related consequences. Compared to the school age period, the social domains in which adolescents participate are more numerous, more complex, more challenging, and potentially more exciting and dangerous. In these domains, adolescents think, feel, act, and interact with others in ways that are new to them. It can be a period of intense interest, excitement, achievement, and happiness. It can be a time of confusion, anxiety, sadness, and disruption. For many youngsters, adolescence represents a time of accomplishments, health, positive growth, and well-being; for others it is a time of insurmountable challenges that lead to an unsatisfying, troubled, and frustrating adulthood.

KEY CHARACTERISTICS OF DEVELOPMENT

What are the major characteristics of social and personality development in adolescence? Social development in adolescence has three central features. They are *growth*, *differentiation*, and *synthesis*. By *growth* we mean that adolescents develop new skills and concepts, experience new emotions, and begin to function in a larger number of social and personal domains. They display a wider repertoire of behaviours and experience a significant broadening of their social worlds. Certainly, some of the most pronounced forms of growth in adolescence are the quantitative and qualitative physical changes that result from puberty. Of the transformations that occur during adolescence, many are characterised by *differentiation*. That is, one's range of activities, behaviours, skills, ideas, social contacts, and emotions becomes broader, or more different, during adolescence than in childhood. Moreover, the differences, or variability, between individuals become larger as individual adolescents set off on their own developmental trajectories. As the range of an adolescent's behaviour, thoughts, and experiences becomes larger and more complex, the adolescent is confronted with the challenge of bringing this diversity together. That is, adolescents need to *synthesise* this 'newness' into a comprehensible and coherent approach to the world. Adolescents who can bring these new experiences and challenges together are likely to be on a trajectory toward a healthy and rewarding adulthood, whereas failing to do so may add to the challenges of becoming an adult.

Just as there are central features to adolescent development, there are also central goals or challenges that adolescents need to address. By the time they are ready to enter adulthood, adolescents should (1) be *autonomous* and *emotionally regulated*; (2) have a *sense of their identity*; and (3) be *able to form close relationships* with both same- and other-sex **peers**. These developments occur within five types of domains. They are the *social environment*, *puberty*, the *family*, the *peer group*, and the *self*. Separate sections of this chapter are devoted to each of these domains. Within each section, we use the intellectual biographies of the pioneering theorists to introduce the important issues of adolescent development. Their ideas provide the conceptual groundwork for our discussion of current research on adolescent social development.

Before we begin this discussion it should be stated that one cannot understand social development in adolescence without understanding parallels in cognitive development during this time. It comes as little surprise that many of the ways in which adolescents come to think about themselves and others, about the way they behave, and about the emotions they experience can be traced to changes in cognition. It is likely also that experiences with parents and peers can challenge adolescents to think in new ways. Certainly, one cannot think about social and cognitive development as independent of each other.

We begin our discussion of social development in adolescence by considering an idea that has formed the foundation for the study of adolescence, proposed first by G. Stanley Hall. It is the idea that adolescence represents a period of storm and stress. We explain this idea and then evaluate it according to the data that are currently available. Following this we discuss the changes in the social domains in which adolescents function. To begin this discussion, we present the ideas of Kurt Lewin (see Smith, 2009). We then discuss the question of how puberty affects the behaviour and emotions of adolescents. This section is introduced with a discussion of the ideas of Anna Freud. Next, we focus on adolescent development within the family. The ideas of Peter Blos serve as the point of departure for this discussion. We next consider the peer system during adolescence, using the ideas of Harry Stack Sullivan as the foundation for this discussion. The last domain we consider is the self. Here we rely heavily on the ideas of Erik Erikson and his concept of identity.

G. STANLEY HALL: ADOLESCENCE AS STORM AND STRESS

If any idea has dominated the study of adolescent development, it is G. Stanley Hall's pronouncement that adolescence is a time of storm and stress. According to this theory, human development is sequenced according to an evolutionary timeline. That is, each individual retraces the historical record of their species development (**phylogeny**) in their own growth (**ontogeny**) (Grinder, 1969, p. 357). Hence, according to Hall, ontogeny **recapitulates** phylogeny. Based on the notion that human development runs through the successive stages through which the human species has passed (Averill, 1982), Hall argued that normal human development follows a progression from animal-like dispositions to 'civilised' higher-order functioning described as the 'attainment of a superior mode or social existence or way of life' (White, 1992, p. 31). Believed to be mediated by biology, Hall argued that recapitulation occurs by virtue of the fact that more primitive areas of the brain mature before the ones that appeared more recently in our evolutionary past (White, 1992).

phylogeny the evolutionary growth and development of a species.

ontogeny the personal growth of an individual living being from conception.

recapitulation the process of repeating again. The expression 'ontogeny recapitulates *phylogeny*' refers to the repetition of evolutionary stages in the growth of the foetus and young mammal.

Adolescence as a second birth

Hall depicts adolescence as the developmental period in which evolutionary momentum begins to subside – in which recapitulatory instincts, so important during childhood, begin to give way for new acquired characters to develop. It is in this capacity that adolescence is perceived as a second 'birth', a second point of initiation and socialisation in which individuals struggle to shed their primitive ways. He portrayed adolescence as a turbulent time of transition between what is coarse and what is refined – a struggle between behavioural patterns of opposing poles. In the words of White (1992, p. 31), Hall viewed adolescence as 'a time of oscillation and oppositions between inertness and excitement, pleasure and pain, self-confidence and humility, selfishness and altruism, society and solitude'. Given the proper educational influences and environment, it is during this crucial period that ontogeny can begin to surpass phylogeny and, as a result, the personality and intellect of the adolescent begin to blossom. The role of educators becomes to stimulate, nurture, guide, and prevent the arrest of social intellectual growth (Grinder, 1969); in brief, to foster adolescents' increased preparedness for selflessness, sacrifice, religion, and the appreciation of nature and science.

Criticism of Hall's account

Hall's notion that storm and stress are the central features of adolescence was at one time largely accepted as truth. More recently, however, empirical scrutiny of this concept has questioned its validity. This research, summarised by Arnett (1999), shows that although adults typically perceive adolescence as a time of upheaval and disorder, the actual occurrence of storm and stress in adolescence has been largely exaggerated. Together, studies of family relations and changes in emotion over time have failed to provide much support for the argument that adolescence is a universally difficult and disruptive period of the lifespan. As Arnett shows, however, although adolescence is not a universally stressful period, the evidence indicates that storm and stress are more likely during adolescence than at other times of the lifespan. Nevertheless, these characteristics are not necessarily characteristic of all adolescents. Whereas adolescence can be stressful for some youngsters, it is not so for all of them. Most of the discussion in this chapter will be oriented toward this modified storm and stress view of adolescence.

THE ADOLESCENT SOCIAL ENVIRONMENT: KURT LEWIN

Before considering further ideas about adolescent development and the empirical evidence related to these concepts, it may be useful to ask, 'What do adolescents do?' A conceptual basis to this question can be found in the work of Kurt Lewin. Inspired by the gestalt school of thought, Lewin was a German social scientist who rejected the common **zeitgeist** that psychological phenomena such as needs, hopes, and fears were beyond experimental reach. He challenged traditional thinking and methodologies by manipulating the intangible and doing what all contemporary psychologists aspire to do – to understand and predict 'molar behaviour patterns from information about the person (needs, motives) and about the situation (its opportunities, goal objects)' (Kelley, 1991, p. 211).

zeitgeist the thinking or feelings peculiar to a generation or period – as in 'the prevailing Zeitgeist' or 'the spirit of the age.'

Field theory

Lewin's ideas were expressed as a coherent set of concepts known as **field theory**. Field theory, undoubtedly Lewin's most famous contribution, rests on the assumption that behaviour (B) is a function (F) of an interaction between a person (P) and that person's environment (E), thus, expressed mathematically, $B = F (P,E)$. Stated somewhat differently, behaviour can be predicted by the interactional forces between the individual and their environment. The Lewinian environment, or field, 'is a perceptual or psychological environment' that has certain structural and dynamic properties (M.A. Lewin, 1998, p. 105). The structure of the environment is made up of regions that correspond roughly to physical areas and objects (the home), social entities (family, religious affiliations), and even concepts such as abstract art and morality. Regions are defined by boundaries that may separate them sharply, for example, 'religious affiliation may have nothing to do with abstract art' (M.A. Lewin, 1998, p. 106). On the other hand, boundaries may overlap – religious affiliation and morality may be deeply interdependent. Regions within the field have attracting or repelling properties, respectively known as positive or negative valences. It is these valences that orient and propel an individual into movement within the field. A person's movement toward or away from a valenced region is called *locomotion*. Lewinian theory suggests that conflicts arise when (1) different goals compete for the individual's locomotion, and (2) when goals carry both positive and negative valences. For example, being offered a highly desired job (positive valence) that involves long-term separation from loved ones (negative valence) may foster feelings of conflict within the individual.

field theory Lewin's theory that behaviour results from the interaction between a person and that person's environment.

The concept of life space

The person, like the environment, is also divided into regions that are separated by more or less permeable boundaries which correspond to the individual's characteristics, needs, and perceptions of the environment (M.A. Lewin, 1998). The number of regions within the person speaks to the complexity of the individual and the 'permeability of boundaries reflect the degree to which the different regions communicate with one another' (M.A. Lewin, 1998, p. 107). The activation of a region (i.e. when a person tries to solve a problem) puts that region under tension. This tension can alter the boundaries, paths, valences, and goals of the particular region. Thus, the make-up of the person and environment are ever-changing, creating the dynamic

life space a person's environment can be divided into regions corresponding to the individual's characteristics, needs, and perceptions of the environment. The person and the environment represent inseparable constructs, which together constitute the life space.

life space. One's life space, expressed as B = F (life space), represents the dynamic interchange between person and environment (M.A. Lewin, 1998). In sum, the person and the environment represent inseparable constructs, which together constitute the life space.

The development of life space

As a person matures, they become increasingly differentiated: 'regions become more numerous and the boundaries between them become less permeable' (M.A. Lewin, 1998, p. 108). During adolescence, change is characterised by increased locomotion from one region to another. Increased locomotion promotes, and is promoted by, the widening of the life space (new geographical and social regions), and the entry into new situations that are 'cognitively unstructured' (K. Lewin, 1939/1953, p. 41). More specifically, adolescents find themselves in a social position between that of the child and that of the adult, which, according to the author, can be paralleled to that of a marginal member of an underprivileged minority group. This transient shift in group belongingness, or locomotion within the field, is what alters and shapes the adolescent's behaviour. Because the move is toward an unknown region, behavioural uncertainty likely ensues. The adolescent may experience emotional instability and sensitivity. Moreover, they may be prone to unbalances in behaviour, 'to either boisterousness or shyness, exhibiting too much tension, and a frequent shift between extremes of contradictory behavior' (1939/1953, p. 40).

Besides locomotion toward cognitively unstructured regions, Lewin also describes how once familiar regions also change during adolescence. For example, body change (i.e. puberty) and new physical experiences are also highlighted as 'a baffling change of a central region of the established life space' (Lewin, 1939/1953, p. 41). These factors are also pivotal in predicting adolescent behaviour. Based on these changes in the life space (through locomotion, and changes that occur in once familiar central regions), Lewin predicts that adolescents are susceptible to specific behavioural patterns. Because they are uncertain in which group they belong, and because of the instability of their position, they experience conflict due to competing goals which relate to attitudes, values, ideologies, and styles of living. These conflicts in turn give rise to emotional tension (i.e. as exhibited by shyness, sensitivity, and aggression). Moreover, the adolescent is expected to display a 'readiness to take extreme attitudes and actions and to shift his/her position radically' (Lewin, 1939/1953, p. 41). Finally, field theory predicts that the 'adolescent profile' should appear in anyone (adolescent or otherwise) who is experiencing some of the transitional phenomena noted above. In brief, the degree of any particular type of behaviour should depend upon the degree of recognition and awareness of the nature of the field, and upon the strength of the conflicting forces within the field.

What do adolescents do?

Certainly, many activities occupy adolescents' time. Some of these activities are mandatory or necessary in nature, others are leisurely or recreational (Flammer et al., 1999). Vazsonyi et al. (2002) studied 7000 15–19-year-old adolescents in Hungary, the Netherlands, Switzerland, and the United States. The majority of these adolescents spent most of their time in solitary activities – studying, reading, exercising – followed by interacting with peers, taking part in community/sports activities, and family activities. They reported differences between countries. Hungarian youth spent a much greater amount of time with the family than did adolescents from the other countries whereas Dutch adolescents spent far more time in solitary activities than adolescents from other countries. In adolescence, time allocation strategies may reflect social-cognitive development, and highlight the context in which developmental tasks are achieved.

Time allocation patterns

Building from the premise that within a 24-hour period investment in any one activity takes time away from any other, Bruno (1996) suggests that individuals' time-investment patterns are organised according to personal lifestyle goals which determine how time is spent. Time allocation patterns, thus, may provide insight into individuals' value systems and life goals. In adolescence, time allocation strategies may reflect social-cognitive development, and highlight the context in which developmental tasks are achieved. For example, it is proposed that leisure activities provide adolescents with the opportunity to develop **autonomy** and strengthen their sense of self (Gibbons *et al.*, 1997; Gordon & Caltabiano, 1996). Moreover, by alleviating boredom and increasing adolescents' feelings of well-being, socially accepted leisure activities may operate as deterrents to antisocial activities such as drug use and delinquency (Iso-Ahola & Crowley, 1991). As such, what adolescents do with their time, especially their free time, may have important developmental consequences (Bassi & Delle Fave, 2006; Bruno, 1996).

> **autonomy** being in complete control of one's life.

Gender differences in time allocation

Using time allocation surveys, Bruno (1996) studied adolescent time usage by dividing a 24-hour span into four categories: (1) outer-directed time: the time allocated to achieving external goals such as career/academic pursuits, financial or status-related gains; (2) other-people-directed time: the time allocated to enhancing popularity with others and to developing close relationships; (3) inner-directed time: time allocated to self-development via hobbies, sports, creative expressions, and special interests; and (4) non-directed time: passive or 'relaxation'-driven time allocated for entertainment purposes (e.g. television). Results reveal that, at least in 1996, American adolescent boys spent most of their time in outer-directed activities (35%), followed by other-directed (27%), inner-directed (23%), and finally in non-directed activities (14%). Although the net ranking of time allocation practices was similar for girls, the distribution of time varied as a function of gender. In other words, although girls spent most of their time pursuing outer-directed activities (36%), followed by other-directed (32%), inner-directed (20%), and non-directed activities (9%), they showed a preference for other-directed activities and less inclination toward non-directed activities relative to boys. Thus, girls allocate more time for social relationships compared to boys, whereas boys invest more time in passive entertainment relative to girls. Interestingly, time allocation patterns also varied for adolescents deemed at risk for negative outcomes (e.g. dropping out of school). At-risk adolescents showed the least preference for outer-directed (achievement) activities, and the greatest preferences for other-directed (social) and non-directed activities (passive entertainment).

Cross-cultural comparisons of time allocation

More recently, international **cross-cultural** studies were conducted to gauge the specific activities pursued by adolescents. For example, Alsaker & Flammer (1999) studied how much time adolescents from 13 different cultures allocated to necessary activities such as sleeping, body-care, eating, travelling to school, school attendance, homework, chores, and shopping (a daily errand in many European countries). Results revealed that necessary activities take up an average of 18.90 hours per day, with French adolescents reporting the most time allocated to necessary activities and the Norwegians the least. Using the same sample of participants, Flammer *et al.* (1999) studied the allocation of free time according to seven leisure activities: playing music, leisure reading, sports activities, watching television, hanging around with friends, dating, or working for extra money (an activity considered non-necessary in the present context). Results showed an average of 4.42 leisure hours a day, with Norwegian adolescents reporting the most time invested in leisure, and the French the least. Watching television was the most popular leisure activity in all countries investigated, with Bulgarians watching the most and the French watching the least.

Factors influencing use of free time

Many factors can influence how adolescents spend their free time, such as (1) age, (2) gender, (3) race, (4) geographical, and (5) individual characteristics (Eccles *et al.*, 2003; Larson & Verma, 1999). As adolescents grow, for example, it is well documented that their interests change. For example, older adolescents spend more time with their friends and more time pursuing romantic relationships then do younger adolescents. As for gender differences, research suggests that males and females who adhere to traditional gender roles differed in their leisure preferences during adolescence (Colley *et al.*, 1996). For example, whereas females reported participating in non-competitive sports (i.e. swimming), social activities (i.e. going to parties, to dance clubs), and home-based activities (i.e. watching television), males reported greater participation in more competitive sports (i.e. soccer, rugby), and computer-based activities. Moreover, Gibbons *et al.* (1997) investigated gender-differences in adolescents from Cyprus, India, the Netherlands, and the United States. According to the authors,

FIGURE 17.1 *White adolescents are more likely to value activities such as going on camping trips than are black teens.*
Source: Shutterstock.

boys participated in more group-oriented activities, and, with the exception of Cyprus, participated in more sports. Peer groups shape the leisure activities in which its members take part. Based on a Canadian sample of adolescents, research reveals that girls' peers influence their leisure choices more strongly than do boys (Shaw et al., 1996). It seems that girls feel more pressure to orient their activities to be in synch with their friends.

Evidence also suggests that different racial and ethnic groups, namely black and white youth, come to value different leisure activities (Philipp, 1998). Black teens are more likely to value activities such as basketball, going to the mall, and dancing relative to white teens. White adolescents, on the other hand, are more likely to value activities like soccer, horseback riding, and going on camping trips (Figure 17.1) than are black teens. However, important group similarities also emerged in this study. For example, black and white youth valued watching television, reading for pleasure, visiting museums, and playing a musical instrument to similar degrees. Interestingly, black adolescents showed fewer gender differences than whites on the examined leisure activities (Philipp, 1998).

In addition to variables of age, gender, and race, geographic location can also shape the types of leisure activities pursued by adolescents. Drawing from an Australian sample, teens from rural areas have been found to engage in more sports and passive forms of leisure (e.g. watching television) than urban-dwelling adolescents (Gordon & Caltabiano, 1996). On the other hand, adolescents in urban centres were more likely to engage in more social forms of leisure such as going out to cinemas and nightclubs. Perhaps because they have fewer resources at their disposition, rural youth report more leisure boredom than do those living in urban centres. This is important because leisure boredom has been associated with substance use (Gordon & Caltabiano, 1996) and delinquency (Iso-Ahola & Crowley, 1991). It has been suggested that unless leisure is optimally arousing it is experienced as boredom (Iso-Ahola, 1980), and that this boredom, paired with other factors such as low self-esteem, heightens adolescents' risk for negative outcomes.

Digital culture and youth

The current daily lives of youth from around the world are spent in spaces of **digital culture** that did not exist 10 years ago. Prominent fixtures in the daily reality for many adolescents include online social networking sites for self-presentation and to learn about others, immediate video contact systems to have visual and auditory contact with a friend regardless of where they are, online gaming, and electronic devices such as iPods and iPads, and powerful mobile phones (Figure 17.2). They have vastly altered the way that teens interact with each other, how they show themselves off to their peers, how they learn about others, and how they establish connections with them. How this new way of functioning and spending time will affect the processes of 'coming of age' for adolescents struggling for autonomy and identity as did their predecessors is not yet clear. We know only that they are dealing with these developmental challenges in a world that provides new contexts for communication, relationships, exploration, self-expression and adventure (see Ito et al., 2008).

> **digital culture** online social networking sites, immediate video contact systems, online gaming, and electronic devices such as iPods and iPads, and mobile phones.

Now that we have seen how adolescents spend their time, we will shift our attention to the central question: What are the major events of adolescent

FIGURE 17.2 *Online social networking sites, iPods and mobile phones, amongst others, have become prominent fixtures in the daily reality for many adolescents.*
Source: Shutterstock.

development? As we noted above, we will use the biographies of major theorists as a means of explaining the hallmark ideas about adolescence. Following these discussions we will consider the empirical evidence taken from scientific studies of these theoretical positions. Our discussion begins with the ideas of Anna Freud, Sigmund Freud's youngest child, and Peter Blos. They propose that the central event of adolescence is puberty and that various developmental changes in personality and family relations result from pubertal maturation.

PUBERTY AND PSYCHOLOGICAL DEVELOPMENT: THE WORK OF ANNA FREUD

Anna, the youngest of Martha and Sigmund Freud's six children, was born in Vienna on 3 December 1895, the same year that her father's *Studies on Hysteria* marked the beginning of the history of psychoanalysis. Sharing her birth year with psychoanalysis, Anna grew up to perceive it as a 'sibling' that sparked her interest in understanding the human mind, its socialisation, and its development. Anna, together with her close friend Dorothy Burlingham, acted upon her belief that an appropriate mix of education and psychoanalysis 'promised to create happier children, and thus, a happier world,' a perspective that formed the basis of their close professional and personal relationship over the course of their lifetime (Henrik Peters, 1985). In 1927, the two women launched a small school which adhered to analytic principles. Its wide curriculum, designed to foster children's imagination, was implemented with help from Peter Blos and Erik Erikson, both of whom would later become leading analysts in post-war America. Anna's observation of children in her capacity as teacher, analyst, and mentor was meticulously recorded during these years. These observations would later serve as the foundation for her most celebrated work, *The Ego and the Mechanisms of Defence*, published in 1936.

The ego, defence mechanisms, and libidinal forces

Anna Freud's interest in psychoanalysis revolved around the processes of the ego, which is the part of the psyche concerned with 'directing action, coping with the external world and integrating competing urges within the self' (Stevens, 1983, p. 1). According to her, understanding **defence mechanisms** – designed to protect the ego from noxious thoughts and feelings associated with the **primary drives** – not only provides insight into basic human motivation, but also allows the analyst to assess varying degrees of psychological adjustment. By investigating how individuals guard themselves against their primary instincts, ego maturity and ego integrity can be assessed, allowing the analyst to better understand normative and pathological occurrences. According to Anna Freud, synchronising the biological with the social environmental represents the analyst's true challenge. As reported by Mayes and Cohen (1996), Anna Freud adhered to the notion that biology, through socialisation, becomes psychology, and it is on this level of psychology that appropriate interventions can restore healthy development. Anna Freud felt it ironic that psychoanalysts, who attribute much importance to the development of sexuality in shaping personality, would to a large extent neglect to discuss adolescence, the period of burgeoning genital sexuality (Henrik Peters, 1985). She described adolescence, or more specifically puberty, as a time of severe psychological upheaval. Using analogies of war and battle, she characterised the onset of puberty as a time of libidinal 'invasion.' As **libidinal forces** surge, instinctual pulls become stronger and the integrity of the ego is threatened. It is this disharmony between developmental lines which can make adolescence a time of opposition and paradox.

> **defence mechanism** in Freud's theory, if an individual's rational thought (*ego*) is threatened by their basic desires (*id*) or their conscience (*superego*), then various defence mechanisms are available which mean that, for the short term, the individual does not have to deal with the internal conflict.

> **libidinal forces** sexual desires. Freud thought these were under the control of the *id*.

These developmental challenges of adolescence may lead to a temporary breakdown in ego controls. As a result, the adolescent may become more crude, less 'sophisticated', as well as more primitively aggressive and narcissistic (Kaplan, 1996). According to Anna Freud, these features are an expression of issues surrounding the Oedipal conflict that were not entirely resolved. For this reason, adolescents may find themselves turning away from parents to focus on new 'love objects' to cherish and admire, such as celebrities who become elevated to hero status. Interestingly, Anna Freud pointed out that these heroes are often at an intermediate age between that of the individual and that of their parents (Sayers, 1997).

Clearly, for Anna Freud, adolescence is characterised as a period of ego struggle as a result of the challenges presented by new energies that emerge during puberty, a period where the ego must grow, develop, and adapt to meet the increasing demands of drive regulation. In other words, adolescence is a time when the ego must mature and become more sophisticated at defending itself. Anna Freud contended that the most common defences during adolescence are asceticism (the severe denial of anything *id*), intellectualisation, and identification.

The role of pubertal development

If Anna Freud is right, we should notice drastic changes in personality and behaviour at the time of puberty. So far, the empirical literature has failed to provide much support for this hypothesis. In regard to emotional states, although it may be the case that adolescents are more moody than are children or adults (Csikszentmihalyi & Larson, 1984), mood fluctuations appear to be only modestly related to pubertal changes. How do we know this? We know this from studies that have tracked mood in adolescents on a daily basis and have examined whether mood changes more at the time of pubertal changes than at other times. In a review of this literature, Buchanan et al. (1992) concluded that there may be some increases in variability in mood or in behaviour during the earliest stages of puberty. Otherwise, however, there is little evidence to support the view that puberty per se is related to emotional or behavioural changes.

Another area of research, however, has shown an association between puberty and adolescents' interactions with their parents. Steinberg (1981) followed a group of boys over a period of one year during early adolescence. He kept track of their pubertal development and observed their interactions with their parents. He reported that as these adolescent boys reached the midpoint or height of their pubertal changes, they showed less warmth and more conflict in their interaction with their mothers, while patterns of family interaction became more rigid. These patterns became less pronounced as these boys moved toward the end of puberty.

These findings were replicated in a second study by Steinberg (1987). Using reports from adolescents and their parents, Steinberg found that pubertal maturation was associated with increased emotional distance between adolescents and their parents, and with increased conflict with their mothers. Other studies have shown equally unsupportive findings. Ruble and Brooks-Gunn (1982), for example, reported that menarche was rarely associated with any sort of upheaval for adolescent girls.

Nevertheless, there is much evidence that the timing of puberty, rather than puberty itself, is associated with behavioural changes in adolescence. In general, empirical studies have shown that early puberty in girls and late puberty in boys is associated with problematic indices during adolescence. For example, Savin-Williams and Small (1986) showed that according to parent reports, early puberty in girls led to greater conflict with mothers and fathers, and that there was more stress in the parent–child relationship when puberty was early in girls and late in boys. These findings confirmed earlier reports (Jones, 1957, 1965) that early-maturing boys were more socially poised, more popular, and more likely to be looked up to by their peers, whereas late-maturing boys were seen as unpopular, childish, and more likely to feel incompetent and inadequate. In this same study, early-maturing girls, relative to late-maturing girls, were observed to be lacking in poise and a sense of competence and were more likely to be withdrawn and reserved. Late-maturing girls were seen as being socially skilled, emotionally competent, and well liked. It should be pointed out also that more recent findings have shown that early-maturing girls, relative to girls of their age who mature on time, are at greater risk for psychiatric disturbances (Hayward et al., 2000). Clearly, the timing of puberty matters, but it appears to matter differently for boys and for girls.

These differences between boys and girls may reflect the fact that puberty typically happens earlier for girls than for boys. Therefore, girls who enter puberty early relative to other girls are typically far ahead of virtually all boys. Likewise, boys who enter puberty late are far behind most boys and behind almost all girls. These two sets of adolescents, early-maturing girls and late-maturing boys, are those who are clearly most out of step with their peers. These findings point to the necessity of understanding a biological form of development within a social context. Indeed, the effects of puberty appear to depend on when puberty happens.

There is evidence also that experience within the family can be an antecedent to pubertal development. A study that used a longitudinal design to follow 756 children from childhood into adolescence assessed whether rearing experiences would predict pubertal timing (Belsky *et al.*, 2007). Puberty was assessed with repeated physical measurement starting in late childhood. Measures of parenting, including measures of negative parenting, such as harsh control, had been made on each participant in the study throughout childhood. Their findings showed that for the girls the negative measures of parenting lead to earlier menarche even after the effects of other factors (e.g. age of maternal menarche) had been accounted for. These findings suggest that, in the case of girls, negatively arousing experiences may accelerate the process of entering adolescence and attaining full physical and sexual maturity.

Clearly, more evidence is needed for us to conduct a full evaluation of the validity of Anna Freud's ideas about puberty and psychological development. The current data, however, certainly fail to reveal any general upheaval related to puberty per se. Although research related directly to Anna Freud's ideas is very limited, there exists much more support for related lines of thinking, namely, those proposed by another psychoanalytic theorist, Peter Blos. His ideas are explained in the next section.

THE FAMILY AND ADOLESCENCE: THE WORK OF PETER BLOS

Peter Blos was a psychoanalytically oriented psychiatrist who was particularly interested in adolescence. Blos believed that human development occurred as a result of transitions through sequentially ordered **psychosexual stages** (see Chapter 2). More specifically, he supported the notion that healthy development depended on the successful completion of the psychological tasks associated with each psychosexual stage. Unlike Freud, however, Blos did not believe that personality formation was primarily achieved by early childhood. Instead, he contended that later stages of development, namely, the stages associated with adolescence, played a critical role in mediating adult personality formation. Blos defined adolescence as 'the sum total of accommodations to the condition of puberty' (Blos, 1972, p. 56). He conceptualised adolescence not as a unitary developmental stage but as a series of stages 'defined in terms of drive and ego positions, as well as in terms of phase-specific conflicts and their resolutions' (Blos, 1972, p. 55).

Independence versus maintaining parental bonds

During early adolescence individuals experience a basic struggle between reconciling a desire to break free of parental bonds while still wishing to maintain a certain dependency on parents. It is this essential conflict that leads to so many contradictions in adolescence, such as the observation that adolescent development and 'progression' seem to detour via a series of regressions (Blos, 1972). Early adolescence, according to Blos, is characterised by the reactivation of infantile (i.e. more primitive) desires and ego skills. For example, a boy's successful negotiation of the latency stage (see Chapter 2), in which the ego is distanced from the id, resulting in increased self-awareness and emotional control, seems to 'fall into shambles at the onset of puberty' (Blos, 1972, p. 58). The young adolescent male tends to manifest 'oral greed, smuttiness, oblivion to unkemptness and uncleanliness, motoric restlessness, and experimentation in every direction' (p. 58). Blos contended that boys' regressions are more obvious, concrete, and action oriented than girls', whose regressive tendencies assert themselves more peripherally and secretly (p. 59). Perhaps Blos implied that whereas boys exhibit their regression within public forums, girls' regressions manifest themselves within the private realm of their relationships.

According to Blos, in order to proceed into the stage of adolescence proper, young adolescents or preadolescents need to undergo a second individuation process much like the individuation that took place from mother in early childhood. This second individuation, according to Blos, represents the major developmental challenge during early adolescence. If successfully accomplished, the Oedipal conflict should once again dominate in terms of drive progression, and, concomitantly, push the ego forward in terms of higher levels of differentiation. Stated differently, the process of the second individuation is thought to promote character formation and 'lend enduring and irreversible structures to the adolescent personality' (Blos, 1972, p. 62).

According to Blos, maladjustment occurs when the phase-specific developmental tasks are not completed, or are sidestepped altogether. Thus, accomplishing the psychological tasks central at one stage of development is crucial for successfully negotiating those associated with subsequent stages. As such, Blos warns against hastening normal developmental periods. Although preadolescents may be undergoing pubertal changes at increasingly younger ages (Blos, 1972), biology should not be followed blindly. The postpubescent 13-year-old remains psychologically a preadolescent, not an adult. Blos recommended environmental changes that would prolong the developmental stages associated with childhood and adolescence, and went so far as to claim that this would enhance not only psychological health, but the capacity for complex cognitive functions (Blos, 1972).

Acquisition of autonomy

The question of how adolescents achieve a sense of *autonomy* from their parents has been examined in several studies. An important point of these studies is that the process of achieving autonomy in adolescence is not a process of separating but is instead one of reorganising or transforming relationships within the family (Smetana *et al.*, 2006). Indeed, as Steinberg (1990) has shown, most families that include an adolescent get along quite well. In this respect, although the research on adolescent family relations shows that families do go through some changes during adolescence, it would be difficult to describe these changes as a form of separation. Steinberg and Silverberg (1986), in a study of early adolescence, showed that from 10 to 14 years of age, adolescents showed three important changes related to autonomy. First, they felt a greater sense of individuation. This means that as they grow older, they become more aware of who they are and are more likely to take responsibility for their own behaviours. Second, with age, young people begin to deidealise their parents. That is, they recognise that their parents could have flaws like other human beings. Third, older adolescents were less likely to feel dependent on their parents. It is important to recognise, though, that this is not simply a process of separation. As Ryan and Lynch (1989) showed, adolescents who are emotionally autonomous but who are distant from their parents show lower levels of psychological adjustment than do adolescents who are autonomous but have close relations with their parents. More recently, a longitudinal study that followed over 200 American youth from age 9 to age 20 showed that decision-making autonomy increased gradually across middle childhood and adolescence before rising sharply in late adolescence (Wray-Lake *et al.*, 2010).

The effects of parental style

Adolescents' ability to become autonomous appears to be related to the kind of family environment that is present in their homes. Of the many ways to characterise parents' behaviour toward their children, Diana Baumrind's (1978, 2005) theoretical framework has been among the most useful. According to her work, there are two critical dimensions of parents' behaviour toward their children: *parental responsiveness* and *parental demandingness* (Maccoby & Martin, 1983). Parental responsiveness refers to the extent to which parents respond to the needs of the child in a supportive and accepting manner. Parental demandingness points to the degree to which parents expect mature, responsible behaviour from their adolescents. Furthermore, the degree to which parents are responsive and demanding varies from one family to the next. Some parents are very demanding of their children, yet offer little in the way of responsiveness and warmth. In other families, parents may be unresponsive and rejecting, and expect very little of their children.

Different parenting styles

As a result of parental responsiveness and parental demandingness being largely independent dimensions of parenting, it is possible to look at combinations of these dimensions. Because parents' levels of both responsiveness and demandingness may be characterised as either high or low, four possible combinations of these two dimensions are possible. These particular combinations, labelled **parenting styles** by Baumrind (1978), are known as *authoritative, authoritarian, indulgent*, and *neglectful*.

parenting styles different ways of child rearing.

FIGURE 17.3 *When dealing with matters of discipline, authoritative parents engage their children in dialogue in a rational, issue-oriented manner.*

Source: Shutterstock.

authoritative parenting parents who are high on responsiveness and demandingness, and set clear standards of behaviour for their children. These parents are considered warm and responsive to the needs of their children.

authoritarian parenting parents who are high on demandingness and low on responsiveness. They value obedience as a virtue and favour punitive, forceful means to curb the self-will of their offspring.

indulgent parenting parents who are high on responsiveness, but low on demandingness. They interact with their children in a benign and passive manner and avoid the use of power when dealing with matters of discipline.

Authoritative parents are high on responsiveness and demandingness. They value both expressive and instrumental attributes (e.g. autonomous self-will and discipline conformity), yet they assume the ultimate responsibility for their children's behaviour. They are cognisant of their own rights and also recognise their children's interests and idiosyncratic ways. Further, these parents set clear standards of behaviour for their children which take into account the child's developing capabilities and needs. They guide their children's activities firmly and consistently and require them to participate in family functioning by helping out with household chores. When dealing with matters of discipline, authoritative parents engage their children in dialogue in a rational, issue-oriented manner (Figure 17.3). Moreover, these parents are considered warm and responsive to the needs of their children. They are affectively responsive by being loving, committed, and supportive, and cognitively responsive in the sense that they provide a stimulating and challenging home environment.

Authoritarian parents are high on demandingness and low on responsiveness. They value obedience as a virtue and favour punitive, forceful means (e.g. the coercive use of power) to curb the self-will of their offspring. They attempt to shape, control, and evaluate the behaviour and attitudes of the child in accordance with a set of absolute standards of conduct. Authoritarian parents attempt to inculcate conventional values such as work, respect for authority, and the preservation of order and traditional structure. Because these parents believe that their children should accept their rules and expectations without question, they do not encourage verbal give-and-take of discipline-related issues. They do not foster their children's autonomy, but rather try to restrict independent behaviour.

Indulgent (permissive) parents are high on responsiveness but low on demandingness. They interact with their children in a more benign and passive manner and avoid the use of power when dealing with matters of discipline. They view themselves as resources available to their children, which the children may or may not choose to use. Indulgent parents are likely to view discipline as an infringement upon the freedom of their offspring, which may impinge upon their healthy development. Consequently, these parents attempt to behave in a non-punitive, accepting, and affirmative manner toward their children's impulses, desires, and actions. In summary, they make few maturity demands on the children's behaviour and allow them a high degree of autonomy.

Neglectful (indifferent) parents are low on responsiveness and demandingness. They try to minimise the amount of time and energy required to raise their children. They know little about their children's lives, interact little with them, and do not include them in making decisions that affect the family. Whereas parents of the other types show concern for their children and espouse a set of beliefs oriented toward their healthy development, neglectful parents' concerns are primarily parent-centred. That is, they structure their home lives around their own needs and interests.

neglectful parenting
parents who are low on responsiveness and demandingness. They try to minimise the amount of time and energy required to raise their children.

What makes the categorisations proposed by Baumrind (1978) important? First, parenting style has been found to be associated with a number of markers of psychosocial development. One of the more prominent of these markers is social competence. Children from authoritative homes have been found to be more socially competent than their peers raised in authoritarian, indulgent, or neglectful environments (Baumrind, 1978). In addition to their more developed social skills, children from authoritative households are more self-reliant, self-controlled, responsible, creative, intellectually curious, adaptive, and successful in school. In contrast, children from authoritarian households are less socially skilled, less self-assured and curious, and more dependent and passive. Children from indulgent homes are less mature, less responsible, more easily influenced by their peers, and less able to take on leadership roles. Those from neglectful homes are often impulsive and more likely to be involved in delinquent behaviours such as precocious experimentation with sex, alcohol, and drugs (Baumrind, 1967; Fuligni & Eccles, 1993; Lamborn et al., 1991; Steinberg et al., 1994). And while exceptions to these widely applicable patterns do exist, the majority of studies indicate that authoritative parenting is strongly linked with healthy adolescent development for a wide range of ethnicities and socioeconomic backgrounds (Maccoby & Martin, 1983; Lamborn et al., 1991).

Why does authoritative parenting work so well?

In an effort to understand why authoritative parenting leads to more healthy development and adaptation among adolescents, researchers have attempted to tease apart the main elements of this parenting style (Steinberg, 1990). Consensus among the majority of researchers indicates that there are three main elements: *warmth, structure,* and *autonomy support*. The first of these is related to the responsiveness dimension, whereas the latter two are related to demandingness. Warmth is the degree of affection and acceptance that exists in the parent–child relationship; it has been found to be associated with overall competence. Structure refers to the extent to which rules and expectations for the adolescent's behaviour exist, and is associated with the presence of fewer behavioural problems. Autonomy support denotes the degree to which parents encourage the individuality and independence of the adolescent and is associated with fewer symptoms of psychological distress such as depression or anxiety (Barber et al., 1994; Hutt, Wang, & Evans, 2009; Steinberg, 1990).

Why is it that authoritative parenting is so strongly associated with healthy adolescent development? First, authoritative parents provide an appropriate balance between restrictiveness and autonomy. This balance encompasses both standards and limits for the adolescent's behaviour, which are needed by developing individuals, and the flexibility necessary to allow the adolescent opportunities to develop self-reliance. Second, authoritative parents are more likely to nurture the intellectual development of their children by engaging them in a verbal give-and-take about rules, expectations, and decisions. These discussions help to foster the development of social competence and enhance the adolescent's understanding of social systems and social relationships. Moreover, discussions of this type have also been argued to lead to the development of reasoning abilities, empathy, and more advanced moral judgement (Baumrind, 1978). Third, due to the combination of warmth and control used by authoritative parents, adolescents are more likely to identify with their parents. According to Steinberg (1996), 'one of the strongest predictors of identification between children and their parents is warmth in the parent–child relationship' (p. 164). Moreover, evidence suggests that we are more likely to imitate those who treat us with warmth and affection (Hill, 1980).

The observation that the family environment is related to adolescent adjustment should not be interpreted to indicate that other forms of relationship are not important. As we show in the next section, peers also play a critical role in shaping individuals' psychological development.

PEER RELATIONS: THE IDEAS OF HARRY STACK SULLIVAN

Sullivan believed that human beings, both the healthy and not so healthy, are much more similar than they are different. Highly attuned to the influence of social interactions, experiences, and social inequities in shaping human behaviour, Sullivan suggested that it was *interpersonal* processes (i.e. the exchange processes that happen between individuals), and not Freud's *intrapsychic* processes (i.e. the processes that happen within the individual), that guide development and shape behaviour. In other words, Sullivan proposed that behaviour cannot be understood in a vacuum, but instead must be understood as the end result of a series of interaction processes between the self and others. Thus, according to the interpersonal perspective, the interpersonal 'other' plays a central role in mapping the psychological development of individuals.

Interpersonal needs stimulate psychological growth

Sullivan's most important contribution to developmental theory lies in the notion that it is the motivation to fulfil *interpersonal needs* that stimulates psychological growth. According to Sullivan, development is organised around sequentially ordered interpersonal needs which emerge at specific times of development. For each emerging interpersonal need, there exists a key social relationship designed to satisfy the need. Therefore, Sullivan contended that the reduction of needs through age-appropriate social relationships is what guides healthy psychological development. Conversely, inadequate or deleterious relationships translate into ineffective need fulfilment, and subsequent negative outcomes (i.e. psychological maladjustment).

Developmental stages, divided into epochs, span the period from infancy into adulthood. Sullivan spoke of six epochs, namely, infancy (0–2 years), childhood (2–6 years), the juvenile epoch (6–9 years), preadolescence (9–12 years), early adolescence, late adolescence, and adulthood (the age demarcations of these latter stages are not clear). Each epoch is characterised by an emerging interpersonal need, such as the need for tenderness during infancy, companionship during childhood, acceptance during the juvenile epoch, friendship intimacy during preadolescence, romantic intimacy during early and late adolescence, and the integration of a love relationship during late adolescence and adulthood. Each sequentially ordered interpersonal need may be satisfied by specific social relationships. For example, the infant's interpersonal need for tenderness is designed to be met by parents or primary caregivers, whereas the need for acceptance is met principally through the peer group.

Subperiods of adolescence

Sullivan did not reduce adolescence to a singular, homogeneous period of development. Instead, he differentiated between pre-, early, and late adolescence. During preadolescence, individuals experience a need for intimacy from peers. For the first time in their developmental histories, preadolescents seek close, reciprocal, mutually validating relationships with others of similar status. It is the relationship of friendship with a same-sex peer, or what Sullivan called the 'chumship', which is designed to satisfy emerging needs for intimacy.

During early adolescence, the onset of puberty and genital sexuality promotes the 'psychologically strong interest' in members of the other sex (Barton Evans, 1996). It is at this stage that individuals must 'resolve a complex interplay between the dynamics of lust, security, and intimacy' (Barton Evans, 1996, p. 73). Because these needs are often difficult to negotiate simultaneously, early adolescence is construed by Sullivan as a tense, often turbulent period of human development. The core relationship associated with satisfying emerging interest in genital sexuality, the need for personal security (freedom from anxiety), and the continuing need for intimacy is that of the *romantic relationship*. Although needs of isophilic intimacy (with same-sex others) may continue to be fulfilled by friends, a shift toward heterophilic intimacy (with members of the other sex) is typical during early adolescence.

This shift away from a primary affiliation with same-sex peers toward affiliation with other-sex peers represents a main challenge of adolescent development. It is not that prior needs have diminished; they haven't. But now a new set of needs requires a transformation in peer experiences. During late adolescence, individuals continue to experience needs for intimacy, security, and lust, but in a more integrative and age-appropriate fashion. During this stage, and into adulthood, the task is to integrate these various needs into a love relationship, that is, with another person who becomes as important to one as oneself. It is truly the component of intimacy-seeking which sets the stage for adolescence and shapes much of life's later stages. According to Sullivan (1953, p. 34), intimacy, throughout adolescence and adulthood, is 'not the primary business of life, but is, perhaps, the principal source of satisfaction in life'.

Research supporting Sullivan's account

Although not all of the ideas proposed by Sullivan have been examined thoroughly, support for many of his ideas has been found in empirical studies. One noticeable feature of adolescent peer relations that is consistent with the views of Sullivan is an increase in levels of intimacy in friendship. Interviews and self-reports have shown that adolescents see more intimacy in their friendships than do younger children (Furman & Buhrmester, 1985; Sharabany et al., 1981; Youniss & Smollar, 1985). The importance of friendship for adolescents is also clear. Adolescents with friends report much higher levels of well-being than is shown by adolescents without friends (Newcomb & Bagwell, 1996). In fact, there is evidence that the effect of having a friend may help adolescent boys and girls overcome the problems that would derive from non-optimal family environments. Specifically, Gauze et al. (1996) reported that early adolescents from either chaotic or poorly structured families who had a friend showed the same level of self-perceived adjustment as shown by early adolescents from family environments more likely to promote well-being. Further evidence regarding these issues comes from a study of 166 American early adolescents. This study showed that even after the effects of parental support have been accounted for, friendship quality predicts higher perceptions of global self-worth and social competence and fewer symptoms of anxiety and depression (i.e, internalising) problems (Rubin et al. 2004). In this same study, friendship quality predicted lower rejection and victimisation, but only for girls. High friendship quality buffered the effects of low maternal support on girls' internalising difficulties.

The role of the peer group

In addition to changes in friendship in adolescence, the structure of the peer group changes. In early adolescence youngsters often form small groups of peers organised around particular themes or activities. These 'cliques' replace the broader peer group as the adolescent's primary peer environment. It is within a clique that most teenagers will have most of their relations with friends. Cliques are often part of larger social structures known simply as crowds (Figure 17.4). Crowds are defined by the attitudes or activities their members share. Common crowd labels among American high school students, for example, might include some of the following: jocks (i.e. athletes), brains, loners, druggies, and populars. Crowds often restrict adolescents' social contacts. Crowd labels may force adolescents to associate with particular types of peers, thus limiting their access to other peers who might fall outside their group. In this way, crowd membership is a salient feature of adolescent social life that can either improve or restrict an adolescent's development. Crowd affiliations appear to matter. According to a study of American adolescents, burnouts and non-conformists showed high levels of health-risk behaviours (e.g. smoking and alcohol use) and had the greatest proportions of close friends who engaged in similar behaviours (La Greca *et al.*, 2001). They also had relatively low social acceptance from peers. Brains and their friends engaged in extremely low levels of health-risk behaviours. In this same study, jocks and populars also showed evidence of selected areas of health risk; these teens also were more socially accepted than others.

FIGURE 17.4 *Crowd membership is a salient feature of adolescent social life that can either improve or restrict an adolescent's development.*
Source: Shutterstock.

Romantic relationships

Typically, romantic relationships do not come to mind when one thinks about peer relationships, but romantic relationships are typically relationships between peers (Figure 17.5). Although still in its infancy, developmental research on romantic relations is beginning to blossom, in large part due to recent attempts to strengthen relevant theoretical frameworks. Of particular interest have been the theoretical insights provided by Furman and Wehner (1994, 1997), which stipulate that individuals' conscious and unconscious cognitive representations (i.e. views) of romantic relationships are shaped by experiences across different *types* of close relationships. Unlike earlier perspectives that have uniquely highlighted the role of parent–child relations in influencing subsequent adult love relationships (Hazan & Shaver, 1987), Furman and Wehner have underscored the importance of both parent–child and peer relations as integral socialisation agents in adolescent romantic development. Lessons extracted from experiences with both parents and peers are carried forward to

FIGURE 17.5 *Romantic relationships are typically relationships between peers.*
Source: Shutterstock.

influence how romantic relations are approached, negotiated, and experienced in adolescence.

According to Furman and Wehner (1994, 1997), romantic relationships involve the activation of four distinct behavioural systems, namely, the attachment, caregiving, affiliation, and sexual systems. It has been suggested that complete integration of all four behavioural systems, in which romantic partners become key figures in fulfilling attachment, caregiving, affiliation, and sexual needs, does not typically occur until the development of long-term, stable romantic relationships which usually emerge during late adolescence and early adulthood (Hazan & Zeifman, 1994). In early and middle adolescence, the sexual and affiliative systems are more salient, and thus are expected to play a greater role than the attachment and caregiving systems in shaping views about romantic relationships. Because the affiliative and sexual-behavioural systems are honed primarily within the peer system, age-mates have been shown to exercise a greater influence on romantic views than do parents in early and middle adolescence (Furman & Wehner, 1994). Moreover, evidence suggests that whereas parent–child relations are not strongly related to romantic views in middle adolescence, they become increasingly central to romantic views during late adolescence (Furman & Wehner, 1997).

Brown's model of romantic development

As adolescents' views of romance are subject to important transformations across time, so are the specific functions of, and motives for, romantic relationships. Not unlike Furman and Wehner's (1994) behavioural systems conceptualisation of romantic development, Brown (1999) has discussed romantic functions from a developmental-contextual perspective, that is, uncleaved from the larger social arena in which they are embedded. From this perspective, romantic development is construed as an integral facet of identity formation, a growth process that is inextricable from the social contexts in which it is rooted. Brown's sequential model of romantic development reflects four distinct phases, namely, (1) *initiation*, (2) *status*, (3) *affection*, and (4) *bonding*. This model provides a frame for understanding the changing motives, developmental functions, and psychosocial transformations that characterise romantic growth across adolescence.

At the onset of adolescence, libidinal awakenings advance the relevance of romantic relations. During the *initiation phase*, young adolescents need to negotiate burgeoning sexual needs within the context of larger identity needs, such as those associated with fitting in and being accepted by peers (Brown, 1990, 1999; Erikson, 1963). Used primarily as a means of broadening one's self-concept, romance in adolescence first emerges as an identity issue, that is, as a vehicle of self-expansion and self-exploration, not necessarily as a relational issue (Brown, 1999). With time, however, the focus on the self widens to include the self in relation to others. During the *status phase*, young adolescents become acutely aware that romance is very much a 'public affair' that provides feedback on one's image and reputation among peers (Brown, 1999, p. 308). In brief, romantic activity can become a tool in reputation management, a means by which one's social standing can be manipulated.

Research has shown that status and prestige variables are among the top three most frequently cited reasons for dating among younger adolescents, but are not among the top five reasons given by college-aged adolescents (Roscoe *et al.*, 1987). The power of peers in regulating romantic behaviour is at its pinnacle during the status phase. Peers influence whom one 'can and cannot' date, as well as how one should and should not behave. Social scripts, as well as social sanctions for failure to adhere to these scripts, are transmitted within the peer domain. Concordantly, research has provided clear support for the influence of peers on adolescents' attitudes and beliefs about sex and dating, as well as on actual sexual behaviour.

As adolescents grow, they experience deepening needs for intimacy as expressed through increased desire for closeness, sharing, and support. During the *affection phase*, attention is shifted away from the context in which the relationship exists and onto the relationship itself (Brown, 1999). Although not divorced from the larger peer group, romance during this developmental period, like identity, becomes a personal and relational affair. Adolescents seek new relational depths and substance from their romantic relationships. In general, middle adolescence represents a time when individuals learn how to negotiate true romantic intimacy. As one would expect from adolescents in the affection phase, 15-year-olds most often cite companionship and intimacy as the most important benefits of dating (Feiring, 1996).

Lastly, the need to look beyond the current moment to make plans for the future is characteristic of the *bonding phase*. During this developmental period, individuals are expected to maintain the relational depths typical of the affection phase while 'replacing some of the emotionality associated with earlier periods with increased levels of pragmatism' (Brown, 1999, p. 321). Issues related to commitment, and potentially life-long commitment, are hallmarks of the bonding phase. How confident are partners about building a future together? How willing are partners to embrace or endure each other's strengths and shortcomings? In brief, the bonding phase represents a time of important, sometimes sobering, decision making. Concordantly, relational characteristics such as shared interests and shared goals for the future are the most frequently cited reasons for dating among older adolescents (Roscoe *et al.*, 1987).

An eight-year longitudinal study conducted in Germany with 103 participants provided evidence for a developmental sequence in romance that was consistent with Brown's model (Seiffge-Krenke, 2003). They also showed that at age 13, during the initiation phase, the self-concept contributed significantly to the prediction of bonded love in young adulthood. During the affection phase, at age 17, the quality of the relationship with the romantic partner was predictive of bonded love in early adulthood. These findings are valuable as they point to the importance of seeing romantic love as an experience steeped in one's developmental history.

Connolly and Goldberg's model of romantic development

In a similar vein, Connolly and Goldberg (1999) have also staged romantic growth using the descriptors of (1) *infatuation*, (2) *affiliation*, (3) *intimacy*, and (4) *commitment* in order to illustrate the motivational underpinnings of romantic relations across adolescence. The infatuation phase sparks the interest in romantic relationships which typically becomes manifest during the affiliation stage of development. During that latter stage, mixed-sex peer groups emerge and romantic relations are usually negotiated within the confines of the group. Because individuals develop primarily within sex-segregated peer groups, mixed-sex groups provide heterosexual adolescents a forum to enhance confidence and communication skills with members of the other sex. As needs for intimacy grow, the importance of the mixed-sex peer group as a social context declines, and the emergence of dyadic romantic relationships is observed (Connolly & Goldberg, 1999; Dunphy, 1963). Finally, in joining previous motives of infatuation, affiliation, and intimacy in motivating and defining romantic relationships, commitment leads to the conscious decision to maintain the relationship over the long term via some form of socially recognised partnership (Connolly & Goldberg, 1999). Recent evidence has provided further empirical support for the Connolly and Goldberg model (Connolly & McIsaac, 2009).

Clearly the effects of peer relations can be either positive or negative. A central theme of the study of peer relations in adolescence is the idea that peer relations affect adolescents' views of themselves. This notion that adolescence is a time when youngsters develop a view of themselves is not seen only in theory related to peer relations. In fact, it is the central theme in the approach to adolescence developed by Erik Erikson.

ERIK ERIKSON AND THE DEVELOPMENT OF IDENTITY IN ADOLESCENCE

Erik Homberger (later known as Erik Erikson) was born in Frankfurt, Germany, in 1902. He was raised by his mother, who was Jewish and of Danish descent, and his stepfather, a Jewish pediatrician whose last name Erik bore. Erikson's biological father, who was of Danish descent, left his mother before Erik was born. Growing up, Erikson felt that his physical appearance impeded him from being fully accepted as a Jew: he was tall, blond, and blue-eyed. Yet, at the same time, he was not raised to think of himself as Danish. He later recounted that these early feelings of alienation contributed greatly to his later interests in 'identity' and identity development (Cloninger, 1993). Heavily influenced by classical psychoanalysis, Erikson, like Freud, believed that all living things grow according to a design plan or 'blueprint' of psychological development. This belief, formally called the **epigenetic principle**, stems from the notion that the 'parts' of an organism develop in a sequential order, each part having its own specific 'time of ascendancy,' until the 'functioning whole' is complete (Erikson, 1959, p. 52). Much like physical development in the womb, Erikson believed

epigenetic principle
the notion that the 'parts' of an organism develop in a sequential order, each part having its own specific time of ascendancy, until the functioning whole is complete.

that the ego, defined earlier as the part of personality concerned with 'directing action, coping with the external world and integrating competing urges within the self' (Stevens, 1983, p. 1), also developed according to the epigenetic principle. In other words, for a whole healthy ego to develop, it is thought that several parts, called ego strengths, need to develop in a sequentially ordered fashion. Thus, like Freud, Erikson proposed a stage model of personality development in which each stage is characterised by a specific psychological task, or conflict that must be resolved, in order for an individual to successfully proceed to the next level (Pumpian-Mindlin, 1966).

Adolescence as transition to adulthood

According to Erikson, adoles-cence is a time of transition toward adult roles, where the individual ceases to 'fit' nicely into any particular social role. It is during this time that the indi-vidual 'struggles against a sense of identity confusion to attain a sense of identity' (Cloninger, 1993, p. 129). Simply put, it is a time where individuals ask, 'Who am I?' The psychosocial stage of identity versus identity diffusion (i.e. confusion) rep-resents a time of personal and interpersonal experimentation in which individuals strive to find their own sense of individuality and of self. The adolescent chal-lenge, then, is to reach a sense of ego continuity and sense of

FIGURE 17.6 *Young adolescents identify with different values, beliefs, and ideologies during the period of moratorium. One consequence of this identity crisis may be the development of a negative identity based on undesirable roles in society.*

Source: Shutterstock.

self-awareness vis-à-vis this continuity. In other words, resolving the identity crisis, meaning that the adolescent's identity emerges as more intact (or formed) than dif-fuse, leads to the development of the ego strength of *fidelity* to both one's identity and sense of self.

Until a stable identity is achieved, it is not uncommon for young adolescents to identify with a string of different values, beliefs, and ideologies. This period of search, in which a consistent, stable sense of identity has not yet been achieved, is called a period of **moratorium** and is considered a normal, healthy part of psychosocial development. However, if, after a period of moratorium, a coherent identity cannot be achieved and 'no one identity prevails at the core' of the individ-ual, identity diffusion ensues (Cloninger, 1993). Another unhealthy consequence of the identity crisis is the development of a negative identity; that is, one based on undesirable roles in society (i.e. juven-ile delinquent: Figure 17.6). Society provides clear images of such negative identit-ies, making them attractive alternatives for adolescents who feel that positively valued identities are unattainable (Cloninger, 1993, p. 130).

moratorium period in an individual's life when they identify with a string of different values, beliefs, and ideologies because of the lack of a stable and consistent self-image.

Identity formation and self-concept

Research on identity in adolescence can be found in two different domains, one concerned with the process of identity formation itself, and the other concerned with the development of the self-concept. Research on identity formation has largely confirmed that identity changes during adolescence, especially in the older years of adolescence. For example, in one study, most 15–18-year-olds were either in a state of diffusion or moratorium, with very few students showing any indication of identity achievement (Montemayor *et al.*, 1985). Nevertheless, the exact conditions that promote identity development are still unknown.

Research on the development of the self-concept has shown that in adolescence the self changes in both content and structure (Harter, 1983). Whereas children's sense of themselves is typically defined by observable characteristics, adolescents think about and reflect upon their own thoughts, desires, and motives. They increasingly emphasise internal characteristics, such as beliefs, values, and psychological traits and characteristics, as the basis of self-definition. As a result, in adolescence the self becomes a richer and more pluralistic concept. One of the challenges of the self in adolescence is with identifying the ways that one is unique and how one is similar to others. Maintaining a sense of individuality while trying to fit into the group is an important task for adolescents. Emphasising differences can lead to loneliness and alienation, while emphasising similarities may impede the development of autonomy.

As adolescents become aware of their own inner world of thoughts and feelings, they become more aware that others also possess such an inner world. As a consequence, adolescents can have a heightened awareness of the ultimate isolation of one's inner world from the inner worlds of others. It is during this time that adolescents become increasingly focused on the uniqueness of the self from other (Elkind, 1967). For this reason, adolescents may initially view separation from others as a fundamental condition of human experience and, as a result, they may feel alone in their efforts to develop a new sense of self during adolescence.

In sum, achieving a clear and coherent identity, or sense of self, may represent one of the most central developmental tasks of adolescence.

SUMMARY AND CONCLUSIONS

Adolescent social development is a collection of interrelated changes and challenges. Adolescence refers to the changes in their bodies, in their thoughts and emotions, in their family experiences, in their relations with peers, and in their conceptions of self. Although it is far from the truth to say that adolescence is necessarily a time of storm and stress, it is the case that adolescence is a time of transition and challenge. The interrelated changes of adolescence happen in several domains at once. Just as adolescents are moving through puberty, they are also functioning in a broader set of environments that challenge them in new ways. These challenges are exaggerated not only by their 'newness', but also by the transitions going on with their families.

Adolescents face the task of changing their relations with their parents; this is not a process of separation but is instead a process of achieving autonomy and an interdependent identity. They also must contend with changes in their relations with peers. The peer group takes on a new structure, organised around thematically based cliques and crowds, and new forms of relationships, such as romantic attachments, emerge.

As adolescents become autonomous, form new relations with parents and friends, acquire new forms of competence, and develop new concepts of self, they become ready to confront the challenges of being an adult. Although adolescence may be a time of challenge, and perhaps even some anxiety, one should not forget that adolescence can be a time of much fun and excitement.

DISCUSSION POINTS

1. Taking account of the evidence presented here and referring to your everyday experience, consider whether adolescence is necessarily a period of storm and stress.

2. What do you think are the relative contributions of biological and social factors to the nature of adolescence?

3. To what extent is adolescence a product of the cultural environment?

4. Is it possible to provide evidence to support psychoanalytic interpretations of adolescence? If it is, what sorts of evidence would you be looking for?

5. What factors determine the development of autonomy in adolescence?

6. Thinking about the evidence presented here and arising from everyday experience, how important are peer relationships in adolescent development?

7. Discuss the factors that contribute to the development of romantic relationships in adolescence.

8. How much are the experiences and feelings of adolescence to do with development of a self-concept?

SUGGESTIONS FOR FURTHER READING

Arnett, J.J., & Tanner, J.L. (2006). *Emerging adults in America: Coming of age in the 21st century.* Washington, DC: APA.

Collins, W.A., & Madsen, S.D. (2006). Close relationships in adolescence and early adulthood. In D. Perlman & A. Vangelisti (Eds.) *Handbook of personal relationships* (pp. 191–209). New York: Cambridge University Press.

Collins, W.A., & Steinberg, L. (2006). Adolescent development in interpersonal context. In W. Damon & N. Eisenberg (Eds.) *Handbook of child psychology: Vol. 4: Socioemotional processes* (pp. 1003–1067). New York: Wiley.

Smetana, J.G., Campione-Barr, N., & Metzger, A. (2006). Adolescent development in interpersonal and societal contexts. In *Annual Review of Psychology* (Vol. 57; pp. 255–284). Palo Alto, CA: Annual Review Press.

REFERENCES

Alsaker, F.D., & Flammer, A. (1999). *Time use by adolescents in an international perspective: The case of necessary activities*. The adolescent experience: European and American adolescents in the 1990s (F. Alsaker & A. Flammer, Series Eds.). Mahwah, NJ: Erlbaum.

Arnett, J.J. (1999). Adolescent storm and stress, reconsidered. *American Psychologist, 54*(5), 317–326.

Averill, L.A. (1982). Recollections of Clark's G. Stanley Hall. *Journal of the History of the Behavioral Sciences, 18*, 341–346.

Barber, B., Olsen, J., & Shagle, S. (1994). Associations between parent psychological and behavioral control and youth internalized and externalized behaviors. *Child Development, 65*, 1120–1136.

Barton Evans, F., III. (1996). *Harry Stack Sullivan: Interpersonal theory and psychotherapy*. London: Routledge.

Bassi, M., & Delle Fave, A. (2006). The daily experience of Italian adolescents in family interactions: Gender and developmental issues. In A. Delle Fave (Ed.) *Dimensions of well-being. Research and intervention* (pp. 172–190). Milano: Franco Angeli.

Baumrind, D. (1967). Child care patterns anteceding three patterns of preschool behavior. *Genetic Psychology Monographs, 75*, 43–88.

Baumrind, D. (1978). Parental disciplinary patterns and social competence in children. *Youth and Society, 9*, 239–276.

Baumrind, D. (2005). Patterns of parental authority and adolescent autonomy. In J. Smetana (Ed.) *New directions for child development: Changes in parental authority during adolescence* (pp. 61–69). San Francisco: Jossey-Bass.

Belsky, J., Steinberg, L.D., Houts, R.M., Friedman, S.L., DeHart, G., Cauffman, E., Roisman, G.I., Halpern-Felsher, B.L., & Susman, E. (2007). Family rearing antecedents of pubertal timing. *Child Development, 78*, 1302–1321.

Blos, P. (1972). The child analyst looks at the young adolescent. In J. Kagan & R. Coles (Eds.) *12 to 16: Early adolescence*. New York: W.W. Norton.

Brown, B.B. (1990). Peer groups and peer cultures. In S.S. Feldman & G.R. Elliott (Eds.) *At the threshold* (pp. 171–196). Cambridge, MA: Harvard University Press.

Brown, B.B. (1999). 'You're going out with who?': Peer group influences on adolescent romantic relationships. In W. Furman, B.B. Brown, & C. Feiring (Eds.) *The development of romantic relationships in adolescence* (pp. 291–329). New York: Cambridge University Press.

Bruno, J.E. (1996). Time perceptions and time allocation preferences among adolescent boys and girls. *Adolescence, 31*(121), 109–126.

Buchanan, C., Eccles, J., & Becker, J. (1992). Are adolescents the victims of raging hormones? Evidence for activational effects on mood and behavior at adolescence. *Psychological Bulletin, 111*, 62–107.

Cloninger, S.C. (1993). *Theories of personality: Understanding persons*. Englewood Cliffs, NJ: Prentice-Hall.

Colley, A., Griffiths, D., Hugh, M., Landers, K., & Jaggli, N. (1996). Childhood play and adolescent leisure preferences: Association with gender typing and the presence of siblings. *Sex Roles, 36*(3/4), 233–245.

Collins, W.A., & Steinberg, L. (2006). Adolescent development in interpersonal context. In W. Damon & N. Eisenberg (Eds.) *Handbook of child psychology: Vol. 4: Socioemotional processes* (pp. 1003–1067). New York: Wiley.

Connolly, J., & Goldberg, A. (1999). Romantic relationships in adolescence: The role of friends and peers in their emergence and development. In W. Furman, B.B. Brown, & C. Feiring (Eds.)

The development of romantic relationships in adolescence (pp. 266–290). New York: Cambridge University Press.

Connolly, J., & McIsaac, C.M. (2009). Adolescents' explanations for romantic dissolutions: A developmental perspective. *Journal of Adolescence, 32*, 1209–1233.

Csikszentmihalyi, M., & Larson, R. (1984). *Being adolescent*. New York: Basic Books.

Dunphy, D. (1963). The social structure of urban adolescent peer groups. *Sociometry, 26*, 230–246.

Eccles, J.S., Barber, B.L., Stone, M., & Hunt, J. (2003). Extracurricular activities and adolescent development. *Journal of Social Issues, 59*, 865–889.

Elkind, D. (1967). Egocentrism in adolescence. *Child Development, 38*, 1025–1034.

Erikson, E.H. (1959). *Identity and the life cycle: Selected papers*. Psychological Issues, 1 (Monograph 1). New York: International Universities Press.

Erikson, E.H. (1963). *Childhood and society* (2nd edn). New York: W.W. Norton.

Feiring, C. (1996). Concepts of romance in 15-year-old adolescents. *Journal of Research on Adolescence, 6*, 181–200.

Flammer, A., Alsaker, F.D., & Noack, P. (1999). *Time use by adolescents in an international perspective: The case of leisure activities*. The adolescent experience: European and American adolescents in the 1990s (F. Alsaker & A. Flammer, Series Eds.). Mahwah, NJ: Erlbaum.

Fuligni, A., & Eccles, J. (1993). Perceived parent–child relationships and early adolescents' orientation toward peers. *Developmental Psychology, 29*, 622–632.

Furman, W., & Buhrmester, D. (1985). Children's perceptions of the personal relationships in their social networks. *Developmental Psychology, 21*, 1016–1022.

Furman, W., & Wehner, E.A. (1994). Romantic views: Towards a theory of adolescent romantic relationships. In R. Montemayor, G.R. Adams, & G.P. Gullota (Eds.) *Advances in adolescent development. Vol. 6. Relationships during adolescence* (pp. 168–195). Thousand Oaks, CA: Sage.

Furman, W., & Wehner, E.A. (1997). Adolescent romantic relationships: A developmental perspective. In S. Shulman & W.A. Collins (Eds.) *Romantic relationships in adolescence: Developmental perspectives* (pp. 21–36). San Francisco: Jossey-Bass.

Gauze, C., Bukowski, W.M., Aquan-Assee, J., & Sippola, L.K. (1996). Interactions between family environment and friendship and associations with self-perceived well-being during early adolescence. *Child Development, 67*, 2201–16.

Gibbons, J.L., Lynn, M., & Stiles, D.A. (1997). Cross-national gender differences in adolescents' preferences for free-time activities. *Cross-Cultural Research: The Journal of Comparative Social Science, 31*, 55–69.

Gordon, W.R., & Caltabiano, M.L. (1996). Urban–rural differences in adolescent self-esteem, leisure boredom, and sensation-seeking as predictors of leisure-time usage and satisfaction. *Adolescence, 31*(124), 883–901.

Grinder, R.E. (1969). The concept of adolescence in the genetic psychology of G. Stanley Hall. *Child Development, 40*(2), 355–369.

Harter, S. (1983). Developmental perspectives on the self-system. In C.M. Hetherington (Ed.) *Handbook of child psychology. Vol. 4. Socialization, personality, and social development* (pp. 275–386). New York: Wiley.

Hayward, C., Killen, J.D., Kraemer, H.C., & Taylor, C.B. (2000). Predictors of panic attacks in adolescents. *Journal of the American Academy of Child and Adolescent Psychiatry, 39*, 207–214.

Hazan, C., & Shaver, P. (1987). Romantic love conceptualized as an attachment process. *Journal of Psychology and Social Psychology, 52*, 511–524.

Hazan, C., & Zeifman, D. (1994). Sex and the psychological tether. In K. Bartholomew & D. Perlman (Eds.) *Advances in personal relationships. Vol. 5. Attachment processes in adulthood* (pp. 151–180). London: Jessica Kingsley.

Henrik Peters, U. (1985). *Anna Freud, a life dedicated to children.* New York: Schocken Books.

Hill, J. (1980). The family. In M. Johnson (Ed.) *Toward adolescence: The middle school years* (79th yearbook of the National Society for the Study of Education). Chicago: University of Chicago Press.

Hutt R.L., Wang, Q., & Evans, G.W. (2009). Relations of parent–youth interactive exchanges to adolescent socioemotional development. *Social Development, 18,* 785–797.

Iso-Ahola, S.E. (1980). *The social psychology of leisure and recreation.* Dubuque, IA: Brown.

Iso-Ahola, S.E., & Crowley, E.D. (1991). Adolescent substance abuse and leisure boredom. *Journal of Leisure Research, 23*(3), 260–271.

Ito, M., Horst, H. A., Bittanti, M., Boyd, D., Herr-Stevenson, B., & Lange, P. (2008). *White paper – living and learning with new media: Summary of findings from the Digital Youth Project.* Chicago: The John P. and Catherine T. MacArthur Foundation.

Jones, M.C. (1957). The later careers of boys who were early- or late-maturing. *Child Development, 28,* 113–128.

Jones, M.C. (1965). Psychological correlates of somatic development. *Child Development, 36,* 899–911.

Kaplan, L.J. (1996). The stepchild of psychoanalysis, adolescence. *American Imago, 53*(3), 257–268.

Kelley, H.H. (1991). Lewin, situations, and interdependence. *Journal of Social Issues, 47,* 211–233.

La Greca, A., Prinstein, M., & Fetter, M. (2001). Adolescent peer crowd affiliation: Linkages with health-risk behaviors and close friendships. *Journal of Pediatric Psychology, 26,* 131–43.

Lamborn, S.D., Mounts, N.S., Steinberg, L., & Dornbusch, S.M. (1991). Patterns of competence and adjustment among adolescents from authoritative, authoritarian, indulgent, and neglectful families. *Child Development, 62,* 1049–1065.

Larson, R., & Verma, S. (1999). How children and adolescents around the world spend time: Work, play, and developmental opportunities. *Psychological Bulletin, 125,* 701–736.

Lewin, K. (1939/1953). Field theory and experiment in social psychology. In J.M. Seidman (Ed.) *The adolescent: A book of readings.* Fort Worth, TX: The Dryden Press. (Originally published in the *American Journal of Sociology, 44,* 868–897.)

Lewin, M.A. (1998). Kurt Lewin: His psychology and a daughter's recollections. In G.A. Kimble, & M. Wertheimer (Eds.) *Portraits of pioneers in psychology* (pp. 105–118). Mahwah, NJ: Erlbaum.

Maccoby, E.E., & Martin, J.A. (1983). Socialization in the context of the family: Parent–child interaction. In C.M. Hetherington (Ed.) *Handbook of child psychology. Vol. 4. Socialization, personality, and social development* (4th edn; pp. 1–101). New York: Wiley.

Mayes, L.C., & Cohen, D.J. (1996). Anna Freud and developmental psychoanalytic psychology. *The Psychoanalytic Study of the Child, 51,* 117–141.

Montemayor, R., Brown, B., & Adams, G. (1985, April). *Changes in identity status and psychological adjustment after leaving home and entering college.* Paper presented at the Biennial Meetings of the Society for Research in Child Development, Toronto.

Newcomb, A.F., & Bagwell, C. (1996). The developmental significance of children's friendship relations. In W.W. Bukowski, A.F. Newcomb, & W.W. Hartup (Eds.) *The company they keep: Friendship in childhood and adolescence* (pp. 289–321). New York: Cambridge University Press.

Philipp, S.F. (1998). Race and gender differences in adolescent peer group approval of leisure activities. *Journal of Leisure Research, 30*(2), 214–232.

Pumpian-Mindlin, E. (1966). Anna Freud and Erik H. Erikson: Contributions to the practice of psychoanalysis and psychotherapy. In F. Alexander, S. Eisenstein, & M. Grotjahn (Eds.) *Psychoanalytic pioneers.* New Jersey: Transaction.

Roscoe, B., Diana, M.S., & Brooks, R.H. (1987). Early, middle, and late adolescents' views on dating and factors influencing partner selection. *Adolescence, 22,* 59–68.

Rubin, K.H., Dwyer, K.M., Booth-LaForce, C.L., Kim, A.H., Burgess, K.B., & Rose-Krasnor, L. (2004). Attachment, friendship, and psychosocial functioning in early adolescence. *Journal of Early Adolescence, 24,* 326–356.

Ruble, D., & Brooks-Gunn, J. (1982). The experience of menarche. *Child Development, 53,* 1557–1566.

Ryan, R., & Lynch, J. (1989). Emotional autonomy versus detachment: Revisiting the vicissitudes of adolescence and young childhood. *Child Development, 60,* 340–356.

Savin-Williams, R.C., & Small, S.A. (1986). The timing of puberty and its relationship to adolescent and parent perceptions of family interactions. *Developmental Psychology, 22,* 342–347.

Sayers, J. (1997). Adolescent identity and desire: History, theory and practice. Essays in honor of Paul Roazan. In T. Dufresne (Ed.) *Freud under analysis.* New Jersey: Jason Aronson.

Seiffge-Krenke, I. (2003). Testing theories of romantic development from adolescence to young adulthood: Evidence of a developmental sequence. *International Journal of Behavioral Development, 27,* 519–531.

Sharabany, R., Gershoni, R., & Hofman, J. (1981). Girlfriend, boyfriend: Age and sex differences in intimate friendship. *Developmental Psychology, 17,* 800–808.

Shaw, S.M., Caldwell, L.L., & Kleiber, D.A. (1996). Boredom, stress and social control in the daily activities of adolescents. *Journal of Leisure Research, 28*(4), 274–292.

Smetana, J.G., Campione-Barr, N., & Metzger, A. (2006). Adolescent development in interpersonal and societal contexts. In *Annual Review of Psychology* (Vol. 57; pp. 255–284). Palo Alto, CA: Annual Review Press.

Smith, B. (2009). Toward a realistic science of environments. *Ecological Psychology, 21,* 121–300.

Steinberg, L. (1981). Transformations in family relations at puberty. *Developmental Psychology, 17,* 833–840.

Steinberg, L. (1987). Bound to bicker: Pubescent primates leave home for good reasons. Our teens stay with us and squabble. *Psychology Today, 87,* 36–39.

Steinberg, L. (1990). Interdependency in the family: Autonomy, conflict, and harmony. In S. Feldman & G. Elliot (Eds.) *At the threshold: The developing adolescent* (pp. 255–276). Cambridge, MA: Harvard University Press.

Steinberg, L., Lamborn, S., Darling, N., Mounts, N., & Dornbusch, S. (1994). Over-time changes in adjustment and competence among adolescents from authoritative, authoritarian, indulgent and neglectful families. *Child Development, 65,* 754–770.

Steinberg, L., & Silverberg, S. (1986). The vicissitudes of autonomy in early adolescence. *Child Development, 57,* 841–851.

Stevens, R. (1983). *Erik Erikson.* Milton Keynes: Open University Press.

Sullivan, H.S. (1953). *The interpersonal theory of psychiatry.* New York: W.W. Norton.

White, S.H. (1992). G. Stanley Hall: From philosophy to developmental psychology. *Developmental Psychology, 28*(1), 25–34.

Vazsonyi, A.T., Pickering, L.E., Lara, L.M., Belliston, D.H., & Junger, M. (2002). Routine activities and deviant behaviors: American, Dutch, Hungarian, and Swiss Youth. *Journal of Quantitative Criminology, 18,* 397–422.

Wray-Lake, L., Crouter, A.C., & McHale, S.M. (2010). Developmental patterns in decision making autonomy across middle childhood and adolescence: European American parents' perspectives. *Child Development, 81,* 636–651.

Youniss, J., & Smollar, J. (1985). *Adolescent relations with mothers, fathers, and friends.* Chicago: University of Chicago Press.

Part V
Practical Issues

18 Educational Implications

Alyson Davis and Naomi Winstone

KEY TERMS

attainment targets • bidirectional processes • cognitive conflict • cognitive development • collaborative learning • conservation • construction • control group • criterion referencing • curriculum • discovery learning • dynamic assessment • egocentric • egocentrism • experimental group • formative testing • heuristics • intermental ability • intramental ability • key stages • meta-analysis • National Curriculum • norm referencing • paradigm • pedagogy • peer facilitation effects • perspective-taking • preoperational stage • scaffolding • single-level testing • sociocognitive conflict • Student Teams Achievement Divisions (STAD) • Tower of Hanoi task • transactional processes • zone of proximal development

CHAPTER OUTLINE

OVERVIEW

In addition to providing evidence and testing theories on how children develop, it is generally expected that developmental psychology will have things to say about applied issues concerning children. A prime example is the contribution of developmental psychology to educational practice. This chapter outlines the different images of the child created by two major developmental theorists: Jean Piaget and Lev Semenovich Vygotsky.

Piaget depicts the child as constructing their own understanding through spontaneous activity on the physical world. He also identifies a role for social interaction with peers in the construction of knowledge, but argues that interaction with parents and teachers is of little value, because the difference in status and in intellectual levels is too great for children to benefit from these experiences. Thus, Piaget's major contribution to education theory is the concept of discovery learning. The chapter reviews evidence on the effects of peer interaction, showing that the presence of peers can have lasting effects on task performance, even when the peers are no longer present.

By contrast, Vygotsky's theory identifies a clear role for adults and teachers, seeing development as a process where children's ability is *drawn forward* through both informal and formal education. A popular term emerging from this view is scaffolding: the adult provides vital support and structure for the child's learning. Evidence is reviewed pointing to the ways in which parents and teachers support children's development, and identifying the characteristics of effective spontaneous teaching by parents.

The final section of the chapter evaluates the impact of developmental psychology on methods of assessing children's learning, and the chapter ends on a positive note regarding the continuing influence of developmental psychology on educational practice.

INTRODUCTION

Most developmental psychologists agree that the task of developmental psychology is two-fold: first, to provide a good description of the developmental changes which take place from infancy into adulthood, and second, to offer sensible theoretical explanations of what causes these changes to take place. If we suppose that we are some way towards achieving this then we ought to be in a position to make a substantial contribution to educational provision and practice. At the broadest level, knowing children's competencies and weaknesses at certain ages should let us have something to say about what we might expect children to be able to achieve or find difficult within a formal educational setting. Similarly, if we have powerful theories to explain why children's competencies change over time, it should also be possible to comment on the best ways of introducing children to a **curriculum**. In other words we could define what constitutes 'good' teaching and effective learning.

curriculum the set of courses, and their content, offered at a school or university

The above is of course just a characterisation of a possible, rather optimistic model of the relationship between developmental psychology and education. One simple example will serve to show that our ability to apply psychology to practice is not just a function of the health of our research base. Teaching in primary schools continues to be a popular career choice for psychology graduates, yet until recently psychologists were frequently rejected for teacher training places because psychology is not one of the specified UK **National Curriculum** subjects. However, 2008 saw the introduction of the first PGCE teacher training course in psychology, following the classification of psychology as a science subject by the UK Qualifications and Curriculum Authority. Nevertheless, this example serves to make the point that any account of how psychology might contribute to education is necessarily constrained by other factors such as educational policy and broader politics.

National Curriculum the curriculum that is followed in all state schools in England, Wales, and Northern Ireland. The government sets the particulars of the subjects covered by the National Curriculum.

Despite these difficulties it can be argued that developmental psychology has a great deal to offer in the field of educational practice. It is important to note, however, that the relationship between psychology and education is not necessarily best characterised as prescriptive. In other words, it is not the case that psychology should tell educators the 'best' way of educating children. Instead, it can be far more productive to see the relationship as **bidirectional** or **transactional**. This might be at a theoretical level, where both psychological and educational models inform each other, or at a policy level. For example, it is now common for research fund providers to tender for research funding aimed at addressing a particular educational policy issue, such as the impact of information technology on learning.

bidirectional/transactional processes children socialise parents just as parents socialise children. They are seen as influencing one another reciprocally.

In this chapter we aim to give a selective account of a few key areas in mainstream developmental psychology which have already impacted on or have the potential to impact on the education of children. In particular, we shall address research that can contribute to the question of facilitating children's learning, and shall consider what we know about the nature of development and learning that allows us to contribute to the debate on how to promote learning, how best to teach, and how to assess the product of children's learning. Toward the end of the chapter, we shall examine some of the issues imposed by the fact that since 1988 there has been a compulsory National Curriculum in the UK to explore the implications for the future relationship between psychology and education in the context of the British system. The latter differs quite markedly from the American education system, which benefits from a broad research base of evaluating different kinds of educational practice.

CHILD-CENTRED PSYCHOLOGY AND EDUCATION

If you were to visit a class of 5-year-olds during a typical day you would find a very 'child-friendly' environment – child-sized tables and chairs arranged in groups, walls covered in the children's work at child's eye level, a sand pit and water tray and perhaps even a play house or shop. The children would typically be working in pairs or small groups using concrete materials such as building blocks to solve problems set them by the teacher while others might be playing on their own building models or engaging in pretend play with other children. The teacher might be working with a small group of children or with an individual child and would rarely address the whole class other than to control noise levels or make an announcement relating to events such as lunchtime. What you would be very unlikely to find is a room full of children sitting in silence at rows of desks, while the teacher stands at the front of the class writing instructions on a blackboard for children to meticulously copy into their workbooks.

These two pedagogical scenarios are familiar to most of us, and we can ask why the first has remained dominant in the UK primary education system for the last 40 to 50 years. The 1960s witnessed a huge shift from so called 'chalk and talk' **pedagogy** toward a 'child-centred' one. Such child-centred approaches had many advocates in educational philosophers such as Froebel, and were therefore readily welcomed by primary teachers.

> **pedagogy** any aspect of theory or practice related to teaching.

However, child-centredness may well have remained influential precisely because it maps so closely onto ideas from cognitive developmental theory, particularly Piagetian theory. Piaget's account of development could, as one of us has argued elsewhere (Davis, 1991), be used by those involved in early education as a formalisation of many of the assumptions underlying child-centred education.

One central tenet of Piagetian theory is the characterisation of children being active in the **construction** of their own development through interaction with the largely physical environment. Such direct activity is essential not only in infancy during sensorimotor development but remains important during later stages as well. This suggests that in order to learn effectively, the child should be an active participant in the learning process, rather than a passive receiver of knowledge. Paradoxically, Piaget wrote very little on the educational implications of his work but where he did the emphasis was on the teacher's role in providing the best physical environment within which children could overcome their **egocentrism** and gain a decentred perspective on principles such as number **conservation** and transitivity. In educational practice such so called **discovery learning** or learning through play became widespread. A second aspect of Piaget's theory that has implications for educational practice is the idea that development proceeds in a number of stages, where children's thinking is qualitatively different at each stage. Thus, children of different ages not only differ in the extent of their knowledge, but also in their way of thinking. This has important implications for curriculum design and teaching strategies.

> **construction** a developmental process in which the child is an active participant in the process through interaction with the environment, rather than a passive receiver of knowledge.

> **discovery learning** encouraging children to learn by discovering information for themselves.

SOCIAL INTERACTION, LEARNING AND DEVELOPMENT

So far we have discussed in fairly general terms how psychological theory might be mapped onto educational practice. We now turn to a more empirically led investigation and consider experimental evidence from developmental psychology that has direct relevance on how we promote learning and introduce effective teaching. The area we have selected is the role of social interaction on **cognitive development**, specifically **peer** interaction and adult–child interaction. This provides an ideal springboard for our present purposes, for two main reasons. First, the developmental literature on the effects of social interaction contains a lively theoretical debate on why interaction effects emerge in the first place. Within this debate, arguments remain as to the relative merits of cognitive theory and social constructionist theories based on the work of Vygotsky in explaining why it is that social interaction appears to exert such a powerful influence on learning. Second, although not always separated in the developmental literature, there are important educational reasons for understanding whether effective learning outcomes for children can best be achieved in individual interaction with an adult (teacher), or whether interaction with peers in groups can be similarly or more beneficial.

The effects of peer interaction

Piaget's interest in interaction was predominantly in the importance of interaction with the physical rather than interpersonal environment. This is definitely the case in relation to his later writing, but in his earlier work (e.g. Piaget 1926, 1932) Piaget outlined a case for the importance of social interaction not only as a means to encourage learning but also as a direct cause of development itself. The primary intellectual deficit of the **preoperational** child, according to Piaget, is the child's inability to decentre or take account of alternative perspectives on the world to their own. However, Piaget argued that this egocentrism could be overcome via a particular type of interaction – interaction with peers. Interaction with adults, be they parents or teachers, was considered to be of little value because the gap, both intellectually and in terms of status, between adult and child is simply too great. Peers, on the other hand provide the ideal potential source of **sociocognitive conflict** necessary for development to take place. Two preoperational children may each hold opposing **egocentric** views on a situation which results in **cognitive conflict**, or disequilibrium, within the child. According to Piaget, such cases of conflict are crucial, because through interaction with peers the child questions their own understanding, leading to a resolution of the conflict and a cognitive advance. Thus, peers are an important influence on the child's own construction of knowledge and their cognitive development. More recently, Bryant (1990) has pointed out the fatal flaw in Piaget's position, namely that while conflict resolution may well take place, there is no logical reason why it should be in the direction of developmental advance. For example, conflict resolution can occur in the opposite direction to cognitive advance if one partner is overconfident that their (incorrect) solution is correct (e.g. Puncochar & Fox, 2004), or where one partner dominates the interaction (e.g. Leman, 2002). Nevertheless, Piaget's claims about cognitive conflict have inspired some important empirical work about the potential impact of peer interaction on development.

sociocognitive conflict
a *cognitive conflict* that arises as a result of a social interaction, e.g. two *peers* having a different understanding of a mathematical problem.

cognitive conflict
cognitive conflict arises when there are two or more competing solutions to a situation or problem.

Working in pairs can promote performance on Piagetian tasks

The initial experimental work was carried out by Willem Doise and colleagues in Geneva in the 1970s and early 1980s (Doise & Mugny 1984). The experiments hinged on two fundamental tests of pre-operational think-ing, the **perspective-taking** task and the conservation task. The perspective-taking task was based on the classic three mountains task originally designed by Piaget and Inhelder (1956), in which children are presented with a three-dimensional display of three mountains with distinguishing features on each (see Chapter 9, Figure 9.1). The child's task is either to select a picture or to reconstruct the array to show how the mountains would appear from an alternative perspective. Young children find the three mountains task exceptionally difficult and a common response of children of around 5 years is to select the picture depicting their own view of the scene. This was taken by Piaget and Inhelder as good evidence for egocentrism in the preoperational child (see Chapter 9 for a fuller description of Piaget's theory).

> **perspective-taking**
> the ability to take some-one else's perspective when it differs from one's own.

Doise and Mugny (1984) modified the materials to include buildings and features of a village rather than three mountains. The important modification to the task was the change in design to allow a test of peer interaction on perspective-taking ability. Doise and Mugny introduced a three-stage design that has become a common **paradigm** in the work on peer interaction effects. In Stage 1, all the children (aged 5–7 years) are tested on the task to assess their individual performance. At Stage 2, the children are divided into two groups – **experimental** and **control**. The children acting as controls are again tested on their individual performance. In contrast, the experimental group are divided into pairs and their performance as a pair is assessed. In the third and final stage, children are tested on their individual performance as they had been at Stage 1. This pre-test, test, post-test design allows two questions to be addressed. First, does the performance of the children working in pairs at Stage 2 exceed that of those work-ing alone? Second, are there any pre-test to post-test gains measurable for the experi-mental group relative to the controls? In other words, a critical test of this design is whether children's individual performance on the Stage 3 post-test is influenced by whether or not they worked alone or in pairs at the second experimental stage.

The results from this experiment showed that for the weakest children, namely those who were totally egocentric at pre-test, working in pairs at the test stage did indeed result in improvements on their individual post-test performance. The effect was strongest when these children were paired with other children who showed evidence of perspective taking but whose performance was not at ceiling. Pairings of two children, both of whom were highly egocentric, did not in this instance show dramatic improvement in individual post-test performance. This said, other stud-ies (e.g. Glachan & Light, 1982), and Doise and Mugny themselves, have found good evidence that the pairing of two weaker children can have a dramatic positive impact on the children's later individual performance compared to children who are never given the opportunity to work in a pair.

These so-called **peer facilitation effects** are by no means con-fined to perspective-taking tasks. Perret-Clermont (1980) reports similar findings using the standard conservation of liquid paradigm (see Chapter 9). Typically, preoperational non-conserving children

> **peer facilitation effects**
> pairing of two children can have a positive impact on children's later individual performance.

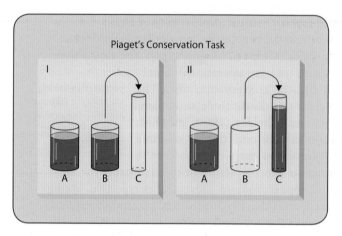

FIGURE 18.1 *Piaget's conservation of liquid task.*

Source: tba

will report a change in quantity when liquid is poured from one container to a container of a different shape. In contrast, conserving children will claim that the amount of liquid remains the same and justify their responses. In her work, Perret-Clermont used the same three-stage, pre-test, test, post-test design as in the work by Doise and Mugny (1984). In the experimental group, a non-conserving child was paired with either another non-conserving child or a conserving child. Their task was to agree how to share juice equally between themselves, each having differently shaped beakers. In this situation it is argued that sociocognitive conflict arises from the contradictions in the children's beliefs about the conservation of liquid. The social interaction required to reach a common understanding forces the child to examine their own understanding and compare it to that of the other child, helping them to overcome their own egocentrism. Again, the results indicated that the non-conserving children were benefitting from interaction, in so far as they did significantly better on the individual post-test than children who had not experienced interaction. Interestingly, the performance of the non-conserving children on the post-test did not differ according to whether they had been paired with a non-conserving or conserving child during the interaction. It therefore seems that in tasks such as these, the process of interaction and working towards a common understanding facilitates the development of children's thinking.

Peer effects are persistent

In both of the perspective taking and conservation studies outlined above, the time delay between the children's interaction sessions and individual post-test was around a week to 10 days. This makes the results even more dramatic because it appears that not only can a relatively short exposure to paired interaction improve children's performance when subsequently working on their own, but these effects are relatively long-lasting. Furthermore, the results can be explained in terms of sociocognitive conflict, whereby children faced with different ways of thinking are forced to challenge and modify their own understanding. Indeed, in some cases the benefits of peer interaction are not observed until after a delay – most probably because the changes in thinking promoted by sociocognitive conflict help children to benefit from subsequent learning experiences (Howe *et al.*, 2005). Research also demonstrates that the positive and persistent effects of peer interaction extend beyond advances in cognitive development to advances in social development (e.g. Gillies, 2002). The very process of working with a partner, and considering a position different to one's own, fosters the development of cooperation skills that can be applied to many areas of the child's life. Taken as they stand, these results are a potential goldmine for extracting educational implications. Teachers frequently ask children to work in pairs or small groups both for pragmatic reasons and because they can see the potential for children learning from each other when working on a task. The Genevan studies outlined above go beyond providing empirical justification for group work in the classroom as they suggest that such group activity has long-lasting effects which are measurable at the individual level. Given that the British educational system from infant school to university assesses understanding and knowledge at an individual level, these findings would be powerful indeed in their educational implications. However, first we must establish that these effects are not confined to these very young children on these very specific sorts of tasks.

Peer effects in older children: Computer-based tasks

Much of the experimental work on the effects of peer interaction on children's learning in middle childhood has centred on computer-based tasks (Figure 18.2). Initially this was for pragmatic reasons rather than because computers were thought to afford any special qualities for promoting interaction. For example, Glachan and Light (1982) found that 7- to 9-year-olds benefitted from interacting with another child when working on the classic **Tower of Hanoi** problem-solving task (see Figure 18.3). The task involves reconstructing a tower of three seriated blocks from peg A to peg C in as few moves as possible without moving more than one block at a time or placing a larger block on top of a smaller one. However, their results also suggested that such benefits may only manifest themselves when children literally cooperate by physically moving the materials together following

FIGURE 18.2 *Computer-based tasks are used in research to examine the effects of peer interaction on children's learning in middle childhood.*
Source: Shuttershock.

verbal decision-making over the appropriate next step. In order to follow this up, Light and colleagues devised a computer-based version of the task which allowed tight control over the children's decision-making and actions, while at the same time allowing the children's responses to be recorded directly into the computer. Computer based tasks also lend themselves to the three stage, pre-test, test, post-test design used earlier by the neo-Piagetians working in Geneva.

Tower of Hanoi task
A task that involves reconstructing a tower of three seriated blocks from peg A to peg C in as few moves as possible without moving more than one block at a time or placing a larger block on top of a smaller one.

During the 1980s and early 1990s a body of evidence emerged which looked very promising indeed in terms of the possible positive effects of paired learning. For example, Blaye, Light, Joiner and Sheldon (1991) presented junior school children with a computer-based complex adventure game

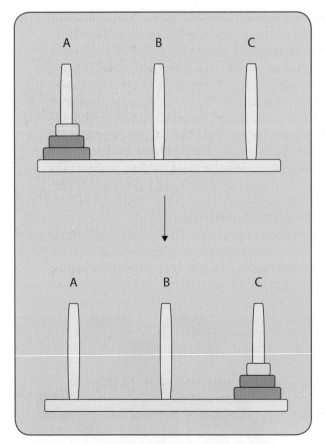

FIGURE 18.3 *The Tower of Hanoi problem-solving task. The three blocks on peg A must be reconstructed on peg C in as few moves as possible, moving one block at a time, and without placing a larger block on top of a smaller block.*

that involved a good deal of planning. The experimental design, as before, involved children working initially individually, then either alone or in pairs at the test stage before being post-tested individually. The results showed that those children who worked in pairs fared better on their individual post-test than those children who did not have the opportunity for collaboration at the test phase. Furthermore, this type of evidence seemed to suggest that peer interaction not only improved how quickly children arrived at the correct solution, but also positively affected the kinds of strategies these children used. Taken together, this evidence coupled with that from workers such as Doise and Mugny could be summarised as follows. Positive peer interaction effects are not restricted to very young children working on Piagetian-based tasks. Instead, they have also been found on more complex problem-solving tasks in children as old as 11–12 years. Furthermore, the process by which these effects comes about could fairly readily be attributable to a cognitive explanation such as sociocognitive conflict. Indeed, there is considerable empirical evidence that peer interaction has beneficial effects at different stages of the educational system, on a variety of tasks, and across a broad range of learner groups (e.g. Dimant & Bearison, 1991; Druyan, 2001; Golbech & Sinagra, 2000; Samaha & DeLisi, 2000; Yarrow & Topping, 2001).

This constitutes an ideal base for approving group work in schools. Teachers rely out of necessity on children working together in small groups, because class sizes prevent one-to-one teaching, but also institute such work patterns for constructive reasons. It is widely believed by primary school teachers that the process of children working together produces social benefits as children learn the social skills for effective cooperation. Therefore, the psychological evidence which suggests that group work may have a significant intellectual outcome should lend further support to this type of educational practice. We can already see evidence of the influence that this area of research is having on learning practices in classrooms. For example, Littleton *et al.* (2005) report positive results from the Thinking Together programme aimed at primary school children in the UK. This intervention develops speaking and listening skills that facilitate exactly the kind of collaborative discussion that can lead to gains in children's thinking. Whilst there is still a way to go, both in the UK and elsewhere, to fully translate our knowledge of peer interaction effects into classroom groupwork (Blatchford *et al.*, 2006), there is clear evidence of positive transfer between psychological knowledge and educational practice.

Although there is clear evidence for the benefits of peer interaction, it has also become apparent that important qualifications must be applied to conclusions arising from computer-based, peer-assisted learning. Marked gender differences began to emerge in those studies using computers as the basis for interaction as well as differences in interactive style.

Gender effects in computer-based tasks

With hindsight, it was perhaps not surprising that gender should become an issue in interaction studies. Since home computers began to be used in the 1980s, evidence emerged that boys had greater access to and more confidence with computers when compared with girls (Hughes, 1986). The massive increase in the number of computers in both the home and school since the 1980s has done little to alleviate this inequality. Culley (1993) found that boys are more positive about computers, are more likely to use them, and moreover use them for more diverse purposes than girls. Furthermore, studies of children working with the programming language LOGO revealed gender differences again in favour of boys (Hughes, 1986). Interestingly, these differences seem to arise not because girls are less able at computer-based tasks or less spatially adept but out of differences in interactive style between boys and girls, with boys tending to dominate and take control of the keyboard and mouse when children are working in mixed-gender pairs (Barbieri & Light, 1992; Light, 1997; Littleton *et al.*, 1992). One might expect that by now such gender differences would have disappeared, but more recent research suggests otherwise. In the UK, children still differ in their perceived self-efficacy in terms of computer use. Boys believe that their computer abilities are superior to those of girls, whereas girls believe their ability to use computers is inferior to that of boys (Oosterwegel, Littleton & Light, 2004). Whilst this study found no overall gender differences in attitudes to computers, and North & Noyes (2002) also report little evidence for a 'technological gender gap' in children, the increased prevalence of computers in the home and children's increased access to computers in school have not succeeded in eradicating gender differences entirely. Colley and Comber (2003) report a comparison between attitudes towards computers in UK schoolchildren in the early 1990s and the beginning of the 21st century. Whilst there were few differences between boys and girls in the degree of computer use, boys reported liking to use computers to a greater degree than girls and boys also reported greater feelings of self-confidence in computer use relative to girls.

This type of gender inequality presents a serious educational challenge because girls enter school already disadvantaged in terms of their attitudes to computers, and this can then be compounded by differences in interactive styles and more subtle factors such as the nature of software (Barbieri & Light, 1992; Crook, 1994). Littleton *et al.* (1998) found that minor modifications to the software had a dramatic impact on gender differences. For example whereas their standard adventure game paradigm involving pirates capturing treasure resulted in superior performance in boys, replacing pirates by 'honey bears' resulted in no gender differences. Interestingly, this change in software reduced the gender inequality by improving the performance of girls without reducing that of boys. This is an important finding because selecting appropriate software is a relatively straightforward means by which at least some of the disadvantage experienced by girls can be rectified. Interventions aimed at differences in interactive style are more likely to pose a greater research challenge.

collaborative learning
any learning that occurs when two or more people work together on a problem.

In an overview on **collaborative learning**, Underwood and Underwood (1999) report that when girls are paired with each other they perform at a level equal to if not better than boys. Mixed pairs appear to fail because in this situation girls are less likely to discuss ideas and contribute to the planning often required to solve complex reasoning tasks (Barbieri & Light, 1992; Underwood & Underwood, 1999). For example, Underwood et al. (1993) analysed children's dialogue when engaged in a computer-based problem-solving task in single-sex or mixed-sex dyads. When boys and girls worked in mixed-sex pairs, there was more disagreement, tension, and antagonism in their discussion. In a further study, Underwood et al. (2000) gave children in either single-sex or mixed-sex pairs a computer-based task, where they had to complete missing letters in a passage of text. In comparison to single-sex pairs, the mixed pairs made fewer attempts to fill in missing letters and in terms of collaborative dialogue, made fewer suggestions and showed lower levels of verbal interaction. Girls' access to the keyboard in the mixed pairs was less than half that of girls in same-sex pairs, supporting the proposition that one of the main problems posed in mixed-sex peer interaction on computer-based tasks is boys' dominance of the computer itself. When this occurs, focus turns away from positive interaction that might promote cognitive advance to practical issues of access and sharing.

However, the findings from the study by Underwood et al. (2000) give us reason to be optimistic about future interventions related to peer interaction on computer-based tasks. Whilst children in the mixed-sex pairs attempted fewer letters in the word-completion task, their overall task performance was not significantly inferior to that of single-sex pairs. In fact, analysis of children's dialogue revealed that some mixed pairs worked well together. This leaves us with clear implications for educational practice: girls and boys can work well together on computer-based tasks if positive collaboration is actively promoted and encouraged. These gender differences affecting productive learning will need to remain a central research question because it appears that they are not specific to childhood but have been found in experiments looking at interaction and learning in undergraduate students (Howe & Tolmie, 1999).

Taken together, this review of some key evidence on the effects of peer interaction on learning must lead us to conclude positively with regard to future prospects for educational practice. Overall the findings suggest that children can learn effectively from collaboration with their peers. Even cases where peer interaction does not seem to lead to direct benefits for children (e.g. Leman & Oldham, 2005; Levin & Druyan, 1993) provide useful information that can be applied to educational practice. Where collaborative learning is to take place, consideration needs to be given to providing the optimum conditions to foster positive collaboration. The research clearly tells us that it is cognitive conflict between peers that is important – social conflict between peers can have negative effects (e.g. Azmitia, 1988). Even the findings regarding gender differences give rise to fairly clear indications as to how inequalities may arise and how they might be reduced. Research from developmental psychology that demonstrates how the benefits of collaborative learning are prevented is as important for educational practice as those findings that provide clear suggestions for promoting effective collaboration.

What is effective teaching?

Vygotsky's theory

An essential aspect of how developmental psychology might contribute educationally relevant implications is to go beyond providing evidence demonstrating where learning may be enhanced (such as through peer interaction) by having something to say about the process of teaching and learning itself. Paradoxically, research which has been predominantly inspired by Piagetian theory is unlikely to do this, because, as has been argued earlier, Piaget simply was not interested in this question. Nevertheless, there are alternative highly influential theories of child development which have at their core the question of the nature of learning and the role of direct teaching in promoting learning. The key theorist here is the Russian psychologist Lev Semenovich Vygotsky. In contrast to Piaget, who focused on mental activity at the individual level, Vygotsky's account prioritises the social nature of learning, and the co-construction of knowledge and understanding. According to Vygotsky, knowledge exists **intermentally** between individuals before it can exist **intramentally** within an individual:

> **intermental plane** concerning knowledge that is possessed between people (also known as the interpsychological plane).

> **intramental plane** concerning knowledge that has been internalised and is possessed by the individual (also known as the intrapsychological plane).

> Any function in the child's cultural development appears twice, or on two planes. First it appears on the social plane and then on the psychological plane. First it appears between people as an interpsychological category and then within the child as an intrapsychological category. This is equally true with regard to voluntary attention, logical memory, the formation of concepts and the development of volition.
>
> *(Vygotsky, 1981, p. 163)*

By emphasising the social nature of development, Vygotsky's theory is not only a theory of learning, it also offers a theory of teaching, because language is the prime medium for sharing knowledge in formal contexts such as schools, and informally in the home. Adults control the child's representation of the world from birth onwards and the presence of more knowledgeable others is a crucial condition for the development of higher mental functions. Over the last 30 years, Vygotsky's work has been highly influential on researchers as a framework for studying the importance of adult–child interaction on development. Two concepts in particular have attracted attention, namely the **zone of proximal development** and **scaffolding**.

The zone of proximal development and scaffolding

The zone of proximal development (ZPD: see Figure 18.4) is 'the distance between the actual developmental level as determined by independent problem solving and the level of potential development as determined through problem solving under adult guidance or in collaboration with more able peers' (Vygotsky, 1978, p. 86; see Figure 18.3). This definition carries with it two important implications. First, the concept of the ZPD characterises learning through guidance or assistance as a normal but important part of development because the child's intermental ability ultimately becomes intramental ability by appropriate interaction. Second, it supposes that learning can be made more effective through the most appropriate form of teaching. Teaching should be aimed towards those aspects of a child's cognitive functioning that are in an active state of development (i.e. their ZPD), rather than towards those that already exist (Black & Wiliam, 2009). The essential question is whether adults can or do pitch their interventions at the appropriate level when interacting with children so as to make effective teachers. We shall describe some of the research evidence relating to this question, but first let us consider a concept related to the ZPD – *scaffolding*. Scaffolding is a metaphor originally used by Jerome Bruner and colleagues (Bruner, 1983; Wood *et al.*, 1976). It is the means by which adults structure and simplify the environment to facilitate children's learning and to guide them through their ZPD. Scaffolding may occur in a variety of contexts, for example by pointing out the next piece in a jigsaw puzzle or offering the child a sock rolled down to make it easier to put on.

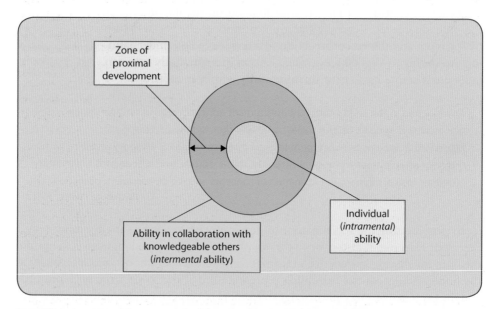

FIGURE 18.4 *Vygotsky's zone of proximal development (ZPD). The inner circle indicates the limit of a child's ability working on his or her own. The outer circle indicates the child's ability working in collaboration with a knowledgeable other. The area between the two is the ZPD.*

Are adults effective natural teachers?

As can be seen, the concepts of the ZPD and scaffolding are closely related because if we observe an adult providing appropriate scaffolding, this implies that they have appropriately assessed the ZPD. But do adults know the best ways of structuring the child's world and the most appropriate time and course of intervention? In other words, do adults make effective teachers? We shall now consider some of the relevant empirical evidence that addresses this question. A key researcher in this area is David Wood (Wood, 1986; Wood & Middleton, 1975; Wood *et al.*, 1978). We have selected his work because it represents a clear attempt to actually measure what goes on in adult–child interaction and specify what constitutes effective and ineffective teaching and learning.

The task employed in Wood's research was intentionally devised so that the 4-year-old children being tested could not solve it without help from their mothers. It involved the construction of a pyramid comprising 21 wooden blocks of different shapes and sizes that could be joined together with pegs if correctly orientated. The mothers were shown in advance how to construct the pyramid one layer at a time, using blocks of decreasing size, and were told to teach their children how to make it so that the children would be able to reconstruct it for themselves. The results from this experiment allowed Wood and Middleton to identify five categories of the mothers' behaviour to account for how they teach their children this particular task. One notable feature of these categories is that they are hierarchically organised in terms of the degree of control the mother takes of the situation. The first category identified was 'General Verbal Prompts' such as 'Now you make something'. Here the mother suggested action on the child's part but did not specify what to do. The level 2 category that emerged was termed 'Specific Verbal Instructions' and includes remarks of the type 'Get four big blocks'. These comments identify relevant features of the task to be taken into account in the next move. The third-level category, 'Indicates Materials' referred to mothers who helped their child by literally pointing out which block was needed next. Level 4 behaviour referred to where the mother literally prepared the block for assembly by correctly orientating the block so that the hole faced the peg; if the mother actually demonstrated by attaching the block herself, this was described as level 5.

Wood's two rules of effective teaching

As can be seen, level 1 interventions involve a very low level of maternal control whereas by level 5 the mothers have taken total control. On the basis of evidence taken from a series of studies, Wood (1986) was able to conclude that children were more likely to succeed on the task if their mothers followed what he terms the 'two rules' of teaching: 'the first dictates that any failure by a child to bring off an action after a given level of help should be met by an immediate increase in the level of control' (Wood, 1986, p. 163). Thus, for example, if the child does not respond appropriately to a general verbal prompt the mother needs to use a specific prompt.

The second of Wood's rules of teaching is that when a child is successful then the adult needs to decrease the level of control. Teaching in line with these two rules is termed 'contingent' and those mothers who showed contingent behaviour were those whose children were subsequently more able to complete the task alone. In other words, effective teaching can lead to effective learning. Wood's emphasis on contingency is closely linked to the concept of ZPD because contingent behaviour on the adult's part implies successful assessment of the ZPD.

Other researchers who also work within a neo-Vygtoskian framework have been critical of the concept of contingency. For example Hoogsteder *et al.* (1996) argue that Wood's approach minimises the child's role in the interaction and assumes the adult takes control in a piecemeal fashion. Hoogsteder *et al.* (1996) propose that adult–child interactions are far more dynamic with the child having a key role to play in their own learning. Thus even in a highly controlled setting such as Wood has used, the way in which the child might influence the adult's behaviour should not be underestimated.

Thus, to be effective teachers, adults need to make an accurate assessment of the child's current level of functioning, and of their potential level of functioning (their ZPD). Only then can an optimum level of scaffolding be provided, being neither insufficiently directive so as to prevent the child making an advance, nor too directive so as to minimise the child's active role in the process. Recent research demonstrates that the level of scaffolding children are exposed to influences their later education, by setting up expectations of learning and the role that they need to take in the process (Neitzel & Stright, 2003; Salonen *et al.*, 2007). With educational methods becoming more and more technologically advanced, the opportunities for teachers to provide scaffolding through information communications technology (ICT) present an important area for future research (Yelland & Masters, 2007).

Are children effective teachers?

We have considered how adults can be teachers for children by providing support through scaffolding to guide the child through their ZPD. However, it is not only adults that have the potential to be teachers: research evidence demonstrates that children can provide scaffolding to less developmentally advanced peers and guide them through their ZPD. Vygotsky's ideas about learning specify that the relationship should be one between an expert and a novice, without specifying that the expert has to be an adult and the novice a child.

Many studies using the neo-Piagetian pre-test, test, post-test design discussed earlier have investigated the effects of peer collaboration on post-test performance where the dyad consists of one less – and one more – developmentally advanced partner. For example,

FIGURE 18.5 *A child teaching another child how to build a brick tower.*

Source: Shuttershock.

Azmitia (1988) demonstrated that when 5-year-old children with little experience of LEGO® construction were paired with a more experienced partner, they showed greater improvements when subsequently completing a more complex building task than children who had been paired with a child of similar ability (Figure 18.5). Similar findings were reported by Garton and Pratt (2001) with a sorting task: post-test improvements were only observed in those children that had been paired with a child of higher ability. Fawcett and Garton (2005) extended these findings by showing that not only is it important that dyads are of mixed ability, but that children actively exchange ideas when working together. This suggests that the more able child is guiding the less able child through their ZPD; the dialogue first operating on an intermental level before being internalised to become intramental.

How might educational practice benefit from these findings? The focus of research is now shifting to gain a deeper understanding of how children should be grouped in order to facilitate cognitive advances. Findings from Schmitz and Winskel (2008) appear to suggest that the higher-ability child should be operating just beyond the lower-ability child's current (intramental) level of functioning. If the higher-ability child is functioning too far beyond this level, the gains for the lower-ability child are not as significant. Whether low-ability children benefit from working with children of higher ability also depends on the quality of the scaffolding that the partner provides and the potential to be actively involved in the task (Gabriele, 2007). Just as with adult teachers, scaffolding should not be so directive as to prevent the low-ability child from being an active participant in the process. Whilst peers can make good teachers, it is probably not surprising that adults have been found to produce both greater quality and quantity of verbal information in scaffolding exchanges (Ellis & Rogoff, 1982).

This brings us back to the questions for educational practice raised by Piaget's view of peer interaction. Although for different theoretical reasons, both Piaget and Vygotsky argued that undertaking tasks with peers can be itself an important mechanism of cognitive development. For Piaget, collaboration could lead to changes in the internal structures of thought, which would then influence the child's own construction of subsequent knowledge. For Vygotsky, dialogue on an intermental level (between minds), through interactions with more cognitively advanced partners, becomes intramental (within the mind). If working together can be more effective than working alone, the task facing developmental psychologists and teachers is to obtain a deeper understanding of the mechanisms of development during peer interaction, and perhaps more importantly, a clearer knowledge of the conditions under which few benefits emerge from peer interaction.

Implications for educational practice and assessment

In the United States there is already empirical evidence to support the efficacy of peer interaction and Vygotskian principles being put into educational practice. Work by Robert Slavin using a method known as **Student Teams Achievement Divisions (STAD)** has

Student Teams Achievement Divisions (STAD) a method used to show how cooperative learning can work. Children are allocated to work in small groups comprising children of varying ability, gender, and ethnic backgrounds. The teacher introduces a topic and the group members discuss this until they agree that they fully understand the topic.

FIGURE 18.6 *A group of school children taking part in cooperative learning.*
Source: Shutterstock.

shown how cooperative learning can work. Children working within the STAD technique are allocated to work in small groups (Figure 18.6). Each group intentionally comprises children of varying ability, gender, and ethnic backgrounds. The teacher introduces a topic to the group and the group's task is to discuss the problem and query each other until members of the group as a whole agree that they understand the topic. Research shows that children operating within STAD show greater achievement than control children taught using more conventional methods (Slavin, 1990).

Further approaches such as Peer Assisted Learning Stratgies (PALS; Fuchs *et al.*, 1999), Peer-Assisted Learning (PAL; Ginsburg-Block *et al.*, 2006) and Paired Thinking (Topping & Bryce, 2004) are clear examples of Vygotskian principles at work in the classroom in both the United States and the UK. The peer interaction involved is an important component of the success of these methods.

Another example of how Vygotsky's ideas have been put into practice is the development of 'reciprocal teaching' (Palincsar & Brown, 1984, 1988, 1989). This technique has been particularly successful on students who, while competent at reading, have difficulty with comprehending text. The teacher's role is to introduce strategies that improve comprehension such as how to précis a passage of text, asking relevant questions, and making predictions about the storyline. Although the teacher models these strategies, the children are required to take on increasing responsibility for the teaching role. One key aspect of reciprocal teaching to have emerged from research aimed at measuring its success is the importance of the teacher offering the right level of support relative to a student's current level of understanding (Palincsar & Brown, 1984). This is a very similar effect to that found in Wood's work described earlier in relation to contingency and mother–child interactions.

All of these approaches provide very convincing evidence that psychological principles can be used to good educational effect. However, how feasible is it that these principles will influence educational practice across the whole curriculum and the way that children's learning is assessed? Mercer and Fisher (1998) argue that one reason why research on actual classroom activity may not embrace concepts such as the ZPD is a practical one. The ZPD is highly specific not only to particular children, but also to particular situations. Therefore, the demands on teachers who plan activities for groups or whole classes would simply be too great. In recognition of these constraints, Mercer and Fisher argue that we should radically revise the way we think about research and classroom practice away from our traditional focus on individual learning toward how groups of learners may advance.

Interestingly, this conclusion is similar to those put forward by Littleton and Light (1999) in their review of children interacting with computers. It is certainly the case that those researchers taking a Vygotskian perspective present a much more serious challenge to educational practice than those who take a more traditional neo-Piagetian cognitive view. Our own view is that while children's learning environments may radically change as a result of developmental theorising and research, other aspects of educational practice will not change in the foreseeable future. In relation to the assessment of children's learning, we suspect that we are a long way off from seeing major changes in the way that children are assessed in the manner being asked for by Mercer and Fisher. While collaborative learning may well increase and become more structured in classrooms, the assessment of pupils at the individual level will, in our opinion, remain with us for some time to come. There are two grounds for risking this prediction. First, much of the support for assessment which is not at the individual level is still at a theoretical level. We simply do not, as yet, have the tools available to us to know how we might go about assessing children in groups or classes which would fulfil the usual demands for reliability and validity. In order to do this we will have to put in a good deal of empirical effort. The second reason for supposing that radical change is unlikely is far more beyond the control of psychological researchers, and that is the political forces involved in educational policy. The last 20 years has already witnessed radical educational reform, for example with the introduction of the National Curriculum in the UK. This reform is very much rooted in the principle of the assessment of individual learning, and debate continues over the most appropriate methods of assessing learning. It is to a discussion of this reform that we now turn.

PSYCHOLOGY, SCHOOLS AND EDUCATIONAL REFORM

The question of the relationship between the content of a school curriculum and the nature of children's learning is key in all developed countries. The tension between curriculum and learning processes is often most apparent when the issue of assessment arises. One clear example of this comes from the United States, when in 1988 the state of Georgia instituted a required test that had to be passed before children could move from kindergarten to first grade. Despite the fact that this is now common practice across America, the move resulted in public outcry regarding the purpose of assessment and its relationship to learning (Woolfolk, 1998). Furthermore, the debate extended to the thorny issue of whether there should be national standards and a national test, and, if so, what such standards and tests should be. In the UK the past 30 years have brought about an almost complete U-turn in educational practice, with the emphasis shifting from child-centred education to curriculum-centred education. The 1967 Plowden Report, entitled *Children and Their Primary Schools,* stated that 'at the heart of the educational process lies the child'. In the mid-1980s the then UK secretary of state for education, Kenneth Baker, remarked that 'at the heart of the educational process lies the curriculum'. Such a radical shift must have an impact on how psychological research might and does influence educational practice.

attainment targets descriptions of the knowledge that children should have acquired as they work their way through the education system.

The UK Education Reform Act of 1988 introduced a compulsory National Curriculum for all children between 5 and 16 years. It defined 'foundation' subjects that would have to be taught, namely, English, mathematics, science, technology, history, geography, art, music, and physical education. Of these, English, mathematics, and science are considered 'core' subjects demanding the majority of curriculum time and effort. Importantly the National Curriculum specified 'Attainment Targets', or descriptions of the knowledge that children should have acquired as they work their way through the education system. It is these **attainment targets** at **key stages** that provide the benchmark for assessment of children's performance throughout their school lives.

key stages stages of the state education system in England, Wales, and Northern Island: KS1 5–7-year-olds; KS2 7–11 years; KS3 11–14 years; KS4 14–16 years; KS5 16–18 years.

Assessing children's learning

Two crucial aspects of the assessment procedures introduced by the National Curriculum are relevant here. First, they represented the first compulsory assessment of children as young as 7 after only two or three years of formal schooling, and, second, the method of testing was intentionally different from standard forms of testing. Most scholastic tests are **norm referenced**; that is, they provide a measure of a given child's performance only relative to other children. However, the tests introduced with the National Curriculum are **criterion referenced** in that they give a measure of the child's performance relative to a specified criterion, in this case a given attainment target in a core curriculum subject. Criterion-referenced testing brings with it both advantages and disadvantages. From a statistical point of view, there are no standard measures of reliability for criterion-referenced tests like those that exist for norm-referenced tests, but new models are being developed which can overcome this (e.g. Schagen & Hutchinson, 1994). The main advantage of criterion-referenced testing is that it gives a description of what the child actually knows in a given area rather than an indication of whether the child is performing better or worse than other children. This **formative** nature of testing, at least in principle, indicates to teachers where their efforts need to be concentrated. Indeed, one of the principle aims of the National Curriculum was that testing children using criterion-referenced Standard Assessment Tasks (SATs) would result in a significant increase in educational standards.

norm referencing tests based on the average scores for the population, and hence provide a reference point to indicate how individual children perform relative to the scores of other children.

criterion referencing the measure of a child's performance relative to a specified criterion.

formative testing a form of assessment where the purpose is to provide guidance for further learning, rather than measuring the outcomes of learning.

Unfortunately, the testing process has been met with much criticism, most notably over the pressure it puts on such young children (e.g. Reay & Wiliam, 1999). The whole concept of assessing children against attainment targets they should have reached by a particular age is itself contentious. There are echoes of Piaget's approach here – that all children develop through a fixed number of developmental stages at specified times. For example, in mathematics, the age at which many concepts are introduced into the curriculum is in line with the age at which Piaget suggested children possess the necessary conceptual understanding. The problem is that a child's true level of understanding of a given concept and the level of understanding they appear to demonstrate based upon their performance on a particular task are not always the same. Correct answers on some experimental tasks can be reached through the use of simple strategies, or **heuristics**, rather than through the correct application of conceptual understanding (Worsfold *et al.*, 2008). It might also be incorrect to assume that all children's understanding develops in line with strict chronological age increases. So what are the alternatives to standard criterion-referenced assessment? There are currently two forms of assessment that are stimulating a significant amount of research and discussion.

heuristics simple strategies for reaching solutions.

The first, **single-level testing**, is the proposed alternative to criterion-referenced National Curriculum assessment. In the criterion-referenced system, children are given a 'level' according to the understanding they demonstrate against attainment targets. All children of a given age are assessed against the same criteria, at the same point in time. Single-level testing is part of a UK government consultation termed 'Making Good Progress', and is a more personalised learning and assessment approach. Children are not all expected to reach a given educational level at a fixed chronological age; instead, children are assessed when they are ready to achieve that level. Single-level testing is currently in the pilot stage, but is promising in its recognition of individual differences in the rate of development of ability.

single-level testing a form of testing in which children are not all expected to reach a given educational level at a fixed chronological age and instead are assessed when they are ready to achieve that level.

The second alternative, receiving increasing research interest, is **dynamic assessment** (Elliott, 2003; Kozulin & Falik, 1995). This approach is rooted in the Vygotskian tradition: many standardised tests assess current levels of performance, whereas proponents of dynamic assessment argue that it is far more beneficial to assess the child's potential for proceeding beyond their current level of performance. Thus, dynamic assessment makes a measurement of the child's dynamic potential for learning, akin to their ZPD, rather than assessing the product of learning, which is static. Two children could appear to be functioning at the same cognitive level if current levels of performance are assessed, but could differ markedly in their potential for learning, in other words, in the 'size' of their ZPD. Dynamic assessment measures a child's cognitive modifiability, that is, their potential to advance their thinking as a result of structured input in a testing situation. It could be argued that assessing the child's response to such scaffolding could be a better criterion for educational success.

dynamic assessment this method of assessment is based on the view that it is beneficial to assess the child's potential for proceeding beyond their current level of performance.

The principles of dynamic assessment are exemplified in Feuerstein's (1979) Learning Propensity Assessment Device (LPAD). This instrument is based on Feuerstein's theory of mediated learning experience, where a mediator (parent, teacher, more-able peer) plays an important role in the relationship between the learner and the material to be learned, guiding the learner's understanding and interpretation of the material. By administering the LPAD tasks, and observing and directing the child's functioning, the assessor can build up a profile of the child's cognitive modifiability, including details about how much cognitive change the child is capable of, what barriers the child may face in achieving this level, and how likely it is that the change will generalise to other areas of understanding (Kozulin & Falik, 1995). The prospective nature of this form of assessment offers teachers the opportunity to direct their teaching towards a child's ZPD, and for the child, shifts the focus from how their current cognitive level places them amongst their peers and against attainment targets to what they have the potential to achieve.

SUMMARY AND CONCLUSIONS

In this chapter we have reviewed some of the theories and evidence from developmental psychology and highlighted a few key areas that we believe to be of direct relevance to those involved in children's education. In conclusion, we must ask whether developmental psychology as a discipline is sufficiently healthy to remain optimistic about possible future changes in educational practice and policy. We think there are two reasons why a reasonable degree of optimism is justified. First, there are no indications that developmental psychologists are losing interest in fundamental questions about the nature of learning and the factors that influence learning. There is lively theoretical debate coupled with solid empirical effort. The ever increasing interest in more socially based models of development such as Vygotsky's can only be a good thing for the potential of our discipline to inform educational practice. It forces us to recognise the importance of children's learning both in and out of school, and accept that learning, like teaching, is rarely a solitary individual activity but involves interaction with adults and peers alike. The second reason to remain optimistic is that there is a growing body of developmental research tackling specific curriculum areas such as reading and mathematics (see Chapter 11). This research is already having a direct impact on the way that the curriculum is presented to children and will continue to do so. It is the development of a strong reciprocal relationship between academic psychology, educational practitioners and the policy makers that will lead to the greatest advances in the translation of knowledge about how children learn, into rich and effective learning environments.

DISCUSSION POINTS

1. Compare the implications of Piaget's and Vygotsky's theories for educational practice.
2. List and consider the factors that might lead to peer presence effects on children's performance.
3. How might gender differences in performance on computer-based tasks be minimised?
4. Why is the zone of proximal development difficult to measure?
5. Considering in particular Vygotsky's theory, how can adults and parents best support children's learning?
6. Can children teach children?
7. How might positive educational effects of peer interaction be encouraged in the classroom?

SUGGESTIONS FOR FURTHER READING

Faulkner, D., Littleton, K., & Woodhead, M. (1998). *Learning relationships in the classroom*. London: Routledge.

Langford, P.E. (2005). *Vygotsky's developmental and educational psychology*. Hove: Psychology Press.

Slavin, R.E. (2004). When and why does cooperative learning increase achievement? Theoretical and empirical perspectives. In H. Daniels & A. Edwards (Eds.) *The RoutledgeFalmer reader in psychology of education* (pp. 271–293). London: RoutledgeFalmer.

Whitebread, D. (2010). *Developmental psychology and early childhood education*. London: Sage.

REFERENCES

Azmitia, M. (1988). Peer interaction and problem-solving: When are two heads better than one? *Child Development, 59*, 87–96.

Barbieri, J.S., & Light, P.H. (1992). Interaction, gender and performance on a computer-based problem solving task. *Learning and Instruction, 2*, 199–214.

Black, P., & Wiliam, D. (2009). Developing the theory of formative assessment. *Educational Assessment, Evaluation and Accountability, 21*, 5–31.

Blatchford, P., Baines, E., Rubie-Davies, C., Bassett, P., & Chowne, A. (2006). The effect of a new approach to group work on pupil–pupil and teacher–pupil interactions. *Journal of Educational Psychology, 98*, 750–765.

Blaye, A., Light, P.H., Joiner, R., & Sheldon, S. (1991). Collaboration as a facilitator of planning and problem solving on a computer-based task. *British Journal of Developmental Psychology, 9*, 471–483.

Bruner, J.S. (1983). *Child's talk: Learning to use language*. Oxford: Oxford University Press.

Bryant, P.E. (1990). Empirical evidence for causes in development. In G. Butterworth & P. Bryant (Eds.) *Causes of development* (pp. 33–45). Brighton: Harvester Wheatsheaf.

Colley, A., & Comber, C. (2003). Age and gender differences in computer use and attitudes among secondary school students: What has changed? *Educational Research, 45*, 155–165.

Crook, C.K. (1994). *Computers and the collaborative experience of learning*. London: Routledge.

Culley, L. (1993). Gender equity and computing in secondary schools: Issues and strategies for teachers. In J. Benyon & H. Mackay (Eds.) *Computers into classrooms: More questions than answers* (pp. 147–159). London: Falmer Press.

Davis, A.M. (1991). Piaget, teachers and education. In P. Light, S. Sheldon, & M. Woodhead (Eds.) *Child development in social context. Vol 2. Learning to think* (pp. 16–31). London: Routledge.

Dimant, R.J., & Bearison, D.J. (1991). Development of formal reasoning during successive peer interactions. *Developmental Psychology, 27*, 277–284.

Doise, W., & Mugny, G. (1984). *The social development of the intellect*. Oxford: Pergamon.

Druyan, S. (2001). A comparison of four types of cognitive conflict and their effect on cognitive development. *International Journal of Behavioral Development, 25*, 226–236.

Elliott, J. (2003). Dynamic assessment in educational settings: Realising potential. *Educational Review, 55*, 15–32.

Ellis, S., & Rogoff, B. (1982). The strategies and efficacy of child versus adult teachers. *Child Development, 53*, 730–735.

Fawcett, L.M., & Garton, A.F. (2005). The effect of peer collaboration on children's problem-solving ability. *British Journal of Educational Psychology, 75*, 157–169.

Feuerstein, R. (1979). *The dynamic assessment of retarded performers: Learning Potential Assessment Device*. Baltimore, MD: University Park Press.

Fuchs, L.S., Fuchs, D., Kazdan, S., & Allen, S. (1999). Effects of peer-assisted learning strategies in reading with and without training in elaborated help giving. *Elementary School Journal, 99*, 201–219.

Gabriele, A.J. (2007). The influence of achievement goals on the constructive activity of low achievers during collaborative problem solving. *British Journal of Educational Psychology, 77*, 121–141.

Garton, A.F., & Pratt, C. (2001). Peer assistance in children's problem solving. *British Journal of Developmental Psychology, 19*, 307–318.

Gillies, R.M. (2002). The residual effects of cooperative-learning experiences: A two-year follow-up. *Journal of Educational Research, 96*, 15–20.

Ginsburg-Block, M.D., Rohrbeck, C.A., & Fantuzzo, J.W. (2006). A meta-analytic review of social, self-concept, and behavioural outcomes of peer-assisted learning. *Journal of Educational Psychology, 98*, 732–749.

Glachan, M., & Light, P.H. (1982). Peer interaction and learning. In G.E. Butterworth & P.H. Light (Eds.) *Social cognition: Studies of the development of understanding* (pp. 233–260). Brighton: Harvester Press.

Golbech, S.L., & Sinagra, K. (2000). Effects of gender and collaboration on college students' performance on a piagetian spatial task. *Journal of Experimental Education, 69*, 22–36.

Hoogsteder, M., Maier, R., & Elbers, E. (1996). The architecture of adult–child interaction: Joint problem solving and the structure of cooperation. *Learning and Instruction, 6*, 345–358.

Howe, C., McWilliam, D., & Cross, G. (2005). Chance favours only the prepared mind: Incubation and the delayed effects of peer collaboration. *British Journal of Psychology, 96*, 67–93.

Howe, C., & Tolmie, A. (1999). Productive interaction in the context of computer-supported collaborative learning in science. In K. Littleton & P. Light (Eds.) *Learning with computers: Analysing productive interaction* (pp. 24–45). London: Routledge.

Hughes, M. (1986). *Children and number: Difficulties in learning mathematics*. Oxford: Blackwell.

Kozulin, A., & Falik, L. (1995). Dynamic cognitive assessment of the child. *Current Directions in Psychological Science, 4*, 192–196.

Leman, P. (2002). Argument structure, argument content, and cognitive change in children's peer interaction. *Journal of Genetic Psychology, 163*, 40–57.

Leman, P.J., & Oldham, Z. (2005). Do children need to learn to collaborate? The effect of age and age differences on collaborative recall. *Cognitive Development, 20*, 33–48.

Levin, I., & Druyan, S. (1993). When sociocognitive transaction between peers fails: The case of misconceptions in science. *Child Development, 64*, 1571–1591.

Light, P.H. (1997). Computers for learning: Psychological perspectives. *Journal of Child Psychology and Psychiatry, 38*, 1–8.

Littleton, K., & Light, P. (Eds.) (1999). *Learning with computers: Analysing productive interaction*. London: Routledge.

Littleton, K., Light, P., Barnes, P., Messer, D., & Joiner, R. (1992). Pairing and gender effects in computer based learning. *European Journal of Psychology of Education, 7*, 1–14.

Littleton, K., Light, P., Joiner, R., Messer, D., & Barnes, P. (1998). Gender and software effects in computer-based problem solving. *Educational Psychology, 7*, 327–340.

Littleton, K., Mercer, N., Dawes, L., Wegerif, R., Rowe, D., & Sams, C. (2005). Talking and thinking together at key stage 1. *Early Years, 25*, 165–180.

Mercer, N., & Fisher, E. (1998). How do teachers help children to learn? An analysis of teachers' interventions in computer-based activities. In D. Faulkner, K. Littleton, & M. Woodhead (Eds.) *Learning relationships in the classroom* (pp. 111–130). London: Routledge.

Neitzel, C., & Stright, A.D. (2003). Mothers' scaffolding of children's problem solving: Establishing a foundation of academic self-regulatory competence. *Journal of Family Psychology, 17*, 147–159.

North, A.S., & Noyes, J.M. (2002). Gender influences on children's computer attitudes and cognitions. *Computers in Human Behaviour, 18*, 135–150.

Oosterwegel, A., Littleton, K., & Light, P. (2004). Understanding computer-related attitudes through an idiographic analysis of gender- and self-representations. *Learning and Instruction, 14*, 215–233.

Palincsar, A.S., & Brown, A.L. (1984). Reciprocal teaching of comprehension-fostering and monitoring activities. *Cognition and Instruction, 1*, 117–175.

Palincsar, A.S., & Brown, A.L. (1988). Teaching and practicing thinking skills to promote comprehension in the context of group problem solving. *Remedial and Special Education, 9*, 53–59.

Palincsar, A.S., & Brown, A.L. (1989). Classroom dialogues to promote self-regulated comprehension. In J. Brophy (Ed.) *Advances in research on teaching* (Vol. 1; pp. 35–67). Greenwich: JAI Press.

Perret-Clermont, A.N. (1980). *Social interaction and cognitive development in children*. London: Academic Press.

Piaget, J. (1926). *The language and thought of the child*. London: Routledge & Kegan Paul.

Piaget, J. (1932). *The moral development of the child*. London: Routledge.

Piaget, J., & Inhelder, B. (1956). *The child's conception of space*. New York: W.W. Norton.

Plowden Report. (1967). *Children and their primary schools*. London: HMSO.

Puncochar, J.M., & Fox, P.W. (2004). Confidence in individual and group decision making: When 'two heads' are worse than one. *Journal of Educational Psychology, 96*, 582–591.

Reay, D., & Wiliam, D. (1999). 'I'll be a nothing': Structure, agency, and the construction of identity through assessment. *British Education Research Journal, 25*, 343–354.

Salonen, P., Lepola, J., & Vauras, M. (2007). Scaffolding interaction in parent–child dyads: Multimodal analysis of parental scaffolding with task and non-task oriented children. *European Journal of Psychology of Education, 22*, 77–96.

Samaha, N.V. & DeLisi, R. (2000). Peer collaboration on a nonverbal reasoning task by urban, minority students. *Journal of Experimental Education, 69*, 5–23.

Schagen, I., & Hutchinson, D. (1994). Measuring the reliability of National Curriculum Assessment. *Educational Research, 36*, 211–221.

Schmitz, M.J., & Winskel, H. (2008). Towards effective partnerships in a collaborative problem-solving task. *British Journal of Educational Psychology, 78*, 581–596.

Slavin, R.E. (1990). *Co-operative learning: Theory, research and practice*. Englewood Cliffs, NJ: Prentice Hall.

Topping, K.J., & Bryce, A. (2004). Cross-age peer tutoring of reading and thinking: Influence on thinking skills. *Educational Psychology, 24*, 595–621.

Underwood, J., & Underwood, G. (1999). Task effects on co-operative and collaborative learning with computers. In K. Littleton & P. Light (Eds.) *Learning with computers: Analysing productive interaction* (pp. 10–23). London: Routledge.

Underwood, G., Underwood, J., & Turner, M. (1993). Children's thinking during collaborative computer-based problem solving. *Educational Psychology, 13*, 345–358.

Underwood, J., Underwood, G., & Wood, D. (2000). When does gender matter? Interactions during computer-based problem solving. *Learning and Instruction, 10*, 447–462.

Vygotsky, L.S. (1978). *Mind in society*. Cambridge, MA: Harvard University Press.

Vygotsky, L.S. (1981). The genesis of higher mental functions. In J.V. Wertsch (Ed.) *The concept of activity in Soviet psychology* (pp. 144–188). New York: Sharpe.

Wood, D. (1986). Aspects of teaching and learning. In M. Richards and P. Light (Eds.) *Children of social worlds* (pp. 191–212). Cambridge: Polity.

Wood, D.J., Bruner, J.S., & Ross, G. (1976). The role of tutoring in problem solving. *Journal of Child Psychology and Psychiatry, 17,* 89–100.

Wood, D.J., & Middleton, D.J. (1975). A study of assisted problem solving. *British Journal of Psychology, 66,* 181–191.

Wood, D.J., Wood, H.A., & Middleton, D.J. (1978). An experimental evaluation of four face to face teaching strategies. *International Journal of Behavioral Development, 1,* 131–147.

Woolfolk, A.E. (1998). *Educational Psychology.* Boston, MA: Allyn & Bacon.

Worsfold, N., Davis, A., & De Bruyn, B. (2008). The effect of horizontal versus vertical task presentation on children's performance in coordinate tasks. *Perception, 37,* 1667–1676.

Yarrow, F., & Topping, K.J. (2001). Collaborative writing: The effects of metacognitive prompting and structured peer interaction. *British Journal of Educational Psychology, 71,* 261–282.

Yelland, N., & Masters, J. (2007). Rethinking scaffolding in the information age. *Computers and Education, 48,* 362–382.

19 Risk and Resilience in Development

LESLIE MORRISON GUTMAN AND EIRINI FLOURI

KEY TERMS

Adverse Life Events Scale • asset-focused programmes • authoritative parenting • childhood income poverty • cumulative risk theory • external support systems • externalising behaviour problems • intergenerational cycle of difficulties • internalising behaviour problems • locus of control • main effects models • mediator effects models • moderator (interactive) effects models • process-oriented programmes • protective factor • resilience • risk accumulation • risk factors • risk specificity • secure attachment • vulnerability factors

CHAPTER OUTLINE

OVERVIEW

Although it is our hope that children will grow up in a happy supportive environment, this is not always the case. Thus it is vital to develop an understanding of the effects different adverse experiences may have on children's development, but also to understand the other side of the coin, children's resilience in the face of these adverse events. Risk factors can arise from within the family, but also from the peer group, school, community, and wider society, and range from bereavement and divorce through lack of school resources, to racism and prejudice. The chapter reviews the effects of these risk factors on children's developmental outcomes, particularly the level of school achievement and social development. Unfortunately, many children encounter more than one risk factor. Under these circumstances, the effect of risk factors is cumulative, and may lead to dysfunction when the adaptive capacity of the individual child is overwhelmed.

Not all children are affected in the same way by a particular risk factor or combination of factors, and some of the research focuses on the processes that support resilience, or undermine it. Protective factors such as a warm cohesive family structure or external support systems can do much to offset the negative effects of risk factors. Additionally, the child's personality and level of self-esteem affect how they respond to risk factors. The chapter reviews different models to explain the degree of resilience an individual child shows in the face of risk factors. Although one might be forgiven for reaching a pessimistic view of the outcome for children faced with severe adversity, the evidence points to astonishing resilience in the face of these factors and marked capacity for recovery. However, relying on children's resilience is clearly no solution, and there is a continuing need for positive family and community based interventions to provide children with the support they need.

INTRODUCTION

Why do some children do well despite facing life adversities? For more than three decades, child psychologists have been interested in the study of risk and **resilience**. Risk has been defined as those stressors that have proven or presumed effects on increasing the likelihood of maladjustment in children, such as poverty, maltreatment, and family dissolution (Rolf & Johnson, 1990). Resilience occurs when children experience positive outcomes despite experiencing significant risk. To infer resilience, two coexisting conditions must apply: (1) exposure to threat or severe adversity and (2) achievement of positive adaptation (Masten & Coatsworth, 1998). In this sense, resilience is not an attribute or personality trait that some children possess and others do not. Rather, resilience is a developmental process which refers to the fact of maintaining adaptive functioning in spite of serious risk (Rutter, 1987).

> **resilience** occurs when children experience positive outcomes despite experiencing significant risk.

Resilience does not mean invulnerability. Children may experience resilience yet still suffer from the residual effects of trauma. Furthermore, resilience is not indefinite. Children who meet the criteria for resilience may not necessarily be doing well continually, in every possible circumstance, and in totality. Rather, resilience is demonstrated by adaptive behaviours and life patterns. In this sense, resilience is a process that can be modified as new risks and/or strengths emerge with changing life circumstances.

HISTORICAL BACKGROUND

The historical roots of resilience research can be traced to research on individuals with psychopathology. The work of Norman Garmezy and his colleagues was particularly important in this regard. During the 1940s and 1950s, Garmezy examined the history and prognosis of patients with serious mental disorders such as schizophrenia. In the 1960s, Garmezy was interested in understanding the antecedents of mental illness and thus began to focus on the children of mentally ill parents due to their elevated risk of developing disorders. He was surprised to discover that many of these children were doing well. By the early 1970s, Garmezy and his research team shifted their focus to the study of competence in children who were at risk due to parental mental illness, poverty, and stressful life experiences. In 1976, Ann Masten joined the research team which was named Project Competence. Their research represents one of the earliest efforts to define the positive factors that compensate for the presence of risk in children's lives.

Another landmark study was conducted by Emmy Werner and Ruth Smith. This longitudinal study spanning more than four decades followed the development of nearly 700 children born on the Hawaiian island of Kauai in 1955. Although most of the children experienced some level of risk such as poverty and low parental education, one-third experienced multiple risks. Despite these risks, one-third of the children with more than four risks developed well in terms of getting along with their parents and peers, doing well in school, and having good mental health. This resilient group had more resources such as good temperaments and positive parenting in their lives. Most of these children grew up to be successful adults – in stable marriages and jobs and satisfied with their relationships and life circumstances.

These early efforts played a crucial role in the recognition of childhood resilience as a major theoretical and empirical field of study. These endeavours enhanced our understanding of the pathways to psychopathology and the processes that lead to normal development. More importantly, this body of work challenged deficit models that characterised the developmental course of disadvantaged children as deterministic, with an inevitable trajectory leading to maladjustment and pathology. This early work inspired others to focus on how resilience research may inform social policy and shape prevention and intervention programmes to improve the lives of at risk children and families.

Following this earlier research, scholarly interest in the study of resilience burgeoned. More contemporary researchers, however, have criticised some of the conceptualisations and methods used by early resilience researchers. One of the main criticisms concerns the absence of a unifying conceptual framework across disciplines and specialised areas (Luthar *et al.*, 2000). A scientific basis for intervention research necessitates precise terminology to build upon earlier classifications and to ensure its continued vitality. A consistent and systematic framework is essential to facilitate the work of researchers and practitioners who pursue work in this area, to integrate findings across diverse fields, as well as provide guidance for the identification and implementation of age-appropriate, optimal targets for preventive interventions (Masten & Powell, 2003). For these reasons, it is essential to delineate the main concepts involved in the study of resilience, such as **risk factors** and **protective/vulnerability factors**, as well as to describe models of risk and resilience and definitions of successful developmental outcomes.

risk factors catastrophic events such as war and natural disasters, family adversities such as bereavement and divorce, economic conditions such as poverty, and exposure to negative environments such as impoverished neighbourhoods.

RISK FACTORS

Risk factors include catastrophic events such as war and natural disasters, family adversities such as bereavement and divorce, economic conditions such as poverty, and exposure to negative environments such as impoverished neighbourhoods. Table 19.1 provides a list of examples of risk factors for children. Risk factors pose a pervasive threat through the deprivation of children's basic needs such as physical sustenance and protection, emotional security and attachment, and social interaction. As a result, exposure to risk factors predicts a variety of difficulties in adjustment and adaptation both concurrently and across the lifespan.

protective factor
anything that prevents or reduces vulnerability for the development of a disorder.

vulnerability factors
those attributes of the individual that contribute to maladjustment under conditions of adversity.

Table 19.1 *Examples of risk factors for children*

Domain	Factor
Family processes	Bereavement Family dissolution Maltreatment Harsh parenting Inter-parental conflict
Parent characteristics	Poor mental health Substance abuse Low education
Family context	Single parenthood Numerous stressful life events Household crowding Poverty
Peers	Peer rejection Deviant peers
Schools	Lower qualified teachers Lack of school resources
Community	Violence Poverty Crime Victimisation Societal discrimination Racism Prejudice
Environment	War Catastrophic natural events

Children's exposure to risk varies according to age. Children in the first few years of life have not established any independent functioning and therefore are highly dependent on their families. As a result, young children are particularly vulnerable to adversities involving their parents and caregivers. However, infants are less likely to suffer from difficulties involving their social environment such as atrocities of war or the significance of major disasters by their lack of understanding of what is happening. Adolescents, on the other hand, have larger and more varied social communities and therefore may have access to supportive environments other than their family. Yet, adolescents are more influenced by the loss and devastation involved in war and natural disasters. They have a greater understanding of what these events signify for their future, a realisation that extends beyond the mental capabilities of young children.

Parental bereavement

One of the most immediately traumatising events for children and adolescents is the death of a parent (Ribbens & McCarthy, 2006). Parental bereavement represents a permanent loss and separation from a primary caregiver (Figure 19.1). The process of bereavement can be aggravated by additional stressors such as family restructuring, new expectations of children's behaviour, parental grief and distress, and death reminders (Sandler *et al.*, 2003). On the other hand, there is evidence that parental death typically has a smaller (less negative) effect on children than the effect of parental divorce (Biblarz & Gottainer, 2000), which, as will be discussed below, also has relatively modest, in general, effects on child adjustment, particularly in the long term.

Parental separation/divorce and inter-parental conflict

FIGURE 19.1 *One of the most immediately traumatising events for children and adolescents is the death of a parent.*
Source: Shutterstock.

Family dissolution from parental divorce increases children's risk for psychological, behavioural, social, and academic problems. Research suggests that children who grow up in single-parent homes are less successful, on average, than children who grow up in two-parent homes. These differences have been found to relate to a broad range of outcomes (Hetherington & Kelly, 2002). Risk is greatest for children of divorced parents who experience high inter-parental conflict, loss of contact with one parent, problems with the mental

health of parents, less economic stability, and whose parents have multiple marital transitions (Hetherington & Elmore, 2003). Although the intensity diminishes
across time, offspring of divorced and remarried families experience difficulties that
extend into adolescence and young adulthood (Hetherington, 1989; Hetherington
& Kelly, 2002). Particularly disturbing is the **intergenerational cycle**
of difficulties in relationships with others. Children of divorced
parents are more likely to have problems with family members, in
intimate relations, in marriage, and in the workplace. Their divorce
rate is also higher, and their reports of general well-being and life
satisfaction are lower (Hetherington, 1989, 1999; Hetherington
& Kelly, 2002). Nevertheless, resilience is the normative outcome
for children who are faced with their parents' marital transitions.
In the absence of additional adversities, the vast majority of children of divorced
parents usually develop into competent well-adjusted adults (Hetherington &
Elmore, 2003). The general consensus is that the deterioration of economic conditions that usually results from family disruption (McLanahan, 1999) is the major
explanation for these children's lower ability and achievement, although not necessarily for their emotional and behaviour problems (Duncan *et al.*, 1998).

> **intergenerational cycle**
> **of difficulties** the vari-
> ous implicit and explicit
> non-verbal and verbal
> ways parents commu-
> nicate their traumatic
> experiences and their
> experiences of shared
> events traumatically.

Abuse and maltreatment

Abuse and maltreatment pose a severe threat to children's development. Child abuse
involves a significant deviation from the normative environment required for children's successful development, and, as a result, few maltreated children experience
resilience (Cicchetti & Lynch, 1995). Child maltreatment also tends to co-occur with
other environmental risks such as inter-parental conflict, parental psychopathology,
parental substance abuse, and poverty (Lynch and Cicchetti, 1998). Another issue that
hinders resilience is the lack of protective factors in maltreated children's lives. For
example, parenting quality may be a protective factor for at-risk children, but maltreated children, by definition, are unlikely to receive quality parenting (Bolger &
Patterson, 2003). Despite this, there are maltreated children who achieve higher levels
of adaptation than others (Cicchetti & Rogosch, 1997). This is likely due to the heterogeneity of maltreatment experiences. Children who are older at the age of onset of
maltreatment and who are exposed to shorter, less severe and pervasive experiences
of abuse are more likely to experience resilience (Bolger & Patterson, 2003).

Parental psychological disturbances

Parental mental health problems and drug/alcohol use have also been linked to a
variety of behavioural, socio-emotional, and cognitive problems in children (Luthar *et*
al., 2003; Rutter, 1979; Sameroff & Seifer, 1987; Sameroff *et al.* 1993; Werner, 1993). Many
of these disorders co-exist and therefore it is often difficult to disentangle their effects
on children. For instance, drug-abusing parents also tend to report a higher degree of

psychological disturbances, stressful life events, and financial problems (Luthar, D'Avanzo, & Hites, 2003). For many of these, exposure to traumatic life experiences also exacerbates their vulnerability to psychological problems such as anxiety (Luthar *et al.*, 1998). Parental psychological disturbances also interfere with interpersonal relationships within the family as well as compromise family functioning (e.g. when daily tasks are not accomplished).

Most of the studies examining the risks associated with parental psychiatric disturbance have focused on depression, particularly of mothers. This is because depression is more common in women than in men, but also because women are more likely to serve as the primary caregiver. Findings consistently show that children of depressed mothers are at greater risk of poor adjustment compared to youth of similar socioeconomic backgrounds (see Hammen, 2003, for a review). For example, the risk of major depression is more than twice as high in children of depressed parents as in children of non-depressed parents. This leads to the question of what is more important in the transmission of depression: genetic or environmental factors? Although the genetic effects appear to be significant, non-genetic factors are better predictors of depression. Furthermore, there is no evidence of a single depressive gene or defect and, most likely, there never will be given the heterogeneity of depression and its multiple pathways. Also, it is not clear what is transmitted. For example, environmental factors such as parenting quality, life stress, and marital conflict that increase children's risk of depression may themselves be inheritable (Goodman & Gotlib, 1999).

Apart from genetic mechanisms of risk, the quality and quantity of parenting behaviours are likely the key determinants relating to the poor functioning of children and adolescents with depressed mothers. According to a review by Lovejoy *et al.*, (2000), in interacting with their children depressed mothers show more negative/hostile behaviours (negative emotions, criticism, and negative facial expressions), fewer positive behaviours (pleasant emotions, praise, affectionate facial expressions), and more disengagement (ignoring, silence, gaze aversion) than non-depressed mothers. The effects of maternal depression on positive parenting were strongest for socioeconomically disadvantaged mothers and mothers of children under 1 year of age. This suggests that the youngest children, particularly babies, who are most dependent on their parents, experience the most impaired parenting associated with maternal depression. Such negative interactions may lead to insecure attachment and discourage the acquisition of important interpersonal skills and problem-solving abilities, which eventually may lead to impaired social and psychological functioning (Goodman & Gotlib, 1999).

Socioeconomic risks

childhood income poverty living in a family whose income falls below a specified level necessary for minimum coverage of basic expenses has been shown to increase the risk of negative child outcomes.

Childhood income poverty – defined by living in a family whose income falls below a specified level necessary for minimum coverage of basic expenses – has been shown to increase the risk of negative child outcomes. Poverty has more detrimental effects if it is extreme and chronic (Figure 19.2). Such negative effects include poor physical health, lower academic and school performance and attainment, and increased likelihood of social, emotional and behavioural difficulties (see McLoyd, 1990, 1998, for reviews). The evidence for the role of the timing of poverty or socio-economic adversity in general effects is less conclusive (Duncan *et al.*, 1994). However, some researchers have shown that poverty in early childhood is more deleterious to long-term achievement outcomes than poverty in middle childhood or adolescence. Duncan *et al.* (1998), for example, showed that for low-income American children a $10,000 increase in mean family income between birth and age 5 was associated with nearly a one-year increase in completed schooling. Similar increments to family income later in childhood had no statistically significant impact. Similarly in the UK, Schoon *et al.* (2002), using data collected from both the 1958 British birth cohort and the 1970 British birth cohort, found that for both cohorts the influence of concurrent disadvantage on academic achievement and subsequent social class attainment was greatest during early childhood.

FIGURE 19.2 *Childhood poverty has been shown to increase the risk of negative child outcomes.* *Source:* Shutterstock.

Another socioeconomic risk for children's cognitive and social development that has attracted a lot of research is low parental socioeconomic status and low parental education. Parental education influences the educational advantages of the family and their access to key educational resources and opportunities. A larger family size, or greater number of children living in the home, also increases the risk of negative outcomes for children (Rutter, 1979; Sameroff *et al.* 1987, 1993). This is most likely due to the fact that a greater number of family members decreases the amount of resources that is available per person.

Although all these risk factors are, in general, associated with children's poor functioning, there is increasing evidence that different socioeconomic risks are differently associated with child outcomes. For example, Goodman (1999) who explored the role of household income, parental education, and parental occupation in US adolescents' mental health showed that even after adjustment for other factors, education and income remained independent correlates of depression but only income remained an independent correlate of attempted suicide. More recently, Goodman *et al.* (2003) examined the public health impact of parental socioeconomic status on adolescents' depression. They showed that although both low household income and low parental education predicted depression across each gender and race/ethnicity group, the risk associated with low education significantly exceeded the risk associated with low income (40% and 26%, respectively). Together, these studies suggest that the effects of low parental education versus low parental income on children will likely vary according to the particular child outcome examined.

Even when the same socioeconomic risk indicator is used, however, specificity in both child outcomes and child populations must be considered. Costello *et al.* (2003), for instance, found that an income intervention that moved rural American families out of poverty significantly improved children's externalising but not **internalising behaviour problems**. Earlier, McGauhey and Starfield (1993) had shown that while low family income was a consistent risk factor for poor health among white children, low income alone was not a risk factor for black children. Among black children, other social risks that are associated with poverty, such as low maternal education, increased the probability of poor child health status.

> **internalising behaviour problems** withdrawal, inhibition, anxiety, and/ or depression.

Stressful life events

The number of stressful life events encountered by the child and/or family has received a lot of attention in developmental psychopathology (Grant *et al.*, 2006, for a review). Stressful life events range from the trivial to severe and from desirable to undesirable. For example, moving home may be stressful even if it is to a more desirable location. Daily hassles – or the irritating, frustrating experiences that happen nearly every single day – can also exacerbate stress. Although stressful life events may have more of an impact on parents, both major and minor events contribute to variation in children's well-being (Armstrong & Boothroyd, 2008; Ford *et al.*, 2007; Wells & Evans, 2003). For example, a recent study of 125 adolescent girls aged 13 to 17 in the United States found that stressful life events was a significant predictor of emotional problems, even controlling for a number of other factors such as demographic characteristics, school performance, perceived safety, neighbourhood quality, religiousness, family functioning, and self-esteem (Armstrong & Boothroyd, 2007). Girls who experienced more stressful life events had more psychological problems including depression, impaired psychosocial functioning, and mental health symptoms. In a fascinating experiment, Evans *et al.* (2007) recently showed that cumulative stress increased children's levels of allostatic load, a physiological marker of cumulative wear and tear on the body caused by the mobilisation of multiple physiological response systems. Evans *et al.* (2007) showed that cumulative stress was also associated with dynamic cardiovascular processes in response to an acute stressor (a mental arithmetic task in their study). Higher levels of cumulative stress were associated with muted reactivity and slower, less efficient recovery in blood pressure. These findings suggest that chronic life stress impacts on children's ability to respond effectively to new stressors. Chronic stress elevates allostatic load, and elevated allostatic load may be implicated in how early childhood exposure to cumulative stressors translates into poorer adjustment and elevated morbidity across the lifespan.

Children's social context

Children living in impoverished urban areas are particularly at risk for experiencing a variety of difficult circumstances. Children living in poor inner-city environments are more likely to live in inadequate housing, to have less access to good quality schools and other social resources, and to be exposed to delinquent peers and multiple violent events. Recent attention has particularly been focused on area socioeconomic deprivation. A growing body of research links neighbourhood deprivation to both psychological and behavioural problems and school underachievement (see Gorman-Smith & Tolan, 2003). Xue *et al.* (2005) in the United States, for example, showed that neighbourhood disadvantage was associated with more internalising behaviour problems and a higher number of children in the clinical range, even after accounting for family demographic characteristics, maternal depression, and earlier child mental health scores. Similarly, McCulloch's (2006) British study showed that in predicting levels of **externalising behaviour problems**, residence in a deprived area was as significant as the family factors. A lot of research has also been carried out to uncover the mechanisms through which area socioeconomic deprivation affects child development. There is now a lot of evidence to suggest that area socioeconomic disadvantage can, via the resources or services available in deprived neighbourhoods to the kinds of role models that less affluent neighbourhoods can provide, strongly influence children's psychiatric outcomes (Leventhal & Brooks-Gunn, 2000). The peer group, in particular, is one of the primary agents through which neighbourhood socialisation adversely affects children's outcomes. Young people growing up in high-crime, dangerous neighbourhoods are exposed to more delinquent peer groups than other adolescents (Wikstrom, 1998).

externalising behaviour problems delinquent activities, aggression, and hyperactivity. Externalising behaviours are directly linked to violent episodes such as punching and kicking often learned from observing others.

Societal mechanisms

Also important is the larger social context. For example, societal mechanisms of discrimination, racism, and prejudice have been shown to negatively influence the lives of ethnic minority children. Racial and ethnic discrimination has been linked to a number of psychological symptoms such as low perceived control, anxiety, and frustration (Simons *et al.*, 2002; Szalacha *et al.*, 2003). Many ethnic minority children experience discrimination in everyday exchanges and this greatly undermines their mental health, particularly when their family's acculturation is low (Wiking *et al.*, 2004). Racism and discrimination also influence other resources in children's lives. For example, research indicates that some teachers have lower expectations for, and respond less positively to, ethnic minority students (see McLoyd, 1998, for a review). These experiences undoubtedly play a role in the underachievement of many ethnic minority children.

Catastrophic events

On a broader scale, catastrophic events such as war, extreme privation, and natural disasters (Figure 19.3) clearly disrupt children's development. In such severe trauma, children experience devastation on an extreme and massive scale. Children are often less capable of coping with the consequences of such catastrophes – including the lack of

FIGURE 19.3 *Catastrophic events such as floods can result in children experiencing devastation on an extreme and massive scale.*

Source: Shutterstock.

basic necessities for existence. These children experience loss of their loved ones and witness unimaginable atrocities. Yet, studies of children who have experienced such catastrophes suggest that most, when placed in new environments, can lead normal, competent lives (Betancourt *et al.*, 2010).

MEASUREMENT OF RISK

The issue of how to best measure contextual risk has generated a lot of debate in psychology and psychiatry. Early studies of risk often focused attention on a single risk factor such as child poverty or maltreatment. Many investigators soon realised that the examination of a single risk factor does not address the reality of most children's lives. Children rarely experience risk in isolation; rather, risks tend to cluster (Masten & Coatsworth, 1998). For example, child maltreatment tends to co-occur with other environmental threats to children's development such as parental mental illness, parental substance abuse, poverty, inter-parental conflict, and community violence.

Where scientists usually see their task as a search for causes, research on risk factors may be a substitute for a more basic understanding of why individuals succeed or fail: risks are probabilistic whereas causes are thought to be deterministic (Sameroff *et al.*, 2003). We now know that it is not a single risk factor that causes difficulties, but the combination of various contextual risk factors that portends numerous negative child outcomes. In fact, the evidence so far suggests that the effects of an isolated risk factor tend to be rather modest. The exposure to a specific risk factor does not necessarily cause difficulties, but rather it is a life history characterised by the accumulation of family disadvantages, economic difficulties, and adverse conditions that reduces developmental competence (Sameroff *et al.*, 2003). For these reasons, many investigators have taken a broader perspective when examining the risk factors that impact on children's development.

Risk accumulation

Given the importance of studying multiple influences simultaneously, a number of researchers have employed **cumulative risk** models that incorporate large sets of risk factors. In Michael Rutter's (1979) approach to risk in child psychiatry, individual characteristics as well as qualities of the environment are examined together. Each risk factor is dichotomised into two groups, representing the presence (1) or absence (0) of an event or

risk accumulation
the way in which multiple risk factors have a cumulative effect on child outcomes.

risk. This dichotomous classification of risk exposure is determined typically by a statistical cut-off (e.g. greater than one standard deviation above the mean, upper quartile) or on the basis of a conceptual categorisation (e.g. being below the poverty line, single parenthood). Cumulative risk is then calculated by a simple summation of these multiple risk categories. These risk categories are not weighted for two reasons (Evans, 2003). First, the foundation of **cumulative risk theory** is that the sum of risk factors rather than any single risk, regardless of its context, is what leads to dysfunction because it overwhelms the adaptive capacities of the individual. In this framework, therefore, no one risk factor is seen as more important than another. This depicts the theoretical notion of mass accumulation, or the idea that the total effect of individual risk factors is greater than the sum of their individual effects. Second, weighted models do not outperform unweighted models over repeated applications. In other words, in this approach risk is viewed as an accumulation of stressors, and the assumption is that the number of risk factors that children experience carries more gravity than the experience of any particular risk factor. The evidence, as will be discussed in detail below, broadly supports this assumption. In any case, cumulative risk indexes have been noted for their potential to capture the natural co-variation of risk factors. For example, physical risk factors such as poor housing quality, noise, and pollution are highly interrelated as are psychosocial risk parameters such as family turmoil and violence (Evans, 2003). Furthermore, aggregate variables of risk are more stable than any individual measure, and there is increased power to detect effects (Burchinal et al., 2000). Cumulative risk measures are consistently found to explain more variance in children's outcomes than single factors (Atzaba-Poria et al., 2004; Deater-Deckard et al., 1998; Sameroff et al., 1993).

> **cumulative risk theory** the sum of risk factors rather than any single risk is what leads to dysfunction because it overwhelms the adaptive capacities of the individual.

In general, studies using cumulative risk models show that the higher the number of risks children experience, the worse their developmental outcomes. In his study of 10-year-old children of mothers with a psychiatric disorder, for example, Rutter (1979) computed a cumulative risk score based on six factors including severe marital distress, low socioeconomic status, large family size or overcrowding, paternal criminality, maternal psychiatric disorder, and placement of the child in foster care. Rutter found that it was not any particular risk factor but the number of risk factors in a child's background that led to the diagnosis of a disorder. Psychiatric risk rose from 2 per cent for children in families with zero or one risk factors to 20 per cent for children in families with four or more risk factors.

Similar findings were evident in research conducted by Arnold Sameroff and his colleagues. These researchers followed a sample of children of families, named the Rochester Longitudinal Study (RLS), with a high level of maternal psychopathology from birth (Baldwin et al., 1993; Sameroff et al., 1982). Ten environmental risk factors were examined:

1. a history of maternal mental illness;
2. high maternal anxiety;
3. parental perspectives that reflected rigidity in the attitudes, beliefs, and values that mothers had in regard to their child's development;
4. few positive maternal interactions with the child observed during infancy;

5. head of the household in an unskilled occupation;
6. minimal maternal education;
7. disadvantaged minority status;
8. single parenthood;
9. stressful life events;
10. large family size.

Once the total risk score was computed, the researchers found that the greater the number of risks, the worse the cognitive and mental health outcomes for children. On an intelligence test, children with no environmental risks scored more than 30 points higher than children with eight or nine risk factors. Furthermore, no children in the zero-risk group had IQs below 85; in contrast, 26 per cent of those in the high-risk group did. A later study of the RLS sample, using the same risk score as the earlier study did, found similar results examining school grades and number of absences from first to twelfth grade (Gutman et al., 2003). High-risk children had lower grades and more absences than low-risk children. Furthermore, the gap between children's school outcomes widened across the school years, suggesting that children from disadvantaged backgrounds fell further and further behind their peers as they progressed through school.

Risk specificity

risk specificity the specific characteristics of an individual risk factor, both in terms of its specific effect and in terms of how it interacts with specific child outcomes.

A drawback of the cumulative risk approach is, however, the assumption that each risk factor carries the same weight in children's lives, and that risk factors are interchangeable. Although several investigators have shown that the explanatory power of the cumulative risk metric in explaining development and behaviour is far greater than that of individual risk effects (e.g. Ackerman et al., 1999), individual risk factors do vary in their respective impacts. Therefore, one needs to also assess the influence of individual risk factors so that they can be examined simultaneously without losing their particular salience. For example, although scores on Ackerman et al.'s (1999) risk metric of 11 risk factors were significantly associated with child behaviour problems; parental alcohol/drug abuse was the only individual risk factor that accounted for a significant amount of unique variance. Furthermore, risk indicators underlying the development of problem behaviour in one child adjustment domain might not be the same as those underlying the development of problem behaviour in another child adjustment domain, which raises questions about the legitimacy of the cumulative risk perspective. In other words, the importance of testing for specificity or the role of specific risk factors in specific child behaviour outcomes should, equally, not be underestimated (McMahon et al., 2003).

This question of whether the quality or the quantity of risk matters for children's outcomes was also explored by Sameroff and his colleagues (Sameroff et al., 1987). Data from the RSL families that experienced a moderate number of risks (3 to 5 out of 10) were examined in order to determine whether specific combinations of risk factors had worse effects than others. The families fell into five groups with different combinations of high risk conditions. Despite these differences, the children had similar developmental outcomes across the five groups. The authors therefore concluded that it was the quantity, but not the combination, of risk factors that was important in predicting children's outcomes. However, they pointed out that it is unlikely that the same intervention could be successful for all families. For each family, a unique combination of risk factors would require a specific set of intervention strategies to address the specific risks facing that family.

More recently, Flouri and her colleagues in the UK revisited the issue of whether the number or the type of risk children experience is more important in determining emotional and behavioural outcomes, which they measured with the Strengths and Difficulties Questionnaire (SDQ). The SDQ is a 25-item 3-point (ranging from 0–2) scale measuring four difficulties (hyperactivity, emotional symptoms, conduct problems, and peer problems), as well as prosocial behaviour (Goodman, 1994, 1997). Each subscale had five items such as 'constantly fidgeting or squirming' (hyperactivity), 'many worries, often seems worried' (emotional symptoms), 'steals from home, school or elsewhere' (conduct problems), 'rather solitary, tends to play alone' (peer problems), and 'helpful if someone is hurt, upset or feeling ill' (prosocial behaviour). A total difficulties scale is calculated by summing the scores for hyperactivity, emotional symptoms, conduct problems, and peer problems. The prosocial scale is examined separately.

To test this Flouri and her colleagues used different measures of multiple risk, many and different samples of children, and different developmental stages of children. Their conclusion across all their studies was also that the number rather than the type of risk was consistently more important in determining children's emotional and behavioural outcomes. For example, they compared the effect of specific life stressors with the effect of cumulative life stress on adolescents' emotional and behavioural problems controlling for total previous life stress and other known important factors such as gender, age, and parental education (Flouri & Tzavidis, 2008). The measure of life stress used in that study was Tiet et al.'s (1998) **Adverse Life Events Scale**. This scale is composed of 25 possible events occurring in the last year which children had little or no control over (e.g. 'someone in the family died', 'someone in the family was arrested', 'negative change in parents' financial situation'), and is a modification of the Life Events Checklist (LEC; Brand & Johnson, 1982; Coddington, 1972a, 1972b), a measure with very good psychometric qualities (Brand & Johnson, 1982). The LEC is a measure of exposure to potentially traumatic events and was developed at the National Center for Posttraumatic Stress Disorder (PTSD) to facilitate the diagnosis of PTSD. The research team showed that none of the individual 25 life events experienced in the past year was statistically significant in predicting total difficulties. The only statistically significant factor predicting total difficulties was total previous life stress. However, when overall number of adverse life events experienced in the past year was used, its effect was strong and statistically significant.

Their more recent work with different measures of cumulative risk and different developmental stages did not change their conclusion that the number rather than

Adverse Life Events Scale a measure of life stress – composed of 25 possible events occurring in the last year over which children had little or no control of some adverse life effect.

the type of risk is more important in determining children's emotional and behavioural outcomes. For example, Flouri, Mavroveli *et al.* (2010) showed that none of their five specific indicators of family level socioeconomic disadvantage (overcrowding, lack of home ownership, receipt of income support, income poverty, and lack of access to a car or van) was significant, after adjustment, in predicting emotional and behavioural problems in their sample of some 5000 preschool children. Rather, the total number of socioeconomic disadvantage indicators present in the child's family was a strong and statistically significant predictor of emotional and behavioural difficulties. In a later study of the same initial sample (Flouri, Tzavidis, & Kallis, 2009) the team showed that none of their eight family adverse life events that took place during the first year of the child's life predicted, after adjustment, children's emotional and behavioural difficulties three years later. The eight family adverse life events were a subsample of the original 25 items used in their earlier study with school age children discussed above, selected to be developmentally appropriate for preschool children. The events were: 'family member died', 'family member was seriously injured', 'negative change in parents' financial situation', 'family member had mental/emotional problem', 'family moved', 'got a new brother or sister', 'one of the parents went to jail', and 'parents separated'. Instead, it was again the number rather than the type of events that significantly predicted children's emotional and behavioural difficulties.

Equifinality and multifinality

Further evidence that a focus on risk specificity can be problematic comes from studies in developmental psychopathology testing full specifity models of associations between risks and child outcomes. These studies conclude, through the examination of associations between multiple risk factors and multiple psychopathological outcomes (McMahon *et al.*, 2003), that risk specificity oversimplifies the complex interactions between risk factors and outcomes. In general, these studies show little evidence for specificity. Rather, they demonstrate that a risk factor can influence multiple child outcomes (multifinality), and, conversely, a child outcome can be influenced by multiple risk factors (equifinality). Studies of single risk factors and single outcomes neglect the contribution and congruence of multiple risk and multiple outcomes. The complexity of the developmental process requires a broader perspective in order to avoid a distorted view of the importance of any single factor.

Levels of risk

Another issue that has generated a lot of debate in child psychology is around deciding the appropriate level of contextual risk. Should contextual risk best be measured at the family or the area/neighbourhood/community level (Leventhal & Brooks-Gunn, 2000; McCulloch, 2006; McCulloch & Joshi, 2001)? Very few studies have used appropriate data to compare family and community influences on children's psychopathology. Flouri, Tzavidis *et al.* (2010b) explored this using longitudinal data from some 19,000 preschool-aged children and their older siblings in the UK. The children were clustered in neighbourhoods and there was detailed information about each neighbourhood's level of poverty and socioeconomic disadvantage. The research team showed that, as expected, in some neighbourhoods children had a lot of emotional and behavioural problems, whereas in others children had few emotional and behavioural problems. Most of this association was explained by the neighbourhood's level of socioeconomic disadvantage – the higher the level of the neighbourhood's socioeconomic disadvantage the greater the level of emotional and behavioural problems. However, the research team showed that once adjustment was made for the socioeconomic characteristics, particularly education, of the children's parents, the association between neighbourhood disadvantage and child psychopathology became statistically non-significant. This suggests that contextual risk measured at the family rather than the neighbourhood/community level influences children's emotional and behavioural outcomes.

PROTECTIVE/VULNERABILITY FACTORS

The examination of children who experience developmental success despite experiencing risk has led to an investigation of the mechanisms that either support or undermine resilience. For children who succeed despite risk experiences, the presence of protective factors may compensate for the risks that exist in their lives and environments. Protective factors are those attributes of persons, environments, situations, and events that relate to positive adaptation under conditions of adversity (Garmezy, 1983). Vulnerability factors, on the other hand, are those attributes that relate to maladjustment under conditions of adversity. Protective and vulnerability factors are the opposite ends of the same construct; they are not different constructs. For example, if level of parental affection is found to affect the adaptation of children experiencing adversity, parental warmth as the 'positive end' is the protective factor, whereas parental coldness as the 'negative end' is the vulnerability factor.

On the basis of his review of research in the area, Garmezy (1993) identified three broad sets of variables that have been found to operate as protective factors: (1) personal characteristics of the child, such as gender, intelligence, and personality traits; (2) family characteristics such as warmth, cohesion, and structure; and (3) **external support systems** such as peers and schools. Table 19.2 provides examples of protective factors for children.

external support systems support systems in the social environment such as friendships that contribute to resilience in adversity.

Nevertheless, it is important to note that there are few universal protective factors for children. Rather, factors that promote competence may vary according to the age of the child, the developmental outcome being targeted, or even the general context (Sameroff & Gutman, 2004). For example, although democratic, *authoritative parenting* may be successful in increasing the positive outcomes of middle-class children, those who live in more dangerous neighbourhoods may benefit from higher levels of parental control. Conversely, children living in more affluent neighbourhoods may experience negative effects from such restrictive control (Gutman, Sameroff, & Eccles, 2002). To truly appreciate the determinants of competence requires attention to the broad ecological system in which children and families are embedded.

Table 19.2 *Examples of protective factors for children*

Domain	Factor
Personal Characteristics	Gender Intelligence Temperament Sociability Perceived control Self-esteem Coping style
Family characteristics	Attachment style Parent–child Interactions Parenting style Family cohesion Family routines Family support Family resources
External support Systems	Friendships Teacher support School resources Organised activities Neighbourhood cohesion

Personal characteristics

Personal attributes suggested to operate as protective factors include both genetic and constitutional factors such as gender, intelligence, temperament, and personality traits. Personal characteristics are always active in a child's life, but they can also influence the way children react when negative situations occur. A similar situation or event will elicit different reactions and responses from children depending on these characteristics. Some children may be more upset than others even when experiencing exactly the same event and these responses will influence the way they can handle such stress.

There have been a number of suggestions in the literature that gender may modify or influence children's responses to adversity. Specifically, evidence indicates that girls are less susceptible to emotional and behavioural disturbances than boys when exposed to family stress, such as family discord. Hetherington (1989) showed that boys did not simply have a higher rate of disturbances in general but rather their risk was much greater when exposed to family discord compared to girls. Rutter (1979) has noted that there are several reasons why boys may be more vulnerable than girls. First, boys may have more direct experiences of family discord; for example, parents may argue more in front of boys than in front of girls. Second, when families break up, sons are more likely than daughters to be placed in institutional care, which exacerbates emotional and behavioural difficulties. For these reasons, girls' lower vulnerability may be simply the result of a reduced exposure to risk factors.

More recent studies, however, have reported less pronounced and consistent gender differences in response to divorce (e.g. Amato, 2000). This decline in gender differences likely reflects the more recent trends of greater father involvement following divorce (Hetherington & Elmore, 2003). Furthermore, the protective effect of gender also appears to lessen with age, and is usually found with young children. In their study of Hawaiian youth, for example, Werner and Smith (2001) found that boys showed greater vulnerability than girls during the first decade of life, but this lessened during the second and third decades.

One of the most widely investigated variables in resilience research is children's intellectual ability. Although earlier studies found that intelligence has protective effects on the academic outcomes of high-risk children (Easterbrooks *et al.*, 1993; Garmezy *et al.*, 1984), other studies have shown that children with multiple risks do not experience any advantage to their academic achievement as a result of their higher intelligence (Gutman *et al.*, 2003; Luthar, 1991). Some researchers have suggested that higher intelligence may be positively related to school achievement at low levels of risk but that children with higher intelligence lose their advantage at high levels of risk. Others have suggested that intelligence may serve a protective function for the academic achievement of younger children. As high-risk children mature into adolescents, they may be more likely to use their talents in areas other than educational achievement (Luthar, 1991). Further studies find that language abilities, more than general intelligence, serve as a protective factor for the academic skills of high-risk children (Burchinal, Roberts, Zeisel, & Rowley, 2008). However, when examining outcomes other than academic achievement including social, emotional, and behavioural adjustment, general ability has been shown to serve as a protective factor for both young (Flouri, Tzavidis *et al.*, 2010a), and older children (Flouri *et al.*, 2011; Flouri & Kallis, 2007; Luthar, 1991) experiencing high levels of adversity.

Research has also suggested that temperament and personality characteristics operate as protective factors for children. Children who have a positive constellation of characteristics such as easy temperament, social responsiveness, and humour may be more likely to elicit positive responses and support from other people, which, in turn, may help in counteracting the risk effects. Child temperament – measured by characteristics such as mood, activity level, attention span or distractibility, adaptability or malleability, and emotion reactivity – has received much attention as a protective factor (Masten & Coatsworth, 1998). Evidence suggests that babies with an easier temperament are more likely to elicit positive responses from mothers than shy or difficult babies (Werner & Smith, 1992). Infant temperament, however, may also act as a risk factor. Children's negative temperaments, for example, may influence the amount of family discord and increase the likelihood that children will experience its adverse effects (Rutter, 1987). In this sense, parents who are experiencing more distress may be more likely to release their negativity on children with difficult temperaments.

Several researchers have also suggested that psychological characteristics such as perceived **locus of control**, self-esteem, and coping style may be key protective factors. Perceived locus of control refers to beliefs about the sources of one's successes and failures. Children with high levels of perceived internal locus of control believe that their successes and failures are due to their own attributes or actions, whereas children who have high levels of external locus of control believe that other people, luck or fate account for such outcomes. High risk children who perceive more control over their lives may have better mental health and higher functioning than their high-risk peers with a more external locus of control (Luthar, 1991; Seifer *et al.*, 1992; Werner, 1993). Low levels of perceived internal control, however, might act as a vulnerability factor by increasing depression and anxiety (Peterson & Seligman, 1984).

Self-esteem has also been suggested to operate as a protective factor for children exposed to risk (Rutter, 1987). A positive sense of self can have a positive impact on children experiencing stress and may facilitate the development of other characteristics, such as perceived internal control, which mitigate the effects of risk. Adaptive coping strategies may also influence children's response to negative life situations. Children who have more active coping skills such as problem-solving and social support seeking are more apt at handling difficult situations. For example, a study of adolescents found that those labelled as resilient had higher scores on problem-solving coping strategies compared to well-adjusted and vulnerable adolescents (Dumont & Provost, 1999). In addition, resilient adolescents had higher self-esteem than vulnerable adolescents. Children who do not learn to cope with stress and use ineffective skills such as distraction and avoidance are more likely to be overwhelmed by adverse circumstances.

Studies also have focused on the role of ethnic identity as a protective factor for minority youth. Evidence indicates that ethnic identity may help facilitate the development of competencies such as academic achievement (Miller & MacIntosh, 1999) and protect against the prevalence of depressive symptoms for children exposed to crime (Simons *et al.*, 2002). For example, a study of 131 urban African-American adolescents found significant main and interactive effects of ethnic identity on school grades. Further analyses suggested daily hassles related to racism were a significant barrier to academic achievement for those adolescents who had a weak ethnic identity. These results indicate that in the presence of increasing hassles, a strong ethnic identity may provide African-American adolescents with the ability not to let those hassles interfere with their academic performance (Miller & MacIntosh, 1999).

Lastly, there is evidence that factors that moderate the effect of risk may be themselves moderated by other factors. For example, protective factors within the individual (e.g. temperament, self-esteem, and locus of control) make a greater impact on the quality of adult coping for high-risk females than high-risk males, whereas external sources of support appear to be more important for high-risk men compared to high-risk women (Werner, 1993).

Family characteristics

secure attachment
responsive, supportive, structured, and affectively stimulating relationship between parent and child that contributes to children's positive development.

A number of studies have examined the protective effects of both proximal family characteristics, such as parent–child interactions, and distal family characteristics, such as parents' financial and educational status. One of the most researched proximal factors is a secure parent–child attachment particularly during infancy and early childhood. Research consistently demonstrates that a **secure attachment** defined by a responsive, supportive, structured, and affectively stimulating relationship between parent and child contributes to children's positive development. A secure attachment has been shown to be particularly important for children exposed to adversity. The security of attachment between child and mother has been shown to differentiate between positive and negative outcomes in children experiencing risk (Masten & Coatsworth, 1998). A sensitive, securely attached caregiver–child relationship also fosters the development of children's sense of self worth and their capabilities to adapt to changing circumstances with positive coping strategies, problem-solving skills, and social competence. In this way, a secure parent–child attachment may not only operate as a protective factor for children exposed to risk, but also enable children to develop their capacity for resilience in the future (Masten & Coatsworth, 1998).

FIGURE 19.4 *Family cohesion may enhance children's perceived internal control and their coping strategies.*
Source: Shutterstock.

The quality of parenting can also play an essential role in children's responses to stressful situations. Parenting may either protect children from difficult life circumstances or make them more vulnerable to adversities. Research suggests that authoritative parenting provides the most beneficial environment for children's development (Baumrind, 1989). Authoritative parents create a warm and supportive environment for their children with the appropriate amount of structure and with consistent discipline. Although authoritative parenting is optimal for most children, it may serve a protective function particularly for children who are experiencing stressful events and situations. For example, research suggests that children who are exposed to family-level stress such as family dissolution or other adversities may be more likely to need additional emotional support and structure that authoritative parents provide (Hetherington, 1999).

Family-level resources such as cohesion, positive interactions, and support (Figure 19.4) may also operate as protective factors. Adversity makes it difficult for families to maintain their normal family-level interactions and routines. For example, parental divorce disrupts family life and decreases interaction with the non-custodial parent. However, children exposed to stressful events such as family disruption and bereavement may have a greater need for these family-level resources in order to maintain a sense of normality and structure (Sandler *et al.*, 2003). These family-level resources may also exert their protective effects by influencing children's psychological adjustment and parent–child interactions. For instance, family cohesion may enhance children's perceived internal control and their coping strategies. Alternatively, family routines such as eating meals together create a context where warm, supportive parenting can occur.

More distal characteristics of families may also operate as protective factors. For example, some researchers have demonstrated the protective effects of household income for specific adverse conditions. For example, children of divorced parents benefit when their fathers provide more financial support. Research indicates that children in mother-custody families who receive child-support payments from their fathers tend to have better relationships with their fathers and experience more positive outcomes (Emery, 1999). Parents' level of education may also serve as a protective factor for children through the increased access to resources and advantages that higher education affords (Masten & Coatsworth, 1998).

External support systems

As children mature, external support systems play an increasingly significant role in their capacity for resilience. Friendships may be particularly important for older children experiencing adverse life circumstances. Reciprocal, positive friendships may provide additional avenues of self-esteem and emotional support for children whose families offer less positive engagement and interaction. Studies suggest that friendships may be particularly important for maltreated children as these children often have fewer opportunities to learn and practice social skills in their family setting (Bolger & Patterson, 2003). The academic achievement of high-risk children may also benefit from having academically supportive friends (Gutman et al., 2002). On the other hand, peer rejection has been shown to exacerbate the deleterious consequences of many life stresses such as divorce (Hetherington & Elmore, 2003). Another vulnerability factor regarding peer relationships is the association with deviant friends. When children spend more time with deviant friends, they are at greater risk for the development of antisocial behaviour and academic problems (Dryfoos, 1990).

Good school environments have also been shown to be beneficial for children experiencing risk. In early childhood, high-quality child care is a protective factor particularly for those children living in low-income environments (Caughy et al., 1994). Children from impoverished homes who started attending day care before their first birthday had higher scores on reading recognition tests than children from comparable home environments who did not attend day care at all. Day care attendance in a centre or school was also related to the best performance on mathematics tests for children from impoverished environments.

Supportive teachers are also consequential for children's development (Rutter, 1987). Teachers can play a crucial role as caring adults or mentors for those students who need additional support (Gutman & Midgley, 2000). There is evidence that these relationships may be protective for some young people (Figure 19.5). For example, a study of adolescents found that the risk associated with having deviant friends was reduced for young people who were close to their teacher, had high achievement motivation, and had high academic achievement (Crosnoe et al., 2002).

There is also increasing evidence that communities can play a protective role for high-risk children (Garbarino, 2001; Gorman-Smith & Tolan, 2003). Social processes within a neighbourhood may be particularly important. Social processes refer to the perceived social support and cohesion among neighbours, supervision of children and adolescents by other adults in the community, participation in voluntary organisations, and a general sense of belonging to the community by its members (Gorman-Smith & Tolan, 2003). These neighbourhood social processes have been shown to help protect against structural disadvantages (e.g. poverty and violence) even in more impoverished communities (Furstenberg, 1993).

Youth-serving community organisations such as churches, community centres, and neighbourhood youth-serving organisations have also been found to influence young people in a positive manner (Masten & Coatsworth, 1998). Participation in organised after-school activities may also provide some protection from the structural disadvantages of a

FIGURE 19.5 *A supportive teacher can be an important protective factor for a child at risk.* Source: Shutterstock.

neighbourhood (Seidman & Pederson, 2003). Unfortunately, youth-serving programmes are less likely to exist in those neighbourhoods with the greatest need for such organisations (Seidman & Pederson, 2003). Participation in organised after-school activities is also lower for low-income families compared to their more advantaged peers because of the overall unavailability of such activities in poorer areas (Mahoney & Eccles, 2007).

THEORETICAL MODELS OF RISK AND RESILIENCE

As resilience cannot be determined in the absence of risk, the theoretical models of resilience consider, by definition, both risk and protective/vulnerability effects. As shown in Table 19.3, researchers have employed different models, each with different implications for the identification of resilience.

Table 19.3 *Models of risk and resilience*

Model	Factor	Risk–resilience relation
Moderator (interactive) effects	Protective/ vulnerability	Resilience is determined by the presence of a significant interactive relationship with risk whereby the factor either has no effect among the low-risk population or its effect is magnified in the high-risk population
Main effects	Promotive	If the study population is high risk, resilience is determined by a significant main effect of the factor on the outcome. If the study population is both high risk and low risk, individuals' resilience cannot be demonstrated in these models
Mediator effects	Deterioration/ mobilisation	Resilience cannot be demonstrated in these models. The factor explains how, in general, risk is related to outcome

Moderator (interactive) effects models

The earliest models of resilience used the term 'protective factors' to refer to factors promoting resilience. The term was first systematically defined by Rutter (1979) who argued that to be meaningful, protective/vulnerability factors must be evident only in combination with a risk factor. In this framework, the essential question of resilience research is: what factors explain positive development in the face of adversity but have little or no positive impact on development in the absence of adversity? To address this question, protective/vulnerability factors are required to have an interactive relationship with the risk factor(s) thereby either having no effect in low-risk populations or their effect being magnified in the presence of risk. Whether a variable is considered a protective or vulnerability factor depends on its connection with the risk variable, not in terms of whether it has positive or negative qualities. Protective factors decrease the effect of risk, whereas vulnerability factors increase the effect of risk. A protective factor may not necessarily be a socially desirable characteristic of the individual or a positive event. Therefore, protection for a high-risk child may even come from a factor that in and of itself is a risk to the mental health or social functioning of a low-risk child. On the other hand, a vulnerability factor for high-risk children may be related to positive development for low-risk children.

In a hypothetical example of an **interactive effects model**, a researcher may want to compare the effects of child care quality on the cognitive development of young children with varying degrees of risk. Therefore, the possible combinations of these two factors (risk and quality of child care) are: (1) high risk, low quality; (2) low risk, low quality; (3) high risk, high quality; and (4) low risk, high quality. High quality of child care would be a protective factor if high-risk children in a

moderator (interactive) effects models models based on interactive relationships between protective/vulnerability factors and risk factor(s)

high-quality child-care environment had significantly higher cognitive development than high-risk children in a low-quality child care environment and there were no differences in the cognitive development of low-risk children regardless of the quality of child care. According to Rutter (1979), this interactive process must be determined empirically, in order to differentiate risk from vulnerability factors.

Main effects models

Main effects models may be differentiated in terms of whether homogeneous or heterogeneous risk samples are examined. Researchers focusing on a homogeneous risk sample, such as children living in poverty, may examine differences between high- and low-competence children experiencing adversity. In this case, protective factors are those variables that differentiate high-risk children who are experiencing positive adaptation from those high-risk children who are not. These study designs may be better at detecting processes that are protective for a specific risk condition, showing that the meaning or definition of resilience can differ among high-risk populations. Maltreated children, for instance, rarely approach the functioning of non-maltreated children. Yet, variation in adaptation does exist suggesting that some maltreated children achieve better than expected outcomes. Studies focusing on a within-group sample, such as maltreated children, can examine more closely profiles of resilient adaptation rather than specific, isolated attributes to understand the meaning of such variability.

main effects models models of resilience in which single factors are identified as determining whether a given child exposed to a risk has a good or a poor outcome.

Rather than examining individuals experiencing high levels of risk, other studies identify factors that are associated with positive outcomes for a heterogeneous sample of individuals. These studies cannot infer resilience but they are useful as they identify factors that are associated with desirable outcomes independent of the occurrence of risk. For example, athletic talent does not necessarily insulate children from adverse circumstances, but instead may provide opportunities for additional successes. For such factors, more appropriate terms, such as 'promotive' which do not suggest resilience, have been proposed (Sameroff, 1999).

Mediator effects models

Mediator effects models cannot infer resilience but they are useful as they show the pathways through which risk factors are related to outcomes. These models explore, therefore, the role of intervening or intermediate variables. There are two forms of mediation with respect to how risk operates to influence outcomes: deterioration and mobilisation. In the deterioration model of mediation, the occurrence of risk decreases the ability to function effectively. For example, impoverished parents may experience greater depression which, in turn, decreases their ability to use effective parenting strategies. In the mobilisation model of mediation, the occurrence of risk increases the ability to function effectively. For example, some girls in divorced, mother-headed households become exceptionally resilient individuals, enhanced by confronting the challenges and responsibilities that follow divorce (Hetherington, 1989). Many divorced mothers also report greater personal growth, autonomy, and

mediator effects models models that explore the role of intervening or intermediate variables on the effects of risks.

educational/career attainments and decreased depression compared to those women who remained in unhappy marriages (Hetherington & Kelly, 2002).

Moderator versus main/mediator effects models

Many researchers agree that interaction effects are the distinguishing feature of resilience research (Roosa, 2000; Luthar *et al.*, 2000). Interaction effects identify which factors are associated with positive adaptation in high-risk groups, while having little or negligible effects in low-risk groups. However, this does not imply that main effects models lack insight into protective processes. In fact, Roosa (2000) argues that, in many cases, interactions are disguised as main effects. As discussed earlier, in high-risk samples, for example, main effect differences between those who are well-adjusted and those who are not may represent interactions in other samples with a wider distribution of risk. According to Luthar *et al.* (2000), it would be mistaken to conclude that main effects models explaining a high proportion of variance are not pertinent to research on protective factors.

Yet, main effects and mediator effects models do not address the essential question of resilience research. That is, what factors explain positive development in the face of adversity but have little or no positive impact on development in the absence of adversity? The unique contribution of resilience research to our understanding of human development lies in its expectations of interactions that lead to competence when other developmental models predict poor adaptation (Rutter, 1987). To maximise the efficacy of intervention efforts to foster development, differentiation between factors that are positive for a broad spectrum of youth versus those young people facing multiple risks is necessary to understand the processes that lead to more or less successful outcomes (Gutman *et al.*, 2002).

DEVELOPMENTAL OUTCOMES: COMPETENCE AND MALADJUSTMENT

The definition of resilience depends on the outcome being assessed. In the past, resilience has been defined according to the absence of social deviance or psychopathology. Although the importance of competence was recognised in developmental research, the medical model which emphasises symptoms, diseases, and treatments dominated the field. More recently, there has been a return toward positive psychology. This has encouraged a shift in focus from maladjustment to more positive developmental outcomes. Several researchers have examined social competence, for instance. Social competence is defined according to the success of a person in meeting societal expectations. Other criteria include personal development and self-actualisation. Studies have measured social competence on the basis of observable, behavioural criteria often assessed by multiple sources including the children themselves and their parents, teachers, and peers, as these multiple informant assessments have greater validity. The definition of social competence also depends on the developmental stage being assessed. For example, social competence in infancy may be operationalised as having a secure mother–child attachment and positive affect. In early childhood, social competence may include measures of autonomous functioning and behavioural and emotional functioning. In middle childhood and adolescence, social competence can be defined according to positive friendships and academic achievement.

Research in resilience has traditionally focused on defining competence in a single domain such as academic achievement. However, studies focusing on multiple dimensions of competence have realised that children who may be doing well in one area of development may suffer in another. Researchers who distinguished between externalising (i.e. acting out) and internalising (i.e. thought-centred) children's behaviours showed that so-called resilient children may react to their stressful experiences in a more covert, internal manner. In resilience research, there is the tendency to assume that if children are doing well in more external behaviours, they have managed to overcome adversity. However, many so-called resilient children who have outstanding behavioural profiles may also experience emotional difficulties. For example, in a study of inner-city adolescents, high-stress children who showed impressive behavioural competence were highly vulnerable to emotional distress over time (Luthar et al., 1993). Furthermore, most of the high-stress children who seemed resilient based on at least one domain of social competence had significant difficulties in one or more domains when assessed at a later point in time. Since resilient children tend to be at higher developmental levels, as reflected in their intellectual maturity, their pathology is more likely to be expressed with internal symptoms rather than behavioural disturbances. For these reasons, some researchers have suggested that in order for high-risk children to be labelled as resilient, they must excel in multiple domains of competence.

There has also been some disagreement over whether competence should be defined according to a representative, heterogeneous sample or within a high-risk, homogeneous group. Some researchers consider high risk children to be resilient when they demonstrate behaviour within the expected average range of a normative cohort. Other researchers examine competence within a high risk sample and define resilience in terms of doing better than other equally disadvantaged counterparts. The latter method considers specific adversities and takes into account that the expression and definition of competence may differ according to the risk condition. Yet, the level of positive adaptation in a high-risk sample often does not equate with competence compared to a normative cohort.

The definition of resilience is also dynamic and developmental in nature. Competence at one stage in development can have a protective effect at a later point in time. For example, high-risk children who are socially competent may have a greater capacity to elicit positive and support responses from others which, in turn, promotes their positive development. Children may be better able to benefit from protective factors in the future when they possess the capacity to engage in their environments in the present. On the other hand, there may be a cascade effect where maladjustment at one stage may contribute to the development of later problems. For example, antisocial behaviour in childhood may undermine academic achievement which, in turn, contributes to later problems. Developmental research explores the dynamic, ongoing processes involved in children's capacity for resilience. A key aim of developmental research is to understand the integration and organisation of experiences that enable children to become successful, competent individuals.

CONTRIBUTIONS OF RISK AND RESILIENCE RESEARCH TO THE DESIGN OF SUCCESSFUL INTERVENTIONS

Studies on risk and resilience have provided a new framework for research with implications for policies and practice concerning vulnerable children and families (Masten & Powell, 2003). Rather than focusing on maladaptive functioning and psychopathology, a resilience framework emphasises the promotion of competent functioning and fosters the development of policies and interventions that reflect the belief in resilient adaptation (Masten, 2001). In a resilience framework, intervention programmes are also more developmental in nature in that they focus on redirecting children's trajectories and strengthening cumulative protective processes in children's lives. Developmental models of intervention consider the risks, protective processes, and competencies that are relevant to a specific age group and conceptualise interventions in terms of dynamic, ongoing processes that evolve and adapt to new developmental tasks and challenges (Masten & Powell, 2003).

risk-focused programmes intervention programmes that attempt to reduce risk exposure.

asset-focused programmes programmes that attempt to directly provide higher quality and/or more quantity of assets in children's lives.

process-orientated programmes programmes that attempt to improve the most important adaptational systems for children such as key relationships, intellectual functioning, and self-regulation systems.

Within the resilience framework, there are several issues to consider when developing interventions. Masten and Powell (2003) outlined three types of intervention designs: **risk-focused, asset-focused,** and **process-orientated**. Risk-focused programmes attempt to reduce the level of risk exposure, as the more risk factors that can be eliminated, the lower the probability of difficulties (Sameroff & Gutman, 2004). For example, risk-focused interventions would give low-income mothers more prenatal care to prevent low birth-weight infants. However, the reality is that for most children, these risks are embedded in the context of many other risks (Sameroff & Gutman, 2004). Therefore, to prevent poor outcomes, other risk factors in the family and community need to be addressed as well.

Asset-focused programmes attempt to directly provide higher quality and/or more quantity of assets in children's lives. They may also attempt to increase the presence and ability of individuals who are assets in the lives of children, such as parents and teachers. For example, asset-focused designs would include teaching job skills to parents, training teachers to enhance the learning and achievement of their students, and increasing the after-school activities available in the neighbourhood.

Process-orientated programmes attempt to improve the most important adaptational systems for children such as key relationships, intellectual functioning, and self-regulation systems. Process-orientated programmes can focus on different system levels such as children, families, schools, and neighbourhoods as well as their interactions such as parent–school involvement, children's self-monitoring of school tasks, and student–teacher mentoring relationships. Intervention programmes may also involve more than one design, such as drug treatment and programmes to increase parent–infant attachment that may help reduce the risks facing infants of drug-abusing mothers, for instance.

SUMMARY AND CONCLUSIONS

According to Masten (2001), resilience arises from 'ordinary magic' in the sense that children are capable of astonishing resistance, adaptation, recovery, and success in the face of adversity using only the normal capacities and resources that individuals rely on to function every day. Despite these strengths and capacities, however, children cannot simply make themselves enduringly resilient in the face of continuous adversities in their environments. As Emmy Werner (1993) has noted, when risk factors outweigh protective processes even the most resilient child will experience difficulties. With this in mind, research in resilience is shifting away from describing individual characteristics of resilient children to instead focusing more sharply on how children's environments – families, peers, schools, and neighbourhoods – can be adapted to meet the needs of children facing adversity. Evidence indicates that effective and effortful family-based and community-level interventions play an essential role in promoting resilience in the lives of vulnerable children.

Yet, as Masten (2001) has noted, there is no magic bullet for resilience. That is, there is no one solution that can be adapted to promote children's resilience in any and all circumstances. Risks are multifaceted and thus interventions must also be multifaceted to reflect the diverse experiences and environments of a child's life (Sameroff et al., 2003). At the same time, we know that a number of risks in children's lives – e.g. premature birth, malnutrition, and homelessness – are preventable. Policies that provide families and children their basic needs such as health care, food, and shelter remain critical in order to maximise the potential of the future generations.

DISCUSSION POINTS

1. Identify as many risk factors in children's development as you can, and identify those that are likely to co-occur.
2. Consider the factors that contribute to resilience in some children.
3. Compare and evaluate different models of risk and resilience.
4. Consider how various protective factors may contribute to positive outcomes for children.
5. Taking account of the evidence presented in this chapter, design an intervention programme aimed at improving developmental outcomes for children at risk.

SUGGESTIONS FOR FURTHER READING

Glanz, M., & Johnson, J.L. (Eds.) (1999). *Resilience and development: Positive life adaptations.* New York: Plenum.

Luthar, S.S. (Ed.) (2003). *Resilience and vulnerability: Adaptation in the context of childhood adversities.* Cambridge: Cambridge University Press.

Masten, A. (2001). Ordinary magic: Resilience processes in development. *American Psychologist, 56,* 227–238.

Rutter, M. (1987). Psychosocial resilience and protective mechanisms. *American Journal of Orthopsychiatry, 57,* 316–331.

Werner, E.E., & Smith, R.S. (2001). *Journeys from childhood to midlife: Risk, resilience, and recovery.* Ithaca, NY: Cornell University Press.

REFERENCES

Ackerman, B.P., Izard, C.E., Schoff, K., Youngstrom, E.A., & Kogos, J. (1999). Contextual risk, caregiver emotionality, and the problem behaviors of six- and seven-year-old children from economically disadvantaged families. *Child Development, 70,* 1415–1427.

Amato, P.R. (2000). The consequences of divorce for adults and children. *Journal of Marriage and the Family, 55,* 23–38.

Armstrong, M.I., & Boothroyd, R.A. (2008). Predictors of emotional well-being in at-risk adolescent girls: Developing preventive intervention strategies. *Journal of Behavioral Health Services and Research, 35*(4), 435–453.

Atzaba-Poria, N., Pike, A., & Deater-Deckard, K. (2004). Do risk factors for problem behaviour act in a cumulative manner? An examination of ethnic minority and majority children through an ecological perspective. *Journal of Child Psychology and Psychiatry, 45,* 707–718.

Baldwin, A.L., Baldwin, C. Kasser, T., Zax, M., Sameroff, A., & Seifer, R. (1993). Contextual risk and resiliency during late adolescence. *Development and Psychopathology, 5,* 741–761.

Baumrind, D. (1989). Rearing competent children. Child development today and tomorrow. In D. William (Ed.) *Child development today and tomorrow. The Jossey-Bass social and behavioral science series* (pp. 349–378). San Francisco, CA: Jossey-Bass.

Betancourt, T.S., Borisova, I.I., Williams, T.P., Brennan, R.T., Whitfield, T.H., de la Soudiere, M., et al. (2010). Sierra Leone's former child soldiers: A follow-up study of psychosocial adjustment and community reintegration. *Child Development, 81,* 1077–1095.

Biblarz, T.J., & Gottainer, G. (2000). Family structure and children's success: A comparison of widowed and divorced single-mother families. *Journal of Marriage and Family, 62,* 533–548.

Bolger, K.E., & Patterson, C.J. (2003). Sequelae of child maltreatment: Vulnerability and resilience. In S.S. Luthar, (Ed.) *Resilience and vulnerability: Adaptation in the context of childhood* (pp. 156–181). New York: Cambridge University Press.

Brand, A.H., & Johnson, J.H. (1982). Note on reliability of the Life Events Checklist. *Psychological Reports, 50,* 1274.

Burchinal, M., Roberts, J., Hooper, S., & Zeisel, S. (2000). Cumulative risk and early cognitive development: A comparison of statistical risk models. *Developmental Psychology, 36,* 793–807.

Burchinal, M., Roberts, J., Zeisel, S., & Rowley, S. (2008). Social risk and protective factors for African American children's academic achievement and adjustment during the transition to middle school. *Developmental Psychology, 44,* 286–292.

Caughy, M.O., DiPietro, J.A., & Strobino, D.M. (1994). Day-care participation as a protective factor in the cognitive development of low-income children. *Child Development: Special Issue: Children and poverty*, 65, 457–471.

Cicchetti, D., & Lynch, M. (1995). Failures in the expectable environment and their impact on individual development: The case of child maltreatment. In D. Ciccheti & D.J. Cohen (Eds.) *Developmental psychopathology, Vol. 2: Risk, disorder, and adaptation* (pp. 32–71). New York: Wiley.

Cicchetti, D., & Rogosch, F.A., (1997). The role of self-organization in the promotion of resilience in maltreated children. *Development and psychopathology*, 9, 797–815.

Coddington, R.D. (1972a). The significance of life events as etiologic factors in the diseases of children: I. A survey of professional workers. *Journal of Psychosometric Research*, 16, 7–18.

Coddington, R.D. (1972b). The significance of life events as etiologic factors in the diseases of children: II. A study of a normal population. *Journal of Psychosometric Research*, 16, 205–213.

Costello, E.J., Compton, S.N., Keeler, G., & Angold, A. (2003). Relationships between poverty and psychopathology: A natural experiment. *Journal of American Medical Association*, 290, 2023–2029.

Crosnoe, R., Erickson, K.G., & Dornbusch, S.M. (2002). Protective functions of family relationships and school factors on the deviant behavior of adolescent boys and girls: Reducing the impact of risky friendships. *Youth Society*, 33, 515–546.

Deater-Deckard, K., Dodge, K.A., Bates, J.E., & Pettit, G.S. (1998). Multiple risk factors in the development of externalizing behavior problems: Group and individual differences. *Development and Psychopathology*, 10, 469–493.

Dryfoos, J.G. (1990). *Adolescents at risk: Prevalence and prevention*. Oxford: Oxford University Press.

Dumont, M., & Provost, M. (1999). Resilience in adolescents: Protective role of social support, coping strategies, self-esteem, and social activities on experience of stress and depression. *Journal of Youth and Adolescence*, 28, 343–363.

Duncan G.J., Brooks-Gunn J., & Klebanov, P.K. (1994). Economic deprivation and early childhood development. *Child Development*, 65, 296–318.

Duncan, G.J, Brooks-Gunn, J., Yeung, W.J., & Smith, J.R. (1998). How much does childhood poverty affect the life chances of children? *American Sociological Review*, 63, 406–423.

Easterbrooks, M.A., Davidson, C.E., & Chazan, R. (1993). Psychosocial risk, attachment, and behavior problems among school-age children. *Development and Psychopathology*, 5, 389–402.

Emery, R.E. (1999). *Marriage, divorce, and children's adjustment* (2nd edn). Thousand Oaks, CA: Sage.

Evans, G.W. (2003). A multimethodological analysis of cumulative risk and allostatic load among rural children. *Development Psychology*, 39, 924–933.

Evans, G.W., Kim, P., Ting, A.H., Tesher, H.B., & Shannis, D. (2007). Cumulative risk, maternal responsiveness, and allostatic load among young adolescents. *Developmental Psychology*, 43, 341–351.

Flouri, E., Hickey, J., Mavroveli, S., & Hurry, J. (2011). Adversity, emotional arousal, and problem behaviour in adolescence: The role of non-verbal cognitive ability as a resilience promoting factor. *Child & Adolescent Mental Health*, 16, 22–29.

Flouri, E., & Kallis, C. (2007). Adverse life events and psychopathology and prosocial behavior in late adolescence: Testing the timing, specificity, accumulation, gradient, and moderation of contextual risk. *Journal of the American Academy of Child & Adolescent Psychiatry*, 46, 1651–1659.

Flouri, E., Mavroveli, S., & Tzavidis, N. (2010). Modeling risks: Area deprivation, family socio-economic disadvantage, and adverse life events effects on young children's psychopathology. *Social Psychiatry and Psychiatric Epidemiology*, 45, 611–619.

Flouri, E., & Tzavidis, N. (2008). Psychopathology and prosocial behavior in adolescents from socio-economically disadvantaged families: The role of proximal and distal adverse life events. *European Child & Adolescent Psychiatry*, 17, 498–506.

Flouri, E., Tzavidis, N., & Kallis, C. (2010a). Adverse life events, area socio-economic disadvantage, and psychopathology and resilience in young children: The importance of risk factors' accumulation and protective factors' specificity. *European Child & Adolescent Psychiatry*, *19*, 535–546.

Flouri, E., Tzavidis, N., & Kallis, C. (2010b). Area and family effects on the psychopathology of the Millennium Cohort Study children and their older siblings. *Journal of Child Psychology and Psychiatry*, *51*, 152–161.

Ford, T., Collishaw, S., Meltzer, H., & Goodman, R. (2007). A prospective study of childhood psychopathology: Independent predictors of change over three years. *Social Psychiatry and Psychiatric Epidemiology*, *42*(12), 953–961.

Furstenberg, F. (1993). How families manage risk and opportunities in dangerous neighborhoods. In W.J. Wilson (Ed.) *Sociology and its public agenda* (pp. 231–258). Newbury Park, CA: Sage.

Garbarino, J. (2001). An ecological perspective on the effects of violence on children. *Journal of community psychology*, *29*, 361–378.

Garmezy, N. (1983). Stressors of childhood. In N. Garmezy & M. Rutter (Eds.) *Stress, coping and development in children* (pp. 43–84). New York: McGraw-Hill.

Garmezy, N. (1993). Children in poverty: Resilience despite risk. *Psychiatry*, *56*, 127–136.

Garmezy, N., Masten, A.S., & Tellegan, A. (1984). The study of stress and competence in children: A building block of developmental psychopathology. *Child Development*, *55*, 97–111.

Goodman, R. (1994). A modified version of the Rutter parent questionnaire including extra items on children's strengths: A research note. *Journal of Child Psychology and Psychiatry*, *35*, 1483–1494.

Goodman, R. (1997). The Strengths and Difficulties Questionnaire: A research note. *Journal of Child Psychology and Psychiatry*, *38*, 581–586.

Goodman, E. (1999). The role of socioeconomic status gradients in explaining differences in US adolescents' health. *American Journal of Public Health*, *89*, 1522–1528.

Goodman, E., Slap, G.B., & Huang, B. (2003). The public health impact of socioeconomic status on adolescent depression and obesity. *American Journal of Public Health*, *93*, 1844–1850.

Goodman, S.H., & Gotlib, I. (1999). Risk for psychopathology in the children of depressed mothers: A developmental model for understanding mechanisms of transmission. *Psychological Review*, *106*, 458–490.

Gorman-Smith, D., & Tolan, P.H. (2003). Positive adapation among young exposed to community violence. In S.S. Luthar, (Ed.) *Resilience and Vulnerability: Adaptation in the Context of Childhood* (pp. 392–413). New York: Cambridge University Press.

Grant, K.E., Compas, B.E., Thurm, A.E., McMahon, S.D., Gipson, P.Y., Campbell, A.J., *et al.* (2006). Stressors and child and adolescent psychopathology: Evidence of moderating and mediating effects. *Clinical Psychology Review*, *26*, 257–283.

Gutman, L.M., & Midgley, C. (2000). The role of protective factors in supporting the academic achievement of poor African American students during the middle school transition. *Journal of Youth and Adolescence*, *29*, 223–248.

Gutman, L.M., Sameroff, A.J., & Cole, R. (2003). Academic trajectories from first to twelfth grades: Growth curves according to multiple risk and early child factors. *Developmental Psychology*, *39*, 777–790.

Gutman, L.M., Sameroff, A.J., & Eccles, J.S. (2002). The academic achievement of African American students during early adolescence: An examination of multiple risk, promotive, and protective factors. *American Journal of Community Psychology*, *30*, 367–399.

Hammen, C. (2003). Risk and protective factors for children of depressed parents. In S.S. Luthar, (Ed.) *Resilience and Vulnerability: Adaptation in the Context of Childhood* (pp. 50–75). New York: Cambridge University Press.

Hetherington, E.M. (1989). Coping with family transitions: Winners, losers, and survivors. *Child Development, 60*, 1–14.

Hetherington, E.M. (1999). Should we stay together for the sake of our children? In E.M. Hetherington (Ed.) *Coping with divorce, single parenting, and remarriage: A risk and resiliency perspective.* (pp. 93–116). Mahwah, NJ: Erlbaum.

Hetherington, E.M., & Elmore, A.M. (2003). Risk and resilience in children's coping with their parents' divorce and remarriage. In S.S. Luthar, (Ed.) *Resilience and vulnerability: Adaptation in the context of childhood* (pp. 182–212). New York: Cambridge University Press.

Hetherington, E.M., & Kelly, J. (2002). *For better or for worse: Divorce reconsidered.* New York: Norton.

Leventhal, T., & Brooks-Gunn, J. (2000). The neighborhoods they live in: The effects of neighborhood residence on children and adolescent outcomes. *Psychological Bulletin, 126*, 309–337.

Lovejoy, M.C., Graczyk, P.A., O'Hare, E.O., & Neuman, G. (2000). Maternal depression and parenting behavior: A meta-analytic review. *Clinical Psychology Review 20*(5), 561–592.

Luthar, S.S. (1991). Vulnerability and resilience: A study of high-risk adolescents. *Child Development, 62*, 600–616.

Luthar, S.S., Cicchetti, D., & Becker, B. (2000). The construct of resilience: A critical evaluation and guidelines for future work. *Child Development, 71*, 543–562.

Luthar, S.S., Cushing, G., Merikangas, K.R., & Rounsaville, B.J. (1998). Multiple jeopardy: Risk/protective factors among addicted mothers' offspring. *Development and Psychopathology, 10*, 117–136.

Luthar, S.S., D'Avanzo, K., & Hites, S. (2003). Maternal drug abuse versus other psychological disturbances: Risks and resilience among children. In S.S. Luthar, (Ed.) *Resilience and vulnerability: Adaptation in the context of childhood* (pp. 104–129). New York: Cambridge University Press.

Luthar, S.S., Doernberger, C.H., & Zigler, E. (1993). Resilience is not a unidimensional construct: Insights from a prospective study on inner-city adolescents. *Development and Psychopathology, 5*, 703–717.

Lynch, M., & Cicchetti, D. (1998). An ecological-transactional analysis of children and contexts: The longitudinal interplay among child maltreatment, community violence, and children's symptomatology. *Development and psychopathology, 10*, 235–257.

Mahoney, J.L. & Eccles, J.S. (2007). Organized activity participation for children from low- and middle-income families. In A. Booth & A.C. Crouter (Eds.) *Disparities in school readiness: How do families contribute to successful and unsuccessful transitions into school?* (pp. 207–222). New York: Lawrence Erlbaum.

Masten, A. (2001). Ordinary magic: Resilience processes in development. *American Psychologist, 56*, 227–238.

Masten, A., & Coatsworth, J. (1998). The development of competence in favorable and unfavorable environments: Lessons from successful children. *American Psychologist, 53*, 205–220.

Masten, A., & Powell, J.L. (2003). A resilience framework for research, policy, and practice. In S.S. Luthar, (Ed.) *Resilience and vulnerability: Adaptation in the context of childhood* (pp. 1–28). New York: Cambridge University Press.

McCulloch, A. (2006). Variation in children's cognitive and behavioural adjustment between different types of place in the British National Child Development Study. *Social Science and Medicine, 62*, 1865–1879.

McCulloch, A., & Joshi, H.E. (2001). Neighborhood and family influences on the cognitive ability of children in the British National Child Development Study. *Social Science and Medicine, 53*, 579–591.

McGauhey, P.J., & Starfield, B. (1993). Child health and the social environment of white and black children. *Social Science Medicine, 36*, 867–874.

McLanahan, S.S. (1999). Father absence and the welfare of children. In E.M. Hetherington (Ed.) *Coping with divorce, single parenting, and remarriage* (pp. 117–145). Mahwah, NJ: Lawrence Erlbaum.

McLoyd, V.C. (1990). The impact of economic hardship on black families and children: Psychological distress, parenting, and socioeconomic development, *Child Development, 61*, 311–346.

McLoyd, V.C. (1998). Socioeconomic disadvantage and child development. *American Psychologist, 53*, 185–204.

McMahon, S.D., Grant, K.E., Compas, B.E., Thurm, A.E., & Ey, S. (2003). Stress and psychopathology in children and adolescents: Is there evidence of specificity? *Journal of Child Psychology and Psychiatry, 44*, 107–133.

Miller, D.B., & MacIntosh, R. (1999). Promoting resilience in urban African American adolescents: Racial socialization and identity as protective factors. *Social Work Research, 23*, 159–169.

Peterson, C., & Seligman, M.E.P. (2004). *Character strengths and virtues: A classification and handbook.* New York: Oxford University Press/Washington, DC: American Psychological Association.

Ribbens, J., & McCarthy, J. (2006). *Young people's experiences of loss and bereavement: Towards an interdisciplinary approach.* Berkshire: Open University Press.

Rolf, J., & Johnson, J. (1990). Protected or vulnerable: The challenges of AIDS to developmental psychopathology. In J. Rolf, A.S. Masten, D. Cicchetti, K.H. Nuechterlein, & S. Weintraub (Eds.) *Risk and protective factors in the development of psychopathology* (pp. 384–404). Cambridge: Cambridge University Press.

Roosa, M.W. (2000). Some thoughts about resilience versus positive development, main effects versus interactions, and the value of resilience. *Child Development, 71*, 567–569.

Rutter, M. (1979). Protective factors in children's responses to stress and disadvantage. In M.W. Kent & J.E. Rolf (Eds.) *Primary prevention of psychopathology: III: Promoting Social Competence and Coping in Children* (pp. 49–74). Hanover, NH: University Press of New England.

Rutter, M. (1987). Psychosocial resilience and protective mechanisms. *American Journal of Orthopsychiatry, 57*, 316–331.

Sameroff, A.J. (1999). Ecological perspectives on developmental risk. In J.D. Osofsky & H.E. Fitzgerald (Eds.) *WAIMH Handbook of Infant Mental Health: Vol. 4. Infant Mental Health Groups at Risk* (pp. 223–248). New York: Wiley.

Sameroff, A.J., & Gutman, L.M. (2004). Contributions of risk research to the designs of successful interventions. In P. Allen-Meares & M.W. Fraser (Eds.) *Intervention with children and adolescents: An interdisciplinary perspective* (pp. 9–26). Boston, MA: Allyn-Bacon.

Sameroff, A.J., Gutman, L.M., & Peck, S. (2003). Adaptation among youth facing multiple risks: Prospective research findings. In S.S. Luthar, (Ed.), *Resilience and vulnerability: Adaptation in the context of childhood* (pp. 364–391). New York: Cambridge University Press.

Sameroff, A.J., & Seifer, R. (1987). Multiple determinants of risk and invulnerability. In E.J. Anthony (Ed.) *The invulnerable child* (pp. 51–69). New York: Guilford Press.

Sameroff, A.J., Seifer, R., Barocas, R., Zax, M., & Greenspan, S. (1987). Intelligence quotient scores of 4-year-old children: Social-environmental risk factors. *Pediatrics, 79*, 343–350.

Sameroff, A.J., Seifer, R., Baldwin, A., & Baldwin, C. (1993). Stability of intelligence from preschool to adolescence: The influence of social and family risk factors. *Child Development, 64*, 80–97.

Sameroff, A.J., Seifer, R., & Zax, M. (1982). *Early development of children at risk for emotional disorder.* Monographs of the Society for Research in Child Development, 47(7, Serial No. 199).

Sandler, I., Wolchick, S., Davis, C., Haine, R., & Ayers, T. (2003). Correlational and experimental study of resilience in children of divorce and parental bereaved children. In S.S. Luthar, (Ed.) *Resilience and vulnerability: Adaptation in the context of childhood* (pp. 213–242). New York: Cambridge University Press.

Schoon, I., Bynner, J., Joshi, H., Parsons, S., Wiggins, R.D., & Sacker, A. (2002). The influence of context, timing, and duration of risk experiences for the passage from childhood to midadulthood. *Child Development, 73*, 1486–1504.

Seidman, E., & Pederson, S. (2003). Holistic contextual perspectives on risk, protection, and competence among low-income urban adolescents. In S.S. Luthar, (Ed.) *Resilience and vulnerability: Adaptation in the context of childhood* (pp. 318–342). New York: Cambridge University Press.

Seifer, R., Sameroff, A.J., Baldwin, C.P., & Baldwin, A. (1992). Child and family factors that ameliorate risk between 4 and 13 years of age. *Journal of American Academy Child Adolescent Psychiatry, 31*, 893–903.

Simons, R.L., Murray, V., McLoyd, V.C., Lin, K., Cutrona, C., & Conger, R.D. (2002). Discrimination, crime, ethnic identity, and parenting as correlates of depressive symptoms among African American children: A multilevel analysis. *Development and Psychopathology, 14*, 371–393.

Szalacha, L.A., Erkut, S., Coll, C.G., Fields, J.P., Alarcon, O., & Ceder, I. (2003). Perceived discrimination and resilience. In S.S. Luthar, (Ed.) *Resilience and Vulnerability: Adaptation in the Context of Childhood* (pp. 414–435). New York: Cambridge University Press.

Tiet, Q.Q., Bird, H.R., Davies, M., Hoven, C., Cohen, P., Jensen, P.S., & Goodman, S. (1998). Adverse life events and resilience. *Journal of the American Academy of Child & Adolescent Psychiatry, 37*, 1191–1200.

Wells, N.M., & Evans, G.W. (2003). Nearby nature: A buffer of life stress among rural children. *Environment and Behavior, 35*, 311–330.

Werner, E.E. (1993). Risk, resilience, and recovery: Perspectives from the Kauai Longitudinal Study. *Development and Psychopathology, 5*, 503–515.

Werner, E.E., & Smith, R.S. (1992). *Overcoming the odds: High risk children from birth to adulthood*. Ithaca, NY: Cornell University Press.

Werner, E.E., & Smith, R.S. (2001). *Journeys from childhood to midlife: Risk, resilience, and recovery*. Ithaca, NY: Cornell University Press.

Wiking, E., Johansson, S.E., & Sundquist, J. (2004). Ethnicity, acculturation, and self reported health: A population based study among immigrants from Poland, Turkey, and Iran in Sweden. *Journal of Epidemiology and Community Health, 58*, 574–582.

Wikstrom, P. (1998). Communities and crime. In M.H. Tonrey (Ed.) *The handbook of crime and punishment* (pp. 269–304). New York: Oxford University Press.

Xue, Y.G., Leventhal, T., Brooks-Gunn, J., & Earls, F.J. (2005). Neighborhood residence and mental health problems of 5- to 11-year-olds. *Archives of General Psychiatry, 62*, 554–563.

20 Social Problems in Schools

PETER K. SMITH AND JULIAN ELLIOTT

KEY TERMS

bias bullying • bullying • ChildLine in Partnership with Schools (CHIPS) • cognitive-behavioural therapy (CBT) • cyberbullying • Diagnostic and Statistical Manual of Mental Disorders (4th edn) (DSM-IV) • emotive imagery • Kidscape • Life in Schools questionnaire • Method of Shared Concern • negative reinforcement • Olweus bully victim questionnaire • Olweus Bullying Prevention Program • positive reinforcement • quality circles (QCs) • restorative justice • retributive justice • Safe to Learn • school phobics • School Refusal Assessment Scale • school tribunal (or bully court) • self-worth protection • separation anxiety • Social and Emotional Aspects of Learning (SEAL) • specific phobia • Support Group Method • systematic desensitisation

CHAPTER OUTLINE

OVERVIEW

Bullying is one of the biggest social problems affecting children in our schools, and at sadly regular intervals we read of another suicide by a victim of persistent bullying. The study of bullying in schools has expanded greatly worldwide over the last two decades, the hope being that by understanding it we can introduce effective strategies to reduce its prevalence and its effects on the victims. Such strategies began in the early 1980s in Norway, which introduced the first national campaign against bullying. The success of this programme inspired many other programmes, and from the 1990s there has been widespread circulation of anti-bullying materials plus, in some countries, legal requirements on schools to have an anti-bullying policy or to tackle bullying effectively.

Incidence figures for the extent of bullying vary depending on how it is measured but it is thought that in Westernised industrial countries some 5 per cent of children are regular or severe bullies, and around 10 per cent are regular or severe victims. There are many types of bullying, which include physical, verbal and indirect/relational, the latter including systematic social exclusion. A fairly recent and often insidious form of bullying is cyberbullying, which uses electronic devices such as mobile phones and the internet: this typically occurs outside of school, but often involves those known from school.

The chapter describes the various types of bullying, with descriptions of typical bullies and the risk factors for becoming victims. The several types of interventions and strategies to reduce bullying and their effectiveness are also described. The chapter then considers school refusals, that is, student/pupil absence from school. Unsurprisingly, most absence from school is as a consequence of a physical malady, and these absences are seen as unavoidable. In other cases of school absences, major factors include students' dislike of school life, boredom, the possibility of undertaking more enjoyable activities elsewhere, anxiety associated with attending school, or an outright rejection of adult authority. The prevalence and types of school refusers are described, as are several types of intervention to reduce truancy and school refusal.

Children spend a great deal of time at school. They are with a large peer group with whom they engage in intense social relationships and social comparison processes. Sadly, and despite the aphorism about schooldays being the happiest days of one's life, Shakespeare's image of the schoolboy heading unwillingly to school may often present a more accurate picture for many children.

INTRODUCTION

From around 4 to 7 years of age, and usually at 5 or 6 years (depending on the country they live in), children start compulsory schooling. Apart from a very small percentage of children who receive home schooling or private tuition, this means attending school with many other pupils, for a large part of the day, many days of the year. For example in the UK, virtually all children start school as 'rising fives' (i.e. the term in which they become 5 years of age), and continue at least until age 16. Through these 11 years they are at school for around 8 hours a day, and for around 200 days per year. We start this chapter by summarising the nature of the school context.

The peer group in school becomes a major source of children's friendships, as well as possible difficulties and conflicts. General issues around peer relationships and friendship are discussed in Chapter 14 on play and peer relations, so those topics are not covered again here, but we do pay particular attention to victimisation and

bullying term used to define an individual's repeated exposure to negative actions by one or more other people.

bullying in school, and how such problems in social relationships can be tackled. An inability to cope with the demands of school, leading to such levels of anxiety that the child refuses to attend, is a major issue that affects future life chances, and this is examined in the final part of the chapter.

THE SCHOOL CONTEXT

Despite the aphorism about schooldays being the happiest days of one's life, Shakespeare's image of the schoolboy heading unwillingly to school may often present a more accurate picture for many children (Figure 20.1). Successfully navigating the many academic and social demands of life in school is difficult for most and highly stressful for many. The fearsome image of the sadistic and uncaring teacher inflicting misery upon their charges is now largely an historical image that bears little resemblance to most classrooms, yet other sources of anxiety, in particular, meeting and coping with the perceptions and expectations of parents, teachers, and peers have taken precedence over the fear of physical chastisement.

Social pressures in the classroom

There are myriad social pressures that operate in the classroom. One key factor is the process of social comparison whereby the child compares their performance with classmates. A recent comprehensive review of relevant research (Dijkstra *et al.*, 2008) suggests that comparison is usually upward, that is, with students who perform better than themselves but who seem similar to them on a range of related and unrelated attributes. Such comparison can raise the child's level of academic performance but can also result in negative self-perceptions.

In Western society, human value is closely related to one's ability to achieve in competition with others (Gardner, 1961). Negative self-perceptions of one's ability can lead some students to try to conceal this from peers in order to minimise any sense of shame. This is not necessarily a universal phenomenon, however, as in some Asian cultures, students may be judged rather more by their level of effort than ability (Grant & Dweck, 2001). However, to protect their sense of self-worth,

FIGURE 20.1 *The child heading unwillingly to school may often present a more accurate picture for many children.*
Source: Shutterstock.

some students may engage in a number of strategies to conceal their own perceived lack of ability. Covington (1992) has coined the term **self-worth protection** to describe the tendency of some students to reduce their levels of effort so that any subsequent poor academic performance will be attributed to low motivation rather than to a lack of ability. A detailed account of some of the specific strategies that are employed can be found in Covington (1998) and Thompson (1999). Given that effort is usually seen as worthy by parents and teachers, it is unsurprising that those who do not try hard may feel guilty. However, this may be preferable to possible alternative outcomes. Thus, Covington and Omelich (1985) have shown that while failure as a consequence of low effort may lead to a sense of guilt, failure following high effort can result in humiliation. In many cases, fear of humiliation is the stronger source of motivation, particularly for males (Craske, 1988; Miller, 1986). As a result, many students seek to preserve:

> **self-worth protection** the tendency of some students to reduce their levels of effort so that any subsequent poor academic performance will be attributed to low motivation rather than to a lack of ability.

> a sense of dignity in school by engaging in a series of 'ruses and artful dodges' that 'reflect a primordial struggle for self-protection so elemental that many students are prepared to sacrifice even good grades for the sake of appearances'.
>
> *(Covington, 1998, p. 100).*

Ultimately, however, such strategies are doomed to failure and these students will often feel angry, incompetent, hopeless and emotionally burnt-out (see Thompson, 1999, pp. 29–43).

Peer pressure to work, or not!

A further important social factor in school concerns peer pressure to work, or alternatively, not to work, hard in class and on homework. In a series of publications Elliott and his colleagues (Elliott *et al.*, 2005; Elliott & Nguyen, 2008; Elliott & Tudge, 2007) have outlined the very different nature of peer pressures in a number of Eastern and Western cultures. Unlike their peers in many Eastern cultures, where striving is typically seen as praiseworthy, children in classrooms in the UK and the United States, (particularly adolescents) often discourage any overt display of academic engagement by their classmates. It is important to note that academic success in itself is not necessarily problematic for acceptance in US and UK contexts; effortless success is generally admired by students. It is the visible demonstration of a student's attempt to excel academically that runs social risks. To demonstrate levels of enthusiasm or interest considered by peers as excessive can result in disapprobation and ridicule. These possible outcomes can result in reduced striving (Howley *et al.*, 1995; Steinberg, 1996). This problem may not be so influential in other Western societies, however. For example, in comparing primary school children in France and England, Osborn (1997) noted that this seemed to be more of an Anglo problem. It was only the English children she studied who seemed reluctant to succeed academically:

> many English children did not want to be the best in the class, and felt lukewarm about getting a good mark or even praise for good work. Some children actually said that they did not want to be seen as too good by the teacher; no French child said this.
>
> *(Osborn, 1997, p. 49)*

As high stakes testing in many countries increasingly leads teachers, parents and students to focus upon success on a variety of externally regulated tests and examinations, it is not surprising that student stress levels in relation to academic performance can often be high (Connor, 2001, 2003; Denscombe, 2000). In a self-report study of UK students, for example, Putwain (2008) estimated that 13 per cent of students aged 14–16 were 'highly' anxious with respect to their forthcoming examinations. Working hard enough to gain academic success but not so much as to attract peer disapprobation is, for many students, a daunting, if not impossible, task.

VICTIMISATION AND BULLYING IN SCHOOL

What do we mean by 'bullying'?

Bullying is usually taken to be a subset of aggressive behaviour, characterised by repetition and an imbalance of power (e.g. Olweus, 1999). The behaviour is repetitive, that is, a victim is targeted a number of times. Also, the victim cannot defend themselves easily, for one or more reasons: they may be outnumbered, be smaller or less physically strong, or be less psychologically resilient, than the person(s) doing the bullying (Figure 20.2). The definition 'a systematic abuse of power' (Smith & Sharp, 1994) also captures these two features.

Although these two criteria (repetition, and power imbalance) are not universally accepted, they are now widely used. Bullying, by its nature, is likely to have particular characteristics (such as fear of telling by the victim), and particular outcomes (such as development of low self-esteem, and depression, in the victim). The relative defencelessness of the victim implies an obligation on others to intervene, if we take the democratic rights of the victim seriously.

Over the last two decades research on school bullying has expanded greatly worldwide, and especially in Europe, North America, Japan, and Australasia. This growth in knowledge, combined with media interest that has at times been intense, has led to action to reduce school bullying and its effects. This started in the early 1980s in Norway, with

FIGURE 20.2 *The victims of bullying are often lonely and abandoned at school.*
Source: Shutterstock.

the first national campaign against bullying. The reported success of this inspired many other projects. During the 1990s, there has also been widespread circulation of anti-bullying materials, plus, in some European countries, legal requirements on schools to have an anti-bullying policy or to tackle bullying effectively.

Bullying can happen in many contexts – the workplace, the home, the armed forces, prisons, and so on (Monks *et al.*, 2009). Indeed, topics such as workplace bullying are growing research areas. In school, too, we can think of teacher–teacher, teacher–pupil, pupil–teacher as well as pupil–pupil bullying. However it is mainly pupil–pupil bullying which has been the focus of research up until now.

How do we find out about bullying?

There are obvious difficulties in getting data on school bullying. Nevertheless a number of methods can be used. The main methods are:

- Teacher and parent reports. These are of limited value, however, as teachers and parents are usually unaware of a lot of the pupil–pupil bullying which is occurring.

- Self-reports by pupils as to whether they have been bullied, or taken part in bullying others (usually, over a definite time period). These are widely used in anonymous questionnaires, such as the **Olweus Bully Victim questionnaire** (Olweus, 1999) and the **Life in Schools questionnaire** (Arora, 1994).

- Peer nominations, in which classmates are asked who is a bully, or a victim. This may be the most reliable method for class-based work. Two common instruments are those of Rigby and Slee (1991) and the Salmivalli Participant Role Scale (Salmivalli *et al.*, 1996).

- Direct observations of behaviour, for example in the playground. Pepler and Craig (1995), for example, use radio microphones plus a telephoto camera. Observations have high validity but are expensive and time-consuming to carry out and analyse.

- Interviews with individuals, focus groups with say 4–8 pupils, and incident reports kept by a school, are other ways of getting information.

Olweus Bully Victim questionnaire a 40-item anonymous questionnaire for school children (ages 8 to 16 years) which assesses whether they have been bullied, or taken part in bullying others.

Life in Schools questionnaire a 40-item anonymous questionnaire filled in by school children which is used to gauge the extent of bullying, other types of aggressive behaviour and friendly behaviour in a class or school at a particular point of time.

Incidence figures for bullying

Incidence figures for bullying vary greatly depending on measurement criteria (for example, what frequency and time span are asked about; whether the information comes from self, peer, teacher, or parent report), but broadly speaking, in the UK and similar Western industrialised countries, some 5 per cent of children might be

FIGURE 20.3 *Bullying has many negative effects on its victims.*
Source: Shutterstock.

bias bullying bullying in which the victim is a member of a particular group, for example race, gender, faith/religion, rather than their victim's individual characteristics

FIGURE 20.4 *Physical bullying includes hitting, kicking or punching.*
Source: Shutterstock.

seen as regular or severe bullies, and some 10 per cent as regular or severe victims. These are appreciable minorities of children and young people, and are of concern because of the suffering caused by bullying, and the long-term effects (Figure 20.3).

Types of bullying

What might be called the 'traditional' forms of bullying include physical, verbal, and indirect/relational, as found in typologies of aggression generally. Physical bullying includes hitting, kicking, punching, and taking or damaging someone's belongings (Figure 20.4). Verbal bullying includes teasing, taunting, and threats. Indirect/relational includes spreading nasty rumours (done indirectly rather than face-to-face) and systematic social exclusion ('you can't play with us'); these damage a person's relations or social network, rather than being a direct physical or verbal attack.

Some bullying is based on (or justified by) the victim being a member of a particular group, often a marginalised or disadvantaged one; rather than on individual characteristics. This has been referred to as **bias bullying**; it includes bullying related to, for example, gender, race/ethnicity, sexual orientation, faith/religion, and disability. For example, children can experience racist teasing and name-calling, and those of non-white ethnic origin have been shown to experience more racist name-calling (though not necessarily other forms of bullying) than white children of the same age and gender. In secondary schools, children may be teased about their sexual orientation, and even physically assaulted or ridiculed about this by other pupils or teachers (Rivers, 1995).

Cyberbullying

A relatively new type of bullying is now commonly called **cyberbullying**. This describes forms of bullying using electronic devices, mainly mobile phones and the internet. One study (Smith, Mahdavi *et al.*, 2008) identified seven types of cyberbullying: text message bullying; mobile phone call bullying; picture/video clip bullying (via mobile phone cameras); email bullying; chat-room bullying; bullying through instant messaging; and bullying via websites. In contrast to other forms of bullying, prevalence rates of cyberbullying were greater outside of school than inside, but often involved those known from school. New forms of cyberbullying are likely to appear as electronic technologies develop further, and, unlike traditional bullying, cyberbullying in the UK appears to be on the increase (Figure 20.5). Rivers and Noret (2010) studied over 11,000 pupils from 2002 to 2005, and asked them 'How often have you received any nasty or threatening text messages or emails?' The percentage answering 'once in a while' or more often rose from 5.8 per cent in 2002 to 7.0 per cent in 2005.

> **cyberbullying** a type of bullying which uses electronic devices, mainly mobile phones and the internet.

No place to hide

There are some distinctive features of cyberbullying. One is *No place to hide*: Unlike traditional forms of bullying, where once the victim gets home they are away from the bullying until the next day, cyberbullying is more difficult to escape from; the victim may continue to receive text messages or emails, or view nasty postings on a website, wherever they are. Another is the breadth of audience: Cyberbullying can reach particularly large audiences in a peer group compared with the normally small groups that are onlookers of traditional bullying. For example when nasty comments are posted on a website, the audience that may see these comments is potentially very large. In addition, those doing the bullying often have more anonymity than in traditional physical or verbal bullying. Online pseudonyms may be used on the internet.

FIGURE 20.5 *Cyberbullying is on the increase.*
Source: Shutterstock.

Roles in bullying

The traditional roles derived from questionnaire and peer nomination data are *bully, victim, non-involved* (neither a bully nor a victim), plus *bully–victim* (pupils who are both a bully and a victim). In addition, victims are often divided into *passive victims*, and *provocative victims*, depending on their typical response; the latter category may overlap with *aggressive victims* or *bully–victims*. Salmivalli *et al.* (1996) refined this process further by describing six participant roles in bullying: *ringleader bullies* (who take the initiative), *follower bullies* (who then join in), *reinforcers* (who encourage the bully or laugh at the victim), *defenders* (who help the victim) and *bystanders* (who stay out of things), as well as the *victims* themselves.

Some structural features of bullying

A great deal has been found out about the nature of bullying, mainly from large-scale surveys using anonymous self-report questionnaires. Many findings replicate across studies and across cultures. One finding, very important for intervention work, is that a substantial proportion of self-reported victims say that they have not told a teacher, or someone at home, about the bullying. This proportion who have not told increases with age. Also, boy victims are less likely to tell anyone, than girl victims. A second finding relates to attitudes about bullying in the peer group as a whole. Although most pupils say they do not like bullying, a significant minority do say they could join in bullying. Perhaps surprisingly, these 'pro-bullying' or 'anti-victim' attitudes increase with age up to 14–15 years (after which they start to decline). Such anti-victim attitudes are more marked in boys than girls – and especially for boys as regards boy victims (Olweus & Endresen, 1998).

Effects of being bullied

Victims of bullying often experience anxiety and depression, low self-esteem, physical and psychosomatic complaints (Williams *et al.*, 1996). In extreme cases, they may commit suicide (Kaltiala-Heino *et al.*, 1999). In a meta-analysis of many studies, Hawker and Boulton (2000) found that victimisation was most strongly related to depression, moderately associated for social and global self-esteem, and less strongly associated with anxiety. It is often assumed that victimisation causes these negative effects, but it could be that being depressed and having low self-esteem make a pupil more susceptible to being bullied (see the next section on causes). In fact, longitudinal studies suggest both processes may be at work (Kochenderfer & Ladd, 1996). Retrospective studies with adults strongly suggest that prolonged victimisation in childhood can have long-term effects (Hugh-Jones & Smith, 1999; Rigby, 2003).

Causes of bullying

Many levels of causation are typically invoked in understanding bullying and victimisation. At the broadest level are society factors, such as tolerance of violence, bullying and abuse of power in society, and portrayals in the mass media. At the community level, relevant factors are neighbourhood levels of violence and safety, and socioeconomic conditions. At the school level, the school climate and quality of teacher and pupil relationships can have powerful effects (Anderson *et al.*, 2001; Utting, Monteiro & Ghate, 2007). It is through the school and the peer group that most anti-bullying interventions have tried to operate, although work with parents and families is clearly also relevant.

Regarding young people who bully others, aggressive behaviour and inequalities of power are commonplace in human groups, including peer groups in school, so bullying can be a temptation. It has been suggested that school bullying may be an early stage in the development of later antisocial behaviour (Baldry & Farrington, 2000; Kumpulainen & Räsänen, 2000). School bullies are up to four times more likely to become chronic offenders than non-bullies and are also more likely to father children who become bullies themselves (Farrington, 1993; Olweus, 1991). Particularly at risk appear to be the 'bully–victims' (those who score or are labelled as both bullies and victims), who comprise perhaps 1 or 2 per cent of the school population.

Parental maltreatment and abuse

Both bullying and more general antisocial behaviour have similar background risk factors. For example, involvement in bullying others is associated with family predictors such as insecure attachment, harsh physical discipline, and being a victim with over-protective parenting (Curtner-Smith *et al.*, 2010). Parental maltreatment and abuse is a likely risk factor in the bully–victim or aggressive victim group (Schwartz *et al.*, 2000; Shields & Cicchetti, 2001).

Risk factors for being a victim

Complementary factors may increase the risk of being a victim for certain pupils. At an interpersonal level, the attitudes of the main peer groups in the school, as well as the nature and quality of friendships that a child has, are amongst the most important risk factors for victimisation. For example, Hodges *et al.* (1997) found that having few friends, or friends who cannot be trusted or who are of low status, and sociometric rejection (dislike by peers), are risk factors for being a victim. Within the family, some victims come from over-protective or enmeshed families (Curtner-Smith *et al.*, 2010). Having a disability or special educational needs is another risk factor for being a victim. Children with special needs are two to three times more at risk of being bullied; they are also more at risk of taking part in bullying others (Mishna, 2003). Possible reasons for this include:

- particular characteristics that may make them an obvious 'target';
- in mainstream settings these children are usually less well integrated socially and lack the protection against bullying which friendship gives;
- those with behavioural problems may act out in an aggressive way and become 'provocative victims'.

INTERVENTIONS TO REDUCE BULLYING

Many sources of advice and support exist for anti-bullying work, and in England the Department for Children, Schools and Families (DCSF; now the Department for Education (DfE)) issued guidelines in **Safe to Learn** (DCSF, 2007). Bullying in school is a systemic problem. Different components of school-based interventions may address different aspects of the system: the whole school level, including the school ethos; the environment of the school; the peer group; and individual pupils, including not only bullies, and victims, but also those involved as bystanders or outsiders to the bullying.

Safe to Learn guidelines issued by the UK Department for Children, Schools and Families (DCSF; now the Department for Education (DfE)), intended to encourage good behaviour and respect for others on the part of school children, and to prevent bullying.

A whole-school policy

Within the UK, a whole-school policy against bullying is taken as a basic first step, and since 1999 it has been a legal requirement in England and Wales for all schools to have some form of anti-bullying policy. It is a written document that should define the issue comprehensively, and state the responsibilities of all concerned in the school and what actions will be taken to reduce bullying and deal with incidents when they occur. School policies vary in scope (Smith, Smith *et al.*, 2008), but provide a framework for the school's response involving the whole school community: pupils, teachers, learning mentors, school support staff, governors and parents/carers. In Welsh schools, a significant association was reported between lower levels of bullying, and pupils reporting that the school had clear rules on bullying (Lambert *et al.*, 2008), although Woods and Wolke (2003) found few associations of policy scores with measures of bullying in 34 English primary schools.

Curriculum work

Classroom activities can be used to tackle issues associated with bullying, progressively and in an age, gender and culturally appropriate way. These can include literature, audiovisual materials, videos, drama/role play, music, debates, workshops, puppets and dolls (in early years), and group work. Such curricular approaches can raise awareness of bullying and the schools' anti-bullying policy, and develop skills, empathy, and assertiveness in confronting bullying. There is some evidence for these effects, but only temporarily if curriculum work is not backed up by continuing anti-bullying work and policy (Smith & Sharp, 1994).

Methods and programmes

quality circles (QCs) small groups of children who meet to problem-solve issues such as bullying.

Some particular methods and programmes can be helpful. For example, **quality circles (QCs)** are small groups of pupils formed for regular classroom sessions. The groups problem-solve particular issues – such as bullying – through standard procedures, including information gathering – and present findings to a wider audience. One evaluation in primary schools found that 95 per cent of pupils liked the experience and felt that the QC group had worked well together. Over half stated that they had become more aware of bullying and that they now tried to stop it (Smith & Sharp, 1994). One curriculum approach that can enhance interpersonal relationships and may reduce victimisation, is cooperative group work. Here, small groups of pupils cooperate in a common task – for example, designing the front page of a class newspaper. Such methods appear to be positive for academic achievement (Johnson *et al.*, 2000), but can also involve/integrate vulnerable children (victims) and children from ethnic minorities; although unless handled carefully, it can be disrupted by bullying children (Cowie & Berdondini, 2001).

Social and Emotional Aspects of Learning (SEAL)

An example of a relationships curriculum in England is **Social and Emotional Aspects of Learning (SEAL)**. The primary SEAL programme is based around seven themes, one of which is 'Say No to Bullying'; this focuses on: what bullying is; how it feels; why people bully; how schools can prevent and respond to it; and how children can use their social and emotional skills. An external evaluation of the primary SEAL pilot (Hallam *et al.*, 2006) found evidence of improvement in pupils' social skills, relationships, and awareness of emotions, although the lack of a control group meant these findings could not be fully validated. The Secondary SEAL programme was launched as a pilot in 2005 under the title *Developing Social, Emotional and Behavioural Skills (SEBS)*. It includes a Year 7 learning and teaching resource, with four themes: 'A place to learn' (setting the context for learning); 'Learning to be together' (social skills and empathy); 'Keep on learning' (motivation); and 'Learning about me' (understanding and managing feelings). Both the UK government's Office for Standards in Education (OFSTED 2007) and Smith, O'Donnell *et al.* (2007) reported that the greatest impact of the pilot was on improving teachers' understanding of social, emotional and behavioural skills. The evaluations do not specifically address the support provided for pupils who bully, or any individual level improvements in their behaviour.

> **Social and Emotional Aspects of Learning (SEAL)** a UK-based relationships curriculum to developing social and emotional skills. It has seven themes, one of which is 'Say No to Bullying'.

Assertiveness training

Victims of bullying tend to have low self-esteem and sometimes poor ways of coping with attempts to bully them. Assertiveness training has been recommended as a way to help victims, or potential victims, of bullying cope in non-passive but non-aggressive ways. These techniques can be taught to pupils and appear to be helpful at least to some pupils. It is not reasonable to use this as the only strategy, but it can be one part of a more comprehensive package.

Peer support systems

Peer support uses the knowledge, skills and experience of children and young people themselves in a planned and structured way to tackle and reduce bullying through both proactive and reactive strategies. There are a wide variety of forms, many of which involve some training of the peer supporters, for example by ChildLine in their **ChildLine in Partnership with Schools (CHIPS)** programme. They include *circle time*, as an arena in which the class can address particular problems, for example relationships with one another, including dealing with anger, fighting and bullying (Figure 20.6); *circles of friends*, which aims to provide a support team of peers to work with a vulnerable pupil; *befriending*, which involves the assignment of a pupil

> **ChildLine in Partnership with Schools (CHIPS)** a UK peer support system founded in 1998 which works in schools, youth clubs and other settings with children, and uses their knowledge, skills and experience to tackle problems which include bullying.

FIGURE 20.6 *Circle time is an arena in which the class can address problems to do with bullying.*

Source: Shutterstock.

or pupils to 'be with' or 'befriend' a peer; *conflict resolution/mediation*, a structured process in which a neutral third party assists voluntary participants to resolve their dispute, using a step-by-step process that helps pupils agree to a mutually acceptable solution; and *active listening/counselling-based approaches*, which extend the befriending and mediation approaches into interventions that are based more overtly on a counselling model, with pupil helpers trained and supervised to use active listening skills to support peers in distress.

Peer-support systems evaluated

In reviewing peer support methods, Cowie and Smith (2009) argue that evaluations so far suggest clear benefits for the peer supporters themselves, and general improvement of school climate; but specific benefits for victims of bullying are more variable or uncertain. Users report that peer supporters offer helpful interventions, and most pupils and teachers believe that such approaches have an impact on the school as a whole. A peer mediation scheme in three Canadian primary school playgrounds helped reduce physically aggressive playground behaviour by over a half (Cunningham *et al.*, 1998).

However if regular supervision is not provided for peer helpers, if there are not enough peer supporters to tackle the problem, or if the problem is particularly severe, the system is likely to be ineffective. In one school with high levels of aggression, the small number of peer supporters was not strong enough to challenge the culture of bullying; its impact was confined to a few victimised pupils and did not reach the school as a whole. Furthermore, there is a sharp gender divide in recruitment of peer supporters, with typically over 80 per cent being girls and only 20 per cent being boys; sometimes male peer supporters can be teased about their role and this gender difference in attitudes is stronger in secondary schools (Smith & Watson, 2004).

Working in the playground

Pupil–pupil bullying predominately takes place outside the classroom in corridors, school grounds and outside the school gates (Blatchford, 1998). An effective playground policy and well designed play area can significantly help to reduce bullying (DCSF, 2007). OFSTED (2003) identified features of good practice including the efficient checking of the school site, setting up safe play areas or quiet rooms, and close supervision at the start and finish of the school day. Work on the physical environment of the playground – structuring or redesigning it to provide more creative opportunities for pupils during break and lunch times, and reduce boredom and bullying – can be a participatory and inclusive process for pupils (Smith & Sharp, 1994). Lunchtime supervisors have a pivotal role in implementing any playground or school anti-bullying policy, but often receive little or no training for this. Training sessions can provide them with additional skills in organising games, recognising bullying behaviours, interviewing pupils, and dealing with bullying and conflict situations. An important aspect is distinguishing bullying from playful fighting. One study found that trained lunchtime supervisors brought about a clear decrease in bullying in the playground in primary schools (Boulton, 1994).

Reactive strategies

Reactive strategies deal with bullying situations when they have arisen. They range from more punitive or direct sanctions-based approaches, through restorative practices, to more indirect and non-punitive approaches. In England the official government view has tended to be that bullying should always incur some form of sanction. Many professionals however prefer less direct approaches, at least for less severe cases of bullying.

Direct sanctions

Direct sanctions may vary in severity and be used on a graded scale if bullying persists. They can range through reprimands / serious talks; involving parents or carers, temporary removal from class, withdrawal of privileges and rewards, disciplinary measures such as detentions, punishment such as litter-picking / school clean-ups, through to temporary or permanent exclusion. Direct sanctions are expected to impress on the perpetrator that what they have done is unacceptable and promote understanding of the limits of acceptable behaviour; give an opportunity for pupils who bully to face up to the harm they have caused and learn from it; deter them from repeating that behaviour; signal to other pupils that the behaviour is unacceptable and deter them from doing it; and demonstrate publicly that school rules and policies are to be taken seriously.

School tribunals – 'bully courts'

A variant of direct sanctions is the use of a **school tribunal**. In a school tribunal or '**bully court**', pupils are elected to hear evidence and decide on sanctions or punishments for those involved in bullying. The UK based charity **Kidscape** issued a one-page sheet of advice and guidance headed 'Bully courts' in 1990; it was claimed that 30 schools were using them, and that in 8 schools being monitored, reports of being bullied dropped from 70 per cent to 6 per cent. However, it has been impossible to verify these claims in a publicly accountable way. School tribunals are not usually popular with teachers, as they feel too much power is being given to pupils. But a case study of a UK secondary school, in which a school tribunal was used together with a peer mentoring support scheme, did find some evidence for effectiveness (Mahdavi & Smith, 2002).

school tribunal (or bully court) pupils are elected to hear evidence and decide on sanctions or punishments for those involved in bullying.

Kidscape a UK-based charity which was established in 1985, whose focus is on children's safety, with an emphasis on the prevention of harm and child protection issues, and identified with the effort to reduce or quell bullying.

Restorative justice

retributive justice
direct sanctions against
bullies that are intended
to reduce the incidence
of bullying.

restorative justice a
range of practices which
focus on the offender
or bullying child being
made aware of the vic-
tim's feelings and the
harm they have caused,
and making some
agreed reparation.

Direct sanctions are seen as a form of **retributive justice**; this contrasts with the idea of **restorative justice** (Braithwaite, 2002). Restorative justice refers to a range of practices which focus on the offender or bullying child being made aware of the victim's feelings and the harm they have caused, and making some agreed reparation. Although originally developed in the area of youth justice and criminal behaviour, restorative approaches are wide ranging and can be used for a variety of difficulties in schools, including bullying, vandalism, theft, assault, and conflicts between teachers and pupils.

Restorative justice is based around three main principles: *responsibility* (the offender, along with their parents, learns to accept responsibility for the offence caused through their actions); *reparation* (the victim is involved through consultation, mediation, and participation, and reparative activities are devised to help the offender alleviate some of the damage and distress they have caused); and *resolution* (successfully ending a dispute so that pupils and their families are free to interact without threat of further conflict). The actual restorative practices used will depend on the nature and severity of the bullying incident, ranging from simple pupil based discussions through to a full restorative conference. Effective use of restorative justice depends on pupils being able to talk about feelings and relationship issues. Restorative approaches are being increasingly used in schools; Tinker (2002) evaluated 105 conferences carried out in Nottingham schools: 78 per cent finished fully successfully, with a further 16 per cent partially successful. A Scottish study has indicated that restorative justice 'can offer a powerful and effective approach to promoting harmonious relationships in school and to the successful resolution of conflict and harm' (Kane *et al.*, 2007).

Counselling-based approaches

At the opposite pole to direct sanctions are approaches in which the bullying child(ren) do not have to directly acknowledge their responsibility, although there is encourage-

**Method of Shared
Concern** a counselling-
based approach for
resolving bullying, which
aims to sensitise bully-
ing children to the harm
they are doing to the
victim and encourage
positive behaviours to
the victim.

ment to recognise the plight or suffering of the victim, and pressure on them to do something helpful to ease this. In Sweden, Pikas (1989, 2002) developed a **Method of Shared Concern**. This is a counselling-based approach for resolving bullying, designed for situations where a group of pupils have been bullying one or more pupils on a regular basis for some time. It uses a combination of individual and group meetings, structured around five consecutive phases: individual talks with suspected bullies; individual talk with the victim; preparatory group meeting; summit meeting; and follow up of the results. This approach is expected to sensitise bullying children to the harm they are doing to the victim (enabled by a lack of hostile blaming attitude on the part of the interviewer), encourage positive behaviours to the victim, and also encourage provocative victims to change their behaviour in positive ways. Although used rather widely in Sweden, there is little evaluation of the technique.

In the UK, the **Support Group Method**, developed by Robinson and Maines (2007), has a similar philosophy. It is a non-punitive approach which aims to change problem behaviours through a mixture of peer pressure to elicit a prosocial response, and self realisation of the harm and suffering caused to the victim. There are seven steps:

> **Support Group Method** in the UK, a non-punitive approach which aims to change problem behaviours through a mixture of peer pressure to elicit a prosocial response, and self realisation of the harm and suffering caused to the victim.

1. The facilitator talks individually to the bullied pupil.
2. A group meeting of six to eight students is set up, some suggested by the victim but without their presence.
3. The facilitator explains to the group that the victim has a problem, but does not discuss the incidents that have taken place.
4. The facilitator assures the group no punishment will given, but instead all participants must take joint responsibility to make the victim feel happy and safe.
5. Each group member gives their own ideas on how the victim can be helped.
6. The facilitator ends the meeting, with the group given responsibility for improving the victim's safety and well-being.
7. Individual meetings are held with group members one week after the meeting to establish how successful the intervention has been.

Smith, Howard, *et al.* (2007) ascertained the use of and support for the Support Group Method within schools and local authorities across the UK. Over half of the schools surveyed (53%) rated the effectiveness of the method as very satisfactory, while 30 per cent said it was rather satisfactory and the remainder were neutral. The method was found to be adapted considerably in use, so that the 'seven steps' were not always followed as above. No direct evidence was provided as to whether the method was able to support and improve the behaviour of children who bullied others.

Not everyone agrees that bullying children should not be blamed; the alternative view is that bullying children must acknowledge their own responsibility in the bullying, and accept any negative sanctions that follow when this is discovered. This is an issue that needs to be handled carefully, bearing in mind the age of the pupils, the duration of the bullying, and the ethos of the school.

Large-scale school-based interventions

There have been quite a number of large-scale school-based anti-bullying interventions, which have been carefully evaluated. Reviews of such studies (Smith *et al.*, 2004; Ttofi *et al.*, 2008) suggest that they are often effective, although the degree of effectiveness does vary markedly. In the most successful programmes, reductions in bullying of about 50 per cent are achieved.

Norwegian intervention campaign

The first large-scale school-based intervention campaign was launched at a nationwide level, in Norway, in 1983. There was a survey in schools, materials, and video for teachers, advice for parents, and mass publicity. Olweus (1991) monitored 42 schools in Bergen that

Olweus Bullying Prevention Program a programme which aims to reduce and prevent bullying problems among school children and to promote pro-social behaviour.

took part; these schools also benefitted from support by the research team, and the early development of what is now the **Olweus Bullying Prevention Program** (Olweus, 2004). Using his self-report question-naire, and comparing equivalent age-groups, he found that from 1983 to 1985, reported bullying fell by 50 per cent, for both boys and girls. There were also falls in reported antisocial behaviour. There was no increase in reported bullying outside school. This encouraging finding has been widely reported and has inspired much subsequent work. Recent work by Olweus (2004) in the second Bergen project (1997–98) and Oslo project (1999–2000) also finds reductions in the range of 30–50 per cent. Other work in Norway directed by Roland (2000) is directed to class climate and makes more use of pupils.

UK intervention programme

The largest intervention programme in the UK has been the Sheffield project from 1991–94 (Smith & Sharp, 1994). The team worked with 23 schools over four terms. Each school developed a whole school policy and chose from a range of other interventions. There was a mean 17 per cent reduction in being bullied for primary schools, with smaller reductions (around 3–5 per cent) in five of the seven secondary schools. In addition there was a strong positive correlation between amount of effort (as assessed by both research team and pupils) and outcomes achieved.

Other wide-scale interventions

Other wide-scale interventions have taken place in many countries including Australia, Belgium, Canada, Finland, Germany, Ireland, Italy, Spain, Switzerland, and the United States (Smith et al., 2004). In general results appear to be mixed and do not replicate the degree of success of the Bergen findings. Another highly successful outcome was with a project in Andalucia (Ortega, del Rey & Mora-Merchan, 2004), where a broad based intervention was sustained over a four-year period. An ongoing programme in Finland, the KiVa Koulu programme, is innovative in its methods. It has universal interventions, including an anti-bullying virtual learning environment (a computer game using simulated characters and episodes whereby pupils learn facts and try out strategies, which can then be applied to everyday life at school) and tar-geted interventions (individual discussions with victims and bullying children, and using prosocial, high-status peers to be defenders). Evaluations have been encourag-ing, with reductions in victimisation of around 40 per cent (Salmivalli et al., 2010).

Some factors that may explain the variability in findings are the nature of the intervention; the extent of external support; the length of intervention; ownership by school and effective implementation; age of pupils (several projects find reduc-tions easier to obtain in primary than in secondary schools); and neighbourhood, community, and societal context (Benbenishty & Astor, 2005).

SCHOOL REFUSAL

Student absence from school has received considerable attention in recent years, par-ticularly as school attendance rates are now seen in the UK as an important indicator of a school's performance. Unsurprisingly, most absence from school is the result of a physical malady of some kind and while lengthy absences for genuine illnesses can seriously undermine children's educational progress, these are generally regarded as unavoidable. In other cases of school absence, a major factor concerns students' dislike of school life, boredom, the promise of undertaking more enjoyable activities elsewhere, or an outright rejection of adult authority (Guare & Cooper, 2003; King and Bernstein, 2001). However, many will also miss occasional periods of schooling because of fears and anxieties about specific events. These can include problems with teachers (e.g. homework has not been completed), peers (a result of anxiety about bullying), friends (e.g. one's best friend has moved away), or concern about potentially embarrassing or humiliating circumstances (e.g. performing in the gym or playing fields, taking a shower in public). Some children strongly dislike school throughout their lives but generally accept the requirement to attend sufficiently regularly to avoid the attentions of external agencies. A much smaller proportion have prolonged absences from school that typically lead to systematic attempts to intervene.

Truancy or school refusal?

In considering the problems of chronic non-attenders, a distinction has often been drawn between truants and *school refusers* (also commonly known as **school phobics**). While not always falling into clear-cut groups, truants are generally perceived as having no major

> **school phobics** children who have a strong aversion to attending school. Also known as *school refusers*.

psychological problem in attending school; rather, they simply choose not to. In contrast, school refusers often (but not always) seem eager to attend school, but because of the high levels of anxiety associated with this action, find that they cannot. Whereas the truant may often present with a range of conduct disorders, including disruptiveness in class, delinquency, and inappropriate sexual activity, the school refuser is often portrayed as someone who has a good record of behaviour in school and whose problem is essentially that of an emotional disorder, with anxiety more prominent than depressive symptoms (King & Bernstein, 2001). Truants are more likely to attend school on a sporadic basis and will typically seek to conceal their absences, In contrast, the school refuser will often have prolonged absences and will typically remain at home during school hours with the knowledge (if not the consent) of parents.

Emotional and psychosomatic problems

School refusers will often demonstrate severe emotional and psychosomatic upset:

> The problem often starts with vague complaints about school or reluctance to attend progressing to total refusal to go to school or to remain in school in the face of persuasion, entreaty, recrimination and punishment by parents and pressure from teachers, family doctors and education welfare officers. The behaviour may be accompanied by overt signs of anxiety or even panic when the time comes to go to school and most children cannot even leave home to set out for school. Many who do, return home halfway there, and some children, once at school, rush home in a state of anxiety. Many children insist that they want to go to school and are prepared to do so but cannot manage it when the time comes.
>
> *(Hersov, 1977, pp. 458–459)*

In addition to anxiety, there may also be signs of depression, with displays of tearfulness, sleeping difficulties, irritability and general indicators of low self-esteem. In addition to physical distress, these children often display a variety of physical illnesses such as stomach pains, headaches, dizziness, and vomiting for which there is rarely an organic cause. Often these ailments recede when the child is permitted to stay at home. However, to the child, and their parents, this physical distress is very real (psychosomatic illness feels as unpleasant as that of organic origin) and thus often renders it difficult for parents to insist upon school attendance. This is compounded by the tendency for bouts of refusal to re-emerge after the child has been absent from school for a genuinely physical illness.

Kearney (2008) suggests that the child's distress can be divided into physical, cognitive, and behavioural components. Thus, allied to the physical symptoms described above, the child's cognitive behaviour concerns thoughts and questions about the need to attend school and the likely repercussions of attendance or refusal. Behavioural components involve tearfulness, tantrums, social withdrawal, and problems concentrating. The order in which these three components come into operation may vary, for example, refusal may follow a long period of illness or social withdrawal may precede thoughts about peer rejection.

Prevalence

Because multiple agencies are involved in school attendance issues and differing criteria are employed to define the term, it is difficult to provide consistent estimates as to the prevalence of school refusal. In addition, some writers (e.g. Kearney, 2001) use the term school refusal as a broad categorisation that includes both truants and those whose absences are prompted by anxiety. Kearney's (2001) review provides a 'best guess' that between 5 and 28 per cent of children and adolescents display some aspect of school refusal behaviour, but this includes all forms of truancy. Where estimates that exclude truancy are employed, figures in the UK and United States generally range from 0.4 per cent to 2 per cent of the population.

Types of school refuser

Separation anxiety? While conceived of as a form of delinquency at the beginning of the twentieth century, it became gradually recognised during the 1930s that prolonged absence from school could be the result of some form of neurosis. Broadwin (1932) is considered to be the first writer to describe a pattern of persistent school absence characterised by fearfulness. Shortly afterwards, Johnson et al. (1941) coined the term school phobia. Historically, the problems underlying school refusal were seen by theorists and clinicians as relating to the home rather than the school. The school refuser was typically categorised as a child who was anxious about separation from loved ones at home, rather than being directly anxious about features of school life. According to the thinking of this time, such children had an excessively strong attachment to the parent (usually the mother), and fantasised about returning to the secure and nurturing relationship experienced in infancy. The mothers of these children were often perceived as having their own unfulfilled emotional needs and, as a result, lavished their children with excessive attention and protection. Strong emotions resulting from the child's attempt to resolve desires for dependence/independence were seen as leading to high levels of anxiety that were then channelled into the act of school refusal.

It is now widely accepted that **separation anxiety** is insufficient to explain all cases of school refusal. The theory does not explain why the peak age for school refusal is 11 to 13 years (Last *et al.*, 1987) rather than the earlier years of schooling as one would expect. Of course, this is the age when the world (and school life, in particular) may appear increasingly threatening to the young person, with the security of home and parental nurturance appearing to be a highly attractive alternative. Another challenge to the notion of separation anxiety is that many school refusers experience little difficulty in leaving their parents for recreational activities. Indeed, one common puzzle is why some school refusers appear so anxious about meeting up with peers (and even friends) in school but don't always manifest this problem in other community settings where young people group together. It appears that school refusers can be located into three broad categories: those with separation anxiety, those who have a specific phobia, and those who are suffering from more generalised anxiety or depression.

> **separation anxiety** a fear of the loss of parental nurturance.

Acute and chronic school refusal A further distinction has also been made between acute and chronic school refusal. Berg *et al.* (1969) suggest that it may be deemed acute where absence is preceded by at least three years' sound attendance, irrespective of current attendance patterns. These tend to be associated with higher levels of depression. Other cases, considered as chronic, tend to be associated with greater levels of neurosis, dependency, parental mental illness, and lower self-esteem and sociability. The prognosis for chronic cases tends to be poorer than for acute cases (Berg, 1970) although, of course, many chronic cases are likely to have started as initially acute.

School refusal is not seen as a specific psychiatric diagnosis in American Psychiatric Association's **Diagnostic and Statistical Manual of Mental Disorders (4th edn)** *(DSM-IV*; American Psychiatric Association, 1994). While not perceived as a 'clinically significant behavioural or psychological syndrome', it is listed as a symptom of separation anxiety. Another DSM-IV diagnosis, **specific phobia**, involves 'marked and persistent fear of clearly discernible, circumscribed objects or situations' (American Psychiatric Association, 1994, p. 405). However, for many children, the nature of the refusal may be more generalised and one or more alternative anxiety-related diagnoses may be employed.

> **Diagnostic and Statistical Manual of Mental Disorders (4th edn) (DSM-IV)** a manual published by the American Psychiatric Association in 1994 that gives diagnostic criteria for all currently recognised mental health disorders. The next edition is DSM-V (2012).

> **specific phobia** a 'marked and persistent fear of clearly discernible, circumscribed objects or situations' (DSM-IV).

Sex and age differences Research studies have not pointed to clear age and sex differences in relation to school refusal although there is some evidence that separation anxiety is more likely to be found in young girls while a specific fear of school may be more prominent in adolescent boys (Last *et al.*, 1987). As noted above, cases appear to peak between the ages of 11 and 13 when children in those countries where studies are most widely conducted (primarily, the United States) transfer from primary to secondary education. It seems that children are at particular risk for school refusal behaviour during their first year at a new school and, indeed, Kearney and Albano (2000) note that most referrals for school refusal occur in the autumn months. In general, it appears that adolescent refusers tend to have more severe disorders and have a poorer prognosis (Atkinson *et al.*, 1985). While many truants experience learning difficulties (in part, exacerbated by prolonged absences) there appears to be no clear relationship between school refusal and intellectual functioning (Trueman, 1984).

A functional approach to understanding school refusal

It is interesting to note that research publications focusing primarily upon school refusal have not been widely in evidence this century. Arguably, the most significant work in the area of school refusal, particularly in relation to clinical issues, during this time has been that conducted by Kearney and his colleagues (2001, 2008). Kearney (2001) argues that categorical distinctions, for example, refusal versus truancy, or separation anxiety versus school phobia, are often unhelpful as there is often significant symptom overlap. As a result, the use of such terms renders it difficult for clinicians to conceptualise the problem and suggest an appropriate intervention.

Kearney argues that rather than diagnosing a category of some kind it may be more useful clinically to examine the functions that refusal serves. Understanding what the child gains from their school refusal in any particular case may prove more helpful in planning an intervention than providing a diagnostic label. On the basis of work with Silverman (Kearney & Silverman, 1990), he has concluded that, for any individual child, refusal is maintained by one or more of four functional categories which are described below. The first two of these are promoted by **negative reinforcement**, that is, avoiding the feared situation becomes reinforced over time. The second two are subject to **positive reinforcement**, whereby the experience outside of school becomes reinforced by positive experiences.

negative reinforcement the avoidance of a negative or disliked event (such as going to school) and the avoidance is reinforcing or rewarding. The term 'negative' does not mean 'unpleasant'.

positive reinforcement an action or outcome following a behaviour that makes the behaviour more likely to be repeated.

Avoidance of stimuli that provoke a sense of general negative affectivity   This includes situations where one or more school-related features such as a specific teacher or toilets are a source of concern, as well as more generalised anxiety. While some children are aware of what it is that causes such fear (although, because of embarrassment over the issue, may not freely divulge this), many children appear unaware of specific factors. When pushed, such children may nominate features of school life but, upon closer examination, these are often seen to be readily insignificant.

Escape from aversive social or evaluative situations   This involves those situations where the child is anxious about their relationships with others (both peers and adults). Often there is an evaluative element associated with this, for example, being asked to read aloud in front of classmates, walking through crowded school corridors, or performing in physical education. Such children will often show significant social phobia, generalised anxiety, and depressive symptoms.

Attention-seeking behaviour   Here, the young person typically finds one or more positive outcome resulting from the refusal. These may be in the form of additional attention or sympathy from family members or friends. Separation anxiety is often a component here but this is solely one aspect underpinning the child's manipulative attempts to gain attention.

Pursuit of tangible reinforcement outside of school   Within this grouping Kearney includes those whose absence is often defined as truancy. Here, the young person may find more gratification staying at home watching television, playing on the computer, shopping, or socialising. While there may be features of generalised anxiety and depression, such symptoms are far less common than for the other groups.

It is important to note that not only may several functions be served by the refusal but also that the functions may change over time. For example, the child may initially refuse school because of some feared event but, as this factor recedes in importance, the refusal may be sustained by the pleasurable experience of staying at home all day playing on the internet. The advantage, according to Kearney, of considering school refusal in terms of the functions it serves, is that such analyses serve to point to more effective forms of intervention.

Assessment

Clinical assessment will typically involve a range of procedures such as interviews (both individually with the child and with the wider family grouping) and self-report instruments (typically gauging levels of anxiety and depression). It is important to recognise, however, that self-report measures may not provide a wholly accurate picture as social desirability issues may lead the child to accentuate or minimise their true feelings.

Kearney's functional approach employs the **School Refusal Assessment Scale** – Revised (SRAS-R) which provides a measure of the strength of each of the four functions outlined above. Some form of direct observation of the child at home, ideally before the beginning of the school day, is often helpful.

> **School Refusal Assessment Scale** An instrument designed to identify four of the variables that are associated with difficulty in attending school: fearfulness/general anxiety, escape from aversive social situations, attention-getting or *separation anxiety*, and *positive reinforcement*.

Intervention

As with many forms of psychological intervention, in treating school refusal, a distinction is often made between cognitive approaches which involve some form of individual, group or family therapy, and behavioural approaches which are predicated on the premise that behaviour is learned and can thus be unlearned by controlling the child's interaction with their immediate environment. However, approaches that are most commonly employed tend to involve both aspects (*cognitive-behavioural strategies*), that is, they seek to help children reduce and manage the unpleasant symptoms of anxiety and fear, reconfigure maladaptive and irrational thoughts about attending school, and slowly shape the child's behaviour in relation to attendance. For a more detailed summary, see Elliott (1999).

Systematic desensitisation and emotive imagery

systematic desensitisation an approach that aims to reduce or eliminate certain phobias in which the child is firstly taught how to relax and subsequently is encouraged to employ this ability when asked to consider the objects of their fear.

A range of approaches exist to reduce the fear and anxiety associated with schooling. These include **systematic desensitisation**, where the child is first taught how to relax and subsequently is encouraged to employ this ability when asked to consider the objects of their fear. A hierarchical approach is employed whereby minor fears are addressed first. A similar approach, **emotive imagery**, involves the child associating fearful situations with imagined scenes which conjure up feelings of pride, self-assertion or amusement. Behind both of these approaches is the notion, derived from classical conditioning, that the fearful situation will become associated with positive emotions and a relaxed state and, as a result, anxiety will be reduced.

emotive imagery an approach which aims to reduce fear and anxiety and involves associating fearful situations with imagined scenes which conjure up feelings of pride, self-assertion or amusement, so that the fearful situation becomes associated with positive emotions and a relaxed state and, as a result, anxiety will be reduced.

Cognitive-behavioural therapy (CBT)

Cognitive-behavioural therapy (CBT) is a popular approach that has, as a major focus, the negative and irrational cognitions that are often witnessed on the part of anxious or depressed individuals. CBT involves the child and the clinician exploring and challenging such thoughts and then replacing them with new understandings. Thus, where the child is overly concerned with peer evaluation, the perception that 'Everyone will laugh at me if I fail to answer a teacher's question correctly' is contrasted with the more positive, 'Everyone makes mistakes from time to time. Other children are unlikely to take much notice of me if I make mistakes'. During the CBT sessions, the child is shown how one set of cognitions can lead to raised levels of anxiety while other views can reduce stress.

cognitive-behavioural therapy (CBT) psychological therapy which aims to help patients change the way they think, feel and behave. CBT is effective in treating a variety of disorders or problems which include mood, eating, anxiety, personality, substance abuse, and psychotic disorders.

While there is some support for the above approaches (Barnes et al., 2003; King et al., 1998) much of the support offered in the literature has been as a result of case studies. There continues to be a dearth of high-quality randomised clinical trials and, of those that do exist, the evidence is not incontrovertible. (cf. Last et al., 1998).

Choice of treatment

Kearney (2001, 2008; Kearney & Silverman, 1990) argues that the choice of treatment depends significantly upon which of the four functions is being served by the child's refusal to attend school. Thus, where there is a strong phobic reaction, the goal is to utilise desensitisation approaches that reduce the high levels of emotional reaction. Where the refusal serves as a means to avoid social or evaluative situations, social skills training, modelling, and role play can be used alongside counselling that seeks to amend or reframe the child's maladaptive perceptions, thoughts, and beliefs. In cases where a desire to gain attention is a crucial factor, the careful granting (and withdrawal) of attention at appropriate times, together with the deployment of other forms of reward, is advocated. Finally, where refusal is prompted or sustained by the rewarding nature of life at home, family therapy (e.g. to ensure consistency of family demand and response) and the use of strict systems of rewards and sanctions is recommended. Of course, such responses should not be too rigidly linked to each of the four functions, particularly as these often overlap in combination.

Treatment for the high levels of anxiety and depression symptomatic of much school refusal may often include some form of drug treatment. Their use is often seen as a last resort and the likelihood of prescription will vary substantially according to the child's country of residence (the United States is typically considered to be a high prescribing nation to children, for example) and the particular practices of the professional concerned. Of course, many professionals who work closely with school refusers are not empowered to prescribe medication and a significant proportion of medical and non-medical practitioners would seek to avoid their use with children wherever possible.

What can be done by the school?

As much of the research literature on school refusal has been produced by psychiatrists and psychologists, it is, perhaps, not surprising that the ways by which the school can support school refusal are seemingly underplayed in academic studies. However, it is also the case that teachers do not always recognise the contribution that the school can make to refusal behaviour (King et al., 1995). Pilkington and Piersel (1991) suggest that too much emphasis has been placed upon separation anxiety as the typical cause, and refusal as a form of neurotic behaviour. Instead, they suggest, 'An alternative conceptualization . . . that views school refusal as a normal avoidance reaction to an unpleasant, unsatisfying, or even hostile environment' (p. 290).

The role of school personnel is important both in initially identifying potential difficulties at an early stage and in providing supportive and flexible arrangements to assist the child's gradual return to full attendance (Elliott & Place, 2004). Often some form of graduated return and reduction in the child's exposure to large numbers of children is necessary. Special arrangements may include late arrival or early departure, partial attendance in mainstream lessons, and alternative operation of break and lunchtimes. School staff also need to be sensitive to, and address, those situations where anxiety is related to academic concerns, peers or teachers (Blagg, 1987).

Prognosis

Gauging the outcomes of school refusal is complicated by the differing definitions given to this term, particular the inclusion in many studies of those whose behaviour is often widely understood as truancy. It would appear that important factors include the severity of the disorder, the age of onset, and how quickly intervention is put into place once the refusal occurs. Treatment is less likely to prove effective if the refusal has persisted for more two or more years (Kearney & Tillotson, 1998). McShane *et al.* (2004) conducted a long-term follow-up with 117 adolescents whose refusal had resulted in inpatient or outpatient intervention. Of these, 22 per cent remained in school and 18 per cent were in full employment. Three years later, approximately 70–76 per cent had a satisfactory outcome. This finding supports several studies (Flakierska *et al.*, 1988, 1997; Kearney, 2001; McCune & Hynes, 2005) which suggest that about one third of young people with school refusal continue to experience serious adjustment problems in later life.

SUMMARY AND CONCLUSIONS

Children spend a great deal of time at school. They are with a large peer group, with whom they engage in intense social relationships (Chapter 8) and social comparison processes. In this chapter we have examined two main problematic aspects of life in school: bullying, and truancy and school refusal.

Bullying refers to repeated attacks against a victim who cannot easily defend themselves. It can be physical, verbal, relational, and increasingly via mobile phones or the internet. We examined the main structural features of bullying, and some explanations of why it happens. Schools can tackle bullying in various ways, and we looked at a range of different approaches, and the evidence for their effectiveness. There is still much to learn about school bullying, but many positive steps can be, and in many schools have been, and are being, taken.

DISCUSSION POINTS

1. What can teachers and parents do to reduce social pressure upon students to appear uninterested and disengaged?

2. To what extent are pressures not to demonstrate significant interest and enthusiasm on academic tasks similarly present in colleges and universities?

3. Given what we know about the causes of bullying, what kinds of strategies are most likely to be effective in reducing it?

4. Can effective strategies be expected to vary by age, gender, or culture?

5. What arguments can be advanced in the debate between sanctions-based, restorative and non-punitive approaches to bullying incidents?

6. What are some important ways in which schools can reduce anxiety-provoking situations?

7. Is the distinction between the conduct disordered truant and the anxious school refuser meaningful and helpful?

8. To what extent can clinicians be guided in their practice by case study illustrations?

SUGGESTIONS FOR FURTHER READING

Alexander, J. (2003). *Bullies, bigmouths and so-called friends*. Oxford: Hachette Children's Books.

Anti-Bullying Alliance. (n.d.). Retrieved from www.anti-bullyingalliance.org.uk

DCSF. (2009). *Staying safe survey*. Retrieved 7 April 2011, from www.education.gov.uk/publications/standard/publicationdetail/page1/DCSF-RR192

McGrath, H., & Noble, T. (Eds.) (2006). *Bullying solutions: Evidence-based approaches to bullying in Australian schools*. Frenchs Forest, NSW: Pearson Education.

Shariff, S. (2009). *Confronting cyberbullying: What schools need to know to control misconduct and avoid legal consequences*. Cambridge: Cambridge University Press.

Smith, P.K., Pepler, D., & Rigby, K. (Eds.) (2004). *Bullying in schools: How successful can interventions be?* Cambridge: Cambridge University Press.

Stone, R. (2005). *Don't pick on me: How to handle bullying*. London: Piccadilly Press.

REFERENCES

American Psychiatric Association. (1994). *Diagnostic and statistical manual of mental disorders* (4th edn) (DSM-IV). Washington, DC: American Psychiatric Association.

Anderson, B., Beinart, S., Farrington, D., Longman, J., Sturgis, P., & Utting, D. (2001). *Risk and protective factors associated with youth crime and effective interventions to prevent it*. London: Youth Justice Board.

Arora, T. (1994). Measuring bullying with the 'Life in School' checklist. *Pastoral Care in Education*, *12*, 11–15.

Atkinson, L., Quarrington, B., & Cyr, J.J. (1985). School refusal: The heterogeneity of a concept. *American Journal of Orthopsychiatry*, *55*, 83–101.

Baldry, A.C., & Farrington, D.P. (2000). Bullies and delinquents: Personal characteristics and parental styles. *Journal of Community and Applied Social Psychology*, *10*, 17–31.

Barnes, V.A., Bauza, L.B., & Treiber, F.A. (2003). Impact of stress reduction on negative school behavior in adolescents. *Health and Quality of Life Outcomes*, *1*, 10.

Benbenishty, R., & Astor, R.A. (2005). *School violence in context*. Oxford & New York: Oxford University Press.

Berg, I. (1970). A follow-up study of school phobic adolescents admitted to an inpatient unit. *Journal of Child Psychology and Psychiatry*, *11*, 37–47.

Berg, I., Nichols, K., & Pritchar, C. (1969). School phobia – its classification and relationship to dependency. *Journal of Child Psychology and Psychiatry*, *10*, 323–328.

Blagg, N. (1987). *School phobia and its treatment*. London: Croom Helm.

Blatchford, P. (1998). *Social life in school: Pupils' experiences of breaktime and recess from 6 to 16*. London: Routledge.

Boulton, M. (1994). Understanding and preventing bullying in the junior school playground. In P.K. Smith & S. Sharp (Eds) *School bullying: Insights and perspectives*. London: Routledge.

Braithwaite, J. (2002). *Restorative justice & responsive regulation*. New York: Oxford University Press.

Broadwin, I.T. (1932). A contribution to the study of truancy. *American Journal of Orthopsychiatry*, *2*, 253–259.

Connor, M.J. (2001). Pupil stress and standard assessment tests (SATS). *Emotional and Behavioural Difficulties*, *6*, 103–111.

Connor, M.J. (2003). Pupil stress and standard assessment tests (SATS): An update. *Emotional and Behavioural Difficulties*, *8*, 101–107.

Covington, M. (1992). *Making the grade: A self-worth perspective on motivation and school reform.* Cambridge, MA: Cambridge University Press.

Covington, M. (1998). *The will to learn: A guide to motivating young people.* Cambridge, MA: Cambridge University Press.

Covington, M., & Omelich, C.E. (1985). Ability and effort evaluation among failure-avoiding and failure-accepting students. *Journal of Educational Psychology*, *76*, 1199–1213.

Cowie, H., & Berdondini, L. (2001). Children's reactions to cooperative group work: A strategy for enhancing peer relationships among bullies, victims and bystanders. *Learning and Instruction*, *6*, 517–530.

Cowie, H., & Smith, P.K. (2009). Peer support as a means of improving school safety and reducing bullying and violence. In B. Doll, W. Pfohl, & J. Yoon (Eds.) *Handbook of youth prevention science.* New York: Routledge.

Cowie, H., & Wallace, P. (2000). *Peer support in action – from bystanding to standing by.* London: Sage.

Craske, M.L. (1988). Learned helplessness, self-worth motivation and attribution retraining for primary-school children. *British Journal of Educational Psychology*, *58*, 152–164.

Cunningham, C.E., Cunningham, L.J., Martorelli, V., Tran, A., Young, J., & Zacharias, R. (1998). The effects of primary division, student-mediated conflict resolution programs on playground aggression. *Journal of Child Psychology and Psychiatry*, *39*, 653–662.

Curtner-Smith, M.E., Smith, P.K., & Porter, M. (2010). Family level intervention with bullies and victims. In E. Vernberg & B. Biggs (Eds.) *Preventing and treating bullying and victimization* (pp. 177–193). Oxford: Oxford University Press.

Denscombe, M. (2000). Social conditions for stress: Young people's experience of doing GCSEs. *British Educational Research Journal*, *26*, 359–374.

DCSF. (2007). *Safe to learn: Embedding anti-bullying work in schools.* London: Department of Children, Schools and Families.

Dijkstra, P., Kuyper, H., van der Werf, G., Buunk, A.P., & van der Zee, Y.G. (2008). Social comparison in the classroom: A review. *Review of Educational Research*, *78*, 828–879.

Elliott, J.G. (1999). School refusal: Issues of conceptualisation, assessment and treatment. *Journal of Child Psychology and Psychiatry*, *40*, 1001–1012.

Elliott, J.G., Hufton, N., Illushin, L., & Willis, W. (2005). *Motivation, engagement and educational performance.* London: Palgrave Press.

Elliott, J.G., & Nguyen, M. (2008). Western influences on the East: Lessons for the East and West. In T. Oon Seng & D.M. McInerney (Eds.) *Research on multicultural education and international perspectives Vol. 7: What the West can learn from the East: Asian perspectives on the psychology of learning and motivation.* Greenwich, CT: Information Age Publishing.

Elliott, J.G., & Place, M. (2004). *Children in difficulty: A guide to understanding and helping* (2nd edn). London: Routledge.

Elliott, J.G., & Tudge, J. (2007). The impact of the West on post-Soviet Russian education: Change and resistance to change. *Comparative Education*, *43*, 93–112.

Farrington, D.P. (1993). Understanding and preventing bullying. In M. Tonry & N. Morris (Eds.) *Crime and Justice Vol. 17.* Chicago: University of Chicago Press.

Flakierska, N., Linstrom, M., & Gillberg, C. (1988). School refusal: A 15–20 year follow-up study of 35 Swedish urban children. *British Journal of Psychiatry*, *152*, 834–837.

Flakierska, N., Linstrom, M., & Gillberg, C. (1997). School phobia with separation anxiety disorder: A comparative 20–29 year follow-up study of 35 school refusers. *Comprehensive Psychiatry*, *38*, 17–22.

Frankham, J., Edwards-Kerr, D., Humphrey, N., & Roberts, L. (2007). *School exclusions: Learning partnerships outside mainstream education*. York: Joseph Rowntree Foundation.

Gardner, J. (1961). *Excellence: Can we be equal and excellent too?* New York: Harper & Row.

Grant, H., & Dweck, S. (2001). Meaning systems: Attributions, goals, culture and motivation. In F. Salili, C. Chiu, & Y.Y. Hong (Eds.) *Student motivation: The culture and context of learning*. New York: Plenum.

Guare, R.E., & Cooper, B.S. (2003). *Truancy revisited: students as school consumers*. Lanham, MD: Scarecrow.

Hallam, S., Rhamie, J., & Shaw, J. (2006). *Evaluation of the primary behaviour and attendance pilot* (DCSF ref: RR717). London: Institute of Education.

Hawker, S. J., & Boulton, M.J. (2000). Twenty years' research on peer victimization and psychosocial maladjustment: A meta-analytic review of cross-sectional studies. *Journal of Child Psychology and Psychiatry, 41*, 441–455

Hersov, L. (1977). School refusal. In M. Rutter & L. Hersov (Eds.) *Child psychiatry: Modern approaches*. Oxford: Blackwell.

Hodges, E.V.E., Malone, M.J., & Perry, D.G. (1997). Individual risk and social risk as interacting determinants of victimisation in the peer group. *Developmental Psychology, 33*, 1032–1039.

Howley, C.B., Howley, A., & Pendarvis, E.D. (1995). *Out of our minds: Anti-intellectualism and talent development in American schooling*. New York: Teachers College Press.

Hugh-Jones, S., & Smith, P.K. (1999). Self-reports of short and long-term effects of bullying on children who stammer. *British Journal of Educational Psychology, 69*, 141–158.

Johnson, A.M., Falstein, E.I., Szurek, S.A., & Svendsen, M. (1941). School phobia. *American Journal of Orthopsychiatry, 11*, 702–711.

Johnson, D., Johnson, R., & Stanne, M. (2000). *Cooperative learning methods: A meta-analysis*. University of Minnesota. Retrieved 6 April 2011, from www.tablelearning.com/uploads/File/EXHIBIT-B.pdf

Kaltiala-Heino, R., Rimpela, M., Marttunen, M., Rimpela, A., & Rantenan, P. (1999). Bullying, depression, and suicidal ideation in Finnish adolescents: School survey. *British Medical Journal, 319*, 348–351.

Kane, J, Lloyd, G., McCluskey, G., Riddell, S., Stead, J., & Weedon, E. (2007). *Restorative practices in three Scottish councils: Final report of the evaluation of the first two years of the pilot projects 2004–2006*. Edinburgh: Scottish Executive.

Kearney, C.A. (2001). *School refusal behaviour in youth: A functional approach to assessment and treatment*. Washington, DC: American Psychological Association.

Kearney, C.A. (2008). *Helping school-refusing children and their parents: A guide for school-based professionals*. London: Oxford University Press.

Kearney, C.A., & Albano, A.M. (2000). *Therapist's guide to school refusal behavior*. San Antonio, TX: Psychological Corporation.

Kearney, C.A., & Silverman, W.K. (1990). A preliminary analysis of a functional model of assessment and treatment of school refusal behaviour. *Behavior Modification, 14*, 340–366.

Kearney, C.A., & Tillotson, C. (1998). School attendance. In D. Watson & M. Gresham (Eds.) *Handbook of child behavior therapy* (pp. 143–161). New York: Plenum Press.

King, N., & Bernstein, G.A. (2001). School refusal in children and adolescents: A review of the past 10 years. *Journal of the American Academy of Child and Adolescent Psychiatry, 40*, 197–205.

King, N., Ollendick, T.H., Murphy, G.C., & Molloy, G.N. (1998). Relaxation training with children. *British Journal of Educational Psychology, 68*, 53–66.

King, N., Ollendick, T.H., & Tonge, B.J. (1995). *School refusal: Assessment and treatment*. Massachusetts: Allyn & Bacon.

Kochenderfer, B.J., & Ladd, G.W. (1996). Peer victimization: Cause or consequence of school mal-adjustment? *Child Development*, *67*, 1305–1317.

Kumpulainen, K., & Räsänen, E. (2000). Children involved in bullying at elementary school age: Their psychiatric symptoms and deviance in adolescence. An epidemiological sample. *Child Abuse and Neglect*, *24*, 1567–1577.

Lambert, P., Scourfield, J., Smalley, N., & Jones, R. (2008). The social context of school bullying: Evidence from a survey of children in South Wales. *Research Papers in Education*, *23*, 269–291.

Last, C.G., Francis, G., Hersen, M., Kazdin, A.E., & Strauss, C. (1987). Separation anxiety and school phobia: A comparison using DSM-III criteria. *American Journal of Psychiatry*, *144*, 653–657.

Last, C.G., Hansen, M.S., & Franco, N. (1998). Cognitive-behavioral treatment of school phobia. *Journal of the American Academy of Child and Adolescent Psychiatry*, *37*, 404–411.

Mahdavi, J., & Smith, P.K. (2002). The operation of a bully court and perceptions of its success: A case study. *School Psychology International*, *23*, 327–341.

McCune, N., & Hynes, J. (2005). Ten year follow-up of children with school refusal. *Irish Journal of Psychological Medicine*, *22*, 56–58

McShane, G., Walter, G., & Rey, J.M. (2004). Functional outcome of adolescents with 'school refusal'. *Clinical Child Psychology and Psychiatry*, *9*, 53–60.

Miller, C.T. (1986). Categorization and stereotypes about men and women. *Personality and Social Psychology*, *12*, 502–512.

Mishna, F. (2003). Learning disabilities and bullying: Double jeopardy. *Journal of Learning Disabilities*, *36*, 336–347.

Monks, C.P., Smith, P.K., Naylor, P., Barter, C., Ireland, J.L., & Coyne, I. (2009). Bullying in different contexts: Commonalities, differences and the role of theory. *Aggression and Violent Behavior*, *14*, 146–156.

OFSTED. (2003). *Bullying: Effective action in secondary schools*. London. OFSTED.

OFSTED. (2007). *Developing social, emotional and behavioural skills in secondary schools. A five year longitudinal evaluation of the Secondary National Strategy pilot*. London. OFSTED.

Olweus, D. (1991). Bully/victim problems among schoolchildren: Basic facts and effects of a school-based intervention program. In D.J. Pepler & K. Rubin (Eds.) *The development and treatment of childhood aggression*. Hillside, NJ: Erlbaum.

Olweus, D. (1999). Sweden. In P.K. Smith, Y. Morita, J. Junger-Tas, D. Olweus, D. R. Catalano, & P. Slee (Eds.) *The nature of school bullying: A cross-national perspective* (pp. 7–27). London & New York: Routledge.

Olweus, D. (2004). The Olweus Bullying Prevention Program: Design and implementation issues and a new national initiative in Norway. In P.K. Smith, D. Pepler, & K. Rigby (Eds) *Bullying in schools: How successful can interventions be?* (pp. 13–36). Cambridge: Cambridge University Press.

Olweus, D., & Endresen, I.M. (1998). The importance of sex-of-stimulus object: Age trends and sex differences in empathic responsiveness. *Social Development*, *3*, 370–388.

Ortega, R., del Rey, R., & Mora-Merchan, J. (2004). SAVE model: An anti-bullying intervention in Spain. In P.K. Smith, D. Pepler, & K. Rigby (Eds.) *Bullying in schools: How successful can interventions be?* (pp. 167–185). Cambridge: Cambridge University Press.

Osborn, M. (1997). Children's experience of schooling in England and France: Some lessons from a comparative study. *Education Review*, *11*, 46–52.

Pepler, D.J., & Craig, W.M. (1995). A peek behind the fence – naturalistic observations of aggressive-children with remote audiovisual recording. *Developmental Psychology*, *31*, 548–553.

Pikas, A. (1989). A pure concept of mobbing gives the best results for treatment. *School Psychology International*, *10*, 95–104.

Pikas, A. (2002). New developments of the Shared Concern Method. *School Psychology International*, *23*, 307–326.

Pilkington, C., & Piersel, W.C. (1991). School phobia: A critical analysis of the separation anxiety theory and an alternative conceptualisation. *Psychology in the Schools*, *28*, 290–303.

Putwain, D.W. (2008). Supporting assessment stress in key stage 4 students. *Educational Studies*, *34*, 83–95.

Rigby, K (2003). Consequences of bullying in schools. *Canadian Journal of Psychiatry*, *48*, 583–591.

Rigby, K., & Slee, P.T. (1991). Bullying among Australian schoolchildren: Reported behavior and attitudes to victims. *Journal of Social Psychology*, *131*, 615–627.

Rivers, I. (1995). Mental health issues among young lesbians and gay men bullied in school. *Health and Social Care in the Community*, *3*, 380–383.

Rivers, I., & Noret, N. (2010). 'I h8 u': Findings from a five-year study of text and email bullying. *British Educational Research Journal*, *36*, 643–671.

Robinson, G., & Maines, B. (2007). *Bullying: A complete guide to the Support Group Method*. Bristol: Lucky Duck Publishing.

Roland, E. (2000). Bullying in school: Three national innovations in Norwegian schools in 15 years. *Aggressive Behavior*, *26*, 135–143.

Salmivalli, C., Kärnä, A., & Poskiparta, E. (2010). From peer putdowns to peer support: A theoretical model and how it translated into a national anti-bullying program. In S. Jimerson, S. Swearer, & D. Espelage (Eds.) *Handbook of bullying in schools: An international perspective* (pp. 441–454). New York: Routledge.

Salmivalli, C., Lagerspetz, K., Björkqvist, K., Österman, K., & Kaukiainen, A. (1996). Bullying as a group process: participant roles and their relations to social status within the group. *Aggressive Behavior*, *22*, 1–15.

Schwartz, D., Dodge K.A., Pettit G. S., & Bates J.E. (2000). Friendship as a moderating factor in the pathway between early harsh home environment and later victimization in the peer group. *Developmental Psychology*, *36*, 646–662.

Shields, A., & Cicchetti, D. (2001). Parental maltreatment and emotion dysregulation as risk factors for bullying and victimization in middle childhood. *Journal of Clinical Child Psychology*, *30*, 349–363.

Smith, P.K., O'Donnell, L., Easton, C., & Rudd, P. (2007). *Secondary social, emotional and behavioural skills (SEBS) pilot evaluation*. (DCSF ref: RR003). Nottingham: DfES.

Smith, P.K., Howard, S., & Thompson, F. (2007). Use of the Support Group Method to tackle bullying, and evaluation from schools and local authorities in England. *Pastoral Care in Education*, *25*, 4–13.

Smith, P.K., Mahdavi, J., Carvalho, M., Fisher, S., Russell, S., & Tippett, N. (2008). Cyberbullying: Its nature and impact in secondary school pupils. *Journal of Child Psychology and Psychiatry*, *49*, 376–385.

Smith, P.K., Pepler, D.J., & Rigby, K. (Eds.) (2004). *Bullying in schools: How successful can interventions be?* Cambridge: Cambridge University Press.

Smith, P.K., & Sharp, S. (Eds.) (1994). *School bullying: Insights and perspectives*. London: Routledge.

Smith, P.K., Smith, C., Osborn, R., & Samara, M. (2008). A content analysis of school anti-bullying policies: Progress and limitations. *Educational Psychology in Practice*, *24*, 1–12.

Smith, P.K., & Watson, D. (2004). *Evaluation of the CHIPS (ChildLine in Partnership with Schools) programme* (Research report RR570). London: DfES.

Steinberg, L. (1996). *Beyond the classroom: Why school reform has failed and what parents need to do*. New York: Touchstone Books.

Thompson, T. (1999). *Underachieving to protect self-worth: Theory, research and interventions*. Aldershot: Ashgate Publishing.

Tinker, R. (2002). *The evaluation of the Nottingham Restorative Conferencing Project*. Nottingham: Nottingham City Anti-Bullying Support Team.

Trueman, D. (1984). What are the characteristics of school phobic children? *Psychological Reports*, *54*, 191–202.

Ttofi, M.M., Farrington, D.P., & Baldry, A.C. (2008). *Effectiveness of programmes to reduce school bullying: A systematic review*. Report to Swedish National Council on Crime Prevention.

Utting, D., Monteiro, H., & Ghate, D. (2007). *Interventions for children at risk of developing antisocial personality disorder: Report to the Department of Health and Prime Minister's Strategy Unit*. London: Policy Research Bureau.

Williams, K., Chambers, M., Logan, S., & Robinson, D. (1996). Association of common health symptoms with bullying in primary school children. *British Medical Journal*, *313*, 17–19.

Woods, S., & Wolke, D. (2003). Does the content of anti-bullying policies inform us about the prevalence of direct and relational bullying behaviour in primary schools? *Educational Psychologist*, *23*, 381–402.

21 Atypical Development

Sarah Norgate

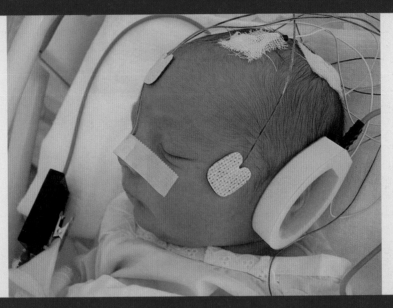

KEY TERMS

amniocentesis • attention deficit hyperactivity disorder (ADHD) • atypical trajectories • autism spectrum disorders • Bronfenbrenner's ecological model • central coherence hypothesis of autism • chromosomal structural abnormalities • chronosystem • congenital blindness • developmental delay • developmental difference • Diagnostic and Statistical Manual of Mental Disorders (DSM-IV) • Down's syndrome • ecosystem • event-related potential (ERP) • executive function hypothesis of autism • exosystem • eye-tracking methodology • functional magnetic resonance imaging (fMRI) • genetic diversity • Human Genome Project • inhibitory control • International Classification of Disease (e.g. ICD-10) • joint attention • lexical development • macrosystem • magnetoencephalography (MEG) • mesosystem • microsystem • neuroimaging • positron emission tomography (PET) • pragmatics • saccades • specific language impairment (SLI) • theory of mind hypothesis of autism • Williams syndrome

CHAPTER OUTLINE

OVERVIEW

Most of the chapters in this book cover research on the typical course of development. However, there are two ways in which development may be atypical. First, development may be exceptionally advanced or particularly slow. In effect, this form of atypical development refers to the extremes of individual differences in development. Second, atypical development may be qualitatively different from typical development. For instance, a blind child has no access to visual perception and must draw on information from other senses in developing knowledge of the world. The gold standard used to assess whether we are dealing with delay or a difference in development is to include two control groups, one matched to the atypical group on chronological age and the other matched on mental age. Investigation of the causes and nature of atypical development is clearly important as a means of improving the lot of affected children, but can also help to throw light on typical developmental processes.

The chapter indicates how progress on the Human Genome Project, and advances in brain imaging and eye tracking have impacted on understanding of atypical development. Consideration is then given to explanations of developmental pathways encountered in Williams syndrome, autism, and attentional deficit hyperactivity disorder (ADHD). Such conditions are often described as disorders, and although we would not generally describe blindness or deafness as a psychological disorder, the chapter indicates how these sensory deficits lead to atypical psychological development.

The final section of the chapter considers how environmental risk factors (the topic of Chapter 20) may lead to atypical development, and presents Bronfenbrenner's ecological model as a means through which the influences of multiple factors can be understood. This framework may also be valuable in explaining conditions such as autism, where there is possibly too much emphasis at present on the individual child isolated from their environment.

INTRODUCTION

Describing and explaining human development that is *typical* continues to characterise the majority of developmental psychology activity. Reflecting this, many of the earlier chapters in the book reviewed the general developmental processes and outcomes associated with perceptual, socio-emotional, cognitive, language, and memory development focused on typically developing children. As well as focusing on characterising general processes of development, the quest of developmental psychology is to simultaneously explain differences between children. It is this narrative around differences which forms the main thread of the current chapter. It is perhaps hardly unsurprising that individual variation between children is readily observable in a variety of areas of development. For instance, in motor development, several months can separate infants in the age at which they first walk unsupported. In communicative development, the age of onset at which a child uses the past tense in speech may vary by a number of months.

If there turns out to be a substantial delay in the emergence of a particular behaviour, this area of development is classifiable as 'atypical'. Alternatively, behaviour may be 'atypical' due to being *qualitatively* different. Patterns of behaviour may present 'differently'. For instance, a toddler may produce different patterns of visual behaviour compared with other sighted toddlers. That is, they could turn out to follow the gaze direction of their caregiver towards points of interest only rarely. To offer a handle on this, if child development is referred to as 'atypical', either the age-of-onset is exceptional or the patterns of behaviour are atypical. It may be worth pointing out from the outset that it is not unusual for researchers to use a variety of expressions – sometimes interchangeably – to reflect different approaches to the study of atypical development. 'Exceptional' or 'disordered' development are two descriptors you may come across in further reading.

Over the last three decades, there have been dramatic advances in theorising and research relating to *atypical* development. Although there have been notable exceptions (see later on the autistic spectrum), these advances in the study of atypical development have tended to be reported somewhat 'partitioned' from research about typical development. This runs the risk of limiting the scope for the cross-infusion of theory mutually informed by research from typically developing and atypically developing children. Encouragingly, though, there are now a number of signs that the boundaries between the study of typical and atypical development will become increasingly porous. And as we shall now see, this progress is facilitated by exciting advances in at least three areas of science.

First, there has been substantial progression in understanding the impact of prenatal events on later development. For instance, infants who are prenatally exposed to cigarettes show increased levels of specific types of early problem behaviours relative to controls. These infants are more likely to show aggression to adults (e.g. disobedience) and peers (e.g. biting, hitting, kicking), even when other confounding factors such as family risk factors (e.g. life stress) are held constant (Wakschlag *et al.*, 2006). Looking at the extent to which antecedents such as drug exposure during foetal development impact on the emergence of atypical behaviours in infancy is an important first step in understanding development 'at risk' across the course of the entire lifespan.

A second advance in the integration of work on typical and atypical development is that there is now unprecedented opportunity to understand how the genotypes of specific disorders map onto the observable expressions in both behaviour and physical features (phenotypes) and associated atypical pathways. This is particularly

Williams syndrome a rare neurodevelopmental disorder caused by deletion of about 26 genes from the long arm of chromosome 7.

the case in the study of **Williams syndrome**, where the characteristic gene set – namely, genes deleted on a region of chromosome 7 – allows new insights into the unfolding of brain and behavioural pathways across the lifespan. In turn, given the genetic 'knowns', this allows developmental scientists to elucidate the role of various non-genetic sources of influence (e.g. culture) on human development (see Chapter 3 for further details). Additionally, outcomes from this work feed back onto what is understood about relative influences (i.e. genetic, brain, social, cultural, etc.) on pathways in typical development.

Finally, a further facilitator of integration is recent progress in research methodology. One difficulty of researching atypical development is that many disorders are extremely rare, and therefore there is a challenge to establish samples with sufficient size to make meaningful interpretation of the findings. However, there is now increased recognition of the opportunities to pool data derived from studies of rare atypical conditions of childhood from research teams around the globe (e.g. Belmonte *et al.*, 2008), which will, in turn, provide greater power and generalisability of research findings.

As was said earlier, given that the field of atypical development still has some distance to go before presenting a more integrated approach across theorising and research capable of bridging atypical and typical development, this chapter primarily treats the study of atypical development independently from typical development. A notable exception is how the study of developing awareness of the theory of mind in typically developing children subsequently informs theorising about atypical development (e.g. Pellicano *et al.*, 2005), and this is illustrated later in the chapter (autistic spectrum).

As is the case with the study of typical development, currently more is known about the early portion of the lifespan than in adolescence and beyond. Reflecting this bias, this chapter largely revolves around the period of childhood, discussing different examples of atypical development. The main theories associated with these examples are outlined, and some implications for interventions and educational practice are presented.

WHAT IS ATYPICAL DEVELOPMENT?

A classic position adopted by developmental psychologists studying atypical development is to consider whether child development is **delayed** or **different**. That is, although a delay refers to development that is behind timetable, it is recognised as passing through the same sequence, without necessarily reaching such an advanced stage as development in *typically* developing children. In contrast, development that is 'different' refers to processes, behaviours and outcomes

developmental delay a delayed but normal path of development.

developmental difference a qualitatively different path of development.

which qualitatively contrast to those of typically developing children. To illustrate these concepts through the vehicle of research, let's now look at the case of prematurity, and any effect on development.

Evidence suggests that children born prematurely show evidence of a *delay* in language development in the preschool period (e.g. Gayraud & Kern, 2007). These researchers showed that premature children produce fewer words at age 24 months than compared with full-term children. However, if we now turn to look at a different area of development in this population – namely, visuomotor

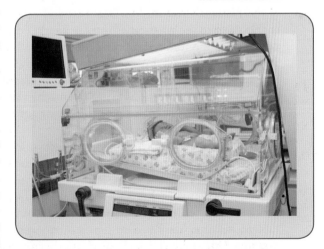

FIGURE 21.1 *Research suggests that there are delays and differences in various areas of development of children born prematurely*

Source: Shutterstock.

functioning – children born prematurely show a pattern of *difference* (van Braeckel *et al.*, 2010). That is, children aged 7 to 11 years born prematurely showed a different pattern of movement control. This outcome came to light from a computer-based task which revealed that these children showed lowered movement speed and accuracy compared to children born full-term. Finally, an intriguing research outcome emerges in relation to perceptual development in preterm children. Janssonn-Verkasaol *et al.* (2010) investigated early auditory perceptual development in Finnish infants and found that for pre-term infants (tested at age 6 months and again at 1 year) the normal perceptual narrowing effect, in which infants gradually lose the ability to discriminate non-native speech sounds, was delayed. They interpret this as due either to delayed or atypical language development in this group.

As you can see, whether the performance of this group is 'delayed' or 'different' or 'unknown' depends on the area of development under scrutiny. This observation underscores the need to avoid making generalisations at the level of a particular group. Instead it is important to undertake research in different areas of development.

Let's now focus on the concept of a delay, and some different scenarios around how this is quantified according to who is using the information (e.g. caregivers, clinicians, or researchers). Clearly, in 'typical' development there is a great deal of variation in the age at which children acquire developmental milestones. The emergence of the ability to sit up unaided, learning to point to objects, producing the first word, and so on, all span a number of months. Expectations about the age at which children should achieve milestones often lead caregivers to seek guidance from peers and/or other resources, especially for first-born children. Caregivers may have questions about their child being perceived ahead of schedule, or because of non-emergence or perceived delay of a particular skill. Some information sources, particularly those available on the internet, cite developmental milestones associated with particular specific ages rather than giving a general age band in which a particular ability or skill is likely to appear in typically developing children. In contrast, specialist sites such as the National Institute on Deafness and other Communication Disorders (1995) enable users to see what milestones in hearing develop within a time frame spanning a number of months. For example, in the band 'birth to 5 months' cited items include 'reacts to loud sound'; 'turns head toward sound source'; 'watches face when speaks' and 'makes noise when talked to'. Parents/guardians are advised to consult medical advice if any of the items have not been achieved within the timeframe expected for normal development. In this way, the use of age bands allows more tolerance of variation before a delay is identified.

Other approaches to quantifying a delay include looking at the extent to which individual children perform relative to a level expected for their chronological age on standardised assessment tests. For example, one commonly used clinical marker of language impairment is a subtest on the Clinical Evaluation of Language Fundamentals (CELF-3UK; Semel *et al.*, 2000) called 'Recalling Sentences'. On this subtest, children are asked to repeat sentences which are of increasing length and grammatical complexity. A clinician or other professional may compare a child's score at a given chronological age with norms published in the test manual. For example, a child who is 12 years old but performs with an age-equivalent score of 10 years 6 months has an age differential of 18 months' delay in this aspect of communication. A programme of intervention could then be devised.

A further way of quantifying a delay (or accelerated development) is in terms of the size of the difference between the child's score and the norms established for the population. This approach is often needed by researchers. A researcher who wishes to identify a sample of children with impaired performance on a particular measure needs to identify the appropriate inclusion criteria for their sample to answer their research question. Researchers wish to identify children performing a set number of standard deviations below the mean. That is, according to the properties of a normal distribution, most children tested will score on or around the average or mean. Scores falling further from the mean – in either direction – are fewer. And at the extremes, only a minority of scores will be located. Mapping the more 'extreme' scores onto statistical convention, a score of 2 standard deviations below the mean would suggest that the child's performance was better than only 2 per cent of the total population. Conversely, in the case of exceptional performance, a score of 2 standard deviations above the mean would suggest the child's performance was better than 98 per cent of the population. In practice, researchers will often use an 'inclusion criterion' for an 'atypical' group as a score 1.5 standard deviations below the mean.

The concept of a delay in itself is under scrutiny in the field of atypical development. Researchers seek tools to distinguish between different *types* of delay (Thomas *et al.*, 2009). One rationale is that simply concluding that a particular aspect of development is delayed tells the researcher little about what underlies the delay. For example, imagine you are a researcher investigating a new developmental disorder. You suspect that there is a delay in language development associated with this disorder. How do you know if any delay relates to the onset of first words or to a slower rate of **lexical development** – or both? One way to investigate this would be to look at both the onset and acceleration of early language development, in this way taking multiple measures of productive speech. This approach lends itself to investigations of different types of delay in various areas of development. This reduces the scope for oversimplification of developmental processes.

> **lexical development** the development of vocabulary.

Assessments of delay are not confined exclusively to norms for typical populations. Standardised assessment scales have been designed for use with specific exceptional populations. For example, practitioners who work with children with congenital visual impairment may use scales revolving around assessment of haptic and verbal skills. The Intelligence Test for Visually Impaired Children (Dekker, 1993) is one such example. In this way, the performance of children with visual impairment is compared with those of other children with visual impairment.

Now that we have looked at the various approaches available to conceptualise delays in development, let's now consider a further example of how developmental psychologists study patterns of 'difference' in development. One approach is to compare behaviours and attributes across the population in question with typically developing children. In this way, characteristics associated with the condition in question are identified. For example, how does the development of HIV-affected children compare to that of non-affected children? With an increase in the number of HIV-infected children, researchers seek answers to this question in order to try to improve the quality of life for these children. As HIV is known to affect the brain, researchers seek to ascertain the extent to which children's learning and behaviours are different from those of unaffected children. A study by Koekkoek *et al.* (2008) looked at cognitive functioning in HIV-infected children, thought to be affected through perinatal transmission by HIV-positive mothers. The children were mean age 9.46 years (range 6.09–13.50) on participation in the study. On the one hand, Koekkoek *et al.* (2008) found that general cognitive functioning (as measured by IQ) was within the average range. However, on a battery of tests looking at the speed and accuracy of cognitive processing, HIV-infected children performed statistically significantly worse than norms. For instance, HIV-infected children were less alert and also slower to respond and less accurate when carrying out tasks of pattern recognition. These outcomes enabled the researchers to conclude that the findings in their study lent support for the idea that although the general cognitive profile was similar to unaffected children, yet it was shown to be weaker on a cluster of specific cognitive measures. Overall, patterns of 'difference' in cognitive functioning were associated with this group. The focus on children who are HIV infected serves to illustrate the concept of 'difference' within the context of one area of development.

So far, we have considered this concept of 'difference' in relation to children born pre-term as well as those who are HIV infected. Other populations featured later in this chapter will not only continue to draw on this concept of 'difference', but also the concept of 'delay'.

WHY STUDY ATYPICAL DEVELOPMENT?

The study of atypically developing children provides a profile of the main behaviours associated with a condition within the context of development across the human lifespan. Vitally, this profile has the potential to generate a new knowledge base from which to design and deliver interventions. Unfortunately, in the context of a relatively young field, there remains insufficient description of the **atypical trajectories** associated with particular disorders to warrant a sufficiently robust evidence base to inform the design and delivery of interventions fit-for-purpose. If effective, interventions – given appropriate resourcing – can work to enhance the life prospects of children and families, particularly if introduced at a particular developmental point when likely to deliver optimal impact. Later on, we offer a flavour of some of the interventions used with specific populations and their families.

atypical trajectory a sequence of development that departs from the typical sequence.

Another reason to study atypical development is that studying development that is considered 'atypical' can inform us about development that is 'typical', and vice versa (e.g. Cicchetti, 1984). To illustrate, let's look at an example from research involving people with Williams syndrome. Williams Syndrome is an extremely rare genetic disorder that occurs as a result of a deletion of one gene and surrounding DNA on chromosome 7 (7q11.23) (Korenberg *et al.*, 2000). The psychological profile associated with this syndrome is that individuals have a low non-verbal IQ, a profound impairment in visuospatial and visuomotor skills, yet relatively intact skills in language and face processing (Mervis *et al.*, 1999).

Observing how children with Williams syndrome represent the world can inform us about the development of drawing in typical children. Mervis (2003) reviews a fascinating case of the contribution made by investigating drawings made by children with William's syndrome. Mervis (2003) reports observations of the nature of drawings by children with William's syndrome, specifically that they scatter parts around the page, not demonstrating integration of drawings. An example from another research study is presented in Figure 21.2. Further, Mervis (2003) recounts how originally, the interpretation was that these outputs could be compared to those of adults with right hemisphere brain damage with onset in adulthood. A fascinating breakthrough came when Bertrand *et al.* (1997) provided evidence that, in fact, these types of drawings were simply part of the normative developmental sequence of learning to draw, with typically developing preschoolers readily producing similar errors. This suggests that this way of drawing was only discovered in typical development through first identifying it in an atypical population. In this way, it contributes to knowledge about the typical pathways of visual-motor integration. A further example of how the study of Williams syndrome is contributing to our understanding of typical human development is featured later.

This focus on Williams syndrome clearly forms one isolated example, and you will be able to find others in further reading about different conditions. More generally, this approach of studying atypical development to inform the study of typical development is now so well established that it

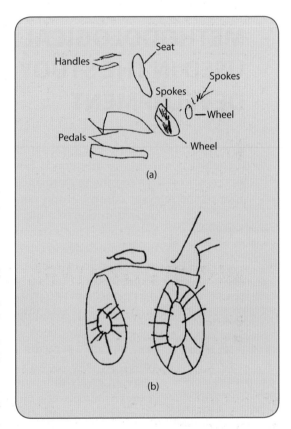

FIGURE 21.2 *Two drawings of a bicycle by the same girl with William's syndrome, aged 9 years 7 months (a), and 12 years 11 months (b). On both occasions, the child was given a blank piece of paper and asked to draw the best bicycle she could. The labels on drawing (a) were provided spontaneously by the child.*

Source: Mervis, C.B. & Klein-Tasman, B.P. (2000). William's syndrome: Cognition, personality, and adaptive behavior. *Mental Retardation and Developmental Disabilities Research Reviews*, 6: 148–158. Reproduced with permission from John Wiley.

underpins the recognised discipline of *developmental psychopathology*. This discipline has grown from the integration of two 'parent' fields – namely, developmental psychology and psychopathology. This new discipline of developmental psycho-pathology is concerned with 'understanding relations between development and its maladaptive deviations' (Achenback, 1990, p. 3), and it is notable that it is the developmental component which has been driving the field (Braet and van Aken, 2006).

METHODOLOGICAL APPROACHES USED IN THE STUDY OF ATYPICAL DEVELOPMENT

One conventional methodological approach to help determine whether or not the particular population in question is exhibiting a delay or a difference is to make a comparison between the performance of the atypical sample and the perform-ance of the relevant control group sample. This would be on a measure reflect-ing acquisition of a specific behaviour. Take, for example, the false belief task. This is one measure originally developed to investigate mind knowledge in typical development, but which is now increas-ingly used in investigations of atypical development. Despite the controversies over its status (e.g. Bloom and German, 2000), the false belief task is frequently used to assess atypically developing children's understanding of mental states (see Chapter 11). In fact, this task has now been used with a number of different disabilities (e.g. **autism spectrum disorders**; **congenitally blind**; Williams syndrome, and Down's syndrome) to assess the degree of delay or qualitatively different pattern of responses. Typically, there is comparison between one group and one or more control groups. Thomas *et al.* (2009) point out that a common practice is to com-pare a clinical group with two control groups, both of which are typically developing. Using a standardised test, the principle is for one control group to be matched on chronological age and the other to be matched on mental age. The matching across groups could potentially be achieved at the level of the individual or the level of the group. The rationale is that if the clinical group underperform compared with the chronological age matched group – but not with the mental age matched group – then the individuals in the clinical sam-ple are concluded to demonstrate a delay. Alternatively, if the clinical group show an underperformance relative to both groups then the clinical group is regarded as showing qualitatively different behaviour. In this way, it is possible to identify a difference or a delay.

autism spectrum disorders a spectrum of psychological conditions characterised by wide-spread abnormalities of social interactions and communication, as well as severely restricted interests and highly repetitive behaviour.

congenital blind-ness the condition of being born unable to see or with severe visual impairment.

However, although on paper these approaches would appear to make sense, in reality, regardless of any identified 'gold standard' in method, criticisms reveal that the use of multiple control groups is far from being routinely used in practice.

IMPACT OF SCIENTIFIC DISCOVERY AND TECHNOLOGICAL INNOVATION ON THE STUDY OF PATHWAYS IN ATYPICAL DEVELOPMENT

Scientific breakthroughs and technological innovation offer potential new opportunities to chart pathways in atypical development. As we shall see, this progress can also raise contentious issues, including ethical concerns. Three major developments having an impact on our understanding of pathways in atypical development are now outlined below. First, there are impacts of the discoveries from the **Human Genome Project**. Second, new techniques in brain imaging are allowing researchers insights into both the location and function of neural substrates relevant to atypical pathways. Finally, increasingly widespread uptake of **eye-tracking** technology by human development laboratories allows researchers to understand how visual behaviours can be potentially useful in contributing to our understanding of a range of different disorders of development.

Human Genome Project one of the biggest research projects in the world. The research found that the number of genes was fewer than previously thought and was a strong indicator that there was more to specifying humanity than action of individual genes in isolation.

eye-tracking methodology the technology of eye-tracking allows automated recording of eye-movements, and allows precise measures of visual behaviour.

The impact of the Human Genome Project on the study of atypical development

Heralded as 'one of the biggest research projects on earth' (Döring, 2005), what impacts do the outcomes from the Human Genome Project have on our understanding of human development, including atypical development?

The global media coverage of the international Human Genome Project reached a crescendo on 27 June 2000 when a press conference held at the White House announced that 90 per cent of the list of instructions encoded in DNA had been 'decoded'. Although the concept of the human genome is popularly described as a 'map' or 'blueprint' of humanity, use of such 'metaphors' are now regarded as being misplaced (Nerlich & Hellsten, 2004). Reflecting this, Craig Venter, director of private company Celera Genomics who carried out the second phase of the Human

Genome Project announced (BBC, 2001): 'The small number of genes – 30,000 instead of 60,000 – supports the notion that we are not hard wired. We now know that the notion that one gene leads to one protein and perhaps one disease is false.' As it happens, later on the revised conclusion was that the human genome actually contained only 21,000 genes. Interestingly, this quantity apparently puts humans on a par with some species of weeds (Commoner, 2009). That the number of genes was still fewer than previously thought was a strong indicator that there was more to specifying humanity than action of individual genes in isolation (for more on this in relation to intelligence, see Chapter 3). What is the relevance of this for the study of human development, including atypical development?

The assumption that there is usually a one-to-one mapping between a particular human DNA gene to a specific protein and, in turn to an associated inherited trait (e.g. genetic disease) rarely holds. Instead, information contained in the separate genes is thought to 'mingle' in complex ways, resulting in a transformation of genetic information. Therefore, it seems that a multitude of pathways are possible between genotype and expression, let alone before any factors around the time of birth or environmental factors exert an influence. Therefore, trying to disentangle the impact of genes in isolation is rarely going to be a fruitful enterprise. Instead, one area of focus, as a direct result of the Human Genome Project, is for researchers to shine the torch at the level of **chromosomal structural abnormalities**. By doing this, they are able to identify the breakpoints on chromosomes (Kurahashi *et al.*, 2009). This type of activity means that there is likely to be growing emphasis on the distinction between 'typical' and 'atypical' genetic mechanisms. What are the risks associated with this?

One serious risk of popularising the concept of 'genetically abnormal' in contrast to 'genetically normal' is that **genetic diversity** is not valued. The issue of genetic diversity is not just academic in nature. In the 1920s and 1930s, eugenic campaigns in the USA were at their peak, with involuntary sterilisations of people deemed as mentally inferior, particularly those enforced into institutions or workfarms (Munger *et al.*, 2007). In this new era of prenatal testing, some view the increased accessibility of genetic testing as simply a contemporary reformulation of the events of the eugenic era. Disability rights activists have raised a number of concerns including the salient point that if prenatal testing prevents the birth of an infant, then one atypical characteristic has become the basis for rejecting the whole infant.

Already, numerous countries are changing the guidelines on availability of prenatal tests. In an increasing number of countries pregnant women are offered screening for **Down's syndrome**. Down's syndrome arises from having an extra chromosome. At conception, normally 23 chromosomes derive from the mother and 23 from the father. The addition of an extra chromosome makes 47 and this is located on 21 causing cognitive disabilities, delayed language production, and characteristic motor differences (e.g. low muscle tone known as hypotonia). Although screening for Down's syndrome has been available through **amniocentesis** since the 1970s, new genomic

chromosomal structural abnormalities an atypical number of chromosomes or a structural abnormality in one or more chromosomes.

genetic diversity the total number of genetic characteristics in the genetic make-up of a species. It is distinguished from genetic variability, which describes the tendency of genetic characteristics to vary.

amniocentesis a medical procedure used in prenatal diagnosis of chromosomal abnormalities and fatal infections, in which a small amount of amniotic fluid, which contains foetal tissues, is extracted from the amnion or amniotic sac surrounding a developing foetus, and the foetal DNA is examined for genetic abnormalities.

profiling technologies now allow the rapid detection of genetic defects. Pregnant women can access information about the statistical chances of having a foetus with Down's syndrome.

In the next decade, the expectation is that pregnant women will have the option of non-invasive testing in the first trimester (i.e. in the first three months of pregnancy) (Fan *et al.*, 2008). However, the ethics of the repercussions of this practice has raised serious questions regarding the condition of Down's syndrome disappearing (Skotko, 2009). As has been pointed out by Munger *et al.* (2007) new technologies in prenatal testing have become available at the same time as life potential for people with Down's syndrome and other disabilities was expanding. As Buckley (2007) states, 'there still may be a need to raise expectations of what young people with Down's syndrome can achieve amongst parents, professionals and the wider community'. Although clearly this could be across any area of life, it is salient that research has shown some of the advances of children with Down's syndrome are in motor skills, one area of development conventionally known to be compromised for these children. For example, interventions in the form of treadmill training (Lloyd *et al.*, 2010) have been shown to enable infants with Down's syndrome to walk earlier. In turn, such interventions are likely to enable earlier independence in exploring the environment. Later in the lifespan, some young people with Down's syndrome excel in terms of their motor abilities. For example, some train their body and mind, to compete at world-class level in their chosen sport, (see Figure 21.3). One salient observation (Balic *et al.*, 2000) is that physical muscle strength in competing athletes with Down's syndrome in the Special Olympics is at least on a par with that of sedentary, non-disabled peers. Presumably then, it may also exceed it.

FIGURE 21.3 *Joanne Kempley – Triple European Swimming Champion (Down's syndrome European Swimming Championships) three gold medals for breaststroke (50 m, 100 m and 200 m)*

Source: Borough of Kirklees Special Needs Swimming Club. Reproduced with permission of Joanne's parents.

How advances in brain imaging are aiding understanding of pathways in atypical development

Neuroimaging tools aid localisation of brain activity that, in turn, enable developmental psychologists to understand more about the pathways associated with atypical development. Although a number of different multiple brain imaging techniques are available, only some of these are typically used with children. For example, **positron emission tomography** (PET) involves the creation of three-dimensional colour images of the body – including the brain. A more common technique

neuroimaging the use of various techniques to either directly or indirectly image the structure, function/pharmacology of the brain.

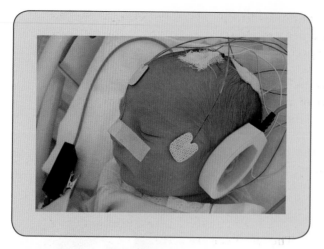

FIGURE 21.4 *Recording infant wearing ERP.*

Source: © Dr Gabor Stefanics (Photographer). Reproduced with permission.

used with children is a version of EEG recording known as **event-related potential** (*ERP*) recording, in which brain activity is monitored during the presentation of specific visual or auditory events. As can be seen from Figure 21.4, ERPs are recorded from electrode nets designed to fit children's head sizes.

ERP works non-invasively to monitor the currents generated by neurons. Laboratories with ERP equipment have frequently looked at cognitive functions in typical children – particularly looking at the development of visual attention. In turn, ERP studies have informed our understanding of atypical pathways where attentional development is at risk. For example, **attention deficit hyperactivity disorder** (**ADHD**) is the most common psychiatric disorder, affecting 3–5 per cent of all school-aged children (Spronk *et al.*, 2008). These children have symptoms in the form of behavioural impairments, inattention, impulsivity, and hyperactivity. Children with ADHD are known to be at much greater risk of school failure and delinquency. ERP studies (e.g. Liotti *et al.*, 2010) of ADHD are starting to highlight the neural basis of the deficiencies in attention processing. For instance, there is evidence of abnormalities in aspects of electrical activity in the frontal cortex, a region known to have a central role in the control of action (*executive function*; see the sections on autistic spectrum disorder and ADHD).

magnetoenceph-alography (MEG) a neuroimaging technique that measures the magnetic fields generated around the head.

One neuroimaging technique with the capacity for tremendous potential in research with clinical populations is **magneto-encephalography** (**MEG**). MEG measures – non-invasively – the magnetic fields generated around the head. Figure 21.5 shows the participant sitting in a device which looks like a very large salon hairdryer – inside the helmet sit magnetic field sensors. Although some children with certain conditions – particularly, children with autistic spectrum

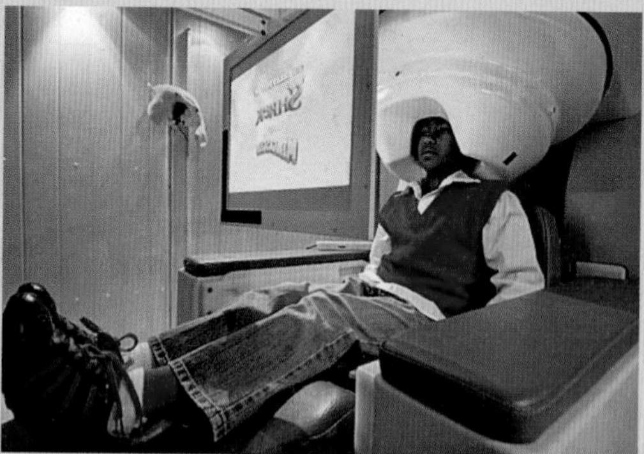

FIGURE 21.5 *MEG recording of a child who is participating in a study.*

Source: Reprinted with permission from the Press Association.

disorders – would understandably find it challenging to tolerate sitting within the confines of a small, unfamiliar space (as would some non-disabled adults), some studies have already involved these groups. Roberts *et al.* (2010) has found that data acquired from MEG reveals the brains of children with autistic spectrum disorders to process auditory tones more slowly than in typically developing children. The technology of MEG may play a role in advancing understanding about communication disorders in this group.

Use of eye-tracking methodology in studies of atypical development

The eyes offer a unique and convenient window from which to understand some of the processes of atypical development. The technology of eye-tracking allows automated recording of eye movements, and allows precise measures of visual behaviour. Experienced researchers use these methods with infants, although the initial process of calibration requires the infant to gaze at particular points on a screen, something that requires attention-catching stimuli to be sufficiently captivating for the experimenter to have sufficient time to map the position of the infant's eye to various calibrated targets on-screen.

One advantage of using eye-tracking is that it serves to capture attention with no overt task demands or explicit language requirements (Norbury *et al.*, 2009). This technology is particularly relevant in conditions with an atypical profile of communication (e.g. autistic spectrum disorder). This technology also offers the researcher the benefit of being able to exert control over the choice of scenes or stimuli to show participants. In this way it is possible to make comparisons across eye movements in response to only subtle shifts in the visual array.

One class of eye movements measured with eye-tracking technology is **saccades**. Saccades are the fast movements of the eye that function to shift fixation to an object of interest, so that its image is projected to the fovea (the part of the eye responsible for sharpest central vision). Having control of eye movements allows humans to make saccades to suddenly appearing targets in the periphery (i.e. when they are important to the task) and also to suppress such attentional shifts when it would distract from the task in hand. Such measures, as we shall see later, are of particular relevance to the study of children with ADHD.

> **saccades** eye movements in which the fast movement of the eye functions to shift fixation to an object of interest, so that its image is projected to the fovea (the central part of the retina responsible for sharpest vision).

UNDERSTANDING ATYPICAL PATHWAYS

Advances in the field of atypical development now mean that atypical conditions of childhood can be characterised according to the type of causal pathways involved. On the one hand, Down's syndrome and Williams syndrome are specific genetic conditions, and serve as models from which to pursue understanding of the relationship between genome and corresponding brain and behavioural expression. In contrast, other disorders, which have no known specific genetic defects per se, are thought to involve multiple causal pathways. In these situations, developmental psychologists work with a range of other collaborators (e.g. neuroscientists, neuropsychologists, practitioners and caregivers), not only to identify the areas of development most at risk but also to design and deliver interventions.

Williams syndrome

One reason why it is a challenging task to establish the nature of developmental pathways associated with the Williams syndrome concerns the limited participant pool. Williams syndrome is an extremely rare condition. The estimated prevalence of the disorder is between 1 in 7500 and 1 in 20,000 (Stromme *et al.*, 2002). Reflecting this outcome, it is not unusual for many studies, particularly the older ones, to have involved as few as 4–6 participants. Although preliminary studies involving small numbers of participants are known to hold great value – particularly in the way that they pave the way for the focus of larger-scale studies – nevertheless, they do tend to lack generalisability. Further, a substantial age band (e.g. sometimes of the order of 10–20 years) is often cited in the 'methodology' sections of studies. This is not due to the study design being intentionally focused across the lifespan. Rather, it reflects the difficulties of recruitment. And this is problematic because even small-scale pilot studies of more common disorders (e.g. ADHD) tend to focus on a research question within a particular developmental period (e.g. infancy; early childhood; adolescence).

A further significant methodological issue is that data sets are typically cross-sectional rather than longitudinal, which presents further difficulties with isolating patterns associated with the pathway linked with chromosome 7 (7q11.23) and insights into the causal nature of developmental mechanisms in the links between genome, environment, and phenotype.

Despite these various methodological challenges, nevertheless, tremendous strides forward have been made in terms of synthesising data from available studies (see Martens *et al.*, 2008). One reason why it is incredibly important to synthesise findings from a range of different studies in a low incidence population is that it enables triangulation from multiple data sets obtained from separate studies. As we shall see, this is important as there is a contentious outcome regarding their profile of abilities across language and cognition.

Frequently, developmental scientists characterise Williams syndrome in terms of making a differentiation between language and cognitive domains. That is, whereas cognition in this group is regarded as 'atypical', language skills are viewed as 'spared'. Salient examples of measures of cognitive impairment include low non-verbal IQ, difficulties in planning, problem-solving and spatial cognition. In contrast, popular views held about language ability revolve around the notion that individuals with Williams syndrome are highly sociable and communicative. Notably, it is this differentiation between performance on verbal and cognitive domains which fuels the topic of an intense debate in developmental science and beyond (e.g. philosophy). Some influential thinkers (e.g. Pinker, 1999) argue that evidence of such a clear dissociation between language and cognition provides support for the view that language abilities are innate and that these develop in isolation from general cognitive abilities. However, this argument has been called into question by those who view communicative and language abilities in Williams syndrome to be less intact than previously thought. One area of language functioning where evidence suggests performance is impaired is **pragmatics** (Mervis & John, 2010). Pragmatics refers to the competence of speakers to communicate in socially appropriate ways. Here are a few examples. If one speaker struck up a conversation about the speed of a passing car, whilst the other conversational partner responded with talk about their recent trip to Mexico, the second speaker would clearly not be following up appropriately in the conversational thread. Another example would be if two strangers started a conversation and one made a number of references to a 'Mike', not taking into account whether or not the listener knew about Mike. In this way, they were not sensitive to the needs of the listener. Pragmatics also refers to the capacity to use humour and to observe cultural conventions around politeness (e.g. ask appropriate questions). In essence, as is shown by these examples, pragmatics refers to the ability to use language appropriately in social context.

One study by Stojanovik (2006) found that when children with Williams syndrome were compared to children with **specific language impairment (SLI)** on a task involving talk with an adult about photos depicting everyday scenes (e.g. going on holiday), there was a difference in their ability to use pragmatics. Children with Williams syndrome showed a number of difficulties, such as their speech was overly dependent on the adult's leads and contributions, with difficulties in leading the conversation forwards reflected in inability to add new

specific language impairment (SLI) a developmental language disorder that can affect both production and comprehension and that is unrelated to other atypicalities in development.

information and respond to requests for new information. These issues did not affect the group with SLI. The rationale for Stojanovik (2006) making the comparison between these two particular groups concerned the difference between the two groups in terms of cognitive functioning. Children with SLI have difficulties with language structure, but they do not have compromised cognitive ability. In contrast, as seen above, children with Williams syndrome have compromised cognitive abilities. Given that the Williams syndrome group performed worse than the group with SLI, although the data were from a small sample, it is plausible to infer that levels of cognitive functioning appear to interfere with social and pragmatic aspects of communication. That children follow an atypical path provides some support for the notion that language skills cannot develop independently from cognitive abilities. In future, longitudinal studies of language and communicative development should shed more light on the extent to which this assertion is supported.

Not all the theoretical debate regarding Williams syndrome has revolved around this issue of the dissociation between language and cognition. Zitzer-Comfort *et al.,* (2007) carried out an intriguing study of the impact of culture on the phenotype of Williams syndrome, specifically, the extent of variation in the social behaviour in Williams syndrome across individuals in Japan and the United States. In Japan, children with Williams syndrome and typically developing children were rated lower in sociability than individuals in the United States. This outcome is extremely illuminating because it demonstrates that the social phenotype varies across cultures, thereby revealing a role for the contribution of environmental input. In particular, this opens up possibilities for interventions, and children with Williams syndrome often access speech language therapy as this can improve social use of language.

Autistic spectrum

Use of a single label 'autism' to describe such a complex, heterogeneous human condition runs the risk of conjuring up an image of a condition that is either categorically 'present' or 'absent' revolving around a tightly defined set of characteristics which run fixed across the course of the lifespan. Of course, this concern around use of a single label could equally apply to any label used to describe a human condition. As we shall see, this is particularly the case with autism because, relative to other disorders, the condition is known to be particularly heterogeneous in terms of how it manifests itself.

The prevalence of autism spectrum disorder is around 1 in 100 (Baron-Cohen, 2008). The core diagnostic features are currently defined at the level of *behaviour*. That is, currently there are no entirely reliable biological indicators such as brain abnormalities that can diagnose autism. However, post-mortems using PET or MRI reveal evidence of cerebellar deficits (Allen & Courchesne, 1993), and some studies report a genetic predisposition (e.g. Curran *et al.*, 2006).

One way to depict autism is according to the triad of atypical behaviours outlined in the US **Diagnostic and Statistical Manual of Mental Disorders (DSM-IV**; American Psychiatric Association, 1994, 2000) or the World Health Organization **International Classification of Disease (ICD-10**; **World Health Organization, 2005**), namely, impairments in social interaction, impairments in communication, and repetitive behaviour within a narrow set of interests.

International Classification of Disease (ICD-10) a coding of diseases and signs, symptoms, abnormal findings, complaints, social circumstances and external causes of injury or diseases, as classified by the World Health Organisation (WHO).

Although each of the three behavioural areas has been intensively researched, the advent of eye-tracking technology is providing new insights into the nature of the impairments in social interaction as indicated by unusual visual behaviour. One of the specific behaviours associated with impairments in social interaction is atypical eye contact. This could take the form of either extremely little eye contact or staring for protracted periods.

Informed by multiple disciplines (e.g. medicine, neurology, genetics, education), researchers and practitioners commonly distinguish between six major subgroups on the autistic spectrum (Baron-Cohen, 2008). As can be seen in Table 21.1, the subgroups are differentiated by cognitive ability level as measured by IQ and the extent to which there has been any delay in learning to talk.

Acknowledging the heterogeneity of the autistic spectrum population in the design of their study, Norbury *et al.* (2009) aimed to look at the patterns of eye movement in 27 male adolescents with autistic spectrum disorder who were either with or without

Table 21.1 *The six major subgroups on the autistic spectrum*

Subgroup	Cognitive ability measured by IQ	Language delay
Asperger syndrome	IQ > 85	None
High-functioning autism	IQ > 85	Delay
Medium-functioning autism	IQ 71–84	Yes/no
Low-functioning autism	IQ < 70	Yes/no
Atypical autism	Late onset	?
Pervasive developmental disorder	Some mild	?

Source: Adapted from Baron-Cohen, S. (2008)

language impairments when compared to 18 controls with no language impairment matched for age and non-verbal ability. They created a series of five professionally produced videos involving two to three characters in a storyline containing emotional responses for up to 36 seconds (e.g. two girls sitting at a cafe table showing disgust at cafe food, talking about sending it back). The hypothesis was that as both autistic spectrum disorder groups would show social impairments, this would be reflected in spending less time fixating on the eyes of the characters in the videos. The mean percentage of visual fixation time adolescents spent on eyes, mouth, body, and elsewhere was compared across the different groups. Whereas, compared with controls, the autistic spectrum disorder children with no language impairment spent a statistically lower proportion of time focusing on the eyes of the characters in the films, there was no difference between autistic spectrum disorder children with language impairment and the controls. Thus there were differences in viewing patterns across subgroups between language impaired and non-language impaired. Crucially, and surprisingly, there was evidence of typical viewing patterns in language-impaired adolescents with autistic spectrum disorder. Of course, although the same viewing patterns occurred, this does not necessarily mean that the observer accessed the same meaning from social stimuli. Future research will try to pinpoint how typical eye movement patterns are related to atypical social impairment. Also, there is a need to examine abilities across the lifespan so as to determine where best to target interventions.

Explaining autism

What have developmental psychologists contributed in the way of theories relating to autism? One way for psychologists to approach this is to propose theories that account for the pattern of the three main deficits associated with autism. Predominantly, cognitive theories have dominated, with three main theories being

theory of mind hypothesis of autism the view that people with autism have difficulties in understanding that others have thoughts and beliefs.

executive function hypothesis of autism the view that autism is due to a deficit in executive function (i.e. skills pertaining to inhibiting inappropriate responses, planning, being mentally flexible, and generating novel ideas).

central coherence hypothesis of autism the view that autism is due to lack of central coherence, which is reflected in the tendency to process information piecemeal rather than to integrate it.

(1) **theory of mind hypothesis**; (2) **executive function hypothesis**; and (3) **central coherence hypothesis**.

One question posed is about the extent to which atypicalities in cognitive processes characterise all individuals with an autistic condition across the lifespan (Loth, 2008). The theory of mind hypothesis revolves around the idea that people with autism have difficulties in understanding that others have thoughts and beliefs. Earlier, in Chapter 11, the development of skills in theory of mind were examined in the case of typical populations. Also, an example was provided of a theory of mind task. One common measure of theory of mind is whether or not children pass the 'litmus' false belief task. Whereas typically developing children will pass this around the age of 3 years, people with autism generally fail. This is interpreted as indicating that they have an impoverished level of social understanding. But not all fail, so what about children with autism who pass the false belief task? One interpretation is that these children have a 'weaker' form of autism (Hughes & Leekham, 2004). There have been observations that individuals who are high functioning pass theory of mind tasks. As pointed out by Loth (2008, p. 84), if impairments in theory of mind were the underlying cause for social and communication deficits characteristic of these groups, it would be reasonable to assume that those individuals who passed theory of mind tasks might also fare better at understanding others in everyday social situations. Evidence from Peterson *et al.* (2009) does not support this conclusion. Their study showed that children with autism who passed laboratory theory of mind tasks were rated by teachers as having *more* mind reading difficulties than those younger typically developing children who failed the task. It would seem, then, that the capacity to understand mental states does not necessarily coincide with, or lead to, social functioning that is unperturbed. Recent research has cast further doubt on the 'theory of mind deficit' explanation of autism. Reasoning impairments in autism relative to typical development reach beyond reasoning about other people's mental states and have been shown in physical problems as well, such as predicting the relation between weight and speed in freefall (Baker *et al.*, 2009). It seems that a deficit in social functioning might not be the full explanation for autism.

What main theoretical developments have fuelled the evidence around social functioning? Central coherence theory (Frith, 1989) was proposed to account for the pattern of deficits associated with autism, including social deficits. This theory relates to the tendency to process information piecemeal rather than to integrate it (Frith & Happé, 1994). Evidence of this processing tendency has been sought from a number of areas of development (e.g. semantic processing). One area which particularly lends itself to this analysis is performance on visuospatial tasks (Pellicano *et al.*, 2005). For example, individuals with autism tend to perform superior to norms on a standardised test called the Embedded Figures Test where the task is to locate a 'hidden' figure (e.g. triangle) from a larger, complex design, as shown in Figure 21.6. Individuals who succeed at locating the shape more quickly have a tendency towards a cognitive processing style that is 'field-independent'. Evidence suggests that they are more ready to perceive the constituent parts of the shape. In contrast, those who are more 'field-dependent' tend to process the 'whole', and are less likely to perceptually deconstruct the visual array into constituent parts. Evidence that individuals with autism tend towards the 'field-independent' end of the continuum on this task as well as others is seen as lending support for theory of weak central coherence. That is, their tendency towards processing the details is viewed as a processing bias, though not necessarily an impairment. Happé and Frith's (2006) central coherence theory essentially repackaged the

FIGURE 21.6 *Example of items from an Embedded Figures Test. The child's task is to identify the triangle in the figures.*

relative strengths and weaknesses of the performance of individuals with autism. The general view now is that some abilities to integrate – to engage at a 'global' – level are spared in this group, but that this may be dependent on the type of task presented, as well as individual differences in performance.

Research with typically developing preschoolers has cast findings into new light. Pellicano *et al.* (2005) deconstructed the concept of central coherence with this age-group and found that performance on the task was related to children's performance on a battery of tasks requiring skills in executive functioning. Executive functioning is an 'umbrella term' which refers to a collection of skills – namely, inhibiting inappropriate responses, planning, being mentally flexible, and generating novel ideas, and is measured by various conventional tasks (e.g. Stuss & Knight, 2002). Evidence suggests a mix of difficulties in this area, with impairments detected later in childhood rather than being particularly visible in the preschool period (Hill, 2004). Also, there is a variable profile of performance dependent on the tests used and the conditions under which the tests are performed. Neuroimaging research relating performance on specific executive functioning tasks to brain activity measured through **functional magnetic resonance imaging (fMRI)** demonstrates that different areas within the prefrontal cortex are involved as a function of which test is being used (Gilbert *et al.*, 2008). These researchers used two different tests known to capture executive function skills. Even within the same individuals, depending on which of two tasks was being used, there was variation in the areas of the brain shown to be functioning abnormally.

In future, the study of autism will be advanced by the capacity to pool data across the breadth of the autistic spectrum. Also, being able to deconstruct appropriate tasks into constituent components that can be simultaneously tracked with neuroimaging and eye-tracking technology by group will permit a more systematic approach to establishing atypical developmental trajectories. In turn, this will allow a more systematic approach to the design and delivery of interventions appropriate to the different subgroups of autistic spectrum disorder. An area already showing promise is in

joint attention an activity in which two individuals attend to the same object or event.

the area of communication. Data available from one of the first randomised controlled trials shows the efficacy of a short-term parent-facilitated intervention in joint engagement in toddlers with autism (Kasari *et al.*, 2010). Compared to toddlers on a waiting list, the experimental group still showed an increased ability to engage in interactive episodes of **joint attention** one year later.

Attention deficit hyperactivity disorder (ADHD)

FIGURE 21.7 *In the classroom, compared with peers, children with ADHD show considerable difficulties in maintaining visual attention, and are frequently involved in 'off task' behaviour.*

Source: Shutterstock.

inhibitory control the ability to overcome a prepotent motor response.

Relative to typically developing children, those diagnosed with ADHD – an estimated 3–7 per cent of school-age children – are excessively hyperactive or impulsive (e.g. they fidget, and have difficulties waiting their turn) and inattentive (e.g. making careless mistakes in schoolwork and failing to give close attention to details) (American Psychiatric Association, 2000). In the classroom, compared with peers, they show considerable difficulties in maintaining visual attention relative to peers (Kofler *et al.*, 2008), and are frequently involved in 'off task' behaviour. Usually first diagnosed by age 7, the symptoms of ADHD are known to manifest across the lifespan (DSM-IV-TR, American Psychiatric Association, 2000) and frequently co-occur with conduct disorder, and other behavioural disorders (American Psychiatric Association, 2000).

What is the underlying cause of ADHD? The challenge is that although researchers (e.g. Spronk *et al.*, 2008) have reached agreement about the behavioural level characteristics, much remains to be resolved about the underlying causes of the condition. One influential hypothesis was that ADHD reflects a core deficit in **inhibitory control** (Barkley, 1997), an aspect of executive function. That is, the child has an inability to overcome a prepotent motor response. A task presumed to measure executive inhibition is popularly referred to as the 'Stop Task'. In the laboratory, on 'start' trials children are requested to press a specific response bar on the computer as soon as they have seen a letter appear on the screen. On other trials children hear a tone (or other signal) that signals them to inhibit their bar-press response. In other words, there is a conflict between being poised to execute a response on some trials and to inhibit it on others. Although a number of studies reported a significantly longer response time in the Stop component of the task, it is difficult to fully interpret the data. One reason for this is that an alternative explanation is that children with ADHD may find it difficult to remember task instructions. Further, a large-scale study of severe ADHD, using a simpler task, found similar levels of errors in ADHD boys and age-matched controls (Rhodes *et al.*, 2005). Collectively, these observations led to doubts that the main cognitive deficit of ADHD is attributable to a deficit in inhibition.

There is a growing shift in emphasis away from traditional common single pathway deficits to a preference for accounts based on multiple developmental pathways in ADHD (Sonuga-Barke, 2005). One rationale here is that not only do a number of symptoms – the impulsiveness, inattention, and hyperactivity – have to be explained by the model, but also there appear to be a cluster of related clinical features to be explained, such as time management and task organisation. On this basis, Sonuga-Barke (2003) proposes a dual pathway hypothesis that takes into account not only the cognitive components but also the affective components in ADHD. Castellanos *et al.* (2006) specifically differentiate the underpinnings of the symptoms of ADHD. They propose that the symptoms of inattention and hyperactivity / impulsivity may be associated with different brain pathways that are nevertheless both associated with executive function. Specifically, they suggest that the more cognitively oriented aspects of executive function are associated with dorsolateral prefrontal cortex, whereas the more affective aspects are handled by the orbital and medial prefrontal cortex; that more than one region is involved supports the notion that multiple pathways are involved developmentally.

IMPACT OF THE ABSENCE OF A SENSORY INPUT ON DEVELOPMENTAL PATHWAYS

So far, the focus has been on various disorders characterised by patterns of deficits resulting from underlying genetic, cognitive, or brain deficits – as illustrated by Down's syndrome, Williams syndrome, autistic spectrum disorders and ADHD. Now, we turn to the impact of the loss of one or more sense on particular developmental pathways. To do so, we start with the case of childhood blindness, before considering children with a dual sensory loss. Ordinarily, the development of children with visual impairment would not characteristically be classed as 'disordered'. However, to illustrate the degree of fuzziness of the boundaries between typical and atypical development, it is important to expand:

- First, it is important to note that certain forms of visual impairment are caused by genetic abnormalities. Earlier we related genetic underpinnings to developmental outcomes, in the context of 'disorder'. As to date the relationship between specific causes of visual impairment and developmental outcomes has not been elucidated, it remains to be seen whether this could class as atypical development. However, it is certainly the case that sensory impaired children have atypical experience, so it appears reasonable to include sensory impairment as a category of atypical development.

- Second, a certain proportion of children who are sensory impaired due to congenital blindness also show behavioural symptoms of autism. It remains to be seen whether the absence of vision per se leads to behaviours associated with autism or whether there is a more complex relationship traceable to the visual loss and other risk factors.

- Finally, there is a point relating to theory and the extent to which children who are congenitally blind or severely visually impaired make developmental progress. It is important to note that some accounts of typical development assign vision a major driving role in, for example, early communicative development in the first year. Yet, we do know that the absence of vision does not prevent congenitally blind infants from learning to talk. Therefore, it clearly follows that infants who are blind make their ways into communication through non-visually mediated mechanisms. A logical conclusion is that this would at least partially involve atypical pathways in communicative development.

A fundamental point is that once congenitally blind infants have learnt to understand language and to speak, they have greater access to the environment through hearing the speech of others relating to what is going on around them and in using their own language to elicit information from others about what is going on. In the light of this, in terms of considering the case of development in the absence of a sensory modality, it makes sense to choose to focus on the development of early communication as a case study.

As with all special populations, populations of children who are blind are heterogeneous. To reflect the composition of samples used in research studies, children who are blind will be defined as those who have been blind since birth, rather than those who have acquired blindness later in life. Also, the majority of research on blindness involves samples of children or infants who have no vision or at best light perception. Thus, for the purpose of this discussion, this group will be the main focus.

In Chapter 7 it was observed that many of the mechanisms of pre-linguistic communication are visually based: eye contact is used to establish and maintain exchanges between caretaker and infant; gaze is used to establish joint attention; and gestures such as reaching and pointing provide information about the intentions of the speaker (e.g. Stern, 1974, 1977). Yet evidence suggests that by six months of age blind infants are able to establish a rapport with their caretakers. Preisler, (1991) reports that infants in her study engaged in imitation, smiling, and were generally 'social and attentive to their mothers'. This suggests that non-visual perceptual information is sufficient for establishing exchanges between blind infants and their parents. Typically, interactions revolve around rhymes and touching routines (e.g. tickling). In support of this, close examination of the interaction between blind infants and their parents reveals special ways of communicating (Fraiberg, 1977; Urwin, 1978a). In particular, Fraiberg draws attention to the way that blind infants' hands are an important source of information about affective states. For instance, with positive emotion, infants may wave and flap their hands rapidly. In addition, a number of studies have drawn attention to the tendency of blind infants and their parents to engage in communication through focusing on rhymes and routines; it appears that such activities permit a blind infant and their parent to focus on the same thing for a period of time using touch and sounds (Dunlea, 1989; Fraiberg, 1977; Norgate *et al.*, 1998; Pérez-Pereira and Castro, 1992; Urwin, 1978b).

Observations suggest that up until 6 months of age sighted infants engage largely in social behaviour which does not involve objects: they smile, vocalise at others and share gaze (Stern, 1985). At around 5 months of age, sighted infants start to reach out towards objects and then, around 6 months, they shift from being interested in people to being interested in people and objects. Between 7 and 15 months, sighted infants discover that others have minds in addition to their own and start to share the focus of attention with others by following another's pointing gesture and establishing their own (Murphy & Messer, 1977). Thus around half way through their first year, sighted infants are not only in a position to become more active in controlling their physical environment, but are also able to start combining different aspects of their physical and social environments. In contrast, Preisler (1991) observed that at 9 months, when sighted infants start to establish joint attention either by following the direction of their partner's gaze towards an object or by pointing at the object, blind infants were not able to engage in joint attention. At 8 months of age, Preisler notes that for all five of the blind infants participating in her study, more than half of the video-recorded interactions were focused on the parent and infant rather than objects. Thus in contrast to sighted infants, person–person–object style interactions were not established in a reliable way until around 21 months.

Of importance, more recent conceptualisations of joint attention in the typical literature operationalise more effectively the notion of 'established joint attention' (EJA) as comprising a sequence of four behaviours (Tasker & Schmidt, 2008). First, an initiating partner makes a bid for attention to a particular object or event. Next the recipient makes an appropriate behavioural response. After that, the initiator follows with a response that indicates that the initiator is aware of the recipient's attention. Then, the dyad focus visually on the object/event and 'attentionally engage one another and the object through, for example, the exchange of smiles, vocalizations, verbalizations, or "eye talk"' (Tasker & Schmidt, 2008, p. 276). Thus much is known about the ways sighted infants and their caregivers use vision to engage in EJA. What happens when there is no access to a shared channel of visual information?

To what extent does it make sense to consider whether the components of EJA are represented through non-visual means? Although the nature of person–person–object interactions within dyads where one member of the partner is blind has been described in relation to the case of sighted mothers and blind infants (e.g. Preisler, 1991), no study to date has systematically documented any 'engagement state' (Bakeman and Adamson, 1984) revolving around the modalities of touch and audition. Norgate (2009) examined how sighted caregivers attempted to direct the attention of their congenitally blind infant towards objects. The objective was to investigate what actions and gestures caregivers used to accompany verbal deixis (e.g. here vs. there; this vs. that) in interaction. Four sighted caregivers and their congenitally blind infants were matched with sighted control dyads for infant verbal comprehension, socioeconomic status, birth order, and maternal age. Longitudinal data were obtained with dyads video-recorded at home twice during their second year. Videos were coded for caregiver action and gesture accompanying deixis (e.g. *that one, this one, that's a . . . , this is a, there's the, here's the*). Based on a total of 41 cases of deixis, findings showed that caregivers of sighted children either displayed objects across the room, pointed to objects, or restricted use to them without any action or gesture. In the case of drawing attention to parts of objects, these caregivers introduced target parts of objects by pointing with actual contact with the object part. A total of 61 deictic episodes were observed in caregivers of blind infants. These caregivers usually positioned themselves in full body contact behind the infant and took the responsibility for physically introducing objects to their infant's hand (or, if the infant was already holding an object, tapping their chest or arm). Caregivers relied on a range of strategies to direct infant attention to parts of objects – they shifted the infant's hand to the target location or if the infant's hand was already in contact with the target location, they carefully timed it with the deictic word.

Children with a dual sensory impairment

Around 50 per cent of children who are registered blind have other disabilities, for example a hearing impairment. For those children with dual sensory impairments it is vital to encourage independence across all areas of development – especially in communication and in mobility. Let's consider interventions tailored towards a child's cognitive level in terms of the provision of mobility training. The provision of resources for those who are sensory impaired is under-resourced, yet the value of *early* interventions in both mobility and way-finding is recognised to lead to enhanced proprioceptive-spatial abilities (Fiehler *et al.*, 2009) that, in turn, lead to an improved quality of life.

Typically, interventions take place in educational settings which currently vary in the extent to which the environment has been adapted to promote both children's understanding of space and their locomotion within it. Hazelwood School (Glasgow, Scotland) is the first 'custom built' school in Europe for children and young people with a dual sensory impairment, and the product of collaboration between parents, staff, stakeholders (e.g. SENSE Scotland) and the architects, Murray Dunlop. The school enshrines the principles of access and sensory awareness in its work through the inclusion of a number of mobility and navigational features: (1) large-scale navigational tool running through the school covered with 'trail rails' and a 'sill' to guide a cane or side of foot; (2) curvilinear corridors, rather than orthogonal layout; (3) use of olfactory cues; (4) ambient temperature as indicators for areas within the school; (5) signage using four different methods of communication. These adaptations of the environment within an educational setting are thought to facilitate the child's independence in moving around their learning environment.

Although it is possible to shape the built environment to help a dual sensory impaired child to achieve good mobility, of course this does not guarantee satisfactory outcomes. For instance, 75 per cent of deafblind children do not receive any one-to-one input outside school, which means that they often do not participate in leisure activities (Bawden, 2008). Article 31 of the UN Convention of the Rights of the Child stipulates the 'right to play and informal recreation'. One aid to independence in this population is access to mobility aids. However, access to mobility aids alone is insufficient, as those work as mobility and independence specialists in education play a particularly key role in facilitating the intregration of these aids into the live of young visually impaired and multidisabled children. Relative to other populations of comparable incidence, this population of dual sensory impaired children remain under-researched.

ENVIRONMENTAL RISK FACTORS: THE CASE OF EMOTIONAL DISTURBANCE

So far, atypical development has been talked about solely in terms of the extent to which behaviours are to be categorised as either delayed or disordered. This puts the emphasis on individual characteristics and can falsely give the impression that atypical development occurs somewhat in isolation, within a vacuum. However, while some forms of atypical development have a clear genetic basis, for others, environmental input is likely to be at least a major contributory factor. One influential model that places individual human development into the wider context of interaction with the immediate environment, as well as the larger context is **Bronfenbrenner's ecological model** (Bronfenbrenner, 1986, 2004; Bronfenbrenner & Morris, 2006). The theoretical underpinning of the model is captured in Figure 21.8, with interpersonal processes nested in five different levels of environmental structure. Although there is no explicit distinction between atypical and typical development made in the model, as we shall see, as the various levels of the model are described it is a logical progression to ask about the absence or atypicality of experiences that may influence the path of individual development.

Bronfenbrenner's ecological model an influential model that places individual human development into the wider context of interaction with the immediate environment, as well as the larger context.

At the heart, the **microsystem** refers to the individual child, their characteristics (e.g. sex, age, health), and the settings where interpersonal relationships relevant at different points in the lifespan take place. For example, in infancy the interpersonal relationships within the family are emphasised. Then, increasingly, across childhood, school, health services, neighbourhood, play areas, religious influences, and so on, become influential as the child moves more independently around their environments.

microsystem in Bronfenbrenner's ecological model, refers to the individual child, their characteristics (e.g. sex, age, health) and the settings where interpersonal relationships relevant at different points in the lifespan take place.

What is the impact on child development if an infant lacks interpersonal relationships and family, due to adverse early deprivation? Children living in institutions, refugee camps or conflict zones clearly do not have access to stable interpersonal relationships or a family context (World Health Organization, 2004). One significant example from Europe in the latter half of the 20th century concerns Romania, under the dictatorship of Ceausescu in the early 1980s. The economic plight meant rationing, and lack of domestic energy for lighting and heat because the energy was diverted to industrial development. Also, Ceausescu had a policy of increasing the birth rate

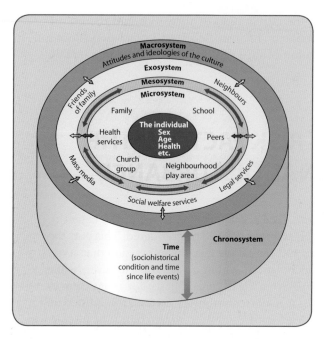

FIGURE 21.8 *A version of Bronfenbrenner's Ecological Model.*

Source: http://www.aifs.gov.au/growingup/pubs/reports/krq2009/images/fig2/gif.

by penalising small families, banning birth control and criminalising abortion (Castle *et al.*, 1999). As a result, many unwanted children remained uncared for and went to Romanian institutions. At the fall of the regime, many institutions were closed and there was a rush for agencies and individuals to adopt children. The quality of institutions was rated from 'poor' to 'abysmal', with an example shown in Figure 21.9.

Generally, children experienced frequent changes of staff. In the worst places, most staff were untrained and the ratio of staff to children was 1 to 20, with children kept in confined spaces and subjected to sedation (Reich, 1990, p. 12). The following quote (Ames, 1990) captures the appalling conditions:

> ... in Vaslui children were sometimes two in a crib, and all wore sweaters and knitted caps in their beds to keep them warm. In that, dirty, foul-smelling orphanage there were no pictures, no heating ovens, no outside play equipment, and it was there that we saw a child who had pulled out hunks of her own hair, another ... who rocked back and forth hitting his

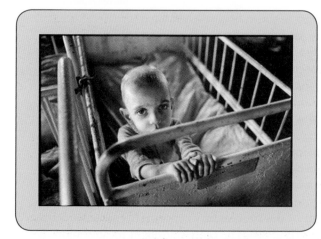

FIGURE 21.9 *A scene from one Romanian Orphanage in the late 1990s.*

Source: Reproduced by permission of Josef Polleross (Photographer).

> head against the metal bars of the crib, and at least three ... children who shrank away from my hand when I extended it towards them ... In the worst orphanage I saw, 2- and 3-year-olds sat on plastic potties placed on small individual chairs four times a day for half-hour each time. And the amazing thing was that they did just sit.
>
> *(Ames, 1990, pp. 9–10).*

Following the downfall of Ceausescu, infants started to be removed from institutions. As many had been adopted in infancy at an average age of one month (Castle *et al.*, 1999), a series of studies looked at child development post-adoption. A longitudinal study involving child assessments took observations and cognitive measures at fourth, sixth and eleventh birthdays. A significant finding was that for children living in institutions at least across their first 6 months, the longer-term impact was an attachment disorder in the form of 'disinhibited attachment' (see Chapter 6 for more on attachment). This was characterised by, among other things, children having a lack of close relationships and having difficulties in social relationships as manifested by being over friendly to unfamiliar people (Rutter *et al.*, 2007). A further key finding of impact on development was that children adopted before the age of 6 months had significantly improved cognitive outcomes compared with children after this age (Beckett *et al.*, 2006). One possible explanation for this is that reduced exposure to early psychosocial stressors is

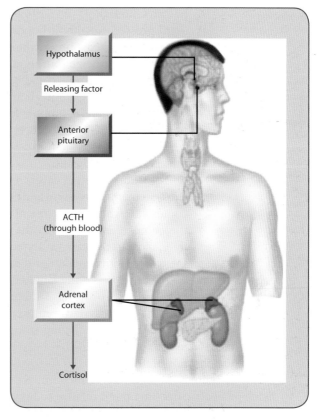

FIGURE 21.10 *Hypothalamic–pituitary–adrenal axis.*
Source: http://www.vitalifenetworks.com/images/Cortisol_image.jpg

thought to have prevented atypical functioning in pathways in the brain – in particular, a brain system known as the hypothalamic–pituitary–adrenal axis (Figure 21.10; see Marshall & Kenney, 2009, for review). However, it is challenging to tease apart the impact of early psychosocial conditions from a range of alternative factors. For example, presumably the more rapidly an infant accesses sufficient nutrients, the lesser the impact of poor nutrition on cognitive ability.

Returning to Bronfenbrenner's theory, the next level up is the **mesosystem**. This refers to the relation between the different microsystems, for instance, the relation between school and family, peers and religious activity, neighbourhood and health, and so on. One study illustrating the relationships between neighbourhood and health was undertaken by Meltzer *et al.* (2007) on 3340 11- to 16-year-olds living in Britain. The researchers used the Development and Well-Being Assessment (DAWBA) to assess for the prevalence of two types of disorders – emotional disorders and conduct disorders. The team discovered a striking outcome. They found that even after taking account of the type of area in which the young people lived (e.g. whether the young

mesosystem in Bronfenbrenner's ecological model, refers to the relation between different *microsystems*, for instance, the relation between school and family, peers and religious activity, neighbourhood and health, and so on.

exosystem in Bronfenbrenner's ecological model, this refers to the variety of influences like the mass media, the neighbours and family friends.

macrosystem in Bronfenbrenner's eco-logical model, this refers to the cultural level of influence.

chronosystem Bronfenbrenner's ecological model, refers to the sociocultural events over the life course.

person's household was situated amongst prosperity or amongst 'hard pressed' neighbourhoods), the odds of having an emotional disorder increased 8 times when contrasting children who perceived no one in their neighbourhood could be trusted with children who perceived many people could be trusted. There was also an increase for conduct disorders, of about 2.5 times. One implication of this study is that there is support for the idea that regeneration of less prosperous neighbourhoods is likely to increase children's positive perceptions of trust and safety, which in turn can have a positive impact on mental health.

The three external layers of the Bronfenbrenner model – the **exosystem**, **macrosystem** and **chronosystem** – all refer to the broader contexts in which development takes place. The exosystem refers to the variety of influences like the mass media, the neighbours, and family friends. In the case of atypical development, the extent to which there are positive models of disability on the television – say, cerebral palsy or a stutterer – may influence the family experiences of living with a child who has, for example, cerebral palsy or who is a stutterer.

At the next level, the macrosystem refers to the cultural level of influence. For example, the rise of deaf culture, giving recognition to the rights of people who use sign language and/or lip reading has been particularly active in North America. Finally the chronosystem refers to the sociocultural events over the life course – for example, changes to legislation which impact on the quality of life for individuals living at a particular time-point relative to how they were say 10 or 20 years ago.

One strength of Bronfenbrenner's model is that it anchors human development – be it atypical or typical – in the real world. The model potentially provides a convenient handle from which to start to conceptualise the various levels of influence on atypical development. Arguably, because the study of atypical development is still a relatively young field, researchers are still largely working to characterise the patterns of child development at the level of the microsystem. In any case, one criticism of Bronfenbrenner's work is its testability (Ceci, 2006), as the systems approach does not readily lend itself to testing. In future, it may make sense to adopt the framework in a systematic way, though while developmental scientists worldwide are grappling with describing characteristics of different disorders – the focus has predominantly been on the individual child. But there are exceptions, as we have seen (e.g. the impact of culture on development of children with Williams syndrome).

SUMMARY AND CONCLUSIONS

This chapter presented topical issues in the contemporary study of atypical development and children at risk. First, it was pointed out that there were advantages to situating the study of atypical development alongside typical development.

However, whilst there have been some exceptions, the study of atypical development remains somewhat partitioned from the study of typical development. The start of the chapter conceptualised atypical development in terms of focusing on the individual child, looking at the extent to which development was different or delayed, and the methods used to achieve this. As current directions in the field of atypical development are being directly shaped by the available tools and advances in science, the impact of genetic testing, eye-tracking and neuroimaging were reviewed. Related to genetic testing, the ethical issues involved in screening for Down's syndrome were raised.

Throughout the chapter, a variety of examples were used to illustrate points – the case of the premature infant and HIV-infected child. To gain further insight into developmental pathways involved in atypical development, three populations of atypically developing children were also considered: autistic spectrum disorder, William's syndrome, and ADHD. In each case, key characteristics (e.g. incidence, features) of each condition were outlined before presenting some of the latest research and debate relating to the underlying genetic, cognitive, or brain deficits. The chapter then moved away from these groups to offer insights into the impact of one or more senses on particular developmental pathways. The last part of the chapter took the emphasis away from the individual child, using the framework of Bronfenbrenner (e.g. 1979) to illustrate that child development does not occur within a vacuum. The case of emotional disturbance was central, featuring adverse environments which led to suboptimal developmental outcomes.

There is a need to continue to recognise the diversity of human development, with variation visible in core domains of cognition, language, communication, social development, and motor skills. However, the opportunities provided by the design and delivery of effective intervention, with appropriate resourcing will enable more children to achieve a better quality of life.

DISCUSSION POINTS

1. Consider the distinction between delayed development and development that is qualitatively different. Is the latter really just a pattern of delay in specific aspects of development?

2. When investigating atypical development, why is it often considered important to include two control groups matched for chronological age and mental age respectively?

3. Consider how advances in brain scanning and eye-tracking techniques have advanced our understanding of atypical development.

4. Consider different explanations of autism, and reach an evidence-based conclusion regarding which account you find most convincing.

5. Think about the sensory worlds of blind children and deaf children, considering the impact of absence of auditory or visual information on development of social interaction.

SUGGESTIONS FOR FURTHER READING

Herbert, M. (2007). *Typical and atypical development: From conception to adolescence* (2nd edn). Oxford: Wiley-Blackwell.

Hulme, C.J., & Snowling, M.J. (2008). *Developmental Disorders Of Language Learning And Cognition*. Oxford: Wiley-Blackwell.

Lewis, V. (2002). *Development and disability* (2nd edn). Oxford: Wiley-Blackwell.

McGregor, E., Nuñez, M., Cebula, K., & Gómez, J.C. (2008). *Autism: An integrated view from neuro-cognitive, clinical, and intervention research*. Oxford: Wiley-Blackwell.

Webster, A., & Roe, J. (1998) *Children with visual impairment: Social interaction, language and learning*. London: Routledge.

REFERENCES

Achenback, T.M. (1990). What is 'developmental' about developmental psychopathology? In J. Rolf, A.S. Masten, K. Nuechterlain, & S. Weintraub (Eds.) *Risk and protective factors in the development of psychopathology* (pp. 29–48). New York: Cambridge University Press.

Allen, G., & Courchesne, E. (1993). Differential effects of developmental cerebellar abnormality on cognitive and motor functions in the cerebellum: An fMRI study of autism. *American Journal of Psychiatry, 160*(2), 262–273.

American Psychiatric Association. (1994). *Diagnostic and statistical manual of mental disorders* (4th edn) (DSM-IV-TR). Washington, DC: American Psychiatric Association.

American Psychiatric Association. (2000). *Diagnostic and statistical manual of mental disorders* (4th edn, text rev.) (DSM-IV). Washington, DC: American Psychiatric Association.

Ames, E.W. (1990). Spitz revisited: A trip to Romanian 'orphanages'. *Canadian Psychological Association Developmental Psychology Section Newsletter, 9*, 8–11.

Bakeman, R., & Adamson, L. B. (1984). Coordinating attention to people and objects in mother–infant and peer–infant interaction. *Child Development, 55*, 1278–1289.

Baker, S., Murray, K., & Hood, B. (2009, October). *Entrenched folk physical beliefs held by typically developing children and children with autism*. Poster presented at the Cognitive Development Society Biennial Meeting, San Antonio, USA.

Balic, M.G., Mateos, E.C., & Blasco, C.G. (2000). Physical fitness levels of physically active and sedentary adults with Down syndrome. *Adapted Physical Activity Quarterly, 17*, 310–321.

Barkley, R.A., (1997). Behavioral inhibition, sustained attention, and executive functions: Constructing a unifying theory of ADHD. *Psychological Bulletin, 121*, 65–94.

Baron-Cohen, S. (2008). *Autism and Asperger syndrome*. Oxford: Oxford University Press.

Bawden, A. (2008). Survey reveals gaps in care for deafblind children. *The Guardian*, 24 June.

BBC. (2001). Who owns the map of the human body? Retrieved 25 September 2010, from news.bbc.co.uk/1/hi/events/newsnight/1173801.stm

Beckett, C., *et al.* (2006). Do the effects of early severe deprivation on cognition persist into early adolescence? Findings from the English and Romanian Adoptees study. *Child Development, 77*, 696–711.

Belmonte, M.K. *et al.* (2008). Offering how to put heads together in autism: Neuroimaging. *Journal of Autism and Developmental Disorders, 38*, 2–13.

Bertrand, J., Mervis, C.B., & Eisenberg, J.D. (1997). Drawing by children with Williams syndrome: A developmental perspective. *Developmental Neuropsychology, 13*, 41–67.

Bloom, P., & German, T.P. (2000). Two reasons to abandon the false belief task as a test of theory of mind. *Cognition, 77*(1), 25–31.

Braet, C., & van Aken, M.A.G. (2006). Developmental psychopathology: Substantive, methodological and policy issues. *International Journal of Behavioral Development, 30*(1), 2–4.

Bronfenbrenner, U. (1986). Ecology of the family as a context for human development: Research perspective. *Developmental Psychology, 22*, 723–742.

Bronfenbrenner, U. (2004). *Making human beings human*. Thousand Oaks, CA; Sage.

Bronfenbrenner, U., & Morris, P.A., (2006). The ecology of developmental processes. In W. Damon & R. Lerner, (Eds.) *Handbook of child psychology* (6th edn; pp. 793–825). New York: Wiley.

Buckley, S. (2007). Increasing opportunities for physical activity. *Down Syndrome Research and Practice, 12*(1), 18–19.

Castellanos, F.X., Sonuga-Barke, E.J.S., Milham, M.P., & Tannock, R. (2006). Characterizing cognition in ADHD: Beyond executive dysfunction. *Trends in Cognitive Sciences, 10*(3), 117–123.

Castle, J., Groothues, C., Bredenkamp, D., Beckett, C., O'Connor, T., & Rutter, M. (1999). Effects of qualities of early institutional care on cognitive attainment. *American Journal of Orthopsychiatry, 69*(4), 424–437.

Ceci, S.J. (2006). Urie Bronfenbrenner (1917–2005). *American Psychologist, 61*(2), 173–174.

Cicchetti, D. (1984). The emergence of developmental psychopathology. *Child Development, 55*, 1–7.

Commoner, B. (2009). Molecular genetics: An example of faulty communication between science and the public. *Organization and Environment, 22*(1), 19–33.

Curran, S., Powell, J., Neale, B.M., Dworzynski, K., Li, T., Murphy, D., *et al.* (2006). An association analysis of candidate genes on chromosome 15 q11–13 and autism spectrum disorder. *Molecular Psychiatry, 11*(8), 709–713.

Dekker, R. (1993). Visually impaired children and haptic intelligence test scores: Intelligence test for visually impaired children (ITVIC). *Developmental Medicine and Child Neurology, 35*(6):478–489.

Döring, M. (2005), A sequence of 'factishes': the media-metaphorical knowledge dynamics structuring the German press coverage of the human genome. *New Genetics & Society, 24*, 317–336.

Dunlea, A. (1989). *Vision and the emergence of meaning*. Cambridge: Cambridge University Press.

Fan, H.C., Blumenfeld, Y.J., Chitkara, U., Hudgins, L., & Quake, S.R., (2008). Noninvasive diagnosis of fetal aneuploidy by shotgun sequencing DNA from maternal blood. *Proceedings of the National Academy of Sciences USA, 105*(42), 16266–16271.

Fiehler, K., Reuschel, J., & Rösler, F., (2009). Early nonvisual experience influences proprioceptive spatial discrimination acuity in adulthood. *Neuropsychologia, 47*, 897–906.

Fraiberg, S. (1977). *Insights from the blind*. New York: Basic Books.

Frith, U. (1989). *Explaining the enigma*. Oxford: Basil Blackwell.

Frith, U., & Happé, F. 1994). Autism: beyond 'theory of mind'. *Cognition, 50*(1–3), 115–132.

Gayraud, F., & Kern, S. (2007). Influence of preterm birth on early lexical and grammatical acquisition. *First Language, 27*, 329–346.

Gilbert, S.J., Bird, G., Brindley, R., Frith, C.D., & Burgess, P.W. (2008). Atypical recruitment of medial prefrontal cortex in autism spectrum disorders: An fMRI study of two executive function tasks. *Neuropsychologia, 46*, 2281–2291.

Happé, F., & Frith, U. (1996). The neuropsychology of autism. *Brain, 119*, 1377–1400.

Happé, F., & Frith, U. (2006). The weak coherence account: Detail-focused cognitive style in autism spectrum disorders. Journal of Autism & Developmental Disorders, 36, 5–25.

Hill, E.L. (2004). Evaluating the theory of executive dysfunction of autism. *Developmental Review*, *24*, 189–233.

Hughes, C., & Leekham, S. (2004). What are the links between theory of mind and social relations? Review, reflections and new directions for studies of typical and atypical development. *Social Development*, *13*(4), 590–619.

Jansson-Verkasalo, E. *et al.* (2010). Atypical perceptual narrowing in prematurely born infants is associated with comprised language acquisition at 2 years of age. BMC Neuroscience, 11:88.

Kasari, C., Guslrud, A.C., Wong, C., Kwon, S., & Locke, J. (2010). Randomized controlled caregiver mediated joint engagement intervention for toddlers for autism. *Journal of Autism and Developmental Disorders*, *40*(9), 1045–1056.

Koekkoek, S., de Sonneville, L.M.J., Wolfs, T.F.W., & Licht, R., (2008). Neurocognitive function profile in HIV-infected school-age children. *European Journal of Paediatric Neurology*, *12*, 290–297.

Kofler, M.J., Rapport, M.D., & Alderson, R.M. (2008). Quantifying ADHD classroom inattentiveness, its moderators, and variability: A meta-analytic review. *Journal of Child Psychology and Psychiatry*, *49*, 59–69.

Korenberg, J., Chen, X.-N., Hirota, H., Lai, Z., Bellugi, U., Burian, D., *et al.* (2000). Genome structure and cognitive map of Williams syndrome. *Journal of Cognitive Neurosciences*, *12*, 89–107.

Kurahashi, H., Inagaki, H., Kato, T., Hosoba, E., Kogo, H., Ohye, T., Tsutsumi, M., Bolor, H., Tong, M., & Emanuel, B.S. (2009). Impaired DNA replication prompts deletions within palindromic sequences, but does not induce translocations in human cells. *Human Molecular Genetics*, *18*, 3397–3406.

Liotti, M., Pliszka, S.R., Higgins, K., Perez III, R., & Semrud-Clikeman, M., (2010). Evidence for specificity of ERP abnormalities during response inhibition in ADHD children: A Comparison with reading disorder children without ADHD. *Brain and Cognition*, *72*, 228–237.

Loth, E. (2008). Abormalities in 'cultural knowledge' in autism spectrum disorders: A link between behaviour and cognition? In E. McGregor, M. Nuñez, K. Cebula, & J.C. Gómez (Eds.) *Autism: An integrated view from neurocognitive, clinical, and intervention research*. Oxford: Blackwell.

Lloyd, M., Burghardt, A., Ulrich, D.A., & Angulo-Barroso, R. (2010). Physical activity and walking onset in infants with Down syndrome. *Adapted Physical Activity Quarterly*, *27*, 1–16.

Marshall, P.J., & Kenney, J., (2009). Biological perspectives on the effects of early psychosocial experience. *Developmental Review*, *29*, 96–119.

Martens, M.A. Wilson, S.J., & Reutens, D.C., (2008). Research review: Williams syndrome: a critical review of the cognitive, behavioural, and neuroanatomical phenotype. *The Journal of Child Psychology and Psychiatry*, *49*(6), 576–608.

Meltzer, H., Vostanis, P., Goodman, R., & Ford, T. (2007). Children's perceptions of neighbourhood trustworthiness and safety and their mental health. *Journal of Child Psychology and Psychiatry*, *48*(12), 1208–1213.

Mervis, C.B. (2003). Williams Syndrome: 15 years of psychological research. Developmental *Neuropsychology*, *23*(1&2), 1–12.

Mervis, C.B., & John, A.E. (2010). Cognitive and behavioral characteristics of children with Williams syndrome: Implications for intervention approaches. *American Journal of Medical Genetics Part C: Seminars in Medical Genetics*, *154C*(2), 229–248.

Mervis, C.B., Morris, C.A., Bertrand, J., & Robinson, B.F. (1999). Williams syndrome: Findings from an integrated program of research. In H. Tager-Flusberg (Ed.) *Neurodevelopmental disorders* (pp. 65–110). Cambridge, MA: MIT Press.

Munger, K.M., Gill, C.J, Ormond, K.E., & Kirschner, K.L. (2007). The next exclusion debate: Assessing technology, ethics, and intellectual disability after the human genome project. *Mental Retardation and Developmental Disabilities Research Reviews*, *13*, 121–128.

Murphy, C.M., & Messer, D.J., (1977). Mothers, infants and pointing: A study of a gesture. In H.R. Schaffer (Ed.) *Studies in mother-infant interaction* (pp. 325–354). London: Academic Press.

National Institute on Deafness and Other Communication Disorders. (1995). *Your child's hearing development checklist* (updated June 2010). Retrieved 25 September, from www.nidcd.nih.gov/health/hearing/silence.htm

Nerlich, B., & Hellsten, I., (2004). Genomics: Shifts in metaphorical landscapes between 2000 and 2003. *New Genetics and Society*, 23(3), 255–268.

Norbury, C.F., Brock, J., Cragg, L., Einav, S., Griffiths, H., & Nation, K. (2009). Eye-movement patterns are associated with communicative competence in autistic spectrum disorders. *Child Psychology and Psychiatry*, 50(7), 834–842.

Norgate, S.H. (2009). *How do sighted caregivers direct the attention of congenitally blind infants towards objects*. Paper presented at Joint Attention: Developments in Developmental and Comparative Psychology, Philosophy Of Mind, and Social Neuroscience, Bentley University, Boston, MA, USA.

Norgate, S.H., Collis, G.M., & Lewis, V., (1998). The developmental role of rhymes and routines for congenitally blind children, *Cahiers de Psychologie Cognitive/Current Psychology of Cognition*, 17(2), 451–479.

Pellicano, E., Maybery, M., & Durkin, K., (2005). Central coherence in typically developing pre-schoolers: Does it cohere and does it relate to mindreading and executive control? *Journal of Child Psychology and Psychiatry*, 46(5), 533–547.

Pérez-Pereira, M., & Castro, J. (1992). Pragmatic functions of blind and sighted children's language: A twin case study. *First Language*, 12, 17–37.

Peterson, C.C., Garnett, M., Kelly, A., & Attwood, T., (2009). Everyday social and conversation applications of theory-of-mind understanding by children with autism-spectrum disorders or typical development. *European Child Adolescent Psychiatry*, 18, 105–115.

Pinker, S. (1999). *Word and rules*. London: Weidenfield and Nicolson.

Preisler, G. (1991). Early patterns of interaction between blind infants and their sighted mothers. *Child: Care, Health and Development*, 17, 65–90.

Roberts, T.P.L., Khan, S.Y., Rey, M., Monroe, J.F., Cannon, K., Blaskey, L., *et al.* (2010). MEG detection of delayed auditory evoked responses in autism spectrum disorders: towards an imaging biomarker for autism. Autism Research, Vol. 3(1), 8–18.

Reich, D. (1990). Children of the nightmare. *Adoption and Fostering*, 14, 9–14.

Rutter, M., *et al.* (2007). Early adolescent outcomes for institutionally-deprived and non-deprived adoptees. I: Disinhibited attachment. *Journal of Child Psychology and Psychiatry*, 48(1), 17–30.

Semel, E., Wiig, E., & Secord, W. (2000). *Clinical evaluation of language fundamentals* (3rd UK edn). London: Harcourt.

Skotko, B.G. (2009). With new prenatal testing, will babies with Down syndrome slowly disappear? *Archives Disease of Childhood*, 94, 823–826.

Sonuga-Barke, E.J.S. (2003). The dual pathway model of AD/HD: An elaboration of neuro-developmental characteristics. *Neuroscience and BioBehavioral Review*, 27, 593–604.

Sonuga-Barke, E.J.S. (2005). Causal models of ADHD: from common simple deficits to multiple developmental pathways. Biological Psychiatry, 57, 1231–1238.

Stojanovik, V., (2006). Social interaction deficits and conversational inadequacy in Williams syndrome. *Journal of Neurolinguistics*, 19, 157–173.

Stromme, P., Bjornstad, P.G., & Ramstad, K. (2002). Prevalence estimation of Williams syndrome. *Journal of Child Neurology*, 17, 269–271.

Spronk, M., Jonkman, L.M., & Kemner, B. (2008). Response inhibition and attention processing in 5- to 7-year-old children with and without symptoms of ADHD: An ERP study. *Clinical Neurophysiology*, 119, 2738–2752.

Stern, D.N. (1974). Mother and infant at play: The dyadic interaction involving facial, vocal and gaze behaviours. In M. Lewis & L.A. Rosenblum (Eds.) *The effect of the infant on its caregiver*. New York: Wiley.

Stern, D.N. (1977). *The first relationship: Infant and mother*. Cambridge, MA: Harvard University Press.

Stern, D.N. (1985). *The interpersonal world of the human infant*. New York: Basic Books.

Stuss, D.T., & Knight, R.T. (2002). *Principles of frontal lobe function*. New York: Oxford University Press.

Tasker, S.L., & Schmidt, L.A. (2008). The 'dual usage problem' in the explanations of 'joint attention' and children's socioemotional development: A reconceptualization. *Developmental Review, 28*, 263–288.

Thomas, M.C., Annaz, D., Ansari, D., Scerif, G., Jarrold, C., & Karmiloff-Smith, A. (2009). Using developmental trajectories to understand developmental disorders. *Journal of Speech, Language and Hearing Research, 52*, 336–358.

Urwin, C. (1978a). The development of communication between blind infants and their parents. In A. Lock (Ed.) *Action, gesture and symbol: The emergence of language* (pp. 79–108). New York: Academic Press.

Urwin, C. (1978b). *The development of communication between blind infants and their parents: Some ways into language*. Unpublished PhD dissertation, University of Cambridge, UK.

van Braeckel, K., Butcher, P.R., Geuze, R.H., van Dujin, M.A.J., Bos, A.F., & Bourma, A. (2010). Difference rather than delay in development of elementary visuomotor processes in children born preterm without cerebral palsy: A quasi-longitudinal study. *Neuropsychology, 24*(1), 90–100.

Wakschlag, L.S., Levanthal, B.L., Pine, D.S., Pickett, K.E., & Carter, A.S. (2006). Elucidating early mechanisms of developmental psychopathology: The case of prenatal smoking and disruptive behavior. *Child Development, 77*(4), 893–906.

World Health Organization. (2004). *The importance of caregiver–child interaction for the survival and healthy development of young children*. A review. Geneva: WHO Dept. Of Child and Adolescent Health and Development.

World Health Organization. (2005). *The ICD-10 classification of mental and behavioural disorders: Clinical description and diagnostic guidelines* (8th edn). Geneva: WHO.

Zitzer-Comfort, C., Doyle, T., Masataka, N., Korenburg, J., & Bellugi, U. (2007). Nature and nurture: Williams syndrome across cultures. *Developmental Science, 10*(6), 755–762.

Glossary

A

A not B error An object-searching error that is often made by 8–12-month-olds. Infants making this error will look for an object where they have most often found it (location A) rather than where they last saw it hidden (location B).

absolute coding *See* **relative coding**.

abstraction principle The principle that the number in a set is independent of any qualities of the members in that set, so it doesn't matter if you are counting the number of butterflies or the number of different animals, the counting principles will be the same.

accommodation The cognitive process through which children adapt to new experiences by modifying their preexisting *schemas*. An important process in Piaget's theory. *See also* **assimilation**, **functional invariants** and **visual accommodation**.

adaptation Piaget believed that adaptation is composed of two processes, *assimilation* and *accommodation*, which work together to drive development forward.

Adult Attachment Interview A semi-structured interview in which adults are asked to describe their childhood relationships with mother and father, and to recall times when they were separated from their parents or felt upset or rejected. According to their responses, adults are placed into one of four attachment categories, *autonomous*, *dismissing*, *preoccupied* and *unresolved*.

Adverse Life Events Scale A measure of life stress – composed of 25 possible events occurring in the last year over which children had little or no control (e.g. 'someone in the family died', 'someone in the family was arrested', 'negative change in parents' financial situation'), and is a modification of the Life Events Checklist (LEC), a measure with very good psychometric qualities.

affect Emotional state or feelings. Contrast with behaviour (what one does in a situation) and *cognition* (how one thinks about a situation).

affect attunement Characteristic of the sensitive mother who is attuned to all of her infant's emotions, accepting and sharing in their affective content.

age-cohort design *See* **sequential design**.

alleles Genes for the same characteristic located in the same place on a pair of *chromosomes*.

alphabetic script A writing system in which written symbols (letters) correspond to spoken sounds; generally, individual *phonemes* represent the individual letters of an alphabetic script.

alternative splicing A process used to code for more than one protein in genes - in which chunks of the mRNA transcript are removed and/or rearranged before leaving the nucleus to be translated into protein.

ambiguous figure A figure that can be perceived in two (or more) different ways.

amniocentesis A medical procedure used in prenatal diagnosis of chromosomal abnormalities and fatal infections, in which a small amount of amniotic fluid, which contains foetal tissues, is extracted from the amnion or amniotic sac surrounding a developing foetus, and the foetal DNA is examined for genetic abnormalities..

analogical reasoning Resolving a problem by comparing it to a similar problem that has been solved previously.

animism A characteristic of children's thinking in Piaget's *preoperational stage* in which they tend to attribute life and life-like qualities to inanimate objects, particularly those that move and are active, such as the wind and the clouds, and sometimes toys and other objects.

antisocial behaviour Any behaviour that shows scant concern about other people's feelings and needs. There is little morality associated with this behaviour.

apoptosis Programmed cell death.

appearance–reality distinction An awareness that things are not always what they appear to be. Young children often fail to make this distinction and when shown an object that looks like something else (e.g. a sponge that looks like a rock), they will often give either *phenomenism* answers and report the appearance ('it's a rock'), or *realism* answers and report the reality of the object ('it's a sponge').

asset-focused programmes Programmes that attempt to directly provide higher quality and/or more quantity of assets in children's lives. They may also attempt to increase the presence and ability of individuals who are assets in the lives of children, such as parents and teachers.

assimilation The process through which children incorporate new experiences into their preexisting *schemes* – that is, they *assimilate* the new to their already-existing schemes of thought. An important process in Piaget's theory. *See also* **accommodation** and **functional invariants**.

associative activity An activity in which children interact with one another, performing similar tasks.

attachment behaviour Any behaviour that helps to form or establish an emotional bond between two individuals. Strong attachment bonds are usually formed between an infant and his or her caregiver. Children with *autism* typically display few, and odd, attachment behaviours.

attainment targets Descriptions of the knowledge that children should have acquired as they work their way through the education system.

attention deficit disorder (ADD or ADHD) A disorder that is characterised by an inability to concentrate on one task at a time and a pervasive impulsivity, which often results in severe behavioural problems and *developmental delay*. Hyperactivity commonly accompanies this disorder, hence ADHD.

attribution theory A conglomerate of theories put forward by social psychologists aiming to encapsulate the allegedly systematic way in which individuals try to explain their own and others' behaviour. The theories are based upon the idea that not only do we look for causes in the world around us but we also think we know what causes our behaviour and the behaviour of others, i.e. we attribute motives, etc., to them. The key word is 'think' because attributions are inferences not actualities about our and others' behaviour. The inferences are based upon needs and expectations drawn from prior experiences.

attribution The belief one holds as to why people carry out a particular action or behaviour.

atypical trajectory A sequence of development that departs from the typical sequence.

authoritarian parenting Authoritarian parents are high on demandingness and low on responsiveness. They value obedience as a virtue and favour punitive, forceful means to curb the self-will of their offspring. They do not foster their children's autonomy, but rather try to restrict independent behaviour. In contrast with children raised by authoritative parents, children raised by authoritarian parents are less socially skilled, less self-assured, less curious, more dependent, and more passive. *See also* **authoritative parenting, indulgent parenting**, and **neglectful parenting**.

authoritative parenting Authoritative parents are high on responsiveness and demandingness. They set clear standards of behaviour for their children that take into account the child's developing capabilities and needs. These parents are considered warm and responsive to the needs of their children. Children raised by authoritative parents tend to be more socially competent, self-reliant, self-controlled, more responsible, creative, and intellectually curious than their *peers*. *See also* **authoritarian parenting, indulgent parenting, and neglectful parenting**.

autism A disorder that affects a person's ability to relate to others. Autistic individuals typically have problems with communication, forming attachments with other people *(attachment behaviour)*, and lack a *theory of mind*. Autistic people usually avoid social contact and may seek a monotony of environment and action (resulting in repetitive stereotyped movements) which appear to provide some comfort. These problems are often referred to as *Wing's triad of impairments*. Occasionally, some autistic individuals demonstrate extreme talents *(savant skills)* in certain activities (e.g. the ability to accurately draw a building, or to mentally compute seven-figure prime numbers); however, these talents are uncommon. Autism is a rare condition (approximately 4 per 10,000 live births) that is usually inherited but can result from brain damage.

autism spectrum disorders A spectrum of psychological conditions characterised by widespread abnormalities of social interactions and communication, as well as severely restricted interests and highly repetitive behaviour.

autonomous attachment Adults who give a coherent, well-balanced account of their attachment experiences, showing a clear valuing of close personal relationships.

autonomy Being in complete control of one's life.

autosomal genetic disorders Disorders resulting from a mutation in a gene in one of the non-sex *chromosomes*. Well-known examples are cystic fibrosis (a recessive type) and achondroplasia (dwarfism, a dominant type).

autosomes The 22 pairs of human *chromosomes*, with the exception of the sex chromosomes. *See also* **autosomal genetic disorders**.

axon The tail-like part of a *neuron* which transmits impulses (the actual message) away from the cell body.

B

babbling The first types of controlled vocalisations produced by infants typically between the ages of 4 and 6 months. *See also* **canonical** and **modulated babbling**.

baby biographies Diaries detailing an infant's development, usually kept by the infant's parents or caregiver. Charles Darwin's biography of his eldest son's development is a well-known example.

baseline group *See* **control group**.

basic emotions *See* **emotion**.

basic level categories *See* **categorisation**.

beginning of thought The final substage in Piaget's account of *sensorimotor* development from approximately 18–24 months, when children become able to form enduring mental representations. This capacity is clearly demonstrated in toddlers' ability to engage in deferred imitation.

behaviour genetics The study of how genetic factors influence behaviour and, more generally, differences between individuals.

behaviourism The theoretical view, associated with J.B. Watson and B.F. Skinner, that sees directly observable behaviour as the proper focus of study, and that sees the developing child as a passive respondent to conditioning, reinforcement, and punishment. Emphasises the role of learning (*nurture*) in causing development rather than inherited factors (*nature*).

bias bullying Bullying in which the victim is a member of a particular group, rather than their individual characteristics. This includes bullying related to, for example, gender, race/ethnicity, sexual orientation, faith/religion, disability.

bidirectional processes Children socialise parents just as parents socialise children. For example, the interaction of mothers and their infants is sometimes symbolised as a dance or dialogue in which following actions of the partners are closely coordinated. *See* **transactional processes**.

Big Five Inventory (BFI) Personality outcomes measurement that assesses on extraversion, agreeableness, conscientiousness, emotional stability, and openness to experience.

bottom-up structures A cognitive development process beginning with the 'input' or uptake of information by the child, and building complex systems of knowledge from simpler origins. *See also* **top-down structures**.

Bronfenbrenner's ecological model An influential model that places individual human development into the wider context of interaction with the immediate environment, as well as the larger context.

bully court *See* **school tribunal**.

bullying Term used to define an individual's repeated exposure to negative actions by one or more other people. There are two types of bullying, direct and indirect. *Direct bullying* refers to cases where there are open attacks on the victim that are often physical in nature but also include taunting or verbal abuse. *Indirect bullying* refers to cases where individuals are socially isolated and intentionally excluded from a group. *See also* **provocative victim** and **passive or submissive victim**.

C

canonical The usual, normal, or natural state of things. *Canonical babbling* refers to *babbling* sounds made by the infant around 6–10 months, when vowels and consonants are combined in such a way that they sound like words. However, there is no evidence that infants actually attach meaning to these sound combinations. *See also* **modulated babbling**.

cardinality The numerical principle that states that any set of items with a particular number is equal in quantity to any other set with the same number of items in it. Therefore, a set of four cars and a set of four buttons may look very different, but cardinality states that there is the same number in each set despite obvious visual differences.

castration complex In Freud's *psychoanalytic theory* where the young boy fears castration at the hands of his father. *See* **Oedipus complex**.

catharsis hypothesis The argument that watching aggressive tendencies in others will reduce your own feelings of aggression.

categorical perception Where perceptually discriminable stimuli are treated as belonging to the same category – e.g. domestic cats may be readily discriminable in terms of size, colour, etc., but all are reliably categorised as 'cats'; the sound 'ba' is discriminably different if spoken by many different people, but is reliably recognised as 'ba' and readily distinguished from 'pa'.

categorical self Those aspects of self, e.g. gender and nationality, which define a person. Whilst children place themselves in particular categories, other people also place children in particular categories. The sum of the categories as perceived by the individual comprises the categorical self.

categorisation The grouping together of items that have some characteristic or characteristics in common. There are several levels of categories which include *basic level* or lower level, e.g. cat, monkey, dog, and *superordinate*, e.g. animal.

central coherence hypothesis of autism The view that autism is due to lack of central coherence. This is reflected in the tendency to process information piecemeal rather than to integrate it. Evidence of this processing tendency has been sought from a number of areas of development. One area which particularly lends itself to this analysis is performance on visuospatial tasks.

centration The focusing or centring of attention on one aspect of a situation to the exclusion of others.

cephalocaudal trend Development that proceeds from head to foot along the length of the body – that is, control of the head is first, then the arms and trunk, and finally control of the legs. *See also* **proximodistal trend** and **cranial-caudal**.

cerebral cortex The area of the brain that is associated with complex tasks such as memory, language, and thoughts and the control and integration of movement and the senses.

chemosensory system Encompasses both the gustatory (taste) and olfactory (smell) senses.

childhood amnesia *See* **infantile amnesia**.

childhood income poverty Living in a family whose income falls below a specified level necessary for minimum coverage of basic expenses has been shown to increase the risk of negative child outcomes.

ChildLine in Partnership with Schools (CHIPS) A UK peer support system founded in 1998 which works in schools, youth clubs and other settings with children, and uses their knowledge, skills and experience to tackle problems which include bullying.

chromosomal structural abnormalities An atypical number of chromosomes or a structural abnormality in one or more chromosomes.

chromosomes Strands of DNA (deoxyribonucleic acid) and protein that contain the genes and provide the genetic blueprint for the animal or plant. In humans there are 23 pairs of chromosomes, 22 *autosomes* and one pair of sex chromosomes, the latter often referred to as X and Y genes.

chronological age (CA) A person's actual age, as opposed to their *mental age*.

chronological age matching Involves comparing typical and atypical groups of the same chronological age.

chronosystem In Bronfenbrenner's ecological model, this refers to the sociocultural events over the life course – for example, changes to legislation which impact on the quality of life for individuals living at a particular time-point relative to how they were say 10 or 20 years ago.

circadian rhythm Bodily cycles within the body that occur on a 24-hour cycle, such as patterns of sleeping/waking.

class inclusion The ability to coordinate and reason about parts and wholes simultaneously in recognising relations between classes and subclasses.

classical conditioning A method of learning first investigated by the Russian physiologist Ivan Pavlov in the early part of the 20th century. In this form of conditioning, certain behaviours can be elicited by a neutral (normally unstimulating) stimulus because of its learned association with a more powerful stimulus. In Pavlov's experiments dogs learned to salivate at the sound of a bell. An important form of learning in *behaviourism*. *See also* **operant conditioning**.

clinical method Research method first used by Piaget whereby natural behaviour is observed and then the individual's environment is changed in order to understand better the behaviour of interest.

cluster effect Memory for test items is significantly improved if the items can be grouped together according to some category or principle, e.g. items of furniture; cutlery used to eat with; animals, etc.

cochlea The inner ear, a structure encased in bone that contains the receptors for sound.

cognition Mental activity, such as attention, memory, problem-solving, thinking, intelligence.

cognitive adaptations Children's developing cognitive awareness of the world. As a result of cognitive adaptations they become better able to understand their world.

cognitive-behavioural therapy (CBT) Psychological therapy which aims to help patients change the way they think, feel and behave. CBT is effective in treating a variety of disorders or problems which include mood, eating, anxiety, personality, substance abuse, and psychotic disorders.

cognitive conflict Cognitive conflict arises when there are two or more competing solutions to a situation or problem.

cognitive development The development of behaviours that relate to perception, attention, thinking, remembering, and problem-solving.

cognitive functioning *See* **cognition**.

cohort A group of people who were raised in the same environment or who share certain demographic characteristics, for example a group of people born at approximately the same time.

collaborative learning Any learning that occurs when two or more people work together on a problem.

collectivist societies Those that emphasise the sameness and belongingness of individuals. *See also* **individualist societies**.

colostrum The breast fluid that precedes true milk. It is rich in minerals and antibodies, and it helps populate the newborn's gut with 'good' bacteria.

combinatory thought Before a child can pass a *conservation task*, they must possess combinatory thought, i.e. they must be able to take more than one factor into consideration. For example, when given the conservation of continuous quantity task where water is poured from one beaker to a different-sized beaker, the child must consider both the height and the width of the beakers before making judgements about the volume of water contained within them.

competence The child's underlying ability, which is often not reflected in their *performance* on tasks.

complex emotions *See* **emotion**.

components of phenotypic variance Components of phenotypic variance are those parts of the total trait variance that can be attributed to different sources of individual differences in a phenotype. In quantitative-genetic models, the total phenotypic variance is partitioned, in general terms, into environmental and genetic variance components and an error term.

comprehension In language development, the language children can understand, distinguished from *production*, which is the language they can produce. Comprehension almost always exceeds production.

conceptual shift A large qualitative change in an individual's cognitive processes.

concrete operations stage The third Piagetian stage of development in which reasoning is said to become more logical, systematic, and rational in its application to concrete objects. However, abstract thinking is still not fully developed. The concrete operations stage is characteristic of children between about 7 and 11 years of age. *See also* **conservation** and **reversibility**.

conditional spelling rules Rules which determine that a letter, or a group of letters, represent one sound in one context and another sound in a different context; for example, the final 'e' or the 'split digraph' rule, as it is sometimes known, determines that the vowel sound is usually long if the letter sequence is followed by an 'e' and usually short if it is not followed by an 'e'. ('hope' and 'mate' as opposed to 'hop' and 'mat'). There are usually many exceptions to these conditional rules.

cones and rods *See* **rods** and **cones**.

configural processing Any processing that pays particular attention to the overall configuration of the smaller elements within the object being perceived rather than the individual features or elements. Attention to the individual elements is known as *featural processing*. *See also* **encoding switch hypothesis**.

congenital blindness The condition of being born unable to see or with severe visual impairment.

connectionism A modern theoretical approach that developed from *information processing* accounts in which computers are programmed to simulate the action of the brain and nerve cells (*neurons*). The programs create so-called artificial neural networks. Connectionist models have been applied to many areas of child development, e.g. perception, attention, learning, memory, language, problem-solving, and reasoning.

conservation The recognition that certain properties of objects (such as number, liquid (or continuous quantity), length, mass (or weight), and volume) are not altered by superficial transformations in appearance, such as changes in length or shape. Children become able to conserve in Piaget's *concrete operations stage*. *See also* **conservation tasks**.

conservation tasks Tasks that examine children's ability to understand that physical attributes of objects, such as their mass and weight, do not vary when the object changes shape. An example would be to show a child two identical beakers containing equal volumes of water. The content of one beaker is then poured into a smaller but broader beaker. One beaker's water level is now much higher, but obviously they both contain the same amount of water. A child who understands the fact that the volume has not changed, despite its change in appearance, will tell you both beakers contain the same amount of water, whereas a child who does not have this knowledge will point to one of the beakers thinking that one has the most water.

construction A developmental process in which the child is an active participant in the process through interaction with the environment, rather than a passive receiver of knowledge.

constructivism Piaget's theoretical view that infants are not born with knowledge about the world, but instead gradually construct knowledge and the ability to represent reality mentally.

continuity in social development Some behaviours show a very strong consistency throughout development, for example the tendency for children to be aggressive shows considerable continuity: the child who fights with other children a lot is likely to be the adolescent who is judged by *peers* to be aggressive.

continuity versus discontinuity Whether development is *continuous*, and therefore an accumulation of 'more of the same', or *discontinuous* and marked by qualitative changes. Piaget's theory is an example of a *discontinuous* theory of development.

continuous function – decreasing ability Behaviour that gets worse as we age. For example, young infants can initially distinguish non-native speech sounds very easily; however, for many sounds they lose this ability after their first year of life. *See also* **continuous function – increasing ability, discontinuous (step) function**, and **U-shaped functions**.

continuous function – increasing ability Behaviour that improves with age. For example, during the first year of life the precision with which infants reach for objects increases. *See also* **continuous function – decreasing ability, discontinuous (step) function**, and **U-shaped functions**.

control group In order to evaluate the effectiveness of a particular treatment or manipulation, the control group is that group of individuals in an experiment who do not receive the treatment. Their behaviour is then compared with that of the *experimental group*, which does receive the treatment.

cooperative activity An activity in which children interact together in complementary ways; for example, one child gets blocks out of a box and hands them to another child, who builds a tower.

coordination of secondary schemes The fourth substage in Piaget's period of *sensorimotor* development, from approximately 10–12 months. Infants begin to deliberately combine schemes to achieve specific goals.

core knowledge Basic information about the world, particularly knowledge about the physical properties of objects, available to the very young infant and probably *innate*.

correlation coefficient A statistical measure ranging from +1.00 to −1.00 that indicates the strength, as well as the direction, of the relationship between two variables. A correlation coefficient varies between +1 (high positive correlation) through zero (no relationship) to −1 (high negative correlation).

correlational studies Studies that examine whether two variables vary systematically in relation to each other, e.g. as height increases, will weight reliably increase also?

cranial-caudal The direction of development beginning with the head end and moving toward the opposite end or feet in humans. *See also* **cephalocaudal trend**.

criterion referencing The measure of a child's performance relative to a specified criterion

critical period A limited period, usually early in an animal's life, in which the young have to be exposed to a particular skill or experience in order for it to be learned. *Imprinting* was thought to occur only during a brief critical period, but it is now known that this can be extended and the concept of *sensitive period* is often used instead.

cross-cultural study A study which aims to examine differences that arise purely from culture. An example would be to examine whether there are different developmental milestones in different regions of the world.

cross-sectional design A study where children of one or more ages are observed at a single point in time. *See also* **longitudinal design**.

crystallised intelligence The store of information, skills, and strategies acquired through education and prior experience. Knowing the capital cities of every country is an example of crystallised intelligence. *See also* **fluid intelligence**.

cultural tools Any tools that help us to calculate, produce models, make predictions, and understand the world more fully, e.g. abacuses, slide rules, calculators, and computers.

cumulative risk theory According to this theory, the sum of risk factors rather than any single risk is what leads to dysfunction because it overwhelms the adaptive capacities of the individual. In this framework, therefore, no one risk factor is seen as more important than another.

cyberbullying A type of bullying which uses electronic devices, mainly mobile phones and the internet.

curriculum The set of courses, and their content, offered at a school or university.

D

deceptive box task This task involves showing children a characteristic box that they will have had some experience with before (e.g. a tube or box that usually contains sweets/candies). The child must say what they think is in the box. Usually they will reply 'sweets'. The child is then shown that the box actually contains pencils. The child is then asked, 'What did you originally think was in the box?' Children under the age of 4 will typically say, 'Pencils'. This task is used to determine whether a child possesses a *theory of mind* or not. *See also* **posting version of the deceptive box test**, **state change test**, and **unexpected transfer test**.

deductive reasoning The outcome of a specific example is calculated from a general principle, that is, deductive reasoning involves drawing specific conclusions from general premises. *See also* **inductive reasoning**.

defence mechanisms In Freud's theory, if an individual's rational thought (*ego*) is threatened by their basic desires (*id*) or their conscience (*superego*), then various defence mechanisms are available which mean that, for the short term, the individual does not have to deal with the internal conflict. An example of a defence mechanism is repression, whereby an unpleasant thought or memory is blocked and the individual has no memory of the problem. *See also* **ego**, **id**, and **superego**.

deferred imitation the ability to copy or mimic the actions of others, some time after they have seen these actions, an important learning in humans, and facilitated by *mirror neurons*.

demand characteristics Cues that are perceived as telling participants how they are expected to behave or respond in a research setting, i.e. social factors that 'demand' a certain sort of response. Demand characteristics include the tendency of participants to behave in the way they think the experimenter expects them to behave.

dependent variable The behaviour that is measured or observed in a study. Changes in the behaviour are dependent on, that is, caused by, changes to the *independent variable*.

derivational morphemes Affixes that create new words which are called 'derived' words. 'Health' is a noun which is created by adding the derivational suffix 'th' to the verb 'heal', and 'logical' is an adjective created by adding '–al' to the noun 'logic'. In both these examples the derived and the base words belong to different grammatical classes, but in other instances the derived and the base words have different meanings but are in the same grammatical class as each other. For example, 'un-' is a derivational prefix that creates a derived word with the opposite meaning to the baseword. Thus, 'unhappy' is an adjective derived from another adjective 'happy', and 'unbeliever' is a noun from another noun 'believer', by adding the prefix 'un-' to each base word.

developmental delay A delayed but normal path of development.

developmental difference A qualitatively different path of development.

developmental functions Typical trends in development; for example, we typically get more intelligent as we age. *See* **continuous function – decreasing ability**, **continuous function – increasing ability**, **discontinuous (step) function**, **stage-like changes in development**, and **U-shaped functions**.

developmental programming the hypothesis that prenatal conditions have detrimental effects on health into adulthood.

developmental quotient (DQ) An index of children's development, calculated in the same way as *intelligence quotient (IQ)*. DQ is usually based on perceptual and motor performance rather than on general intellectual development.

Diagnostic and Statistical Manual of Mental Disorders (4th edn) (DSM-IV) A manual published by the American Psychiatric Association in 1994 that gives diagnostic criteria for all currently recognised mental health disorders. The next edition, DSM-V, will be published in 2012.

differential psychology The branch of psychology that deals with individual differences between people.

digital culture online social networking sites for self-presentation and to learn about others, immediate video contact systems to have visual and auditory contact with a friend regardless of where they are, online gaming, and electronic devices such as iPods and iPads, and mobile phones. They have vastly altered the way that teens interact with each other, how they show themselves off to their peers, how they learn about others, and how they establish connections with them.

direct bullying *See* **bullying**.

discontinuous (step) function Development that takes place in a series of stages or steps. Each new stage is qualitatively different from the preceding and following stages. The moral judgement stages described by Piaget and Kohlberg are examples of a discontinuous (step) function. *See* **continuous function – decreasing ability**, **continuous function – increasing ability**, and **U-shaped functions**.

discovery learning Encouraging children to learn by discovering information for themselves. Often teachers will tailor the child's environment in order to maximise this type of learning.

dishabituation *See* **habituation**.

dismissing attachment adults who deny the importance of attachment experiences and insist they cannot recall childhood events and emotions, or provide idealised representations of their attachment relationships that they are unable to corroborate with real life events.

dizygotic (fraternal) twins Individuals who are conceived at the same time but result from two eggs being fertilised by different sperm. Thus, they are like regular siblings and share half of their genes. *See also* **monozygotic twins.**

domain-specific Knowledge that can only be applied to specific situations that fall within the same domain.

dominance Getting one's own way or influencing others in interpersonal encounters.

Down's syndrome (DS) A chromosomal condition caused by the presence of all or part of an extra 21st *chromosome.* Often Down's syndrome is associated with some impairment of cognitive ability and physical growth, and a particular set of facial characteristics.

d-structure (or deep structure) The abstract representation of a sentence, or the actual meaning that the sentence is trying to convey. *See also* **s-structure.**

dynamic assessment This method of assessment is based on the view that it is beneficial to assess the child's potential for proceeding beyond their current level of performance.

dynamic systems theory A theoretical approach applied to many areas of development which views the individual as interacting dynamically in a complex system in which all parts interact. As applied to motor development in infancy, dynamic (or dynamical) systems theory views every new developing ability or skill as being jointly influenced by nervous system development, the movement capabilities of the body, and environmental supports for the task or skill the child wants to accomplish.

E

ecological validity The results obtained from a study are ecologically valid if they are meaningful in the real world.

ectoderm The outermost of the three primary germ layers of an *embryo.* The central nervous system and skin, among other structures, develop from ectoderm.

ego In Freud's theory, the ego can be thought of as the rational thought that evolved to control the urges of the *id* in order to meet the demands of reality and maintain social approval and esteem. *See also* **id, defence mechanisms,** and **superego.**

egocentric An egocentric child is one who finds it difficult to see things from another person's point of view. Not to be confused with egotistical.

egocentrism The difficulty or inability of young children to distinguish between their own perspective and that of others. A major characteristic of children's thinking in the *preoperational stage* in Piaget's theory. Widely investigated under the topic of *theory of mind.*

Eight Stages of Man Eight distinct stages in life which, according to Erikson, are each characterised by a social challenge or conflict. If a stage-related conflict is successfully resolved the individual is ready for the social challenge in the next stage. If the conflict has a negative outcome the challenge may be revisited and resolved at a later stage.

elaboration A memory *mnemonic* that works by making connections between items that have to be remembered. For example, if a child has to remember the pair *fish–fork* in a *paired-associate memory task,* she might imagine eating the fish with a fork. The spontaneous use of this strategy does not appear until adolescence.

electra complex In Freud's *psychoanalytic theory* this is where little girls develop feelings towards their father and fear retribution at the hands of their mother. *See* **Oedipus complex.**

electroencephalogram (EEG) A scalp recording done with electrodes that measure electrical activity produced by neurons. The EEG is often measured when it is time-locked to a stimulus event, producing an *event-related potential (ERP).*

embedded shapes Complete shapes that have been used to form part of a different, larger shape. For example, four triangles can be arranged to form a square. Initially we may just perceive the square, but closer inspection will reveal the triangles also. The Embedded Shapes Test is used to test individuals' visuo-spatial skills.

embryo the developing organism during the period when organs are forming. In humans from first cell divisions until about 10 weeks.

emotion Emotion ranges from simple emotions such as happiness, sadness, fear, and anger, to more complex emotions such as self-consciousness and jealousy.

emotion regulation Adjusting one's emotional state to a suitable level of intensity. This prevents emotional 'overload' and allows one to function in a consistent manner.

emotional ambiguity The realisation that a person's feelings may not be clear-cut or match your own emotional response.

emotive imagery An approach which aims to reduce fear and anxiety and involves associating fearful situations with imagined scenes which conjure up feelings of pride, self-assertion or amusement, so that the fearful situation becomes associated with positive emotions and a relaxed state and, as a result, anxiety will be reduced. *See also* **systematic desensitisation**.

empiricism The belief that psychological abilities are acquired primarily through experience. *See also* **nativism** and **nature–nurture issue**.

encoding switch hypothesis In face perception, this hypothesis argues that different information about faces is represented in memory by children at different ages. It is suggested that young children rely on information about individual features (e.g. eyes, nose, mouth) in recognising faces, whereas older children and adults use information about the configuration of the features, that is, the spatial layout. *See also* **configural processing** and **featural processing**.

encoding The first stage in the memory system. Information that is attended to gets placed (*encoded*) in the memory storage system. Encoded information enters the *short-term memory* store.

environmentalism The hypothesis that people learn to be the way they are, that the person we become is a consequence of the experiences we have had throughout life. *See also* **genetic determinism** and **nature–nurture issue**.

environmentality The extent to which variations within a population are caused by environmental factors. Often expressed as e^2. *See also* **heritability**.

environment–gene correlation *See* **gene–environment correlation**.

epigenetic principle (Erikson) The notion that the 'parts' of an organism develop in a sequential order, each part having its own specific time of ascendancy, until the functioning whole is complete.

epigenetic theory A theory of development concerning changes in phenotype (appearance) resulting from the dynamic interaction between genetic and environmental forces.

episodic memory Memory for specific personally experienced events, including their temporal and spatial contexts. Thus, the episodic memory for 'market' would represent the trips to the market and where you can buy (for instance) the best cheese; remembering your first lecture/class is another example of an episodic memory.

epistemology The study of the origins of knowledge and how we know what we know.

equilibrium In Piagetian theory, a state in which children's *schemes* are in balance and are undisturbed by conflict.

ethnic identity An awareness of which racial, national, linguistic, or religious group one belongs to.

ethological approaches Approaches which emphasise the evolutionary origins of many behaviours that are important for survival, such as *imprinting*.

event-related potential (ERP) Scalp recordings in which brain activity is monitored during the presentation of specific perceptual events.

event sampling An *observational study* which records what happens during particular events. Events studied include playing, bathtime, feeding, and reading.

evolutionary adaptation A process whereby a population becomes better suited to its habitat.

executive functioning The process whereby behaviour is directed and controlled in order that the desired goal will be achieved.

executive function hypothesis of autism The view that autism is due to a deficit in executive function. Executive function refers to a collection of skills – namely, inhibiting inappropriate responses, planning, being mentally flexible, and generating novel ideas, and is measured by various conventional tasks.

existential self A sense of personal existence, uniqueness and autonomy which develops through the child's interactions with the social and physical world.

exosystem In Bronfenbrenner's ecological model, this refers to the variety of influences like the mass media, the neighbours and family friends.

experimental group The group of individuals who receive a particular treatment or manipulation. In order to measure the effectiveness of the treatment, their results are compared with those from a *control group* that does not receive the treatment.

experimental methods Experimental methods control an individual's environment in systematic ways in an attempt to identify which variables influence the behaviour of interest.

explicit memory Memory for an experience or event that is easily accessible.

external support systems Support systems in the social environment such as friendships that contribute to resilience in adversity.

externalising behaviour problems Externalising behaviours refer to delinquent activities, aggression, and hyperactivity. Externalising behaviours are directly linked to violent episodes such as punching and kicking, often learned from observing others.

extraversion A personality variable. Someone who scores highly on an extraversion scale will typically be an outgoing and confident person. *See also* **introversion**.

eye-tracking methodology The technology of eye-tracking allows automated recording of eye-movements, and allows precise measures of visual behaviour. Experienced researchers use these methods with infants, although the initial process of calibration requires the infant to gaze at particular points on a screen, something that requires attention-catching stimuli to be sufficiently captivating for the experimenter to have sufficient time to map the position of the infant's eye to various calibrated targets on screen.

F

false belief Incorrectly believing something to be the case when it is not. Often used in *theory of mind* research.

false positive Believing something to be true, when in fact it is false.

familial resemblance The resemblance between relatives whose genetic relationship to each other is known.

featural processing In face perception, this refers to a tendency to process the separate features of the face, as opposed to perceiving the relationship between the parts, or *configural processing*. *See also* **encoding switch hypothesis**.

field theory Lewin's theory that behaviour results from the interaction between a person and that person's environment.

foetus In human *prenatal development*, the organism 12 weeks after conception until birth.

formative testing A form of assessment where the purpose is to provide guidance for further learning, rather than measuring the outcomes of learning.

field theory Lewin's theory that behaviour results from the interaction between a person (their genetic influences) and that person's environment (*nurture*).

fluid intelligence Intellectual ability that cannot be taught easily, general ability to grasp new concepts and to think and reason abstractly. This type of intelligence is said to be culture free because it does not depend upon previous experience. *See* **crystallised intelligence**.

Flynn effect An increase in the average intelligence quotient (IQ) test scores over generations. The effect has been observed in many parts of the world, and is thought to be related to improvements in diet, health and education, and smaller family sizes.

'Folk' theories of development Ideas held about development that are not based upon scientific investigation.

formal operations stage The fourth Piagetian stage in which the individual acquires the capacity for abstract scientific thought. This includes the ability to theorise about impossible events and items. This stage, which appears from around 11 years, sees the beginnings of *hypothetico-deductive reasoning, propositional thought*, and improvements in the capacity for *combinatory thought*.

fraternal twins *See* **dizygotic twins**.

frontal cortex One of the four main lobes of the *cerebral cortex* (the others being parietal, temporal, and occipital), located behind the eyes and forehead. The frontal cortex is involved in emotional experiences and many cognitive abilities, such as problem-solving, planning, and judgement.

functional magnetic resonance imaging (fMRI) An imaging method measuring cortical activity, which works by measuring blood flow, and involves no invasive procedures. Instead it records by means of a strong magnetic field in which the participant is placed, which detects differences in oxygen concentration throughout the brain.

functional invariants Processes that do not change during development, such as *accommodation* and *assimilation* in Piaget's theory. What do change are the cognitive structures (often called *schemes*) that underlie *cognitive development* and allow the child to comprehend the world at progressively higher levels of understanding.

G

g The term used to denote general intelligence. Note that it is always written as g and never G.

gender constancy The awareness, in early childhood, that one is either a boy or a girl, and that this is unchangeable – once a girl (boy), always a girl (boy).

gender development The developing understanding by a child that it is either a girl or a boy and that there are gender-appropriate behaviours associated with this difference.

gender identity The awareness that one is a boy, or a girl.

gene–environment correlation The ways in which children's genetic inheritance affects the environment they experience, and vice versa (also known as *environment–gene correlation*).

gene expression The process by which information from a gene is used in the synthesis of a functional gene product.

genetic diversity The total number of genetic characteristics in the genetic make-up of a species. It is distinguished from genetic variability, which describes the tendency of genetic characteristics to vary.

genetic variant The contribution of different versions of the human genome to individual differences. The best way to understand this concept is to think about faces. Everyone has two eyes, a nose, and a mouth. These features are often minimally different between individuals of similar ethnic backgrounds. However, those subtle differences are what make us unique – what allow us instantly to recognise the faces of people we know, and even to tell identical twins apart!

generalisations *See* **overgeneralisations**.

genetic determinism The hypothesis that people become who they are as a consequence of their genetic code. *See also* **environmentalism, maturation** and **nature–nurture issue**.

genitive A possessive word, for example the apostrophe + 's' in 'the boy's jumper' indicates that the jumper belongs to the boy.

genotype The genetic composition of the individual. *See also* **phenotype**.

gestural babbling *See* **manual babbling**.

guided participation Children's ability to learn from interaction with others. *See also* **scaffolding** and **zone of proximal development**.

gyri The prominent ridges on the outer surface of the brain.

H

habituation The process by which a response to a stimulus gradually declines over time. For example, infants will initially be very interested in an auditory or visual stimulus and will spend a lot of time attending to it; however, over time they will become bored with the stimulus and their attention to it will decrease. Recovery of attention to a novel stimulus is called dishabituation.

Head Start A federally supported programme in the United States with five components: (1) preschool enrichment education; (2) health screening and referral services; (3) nutrition education and hot meals; (4) social services; and (5) parent education and involvement. Research has indicated that children's cognitive and language development is enhanced during the period that they are participating in a Head Start programme. The British equivalent is called Sure Start.

heritability The extent to which variations within a population are genetically determined. Estimates of heritability range between 0 and 1 – values close to 1 indicate a strong genetic contribution. Often expressed as h^2. *See also* **environmentality**.

hermaphrodite An organism or individual with both male and female sexual organs.

heteronomous morality The first of Kolberg's stages of moral reasoning in which children believe that 'right' and 'wrong' are determined by powerful adult figures. Little consideration is given to the intentions or desires of individuals other than the self when making moral judgements. This is followed by the stage if instrumental morality

heuristics Simple strategies for reaching solutions.

hierarchy of needs Stages of needs or desires in Abraham Maslow's *humanistic theory* which go from the basic physiological needs for food and water to the ultimate desire for *self-actualisation* or the desire to fulfil one's potential.

hindsight bias The inclination to see events that have already happened as being more predictable than they were before they took place.

horizontal décalage Refers to the non-synchronous development of children on Piagetian tasks (e.g. cases in which children may succeed on conservation of number tasks but not on conservation of continuous quantity).

hot cognition The inextricable link between emotion (probably strong emotion) and cognition. Feelings influence thoughts and thoughts influence feelings. In particular when emotion is strong, e.g. in relation to aspects of identity, perception is selective, selectively organised and accompanying thoughts are likely to be strongly influenced.

Human Genome Project One of the biggest research projects in the world. The research found that the number of genes was fewer than previously thought and was a strong indicator that there was more to specifying humanity than action of individual genes in isolation.

human rights and social welfare morality Kohlberg's final stage of moral judgement, also called the *social contract orientation stage*. Individuals who have reached this stage make use of ethical principles to guide moral judgements. Moral decisions are made with reference to the rules one would like to see in an ideal, as opposed to the real, world. Therefore, stealing is acceptable if it is the only way to save another person's life.

humanistic theory Theory which assumes that growth in the developing child is influenced by the fulfilment of a set of basic needs that constitute a hierarchy, and that higher needs appear when lower, more compelling ones are satisfied. It is argued that healthy children have satisfied their lower, basic needs (for life, safety, love, and esteem) and are motivated by trends toward self-actualisation.

hunter–gatherer tribe A tribe of people who live in the traditional fashion of hunting and gathering. In such tribes, it is typical that the individual members will live in small communities and they depend upon one another for survival. Typically, the males will leave the home base periodically to hunt wild animals, while the females, children, and infirm stay close to the base and gather various fruits and berries for eating also.

hypothetico-deductive reasoning The ability to develop theories in an attempt to explain certain phenomena, generate hypotheses based on these theories, and systematically devise tests to confirm or refute these hypotheses.

I

id In Freud's theory, a primitive collection of urges with which an individual begins life. The id is responsible for an individual's 'primitive' instincts, such as eating and reproducing. *See also* **defence mechanisms, ego,** and **superego**.

identical twins *See* **monozygotic twins**.

identification A psychological process in which an individual identifies closely with another person, and may attempt to transform themselves to be like the other (usually admired or idolised) person. Derives from Freudian *psychoanalytic theory*. *See also* **personal modelling**.

imaginary companion A companion who does not exist but who can appear very real to children. The companion may follow the child around, or need to be fed at mealtimes, or tucked up in bed with the child. Some one-quarter to one-half of children have some form of imaginary companion, especially between 3 and 8 years (they are mostly abandoned by age 10). *See also* **paracosm**.

imaging methods Methods of recording brain activity.

implicit memory Memory for events that we cannot *consciously* remember.

imprinting A period soon after birth or hatching in which the young of *precocial species* of animals (which includes ducks, geese, sheep, horses) follow the first moving objects they see. Since this is usually the mother, a parent–infant bond is formed and the following response is adaptive (adds to survival value) because it leads to a physical proximity between parent and offspring. The term is also used in Bowlby's theory of attachment to refer to the formation in the early months of the human infant–mother bond.

independent variable A factor or variable in a study or experiment which can be systematically controlled and varied by the experimenter to see if there are changes in the child's response. The behaviour that changes is called the *dependent variable*.

indirect bullying *See* **bullying**.

individualist societies Those in which there is an emphasis on the individualistic and uniqueness of individuals. *See also* **collectivist societies**.

inductive reasoning Creating a general principle or conclusion from specific examples, that is, drawing a general conclusion from specific premises. *See also* **deductive reasoning**.

indulgent parenting Indulgent parents are high on responsiveness, but low on demandingness. They interact with their children in a benign and passive manner and avoid the use of power when dealing with matters of discipline. They make few maturity demands on the children's behaviour and allow them a high degree of autonomy. Children from indulgent homes are less mature, less responsible, more easily influenced by their peers, and less able to take on leadership roles. *See also* **authoritarian parenting, authoritative parenting,** and **neglectful parenting**.

inflectional morphemes affixes whose presence, and also whose absence, provide essential information about words. In English the presence of the suffix 's' at the end of a noun tells you that the noun is in the plural and its absence tells you that it is in the singular e.g. 'dog' (singular) 'dogs' (plural). In English there are inflections for nouns, verbs (e.g. the past tense ending '-ed') and adjectives (the comparative '-er' and the superlative '-est'). Many languages are much more inflected than English. For example, in Greek there are different inflections for singular and plural adjectives which is not the case in English.

intuitive scientists The idea that we are all capable of constructing commonsense theories to explain how the world works, and are able to conduct 'experiments' to test them.

intuitive substage The second part of Piaget's *preoperational stage* of thinking, from approximately 4 to 7 years. Children begin to classify, order, and quantify in a more systematic manner. Piaget called this sub-stage intuitive because although children can carry out such mental operations they remain largely unaware of the underlying principles and what they know. *See also* **symbolic function substage**.

infant-directed speech The speech that adults and children over 4 years old use when addressing an infant. When compared to speech directed to adults, infant-directed speech has shorter sentences, a higher pitch, more exaggerated pitch contours, a larger pitch range, and is more rhythmic in nature. It is thought that this type of speech helps infants to segment the speech stream into individual words. Also known as motherese.

infantile amnesia Inability to remember events during early childhood (first 3 years). Also called *childhood amnesia*.

inferiority complex A feeling of self-worthlessness, and that one is inferior to others in some way(s). Such feelings can arise from an actual or an imagined inferiority in the afflicted person.

information processing The view that cognitive processes are explained in terms of inputs and outputs and that the human mind is a system through which information flows, i.e. information is received and processed by the brain, which then determines how that information will be used. Information processing is a term borrowed from computer programming.

inhibitory control The ability to overcome a prepotent motor response.

innate mechanism A mechanism or ability that does not need to be learned, something we are born knowing.

insecure-avoidant A particular type of attachment behaviour exhibited in the strange situation measure. Insecure-avoidant infants appear indifferent toward their caregiver, and treat the stranger and caregiver in very similar ways. They show very little, if any, distress at being left with the stranger. *See also* **insecure-resistant** and **securely attached**.

insecure-resistant A particular type of attachment behaviour exhibited in the strange situation measure. Insecure-resistant infants are over-involved with the caregiver, showing attachment behaviour even during the pre-separation episodes, with little exploration or interest in the environment. These infants become very distressed upon separation, but the over-activation of their attachment systems hampers their ability to be comforted by the caregiver upon reunion. *See also* **insecure-avoidant** and **securely attached**.

instinct (1) Behaviour that is genetic in its origin, e.g. human sexual desire; (2) a feeling or emotion that has no basis in fact, e.g. 'My instinct tells me he's not to be trusted'.

instrumental morality The second of Kohlberg's moral judgement stages. In this stage individuals (usually children) become aware that other people have intentions and desires, and that there are two sides to every argument. Moral decisions are made by referring to the side that provides the greatest benefit. Therefore, if someone is very helpful to you, it is acceptable to steal in order to save that person's life.

intelligence quotient (IQ) An IQ score gives an indication of an individual's intelligence compared with other individuals of the same chronological age. Originally, IQ was calculated in children by dividing a child's mental age by his or her chronological age and multiplying by 100, although a slightly different calculation is now used. Intelligence test scores stabilise in adolescence and a different calculation is used for older children and adults. A score of 100 denotes a person as having average intelligence for his or her age.

intelligence test Any test that aims to measure an individual's intellectual ability. These tests have traditionally concentrated on intelligence quotient (IQ), but modern tests now examine both crystallised and fluid intelligence.

intergenerational cycle of difficulties The various implicit and explicit non-verbal and verbal ways parents communicate their traumatic experiences and their experiences of shared events traumatically.

intermental plane Concerning knowledge that is possessed between people (also known as the interpsychological plane). *See also* **intramental plane**.

internal working model (IWM) Develops through day-to-day interactions with the primary caregiver(s) early in life. It comprises the child's picture of self, others and relationships (self in relation to others) and has both an affective (emotional) component and a cognitive component (mental representation). According to Bowlby, the IWM determines the child's continuing view of self, other and relationships between self and others.

internalising behaviour problems Withdrawal, inhibition, anxiety, and/or depression.

International Classification of Disease (ICD-10) A coding of diseases and signs, symptoms, abnormal findings, complaints, social circumstances and external causes of injury or diseases, as classified by the World Health Organisation (WHO).

interpersonal normative morality This third stage of Kohlberg's moral judgement stages is sometimes referred to as the 'good boy/good girl orientation'. Individuals in this stage seek to be viewed as 'good' and feel guilt when it is likely that others will condemn their behaviour. Therefore, an action is acceptable if it can be said that someone's heart was in the right place, even if that person breaks rules. For example, stealing to save your wife's life is acceptable as long as you want to be a good husband.

interpropositional thinking Characterisitic of the abstract thought of the adolescent in Piaget's *formal operations stage* where the individual is able to relate one or more parts of a proposition to another part to arrive at a solution to a problem. The propositions are symbolic, and hence, abstract.

intersubjectivity Taking account of other people's intentions, thoughts, emotions, and feelings in deciding what to do. When this involves shared attention with both objects and another person(s), it is termed secondary intersubjectivity.

intervention group *See* **experimental group**.

intonation The rhythmic pattern of speech. For example, the meaning of a sentence is changed when the ending has a raised pitch, e.g. 'He didn't come' versus 'He didn't come?'

intramental plane Concerning knowledge that has been internalised and is possessed by the individual (also known as the intrapsychological plane). *See also* **intermental plane**.

intrapropositional thinking Characterisitic of the thought of the child in Piaget's *concrete operations stage* of development, which includes concrete content rather than abstract symbols.

intrasyllabic units Units of speech that are smaller than syllables but larger than phonemes. Onset and rime are two examples of intrasyllabic units.

introspectionism An approach to psychology common in the nineteenth century in which observers were asked to reflect on their thoughts, feelings, and perceptions.

introversion A personality variable. Someone who scores highly on an introversion scale will typically be very quiet and reserved. *See also* **extraversion**.

intuitive psychology The awareness some people have regarding others' desires, motives, and beliefs; they appear able to anticipate others' reactions and behaviour.

intuitive scientists The idea that we are all capable of constructing commonsense theories to explain how the world works, and are able to conduct 'experiments' to test them.

invariance, principle of As used in connection with conservation, the principle that quantities remain unchanged if nothing is added or subtracted.

IQ test *See* **intelligence test**.

J

joint attention An activity in which two individuals attend to the same object or event.

K

key stages Stages of the state education system in England, Wales and Northern Island: KS1 5–7-year-olds; KS2 7–11 years; KS3 11–14 years; KS4 14–16 years; KS5 16–18 years.

Kidscape A UK-based charity which was established in 1985, whose focus is on children's safety, with an emphasis on the prevention of harm and child protection issues, and identified with the effort to reduce or quell bullying.

L

last-number-counted principle The principle that the last number counted represents the value for that set.

law of effect Law or rule devised by the American psychologist Edward Lee Thorndike which states that the likelihood of an action being repeated is increased if it leads to a pleasant outcome, and decreased if it leads to an unpleasant outcome.

letter–sound associations Where one letter represents one sound or phoneme.

lexical development The development of vocabulary.

lexical skills The understanding of what constitutes acceptable speech and language, including understanding words and grammar.

libidinal forces Sexual desires. Freud thought these were under the control of the *id*.

life space Lewin argues that a person's environment can be divided into regions that are separated by more or less permeable boundaries that correspond to the individual's characteristics, needs, and perceptions of the environment. The person and the environment represent inseparable constructs, which together constitute the life space.

Life in Schools questionnaire A 40-item anonymous questionnaire filled in by school children which is used to gauge the extent of bullying, other types of aggressive behaviour and friendly behaviour in a class or school at a particular point of time.

locus of control People who develop an internal locus of control believe that they are responsible for their own failures and successes. Those with an external locus of control believe that external forces, such as luck or fate, determine their outcomes.

longitudinal design A study where more than one observation of the same group of children is made at different points in their development. *See also* **cross-sectional design**.

long-term memory Items stored in the long-term memory have passed through the *short-term memory* and are now stored for an extended period of time.

M

macrosystem In Bronfenbrenner's ecological model, this refers to the cultural level of influence.

magnetoencephalography (MEG) A neuroimaging technique with the capacity for tremendous potential in research with clinical populations. MEG measures the magnetic fields generated around the head.

main effects models Models of resilience in which single factors are identified as determining whether a given child exposed to a risk has a good or a poor outcome.

manual babbling The manual equivalent of vocal *babbling* which is found in deaf children and hearing children learning to sign. The presence of manual babbling has led to the proposition that a manual communication system may have evolved before our vocal-based system.

marker task A method designed to elicit a behaviour with a known neural basis. Often the neural basis is discovered through experiments with animals, for which experiments on brain function present fewer ethical hurdles than experiments with humans. For example, much is known about the neural basis of visual function from experiments with monkeys.

maternal deprivation A term to describe the deprivation infants experience as a result of long-term separation from their mother, or from being orphaned.

Material me According to William James, one of three constituents of self as a subject of experience (*existential self*). There is self-awareness of the body, clothes, close family, home and material possessions. The other two constituents of existential self are Social me and Spiritual me.

maturation Aspects of development that are largely under genetic control, and hence largely uninfluenced by environmental factors. Not to be confused with maturing, which means development into the mature or adult state, however caused.

mechanistic world view The idea that a person can be represented as being like a machine (such as a computer), which is inherently passive until stimulated by the environment. This viewpoint argues that a child's development is controlled only through environmental input and is little influenced by genetics. Behaviourism is an example of this world view. *See also* **organismic world view**.

medial temporal (MT) area A specific area of the visual system. The development of this area and its connections with other parts of the visual system is responsible for the onset of smooth pursuit in humans. Damage to monkey MT causes deficits in motion tracking.

mediator effects models Models that explore the role of intervening or intermediate variables on the effects of risks.

meiotic cell division The type of cell division that occurs in sexually reproducing organisms which halves the number of *chromosomes* in reproductive cells (sperm and ova), leading to the production of *gametes*.

mental age (MA) The level of mental skills that is average for a particular age group. If a child has a developmental delay, then their mental age will be lower than their chronological age, and vice versa for bright children.

mental representation An internal description of aspects of reality that persists in the absence of these aspects of reality.

mesosystem In Bronfenbrenner's ecological model, this refers to the relation between different *microsystems*, for instance, the relation between school and family; peers and religious activity; neighbourhood and health and so on.

meta-analysis An analysis of many studies on the same topic in order to draw general or overall conclusions.

metacognition Knowledge of one's state of mind, reflective access to one's cognitive abilities, thinking about how one is feeling or thinking.

metamemory Understanding one's own memory and having an awareness of the ways in which memory works and can be improved.

Method of Shared Concern A counselling-based approach for resolving bullying, which aims to sensitise bullying children to the harm they are doing to the victim, encourage positive behaviours to the victim, and also encourage *provocative victims* to change their behaviour in positive ways.

microgenetic method A method that examines change as it occurs and involves individual children being tested repeatedly, typically over a short period of time so that the density of observations is high compared with the typical longitudinal study. Thus, the method provides detailed information about an individual, or individuals, over a period of transition.

microsystem In Bronfenbrenner's ecological model, this refers to the individual child, their characteristics (e.g. sex, age, health) and the settings where interpersonal relationships relevant at different points in the lifespan take place.

mind-mindedness Caregivers who are able to 'read' their infant's signals appropriately. Maternal mind-mindedness is a good predictor of attachment security.

mirror neurons A distinctive class of neurons that discharge both when an individual executes a motor act and when they see another individual performing a motor act. Believed to underlie many human abilities such as imitation of manual and vocal gestures.

mnemonic strategy Any strategy that helps to improve one's own memory. Mnemonic strategies include *elaboration*, *organisation*, and *rehearsal*.

moderator (interactive) effects models Models based on interactive relationships between protective/vulnerability factors and risk factor(s)

modularity The view that we have separate modules for different abilities, e.g. face perception, understanding minds (*see* **theory of mind**), numerical abilities.

modulated babbling This is the final period of babbling and language play and appears from around 10 months on. This period is characterised by a variety of sound combinations, stress and intonation patterns, and overlaps with the beginning of meaningful speech. Modulated babbling may play an important role in the acquisition of the intonation patterns that are important for the infant's native language. *See also* **babbling** and **canonical**.

monotropy The view that the infant has a basic need to form an attachment with one significant person, usually the mother. A central claim in Bowlby's early theory of attachment formation.

monozygotic (identical) twins Genetically identical twins, developed from one ovum and one sperm which divides into two shortly after conception. Such twins have the same genetic make-up. *See also* **dizygotic twins**.

mora A rhythmic unit in languages like Japanese and Tamil that can be either a syllable or part of a syllable. In English a mora roughly corresponds to a consonant–vowel syllable with a short vowel, e.g. 'the' as opposed to 'thee', which has a long vowel, or to 'them', which ends with a consonant. 'Thee' and 'them' each consist of two moras.

moral dilemmas Situations in which people must choose and justify a course of action or reasoning with respect to a moral issue. Hypothetical moral dilemmas are often used as research tools to examine the development of moral reasoning.

moral judgement stages Piaget described two stages in the development of moral reasoning, the heteronomous stage and the autonomous stage. Kohlberg described five stages, the earlier of which overlap with Piaget's. The five stages are punishment and obedience orientation, instrumental morality, interpersonal normative morality, social system morality, and human rights and social welfare morality.

moratorium Period in an individual's life when they identify with a string of different values, beliefs, and ideologies because of the lack of a stable and consistent self-image.

morpheme A unit of meaning. The past verb 'cooked' has two morphemes, the stem 'cook' and the /t/ sound at the end, which tells you that it is about a past action. The plural 'dogs' also has two morphemes, 'dog' and 's'.

morpho-phonemic A description of orthographies in which there are regular relationships between letters or groups of letters and morphemes as well as sounds. The representation of the past tense ending as '-ed' is an example of a regular relation between an affix morpheme and a group of letters.

motherese Another name for infant-directed speech.

motor milestones The basic motor skills acquired in infancy and early childhood, such as sitting unaided, standing, crawling, walking.

myelin A fatty insulator which prevents leakage of the messages travelling along the nerves, and increases the speed of neural transmission.

myelination The process by which *myelin* is formed around the *neurons*. Myelination begins in the sixth month of life in the *foetus* but continues through childhood.

N

National Curriculum The curriculum that is followed in all state schools in England, Wales, and Northern Ireland. The government sets the particulars of the subjects covered by the National Curriculum.

nativism The belief that psychological abilities are the product of genetic inheritance – we are simply the product of our genes. According to nativism attributes such as intelligence or personality are inherited, and therefore cannot be changed. *See also* **empiricism, maturation,** and **nature–nurture issue.**

nature–nurture issue Ongoing debate on whether development is the result of an individual's genes (nature) or the kinds of experiences they have throughout their life (nurture). *See also* **empiricism, environmentalism, environmentality, genetic determinism, heritability, nativism.**

negative reinforcement The avoidance of a negative or disliked event (such as going to school) and the avoidance is reinforcing or rewarding. The term 'negative' does not mean unpleasant. *See also* **positive reinforcement.**

neglectful parenting Neglectful parents are low on responsiveness and demandingness. They try to minimise the amount of time and energy required to raise their children. They know little about their children's lives, interact sparingly with them, and do not include them in making decisions that affect the family. Children from neglectful homes are often impulsive and more likely to be involved in delinquent behaviours such as precocious experimentation with sex, alcohol, and drugs. *See also* **authoritarian parenting, authoritative parenting,** and **indulgent parenting.**

neo-cortex In evolutionary terms, the most recently developed area of the *cerebral cortex.*

neonate An infant less than a month old.

neural plate A thickening of endoderm cells that will give rise to the brain.

neural tube A hollow structure in the embryo that gives rise to the brain and spinal column.

neurogenesis The birth of neurons.

neuroimaging The use of various techniques to image the structure, function/pharmacology of the brain.

neurons Nerve cells within the central nervous system which transmit information in the form of electrochemical impulses.

neuropsychological deficits Disorders that originate in the brain and that affect a person's behaviour or *cognitive functioning.*

norm referencing Tests based on the average scores for the population, and hence provide a reference point to indicate how individual children perform relative to the scores of other children.

non-nutritive sucking Infant sucking that does not provide nourishment, as when the baby is sucking on a dummy or pacifier. Gives a different pattern of burst–pause sucking from *nutritive sucking.*

nucleotides The structural units of DNA which act like a genetic 'alphabet' and encode information. Molecules that when joined together make up the structural units of RNA and DNA.

nutritive sucking Infant sucking that provides nourishment, as when the baby is breast or bottle fed. Gives a different pattern of burst–pause sucking from *non-nutritive sucking.*

O

object permanence The ability to understand that even if an object is no longer visible, it continues to exist.

object unity When two parts of an object are visible but its centre is hidden by another object – do infants perceive the visible parts to be connected?

observational learning Situation in which people (especially children) learn by observing others and then copying (imitating) the observed acts. Such learning is often influenced by vicarious reinforcement, which is seeing if others are rewarded for producing the behaviours or acts that are observed. A key concept in *social learning theory.*

observational studies Studies in which behaviour is observed and recorded, and the researcher does not attempt to influence the individual's natural behaviour in any way.

Oedipus complex An important stage of development in Freud's *psychoanalytic theory*. This expression derives from the Greek myth in which Oedipus became infatuated with his mother. In the Freudian account, the young boy develops sexual feelings toward his mother but realises that his father is a major competitor for her (sexual) affections. He then fears castration at the hands of his father (the *castration complex*), and in order to resolve this complex he adopts the ideals of his father and the *superego* (the conscience) develops. For young girls the *Electra complex* is when they develop feelings toward their father and fear retribution at the hands of their mother. They resolve this by empathising with their mother, adopting the ideals she offers, and so the girl's superego develops.

Olweus Bullying Prevention Program A programme which aims to reduce and prevent bullying problems among school children and to promote prosocial behaviour. It was developed in Norway and has been implemented in more than a dozen countries, including the UK and the United States.

Olweus Bully Victim questionnaire A 40-item anonymous questionnaire for school children (ages 8 to 16 years) which assesses whether they have been bullied, or taken part in bullying others.

one-to-one correspondence Two sets are in one-to-one correspondence if each object in one set has a counterpart in the other set. If the objects in two sets are in one-to-one correspondence, they are equal in number.

one-to-one principle The principle that when counting a set of objects, each object must be counted once and once only and that each must be given a unique number tag.

onset The onset of a *syllable* is the consonant, cluster of consonants, or vowel at the beginning of a syllable. The onset of 'hat' is 'h,' and 'st' is the onset of 'stair'. *See also* **rime**.

ontogeny The personal growth of an individual living being from conception. *See also* **phylogeny**.

operant conditioning A form of conditioning investigated by B.F. Skinner. The training, or shaping, of an animal or human by reinforcing them for producing the desired behaviour (or a close approximation to it) and/or either ignoring or punishing undesirable behaviours in order to stop them. An important form of learning in *behaviourism. See also* **classical conditioning**.

order irrelevance principle The principle that it does not matter in which order members of a set are counted: if one person starts at the top and works down, they should get the same result as someone who starts at the bottom and works up.

ordinality The numerical principle that states that numbers come in an ordered scale of magnitude: 2 is more than 1, and 3 is more than 2, and as a logical consequence 3 is more than 1.

organismic world view The idea that people are inherently active and continually interacting with the environment, and therefore helping to shape their own development. Piaget's theory is an example of this world view. *See also* **mechanistic world view**.

organisation A *mnemonic strategy* that reduces the load on memory by organising items into meaningful categories. *See* **cluster effect**.

organogenesis The process of organ formation in very early development. In humans this is from first cell divisions until about 10 weeks.

orthography A writing system. Orthography is used to describe any aspect of print or, more loosely, spelling.

overextension Extending the meaning of a word too broadly, for example using the word 'bird' to refer to birds, aeroplanes, and hot air balloons. *See also* **underextension**.

overgeneralisation Creating a new verb by treating a noun as if it were a verb, for example 'I am ballereening', meaning 'I am dancing like a ballerina'.

overlapping waves A central concept in Siegler's theory of development in which at any one time the child has a number of strategies that can be used to solve problems. Over time less efficient strategies are replaced by more effective ones.

overregularisation The name given when a previously learned rule is applied in the wrong situation. For example, a child learning English might say 'thinked' rather than 'thought' because the child is using the regular past tense rule (attach '-ed' to the end of the verb) rather than the correct exception to the rule ('thought').

P

paired-associate task A memory test in which participants must remember pairs of unrelated items. For example, the participant is told to link the picture of a house with the picture of an elephant. During the testing phase, they are shown the elephant picture, and their task is to link this to the house. *See also* **elaboration**.

paradigm Literally, a pattern or sample, the term is now frequently applied to a theoretical or philosophical framework in any scientific discipline. Often wrongly used to mean a specific research method.

paracosm An imagined, detailed fantasy world invented by a child or perhaps an adult, involving humans and/or animals, or perhaps even fantasy or alien creations. Often having its own geography, history, and language, it is a fantasy that may continue over a long period of time: months or even years.

parallel activity A type of activity where children play near each other with the same materials, but do not interact much.

parenting styles Different ways of child rearing. One of the best known theories of parenting style was developed by Diana Baumrind. She proposed that parents fall into one of four categories: *authoritarian*, *indulgent*, *authoritative*, and *neglectful* parents. Two dimensions (levels of parental responsiveness and parental demandingness) result in these four different parenting styles.

passive or submissive victim Passive or submissive victims are individuals who are not aggressive or teasing in their behaviour, and who are often cautious, sensitive, and quiet. They usually react to bullying by crying or withdrawing from the situation, often do not have any friends, and have a very negative attitude toward violence and the use of violent means. *See also* **bullying** and **provocative victim**.

pedagogy Any aspect of theory or practice related to teaching.

peer Companion of approximately the same age and developmental level.

peer facilitation effects Pairing of two children can have a positive impact on children's later individual performance.

percentile Location of an individual's development or achievement along a percentage scale. For example, if an individual is at the 60th percentile on height, they are taller than 60 per cent of their peers.

perception of causality Perception of the causal nature of interactions between objects and between people. For instance, when one object collides with another it causes it to move. Two parameters are especially important to perceive causality: temporal and physical contiguity. When a billiard ball strikes another and makes it move, contact takes place and, the second ball moves immediately upon contact.

perceptual defence A defence mechanism in which the individual doesn't see, or hear, etc., stimuli or events that are personally threatening, e.g. obscene words are not heard correctly, or violent acts are not seen accurately.

performance limitations Limitations that are associated with the task being asked, rather than a deficiency in competence, so that the child's performance may not reflect their underlying competence.

perinatal The period just before and after birth.

perseveration *See* **response perseveration**.

personal modelling Occurs when the child feels emotionally attached to a person and wants to be like them. This is akin to the concept of *identification* used by the psychoanalytic theorists. *See* **positional modelling**.

personality trait Facet of a person's character that is relatively stable. Examples of personality traits include shyness, *extraversion*, and confidence.

perspective-taking The ability to take someone else's perspective when it differs from one's own. Young children tend to be *egocentric* and often have difficulty in understanding a situation from someone else's point of view.

phallic stage A stage in Freud's *psychoanalytic theory* in which the young boy's interest centres on his penis and he develops feelings of sexual attraction towards his mother. The resulting conflict is resolved by identifying with his father. *See* **Oedipus complex**.

phenomenism Knowledge that is limited to appearances such that, in tasks that involve distinguishing reality from appearance, children report only appearance. *See also* **appearance–reality distinction** and **realism**.

phenotype The apparent, observable, measurable characteristics of the individual. *See also* **genotype**.

phimosis A condition where the male foreskin cannot be fully retracted from the head of the penis, and typically causes problems with urinating. A treatment may be circumcision.

phoneme The smallest unit of speech that affects meaning. It is really a set of sounds that are not physically identical to one another, but which speakers of a language treat as equivalent sounds. So whilst the sound 'ba' will sound very different if spoken by a man and a woman, English speakers will still perceive both instances as examples of the same phoneme.

phonological skills An awareness of sounds at the phonetic level, the ability to detect and manipulate sounds at the phonetic, syllabic and intra-syllabic levels; being able to detect the individual sounds (*phoneme, onset* and *rime, syllable*) in words. Phonology is the aspect of language that is concerned with the perception and production of sounds that are used in language. In order for effective communication to occur, children must learn which sounds are important in the language that they hear.

phylogeny The evolutionary growth and development of a species. *See also* **ontogeny**.

play hierarchy A scheme used for coding children's activities, based on social participation and level of play.

play tutoring Where parents or other adults, such as preschool teacher, model or *scaffold* types of play, such as social *pretend play* that may be limited or absent in the child's spontaneous play.

positional modelling Occurs when the child perceives a similarity between themselves and the role model who may not be personally known to the child. *See* **personal modelling**.

positive reinforcement An action or outcome following a behaviour that makes the behaviour more likely to be repeated.

positron emission tomography (PET) An imaging method measuring cortical activity. PET works by measuring blood flow to tissues in the body, including tissues in the brain; blood flow is localised to regions of high activity. PET requires injection of a short-lived radioactive isotope, however, limiting its use to high-risk populations, and as such it is rarely used with infants and children.

posting version of the deceptive box test A version of the *deceptive box task* where the child posts an illustration of what they think is in a box. *See* **state change test**, **theory of mind**, and **unexpected transfer test**.

postnatal development The development of a human individual after he or she is born, particularly during early infancy.

pragmatic system The cognitive and social skills that enable us to communicate effectively. For example, the abilities involved in *turn-taking*, initiating new topics and conversations, sustaining a dialogue, and repairing a faulty communication are all important aspects of the pragmatic system. *See also* **pragmatics**.

pragmatics Pragmatics refers to the competence of speakers to communicate in socially appropriate ways. Pragmatics also refers to the capacity to use humour and to observe cultural conventions around politeness (e.g. ask appropriate questions).

precocial species Those species of animals where the young are able to locomote almost immediately after birth or hatching. These include ducks, geese, sheep, and horses. The young will often *imprint* on and follow their mother, an instinctive response which has clear survival value for the young. *See also* **critical period**.

prenatal development The development of human individuals before they are born.

preoccupied attachment Adults who are unable to move on from their childhood experiences, and are still over-involved with issues relating to their early attachment relationships.

preoperational stage A stage of development described by Piaget in which children under the age of approximately 7 years are unable to coordinate aspects of problems in order to solve them. Preoperational children fail *conservation tasks* and display *animism* in their thinking.

pretend play 'Make-believe play' in which the child may pretend to be other people or act out real-life situations, e.g. playing 'mummies and daddies,' or may pretend that one object (e.g. a banana) is another (e.g. telephone). Sometimes called *symbolic play*.

preterm Born prematurely. Human infants are regarded as preterm if they are born before 38 weeks of pregnancy.

primary caregiver The individual, usually but not always the mother, who satisfies the baby's biological and psychological needs. *See also* **monotropy**.

primary drives Basic needs which include hunger, thirst, and the need for warmth. Bowlby and others have argued that an infant's need for attachment is also a primary drive.

primary circular reactions The second stage in Piaget's period of sensorimotor development, from approximately 1 to 4 months. Repetitive actions based around the infant's body to exercise and coordinate reflexes that develop in the earlier period.

private speech As children master language they can use internal self-directed speech to guide their thinking and planning.

procedural skills Applying certain routines or procedures in order to solve certain problems and tasks, such as counting the number of objects in a set.

process-orientated programmes programmes that attempt to improve the most important adaptational systems for children such as key relationships, intellectual functioning, and self-regulation systems. Process-orientated programmes can focus on different system levels such as children, families, schools, and neighbourhoods as well as their interactions such as parent–school involvement, children's self-monitoring of school tasks, and student–teacher mentoring relationships.

profound visual impairment (PVI) An inability to see anything more than shades of light and dark. *See also* **severe visual impairment**.

projection A psychological defence mechanism which derives from psychoanalysis in which the individuals see their own traits in others.

projective techniques Personality tests which attempt to identify *personality traits* through the use of sub-jective measures. Examples of these would be asking an individual to write a story, draw a picture, or say what she sees in inkblots. The theory is that the individual expresses aspects of her personality through her writing, drawing, or interpretations.

propositional thought The ability to express relationships in terms of symbolic (and hence abstract) propositions.

prosocial behaviour Any behaviour that is enacted in order to benefit others.

prosody The intonations, stress, and rhythm of speech that are used to communicate meanings, e.g. 'this is correct' becomes a question as opposed to a statement when 'correct?' ends in a raised inflection.

protective factor Anything that prevents or reduces vulnerability for the development of a disorder.

proto-conversations Interactions between adults and infants in which the adults tend to vocalise when the infants are not vocalising, or after the infant has finished vocalising. Proto-conversations may be important precursors to the *turn-taking* observed in early conversations.

proto-declarative Occurs when an infant uses pointing or looking to direct an adult's attention toward an object. *See also* **proto-imperative**.

proto-imperative Occurs when infants point to an object and then alternate their gaze between the object and the adult until they obtain the desired object. *See also* **proto-declarative**.

prototypical face The most typical example of a face. Produced when many different faces are averaged. For example, the distance between the eyes on the prototypical face will be the average distance between the eyes of all the faces used.

provocative victim Provocative victims are individuals who are both anxious and aggressive in their behav-iour. They often have problems concentrating and they behave in ways that causes irritation and tension around them. They can often be characterised as hyperactive and their behaviour often provokes other students, thus resulting in negative reactions from their *peers*. *See also* **bullying** and **passive or submis-sive victim**.

proximodistal trend The development of motor control in infancy which is from the centre of the body out-wards to more peripheral segments – that is, the head, trunk, and pelvic girdle are brought under control before the elbow, wrist, knee, and ankle joints, which leads to finer control over the hands and fingers. *See also* **cephalocaudal trend**.

pseudo-word A nonexistent but pronounceable non-word, such as 'tibudo' or 'wug', often used in psycho-logical experiments. Pseudo-words are used to test for spelling, grammar, or other aspects of understand-ing language where we can be sure that the participants have not heard the 'words' before.

psychoanalysis The theoretical view, first developed by Sigmund Freud, that much of our behaviour is deter-mined by unconscious factors. According to this view, the child goes through *psychosexual stages* of devel-opment – oral, anal, phallic, latency, and genital.

psychoanalytic theory Most prominently associated with Sigmund Freud. Freud suggested that there are three main personality structures. The *id* is present in the newborn infant and consists of hidden impulses, emotions, and desires. It demands instant gratification of all its wishes and needs. As this is impractical, the *ego* develops to act as a practical interface or mediator between reality and the desires of the *id*. The final structure to develop is the *superego*, which is the sense of duty and responsibility – in many ways the conscience. *See also* **psychosexual stages**.

psychological tests Instruments for the quantitative assessment of some psychological attribute or attributes of a person. The developmental psychologist will use such testing to measure such things as motor development, motivation, reading ability, or general intelligence.

psychopathology A psychological imbalance such that the individual has difficulties in functioning in the real world.

psychosexual stages Freud argued that there were five stages of human development. All but the latency stage are centred around the stimulation of an erogenous zone. The stages develop in the following order: oral (0–1 year), anal (1–3 years), phallic (3–6 years), latency (6 years–adolescence), and genital (adolescence onwards).

psychosocial stages Stages of development put forward by Erik Erikson. The child goes from the stage of 'basic trust' in early infancy to the final stage in adult life of maturity with a sense of integrity and self-worth. There is little empirical evidence for these stages, and it is more a matter of belief than fact (as is the case for *psychoanalytic theory*).

punishment and obedience orientation This is the first of Kohlberg's *moral judgement stages* and is very similar to Piaget's *heteronomous stage*. This stage is characterised by an unquestioning belief that some-thing is wrong if a law or an authority figure prohibits it.

Q

quality circles (QCs) Small groups of pupils who meet for regular classroom sessions, which aim to problem-solve issues such as bullying.

R

racial prejudice A negative evaluation of someone as a consequence of their being in a certain racial or ethnic group.

reaction formation A term used in *psychoanalytic theory*. The individual may react, often unconsciously, to negative aspects of their personality so that, for example, the person whose upbringing destines her to become a miser may react against this and become generous.

realism In Piagetian theory, characteristic of children who are *egocentric* and assume that others share their own perspective. Also used to refer to children's responses in appearance–reality tasks (e.g. in tasks that involve distinguishing appearance from reality, children report only reality). *See also* **appearance–reality distinction** and **phenomenism**.

recall After witnessing an event, or learning test items, a participant is asked to report what they remember about the event or the test items once they are no longer present. *See also* **recognition**.

recapitulation The process of repeating again. The expression '*ontogeny* recapitulates *phylogeny*' refers to the repetition of evolutionary stages in the growth of the foetus and young mammal.

recognition After witnessing an event, or learning test items, a participant is shown a list of items and asked to identify (recognise) any that were present during the event or initial learning. *See also* **recall**.

reductionism The claim that complex behaviours and skills such as language and problem-solving are formed from simpler processes, such as neural activity and conditioning, and can ultimately be understood in these simpler terms.

reflexive schemes In Piaget's theory the basis for the first substage of *sensorimotor* development, which covers the period from birth to 1 month of age. During this substage infants use their innate reflexes (e.g. sucking, grasping) to explore their world.

reflexive vocalisations The first sounds produced by infants, including cries, coughs, burps, and sneezes.

rehearsal A *mnemonic strategy* that involves the repetition of the items or information that have to be remembered. An example is repeating a telephone number so as not to forget it before dialling.

relative coding Coding based on relative attributes, e.g. I am taller than him, I have fairer hair than her. Contrast with *absolute coding*, e.g. I am 5′5′ (1.7 m) tall, I have blond hair.

representational ability The ability to form a mental representation of an event or an object.

resilience This occurs when children experience positive outcomes despite experiencing significant risk. To infer resilience, two coexisting conditions must apply: (1) exposure to threat or severe adversity and (2) achievement of positive adaptation.

response perseveration Repeating a previously learned response usually when it is no longer appropriate. For example, when infants incorrectly search at location A when making the *A not B error*, they may be repeating the previously successful response to search at A.

restorative justice In relation to bullying, a range of practices which focus on the offender or bullying child being made aware of the victim's feelings and the harm they have caused, and making some agreed reparation. *See also* **retributive justice**.

retinal image size The size of a visually perceived object on the retina of the eyes. This image will vary depending on the real size of the object and its distance from the observer.

retributive justice Direct sanctions against bullies that are intended to reduce the incidence of bullying. *See also* **restorative justice**.

retrieval demands Cognitive demands made when attempting to remember information. Retrieval demands are greatest in *recall* tasks, and easiest in *recognition* tasks where the task provides retrieval cues by showing the items to be recognised.

retroactive interference The process through which information received after an event can interfere with and alter one's memory for the event.

reversibility The ability to imagine a series of steps in both forward and reverse directions. Characteristic of thinking in Piaget's *concrete operations stage*.

rhyme Words rhyme with each other when they share a *rime* – 'cat' and 'hat' rhyme because they have the *rime* 'at' in common.

rime The vowel sound of a *syllable* plus any consonants that follow. The rime of 'hat' is 'at', and the rime of 'stair' is 'air'. *See also* **onset**.

risk-focused programmes Intervention programmes that attempt to reduce risk exposure.

risk accumulation Given the importance of studying multiple influences simultaneously, cumulative risk models assess the overall effect of large sets of risk factors.

risk factors Catastrophic events such as war and natural disasters, family adversities such as bereavement and divorce, economic conditions such as poverty, and exposure to negative environments such as impoverished neighbourhoods.

risk specificity The specific characteristics of an individual risk factor, both in terms of its specific effect and in terms of how it interacts with specific child outcomes.

rods and cones Light-sensitive cells found in the retina of the eye which translate light into electrical signals that are then transferred to the brain so that the image can be interpreted. Rods are more sensitive and support perception in low light conditions. Cones are concentrated near the central retina (fovea) and support colour vision.

rooting reflex The reflex that causes newborn babies to respond to one of their cheeks being touched by turning their head in that direction. This reflex helps infants to find a nipple with their mouth.

rouge test A test to examine an infant's self-concept. A small amount of rouge (or some other colour) is placed on the infant's nose before they are placed in front of a mirror. If the infant touches their own nose, as opposed to the reflection in the mirror, they are said to have acquired a self-concept.

rough-and-tumble play A friendly type of play that involves play-fighting with a partner.

S

saccades One class of eye movements measured with eye tracking technology. Saccades are the fast movement of the eye that functions to shift fixation to an object of interest, so that its image is projected to the fovea (the central part of the retina responsible for sharpest vision).

Safe to Learn Guidelines issued by the UK Department for Children, Schools and Families (DCSF – now the Department for Education (DfE)), intended to encourage good behaviour and respect for others on the part of school children, and to prevent bullying.

scaffolding The process whereby adults structure and simplify a child's environment in order to facilitate his or her learning. Scaffolding may occur in a variety of contexts, for example by pointing out the next piece in a jigsaw puzzle or offering the child a sock rolled down to make it easier to put on.

schemes Mental structures in the child's thinking that provide representations and plans for enacting behaviours. *See also* **accommodation** and **script**.

school phobics Children who have a strong aversion to attending school. Also known as *school refusers*.

School Refusal Assessment Scale An instrument designed to identify four of the variables that are associated with difficulty in attending school: fearfulness/general anxiety, escape from aversive social situations, attention-getting or *separation anxiety*, and *positive reinforcement*.

school refusers *See* **school phobics**.

school tribunal Pupils are elected to hear evidence and decide on sanctions or punishments for those involved in bullying. Also known as *bully courts*.

script A generalised framework for commonly experienced events or situations, with a stored representation of what one would expect to happen in such situations. An example of an event that would typically have a stored script would be going to a restaurant.

social and emotional aspects of learning (SEAL) A UK-based relationships curriculum to developing social and emotional skills. It has seven themes, one of which is 'Say No to Bullying'.

secondary circular reactions The third substage in Piaget's sensorimotor development, from approximately 4–10 months. Infants repeat actions that have had an interesting effect on their environments, and manipulation and an understanding of the environment begins.

secondary drive A term used in *behaviourism* to refer to the fact that objects can acquire reinforcing properties by being associated with the satisfaction of an individual's *primary drives*. It is thought that many fetishes can be acquired this way.

secondary intersubjectivity Involving both objects and other people in one's interaction with the world. For example, a 9-month-old infant will begin to share the experience of a new object with other people, she may point to the object or make vocalisations in order to direct another's attention toward it. This behaviour indicates that the infant understands that both she and another can attend to the same object, and that she can influence and direct another person's attention. *See also* **intersubjectivity**.

second-order analogy An analogy that requires the use of *crystallised intelligence*. In order to make the connections, one must be able to derive a relationship that is not inherent within the analogy. An example of a second-order analogy is (Bert and Ernie):friendship:: (Romeo and Juliet):love. Note that understanding the analogy requires that the relationships of Sesame Street's Bert and Ernie, and Shakespeare's Romeo and Juliet, be derived: only then does the analogy reduce to 'friends are to friendship as lovers are to love'.

secure attachment Responsive, supportive, structured, and affectively stimulating relationship between parent and child that contributes to children's positive development. A secure attachment has been shown to be particularly important for children exposed to adversity.

securely attached Descriptive of children who find comfort and consolation in the presence of a parent or caregiver, and who seek comfort from that person after a separation or other aversive event. Whilst the caregiver is present, securely attached infants use the caregiver as a secure base to explore the environment. See **insecure-avoidant**, **insecure-resistant**, and **strange situation**.

selective attention The ability to allocate attentional resources and to focus on (a) specific topic(s).

self-actualisation Fulfilment of needs beyond those deemed necessary for survival. When the need for life, safety, love, and esteem is being met, individuals are free to seek the fulfilment of higher needs, such as pursuing talents and dreams. *See also* **humanistic theory**.

self-concept One's awareness and evaluation of one's self.

self-efficacy A person's evaluation of their ability to achieve a goal or an outcome in particular tasks. Different from *self-esteem* in that you may feel that you would perform poorly in tasks that are of little interest to you, so that your self-esteem is not dented.

self-esteem A person's overall evaluation or appraisal of his or her worth.

Self-Esteem Inventory A checklist of self-esteem items examining how children see themselves in relation to peers, parents, school and personal interests.

Self Perception Profile Designed by Harter and aims to measure five specific domains of self-esteem: perceived athletic competence, behavioural conduct, physical appearance, scholastic competence, social acceptance and also overall self-worth.

self-socialisation The idea that children attend to and imitate same-sex models, and follow sex-appropriate activities, because they realise that this is what a child of their own sex usually does.

self-worth protection The tendency of some students to reduce their levels of effort so that any subsequent poor academic performance will be attributed to low motivation rather than to a lack of ability.

semantic memory *Long-term memory* of all of our world knowledge, including concepts, algorithms, definitions of words and the relations between them. The semantic memory for 'market,' for example, includes the knowledge that it is a place for buying and selling goods.

semantic system A system that categorises words in relation to their meaning.

sensitive period A period of development, usually early in life, during which the individual is most sensitive to certain types of experience or learning. Refers to a period of time that is more extended than a *critical period*.

sensorimotor play Refers to play with objects, making use of their properties (falling, making noises) to produce pleasurable effects – pleasurable for the infant, that is! The kinds of secondary circular reactions described by Piaget as part of his sensorimotor period appear to be playful in this way.

sensorimotor stage In Piaget's theory, the first stage of *cognitive development*, whereby thought is based primarily on perception and action and internalised thinking is largely absent. This stage is characteristic of infants from birth to about 2 years old.

separation anxiety A fear of the loss of parental nurturance.

sequential design A combination of longitudinal and cross-sectional designs that examines the development of individuals from different age *cohorts*. Additionally, a cross-section of ages is also examined in order that any cohort effects may be identified. Sometimes called age-cohort design. *See also* **cross-sectional design** and **longitudinal design**.

seriation Putting items in a coherent or logical order.

severe visual impairment (SVI) Whilst still having very poor vision, individuals with SVI do have some limited visual perception of form and shape. *See also* **profound visual impairment**.

sex-role stereotypes Beliefs held about what roles are most appropriate for one sex or the other.

shape constancy Understanding that an object remains the same shape even though its *retinal image shape* changes when it is viewed from different angles. Therefore, when we view a square tilted on one axis, we do not perceive the shape as a rectangle but as a square tilted away from us. *See also* **size constancy**.

short-term memory *Encoded* events enter the short-term memory first, and can then progress to the *long-term memory*. Short-term memory can typically only hold a limited number of items (about seven) for a short period of time. Also called *working memory*.

single-level testing A form of testing in which children are not all expected to reach a given educational level at a fixed chronological age and instead are assessed when they are ready to achieve that level.

size constancy Understanding that an object remains the same size despite its *retinal image size* changing as it moves closer to or away from us. Therefore, when we see a car driving down the road away from us, we do not see it as shrinking despite the fact that its retinal image size decreases. *See also* **shape constancy**.

social cognition The comprehension of social situations.

social cognitive theory A theory that emphasises social factors in cognitive development.

social contract orientation stage *See* **human rights and social welfare morality**.

Social Identity Theory (SIT) Recognises the importance of social processes in the development of self-image. An individual belongs to many groups and this membership can become internalised as part of self-image. The theory was originally formulated to explain how a positive self-image can be maintained – membership of 'in-groups' and non membership of 'out-groups' enhances positive self-image. More recently developmental psychologists have used SIT as an explanation of self development so that children's group membership, their increasing ability to distinguish between groups and their feelings towards groups helps to embed their identity 'I am like this group and I like them but I am not like that group and I do not like them'.

social learning theory Describes psychological factors that lead to behaviour change and emphasises humans' ability to exercise control over the nature and quality of their lives and to be 'self-reflective about one's capabilities, quality of functioning, and the meaning and purpose of one's life pursuits'.

social policies Actions, rules, and laws aimed at solving social problems or attaining social goals, in particular intended to improve existing conditions.

social referencing Infants and young children look to their caregiver for 'advice' when faced with a difficult or uncertain situation and seek social cues (such as smiling or frowning) to guide their actions.

social signalling devices Devices such as smiling and crying that signify someone's emotional state.

social system morality The fourth of Kohlberg's *moral judgement stages*, also called the *law and order orientation stage*. In this stage individuals recognise that all members of society have intentions and pursue goals, but they understand that rules and laws are necessary in order for society to function and to prevent anarchy. It is therefore necessary for them to always side with whoever is more within the law, even if this causes great regret. Therefore, it is never acceptable to steal because this is against the law; however, one may still feel sympathy for a man who steals in order to save his wife.

sociocognitive conflict A *cognitive conflict* that arises as a result of a social interaction, e.g. two *peers* having a different understanding of a mathematical problem.

sociogram A visual representation of interpersonal relationships within a group. Often used in an educational context in order to help teachers and staff understand more about pupils' peer relationships.

sociodramatic play *Pretend play* involving social role-playing in an extended story sequence.

socio-economic status (SES) A scale that gives an indication of someone's social class and income bracket.

sociometric status A categorisation of children as popular, controversial, rejected, neglected, or average, according to whether they are high or low on positive and negative nominations.

sociometry A picture of the social structure in a group, derived from observation, questionnaire, or interview.

specific language impairment (SLI) A developmental language disorder that can affect both production and comprehension and that is unrelated to other atypicalities in development.

specific phobia A 'marked and persistent fear of clearly discernible, circumscribed objects or situations' (*DSM-IV*).

speech stream The undifferentiated series of words that are produced when we communicate. In order to understand the meaning conveyed when someone speaks, we must first break the speech stream into the individual words contained within it.

speed of processing The time it takes for the brain to either receive or output information, or the speed with which a mental calculation can be carried out.

s-structure (or surface structure) The *syntax* of a sentence. However, one s-structure can have more than one meaning. In order to understand the intended meaning of a sentence, one must examine the *d-structure*.

stability versus change The question of whether individuals are stable in the sense of maintaining their rank order across age, e.g. does the bright 2-year-old become a bright 10-year-old?

stable order principle The principle that number words must be produced in a set order: if you count 1–2–3 on one occasion, you must never then count 3–2–1 on another.

stage-like changes in development Changes in development that can be categorised into qualitatively different stages, so that a child's abilities will remain relatively stable and then, often suddenly, move up to the next stage. Development of this kind is usually nonreversible; once a child has reached a particular stage, she does not fall back to the previous stage's thinking or behaviour. A major characteristic of Piaget's theory of intellectual development.

stages of moral reasoning *See* **moral judgement stages**.

standard deviation Statistical term that indicates the spread of scores from the mean. A high standard deviation would indicate that there is a large variability within the data. A low standard deviation indicates that there is little variability in the data, i.e. many of the scores have values that are very close to the overall mean.

standardisation The development of a test or procedure by administering it to a large group of individuals in order to develop uniform instructions and group norms. A *standardised test* is one that can be given to children (or adults) to compare their performance with that of others of the same age or background.

standardised score A score that has been converted to fit a distribution with a given mean and *standard deviation*. Standardised scores make it easy to compare two individuals, since their scores are being converted in the same manner and are therefore relative to each other. *Intelligence tests* use standardised scoring.

standardised test A test of a psychological characteristic, such as personality, aptitude, or intelligence, that has been *standardised* on a representative sample of the population.

state change test Used in *theory of mind* research. A variation of the *deceptive box task*. The child is shown a tube or box of sweets/candies and has to guess what it contains. The box is then opened and the child sees the sweets/candies being removed and replaced by a pencil. The box is then closed again. The question asked is, 'When you first saw the box, before we opened it, what did you think was inside?' Using this method, a much larger per centage of 3- and 4-year-old children give the correct response of 'sweets' (80 per cent versus 40 per cent in the original deceptive box task). *See also* **posting version of the deceptive box test** and **unexpected transfer test.**

still-face procedure This procedure is used to examine how changes to infants' social surroundings affect their behaviour. Mothers are asked not to respond to their infants as they normally would, but to remain silent and expressionless. Infants respond to this situation with signs of distress, they gaze warily at their mother, give brief smiles followed by sobs, look away for long periods of time, and eventually become very withdrawn and distressed.

strange situation Measure, devised by Ainsworth, of the level of attachment a child has with their parent. It is typically conducted when the infant is between 1 and 2 years of age and assesses infants' responses to separation from, and subsequent reunion with, their mother, and their reactions to an unfamiliar woman (the so-called stranger). *See also* **insecure-avoidant, insecure-resistant**, and **securely attached**.

stranger anxiety Unhappiness felt by many infants when they encounter an unfamiliar person. Stranger anxiety begins to emerge at around 7 months of age.

strategies Knowledge used to solve particular problems.

structured observation An *observational study* in which the *independent variable* is systematically controlled and varied, and the investigator then observes the child's behaviour. Similar to an experiment but the degree of control is less precise than in a laboratory setting.

Student Teams Achievement Divisions (STAD) A method used to show how cooperative learning can work. Children working within the STAD technique are allocated to work in small groups. Each group intentionally comprises children of varying ability, gender, and ethnic backgrounds. The teacher introduces a topic to the group and the group's task is to discuss the problem and query each other until members of the group as a whole agree that they understand the topic.

subitising The ability to perceive directly the number of items without consciously counting them or using another form of calculation. This ability only applies to very small numbers.

sulci The deep narrow grooves of the outer surface of the brain.

subjective contours When only parts of an object are presented, the remaining contours are 'filled in' in order that the complete shape can be perceived. The lines that are 'filled in' are referred to as subjective contours since they are not really there.

suggestibility A child's (or adult's) tendency to change their memories and beliefs, often in response to interrogation. This is likely to result in inaccurate recall of events.

superego In Freud's theory, a collection of ideals, an individual's morality. This is what we refer to as our conscience and it is often in conflict with our *id*. *See also* **defence mechanisms** and **ego**.

superordinate categories *See* **categorisation**.

Support Group Method In the UK, a non-punitive approach which aims to change problem behaviours through a mixture of peer pressure to elicit a prosocial response, and self realisation of the harm and suffering caused to the victim.

Sure Start *See* **Head Start**.

syllabary The name given to a language that relies heavily on *syllables* for meaning.

syllable The smallest unit of a word whose pronunciation forms a rhythmic break when spoken.

syllogism Comprises two statements (called premises) and a conclusion that is derived from the previous statements. For example: If A is a subset of B, and B is a subset of C, A must also be a subset of C.

symbolic function substage The first substage in Piaget's *preoperational stage* of reasoning, in which children acquire the ability to mentally represent objects that are not physically present.

symbolic play *See* **pretend play**.

synapse The connections between *neurons* which enable them to transmit information.

synaptogenesis The building of connections (*synapses*) between nerve cells.

syntax The manner in which words and parts of words are related to one another to produce grammatical sentences: the production of sentences is governed by grammatical structures and rules.

systematic desensitisation An approach that aims to reduce or eliminate certain phobias, and can be used to reduce fear and anxiety associated with schooling, in which the child is firstly taught how to relax and subsequently is encouraged to employ this ability when asked to consider the objects of their fear. A hierarchical approach is employed whereby minor fears are addressed first. *See also* **emotive imagery**.

T

tachistoscope A device for presenting visual stimuli for very brief and precisely controlled times. Such devices are now obsolete and computers are used to control such presentations.

tadpole stage An early stage in children's drawings of the human figure in which there is no differentiation between the head and the body, and body parts such as the arms and legs are typically drawn as though they grow directly from the head, and the naval may be drawn inside the head. It is doubtful that children actually perceive people as being like their drawings!

term The end of pregnancy.

tertiary circular reactions The fifth substage in Piaget's account of *sensorimotor* development from approximately 12–18 months. The child begins to search for novelty and uses trial and error to explore the characteristics and properties of objects, and develops new ways of solving problems.

theory of development A scheme or system of ideas that is based on evidence and attempts to explain, describe, and predict behaviour and development.

theory of mind The understanding that different people may have different emotions, feelings, thoughts, and beliefs from one's own.

theory of mind hypothesis of autism The view that people with autism have difficulties in understanding that others have thoughts and beliefs.

three mountains task A task used by Piaget to investigate *egocentricity* in *preoperational* children. The child is shown a model of three mountains and asked to choose the view that would be seen by someone in a different location from themselves, and the preoperational child typically chooses the view from their own location.

time sampling An *observational study* that records an individual's behaviour at frequent intervals of time.

top-down structures A cognitive development process in which the state of the system is specified or presumed, and then working to discover its components and their development, a view more consistent with nativist theory. See also **bottom-up structures**.

Tower of Hanoi task A task that involves reconstructing a tower of three seriated blocks from peg A to peg C in as few moves as possible without moving more than one block at a time or placing a larger block on top of a smaller one.

transactional processes Processes in which parent and child are seen as influencing one another reciprocally. According to this model, child problems can develop if the relationship between parent and child goes bad as the two interact over time. Optimal child development is likely to result when parent–child transactions evolve in more positive directions.

transcription A process of creating an equivalent RNA copy of a sequence of DNA.

transitive inference The relation between two (or more) premises (e.g., A > B, B > C) that leads to an inference that is logically necessary (A > C). *See also* **transitivity task**.

transitivity task A task that examines a person's ability to infer a relationship between two or more items that usually cannot be directly compared. For example, given four sticks of different lengths seen in pairs A and B, B and C, C and D, the relationship between A and D can be calculated if one knows that A > B, B > C, and C > D, namely, that A > D. *See also* **syllogism**.

translation Turning an mRNA transcript into a protein.

transnatal learning Learning that occurs during the *prenatal* period which is remembered during the *postnatal* period.

transsexual An individual who identifies with a gender inconsistent or not culturally associated with their biological sex.

trimester A period of three months. The course of human pregnancy is divided into three trimesters.

turn-taking The understanding that during a communicative exchange each participant takes turns to communicate in an alternating fashion.

Twenty Statements Test (TST) A tool to facilitate self-awareness devised by Kuhn and McPartland. An individual asks the question 'Who am I?' 20 times and then reflects upon their responses in order to draw up a prioritised list of self-attributes.

U

ultradian rhythm Rhythms or cycles that repeat in less than a 24-hour period.

underextension Extending the meaning of a word to too few instances, as when a child restricts their use of a word such as 'duck' to situations in which the child is playing with a toy while in the bath, therefore failing to refer to the animals at the park as 'ducks'. *See also* **overextension**.

unexpected transfer test A third-person version of the *deceptive box task* as a measure of *theory of mind*. In this test a child sees an object put in one place and it is later moved to another location without the child being aware of the move. The children who are tested are asked where the child will look for the object when they want to find it. Those children who fail the *deceptive box task* are more likely to fail this test also and say that the child will search in the place where the object has been moved to. *See also* **posting version of the deceptive box test** and **state change test**.

universal counting principles A set of principles that must be obeyed in order for our number system to work. These principles are the *abstraction principle*, the *last-number-counted principle*, the *one-to-one principle*, the *order irrelevance principle*, and the *stable order principle*.

universality The notion that certain developmental principles apply across all cultures. For example, moral stages that are used to characterise moral judgement development in the United States can also be used to understand moral judgement in all other cultures.

unresolved attachment Adults who have not been able to resolve feelings relating to the death of a loved one or to abuse that they may have suffered.

U-shaped functions Behaviour where ability is initially very good, then decreases, and then increases again follows a U-shaped function of development. An inverted U-shaped function follows the opposite trend, initially poor, then getting better, and then becoming poor again.

V

vertical décalage Within Piagetian terminology this is where the child has a level of understanding at one level (perhaps at the level of action) that has to be reconstructed at a later age at a different stage or level of understanding (perhaps at the level of thought).

vestibular system The sensory system that contributes to balance and spatial orientation.

violation of expectation technique This technique is used to examine whether infants have any expectations about the world around them. They are typically familiarised with an event sequence, and then presented with two test trials that are variants on the original, one involving a possible event and the other involving an impossible event. If the infants look longer at the impossible event, this is taken as evidence that they have detected the impossibility of the event sequence.

visual accommodation The ability to focus on objects irrespective of their distance from the eye. Therefore, as an object moves closer toward us, it does not appear to go in and out of focus.

visual acuity The ability to make fine discriminations between the elements in the visual array. When an object is in focus, acuity is constrained by the density of receptors in the retina, which is low at birth and increases in the early months of life, particularly in central vision.

visual cliff A piece of apparatus used to study depth perception in infants. The apparatus consists of a glass table with a checkerboard pattern beneath it. At one half of the table the checkerboard pattern is directly below the glass (the 'solid' half). At the other half the checkerboard is several feet below the glass top (the 'deep' half). Infants are placed on the 'solid' half and encouraged by their mothers to crawl to the end of the 'deep' half. Infants crawl to the edge of the 'solid' half, but usually refuse to crawl on to the 'deep' half (although in reality it would be perfectly safe to do so). This indicates that infants perceive (and fear) depth from visual information alone.

visual preference method This technique is used to examine whether infants have preferences for certain stimuli. Infants are shown two objects (usually 2-D pictures) side by side, and the amount of time they spend looking at each one is then compared. A consistent preference for one over the other is defined as a visual preference.

vulnerability factors Those attributes of the individual that contribute to maladjustment under conditions of adversity.

W

Williams syndrome A rare neurodevelopmental disorder caused by deletion of about 26 genes from the long arm of chromosome 7.

Wing's triad of impairments Impairments of (1) social relationships, (2) communication, and (3) imagination characteristic of *autistic* behaviour.

working memory *Short-term memory* store in which mental operations such as *rehearsal* and *categorisation* take place.

Z

Zeitgeist The thinking or feelings peculiar to a generation or period – as in 'the prevailing Zeitgeist' or 'the spirit of the age.'

zone of proximal development The distance between the actual developmental level as determined by independent problem solving and the level of potential development as determined through problem solving under adult guidance or in collaboration with more able *peers*.

Names Index

UNIVERSITY
OF
GLASGOW
LIBRARY

BPS Textbooks in Psychology

The only series to be approved by the BRITISH PSYCHOLOGICAL SOCIETY

no other series bears the BPS seal of approval!

BPS Blackwell presents a comprehensive and authoritative series covering everything a student needs in order to complete an undergraduate degree in psychology. Refreshingly written to consider more than North American research, this series is the first to give a truly international perspective. Every title fully complies with the BPS syllabus in the topic.

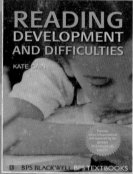

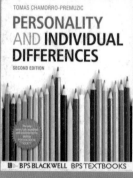

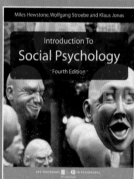

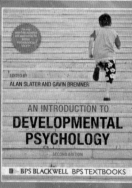

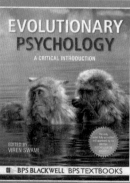

Each book is supported by a companion website, featuring additional resource materials for both instructors and students.

For further information and to view our entire list of BPS Textbooks in Psychology, go to:

www.wiley.com/go/bps

BPS BLACKWELL